MW00667081

. . . TO WORK

USING THE NEWS . . .

Finding Up-to-Date Information on Money 27
Keeping Up with Bond Prices and Yields 84
Using Bond Yields to Assess Risk 148
How to Read the Yield Curve 161
Reading Exchange Rates 185
Reading Financial Futures Listings 213
Reading Options Listings 219
A Tombstone for Something New? 283
Federal Reserve Data and Change in the Monetary Base 477
The U.S. Balance of Payments 578

CASE STUDIES

Where Do Households Put Their Savings? 47
How Much Risk Should You Tolerate in Your Portfolio? 103
Modeling Risk Premiums in Financial Markets 108
Should You Bank on International Investment? 197
Citron Pressed—The Orange County Fiasco 222
Barings Lost—The Queen's Banker Goes Bust 223
What Goes Up . . . 249
What Kind of Financial Institution Is a Hedge Fund? 302
What Kind of Financial Institution Is a Venture Capital Fund? 303
Is Banking a Declining Industry? 369
Using the Money Supply Equation to Predict Money Growth 461
Is Inflation Targeting a Good Idea? 560
Do Sterilized Interventions Affect the Exchange Rate? 577
Financial Collapse in Mexico 596
Financial Collapse in Asia 597
How Does Money Affect Aggregate Demand in the New Keynesian View? 699

MOVING FROM THEORY TO PRACTICE . . .

E-Cash 2.0 30
Mrs. Watanabe Learns to Invest 56
A Bond Anybody Can Love 92
Sex Matters 112
Interest Rates: Up or Down? 140
What If Treasury Debt Disappears? 172
The Euro Recovers 206
Futures of Pollution 226
So, Is the Stock Market Overvalued? 254
On the Cutting Edge of Corporate Control in China 274
Federal Credit Agencies: Is "Too Much" Lending Possible? 308
Banking: "Clicks" or "Bricks"? 340
The Bigger They Come . . . 376
Crisis and Response in Japan 406
New Basle Committee Proposals 428
The Fed and the Monetary Base: Thwarting a Slowdown 464
ECB Warns on Budget Deficits 488
The ECB's Terrible Twos 508
Fed Rate Cut Combats a Contagion 534
The Chairman's Upbeat View 566
Central Banks Boost the Euro 600
A Legal Tender of One's Own 622
Productivity: The Magic Elixir 654
Memo to Tokyo: Print Money 686
Will the Fed Step on the Gas? 708
A New Credit Crunch for Japan? 734
Growth or Inflation? 762

Is Something Missing?

If the tear-out card is missing from this book, then you're missing out on an important part of your learning package. Choose to buy a new textbook, or visit www.aw.com/hubbard for information on purchasing a subscription.

CONGRATULATIONS!

As a student purchasing Hubbard's *Money, the Financial System, and the Economy*, you are entitled to a prepaid subscription to premium services on our Companion Web Site at www.aw.com/hubbard.

The duration of your subscription is 6 months.

TO ACTIVATE YOUR PREPAID SUBSCRIPTION:

1. Launch your Web browser and go to www.aw.com/hubbard.
2. When you select a protected section of the Web site, you will be asked to log in.
3. Follow the instructions on the screen to register yourself as a new user. Your pre-assigned Access Code is located underneath the scratch-off area below:

Access Code:

4. During registration, you will choose a personal User ID and Password for use in logging into the Web site.
5. Once your personal User ID and Password are confirmed, you can begin using the Web site.

This Access Code can be used only once to establish a subscription. This subscription is not transferable.

If you did not purchase a new textbook, this Access Code may not be valid!

Money, *the* Financial System, *and the* Economy

Fourth Edition

The Addison-Wesley Series in Economics

Abel/Bernanke
Macroeconomics

Bade/Parkin
Foundations of Economics

Bierman/Fernandez
Game Theory with Economic Applications

Binger/Hoffman
Microeconomics with Calculus

Boyer
Principles of Transportation Economics

Branson
Macroeconomic Theory and Policy

Bruce
Public Finance and the American Economy

Burgess
The Economics of Regulation and Antitrust

Byrns/Stone
Economics

Carlton/Perloff
Modern Industrial Organization

Caves/Frankel/Jones
World Trade and Payments: An Introduction

Chapman
Environmental Economics: Theory, Application, and Policy

Cooter/Ulen
Law and Economics

Eaton/Mishkin
Online Readings to Accompany The Economics of Money, Banking, and Financial Markets

Ehrenberg/Smith
Modern Labor Economics

Ekelund/Tollison
Economics: Private Markets and Public Choice

Fusfeld
The Age of the Economist

Gerber
International Economics

Ghiara
Learning Economics: A Practical Workbook

Gordon
Macroeconomics

Gregory
Essentials of Economics

Gregory/Stuart
Russian and Soviet Economic Performance and Structure

Hartwick/Olewiler
The Economics of Natural Resource Use

Hubbard
Money, the Financial System, and the Economy

Hughes/Cain
American Economic History

Husted/Melvin
International Economics

Jehle/Reny
Advanced Microeconomic Theory

Klein
Mathematical Methods for Economics

Krugman/Obstfeld
International Economics: Theory and Policy

Laidler
The Demand for Money: Theories, Evidence, and Problems

Leeds/von Allmen
The Economics of Sports

Lesser/Dodds/Zerbe
Environmental Economics and Policy

Lipsey/Courant/Ragan
Economics

McCarty
Dollars and Sense: An Introduction to Economics

Melvin
International Money and Finance

Miller
Economics Today

Miller/Benjamin/North
The Economics of Public Issues

Mills/Hamilton
Urban Economics

Mishkin
The Economics of Money, Banking, and Financial Markets

Parkin
Economics

Parkin/Bade
Economics in Action Software

Perloff
Microeconomics

Phelps
Health Economics

Riddell/Shackelford/Stamos/Schneider
Economics: A Tool for Critically Understanding Society

Ritter/Silber/Udell
Principles of Money, Banking, and Financial Markets

Rohlf
Introduction to Economic Reasoning

Ruffin/Gregory
Principles of Economics

Sargent
Rational Expectations and Inflation

Scherer
Industry Structure, Strategy, and Public Policy

Schotter
Microeconomics: A Modern Approach

Sherman/Kolk
Business Cycles and Forecasting

Smith
Case Studies in Economic Development

Studenmund
Using Econometrics: A Practical Guide

Su
Economic Fluctuations and Forecasting

Tietenberg
Environmental and Natural Resource Economics

Tietenberg
Environmental Economics and Policy

Todaro
Economic Development

Waldman/Jensen
Industrial Organization: Theory and Practice

Williamson
Macroeconomics

Money, *the* Financial System, *and the* Economy

Fourth Edition

R. GLENN HUBBARD
COLUMBIA UNIVERSITY

Addison Wesley

Boston San Francisco New York
London Toronto Sydney Tokyo Singapore Madrid
Mexico City Munich Paris Cape Town Hong Kong Montreal

For Constance, Raph, and Will

Editor-in-Chief: *Denise Clinton*
Executive Development Manager: *Sylvia Mallory*
Senior Production Supervisor: *Juliet Silveri*
Production Coordinator: *Heather Bingham*
Supplements Editor: *Meredith Gertz*
Marketing Manager: *Adrienne D'Ambrosio*
Cover and Interior Designer: *Joyce Cosentino*
Design Supervisor: *Regina Hagen*
Copyeditor: *Jill Hobbs*
Proofreader: *Jan Cocker*
Senior Prepress Supervisor: *Caroline Fell*
Manufacturing Supervisor: *Hugh Crawford*
Typesetter: *Lynn Lowell, Electronic Publisher*

Library of Congress Cataloging-in-Publication Data
Hubbard, R. Glenn.
Money, the financial system, and the economy / R. Glenn Hubbard.—4th ed.
p. cm.
Includes index.
ISBN 0-201-72614-9 (hardbound)
1. Finance. 2. Money. 3. Banks and banking. 4. Monetary policy—United States.
5. International finance. I. Title.

HG173 .H8 2001
332.1—dc21 2001033494

3 4 5 6 7 8 9 10—QWT—05 04 03 02

Preface

Thinking About the Book

When I studied money and banking as an undergraduate in 1979, the course emphasized real-world topics: Why is inflation high (as it was in those days), and where does it come from anyway? Why does a boom in the stock or bond market excite news commentators, and how are prices of stocks and bonds determined in the first place? What do banks do with my money? How do economic events in other nations affect financial markets and interest rates in the United States? Like me, students often come to this course expecting to learn simple answers to such questions. The answers were not simple in 1979, and they are even more complex in the early twenty-first century. Today's students face an even greater challenge: trying to understand the organization of U.S. financial markets and institutions and the Federal Reserve System in the face of domestic and global change.

Having taught money and banking courses to undergraduate and graduate students over many years, I was frustrated that existing books simply stressed the current organization of the financial system and failed to give students a coherent framework for understanding new regulations and events. Adding to my dissatisfaction was the way these texts included new developments: They simply increased the number of topics to be covered during an already crowded term. Even with all this material, students still lacked the tools to predict the effects of changes to the financial system.

A Better Approach

My goal in writing this text is to present to students underlying economic explanations for why the financial system is organized as it is and to show them the interconnection of the financial system and the economy. With this presentation, the student learns a paradigm for interpreting events, not a laundry list of facts that quickly becomes outdated. I wanted to go beyond the traditional approach and teach students how to apply the theory that they learn in the classroom to the practice of the real world. To achieve this goal, I have built three advantages into this text: (1) a framework for understanding, evaluating, and predicting; (2) a contemporary economic approach; and (3) integration of international material throughout the book.

Framework of the text: understand, evaluate, predict. The framework underlying all discussion in this text has three levels: First, the student learns to *understand* economic analysis. "Understanding" refers to the development of economic intuition for organizing concepts and facts. Second, economic analysis is used to *evaluate* current developments and the financial news, challenging the student to use financial data and to think critically about interpretations of current events. Finally, the student uses economic tools and principles to *predict* future events, applying economic analysis to anticipate the effects of changes in the economy and the financial system.

This presentation offers students a way to think critically about developments in financial markets and institutions and in monetary institutions and policy. Students then can interpret current events as the logical outcome of principles. For example, Parts 2, 3, and 4, which examine the roles of financial markets and institutions in the economy, repeatedly use the concepts of risk-sharing, liquidity, and information services demanded of and supplied by the financial system to explain such topics as how different financial arrangements bring together borrowers and savers (Chapters 3, 12, and 13), how they respond to changes in regulation (Chapter 15), why they differ in different countries (Chapter 16), and how their functioning affects the macroeconomy (Chapter 27).

A contemporary approach. Throughout this text, I incorporate recent research in a way that is accessible to students. Current research on monetary policy, financial institutions, and inflation is used to develop a general model for how monetary policy affects the economy (Chapter 26). The examination of credit crunches (Chapter 27) integrates the economic role of financial institutions in a simple macro model. Efficient markets are covered early (Chapter 10) to lay a groundwork for the discussion of information problems in financial markets (Chapters 11, 12, 13, and 27).

Integration of international topics. Students today are keenly interested in the workings of the international financial system and in differences in financial systems across countries. To address this issue, international applications have been integrated throughout the text. For example, international comparisons of financial systems and international constraints on central bank decision making are discussed concurrently with events in the United States (Chapter 22). Separate, optional chapters on exchange rates (Chapter 8), international banking (Chapter 16), and the international monetary and financial system (Chapter

22) appear where they fall naturally. Instructors who wish to omit these topics or cover them later in the course can easily do so.

New Developments in the Fourth Edition

I established three objectives in revising the content of the fourth edition.

The first objective is the integration of recent developments in financial markets and institutions and the international monetary and financial system with the text's analytical foundations. The major changes in the regulation of U.S. financial institutions in the wake of the Gramm-Leach-Bliley Financial Services Modernization Act of 1999 offer the opportunity to apply ideas of how financial institutions evolve to provide risk-sharing, liquidity, and information services and to understand the current blurring of lines among financial institutions. The debate over reform of the International Monetary Fund in the aftermath of the Asian financial crisis of the late 1990s provides a backdrop for emphasizing the economics of banking and financial regulation, as well as illuminating currency crises and monetary policy and economic performance. The banking and financial crisis in Japan gives students an opportunity to link lessons of the U.S. S&L crisis of the 1990s with current financial developments. The rise of hedge funds and the collapse of Long-Term Capital Management offer a window on the economic analysis of financial institutions and on the prospects for success of emerging institutions. I use the early years of the euro and the European Central Bank to explore exchange rate determination, central bank organization, monetary policy tools, and monetary policy effectiveness. The U.S. productivity boom of the late 1990s is a useful case study for illustrating determinants of output growth and inflation in the economy. Finally, many innovations—from on-line banking to U.S. Treasury inflation-indexed bonds to new futures markets to institutional reform in Japan to corporate control in China to consequences of U.S. government budget surpluses—are discussed using the text's economic tools.

Second, the framework of risk sharing/liquidity/information, which was so successful in linking diverse topics in the first, second, and third editions, has been expanded in the fourth edition. I believe that this framework is successful because it helps students understand what services financial markets and institutions provide—and why—and how markets and institutions evolve over time. In the fourth edition, applications of the framework relate developments in financial markets and institutions, regulation, and macroeconomic model building to economic principles.

Third, I wanted to maintain the sense of dynamism in the financial system introduced in the text through examples and boxed features. To achieve this, all of the *Moving from Theory to Practice* news spreads have been updated to include significant financial events that have occurred over the past year or so and analyses of these events that reinforce the chapter theory. Similarly, the *Using the News* sections, in which students observe patterns in reported financial data, have been updated. Examples describing new developments in markets, institutions, regulation, and public policies are cited liberally throughout each chapter.

I made these content changes on the basis of economic events, reactions of my own and other students, suggestions from users of the previous editions, and reviewer comments.

The fourth edition allows significant flexibility for use in undergraduate courses in two-year and four-year institutions and in graduate courses in economics, finance, and public policy. The *Instructor's Resource Manual* describes several alternative paths through the text. Some sample course sequences include the following:

General Money and Banking Course: Chapters 1–7, 10–15, 17, 19, 22, 27
General Course with International Topics: Chapters 1–8, 10–17, 19–23, 27
Financial Markets and Institutions: Chapters 1–15, 8–9 (optional), 16
Monetary Institutions and Policy: Chapters 1–3, 13, 14, 17–21, 22 (optional)
Monetary Economics: Chapters 13–15, 17–21, 22 (optional), 23–28

Putting the Book to Work: Chapter Pedagogy

The features of this text are intended to help the student learn to view the financial system and the economy as an economist does. As much as possible, I have placed the student in the role of decision maker. In addition, I use real-world situations throughout the text so that students see the usefulness of economic analysis in interpreting events.

Chapter openers. The episode that begins each chapter shows students the real-world relevance and application of the material. The opening scenario is followed by an overview of the topics to be studied in the chapter. The chapter opener provides the student with an application to consider as the chapter develops its themes.

Checkpoints. These features test students' understanding by applying the chapter's economic approach to real-world situations. They address such issues as why some firms in cyclical industries don't rely on debt (p. 269) and how one can discern the Fed's goals from its actions (p. 522). These study aids help students prepare to answer the end-of-chapter exercises.

Consider this. I have drawn these topical illustrations of the chapter's economic approach from current events or research. Included are discussions of "rock star bonds" as a financial innovation (p. 50), behavioral finance (p. 242), whether bank consolidation is good for business (p. 362), whether currency boards are likely to be successful (p. 598), and ways in which the different sensitivity of economic activity to interest rates makes the job of the European Central Bank more difficult (p. 698).

Other times, other places. These features extend the chapter's economic approach to historical events or to developments in other countries. Examples include learning about money from Moscow cab drivers (p. 22), ways in which the Asian financial crisis affected European bond markets (p. 160), links between financial regulation and financial crisis in Russia and Japan (p. 403), and how the conduct of monetary policy responds to political pressures (p. 556).

Using the news. These excerpts present data from *The Wall Street Journal* and other sources. Students learn not only how to read and interpret such information, but also how to use it for predicting changes within the financial system and the economy.

Case studies. Many chapters conclude with detailed descriptions of recent events that extend the theory in the chapter. These longer applications are developed from recent events, adding to the currency of the revision. Included are discussions of what happened in the Orange County derivatives crisis (p. 222), the rise of hedge funds and the fall of Long-Term Capital Management (p. 302), whether the U.S. banking industry is in decline (p. 369), the Asian financial crisis (p. 597), and how monetary policy affects aggregate demand (p. 699).

Moving from theory to practice. In my experience, students are especially interested in applying the economic tools that they acquire to analyze events and policy developments in the news. To help students learn how to read news about the financial system and the economy critically, I have included an application feature at the end of each chapter. It consists of an actual news article (often from *The Wall Street Journal*) followed by a section that uses the chapter's economic principles to evaluate the argument of the article. Articles deal with both domestic and international situations, including differences in men's and women's attitudes toward stock ownership (p. 112), consequences of sharp reductions in outstanding Treasury debt (p. 172), "clicks" versus "bricks" in banking (p. 340), the European Central Bank in the "terrible twos" (p. 508), advice to the Bank of Japan (p. 686), and the debate in 2000 over whether the new economy should change the Fed's outlook for the U.S. economy's growth potential (p. 762).

Summary tables. These pedagogical aids present easy-to-understand explanations of the causes and effects of changes within the financial system and the economy. They frequently use small analytical diagrams to reinforce relationships visually.

Process diagrams. Because many students learn visually, the text has many process diagrams that illustrate the underlying economic forces that shape events, institutions, and markets. For example, I introduce a basic diagram in Chapter 3 (p. 38) showing that savers and borrowers value risk-sharing, liquidity, and information services. The basic diagram, shown there, is modified and repeated so that students internalize the model and can begin to make predictions based on it.

Analytical graphs. To aid students in seeing the principles and factors underlying events in the financial system and the economy, I use color functionally in analytical graphs. For example, on page 150, the initial conditions are consistently indicated by blue curves, and the final state by red curves. A blue-to-red shift arrow highlights the curves' movement, and beige "shock" boxes are numbered, allowing students to follow the sequence of events easily by referring to the numbers in the captions that accompany the graphs. These captions explain the economic factors fully so that students do not have to search for explanations within the text.

End-of-chapter summary. An aid for exam review, this summary feature presents the key terms and concepts and summarizes the main points of the chapter.

End-of-chapter exercises. Each chapter concludes with three types of exercises. *Review Questions* test students' recall of concepts and events. *Analytical Problems* give students a chance to apply the chapter's economic approach to specific cases and events. *Data Questions* ask students to collect data from specific sources in the library and use them to evaluate an economic argument. I have provided numerous questions to give the instructor maximum flexibility in making assignments. In addition, review questions and analytical problems in each chapter highlight the applicability of the chapter's economic approach to current events.

Content and Organization

The text's consistent theoretical approach and thorough coverage of contemporary events, institutions, and data offer students a well-balanced picture of the interactions among money, the financial system, and the economy. Within each part, the presentation develops economic models and then offers applications and analysis to help the student understand, evaluate, and predict financial events. Although related economic models are used throughout the book, instructors can easily use individual parts and chapters of the book independently. It is not necessary to cover the chapters in sequence.

Part 1: Introduction (Chapters 1–3). This introduction to the text includes the reasons for using an economic approach to studying money, financial markets and institutions, and the economy (Chapter 1); the role of money within the financial system (Chapter 2); and an overview of the role played by different elements of the financial system in matching savers and borrowers and providing risk-sharing, liquidity, and information services (Chapter 3).

Part 2: Interest Rates (Chapters 4–7). In Part 2, the focus shifts to how interest rates are determined. The student observes how the decisions of thousands of individual lenders and borrowers in the United States and around the world set the market interest rates that we read about in the newspaper. (Later, Part 5 explores how decisions of the Federal Reserve affect interest rates.) Chapter 4 explains what interest rates are, how they are measured, and where students can obtain information about interest rates to inform their financial decisions. Chapter 5 looks at how savers compare interest rates and returns on assets to allocate their savings in a portfolio, or collection of assets. Chapters 6 and 7 are the key analytical chapters. Chapter 6 studies how decisions about lending and borrowing determine bond prices and market interest rates in the United States and the international capital market. Chapter 7 extends the analysis to encompass the hundreds of interest rates that are reported each business day. That chapter examines how differences in risk, liquidity, information costs, taxation, and maturity affect interest rates.

Part 3: Financial Markets (Chapters 8–11). Whereas Part 2 concentrates on interest rates and the bond market, these chapters extend the analysis to encompass financial markets more broadly. Chapter 8 investigates the market for foreign exchange, focusing on how exchange rates are determined and how movements in exchange rates and interest rates are related. Chapter 9 examines the operation of derivative markets, looks at the services they provide, and studies why market prices fluctuate. Chapters 10 and 11 consider how financial markets evaluate and communicate information. Chapter 10 theorizes why prices of stocks, bonds, foreign-exchange, and derivative instruments contain information about assets' fundamental value for savers and borrowers. It also checks whether the evidence from financial markets supports the theory. Chapter 11 examines the costs that are imposed on financial markets by asymmetric information, and observes how financial markets respond to information problems.

Part 4: Financial Institutions (Chapters 12–16). Part 4 continues to use the concepts of risk sharing, liquidity, and information to explain why and how financial institutions and instruments evolve. Chapter 12 explains how the provision of risk-sharing, liquidity, and information services results in the development of different financial institutions. Chapter 13 examines the activities of banking firms and concludes with an analysis of how banks have exploited transactions cost and information cost advantages to enter new lines of business. Chapter 14 analyzes the development and current organization of the U.S. banking industry (and banking industries in other countries) and summarizes economic arguments for and against regulation. Chapter 15 examines financial regulation using a model of crisis, regulation, financial innovation, and regulatory response. This chapter also offers an up-to-date description of the regulatory debate surrounding the passage of the Riegle-Neal Interstate Banking and Branching Efficiency Act of 1994, as well as the implementation of the Gramm-Leach-Bliley Financial Services Modernization Act of 1999. Chapter 16 focuses on banks' provision of risk-sharing, liquidity, and information services in international transactions and introduces students to Euromarkets and global trends.

Part 5: The Money Supply Process and Monetary Policy (Chapters 17–22). This part opens the discussion of the links between the financial system and the macroeconomy. It begins with the money supply process, focusing on the role of the Fed, banks, and the nonbank public in determining the monetary base and the money multiplier (Chapter 17). Next is an optional chapter on the determinants of changes in the monetary base (Chapter 18). Chapter 19 analyzes the organization of the Fed and offers comparisons with the central banks of other countries. Chapter 20 introduces the tools of monetary policy and offers a simple graphical analysis of the reserves market so that students can apply their understanding. The conduct of monetary policy and contemporary developments in central banking such as inflation targeting are explored in Chapter 21. Chapter 22, an optional chapter, examines constraints on the conduct of monetary policy in an open economy using the model of exchange rate determination that was introduced in Chapter 8; Chapter 22 applies the model to analyze the currency crises that rocked the international financial system in the late 1990s.

Part 6: The Financial System and the Macroeconomy (Chapters 23–28). The final part studies the impact of monetary policy on the macroeconomy. Chapter 23 explains the demand for money based on the determinants of portfolio allocation and discusses the measurement of money. For those instructors who wish to use the *IS-LM* model, Chapter 24 presents a modern development of the model using the full-employment output line and a synthesis of the models of lending and borrowing, portfolio allocation, and money demand that were developed earlier in the book. For instructors who wish to use the aggregate demand–aggregate supply model, Chapter 25 intuitively derives the *AD* curve and presents a modern development of aggregate supply and the *AS* curve in the short run and the long run. Chapter 26 provides a concise treatment of short-run economic impacts of monetary policy, with analysis of competing approaches and empirical evidence. Chapter 27 expands the analysis of the role of financial institutions in macroeconomic models, including the debate over the extent to which a credit crunch worsened the 1990–1991 recession in the United States and the Japanese economic downturn of the late 1990s and early 2000s. Chapter 28 uses the *AD-AS* framework to analyze determinants of inflation in the short run and the long run.

Supplements

We are pleased to introduce with this fourth edition of the textbook an all-new **Mini-Cases** supplement. Written by Michael Brandl of the University of Texas at Austin, the nine original mini-cases involve students in applying the concepts covered in the textbook to real-world decision-making situations from the realms of business and financial markets. The task of the students is to analyze each of the potential decisions carefully and to conduct an informed cost-benefit analysis of each decision. Allowing the course to move beyond the lecture format, the mini-cases promote student interaction and discussion.

The **Study Guide** has been updated and expanded by Michael R. Redfearn of the University of North Texas. Carefully coordinated with the main text, it contains chapter overviews, a summary of key points, practice exercises, and analytical problems. This student resource also has two midterm and final exams that allow students to test their cumulative understanding of the material, as well as a comprehensive glossary.

Fully updated for the new edition, the **Instructor's Resource Manual, Teaching Notes for the Mini-Cases, and Test Bank,** by Anthony O'Brien of Lehigh University and Michael Brandl of the University of Texas at Austin, has three sections. The **Instructor's Resource Manual** section, written by Professor O'Brien, features chapter outlines, solutions to end-of-chapter questions and problems in the main text, essay and discussion questions, references for additional readings, and thumbnail printouts of all the PowerPoint lecture slides. The **Teaching Notes for the Mini-Cases** section comprises a wealth of tips and ideas for instructors on using the new mini-cases supplement described above. In particular, these notes, written by Michael Brandl, give advice and insight to instructors as to possible directions for discussion of the cases in class. The notes are designed to be useful to novices as well as to experienced case discussion leaders. Finally, the **Test Bank** portion of the manual, also by Professor O'Brien, contains over 2,300 multiple-choice questions, more than 200 of which are new to this edition.

The **Instructor's Resource CD-ROM** contains the Test Bank in **Test Generator Software** (TestGen-EQ with QuizMaster-EQ) for Windows and Macintosh. TestGen-EQ's updated and revised graphical interface enables instructors easily to view, edit, and add questions; transfer questions to tests; and print different forms of tests. Search and sort features allow the instructor to locate questions and arrange them in a preferred order quickly. QuizMaster-EQ, designed for your school's computer network, automatically grades the exams, stores results on disk, and allows the instructor to view and print a variety of reports.

Also on the **Instructor's Resource CD-ROM** are **PowerPoint Lecture Slides** by David Macpherson of Florida State University. The PowerPoint lectures have been updated and enhanced to include key figures in the text, along with detailed lecture notes. The **Instructor's Resource CD-ROM** may be obtained through your Addison-Wesley representative.

The text's **Companion Web site** is available at http://www.aw.com/hubbard. This site offers multiple-choice and essay quizzes as well as additional resources and numerous Web links for each chapter.

We are pleased, too, to offer the flexible, state-of-the art online course-management system **CourseCompass™** with the new edition of Hubbard. CourseCompass™ combines the strength of Addison-Wesley content with today's best e-learning tools. CourseCompass™ is a nationally hosted, dynamic, interactive system powered by Blackboard, a leader in the development of Internet-based learning tools. This easy-to-use and customizable program enables professors to tailor content and functionality to meet individual course needs. Every CourseCompass™ course includes a range of pre-loaded content such as testing and assessment question pools, chapter-level objectives, chapter summaries, photos, illustrations, videos, animations, and Web activities—all designed to help students master core course objectives. For more information or to see a demo, visit http://www.coursecompass.com or contact your local Addison-Wesley sales representative.

Addison-Wesley's **Product Support Web site**, located at http://www.aw.com /techsupport, provides media product information and technical help for all technology-oriented supplements. In addition to information about how to contact product support staff, the site includes product descriptions, answers to frequently asked questions, hardware requirements, and software downloads.

Acknowledgments

In the years during which I developed the material for this book, I learned much from the reactions of my students at Northwestern University and Columbia University. I have also received critical, substantive suggestions from the following reviewers and focus group participants, to whom I extend sincere thanks:

Douglas Agbetsiafa
Indiana University at South Bend

Ehsan Ahmed
James Madison University

Christine Amsler
Michigan State University

David Aschauer
Bates College

John W. Bay
University of Southern Maine

Teresa Beckham
Rhodes College

Willie Belton
Georgia Institute of Technology

Ben Bernanke
Princeton University

Robert W. Boatler
Texas Christian University

Frank J. Bonello
University of Notre Dame

Michael Brandl
University of Texas at Austin

Maureen Burton
California Polytechnic State University

Charles Calomiris
Columbia University

Doug Cho
Wichita State University

Steven Cobb
Xavier University

Doug Copeland
Johnson County Community College

Hugh Courtney
McKinsey and Company

Dean Croushore
Federal Reserve Bank of Philadelphia

Steven Cunningham
University of Connecticut

Edward Day
University of Central Florida

Robert Defina
Villanova University

Don Dutkowsky
Syracuse University

Stephanie Ellis
University of Michigan, Dearborn

Mary English
DePaul University

Gerald Epstein
University of Massachusetts, Amherst

Martin D. Evans
Georgetown University

Marjorie Flavin
University of California, San Diego

Garry Fleming
Roanoke College

Peter Frevert
Kansas University

Edward N. Gamber
Lafayette College

Neil Garston
California State University, Los Angeles

Mark Gertler
New York University

Joshua A. Gotkin
University of Arizona

Harry Greenbaum
South Dakota State University

Owen Gregory
University of Illinois at Chicago

David R. Hakes
University of Northern Iowa

Bassam Harik
Western Michigan University

John T. Harvey
Texas Christian University

Thomas Havrilesky
Duke University

Robert Herren
North Dakota State University

Melissa J. Hieger
Boston University

Ferdaus Hossain
Iowa State University

Regina Hughes
University of Texas, Austin

Nancy Jianakoplos
Colorado State University

Karen Johnson
Baylor University

Fred Joutz
George Washington University

Magda Kandil
University of Wisconsin at Milwaukee

Jules Kaplan
University of Colorado, Boulder

Anil Kashyap
University of Chicago

Thomas Kopp
Siena College

Faik Koray
Louisiana State University

Viju C. Kulkarni
San Diego State University

Patricia Kuzyk
Washington State University

John Lapp
North Carolina State University

Chris Lawrey
Williams Baptist College

Charles Leathers
University of Alabama

Sung Lee
St. John's University

Robert D. Ley
Bemidji State University

Ron Liggett
University of Texas, Arlington

Richard MacDonald
Saint Cloud State University

David Macpherson
Florida State University

Michael Marlow
California Polytechnic State University

V. T. Mathews
Seton Hall University

Stephen McCafferty
Ohio State University

Hal McClure
Villanova University

W. Douglas McMillin
Louisiana State University, Baton Rouge

Ron McNamara
Bentley College

Paul A. Meyer
University of Maryland

Steve Miller
University of Connecticut at Storrs

Frank Mixon
University of Southern Mississippi

Anthony O'Brien
Lehigh University

Rowena Pecchenino
Michigan State University

Chung Pham
University of New Mexico

Dean Popp
San Diego State University

Prosper Raynold
Miami University

Michael Redfearn
University of North Texas

Walter Rogers
Middle Tennessee State University

Steven Russell
Indiana University–Purdue University at Indianapolis

Robert S. Rycroft
Mary Washington College

Ira Saltz
Florida Atlantic University

Eugene Sarver
Pace University

Richard Schiming
Mankato State University

Calvin Siebert
University of Iowa

Frank Steindl
Oklahoma State University

Fred Thum
University of Texas at Austin

Robert Tokle
Idaho State University

Steven Tomlinson
University of Texas at Austin

Richard J. Torz
St. Joseph's College

Paul Wachtel
New York University

John Wassom
Western Kentucky University

Eugene White
Rutgers University

I am also fortunate to have worked with the individuals who prepared the supplements that accompany the text: Michael Redfearn, David Macpherson, Anthony O'Brien, and Michael Brandl.

The publication of the book is a team effort in the truest sense, and I have been gratified to work with so many talented professionals at Addison-Wesley. Editor-in-chief Denise Clinton and especially executive development manager Sylvia Mallory contributed challenging and valuable input at every stage; the book has been greatly improved by their efforts. I would also like to thank the production supervisors, Heather Bingham and Juliet Silveri; the supplements editor, Meredith Gertz; the Web project editor, Melissa Honig; and the marketing manager, Adrienne D'Ambrosio, for all of their hard work and enthusiasm about the book.

It is traditional to conclude acknowledgments by thanking one's family members for their support. I cannot begin to thank my wife Constance for her emotional support, patience, ideas, and countless hours of assistance in preparing the manuscript. She often reminded me that my reason for writing and revising this book was to synthesize ideas from my research and teaching that I believed would further the development of the course. Our sons Raph and Will have taken it all in stride. I can only hope that this book will please them.

R.G.H.
New York, New York

Brief Contents

Part 1 **Introduction** 1

1 Introducing Money and the Financial System 2
2 Money and the Payments System 14
3 Overview of the Financial System 35

Part 2 **Interest Rates** 67

4 Interest Rates and Rates of Return 68
5 The Theory of Portfolio Allocation 97
6 Determining Market Interest Rates 116
7 Risk Structure and Term Structure of Interest Rates 146

Part 3 **Financial Markets** 177

8 The Foreign-Exchange Market and Exchange Rates 178
9 Derivative Securities and Derivative Markets 210
10 Information and Financial Market Efficiency 234
11 Reducing Transactions Costs and Information Costs 258

Part 4 **Financial Institutions** 277

12 What Financial Institutions Do 278
13 The Business of Banking 312
14 The Banking Industry 346
15 Banking Regulation: Crisis and Response 380
16 Banking in the International Economy 411

Part 5 **The Money Supply Process and Monetary Policy** 433

17 The Money Supply Process 434
18 Changes in the Monetary Base 471
19 Organization of Central Banks 491
20 Monetary Policy Tools 512
21 The Conduct of Monetary Policy 539
22 The International Financial System and Monetary Policy 569

Part 6 **The Financial System and the Macroeconomy** 605

23 The Demand for Money 606
24 Linking the Financial System and the Economy: The *IS-LM-FE* Model 627
25 Aggregate Demand and Aggregate Supply 662
26 Money and Output in the Short Run 690
27 Information Problems and Channels for Monetary Policy 714
28 Inflation: Causes and Consequences 739

Contents

PART 1 **Introduction** 1

CHAPTER 1 Introducing Money and the Financial System 2

Getting Started 3
The Financial System and the Economy 3
Financial Markets 5
Financial Institutions 7
Money 8
Economic Analysis as a Tool 9
Developing an Economic Approach 10
Applying an Economic Approach 10
Review Questions 12
Analytical Problems, Data Question 13
Other times, other places . . . The Only Thing Constant in the Financial System Is Change 6
Consider this . . . Is the Financial System Truly Global? 7

CHAPTER 2 Money and the Payments System 14

Meeting the Needs of Exchange with Money 14
Barter 15
Government Allocation 16
Money 16
What Can Serve as Money? 19
The Payments System 20
Commodity Money 21
Fiat Money 21
Checks 22
Electronic Funds and Electronic Cash 23
Measuring the Money Supply 25
Measuring Monetary Aggregates 25
Selecting Monetary Aggregates 28
Review Questions, Analytical Problems 32
Data Questions 33
Appendix: Calculating Price Indexes 34
Other times, other places . . . Will the Euro Be a Success? 20
Consider this . . . What's Money? Ask a Taxi Driver! 22
Using the news . . . Finding Up-to-Date Information on Money 27
Moving from theory to practice . . . E-Cash 2.0, *The Economist,* 2/19/00 30

CHAPTER 3 Overview of the Financial System 35

What Is the Purpose of the Financial System? 35
Key Services Provided by the Financial System 38
Risk Sharing 39
Liquidity 39
Information 40

Financial Markets in the Financial System 41
Matching Savers and Borrowers: Debt and Equity 41
Providing Risk-Sharing, Liquidity, and Information Services 43
Financial Intermediaries in the Financial System 45
Matching Savers and Borrowers 46
Providing Risk-Sharing, Liquidity, and Information Services 46
Competition and Change in the Financial System 48
Financial Innovation 49
Changes in Financial Integration and Globalization 49
Financial Regulation 51
Provision of Information 52
Maintenance of Financial Stability 52
Advancement of Other Policy Objectives 53
Effects of Regulation 54
Review Questions 58
Analytical Problems, Data Question 59
Appendix: Financial Instruments 60
Case Study Where Do Households Put Their Savings? 47
Consider this . . . Financial Innovation: Home Mortgages or Rock Star Bonds? 50
Other times, other places . . . The Growth of International Bond and Stock Markets 51
Moving from theory to practice . . . Mrs. Watanabe Learns to Invest, *The Economist,* 12/18/99 56

PART 2 Interest Rates 67

CHAPTER 4 Interest Rates and Rates of Return 68

Comparing Debt Instruments 68
Timing of Payments 69
Present Value 72
Using Yield to Maturity as a Yardstick 75
Bond Yields and Prices 80
Why Can Price and Face Value Differ? 80
How Are Bond Yields and Prices Related? 82
Finding the Total Rate of Return 86
Real versus Nominal Interest Rates 87
Review Questions, Analytical Problems 94
Data Questions 96
Consider this . . . Can They STRIP? Creating New Financial Instruments 71
Consider this . . . Who Will Buy Those Fabulous Fifties? 82
Using the news . . . Keeping Up with Bond Prices and Yields 84
Other times, other places . . . Principal Derailed: Inflation and Long-Term Bond Prices 88
Moving from theory to practice . . . A Bond Anybody Can Love, *Business Week,* 6/19/00 92

CHAPTER 5 The Theory of Portfolio Allocation 97

Determinants of Portfolio Choice 97
Wealth 99
Expected Returns on Assets 100
Risk Associated with Asset Returns 101
Liquidity of Assets 102
Costs of Acquiring Information 102
Advantages of Diversification 104

Putting It All Together: Explaining Portfolio Allocation 108
Review Questions 111
Analytical Problems 114
Data Questions 115
Case Study How Much Risk Should You Tolerate in Your Portfolio? 103
Case Study Modeling Risk Premiums in Financial Markets 108
Other times, other places . . . Are Investors (Globally) Well Diversified? 110
Moving from theory to practice . . . Sex Matters, *Mutual Funds,* 4/00 112

CHAPTER 6 Determining Market Interest Rates 116

Supply and Demand in the Bond Market and Loanable Funds 116
- The Demand Curve 117
- The Supply Curve 119
- Market Equilibrium 119

Explaining Changes in Equilibrium Interest Rates 121
- Shifts in Bond Demand 122
- Shifts in Bond Supply 127
- Using the Model to Explain Changes in Interest Rates 132
- Back to the Bond Market's Votes 135

The International Capital Market and the Interest Rate 136
- Small Open Economy 137
- Large Open Economy 138

Review Questions 143
Analytical Problems 144
Data Questions 145
Consider this . . . Where Do Savings Come from? 125
Other times, other places . . . Do Interest Rates Rise During Wartime? 131
Moving from theory to practice . . . Interest Rates: Up or Down?, *The Economist,* 12/2/00 140

CHAPTER 7 Risk Structure and Term Structure of Interest Rates 146

Risk Structure of Interest Rates 146
- Default Risk 147
- Liquidity 152
- Information Costs 153
- Taxation 156
- Using the Risk Structure for Forecasting 158

Term Structure of Interest Rates 159
- Segmented Markets Theory 161
- Expectations Theory 162
- Preferred Habitat Theory 166
- Using the Term Structure for Forecasting 168

Review Questions, Analytical Problems 174
Data Question 176
Using the news . . . Using Bond Yields to Assess Risk 148
Consider this . . . Will a Consumption Tax Kill Munis' Allure? 159
Other times, other places . . . Asian Flu for European Bonds? 160
Using the news . . . How to Read the Yield Curve 161
Consider this . . . Can the Treasury Change the Shape of the Yield Curve? 170
Moving from theory to practice . . . What If Treasury Debt Disappears?, *The Wall Street Journal,* 8/3/00 172

PART 3 Financial Markets 177

CHAPTER 8 The Foreign-Exchange Market and Exchange Rates 178

Exchange Rates and Trade 179
Nominal versus Real Exchange Rates 180
Foreign-Exchange Markets 182
Determining Long-Run Exchange Rates 183
Supply and Demand 183
Economic Fundamentals and Long-Run Exchange Rate Trends 184
The Law of One Price and the Purchasing Power Parity Theory 186
Does the Theory Match Reality? 187
Determining Short-Run Exchange Rates 188
Comparing Expected Returns on Domestic and Foreign Assets 190
Foreign-Exchange Market Equilibrium 192
Interest Rate Parity 194
Exchange Rate Fluctuations 196
Changes in Domestic Real Interest Rates 196
Changes in Domestic Expected Inflation 198
Changes in Foreign Interest Rates 199
Changes in the Expected Future Exchange Rate 200
Currency Premiums in Foreign-Exchange Markets 202
A (Big) New Kid on the Block: The Euro 204
Review Questions 205
Analytical Problems 208
Data Question 209
Using the news . . . Reading Exchange Rates 185
Case Study Should You Bank on International Investments? 197
Other times, other places . . . Interest and Exchange Rates in the 1980s 203
Moving from theory to practice . . . The Euro Recovers, *Financial Times,* 12/16–17/00 206

CHAPTER 9 Derivative Securities and Derivative Markets 210

Forward Transactions and Derivatives 210
Futures 212
Futures Pricing 212
Using Futures to Manage Risk 214
Options 217
Options Pricing 218
Using Options to Manage Risk 220
Benefits of Derivative Markets for the Financial System 221
Standardization and Liquidity 224
Anonymous Trading and Information 224
Review Questions 228
Analytical Problems 229
Data Question 230
Appendix: Swaps 230
Using the news . . . Reading Financial Futures Listings 213
Using the news . . . Reading Options Listings 219
Other times, other places . . . Futures Trading, Index Arbitrage, and the Stock Market Crash of 1987 221
Case Study Citron Pressed—The Orange County Fiasco 222
Case Study Barings Lost—The Queen's Banker Goes Bust 223
Moving from theory to practice . . . Futures of Pollution, *The Banker,* 10/99 226

CHAPTER 10 Information and Financial Market Efficiency 234

Rational Expectations 235
The Efficient Markets Hypothesis 237
Determining an Asset's Expected Price 238
Price Fluctuations 239
Investment Strategies 241
Actual Efficiency in Financial Markets 244
Pricing Anomalies 245
Mean Reversion 246
Excessive Volatility 246
Market Efficiency and the Crash of 1987 247
Value Investing versus Efficient Markets 250
Costs of Inefficiency in Financial Markets 251
Costs of Excessive Price Fluctuations 251
Information Costs 252
Review Questions, Analytical Problems 256
Data Question 257
Consider this . . . Are Investors Really Rational? 242
Other times, other places . . . Charting the Civil War with the Gold Market 243
Case Study What Goes Up . . . 249
Moving from theory to practice . . . So, Is the Stock Market Overvalued?, *The Wall Street Journal*, 3/17/99 254

CHAPTER 11 Reducing Transactions Costs and Information Costs 258

Obstacles to Matching Savers and Borrowers 258
Transactions Costs 259
Asymmetric Information and Information Costs 260
Adverse Selection 260
"Lemons Problems" in Financial Markets 261
Reducing Information Costs 262
Moral Hazard 264
Moral Hazard in Equity Financing 264
Moral Hazard in Debt Financing 266
Information Costs and Financial Intermediaries 269
Financial Intermediaries and Adverse Selection 270
Financial Intermediaries and Moral Hazard 270
Review Questions 273
Analytical Problems, Data Question 276
Consider this . . . Are Stock Market Signals Affected by Adverse Selection? 265
Consider this . . . Can Falling Prices Raise Information Costs? 268
Other times, other places . . . Investor Protection and Economic Growth 271
Moving from theory to practice . . . On the Cutting Edge of Corporate Control in China, *The Economist*, 6/3/00 274

PART 4 Financial Institutions 277

CHAPTER 12 What Financial Institutions Do 278

Securities Market Institutions 279
Information: Investment Banking 280
Liquidity and Risk Sharing: Secondary Markets 282

Investment Institutions 285
Mutual Funds 285
Finance Companies 288
Contractual Saving: Insurance Companies 289
Principles of Insurance Management 289
Life Insurance Companies 292
Property and Casualty Insurance Companies 293
Regulation of Insurance Companies and Recent Trends 295
Contractual Saving: Pension Funds 295
Ownership of Pension Funds Assets 296
Funding of Pension Plans 297
Regulation of Private Pension Plans 297
Public Pension Plans 298
Recent Trends 298
Depository Institutions 299
Commercial Banks 299
Savings Institutions 300
Credit Unions 300
Government Financial Institutions 301
Direct Role: Federal Credit Agencies 301
Indirect Role: Loan Guarantees 305
Recent Trends 305
Financial Institutions: Blurring the Lines 305
Review Questions 310
Analytical Problems, Data Question 311
Using the news . . . A Tombstone for Something New? 283
Consider this . . . Can Investors Keep "Captives" at Bay? 291
Case Study What Kind of Financial Institution Is a Hedge Fund? 302
Case Study What Kind of Financial Institution Is a Venture Capital Fund? 303
Moving from theory to practice . . . Federal Credit Agencies: Is "Too Much" Lending Possible?, *The Wall Street Journal,* 7/14/00 308

CHAPTER 13 The Business of Banking 312

How Banks Earn Profits 313
Bank Liabilities 313
Bank Assets 316
Bank Net Worth 317
Bank Failure 317
Determining Bank Profits 318
The Relationship Between Banks and Savers 320
Managing Moral Hazard 321
Managing Liquidity Risk 323
The Relationship Between Banks and Borrowers 325
Managing Credit Risk 326
Managing Interest Rate Risk 330
Expanding the Boundaries of Banking 333
Opportunities and Financial Innovation 334
Off-Balance-Sheet Activities 334
Review Questions 342
Analytical Problems 343
Data Questions 344
Appendix: Measuring the Duration of Bank Assets and Liabilities 344
Consider this . . . How Do Banks Account for Loan Losses? 319
Consider this . . . When Is Credit-Risk Analysis "Discrimination"? 327

Consider this . . . Grading Bank Derivatives: Extra Credit? 338
Moving from theory to practice . . . Banking: "Clicks" or "Bricks"?, *The Economist,* 11/11/00 340

CHAPTER 14 The Banking Industry 346

Origins of Today's U.S. Banking Industry 347
Who Regulates Banks 348
Chartering and Examination 349
Regulating Commercial Banks 349
Regulating Savings Institutions 350
Regulating Credit Unions 350
Why the Banking Industry Is Regulated 351
Bank Runs 352
The Cost of a Bank Run 352
Government Intervention in the Banking Industry 354
Lender of Last Resort 355
Federal Deposit Insurance 356
Restrictions on Banking Industry Competition 361
The Banking Industry in Other Countries 368
Japanese Banking 371
German Banking 373
Integration of European Banking 374
Review Questions, Analytical Problems 378
Data Question 379
Other times, other places . . . Lessons from the Free Banking Period 348
Consider this . . . Is Bank Consolidation Good for Business? 362
Case Study Is Banking a Declining Industry? 369
Moving from theory to practice . . . The Bigger They Come . . . , *The Economist,* 10/28/00 376

CHAPTER 15 Banking Regulation: Crisis and Response 380

The Pattern of Regulation 381
Lender of Last Resort 381
The Great Depression 381
Success in Recent Years 383
Concluding Remarks 385
Anticompetitive Bank Regulation 385
The Credit Crunch of 1966 387
Banks' Response 387
Regulatory Response 389
Concluding Remarks 390
The U.S. Deposit Insurance Crisis of the 1980s 391
Beginning of the Crisis: Worsening Conditions in S&Ls 391
Financial System Response 391
Regulatory Response: The S&L Bailout 394
The Widening Crisis: Commercial Banks 395
Options for Regulatory Reform 397
Current Issues in Regulatory Reform 401
Concluding Remarks 402
Lessons from Banking Regulation for Other Institutions 404
Insurance Regulation 404
Pension Fund Regulation 405
Review Questions 408

Analytical Problems 409
Data Question 410
Consider this . . . How Does a Lender of Last Resort Protect the Payments System? 384
Other times, other places . . . The Cycle of Crisis and Response: Russia and Japan 403
Moving from theory to practice . . . Japanese Bank Reform, Vital to the Economy, Snags on Political Reef, *The Wall Street Journal*, 12/11/00 406

CHAPTER 16 Banking in the International Economy 411

Organization of International Banks 412
Overseas Organization of U.S. Banks 413
Organization of Foreign Banks in the United States 414
Leaders in Global Banking 415
Managing Exchange Rate Risk 415
Services Provided by International Banks 417
Reducing Transactions Costs 417
Providing Information Services 418
The Rise of Euromarkets 420
Euromarket Customers 422
Loans in Euromarkets 423
Financial Regulation in International Banking 424
Capital Requirements 425
Deposit Insurance 426
Central Bank Intervention 427
International Coordination 427
Review Questions 430
Analytical Problems, Data Question 431
Consider this . . . Why Did Closing BCCI Take So Long? 416
Consider this . . . Will Europe Kill the Eurobond? 423
Other times, other places . . . Do Sovereigns Default? 425
Moving from theory to practice . . . New Basle Committee Proposals, *The Financial Times*, 2/17/01 428

PART 5 The Money Supply Process and Monetary Policy 433

CHAPTER 17 The Money Supply Process 434

The Fed and the Monetary Base 435
The Fed's Liabilities 435
The Fed's Assets 436
How the Fed Changes the Monetary Base 437
Comparing Open Market Operations and Discount Loans 441
The Simple Deposit Multiplier 443
Multiple Deposit Expansion 443
Multiple Deposit Contraction 448
The Money Multiplier and Decisions of the Nonbank Public 450
Determinants of Portfolio Choice 450
Concluding Remarks 452
Bank Behavior: Excess Reserves and Discount Loans 453
Excess Reserves 454
Discount Loans 455
Deriving the Money Multiplier and the Money Supply 456

Review Questions 466
Analytical Problems 467
Data Question 469
Appendix: The Money Supply Process for *M2* 469
Consider this . . . What Are the Origins of Multiple Deposit Expansion? 445
Other times, other places . . . The Money Multiplier and Money Supply During the Early 1930s 459
Case Study Using the Money Supply Equation to Predict Money Growth 461
Moving from theory to practice . . . The Fed and the Monetary Base: Thwarting a Slowdown, *The New York Times,* 1/4/01 464

CHAPTER 18 Changes in the Monetary Base 471

Balance Sheet of the Federal Reserve System 471
The Fed's Assets 472
The Fed's Liabilities 473
Determining the Monetary Base 474
Changes in the Monetary Base 475
Determinants That Increase the Monetary Base 476
Determinants That Decrease the Monetary Base 479
Concluding Remarks 480
The Federal Budget Deficit and the Monetary Base 481
Alternative Strategies 483
The Government Budget Constraint and the Monetary Base 485
Review Questions, Analytical Problems 487
Data Questions 490
Using the news . . . Federal Reserve Data and Change in the Monetary Base 477
Other times, other places . . . Dealing with the Debt: The Treasury–Federal Reserve Accord 482
Moving from theory to practice . . . ECB Warns on Budget Deficits, *The Financial Times,* 3/18/99 488

CHAPTER 19 Organization of Central Banks 491

Power Sharing in the Federal Reserve System 492
Creation of the System 492
Federal Reserve Banks 493
Member Banks 495
Board of Governors 495
Federal Open Market Committee 496
Power and Authority Within the Fed 497
How the Fed Operates 498
Handling External Pressure 499
Examples of Treasury–Fed Conflict 500
Factors That Motivate the Fed 501
Fed Independence 503
Central Bank Independence in Other Countries 505
Organization and Independence of the European Central Bank 506
Review Questions, Analytical Problems 510
Data Questions 511
Consider this . . . Importance of Selecting a Fed Chairman 501
Other times, other places . . . Conflicts Between the Treasury and the Central Bank in Japan over Independence 504
Moving from theory to practice . . . The ECB's Terrible Twos, *The Economist,* 1/6/01 508

CHAPTER 20 Monetary Policy Tools 512

Open Market Operations 512
- Implementing Open Market Operations 513
- Open Market Operations versus Other Policy Tools 516
- Fed Watching and FOMC Directives 516
- Open Market Operations in Other Countries 517

Discount Policy 518
- Using the Discount Window 518
- Policing the Discount Window 519
- Benefits of Discount Policy 520
- Drawbacks of Discount Policy as a Monetary Policy Tool 522
- Discount Policy in Other Countries 522

Reserve Requirements 522
- Changes in Reserve Requirements 523
- Measurement and Compliance 524
- Criticism of Reserve Requirements 524
- Reserve Requirements in Other Countries 527

Fed Watching: Analyzing the Policy Tools 527
- The Federal Funds Market 527
- Open Market Operations 528
- Changes in the Discount Rate 529
- Changes in Reserve Requirements 529
- Other Disturbances of the Monetary Base 530
- The Federal Funds Rate and Monetary Policy 531
- Concluding Remarks 533

Review Questions 536
Analytical Problems 537
Data Question 538
Consider this . . . A Day's Work at the Open Market Trading Desk 515
Consider this . . . How Do You Decode FOMC Statements? 517
Other times, other places . . . An Early Mistake in Setting Reserve Requirements 526
Moving from theory to practice . . . Fed Rate Cut Combats a Contagion, *The Wall Street Journal,* 2/1/01 534

CHAPTER 21 The Conduct of Monetary Policy 539

Goals of Monetary Policy 539
- Price Stability 540
- High Employment 540
- Economic Growth 541
- Financial Market and Institution Stability 541
- Interest Rate Stability 542
- Foreign-Exchange Market Stability 542

Problems in Achieving Monetary Policy Goals 542
- Using Targets to Meet Goals 543
- Monetary Aggregates and Interest Rates as Targets 545
- Selecting Intermediate Targets 547
- Selecting Operating Targets 550

The Monetary Policy Record 550
- Early Interest in Targets: 1951–1970 551
- Experimenting with Monetary Targets: 1970–1979 552
- De-emphasizing Interest Rates: 1979–1982 553
- Policy After 1982: Back to Interest Rates 554

Increasing International Concerns: The 1980s and 1990s 556
Concluding Remarks 557
Reevaluating Fed Targeting Policy 557
Alternative Intermediate Targets 557
The Taylor Rule 558
The Future of Targeting 559
International Comparison of Monetary Policy Conduct 562
Review Questions 565
Analytical Problems, Data Question 568
Other times, other places . . . Does the Conduct of Monetary Policy Respond to Political Pressures? 556
Case Study Is Inflation Targeting a Good Idea? 560
Moving from theory to practice . . . The Chairman's Upbeat View, *The Wall Street Journal,* 2/14/01 566

CHAPTER 22 The International Financial System and Monetary Policy 569

Foreign-Exchange Intervention and the Money Supply 570
Foreign-Exchange Intervention and the Exchange Rate 572
Unsterilized Intervention 572
Sterilized Intervention 574
Capital Controls 575
Recent Fed Interventions 576
Balance of Payments 577
The Current Account 579
The Capital Account 580
The Official Settlements Balance 580
Relationships Among the Accounts 581
Exchange Rate Regimes and the International Financial System 582
Fixed Exchange Rates and the Gold Standard 582
Adapting Fixed Exchange Rates: The Bretton Woods System 584
Central Bank Intervention After Bretton Woods 591
Fixed Exchange Rates in Europe 593
How Successful Are Fixed Exchange Rates Likely to Be in the Long Run? 599
Review Questions 602
Analytical Problems 603
Data Questions 604
Case Study Do Sterilized Interventions Affect the Exchange Rate? 577
Using the news . . . The U.S. Balance of Payments 578
Consider this . . . Are the IMF and the World Bank Obsolete? 586
Other times, other places . . . Speculative Attack: 1990s Style 595
Case Study Financial Collapse in Mexico 596
Case Study Financial Collapse in Asia 597
Consider this . . . Back to the (Currency) Drawing Board 598
Moving from theory to practice . . . Central Banks Boost the Euro, *The Wall Street Journal,* 9/25/00 600

PART 6 The Financial System and the Macroeconomy 605

CHAPTER 23 The Demand for Money 606

Transactions Motives 606
Real Money Balances 607
Velocity and the Demand for Real Balances 608

Changes in Velocity over Time 609
Portfolio Allocation Motives 614
Motives for Holding Money: Keynes's Liquidity Preference Theory 615
Broader Portfolio Factors: Friedman's Money Demand Model 617
Comparing the Two Models: Keynes versus Friedman 617
Explaining Money Demand 618
The Money Demand Function 619
Measuring Money Demand 619
Review Questions 624
Analytical Problems 625
Data Question 626
Consider this . . . The Money Growth Slowdown in the Early 1990s: Was Velocity the Culprit? 610
Other times, other places . . . The Case of the Missing Money 621
Moving from theory to practice . . . A Legal Tender of One's Own, *The New York Times*, 1/30/01 622

CHAPTER 24 Linking the Financial System and the Economy: The *IS-LM-FE* Model 627

A Model for Goods and Asset Markets: Assumptions 628
The *IS* Curve 629
Saving, Investment, and Aggregate Demand 629
Determinants of National Saving 630
Determinants of National Investment 631
Constructing the *IS* Curve 632
The *IS* Curve for an Open Economy 634
Shifts of the *IS* Curve 636
Determining Output: The Full Employment Line 637
The *LM* Curve 639
Asset Market Equilibrium 640
Constructing the *LM* Curve 641
Shifts of the *LM* Curve 645
The Financial System and the Economy: The *IS-LM-FE* Model 647
Using the Model to Explain the Economy's Equilibrium 648
Restoring Equilibrium: Price-Level Adjustment 650
Money, Output, and Prices in the Long Run 652
Review Questions, Analytical Problems 656
Data Question 658
Appendix: Derivation of the *IS* Curve 659
Consider this . . . Are Savings Internationally Mobile? 636
Other times, other places . . . The Gulf War and "Confidence" 638
Moving from theory to practice . . . Productivity: The Magic Elixir, *The Wall Street Journal*, 2/15/01 654

CHAPTER 25 Aggregate Demand and Aggregate Supply 662

The Aggregate Demand Curve 662
Deriving the Aggregate Demand Curve 663
Shifts of the Aggregate Demand Curve 664
The Aggregate Supply Curve 668
Short-Run Aggregate Supply Curve 668
Long-Run Aggregate Supply Curve 674
Shifts in the Short-Run Aggregate Supply Curve 674
Shifts in the Long-Run Aggregate Supply Curve 675

Equilibrium in Aggregate Demand and Aggregate Supply 677
Short-Run Equilibrium 678
Long-Run Equilibrium 679
The Real Business Cycle View 680
Economic Fluctuations in the United States 681
Shocks to Aggregate Demand, 1964–1969 682
Supply Shocks, 1973–1975 and 1995–2000 682
Credit Crunch and Aggregate Demand, 1990–1991 683
Are Investment Incentives Inflationary? 684
Review Questions, Analytical Problems 685
Data Questions 689
Consider this . . . Do Tax Cuts Stimulate Aggregate Demand? 666
Other times, other places . . . Shock Therapy and Aggregate Supply in Poland 676
Consider this . . . Can Shifts in Aggregate Demand Affect Output in the Long Run? 679
Moving from theory to practice . . . Memo to Tokyo: Print Money, *The Financial Times*, 2/7/00 686

CHAPTER 26 Money and Output in the Short Run 690

Tracking Money and Output Movements in the Short Run 690
The Real Business Cycle Model 692
Money and Output: The New Classical Model 694
Money and Output: The New Keynesian Model 696
Should Public Policy Stabilize Economic Fluctuations? 700
The Real Business Cycle and New Classical Views 700
The New Keynesian View 701
Explaining Events of the 1980s and 1990s 704
Effects of Policy Shifts in the Early 1980s 705
Effects of Policy Shifts in the Early 1990s 706
Concluding Remarks 707
Review Questions 710
Analytical Problems 711
Data Questions 713
Consider this . . . Can One Size Fit All in Europe? 698
Case Study How Does Money Affect Aggregate Demand in the New Keynesian View? 699
Other times, other places . . . Yasushi Mieno and the Stabilization Policy Debate in Japan 703
Moving from theory to practice . . . Will the Fed Step on the Gas?, *The Financial Times*, 2/5/01 708

CHAPTER 27 Information Problems and Channels for Monetary Policy 714

Macroeconomic Costs of Information Problems 715
Information Problems in Lending: Role of Financial Intermediaries 716
Information Problems in Lending: Role of Net Worth 716
Consequences of a Drop in Bank Lending 717
Consequences of a Fall in Borrowers' Net Worth 718
Financial Panics 719
Credit Controls and Credit Crunches 720
Expanded Channels for Monetary Policy 722
The Money Channel: Monetary Policy and Interest Rates 722
The Bank Lending Channel: Monetary Policy and Banks 724
Money Channel and Bank Lending Channel Predictions 724
The Balance Sheet Channel: Monetary Policy and Net Worth 727
Validity of the Bank Lending and Balance Sheet Channels 729
Implications for Public Policy 733
Review Questions, Analytical Problems 737
Data Question 738

Other times, other places . . . The Global Banking Crisis and the Great Depression 721
Consider this . . . Was There a Credit Crunch During the 1990–1991 Recession? 732
Moving from theory to practice . . . A New Credit Crunch for Japan?, *The Financial Times,* 12/22/00 734

CHAPTER 28 Inflation: Causes and Consequences 739

Explaining Price Level Changes 739
- Causes of Price Level Changes 740
- Causes of Price Level Fluctuations 741
- Sustained Changes in the Price Level: Inflation 744

Costs of Inflation 746
- Expected Inflation 746
- Unexpected Inflation 747
- Inflation Uncertainty 748

Inflation and Monetary Policy 749
- Cost-Push Inflation 749
- Demand-Pull Inflation 750

Costs of Reducing Inflation 752
- New Classical Disinflation: Reducing Inflation Cold Turkey 752
- New Keynesian Disinflation: Reducing Inflation Gradually 753

Central Bank Credibility 754
- Strategies for Building Credibility 755
- Rules versus Discretion 758
- Price Controls and Credibility 760

Review Questions 761
Analytical Problems 764
Data Questions 765
Appendix: Inflation versus Unemployment: The Phillips Curve 766
Other times, other places . . . Central Bank Credibility in the United States and Japan 755
Consider this . . . Can Credibility Enhance Central Bank Flexibility? 759
Moving from theory to practice . . . Growth or Inflation?, *The New York Times,* 1/30/00 762

Glossary A-1
Answer Section A-17
Index A-39

About the Author

Currently the Chairman of President George W. Bush's Council of Economic Advisers, Russell L. Carson Professor of Economics and Finance at the Graduate School of Business, and Professor of Economics in the Department of Economics at Columbia University, Glenn Hubbard received his B.A. and B.S. from the University of Central Florida and A.M. and Ph.D. in economics from Harvard University, where he was honored with both National Science Foundation and Alfred P. Sloan Foundation fellowships. He served as deputy assistant secretary of the U.S. Treasury Department in Washington, D.C., during the administration of George H. W. Bush.

Hubbard has published numerous articles—on financial economics, public finance, macroeconomics, industrial organization, energy economics, and public policy—in such journals as *American Economic Review; Annales d'Economie et de Statistique; Brookings Papers on Economic Activity; European Economic Review; Journal of Banking and Finance; Journal of Business; Journal of Finance; Journal of Financial Economics; Journal of Industrial Economics; Journal of Law and Economics; Journal of Money, Credit, and Banking; Journal of Political Economy; Management Science; National Tax Journal; Quarterly Journal of Economics; Rand Journal of Economics;* and *Review of Economics and Statistics*. He has been a research consultant for the Federal Reserve Board, the Federal Reserve Bank of New York, the Internal Revenue Service, the Social Security Administration, the U.S. Department of the Treasury, the U.S. International Trade Commission, the National Science Foundation, and the World Bank. Hubbard has also advised numerous private financial institutions on developments in public policy and regulation.

He has also served as a visiting professor at Harvard's John F. Kennedy School of Government and Harvard Business School, as a John M. Olin Visiting Professor at the Graduate School of Business at the University of Chicago, and as a John M. Olin Fellow at the National Bureau of Economic Research, where he remains a research associate. He has also been a visiting scholar at the American Enterprise Institute.

Hubbard has also been honored with research grants from the National Bureau of Economic Research, the National Science Foundation, the U.S. Department of Energy, the Bradley Foundation, and the Institute for Fiscal Studies.

Hubbard, his wife Constance, and their sons Raph and Will live in New York City.

PART 1

Introduction

Part 1 provides the background you need to study money and the financial system. In this book, we use economic analysis to explain today's developments and predict tomorrow's developments. The three chapters in Part 1 introduce this economic approach to the major topics of the book. Chapter 1 describes the benefits of using an economic approach to studying money, financial market and institutions, and the economy. In Chapter 2, we see why modern economies use money, explain how money affects your decisions, and find easy sources of information about measures of money. Chapter 3 offers an overview of the role played by different elements of the financial system in matching savers and borrowers and providing risk-sharing, liquidity, and information services. Understanding these services will help you to see how the financial system has developed and how it will change in the future.

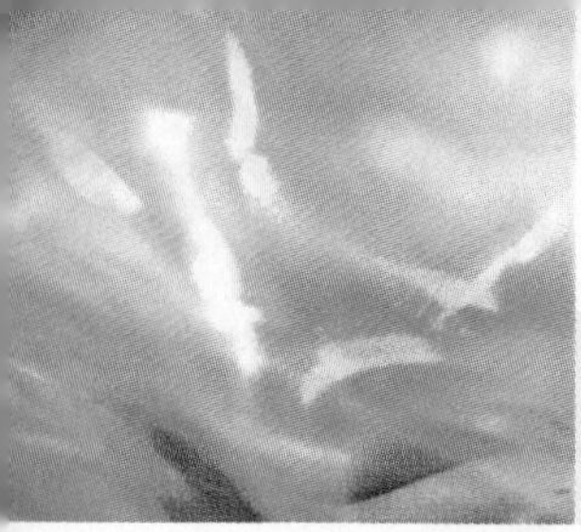

CHAPTER 1

Introducing Money and the Financial System

Investors around the world—from small savers to wealthy financiers, from local entrepreneurs and owners of small businesses to the leadership of Exxon and Nissan—were nervous about how financial markets were behaving. In late 1998, Russia was back in the news as the Evil Empire—not for military action but for defaulting on its debt. The Russian default added to the storm clouds caused by the Asian crisis that had begun with Thailand's currency woes in 1997. Stock markets in the United States and other major economies had a rocky second half of 1998. Foreign currency analysts worried about the emergence of the euro, the eventual common currency of the European monetary union, in 1999. Fears of a "credit crunch" on lending to small businesses in the United States as well as Asia were widespread. Investors, business managers, and policymakers shrugged off discussion of impeachment of embattled U.S. president Bill Clinton but wondered what lay ahead in the century's last election campaign. The financial media were full of suggestions for reform of the country's banking system, and big bank mergers made headlines. Editorial writers and pundits regularly discussed what the Federal Reserve System, the U.S. central bank, should do about the nation's money supply and what the President and the new Congress should (and could) do about a budget surplus and reform of the country's tax system.

The extensive media coverage of financial system events—prices of stocks and bonds, the health of the banks, what the Federal Reserve chairman did or didn't say—reflects the influence of money and the financial system on the U.S. economy and other economies around the world. Financial markets react to the performance of the economy and the changes in fortunes of individual businesses, and changes in financial markets determine the rewards to savers and borrowers—and the ability of individuals to achieve wealth and prosperity. Using economic tools, we analyze changes observed in the past and use this information to predict future changes in the financial system. Understanding the workings of financial markets and financial institutions within the financial system will help you interpret current events, predict future developments, and make better-informed decisions as a consumer, saver, borrower, or business manager. You also will learn to use some economic ideas, principles, and models to make sense of complex and, at times, confusing news accounts, reports, and statistics.

We begin our investigation by introducing the financial system and the role of money in the economy. We also describe the economic tools used to analyze the behavior observed in the financial system.

GETTING STARTED

In this chapter, we introduce five topics that are important to economists, businesspeople, policymakers, and individuals making their own financial decisions. First, we describe briefly how the financial system and the economy are connected in the United States and around the world. Second, we examine the role played in the financial system by **financial markets,** which are markets for buying and selling bonds, stocks, foreign exchange, and other financial instruments. Third, we consider the functions of **financial institutions,** such as banks or insurance companies, which are the go-betweens for savers and borrowers. Fourth, we identify ways in which money influences economic variables that affect our daily lives, such as economic activity, prices, and interest rates. Fifth, we introduce an economic approach that offers a roadmap for interpreting today's information and decisions and that can help you predict future events and the effects those events can have on your own decisions. We focus on tools for analyzing information and making decisions rather than on just describing the mechanics of money, the financial system, and the economy. In particular, we help you develop the tools necessary for answering questions such as the following and applying the answers in making your own decisions.

- Why should you care about money? Are changes in the money supply responsible for booms and busts in the economy?
- What does the financial system do?
- How are interest rates determined?
- Why do banks and other financial institutions exist? How do they affect your financial decisions?
- Should financial markets and institutions be regulated? Who wins and who loses from financial regulation?
- What causes inflation?
- Living in a global economy, what do you need to know as a saver and a borrower about financial developments outside the United States?

THE FINANCIAL SYSTEM AND THE ECONOMY

The massive changes in Eastern Europe and the former Soviet Union in the late 1980s and early 1990s startled even geopolitical experts. The sudden collapse of a system in which the government decided how much people would save, how many goods businesses would produce, and how much workers would be paid left those economies in a vacuum. For example, how would individuals invest their savings? How would consumers borrow to buy new cars and homes? Who would decide which business enterprises should be funded and for how much?

Those Eastern European countries are engaged in a struggle to create a **financial system,** a network of markets and institutions to bring savers and borrowers together. In the U.S. economy and the economies of other industrialized countries, the financial system already brings savers and borrowers together. Consider how the financial system works for you. At some points in your life, you will be a saver. You may want to put aside some of your income to buy a new car, to finance your retirement, or to pay for your children's education. Through the financial system, you can save by opening bank accounts, purchasing mutual funds, or buying stocks. At other points in your life, you will be a borrower, spending more than you currently have. You may borrow to buy a house, to open a business, or to buy that car now instead of saving for it. Most individuals who are borrowers take out loans from financial institutions—major players in the financial system. Without the financial system, you would be stuck trying to make the most of the funds you had on hand and didn't spend, and you would be restricted to purchases that you could buy for cash.

The three groups of potential savers and borrowers in an economy are households, businesses, and governments. The financial system transfers savers' funds to borrowers and provides savers with payments for the use of their funds. The financial system achieves this transfer by creating IOUs known as **financial instruments,** which are assets for savers and liabilities for (claims on) borrowers. A familiar example of a financial instrument is a car loan, which is a liability for you—you owe money to the bank—and an asset for the bank—it owns the right to receive future payments from you.

As an individual saver, you could seek out potential borrowers yourself, but that would be cumbersome and costly. For example, suppose you wanted to lend someone money to buy a car. How could you locate such a person? Would you advertise that you were willing to lend a potential car buyer $10,000? How would you be sure that the lender could repay your loan or that you could ask for repayment suddenly if you found you needed the money? Instead, it is much easier and cheaper to save your money in a bank account and let the bank act as your go-between by making loans to worthy car buyers.

Funds can be transferred between savers and borrowers in several ways. One option is for the government to allocate funds among the sectors of the economy. The recent experiences of Eastern Europe and the former Soviet Union demonstrated the folly of this approach. In the U.S. economy and other industrial economies, private networks in the financial system generally channel funds between savers and borrowers.

Savers and borrowers use the financial system because each gets something in return: Borrowers can use savers' funds productively until the savers themselves need the funds, and borrowers are willing to pay savers for that privilege. Moreover, the financial system provides three key **financial services:** risk sharing, liquidity, and information.

Risk is the degree of uncertainty of an asset's return. Most people do not gamble with their savings, seeking a relatively steady return on their assets as a whole. When they borrow, they also want the cost of borrowing to be predictable. The financial system provides **risk sharing** by giving savers and borrowers ways to reduce the uncertainty to which they are exposed.

Second, most people care about how easily they can exchange their assets for cash. **Liquidity** is a measure of how readily one asset can be converted to cash. If you used all your savings to buy a plot of land in Arizona, you might find it difficult to sell the land quickly if you needed money to fix your car or pay your tuition, because land is not a liquid asset. The financial system enables people to convert their savings to such liquid assets as checking accounts, stocks, and bonds.

Finally, the financial system gathers and communicates **information** about borrowers' circumstances so that individual savers do not have to search out prospective borrowers. In this way, the financial system allocates funds efficiently because it reduces the cost of information in matching savers with borrowers.

Delivery of these three key services helps to explain how the financial system has developed and how it will likely change in the future. Changes in the financial system may well affect your opportunities to save or borrow or even your career choices.

The financial system is a relatively small but important source of jobs and income for the U.S. economy and other major economies. By 2000, the U.S. financial system accounted for almost 22% of the economy's value added (GDP). As did the United States, most other major economies experienced an increase in the contribution of the financial services sector to employment and value added, though the sector's relative importance varies across countries. In addition, jobs in the financial services sector pay relatively well. Averaging much higher than the national average, the pay in the financial services sector is better than the average in wholesale and retail trade, manufacturing, agriculture, mining, construction, and government. New jobs in financial markets and institutions are highly sought by college graduates and business school students.

The financial system matches savers and borrowers and provides risk-sharing, liquidity, and information services through two channels: financial markets and financial institutions. In this chapter we briefly describe the workings of these two channels. You will learn more about both as you read on in this text.

Financial Markets

Events in the world of high finance in the fall of 1997 and into 1998 resembled a thriller novel. Confusion seemed to dominate international financial markets. As Asian currencies sank in foreign-exchange markets, the U.S.

OTHER TIMES, OTHER PLACES . . .

The Only Thing Constant in the Financial System Is Change

The pace of change in the activities of financial intermediaries accelerated in the 1980s, 1990s, and early 2000s. As recently as 1979, when I was an undergraduate student in money and banking, small savers could invest in a checking account (which paid no interest) and passbook savings accounts (which paid a low rate of interest limited by regulation). Higher-yielding Treasury bonds and corporate bonds were available only in large denominations to wealthy savers. By contrast, by the late 1990s, financial intermediaries offered an array of products with market yields for small savers, including money market mutual funds and interest-bearing checking accounts. These new products were the result of financial innovation by, and competition among, banks and other financial intermediaries.

In 1979, government tightly regulated the lines of business of banks and other financial intermediaries. However, the pace of competitive innovation by financial intermediaries has led to calls for major changes in regulation. Understanding the risk-sharing, liquidity, and information services provided by intermediaries helps in understanding the types of regulation needed and predicting how those intermediaries will respond to new regulation. Because the pace of change in the financial system is so rapid, that understanding provides a way to assess developments in financial intermediaries in order to analyze new financial products, to get a job in the financial services industry, or to be informed about investment opportunities.

dollar and German mark rose. Stock prices fluctuated around the world, and interest rates on bonds rose and fell as traders, bankers, and finance ministers tried to maintain stability. Also, the 1980s and 1990s were volatile times in financial markets in the United States. In financial markets, interest rates on bonds, stock prices, and the value of the U.S. dollar relative to other currencies fluctuated significantly. To understand the roller-coaster behavior of domestic and global financial markets, you need to understand the role that financial markets play in the economy and what movements in financial markets tell savers and borrowers.

Financial markets such as the stock and bond markets are one arena in which savers' surpluses are transferred to borrowers. Savers can buy stocks and bonds. Business borrowers can obtain funds by issuing stocks and bonds. Moreover, financial markets extend beyond any single country's borders. Indeed, the **international capital market**—that is, the market for lending and borrowing across national boundaries—grew rapidly during the past 20 years. In addition to helping businesses and governments around the world raise funds, financial markets communicate important information through the prices of financial assets. In Parts 2 and 3, we show how interest rates, stock prices, and exchange rates are determined and can influence decisions by individuals and managers. As an individual, should you buy a U.S. Treasury bond or invest in a new business? As a manager, should your company build a new factory?

CONSIDER THIS . . .

Is the Financial System Truly Global?

Although an international capital market for certain types of lending has existed for centuries, analysts point to the 1980s and 1990s as a time when the greatest number of boundaries seperating national financial markets in the United States, Europe, Japan, and emerging economies dissolved. These changes mean that the money in your savings account might go to help finance a new factory in Germany. They also mean that your job prospects may depend as much on movements in the Japanese stock market or actions of the German central bank as on events in the United States.

Three trends toward globalization are of interest. First, business is global: At the end of the 1990s, the global investment in the stock of some 35,000 multinational corporations exceeded $2 trillion. Second, financial markets are global: During the 1980s, the volume of worldwide cross-border transactions in stocks and bonds grew at an annual rate of 28%. Finally, lending is global: During the 1980s and 1990s international bank lending grew more than 20-fold. Throughout this book, you will encounter reasons for those developments and what they mean for households, businesses, and governments and for U.S. banks and financial markets.

Financial Institutions

Every day, people lend money to a large number of borrowers, including the U.S. government, IBM, the local hardware store, or their neighbors, without even knowing it. They approach these borrowers not directly through financial markets, but indirectly through financial institutions that act as intermediaries. **Financial intermediaries** are institutions such as commercial banks, credit unions, savings and loan associations, mutual savings banks, mutual funds, finance companies, insurance companies, and pension funds that borrow and pool funds from savers and lend them to borrowers. When you deposit money in a savings account, the bank can lend it to a local business. Similarly, when you contribute to a pension plan, the fund managers invest your retirement savings in shares of Mitsubishi, U.S. Treasury bonds, or other financial instruments.

Problems in financial institutions have been big news in the United States, particularly the deposit insurance crisis in the 1980s and early 1990s, a debacle that seemed so familiar during Japan's banking crisis in the late 1990s and early in the new century. The eventual cost to taxpayers for the U.S. crisis is estimated to be as high as $150 billion; estimates for Japan are even higher. The U.S. crisis led to bank regulatory reforms, the effects of which are the subject of vigorous political debate. Some of these regulation reforms have facilitated an unprecedented consolidation of the U.S. banking industry, with megabank mergers making headlines. Another controversy has arisen over whether other financial institutions, especially pension funds, insurance companies, and mutual funds, may also be heading for financial crises that would require even more tax dollars to resolve.

Why should you study the role of financial institutions as intermediaries between savers and borrowers? After all, you hear and read much more about the bond market and the stock market daily. Despite their visibility, the bond and stock markets are not the most important means for businesses to raise money. Figure 1.1 shows that during the 1970s, 1980s, and 1990s, new stock issues accounted for only about 2% of funds raised externally by firms (that is, funds raised over and above firms' own profits). Bonds account for more of the funds raised externally but still account for only about 30%. The majority of funds that borrowers raise—nearly two-thirds—comes from loans from banks and other financial institutions. Households also raise most of the funds they borrow through financial institutions. This role for financial institutions as go-betweens for savers and borrowers is true not only in the United States but also in most industrialized countries.

As you study financial institutions in Part 4, you will learn why they play such a major role in the financial system. In this book we emphasize the activities of banks for two reasons: (1) They are the largest financial intermediaries, and (2) they lend to many sectors of the economy, including households and small and medium-sized businesses. In particular, we describe what goes on in the business of banking, how and why banks are regulated by the government, and why the banking industry went through a crisis and transformation in the 1980s and 1990s. Our economic analysis explains how banks and other financial institutions provide risk-sharing, liquidity, and information services to savers and borrowers. Our analysis also addresses how and why banks and other financial institutions compete with one another and what consequences that competition brings for the financial system, savers and borrowers, and the economy.

MONEY

Throughout 1998, the Federal Reserve made headlines. Some commentators blamed the Fed for cutting interest rates too slowly that year, thereby slowing

Figure 1.1

Sources of Funds for Nonfinancial Businesses: Markets versus Institutions

Most external funds raised by nonfinancial businesses are loans from financial institutions (mainly banks), with far less reliance on funds raised through bond and stock issues in financial markets. Data are averaged for 1970–2000.

Source: Board of Governors of the Federal Reserve System, *Flow of Funds Accounts*, various issues.

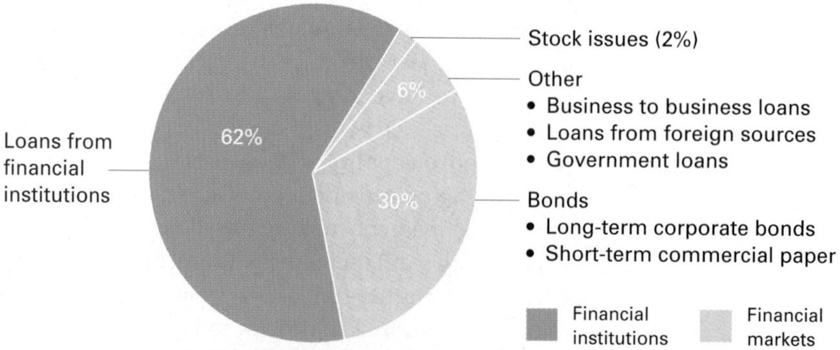

the fall in the cost of loans to purchase homes, cars, and business investment goods. Others praised the Fed for its concern about inflation. Interest rates and inflation are among many economic variables tied to changes in the money supply, a key topic in this book.

To understand these events, the Fed's actions and their consequences, and the impact of changes in the money supply on the economy, we need to start with a few definitions. **Money** is anything that people are willing to accept in payment for goods and services or to pay off debts. The **money supply** is the total quantity of money in the economy. The **Federal Reserve System** (often called the **Fed**) collects data on various measures of the money supply, and it is the central bank in the United States.

Talk about money is prominent in the news media, in which reports of changes in the money supply are reported with fanfare. The reason is that such changes are associated with current and future changes in economic variables, including the economy's output of goods and services. These changes have an impact on your daily life, affect the prices you pay for goods and services, and determine the interest rates you earn on savings or pay on borrowed funds.

As individuals or managers, we want to predict movements in economic variables. Because money supply movements are associated with movements in many economic variables, many private analysts focus their attention on predicting changes in the money supply. They are not the only ones; government policymakers and the Fed actively try to manage the quantity of money. **Monetary policy** refers to the management of the money supply and its links to prices, interest rates, and other economic variables. In Part 5, we show that the Federal Reserve System, banks, businesses, and consumers together are responsible for determining the money supply. Nonetheless, the Fed is the most influential of those responsible. We give you the basic tools of Fed watching so that you can predict changes in the money supply and their effects on variables that concern you as an investor, businessperson, or interested student of current events.

In Part 6, we focus on **monetary theory**, which explores the relationships linking changes in the money supply to changes in economic activity and prices. In discussing monetary theory in this book, we also examine the ways in which changes in the health of financial intermediaries, especially banks, affect economic activity. Many analysts believe, for example, that a collapse in bank lending worsened the U.S. economic downturn in the early 1990s; fears of a credit crunch also surfaced during the Asian financial crisis in 1998.

ECONOMIC ANALYSIS AS A TOOL

To organize your thoughts as you study the financial system and money and to see the relationships among the variables we introduce, we use economic analysis as a tool. Economic analysis allows you to (1) *explain* current developments or events and (2) *predict* future developments or events.

Developing an Economic Approach

The following example demonstrates how economic analysis helps you develop a framework for explaining and predicting. Suppose that you want to explain why graduates of your college or university choose a particular mix of careers; that is, you want to determine what influences students to major in law, medicine, business, engineering, or teaching. You know that income is not the only factor explaining career choice. Some individuals choose a career on the basis of the years of schooling needed to qualify for an entry-level job, opportunities for self-fulfillment, or other nonmonetary aspects. Even though real-world decisions are complex, a simple model based on key assumptions can identify reasons for an individual's choice. You can determine how appropriate your assumption that income motivates career choice is by *testing* it—that is, by comparing its predictions to actual data. To develop a simple model, you need to focus on a few key factors. You could start, for example, by theorizing that graduates choose the careers that offer the greatest incomes; that is, if lawyers' incomes rise relative to incomes in other fields, a greater proportion of your school's graduates will enter the field of law.

To start your investigation, you must collect data. From your college alumni office, you can learn the proportion of graduates entering different careers along with information on average income by career. You can compare your theory—that the careers with the highest incomes in a given year should attract the greatest percentage of students—to the actual data. If the data match your theory, the theory is reasonable.

If the data confirm your theory, you have a way of *explaining* current career choices and *predicting* how those choices will evolve as relative incomes of different careers change. If the data from the alumni office do not support your theory, you will have to modify your idea. Perhaps income does influence career choice but cannot explain more than, say, half the actual choices. To investigate further, you must decide whether to make additional assumptions, leading to a more complicated theory, or to settle for simplicity.

How useful is the theory on which you settle? Three criteria can help you assess its usefulness: (1) Are your assumptions reasonable? (2) Does the theory generate predictions that you can verify with actual data? (3) Are the predictions actually corroborated by the data? For a successful theory, the answer to all three questions is yes. Does that mean that there can be only one successful theory for any problem? No. You and other analysts might differ in your assumptions or in evaluating how well your theory stood up to testing. You will discover that economists sometimes differ in their views of the best theory to explain a particular problem or predict a particular event.

Applying an Economic Approach

Developing theories and testing them is the way we use economic analysis to study money, financial markets, and financial institutions in this book. Economic analysis does not have to mean pages of mathematical formulas.

Usually, it simply means organizing a study by setting out what you want to explain (the problem), how you believe it can be explained (the theory), and what actual information, events, and data say about your interpretation (the test). Let's consider three examples of applying an economic approach that are developed later in this book.

1. One reason to study the bond market in a course on money, financial markets, and financial institutions is to understand how interest rates are determined. In Part 2, the economic analysis of interest rate determination focuses on decisions that savers and borrowers make in the bond market. The theory identifies factors that determine the demand for and supply of bonds in order to explain interest rates. We then analyze information about those factors to explain, for example, why interest rates were higher in the early 1980s than in 2001 or why the interest rate on a 30-year General Motors bond is greater than that on a 30-year U.S. Treasury bond. The analysis also allows prediction, for example, of the likely effects on U.S. interest rates from a Japanese decision to spend tens of billions of dollars to rebuild Japan's highways, bridges, and schools.

2. Earlier in this chapter, we noted that the financial system consists of financial markets and institutions that bring savers and borrowers together and provide financial services. In Chapter 3 and in more detail in Part 4, we develop a theory that explains the activities of financial markets and institutions. The theory combines two ideas: (1) savers' and borrowers' desire for risk-sharing, liquidity, and information services and (2) differences in the cost of providing those services in different markets and institutions. We confirm the theory with observations about the activities of actual financial markets and institutions. This use of economic analysis helps to predict how financial markets and institutions adapt to changing conditions in the United States. It also helps to explain why financial systems are organized differently in different countries.

3. We noted that movements in the growth rate of the money supply are often associated with movements in the growth rate of the economy's output, inflation, and interest rates. In Part 6, we evaluate simple theories of these relationships to determine whether their prediction is consistent with actual economic events in the United States and other countries. With a reasonable theory in hand, what information should you look for to forecast changes in the money supply, the economy's output, inflation, and interest rates?

KEY TERMS AND CONCEPTS

Financial institutions
Financial instruments
Financial intermediaries
Financial markets
Financial services
- Information
- Liquidity
- Risk sharing

Financial system
International capital market
Monetary theory
Money
- Federal Reserve System (Fed)
- Money supply
- Monetary policy

SUMMARY

1. The financial system brings together savers and borrowers by channeling funds from savers to borrowers while giving savers claims on borrowers' future income. The financial system also provides three key services for the benefit of savers and borrowers: risk sharing, liquidity, and information.
2. Financial markets match savers and borrowers, and prices of financial assets in those markets affect the financial and spending decisions of individuals and businesses, and the efficiency of the U.S. and global economies.
3. Financial intermediaries are institutions that borrow funds from savers and lend them to borrowers, providing risk-sharing, liquidity, and information services in the process. The principal types of financial intermediaries are commercial banks, credit unions, savings and loan associations, mutual savings banks, mutual funds, finance companies, insurance companies, and pension funds. Competitive innovation by banks and other intermediaries has changed the way these institutions do business.
4. Money is anything that someone is willing to accept in payment for goods and services or to pay off debts. In the United States, measures of the money supply are calculated and published by the Federal Reserve. Households, businesses, and governments are interested in movements in the money supply because those movements are associated with changes in important economic variables, including the economy's output, the price level, inflation, and interest rates.

REVIEW QUESTIONS

1. Could a central planning agency allocate funds between savers and borrowers more efficiently than many different financial institutions can? Explain.
2. Why are financial instruments like IOUs? Explain why financial instruments are assets for savers but liabilities for borrowers.
3. What are the three main services offered by financial institutions? Describe each briefly.
4. Who determines the money supply? Who determines monetary policy?
5. Why is monetary theory important? Why should policymakers at the Federal Reserve System understand monetary theory? Why should you understand monetary theory?

ANALYTICAL PROBLEMS

6. Why do most people want to reduce the risk involved in holding a financial asset? Suppose you own a financial asset that you expect about half the time will yield a return of 5% and about half the time will yield a return of 15%. Would you prefer to own this asset or another asset on which you would always receive a 10% return? Explain your reasoning.
7. Why might you lend money to individuals and businesses in your city through a local bank rather than directly?
8. Suppose that the government prohibited banks from paying interest on checking account deposits. What would you do with the funds in your checking account? What might your bank try to do?
9. Suppose that monetary policy induces a recession (economic downturn) in the United States. How might the economies of Germany or France be affected?
10. What do you think would happen to the economy if new regulations prevented banks from making as many loans to businesses as they previously did? What would the firms try to do in response?

DATA QUESTION

11. In *The Wall Street Journal,* find today's interest rate on three-month Treasury bills. What do you think the interest rate is likely to be in one year? In five years? Now look in the latest *Economic Report of the President* and find a table listing interest rates on three-month Treasury bills for the past several decades. Note how high the interest rate is in some years and how low it is in other years. Do you feel comfortable with your forecast now?

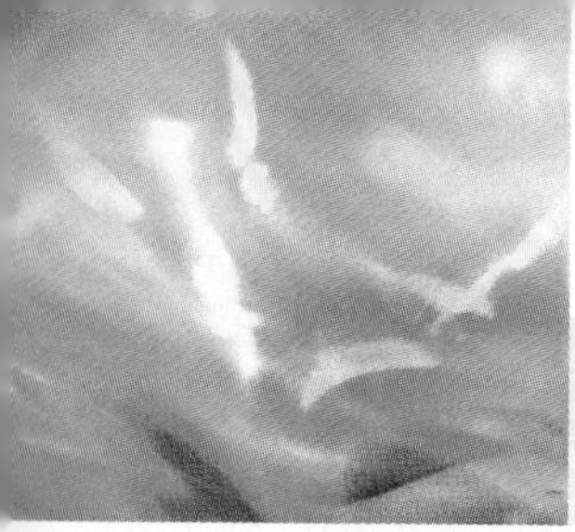

CHAPTER 2

Money and the Payments System

When you hear the word "money," do you conjure up images of cash stacked from floor to ceiling in a bank vault, coins cascading from a slot machine, or a $1 million check presented to a lottery winner? The cash and the check are money—but to an economist, the concept of money includes even more. Whether you are a miser, you like to shop 'til you drop, or you fall somewhere between those extremes, you are undoubtedly familiar with money and its benefits. But to study money, you must know what it is, what it does, and how it is measured. Those are the objectives of this chapter.

Consider how complicated and costly it would be to buy and sell goods and services if each state in the United States had its own money. Worse yet, what if no one could agree on what to use as money? Now imagine how much easier traveling from England to France to Germany to Italy—countries that have used different currencies—would be if each country used the same currency. European countries have been moving toward such a monetary union because many economists argue that the gains from such a union would be significant. The union would eliminate the costs of converting currency in commercial and financial transactions and would unify the European market. The euro—the common currency—made its debut in January 1999, though it had a rough time in its early years.

This example illustrates one use of money that we explore in this chapter: as a vehicle for improving trade between individuals and the well-being of citizens in an economy. To observe the impact of money on the economy, we need to know precisely what money is. Therefore, after describing money and functions, we turn to measures of all the money in the economy—the *money supply*. Movements in the money supply are associated with changes in interest rates, inflation, and output—variables that are of concern to us as households or businesses.

MEETING THE NEEDS OF EXCHANGE WITH MONEY

Money is an integral part of all modern economies. Why? A partial answer is that money allows the economy to operate more efficiently and hence improves the standard of living. To see why this is so, consider what life would be like without money.

In economies in early stages of development, most individuals are self-sufficient. They grow their own food, build their own homes, and make their own clothes and tools. Such societies do not prosper greatly because, in doing everything, an individual does some tasks well and does others poorly.

In more developed economies, individuals rely on **specialization,** producing the goods or services for which they have relatively the best ability. Individuals then *exchange,* or trade the goods or services they produce for those they need. If a furniture maker trades with a boat builder, they produce more and better furniture and boats than if each produced both with no exchange. Moreover, by encouraging production and higher-quality goods—and thus income—an economy's allowance for specialization and trade increases its citizens' standard of living. To reap the benefits of specialization, an economy must develop ways for individuals to exchange goods with one another. Then each person can obtain all the goods he or she needs, or wants, to consume. We next examine three options that societies have developed to meet the needs of trade: barter, government allocation, and the use of money.

Barter

Individuals can exchange goods and services by trading output directly with others. This type of exchange is called **barter.** For example, the furniture maker could trade chairs for a bushel of wheat. The furniture maker and farmer might agree that the price of eight chairs is three bushels of wheat. In a barter system, each such potential trade requires a price to be set in terms of the two goods.

Although individuals can specialize and be better off in a barter economy than in an economy without specialization, this system has several drawbacks. First, effort must be spent searching for trading partners—a type of **transactions cost,** or cost of trade or exchange. A second drawback is that each good has many prices. The furniture maker might be able to exchange eight chairs for three bushels of wheat, ten chairs for a boat, or a table for a wagon. This problem is akin to reading a recipe in which the amounts of some ingredients are in ounces, others in pounds, others in grams, others in liters, and so on. Baking a loaf of bread would take days! In addition, the prices are often inconsistent. One furniture store might quote the price of one type of chair as 100 pens, another as 500 eggs, and still another as 20 movie tickets. Needless to say, you would have to think hard about how to make informed decisions about which is the best buy! A barter economy with only 100 goods would have 4950 prices; one with 10,000 goods would have 49,995,000 prices.[†]

A third complication arises from lack of standardization: A chair and a sack of wheat can vary substantially in quality and size. A fourth drawback is that each individual must have exactly the good that the other wants for the exchange to take place—a situation that economists call a *double coincidence of wants.* Suppose the boat maker wants to buy wine from a wine maker but

[†]These calculations are based on the formula for telling us how many prices we need with N goods—that is, the number of prices when there are N items: Number of prices = $N(N-1)/2$.

the wine maker does not want a boat. Will exchange take place? The wine maker could accept the boat for a lower value than that offered by the boat maker and try to trade it to someone else. The wine maker's willingness to do so depends on whether other traders accept boats in payment for their goods. Finally, imagine the difficulty of storing value when goods are perishable. Tomatoes are valuable in exchange only when they are fresh, for example.

Government Allocation

Another option is to sidestep voluntary trade and use **government allocation** to distribute goods and services. In this system, a central authority collects the specialized output of each individual producer and distributes it to others according to some plan. Although such a system may seem simpler than barter, it is not likely to prove useful in a changing economy (even if the authority could make everyone happy initially). Shifts in the costs of producing individual goods and services or in the value that consumers place on different goods and services will not be reflected in the amount of goods and services allocated to each individual. Ignoring market forces reduces incentives to produce and leaves consumers unhappy with the goods and services they receive. The collapse of economic systems in Eastern Europe and the former Soviet Union during the late 1980s and early 1990s demonstrated that government allocation of goods and services did not successfully replace a market system.

Money

How can people benefit from specialization without incurring the high trading costs of barter or the misallocations associated with government allocation? They can use **money.** Money eliminates the need for people to have a double coincidence of wants. Money has four key functions that make it the most efficient means of trade:

1. It acts as a medium of exchange.
2. It is a unit of account.
3. It is a store of value.
4. It offers a standard of deferred payment.

As Fig. 2.1 shows, the use of money makes it easier for people to trade with one another.

Medium of exchange. **Money** refers to anything that is generally accepted as payment for goods and services or in the settlement of debts, also called the **medium of exchange**. For example, *currency,* such as bills and coins, is one type of money. The amount of food you can buy at Burger King or Pizza Hut is usually limited by the amount of cash you have in your pocket. For many purchases, however, currency is too narrow a definition of acceptable money. You can probably buy books at your local bookstore by writing a check, for example.

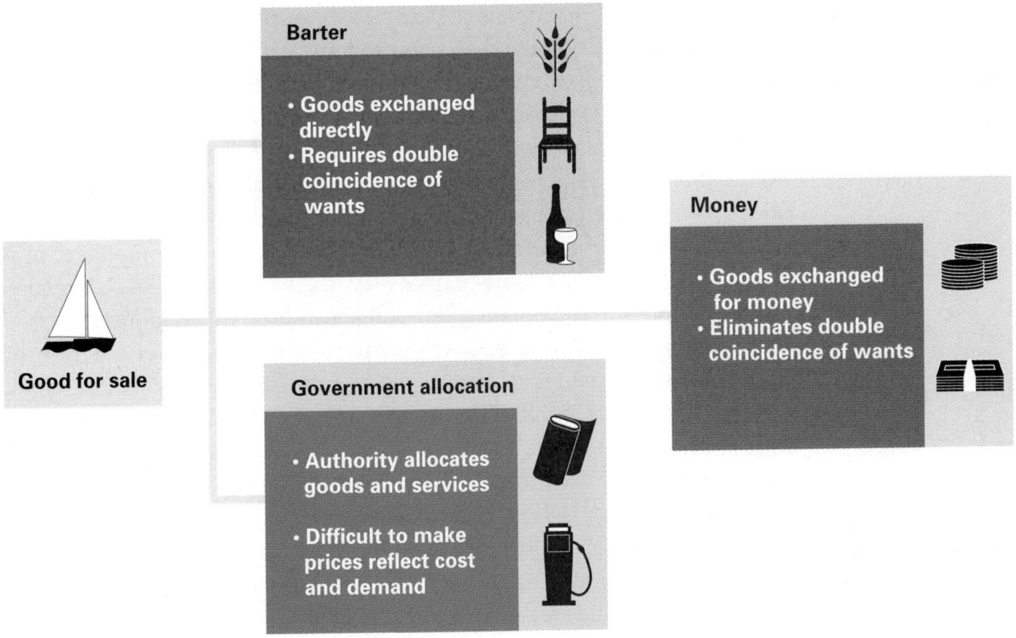

Figure 2.1

Methods of Exchange

Society has developed three methods to gain the efficiency benefits of specialization: barter, government allocation, and the use of money. Money facilitates trade best by being accepted as a medium of exchange.

To go back to our earlier example, the furniture maker would not have to want wheat, and the farmer would not have to want a chair. Both would exchange their products for money. Suppose that a boat maker values gold because other traders do not want to trade their goods for boats. The boat maker would probably give a furniture maker a better deal on a boat if the furniture maker paid in gold instead of chairs. In the same way, if a single good, such as gold, were accepted by many individuals with specialized goods to sell, all would get a better deal in trade. Thus society achieves greater prosperity when a single good is recognized as a medium of exchange.

Unit of account. Using a good as a medium of exchange confers another benefit: It reduces the need to quote so many different prices in trade. Instead of having to quote the price of a single good in terms of many other goods, each good has a single price quoted in terms of the medium of exchange. This function of money gives traders a **unit of account,** a way of measuring value in the economy in terms of money. When an economy uses a commodity such as gold, then each good (such as wheat, chairs, and boats) has a price in terms of gold.

Store of value. Money allows value to be stored easily, resulting in a **store of value:** If you do not use all your accumulated dollars to buy goods and services today, you can hold the rest for future use. In fact, a fisherman and a farmer would be better off maintaining their wealth in money rather than in inventories of their perishable goods. The acceptability of money in future transactions depends on its not losing value over time as its freshness deteriorates.

Hence money is also an **asset,** or a thing of value that can be owned. We often say that individuals in *Forbes* magazine's list of richest Americans have a lot of money. We don't really mean that they have a lot of currency in their pockets (or hidden away in their mansions or yachts) but that they own valuable assets, such as stocks, bonds, or houses. Money, like other assets, is a component of **wealth,** which is the sum of the value of assets less the value of liabilities. However, only if an asset serves as a medium of exchange can it be called money.

Although *wealth* and *income* (the flow of earnings over a period of time) are important measures of value, we do not use these terms interchangeably with *money* in this book. That is, the amount of money an individual has is represented by the stock of currency and currency substitutes (such as checking account deposits or traveler's checks) owned, not by the stock of wealth or a monthly or yearly salary or flow of income.

Money is not the only store of value. Any asset—shares of General Motors stock, Treasury bonds, real estate, or Renoir paintings, for example—represents a store of value. Indeed, financial assets offer an important benefit relative to holding money because they generally pay a higher rate of interest or offer the prospect of gains in value. Other assets (such as a house) also have advantages relative to money, as they provide services (such as a place to sleep).

Why, then, would you bother to hold any money? The answer goes back to *liquidity,* or the ease with which a given asset can be converted into the medium of exchange. When money is the medium of exchange, it is the most liquid asset. You incur transactions costs when you exchange other assets for money. When you sell bonds or shares of stock to buy a car, for example, you pay a commission to your broker. If you have to sell your house on short notice to finance an unexpected major medical expense, you pay a commission to a real estate agent and probably have to accept a lower price to exchange the house for money quickly. To avoid such transactions costs, people are willing to hold some of their wealth in the form of money, even though other assets offer a greater return as a store of value.

Standard of deferred payment. Money is also useful because of its ability to serve as a **standard of deferred payment** in credit transactions. Money can facilitate exchange at a *given point in time* by providing a medium of exchange and unit of account. It can facilitate exchange *over time* by providing a store of value and standard of deferred payment. Hence a furniture maker may be willing to sell the boat builder a chair now in exchange for money in the future.

How important is it that money be a reliable store of value and standard of deferred payment? People care about how much food, clothing, and other goods and services their dollars will buy. The value of money depends on its **purchasing power,** the ability of money to be used to acquire goods and services. A decline in the purchasing power of money is known as **inflation,** a condition in which rising prices cause a given amount of money to purchase fewer goods and services. The opposite condition, in which the value of money increases, indicating falling prices, is called **deflation.**

You have probably heard relatives or friends exclaim, "A dollar doesn't buy what it used to!" They really mean that the purchasing power of a dollar has fallen, that a given amount of money will buy a smaller quantity of the same goods and services in the economy than it once did.

Just how much has the dollar shrunk? Consider the quantity of real goods and services that $1.00 would buy at the beginning of 2001. To buy the same quantity would have cost 56¢ in 1980, 27¢ in 1970, 20¢ in 1960, 16¢ in 1950, and 8¢ in 1940. Less than a dime earned in 1940 would buy $1.00 worth of goods and services today! Obviously, the U.S. economy has experienced significant inflation since 1940.

Changes in the purchasing power of money affect money's usefulness as a store of value and standard of deferred payment and, in turn, individuals' willingness to hold money. In 1989, newly elected Argentine President Carlos Menem faced an inflation rate of 12,000% per year. Very high inflation rates—say, in excess of 50% per month—are referred to as *hyperinflation.* With such rapid inflation, households and firms refused to hold official money. Instead they resorted to barter and the use of U.S. dollars. This example underscores our analysis of what serves as money: For money to be acceptable as a medium of exchange, households and firms must believe that it has value and will be acceptable. In Argentina, rapid erosion of money's purchasing power undermined this belief. Policymakers have significant concerns about maintaining the purchasing power of official money.

The value of money is determined by the quantity of goods and services you can purchase with it. Using a **price index,** a summary statistic that reflects changes in the price of a group of goods and services relative to the price in a base year, you can see how the value of money has changed over time. Some commonly used price indexes are summarized in the appendix to this chapter.

Now that we understand *what* money is, we'll examine *how* money is used to settle transactions in the economy.

What Can Serve as Money?

Having a medium of exchange helps to make transactions easier and thus allows the economy to work more smoothly. The next logical question is, What can serve as money? That is, which assets should be used as the medium of exchange? You learned earlier that an asset must, at a minimum, be generally accepted as payment to serve as money. In practical terms, however, it must be even more.

What makes a good suitable to use as a medium of exchange? There are five criteria.

1. The good must be *acceptable* to (that is, usable by) most traders.
2. It should be of *standardized quality,* so that any two units are identical.

OTHER TIMES, OTHER PLACES . . .

Will the Euro Be a Success?

Effective January 1, 1999, the *euro* entered the world of major currencies. Worth about $0.83 in early 2001 (versus $1.18 at its introduction), the *euro* will in early 2002 circulate as notes and coins. By later that year it will replace national currencies in Austria, Belgium, Finland, France, Germany, Ireland, Italy, Luxem-bourg, the Netherlands, Portugal, and Spain.

Will the use of the euro as a currency benefit Europe? On the one hand, the new currency lowers the transactions costs of exchanging currencies, and a single currency will likely promote competition in the European Union. On the other hand, using a single currency can allow some parts of Europe to boom while other parts languish. In the United States, where the dollar is used in all 50 states, a downturn in one region is cushioned by fiscal transfers (that is, using tax revenues collected in one region to cushion the depressed region), whereas Europe lacks this important cushion. While economists have expressed views on either side, much of the European support for the euro reflects a political belief that a single currency will give Europe a large political role in world affairs.

3. It should be *durable,* so that value is not lost by spoilage.
4. It should be *valuable relative to its weight,* so that amounts large enough to be useful in trade can be easily transported.
5. Because different goods are valued differently, the medium of exchange should be *divisible.*

U.S. Federal Reserve Notes meet all these criteria.

What determines the acceptability of dollar bills as a medium of exchange? Basically, it is through self-fulfilling expectations: You value something as money only if you believe that others will accept it from you as payment. Our society's willingness to use green paper notes issued by the Federal Reserve System as money makes them an acceptable medium of exchange. This acceptability property is not unique to money. Your personal computer has the same keyboard organization of letters as other computer keyboards because manufacturers agreed on a standard layout. You learned to speak English because it is the language that most people around you speak.

THE PAYMENTS SYSTEM

Money facilitates transactions in the economy. The mechanism for conducting such transactions is known as a **payments system.** The payments system has evolved over time from precious metals to currency and checks to electronic funds transfer services. **Definitive money** is money that does not have to be converted into a more basic medium of exchange, such as gold, silver, or Federal Reserve Notes. The use of definitive money for trading goods and services at a point in time or over time, through credit, is the simplest type of payments system.

Commodity Money

In earlier times, traders used precious metals such as gold and silver as media of exchange. These physical goods were the dominant means by which trade was accomplished and were known as **commodity money.** Commodity money meets the criteria for a medium of exchange, but it has a significant problem: Among other factors, its value is related to its purity. Therefore someone who wanted to cheat could mix impure metals with a precious metal. Hence, unless traders trusted each other completely, they needed to check the weight and purity of the metal at each trade. Respected merchants, who were the predecessors of modern bankers, solved this problem by assaying metals and stamping them with a mark certifying weight and purity, earning a commission in the process. Unstamped (uncertified) commodity money was acceptable only at a discount. It wasn't long before rulers became interested in this process. If a profit was to be made from the minting of commodity money of certified purity and weight, why shouldn't the sovereign claim it? Kings and dukes with wars and palaces to finance found this opportunity difficult to resist.

Fiat Money

An economy's reliance on precious metals alone makes for a cumbersome payments system. What if you had to transport gold bullion to settle your transactions? Not only would doing so be difficult and costly, but you would run the risk of being robbed. To get around this problem, private institutions or governments began to store the definitive money and issue paper certificates representing it. In modern economies, paper currency is generally issued by a **central bank,** which is a special governmental or quasi-governmental institution in the financial system that regulates the medium of exchange. If you look at a U.S. dollar bill, you will see that it is actually a Federal Reserve Note, issued by the Federal Reserve System, which is the central bank in the United States. Federal Reserve currency is **legal tender** in the United States; that is, the federal government mandates its acceptance to discharge debts and requires that cash or checks denominated in dollars be used in payment of taxes. Nonetheless, without everyone's acceptance, dollar bills would not be a good medium of exchange and could not serve as money.

The modern U.S. payments system is a **fiat money** system. In such a system, money authorized by a central bank or governmental body is the definitive money and does not have to be exchanged by the central bank for gold or some other commodity money. What this means is that the Federal Reserve System is not required to give you gold or silver (or even aluminum cans) for your dollar bills. You, along with everyone else, agree to accept Federal Reserve currency as money. In the United States, the Federal Reserve System issues dollar bills and holds deposits of banks and the federal government. Banks can use these deposits to settle transactions with one another. In the United States, the Fed has a monopoly on the right to issue currency. Although checks drawn on accounts at private banks are a substitute for Federal Reserve Notes in paying for goods and services, private banks cannot issue their own bank notes.

CONSIDER THIS . . .

What's Money? Ask a Taxi Driver!

Some years ago, I learned a great lesson about money from Russian cab drivers. In August 1989, along with a group of American economists, I traveled to Moscow and Leningrad (now St. Petersburg) to discuss with Soviet economists some economic problems faced by both countries.

Taking taxis in Moscow to and from meetings and dinners was an ordeal. Our hosts had given us rubles (Soviet currency at the time), but Russian merchants and taxi drivers discouraged payments in rubles. A bewildering array of fares were always quoted in terms of U.S. dollars, German marks, or Japanese yen. And the fares varied inconsistently from cab to cab.

When I relayed this frustration to my wife at our hotel one evening, she told me that she had encountered no such difficulty. She used Marlboro cigarettes! When I experimented with her Marlboros the next day (no other brand worked as well), I found my exchange problems vastly simplified. The cigarettes served as a medium of exchange, as well as a unit of account, as all the taxi drivers could easily convert all major currencies to Marlboro equivalents.

Official money (rubles) had been displaced by Marlboros as a medium of exchange. Marlboros are of standardized quality, are easily recognized, and retain their value when unused—a logical money indeed.

As of December 2000, Federal Reserve Notes in circulation totaled about $460 billion. What stops the Fed from issuing as many dollars as it wants? In principle, nothing! In Part 5, we discuss how much money the Fed circulates. For now, however, let's assume that the Fed issues the "right" amount of dollars.

Checks

Paper money can also be expensive to transport for settling large commercial or financial transactions. Imagine going to buy a car with a suitcase full of dollar bills! Another major innovation in the payments system came from the use of a substitute for definitive money: checks. **Checks** are promises to pay definitive money on demand and are drawn on money deposited with a financial institution. They can be written for any amount and are more difficult to use fraudulently than currency or precious metals are. As a result, they are a convenient way to settle transactions. Another benefit of using checks is that traders avoid paying the cost of shipping currency back and forth, as many payments among parties cancel each other. Traveler's checks serve a similar purpose; purchased from a financial institution, they are pieces of paper that can be used to settle transactions.

Settling transactions with checks requires more steps than settling transactions with currency. Suppose that your roommate owes you $50. If she gives you $50 in cash, nothing further is needed to settle the transaction. Suppose, however, that she writes you a check for $50. You first take the check to your bank. Your banker, in turn, must present the check for payment to your roommate's bank, which then must collect the money from her account. This process generally takes several business days. Processing the enormous flow of checks in the United States costs the economy several billion dollars each year.

Checks and other substitutes for definitive money are less liquid than cash, and there is a cost to using checks. The cost of converting checks affects the seller's willingness to accept them in a transaction instead of definitive money. If you had to pay $10 to cash each check you received, you would undoubtedly prefer to receive cash. Another cost is the information cost: the time and effort required for the seller to verify whether the check writer (the buyer) has a sufficient amount of definitive money on deposit to cover the amount of the check. Accepting checks requires more trust on the part of the seller than accepting dollar bills does.

Electronic Funds and Electronic Cash

Electronic telecommunication breakthroughs have improved the efficiency of the payments system, reducing the time needed for clearing checks and the costs of paper flow for making payments. Settling and clearing transactions can now be done with computers in **electronic funds transfer systems,** computerized payment-clearing devices. Important examples include *debit cards* for point-of-sale transfers and *automated teller machines* (ATMs).

Debit cards can be used like checks: Cash registers in supermarkets and retail stores are linked to bank computers, so when a customer uses the debit card to buy groceries or other products, the customer's bank instantly credits the store's account with the amount and deducts it from the customer's account. Such a system eliminates the problem of trust between the buyer and seller that is associated with checks because the bank computer authorizes the transaction. Lest you think that such electronic transactions are just futuristic glimpses of the twenty-first century, the overwhelming majority of the dollar value of transactions among financial institutions is conducted electronically.

Twenty years ago, you had to stand in line at a bank teller's window during working hours to make deposits, withdrawals, and payments. Today, ATMs allow you to perform the same transactions at your bank whenever it is most convenient for you. Moreover, ATMs are connected to networks (such as Cirrus) so that you can make withdrawals of cash away from your home bank. By 1998, the Cirrus network had more than 200,000 ATMs in the United States and 67 other countries and territories, at which more than 1 billion transactions were conducted each month. Hence U.S. travelers can withdraw money in Paris to buy meals and souvenirs. Beyond ATMs, Chemical Bank (before its merger with Chase) and the First National Bank of Boston introduced in 1995 an electronic check that could become widely available for payments between computer users on the Internet.

The boundaries of electronic funds transfers have expanded to include **electronic money** (or e-money), money that is stored electronically on cards or computer accounts. The simplest version of electronic money is a debit card (described earlier), which permits consumers to buy goods and services by transferring funds from their bank accounts to a merchant's bank account. Such cards resemble credit cards and are used with card readers.

Stored-value cards have the physical characteristics of a debit card but contain an amount of digital cash. That amount can be preset or, on so-called smart cards, increased as desired. Stored-value cards are common in Europe, Canada, Chile, Australia, Singapore, and China. Some recent developments by U.K.-based Mondex offer electronic money transfers among individuals. Stored-value cards are in their comparative infancy in the United States.

Finally, electronic cash (or e-cash) is digital cash employed to buy goods and services on the Internet. The e-cash is acquired by a consumer from an Internet bank and transferred to a merchant's computer when a purchase is made. Electronic checks, or Internet banking, make it possible for consumers to pay bills by e-check over the Internet. Electronic checks significantly decrease the cost of transactions relative to the cost of paper checks.

The developments in e-money are exciting and lead some commentators to talk about a "cashless society." In reality, a cashless society is unlikely. First, the infrastructure for an e-payments system will be expensive to build. Second, many households and businesses worry about protecting their privacy in an electronic system that is subject to computer "hackers." While the flow of paper in the payments system is likely to shrink, it is unlikely to disappear.

To summarize, the efficiency of the payments system, which increases as the cost of settling transactions decreases, is important for the economy. Suppose that the banking system broke down and all transactions—commercial and financial—had to be carried out in cash. You would have to carry large amounts of cash to finance all your purchases and would incur additional costs for protecting your cash. No bank credit would be possible, severely harming the financial system's role in matching savers and borrowers. Thus disruptions in the payments system increase the cost of trade and credit. Many economists, for example, blame the collapse of the banking system for the severity of the Great Depression of the 1930s. The efficient functioning of the economy's payments system is a significant public policy concern. Governments typically regulate the medium of exchange and establish safeguards to protect the payments system.

CHECKPOINT

Do you think that cash and checks will one day become obsolete and all payments will be made electronically? What benefits do you see from such an arrangement? What might prevent such an arrangement from being fully realized? In the early 1990s, analysts speculated that debit cards would soon be used for a significant fraction of consumers' purchases by the end of the decade. These electronic transactions are less costly than checks and more convenient for consumers than cash. A cashless society is not likely, however. Cash would still be used for small purchases. In addition, certain legal issues have not been resolved, such as whether you would be liable if someone discovered your secret account access code and illegally transferred funds from your account. Finally, some individuals value the anonymity afforded by using currency. Individuals engaging in illegal transactions (drug deals or tax evasion schemes, for example) would be unlikely debit card users. o

MEASURING THE MONEY SUPPLY

Households, firms, and policymakers are all interested in measuring money because, as we noted in Chapter 1, changes in the quantity of money are associated with changes in interest rates, prices, and economic activity. To understand money's role as an economic variable, we need to measure it.

The definition of money (a medium of exchange for goods and services and the settlement of debts) depends on beliefs about whether others will use the medium in trade now and in the future. This definition offers guidance for measuring money in an economy. Interpreted literally, this definition says that money should include only those assets that function obviously as a medium of exchange: currency, checking account deposits, and traveler's checks. These assets can easily be used to buy goods and services and thus act as a medium of exchange.

This strict interpretation is too narrow as a measure of the money supply in the real world, though. Many other assets can be used as a medium of exchange, but they are not as liquid as a checking account deposit or cash. For example, you can convert your savings account at a bank to cash without paying a large transactions cost. Likewise, if you have an account at a brokerage firm, you can write checks against the value of securities the firm holds for you. Although these alternatives have restrictions and some transactions costs, these assets are plausibly part of the medium of exchange.

Economists have developed several different definitions of the money supply based on the differences in the assets included as money. The definitions range from narrow to broad, depending on how substitutable different assets are for definitive money. Substitutability in this case refers to liquidity, the cost at which an asset can be converted to definitive money. Thus the most narrow money measure is definitive money itself. A broad measure would include other assets that could be easily converted to cash—your checking account or savings account, for example. In the United States, the Fed has defined certain measures of money as part of its effort to estimate the effects of the money supply on prices and economic activity.

The Fed has conducted several studies of the appropriate definition of money. This job has become more difficult during the past two decades as innovation in financial markets and institutions has created new substitutes for the traditional measures of the medium of exchange. During the 1980s, the Fed adapted its definitions of money in response to financial innovation.

Measuring Monetary Aggregates

Charged with regulating the quantity of money in the United States, the Federal Reserve has developed three definitions of money that include assets broader than currency. Figure 2.2 illustrates these definitions—referred to as **monetary aggregates**—graphically. Let's see how the current set of definitions works.

M1* aggregate.** The narrowest aggregate measure of money is ***M1. As Fig. 2.2 shows, *M1* measures money as the traditional medium of exchange. *M1* includes currency, traveler's checks, and checking account deposits. Through the early 1980s, checking accounts were deposits that paid no interest and thus were close substitutes for definitive money. Since then, financial innovation in the banking industry and government deregulation in the 1970s, 1980s, and 1990s have made more types of bank accounts acceptable as close substitutes for checking deposits. These new accounts include checking accounts at savings institutions and credit unions, as well as interest-bearing checking accounts at commercial banks. Measures of *M1* now include these other deposits against which checks may be written, along with non-interest-bearing checking account deposits, traveler's checks, and currency.

Figure 2.2

Measuring Monetary Aggregates, November 2000

Monetary aggregates offer measures of different definitions of money. Each measure includes the content of the level above plus other assets.

Sources: Federal Reserve Bulletin; Monthly Economic Indicators.

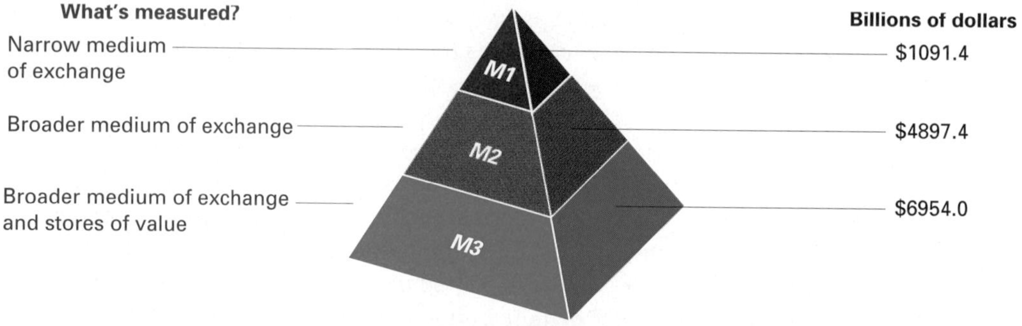

What's included?

M1

Currency in circulation +
- Traveler's checks
- Demand deposits
- Other checkable deposits

M2

M1 +
- Small-denomination time deposits
- Savings deposits
- Money market deposit accounts
- Noninstitutional money market fund shares
- Overnight repurchase agreements
- Overnight Eurodollars

M3

M2 +
- Large-denomination time deposits
- Institutional money market fund balances
- Term repurchase agreements
- Term Eurodollars

USING THE NEWS . . .

Finding Up-to-Date Information on Money

To find out how rapidly the money supply is growing, consult the "Money and Investing" section of *The Wall Street Journal*. On most Fridays, the *Journal* publishes data on *M1*, *M2*, and *M3*. The example shown here summarizes information for November 24, 2000. The *sa* entries have been seasonally adjusted. This adjustment removes seasonal fluctuations in the money supply (such as the increase in money holdings during the summer vacation season or the Christmas shopping season) from the data.

For the week ending November 13, 2000, *M1* averaged $1075.0 billion. Is this an exact count of all components of *M1*? No. It is based on initial estimates by the Fed. As the Fed receives more and better information, it revises its initial estimates. Revisions to money stock estimates can be significant, so initial estimates may not be a reliable guide to short-term movements in the money supply. However, forecasters have found that over longer periods, such as a year, the initial and revised money supply series produce similar longer-term growth rates.

MONETARY AGGREGATES
(daily average in billions)

	1 WEEK ENDED:	
	Nov. 13	Nov. 6
Money supply (M1) sa	1076.2	1087.5
Money supply (M1) nsa	1075.0	1089.2
Money supply (M2) sa	4889.8	4895.0
Money supply (M2) nsa	4900.4	4899.4
Money supply (M3) sa	6954.1	6953.7
Money supply (M3) nsa	6973.2	6955.8
	4 WEEKS ENDED:	
	Nov. 13	Oct. 16
Money supply (M1) sa	1095.1	1095.9
Money supply (M1) nsa	1090.0	1086.8
Money supply (M2) sa	4890.6	4885.0
Money supply (M2) nsa	4876.9	4859.9
Money supply (M3) sa	6946.1	6926.5
Money supply (M3) nsa	6930.9	6883.5
	MONTH	
	Oct.	Sep.
Money supply (M1) sa	1099.9	1095.4
Money supply (M2) sa	4889.7	4871.5
Money supply (M3) sa	6935.4	6909.7

nsa—Not seasonally adjusted. sa—Seasonally adjusted.

Source: The Wall Street Journal, November 27, 2000, Page C17. Republished by permission of Dow Jones, Inc. via Copyright Clearance Center, Inc.

***M2* aggregate.** *M2*, the next measure of money shown in Fig. 2.2, is slightly broader than M1. In addition to the assets included in M1, it covers short-term investment accounts. These accounts can be converted to definitive money but not as easily as the components of *M1*. Originally, *M2* consisted predominantly of small-denomination time deposits (less than $100,000) and savings accounts. Now it also includes some assets that offer check-writing features, such as money market deposit accounts at banks and noninstitutional money market mutual fund shares.

***M3* aggregate.** *M3* includes more assets than *M2* and *M1*. In addition to currency, traveler's checks, checking deposits, and short-term investment accounts, *M3* is composed of such less liquid assets as large-denomination time deposits ($100,000 or more), institutional money market mutual fund balances, term repurchase agreements, and Eurodollars.

In addition to monetary aggregates, the Fed reports information on debt as a store of value. In particular, the Fed reports outstanding credit market debt of domestic nonfinancial sectors. We explore the differences among various debt instruments in Chapter 3.

Figure 2.3

Growth Rates of *M1, M2,* and *M3,* 1960–2000

Monetary aggregates move together broadly over long periods of time. However, their growth rates diverge during some periods.

Source: Federal Reserve Bulletin.

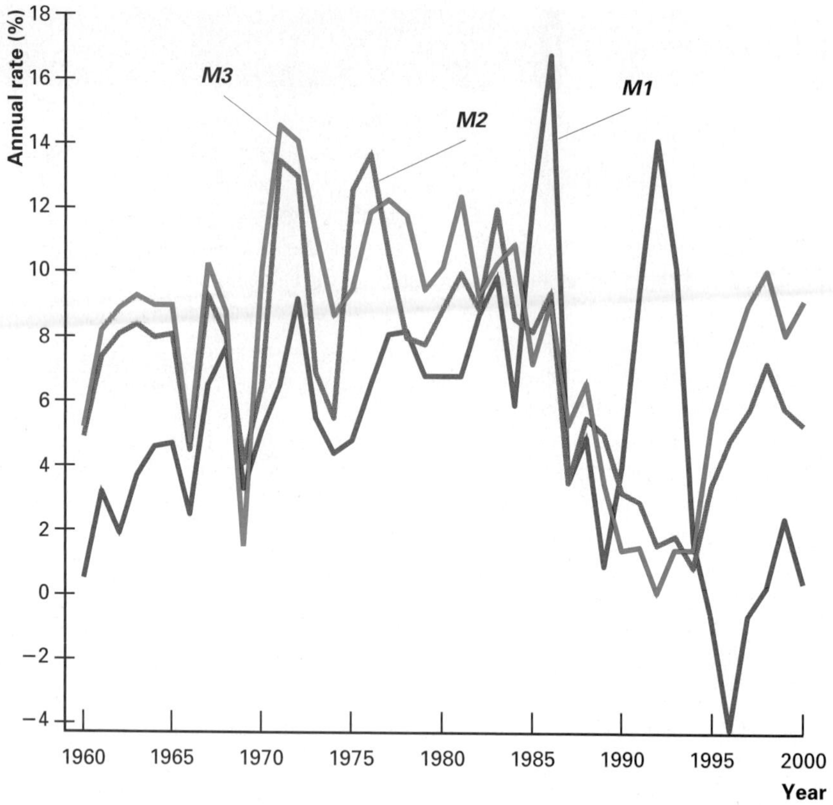

Selecting Monetary Aggregates

Which is the correct measure of money? The answer depends on the purpose of the measurement. Until the 1980s, *M1* was generally accepted as the measure of money. In the 1980s, *M1*'s role as a measure was challenged as the new substitutes for simple checking accounts were included in *M2*. In the 1980s and 1990s, economists and policymakers have generally considered *M2* to be the measure of the money supply, though developments in the financial system during that period have made complicated attempts to define money. The Fed has also experimented with hybrid measures of money using portions of components of the monetary aggregates. For example, if money market mutual fund shares are held for both transactions and investment purposes, they could be allocated in part to an *M1*-type measure and in part to an *M2*-type measure.

Because the Fed's monetary aggregates are attempts to measure some underlying true stock of money, economists and policymakers want to know whether the aggregates move together. For example, if *M1, M2,* and *M3* tend to rise or fall together, the Fed could use any one of them to try to influence the economy's output, prices, or interest rates. If these measures of money do not move together, they may tell different stories about what is happening to money. As a result, policymakers would have difficulty deciding on an appropriate monetary policy.

As is shown in Fig. 2.3, it turns out that monetary aggregates move broadly together over long periods of time. However, some significant differences in monetary aggregate movements have occurred during certain periods. For example, while the growth rate of *M1* rose during the 1970s and mid-1980s, the growth rates of the broader *M2* and *M3* aggregates actually decreased. Hence the different monetary aggregates give a different picture of movements in the money supply over time.

How then do the Fed and private forecasters decide which measures to use? As we noted earlier, the Fed continues to experiment with hybrid measures of money in which different assets have different degrees of liquidity. In addition, Federal Reserve economists, academic economists, and private forecasters conduct research on which monetary aggregates are most closely tied to movements in economic variables, such as the economy's total output, the price level, and interest rates. In Part 6, we examine these empirical approaches more carefully.

KEY TERMS AND CONCEPTS

Asset
Barter
Central bank
Definitive money
Deflation
Electronic money
Government allocation
Inflation
Legal tender
Medium of exchange
Monetary aggregates (*M1, M2, M3*)
Money
Payments system
- Checks
- Commodity money
- Electronic funds transfer systems
- Fiat money

Price index
Purchasing power
Specialization
Standard of deferred payment
Store of value
Transactions cost
Unit of account
Wealth

SUMMARY

1. Specialization increases economic efficiency: Individuals produce things they are good at producing. Because of such specialization, people create surpluses and need ways to trade the things they produce. The three possible allocations rely on barter, government allocation, and money. The problem with barter is that it cannot easily match the highly specific needs of buyers and sellers. Government allocation often fails because it misallocates resources. Money works well in facilitating trade, allocating resources efficiently, and avoiding the need for matching each buyer and seller.
2. In its role as a medium of exchange, money is a generally accepted means of payment. A particular item becomes a medium of exchange because people believe that it will be mutually acceptable.
3. Money provides a unit of account so that all prices can be quoted in monetary terms. Money also reduces the costs of trading over time. As a store of value, money allows people to hold it today and buy things with it in the future. As a standard of deferred payment, money makes credit transactions possible.

THE ECONOMIST FEBRUARY 19, 2000

E-Cash 2.0

Money has always been a sexy topic. As has technology. So the hype that greeted the arrival in the mid-1990s of several digital kinds of cash should not have been surprising. Some predicted that private electronic currencies would swiftly compete with dollars or D-marks. Central bankers began to worry that—perish the thought!—they might become obsolete.

The reality has proved much less exciting, for electronic cash has flopped badly. Its issuers either went bankrupt (DigiCash), dropped the product (CyberCash), or moved into another business (First Virtual Holdings, now MessageMedia). On the Internet, almost all payments are still made by unsexy credit cards. . . .

Despite that sobering experience, a second generation of financial firms is now giving e-cash another go, on-line. Hardly a week passes without a start-up venture—usually American—
a announcing a new form of electronic money. And this time, the prospects look rather better.

There appears now to be a genuine demand for an on-line alternative to credit cards, which the rapid growth of e-commerce is bound to fuel. Sometimes, consumers will wish to remain anonymous. Many, particularly outside America, have no access to plastic money. Some are too young. And auctions and other sorts of consumer-to-consumer e-commerce have created a need for on-line payment between individuals. . . .

Another company, Beenz.com, is taking a different approach. What Phillip Letts, its chief executive, calls its "big gotcha" is that consumers can earn "beenz" simply by being on-line. About 50 Web sites use them to pay people for visiting, filling in on-line surveys, or shopping. . . . The firm sells its currency to partner merchants at a rate of 100 to the dollar, of which half is its commission; so one beenz is worth half a cent. . . .

Schemes such as Beenz . . . are, in essence, rewards programs. David Birch, director of Consult Hyperion, a British e-cash consultancy, argues that, since consumers cannot pay each other with beenz or mileage points, they do not qualify as genuine digital money. One technology that does is PayPal, developed by Confinity. After opening an account on the company's Web site, people can e-mail dollars to others. Or users
can download money to one Palm handheld computer and transfer it to another via infrared signals. . . . b

But the schemes are far from the digital ideal. Most keep track of what users buy, and so fail to meet demands for anonymity and privacy. And many limit how their money can be spent. The products that offer the most anonymity and liquidity—especially if they can also be spent off-line—have the best long-term prospects.

Technology will also make it possible—and cheap—to turn financial assets such as mutual funds into money. There is no reason, argues Hyperion's Mr.
Birch, why consumers should not be able to pay their bills directly with units of a mutual fund, instead of having to go through a bank. . . . c

When you walk into a store to buy a book or a compact disc, you can choose from as many as six ways to pay: cash, check, credit card, debit card, automated clearing house debit, or stored-value card. Now e-commerce brings a new means of payment for cyber-shopping—digital cash. Despite the fact that most Internet payments are currently made by credit cards, some analysts remain hopeful that e-cash will eventually become a major feature of e-commerce transactions.

You may have already used electronic money. Such digital cash lacks the restrictions on credit card access that have limited general participation in electronic commerce. In addition, leading analysts such as Jupiter Communications have noted consumers' dissatisfaction with credit card use for on-line shopping and argued that digital cash's day may soon be dawning.

(a) Will e-cash become a successful alternative to current means of payment? To do so, it must offer value to consumers, merchants, and digital cash issuers—the participants involved. It's too early to imagine some sources of value. Consumers, however, might find e-commerce more appealing with lower credit card charges and anonymity. Merchants would see advantages in saving money and time in handling cash and credit card transactions. Issuers could decrease cash-handling cost and fraud, as well as gain new sources of fee income from consumers and merchants through cross-selling of other products and services.

(b) How would an e-cash system work? While early systems required consumers to install special software, some newer e-cash firms distribute currency through on-line merchant partners or airline frequent-flyer programs. Confinity's approach is even more advanced, allowing participants to e-mail dollars.

(c) Are there any drawbacks? Consumers worry about the lack of anonymity and privacy in some current digital cash solutions. Merchants and issuers worry about the large capital costs to build a well-functioning digital cash system. Nevertheless, many analysts believe that digital cash will eventually become an important part of the way in which we make payments. In today's Finland, users may already beam e-cash to vending machines. In tomorrow's United States, perhaps households will be able to e-pay their bills from financial assets such as a mutual fund, without ever using a bank.

For further thought . . .

How would changes in consumer attitudes toward Internet commerce likely affect potential gains from digital cash?

Source: Excerpted from "E-Cash 2.0," *The Economist,* February 19, 2000. www.economist.com.

4. Definitive money is money that does not have to be converted into a more basic legal medium of exchange. In commodity money systems, commodities (such as gold) are definitive money. In fiat money systems, paper currency and coin issued by the government or central bank are definitive money.
5. The payments system consists of ways to conduct transactions in the economy. Over time, payments systems have changed from simple (paper currency as the main method of payment) to complex (automatic clearing of payments by computer and electronic money).
6. Financial assets are grouped into different monetary aggregates, depending on their liquidity—that is, how easily they can be traded for definitive money. The Federal Reserve System, the central bank of the United States, defines monetary aggregates and collects data on them. These aggregates include measures designed to reflect money's role as a medium of exchange (*M1* and *M2*) and those designed to capture its role as a short-term store of value (*M3*).

REVIEW QUESTIONS

1. What makes a dollar bill money? What makes a personal check money? What factors, if changed, would affect your willingness to accept a dollar bill or a check as money?
2. How does specialization improve an economy's standard of living?
3. What are the costs of a barter system?
4. What are the four main functions of money? Describe each function.
5. What is commodity money? How does it differ from fiat money?
6. How does a monetary system affect the development of a credit system? If legal money is not broadly accepted as a medium of exchange, are credit contracts likely to be expressed in monetary terms? Why or why not?
7. What is a payments system? If there were a decrease in the efficiency of the payments system, what would be the cost to the economy?
8. How does high and accelerating inflation change the value of money? How does it change the usefulness of money as a medium of exchange?
9. Is the store-of-value function unique to money? If not, give some other examples of stores of value. Must money be a store of value to serve its function as a medium of exchange? Why or why not?
10. Which roles of money are adversely affected by inflation?
11. What is the purpose of having several definitions of the money supply? Why doesn't the Federal Reserve simply decide on the best definition of the money supply and discard the other definitions?
12. Why aren't credit cards included in any of the definitions of the money supply?

ANALYTICAL PROBLEMS

13. During the late nineteenth century the United States experienced a period of sustained deflation. How might this have affected money's usefulness?
14. Why might a $20 Federal Reserve Note be more desirable as a form of money than a $20 gold coin from the point of view of an individual? How about from the point of view of the government?
15. Why would someone keep currency in his or her pocket when money in the bank pays interest?
16. Suppose that your bank lowers its minimum balance requirement on a NOW account (a checking account that pays interest). You take $500 out of your NOW account and put it in a passbook savings account (a type of savings deposit) that pays a slightly higher interest rate. What is the overall effect on *M1* and *M2*?

17. If your income increases 10% in a year, are you better off? Why or why not?

18. Suppose that a primitive economy uses a rare stone as its money. Suppose also that the number of stones declines as stones are accidentally destroyed or used as weapons. What happens to the value of the stones over time? What would be the consequence if someone discovered a large amount of new stones?

19. Consider the country of Friedmania, where the money is gold crowns, each of which contains 1 gram of gold. The Royal Mint in Friedmania freely makes crowns out of raw gold. Then one day a new king orders the mint to put only 0.9 gram of gold in all new crowns and orders that the new crowns trade one-for-one with the old crowns. What do you think happens to the use of crowns as a medium of exchange? If you lived in Friedmania and had some old crowns and some new crowns, which would you spend first?

20. During the 1980s, broad price indexes in Germany rose less than those in Italy. What should happen to the value of money in Germany relative to the value of money in Italy? Suppose that Germany and Italy trade freely. What would happen to the purchasing power of Germans buying Italian goods? Of Italians buying German goods?

21. Define "liquidity." Rank the following assets in terms of liquidity, from most to least liquid: money market mutual fund, passbook savings account, corporate stock, dollar bill, house, gold, checking account.

22. Match each of the following items with the smallest monetary aggregate (*M1, M2,* or *M3*) of which it is part: money market deposit account, term repurchase agreement, commercial paper, traveler's check, overnight repurchase agreement, U.S. savings bond, currency, large time deposit, small time deposit, short-term Treasury bond, checking account.

Questions 23 and 24 pertain to the appendix.

23. The consumer price index (CPI) had the value 148.2 for 1994, with 1982–1984 as the base period (that is, the CPI over 1982–1984 is taken as 100). Now suppose that 1994 becomes the base year (that is, the new CPI in 1994 is taken as 100). What is the new CPI for 1982–1984?

24. If the price index was 100 for 1990 and 120 for 2000, and nominal gross domestic product (GDP) was $720 billion for 1990 and $960 for 2000, what is the value of 2000 real GDP in terms of 1990 dollars?

DATA QUESTIONS

Questions 25 through 28 pertain to the appendix.

25. In the latest copy of the *Economic Report of the President,* (a) look up the value of nominal GDP (the value of all final goods and services produced in the economy during the course of a year) for 1990 and 2000; (b) find the value of the GDP implicit price deflator in 1980 and 1990; (c) calculate real GDP for both years; and (d) find the percentage change in real GDP over the decade.

26. Find the consumer price index in the latest copy of the *Economic Report of the President.* Find the value of the index in the years 1960, 1970, 1980, 1990, and 2000. Calculate the inflation rates for the decades of the 1960s, 1970s, 1980s, and 1990s.

27. Repeat Problem 26 for the GDP implicit price deflator and the producer price index. How do the inflation rates compare?

28. In the latest issue of the *Federal Reserve Bulletin,* find the current figures for *M1, M2,* and *M3.* Now look in the *Economic Report of the President* to find the latest data on the population of the United States. Divide the money aggregate numbers by the population to get average money holdings per person. Do the numbers look reasonable to you? Explain why the numbers are so large.

APPENDIX: Calculating Price Indexes

A price index is calculated by dividing the price of selected goods making up a market basket P in some year t by the price of the market basket in a base year 0 (and multiplying by 100 to convert to percentage terms):

$$(\text{Price index})_t = \frac{P_t}{P_0} \times 100.$$

For example, if prices increased by 20% between the year 0 and year t, the index would be $1.20 \times 100 = 120$.

The most commonly watched price indexes in the United States are the following:

GDP deflator: the index of prices of all goods and services included in the gross domestic product (the final value of all goods and services produced in the economy).

Producer price index (PPI): the index of prices that firms pay in wholesale markets for crude materials, intermediate goods, and finished goods.

Consumer price index (CPI): the index of prices of the market basket of goods purchased by urban consumers (used as a measure of the cost of living).

CHAPTER 3

Overview of the Financial System

Throughout 1991 and during the course of the presidential campaign in 1992, many businesspeople complained that the financial system was simply not working during the recession. Small and medium-sized businesses, important sources of jobs for the recovering economy, sent lobbyists to Washington to let the Treasury Department and the Federal Reserve Board know that they could not get the credit they needed to expand. Politicians and economists began to take a hard look at how well the U.S. financial system brought together borrowers with good ideas and savers with money to lend.

Although you might not march to Washington to express your views about the financial system, the way the financial system works affects your well-being. At times in your life, you will be a saver, as when you put aside money for your children's education or your retirement. At other times, you will be a borrower. You may borrow to buy a home or car or to build a factory to produce your great invention. The financial system channels funds from savers to borrowers and makes it possible for both to achieve their objectives. When the financial system works efficiently, it increases the health of the economy: Borrowers obtain funds for consumption and investment, and savers are rewarded by earning extra funds that they might not have otherwise.

What does the financial system do? How does it accomplish its objectives? We begin to answer these questions in this chapter by introducing the playing field—*financial markets*—and some key players—*financial institutions*. To answer these questions in full, we need more than a single chapter. We continue our investigation of financial markets and financial institutions in Parts 2, 3, and 4. This chapter will give you the ground rules and background for your study of the financial system.

WHAT IS THE PURPOSE OF THE FINANCIAL SYSTEM?

You probably don't think you have much in common with a farmer, an inventor, or the federal government. But you do. All of you at one time or another may need more funds than you have on hand. You may want to go to graduate school and delay your entry into the job market. A farmer may need money for spring planting. An inventor may want to finance the start of a new high-technology company. The federal government may run a budget deficit, spending more than it collects in taxes. Those finding themselves with a mismatch between income and desired spending may be willing to pay for the funds they need.

At the same time, others spend less than their incomes. Your parents may save for their retirement or for your education. A business receiving a big payment on a government contract may decide not to spend all the funds at once. Even the federal government currently collects more in taxes than it needs immediately. Those who have surplus funds may be willing to let someone else use their savings if they are compensated for doing so.

The mismatch between income and spending for individuals and organizations creates an opportunity to trade. The inventor can use the funds saved by your parents to start a business now. The inventor would be better off by earning a profit from investing funds in a new venture. Your parents would be better off by receiving the return that the inventor pays them for "renting" their funds. They would not have earned this extra income if they had kept their savings in a shoebox in a closet.

Not all financial transactions involve investing in a new project or business venture. Suppose that you have a good job and decide to buy a house. There's only one problem: You earn $30,000 per year, and the house you want to buy costs $100,000. You could rent an apartment and save your money slowly until you accumulate enough to buy the house. That would probably take many years, though, and you and your family may want to enjoy owning a home sooner. As an alternative, someone could lend you the money to buy the house now. Just as you would be better off by being able to enjoy the benefits of homeownership sooner, the person who loaned you the money would be better off, too. The interest that you pay the lender would be extra income—income that the lender would not have received without making the loan.

Now you can begin to see what functions the financial system provides in the economy. It moves funds from those who want to spend less than they have available to those who have a desire to purchase durable goods or those who have productive investment opportunities. This matching process increases the economy's ability to produce goods and services. In addition, it makes households and businesses better off by allowing them to time purchases according to their needs and desires. A smoothly functioning financial system thus improves the economy's efficiency and people's economic welfare.

The **financial system** provides channels to transfer funds from individuals and groups who have saved money to individuals and groups who want to borrow money. **Savers** (or lenders) are suppliers of funds, providing funds to borrowers in return for promises of repayment of even more funds in the future. **Borrowers** are demanders of funds for consumer durables, houses, or business plant and equipment, promising to repay borrowed funds based on their expectation of having higher incomes in the future. These promises are financial **liabilities** for the borrower—that is, both a source of funds and a claim against the borrower's future income. Conversely, the promises, or IOUs, are financial **assets** for savers—that is, both a use of funds and a claim on the borrower's future income. For example, your car loan is an asset (use of funds) for the bank and a liability (source of funds) for you. If you buy a house, the mortgage is your liability and your lender's asset. If your uncle buys Treasury bonds for his retirement account, the bonds are assets for him and liabilities for the U.S. government.

Figure 3.1 shows that the financial system channels funds from savers to borrowers and channels returns back to savers, both directly and indirectly. Savers and borrowers can be households, businesses, or governments, both domestic and foreign. **Financial markets,** such as the stock market or the bond market, issue claims on individual borrowers directly to savers. **Financial institutions** or **intermediaries,** such as banks, mutual funds, and insurance companies, act as go-betweens by holding a portfolio of assets and issuing claims based on that portfolio to savers. We discuss the participants in these activities and their roles later in this chapter. First, however, let's consider the financial services that motivate savers and borrowers to use the financial system.

Figure 3.1

Moving Funds Through the Financial System

The financial system transfers funds from savers to borrowers. Borrowers transfer returns back to savers through the financial system. Savers and borrowers include domestic and foreign households, businesses, and governments.

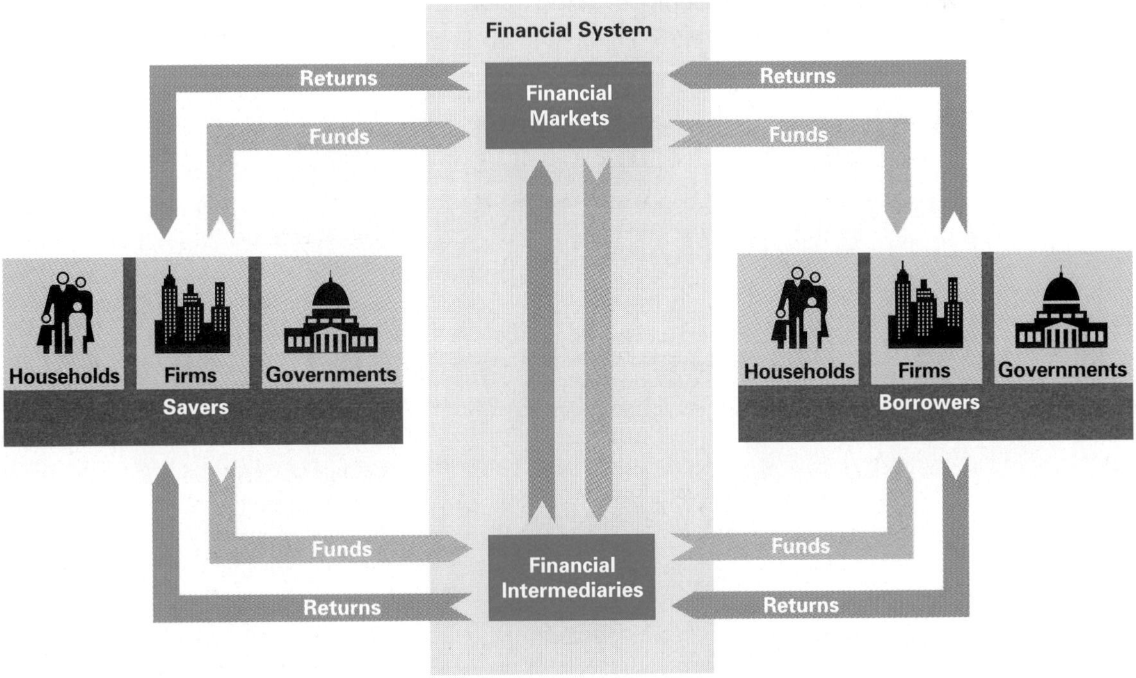

CHECKPOINT

As a saver, what sort of claims might you hold? You can hold claims on many borrowers. Your checking account is a claim on your bank. If you have savings bonds, you own a claim on the U.S. government. Money market accounts with Fidelity, Merrill Lynch, or any of their competitors are claims on a portfolio of assets held by the brokerage firm. If your aunt left you a Disney bond, you own a claim against that firm. o

KEY SERVICES PROVIDED BY THE FINANCIAL SYSTEM

In addition to matching individuals who have excess funds with those who need them, the financial system provides three key services for savers and borrowers. These services are *risk sharing, liquidity,* and *information.* Figure 3.2, a modified version of Fig. 3.1, emphasizes these services. Financial markets and financial intermediaries provide these services in different ways, making various financial assets and financial liabilities more attractive to individual savers and borrowers. Many financial decisions made by savers and borrowers are shaped by the availability of these services.

Figure 3.2 **Key Services Provided by the Financial System**

The financial system provides risk-sharing, liquidity, and information services. These services are valued by savers and borrowers.

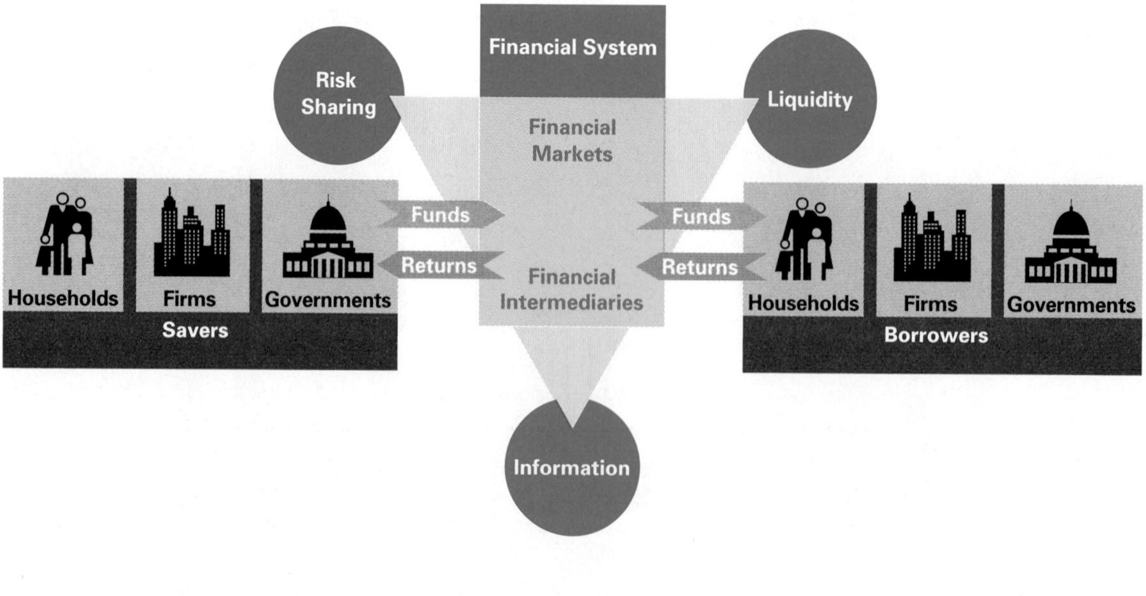

Risk Sharing

Your brother-in-law asks you to invest all your savings in shares of stock in his new company. You know that it's a risky proposition. If the economy booms, sales of the product—glow-in-the-dark earrings—might make you rich. But if the economy sours, those earrings might not be such a great product. You would like to invest in the business, but you're not convinced that you should tie up all your savings in such an investment. Are you being too cautious?

Probably not. One advantage of using the financial system to match individual savers and borrowers is that it allows the sharing of risks. Risk is the chance that the value of financial assets will change relative to what you expect. For example, if you buy a bond of Okayco for $1000, that bond might be worth $900 or $1100 in one year's time, depending on fluctuations in interest rates and Okayco's prospects. Most individual savers are not gamblers and seek a steady return on their assets rather than erratic swings between high and low earnings. Indeed, individuals prefer stable returns on the collection of assets they hold. A collection of assets is called a **portfolio.** For example, you might hold some U.S. savings bonds, some shares of stock, and some shares in a mutual fund. Although one asset or set of assets may perform well and another not so well, overall the returns tend to average out. This splitting of wealth into many assets is known as **diversification.** As long as the individual returns do not vary in the same way, the risk of severe fluctuations in a portfolio's value will be reduced. The financial system provides **risk sharing** by allowing savers to hold many assets.

We demonstrate the advantages of diversification in Chapter 5 and describe ways in which the financial system enables individuals to *transfer risk*. Financial markets can create instruments to transfer risk from savers or borrowers who do not like uncertainty in returns or payments to savers or investors who are willing to bear risk. For example, you might be willing to accept a lower return on your investment in your brother-in-law's business if he or one of his other investors guaranteed you that return. You have transferred some of your risk as a saver to the borrower—but the transfer comes at a cost: the lower return.

The ability of the financial system to provide risk sharing makes savers more willing to buy borrowers' IOUs. This willingness, in turn, increases borrowers' ability to raise funds in the financial system.

Liquidity

The second service that the financial system offers savers and borrowers is **liquidity,** which is the ease with which an asset can be exchanged for money to purchase other assets or exchanged for goods and services. Savers view the liquidity of financial assets as a benefit. When they need their assets for their own consumption or investment, they want to exchange them easily. In general, the more liquid an asset, the easier it is to exchange the asset for something else. You can easily exchange the dollar bill in your pocket for a hamburger because a dollar bill is highly liquid. You could also cash a check within a short period of time to buy clothes. Selling your car, however, takes more time because personal property is not very liquid. By holding financial claims (such as stock or bonds) on a factory, individual investors have more liquid savings than they would if they owned the machines in the factory. The reason is that the investor can more easily sell the claim than a specialized machine in order to buy other assets or goods. Liquid assets allow an individual or firm to respond quickly to new opportunities or unexpected events. Financial assets created by the financial system, such as stocks, bonds, or checking accounts, are more liquid than cars, machinery, or real estate.

Financial markets and intermediaries provide trading systems for making financial assets more liquid. In addition to creating financial assets, the financial system provides systems for increasing the liquidity of financial assets. In the United States, for instance, investors can readily sell their holdings in government securities and stocks and bonds of large corporations, making those assets very liquid. During the past two decades, the financial system has made many other assets liquid besides stocks and bonds. Twenty years ago, for example, financial intermediaries had to hold mortgage loans and loans made to businesses until the loans were paid off. Now, those institutions can sell the loans to other investors and buy loans made by other institutions. As a result, mortgages and other loans have become more desirable assets for savers to hold. Savers are willing to accept a lower return on assets with greater liquidity, reducing the costs of borrowing obligations for less well-known firms. One measure of the efficiency of the financial system is the extent to which it can transform illiquid assets into the liquid claims that savers want.

Information

A third service of the financial system is the collection and communication of **information,** or facts about borrowers and expectations about returns on financial assets. The first informational role the financial system plays is to gather information. That includes finding out about prospective borrowers and what they will do with borrowed funds. Joe's neighbor wants to borrow the money that Joe has set aside for his daughter's education and promises to pay it back when she starts college. Should Joe lend his neighbor his nest egg? To make a wise decision, Joe needs to know more about the loan. What will the neighbor do with the funds? How likely is it that Joe will be paid back in time for the first tuition payment? Obtaining such information would be costly and time-consuming for savers, who of course want all the facts before lending their money. Working through the financial system, Joe is likely to learn more about the borrower than he would if he tried to make the investment on his own.

Another problem that exists in most transactions is **asymmetric information.** This means that borrowers possess information about their opportunities or activities that they don't disclose to lenders or creditors and can take advantage of this information. Sometimes, financial arrangements have to be structured so that borrowers do not take advantage of asymmetric information at the expense of lenders. Fast Eddie might seek a $10,000 loan that he claims he will use to launch a new line of billiard cues, but he really plans to use the funds for a first-class cruise to Europe. Clearly, Fast Eddie knows more about the actual use of the funds than the potential lender. Parts of the financial system specialize in information gathering and monitoring, and specialized arrangements exist for solving problems of asymmetric information.

The second informational role that the financial system plays is *communication* of information. If you read a newspaper headline announcing that a pharmaceutical company had found a cure for cancer, how would you determine the effect of this discovery on the company's financial position? Financial markets do that job by incorporating information into the prices of stocks, bonds, and other financial assets. In this example, the expectation of higher future profits would boost the prices of the pharmaceutical company's outstanding stocks and bonds.

Savers and borrowers receive the benefits of information from the financial system by looking at asset returns. As long as financial market participants are informed, the information works its way into asset returns and prices. Information is communicated to borrowers as well as to savers. For example, if the price of the pharmaceutical company's stock goes up, the company may decide to sell more shares and invest the proceeds in new research projects. The incorporation of available information into asset returns is the distinguishing feature of well-functioning financial markets.

FINANCIAL MARKETS IN THE FINANCIAL SYSTEM

Financial markets bring savers and borrowers together directly. When you buy a new share of Boomco stock for $100, you are investing the $100 directly in Boomco to finance its growth. In this form of finance, known as **direct finance,** an individual saver holds financial claims issued directly by an individual borrower. These direct finance arrangements take place through financial markets, markets in which investors lend their savings directly to borrowers. To analyze the role played by financial markets, we focus on the two principal tasks of the financial system: (1) matching savers and borrowers and (2) providing risk-sharing, liquidity, and information services.

Matching Savers and Borrowers: Debt and Equity

Primary markets are those in which newly issued claims are sold to initial buyers by the borrower. Businesses use primary markets to raise funds for new ventures, and governments use them to finance budget deficits. Borrowers can raise funds in a primary financial market in two ways—by borrowing or by selling shares—which result in different types of claims on the borrower's future income. The first and most commonly used claim is **debt,** which requires the borrower to repay the amount borrowed, the **principal,** plus a rental fee, or **interest.**† The other type of claim is **equity,** which is an ownership claim to a share in the profits and assets of a firm.

Debt instruments are promises to repay the principal and interest, all at once or in periodic payments over a fixed period of time. The length of the period of time before the debt instrument expires is its **maturity,** or term. The maturity can be a short period of time (30 days or even overnight) or a long period of time (30 years or more). **Short-term debt** instruments have a maturity of less than one year. **Intermediate-term debt** instruments have a maturity between 1 year and 10 years. **Long-term debt** instruments have a maturity of 10 years or more. Debt instruments include student loans, government bonds, corporate bonds, and loans by financial institutions.

Debt instruments offer borrowers certain advantages. Suppose that you take out a student loan to study business, and when you graduate, you land a Wall Street position paying $50,000 per year. The fact that you got such a good job does not mean that you have to pay back more than the agreed-upon loan amount. In general, in a debt contract, a lender does not get more than the amount promised even if the borrower does exceptionally well. However, the lender may get less than the amount promised. If, for example, you cannot find a job and consequently can't pay back your loan, the lender gets less than the full amount of the loan. Lenders face the risk that borrowers will **default,** or not be able to repay all or part of their obligations.

The second means of raising funds—equity—allows for variable payments from the borrower to the lender. A good example is common stock, which entitles stockholders in a business to get their share of the firm's profits after all expenses, including payments of principal and interest to debtholders, have been settled. For example, if you own 100 shares of Bigco, which has 1 million shares outstanding, you own the right to 1/10,000 (100/1 million) of the firm's profits and assets. Equity owners generally receive periodic payments (usually once each quarter) from the firm, known as **dividends.** If the business does exceptionally well, equity owners receive more, while the debtholders still get only their promised payment. However, if the business's profits are weak, there may be nothing left after payments to debtholders are made. If you buy shares in Oopsco and it loses money, do you have to pay the firm's losses? No. Shareholders in corporations can lose only the amount of funds they invest in the venture. Firms also have strong reasons for issuing a particular mix of equity and debt. In Chapter 11, we examine the relative merits of using equity or debt to finance businesses, and we use economic intuition to explain major developments in the use of debt or equity.

Although you hear about the stock market's fluctuations each night on the evening news, debt instruments actually account for more of the funds

†The formula for computing how much interest is paid can be either an agreed-upon percentage, as is used for your bank account or student loan, or an indexed percentage, tied to some economic indicator such as the inflation rate or some published interest rate. Many business loans made by banks—especially in international lending—fall into the second category.

raised in the financial system. In late 2000, the value of debt instruments was about $26.5 trillion compared to $19.3 trillion for equities.

Providing Risk-Sharing, Liquidity, and Information Services

Risk-sharing, liquidity, and information services are provided in **secondary markets,** markets in which claims that have already been issued are sold by one investor to another. Suppose, for example, that you start a software company, Hitechco, which after a few years is growing rapidly but is in need of new capital for expansion. If you sell shares in Hitechco, you are turning to a primary market for new funds. Once Hitechco shares are issued, investors trade the shares in the secondary market. Note that as an owner of Hitechco, you do not receive any new funds when your company's shares are traded in secondary markets.

Most of the news about events in financial markets concerns secondary markets rather than primary ones. Most primary market transactions are sales of new debt or equity instruments to initial buyers and are conducted behind closed doors. The most widely reported secondary markets—such as the New York, American, and Tokyo Stock Exchanges—are those in which already-issued equities are traded. Even larger volumes of secondary market transactions take place in the bond market, in which U.S. government and corporate debt instruments are traded. Secondary markets are also important for global foreign-exchange transactions. Regardless of the type of instrument being traded, the buyer of the instrument in a secondary market pays money to the seller. The *initial* seller of the instrument—a corporation or government agency, for example—does *not* receive the proceeds. The initial issuer receives only the proceeds from the sale of the instrument in the primary market.

If the initial seller of a financial instrument raises funds from a lender only in the primary market, why are secondary markets so important? The answer incorporates risk-sharing, liquidity, and information services. Smoothly functioning secondary markets make it easier for investors to reduce their exposure to risk by holding a diversified portfolio of stocks, bonds, and other assets. Secondary markets also promote liquidity for stocks, bonds, foreign exchange, and other financial instruments so that it is easier for investors to sell the instruments for cash. This liquidity makes investors more willing to hold financial instruments, thereby making it easier for the issuing firm or government agency to sell the securities in the first place. Finally, secondary markets convey information to both savers and borrowers by determining the price of financial instruments. When the price of your shares of Hitechco rises, you are richer, which tells you that you can spend more if you want to. Likewise, the managers of Hitechco can get information on how well the market thinks they are doing from secondary market prices. For example, a major increase in Hitechco's stock price conveys the market's good feelings about the firm's investment possibilities and management skills, and the firm may decide to issue new debt or equity and expand. Hence secondary market prices are valuable sources of information for corporations that are considering issuing new debt or equity. As a result, we will focus mainly on secondary markets in our discussion.

There is no single "secondary market." Indeed, we can categorize secondary markets by (1) what maturity level characterizes the claims being traded, (2) how trading takes place, and (3) when settlement takes place.

Maturity: money and capital markets. Debt instruments that have a maturity of greater than one year are traded in **capital markets.** Equities, which have no fixed maturity, are also traded in capital markets. Short-term instruments, with a maturity of less than one year, are traded in **money markets.** Where do these instruments come from? Borrowers seeking funds for long-term investments in housing or business investment issue long-term financial instruments in capital markets. When the government or well-known corporations need funds to finance inventories or to meet short-term needs, they issue money market instruments. (The principal money and capital market instruments are described in the appendix to this chapter.)

How do investors decide which instruments to buy? There are three differences between money market and capital market instruments that result from differences in risk, liquidity, and information. First, short-term instruments have relatively small increases or decreases in price, so they are less risky as investments than long-term instruments are. As a result, financial institutions and corporations typically invest short-term surplus funds in money markets. Some financial institutions, such as pension funds and insurance companies, are willing to hold assets for a long time and risk price fluctuations in capital markets. Second, money market instruments are generally more liquid than capital market instruments because their trading volume is greater and the cost of buying and selling is low. Thus households and businesses can invest their funds for a short period of time relatively cheaply. Finally, information costs are lower for money market instruments because the borrowers are well known and the length of time for which funds are loaned is relatively short.

Trading places: auction and over-the-counter markets. Secondary financial markets can also be categorized according to how assets are traded between buyers and sellers. The first category is **auction markets,** in which prices are set by competitive bidding by a large number of traders acting on behalf of individual buyers or sellers. The most common auction markets are **exchanges,** or central locations at which buyers and sellers trade. They include the New York and American Stock Exchanges, the Tokyo Stock Exchange, the London Stock Exchange, and others.

Secondary markets also can be organized as **over-the-counter (OTC) markets,** in which there is no centralized place for exchanges. Over-the-counter dealers buy and sell stocks and bonds through computerized trading to anyone who is willing to accept their posted prices. Close electronic contact keeps the over-the-counter market competitive. You are unlikely to pay a much higher price for a share of stock of Apple Computer at one dealer than at another.

The equities of the largest corporations are traded on exchanges, as are the bonds of the best-known corporations. The shares of smaller, less well-known firms are generally traded in over-the-counter markets, as are U.S. government bonds. The market for these bonds has the largest trading volume of any debt or equity market. Other major OTC markets include those for foreign exchange, federal funds, and negotiable certificates of deposit.

Settlement: cash and derivative markets. Finally, financial markets can be categorized by whether the claims traded are direct or derivative. **Cash markets** are those markets in which actual claims are bought and sold with immediate settlement: The buyer pays money to the seller in exchange for the asset. Examples include the stock and bond markets. Alternatively, in **derivative markets,** trades are made now, but settlement is made at a later date. For example, an investor could agree to buy a Treasury bond from a bond dealer one year from now at a prespecified price. Why would anyone want to do this? The reason is that households and businesses use derivative markets to reduce their exposure to the risk of price fluctuations in cash markets (and sometimes even to bet on future price fluctuations).

Derivative claims, the value of which is determined by (derived from) underlying assets (such as stocks, bonds, or foreign exchange), include financial futures and options. **Financial futures** require settlement of a purchase of a financial instrument at a specified future date, with the price determined at the outset. **Options** on financial contracts, as the name suggests, confer on the trader the right (or option) to buy or sell a particular asset (shares of stock, bonds, or units of foreign currency, for example) within a specified time at a specified price.

CHECKPOINT

Using the categories describing financial markets, how would you characterize a transaction in which you buy 100 shares of Growthco from someone through a dealer? *Debt or equity:* Shares of stock are equities. *Primary or secondary market:* The stock is already outstanding, so the transaction takes place in a secondary market. *Money or capital market:* The equities have no fixed maturity and so are traded in the capital market. *Auction or over-the-counter market:* The transaction takes place through a dealer rather than through an exchange, so it is conducted in an over-the-counter market. *Cash or derivative market:* You pay money to the dealer and receive the stock now, so the transaction takes place in a cash market. o

FINANCIAL INTERMEDIARIES IN THE FINANCIAL SYSTEM

The financial system also channels funds from savers to borrowers indirectly through intermediaries. These institutions facilitate financial trade by raising funds from savers and investing in the debt or equity claims of borrowers.

This indirect form of finance is known as **financial intermediation.** Like financial markets, financial intermediaries have two tasks: (1) matching savers and borrowers and (2) providing risk-sharing, liquidity, and information services.

Matching Savers and Borrowers

When you deposit funds in your checking account, the bank may lend the funds (together with the funds of other savers) to Jane's Sub Shop to open a new store. In this intermediated transaction, your checking account is an asset for you and a liability for the bank. The loan becomes Jane's liability and the bank's asset. Rather than your holding a loan to Jane's Sub Shop as an asset directly, the bank acts as a go-between for you and Jane. Financial intermediaries, such as banks, insurance companies, pension funds, and mutual funds, also make investments in stocks and bonds on behalf of savers.

Intermediaries pool the funds of many small savers to lend to many individual borrowers. The intermediaries pay interest to savers in exchange for the use of savers' funds and earn a profit by lending money to borrowers and charging borrowers a higher rate of interest on the loans. For example, a bank might pay you as a depositor a rate of interest of 5% while lending the money to a local business at an interest rate of 8%.

Providing Risk-Sharing, Liquidity, and Information Services

Intermediation adds an extra layer of complexity and cost to financial trade. Why don't savers just deal directly with borrowers, bypassing the costs of financial intermediation? Again, the three main reasons are risk sharing, liquidity, and information. First, as a saver, you want to share risk. If you had $5000 in cash, you could loan it to your neighbor. But how do you know that your neighbor will pay you back? If you deposit your $5000 in the bank, the bank puts your money to work by making various loans and investments. Because banks have a large quantity of deposits and access to numerous borrowers and investments, they can diversify and provide risk-sharing services to you at a lower cost than you could obtain on your own. Second, bank deposits and other intermediary claims are liquid. Therefore, if your car breaks down, you can easily withdraw funds from your bank account to pay for repairs. (Your neighbor would probably not be able to pay you back early or appreciate having to do so.) Finally, financial intermediaries provide information services that are important to savers who may not have the time or resources to research investments on their own. You can easily get information about the likely return on a U.S. Treasury bond or a bond issued by a major corporation such as Exxon. More difficult, however, is obtaining information about the likely financial prospects of individuals or small and medium-sized businesses.

Your local bank is an information warehouse. It collects information on borrowers by monitoring their income and spending as reflected in their checking account transactions. Borrowers fill out detailed loan applications, and the bank's loan officers determine how well each borrower is doing financially.

CASE STUDY

Where Do Households Put Their Savings?

The Federal Reserve System publishes quarterly and annual data on assets and liabilities of sectors of the U.S. economy. Clues about trends in direct finance and indirect intermediary finance are provided by examining the Fed's data on household holdings of financial assets.

The table reports holdings of assets in financial markets and of assets supplied by financial intermediaries. These data show the importance of financial intermediation for savers. About one-half of household financial assets are held through financial intermediaries. Note particularly the increasing share of mutual funds and pension funds, which helped to increase the percentage of financial assets in indirect finance from 46.3% in 1978 to 54.0% in 2000.

These data come from the Fed's publication entitled *Flow of Funds Accounts, Financial Assets and Liabilities,* which you can find in the library.

Household Holdings of Selected Financial Assets

(Billions of Dollars, Various Years)

	1978	1985	2000
Financial Assets in Financial Markets			
U.S. government securities	148.6	447.5	806.9
State and local government securities	94.0	305.0	563.4
Corporate bonds	57.0	18.9	764.7
Mortgages	76.0	127.4	110.5
Commercial paper	31.4	128.7	73.7
Corporate equities	663.9	1700.0	7998.5
Equity in unincorporated businesses	1398.9	2040.6	4764.9
Miscellaneous assets	68.0	132.5	696.6
Subtotal	**2537.8**	**4900.6**	**15,779.2**
% in direct finance	*53.7%*	*50.8%*	*46.0%*
Financial Assets in Financial Intermediaries			
Bank deposits	1280.1	2306.7	3497.3
Money market mutual fund shares	9.4	211.1	891.7
Mutual fund shares	41.1	206.9	3155.9
Life insurance reserves	196.0	256.7	802.8
Pension fund reserves	661.5	1794.5	10,139.0
Subtotal	**2188.1**	**4775.9**	**18,486.7**
% in indirect finance	*46.3%*	*49.2%*	*54.0%*
Total Financial Assets	**$4725.9**	**$9676.5**	**$34,265.9**

Because the bank collects and processes information on behalf of you and other depositors, its costs for information gathering are lower than yours would be if you tried to gather information on a pool of borrowers. The intermediary's profits from lending compensate it for investing in information.

Financial intermediaries are the largest group in the financial system. They move more funds between savers and borrowers than do financial markets in the United States and in most other countries. Many economists believe that intermediaries' advantage in reducing information costs accounts for this pattern globally as well as nationally. Even in the United States, where financial markets are the most highly developed, businesses raise about twice as much of their external funds from intermediaries as they do directly from financial markets.

CHECKPOINT

Why might you be willing to buy a bond issued by IBM but prefer to lend to the local computer store through a bank? Your preference results from differences in information costs. Information about IBM is readily available, but you would have to incur significant costs to investigate the creditworthiness of the computer store. A bank can collect information on behalf of many small savers, reducing the cost of lending to the computer store and reducing the chance that you will invest your savings in a losing proposition. o

COMPETITION AND CHANGE IN THE FINANCIAL SYSTEM

Let's say that you've sold your car and have decided not to buy a new one. What will you do with the proceeds from the sale? Your choices are many: Depending on how much you have to invest, you might buy debt or equity claims in a financial market or place your funds in a financial institution. As in other industries, financial markets and financial intermediaries compete for your funds and more generally for market share in the financial system. Their tools for competition are the risk-sharing, liquidity, and information services they offer to savers and borrowers.

Mutual funds and banks, for example, offer savers the chance to hold a diversified portfolio of assets at a lower cost than savers could arrange individually (a risk-sharing service). Mutual funds offer assets that are money market or capital market instruments, whereas a bank's assets are the loans originated and monitored by the bank. Banks and mutual funds compete for savers' funds, and these are but two of many choices savers have.

Borrowers can also choose from an array of financial arrangements. A firm could seek short-term finance through money markets or from an intermediary such as a bank. A firm could raise long-term funds through capital markets or from an intermediary such as a life insurance company.

Financial Innovation

With all the competition among financial markets and institutions, how do savers and borrowers choose among them? They base their decisions on the risk-sharing, liquidity, and information characteristics that are best suited for their needs. A saver who values a low degree of risk, for example, might turn to financial markets that match savers with low-risk borrowers, such as the U.S. government or well-known corporations. Savers who want a diversified portfolio without doing their own research might turn to intermediaries such as banks, which specialize in reducing information costs and have an accumulated stock of information about borrowers. However, the types of services offered by markets and intermediaries change over time.

Changes in costs of providing risk-sharing, liquidity, or information services or changes in demand for these services encourage financial markets and intermediaries to alter their operations and to offer new types of financial assets and liabilities. These improvements in the financial system are called **financial innovation.** Financial innovation can benefit everyone. Indeed, financial markets and institutions that have survived and thrived are those that combine low operation costs with high demand (meeting households' and firms' demand for risk-sharing, liquidity, and information services). Shifts in the cost of and demand for financial services can also alter the competitive balance among markets and institutions in the financial system.

Changes in Financial Integration and Globalization

Financial systems in the United States and around the world become linked more closely every day. The funds in your checking account can help finance a car loan in your hometown, a new drill press in Chicago, a new steel mill in Seoul, or a loan to the government of Brazil. Bringing together savers and borrowers from around the country and around the world helps the global economy.

Integration. One measure of the system's efficiency is its degree of **financial integration,** or the way in which financial markets are tied together geographically. Early nineteenth-century U.S. financial markets were fragmented geographically. Because of the high costs of gathering and communicating information, eastern capital to a large extent was used in the East; similarly, western or southern capital was used in the West or South. Hence interest rates charged to borrowers tended to be different in different parts of the country, making the financing of a high-quality investment project more costly in the West than in the East. As a result, savers sank too much capital in mansions and silver tea sets in Boston while potentially profitable mining and industrial ventures in California lacked funds.

The increasing ease of communicating information has enabled U.S. financial markets to become much more integrated. Now borrowers who raise funds through securities have access to national markets.

CONSIDER THIS . . .

Financial Innovation: Home Mortgages or Rock Star Bonds?

For most of us, the largest transaction we will make is financing the purchase of a home. A generation ago, home mortgage loans were generally made and held by local savings and loan institutions and mortgage bankers. As a result, housing finance tended to be a regional business, making diversification of mortgage loans into different geographical areas difficult for lenders.

In the early 1980s, however, the situation changed. The federal government's credit agencies developed secondary markets to improve the liquidity of home mortgages by increasing their desirability for investors. Mortgage pools could package mortgages from different original lenders and sell claims on the package to savers, a process known as *securitization.* These claims are traded in secondary markets. You may be able to obtain funds from a lender to purchase a house at a lower cost than your parents could obtain 20 years ago.

Securitization has marched on and now includes cash flows beyond mortgages, such as business loans and consumer credit card loans. By 2001, more exotic securitizations included rights to a slice of royalties by rock stars such as David Bowie and Rod Stewart. Pop or flop? Some analysts worry about rock star securitization, which subtracts pooling and adds moral hazard (how hard will the star work when paid up front?) to the old idea.

Globalization. A major development during recent decades has been the global integration of financial markets. Just as capital became more mobile among regions in the United States, moving capital between countries became increasingly important in the 1970s, 1980s, and 1990s. New York's Chase can raise funds in London as easily as it can in Brooklyn, and it can lend money to finance an industrial development project in Queensland, Australia, or in Queens, New York. The globalization of financial markets improves the ability of the financial system to channel savers' funds to the highest-value borrowers, wherever they may be.

Over most of the period following World War II, U.S. financial markets dominated financial markets elsewhere. This dominance eroded substantially during the 1980s and 1990s for two reasons. First, rapid postwar economic growth in Japan and in Europe increased the pool of savings brought to foreign financial markets. Second, during the past decade, many countries lifted regulations that kept their citizens from exporting their savings or foreigners from importing it, thereby enabling savers to transfer their funds to borrowers around the world. In the early 1990s, capital market funds crossed national borders at a rate of several trillion dollars per year. Indeed, the foreign-exchange market now has a volume of trading of more than \$1 trillion per day.

The globalization of financial markets has two effects. First, the easy flow of capital across national boundaries helps countries with productive opportunities to grow, even if their current resources are insufficient. For instance, the U.S. economy grew rapidly in the 1980s, but domestic saving was insufficient to fund the demand for investment. Foreign funds filled the gap between U.S.

investment and U.S. saving. Second, increasing financial integration around the world reduces the cost of allocating savers' funds to the highest-valued uses, wherever they may be. That is what the financial system is supposed to do.

CHECKPOINT

Why do you think many experts have encouraged emerging market economies in Eastern Europe to develop financial intermediaries before relying on financial markets? Financial intermediaries can reduce the information costs of lending in these countries while offering risk-sharing and liquidity services to savers. After information about companies becomes better known to savers, financial markets will become more important. **o**

FINANCIAL REGULATION

Countries' governments around the world regulate financial markets and institutions. This regulation occurs for three reasons. First, governments want to ensure that all participants in the financial system have access to information and that markets and intermediaries give savers and borrowers accurate and

OTHER TIMES, OTHER PLACES . . .

The Growth of International Bond and Stock Markets

Before the 1960s, the term "international bond market" referred to *foreign bonds*, or bonds sold in another country and denominated in that country's currency. Since the 1960s, a new form of finance known as a *Eurobond* has grown rapidly. Unlike foreign bonds, Eurobonds are denominated in a currency other than that of the country where they are sold, usually in U.S. dollars. Currently, about 85% of new issues in the international bond market are Eurobonds, and the value of new issues in the Eurobond market exceeds the value of new issues of the U.S. corporate bond market. Historically the center of foreign borrowing, London has retained its dominance as a center for Eurolending, but competition from other European nations and Japan is expected in the new century.

In the mid-1980s, another new market developed, this time in *Euroequities*, or new equity issues sold to investors abroad. This market has grown rapidly relative to domestic equity issues. Cross-border equity trading is now substantial. The tremendous increase in cross-border equity trading has improved the ability of the financial system to match savers' funds with the highest-value users. But it exposes savers to risks that were unfamiliar a generation ago. For example, a stock market crash in Japan could affect a Japanese bank's ability to pay its creditors around the world.

Global stock and bond transactions are likely to become even more important over the next 10 years. Although bonds continue to account for most financial market capital flows, the multitrillion-dollar equity flows are growing for two reasons. First, equities proved to be lucrative investments in the 1990s. Second, as many countries shift toward private pension schemes, the funds that are available for equity investments are increasing. The internationally integrated financial markets in New York, London, Tokyo, and other cities are making the financial system truly global.

timely information. Without such information, it is difficult to make prudent financial decisions. Second, governments regulate the financial system to maintain financial stability. Stock market crashes, bank failures, and other financial disasters can undermine the efficiency with which the economy's resources are allocated. Finally, the government can advance economic policy by interacting with the financial system. Actions of the Federal Reserve, for example, affect the banking system and promote monetary policy. Over time, regulations imposed by governments change, causing the services and instruments offered by markets or institutions to change.

Provision of Information

The quality of many products—from fish in the supermarket to clothing in a department store—is relatively easy to assess. The quality of other goods and services—from cars to legal services—is more problematic to judge. Even more difficult to evaluate are debt and equity instruments traded in financial markets. A small investor cannot easily judge whether shares or bonds issued by a business are safe investments. The investor could pay a financial analyst or an accounting firm to evaluate corporations that issue stocks and bonds, but the cost of gathering this information is likely to be prohibitive. Because of the demand for this type of service, private firms have organized to collect information on the quality of financial instruments. (Moody's Investor Service and Standard & Poor's Corporation are leading examples.) These firms earn profits by selling the information to individual investors.

However, private firms are not always able to collect truthful information. As a result, the federal government has intervened in financial markets to require issuers of financial instruments to disclose information about their financial condition and to impose penalties on issuers that do not comply. The leading federal regulatory body for financial markets in the United States is the Securities and Exchange Commission (SEC). It was established by the Securities Act of 1933 in response to investors' concerns over the stock market crash of 1929 and fraud by securities dealers during the 1920s. The SEC mandates that corporations issuing bonds or stocks disclose information about earnings, sales, assets, and liabilities. It also limits trading by managers owning large amounts of a firm's stock or others having privileged information (this type of trading is called *insider trading*). These regulations ensure that securities dealers communicate information and that investors are protected from fraud. The SEC prosecuted two leading financiers of the 1980s, Ivan Boesky and Michael Milken, for violating information disclosure and insider trading rules. In derivative markets, the Commodities Futures Trading Commission (CFTC) guards against fraud in futures trading.

Maintenance of Financial Stability

Most regulation of the financial system is concerned with its stability, meaning the ability of financial markets and intermediaries to provide the three key services (risk sharing, liquidity, and information) in the face of economic disturbances. For example, if the stock market were to cease functioning efficiently, stock liquidity would be reduced, and individuals' willingness to hold stocks would diminish. Companies would have difficulty raising capital for investment and job creation. Reductions in the ability of the financial system to provide the three key services raise the cost of moving funds from savers to borrowers. In fact, many economists link the severity of the Great Depression of the 1930s to the breakdown in the banking system's ability to provide financial services. A sudden collapse of a segment of the financial system can lead to sharp reductions in economic activity. Such dramatic instances can prompt new government regulation. Indeed, the length and depth of the Great Depression were responsible for the development of current U.S. financial regulations.

Because most financial assets are held by intermediaries such as banks, pension funds, or insurance companies, policymakers are concerned about the financial soundness of those intermediaries. The federal government has implemented four types of regulations that address such concerns: disclosure of information, prevention of fraud, limitations on competition, and safety of investors' funds. We analyze these regulations in Part 4.

Advancement of Other Policy Objectives

Financial regulation also may be used to further public policy objectives that are unrelated to the efficiency of the financial system. These objectives include controlling the money supply and encouraging particular activities, such as homeownership.

Controlling the money supply. Because banks affect movements in the money supply, which in turn influence the economic variables that affect people's daily lives, policymakers have implemented rules to facilitate control of the quantity of money. For example, the Federal Reserve System requires banks to hold a specified fraction of their deposits in cash or in accounts with the Fed, giving the Fed some control over the money supply.

Encouraging particular activities. Several regulations are designed to promote homeownership, a politically popular objective. One way in which the federal government fosters homeownership is by allowing the deduction of interest paid on a home mortgage from income subject to federal income taxes, something the taxpayer can no longer do for interest on a car loan or credit card debt. In addition, Congress created large government-sponsored financial intermediaries to make home mortgages accessible to many borrowers and, before 1980, restricted savings and loan associations and mutual savings banks to mortgage loans. This restriction was intended to make more funds available for mortgage lending; in fact, it made these institutions vulnerable to certain types of risks. Regulators weakened these limitations in the 1980s. Many economists and policymakers question whether regulations designed to direct savings to finance home mortgages improved the efficiency of the financial system.

The federal government has also intervened in credit markets to subsidize lending for agriculture, college tuition, and other activities that it regards as beneficial to the economy. In each case, the interventions created specialized intermediaries and provided guarantees for certain types of loans.

Effects of Regulation

Regulation affects the ability of financial markets and institutions to provide risk-sharing, liquidity, and information services. Restrictions on the types of instruments that can be traded in markets affect liquidity. Regulations limiting the ability of financial institutions to hold certain types of assets or to operate in various geographic locations affect risk sharing and the potential for diversification. Policymakers should consider the effects of regulation on the financial system's ability to provide risk-sharing opportunities, liquidity, and information. Stringent limits placed on these activities in domestic

TABLE 3.1 **REGULATION OF FINANCIAL INSTITUTIONS AND MARKETS IN THE UNITED STATES**

	Effect of Regulation on Key Services of the Financial System		
Regulatory body	**Risk sharing**	**Liquidity**	**Information**
Securities and Exchange Commission (SEC)	—	Supervises trading in organized exchanges	Mandates information disclosure and financial markets
Commodities Futures Trading Commission (CFTC)	—	Sets rules for trading in futures markets	—
Office of the Comptroller of the Currency (OCC)	Restricts assets held by federally chartered commercial institutions (e.g., banks)	—	Charters and examines federally chartered banks
Federal Deposit Insurance Corporation (FDIC)	Provides insurance to bank depositors	Promotes liquidity of bank deposits	Examines insured banks
Federal Reserve System	Restricts assets of participating financial institutions	Promotes liquidity of bank deposits	Examines commercial banks in Federal Reserve System
State banking and insurance commissions	Impose restrictions on assets held by banks; impose restrictions on	— state-chartered banks and insurance companies bank branching	Charter and examine
Office of Thrift Supervision (OTS)	Restricts assets held by savings and loan	— loan associations associations	Examines savings and
National Credit Union Administration	Restricts assets held by credit unions	— federally chartered credit unions	Charters and examines

markets create opportunities for international competition. Table 3.1 summarizes current regulation of U.S. financial institutions and markets and its effects on their key services.

Financial regulation in other industrial economies, such as Japan, Canada, the United Kingdom, and Western European countries, is broadly similar to that in the United States. The ability of financial markets to provide risk-sharing, liquidity, and information services is enhanced by regulators promoting financial disclosure. The vitality of financial intermediaries is bolstered by licensing and examination of banks and other financial institutions.

These broad similarities notwithstanding, significant differences exist in investor protection in financial markets and in bank regulation. Some industrial countries, among them France, offer weaker protection of creditor claims and outside equity investors, making securities markets for bonds and stocks less important for financing enterprises there than in the United Kingdom or United States. In the area of banking regulation, the United States stands out historically because of its restrictions on branching and on the types of assets banks can hold. Although U.S. branching restrictions were eliminated in 1994, U.S. banks still lack the ability to hold direct equity stakes in firms of the size permitted in Germany or Japan.

KEY TERMS AND CONCEPTS

- Assets
- Asymmetric information
- Auction markets
- Borrowers
- Capital markets
- Cash markets
- Debt
  - Default
  - Interest
  - Intermediate-term debt
  - Long-term debt
  - Maturity
  - Principal
  - Short-term debt
- Derivative markets
- Direct finance
- Diversification
- Dividends
- Equity
- Exchanges
- Financial futures
- Financial innovation
- Financial institutions
- Financial integration
- Financial intermediation
- Financial markets
- Financial system
- Information
- Intermediaries
- Liabilities
- Liquidity
- Money markets
- Options
- Over-the-counter (OTC) markets
- Portfolio
- Primary markets
- Risk sharing
- Savers
- Secondary markets

THE ECONOMIST DECEMBER 18, 1999

Mrs. Watanabe Learns to Invest

"There is only one word to describe the state of mind of the typical Japanese saver," says Yoneo Takeda with a theatrical waggle of his finger: "Turmoil!"

Mr. Takeda is an independent financial adviser, a member of a profession that barely existed in Japan a few years ago. . . .

These advisers are eyeing what is the financial world's biggest pot of gold: ¥1240 trillion ($12 trillion) of household savings, mostly parked in banks, life insurance companies, and the post office. The usual explanation for this lack of adventure is that Mrs. Watanabe, the archetypal housewife who holds the family purse strings, has been averse to risk, especially since the stock market bubble burst in 1990. But there is another explanation—one offering more hope of change: Until now, Japanese households have not taken their investment choices seriously, partly because government rules have stifled both choice and competition.

a

With little variety on offer, savers have simply bought what has been sold to them on the doorstep—life insurance, from Japan's 300,000 "insurance ladies," and time deposits, which graduate recruits at the banks used to sell door-to-door as their first job. . . .

But attitudes are changing. Japan's bookshops are filling their shelves with new *paasonaru fainansu* (personal finance) magazines. . . .

Another force for change is the saturation of Japan's life insurance market. The Japanese have a peculiar penchant for its products, spending around $4000 each year on life insurance, four times as much as Americans or Britons. Takao Ino, an independent financial adviser who used to sell insurance at Sony Life, a subsidiary of the consumer-electronics company, says this is partly because there is a basic confusion in Japan between savings and insurance. Typically, he says, people think of the two as interchangeable—not surprising, since most Japanese life insurance policies blend both. But as people come to understand that they have too much insurance, Mr. Ino thinks they will begin to buy more savings products instead, such as investment trusts (mutual funds). Already, more and more money is going into the stock market, via equity funds. . . . Kathy Matsui of Goldman Sachs compares Japan's mutual-fund industry to that of continental Europe three to five years ago. Savers were also said to be "culturally" more averse to risks than those in Britain and America. Yet in the past three years German mutual funds' assets have grown by nearly 50%. In Italy, they have quadrupled. . . .

b

The effects of these changes are not hard to fathom. Just as in Germany and Italy, Japan could soon witness the virtuous circle of more stock market investment, better corporate governance at its big companies, higher profits, and rising stock prices, which in turn could encourage more investment in the stock market, and so on. . . .

c

The financial system plays a crucial role in economic growth: It brings together savers and borrowers. That is, active financial markets and institutions provide the link between savers' funds and able borrowers.

In a sense, the problems faced by Japan's financial system are difficult to understand. Although the Japanese financial system modernized very slowly in the 1960s and 1970s, rapid change during the 1980s brought the country's financial institutions global prominence. By the late 1990s and into the new century, the system did not seem to be carrying out its key tasks well—in Japan.

a Japan's financial system has not performed its role of matching savers and borrowers. Japanese savers have earned lower returns than U.S. savers in recent years because the Japanese financial system has not allocated funds to their highest-valued users. While Japan is rich—measured by a large pool of savings—poor financial-system performance hinders the ability of the nation to grow by not providing ways for the most promising borrowers to tap into the country's savings.

b Japanese savers may believe that the "mattress" solution is better than supporting value-destroying projects, but other alternatives exist as well. The current problems in matching savers and borrowers create opportunities for competitors. U.S. financial institutions began making inroads in Japan in the late 1990s in consumer lending, commercial lending, and mutual fund management. Japanese household's projected greater relative reliance on mutual funds and equities (as opposed to saving through insurance) is a promising trend. U.S. institutions and some Japanese investors are urging more active investor involvement in corporate governance.

c High information costs impose costs on Japan's economy. In the presence of asymmetric information and weak corporate governance, savers cannot make informed decisions about investments. In principle, financial institutions can step in to gather and monitor information to allocate savers' funds. When banks fail to gather and monitor information effectively, however, savers lose and the cost of funds to good borrowers is unnecessarily high.

For further thought . . .

Using Japan's recent experience as a model, what advice would you give to emerging economies about their developing financial systems?

Source: Excerpted from "Mrs. Watanabe Learns to Invest," *The Economist,* December 18, 1999.

SUMMARY

1. The basic motivation for financial trade, and hence for the development of a financial system, is that individuals, businesses, and governments sometimes need to save and at other times need to borrow. The financial system channels funds from savers to borrowers, giving savers claims on borrowers' future income.
2. The financial system provides three key services: risk sharing, liquidity, and information. These services make financial claims attractive to savers and can lower the cost of finance for borrowers. Differences in the demand for and the cost of providing these services partially explain changes in the U.S. financial system over time, as well as differences among financial systems internationally.
3. The financial system brings together savers and borrowers in two ways. In direct finance through financial markets, individual savers hold the claims issued by individual borrowers. In indirect finance through financial intermediaries, claims held by savers are claims against intermediaries that are backed by their portfolios of assets, which are claims on the borrowers.
4. Financial markets for debt and equity include primary markets, in which claims are newly issued, and secondary markets, in which outstanding claims are traded. In secondary markets, some claims mature in less than one year (money market), whereas others mature in more than one year (capital market); some claims are traded by auction, whereas others are traded over the counter; and some claims are traded in cash markets, whereas others are traded in derivative markets.
5. Financial intermediaries act as go-betweens for savers and borrowers. These institutions acquire funds from savers and then make loans to or purchase financial instruments issued by borrowers. In the process, financial intermediaries provide risk-sharing, liquidity, and information services that especially benefit small savers and borrowers.
6. Changes in the financial system are called financial innovations. Shifts in the demand for and cost of providing risk-sharing, liquidity, and information services lead to changes in the operation of financial markets and institutions.
7. An important measure of the financial system's efficiency is its degree of integration, or the way in which markets are tied together geographically. Financial markets have become much more integrated over many years in the United States and are now becoming integrated globally.
8. Another cause of differences and changes in financial systems is government regulation. Governments regulate financial markets for three reasons: (a) to guarantee provision of information, (b) to maintain the stability of the financial system, and (c) to advance other policy objectives.

REVIEW QUESTIONS

1. Why do households save? Why do businesses borrow? Why are the financial services of risk sharing, liquidity, and information valued by savers and borrowers?
2. Explain why financial assets are considered to be uses of funds from the point of view of savers and sources of funds from the point of view of borrowers.
3. Why are money market assets typically more liquid than capital market assets? Does the relative illiquidity of capital market assets have any consequences for the banking system?
4. Under what circumstances does financial regulation improve the efficiency of the financial system?
5. What is meant by *integration* of financial markets? What effect would increased integration of financial markets, domestically and internationally, have on returns for savers? On costs to borrowers?
6. What are the benefits to savers and borrowers if financial markets communicate all available information about financial instruments via their prices?

In Questions 7–12, categorize the transactions described according to whether they (a) rely on financial markets or intermediaries, (b) occur in the primary or secondary market or, (c) are carried out in the money or capital market.

7. A bank makes a 30-year mortgage loan to a household.
8. The bank sells a mortgage loan to a government-sponsored financial intermediary.
9. ABC Corporation opens for business by selling shares of stock to 10 private investors.
10. Joan Robinson sells her shares of ABC stock to someone else.
11. The DEF money market mutual fund buys $100,000 of three-month Treasury bills in the government's weekly auction.
12. DEF buys $100,000 of three-month Treasury bills from First Bank.

ANALYTICAL PROBLEMS

13. An attribute of financial assets that investors sometimes overlook is the asset's tax treatment. Suppose that you are an investor with a choice among three assets that are identical in every way except in their rate of return and rate of taxation. Which asset yields the highest after-tax return?

    A: interest rate 10%, interest taxed at a 40% rate.

    B: interest rate 8%, interest taxed at a 25% rate.

    C: interest rate 6.5%, no tax on interest.
14. Suppose that asset A in Problem 13 paid 11%. Would your answer change?
15. What is "insider trading"? Analyze the consequences for securities markets of legalizing insider trading.
16. The text states that because of financial integration and globalization: "The funds in your checking account can help finance a car loan in your hometown, a new drill press in Chicago, a new steel mill in Seoul, or a loan to the government of Brazil." Is the possibility that U.S. savings might be loaned to foreign businesses or governments a good or bad development from the point of view of the U.S. economy?
17. Why do people want to share risk? After all, the only way to get rich is to take risks.
18. Do banks and other financial intermediaries like high interest rates? Why or why not?
19. Traditionally, financial markets in Germany and Japan have played a smaller role in financing businesses than markets in the United States and Great Britain, while financial institutions play a larger role as a source of long-term funds. What factors determine whether businesses rely more heavily on financial markets or financial institutions to raise funds needed for investment in plant and equipment?
20. You have not yet studied the effects of financial regulation on incentives for borrowers and savers. Do you think that insuring savers against fluctuations in the value of claims on financial institutions necessarily makes the financial system more efficient? Why or why not?

DATA QUESTION

21. In a current issue of *The Wall Street Journal,* try to find financial instruments traded in money and capital markets, auction and over-the-counter markets, and cash and derivative markets. Compare the yields on these different assets. Can you explain the different yields?

APPENDIX: Financial Instruments

Financial instruments are the vehicles by which financial markets channel funds from savers to borrowers and provide returns to savers. In this appendix, we compare major instruments, or securities, traded in the financial system. For convenience, we analyze money market and capital market instruments separately. (Recall that money market claims mature in less than a year and capital market claims mature in more than a year.) Both money market and capital market assets are actively traded in U.S. financial markets. We describe the issuers and the characteristics of the most widely used instruments here and discuss them in more detail in Parts 2 and 3.

Money Market Instruments

The short maturity of money market assets doesn't allow much time for their returns to vary. Therefore these instruments are safe investments for short-term surplus funds of households and firms. However, in making investment decisions, savers must still consider the possibility of default—the chance that the borrower will be unable to repay all the amount borrowed plus interest at maturity.

U.S. Treasury bills. U.S. Treasury securities are short-term debt obligations of the U.S. government. They are also the most liquid money market instrument because they have the largest trading volume. The federal government can raise taxes and issue currency to repay the amount borrowed, so there is virtually no risk of default.† Treasury securities with maturities of less than one year are called Treasury bills (T-bills). Although individuals can hold them, the largest holders of T-bills are commercial banks, followed by other financial intermediaries, businesses, and foreign investors.

Commercial paper. Commercial paper provides a liquid, short-term investment for savers and a source of funds for corporations. High-quality, well-known firms and financial institutions use commercial paper to raise funds. Because these borrowers are generally the most creditworthy, the default risk is small, but the interest rate is higher than that on Treasury bills. The growth in the commercial paper market during the past two decades is part of a shift by many corporations toward direct finance (and away from bank loans).

Bankers' acceptances. Designed to facilitate international trade, bankers' acceptances are instruments that establish credit between parties who do not know each other. A banker's acceptance is a checklike promise that the bank will pay the amount of funds indicated to the recipient. It is issued by a firm (usually an importer) and is payable on a date indicated. The bank that marks

† Technically, in the United States, the Federal Reserve issues currency.

the draft "accepted" guarantees the payment to the recipient (usually an exporter or its representing bank). The issuing firm is required to deposit funds in the bank sufficient to cover the draft; if it does not do so, the bank is still obligated to make good on the draft. The bank's good name is likely to enable an importer to buy goods from an overseas exporter that lacks knowledge about whether the importer will be able to pay. In recent years, acceptances have generally been resold in secondary markets and held by other banks, households, and businesses.

Repurchase agreements. Repurchase agreements, also known as repos or RPs, are used for cash management by large corporations. They are very short-term loans, typically with maturities of less than two weeks. In many cases, a firm loans a bank money overnight. For example, if a large firm such as IBM has idle cash, it purchases T-bills from a bank that agrees to buy them back the next morning at a higher price, reflecting the accumulated interest. The T-bills serve as collateral; that is, if the borrower defaults, the lender receives the T-bills. Since their inception in 1969, repurchase agreements have become a significant source of funds for banks.

Federal (Fed) funds. Federal funds instruments represent overnight loans between banks of their deposits with the Federal Reserve System (the U.S. central bank). Banking regulations require that banks deposit a percentage of their deposits as reserves with the Fed. If a bank is temporarily low on reserves, it can borrow funds from another bank that has reserves greater than the required level. The federal funds market reflects the credit needs of commercial banks, so money market analysts watch the *federal funds rate* (the interest rate charged on these overnight loans) closely. When it is high, banks need additional funds; when it is low, banks have low credit needs.

Eurodollars. Eurodollars are U.S. dollars deposited in foreign branches of U.S. banks or in foreign banks outside the United States (not necessarily in Europe). Rather than being converted into the currency of the foreign country, the deposits remain denominated in dollars. U.S. banks can then borrow these funds. Eurodollar funds raised abroad have become an important source of funds for U.S. banks.

Negotiable bank certificates of deposit. A certificate of deposit (CD) is a fixed-maturity instrument sold by a bank to depositors; it pays principal and interest at maturity. You might, for example, take the $1000 you earned over vacation and put it in a CD for six months at 5% interest (an annual rate). After six months, your investment would be worth $1025. Before 1961, CDs were illiquid because they were nonnegotiable; that is, the depositors could not sell them to someone else before redemption. In 1961, Citibank created the *negotiable certificate of deposit*—a CD in a large denomination (over $100,000, and today typically over $1,000,000) that could be sold again in a secondary market. Negotiable CDs are an important source of funds for banks today and are held principally by mutual funds and nonfinancial corporations.

Figure 3A.1

Money Market Instruments in the United States

U.S. Treasury bills, commercial paper, and negotiable CDs are the leading money market instruments. Since 1980, commercial paper issues have grown relative to negotiable CD issues.

Sources: Federal Reserve Flow of Funds Accounts; Council of Economic Advisers, *Economic Report of the President; Federal Reserve Bulletin.*

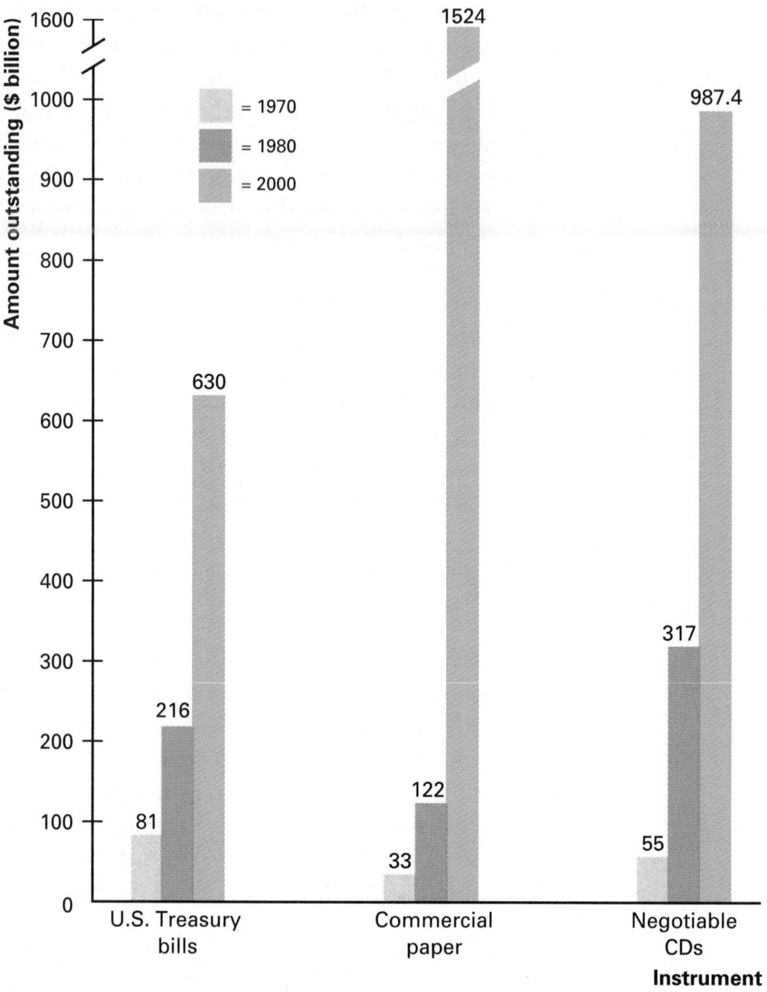

Concluding remarks. Figure 3A.1 shows the amounts of the principal money market instruments outstanding in 1970, 1980, and 2000. Information on interest rates for these instruments appears each business day in the Money Rates column of *The Wall Street Journal.* Note the especially rapid growth in commercial paper and negotiable certificates of deposit. In Part 4, we show that this growth reflects important changes in the business of banking during the past two decades.

Capital Market Instruments

Because capital market instruments have longer maturities than money market instruments, they are subject to greater fluctuations in their returns. For this reason, borrowers who seek to use funds for a long period of time and savers with long investment horizons invest in them. With the exception of U.S. government obligations, all capital market debt instruments contain some risk of default.

U.S. Treasury securities. Intermediate-term and long-term U.S. Treasury securities are bonds issued by the federal government to finance budget deficits. They are widely traded and hence are liquid. Since 1997, these instruments have included inflation-indexed notes and bonds. These government securities are held by domestic banks and households, foreigners, and the Federal Reserve System.

U.S. government agency securities. U.S. government agency securities are intermediate-term or long-term bonds issued by the federal government or government-sponsored agencies. For example, the Farm Credit System issues bonds to raise money to finance agricultural activities, and the Government National Mortgage Association (GNMA) issues bonds to finance home mortgages. Many such securities are officially guaranteed by the government (with a pledge of the government's "full faith and credit"); others are implicitly guaranteed, so the default risk is still low.

State and local government bonds. State and local government bonds (often called municipal bonds) are intermediate-term or long-term bonds issued by municipalities and state governments. These governmental units use the funds borrowed to build schools, roads, and other large capital projects. The bonds are exempt from federal income taxation (and typically also income taxation by the issuing state). These bonds are often held by high-tax-bracket households, commercial banks, and life insurance companies. Although generally considered safe, these instruments do have some default risk. In the early 1930s, for example, many state and local governments defaulted on their bonds. In 1994, Orange County, California's default sent shock waves through the municipal bond market.

Stocks. Stocks are issued as equity claims by corporations and represent the largest single category of capital market assets. However, new stock issues are not a major source of funding for nonfinancial businesses in the United States and many other countries. From the end of World War II through 1980, new share issues accounted for about 5% of total funds raised. During the late 1980s, new share issues were substantially *negative* (–30% of funds raised in 1988, for example), as U.S. corporations used funds raised with debt to buy back shares. That trend reversed in the early 1990s, but share repurchases increased again in the late 1990s.

Corporate bonds. Corporate bonds are intermediate-term and long-term obligations issued by large, high-quality corporations to finance plant and equipment spending. Typically, corporate bonds pay interest twice each year and repay the principal amount borrowed at maturity. There are many varia-

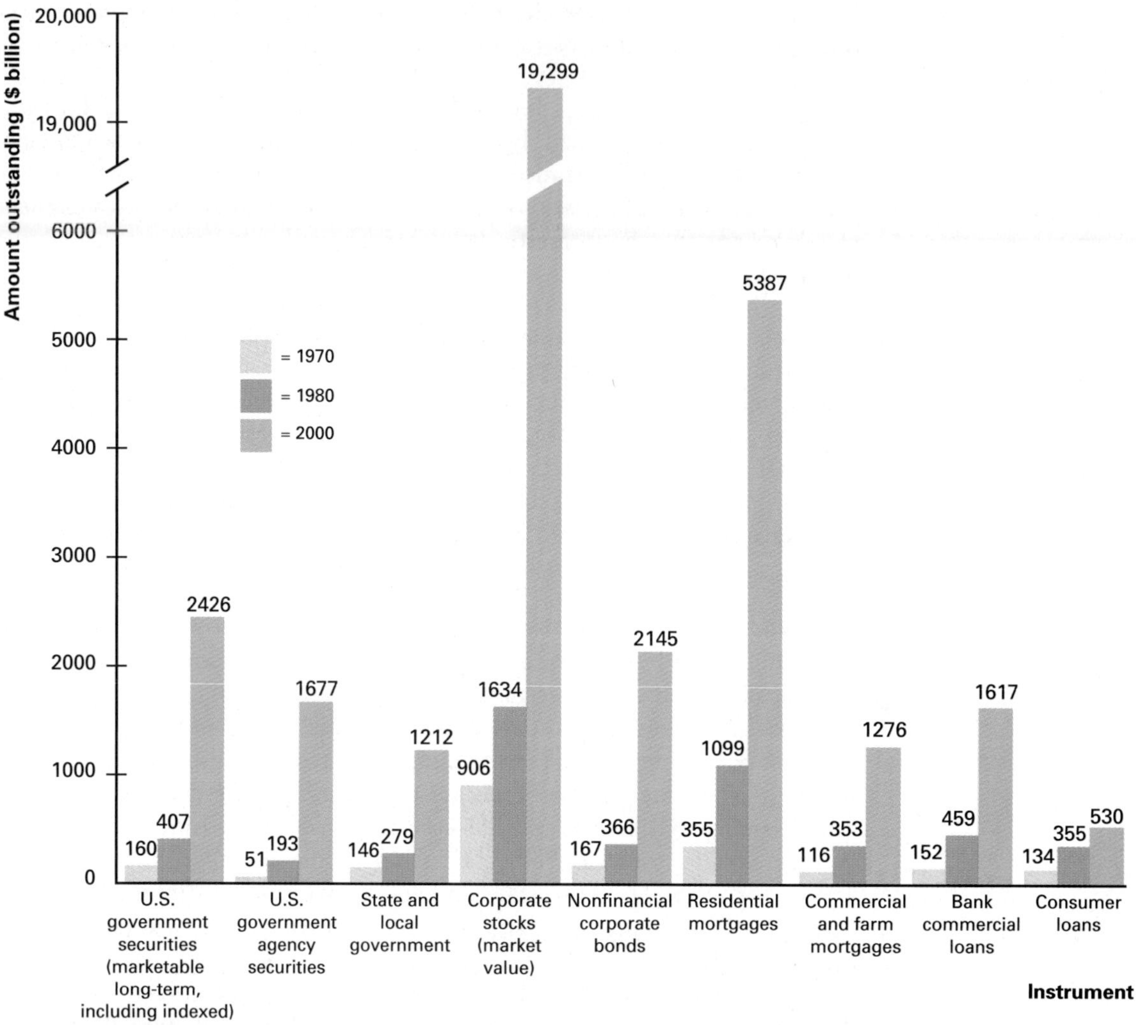

Figure 3A.2

Capital Market Instruments in the United States

The leading capital market instruments are corporate stocks, residential mortgages, and U.S. government securities. Since 1970, the share of outstanding capital market instruments represented by U.S. government securities has doubled.

Sources: Federal Reserve Flow of Funds Accounts; Federal Reserve Bulletin.

tions, however. *Convertible bonds,* for example, allow the holder to convert the debt into equity (for a specified number of shares). By using such variations, firms can sometimes lower their borrowing costs by giving bond buyers an extra return if the firm does exceptionally well. Corporate bonds are not as liquid as government securities because they are less widely traded. Corporate bonds have greater default risk than government bonds, but they generally fluctuate less in price than corporate equities.

Although the corporate bond market is smaller than the stock market in the United States, it is more important for raising funds because corporations issue new shares infrequently. Most funds raised through financial markets take the form of corporate bonds. Investors in corporate bonds are a diverse group, including households, life insurance companies, and pension funds.

Mortgages. Mortgages are loans (usually long-term) to households or businesses to purchase buildings or land, with the underlying asset (house, plant, or piece of land) serving as collateral. In the United States, the mortgage market is the largest debt market. Residential mortgages, the largest component, are issued by savings institutions and commercial banks. Mortgage loans for industrial and agricultural borrowers are made by life insurance companies and commercial banks. Since World War II, the growth of the mortgage market has been spurred by federal government interventions to encourage homeownership by creating a liquid secondary national mortgage market. Three government agencies—Federal National Mortgage Association (FNMA), Government National Mortgage Association (GNMA), and the Federal Home Loan Mortgage Corporation (FHLMC)—borrow in bond markets to provide funds for mortgage financing.

Commercial bank loans. Commercial bank loans include loans to businesses and consumers made by banks and finance companies. Secondary markets for commercial bank loans are not as well developed as those for other capital market instruments, so these loans are less liquid than mortgages. In Chapter 13, we show how recent developments in banking and financial markets are improving the liquidity of these loans.

Concluding remarks. Figure 3A.2 summarizes the amounts of principal capital market instruments outstanding in 1970, 1980, and 2000. Note the enormous growth in U.S. government and government agency securities. This growth reflects the borrowing necessitated by large federal budget deficits in the 1980s and early 1990s and the increasing prominence of federal credit agencies in the capital market.

PART 2

Interest Rates

In Part 2, we focus on how interest rates are determined. In so doing, we study ways in which decisions of thousands of individual lenders and borrowers in the United States and around the world set the market interest rates we read about in the newspaper. (Later, in Part 5, we explore how decisions of the Federal Reserve affect interest rates.) We begin in Chapter 4 by explaining what interest rates are, how they are measured, and where you can obtain information about interest rates to be better informed in making your financial decisions. In Chapter 5, we look at how savers compare interest rates and returns on assets to allocate their savings in a portfolio, or collection of assets.

Chapters 6 and 7 are the key analytical chapters. In Chapter 6, we study how decisions about lending and borrowing determine bond prices and market interest rates in the United States and in the international capital market. Chapter 7 extends the analysis to encompass the hundreds of interest rates that are reported each business day in *The Wall Street Journal*. We will see how differences in risk, liquidity, information costs, taxation, and maturity affect interest rates.

CHAPTER 4

Interest Rates and Rates of Return

The news media report interest rates every day—and with good reason. The interest rate is the borrower's cost on a loan and the lender's reward on the investment. Interest rates affect individuals' decisions about whether to spend more or save to buy a house or for retirement. They also affect businesspeople's decisions about whether to expand operations by building factories and purchasing new equipment or buy Treasury bonds. In 2000, interest rates on bank deposits and money market funds were about 6%, bad news for investors who had obtained double-digit (10% or greater) rates several years earlier. As a result, many individual savers sought higher interest rates from investments, such as long-term Treasury securities and corporate bonds. Savers must evaluate the interest they will earn, and the rate of return on their investment, to select the financial instrument that offers them the best deal.

Decisions facing investors are complex, however, because there are so many alternatives, but investors can use some common techniques to compare the values of different securities. In this chapter, we look specifically at debt instruments to determine their returns. You will learn to measure interest rates and rates of return on different investments and to compare these values on investments offering different repayment schedules. This chapter also provides the background for the further study of interest rates in Chapters 5–7, where you will learn how interest rates are determined and how savers allocate their wealth.

COMPARING DEBT INSTRUMENTS

When you place your savings in a financial market or institution, the financial system channels those funds to borrowers. The funds are assets to you (the saver) and liabilities, or claims on future income, to the borrowers. If you save through a bank, the bank pays you interest, and borrowers pay the bank interest for the indirect use of your funds. Likewise, if you buy a Treasury bond, the U.S. government pays you interest for the use of your money.

Debt instruments (also called **credit market instruments**), such as those issued by banks, the government, and corporations were introduced in Chapter 3. Although debt instruments might vary in the timing of their payments, the guarantees made by borrowers to lenders, and restrictions in the loan agreement, all are IOUs, or promises by the borrower to pay interest and repay principal to a lender. Debt instruments take different forms because lenders and borrowers have different needs. In this section we compare debt instruments by grouping them into four general categories: simple loans, discount bonds, coupon bonds, and fixed-payment loans. We first look at the differences in the timing of their payments, and we then describe techniques that investors can use to compare their values.

Timing of Payments

We use the categories of bonds to identify the variations in the timing of payments that bond issuers make to lenders. Borrowers issuing simple loans and discount bonds pay interest in a single payment. In contrast, issuers of coupon bonds and fixed-payment loans pay investors in multiple payments of interest and principal. In addition to describing each bond type, we represent the payments on a time line to make it easier to measure the inflows and outflows of funds.

Simple Loan. With a simple loan, the borrower receives from the lender an amount of funds called the *principal* and agrees to repay the lender the principal plus an additional amount called *interest* (as a fee for using the funds) at a given date (maturity). For example, suppose that Sunbank makes a one-year simple loan of $10,000 at 10% interest to Nelson's Nurseries. We can illustrate this transaction on a time line to show the return to the lender (saver), or payment of interest and principal by the borrower. After one year, Nelson's would repay the principal plus interest: $10,000 + (0.10) ($10,000), or $11,000. On a time line, the lender views the transaction as follows:†

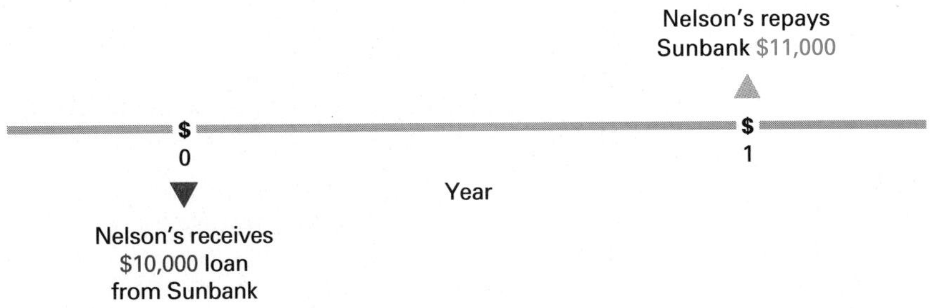

We can express this transaction more generally in an equation for computing the total payment to a lender of principal P and interest at the interest rate i for a simple loan:

$$\text{Total payment to lender} = \underset{\text{Principal}}{P} + \underset{\text{Interest}}{iP} = P(1 + i),$$

The most common simple loan is a short-term commercial loan from a bank.

† Although we illustrate the payments from the saver's perspective, the interest rate concepts that we develop in the chapter are important for both savers' and borrowers' decisions.

Discount bond. A borrower also repays a **discount bond** in a single payment. In this case, however, the borrower pays the lender the amount of the loan, called the *face value* (or par value), at maturity but receives less than the face value initially. Suppose Nelson's Nurseries issued a one-year discount bond with a face value of $10,000, and received $9091, repaying $10,000 after one year. Hence the time line for Nelson's Nurseries discount bond is

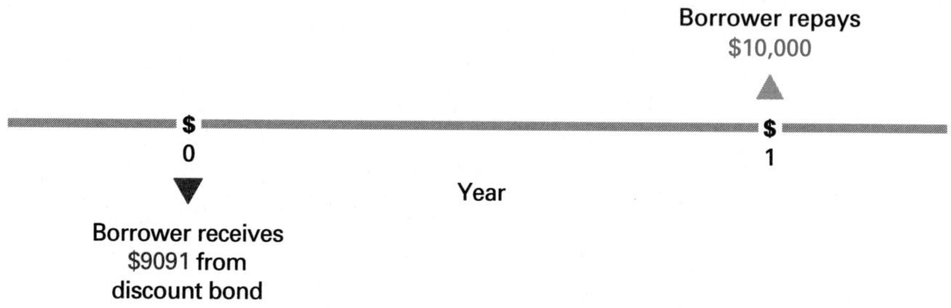

The lender receives interest of $10,000 − $9091 = $909 for the year; the implicit interest rate is 909/9091 = 10%. The most common types of discount obligations are U.S. savings bonds, U.S. Treasury bills, and zero-coupon bonds.

Coupon bond. Borrowers issuing a coupon bond make multiple payments of interest at regular intervals, such as semiannually or annually, and repay the face value at maturity. A coupon bond specifies the maturity date, face value, issuer (a governmental unit or private corporation), and coupon rate. The coupon rate equals the yearly coupon payment divided by the face value. For example, if Pond Industries issued a $10,000, 20-year bond, promising a coupon rate of 10%, it would pay $1000 per year for the 20 years and a final payment of $10,000 at the end of 20 years (the face value). The time line of payments on the Pond Industries' coupon bond is

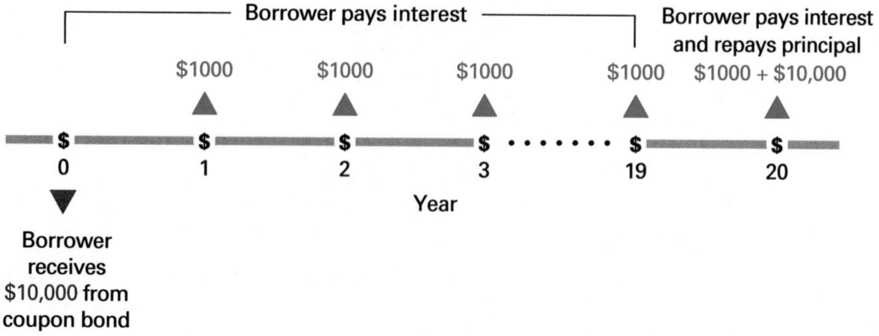

Long-term U.S. Treasury bonds and notes and long-term corporate bonds of relatively well-known firms are examples of coupon bonds.

CONSIDER THIS . . .

Can They STRIP? Creating New Financial Instruments

In the late 1970s and early 1980s, the U.S. Treasury issued only two types of instruments: Treasury bills, which are discount bonds, and long-term Treasury bonds, which are coupon bonds. However, interest rates began fluctuating significantly, and investors could not predict whether they would rise or fall from their current level. Investors were concerned that if interest rates fell over the life of a coupon bond, they would have to reinvest their coupon payments at an interest rate lower than the original coupon rate. Therefore investors demanded longer-term discount bonds, on which they would know the exact return if they held the instruments to maturity.

With the hope of earning a profit, financial markets responded to investors' demands. In 1982, Merrill Lynch created a new instrument called a TIGR (Treasury Investment Growth Receipt), which works like Treasury bills (discount bonds). Merrill Lynch buys $1 million of 20-year Treasury bonds with a coupon rate of, say, 9%. Merrill Lynch is then entitled to receive $90,000 each year for 20 years from the Treasury, plus the $1 million face value after 20 years. However, Merrill Lynch does not hold the bonds. Instead, it sells $90,000 of one-year TIGR bills, which are fully backed by the underlying $1 million of 20-year bonds, to investors. The rights to these individual interest payments received by investors are known as Treasury "Strips."

The Treasury soon realized the potential profits of offering longer-term bills and, in 1984, introduced its own version of Merrill Lynch's innovation. Called STRIPS (Separate Trading of Registered Interest and Principal of Securities), the new instrument allowed investors to register and trade ownership for each interest payment and for the face value. Hence individuals can effectively obtain long-term discount bonds or coupon bonds from the government, increasing their options for investment.

Fixed-payment loan. In a **fixed-payment loan,** the borrower makes regular periodic payments (monthly, quarterly, or annually) to the lender. The payments includ33e both interest and principal; thus at maturity there is no lump-sum payment of principal. Common fixed-payment loans are home mortgages, student loans, and installment loans (such as automobile loans). For example, repaying a $10,000, 10-year student loan with a 9% interest rate means a monthly payment of approximately $127. The time line of payments from the lender's perspective would be

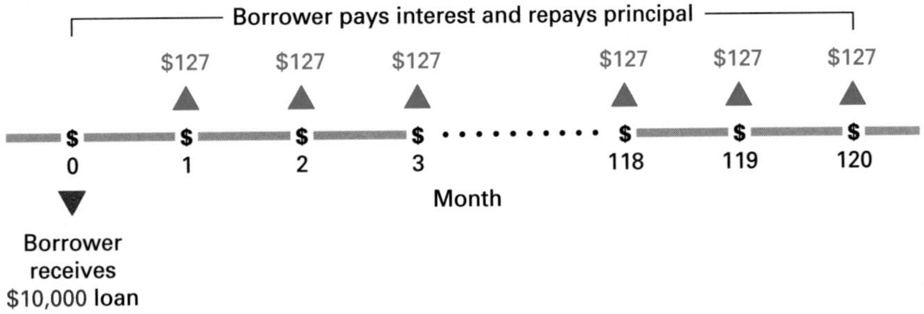

Although most credit market instruments fall into these four categories; the changing needs of savers and borrowers have spurred the creation of new instruments having characteristics of more than one category.

Present Value

We can now turn to the important task of comparing the returns from simple loans, discount bonds, coupon bonds, and fixed-payment loans. This comparison is not easy because each type of instrument makes payments to lenders (savers) in different amounts at different times. The solution to this problem is the concept of **present value,** a measure that provides a way to compare interest rates on different instruments.

Using present value, we can answer questions such as these: Is a 30-year, \$10,000 Treasury bond with an annual coupon payment of \$800 a better investment than a six-month Treasury bill that gives you \$10,000 for an investment of \$9500? Would you be better off financing your new home with a 15-year mortgage at 9% or by borrowing for five years at 8% and refinancing thereafter? How can a saver determine which debt instrument offers the best return?

The problem is this: Dollars paid in different periods are not in the same units. Suppose, for example, that a friend offers you a dollar and says that you can have it either today or a year from today. Which would you pick? Most people would take the dollar today. A dollar received in the future is worth less than a dollar received today. Because credit market instruments pay different amounts in different periods, we need a way to compare amounts paid at different times.

You have no doubt solved the problem of comparing different quantities already. To find the total weight of three items weighing 1 pound, 8 ounces, and $\frac{1}{4}$ ton, you converted them to a common unit. If you express each in pounds, you can then add them. That is, $1\text{ lb} + \frac{1}{2}\text{ lb} + 500\text{ lb} = 501\frac{1}{2}\text{ lb}$. Just as you cannot add weights in different units, you cannot add measures of money paid in different periods. To find a common unit to measure funds at different times, we must find the present value of each payment by putting all payments in *today's dollars*. Then we can compare each payment.

Let's see how present value works. Suppose that you have just won \$6500 in a contest. You would like to save the winnings so that eventually you can buy a car. You take the money to your bank, which offers you 5% interest each year. After one year, you have a total of \$6825, or your original \$6500 plus interest of \$325. The time line is

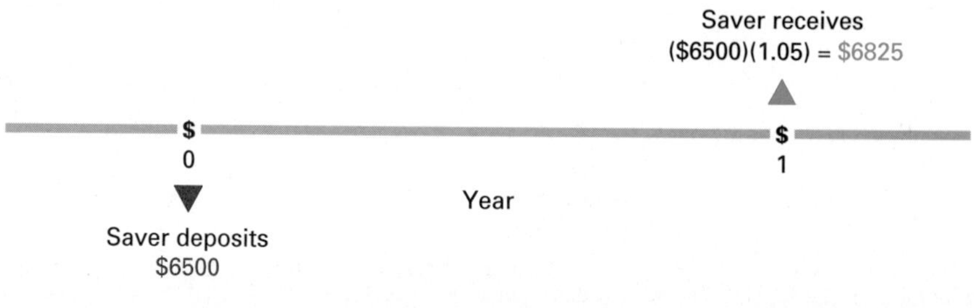

What if you want and can afford to save the money for longer than one year? If the interest rate remained constant at 5% and you reinvested, or rolled over, your principal and accumulated interest, you would earn 5% interest on your accumulated savings each period. This process of earning interest on the interest (as well as on the principal) is known as **compounding.** At the end of two years you would have (\$6825)(1.05) = \$7166. At the end of five years, you would have $(\$6500)(1.05)^5$, or approximately \$8300. At the end of n years, you would have $(\$6500)(1.05)^n$, as shown on this time line:

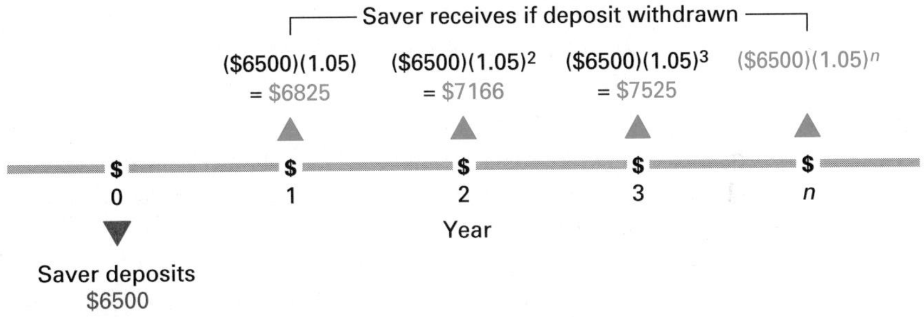

Looking at interest payments on a time line helps to explain the value that savers and borrowers put on debt instruments. The next step is to develop a general procedure to use in comparing different instruments.

Let's return to the example of saving for a car, in which you put aside \$6500 today. At an interest rate of 5%, you could buy an \$8300 car five years from now. If 5% is the prevailing interest rate for savers, \$6500 today and \$8300 in five years have the same present value. That is, at a 5% annual interest rate, you would be indifferent about receiving \$6500 today or \$8300 in five years.

Now let's write a general expression that allows us to find the present value of \$1 received n years in the future. If we assume that the interest rate is constant at rate i over the n years, the present value is

$$\text{Present value of future } \$1 = \frac{\$1}{(1+i)^n}. \tag{4.1}$$

Equation (4.1) shows that a future dollar is worth less than a current dollar because the denominator is greater than 1. In other words, you can invest a dollar today and earn interest at rate i.

Applying this present value expression to the sum of payments made over time allows us to value those payments today. Suppose that Mary Lucky wins \$2 million in the state lottery, to be paid in \$100,000 installments each year for 20 years. If the interest rate is currently 10% and is expected to remain at 10% for the next 20 years, Ms. Lucky is not as rich as she thought. The \$100,000 she receives this year has a present value of \$100,000, but next year's payment is worth only \$100,000/1.10, or \$90,909 in today's dollars. Hence the sum of the payments over 20 years has a present value of \$936,492, or less than half of the stated value of the prize (although we would likely shed no tears for Ms. Lucky).

We use present value as a measure to evaluate savers' returns from different credit market instruments that have different time patterns for payments. Because each payment has a different present value, savers cannot simply add up total payments to determine which instrument is the best investment. They must find the present value of each payment and add the present values: The sum of these individual present values equals the present value of the cash flows from holding the instrument.

To demonstrate how we can use the present value equation to assess two alternative debt securities, suppose that the interest rate is 10% and you are offered either a discount bond paying you \$1000 in five years or a fixed-payment loan paying you \$150 per year for five years for a price of \$600. Which should you buy? To answer the question, you need to calculate the present value of the payments from the two financial instruments. The present value of the discount bond's payments is

$$\begin{matrix}\text{Present value}\\ \text{(discount bond)}\end{matrix} = \frac{\$1000}{1.10^5} = \$620.92,$$

whereas the present value of the payments from the fixed-payment loan is

$$\begin{matrix}\text{Present value}\\ \text{(fixed-payment bond)}\end{matrix} = \frac{\$150}{1.10} + \frac{\$150}{1.10^2} + \frac{\$150}{1.10^3} + \frac{\$150}{1.10^4} + \frac{\$150}{1.10^5} = \$568.62.$$

Because the present value of the payments from the discount bond is greater than \$600 and that of the payments on the fixed-payment loan is less than \$600, you would be willing to buy the discount bond at the \$600 offering price.

Figure 4.1 summarizes payment schedules for the four main categories of credit market instruments—simple loan, discount bond, coupon bond, and fixed-payment loan—from the lender's perspective. Each has the same present value: \$1000 for a five-year loan at an interest rate of 10%. Note that although the four instruments have the same present value, the time patterns of the payments differ significantly. In the case of a simple loan or discount bond, for example, no payment is received until year 5. For the coupon bond and the fixed-payment loan, however, the lender receives payments each year. Using the present value equation, the lender can compare the present values of returns on different credit market instruments, even though the returns in any given period need not be comparable.

CHECKPOINT

Suppose that *Business Week* magazine offers you a deal: a two-year subscription for \$50 or a subscription this year for \$30 and another next year for an additional \$30. Which deal should you choose? To make the two methods of payment comparable, you

Figure 4.1

Time Lines for Credit Market Instrument Repayment

The four main categories of credit market instruments (shown from the lender's perspective) have the same present value but different time patterns of repayment.

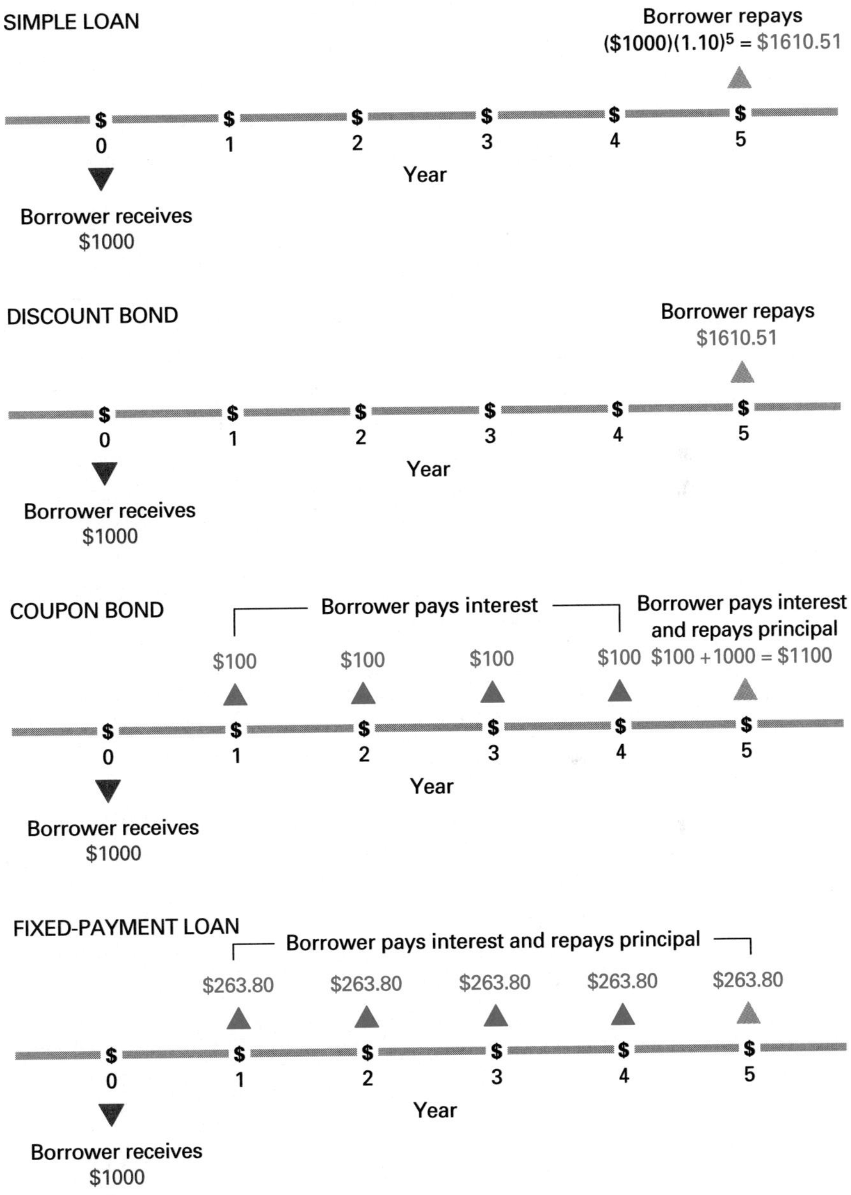

value them in today's dollars. At an interest rate of 5%, the present value of the two one-year subscriptions is \$30 + (\$30/1.05) = \$58.57. Because the present value of the two-year subscription is \$50, it is the better deal. o

Using Yield to Maturity as a Yardstick

In determining the present value of a debt instrument in the previous discussion, we were given an interest rate. In reality, we often know the price of a debt instrument in today's dollars and the future payment schedule; we don't always know the interest rate. More typically, the problem confronting a saver is one like this: Which is a better investment to buy, a $10,000 coupon bond for $10,220 with a coupon rate of 8% or a six-month, $10,000 Treasury bill for $9600? How can the saver evaluate which is the better deal in the financial marketplace? The solution is to use a present value calculation to find interest rates. Instead of asking, "At the going interest rate, what payment today puts me in the same financial position as some set of payments in the future?", ask, "If I pay a price P today for a set of future payments, what is the interest rate at which I could invest P and get the same set of future payments?" For example, instead of calculating the present value of the payments to be received on a 30-year Treasury bond, we calculate the interest rate at which the money paid for the bond could be invested for 30 years to get the same present value.

The interest rate that equates the present value of the asset's returns with its price today is called the **yield to maturity.** The yield to maturity comes from the economically sensible concept of present value and is the interest rate measure that is used most often in financial markets. Calculating yields to maturity for alternative investments allows savers to compare any type of credit market instrument. For example, you can compare the yield to maturity on a 30-year Treasury bond with a 20-year fixed-payment loan to determine which investment gives you the greatest return. Let's calculate the yield to maturity for each of the four types of credit market instruments.

Simple loans. Finding the yield to maturity for a simple loan is straightforward. We seek the interest rate that makes the lender indifferent about having the amount of the loan today or the final payment at maturity. Consider again the $10,000 loan to Nelson's Nurseries. The loan requires payment of the $10,000 plus $1000 in interest one year from now. We calculate the yield to maturity as follows:

$$\text{Value today} = \text{Present value of future payment}$$

$$10{,}000 = \frac{10{,}000 + 1000}{1 + i},$$

from which we solve for i:

$$i = \frac{11{,}000 - 10{,}000}{10{,}000} = 0.10, \text{ or } 10\%.$$

Note that the yield to maturity, 10%, is the same as the simple interest rate. From this example, we can come to the general conclusion that, for a simple loan, the yield to maturity and the specified interest rate are equivalent.

Discount bonds. Calculating the yield to maturity of a discount bond is similar to finding that of a simple loan. Let's calculate the yield to maturity on a one-period discount bond, where a period may be a quarter or a year. The yield to maturity is the interest rate that equates the current purchase price with the present value of the future payment. We use the same equation to find the yield to maturity on the $10,000 discount bond of Nelson's Nurseries as we did in the case of a simple loan. If Nelson's Nurseries receives $9200 today, we calculate the yield to maturity by setting the present value of the future payment equal to the value today, or $\$9200 = \$10{,}000/(1+i)$. Solving for i gives

$$i = \frac{10{,}000 - 9200}{9200} = 0.087 \quad \text{or} \quad 8.7\%.$$

From this example we can write a general equation for a one-period discount bond at price D with face value F. The yield to maturity i is

$$i = \frac{F - D}{D}. \tag{4.2}$$

Coupon bonds. Coupon bonds have many payment periods. Because the yield to maturity equates the present value of all the bond's payments with its price today, we write an expression for the present value of each payment, calculate each amount, and add them. For example, suppose that Growthco issued a 10-year, $10,000 coupon bond with an annual coupon payment of $1000. What is the present value of the $1000 received next year? If i is the yield to maturity,

$$\text{Present value of \$1000 payment in one year} = \frac{\$1000}{1+i}.$$

Similarly, the present value of the second year's coupon payment would be

$$\begin{array}{c}\text{Present value of \$1000 payment}\\ \text{in two years}\end{array} = \frac{\$1000/(1+i)}{1+i} = \frac{\$1000}{(1+i)^2}.$$

The last year's payment includes a coupon payment of $1000 plus the face value of $10,000, for a present value of $\$11{,}000/(1 + i)10$. So the present value of the coupon bond is the sum of all 10 future coupon payments plus the payment of the face value at the end.

$$\begin{array}{c}\text{Present value}\\ \text{of coupon bond payments}\end{array} = \frac{\$1000}{1+i} + \frac{\$1000}{(1+i)^2} + \cdots + \frac{\$1000}{(1+i)^{10}} + \frac{\$10{,}000}{(1+i)^{10}}.$$

To calculate the yield to maturity, we find the interest rate that equates this present value to the current price of the bond. Typically, this calculation is complex, requiring either a published present value table or a programmable calculator to find the yield to maturity.[†] In general, for a coupon bond with coupon payment C, face value F, and maturity after n periods,[††]

$$\text{Price of coupon bond} = \frac{C}{1+i} + \frac{C}{(1+i)^2} + \dots + \frac{C}{(1+i)^n} + \frac{F}{(1+i)^n}. \quad (4.3)$$

In Eq. (4.3), we can solve for the yield to maturity i because the coupon payment C, face value F, and number of periods n are known variables. For example, we can use Eq. (4.3) to find the yield to maturity on a 10-year, \$1000 bond with a coupon rate of 10% currently selling for \$955. Using a programmable calculator or published bond tables, you can calculate the yield to maturity to be about 10.75%. Note that if the bond were selling for \$1000, the yield to maturity would be the same as the coupon rate, 10%. To summarize, if i is the yield to maturity of a coupon bond, the price of the coupon bond today equals the present value of the coupon bond payments discounted at rate i.

Fixed-payment loans. The calculation of the yield to maturity for a fixed-payment loan closely resembles that for a coupon bond. Recall that fixed-payment loans require periodic payments of interest and principal but no face value payment at maturity. Consider the example of a 20-year commercial mortgage with annual payments of \$12,731. If the loan's value today is \$100,000, the yield to maturity can be calculated as the interest rate that solves the equation

$$\text{Value today} = \text{Present value of payment}$$

$$\$100{,}000 = \frac{\$12{,}731}{1+i} + \frac{\$12{,}731}{(1+i)^2} + \dots + \frac{\$12{,}731}{(1+i)^{20}}.$$

[†]Using algebraic manipulation, we can simplify the required expression to

$$\text{Price of coupon bond} = \frac{C}{1+i}\left[\frac{(1+i)^{-n}-1}{(1+i)^{-1}-1}\right] + \frac{F}{(1+i)^n}$$

$$= \frac{C}{i}\left[1-(1+i)^{-n}\right]\frac{F}{(1+i)^n}.$$

Using published present value tables or most programmable calculators, you can calculate the yield to maturity i if you know C, F, n, and the current price.

[††]The case of a coupon bond with infinite maturity—a perpetual, or *consol*, bond—generates a simpler expression. Note that as n increases toward infinity, the present value of the final (face value) payment approaches zero; it is received too far in the future to have any value today. For example, if $i = 10\%$ and $n = 100$ years, today's value of a \$1000 payment 100 years from now equals $\$1000/(1+i)^{100}$, or less than a penny. Hence the price of the bond comes from the present value of the coupon payments:

$$\text{Present value of payments} = \text{Price of consol} = C/i.$$

Using a calculator to solve this equation for i, we find that $i = 11.2\%$. In general,[†] for a fixed-payment loan with fixed payments FP, interest rate i, and maturity at period n,

$$\text{Loan value} = \frac{FP}{1+i} + \frac{FP}{(1+i)^2} + \cdots + \frac{FP}{(1+i)^n}. \tag{4.4}$$

Bankers use computer programs, programmable calculators, or published tables to calculate alternative mortgage payments for loan applicants at different interest rates and numbers of periods until maturity. To summarize, if i is the yield to maturity of a fixed-payment loan, the amount of the loan today equals the present value of the loan payments discounted at rate i.

Concluding remarks. The concept of present value allows us to explain why a dollar received today is more valuable than a dollar received in the future. A dollar today can be invested to earn interest; a dollar received n years from now has a value of $\$1/(1+i)^n$, or less than \$1 today. To obtain the present value of payments for a debt instrument, we calculate the present value of each future payment and then add all of these values. In this way, investors can compare returns on alternative financial instruments using the yield to maturity, or the interest rate that equates the value of the instrument today with the total present value of future payments.

CHECKPOINT

To test your skill with yield to maturity calculations, write the equations to solve for the yield to maturity

(a) for a simple loan for \$500,000 that requires a payment of \$700,000 in four years

(b) for a discount bond for which \$9000 is initially received by the borrower, who must pay the lender \$10,000 in one year

(c) for a corporate bond with a face value of \$10,000 and a coupon payment of \$1000 with five years until maturity

(d) for a student loan of \$2500 to finance tuition for which \$315 per year must be paid for 25 years, starting two years after graduation this year

Answers:

(a) $\$500{,}000 = \$700{,}000/(1+i)^4$

(b) $i = (\$10{,}000 - \$9000)/\$9000$

[†]This expression can be simplified to

$$\text{Value} = \frac{FP}{i}\left[1 - (1+i)^{-n}\right].$$

(c) $\$10{,}000 = 1000/(1 + i) + \$1000/(1 + i)^2 + \$1000/(1 + i)^3 + \$1000/(1 + i)^4 + \$11{,}000/(1 + i)^5$

(d) $\$2500 = \$315/(1 + i)^2 + \$315/(1 + i)^3 + \cdots + \$315/(1 + i)^{26}$ o

BOND YIELDS AND PRICES

The present value equation told us how much the future cash flows from an investment are worth today. A prudent lender would not pay more for a bond than its present value, and that should be the price a lender would pay for the investment. In effect, the price of a debt instrument is equal to its present value.

The bonds we have described so far are original-issue bonds—bonds issued by a borrower who receives the proceeds from selling the instrument. Many investors hold their bonds to maturity and receive interest and principal payments directly from the borrower—but other investors may sell their bonds before maturity, and the price that they receive for the bonds is influenced by factors other than the future cash flows of the bond. In particular, market interest rates change over time, and these changes affect the value of the bonds an investor holds.

Suppose that you are holding a 20-year bond of Bigco with a coupon rate of 9%, and market interest rates rise to 12% for several years. What happens to the price of your bond? Suppose that you expect interest rates to fall during the next several years. Is it a good time to buy 30-year Treasury bonds or three-month Treasury bills? In this section, we demonstrate how the yield to maturity and the price of a credit market instrument are linked. We also show that current and expected future changes in yields lead to changes in the prices of financial instruments, affecting, for example, the value of savings or the cost of a mortgage. We discuss the relationship between prices and yields using coupon bonds, but the points that we make apply generally to all instruments.

Let's begin by asking why a bond's price might change over time. Then we can get more precise about the relationship between yields and prices.

Why Can Price and Face Value Differ?

Joe Romano bought a 20-year bond for a face value of $1000 with a yield to maturity of 5%, but Joe finds that after five years he must sell the bond to meet an unexpected expense. Over the five years Joe has owned the bond, market interest rates have increased to 10%. What is the impact of this change on the price he will realize from the sale of his bond? Nobody would pay $1000 for his bond because doing so results in a 5% yield. An investor could purchase a newer bond that offers a 10% yield. To be competitive with the now higher market interest rates, Joe must lower the asking price for his bond. Only if someone pays a lower price for his bond's future stream of payments will the investor's rate of return rise above 5%. Indeed, Joe will have to keep lowering the price of his bond until its return rises to 10% and is competitive with the market. Thus, as market interest rates change, the market price of the bond may no longer equal the face value.†

† As we show in Chapter 7, the price of a bond also may change in response to a change in the borrower's ability to repay the loan. Here we focus only on price changes due to interest rate movements.

How can we use the yield to maturity to measure both the initial interest rate and a change in the price of the bond that results from a change in market interest rates? To begin, we express the yield to maturity for a coupon bond or a fixed-payment loan as the sum of two components. The first component is the **current yield,** which equals the coupon payment C divided by the current price of the bond P:

$$\text{Current yield} = \frac{C}{P}. \tag{4.5}$$

Consider a \$1000 coupon bond that has an annual coupon payment of \$100 and is selling for \$750. Although the coupon rate is \$100/\$1000, or 10%, the current yield is

$$\frac{C}{P} = \frac{\$100}{\$750}, \quad \text{or} \quad 13.3\%.$$

Should you compare the 13.3% current yield on this bond with current yields on other bonds to determine how you should invest your savings? To look ahead for a moment, the answer is *no*. Recall that the interest rate used to compare returns on financial instruments is the yield to maturity. The current yield is one component of the yield to maturity, but a second component measures the future cash flows you will have if you hold the bond to maturity. For example, if you hold the bond to maturity, you expect to receive \$1000, realizing a capital *gain* of \$250 because you bought the bond for \$750. (However, if the price of the bond were greater than \$1000, you would still expect to receive only \$1000 at maturity, realizing a capital *loss*.)

From this analysis, we can make three observations about the relationships among the yield to maturity, the current yield, and the coupon rate of the bond:

1. If the current price of the bond P equals the face value F, there is no capital gain or loss from holding the bond until maturity. Hence the yield to maturity i equals the current yield C/P, which is equal to the coupon rate C/F.

2. If the current price is less than the face value, $P < F$, an investor receives a capital gain by holding the bond until maturity. Hence the yield to maturity i is greater than the current yield C/P, which in turn is greater than the coupon rate C/F.

3. If the current price is greater than the face value, $P > F$, an investor receives a capital loss by holding the bond until maturity. Hence the yield to maturity i is less than the current yield C/P, which in turn is less than the coupon rate C/F.

These relationships hold for any coupon bond and follow directly from our definition of yield to maturity. If a 10-year bond with a face value of \$1000 and a 10% coupon rate sells for \$1000, you receive an interest rate of 10% if you hold the bond for 10 years. This yield to maturity is equal to the current yield and the coupon rate, which also are 10%. If that same bond sold for \$900, you would realize a capital gain at maturity, so the yield to maturity (which is

11.75%) is greater than the current yield ($100/$900 = 11.1%) and the coupon rate ($100/$1000 = 10%). Finally, if the same bond sold for $1100, you would realize a capital loss at maturity, so the yield to maturity (which, calculated on a programmable calculator, is 8.48%) is less than the current yield ($100/$1100 = 9.09%) and the coupon rate ($100/$1000 = 10%).

The three relationships illustrate how the yield to maturity relates to the current yield or coupon rate, depending on whether the bond price is greater than, less than, or equal to its face value. We can use these observations to ask how bond yields and prices are related.

How Are Bond Yields and Prices Related?

A bond's price and the yield to maturity are inversely related. Thus, as the price falls, the yield to maturity rises because the buyer is paying less for the same future stream of income. Conversely, as the price rises, the yield to maturity falls. This inverse relationship between the yield to maturity and the current price of the instrument is important, and the reason for it can be explained in this way: Discounting future payments at a higher rate necessarily reduces the present value of the payments and hence the value or price of the bond. A lower yield to maturity raises the present value of the future payments and hence the price of the bond.

Moreover, the longer the time until a bond matures, the greater is the potential price change caused by a specific change in the yield to maturity.

CONSIDER THIS . . .

Who Will Buy Those Fabulous Fifties?

In a new offering in April 1992, the Tennessee Valley Authority (TVA), a quasi-governmental agency and utility, sold $1 billion of 50-year bonds. Priced to yield 8.5%, the bonds had an interest rate that was about 0.5% above the yield on the Treasury's 30-year bonds. Institutional investors such as pension funds and insurance companies that seek long-term investments to pay their long-term liabilities found the TVA's bond so attractive that the demand for the bonds exceeded the supply. This phenomenon is known as *oversubscription*. Why would investors buy these "fabulous fifties"?

Our analysis predicted correctly that longer-maturity assets have a greater price sensitivity to interest rate changes than do shorter-maturity assets. Investing in 50-year coupon bonds is not for the faint of heart, because the potential to incur capital losses is great. For example, a two-percentage-point *increase* in the yield to maturity would *reduce* the bond's price by about 19%, whereas a two-percentage-point *decrease* in the yield to maturity would *raise* the bond's price by about 26%. In the case of the TVA's 50-year bonds (which would pay no interest for 20 years, then pay interest for the next 30 years), a $1000 bond sold for $160, with an initial yield to maturity of 8.5%. Thus a two-percentage-point increase in the yield to maturity would reduce the bond price by about 47%, whereas a two-percentage-point decrease in the yield to maturity would raise the bond price by 78%! Of course, the potential gains in response to a fall in the yield to maturity are also large; perhaps this explains why the issue was oversubscribed.

Let's examine why this is so. Suppose that the initial yield to maturity and current yield on a $10,000 bond are 10%. Because of a boom in investment opportunities and a higher demand for funds, the yield to maturity for this bond is expected to rise to 15% one year from now. What happens to the price of the bond? The price can fall dramatically in response to the increase in yield. As Fig. 4.2 shows, for a bond that matures one year from now, the price is unaffected because the current price equals the face value. For a bond that matures five years from now, we use Eq. (4.3) to calculate that the price of the bond *falls* by $1298 because the future interest payments are worth less. Even more striking is the current capital loss for a bond that matures 20 years from now, because the bond's payments occur well into the future. Using Eq. (4.3), we calculate that the bond's price falls by $2817.

Thus, when yields to maturity change, investors face the risk of a change in bond price. For example, even though U.S. Treasury obligations carry no risk of default on either the principal or interest, these obligations still are risky in that changes in the yield to maturity can affect the value of the instruments.

Thus credit market instruments display differing price sensitivities to fluctuations in the yield to maturity, depending on their time to maturity. The present value expressions derived earlier show that the present value of short-term instruments is relatively unaffected by an increase or decrease in the interest rate. As time to maturity increases, prices become more sensitive to changes in the yield to maturity.

From the preceding discussion, it might seem that investors could reduce their risk of fluctuating market interest rates by holding only short-term instruments. If that is the case, why would anyone want to hold a long-term bond? To demonstrate, consider the choices that face Suzanne Midlife. Suzanne Midlife plans to retire in 30 years. On the one hand, if she holds a

Figure 4.2

Sensitivity of Bond Prices to Changes in Interest Rates

The price of a bond and the yield to maturity are negatively related. Suppose that the yield to maturity for a bond is expected to rise from 10% to 15% one year from now. What happens to the price of the bond? A change in the yield to maturity affects the prices of long-term bonds more dramatically than it affects the prices of those closer to maturity.

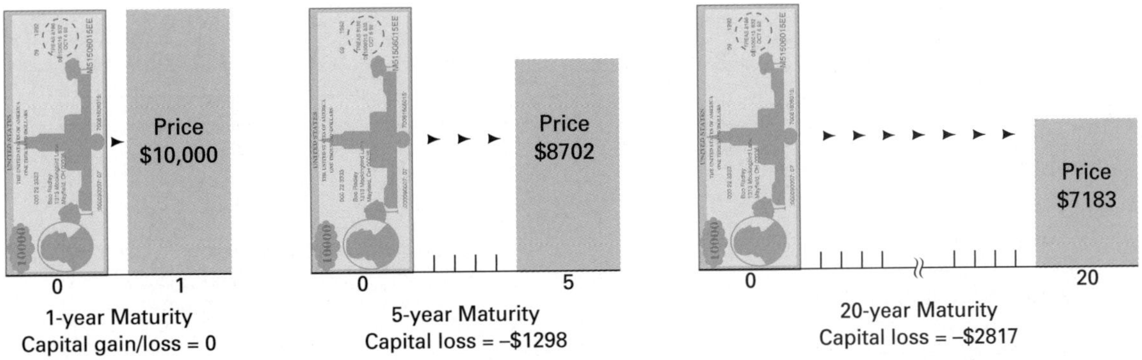

USING THE NEWS . . .

Keeping Up with Bond Prices and Yields

Each day, the *Money and Investing* section of *The Wall Street Journal* lists information on bond prices and yields. We use several examples to show you how to extract the information you need to compare yields. The categories illustrated are Treasury notes and bonds, Treasury bills, and New York Stock Exchange Corporation bonds.

Panel 1

Panel 1 contains data on U.S. Treasury bonds and notes. These obligations are coupon bonds with different maturities. Treasury notes have a maturity of less than 10 years from their date of issue; Treasury bonds have a maturity of more than 10 years from their date of issue.

The first two columns tell you the coupon rate and maturity date, respectively. Bond A, for example, has a coupon rate of 5.5%, so it pays $55.00 each year on a $1000 face value bond; its maturity date is February 2003. Some bonds—Bond C, for example—have two maturity dates. In this case, the Treasury has the option of paying off the face value any time between November 2002 and November 2007. Such callable bonds offer more flexible financing for the U.S. Treasury. They present a risk to investors, however, because, if market rates should fall below the coupon rate, the Treasury might redeem the bond early.

The next three columns refer to the bond's price. All prices are reported per $100 of face value; numbers following the colon refer to thirty-seconds of a dollar. For Bond A, the first price listed, 99:11, means "99 and 11/32," or an actual price of $993.44 for a $1000 face value bond. The *bid* price is the price you will receive from a government securities dealer if you sell the bond; the *asked* price is the price you must pay the dealer for the bond. The difference between the asked price and the bid price (known as the *bid-asked spread*) is the profit margin for dealers. Bid-asked spreads are low in the government

TREASURY BONDS, NOTES & BILLS

Wednesday, November 22, 2000
Representative and Indicative Over-the-Counter quotations based on $1 million or more.
Treasury bond, note and bill quotes are as of mid-afternoon.
Source: Telerate/Cantor Fitzgerald.

Panel 1: Treasury Bonds and Notes

GOVT. BONDS & NOTES

	Rate	Maturity Mo/Yr	Bid	Asked	Chg.	Ask Yld.
	5 5/8	Dec 02n	99:20	99:22	+ 3	5.78
	5 1/2	Jan 03n	99:11	99:13	+ 4	5.79
	6 1/4	Feb 03n	100:27	100:29	+ 3	5.80
	10 3/4	Feb 03	109:31	110:01	+ 2	5.87
Bond A	5 1/2	Feb 03n	99:11	99:13	+ 4	5.78
	5 1/2	Mar 03n	99:11	99:13	+ 4	5.77
	5 3/4	Apr 03n	99:28	99:30	+ 4	5.78
	12	May 05	124:12	124:18	+ 8	5.70
	6 1/2	Aug 05n	103:11	103:13	+ 8	5.67
Bond B	10 3/4	Aug 05	120:13	120:19	+ 9	5.71
	5 3/4	Nov 05n	100:23	100:24	+ 9	5.57
	5 7/8	Nov 05n	100:29	100:31	+ 9	5.65
	5 5/8	Feb 06n	99:25	99:27	+ 10	5.66
	9 3/8	Feb 06	116:10	116:14	+ 9	5.69
	6 1/4	Feb 07n	102:31	103:01	+ 12	5.66
	7 5/8	Feb 02-07	101:23	101:25	+ 2	6.08
	6 5/8	May 07n	105:02	105:04	+ 11	5.67
	6 1/8	Aug 07n	102:15	102:17	+ 12	5.67
Bond C	7 7/8	Nov 02-07	103:15	103:17	+ 4	5.95
	3 5/8	Jan 08i	98:17	98:18	+ 1	3.86
	5 1/2	Feb 08n	99:00	99:02	+ 13	5.66
	5 1/8	May 08n	99:22	99:24	+ 12	5.67

Panel 2: Treasury Bills

TREASURY BILLS

Maturity	Days to Mat.	Bid	Asked	Chg.	Ask Yld.
Nov 30 '00	6	6.04	5.96	+0.01	6.05
Dec 07 '00	13	6.11	6.03	+0.01	6.13
Dec 14 '00	20	5.82	5.74	+0.01	5.84
Dec 21 '00	27	6.44	6.36	+0.01	6.48
Dec 28 '00	34	6.20	6.16	+0.01	6.28
Jan 04 '00	41	6.13	6.09	+0.01	6.22
Jan 11 '00	48	6.17	6.13	+0.01	6.27

Panel 3: New York Stock Exchange Bonds

CORPORATION BONDS

Volume, $6,862,000

	Bonds	Cur. Yld.	Vol.	Close	Net Chg.
	AES Cp 8s8	8.7	33	91 7/8	+ 1 3/8
	AMR 9s16	9.0	10	100 1/2	− 1/4
	ATT 5 1/8 01	5.2	25	99 1/16	. . .
	ATT 7 1/8 02	7.1	95	100 1/4	+ 3/8
	ATT 6 1/2 02	6.6	50	98 3/8	+ 1/4
	ATT 6 3/4 04	6.9	60	97 1/2	+ 1/8
	ATT 5 5/8 04	6.0	35	94 5/8	− 1/4
Bond D	ATT 7 1/2 06	7.5	65	99 3/4	+ 3/8
	ATT 7 3/4 07	7.7	2	100 1/2	. . .
	ATT 6s09	6.9	160	87 5/8	. . .
	ATT 8 1/8 22	8.4	219	97	+ 1/2
	ATT 8 1/8 24	8.4	327	96 1/2	+ 3/8
	ATT 8.35s25	8.6	80	96 7/8	+ 1/4
	ATT 6 1/2 29	8.0	81	81 1/8	+ 1 5/8
	ATT 8 5/8 31	8.8	291	98 3/8	+ 3/8
	Alza zr14	. . .	147	99	− 18
	ArmWld 9 3/4 08	39.0	40	25	− 3
	BauschL 7 1/8 28	13.7	5	52	. . .

Source: The Wall Street Journal, November 24, 2000.

USING THE NEWS ***continued***

securities markets, indicating low transactions costs and a liquid and competitive market. The "Chg." column tells you by how much the bid price increased or decreased from the preceding trading day. For Bond A, the bid price rose by 4/32nds from the previous day.

The final column contains the yield to maturity calculated using the method we discussed for coupon bonds and the asked price. *The Wall Street Journal* reports the asked price because readers are interested in the yield from the buyer's—investor's—perspective. Hence you can construct three interest rates from the information contained in the table: the yield to maturity just described, the coupon rate, and the current yield (equal to the coupon rate divided by the price, or 5.50/99.41, or 5.52% for Bond A). Note that the current yield of Bond B is well above the yield to maturity. The current yield, 10.75/120.59, or 8.9%, is significantly greater than the yield to maturity of 5.71%. This illustrates that the current yield is not a good substitute for the yield to maturity for instruments with a short time to maturity, because it ignores the effect of expected capital gains or losses on the yield to maturity.

The Wall Street Journal also lists prices and yields for inflation-indexed Treasury securities; securities issued by U.S. government agencies, such as the Government National Mortgage Association (GNMA), which borrows funds to acquire mortgages; state and local governments; and international credit agencies. Prices and yields for federal agency bonds, Treasury inflation-indexed securities, and state and local government bonds, and bonds of international agencies are reported in the same way as those for Treasury bonds.

Panel 2

Panel 2 shows information about U.S. Treasury bill yields. Recall that Treasury bills are discount bonds, unlike Treasury bonds and notes, which are coupon bonds. Accordingly, they are identified only by their maturity date (first column). The second column gives the number of days to maturity. In the Treasury bill market, yields are quoted on a discount basis.† The bid yield is the discount yield for investors who want to sell the bill to dealers; the asked yield is the discount yield for investors who want to buy the bill from dealers. The dealers' profit margin is the difference between the asked yield and the bid yield. The last column shows the yield to maturity (based on the asked price).

Note that the yield to maturity on short-term Treasury bills is less than that on long-term Treasury bonds. Should you invest all your money in long-term bonds to get the higher yield? Probably not. Remember, an increase in interest rates would drive down the price of the bonds in the secondary (resale) markets. In that case, if you wanted to sell the bond before maturity, you would lose part of the principal. Of course, if interest rates fell, the price of your bonds would increase. You might decide to invest some of your savings in short-term Treasury bills and the balance in longer-term bonds, depending on your guess about whether interest rates will rise or fall.

Panel 3

Panel 3 gives quotations for corporate bonds listed on the New York Stock Exchange (corporate bonds traded on the American Stock Exchange are reported similarly). The first column tells you the name of the corporation issuing the bond—in this case, AT&T, a large telecommunications company. The next column gives you the current yield, 7.5%, for Bond D. The third column reports trading volume; in this case, 65 bonds were traded on the day reported. The last traded price (per $100 of face value) is presented in the "Close" column, 99¾ for Bond D. The last column tells you how much the closing price changed from the preceding trading day: Bond D's price per $100 of value rose by ⅜ from the previous day's close. The yield to maturity is not reported, though you can calculate it using a programmable calculator or published tables. Note that yields on long-term corporate bonds are higher than those on long-term U.S. Treasury bonds.

†The yield on a discount basis for a bond with face value F and a purchase price D is $(F - D)/F \times$ (360/number of days to maturity). Data Question 28 at the end of this chapter compares the yield on a discount basis with the yield to maturity.

30-year discount bond with a yield to maturity of 5%, she knows what her yield will be until retirement. On the other hand, if she buys a sequence of one-year discount bonds, the yield that Suzanne realizes is given by the sequence of one-year yields over the next 30 years. This average may be more than or less than the 5% she could obtain on the 30-year bond. In the strategy of buying a sequence of one-year discount bonds, Suzanne is exposed to *reinvestment risk,* the risk that accompanies periodic reinvestment when future interest rates are not known. What should Suzanne do? Financial planners advise savers to consider their time horizon, whether they are likely to need the money, and their attitude toward risk.[†]

To summarize, the longer the maturity of a bond, the larger will be the price change in response to a change in the yield to maturity. The only case for which the bond price does not react to a change in the yield to maturity is when the holding period is the same as the number of periods until maturity.

FINDING THE TOTAL RATE OF RETURN

The yield to maturity is not the only measure of bond returns that is of interest to investors. Over any given holding period (the length of time for which the bond is held), an investor may receive a different rate of capital gain or loss than expected originally. As a result, the **total rate of return,** which is the sum of current yield and the *actual* capital gain or loss, can differ from the yield to maturity.

Suppose that Swifty Rich buys a \$1000 face value bond in Goodnewsco, which has a coupon rate of 8%, for \$1000. After one year, he sells the bond for \$1100. How well did Swifty do on his investment? The total rate of return R is

$$R = \frac{\$80}{\$1000} + \frac{\$1100 - \$1000}{\$1000}, \text{ or } 18\%.$$

The first term reflects Swifty's current yield: His \$1000 investment brought him \$80 in interest, or an 8% interest return. The second term reflects Swifty's capital gain. Swifty made a profit of \$100 on the Goodnewsco bond, or a 10% additional return on his investment of \$1000. Hence his total rate of return is 8% + 10% = 18%.

Swifty's brother Never B. Rich bought a \$1000 face value bond in Badnewsco at the same time; the bond had a coupon rate of 8% and sold for

---

[†]If an investor's holding period actually exceeds the term to maturity, the investor faces reinvestment risk. The reason is that any funds from the payments of the short-term bond must be invested at a future—uncertain—interest rate. In this case, the investor benefits relative to the base case if interest rates rise (she gets to reinvest the proceeds at a higher interest rate than expected) and loses if interest rates fall (she reinvests the proceeds at a lower rate than expected).

\$1000. After one year he sells the bond for \$900. In this case, the total rate of return actually is negative:

$$R = \frac{\$80}{\$1000} + \frac{\$900 - \$1000}{\$1000}, \text{ or } -2\%.$$

While Never B. earned the same interest return as Swifty, his capital loss of \$100 represented an additional return of −10%. Never B. lost money on his investment.

We can extend these examples for coupon bonds to write a general equation for the total rate of return. The total rate of return R from holding a coupon bond over the period from t to $t + 1$ is equal to the current yield plus the actual capital gain or loss. To find the initial current yield, divide the coupon payment C by the price at time t, or P_t. Thus the initial current yield equals C/P_t. To find the percentage change in price, subtract P_t from $P_t + 1$ and divide by P_t. Thus the percentage change in price, or rate of capital gains, equals $(P_t + 1 - P_t)/P_t$. If the value of this expression is positive, the investor has a capital gain; if it is negative, the investor has a capital loss. The total rate of return is

$$\text{Total rate of return} = \text{Initial current yield} + \text{Rate of capital gains}$$

$$R = \frac{C}{P_t} + \frac{P_{t+1} - P_t}{P_t} \tag{4.6}$$

This return can vary significantly from the current yield, as Fig. 4.2 shows. Indeed, a large enough capital loss on a bond results in a negative total rate of return, even if the current yield is positive, as Never B. Rich found, to his consternation. Hence investors are concerned with the total rate of return over a holding period, not just the current yield.

To understand why capital gains or losses from interest rate changes can be larger than the interest return, you need to recall that a rise in a bond's yield leads to a fall in its price (and a capital loss), and a fall in a bond's yield leads to an increase in its price (and a capital gain). Hence, if you own long-term bonds and you read about a large increase in yields, don't get excited about receiving a greater interest return. You may well have lost on your investment.

REAL VERSUS NOMINAL INTEREST RATES

In the chapter opener and in all the interest rate calculations we made to assess the yield on a particular debt instrument, we expressed our results as **nominal interest rates** and rates of return. That is, our interest rates and rates of return were not adjusted for changes in purchasing power. But inflation can reduce the purchasing power of returns on any investment. For example, suppose that you buy a \$1000 bond that pays you \$50 in interest each year for 20 years. If the purchasing power of the dollars that you receive declines over time, you are losing part of your interest income to inflation. If inflation is 5% per year,

OTHER TIMES, OTHER PLACES . . .

Principal Derailed: Inflation and Long-Term Bond Prices

Holders of very long-term nominal bonds have much to worry about. First, there is the question of whether the borrower will be around to redeem the bond's principal in full. Second, inflation that is higher than that expected when the bond is issued can erode the value of the bond. Higher inflation raises nominal interest rates and reduces the price of the bonds—bad news for bondholders. Long-term bondholders snapped up 100-year bonds issued by Walt Disney Company in 1993, with a coupon interest rate of 7.55 percent. Those purchasers bet on the stability of both Mickey Mouse and inflation.

A reasonable bet? Historical experience suggests caution. In July 1995, bonds that had been issued by the Atchison, Topeka, and Santa Fe Railroad in 1881 were redeemed. The funds that were returned related to an issue of 100-year bonds with a 4% coupon yield during the railway's 1895 reorganization. At one level, the 1995 bondholders breathed a sigh of relief because of the railroad's checkered history. After gunman Bat Masterson helped the railroad to establish important routes in the Southwest, the company experienced hard times in the 1890s, then boomed earlier in the twentieth century. After troubled times during the Depression of the 1930s, the firm recovered.

This silver lining has with it a cloud. Inflation in the United States proved far more significant than that incorporated in the original coupon yield of 4%. Though the bondholders received the face value, each $1000 payment was worth less than $70 at 1881 prices. Especially for very long-term bonds, inflation can give bondholders a wild ride. The bond market's concern about inflation is therefore understandable.

Today, investors can buy long-term *inflation-indexed Treasury securities* as a protection against inflation.

the purchasing power of the $1000 principal falls by $50 each year, offsetting the interest you receive.

Because inflation reduces the purchasing power of interest income, savers and borrowers base their investment decisions on interest rates and rates of returns adjusted for changes in purchasing power. Such adjusted rates are known as **real interest rates.** Because lenders and borrowers don't know what the *actual* real interest rate will be at the maturity of their investment, they must make saving or investment decisions on the basis of the real interest rate that they *expect* at that time. Lenders and borrowers know the nominal interest rate in advance; they estimate the expected real interest rate by guessing about inflation. The **expected real interest rate** r equals the nominal interest rate i minus the expected rate of inflation π^e, or

$$r = i - \pi^e. \tag{4.7}$$

Does a change in expected inflation affect the real interest rate and the decisions of lenders and borrowers? Generally, it doesn't. Suppose, for example, that Tristate Automotive Services Company borrows $10 million for one year from Amalgamated Financial Services at the prevailing *real* interest rate of 5%. Now suppose that borrowers like Tristate and lenders like Amalgamated expect that over the next year, the prices of goods and services in the economy will rise 5%; that is, the expected rate of inflation is 5%. As a return on the loan, Amalgamated expects to earn (\$10,000,000)(0.05) = \$500,000. However, because expected inflation is 5%, the purchasing power of the \$10 million principal is expected to decline by \$500,000. Therefore Tristate will benefit because the money it received from the loan is worth more than the amount it expects to repay, adjusted for changes in purchasing power. Amalgamated's loss in purchasing power is Tristate's gain. Tristate and Amalgamated can secure an expected real interest rate of 5% by agreeing to a nominal interest rate of 10%, which would provide the extra return needed to compensate for the expected decline in the value of the principal.

A noted economist, Irving Fisher, expressed this relationship between interest rates and expected inflation many years ago. The **Fisher hypothesis** states that the nominal interest rate rises or falls point-for-point with expected inflation. Do actual data corroborate the Fisher hypothesis? Nominal interest rates *do* increase when expected inflation increases, but empirical estimates do not generally support a one-for-one movement. Some reasons for this difference are that the basic Fisher hypothesis omits taxes and that quantifying expectations of inflation is difficult. Nonetheless, the likelihood that nominal interest rates reflect changes in expected inflation is not disputed.

The Fisher hypothesis does not imply that the actual real interest rate (the nominal rate less actual inflation) is unaffected by changes in the actual inflation rate. In the preceding example, if the rate of inflation were 10% rather than 5%, the purchasing power of the \$10 million principal would decline by \$1 million, not \$500,000. Tristate (the borrower) would gain at Amalgamated's (the lender's) expense relative to the agreement, with an expected real return of 5%. If actual inflation were less than 5%, this transfer or redistribution would reverse: The lender would gain and the borrower would lose.

Nominal interest rates are not always a good indicator of real interest rates.† For example, how do you know whether a nominal interest rate of 10% is high or low? If expected inflation were 2%, the expected real interest rate, 10% − 2% = 8%, would be high by U.S. standards (real interest rates are normally about 2–3%). If expected inflation were 10%, however, the

†For taxable investments, the relevant interest rate is the real after-tax interest rate. If t is the investor's marginal tax rate, ti is tax paid, and expected inflation is π^e, then a nominal yield i corresponds to a real after-tax interest rate of

$$\text{Nominal yield} = \text{After-tax nominal gains} - \text{Expected inflation}$$
$$i - ti - \pi^e = (1 - t)i - \pi^e.$$

Real after-tax interest rates can be quite low, even negative. In 1981, the nominal (annualized) yield on six-month certificates of deposit averaged 15.8%, compared to 6.5% in 1986. But the real after-tax yield (ATY) for a high-income investor in 1981, using actual inflation π, was

$$\text{ATY} = (1 - t)i - \pi = (1 - 0.59)(15.8\%) - 8.9\%, \quad \text{or} \quad -2.4\%,$$

whereas in 1986 it was

$$\text{ATY} = (1 - 0.45)(6.5\%) - 1.1\%, \quad \text{or} \quad +2.5\%.$$

Figure 4.3

Real and Nominal Interest Rates, Three-Month Treasury Bills, 1960–2000

Nominal interest rates are higher than real interest rates as long as expected inflation is positive. Real and nominal rates do not always move together.

Source: U.S. Department of the Treasury, Office of Economic Policy.

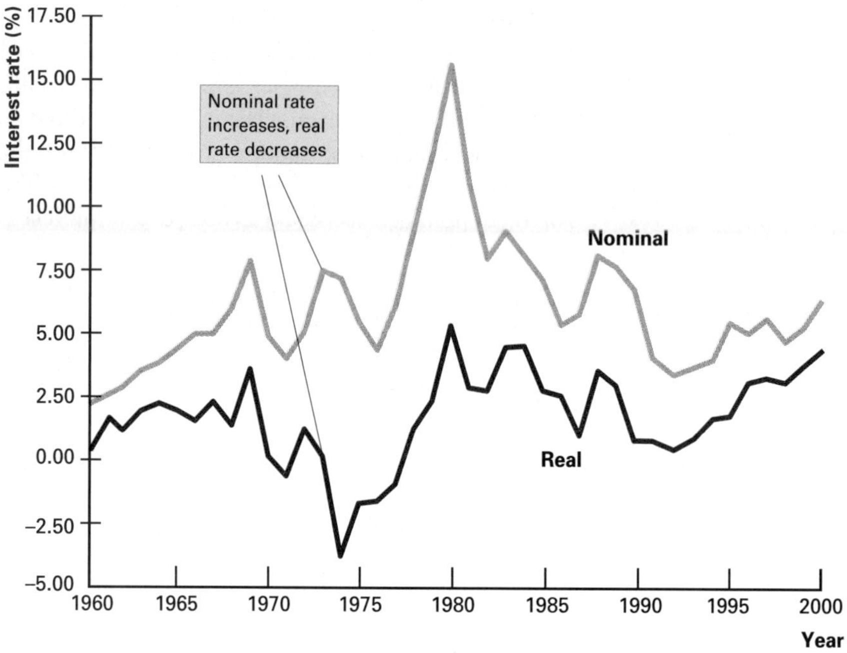

expected real interest rate, 10% − 10% = 0%, would be low by U.S. standards. Figure 4.3 shows that although nominal interest rates on three-month Treasury bills were higher in the 1970s than in the 1960s, real rates were lower (sometimes quite negative). Thus, while nominal interest rates were indicating a high return to lenders and a high cost of funds to borrowers, real interest rates were indicating a low return to savers and a low cost of funds to lenders. Because lenders and borrowers use the expected real interest rate in determining how to allocate their wealth to alternative assets, the low real interest rates spurred spending by businesses and households.

The **real rate of return** reflects the amount of additional goods and services an investor can buy from earnings on a financial instrument. Suppose that your total rate of return (including capital gains) from holding a Treasury bond over the last five years was 40%. However, if inflation had been 22% over the same period, your real rate of return, taking account of the decline in your purchasing power, would have been 40% − 22% = 18%. Just as the real interest rate is the interest rate adjusted for purchasing power of goods and services, the real rate of return equals the nominal rate of return adjusted for expected inflation.

Since January 1997, the real interest rate has been observable in the United States. At that time, the U.S. Treasury started issuing **indexed bonds,** whose payments of principal and interest are adjusted for changes in the price level. The U.S. TIPS (Treasury Inflation Protection Securities) followed the introduction of indexed bonds in Australia, Canada, Sweden, and the United Kingdom. TIPS allow savers, investors, and policymakers to obtain real-time measures of real interest rates and expected inflation. On February 9, 2001, for example, the yield on the 10-year Treasury bond was 5.02 percent versus 3.4 percent on the 10-year TIPS, implying a real rate of 3.4 percent (the TIPS yield) and an expected inflation rate of 1.6 percent.

CHECKPOINT

In the late 1960s and early 1970s, savings and loan institutions traditionally made long-term (20- or 30-year) home mortgage loans at fixed nominal interest rates, when expected inflation and nominal interest rates were low. Most experts believe that an important cause of the savings and loan crisis of the late 1980s was unexpected inflation in the late 1970s and early 1980s. Why might unexpected inflation be costly for mortgage lenders? The unexpected burst of inflation later in the 1970s reduced the real value of the mortgage loans to savings and loan institutions. As a result, for many institutions, the present value of the long-term mortgages they held (their assets) fell below the present value of their short-term liabilities to savers, making the institutions insolvent. o

KEY TERMS AND CONCEPTS

Compounding
Credit market instruments
- Coupon bond
- Discount bond
- Fixed-payment loan
- Simple loan

Current yield
Expected real interest rate
Fisher hypothesis
Indexed bond
Nominal interest rates
Present value

Rate of capital gains
Real interest rates
Total rate of return
Yield to maturity

SUMMARY

1. Credit market instruments are classified into four main categories: simple loans, discount bonds, coupon bonds, and fixed-payment loans. The timing of interest payments from borrowers to lenders varies widely among credit market instruments. Simple loans and discount bonds have a single payment of principal and interest; coupon bonds and fixed-payment loans have multiple payments of interest and principal.
2. To compare returns on assets that have different maturities, we calculate the present value of each asset's expected payments. A variation of the present value equation allows us to find the interest rate on a debt instrument when we know the bond's price in today's dollars and the bond's payment schedule. This interest rate is called the yield to maturity. The yield to maturity is the interest rate that equates the current value of the asset with the present value of its payments.
3. Fluctuations in prices of bonds or loans arise from fluctuations in yields to maturity. If the yield to maturity increases, the price of a bond or loan falls; if the yield to maturity decreases, the price of a bond or loan increases. The longer the maturity of an instrument, the larger is the price change in response to a change in the yield to maturity.

BUSINESS WEEK JUNE 19, 2000

A Bond Anybody Can Love

When a bright guy who is renowned as a long-time bull on stocks recommends a bond, I listen. That happened recently when Jeremy Siegel told *Business Week* that he finds a particular sort of oddball bond to be an attractive hedge against stocks. Siegel, the Wharton School economist whose book, *Stocks for the Long Run,* underpins today's buy-and-hold equities creed, turns out to love a crazy little thing called TIPS.

TIPS is a nickname for Treasury inflation-protected securities, never mind that Uncle Sam's official name for these bonds is Treasury Inflation Protection Securities. Just that much gives you a clue how quickly the world of TIPS turns arcane. That's too bad, because the essence of these things is not that hard to grasp. In any case, I promise you'll be hearing more about TIPS soon.

One reason is that mutual fund giant Vanguard Group is opening its new Vanguard Inflation-Protected Securities Fund, which is devoted to these bonds. A bigger reason is that inflation seems to be picking up. That's bad news for holders of both stocks and bonds—but not TIPS, which are built to withstand inflation. . . .

a How do they work?... [I]n exchange for borrowing your money, the Treasury gives you a TIPS and vows to make up any purchasing power it loses to inflation. . . . Ordinary bonds pay back only the face amount. . . .

Not bad. Yet these bonds are hardly a hot investment. Since coming out in January 1997, they've claimed only a small slice of the total bond market. One drawback is they come in just seven maturities, ranging from 2 to 29 years. A bigger problem is taxes: Buy a TIPS, and you'll have to pay income tax each year on the inflation adjustments, even though you won't get the actual cash until the bond matures. That makes TIPS most useful in tax-deferred accounts. Hurting demand even more is that TIPS just don't appear to pay enough. The guaranteed interest TIPS must pay looks low next to ordinary bonds. A 10-year TIPS recently yielded 4.3%, while a plain 10-year Treasury bond yielded 6.3%.

The thing is, that gap is an illusion. If consumer prices rise by their long-term average of 3%, then the real yield of the ordinary Treasury bond, after inflation, sinks to 3.3%. The yield on TIPS? It holds steady at 4.2%. So, unless inflations stays far under its long-term average, that's a sweet deal.

b For all the beauty at the heart of TIPS, though, their complexity makes them hard to love. A few Web sites I've found help cut through the confusion and explain the details. There also are TIPS mutual funds, which offer an important edge: Thanks to a regulatory quirk, they can pay you, in cash, the inflation adjustment each year that you otherwise wouldn't see until the TIPS mature. Two TIPS funds, Pimco Real Return Bond and American Century Inflation-Adjusted Treasury, have operated since 1997, but the new Vanguard fund is a better bet because its annual operating expense is just 0.25% cheaper by half or more. . . .

Many economists and financial planners urge individuals to consider strongly allocating part of their longer-term savings to Treasury Inflation Protection Securities (TIPS). These Treasury bonds and notes offer returns that compensate savers for changes in the value of the bond caused by inflation. In 2000, the yield on TIPS was about 4%, indicating a healthy default-risk-free real return that a saver could lock in. If you are interested in purchasing TIPS, you can find yield information in *The Wall Street Journal* or at Web sites for Bloomberg, the Bureau of the Public Debt, or Morningstar (for information about TIPS mutual funds).

a The total return on a coupon bond over one period is the sum of the initial current yield and the rate of capital gains. An increase in expected inflation increases nominal yields, reducing the price of a nominal bond. With a nominal Treasury bond, then, higher expected inflation translates into a capital loss for the bondholder. With TIPS, the bondholder is compensated as actual inflation reduces the value of the bond.

How does inflation indexing work in practice? Each year, the Treasury pays the coupon rate plus the rate of consumer price index (CPI) inflation (although the cash associated with the latter is not paid until the bond matures). Hence savers don't encounter nasty surprises in their real bond returns as inflation fluctuates. The Treasury also makes inflation insurance a one-way debt by keeping the saver whole should deflation (a falling CPI) occur.

b Currently, TIPS account for only a small share of the large U.S. Treasury bond market. One complicating factor is taxes. Savers must pay income taxes on the inflation adjustments even though the cash is not received until the bond matures. Financial intermediaries are offering savers the opportunity of annual cash payments and very low operating expenses.

For further thought . . .

TIPS offer low-cost inflation protection in the bond market for households and firms. Does the use of TIPS imply that the bondholder faces no risk from fluctuations in interest rates? Explain.

Source: Excerpted from Robert Barker, "A Bond Anybody Can Love," *Business Week,* June 19, 2000. Reprinted from June 19, 2000 issue of *Business Week* by special permission, copyright © 2000 by McGraw-Hill Companies, Inc.

4. The total rate of return from holding a financial instrument over a period is the sum of the current yield and the rate of capital gain (or loss). The current yield understates the total rate of return when there is a capital gain and overstates the total rate of return when there is a capital loss.
5. The interest rate that is relevant for borrowing and lending decisions is the expected real interest rate. The expected real interest rate is the nominal interest rate minus the expected rate of inflation. Accordingly, for any expected real rate of interest, an increase in the expected rate of inflation raises the nominal interest rate (the Fisher hypothesis). A decrease in the expected rate of inflation decreases the nominal interest rate. Unexpected inflation or deflation leads to a redistri-bution of resources between borrowers and lenders.

REVIEW QUESTIONS

1. How does a discount bond differ from a simple loan?
2. What is the main difference between a coupon bond and a fixed-payment loan?
3. What is the yield to maturity of an asset? How can it be derived?
4. What is the current yield on a bond paying $1000 this year with an initial interest rate of 5% and a current price of $18,000?
5. What is the total rate of return on an asset? How can it be calculated?
6. Define the expected real interest rate. How does it compare to the actual real interest rate?
7. What is the Fisher hypothesis? Is it valid? Explain.
8. Discuss some factors that affect yields on credit market instruments in general and factors that affect yields on particular instruments or groups of instruments. Would you expect yields to vary more among U.S. Treasury obligations or among private corporate bonds? Why?

ANALYTICAL PROBLEMS

9. Suppose you are the agent for a baseball pitcher. Suppose he is offered the following contract by the New York Yankees: a signing bonus of $3,000,000 (to be received immediately), a first year's salary of $6,000,000 (to be received one year from today), a second year's salary of $7,000,000 (to be received two years from today), and a third year's salary of $8,000,000 (to be received three years from today). Suppose he is also offered the following contract by the San Francisco Giants: a signing bonus of $6,000,000, a first year's salary of $5,500,000, a second year's salary of $6,000,000, and a third year's salary of $6,000,000. If you believe the relevant discount rate is 10%, which offer would you advise the pitcher to accept? Would your advice change if you believed the relevant discount rate were 5%?
10. What is the present value of a bond that pays $340 one year from now and $5340 two years from now at a constant interest rate of 6.8%?
11. If the interest rate is 8%, what is the present value of $1000 payable two years from now?
12. Would you prefer to receive (a) $75 one year from now, (b) $85 two years from now, or (c) $90 three years from now if the interest rate is 10%?
13. What would be your answer to Problem 12 if the interest rate is 20%?
14. Would it ever make sense to pay $1100 for a coupon bond with a face value of $1000? Briefly explain.
15. Suppose that you have just bought a four-year, $10,000 coupon bond with a coupon rate of 7% when the market interest rate is 7%. Immediately after you buy the bond, the market interest rate falls to 5%. What happens to the value of your bond?
16. Suppose that in exchange for allowing a road to pass through his farmland, George Pequod has been paid $135 per year by the township he lives in. He had been promised that he and future owners of his

land would receive this payment in perpetuity. Now, however, the township has offered, and he has accepted, a one-time payment of $1125, in exchange for his giving up the right to receive the annual $135 payment. What implicit interest rate have George and the township used in arriving at this settlement?

17. Suppose that you are considering subscribing to *Economic Analysis Today* magazine. You are offered a one-year subscription for $60 or a two-year subscription for $115. You plan to keep getting the magazine for at least two years, and the advertisement says that the two-year subscription saves you $5 compared to two successive one-year subscriptions. If the interest rate is 10%, should you subscribe for one or two years?

18. The British government sells consols that pay interest forever. Suppose that you want to buy a consol that pays 100 pounds sterling every year and the current interest rate is 5%. How much would you be willing to pay for the consol? Suppose that you buy the consol and the interest rate rises suddenly and unexpectedly to 10%. What is the consol worth now?

19. Suppose that you bought 100 shares of stock in Cruella, Inc., on December 31, 1998, for $55 per share. Cruella paid $2 per share in dividends during 1999, and on December 31, 1999, its price was $60 per share. What total return did you receive in 1999?

20. Suppose that you are considering the purchase of a coupon bond that has the following future payments: $600 in one year, $600 in two years, $600 in three years, and $600 + $10,000 in four years.
    a. What is the bond worth today if the market interest rate is 6%? What is the bond's current yield?
    b. Suppose that you have just purchased the bond, and suddenly the market interest rate falls to 5% for the foreseeable future. What is the bond worth now? What is its current yield now?
    c. Suppose that one year has elapsed, you have received the first coupon payment of $600, and the market interest rate is still 5%. How much would another investor be willing to pay for the bond? What was your total return on the bond? If another investor had bought the bond a year ago for the amount you calculated in (b), what would that investor's total return have been?
    d. Suppose that two years have elapsed since you bought the bond, and you have received the first two coupon payments of $600 each. Now suppose that the market interest rate suddenly jumps to 10%. How much would another investor be willing to pay for your bond? What will the bond's current yield be over the next year? Suppose that another investor had bought the bond at the price you calculated in (c). What would that investor's total return have been over the past year?

21. From an investor's point of view, the stock market drop in the mid-1970s actually was *worse* than the stock market crash of 1929, even though stock prices fell by a greater percentage in 1929. How is this result possible?

22. Suppose that you bought an asset that pays a 7% nominal interest rate, you expect the inflation rate to be 3%, and actual inflation is 5%. Calculate the expected real interest rate and the actual real interest rate.

23. Why might the actual real interest rate differ from the expected real interest rate? Would this possible difference be of more concern to you if you were considering making a loan to be paid back in one year or a loan to be paid back in 10 years?

24. Your brother-in-law tells you at a family picnic that investors in the Wild Fund, the bond fund that he manages, have been lucky; they now have a current yield on their portfolio of 20%. At the same time the current yield on the Safe Fund, a competitor, is 10%. Should you join the ranks of Wild Fund investors? Why or why not?

25. In the city of Midborough, two financial institutions have borrowed funds from community residents through notes with a maturity of three months. The first institution invests the proceeds in short-term corporate credit market instruments. The second makes 30-year fixed-rate mortgage loans to local homeowners. Describe the likely effects on the net worth (value of assets less value of liabilities) of the two institutions if the general level of interest rates increases substantially.

DATA QUESTIONS

26. If your library or your professor has the yearbook *Stocks, Bonds, and Inflation* by Ibbotson Associates, you can look up total returns on different assets. Try to find data on the total returns of common stocks, short-term Treasury bills, and long-term Treasury bonds over the past 30 years. What asset pays the highest return? The lowest? What attributes of the assets do you think caused this pattern?
27. In the yearbook *Stocks, Bonds, and Inflation* by Ibbotson Associates, look up the total returns on different assets (Treasury bills, Treasury bonds, and stocks) during each of the 12 months for the past year. If you could switch your portfolio between these different assets each month, how would you do so? What would your total return be from switching, compared to keeping the same asset throughout the year? Suppose that each time you switched, you paid 0.5% of your assets in transactions costs. Would you want to switch as often? What would your total return be if you subtracted transactions costs?
28. As a carryover from the days before computerization, dealers in U.S. Treasury bills often quote a yield measure called "yield on a discount basis." It differs in two ways from the yield to maturity. First, the return is divided by the face value rather than by the purchase price. Second, the number of days in a year (used for annualizing returns on bills with a maturity of less than one year) is set at 360, rather than 365. That is, the yield on a discount basis for a bond with face value F and purchase price D is

$$\left(\frac{F - D}{F}\right)\left(\frac{360}{\text{Number of days to maturity}}\right).$$

The yield for a discount bond in this chapter is

$$\left(\frac{F - D}{F}\right)\left(\frac{365}{\text{Number of days to maturity}}\right).$$

Find a copy of *The Wall Street Journal* and select a Treasury bill with about 90 days to maturity. Calculate the yield on a discount basis and the yield to maturity. Is the yield on a discount basis less than or greater than the yield to maturity? Why? Would you expect the two yield measures to move together? Explain.

CHAPTER 5

The Theory of Portfolio Allocation

If you turn to Section C of *The Wall Street Journal,* you will see ads for financial services companies, offerings for bonds or stocks, and listings of financial assets ranging from the common stock of *Fortune* 500 firms to junk bonds used to finance leveraged buyouts to a staggering array of mutual funds. Each of these assets offers savers the potential for future returns and a reward in the form of interest or capital gains for postponing consumption. How can savers choose among these financial assets in deciding where to invest their funds?

Individuals may be motivated to save for several reasons: to smooth spending over time, to purchase durable goods, to accumulate precautionary (or emergency) funds for retirement, and to leave bequests. In meeting these needs, savers are concerned about the expected return on their savings. They also care about how easily their savings can be converted into a secure and steady source of income to finance future spending.

In this chapter, we explore portfolio allocation to understand how savers decide to allocate their wealth among alternative assets. The theory of portfolio allocation describes why savers behave as they do when selecting one asset rather than another. But this is not the only choice savers must make. Suppose you find the perfect financial asset—bonds issued by Golden Horizons, Inc. Should you put all your savings into Golden Horizons? The answer is no. The second theme of this chapter is to demonstrate why investing in a group of assets, or a *portfolio,* allows investors to reduce their risk. The decisions they make about asset allocation affect the performance of the entire portfolio. A third theme of this chapter is to describe why investing in a portfolio of assets allows investors to reduce their risk. Our subsequent analysis in later chapters of interest rate determination, the behavior of financial institutions, and innovation in financial markets and institutions builds on the concepts presented in this chapter.

DETERMINANTS OF PORTFOLIO CHOICE

The financial system offers savers an array of assets from which to choose. Such assets are stores of value; that is, they can be sold when the saver needs the funds to spend on goods and services. The types of financial assets that savers have held, on average, are shown in Fig. 5.1. Americans in 2000 held 1.3% of their financial assets in checkable deposits, another 10.7% in bank savings and time deposits, 11.0% in equity mutual funds, 27.9% in stocks directly held, 2.8% through life insurance reserves, and 35.3% through pension fund reserves. A generation ago, things were different. In 1970, households kept a larger share of their savings in bank checking and saving accounts and life insurance reserves and a smaller share in mutual funds and pension reserves. Two generations ago, in 1950, households held most of their financial assets in bank accounts, government securities, and stocks; mutual funds and pension reserves were not major stores of household wealth.

Figure 5.1 shows two patterns. The first pattern is that savers divide their assets among different financial assets, and the second pattern is that these allocations change over time. Our focus in this section is on the decisions that an individual saver makes in deciding which assets to include in a portfolio, or collection of assets, and how much a saver will devote to each asset in a portfolio. Later in the chapter, we describe the reason for the changes in asset allocation over time.

To begin, how would you invest $1000? You might choose to invest in stocks, a bond, a money market fund, or physical assets (such as commodities, real estate, gold, machines, or paintings) or hold it as cash. What influences your choice?

Figure 5.1 **Portfolios of U.S. Households: 2000, 1970, 1950**

Source: Board of Governors of the Federal Reserve System, *Flow of Funds Accounts*, various issues.

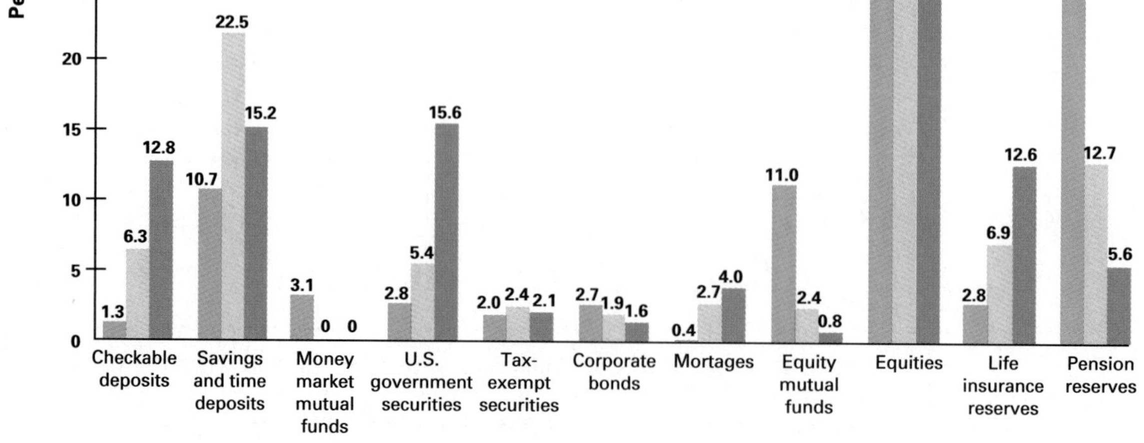

The **theory of portfolio allocation** seeks to answer questions about portfolio choice and predicts how a saver distributes his or her savings across alternative investments. According to this theory, savers evaluate five criteria when deciding what investments to make and how much to invest in each alternative. These **determinants of portfolio choice** are

- the saver's *wealth* or total stock of savings to be allocated,
- the *expected return* from the investment as compared with the expected return from other investments,
- the degree of *risk* of the asset as compared to the risk of other assets,
- the *liquidity* of the asset as compared to other assets, and
- the *cost of acquiring information* about the asset as compared to gathering information about other assets.

Wealth

As people become wealthier, the size of their portfolio of assets increases because they have more savings to allocate to the acquisition of assets. As people grow richer, they do not increase the quantities of all they have in their portfolios; rather, they choose to increase their purchases of some assets rather than others. Which assets do they choose? To begin answering this question, consider the asset mix you would purchase if your total wealth were \$1000; you might hold 10%, or \$100, in cash. If your total wealth were \$1 million, however, you probably would not hold \$100,000 in cash. Cash holdings would make up a smaller percentage of your wealth, and you would increase your relative holdings in other assets, such as stocks. Although holding many shares of different high-quality stocks with wealth of only \$1000 is difficult, you might well own a variety of stocks with \$1 million.

The **wealth elasticity of demand** describes how responsive the percentage change in the quantity of an asset chosen is to a percentage change in wealth. The wealth elasticity of demand does not depend on the actual dollar value of your wealth. Rather, it equals the percentage increase in the quantity of an asset you demand divided by the percentage increase in your total wealth; that is,

$$\begin{array}{c}\text{Wealth elasticity of demand}\\ \text{for an asset}\end{array} = \frac{\text{\% change in quantity demanded of the asset}}{\text{\% change in wealth}}.$$

Let's use this definition to find the wealth elasticity of your demand for cash when your wealth increases from \$1000 to \$1 million. With \$1000, you might hold 10%, or \$100, of your wealth as cash if your total wealth were \$1000. When your wealth reaches \$1 million (be optimistic!), you might hold 0.1%, or \$1000, in cash. Thus your wealth elasticity of demand for cash is 0.01, which is less than 1. Hence an increase in wealth generates a decrease in percentage terms of cash held. However, your wealth elasticity of demand for stocks and other assets is greater than 1. Hence an increase in wealth generates an increase in percentage terms of stocks and other assets held.

A *necessity asset* is one for which the wealth elasticity of demand is less than 1. Savers demand necessity assets, such as cash or checking accounts, in order to conduct regular transactions. A *luxury asset,* however, is one for which the wealth elasticity of demand exceeds 1. What makes some assets luxuries? They are assets, such as stocks, that are held for investment rather than for facilitating transactions. Savers also must consider the high fixed cost of owning a luxury asset, such as real estate taxes and insurance costs for a $1 million house, or the high transactions costs of acquiring the asset, such as stockbroker or dealer fees for stocks. For savers with less wealth, these costs make up a larger percentage of their investment than for savers with more wealth. Thus acquiring some assets, such as buying a famous painting, is feasible only for wealthy individuals.

To summarize, as wealth increases, savers hold more of their wealth in luxury assets and less in necessity assets.

Expected Returns on Assets

What factors determine how savers, whether wealthy or poor, choose to allocate their wealth among assets? Given the choice between two otherwise similar assets, a saver will pick the one with the higher expected return. The correct measure of expected return is the expected *real* rate of return.

Savers must assess the impact of inflation on returns because changes in the value of money will affect the real value of returns. We encountered the problem of converting nominal returns to real returns in Chapter 4 when we studied rates of returns on bonds. The expected real return savers consider equals the nominal return less expected inflation. Savers use real returns as the measure of their gain in an investment because those returns adjust for changes in purchasing power.

Because savers care about expected returns for financing current and future spending, they also focus on the amount that they can keep after taxes; that is, they compare expected real after-tax returns. Taxation of returns on savings varies significantly in the United States. Interest on private corporate bonds, bank deposits, and dividends from holdings of corporate stock are taxed at the federal, state, and local levels. Interest received from U.S. Treasury securities is subject to federal income taxation but not to state and local income taxation. The obligations of state and local governments (called municipal bonds) generally are exempt from all taxation and often are called *tax-exempt bonds.* All such differences affect savers' portfolio decisions.

When assets are similar—that is, all other factors being held constant—an increase in the expected return on one asset relative to other assets makes the asset more desirable to savers. The remaining three determinants of portfolio choice—risk, liquidity, and information costs—are attributes that we use to compare two assets.

CHECKPOINT

Interest received from municipal bonds is tax-exempt in the United States. Should you switch your savings from taxable assets to municipal bonds to take advantage of their favorable tax treatment? Not necessarily. Investors compare expected *after-tax* returns when making their investment decisions. Suppose that a taxable bond pays an interest rate of 10%. If investors face a tax rate of 30%, this after-tax return is equivalent to the return on the tax-exempt bond of 10% − 0.3(10%) = 7%. If the tax-exempt rate were higher (say, 8%), the expected return on the tax-exempt bond would exceed that on the taxable bond. Investors would increase their demand for tax-exempt bonds, bidding up their price and reducing their yield. (Recall that bond prices and yields are inversely related.) At a tax rate of 15%, investors would prefer to invest in the taxable bond because they could receive an expected after-tax return of 10% − 0.15(10%) = 8.5%. This is greater than the 7% expected rate of return on the tax-exempt bond. Investors who are subject to high tax rates are more likely to invest in tax-exempt bonds than are investors who are subject to low tax rates. o

Risk Associated with Asset Returns

In making investment decisions, savers evaluate the variability of (fluctuations up and down in) the expected return as well as the size of the return. Because households use their assets largely to smooth their spending over time, they want to avoid having assets fall in value just when they need funds.

To demonstrate the impact of variability on expected returns, suppose that you have \$1000 to invest in stocks and are comparing the shares of Solid Enterprises and Rollercoaster Industries. Solid Enterprises' shares yield a return of 10% all the time (with certainty), whereas Rollercoaster Industries' shares yield a return of 20% half the time and 0% half the time. We calculate the expected return on Rollercoaster's shares using a weighted average of its possible returns:

$$\left(\frac{1}{2}\right)(0.20) + \left(\frac{1}{2}\right)(0) = 0.10, \quad \text{or} \quad 10\%.$$

Solid's expected return, 10%, is the same. How do you choose between the two investments?

The answer lies in the degree of risk or variability associated with the two investments. Although Solid and Rollercoaster have equal expected returns, the likelihood that an investor in Rollercoaster will earn 10% is less certain than the return from an equivalent investment in Solid. The greater potential variation in Rollercoaster's return means that it is a riskier investment. The investor's view of risk determines which asset the investor will buy. Most people are **risk-averse savers.** They seek to minimize variability in the return on their savings and prefer security in their investments. A risk-averse saver would even accept a lower return from Solid Enterprises because of this desire for stability. **Risk-neutral savers** judge assets only on their expected returns; variability of returns is not a concern. A few individuals are **risk-loving savers,** who actually prefer to gamble by holding a risky asset with the possibility of maximizing returns.

Empirical evidence on expected returns from financial markets confirms the risk-averse behavior of most investors. For example, annual real rates of return (adjusted for inflation) on U.S. common stocks averaged 8.2% from 1926 to 1999, while annual real rates of return on long-term government bonds averaged only 2.0%.[†] Why do investors accept such low returns on government bonds when they could earn more by investing in stocks? The principal reason is that government bonds have less risk. Stocks offer higher potential returns to compensate savers for taking the higher risk associated with equity investment. Nevertheless, many economists have argued that the *equity premium* implied by the gap between the return on stocks and bonds is too large to be explained by risk considerations alone.

Because savers are generally risk-averse, an increase in the risk of one asset relative to other assets leads to a decline in the quantity of that asset chosen.

Liquidity of Assets

Assets with greater liquidity help savers to smooth spending over time or to draw down funds for emergencies. For example, if you maintain some savings in financial assets to meet unanticipated medical expenses, you want to be able to sell those assets quickly if you need the money for an operation.

Obviously, cash is the most liquid asset. Many marketable securities, such as U.S. government bonds or shares of IBM, are very liquid assets because finding a buyer for them with minimal transactions costs is easy. Real estate, coins, and fine paintings are relatively illiquid assets because their sale incurs substantial transactions costs. For example, a saver who wants to sell a house might need to wait months or even years before finding a buyer who is willing to pay the full asking price.

The average investor favors assets that are liquid over those that are not. The investor must weigh the benefits of liquidity against the lower returns that are generally available on liquid assets when selecting assets for a portfolio.

CHECKPOINT

Certificates of deposit (CDs) offered by banks have a penalty for early withdrawal. For example, if you invest $1000 in a one-year CD paying 5% interest, you receive less interest if you withdraw your savings before the end of a year. Why are investors willing to accept a lower interest rate (say, 3.25%) on savings accounts without a penalty for early withdrawal? Savers are generally willing to sacrifice some portion of expected return to be able to convert an asset to cash quickly to finance unplanned or emergency spending.

Costs of Acquiring Information

Savers seek to lower the risk associated with an asset but want to do so without devoting time or resources to assessing the issuer's creditworthiness or monitoring the borrower's actions. For some assets, such as cash or government

---

[†]The calculations are based on data from Roger C. Ibbotson and Rex A. Sinquefield, *Stocks, Bonds, and Inflation: 2000 Yearbook*, Chicago: Ibbotson Associates, 2000.

CASE STUDY

How Much Risk Should You Tolerate in Your Portfolio?

Although all investments are risky, you can take steps to understand and manage risk when building your own portfolio. Financial planners encourage their clients to evaluate their financial situation and their willingness to bear risk in determining whether an investment is appropriate.

In assessing the volatility of returns, financial planners recommend that you determine how far ahead your savings goal extends.

The longer your time horizon, the more you can focus on the growth potential of investments in stocks. Over the period from 1926 to 1999, one-year returns on stocks ranged between −43% and 54%, while 20-year returns ranged between 3% and 18%. For most people an important savings goal is retirement, and retirement savings make up a significant component of their wealth. If your retirement is many years away, you can take advantage of the long-term gains from riskier investments such as common stock without much concern for short-term variability in returns. Then as you approach retirement, you should adopt a more conservative strategy to reduce the risk of losing a substantial portion of your savings. Here are two typical financial plans that differ in the time horizon and savings goal of younger and older savers:

Younger Saver	**Older Saver**
Description:	
Below age 50 and wishes to build his or her net worth over a relatively long time.	Close to retirement age with a portfolio at or near the amount needed to retire.
Goal:	
Accumulate funds by earning high long-term return.	Conserve existing funds to earn a return slightly above the inflation rate.
Portfolio plan:	
Select portfolio based on maximizing expected real return with only limited concern for variability.	Reduce risk by selecting safe assets to earn an expected real return of about zero.

Finally, in assessing the volatility of your returns, you must consider the effects of inflation and taxes. Your investment returns are (generally) subject to taxation, and your real returns lop off inflation. With these considerations in mind, over the period mentioned above, "safe" nominal government bonds would have brought you a much lower and less-than-volatile average annual yield relative to common stocks.[†]

Understanding the types of risk that influence your investment will help you to reduce emotional reactions to market volatility and to make informed investment decisions.

[†]The calculations are based on data from Roger C. Ibbotson and Rex A. Sinquefield, *Stocks, Bonds, and Inflation: 2000 Yearbook,* Chicago: Ibbotson Associates, 2000.

TABLE 5.1 **DETERMINANTS OF ASSET ALLOCATION**

An increase in ...	Causes the quantity of the asset in the portfolio chosen to ...	Because ...
wealth	rise	savers have greater stock of savings to allocate
expected return on asset relative to expected returns on other assets	rise	savers gain more from holding asset
risk (variability of returns)	fall	savers are generally risk-averse
liquidity (ease with which an asset can be converted to cash)	rise	the asset can be cheaply converted to cash to finance consumption
information costs	fall	savers must spend more resources acquiring and analyzing data on the asset and its returns

securities, information is readily available to the public at low cost. For example, if you want to buy a government bond, you can easily find prices and returns in *The Wall Street Journal.* Similarly, savers can gather information about the stocks and bonds of large corporations inexpensively because financial analysts publicize information about these assets.

If a new company issues financial claims, however, investors must spend time and resources to collect and analyze information about the company before deciding to invest. Therefore savers prefer to hold assets with low information costs. An increase in the information cost for an asset raises the required rate of return on the asset; a decrease in information costs reduces the required rate of return. Specialists in the financial system acquire and analyze information about issuers of financial assets and make this information available for a fee. Other factors being held constant, a higher cost of information for an asset relative to other assets leads to a decrease in the quantity of that asset demanded.

Table 5.1 summarizes the principal determinants of portfolio choice. The underlying assumption for the effects listed in the second column of the table is that all other factors remain constant. Given the discussion of each factor, you can think about how these determinants shape your own financial decisions. As we discuss in Part 4, the same factors affect the portfolio allocation decisions of businesses and financial intermediaries.

ADVANTAGES OF DIVERSIFICATION

Savers purchase assets with the expectation that these assets will increase in value over time, but not all assets appreciate in this way. From our description of a saver's behavior in selecting an asset, you might expect that a saver could sort through the maze of available assets and find one that does increase in value and is a "best" choice for the saver's investment dollars. But implicit in our discussion of the theory of portfolio allocation is the importance given to each asset the saver decides to include in a portfolio. Why did we assume that the saver would hold more than one asset if he or she could locate the perfect investment? The answer is that the real world is full of uncertainty, and despite all the analysis and careful decision making, a saver cannot be certain that an asset will perform as expected. To compensate for the inability to find a perfect asset, individuals typically hold various types of assets, including financial instruments, property, and durable goods. Even within categories of financial assets (stocks, for example), investors usually hold many individual issues. Allocating savings among many different assets is known as **diversification.**

In the real world, returns on assets do not move together perfectly because their risks are imperfectly correlated. That is, assets do not all fare well or poorly at the same time. Thus the return on a diversified portfolio is more stable than the returns on the individual assets making up the portfolio. Diversification effectively allows the investor to divide risk into smaller and thus less potentially harmful pieces. Research on the benefits of diversification led to three Nobel Prizes in economics: to James Tobin of Yale University, Harry Markowitz of Baruch College, and William Sharpe of Stanford University.

How does diversification reduce portfolio risk? Let's use an example to answer this question. Suppose that you want to invest \$1000 in stocks and are choosing between two investments—shares in Boomco, Inc., and shares in Bustco, Inc.—whose returns vary with the economy's performance in different ways. Suppose that Boomco does well half the time and not so well the other half. When the economy does well, Boomco prospers. Its shares have a rate of return of 20%, and you earn \$200. But in a weak economy, sales of Boomco's products are poor. Then the stock's rate of return is 0%, and you have nothing. The expected amount you will earn on your \$1000 investment in Boomco is

$$\left(\frac{1}{2}\right)(\$200) + \left(\frac{1}{2}\right)(\$0) = \$100.$$

If you invest only in Boomco, you can expect a rate of return of 10% (100/1000).

Suppose that Bustco's returns follow an opposite pattern. The rate of return on Bustco shares is high (20%) when the economy is weak, and you earn \$200. When the economy does well, you earn nothing (0%). Like Boomco shares, Bustco shares have an expected return of

$$\left(\frac{1}{2}\right)(\$0) + \left(\frac{1}{2}\right)(\$200) = \$100.$$

If you invest only in Bustco, you can expect a rate of return of 10%. Of course, if you invest only in Boomco shares or only in Bustco shares, you incur risk because the returns vary with the economy's performance.

Now consider what happens if you invest equal amounts in Boomco and Bustco shares. In good times, Boomco's rate of return is 20% and Bustco's rate of return is 0%. Therefore your total rate of return in good times is

$$\left(\frac{1}{2}\right)(\text{Boomco return}) + \left(\frac{1}{2}\right)(\text{Bustco return}) = 10\%,$$

or

$$(\$500)(0.20) + (\$500)(0) = \$100.$$

Similarly, in bad times, you earn

$$\left(\frac{1}{2}\right)(\text{Boomco return}) + \left(\frac{1}{2}\right)(\text{Bustco return}) = 10\%,$$

or

$$(\$500)(0) + (\$500)(0.20) = \$100.$$

By this strategy you earn the same expected return (10%) as you would earn from buying the shares of only one of the companies. However, you lessen the risk affecting your portfolio's returns by limiting the influence of one source of variability: the economy. The strategy of dividing risk by holding multiple assets ensures steadier income.

Savers cannot eliminate risk entirely because assets share some common risk called **market** (or **systematic**) **risk.** For example, general fluctuations in economic conditions can increase or decrease returns on stocks collectively. Assets also carry their own unique risk called **idiosyncratic** (or **unsystematic**) **risk.** For example, the price of an individual stock may be influenced by factors such as discoveries, strikes, or lawsuits that influence the profitability of the firm and its share value. Diversification can eliminate idiosyncratic risk but not systematic risk.†

Diversification reduces the riskiness of the return on a portfolio unless assets' returns move together perfectly. The less the returns on assets move together, the greater the benefit savers reap from diversification in reducing portfolio risk. Because savers generally are risk-averse, they amass portfolios containing an array of different assets.

Figure 5.2 illustrates the results of a study to determine how much risk can be eliminated through diversification in a portfolio of stocks traded on the New York Stock Exchange. It illustrates the relationship between the average annual variability on equally weighted portfolios and the different numbers of stocks (selected randomly) in the portfolios. Although a single security had an average annual variability (measured by the standard deviation) of about 49%, holding two stocks reduced the variability by about one-quarter, to just over 37%.†† Holding eight stocks cuts the average annual variability in half, to just less than

† Indeed, even if asset returns are independent (completely uncorrelated), increasing the number of assets held in a portfolio reduces overall risk.

†† The variance of a portfolio return is the squared deviation from the expected return. The standard deviation is the square root of the variance.

Figure 5.2

Reducing Risk through Stock Portfolio Diversification

Increasing the number of New York Stock Exchange–listed stocks held in a portfolio decreases the variability of the portfolio's return. While diversification can reduce individual risk, there is a certain amount of risk that cannot be reduced.

Source: Based on calculations presented in Meir Statman, "How Many Stocks Make a Diversified Portfolio?" *Journal of Financial and Quantitative Analysis,* 22:353–364, 1980.

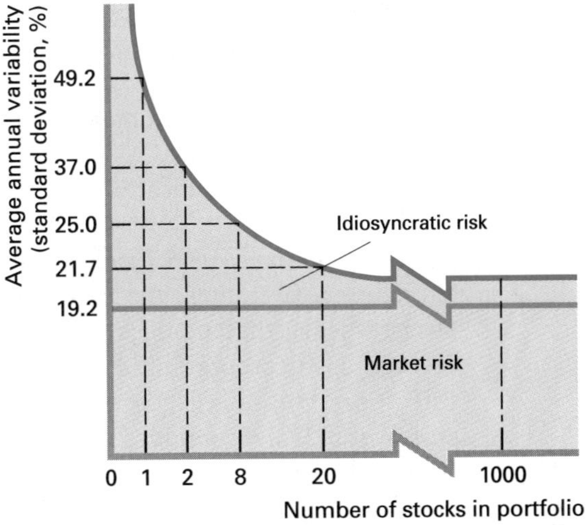

25%. Increasing the number of assets to 20 cuts the average annual variability further to about 21.7%. Holding the entire portfolio of stocks listed on the New York Stock Exchange reduces the average annual variability to 19.2%. This remaining variability is traceable to market risk and cannot be eliminated by holding additional stocks; that is, the risk is nondiversifiable. In the (unlikely) event that returns are perfectly and positively correlated, adding additional assets does not reduce the variability of the portfolio.

To measure systematic risk, financial economists calculate a variable called beta, the responsiveness of a stock's expected return to changes in the value of the complete market portfolio of that stock—that is, the collection of all stocks. For example, if a 1% increase in the value of the market portfolio leads to a 0.5% increase in the value of the asset, the asset's beta is calculated to be 0.5. If the value of the asset rises by 1.5% when the market portfolio rises by 1%, then the asset's beta equals 1.5.

The market portfolio faces no idiosyncratic risk, only systematic risk. Hence, when an asset has a high value of beta, its return has a lot of systematic risk. This systematic risk is scaled by beta; a beta of 1.5 implies three times the systematic risk as a beta of 0.5. Because systematic risk cannot be diversified away, investors are less willing to hold an asset with a high beta, all other factors being equal. Hence assets with higher values of beta must have a higher expected return to compensate investors for their higher risk.

Savers' ability to diversify is limited by the cost of acquiring information about alternative assets and the transactions costs of buying and selling individual assets. Another potential limit to diversification comes from legal restrictions on the assets that can be held by individual savers or by certain financial intermediaries on their behalf. For example, individuals face limits on their investments in derivative securities depending on their net worth and financial sophistication. Commercial banks are not allowed to invest depositors' funds in corporate equities.

PUTTING IT ALL TOGETHER: EXPLAINING PORTFOLIO ALLOCATION

At the beginning of the chapter we looked at current and past patterns of asset allocation by households. We can use the determinants of portfolio choice and the principle of diversification to explain how portfolio composition changes over time.

One pattern in Fig. 5.1 is that, in looking at the allocation of savings to different assets over time, the popularity of some assets has increased among savers, whereas that of others has declined. For example, there has been a sharp decrease in the proportion of savers' portfolios devoted to checkable deposits. One reason for this is the increase in wealth that has occurred over the post–World War II period. Checking accounts are an example of a necessity asset. As U.S. households have become much wealthier over the postwar period, their balances of checking accounts have fallen relative to other asset holdings.

Another reason for the changes is the tax treatment of different assets. Savers compare expected returns on alternative assets when making decisions about portfolio allocation. One component of differences in expected returns is different tax treatment. When a household buys stocks or bonds directly, it pays income taxes on returns. Savings through life insurance reserves receive favorable tax treatment because no tax is paid as earnings on reserves accrue. Pension fund reserves receive similarly favorable tax treatment and an additional benefit: households' contributions to pension plans are from pre-tax dollars; no individual-level tax is paid on the earnings contributed. Since 1950, as pension plan eligibility has expanded, households have held more assets through pension plans to take advantage of higher after-tax returns. Direct holdings of U.S. government bonds, corporate bonds, and equities have declined in relative importance over the same period.

In 1950, U.S. households held less than 1% of their financial assets in stock mutual funds; that figure more than doubled by 1970 to 2.4%, then more than quadrupled again by 2000 to 11.0%. One reason for their increase is that mutual funds reduce risk and information costs for small investors and increase the liquidity of owning stock.

CASE STUDY

Modeling Risk Premiums in Financial Markets

An increase in the risk of an asset's return makes investors less willing to hold the asset, other things being equal. This useful qualitative prescription has stimulated major efforts to model risk premiums. In what follows, we consider two of these developments: the *capital asset pricing model (CAPM)* and the *arbitrage pricing theory (APT)*.

The CAPM was developed by William Sharpe of Stanford University and the late John Lintner of Harvard University in the 1960s. It begins with the idea that the risk contributed by an individual asset (say, Exxon stock) to a well-diversified portfolio of stocks reflects the magnitude of its systematic risk. This magnitude is measured by beta. The larger is beta, the greater is the systematic risk and therefore the higher is the expected return required by investors for being willing to hold the asset. In the CAPM the expected return on asset j, R_j^e, depends on the default-risk-free interest rate, R_f, and the expected return on the market portfolio, R_m^e. Specifically,

$$\underbrace{R_j^e}_{\substack{\text{Expected}\\\text{return on}\\\text{asset } j}} = \underbrace{R_f}_{\substack{\text{Risk-free}\\\text{rate}}} + \underbrace{\underbrace{\beta_j}_{\substack{\text{Beta of}\\\text{asset } j}} \times \underbrace{\left(R_m^e - R_f\right)}_{\substack{\text{Risk premium on}\\\text{the market portfolio}}}}_{\text{Risk premium on asset } j}$$

In other words, the expected return on asset has two components: the default-risk-free rate and the risk premium for that asset. The risk premium compensates the investor for the risk that the security will not generate the expected return. In the CAPM the risk premium equals the risk premium on the market portfolio scaled by beta. Suppose, for example, that an asset has a beta of 1.0. Then its risk premium equals $1.0 \times (R_m^e - R_f)$, or the risk premium on the market portfolio. If the asset has a beta of 1.5, then its risk premium is one and one-half times that of the market portfolio. In this case, for example, if the expected return on the market portfolio is 9% and the risk-free rate is 1%, then the risk premium on the market portfolio is 8%, and the risk premium on the individual asset is $1.5 \times 8\%$, or 12%.

A key element in the simplicity of the CAPM is its assumption of a single source of market risk—that is, the systematic risk of the market portfolio. There may, however, be multiple sources of systematic risk in the economy. Examples include aggregate inflation or aggregate output. In the arbitrage pricing theory, developed by Stephen Ross of Yale University, each of these factors has an associated beta. The beta values are found by estimating how sensitive the expected return is to a change in the factor. To see how the APT refines the CAPM, we can substitute for the market return R_m^e the expected return from each factor R_{FAC}^e. Hence in the arbitrage pricing theory,

$$\underbrace{R_j^e}_{\substack{\text{Expected return}\\\text{on asset } j}} = \underbrace{R_f}_{\substack{\text{Risk-free}\\\text{rate}}} + \underbrace{\underbrace{\beta_{j1}\left(R_{FAC1}^e - R_f\right)}_{\substack{\text{Contribution to risk}\\\text{premium from factor 1}}} + \underbrace{\beta_{j2}\left(R_{FAC2}^e - R_f\right)}_{\substack{\text{Contribution to risk}\\\text{premium from factor 2}}} + \cdots \underbrace{\beta_{jN}\left(R_{FACN}^e - R_f\right)}_{\substack{\text{Contribution to risk}\\\text{premium from factor } N}}}_{\text{Risk premium on asset } j}$$

In this theory, an increase in the sensitivity of the assets to each factor increases the risk premium.

While they have been extended in many ways, both the CAPM and the APT are used by practitioners in financial markets. Although each theory offers technical interpretations for calculating risk premiums, the central insight is common: An increase in systematic risk raises an asset's risk premium and the return investors require for holding the asset.

One way in which mutual funds help savers to reduce overall exposure to risk is by facilitating diversification. One barrier to diversification is the cost of buying and selling financial assets. On the one hand, transactions costs of direct purchases and sales can be high for small savers. For example, brokerage commissions to buy a few shares of GM stock are very high. On the other hand, investors in a mutual fund buy shares in diversified portfolios of assets from financial markets. Because a mutual fund has a great quantity of funds to invest (the collective funds of the individual savers), it offers lower transactions costs. Thus mutual funds can offer diversified portfolios of stocks. Mutual funds offer diversification possibilities beyond stocks—to government or corporate bonds and money market instruments such as Treasury bills or commercial paper.

In addition to offering a way for savers to pool risk, mutual funds allow maintenance of liquidity through low transactions costs and, in some cases, check-writing features. They also reduce savers' information costs by economizing on costs of research and information collection about the assets in the portfolio.

OTHER TIMES, OTHER PLACES . . .

Are Investors (Globally) Well Diversified?

In domestic equity markets, investors can reduce their exposure to risk by diversifying—that is, by holding many individual stocks whose returns do not rise or fall at the same time. Investors can apply this principle even further by diversifying in *international* markets: Because equities in different national markets do not always move precisely together, investors can improve their portfolio diversification by holding stocks from many countries. Kenneth French and James Poterba of M.I.T. have shown that equity returns on stocks from the United States, Japan, United Kingdom, France, Germany, and Canada do not move together, indicating that investors could significantly reduce risk by holding a portfolio made up of stocks from more than one of these countries.†

Although the benefits of global diversification have long been known, most savers nonetheless hold the vast majority of their wealth in domestic assets. The study by French and Poterba of the world's five largest stock markets—United States, Japan, United Kingdom, Germany, and France—indicates that domestic investors account for about 90% of ownership, with the exception of Germany, which has about 80% domestic ownership.

Why are investors missing the potential for significant gains from more global diversification of their portfolios? One possible explanation is *institutional barriers*, such as government regulations that limit investment abroad. Although this explanation may have been plausible in the 1970s when such controls were widespread, capital controls are not widely used by industrial countries today. Another theory suggests that there are different *transactions costs* between domestic and foreign markets and that investors seek the lowest trans- actions costs. However, since such costs are lower in very liquid markets such as New York, this explanation does not fit the fact that most investors keep their investments in their *home* market. The most likely explanation relates to *information costs:* Investors may assign extra "risk" to foreign stocks simply because they know less about foreign firms and markets. Therefore they choose the less risky option of domestic investment. Country-specific mutual funds, which give investors access to broad groups of foreign stocks and have been growing in popularity, might help to overcome this barrier to diversification.

†See Kenneth R. French and James M. Poterba, "Investor Diversification and International Equity Markets," *American Economic Review*, 81:222–226, 1991.

Why do mutual funds provide these services that have accounted for their rapid growth? The funds earn a profit for the fund managers, as investors are willing to sacrifice some of the expected return on investments to obtain these benefits. While diversification is a worthwhile investment goal, be careful not to invest in too many similar funds. When you buy a mutual fund, you are already diversifying by investing in a group of securities. If you invest in too many similar funds, you may be racking up extra costs in fees and recordkeeping.

To summarize, we can explain trends in the way in which savers allocate their funds among different assets by applying the theory of portfolio choice and diversification. As the wealth of the population grows, investors are more likely to substitute luxury assets for necessity assets. Investments that reduce risk and information costs and increase liquidity become popular vehicles for savers who seek high expected returns. Shifts in taxation or differences in taxation among assets cause investors to favor some securities over others.

KEY TERMS AND CONCEPTS

Beta
Determinants of portfolio choice
Diversification
Idiosyncratic (unsystematic) risk
Market (systematic) risk
Risk-averse savers
Risk-loving savers
Risk-neutral savers
Theory of portfolio allocation
Wealth elasticity of demand

SUMMARY

1. The theory of portfolio allocation helps to predict how savers select assets to hold as investment. A saver's allocation of savings in a particular asset is determined by (1) wealth (with greater responsiveness for luxury assets than for necessity assets); (2) expected return on the asset relative to expected returns on other assets; (3) risk of the return on the asset relative to the returns on other assets; (4) liquidity of the asset relative to other assets; and (5) cost of gathering information about the asset relative to information costs associated with other assets.
2. Diversification (holding more than one asset) reduces the risk of the return on a portfolio unless the returns on the individual assets move together perfectly. The less the returns on assets move together, the greater is the reduction in risk provided by diversification. This reduction in risk is valued by risk-averse savers, who are concerned not only about the expected return on their savings (portfolio of assets), but also about the variability of that return.

REVIEW QUESTIONS

1. What are the five key determinants of demand for a particular asset?
2. What is the difference between a necessity asset and a luxury asset? Give some examples of each.
3. What are the differences in being *risk-averse, risk-neutral,* and *risk-loving?* Which type of saver is likely to own only stocks and stock options? Which type of saver is likely to hold more bonds and cash than stocks?
4. U.S. citizens invest mostly in the U.S. stock market; Japanese citizens invest mostly in the Japanese

MUTUAL FUNDS APRIL 2000

Sex Matters

Truth hurts, but here it is: Academic studies and anecdotal evidence alike say women are better investors than men. But they also say the opposite, that men are better investors than women. Which is true? Which are you? And who do you want running your mutual funds—men or women? We've looked into the Adam versus Eve question—naturally—with great interest. . . .

According to a recent study of 35,000 brokerage accounts done by economists at the University of California at Davis, men trade 45% more often than women—and wind up hurting themselves. Men's annual risk-adjusted returns (after trading costs) were 1.5 percentage points lower than women's. . . .

What about professional money managers, as opposed to random investors? Look at portfolio turnover. Female fund managers, on average, replace 83% of their portfolios each year; male managers, 110% (meaning they sell everything they own in less than a year). That's a lot o' trading. Anecdotally, (a) you'll often hear that women, in particular, gravitate toward lower-risk (and, by definition, lower turnover) investing styles, such as value investing. Might this explain their slower trading? If such a tendency exists, it isn't obvious among growth and value funds. Women manage 10% of the former and only 5% of the latter. . . .

Terrance Odean, who co-wrote the turnover study, notes that in the general population, neither gender exhibits superior stock-picking ability. And to the discredit of both sexes, males and females both tend to sell stocks that go on to perform better than the ones they buy.

The only real difference, then—in light of Odean's research—may be that men (b) churn their accounts more, a fact that Odean attributes to male overconfidence…

Some studies go further, suggesting that women have less tolerance for risk than men regardless of what the market is doing. Catherine Eckel, professor of economics at Virginia Tech, has conducted a variety of experiments in which women and men are presented with real money at stake and with an uncertain outcome. (Sound familiar?) "What we've found, across a bunch of different environments, is that women are more risk-averse than men," she says. "It's really true." . . .

All the talk of women's "instinctive" behavior is bunk, says Elizabeth Bramwell, the successful manager of Gabelli Growth back in the late 1980s and early 1990s and of Bramwell Growth since 1994. "Women have historically been risk-averse—savers—for a very good reason: They've had less money than men," Bramwell says. "If they're at home, they're saving cookie-jar money, historically. If they work, (c) they've been paid less. So there are reasons they've been so defensive." But in a world where more women must support themselves (and their families), there's a huge risk for women who are too risk-averse. . . .

And the gentlemen? What should they do to get over their commitment-phobia and stick with their picks?

That's a question women have pondered through the ages.

Investors compare alternative assets by considering expected returns, risk, liquidity, and information costs. Most financial planners in the United States recommend that individuals place a significant portion of their retirement savings (the bulk of households' financial assets) in stock. A majority of households in the United States own stocks either directly or through mutual funds. Some financial commentators have observed that women are less likely to allocate substantial portions of their portfolio to equities, apparently passing up higher expected returns. The determinants of portfolio choice offer some explanations (see below).

Financial observers have another reason to focus on women's portfolio allocation decisions. Attracting women to equity investments is an important and potentially lucrative challenge for brokerage firms and investment advisors. In 2000, the Securities Industry Association (SIA) estimated that about 222,000 women headed households with annual incomes exceeding $100,000; the SIA also estimated that the number of such women would double by 2010, at which time they would control more than $1 trillion of financial assets.

a One possibility is that women as investors have a different attitude toward risk than men as investors—in particular, that women as a group are more risk-averse. If women dislike risk, stocks—with sometimes quite variable returns—will be less preferred than bonds.

b Transactions costs probably do not explain the difference in the portfolio allocation decisions of men and women, as both face the same costs (for a given portfolio size and pattern of trading). Because men trade more often than women on average, they run the risk of lower returns over the long run, because they accumulate substantial transactions costs. The article attributes men's greater trading to "overconfidence," a claim that could be corroborated only by looking at portfolio returns over a long period of time, after controlling for income, wealth, and other individual characteristics.

c At least historically, information costs may be the culprit in explaining the portfolio differences between women and men. For women, increases in labor force participation and exposure to retirement saving plans and financial planning in the workplace may stimulate holdings of equity.

For further thought . . .

Suppose the United States switched from the current Social Security system (in which payroll taxes paid by workers fund their retirement) and instead allowed workers to invest their own contribution and bear the risk of their portfolio choices. Based on the article, what sort of investment guidelines and rules would be needed to integrate the gender-based investing differences suggested in the article?

Source: Excerpted from Barbara Milotek Whelehan, "Sex Matters," *Mutual Funds,* April 2000.

stock market. Why do they do so if there are gains to diversification?

5. The saying "You shouldn't put all your eggs in one basket" is an example of what principle in investing? What does it mean?
6. If the equity premium implied by the gap between the return on stocks and the return on bonds is too large to be explained by risk considerations alone, how might it be explained?
7. What advantages do small investors see in owning stock mutual funds as opposed to holding individual stocks?
8. Despite the stock market boom of the 1990s, the fraction of household financial assets directly invested in equities declined by 10 percentage points between 1970 and 1998. Can you think of reasons why this happened?
9. What is the difference between market risk and idiosyncratic risk? Which type of risk can be reduced by diversification?
10. Why don't all risk-averse investors hold a fully diversified portfolio?
11. Would you expect the variability of returns on individual stocks traded on the New York Stock Exchange to be greater or less than the variability of the return on a portfolio consisting of all stocks traded on the exchange? Why or why not?

ANALYTICAL PROBLEMS

12. Suppose that your wealth elasticity of demand for IBM stock is 2, you own 1000 shares of IBM stock, and your total wealth is $1 million. You earn a $100,000 bonus at work. How much more IBM stock will you buy?
13. Suppose that you are an investor with a choice of three assets that are identical in every way except in their rate of return and taxability. Which asset yields the highest after-tax return?
    Asset 1: interest rate 10%, interest taxed at a 40% rate
    Asset 2: interest rate 8%, interest taxed at a 25% rate
    Asset 3: interest rate 6.5%, no tax on interest
14. Suppose that Asset 1 in Problem 13 had a return of 11%. Would your answer change? If so, in what way?
15. U.S. government bonds with 30-year maturities used to be sold with a call provision: After 25 years, the government could call the bonds and make a final interest payment plus principal repayment. When the government eliminated the call provision in 1985, it found that it could offer a different interest rate on the bonds than it could before. Was the interest rate higher or lower? Why? When was the government likely to call the outstanding callable bonds?
16. Suppose that you have invested $1000 in Acme Widget. Half of the time you earn a 20% return on your Acme shares and half of the time you earn a 0% return. Suppose that you have studied the returns on the shares of Amalgamated Gidget and it turns out that in years when the return on Acme's shares was 20%, half the time the return on Amalgamated's shares was also 20% and half the time the return was 0%. Similarly, in years when the return on Acme's shares was 0%, half the time the return on Amalgamated's shares was 20% and half the time the return was 0%. Would you be better off selling $500 worth of your Acme shares and investing the funds in Amalgamated or would you be better off keeping all of your funds invested in Acme?
17. In the mid-1980s, a new technique was developed that divides payments on government coupon bonds into two parts: One part consists of the coupon interest payments on the bonds, and the other part consists of the principal repayment on the bonds. Sold separately, the two parts are worth more to investors than the entire bond. Why?
18. Suppose that you are investing money in a portfolio of stocks and are choosing from among Badrisk Company, which returns 30% in good years and loses 50% in bad years; Worserisk Company, which returns 30% in good years and loses 75% in bad years; Norisk Company, which returns 10% all the time; and Lowrisk Company, which returns 20% in good years and loses 5% in bad years.

a. If you were completely risk-averse and your only goal was to minimize your risk, which stock(s) would you buy?

b. If you were risk-neutral, and good years and bad years each occurred half the time, which stock(s) would you buy?

c. If you were somewhat risk-averse, would you ever have both Badrisk and Worserisk in your portfolio? Why or why not?

d. If you decided on a portfolio consisting of one- third Badrisk, one-third Norisk, and one-third Lowrisk, what would be your rate of return in good years? In bad years? What would be your average rate of return over all years if good years and bad years each occurred half the time? If good years occurred 80% of the time and bad years 20% of the time?

19. Suppose that you want to hold a stock portfolio for just one year. You have $1000 to invest in stocks, and you can choose to invest in Topgunner, Inc., which has returns of 20% in good years and –10% in bad years, or in Lowrunner, Inc., which has returns of 35% in good years and –15% in bad years.

a. What is your return in a good year if you buy just Topgunner? In a bad year? What is your return in a good year if you buy just Lowrunner? In a bad year? What is your return in a good year if you put half your money in Topgunner and half in Lowrunner? In a bad year?

b. Now suppose that, for every stock you buy, you must pay transactions costs equal to $50. Repeat (a) with your return reduced by these transactions costs. What happens to your portfolio choice?

20. You are a member of an investment club that owns shares in a firm that manufactures men's clothing. Explain the arguments for and against buying

a. shares in a company that manufactures women's clothing.

b. shares in a chemical manufacturing concern.

Which investment is more likely to decrease the overall risk of your club's portfolio? Why?

21. Using the theory of portfolio allocation, state why you would be more willing or less willing to buy a share of IBM stock if you

a. win $1 million in the state lottery.

b. expect that stock prices will become more volatile.

c. expect the price of IBM shares to increase over the next year.

d. read about new developments increasing the liquidity of the bond market.

22. Using the theory of portfolio allocation, state why you would be more willing or less willing to buy corporate bonds if you

a. expect interest rates on bonds to rise.

b. expect a large capital loss next month on the sale of your house.

c. learn that the transactions costs of selling bonds will increase.

d. expect inflation to increase significantly in the future.

DATA QUESTIONS

23. You can find information about mutual funds through advertisements in *The Wall Street Journal.* Such ads invite you to write to the fund manager to obtain a copy of the *prospectus,* which contains information about the fund's portfolio, management strategy, and fees. Find a prospectus on the World Wide Web, or locate one in your library for a fund specializing in equities, and examine the list of stocks held. Is the fund well diversified? How can you tell?

24. The Federal Reserve periodically publishes a summary of assets and liabilities of U.S. households and businesses. Locate a recent copy of *Balance Sheets for the U.S. Economy* in your library. Calculate for the most recent year available the ratio of foreign corporate equities held to total corporate equities held. Using the theory of portfolio allocation, explain why such a small fraction of equity holdings of U.S. residents are in non–U.S. stocks.

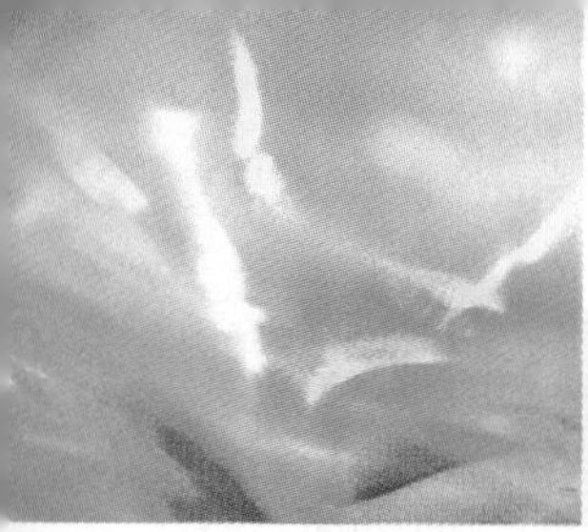

CHAPTER 6

Determining Market Interest Rates

The 2000 presidential campaign was dominated by a struggle between George W. Bush and Al Gore over what to do with the emerging U.S. budget surplus—an event unprecedented in a generation. Indeed, the wait for this surplus had been going on for some time. As far back as 1994, *Washington Post* columnist Bob Woodward's book *The Agenda,* which chronicled U.S. budget planning during 1993, was a best-seller.[†] A notable and perhaps surprising theme was the attention that budget planners paid to the bond market (in particular, the market for long-term bonds issued by the U.S. Treasury). The exhaustive debate between the President's political advisors and economic advisors over a deficit reduction package led one political adviser to inquire, "How many votes does the *!@ bond market have?" The concern over the bond market's "votes" was practical. A rise in bond prices in response to a budget that reduced the deficit would reduce interest rates paid by households, businesses, and the government itself. In this chapter, we describe how lending and borrowing decisions produce a supply of and demand for funds in the financial system. We show how such decisions affect interest rate determination. Using the analysis in Chapter 4, we know that interest rates and bond prices are negatively related; hence explaining movements in bond prices permits us to explain movements in interest rates. As in other markets that you studied in your first economics course, the equilibrium price of bonds and the interest rate depend on supply and demand considerations.

A change in the federal budget deficit is only one of many reasons that market interest rates rise and fall. In this chapter, we describe other reasons for the volatility of market interest rates, beginning with an investigation of what determines market interest rates in the first place.

SUPPLY AND DEMAND IN THE BOND MARKET AND LOANABLE FUNDS[††]

The interest rate that prevails in the **bond market** is determined by the demand for and supply of bonds. To see how this interest rate is set, we begin by

---

[†]Bob Woodward, *The Agenda: Inside the Clinton White House,* New York: Simon & Schuster, 1994. The quotes are taken from page 130.

[††]The author gives special thanks to Steven Tomlinson of the University of Texas at Austin for recommending the joint presentation of the bond market and loanable funds.

focusing specifically on the behavior of bond buyers and sellers. We restrict our investigation to the quantity of bonds in the market and the price of those bonds, holding all other factors equal. Once we observe the basic relationships, we introduce some of those "other factors" and see how they change our basic predictions about how the bond market works.

We can view the buyer (demander) of bonds and the seller (supplier) of bonds in two ways. First, we can consider the bond as the "good." In this case, the lender is buying the bond and the borrower is selling the bond. The amount the lender pays for the bond is the "price" of the bond. In the second view, the use of the funds is the "good." In this case, the borrower is the buyer because the borrower purchases the use of the funds and pays for it with a promise to repay. The seller is the supplier of the funds. The "price" of the funds exchanged is the interest rate. The following chart summarizes the two views of the bond market.

	Bond Is the Good	**Use of Funds Is the Good**
Buyer	Lender who buys bond	Borrower raising funds
Seller	Borrower issuing bond	Lender supplying funds
Price	Bond price	Interest rate

The first step in determining how interest rates are determined in the bond market is to observe how the quantity varies with price. In the case in which the bond is the good, the quantity of bonds will vary with the price of bonds. In the case in which the loanable funds are the good, the quantity of loanable funds will vary with the interest rate. Our analysis illustrates again the relationship between bond prices and interest rates that we studied in Chapter 4.

The Demand Curve

The first relationship we want to establish is the one between the price of bonds and the quantity of bonds demanded by lenders. Let's study the demand for a one-year discount bond that will pay the owner \$10,000 when the bond matures. If the bond has a price of \$8000 (point A in Fig. 6.1(a)), lenders will want to purchase more of these bonds than if it has a price of \$9500 (point B). This relationship between price and quantity produces the demand curve in Fig. 6.1(a). The demand curve slopes down because the lender is willing and able to purchase more bonds when the price of the bond is low than when it is high.

In Fig. 6.1(a), the demand curve illustrates the relationship between the quantity demanded of bonds (on the horizontal axis) and the price of bonds (on the vertical axis), the values of other variables being held constant. Changes in the values of those other variables shift the demand curve, a point we consider later in the chapter.

To construct a demand curve for the bond market when we view the good exchanged as loanable funds rather than bonds, we have to find the interest rates for the discount bonds selling for \$8000 and \$9500. The expected return from holding the bond for one year is its yield to maturity. The formula for the yield to maturity i in this case is i = (Face value − Discount price) / Discount price. The face value is known—$10,000. If the discount price is $8000, then the associated interest rate i equals

$$(10{,}000 - 8000) / 8000 = 25\%.$$

If the discount price is $9500, then the associated interest rate equals

$$(10{,}000 - 9500) / 9500 = 5.3\%.$$

For this interpretation, on the horizontal axis in Fig. 6.1(b), we measure **loanable funds,** L, the quantity of funds changing hands between lenders and borrowers. On the vertical axis, we measure the price. Measuring the price of a loan as a "promise" requires a bit more subtlety than measuring the price of the security. In this case, lenders are concerned about the interest they will earn—the rental rate on their funds. At a bond price of $8000, the interest rate is 25% (point A). At a price of $9500, the interest rate is 5.3% (point B). The demand for bonds is equivalent to the supply of loanable funds. As the interest rate rises from 5.3% to 25%, all other things being equal, lenders are willing and able to increase the quantity of funds supplied to borrowers. As Fig. 6.1(b) shows, the supply curve for loanable funds, L^s, slopes up: An increase in the interest rate makes lenders willing and able to supply more funds, all other things being equal.

Figure 6.1 **Demand for Bonds by Lenders**

As shown in (a):
The bond demand curve, B^d, shows a negative relationship between the quantity of bonds demanded by lenders and the price of bonds, all else being equal.

As shown in (b):
The supply curve for loanable funds, L^s, shows a positive relationship between the quantity of loanable funds supplied by lenders and the interest rate, all else being equal.

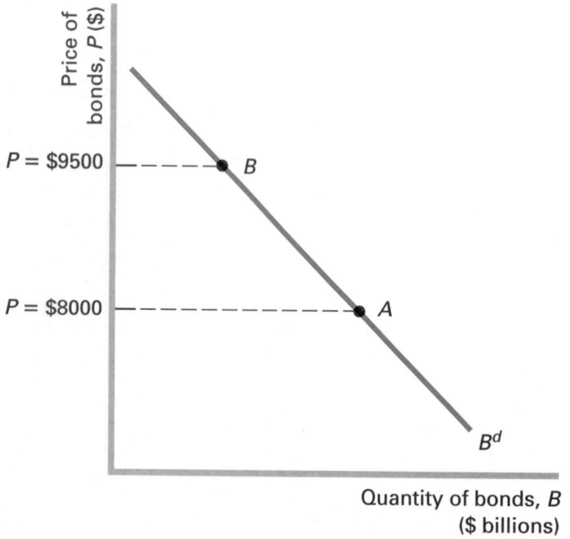

(a) Bond Market Perspective

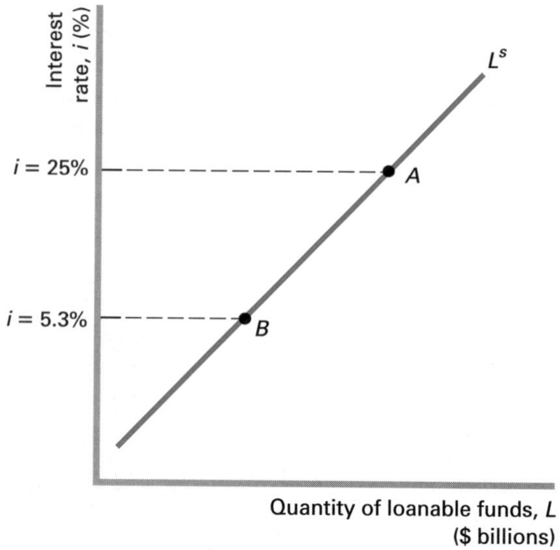

(b) Loanable Funds Perspective

The Supply Curve

The supply curve for bonds shows us how the quantity of bonds supplied by borrowers varies with bond prices, all other things being equal. Figure 6.2(a) plots the quantity of bonds borrowers are willing to supply as bond prices change. Consider again the one-year discount bond with a face value of \$10,000. Borrowers are willing and able to offer more bonds (promises to repay) when the bonds' price is \$9500 (point C) than when it is \$8000 (point *D*). The supply curve for bonds, B^s, slopes up.

To view the bond market as the demand for loanable funds, we look at the behavior of borrowers demanding loanable funds from lenders. Figure 6.2(b) takes this approach. Borrowers are willing to demand more funds when interest rates are low than when they are high. At a price of \$9500, the interest rate on the discount bond is 5.3% (point C); at a price of \$8000, the interest rate is 25% (point *D*). As the interest rate rises from 5.3% to 25%, borrowers are willing and able to borrow less in the market for loanable funds. Hence the demand curve for loanable funds, L^d, slopes down.

Market Equilibrium

We now have enough information to determine a market interest rate in the markets for bonds and loanable funds by combining our demand and supply curves. Let's work with the example of \$10,000 discount bonds to see what bond price and quantity will prevail and observe what the market interest rate will be. To do this, we combine the demand and supply curves in Figs. 6.1 and 6.2 to produce the market diagrams in Fig. 6.3.

Which bond price and interest rate prevail? The equilibrium bond price P^* is determined by the intersection of the bond demand curve, B^d, and the bond supply curve, B^s, which is at point *E* in Fig. 6.3(a). What do we mean by ***equilibrium***? Essentially, in equilibrium, the price of bonds and the volume of bonds tend to remain the same. Neither savers nor borrowers have an incentive to change their buying or selling decisions.

To see why, let's consider what happens when the market is not in equilibrium. We can think of markets in disequilibrium in two ways. We look first at bond prices and quantities, and then at loanable funds.

Suppose that the price of bonds shown in Fig. 6.3(a) is P_1 = \$9500, which is higher than the equilibrium price P^* = \$9091. In this case, the quantity of bonds supplied by borrowers is greater than the quantity of bonds demanded by lenders, so there is an excess supply of bonds. Lenders are buying all the bonds they want at the going price. But some people who want to borrow cannot find lenders of funds. Therefore they have an incentive to reduce their bond price demands so that lenders will buy their bonds. As the bond price falls, two things happen. First, some people who did not want to lend before do so because lenders now earn a greater return. Second, some people who wanted to borrow before are no longer interested in doing so because the cost of borrowing is higher. The price of bonds continues to fall until the excess supply of funds is eliminated. Equilibrium is restored at a price of P^* = \$9091, or point *E*, at which the quantity demanded and quantity supplied of bonds are equal.

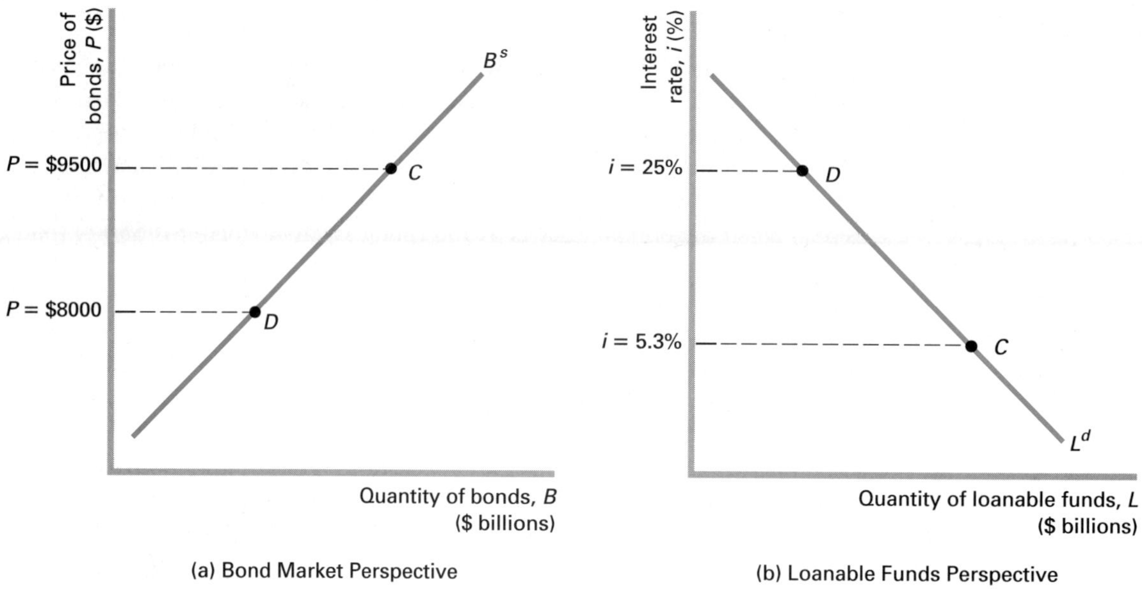

Figure 6.2

Supply of Bonds by Borrowers

As shown in (a):
The bond supply curve, B^s, shows a positive relationship between the quantity of bonds supplied by borrowers and the price of bonds, all else being equal.

As shown in (b):
The demand curve for loanable funds, L^d, shows a negative relationship between the quantity of loanable funds demanded by borrowers and the interest rate, all else being equal.

Suppose, however, that the bond price in Fig. 6.3(a) is $P_2 = \$8000$, which is less than P^*. In this case, the quantity of bonds that lenders demand exceeds the quantity of bonds that borrowers are willing to supply, so there is an excess demand for bonds. Borrowers are selling all the bonds they want at the going price. But some people who want to lend cannot find any bonds to buy at the going price. Therefore they have an incentive to raise the price of the bonds they are purchasing from borrowers. As the bond price rises, two things happen. First, some people who did not want to borrow before do so because the cost of borrowing has declined. Second, some people who wanted to lend before are no longer interested in doing so because they get a lower expected return from lending. The bond price continues to rise until the excess demand for bonds is eliminated at $P^* = \$9091$, at which equilibrium is reached at E. The financial system makes this return to equilibrium possible.

We can consider the same tendency toward equilibrium in the market for loanable funds, as shown in Fig. 6.3(b). At an interest rate of 5.3%, borrowers want more funds than lenders are willing to provide. They must offer a higher interest rate to be able to borrow more. As the interest rate rises, lenders increase their willingness to offer loanable funds, and borrowers reduce their planned spending on investment. The interest rate continues to rise until the excess demand for loanable funds is eliminated at $i^* = 10\%$, with an equilibrium at E.

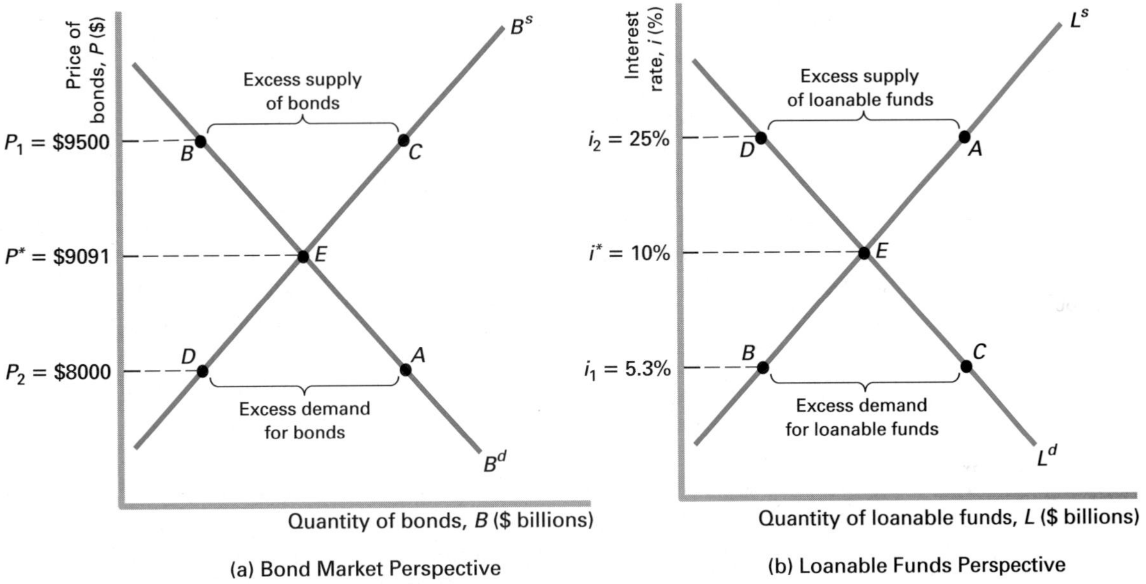

Figure 6.3

Equilibrium in Markets for Bonds and Loanable Funds

As shown in (a):
At the equilibrium bond price, P^*, the quantity of bonds demanded by lenders equals the quantity of bonds supplied by borrowers. At any price above P^*, there is an excess supply of bonds. At any price below P^*, there is an excess demand for bonds. The behavior of bond buyers and sellers pushes the bond price to P^*.

As shown in (b):
At the equilibrium interest rate, i^*, the quantity of loanable funds supplied by lenders equals the quantity of loanable funds demanded by borrowers. At any interest rate below i^*, there is an excess demand for loanable funds. At any interest rate above i^*, there is an excess supply of loanable funds. The behavior of lenders and borrowers pushes the interest rate to i^*.

Also recall that the demand curve for bonds represents the quantity of loanable funds that lenders are willing to supply. Hence an excess demand for bonds at P_2 corresponds to an excess supply of loanable funds at interest rate $i_2 = 25\%$. At this interest rate, lenders are willing to offer more funds than borrowers are willing to borrow. Lenders must lower the interest rate they are willing to accept to attract more borrowers. As the interest rate falls, borrowers increase their willingness to obtain funds, and lenders offer less funds. The interest rate continues to fall until the excess supply of loanable funds is eliminated at $i^* = 10\%$, with an equilibrium at E.

To summarize, the behavior of buyers and sellers leads the bond market to gravitate toward the equilibrium bond price and interest rate.

EXPLAINING CHANGES IN EQUILIBRIUM INTEREST RATES

The basic demand and supply model shows us the relationship between bond quantities and prices in the market for bonds and quantities of loanable funds and interest rates in the loanable funds market. To find the equilibrium interest rate, we made some assumptions. Specifically, we eliminated all other influences on the market from our analysis aside from price and quantity. In the real world, other factors influence the prices of bonds that prevail in the market and change the market interest rate. We describe those factors now and illustrate how they change equilibrium interest rates and bond prices.

When we worked with price and quantity only in our simplified model of the bond market, changes in price or quantity moved us to a different position on the same demand or supply curve. For example, in Fig. 6.1(a), when bond prices fell from \$9500 to \$8000, we moved along the demand curve from point *B* to point *A* and observed the resulting increase in the quantity of bonds demanded by lenders. When we bring "other factors" into the analysis, the entire demand or supply curve shifts to the right or left. The shifts are illustrated in Figs. 6.4 and 6.5 (on pages 124 and 129).

In the market for bonds or loanable funds, factors that increase demand shift the demand curve to the right. Factors that decrease demand for bonds or for loanable funds shift the demand curve to the left. In a similar fashion, factors that increase the supply of bonds or the supply of loanable funds shift the supply curve to the right. Factors that decrease the supply of bonds or loanable funds shift the supply curve to the left. We first describe factors that change the quantity demanded at each price and then those that change the quantity supplied at each price.

Shifts in Bond Demand

The same criteria that savers use to select investments in the theory of portfolio allocation (Chapter 5) are those that cause the demand curve for bonds to shift. These criteria include wealth, expected returns and expected inflation, risk, liquidity, and information costs. As lenders, savers will consider bonds along with other investments. If bonds offer advantages over alternative investments, savers will purchase bonds instead of those other investments, shifting the demand curve to the right. If other investments offer greater benefits than bonds, then savers will substitute those investments for bonds, shifting the demand curve to the left. We describe each factor and its impact on the demand for bonds and on interest rates.

Wealth. Suppose savers are trying to decide how many bonds to buy. The wealthier savers are, the larger the stock of savings they have available to invest in financial assets, including bonds. In Fig. 6.4(a), the bond market is initially in equilibrium at E_0, with an initial equilibrium bond price of P_0. As wealth increases in the economy, savers are willing and able to buy more bonds at any given price. That is, at each bond price, the quantity of bonds demanded rises. As a result, the bond demand curve B^d shifts to the right, from B_0^d to B_1^d. Note that the rightward shift of the bond demand curve leads to a higher equilibrium bond price, $P_1 > P_0$. Starting again at E_0, what happens if aggregate wealth—the economy's stock of savings—falls? The decrease in savings shifts the bond demand curve to the left, from B_0^d to B_2^d. At the new equilibrium E_2, the new bond price P_2 is lower than P_0.

We examine the same effect in the loanable funds market. In Fig. 6.4(b), the loanable funds market is initially in equilibrium at E_0, with an interest rate of i_0. An increase in wealth increases lenders' willingness to lend at any interest rate, and the supply curve for loanable funds shifts to the right, from L_0^s to L_1^s. At the new equilibrium, E_1, the interest rate falls from i_0 to i_1. Note that the lower interest rate (Fig. 6.4(b)) is associated with the higher bond price (Fig. 6.4(a)). Starting again from E_0, a decrease in aggregate wealth reduces lenders' ability to supply funds at any interest rate, shifting the supply curve for loanable funds to the left from L_0^s to L_2^s. At the new equilibrium, E_2, the interest rate rises from i_0 to i_2.

We can generalize these findings. As aggregate wealth expands, the demand for bonds rises; the bond demand curve shifts to the right, raising bond prices and reducing interest rates, all else being equal. As wealth falls, the demand for bonds falls; the bond demand curve shifts to the left, lowering bond prices and raising interest rates, all else being equal.

Expected returns and expected inflation. If expected returns on bonds increase, bonds become a more attractive investment. But this is not the only change in the demand for bonds that occurs when expected returns rise. Bond demand is also affected by changes in the expected returns on *other assets*. For example, if investors become more optimistic about business prospects, expected capital gains on stocks are higher, raising expected returns on equities. If the expected returns on bonds do not change, the higher expected returns on stocks imply that the expected return on bonds has fallen relative to that on stocks, reducing the demand for bonds. This is illustrated in Fig. 6.4(a) by a leftward shift in the bond demand curve. In the new equilibrium, the price of bonds is lower. Hence the decline in the expected return on bonds relative to stocks reduces the price of bonds.

We can illustrate the same example from the perspective of the loanable funds market, as in Fig. 6.4(b). A decline in the attractiveness of lending reduces lenders' willingness to supply loanable funds at any interest rate. The supply curve for loanable funds shifts to the left. In the new equilibrium, the interest rate is higher to induce lenders to lend.

In general, an increase in the expected returns on other assets reduces the demand for bonds, shifting the bond demand curve to the left. The price of bonds falls, and the interest rate rises. A decrease in the expected returns on other assets raises the demand for bonds, shifting the bond demand curve to the right. The price of bonds rises, and the interest rate falls.

Other financial assets are not the only alternative to bonds as investments. Physical assets such as houses, cars, major appliances, or commodities also offer ways to hold wealth. These real assets tend to offer protection against expected inflation. An increase in expected inflation raises expected future prices of physical assets, implying nominal capital gains and higher expected returns from holding these assets. If the expected return on bonds does not change, a rise in the expected return on physical assets reduces the expected return on bonds relative to that on physical assets, causing the demand for bonds to fall. In Fig. 6.4(a), the bond demand curve shifts to the left and the price of bonds falls.

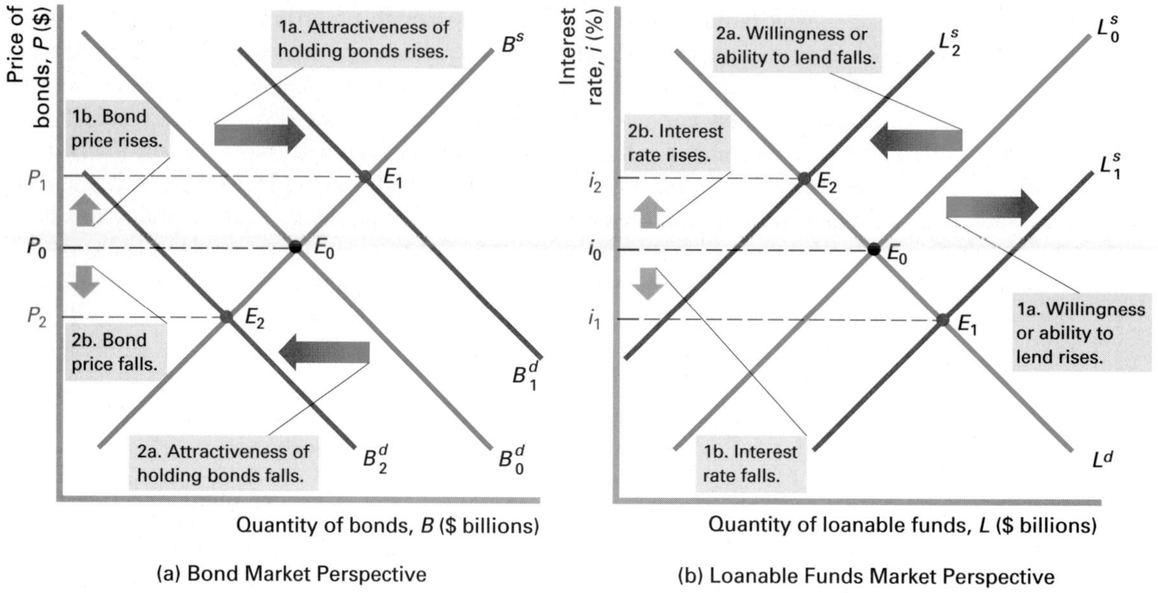

Figure 6.4

Shifts in the Demand for Bonds

As shown in (a):

1. From an initial equilibrium at E_0, as the attractiveness of holding bonds rises, the quantity of bonds demanded at any bond price also rises. The bond demand curve shifts to the right from B_0^d to B_1^d. In the new equilibrium, E_1, the price of bonds rises from P_0 to P_1.
2. From an initial equilibrium at E_0, as the attractiveness of holding bonds falls, the quantity of bonds demanded at any bond price also falls. The bond demand curve shifts to the left from B_0^d to B_2^d. In the new equilibrium, E_2, the price of bonds falls from P_0 to P_2.

As shown in (b):

1. From an initial equilibrium at E_0, an increase in lenders' willingness to lend at any interest rate shifts the supply curve for loanable funds to the right from L_0^s to L_1^s. In the new equilibrium, E_1, the interest rate falls from i_0 to i_1.
2. From an initial equilibrium at E_0, a decline in lenders' willingness to lend at any interest rate shifts the supply curve for loanable funds to the left from L_0^s to L_2^s. In the new equilibrium, E_2, the interest rate rises from i_0 to i_2.

In the loanable funds market, an increase in expected inflation makes lenders less willing to supply funds at any interest rate because they are losing purchasing power. The supply curve for loanable funds shifts to the left, and the interest rate rises to compensate lenders for losses due to inflation.

In general, an increase in expected inflation reduces the demand for bonds, shifting the bond demand curve to the left; the price of bonds falls, and the interest rate rises. A decrease in expected inflation raises the demand for bonds, shifting the bond demand curve to the right; the price of bonds rises, and the interest rate falls.

Risk. There are two ways in which risk affects the demand for bonds. First, an increase in the risk of investments in bonds reduces the demand for bonds, all other things being equal. (Remember that most investors are risk-averse, so a rise in the volatility of asset returns reduces the attractiveness of holding the asset.) In Fig. 6.4(a), the bond demand curve shifts to the left, and the price of

CONSIDER THIS . . .

Where Do Savings Come from?

Increases or decreases in wealth—the stock of savings—affect savers' demand for bonds and the supply of loanable funds. Economic expansions or contractions offer a partial explanation of changes in wealth. To look more deeply, we must consider the decisions that give rise to wealth in the first place: saving decisions. Economists studying wealth accumulation focus on three underlying determinants: life-cycle considerations, precautionary saving, and bequest saving.

Life-Cycle Considerations. For most of us, income and desired spending are not precisely matched at each point in our lifetimes. As you might expect, students and retirees usually are not able to save much. Rather, most individuals save in the middle years of their lives. Accumulating and decumulating wealth helps households to smooth out spending over time. Suppose you think your earnings will rise as you gain experience and fall substantially after retirement. You can borrow money when you are young and broke, pay back debts and save for retirement when you are middle-aged and better off financially, and live on savings and pensions in your retirement. In this life-cycle story about wealth accumulation, demographics and growth are important considerations. Growth in the number of younger savers relative to older dissavers or growth in incomes increases saving.

Precautionary Saving. Another determinant of aggregate wealth of households is the stock of *precautionary saving,* saving in preparation for emergencies, such as sudden health care needs or the loss of a job. Because no one can predict when such emergencies might arise, many people put aside some funds as a precautionary measure. Some economists believe that wealth held for precautionary saving is a significant component of total wealth.

Bequest Saving. Wealth accumulated for bequests is another component of total private wealth. Not all individuals save exclusively to finance their own future spending. Many who can afford to do so save to leave funds to their children and other heirs through *bequests,* or amounts of funds left in a will. Recipients of a bequest inherit savings of the deceased and use the funds to finance their own future spending. In addition, many individuals transfer wealth to their children or other relatives before death (to assist with a down payment on a home, for example).

Shifts in wealth generated by changes in the determinants of saving affect prices and interest rates for securities in the economy.

bonds falls. Second, an increase in the risk of another asset—say stocks—makes bonds relatively more attractive, increasing the demand for bonds. In this case, the bond demand curve shifts to the right, and the price of bonds rises. From the perspective of the loanable funds market, any change decreasing the riskiness of bonds increases lenders' willingness to supply funds at any interest rate, shifting the supply curve for loanable funds to the right and reducing the interest rate. All else being equal, any change that increases the riskiness of bonds reduces lenders' willingness to supply funds at any interest rate, shifting the supply curve for loanable funds to the left and increasing the interest rate to compensate lenders for bearing the additional risk.

In general, an increase in the riskiness of bonds relative to other assets causes the demand for bonds to fall, shifting the bond demand curve to the left; the price of bonds falls, and the interest rate rises. A decrease in the riskiness of bonds relative to other assets causes the demand for bonds to rise, shifting the bond demand curve to the right; the price of bonds rises, and the interest rate falls.

Liquidity. Investors value liquidity in an asset because greater liquidity implies lower costs of selling the asset to raise funds (say, to buy a new car or take a vacation) or to invest in another asset. As a consequence, if liquidity increases in the bond market, people are more willing to hold bonds at any bond price, increasing the demand for bonds. The bond demand curve shifts to the right, and the price of bonds rises. Changes in liquidity in other asset markets also influence the demand for bonds. For example, as governments in many countries have deregulated brokerage commissions for trading stocks, the cost of trading has fallen, increasing stock market liquidity and, all else being equal, making holding stocks relatively more attractive than holding bonds. In this case, the decline in the relative attractiveness of holding bonds shifts the bond demand curve to the left, and the price of bonds falls. All else being equal, from the perspective of the loanable funds market, any change that improves liquidity in the loanable funds market increases lenders' willingness to lend at any interest rate; the supply curve for loanable funds shifts to the right, and the interest rate falls. Any change that reduces liquidity in the loanable funds market reduces lenders' willingness to lend at any interest rate; the supply curve for loanable funds shifts to the left, and the interest rate rises to compensate lenders for the loss of liquidity.

In general, an increase in the liquidity of bonds relative to other assets causes the demand for bonds to rise, shifting the bond demand curve to the right; the price of bonds rises, and the interest rate falls. A decrease in the liquidity of bonds relative to other assets causes the demand for bonds to fall, shifting the bond demand curve to the left; the price of bonds falls, and the interest rate rises.

Information costs. The information costs investors must pay to evaluate assets affect their willingness to buy those assets. For example, the availability of ratings of bonds released by such firms as Standard & Poor's reduces investors' information costs, making bonds more attractive than assets that have higher information costs. As a result, the bond demand curve shifts to the right, and the price of bonds rises. In the loanable funds market, lower information costs increase lenders' willingness to lend at any interest rate. The supply curve for loanable funds shifts to the right, and the interest rate falls.

In general, a rise in the information costs for bonds relative to other assets causes the demand for bonds to fall, shifting the bond demand curve to the left; the price of bonds falls, and the interest rate rises. A fall in the information costs for bonds relative to other assets causes the demand for bonds to rise, shifting the bond demand curve to the right; the price of bonds rises, and the interest rate falls.

Summary. Table 6.1 summarizes reasons that the demand curve for bonds may shift. Remember that the demand for bonds corresponds to the supply of loanable funds. Hence, as Table 6.1 shows, factors that shift the demand curve for bonds to the right—raising the price of bonds—shift the supply curve for loanable funds to the right—reducing the interest rate. Factors that shift the demand curve for bonds to the left—reducing the price of bonds—shift the supply curve for loanable funds to the left—increasing the interest rate.

CHECKPOINT

You read in the morning paper that the Congress has passed a bill eliminating the tax on capital gains from holding stocks. What would you expect to happen to the price and yield of bonds? The cut in the capital gains tax lowers the expected return on bonds relative to stocks; the bond demand curve shifts to the left. If nothing else changes, the price of bonds falls and the yield on bonds rises. **o**

Shifts in Bond Supply

Shifts in the supply curve for bonds result from changes in the willingness and ability of borrowers to issue bonds at any given price or interest rate. Four factors are most important in explaining the shifts in bond supply:

1. expected profitability of capital,
2. business taxation,
3. expected inflation, and
4. government borrowing.

Expected profitability of capital. Most firms borrow (issue bonds) to finance the purchase of capital assets—assets such as plant and equipment that they expect to use over several years to produce goods and services. In planning their needs for investment in capital assets, firms project their current and future profitability. Future profitability depends on the firm's production of innovative products and services, improvements in operations as a result of using new technologies, and projections of future demand. Higher expected profitability leads firms to want to borrow more to finance investment in plant and equipment—that is, to supply more bonds at any price. For example, when deciding whether to invest in the development of a new drug, a pharmaceutical company will consider the likely future demand for the drug. Also, in a period of economic expansion, when expected profitability is high, firms are willing and able to supply more bonds at any price. According to the bond market diagram in Fig. 6.5(a), an increase in expected profitability shifts the supply curve for bonds to the right, from B_0^s to B_1^s, and the price of bonds falls from P_0 to P_1. In the loanable funds diagram in Fig. 6.5(b), an increase in expected profitability increases borrowers' demand for funds to finance investment. The demand curve for loanable funds shifts to the right, from L_0^d to L_1^d, and the interest rate rises from i_0 to i_1.

In general, an increase in expected profitability raises borrowers' willingness to supply bonds; the bond supply curve shifts to the right, reducing the price of bonds and raising the interest rate. A decrease in expected profitability reduces borrowers' willingness to supply bonds; the bond supply curve shifts to the left, raising the price of bonds and reducing the interest rate.

Business taxation. Corporate taxes also affect expectations about future profitability because businesses are concerned only about the profits they retain after taxes. As a result, investment incentives—special tax subsidies for investment—

TABLE 6.1

FACTORS THAT SHIFT THE DEMAND CURVE FOR BONDS

All else being equal, an increase in . . .	Causes the equilibrium quantity of bonds or loanable funds to . . .	Because . . .	Graph of effect on Bonds	Graph of effect on Loanable funds
wealth	increase	more funds are allocated to bonds	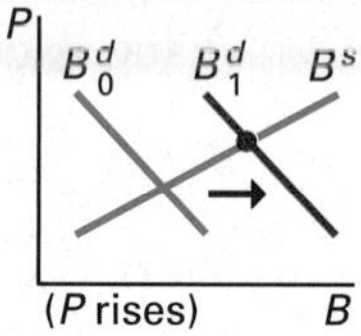	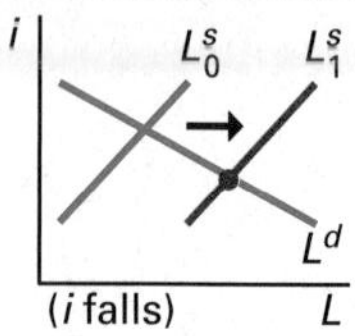
expected returns on bonds, expected interest rate	increase	holding bonds is relatively more attractive	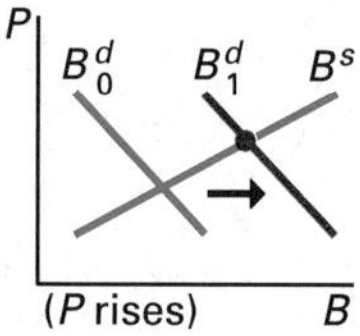	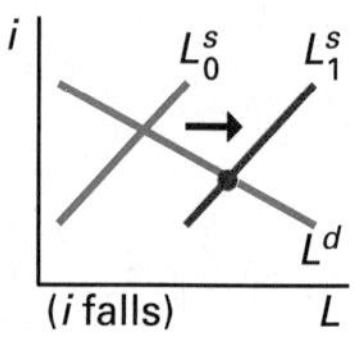
expected inflation	decrease	holding bonds is relatively less attractive	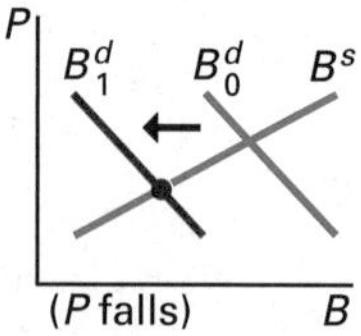	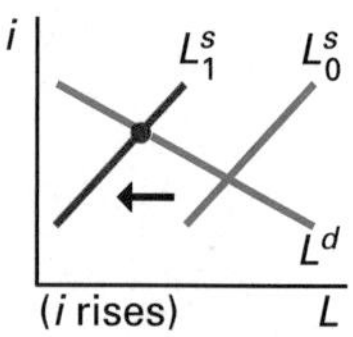
expected returns on other assets	decrease	holding bonds is relatively less attractive	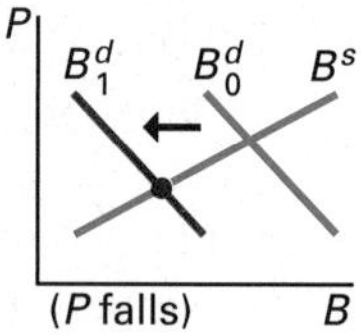	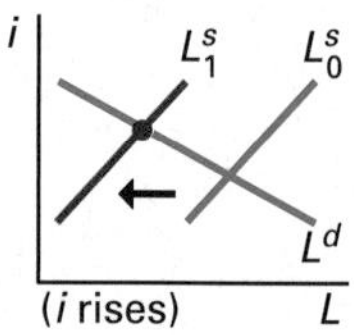
riskiness of bonds relative to other assets	decrease	holding bonds is relatively less attractive	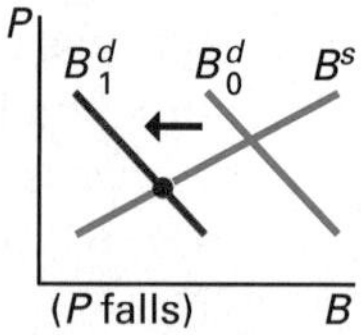	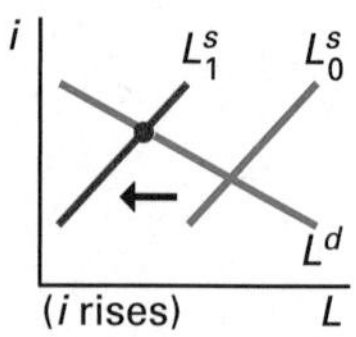
liquidity of bonds relative to other assets	increase	holding bonds is relatively more attractive	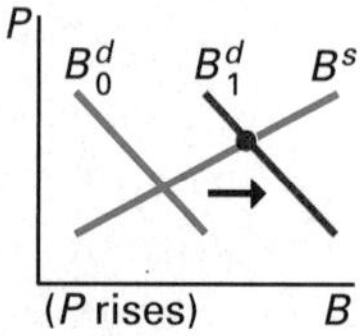	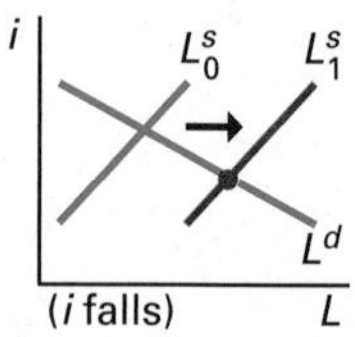
information costs of bonds relative to other assets	decrease	holding bonds is relatively less attractive	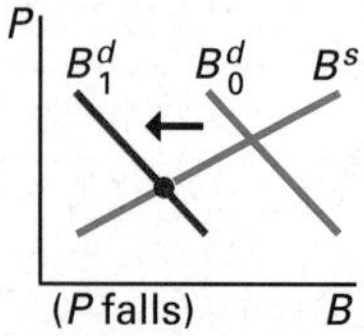	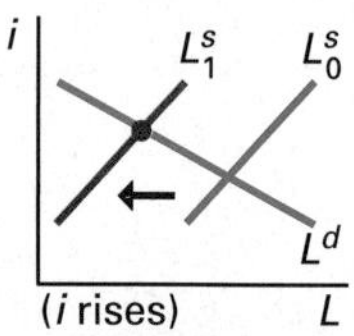

increase the profitability of investment and increase firms' willingness to supply bonds at any given price. Using Fig. 6.5(a), the tax breaks shift the bond supply curve to the right from B_0^s to B_1^s, reducing the price of bonds from P_0 to P_1. In the loanable funds market depicted in Fig. 6.5(b), the tax breaks increase firms' demand for funds at any interest rate. The demand curve shifts to the right from L_0^d to L_1^d, and the interest rate rises from i_0 to i_1. Hence investment incentives, all else being equal, lead to a fall in bond prices and an increase in interest rates. Conversely, higher tax burdens on the profits earned by new investment reduce firms' willingness to supply bonds. As Fig. 6.5(a) shows, higher corporate profits taxes shift the bond supply curve to the left, from B_0^s to B_2^s, increasing the price of bonds from P_0 to P_2. In the loanable funds market, higher corporate tax burdens reduce firms' desire to borrow to finance investments. In Fig. 6.5(b), the demand curve for loanable funds shifts to the left, from L_0^d to L_2^d, and the interest rate falls from i_0 to i_2.

Figure 6.5

Shifts in the Supply of Bonds

As shown in (a):

1. From an initial equilibrium at E_0, an increase in the attractiveness of issuing bonds increases the quantity of bonds supplied by borrowers at any bond price. The bond supply curve shifts to the right from B_0^s to B_1^s. In the new equilibrium, E_1, the price of bonds falls from P_0 to P_1.
2. From an initial equilibrium at E_0, a decrease in the attractiveness of issuing bonds decreases the quantity of bonds supplied by borrowers at any bond price. The bond supply curve shifts to the left, from B_0^s to B_2^s. In the new equilibrium, E_2, the price of bonds rises from P_0 to P_2.

As shown in (b):

1. From an initial equilibrium at E_0, an increase in the willingness to borrow increases the quantity of loanable funds demanded at any interest rate. The demand curve for loanable funds shifts to the right from L_0^d to L_1^d. In the new equilibrium, E_1, the interest rate rises from i_0 to i_1.
2. From an initial equilibrium at E_0, a decrease in the willingness to borrow decreases the quantity of funds demanded at any interest rate. The demand curve for loanable funds shifts to the left, from L_0^d to L_2^d. In the new equilibrium, E_2, the interest rate falls from i_0 to i_2.

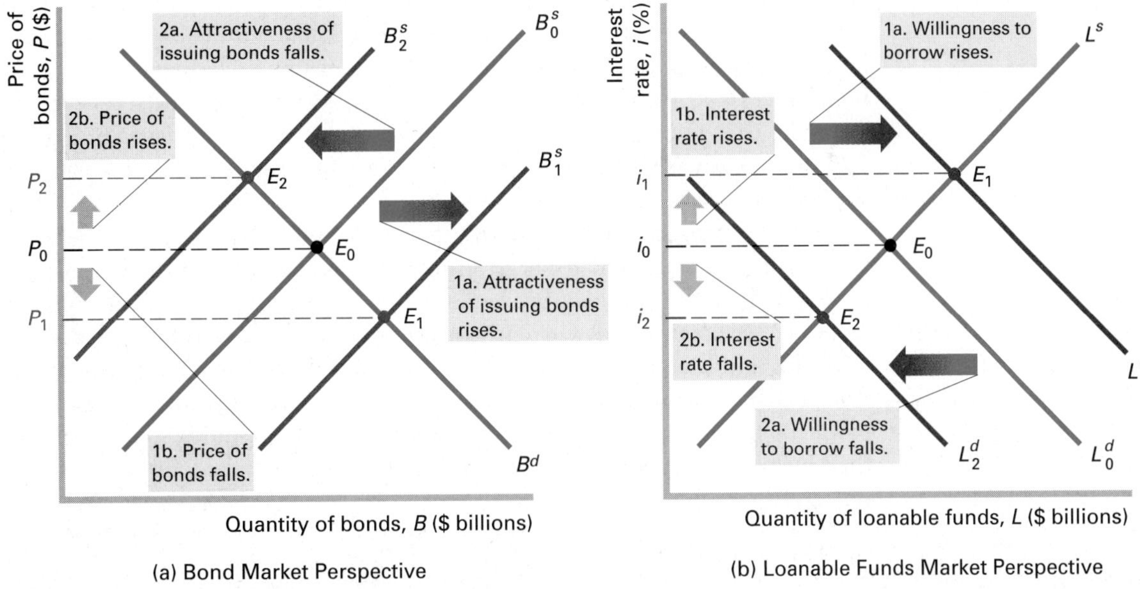

To summarize, an increase in the expected profitability of capital net of taxes increases borrowers' willingness to supply bonds; the bond supply curve shifts to the right, reducing the price of bonds and raising the interest rate. A decrease in the expected profitability of capital net of taxes decreases borrowers' willingness to supply bonds; the bond supply curve shifts to the left, raising the price of bonds and lowering the interest rate.

Expected inflation. An increase in expected inflation reduces the value of existing bonds and raises borrowers' willingness to supply bonds at any bond price. As Fig. 6.5(a) shows, higher expected inflation shifts the bond supply curve to the right, from B_0^s to B_1^s, reducing the price of bonds from P_0 to P_1. In the market for loanable funds, higher expected inflation increases borrowers' demand for funds at any interest rate. This is because, for any given nominal interest rate, an increase in expected inflation reduces the real cost of borrowing.† Hence, as in Fig. 6.5(b), the demand curve for loanable funds shifts to the right, from L_0^d to L_1^d, and the interest rate rises from i_0 to i_1.

In general, an increase in expected inflation leads to an increase in borrowers' willingness to supply bonds; the bond supply curve shifts to the right, reducing the price of bonds and increasing the interest rate. A fall in expected inflation leads to a decrease in borrowers' willingness to supply bonds; the bond supply curve shifts to the left, increasing the price of bonds.

CHECKPOINT

Suppose you read that business optimism is leading to a large increase in borrowers' demand for funds. What do you think will happen to the value of your grandmother's bonds? An increase in expected profitability shifts the bond supply curve to the right. If nothing else happens, the price of bonds falls, and the interest rate rises.

Government borrowing. So far we have emphasized the influence on bond prices and interest rates of decisions by households and businesses and have ignored the role played by governments. Decisions by governments can affect bond prices and interest rates in the economy. Many economists believe, for example, that the series of large U.S. government budget deficits during the 1980s and early 1990s caused the interest rate to be higher than it otherwise would have been.

What is the government sector? It includes not only the federal government, but also state and local governments. Like households and firms, the government sector can be a net lender or borrower. In some periods, income from tax receipts exceeds current expenditures, so the government sector has a surplus and is a net supplier of funds. At other times, the government sector runs a deficit, with expenditures greater than tax receipts, and is a net borrower of funds. In either case, governments, like households, must consider their income and spending over time. Cumulatively, over the long run, the gov-

† The real cost of borrowing for firms is the expected real interest rate, which is the nominal interest rate less expected inflation.

ernment sector cannot spend more than it collects in taxes, although it can have a surplus or deficit in any given year.

From 1970 through 1997, the domestic government sector was a net borrower. The federal budget deficit for fiscal year 1997 was $22 billion; by 1998, the federal budget was in surplus, with surpluses projected for the next several years. How does government net lending and borrowing affect bond prices and interest rates? Let's assume that the government's saving decisions are determined by public policies about taxes and expenditures and are not sensitive to changes in interest rates. We can then add the change in government debt to the bond supply curve.

Suppose the federal government increases its purchases of military equipment and doesn't increase taxes; that is, the government borrows to finance the

OTHER TIMES, OTHER PLACES . . .

Do Interest Rates Rise During Wartime?

In wartime, governments often become temporary borrowers, as purchases of military hardware and expenditures for soldiers' compensation, accommodations, and transport increase. These increased expenditures are temporary, and governments generally do not increase current taxes sufficiently to pay for the war. Instead, they typically borrow during wars, financing them in part by future taxes.

What are the effects of wars on the interest rate? In the bond supply and demand diagram, we note that a temporary increase in government purchases (holding taxes constant) should decrease bond prices. If nothing else changes, then, the interest rate should rise. Thus our analysis predicts that a military buildup raises the interest rate, thereby crowding out (reducing) some private borrowing.

Because the British fought several major and minor wars during the period from 1730 to 1913, British data are particularly useful for analyzing the effects of wars on private lending and borrowing and on the interest rate. Robert Barro of Harvard University analyzed movements in real interest rates during wars, using British data for that period.† He found that inflation was essentially nonexistent over most of this period, making movements in nominal interest rates a good approximation of movements in the real interest rate. Averaging about 3.5% over the period, long-term nominal interest rates in Britain rose to 5.5% during the American Revolution (late 1770s and early 1780s) and 6% during the Napoleonic Wars (early 1800s). Barro's analysis suggests that real interest rates rise during wars. Applying Barro's findings to U.S. wartime experiences is more difficult because, unlike the historical British experience, the U.S. government imposed price controls and direct controls on interest rates. However, during major conflicts such as the Korean War and especially World War II, private investment declined significantly relative to GDP while government purchases rose significantly relative to GDP. The decline of private investment during wartime suggests that interest rates do rise during wars. This result is consistent with the graph in Fig. 6.5(b).

In Fig. 6.5(a), the rightward shift in the bond supply curve from B_0^s to B_1^s reduces the price of bonds from P_0 to P_1. From the perspective of the loanable funds market, the increase in government borrowing increases the total demand for funds at any given interest rate. In Fig. 6.5(b), the demand curve for loanable funds shifts to the right from L_0^d to L_1^d, and the interest rate rises from i_0 to i_1.

†Robert J. Barro, "The Neoclassical Approach to Fiscal Policy." In Robert J. Barro (ed.), *Modern Business Cycle Theory.* Cambridge, Mass.: Harvard University Press, 1989.

new purchases. This government borrowing shifts the bond supply curve to the right. If households do not change their saving in response to the increased borrowing by the government, household wealth does not change and the bond demand curve does not shift. As a result, all other things being equal, the total quantity of bonds rises and the price of bonds falls. This fall in the price of bonds implies that the increase in government borrowing raises the interest rate.

Households could increase their saving when the government borrows in order to pay the future taxes required to pay off the government's debt. In this case, the bond demand curve shifts to the right at the same time that the bond supply curve shifts to the right. The interest rate need not rise in response to the increase in government borrowing. However, studies by economists suggest that households do not increase their current saving by the full amount of the government's dissaving. Interest rates are likely to rise, all else being equal, in response to an increase in government borrowing.

Hence, if nothing else changes, an increase in government borrowing shifts the bond supply curve to the right, reducing the price of bonds and increasing the interest rate. A fall in government borrowing shifts the bond supply curve to the left, increasing the price of bonds and decreasing the interest rate.

Summary. Table 6.2 summarizes factors that shift the supply curve for bonds. Remember that the factors that shift the supply curve for bonds also shift the demand curve for loanable funds. Hence, as Table 6.2 shows, factors that shift the supply curve for bonds to the right (reducing the price of bonds, all else being equal) shift the demand curve for loanable funds to the right (raising the interest rate, all else being equal). Factors that shift the supply curve for bonds to the left (increasing the price of bonds, all else being equal) shift the demand curve for loanable funds to the left (reducing the interest rate, all else being equal).

Using the Model to Explain Changes in Interest Rates

Movements in interest rates occur because the demand for or supply of bonds or loanable funds changes. In this section, we consider two examples: (1) the movement of interest rates over *business cycles,* or periodic fluctuations in economic activity, and (2) the movement of interest rates in response to changes in inflation. In practice, many shifts in bond demand and bond supply occur simultaneously, and analysts try to disentangle explanations. To follow developments in the bond market, you can consult the bond page in *The Wall Street Journal* each day. This analysis appears in the "Money and Investing" section of *The Wall Street Journal.*

Why do interest rates fall during recessions? We can illustrate changes in interest rates over the business cycle using the bond market or loanable funds diagram. At the beginning of a downturn, households and firms expect that economic activity will be lower than usual for a period of time. As Fig. 6.6(a) shows, the fall in household wealth shifts the demand for bonds to the left, from B_0^d to B_1^d. At the same time, firms expect the profitability of capital to be

TABLE 6.2

FACTORS THAT SHIFT THE SUPPLY CURVE FOR BONDS

All else being equal, an increase in . . .	Causes equilibrium quantity of bonds or loanable funds to . . .	Because . . .	Graph of effect on: Bonds	Graph of effect on: Loanable funds
expected profitability	increase	businesses borrow to finance profitable investments	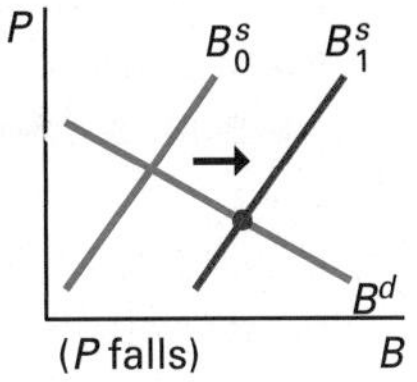	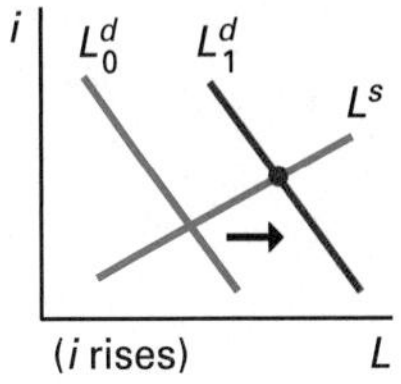
corporate taxes on profits	decrease	taxes reduce the profitability of investment	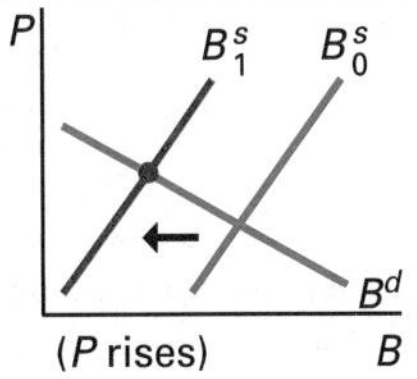	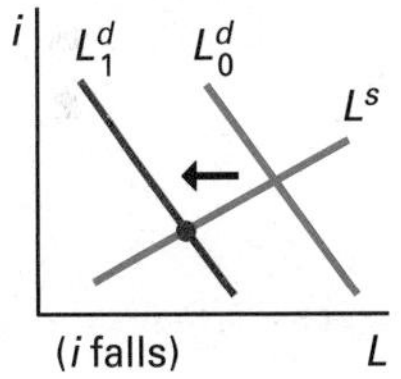
tax subsidies for investment	increase	subsidies lower the cost of investment, thereby increasing the profitability of investing	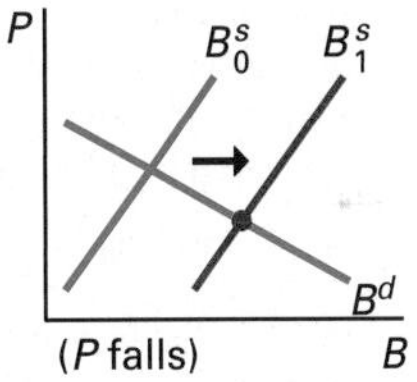	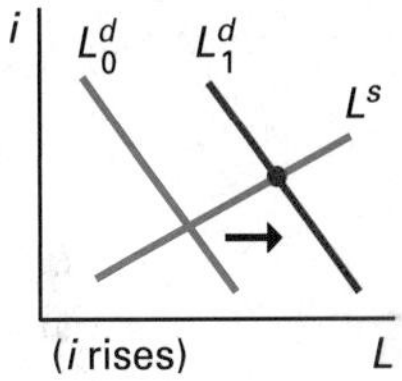
expected inflation	increase	at any given bond price or interest rate, the real cost of borrowing falls	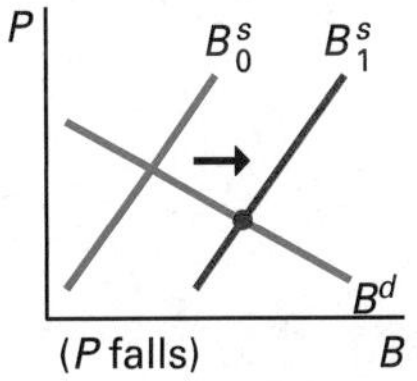	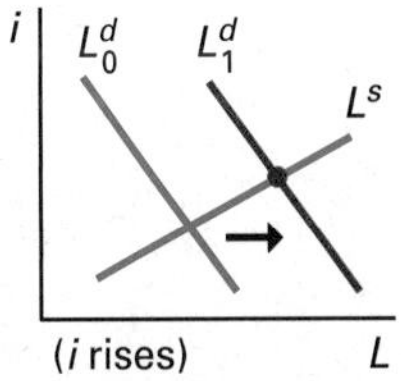
government borrowing	increase	more bonds are offered in the economy at any given interest rate	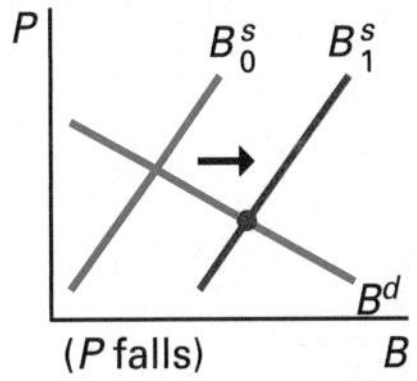	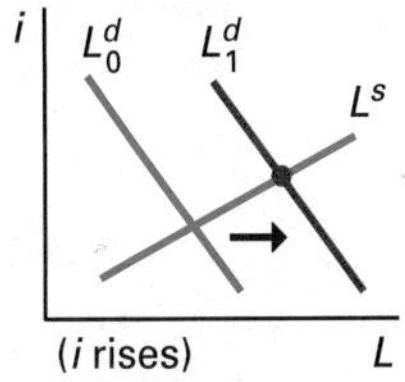

low for a period of time, reducing their willingness to borrow to finance capital investments, so the supply of bonds shifts to the left, from B_0^s to B_1^s. The equilibrium bond price rises from P_0 to P_1. In the market for loanable funds, the fall in wealth reduces lenders' ability to supply funds at any interest rate; the supply curve for loanable funds shifts to the left, from L_0^s to L_1^s, as in Fig. 6.6(b). The fall in expected profitability reduces borrowers' demand for funds at any interest rate; the demand curve for loanable funds shifts to the left, from L_0^d to L_1^d. The equilibrium interest rate rises from i_0 to i_1.

Note that the leftward shift of the bond demand curve reduces bond prices and raises interest rates, all else being equal, whereas the leftward shift of the bond supply curve raises bond prices and lowers interest rates. Evidence from U.S. data indicates that interest rates generally rise during economic upturns and fall during economic downturns, suggesting that the bond supply shift dominates, as shown in Fig. 6.6.

Expected inflation and interest rates. Interest rate forecasters pay significant attention to surveys about any signs of expected inflation. Most economists credit the decline in short-term nominal rates over the 1980s and 1990s to the Federal Reserve's fight against inflation. Let's see why this is so. When we discussed the relationship between real and nominal interest rates in

Figure 6.6 **Interest Rate Changes in an Economic Downturn**

As shown in (a):

1. From an initial equilibrium at E_0, an economic downturn reduces household wealth and decreases the demand for bonds at any bond price. The bond demand curve shifts left, from B_0^d to B_1^d.
2. The fall in expected profitability reduces lenders' supply of bonds at any bond price. The bond supply curve shifts left, from B_0^s to B_1^s.
3. In the new equilibrium, E_1, the bond price rises from P_0 to P_1.

As shown in (b):

1. From an initial equilibrium at E_0, an economic downturn reduces wealth and decreases the supply of loanable funds at any interest rate. The supply curve for loanable funds shifts left, from L_0^s to L_1^s.
2. The fall in expected profitability reduces borrowers' demand for loanable funds at any interest rate. The demand curve for loanable funds shifts left, from L_0^d to L_1^d.
3. In the new equilibrium, E_1, the interest rate falls from i_0 to i_1.

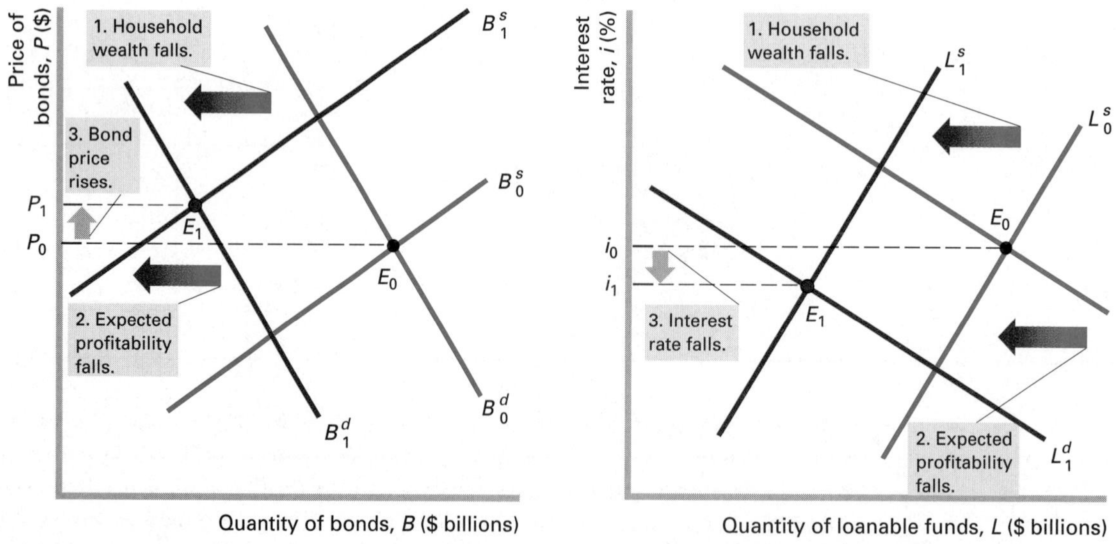

(a) Bond Market Perspective

(b) Loanable Funds Market Perspective

Chapter 4, we considered the Fisher hypothesis, which states that nominal interest rates rise or fall point-for-point with expected inflation. As we noted there, short-term interest rates offer broad support for the Fisher hypothesis.

We can explore the logic of the hypothesis using our graphical analysis of the markets for bonds (in Fig. 6.7(a)) or loanable funds (in Fig. 6.7(b)). Suppose expected inflation is 2% and the market for bonds (or loanable funds) is in equilibrium at E_0. Now suppose that market participants revise upward their expectation of inflation to 6%.

Lenders now realize that at any given bond price (or associated interest rate), the expected real return from lending has fallen. As a result, they decrease their willingness to hold bonds. The bond demand curve shifts to the left in Fig. 6.7(a), from B_0^d to B_1^d, in response to the lower expected return. In the loanable funds diagram (Fig. 6.7(b)), the supply curve for loanable funds shifts to the left.

Borrowers view the increase in expected inflation differently. For them, at any given bond price (or interest rate), the real cost of borrowing has fallen. As a consequence, the quantity of bonds supplied rises at any given bond price; the bond supply curve shifts to the right in Fig. 6.7(a), from B_0^s to B_1^s. In the loanable funds diagram (Fig. 6.7(b)), the demand curve for loanable funds shifts to the right.

In response to the rise in expected inflation, both the demand curve and supply curve for bonds (and loanable funds) shift. The new equilibrium lies at E_1. The increase in expected inflation leads to lower bond prices and higher nominal interest rates. In the figures, the quantity of bonds or loanable funds does not change; the nominal interest rate rises exactly by the increase in expected inflation. More generally, while the nominal interest rates rise with expected inflation, the exact relationship depends on the relative sizes of shifts in the demand curve and the supply curve.

Back to the Bond Market's Votes

Returning to the federal budget deliberations described at the beginning of the chapter, what was the argument regarding the bond market's "votes" about? Many of the President's economic advisors suggested that a budget package that generated lower federal budget deficits over several years would reduce government borrowing. In the bond market diagram, such a change shifts the bond supply curve to the left, raising bond prices (and lowering interest rates). Critics of the plan suggested that tax increases might reduce investment demand and therefore bond supply. While such a shift would also raise bond prices and lower interest rates, it is associated with a fall in the volume of private economic activity, which is not good news.

Bond yields indeed fell during 1993 from about 7.4% on 30-year Treasury bonds in January to just under 6% in October. By November 1994, the long-term bond yield had risen to about 8%. Even with the advantage of hindsight, economists and bond market analysts have no consensus explanation of the events. Candidates include the two scenarios sketched above and a scenario of changes in inflationary expectations. One thing seems clear: The "bond market" has clout, if not votes.

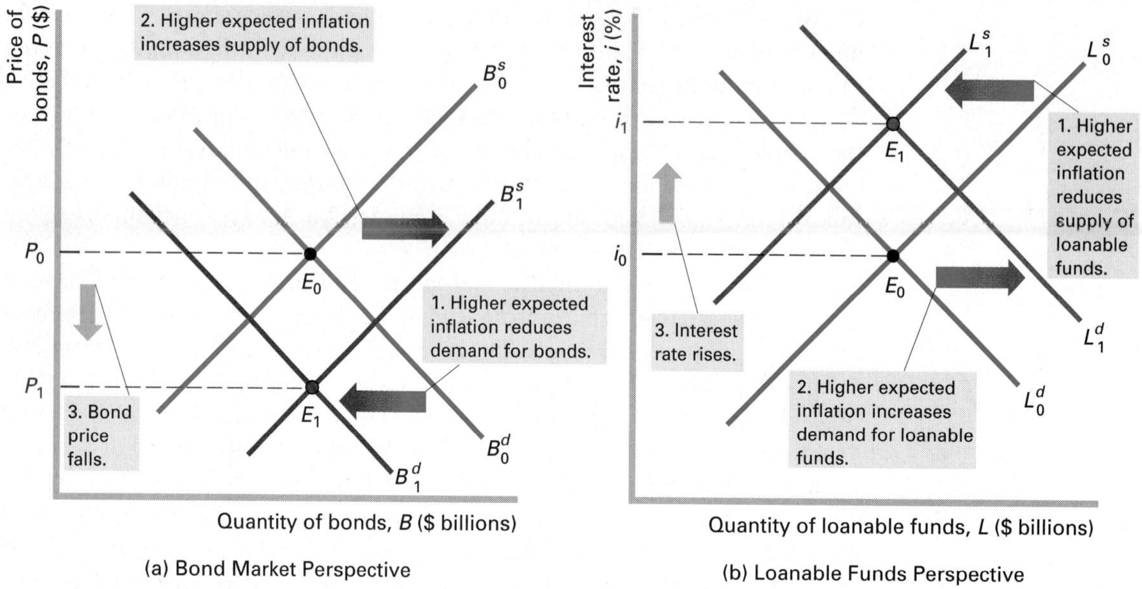

Figure 6.7 **Expected Inflation and Interest Rates**

As shown in (a):

1. From an initial equilibrium at E_0, an increase in expected inflation reduces lenders' expected real return, reducing lenders' willingness to hold bonds. The demand curve for bonds shifts left, from B^d_0 to B^d_1.
2. The increase in expected inflation increases borrowers' willingness to issue bonds at any bond price. The supply curve for bonds shifts right, from B^s_0 to B^s_1.
3. In the new equilibrium, E_1, the bond price falls from P_0 to P_1.

As shown in (b):

1. From an initial equilibrium at E_0, an increase in expected inflation reduces lenders' expected real returns at any interest rate. The supply curve for loanable funds shifts left, from L^s_0 to L^s_1.
2. The increase in expected inflation increases borrowers' demand for loanable funds at any interest rate. The demand curve for loanable funds shifts right, from L^d_0 to L^d_1.
3. In the new equilibrium, E_1, the interest rate rises from i_0 to i_1.

THE INTERNATIONAL CAPITAL MARKET AND THE INTEREST RATE

The foreign sector also influences the amount of funds available for domestic borrowers and market interest rates. So far, we have analyzed the bond market or market for loanable funds for a **closed economy,** an economy that neither borrows from nor lends to foreign countries—a scenario that is unrealistic in today's global economy. Figure 6.8 illustrates the flows of international borrowing and lending. Foreign households, businesses, and governments may want to lend funds to borrowers in the United States if the expected returns are higher there than in other countries. Similarly, if opportunities are more promising outside the United States, loanable funds will be drawn away from U.S. markets to fund borrowings abroad. In the 1980s and 1990s, the United States generally was a net borrower of foreign funds, receiving a net inflow of funds from abroad to finance borrowing by firms and the U.S. government.

To consider international capital mobility, we work with the loanable funds diagram. To keep matters simple, we will assume that the "interest rate" is the expected real interest rate, r—that is, the nominal interest rate less the expected rate of inflation. In this way, we can ignore differences in rates of inflation across countries.

In an **open economy,** capital is mobile internationally. Borrowing and lending take place in the international capital market, the capital market in which households, firms, and governments borrow and lend across national borders. The **world real interest rate** r_w is the interest rate that is determined in the international capital market. The quantity of loanable funds that is supplied in an open economy can be used to fund projects in the domestic economies or abroad. Decisions about the supply of or demand for loanable funds in small open economies, such as those of the Netherlands and Belgium, do not have much effect on the world real interest rate. However, shifts in the behavior of lenders and borrowers in large open economies, such as those of Germany and the United States, do affect the world real interest rate. Let's consider interest rate determination for each case.

Small Open Economy

For a closed economy, the equilibrium interest rate is the rate at which the quantities of loanable funds demanded and supplied are equal; it is determined by the intersection of the supply curve and demand curve for loanable funds. In a **small open economy,** the quantity of loanable funds supplied is too small to affect the world real interest rate, and the economy takes the world interest rate as a given. That is, its domestic real interest rate equals the real interest rate

Figure 6.8

Flow of Funds in an Open Economy

In an open economy, domestic savers can lend to domestic or foreign borrowers, as can foreign savers.

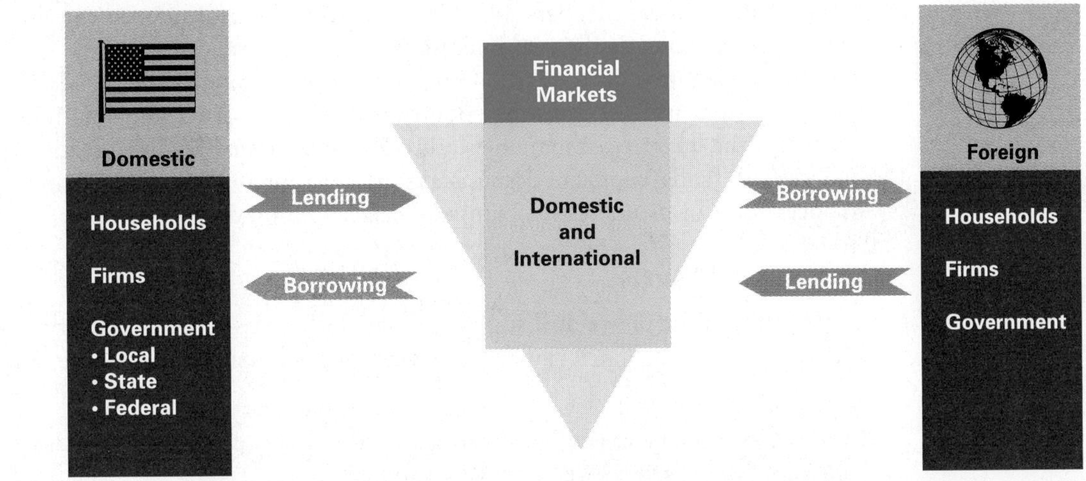

determined in the international capital market. If the principality of Monaco pursued tax policies to increase domestic wealth accumulation, for example, any increase in the volume of loanable funds would have only a trivial effect on worldwide saving and the world interest rate.

For a small open economy, the domestic real interest rate must equal the world real interest rate r_w; otherwise, domestic savers would invest their funds outside the country. Suppose that the world real interest rate is 4% and that the domestic real interest rate in Monaco is 3%. A lender in Monaco would not accept an interest rate of less than $r_w = 4\%$ in the domestic capital market because the lender could easily buy foreign bonds. But if Monaco's real interest rate is 5%, domestic borrowers will be unwilling to pay a real interest rate greater than $r_w = 4\%$, since they have access to the international capital market and can raise funds at 4%.[†]

Because a small open economy takes the world interest rate as a given, we can determine the level of loanable funds and level of international borrowing and lending from the loanable funds diagram. Figure 6.9 shows the supply and demand curves for loanable funds for a small open economy. If the world real interest rate is 3%, the quantities supplied and demanded of loanable funds domestically are equal (point *E*); that is, the country neither lends nor borrows funds in the international capital market.

Suppose instead that the world real interest rate is 5%. In this case, the quantity of loanable funds supplied domestically (*C*) exceeds the quantity of funds demanded domestically (*B*), as shown in Fig. 6.9. Because it is small, however, this economy can lend as much as it wants in the international capital market at the going rate of 5%. Hence it brings the funds that cannot be lent at home to the international capital market, where there are willing borrowers.

But suppose the world real interest rate is 1%. The quantity of loanable funds demanded domestically (*A*) now exceeds the quantity of funds supplied domestically (*D*), as Fig. 6.9 depicts. As a small open economy, the country can borrow as much as it wants in the international capital market at the going rate of 1%. Hence it borrows the funds from the international capital market, where foreign lenders are willing to lend. The real interest rate in a small open economy is the real interest rate in the international capital market. If the quantity of funds domestically supplied exceeds the funds demanded at that interest rate, the country invests some of its loanable funds abroad. If the quantity of loanable funds demanded domestically exceeds the quantity of funds supplied domestically at that interest rate, the country finances some of its domestic borrowing needs with funds from abroad.

Large Open Economy

Shifts in the demand for and supply of loanable funds in many countries—such as the United States, Japan, and Germany—are sufficiently large that

[†]Here we assume that the country imposes no barriers to international lending or borrowing. In Chapter 22, we discuss such barriers.

Figure 6.9

Determining the Real Interest Rate in a Small Open Economy

The domestic real interest in a small open economy is the world real interest rate r_w.

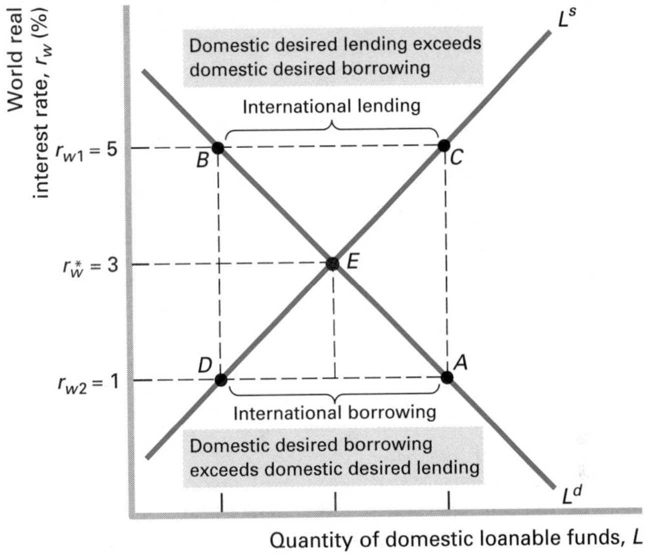

they *do* affect the interest rate in the international capital market. Such a financially powerful country is an example of a **large open economy,** or an economy that is large enough to affect the world interest rate.

In the case of a large open economy, we can no longer assume that the domestic real interest rate is the real interest rate in the international capital market. Recall that in a closed economy, the equilibrium interest rate equates the quantities of loanable funds supplied and demanded. By extension, if we think of the world as two large open economies—the economy of the United States and the economy of the rest of the world—the real interest rate in the international capital market equates desired international lending by the United States with desired international borrowing by the rest of the world.

Figure 6.10 illustrates the process of interest rate determination for a large open economy. Loanable funds diagrams for two economies are presented in the figure, labeled *United States* and *Rest of the World.* If the world real interest rate is 3%, the quantities of loanable funds supplied and demanded domestically in the United States are equal ($L^{s*} = L^{d*}$ in (a)). However, at that interest rate, the quantity of funds demanded in the rest of the world, L_1^d, exceeds the quantity of funds supplied in the rest of the world, L_1^s, by \$100 billion. That is, foreign borrowers want to borrow \$100 billion from the international capital market. If they can obtain a higher real interest rate, domestic lenders will lend funds to foreign borrowers. As long as the domestically supplied loanable funds may be invested at home or abroad, foreign borrowers will agree to pay lenders in the United States a real interest rate greater than 3%.

Figure 6.10 shows that the demand for funds by the rest of the world would push up the real interest rate in the international capital market to 4%. At a real interest rate of 4%, the quantity of funds supplied domestically in the United States, L_1^s, exceeds the quantity of funds demanded domestically, L_1^d, by \$50

THE ECONOMIST DECEMBER 2, 2000

Interest Rates: Up or Down?

The growth in America's third-quarter GDP was revised downward this week to an annual rate of 2.4%, a sharp fall from the 5% growth recorded in the first half of the year. Yet American consumers continue to spend furiously. In the third quarter, and maybe in the fourth, their spending will have exceeded their income for the first time since the 1930s. In other words, they had a negative saving rate. Nobody is storing up for a rainy day. In the early 1990s, American households were saving around 9% of their disposable income.

a That Americans now prefer consuming to saving is a familiar story. Less widely appreciated is the fact that saving is also going out of fashion in many other developed economies. Germany's personal-saving rate has fallen by half, to some 8% over the past decade; Canada's has plunged from 12% to 1%; and Italy's from 19% to 13%. The main exception is Japan, where households still save 12% of their income, exactly the same as they did in 1990. . . .

Some economists argue that the official figures understate the true level of saving. Household saving is measured in the national accounts as the gap between personal disposable income and expenditure. It ignores changes in the value of financial assets, such as shares. Yet, from an individual's point of view, an increase in financial wealth thanks to rising share prices means that less needs to be saved out of current income to build up a desired nest-egg. . . .

b Moreover, consumers are only part of the picture. At the same time that households have been on a spending spree, the American government has become more prudent, moving from a budget deficit of 5% of GDP in the early 1990s to an estimated surplus of 2% of GDP this year. . . .

To many, however, this view seems too complacent. Ed McKelvey, an economist at Goldman Sachs, points out that the historically flat personal-saving rate (once realized capital gains are included) means that households are, in essence, treating such gains as a perfect substitute for disposable income. Yet capital gains are much more volatile than wages, and cannot be guaranteed in future. If share prices plunge, a low personal-saving rate provides less of a cushion than a high one.

c Nor does the fact that overall domestic saving has risen mean that we can all sleep soundly. The problem is that investment by American firms has risen by even more than domestic saving, leaving a large gap to be filled by foreign capital. America's infamous current-account deficit (the gap between domestic saving and investment) has widened to a record level of around 4.5% of GDP. This is the best evidence that America is living beyond its means. So far, capital has been easily lured to the United States by its firms' high profitability. But as America's economy (and so its corporate-profit growth) slows, that money could dry up. . . .

Whereas short-term interest rates rose during 2000, yields on long-term Treasury bonds fell, producing a bond market boom in a year when broad stock market indices declined. As 2001 approached, some analysts worried that underlying trends in saving and investment might put upward pressure on interest rates. Using our analysis of interest rate determination, we can interpret these predictions.

(a) All else being equal, a decline in households' willingness to save is bad news for bondholders. Such a decline causes the bond demand curve to shift to the left, reducing the price of bonds and reducing yields. If the decline in households' willingness to save occurs in other major economies as well, upward pressure on international borrowing by the rest of the world would put additional upward pressure on interest rates in the international capital market and in the United States.

(b) If government saving increases—for example, because of a greater willingness of U.S. policymakers to run federal budget surpluses—some of the upward pressure on interest rates from a decline in households' willingness to save is mitigated. Fiscal restraint implies a reduction in the supply of bonds, shifting the bond supply curve to the left, as shown in Fig. 6.5(a). The resulting increase in the price of bonds implies lower market interest rates.

(c) If business capital investment demand were to boom, the bond supply curve would shift to the right, again putting downward pressure on U.S. bond prices and upward pressure on U.S. interest rates. If business capital investment demand were instead to falter, the bond supply curve would shift to the left, mitigating any upward pressure in interest rates traceable to a decline in households' willingness to save.

On balance, the direction of bond yields in 2001 will depend on the relative importance of changes in households' willingness to save, changes in the government's willingness to run a budget surplus, and changes in businesses' willingness to invest—as well as expected inflation.

For further thought . . .

Suppose that economic growth slows in Europe in 2001. How will U.S. bond prices and market interest rates respond?

Source: Excerpted from "Rainy-Day Blues," *The Economist*, December 2, 2000.

billion. Similarly, at a real interest rate of 4%, the quantity of funds demanded in the rest of the world, L_2^d (in (b)), exceeds the quantity of funds supplied, L_2^s, by \$50 billion. At a 4% real interest rate, then, desired international lending by the United States equals desired international borrowing by the rest of the world. As a result, the international capital market is in equilibrium when the real interest rate in the United States and the rest of the world is 4%. The equilibrium world real interest rate equates international lending by one large open economy with international borrowing by others. Factors that increase desired international borrowing relative to desired international lending raise the world real interest rate. Factors that increase international lending relative to international borrowing lower the world interest rate.

CHECKPOINT

A recent economic study concluded that Japanese households are likely to lend much less after 2000 than they did in the 1970s, 1980s, and 1990s. What, if anything, does this finding imply for real interest rates on home mortgage loans and business loans in the United States? Japan and the United States are large open economies, so shifts in their domestic lending and borrowing patterns affect the world real interest rate. The predicted decline in Japanese lending reduces desired international lending, putting upward pressure on the world real interest rate. A higher world real interest rate increases the cost of funds for home mortgages and business loans. o

Figure 6.10 **Determining the Real Interest Rate in a Large Open Economy**

Saving and investment shifts in a large open economy can affect the world real interest rate. The world real interest rate, r_w, adjusts to equalize desired international borrowing and desired international lending. At a world real interest rate of 4%, desired international lending by the domestic economy equals desired international borrowing by the rest of the world.

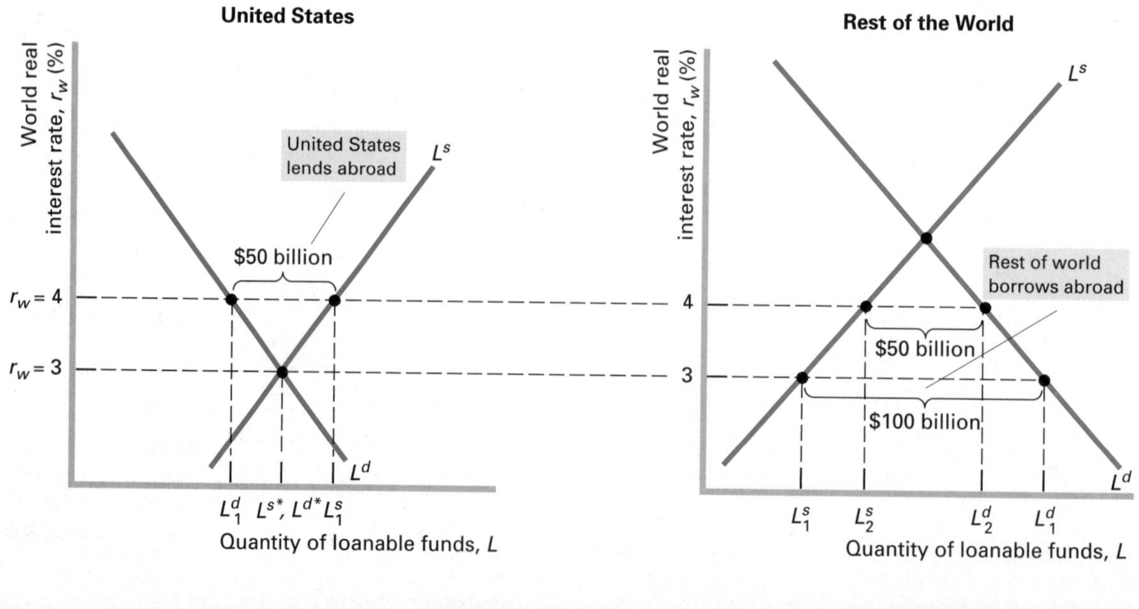

KEY TERMS AND CONCEPTS

Bond market
Closed economy
Loanable funds
Open economy
- Large open economy
- Small open economy

World real interest rate

SUMMARY

1. To understand how bond prices and interest rates are determined, we must focus on the determinants of the demand for and supply of bonds or, equivalently, the supply of and demand for loanable funds. Analysis of the bond market or the market for loanable funds tells us that the equilibrium bond price and interest rate are determined by the intersection of the demand curve and the supply curve. Changes in bond prices and interest rates are accounted for by factors that shift the demand curve or the supply curve.
2. The demand curve for bonds relates lenders' willingness to hold bonds to the price of bonds, other economic variables being held constant. The demand curve shifts in response to changes in wealth, expected returns on bonds relative to other assets, riskiness of bonds relative to other assets, liquidity of bonds relative to other assets, and information costs of bonds relative to other assets. Decisions about the demand for bonds can also be represented as decisions about the supply of loanable funds. Factors that make holding bonds more attractive shift the demand curve to the right, raising the price of bonds and lowering the interest rate, all other things being equal. Factors that make holding bonds less attractive shift the demand curve to the left, lowering the price of bonds and raising the interest rate, all other things being equal.
3. The supply curve for bonds relates borrowers' willingness to offer bonds to the price of bonds, other economic variables being held constant. The supply curve shifts in response to changes in the expected profitability of capital, expected inflation, and government borrowing. Decisions about the supply of bonds can also be represented as decisions about the demand for loanable funds. Factors that make borrowing more attractive shift the supply curve to the right, lowering the price of bonds and raising the interest rate, all other things being equal. Factors that make borrowing less attractive shift the supply curve to the left, raising the price of bonds and reducing the interest rate, all other things being equal.
4. If capital is not internationally mobile, the equilibrium real interest rate lies at the intersection of the demand curve and the supply curve for loanable funds for the country.
5. If capital is mobile internationally (an open economy), desired lending in the economy can be absorbed by domestic borrowing or by lending abroad. A small open economy takes the real rate of interest in the international capital market as given because the amount of its lending or borrowing is not substantial enough to influence the international capital market. Shifts in desired lending or borrowing in a large open economy, however, can affect the real interest rate in the international capital market (the world real interest rate). Factors that increase desired lending or decrease desired borrowing lower the world real interest rate; factors that decrease desired lending or increase desired borrowing raise the world real interest rate.

REVIEW QUESTIONS

1. Explain why each of the following changes might occur:
   a. The bond demand curve shifts to the left.
   b. The bond supply curve shifts to the right.
   c. The loanable funds demand curve shifts to the left.
   d. The loanable funds supply curve shifts to the right.
2. Discuss the relationship between an excess supply of bonds and an excess demand for loanable funds. Discuss how the bond market adjusts to equilibrium from an excess supply of bonds and how the

loanable funds market adjusts to equilibrium from an excess demand for loanable funds.

3. If you looked at actual data, would you expect to find that the real interest rate was the same in all small open economies? Briefly explain.
4. Why does the bond supply curve slope up and the bond demand curve slope down in the bond market diagram?
5. In what types of economies can domestic lending not equal borrowing at equilibrium? How can this occur?
6. How does a change in household wealth affect the price of bonds, all other things being equal?
7. How does a small open economy differ from a large open economy?

ANALYTICAL PROBLEMS

8. When expected inflation rises, many changes in the demand for and supply of loanable funds and the equilibrium interest rate are possible. This happens because the tax system distorts saving and investment decisions, as do certain aspects of the financial structure (such as the criteria that banks use to justify loans). The result is that the demand and supply curves for loanable funds could shift to the left or right in response to a change in expected inflation. Draw a loanable funds diagram to illustrate each of the following scenarios:
   a. In a closed economy, the supply curve for loanable funds shifts to the left and the demand curve shifts to the right, leaving the equilibrium quantity of loanable funds unchanged.
   b. In a closed economy, the supply curve for loanable funds shifts to the left, and the equilibrium real interest rate declines.
   c. In a small open economy that initially neither borrows nor lends abroad, the supply curve for loanable funds shifts to the left, and the demand curve shifts to the right. Does the economy now borrow or lend abroad?
   d. In a small open economy that initially neither borrows nor lends abroad, the supply curve for loanable funds and the demand curve for loanable funds shift to the left, and the economy still neither borrows nor lends.
9. When an economy initially comes out of a recession, people receive higher incomes, so they increase their demand for bonds, and businesses invest more and supply more bonds as they anticipate higher profits. With both the bond demand and bond supply curves shifting to the right in the bond market diagram, the effect on the price of bonds is ambiguous. Data suggest that the interest rate usually rises as the United States comes out of a recession. Draw bond market diagrams that are consistent with this condition for both a closed economy and a large open economy. Is this result possible for a small open economy? Why or why not?
10. In a closed economy, how would each of the following events affect the interest rate?
    a. A natural disaster destroys bridges and roads in California, leading to increased investment spending for rebuilding the infrastructure.
    b. Future taxes of businesses are expected to be increased.
    c. A popular TV miniseries runs every night for a month, causing people to stay home to watch it and spend much less money than usual.
    d. The government proposes a new tax on savings, based on people's balances on December 31 each year.
11. Repeat Problem 10 for a small open economy.
12. Repeat Problem 10 for a large open economy.
13. How would the following events affect aggregate wealth in the United States?
    a. Oil reserves 10 times as large as those in the Middle East are discovered in Montana.
    b. The economy grows twice as fast as expected, owing to higher productivity growth, so unemployment falls substantially.
    c. Reconstruction projects in Eastern Europe require $1 trillion, causing an increase in the world real interest rate.

14. The federal government in the United States has begun to run a budget surplus. Use the loanable funds approach to show the impact of the U.S. budget surplus on the world real interest rate.

15. How would the following events affect the demand for loanable funds in the United States?
    a. U.S. cities nationwide, overburdened with payments for social problems, increase business taxes.
    b. Increased computerization in corporations allows them to decrease substantially inventories and their associated costs.
    c. The tax deduction for home mortgage interest payments is eliminated.

16. Suppose that in a large open economy, the quantity of loanable funds supplied domestically is initially equal to the quantity of funds demanded domestically. Then a change in business taxes discourages investment. Show how this change affects the quantity of loanable funds and the world real interest rate. Does this economy now borrow or lend internationally?

17. Two countries that are alike in all other respects differ markedly in their provision of social insurance. One country provides old-age retirement pensions, unemployment insurance, and catastrophic illness insurance; the other country provides no social insurance. What is your prediction about the difference in average levels of household wealth between the two countries? Why?

18. Throughout the 1980s, the U.S. government had budget deficits (spending greater than current tax receipts), necessitating large amounts of government borrowing. Using the loanable funds diagram, illustrate the effects of government borrowing on the interest rate and business borrowing. What would happen if households believed that deficits would be financed by higher taxes in the near future and increased their saving in anticipation of those higher taxes?

19. Most economists argue that a boom in the stock market is a sign that profitable business opportunities are expected for the future. Describe the likely effects of such a boom on the bond supply and interest rate. What assumptions did you make?

20. Suppose that two countries have completely separate financial systems; that is, funds do not flow between them to finance investment. One country is just beginning to develop, with only limited domestic funds and a small amount of accumulated wealth. The other country is mature, with few new investment opportunities but a large amount of wealth. Using a loanable funds diagram, describe the difference in the expected real interest rates in the two countries. What would happen to the return on savings in the two countries if funds could flow without restriction between them? Would more profitable investment projects be financed and undertaken? Why or why not?

21. During some years in the 1970s, the real rate of interest on many debt securities in the United States was negative; that is, actual inflation exceeded the nominal interest rate. Were lenders willing to accept a negative real return during those years? Why or why not?

DATA QUESTIONS

22. To get some idea of the size of international borrowing and lending by the United States, obtain a copy of the latest *Economic Report of the President* at the library. Look up the table of U.S. international transactions, and find the balance on current account. Except for a few differences, and a fairly large statistical discrepancy, this balance should equal the difference between U.S. investment and saving. What happened to the current account balance in the mid-1980s? What do you think might explain this event?

23. Find the most recent *Economic Report of the President* in the library. Prepare a graph that allows a visual comparison of the New York Stock Exchange composite index and the ratio of personal saving to personal income for each year in the 1990s. How can you account for the relationship between the two series?

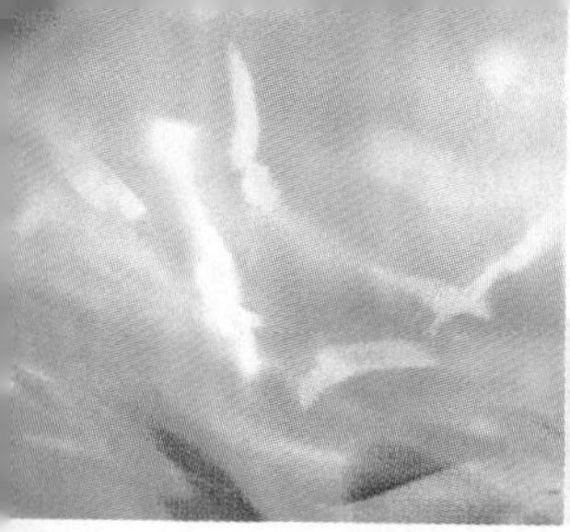

CHAPTER 7

Risk Structure and Term Structure of Interest Rates

On any business day, *The Wall Street Journal* reports interest rates for various financial instruments. Here is a sample of bond yields reported on December 18, 2000:

Bond	Maturity Date	Yield
Treasury bond	February 2020	5.55%
AT&T bond	2022	8.20%
RJR bond	2013	9.90%
Treasury bill	November 2001	5.77%

In Chapter 6, we looked at the way in which interest rates are determined in the bond market, assuming that there was one interest rate that was suitable for all bonds traded. Now we observe that there is more than one "market" interest rate. Does this mean that our analysis was wrong? Not really. The assumptions that we made allowed us to develop a broad picture of market interest rates. When investors enter the bond market to purchase a particular security, they are interested in the yield it will return, and many of the same variables that determine interest rates for bonds in general apply equally to individual bonds.

In this chapter, we refine the analysis presented in Chapter 6 to see how qualities possessed by an individual bond determine the interest rate it must offer an investor. In the first part of the analysis, we look at the *risk structure of interest rates,* which explains differences in yields across securities with similar maturity. In the second part of the chapter, we turn to the *term structure of interest rates*. We compare bonds with similar risk, liquidity, and information-cost characteristics and observe how their yields vary according to their time to maturity. Investors use both types of analyses to forecast the future movement of individual securities and market interest rates, and we describe this process as we study the differences in bonds.

RISK STRUCTURE OF INTEREST RATES

If the bonds listed at the start of this chapter have similar maturity (as they do, except for the Treasury bill), we can attribute the difference in interest rates—and in yields—to differences in default risk, liquidity, information costs, and taxation. The **risk structure of interest rates** summarizes effects of these determinants on yields for a given maturity. In this section, we describe how each determinant affects the interest rate of a credit market instrument and how interest rates can change as savers' perceptions of each determinant change. We also describe how variations in the interest rates reported in the financial media allow investors to forecast financial and economic trends.

Default Risk

Borrowers differ in their ability to repay in full the principal and interest required by a loan agreement. Savers view promises made by O.K. Used Cars, for example, as being less likely to be fulfilled than those made by IBM. As a result, O.K. Used Cars, and other private companies whose ability to repay their obligations in full is uncertain, must offer investors higher yields to compensate them for the risk they take in buying their bonds or making loans. The risk that a creditor cannot fulfill its promised principal and interest payments is called the **default risk.**

Measuring default risk. To determine the default risk on a security, we need a yardstick. U.S. Treasury securities fulfill this need because they are **default-risk-free instruments.** We assume that they have zero risk because the U.S. government guarantees that all principal and interest will be repaid in nominal terms. The government can make this guarantee to settle debts. We measure the default risk of a security by comparing it to default-risk-free Treasury securities.†

The **default risk premium** on a bond is the difference between its yield and the yield on a default-risk-free instrument of comparable maturity, and it measures default risk. The default risk premium is the additional yield that a saver requires for holding a risky instrument. For example, if the yield on Treasury bonds was 8%, you would demand a higher interest rate, say 12%, on a corporate bond issued by Worry Free Company, which has a middling credit history. The default risk premium on the Worry Free bond is 12% − 8% = 4%.

The risk premium has two components. First, for the risk-neutral savers who care only about expected returns and not about the variability of those returns, the interest rate for an instrument that carries default risk must be greater than that for a default-risk-free instrument. The higher rate compensates savers for losses if the bond issuer defaults on either interest or principal, or both. The default risk premium makes the expected return on the investment with default risk equal to the certain return from the default-risk-free instrument. Second, because savers generally are risk-averse and care about the variability of returns as well as about expected returns, yields incorporate an extra premium for bearing default risk.

---

†Nonetheless, the prices of Treasury securities can fluctuate as market interest rates increase or decrease. For example, an increase in market interest rates raises yields on Treasury securities, reducing their prices.

USING THE NEWS . . .

Using Bond Yields to Assess Risk

We can use the bond data at the beginning of the chapter and in the accompanying figure to find the default risk premiums on the AT&T and RJR bonds. The AT&T bond due in 2022 with an 8.125% coupon rate has a current yield of 8.2%, whereas the RJR bond due in 2013 with a 9.25% coupon rate has a current yield of 9.9%. (Because both are very long-maturity bonds, the current yield is approximately equal to the yield to maturity.) On the same day, the yield to maturity on a Treasury bond due in 2020 was about 5.55%. Hence the risk premium on the AT&T bond is 8.2% − 5.55% = 2.65%, and the risk premium on the RJR bond is 9.9% − 5.55% = 4.35%. Since the bonds have similar tax, liquidity, and information characteristics and both have a long maturity, this difference in risk premiums reflects investors' belief that RJR is more likely than AT&T to default on interest or principal payments. Investors use these quotes as a guide to bond market participants' assessment of the risk of different bonds.

NEW YORK BONDS

Quotations as of 4 p.m. Eastern Time
Thursday, December 15, 2000

CORPORATION BONDS
Volume $8,438,000

Volume traded. (Vol)
Current yield. (Cur Yld)
Closing price per $100 of face value. (Close)
Change in price from previous trading day. (Net Chg)

Bonds	Cur Yld	Vol	Close	Net Chg
AES CP 8s8	8.6	19	92 7/8	+ 1 5/8
ATT 5 5/8 04	5.9	19	95 1/2	− 1/4
ATT 7 1/2 06	7.4	14	101	. . .
ATT 7 3/4 07	7.5	1	102 7/8	+ 1
ATT 6s09	6.6	32	91 3/8	+ 3/8
ATT 8 1/8 22	8.2	155	99 1/4	+ 1/4
ATT 8 1/8 24	8.2	230	99	. . .
ATT 8.35s25	8.4	20	99 3/8	+ 3/8
ATT 6 1/2 29	7.8	170	82 7/8	. . .
ATT 8 5/8 31	8.6	80	100	. . .
Apache 9 1/4 02	9.0	10	103 1/4	+ 1/4
AscCp dc6s01	6.0	5	99 7/32	+ 5/8
RalsP 7 7/8 25	8.0	1	99	+ 1
ReynTob 8s01	8.0	10	100	. . .
ReynTob 8 5/8 02	8.2	33	97 1/2	− 7/8
ReynTob 7 5/8 03	8.0	21	95	− 1/2
ReynTob 8 3/4 04	9.1	25	96 1/2	− 1 1/8
ReynTob 8 3/4 05	9.2	200	95 3/8	− 7/8
ReynTob 8 3/4 07	9.3	30	94 1/8	+ 3/8
ReynTob 9 1/4 13	9.9	35	93 5/8	. . .
RobMyr 63	cv	100	98 1/2	− 3/8
Safwy 10s01	9.8	40	102	− 1 1/8

Source: The Wall Street Journal, December 18, 2000. Republished by permission of Dow Jones, Inc. via Copyright Clearance Center, Inc. (Quotes are from December 15, 2000.)

To determine the size of the default risk premium to assign to a bond or loan agreement, lenders try to assess the creditworthiness (the ability to repay) of borrowers. The cost of acquiring information about a borrower's creditworthiness can be high. Accordingly, investors often pay professional analysts to gather and monitor such information. For corporate debt instruments, private firms such as Standard & Poor's Corporation (S&P) and Moody's Investors Service assign ratings that are published and updated periodically (see Table 7.1). A **bond rating** is a single statistic summarizing the rating company's view of the issuer's net worth, cash flow, and prospects—in short, of the issuer's likely ability to meet its debt obligations. Because they are less risky, instruments with high ratings, such as AAA by S&P, have lower yields than do risky instruments with low ratings, such as C by S&P, and this difference in yields is one source of the yield variation in risk structure. Both borrowers and lenders are concerned about ratings. For borrowers, the rating affects their risk premium and hence their cost of funds. Savers look to the rating as a source of information about default risk.

Changes in default risk and the default risk premium. How does a change in default risk affect the interest rate on a particular financial instrument, such as General Electric bonds? The default risk premium can fluctuate as new information about a borrower's creditworthiness becomes available to investors. In other words, shifts in the market's perception of default risk can lead to a change in yield.

We can examine the determination of the price (and expected interest rate) for high-default-risk and low-default-risk instruments with the bond market diagram developed in Chapter 6. Figure 7.1(a) illustrates determination of the market price of a low-default-risk asset, and Fig. 7.1(b) illustrates determination of the market price of a high-default-risk asset. In both diagrams, the willingness to supply bonds rises with the price of the bonds. The demand curves represent lenders' willingness to buy bonds, based on returns available for

TABLE 7.1 **READING THE RATINGS PROVIDED BY MOODY'S AND STANDARD & POOR'S**

	Moody's	S&P's	Meaning
Investment-grade bonds	Aaa	AAA	Bonds of the best quality, offering the smallest degree of default risk. Issuers are exceptionally stable and dependable.
	Aa	AA	Bonds of high quality by all standards. Slightly higher degree of long-term default risk.
	A	A	Bonds with many favorable investment attributes.
	Baa	BBB	Bonds of medium-grade quality. Security appears adequate at present but may become unreliable.
Non-investment-grade bonds	Ba	BB	Bonds with speculative returns. Moderate security of payments; not well safeguarded.
	B	B	Cannot be considered a desirable investment. Small long-term assurance of payments.
	Caa	CCC	Bonds of poor standing. Issuers may be in default or in danger of default.
	Ca	CC	Bonds of highly speculative quality; often in default.
	C	C	Lowest-rated class of bonds. Very poor prospects of ever attaining investment standing.
	—	D	In default.
Commercial paper	P1	A1	Issues of the highest quality, offering the smallest degree of default risk.
	P2	A2	Lower-quality commercial paper.
	P3	A3	Lowest investment-grade quality commercial paper.
Unrated			

Source: Reprinted with the permission of Simon & Schuster from *The Wall Street Journal Guide to Understanding Money and Markets,* by Richard Saul Wurman, Alan Siegel, and Kenneth M. Morris. Copyright © 1989 by Access Press Ltd., and Siegel & Gale, Inc.

other investments. The quantity of bonds demanded falls as the price increases. In Fig. 7.1 (and other figures that follow), we focus on the market for bonds and the price of bonds. Remember that bond prices and yields are inversely related, so a rise in the price of the bond is associated with a fall in the yield, and a fall in the price is associated with a rise in the yield. This relationship allows us to interpret the changes shown in Fig. 7.1. The graph shows changes in bond prices. Thus, once we see that bond prices rise or fall, we can use this price movement to predict what will happen to bond yields. We demonstrate this change in the default risk premium by working through Fig. 7.1.

If lenders anticipate no changes in the other sources of variation in yields (liquidity, information costs, and tax differences), the yield on a risky security should be greater than that on a safe security, and the price of the risky security should be lower than the price of the safe security. Such is the case in Fig. 7.1: The initial price of the safer security, P_{safe0}, exceeds that of the riskier security, P_{risky0}. From the pricing information shown, we can identify the differences in returns on these bonds. The initial interest rate on the riskier security,

Figure 7.1

Determining Default Risk Premium in Yields

The initial default risk premium can be seen by comparing yields associated with the prices P_{safe} and P_{risky}. Because the price of the safer asset exceeds that of the riskier asset, we can infer that the yield on the riskier asset, i_{risky}, exceeds that on the safer asset, i_{safe}, to compensate savers for bearing risk.

1. The initial default risk premium, then, is $i_{risky0} - i_{safe0}$, where i_{risky} and i_{safe} are the yields associated with P_{risky} and P_{safe}, respectively. As lenders revise upward the expected default risk in the high-default-risk market, the B^d curve shifts to the left (from B^d_{risky0} to B^d_{risky1}).

2. The rise of default risk in the high-default-risk market causes investors to shift their funds to less risky markets, causing the B^d curve to shift to the right (from B^d_{safe0} to B^d_{safe1}) in the low-default-risk market, raising the price of low-default-risk bonds and reducing the yield on low-default-risk bonds.

3. Because of the greater gap between prices of low-default-risk and high-default-risk instruments, the premium between the high-default-risk yield and the low-default-risk yield increases to $i_{risky1} - i_{safe1}$.

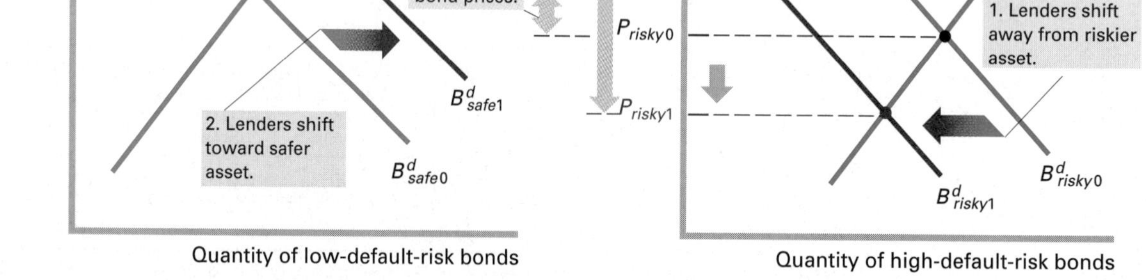

(a) Low-Default-Risk Market

(b) High-Default-Risk Market

i_{risky0}, exceeds that on the safer security, i_{safe0}. The risk premium, $i_{risky0} - i_{safe0}$, compensates lenders for the default risk on the riskier security.

Now suppose that market participants believe that the likelihood of default on the riskier instrument has increased because an anticipated recession lowers profits of high-risk firms. Accordingly, lenders are willing to pay less for the high-risk security (that is, they demand a higher expected return) to compensate them for bearing additional default risk. The demand curve in Fig. 7.1(b) shifts to the left, as investors reduce the volume of funds they channel to that security. The shift in the demand curve reduces the price of risky bonds (and raises the yield on risky bonds).

When lenders perceive an increase in the default risk on risky instruments, they tend to shift their funds to low-risk instruments. This shift is called a *flight to quality*. Note in Fig. 7.1(a) that the demand curve in the safer market shifts to the right because of greater default risk on the riskier security. From the theory of portfolio allocation, we would predict that the increase in the risk of the higher-risk security would increase the demand for the safer bonds. In this case, the price of the safer bond rises, while the price of the riskier bond falls—that is, the default risk premium widens. The yield on a bond with a higher default risk carries a greater default risk premium. An increase in expected default risk reduces lenders' willingness to buy riskier instruments and increases their willingness to buy safer instruments.

In practice, how do changes in default risk work to cause investors to shift funds from one asset to another? Figure 7.2 highlights two shifts in U.S. financial markets. It shows that, although long-term interest rates generally move together (as do short-term rates), episodes do occur in which risk premiums fluctuate. In the early 1980s, when a recession caused concern about corporations' ability to repay, investors reallocated funds away from risky long-term corporate debt and toward safe government debt. Note the dramatic increase in the yield on medium-quality (Baa) bonds relative to the yield on long-term Treasury securities in the early 1980s. The 1974–1975 recession raised investors' concern about default risk in the short-term market. Note the significant increase in the commercial paper rate, which carries some default risk, relative to the Treasury bill rate, which does not. These episodes reflect market perceptions of an increase in default risk, raising the required yield on alternatives to default-risk-free instruments. In August 1998, risk premiums rose as worldwide investors, panicked by the Asian financial crisis, bought up Treasury securities.

Another flight to quality occurred from 1929 to 1931. As expectations of the downturn worsened during the Great Depression, savers shifted their funds away from risky corporate securities. They shifted their savings to government securities, actually pushing yields close to zero. The spread between Baa and long-term government bond rates increased significantly—from 2 percentage points in 1929 to 6 percentage points in 1931. Other changes in default risk premiums occurred in the early 1970s in the commercial paper market. The default of the Penn Central Railroad in 1970 raised the perceived risk on corporate commercial paper. In the municipal

Figure 7.2

Long-Term and Short-Term Yields in the United States, 1960–2000

In periods when investors are concerned about the ability of corporations to repay, investors reallocate funds from corporate debt to safe government debt, seen here in 1974–1975 and again in the early 1980s.

Source: Council of Economic Advisers, *Economic Report of the President,* various issues; after 1997, commercial paper data are for three-month instruments.

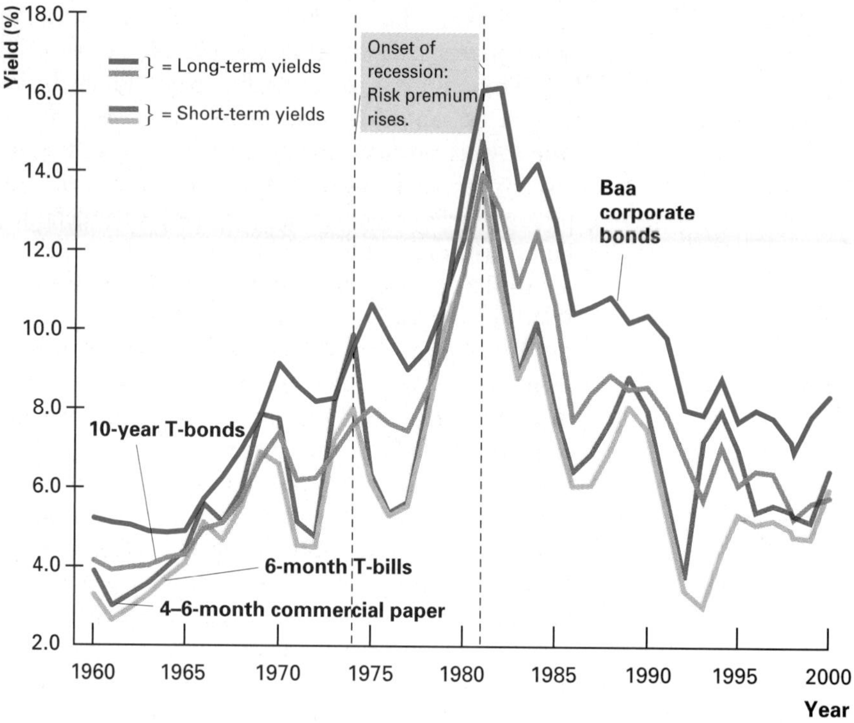

bond market in the early 1980s, the default of the Washington State Public Power System bonds increased the perceived risk of investments in the municipal bond market.

CHECKPOINT

Hitechco, a relatively young technology company, has $10 million in bonds outstanding. You notice in *The Wall Street Journal* that the firm has been awarded a $30 million settlement in a patent dispute with an electronics conglomerate. What would you predict to be the effect of the settlement on the yield on and price of Hitechco's bonds? The news of the settlement reduces the default risk on any Hitechco debt. The default risk premium on Hitechco bonds should then fall, reducing the yield and increasing the bonds' price. o

Liquidity

Differences in *liquidity* are another reason we observe differences in interest rates. Because investors care about liquidity, they are willing to accept a lower interest rate on more liquid investments than on less liquid—illiquid—investments, all other things being equal. Hence a less liquid asset must pay a higher yield to compensate savers for their sacrifice of liquidity. The overall risk premium on an investment includes this liquidity premium as well as the default risk premium.

Liquidity premium. The way in which a financial instrument is traded affects its liquidity. As with default risk, we can use U.S. Treasury securities to compare liquidity among different financial instruments. Markets for Treasury securities are extremely liquid, whereas matching buyers and sellers of corporate bonds is more difficult. Therefore corporate bond markets are much less liquid than government bond markets, and so investors require an additional premium in their yields.

Changes in liquidity and the liquidity premium. How does a change in the liquidity of a financial instrument affect its yield? The theory of portfolio allocation tells us that for any yield, investors prefer to hold more liquid instruments (such as government bonds) than illiquid ones. Therefore, if the market for corporate bonds becomes less liquid, the spread between yields on less liquid and more liquid instruments increases.

Figure 7.3 illustrates the effect of a change in liquidity on bond prices. Figure 7.3(a) shows the determination of the market price of securities in a more liquid market (such as that for U.S. Treasury bonds). Figure 7.3(b) shows the determination of the market price of bonds in a less liquid market (such as that for corporate bonds). Because we want to focus on the consequences of a change in liquidity for the risk premium, for simplicity we assume that the initial prices in the two markets are equal, or $P_{illiq0} = P_{liq0}$; hence the initial yields in the two markets are also equal, or $i_{illiq0} = i_{liq0}$.

Suppose that the less liquid instrument becomes even more illiquid. Savers then will require a higher expected return to compensate them for the loss of liquidity; that is, the demand curve in the illiquid market shifts to the left as the demand for bonds decreases from B^d_{illiq0} to B^d_{illiq1} in Fig. 7.3(b). This shift lowers the price and raises the yield in the illiquid market. As lenders reallocate their funds toward the more liquid market, the demand curve in Fig. 7.3(a) shifts to the right from $B^d_{liq0}$to B^d_{liq1}. As a result, the price rises (from P_{liq0} to P_{liq1}) and the interest rate falls in the more liquid market, while the price falls (from P_{illiq0} to P_{illiq1}) and the interest rate rises in the less liquid market. Associated with the gap between the prices ($P_{liq1} - P_{illiq1}$), the liquidity component of the risk premium rises to $i_{illiq1} - i_{liq1}$. Lenders are less willing to hold the illiquid instrument and require a higher return, and borrowers using that instrument to raise funds will have a higher cost of funds. An increase in the liquidity of an asset reduces its required return; a decrease in liquidity raises the required return.

Information Costs

The third factor influencing the risk structure of interest rates is the *cost of acquiring information.* The activity of an investor who devotes resources—time and money—to acquire information on an asset reduces the expected return on that financial asset. The cost of using those resources thus is included in the borrowing cost charged by the lender, just as the cost of labor is included in the price of a sweater. If two assets have equal default risk and liquidity, investors prefer to hold the asset with lower information costs.

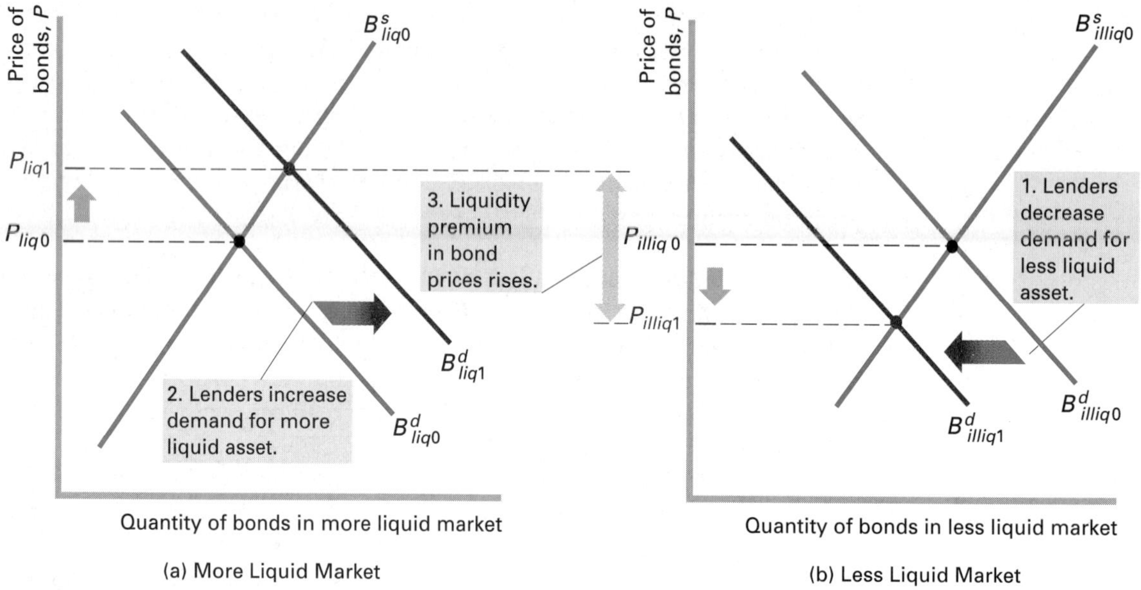

Figure 7.3

Effect on the Risk Premium of a Decrease in Liquidity

Lenders value liquidity. Therefore an instrument traded in a less liquid market will have a lower price and greater required return than an instrument traded in a more liquid market.

1. A decrease in liquidity causes lenders to decrease their demand curve for that asset, shifting the demand curve from B^d_{illiq0} to B^d_{illiq1}.
2. Lenders reallocate their funds from the less liquid market to the more liquid market, shifting the demand curve from B^d_{liq0} to B^d_{liq1}.
3. The liquidity premium embodied in the change in the spread in bond prices—the difference in the yield on the less liquid instruments—equals $i_{illiq1} - i_{illiq0}$.

Measuring information costs. Government obligations, such as Treasury bills and bonds, have the lowest information costs because all savers know with certainty that the principal and interest will be repaid (in nominal terms). Rating agencies reduce the information costs of gathering data on and monitoring well-known borrowers, but such costs are higher for loans made to less well-known borrowers. For example, if you want to start a business of selling customized T-shirts and go to your local bank for a loan, the bank will have to assess your ability to repay on the basis of your income and the chances that your business will succeed. The cost of collecting this information leads to higher costs either directly in terms of a higher interest rate on your loan or indirectly through restrictions on your activities that the bank will write into your loan contract. Financial instruments with high interest rates due to higher information costs also tend to be relatively illiquid. The reason is that without readily available information, trading these instruments in financial markets is difficult.

Changes in information costs and the risk premium. Figure 7.4 illustrates the effect of an increase in information costs on the price of a financial instrument and, by inference, on the risk premium for a financial instrument. Figure 7.4(a) shows the determination of the market price of low-information-cost bonds. Figure 7.4(b) shows the determination of the market price of high-information-cost bonds. Again, for simplicity, let's assume that the prices of the two bonds are initially equal, or $P_{high0} = P_{low0}$, so the yields are equal, $i_{high0} = i_{high1}$. (In practice, of course, $i_{high0} > i_{low0}$. This difference reflects the difference in costs that lenders incur to gather information on the two bonds.)

When information costs rise for the high-information-cost market, lenders are less willing to invest their funds in the market for that instrument at the going price and yield, shifting the demand curve to the left in Fig. 7.4(b). As the funds are reallocated to the low-information-cost market, the demand curve shifts to the right in the market for that instrument, as shown in Fig. 7.4(a). As a result, the price rises (from P_{low0} to P_{low1}) and the interest rate falls in the low-information-cost market, while the price falls (from P_{high0} to P_{high1}) and the interest rate rises in the high-information-cost market. Associated with the gap

Figure 7.4

Effect on Risk Premium of an Increase in Information Costs

An increase in information costs in a high-information-cost market causes the price of bonds in that market to fall and the interest rate to rise; the difference in the interest rate on high-information-cost lending and low-information-cost lending rises.

1. An increase in information costs in the initially high-information-cost market causes lenders to decrease their demand for that asset, shifting the demand curve for that asset to the left from B^d_{high0} to B^d_{high1}, reducing the price of bonds and raising the yield.

2. Lenders reallocate their funds toward the low-information-cost market, shifting the demand curve to the right from B^d_{low0} to B^d_{low1}, raising the price of bonds, and reducing the yield.

3. The difference in the bond prices is matched by a difference in the required returns. The gap between i_{high1} and i_{low1} is the information-cost premium.

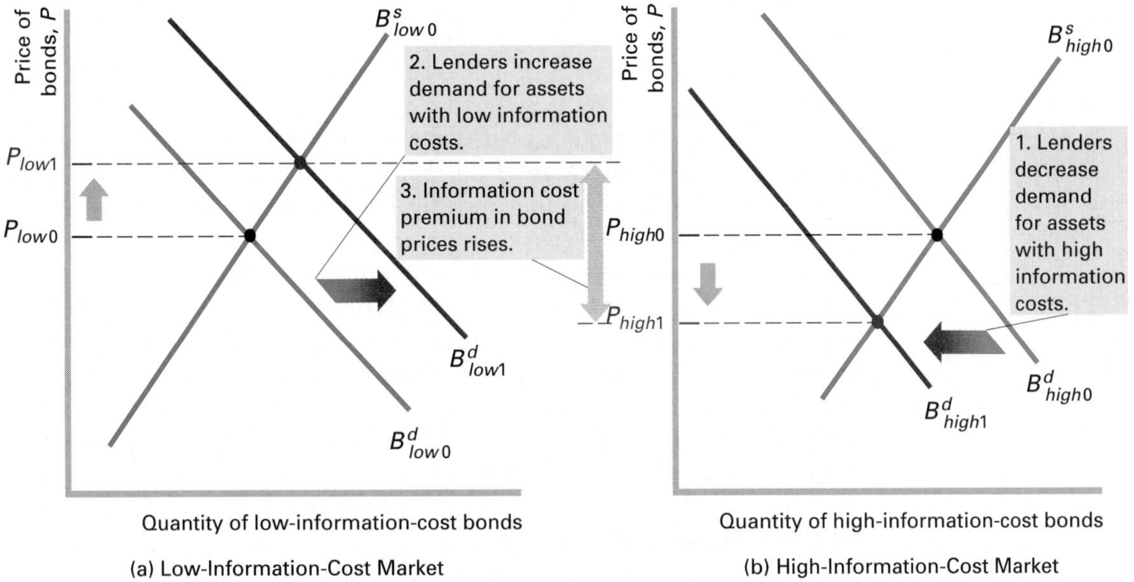

between the prices ($P_{low1} - P_{high1}$), the information-cost component of the risk premium rises to $i_{high1} - i_{low1}$. An increase in information costs increases the required return on a financial instrument. A decrease in information costs decreases the required return on a financial instrument.

Taxation

Another reason for differences in interest rates across credit market instruments is *taxation*. If returns on all instruments were taxed identically, the differences among instruments in terms of default risk, liquidity, and information costs would be the only sources of variation in the risk structure. Differences in the taxation of returns, however, also create differences in yields among credit market instruments.

Measuring tax differences. When savers project the estimated returns from a bond investment, they first determine whether interest payments are taxable and how taxes reduce their returns. For example, interest received on **municipal bonds**, which are obligations of state and local governments, is exempt from federal, state, and local income taxes. Owing to this exemption, many savers are willing to accept a lower interest rate on municipal bonds than on comparable instruments (including some with lower default risk) because the after-tax yield of municipal bonds is greater. To demonstrate, suppose that you are comparing the returns on a \$1000 Treasury bond with a 9% coupon rate and a \$1000 municipal bond paying 7.5% interest. The before-tax yield on the Treasury bond (9%) is greater than that on the municipal bond (7.5%). If your marginal income tax rate is 30%, 30¢ of each additional dollar of interest income goes to the government through taxes. An annual coupon payment of \$90 on the \$1000 taxable Treasury bond provides you with $(90)(1 - 0.3) = \$63$ in after-tax interest income. Alternatively, a \$1000 municipal bond with a \$75 coupon payment and no taxes provides you with \$75 in after-tax interest income. Therefore you might be willing to hold the municipal bond.

In addition to determining whether interest is taxed, savers must compare differing tax rates on the returns from their investments. Under U.S. law, interest and capital gains are taxed differently. Interest income is taxed at the same rate as wage and salary income. Capital gains carry a lower effective tax rate than interest because capital gains are taxed when they are *realized* (when the asset is sold) and not as they accrue; that is, the taxes are deferred. For example, if you hold shares of Boomco for 20 years before you sell them and realize a capital gain, you will not be taxed until you sell the shares. The benefit of a deferred tax obligation is that the *present value* of the tax that is paid on the gain when it is realized is lower than the present value of the tax payments if you paid the tax incrementally as the gain accrued. At times (including currently), capital gains have been subject to a lower explicit tax rate as well as the implicit tax benefit of deferral.

Finally, the exemption of interest returns on U.S. government securities from state and local taxation provides these obligations with favorable tax treatment relative to taxable corporate securities. Because their returns are taxed, part of the risk premium between commercial paper and Treasury bill yields results from this difference in tax treatment. If the attributes of default risk, liquidity, and information costs are held constant, then shifts in the tax treatment of returns on certain obligations will affect before-tax yields. Investors, however, will compare after-tax expected returns in making their portfolio allocation decisions.

Tax exemption and differences in yields. Figure 7.5 depicts the effect of a tax exemption for municipal bond interest on the yields of a U.S. government bond and a municipal bond. For simplicity, suppose that, with no difference in tax treatment, the prices of the two instruments ($P_{tax\text{-}ex0} = P_{tax0}$) are the same, as are the yields ($i_{tax\text{-}ex0} = i_{tax0}$). If yields on municipal bonds become tax-exempt, U.S. government bonds are less attractive to savers because their yields are taxable. Hence the demand curve shifts to the left in Fig. 7.5(b). At the same

Figure 7.5

Effect of Differences in Tax Treatment on Yields

If nothing else changes, a decrease in a bond's tax liability raises its prices and decreases its yield.

1. If municipal bonds become tax-exempt, lenders decrease their holdings of taxable U.S. government bonds, and the demand curve shifts to the left, from B^d_{tax0} to B^d_{tax1} in (b), reducing the price of taxable bonds.

2. Lenders increase their demand for tax-exempt bonds, so that the demand curve shifts from $B^d_{tax\text{-}ex0}$ to $B^d_{tax\text{-}ex1}$ in (a), raising the price of tax-exempt bonds.

3. The difference in the bond prices is matched by a difference in the required returns. The gap between i_{tax1} and $i_{tax\text{-}ex1}$ is the tax component of the difference in yields.

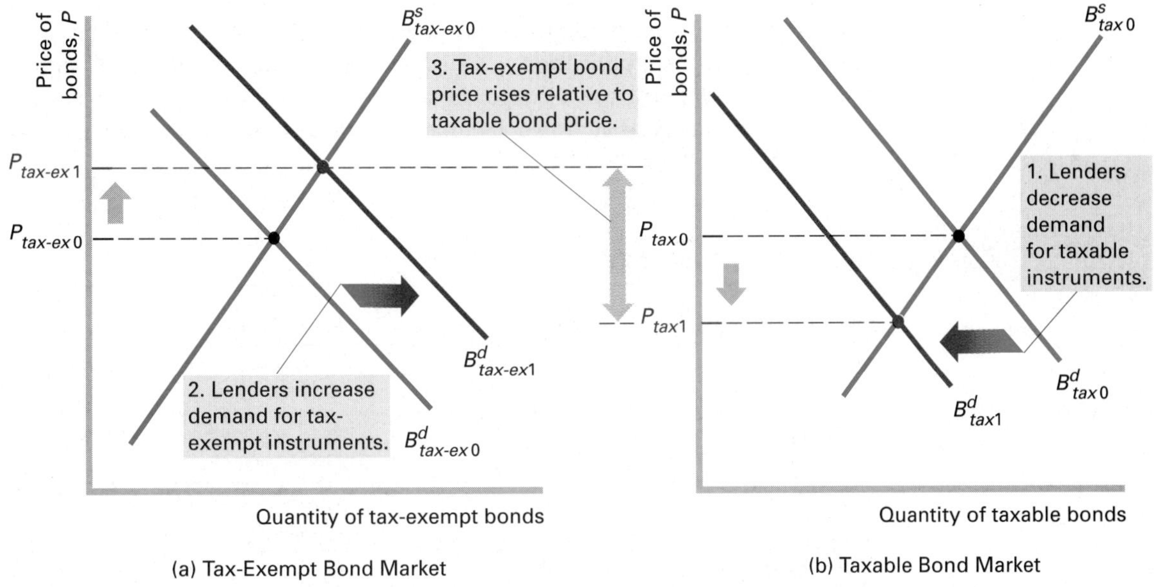

time, lenders will increase their demand for municipal bonds, shifting the demand curve to the right in Fig. 7.5(a). As a result, the price of the tax-exempt bond rises (from $P_{tax\text{-}ex0}$ to $P_{tax\text{-}ex1}$) and its yield falls, while the price of the taxable bond falls (from P_{tax0} to P_{tax1}) and its yield rises. Associated with the gap between the new equilibrium prices, the tax component of the yield difference rises to $i_{tax\text{-}ex1} - i_{tax1}$. At this difference in yields, lenders are indifferent between holding the taxable U.S. government bond and holding the tax-exempt municipal bond.

Table 7.2 summarizes the determinants of the risk structure of interest rates.

CHECKPOINT

Suppose that Congress enacted and the President signed a tax on trading in corporate bonds to reduce the federal budget deficit. What should happen to the difference between the yield on corporate bonds and that on Treasury bonds? The tax on trading raises transactions costs in the corporate bond market relative to the Treasury bond market, reducing the liquidity of corporate bonds relative to Treasury bonds. The liquidity premium in corporate bond yields rises. o

Using the Risk Structure for Forecasting

Many business and government analysts use financial data for forecasting, or predicting, changes in economic variables such as total output of the economy or prices. Businesspeople use forecasts in making investment, production, and employment decisions. Government officials use forecasts to predict future tax revenues and expenditures and to guide policy decisions.

Many commercial forecasting models include changes in the risk structure of interest rates to predict future trends in economic activity. When you think about it, this application is sensible: Risk premiums reflect the difference between the yields of a corporate instrument and a Treasury instrument of similar maturity. They also include assessments of the underlying risk

TABLE 7.2 **THE RISK STRUCTURE OF INTEREST RATES**

An increase in an asset's . . .	Causes its yield to . . .	Because . . .
default risk	rise	savers must be compensated for bearing additional risk
liquidity	fall	savers incur lower costs of exchanging the asset for cash
information costs	rise	savers must spend more resources to evaluate an asset
tax liability	rise	savers care about after-tax returns and must be compensated for the tax liability

CONSIDER THIS . . .

Will a Consumption Tax Kill Munis' Allure?

In late 1994 and through 1995, talk of tax reform swept through Washington. House Majority Leader Dick Armey introduced a flat tax, which would replace the current individual income tax with a flat-rate tax on wage and salary income. Senators Sam Nunn and Pete Domenici introduced a plan to allow individuals an unlimited deduction for funds saved rather than spent. These plans and many other variants share a common theme: they are taxes on consumption, not income. They exempt from taxation returns to savings—interest, dividends, and capital gains.

As serious discussion of the proposals began, financial market participants considered the effects of tax reform on the prices and yields of different types of bonds. Under the income tax, interest income from municipal bonds is exempt from federal, state, and local taxation. As a result of that exemption, yields on municipal bonds were lower than those on comparable taxable bonds. If all forms of interest income were exempt from taxation, then munis would lose their relative tax preference. The prices of existing higher-yield currently taxable bonds would rise—and yields would fall—while muni prices would fall—and yields would rise.

Analysts warned municipal bond buyers of this prospect in 1995 and early 1996, though investors' demand for munis remained healthy. What was going on? One possibility is that investors did not believe that these tax changes would be enacted.

structure—that is, the contribution of default risk, liquidity, information costs, and taxation—to the yields required on different types of securities.

For example, increases in risk premiums may reflect market participants' anticipation of periods of difficulty in servicing debt obligations because of, for example, lower expected future profits. Analysts have successfully used increases in the risk premium of certain broad classes of securities, such as the Baa bond and Treasury bond yield differential or the commercial paper and Treasury bill yield differential, to forecast business recessions (in which the likelihood of default increases). The National Bureau of Economic Research, an independent research organization that is responsible for determining the onset of recessions in the United States, uses risk premiums in formulating its *leading indicators* of future economic activity and for forecasting when a recession will begin or end. Private forecasters widely use these measures to advise financial and business clients.

TERM STRUCTURE OF INTEREST RATES

Let's now turn our attention to variations in yields among instruments with common default risk, liquidity, information cost, and taxation characteristics but with different maturities. The variation in yield for related instruments that differ in maturity is known as the **term structure of interest rates.** Because the risk-structure factors can be held constant most easily for U.S. government obligations, term structure is usually defined with respect to yields on those securities.

OTHER TIMES, OTHER PLACES . . .

Asian Flu for European Bonds?

A well-functioning corporate bond market gives investors information about risk premiums on corporate debt instruments. Until 1994, very few risky bonds for European companies were issued and traded. As those bonds became more popular in the late 1990s, many European firms gained access to public debt markets, frequently lowering their cost of capital relative to bank loans or new equity issues. Europe's "non-investment-grade" bond sector picked up steam for two reasons—the impending European monetary union and the low transactions costs made possible by active debt markets.

Beginning in late 1997, the Asian financial crisis reduced the appetite for risk taking by investors around the world. When Russia defaulted on its domestic bond obligations in August 1998, investors fled the debt of risky firms—even in Europe and the United States—as they stampeded to buy U.S. Treasury obligations. As illustrated in Fig. 7.1, the shift away from European non-investment-grade debt lowered bond prices and raised bond yields and the cost of borrowing for European firms.

The high yields began attracting investors in late 1998 and early 1999, as Europe-based bond funds grew in popularity. Some observers have noted that getting precise information about differences in default risk, liquidity, and information costs from the risk structure of corporate bond yields in Europe remains difficult. Investors are awaiting increased coordination of accounting standards and the activities of rating agencies in Europe. Asian flu or no, optimists predict greater growth in the European non-investment-grade bond market in the new century's first decade than in the U.S. counterpart.

To obtain information about investors' expectations of future credit market conditions, market analysts often study the yields to maturity on different default-risk-free instruments as a function of maturity. The graph of this relationship is known as a **yield curve.** In principle, yield curves can have three shapes. They can be upward sloping, flat, or downward sloping. An upward-sloping yield curve tells us that long-term yields are higher than short-term yields. When a yield curve is flat, short-term and long-term obligations have the same yield. If short-term yields are higher than long-term yields, the yield curve is downward sloping. The yield curve in *The Wall Street Journal* contains valuable information for savers and borrowers.

Since World War II, yield curves for U.S. Treasury securities have exhibited a typical slope and position. First, while not the case for the yield curve shown in "Using the News . . . ," the shape of the yield curve is usually upward sloping, showing that long-term yields are generally higher than short-term yields. Second, yields on default-risk-free instruments with different maturities typically move together, increasing or decreasing collectively. Hence the yield curve typically shifts up or down rather than changing its shape. Understanding the patterns and position can help you to use yield curves to forecast economic variables such as interest rates and inflation rates.

Economists have advanced three theories to explain the appearance of the yield curve: the segmented markets theory, the expectations theory, and the preferred habitat theory. How can we judge these theories? Two criteria help.

USING THE NEWS . . .

How to Read the Yield Curve

Each day in its Credit Markets section, *The Wall Street Journal* plots the yield curve for U.S. Treasury securities. The numbers on the horizontal axis indicate the maturity, ranging from three months (Treasury bills) to 30 years (Treasury bonds). The numbers on the vertical axis indicate yields to maturity at the end of the previous trading day. Comparing the current and four-week-ago yield curves, we see that the general level of yields fell, though more for intermediate-term instruments. In addition, there is considerable variation in yields by maturity. The yield curve slopes down over the range from six months to five years, then rises thereafter.

Should you invest in short-term Treasury bills because their yield is higher than that of long-term Treasury bonds? We answer this question as we discuss the term structure of interest rates.

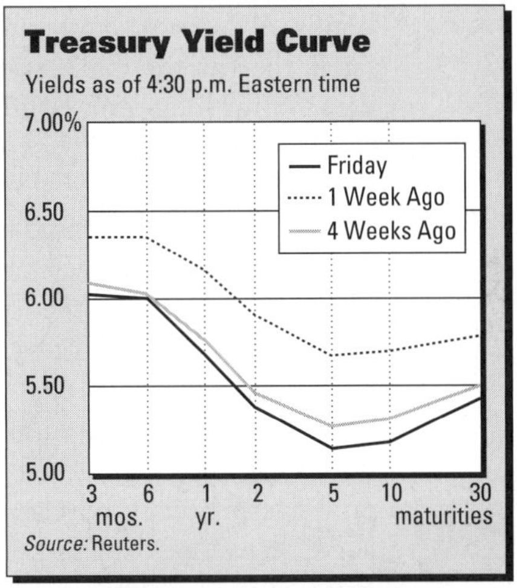

Source: The Wall Street Journal, December 18, 2000. Republished by permission of Dow Jones, Inc. via Copyright Clearance Center, Inc. © 2000 Dow Jones and Company, Inc. All Rights Reserved Worldwide. (Quotes are from December 18, 2000.)

First is logical consistency: *Does the theory offer an internally consistent model of financial markets that explains real-world events?* Second is predictive power: *How well does the theory explain actual data on yield curves?*

Segmented Markets Theory

The **segmented markets theory** holds that the yield on each instrument, from three-month T-bills to two-year notes to 30-year bonds, is determined in a separate market, with a separate market demand and supply. An assumption of this theory is that borrowers have particular periods for which they want to borrow and that lenders have particular holding periods in mind. For example, individuals may want to match maturities and holding periods because they are saving for retirement or their children's education. By doing so, they know exactly what their nominal return is. Or borrowers may have a particular period in mind because they know that a business investment project will pay off over 20 years and the business wants to match its debt repayments with its expected revenues. Under the segmented markets theory, borrowers and lenders are unwilling to move from one market to another, and therefore obligations with different maturities are not substitutable.

According to the segmented markets theory, the yield in each market reflects only demand and supply in that market. The yield curve is plotted from supply and demand behavior in each market for a specific type of security, and it represents many small demand and supply decisions. An upward-sloping yield curve implies that the demand for short-term bonds is high relative to that for long-term bonds. As we showed in Chapter 4, this demand exerts upward pressure on the price and downward pressure on the yield for short-term bonds. A flat yield curve implies that demand and supply conditions are similar in the various markets. A downward-sloping yield curve implies a higher demand for long-term bonds relative to that for short-term bonds.

Does this theory pass the first test of explaining the slope of the yield curve? Because upward-sloping yield curves are most prevalent in post–World War II data for the United States, the segmented markets theory suggests that investors generally prefer to hold short-term bonds rather than long-term bonds. Therefore the theory can explain upward-sloping yield curves as long as investors prefer short-term instruments.

Does this theory pass the second test of explaining the data for yield curves? As we just noted, under the segmented markets theory, demand for a bond typically falls as the bond's maturity increases. In equilibrium, the yields on longer-maturity bonds exceed those on shorter-maturity bonds. The yield curve then slopes upward. Of course, preferences for bonds of different maturities shift on occasion. At times, investors become more willing to hold longer-term bonds. When they do, the equilibrium yields on those bonds fall, causing the yield curve to flatten or slope downward.

However, the segmented markets theory cannot explain the observation that yields on different instruments tend to move together. Because the theory claims that only market-specific demand and supply determine yields, the curves could move together only by coincidence.[†] Thus the theory does not explain why an investor would turn down potentially higher returns in other markets in order to meet a particular holding-period preference.

Expectations Theory

In contrast to the segmented markets theory, the **expectations theory** states that investors view assets of all maturities as perfect substitutes at the same levels of default risk, liquidity, information costs, and taxation. According to this theory, a long-term bond rate equals the average of short-term rates covering the same investment period. In addition, it suggests that the yield curve slope depends on the expected future path of short-term rates.

Let's begin with an example of how you can infer expectations of future short-term rates from current long-term rates. Suppose that the interest rate on a one-year bond is 6%, the interest rate on a two-year bond is 7%, the

[†] Technically, the segmented markets theory can explain the up and down movements in the yield curve if there are movements into and out of the bond market *at all maturities*. This occurrence certainly would be coincidental.

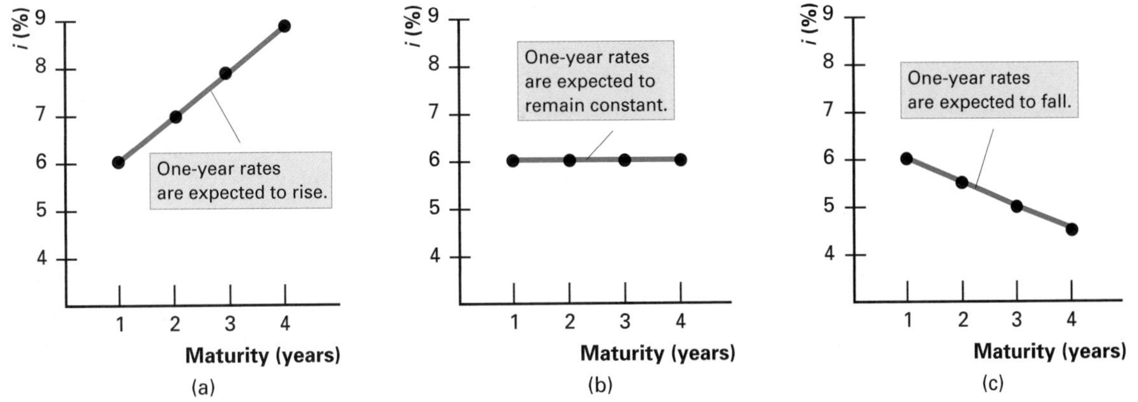

Figure 7.6

Using the Yield Curve to Predict Interest Rates: The Expectations Theory

Under the expectations theory, the slope of the yield curve shows that future short-term interest rates are expected to (a) rise, (b) remain the same, or (c) fall relative to current levels.

interest rate on a three-year bond is 8%, and the interest rate on a four-year bond is 9%. Figure 7.6(a) shows this upward-sloping yield curve. The simple description of the expectations theory tells you how to infer the (unobservable) expectations of future short-term interest rates from this yield curve. The two-year rate (7%) is an average of the current one-year rate (6%) and the expected future one-year rate,† or

$$\frac{6\% + \text{Expected future one-year rate one year ahead}}{2} = 7\%.$$

The expected future one-year rate then is 2(7%) − 6% = 8%.

Similarly, you can infer the expected future one-year rate two periods from now by looking at the three-year bond rate. That rate should be the average of the current one-year bond rate (6%), the expected one-year rate one year ahead (just calculated to be 8%), and the expected one-year rate two years ahead, or

$$\frac{6\% + 8\% + \text{Expected one-year rate two years ahead}}{3} = 8\%.$$

The expected one-year rate two years ahead is 10%. Finally, you can infer the expected one-year rate three years ahead, which is 12%.†† Under the

†This arithmetic average is an approximation to the more precise answer, which is the geometric mean of the current and expected future rates.

††Here

$$\frac{6\% + 8\% + 10\% + \text{Expected one-year rate three years ahead}}{4} = 9\%,$$

so the expected one-year rate three years ahead is 12%.

expectations theory, when short-term rates are expected to rise, the yield curve slopes up.

Figure 7.6(b) shows a flat yield curve, in which the yields on one-year, two-year, three-year, and four-year bonds all are 6%. Thus, under the expectations theory, you can infer that one-year rates will remain unchanged at 6% for the next three years. Under the expectations theory, when short-term rates are expected to remain unchanged, the yield curve is flat.

Figure 7.6(c) shows a downward-sloping yield curve in which the yields are 6% for the one-year bond, 5.5% for the two-year bond, 5% for the three-year bond, and 4.5% for the four-year bond. What would you expect future one-year rates to be one, two, and three years from now? The two-year bond rate is an average of the current one-year rate (6%) and the expected future one-year rate, or

$$\frac{6\% + \text{Expected future one-year rate one year ahead}}{2} = 5.5\%.$$

The expected one-year rate one year from now is 5%. The expected one-year rate two years from now can be found from the following:

$$\text{Rate on three-year bonds} = \frac{6\% + 5\% + \text{Expected one-year rate two years ahead}}{3} = 5\%.$$

The one-year rate that you can infer for two years from now is 4%. Using the same approach, you can find the expected one-year rate three years from now:

$$\text{Rate on four-year bonds} = \frac{6\% + 5\% + 4\% + \text{Expected one-year rate three years ahead}}{4} = 4.5\%.$$

The one-year rate that you can infer for three years from now is 3%. Under the expectations theory, when short-term rates are expected to fall, the yield curve slopes down.

We can generalize from these examples. The perfect substitutability assumption of the expectations theory implies that expected returns for a given holding period must be the same for bonds of different maturities. Otherwise, investors would change their relative demand for instruments with different maturities to take advantage of differences in yields. In addition, the perfect substitutability assumption implies that the yield on a long-term bond will equal an average of expected short-term yields over the life of the bonds. Why? Take a holding period of, say, 10 years. If all instruments are perfect substitutes, investors should get the same expected return from holding a 10-year bond, a sequence of five two-year notes, a sequence of 40 three-month bills, and so on. Under this theory, if the long-term yield is higher than the short-term yield, investors should expect short-term rates to increase over the 10-year period.

Let's further clarify the prediction of the expectations theory about relationships among yields on bonds with different maturities. Suppose that you are considering two strategies for a two-year investment, where i is the interest rate of the bond:

Buy-and-hold strategy
Buy a two-year bond and hold it until maturity. The interest rate today is i_{2t}, where t represents the time period.

Roll-over strategy
Buy a one-year bond today and hold it until maturity. The interest rate today is i_{1t}. After the one-year bond matures ($t + 1$), buy another one-year bond and hold it until maturity. The precise interest rate on that bond is unknown. As of today, we expect that it will be $i^e_{1,t+1}$, where e represents expectation.

What are the expected returns on a \$1 investment after two years for each strategy? If you buy and hold, your \$1 is worth $\$(1 + i_{2t})$ after the first year and $\$(1 + i_{2t})(1 + i_{2t})$ after two years. Under the roll-over strategy, your \$1 is worth $\$(1 + i_{2t})$ after the first year, and as you expect to earn $i^e_{1,t+1}$ on a one-year bond in the second year, your initial \$1 will be worth the following: $\$(1 + i_{1t})(1 + i^e_{1,t+1})$.

Under the expectations theory, the two instruments are perfect substitutes. Therefore their expected net returns over the two-year holding period must be equal:

$$(1 + i_{2t})(1 + i_{2t}) - 1 = (1 + i_{1t})(1 + i^e_{1,t+1}) - 1.$$

Simplifying, we get

$$2i_{2t} + i^2_{2t} = i_{1t} + i^e_{1,t+1} + i_{1t}(i^e_{1,t+1}).$$

Because the product of the two interest rates is small, we can ignore it. (Note, for example, that if $i = 0.08$, then $i^2 = 0.0064$, and the i^2_{2t} and $i_{1t}(i^e_{1,t+1})$ terms can be ignored.) With that approximation, the yield on the two-year bond is an average of the expected yields on the two one-year bonds:

$$i_{2t} = \frac{i_{1t} + i^e_{1,t+1}}{2}. \qquad (7.1)$$

More generally, for an n-period bond, a more precise statement of the expectations theory is

$$i_{n,t} = \frac{i_{1t} + i^e_{1,t+1} + \cdots + i^e_{1i,t+n-1}}{n}.$$

The n-period bond yield is an average of the expected short-term yields over the life of the bond.

Unlike the segmented markets theory, the expectations theory attribute the slope of the yield curve to market expectations, based on the assumption that instruments with different maturities are perfect substitutes. A flat yield curve means that market participants expect future short-term rates to be the same as current short-term rates, making current short-term rates and long-term rates (the average of expected future short-term rates) equal. A downward-sloping yield curve means that investors believe that short-term rates will decline in the future relative to current levels. Finally, an upward-sloping yield curve reflects expectations that short-term rates will be higher in the future, thereby increasing long-term rates today.

How successful is this theory at explaining actual patterns in yield curves? In contrast to the segmented markets theory, the expectations theory offers a logically consistent explanation of movement together by interest rates on bonds of different maturities. For the post–World War II period, movements in U.S. interest rates have been persistent; that is, increases (or decreases) in short-term rates tend to continue for many periods. An increase in short-term rates today increases expected future short-term rates and current long-term rates. Hence the expectations theory can explain movement together by short-term and long-term interest rates.

However, the expectations theory does not explain well the general pattern of an upward-sloping yield curve. If we interpreted the theory strictly, an upward-sloping yield curve would mean that short-term interest rates are expected to rise always. This pattern is inconsistent enough with actual experience to warrant skepticism. Nonetheless, the theory offers a logically consistent foundation for explaining investors' decisions and comovements of interest rates.

CHECKPOINT

Use the expectations theory to answer the following question. Studying *The Wall Street Journal*, you notice that the yield curve slopes upward: Yields on 30-year Treasury bonds are greater than those on seven-year notes, which are in turn greater than those on six-month bills. As all Treasury securities have the same default risk, liquidity, information costs, and tax treatment, should you invest all your money in the 30-year bonds? No. Under the expectations theory, the long-term bond rate is just the average of the expected future short-term rates. You would not earn a higher *expected* return by holding long-term rather than intermediate-term or short-term Treasury instruments. **o**

Preferred Habitat Theory

Neither the segmented markets theory nor the expectations theory provides a complete explanation of the yield curve. Essentially, their shortcomings arise from the extreme position that each takes. Under the segmented markets theory, investors view maturities as completely unsubstitutable; under the expectations theory, investors view maturities as perfect substitutes. A third theory, the preferred habitat theory, seeks a middle ground and thus is able to explain the shape of the yield curve.

The **preferred habitat theory** holds that investors care about both expected returns and maturity; they view instruments having different maturities as substitutes—but not perfect substitutes. Specifically, investors prefer shorter to longer maturities, as in the segmented markets theory. That is, investors have a preferred maturity, called a habitat, but they can be induced to purchase other securities. As a result, investors will not buy a long-term bond if it offers the same yield as a sequence of short-term bonds. Instead, investors require something extra, a **term premium,** to compensate them for investing in a less preferred maturity. An example helps to illustrate this point.

Suppose that one-year bonds currently yield 6% but are expected to yield 8% next year. Would investors be just as happy buying a two-year bond yielding 7%? The two-year bond offers the same yield as the average of two one-year bonds. But as investors *prefer* to buy one-year bonds, they must be given an even higher yield—say, 7.5%—to lure them into the less desirable two-year maturity. If they are offered only 7%, they will choose the one-year bonds. The additional 0.5% that is needed to make the two-year bonds competitive is the term premium.

Let's generalize this example to compare the predictions of the expectations theory and the preferred habitat theory. Let i represent yields as before, n the number of periods until maturity, and h (habitat) the term premium for the particular maturity. Under the preferred habitat theory, the interest rate on an n-period bond (approximately) equals the average of expected future one-period yields over the life of the bond plus a term premium for that maturity. In general, then, the preferred habitat theory predicts that the yield on an n-period bond is

$$i_{n,t} = \frac{i_{1t} + i^e_{1,t+1} + \cdots + i^e_{1,t+n-1}}{n} + h_{n,t}. \tag{7.2}$$

Under the expectations theory, assets are perfect substitutes; there are no habitats, and h is always zero. The term premium $h_{n,t}$ is not a constant under the preferred habitat theory. Data for post–World War II U.S. financial markets reveal, on average, a positive term premium for longer-term securities. Because shorter maturities are preferred to longer maturities, $h_{n,t}$ increases as a bond's maturity increases. Thus the preferred habitat theory predicts a built-in upward slope in the yield curve, regardless of the expected path of short-term rates—an important correction of the strictly interpreted expectations theory. Thus the shape of the yield curve depends on both the expected path of short-term rates *and* the size of the term premium at each maturity.

Under the preferred habitat theory, then, a flat yield curve reflects an expectation of slightly falling future short-term rates, because of the built-in upward tilt in the yield curve. An upward-sloping yield curve reflects a smaller expected increase in future short-term rates than it does under the expectations theory. A downward-sloping yield curve reflects a more significant expected

TABLE 7.3 **THEORIES OF THE TERM STRUCTURE**

Theory	Assumes . . .	Predicts . . .	Evaluation . . .
Segmented markets	Maturities are not substitutable; shorter maturities are preferred to longer maturities	Yields on different maturities are determined in separate markets	Explains shapes of the yield curve but not why short-term and long-term rates move together
Expectations	Maturities are perfect substitutes	Yield on an *n*-period bond equals the average of yields on one-period bonds over the next *n* periods of the yield curve	Explains why short-term and long-term rates move together but not the usual upward slope
Preferred habitat	Maturities are substitutable but not perfectly	Yield on an *n*-period bond equals the average of yields on one-period bonds over the next *n* periods plus a term premium	Explains both the shapes of the yield curve and why short-term and long-term rates move together

decline in future short-term rates than the expectations theory predicts. As with the expectations theory, the slope of the yield curve under the preferred habitat theory provides information on market expectations about future short-term rates. The preferred habitat theory is logically consistent and explains both the usual pattern of an upward-sloping yield curve and the movement together by yields on bonds having different maturities.

Table 7.3 summarizes the segmented markets theory, the expectations theory, and the preferred habitat theory.

Using the Term Structure for Forecasting

Investors, businesspeople, and policymakers also use information contained in the term structure of interest rates for forecasting. Under the expectations and preferred habitat theories, the slope of the yield curve provides information about market participants' expectations about future short-term nominal interest rates. In addition, if fluctuations in expected real interest rates are small, the yield curve provides information about expectations of future inflation rates. Suppose that you want the financial markets' best guess about the rate of inflation in five years. If the real interest rate is expected to remain constant, you can interpret an upward-sloping yield curve to mean that inflation is expected to rise. Indeed, the Fed and many financial market participants use the yield curve to forecast future inflation. Economists and market participants also look to the slope of the yield curve for information on the likelihood of a recession. When short-term rates are higher than long-term rates, the yield curve is said to be "inverted." (Remember that the yield curve is generally upward sloping.) Campbell Harvey of Duke University found that, since the mid-1950s, inverted yield curves (specifically, a three-month

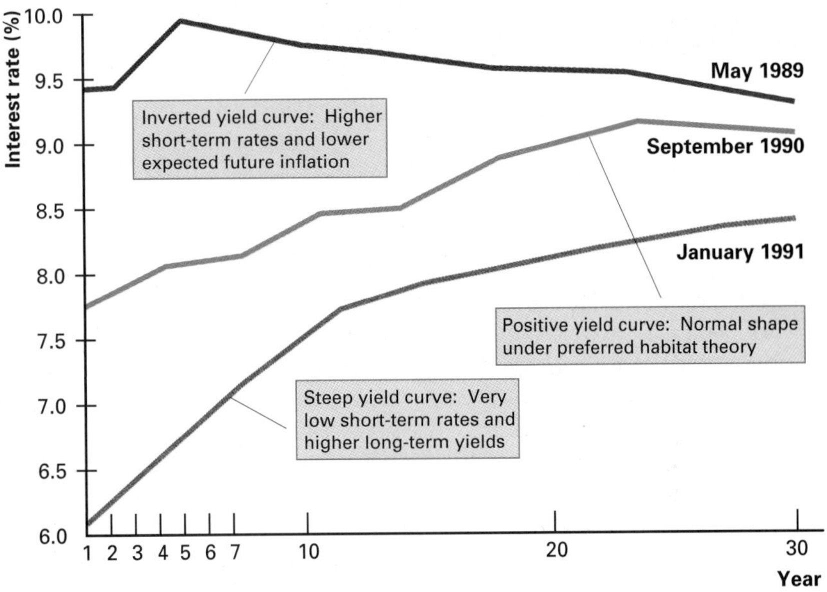

Figure 7.7

Interpreting the Yield Curve

Models of term structure, such as the preferred habitat theory, help analysts use data from *The Wall Street Journal* as a forecasting tool. Understanding the shape of the yield curve makes reading *The Wall Street Journal* data more meaningful.

Treasury bill yield higher than a 10-year Treasury bond yield) have generally predicted recessions four to five quarters hence. More generally, Michael Dotsey of the Federal Reserve Bank of Richmond concluded that the slope of the yield curve is a useful leading indicator of economic activity.†

Figure 7.7 shows three yield curves: one that slopes downward, one that slopes upward slightly, and one that slopes upward steeply. If we apply the preferred habitat theory, these three yield curves—representing three points in time between 1989 and 1991—tell a story about financial markets' expectations and the economy.

The top yield curve characterizes the term structure in the spring of 1989. The belief that the Fed would pursue a policy to reduce inflation led market participants to expect that future short-term rates would be lower than current short-term rates. The preferred habitat theory of the term structure suggests that long-term rates should fall relative to short-term rates. In this case, the yield curve actually is *inverted* from the normal upward-sloping case.

The upward slope shown in the middle curve is characteristic of a normal yield curve under the preferred habitat theory. It characterizes the term structure in the fall of 1990, when the economy was experiencing a recession. However, investors expected that, as economic activity increased in the future, the demand for credit would increase, causing interest rates to increase. In other words, investors expected future short-term rates to rise above current levels.

---

† Campbell R. Harvey, "The Real Term Structure and Consumption Growth," *Journal of Financial Economics* 22 (1988). Michael Dotsey, "The Predictive Content of the Interest Rate Term Spread for Future Economic Growth," Federal Reserve Bank of Richmond, *Economic Quarterly* 84 (Summer 1998): 31–52.

CONSIDER THIS . . .

Can the Treasury Change the Shape of the Yield Curve?

In January 2000, the U.S. Treasury Department announced that it planned to decrease the average maturity of outstanding U.S. Treasury debt by curtailing sales of long-term bonds, particularly 30-year bonds. In May 1993, it had made a similar announcement, with a larger-than-anticipated reduction in the government's issuance of long-term bonds being accompanied by an increase in issuance of short-term debt. The situation in 2000 was somewhat different, as federal budget surpluses permitted the Treasury to retire substantial amounts of debt, something it had not done in many years.

Following the Treasury Department's announcement, market yields on intermediate-term and long-term U.S. Treasury securities—especially the 30-year bond—fell substantially between mid-January and late February 2000. Some market participants argued that the yield changes reflected supply and demand. Investors with long-term commitments, such as pension funds, buy long-term U.S. Treasury securities to hedge future liabilities. To the extent that those investors' increased purchases of securities anticipating lower future supply, long-term bond prices were expected to rise, trimming yields.

This version of events reflects the *preferred habitat theory of the term structure.* That approach argues that investors prefer short-term maturities. Thus the interaction of investor preferences and the supply of Treasury debt at different maturities determines the term premium needed to attract investors. If investor preferences for shorter-term maturities are held constant, a reduction in the quantity of 30-year bonds supplied would raise their price and reduce their yield.

Alternatively, a drop in yields on long-term securities below yields on short-term securities would reflect expectations of lower economic activity and inflation, as many forecasters predicted at the time. Implicitly, such a story reflects the perspective of the *expectations theory of the term structure.* Under this theory, investors view short-term and long-term Treasury obligations as perfect substitutes. As a result, a relatively low long-term bond rate reflects market participants' expectation of lower short-term interest rates in the future (as would be the case with an economic slowdown and lower expected inflation).

Which story is right? We can use the yield spreads between conventional and inflation-protected Treasury securities (TIPS) to shed light on inflationary expectations and to examine reasons for the fall in market yields. Looking at late January and early February, the spread between 30-year conventional securities and TIPS fell substantially, while yield spreads for 5-year and 10-year securities did not. This divergence suggests that the behavior of Treasury bond prices in January and February 2000 was not dominated by changes in expected inflation. While yields incorporate market expectations about future economic activity and inflation, as predicted by the expectations theory, market demand and supply factors can also affect yields in the short run, as predicted by the preferred habitat theory.

The bottom yield curve represents the term structure in early 1991, when the Fed continued to reduce short-term rates. However, concerns about inflation and government budget deficits kept expected future short-term rates—and hence current long-term rates—high. The inflation fears added to the normal upward slope of the yield curve predicted by the preferred habitat theory.

KEY TERMS AND CONCEPTS

Risk structure of interest rates
- Bond rating
- Default risk
- Default-risk-free instruments
- Default risk premium
- Municipal bonds

Term structure of interest rates
- Expectations theory
- Preferred habitat theory
- Segmented markets theory
- Term premium
- Yield curve

SUMMARY

1. There are two ways to categorize the differences in interest rates on different bonds. The risk structure of interest rates describes the variation in yields among financial instruments that have the same time to maturity but differences in default risk, liquidity, information costs, and taxation. The term structure of interest rates distinguishes variation in yields between instruments with the same risk, liquidity, information costs, and taxation but different maturities.
2. The default risk premium is the additional return that a saver requires to hold a risky instrument rather than a default-risk-free instrument with the same maturity. Although the major component of differences in yields on instruments of similar maturity is default risk, differences in liquidity, information costs, and taxation are also important components. U.S. government securities serve as a benchmark against which to calculate risk premiums because they are default-risk-free, are traded in liquid markets, and have low information costs. Differential taxation of returns on credit market instruments affects their risk premiums.
3. Because government securities are instruments for which default risk, liquidity, information costs, and taxation can be held constant most easily, the term structure usually refers to the yields on government securities. A graph of the yields to maturity on default-risk-free instruments as a function of maturity is known as a yield curve.
4. The yield curves for contemporary U.S. Treasury securities have two typical patterns. First, the yield curve usually slopes upward because long-term yields generally are higher than short-term yields. Second, yields on securities that have different maturities often move together.
5. Economists use three theories to explain the two yield curve features. The theories differ in the relative emphasis placed on expected return or maturity. Under the segmented markets theory, borrowers and lenders want only a particular maturity. This theory can explain upward-sloping yield curves as long as investors have a preference for short-term instruments, other factors being held constant. It cannot explain the observation that interest rates tend to move together. Under the expectations theory, borrowers and lenders care only about getting the highest expected return; instruments with different maturities are perfect substitutes. The expectations theory implies that the interest rate on a long-term bond is an average of expected future short-term rates. This approach can explain comovement of interest rates as long as increases (or decreases) in short-term rates continue for many periods. However, an upward-sloping yield curve predicts ever-increasing short-term rates, casting doubt on the theory in its simplest form. The third approach is a hybrid of the first two theories and is based on the assumption that investors care about both maturity and expected returns. Known as the preferred habitat theory, it describes the interest rate on a long-term bond as an average of expected future short-term rates over the life of the bond plus a term premium. The term premium is affected by demand for and supply of the specific maturity. With an investor preference for short-term instruments (all other factors being equal), the yield curve slopes upward even if short-term rates are not expected to rise.

THE WALL STREET JOURNAL AUGUST 13, 2000

What If Treasury Debt Disappears?

Fannie Mae, the nation's biggest mortgage purchaser, yesterday pulled off the largest bond sale in U.S. history outside of the Treasury market.

a The historic sale of $11.5 billion in bonds is a striking sign that vitality has returned to bond markets around the globe. The deal also buoys the effort by Fannie Mae, a quasi-government agency, to become a benchmark security for the entire U.S. bond market. With the U.S. Treasury buying back its debt, Fannie Mae has striven to step into the void and make its securities a bellwether in the bond world.

b But Fannie Mae, based in Washington, whose stock trades on the New York Stock Exchange, had to pay higher interest rates relative to Treasurys than it would have just six months ago. That is because of the continuing controversy about the future of both Fannie Mae and Freddie Mac; the agencies are under scrutiny from banks, politicians, and even Alan Greenspan of the Federal Reserve. Some critics fear the agencies' rapid growth could someday pose a risk to taxpayers if the agencies ever run into problems, while competitors complain the agencies are using their advantages as government-sponsored entities to poach on their turf. . . .

Still, market observers note that the spreads between Fannie Mae securities and 10-year Treasurys are still around one percentage point above comparable Treasurys, much wider than the 0.60 point seen at the beginning of the year, forcing Fannie Mae to pay more when selling bonds. . . .

c A Fannie Mae official said yesterday's high sale is merely a product of a change in the way the company packages its debt. Until the past 2½ years, the company usually sold its debt in smaller increments, often at unscheduled sales. But in an effort to provide more predictability to investors—and some say to mimic Treasurys—the company has begun packaging debt into larger, regularly scheduled sales each month. . . .

There is still widespread nervousness among bond investors and traders. In the fall of 1998 many parts of the bond market froze up, on the heels of the Russian debt default, making it hard to buy and sell bonds. With the memory of that wrenching experience still fresh almost two years later, investors continue to flock to issuers like Fannie Mae that promise big, liquid bond deals that are easier to trade in times of financial stress.

"There's real demand for very large deals that let investors get out easily, not because investors want to sell these securities but because they want the comfort of knowing they can; they want to know there won't be any adverse consequences due to illiquidity, which many suffered in 1998," said Beth Hammack, co-head of agency underwriting and trading at Goldman Sachs.

Economists and financial market participants have traditionally focused on U.S. Treasury yields in constructing the term structure of interest rates. Other bond yields have traditionally been determined based on risk and liquidity premiums relative to yields on comparable-maturity Treasury securities.

But what if the U.S. Treasury debt market did not exist? A far-fetched question? Maybe not. Many analysts predict that the goodbye to the Treasury market will pick up steam under the new Bush administration. In late 2000, outgoing Clinton Treasury officials considered ending the issuance of 30-year bonds. By mid-2000, the one-year Treasury bill was scheduled to be retired, with the two-year note likely following close behind.

Why the change in the Treasury market? Large federal budget surpluses projected by the Congressional Budget Office imply that funds will be used to pay off maturing obligations and even buy back some outstanding obligations.

(a) As a government-sponsored credit entity, the private Federal National Mortgage Association—Fannie Mae—can issue bonds as bellwether securities. With implicit guarantees from the U.S. Treasury, Fannie Mae hopes to provide a default-risk-free benchmark given the shrinking supply of U.S. Treasury securities.

(b) Uncertainty over the future relationship between Fannie Mae and the federal government affects the default risk premium on Fannie Mae securities. In addition to increasing required yields on agency securities, this uncertainty complicates the pricing of other private securities that use Fannie Mae instruments as a benchmark.

(c) An effective bellwether credit-market instrument should be very liquid, so that its yield is not contaminated by a liquidity premium. By offering large, regular issues, Fannie Mae is mimicking the liquidity built up in the U.S. Treasury market. Such liquidity can make the agency securities a resource in the event of a flight to quality to safer securities.

For further thought. . .

Suppose the combination of tax cuts and spending increases, reduces, or eliminates the federal budget surpluses projected by the Congressional Budget Office. What would you predict regarding changes in Treasury bond yields and Fannie Mae bond yields? Explain.

Source: Excerpted from Gregory Zuckerman and Patrick Barta, "Fannie Mae Sells $11.5 Billion in Bonds, Fueling Its Efforts to Become Benchmark," *The Wall Street Journal*, August 13, 2000. Republished by permission of Dow Jones, Inc., via Copyright Clearance Center, Inc.

6. The risk and term structures of interest rates contain important information about expectations of future economic variables and, for that reason, are useful for forecasting. Because risk premiums reflect expectations about default risk, they are good predictors of future levels of economic activity and the ability of firms to meet debt obligations. Under the expectations theory and preferred habitat theory, the term structure includes expectations of future short-term rates in current long-term rates. If real interest rates are expected to be constant over the long run, the term structure may contain information about expected future rates of inflation.

REVIEW QUESTIONS

1. A yield curve shows the relationship between the market interest rates on bonds that are identical except in what aspect?
2. What is the term structure of interest rates?
3. According to the expectations theory of the term structure of interest rates, what happens to long-term interest rates when short-term interest rates are expected to fall in the future?
4. When does the yield curve slope upward, according to the expectations theory? According to the segmented markets theory? According to the preferred habitat theory?
5. Why does the yield curve often slope slightly upward, according to the preferred habitat theory?
6. What theory is being used by analysts who examine the demand for and supply of funds at different maturity levels to predict the term structure of interest rates?
7. Why is the interest rate on a U.S. Treasury bond usually less than that on a corporate bond?
8. What factors affect the interest rate that is paid on a bond?
9. Does a taxable bond or a tax-free bond pay a higher before-tax interest rate?
10. If the risk premium on a corporate bond increases, does its interest rate necessarily rise? In answering this question, be sure to define "risk premium."
11. At the start of the recession in 1990, interest rates on lower-rated corporate bonds rose relative to the interest rate on Treasury bonds. Why did this happen? What is this phenomenon called?
12. Would you expect the yield on a six-month Treasury bill to be higher or lower than that on commercial paper of comparable maturity? Why?
13. Describe factors that affect the difference between a 10-year General Motors bond and a 10-year U.S. Treasury bond. What additional factors would you consider in explaining the difference between a 10-year junk bond and a 10-year U.S. Treasury bond?
14. Suppose that the risk premiums on new issues of corporate bonds and commercial paper increase. Explain how the shifts would affect your guess about the likelihood of an economic downturn in the near future.
15. During the late 1970s Michael Milken convinced many investors that the yields on junk bonds more than compensated for their higher default risk. What do you think happened to the liquidity of these bonds as a result?
16. Why are credit market instruments with high information costs often illiquid?

ANALYTICAL PROBLEMS

17. Suppose that interest rates for one-year bonds are expected to follow this pattern: 3% today, 5% one year from now, and 7% two years from now. What are the current interest rates on two-year and three-year bonds, according to the expectations theory?
18. Suppose that an investor wants to invest for three years to get the highest possible return. The investor has three options: (a) roll over three one-year bonds, which pay interest rates of 8% in the first year, 11% in the second year, and 7% in the third year; (b) buy a two-year bond paying 10%

today, then roll over the amount received when that bond matures into a one-year bond paying 7%; or (c) buy a three-year bond today paying 8.5%. Assuming annual compounding and no transactions costs, which option should the investor choose?

19. Suppose that you have $1000 to invest in the bond market on January 1, 2001. You could buy a one-year bond paying 4%, a two-year bond paying 5%, a three-year bond paying 5.5%, or a four-year bond paying 6%. You expect interest rates on one-year bonds in the future to be 6.5% on January 1, 2002, 7% on January 1, 2003, and 9% on January 1, 2004. You want to hold your investment until January 1, 2005. Which of the following investment alternatives gives you the highest expected return by 2005: (a) buy a four-year bond today; (b) buy a three-year bond today and a one-year bond in 2004; (c) buy a two-year bond today, a one-year bond in 2003, and another one-year bond in 2004; or (d) buy a one-year bond today and then additional one-year bonds in 2002, 2003, and 2004?

20. Answer Problem 19 if a $10 transactions cost is added for every bond you purchase. In other words, if you have $1000 now, you can buy a bond only for $990, as $10 goes for the transactions cost. Which set of bonds should you buy?

21. In June 1981, the yield curve sloped downward, and in June 1984, the yield curve sloped upward. Interpret these slopes according to the expectations theory.

22. Suppose that short-term interest rates fall during recessions and rise during expansions. What would you expect the slope of the yield curve to be (according to the expectations theory) when (a) the economy is at a peak and a recession is beginning; (b) the economy is midway between a peak and a trough; (c) the economy is in a trough, and an expansion is beginning; and (d) the economy is midway between a trough and a peak?

23. In the spring of 1999 it was unclear whether the Japanese economy was expanding or whether it would fall into deeper recession. If it began to expand, then inflation was likely to increase. If it fell into deeper recession, then government borrowing was likely to increase. *The Wall Street Journal* quoted one analyst as arguing: "Either way, the yield curve will steepen." Explain his reasoning.

24. Suppose the presidential election in the year 2000 is won by a candidate who runs on a platform of "soak the rich." After being elected he or she persuades Congress to raise the top marginal tax rate on the federal personal income tax from 39.6% to 65%. Use one diagram to show the impact of this change in tax rates on the municipal bond market and another diagram to show the impact on the market for U.S. Treasury bonds.

25. Suppose that, holding yield constant, investors are indifferent as to whether they hold bonds issued by the federal government or bonds issued by state and local governments (that is, they consider them to have the same degree of default risk and liquidity). Suppose that state governments have issued perpetuities (or consols) with $75 coupons and the federal government has also issued perpetuities with $75 coupons. If the state and federal perpetuities both have after-tax yields of 8%, then what are their pre-tax yields? (Assume for purposes of this problem that the relevant federal income tax rate is 39.6%.)

26. Suppose that your marginal federal income tax rate is 40%. What is your after-tax rate of return from holding to maturity a one-year municipal bond with an 8% yield? What is your return from holding to maturity a one-year corporate bond with a 10% yield? If both securities had the same default risk and liquidity, which would you prefer to own?

27. If you looked at the data on interest rates, you would see less difference between rates on U.S. government bonds and municipal bonds in the 1980s than earlier. Why do you think this happened?

28. What happens to the yields on junk bonds as the level of economic activity rises and falls?

29. You are considering investing in Fred's Fine Furniture Factory. It is an expanding firm with fine prospects whose future looks fabulous. Based on solid information, your analysis of Fred's finances shows that the company is sound. You decide that

the risk of such an investment is small relative to other investments and that the return looks better than average. What other factor might be important to your decision about investing in Fred's?

30. Some aspects of an asset's taxability may cause the yield to maturity to be an inaccurate measure of return. Suppose that Bob's bond was issued some years ago and has one year left to maturity; it has a yield to maturity of 7%, with a current yield of 3% and an expected capital gain of 4%. Suppose that Betty's bond is newly issued and matures in a year, with a yield to maturity equal to the current yield of 8%. If you are an investor with a 33% marginal tax rate on interest income but a 0% tax rate on capital gains, whose bond would you prefer to own? Why?

31. The Federal Reserve System holds many U.S. government bonds. When the yield curve slopes upward sharply, the Fed could earn a higher return by buying long-term bonds instead of short-term bonds. Should it do so?

32. Under what conditions can you infer expectations about future rates of inflation from the yield curve (according to the expectations theory of the term structure)? Are these conditions more likely to hold for short or long time periods?

33. Using the expectations theory, explain why a firm that is borrowing for two years is unlikely to save money (over the two years) by borrowing short-term (and refinancing) instead of borrowing long-term when the current short-term rate is lower than the long-term rate.

DATA QUESTION

34. Look at *The Wall Street Journal* today or sometime this week and find a plot of the yield curve. (It is a regular feature in Section C.) Compare this plot with the yield curves on the same date one, two, and three years ago. How do the yield curves compare? Can you use the theories of the term structure of interest rates to explain why the yield curve has changed over time?

PART 3

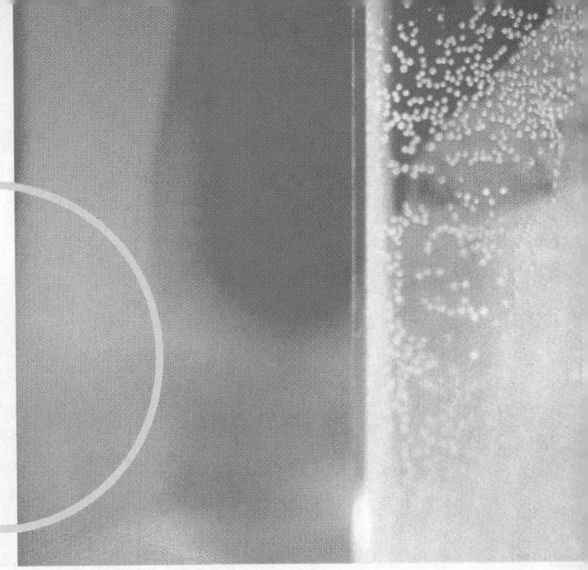

Financial Markets

In Part 2, we studied interest rates and the bond market. In Chapters 8 to 11, we extend our analysis to encompass financial markets more broadly. In Chapter 8, we investigate the market for foreign exchange. In this chapter, you will learn how exchange rates are determined and how movements in exchange rates and interest rates are related. In Chapter 9, we examine the operation of derivative markets, look at the services they provide, and study why market prices fluctuate. Chapters 10 and 11 consider how financial markets evaluate and communicate information. In Chapter 10, we theorize about why prices of stocks, bonds, foreign exchange, and derivative instruments contain information about assets' fundamental value for savers and borrowers. We also check whether the evidence from financial markets supports the theory. In Chapter 11, we examine the costs imposed on financial markets by asymmetric information and observe how financial markets respond to information problems.

Two themes tie together the analysis in Part 3. First, to understand how markets operate, how prices are determined, and what prices mean, we focus on the decisions of individual investors and the ways in which those decisions collectively yield market outcomes. Second, we emphasize how market prices summarize the interaction among market participants and convey information about current and future returns to savers and borrowers.

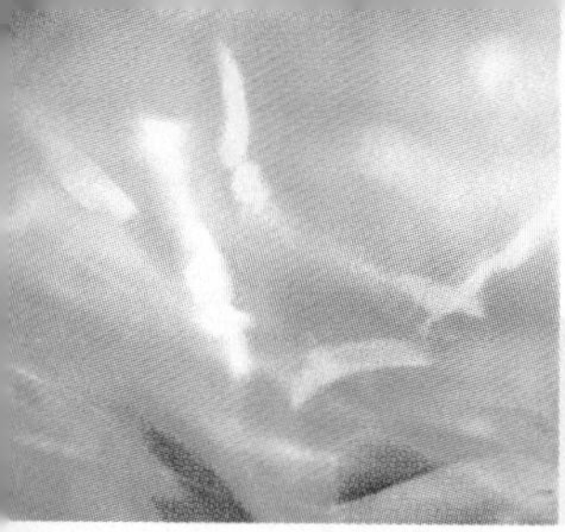

CHAPTER 8

The Foreign-Exchange Market and Exchange Rates

In September 1997, the global financial system trembled. Currency crises spread from Thailand to Indonesia and rocked Asian financial markets. Japan, weakened by a domestic financial crisis, looked on. Russia teetered, with a currency crisis and internal weakness, and subsequently defaulted on its bonds. Business leaders in the United States fretted about the implications of weak Asian economies for U.S. exports and the vaunted U.S. expansion. A flight to U.S. Treasury securities pushed U.S. interest rates in 1998 to their lowest levels in a generation. Why should foreign currency crises and interest rate fluctuations affect the United States? We can answer this question once we learn how transactions take place in global financial markets.

Although the United States uses the dollar as its currency, the dollar is neither a unit of account nor a medium of exchange in Japan, which uses the yen, or in the United Kingdom, which uses the British pound. Nearly every country has its own currency. Hence to buy goods, physical assets, or financial assets in other countries, people must exchange currencies first. When a U.S. business wants to buy foreign goods, it must exchange dollars for the foreign currency. A similar transaction takes place when a U.S. investor purchases a foreign asset. The dollars that the investor has on deposit in a U.S. bank must be converted to bank deposits in the foreign currency. The exchange rate determines how much one currency is worth in terms of another, and it influences the price of international exchanges.

In this chapter we devote our attention to the exchange rate. Specifically, we describe how individuals, businesses, and investors make transactions when the people and organizations are in different countries. In addition to explaining how exchange rates are determined, we learn how and why they change over time. Exchange rates experience long-term trends and short-term fluctuations. Understanding these changes will show you why Germany's desire to keep its high interest rates caused so much turmoil in international financial markets—and it will demonstrate generally the link between interest rates and exchange rates in global economies.

EXCHANGE RATES AND TRADE

In the 1990s and the new century, markets for goods, many services, and financial assets are global. For example, nearly 15% of the goods and services that U.S. consumers, businesses, and governments purchased in 2000 were produced by foreigners, and the United States exported about 11% of U.S. output to foreigners. In 1965, both these proportions were only about 5%. When individuals, businesses, and governments in one country want to trade, borrow, or lend in another country, they must convert their currency into the currency of the other country to complete the transaction. The **nominal exchange rate** is the price of one country's currency in terms of another's: Japanese yen per U.S. dollar or euros per British pound, for example. The nominal exchange rate is usually called the **exchange rate.** That is, when someone says, "the exchange rate," he or she means the *nominal* exchange rate.

How is buying a foreign good different from buying a domestic good? The dollar price of a foreign good, service, or asset, which is what U.S. consumers and investors care about, has two parts: (1) the foreign currency price and (2) the number of dollars needed to obtain the desired amount of foreign currency. When a U.S. citizen buys a Japanese camera or bond, the two parts determining the dollar price are the price of the camera or bond in yen and the exchange rate between the dollar and the yen (¥). If the Japanese camera sells for ¥25,000 and if the yen is worth $0.01, then the dollar price of the camera is $250. If U.S. consumers increase their demand for Japanese cameras, they must buy more yen to purchase the camera. As we will see, this action raises the yen's value against the dollar.

This simple calculation is complicated by the variation in the exchange rate. Exchange rates change over time because the value of each country's currency changes with respect to the values of other currencies. When exchange rates vary, the price of the foreign good to domestic consumers or investors changes. An increase in the value of a country's currency compared to the currencies of other countries is called **appreciation.** A decrease in the value of a country's currency compared to the currency of other countries is called **depreciation.**† To see the effect of a change in the value of the currency and the exchange rate, consider how much the camera costs when the yen appreciates to $0.012 from $0.01. The dollar price of the camera is now $300. The yen's appreciation makes Japanese goods more expensive than comparable non-Japanese goods. The opposite happens if the yen depreciates relative to the dollar. If the value of the yen falls from $0.01 to $0.008, the dollar price of the Japanese camera will fall from $250 to $200. Japanese goods are now more attractive in foreign markets, and the rising dollar makes U.S. goods less attractive in Japan. When a currency appreciates, the price of that country's goods abroad increases, and the

---

†In using the terms "appreciation" and "depreciation," we are treating exchange rates as flexible, or determined purely by market forces. In Chapter 22, we discuss attempts by governments and central banks to fix exchange rates.

price of foreign goods sold in that country decreases. When a currency depreciates, prices of that country's goods abroad decrease, and prices of foreign goods sold in that country increase.

The change in the value of a country's currency can affect domestic manufacturers and workers. When the dollar appreciates significantly, U.S. goods become more expensive abroad, and U.S. exports decline. For firms competing in global markets—which includes many companies in today's economy—this means lower demand for products and layoffs of workers. But the increased value of the dollar does benefit U.S. consumers because foreign products are cheaper.

Nominal versus Real Exchange Rates

Nominal exchange rates are the value of one currency in terms of another, as in the Japanese camera example. They do not, however, measure the purchasing power, or **real exchange rate,** of the currency. For example, suppose that you can exchange \$1.00 for 1818 Italian lira (L). Although L1818 may seem like a large number, in Rome a hamburger costs L4500 and an espresso at a trendy outdoor café costs L5000. In other words, the purchasing power of the lira is substantially less than the purchasing power of the dollar.

Let's find out why. Real and nominal exchange rates are different concepts, but we can compare them in a simple relationship. Suppose that a Big Mac costs \$2.56 in Columbus, Ohio, and L4500 in Rome. If \$1.00 buys L1818 on foreign-exchange markets, we find the real exchange rate, or relative purchasing power of lira to dollars, by comparing the costs of the hamburgers in dollar terms. Let:

EX = nominal exchange rate in foreign currency per dollar (lira per dollar in our example);

P_f = foreign-currency price of goods in the foreign country (lira price of a Big Mac in Rome);

P = domestic-currency price of domestic goods (dollar price of a Big Mac in Columbus, Ohio);

EX_r = real exchange rate (number of comparable goods that domestic consumers can get by trading for a unit of domestic goods).

The real exchange rate EX_r is given by the equation

$$\text{Real exhange rate} = \frac{\text{Nominal exchange rate} \times \text{Domestic price}}{\text{Foreign price}}$$

$$EX_r = \frac{EX \times P}{P_f}. \tag{8.1}$$

To find the cost of the hamburger in dollar terms, we substitute and solve Eq. (8.1):

$$EX_r = \frac{(\text{L}1818/\$)(\$2.56/\text{U.S. Big Mac})}{\text{L}4500/\text{Italian Big Mac}}$$

$$= 1.03 \text{ Italian Big Mac per U.S. Big Mac}$$

Hence at the nominal exchange rate used in the example, \$2.56 buys one Big Mac in the United States but 1.03 Big Macs in Italy. If we use purchasing power to measure the value of a Big Mac, the real exchange rate is 1.03 Italian Big Mac per U.S. Big Mac. In purchasing power terms, Big Macs are more expensive in Columbus, Ohio, than in Rome.

In reality, of course, different countries produce many different goods, so the real exchange rate usually isn't defined by a single good. Instead, it is computed from *price indexes,* which compare the price of a group of goods in one country with the price of a similar group of goods in another country. The consumer price index and the price deflator for the gross domestic product are two examples of price indexes. Just as we did for nominal exchange rates, we can apply the concepts of appreciation and depreciation to real exchange rates. When a currency's real exchange rate rises (its currency appreciates), the country can trade its goods for more units of foreign goods. When a currency's exchange rate falls (its currency depreciates), the country obtains a smaller volume of foreign goods per unit of domestic goods.

The relationship between the nominal and real exchange rates depends on the rates of inflation in the two countries. We know that the real exchange rate EX_r is given by Eq. (8.1). We can calculate the percentage change in the real exchange rate $\Delta EX_r/EX_r$ as the percentage change in the numerator of Eq. (8.1) minus the percentage change in the denominator:

$$\begin{matrix}\text{\% change in} \\ \text{real exchange rate}\end{matrix} = \begin{matrix}\text{\% change in nominal} \\ \text{exchange rate}\end{matrix} + \begin{matrix}\text{\% change in} \\ \text{domestic prices}\end{matrix} - \begin{matrix}\text{\% change in} \\ \text{foreign prices}\end{matrix}$$

or

$$\frac{\Delta EX_r}{EX_r} = \frac{\Delta EX}{EX} + \frac{\Delta P}{P} - \frac{\Delta P_f}{P_f}. \tag{8.2}$$

The *percentage change* in domestic prices $\Delta P/P$ is the domestic rate of inflation π. Similarly, the percentage change in foreign prices is the foreign rate of inflation π_f. Accordingly, we rewrite Eq. (8.2) as

$$\frac{\Delta EX}{EX} = \frac{\Delta EX_r}{EX_r} + (\pi_f - \pi). \tag{8.3}$$

Equation (8.3) shows that the percentage change in the nominal exchange rate has two parts: the percentage change in the real exchange rate and the difference between the foreign and domestic inflation rates. Considering these parts separately reveals two explanations for a rising nominal exchange rate: a rising real exchange rate or a high foreign inflation rate relative to the domestic inflation rate, or both. Similarly, a falling nominal exchange rate reflects some combination of a falling real exchange rate and a high domestic inflation rate relative to the foreign inflation rate.

CHECKPOINT

Bicca and Montblanca are companies in two countries whose currencies are the crown and the royal. Bicca manufactures ballpoint pens that are sold for 2 crowns each. Montblanca manufactures high-quality fountain pens that are sold for 10 royals each. The real exchange rate between Bicca and Montblanca is 10 ballpoint pens per fountain pen. What is the nominal exchange rate? The real exchange rate is 10 ballpoint pens per fountain pen, so, by Eq. (8.1), 20 crowns (the cost of 10 ballpoint pens) equal 10 royals (the cost of one fountain pen), or 1 royal = 2 crowns. o

FOREIGN-EXCHANGE MARKETS

From the perspective of an individual consumer or investor, exchange rates can be used to convert one currency into another. When you go abroad, you must convert U.S. dollars into Japanese yen, euros, British pounds, or other currencies, depending on the country you visit. If the dollar rises in value, you can buy more of other currencies during your travels, enabling you to savor a fine meal or bring back more souvenirs. Likewise, to buy foreign assets, you must convert U.S. dollars into the appropriate currency. Hence if the dollar appreciates, you can buy large amounts of yen-, euro-, or other currency-denominated assets.

Market forces determine the exchange rate that prevails for consumers and investors. International currencies are traded in **foreign-exchange markets** around the world. Foreign-exchange markets are over-the-counter markets; that is, there is no single physical location at which traders gather to exchange currencies, as there is for many domestic stocks and bonds. Computer networks link traders in commercial banks in many countries. Most foreign-exchange trading takes place in London, New York, and Tokyo, with secondary centers in Hong Kong, Singapore, and Zurich. Just as transactions by buyers and sellers in domestic debt markets determine domestic interest rates, transactions in foreign-exchange markets determine the rates at which international currencies are exchanged. Those exchange rates affect costs of acquiring foreign financial assets or foreign goods and services.

With daily turnover in the trillions of dollars, the worldwide foreign-exchange market is one of the largest financial markets in the world. Major market participants are importers and exporters, banks, investment portfolio managers, and central banks. They trade currencies such as the U.S. dollar ($), euro (€), British pound (£), and Japanese yen (¥) around the clock. The busiest trading time is in the morning (U.S. Eastern Standard Time), when the London and New York markets are open for trading, but trading is always taking place somewhere. A trader in New York might be awakened in the middle of the night to adjust foreign-exchange positions in response to events overseas.

Two types of currency transactions are conducted in foreign-exchange markets. In **spot market transactions,** currencies or bank deposits are exchanged immediately (subject to a two-day settlement period). The current exchange rate, or *spot rate,* is analogous to a price quote on a share of GM stock from your broker—the price at which you may buy a share of GM right now. In **forward transactions,** currencies or bank deposits are to be exchanged at a set date in the future. That is, investors sign the contract today for a given quantity of currency and exchange rate. At a specific future date, the actual exchange will take place at a rate known as the *forward rate.*

DETERMINING LONG-RUN EXCHANGE RATES

We begin by examining how exchange rates are determined in the long run and then apply that understanding to their determination in the short run.

Supply and Demand

In the long run, exchange rates are set by economic fundamentals such as price levels or productivity levels in different countries. Given values of these economic variables, we can think of the supply and demand for a currency—let's say dollars—as depending on the price of that currency relative to others—the exchange rate.

The demand for U.S. dollars represents the demand by domestic residents and foreign residents to buy U.S. goods and financial assets. The lower the exchange rate, the higher is the quantity of dollars demanded. For example, if the British pound/dollar exchange rate falls from $1 = £0.64 to $1 = £0.56, it is cheaper to convert pounds into dollars to buy U.S. goods or financial assets, and the quantity of dollars demanded rises.

The supply of U.S. dollars represents the dollars supplied by U.S. and foreign individuals and financial institutions who hold dollars and want to buy non-dollar-denominated goods or assets. Suppliers trade dollars for British pounds and other currencies in the foreign-exchange market. As the exchange rate rises (that is, as the dollar appreciates against the pound), the quantity of U.S. dollars supplied rises. This is because at higher exchange rates, the dollars supplied command a higher price in terms of other currencies in the foreign-exchange market.

In the long run, the equilibrium exchange rate balances the quantity of dollars demanded and supplied. Changes in the long-run value of the exchange rate are due to the reactions of traders in the foreign-exchange market to changes in economic fundamentals.

Figure 8.1

Exchange Rate Between the British Pound and Dollar, 1973–2000

Over the period from 1973 through 1985, the exchange rate exhibited a generally upward trend (with an exception in the late 1970s), as the dollar appreciated against the pound. This trend was reversed between 1985 and 1992, as the dollar depreciated against the pound. Since 1993, the dollar's value has fallen modestly against the pound.

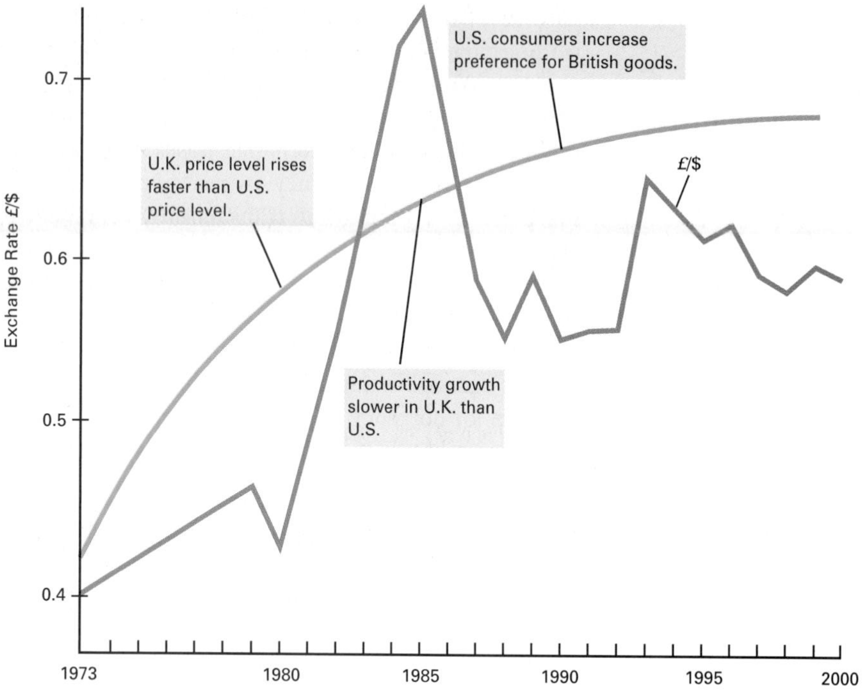

Economic Fundamentals and Long-Run Exchange Rate Trends

Figure 8.1 shows the long-term trends in the exchange rate between British pounds and U.S. dollars. Four key factors account for long-run trends in the supply of and demand for currencies in the foreign-exchange market: price level differences, productivity differences, consumer preferences, and trade barriers.

Price level differences. When the price level increases in the United Kingdom relative to the price level in the United States, U.K. goods or financial assets become more costly compared to similar U.S. goods or financial assets. If the price level rises faster in the United Kingdom than in the United States—that is, if inflation is higher in the United Kingdom than in the United States—the pound is less useful as a store of value than the dollar. A higher price level in the United Kingdom increases the supply of pounds, causing the equilibrium exchange rate to fall. All else being equal, an increase in the price level relative to price levels in other countries causes the country's currency to depreciate. As Fig. 8.1 illustrates, the excess growth of the U.K. price level over the U.S. price level in the late 1970s led the pound to depreciate against the dollar.

Productivity differences. Productivity growth measures the increase in a country's output for a given level of input. When a country has a higher rate of productivity growth, its firms can produce goods more cheaply than its foreign competitors can. As a result, that country's domestic goods can be supplied at prices lower than those of comparable foreign goods, thereby increasing the demand for domestic goods and increasing the demand for domestic currency. But if a

USING THE NEWS . . .

Reading Exchange Rates

Current spot and forward exchange rates for all major currencies are reported each day in *The Wall Street Journal.* The first entry for a country is the spot exchange rate. For Germany, on December 15, 2000, DM1.00 could be exchanged for \$0.4576, or (equivalently) \$1.00 = DM2.1854. However, the 180-day forward exchange rate is \$0.4609 per deutsche mark, so \$1.00 = DM2.1698. This slight difference between the forward and spot rates exists because the investors expect the foreign-exchange value of the dollar to fall slightly relative to the deutsche mark by about 0.7%, or from DM2.1854 to DM2.1698. In general, when the forward rate is greater than the spot rate, investors expect the domestic currency to depreciate. When the forward rate is less than the spot rate, investors expect the domestic currency to appreciate. At its peak in 1985, \$1.00 could be exchanged for DM2.942; that is, the foreign-exchange value of the dollar fell by about 26% between 1985 and December 2000.

CURRENCY TRADING

EXCHANGE RATES

Friday, December 15, 2000

The New York foreign exchange mid-range rates below apply to trading among banks in amounts of \$1 million and more, as quoted at 4 p.m. Eastern time by Telerate and other sources. Retail transactions provide fewer units of foreign currency per dollar.

Name of Country and unit of account. (Argentina (Peso))

Price as of last trading day. (Canada, .6577)

Spot exchange rate. (Germany (Mark))

Forward exchange rate. (Germany, 6-months forward)

	U.S. \$ equiv.		Currency per U.S. \$	
Country	Fri	Thu	Fri	Thu
Argentina (Peso)	1.0011	1.0004	.9989	.9996
Australia (Dollar)	.5445	.5424	1.8376	1.8435
Austria (Schilling)	.06504	.06479	15.376	15.435
Bahrain (Dinar)	2.6525	2.6525	.3770	.3770
Belgium (Franc)	.0222	.0221	45.0750	45.2495
Brazil (Real)	.5088	.5092	1.9655	1.9640
Britain (Pound)	1.4747	1.4731	.6781	.6788
1-month forward	1.4756	1.4740	.6777	.6784
3-months forward	1.4768	1.4752	.6771	.6779
6-months forward	1.4782	1.4767	.6765	.6772
Canada (Dollar)	.6577	.6584	1.5205	1.5189
1-month forward	.6582	.6588	1.5194	1.5178
3-months forward	.6589	.6595	1.5177	1.5162
6-months forward	.6598	.6606	1.5157	1.5138
Chile (Peso)	.001743	.001740	573.85	574.85
China (Renminbi)	.1208	.1208	8.2768	8.2768
Colombia (Peso)	.0004594	.0004584	2176.75	2181.50
Czech. Rep. (Koruna)	...	...	...	...
Commercial rate	.02585	.02561	38.691	39.045
Denmark (Krone)	.1200	.1196	8.3310	8.3627
Ecuador (US Dollar)-e	1.0000	1.0000	1.0000	1.0000
Finland (Markka)	.1505	.1499	6.6436	6.6694
France (Franc)	.1364	.1359	7.3295	7.3579
1-month forward	.1366	.1361	7.3187	7.3472
3-months forward	.1370	.1364	7.3005	7.3290
6-months forward	.1374	.1369	7.2771	7.3054
Germany (Mark)	.4576	.4558	2.1854	2.1939
1-month forward	.4583	.4565	2.1822	2.1907
3-months forward	.4594	.4576	2.1768	2.1852
6-months forward	.4609	.4591	2.1698	2.1782
Greece (Drachma)	.002626	.002616	380.75	382.26
Hong Kong (Dollar)	.1282	.1282	7.7999	7.7998
Hungary (Forint)	.003385	.003367	295.47	296.99

Source: The Wall Street Journal, December 18, 2000. Republished by permission of Dow Jones, Inc. via Copyright Clearance Center, Inc. © 2000 Dow Jones and Company, Inc. All Rights Reserved Worldwide. (Quotes are from December 15, 2000.)

country's productivity growth is lower than that of other countries, the goods it sells become more expensive, and all else being equal, its currency will depreciate. An increase in a country's productivity relative to that of other countries leads to higher demand for the domestic currency, causing the real and nominal exchange rate to increase. During the 1970s and much of the 1980s, the rate of productivity growth in the United States exceeded that of the United Kingdom, providing additional upward pressure on the long-run pound/dollar exchange rate.

Preferences for domestic or foreign goods. If U.S. consumers demand British-made goods (cars, cameras, and so on), they will demand pounds to buy these goods, putting upward pressure on the pound and depreciating the dollar.

Conversely, if U.K. consumers demand U.S. goods (clothes, compact discs, and so on), they will buy dollars, increasing the worldwide demand for dollars and causing the dollar to appreciate. Thus the real exchange rate changes in response to a shift in households' and firms' preferences for domestic or foreign goods. Unless inflation rates change, nominal exchange rates also change. We can hold everything else constant and generalize this connection. A country's currency appreciates in the long run in response to an increase in demand for its exports. An increase in a country's demand for imports from other countries causes its currency to depreciate in the long run. During the mid-1980s, for example, many U.S. consumers considered some British goods to be higher-quality products than comparable U.S.-produced goods. This shift in preferences increased demand for pounds and contributed to the depreciation of the dollar against the pound in the second half of the decade.

Trade barriers. Countries do not always allow goods to be traded freely with no market intervention. One common trade barrier is **quotas,** or limits on the volume of foreign goods that can be brought into a country. Another trade barrier is **tariffs,** or taxes on goods purchased from other countries. Suppose, for example, that the United States places a tariff on U.K. leather goods. U.S. consumers then find U.K.-made leather goods more expensive than U.S.-made leather goods. The trade barrier increases cost-conscious U.S. consumers' demand for U.S.-made leather goods. As a result, the demand for dollars (to buy U.S.-made leather goods) is higher than if there were no tariff. Hence, all else being equal, with trade barriers, the quantity of U.S.-made leather goods sold will remain high even when the dollar's value on foreign-exchange markets is high. Trade barriers increase demand for the domestic currency, leading to a higher exchange rate in the long run for the country imposing the barriers.

As we will see, economists have used information on long-term determinants of the exchange rate to develop a theory of exchange rate levels.

The Law of One Price and the Purchasing Power Parity Theory

Our analysis of exchange rates in the long run begins using the **law of one price.** This law states that if two countries produce an identical good, profit opportunities should ensure that its price is the same in both countries, no matter which country produces the good.[†] Suppose that a yard of cloth produced in the United States sells for \$10 and that the same type of cloth produced by a British manufacturer costs 5 pounds (£) per yard. The law of one price says that the exchange rate between the U.S. dollar and the British pound must be £5/\$10, or £0.5 per \$1. Why? If the exchange rate were £0.25 = \$1, U.S. cloth would be cheaper than British cloth. British consumers would demand dollars to buy the cloth at a bargain. (In the United Kingdom, U.S. cloth would sell for \$10 × 0.25 = £2.50, which is cheaper than the £5 charged by British manu-

[†]There is an important qualification, however: The good should be tradeable, and price differences are allowed to the extent that they reflect transportation costs. In the Big Mac example earlier, trading Big Macs between Rome and Columbus would be difficult.

facturers. In the United States, British cloth would sell for £5/0.25 = \$20 per yard, which is more expensive than U.S.-produced cloth at \$10 per yard. As a result, there would be no demand for British cloth.) The demand for dollars would bid up the value of the dollar, and the exchange rate would eventually return to £0.5 per \$1. But if the exchange rate were £0.75 per \$1, British cloth would be cheaper than U.S. cloth, eliminating the demand for U.S. cloth. The demand for pounds to buy British cloth would rise, pushing up the value of the pound, until the exchange rate was restored to £0.5 per \$1.

When we compare the international prices for an identical good, the law of one price holds. When we extend the concept and apply it to a group of goods, it becomes the purchasing power parity theory of exchange rate determination. The **purchasing power parity (PPP) theory** is based on the assumption that real exchange rates are constant. Differences in inflation rates in the two countries cause changes in the nominal exchange rate between two currencies. We can demonstrate this relationship by rearranging terms in Eq. (8.1):

$$EX = EX_r\left(\frac{P_f}{P}\right).$$

Because the law of one price holds that EX_r is constant, increases or decreases in the nominal exchange rate, EX, reflect changes in relative price levels between the two countries.

In the U.S. and British cloth example, a 5% expected increase in the U.K. price level relative to the U.S. price level should cause the dollar to appreciate by 5% because EX_r is constant:

$$\frac{\Delta EX}{EX} = \frac{\Delta EX_r}{EX_r} + (\pi_f - \pi) = 0 + 0.05, \quad \text{or} \quad 5\%.$$

When British expected inflation exceeds U.S. expected inflation and the real exchange rate doesn't change, the dollar rises in value. Under the PPP theory, the dollar's purchasing power has risen relative to that of the pound.

In general, the PPP theory of exchange rate determination suggests that whenever a country's price level is expected to fall relative to another country's price level, its currency should appreciate relative to the other country's currency. In the preceding example the dollar appreciated by 5% relative to the British pound. Conversely, whenever a country's price level is expected to rise relative to another country's price level, its currency should depreciate, as the U.K. currency did in the example.

Does the Theory Match Reality?

While the PPP theory generally predicts correctly the long-run direction of changes in the exchange rate, researchers have found that actual exchange rate movements reflect more than differences in price levels. That is, movements in exchange rates are not completely consistent with the PPP theory. Part of this failure results from characteristics of the goods traded. Some commodities (oil, steel, and wheat, for example) are pretty much the same regardless of where they are produced, whereas most other goods are differentiated, or not identical. For example, Kodak and Nikon both manufacture cameras, but their products' characteristics are different, and so the prices may differ. For differentiated products, the law of one price doesn't hold.

Another measurement problem with the PPP theory is that not all goods and services are traded in international markets. It might be cheaper to get your shoes repaired in Berlin than in New York, but not many New Yorkers would fly to Berlin for that purpose. Similarly, other services such as child care and haircuts or goods such as meals in restaurants and houses are not tradeable internationally. Thus significant differences in prices of nontraded goods and services in various countries are not completely reflected in exchange rates.

Finally, the PPP theory's underlying assumption that the real exchange rate is constant is not reasonable. As we noted above, the real exchange rate can vary if there are shifts in preferences for domestic or foreign goods and if there are trade barriers. If inflation rates do not change, these factors also can explain shifts in nominal exchange rates.

CHECKPOINT

Suppose that U.S. consumers follow a "Buy American" strategy in their purchases for a long period of time. Predict the consequences for the nominal exchange rate and the value of the dollar. If other determinants of the nominal exchange rate are held constant, an increased preference for domestic goods over imports will raise the nominal exchange rate. The domestic currency will appreciate. o

DETERMINING SHORT-RUN EXCHANGE RATES

Returning to Fig. 8.1, note that if we examine shorter intervals, we see that the exchange rate is very volatile. Indeed exchange rates can fluctuate by several percentage points even during a single day. Hence there must be other reasons that influence nominal exchange rates that we have not accounted for in the purchasing power parity theory and the analysis of changes in demand for domestic and foreign goods.

Figure 8.2 shows that, during the early 1980s, the value of the dollar generally increased substantially relative to other major currencies. The strong dollar was a boon to U.S. tourists, who flocked across the Atlantic to travel in Europe. The strong dollar also enabled U.S. investors to buy more foreign assets. But in the late 1980s and early 1990s, the dollar's value lost ground to other leading currencies, and large numbers of tourists from other countries descended on the United States. To understand why these fluctuations in nominal exchange rates occurred over short periods of time, we first need to focus on the way in which exchange rates are determined in the market for international currencies.

In addition to trade in domestic and foreign goods, financial assets are traded in global financial markets. Because these markets are linked by sophisticated telecommunications systems and trading can occur around the clock,

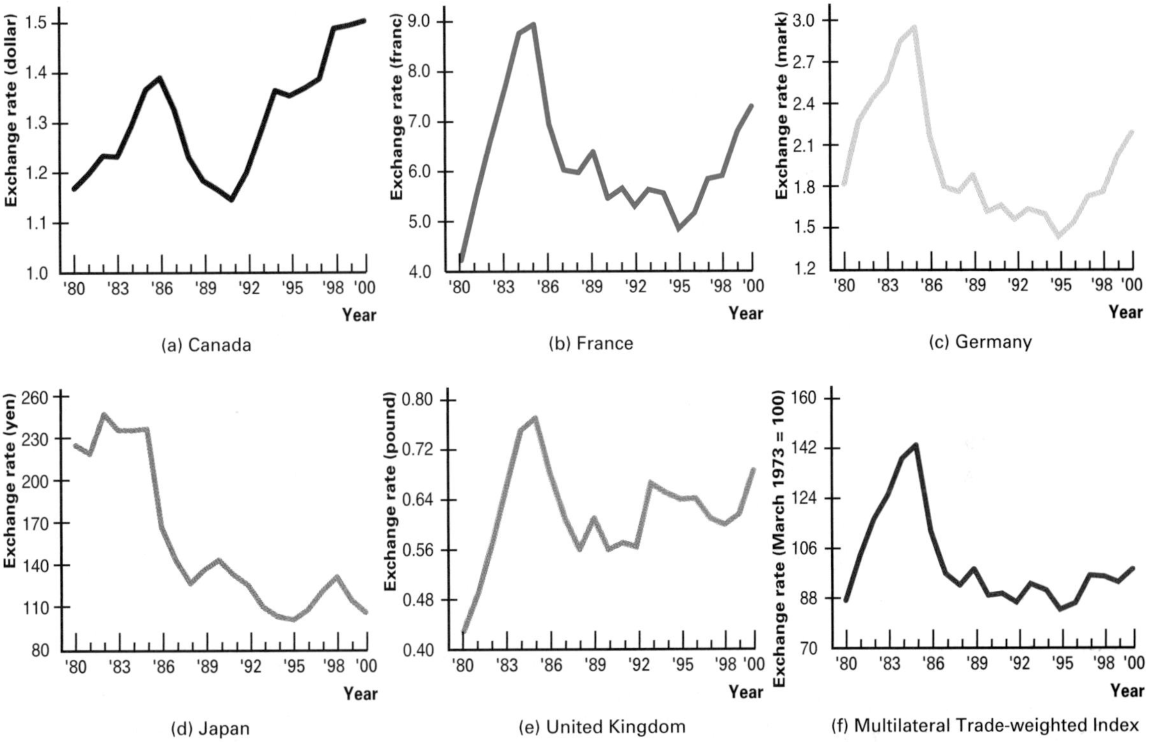

Figure 8.2 **Nominal Exchange Rate: U.S. Dollars versus Other Major Currencies**

The U.S. dollar exchange rate rose in the first half of the 1980s, generally declined through the mid-1990s, and rose again in the late 1990s.

investors in financial assets can trade rapidly and adjust their views of currency values almost instantaneously. Traders of financial assets change their positions as expectations of the currency's value or returns on foreign assets change.

In this section, we focus on the factors that cause the exchange rate to have a particular value at one point in time (the short run). We describe how actions of buyers and sellers of domestic and foreign financial assets and traders in the foreign exchange market determine the short-run equilibrium value of the exchange rate. In the next section, we discuss what might cause this value to vary from one point in time to another.

In the short run, we can express the exchange rate as the price of financial assets in one currency relative to the price of similar financial assets in another currency. In particular, the nominal exchange rate represents the price of domestic financial assets (bank deposits or Treasury bills) denominated in domestic currency in terms of foreign financial assets (foreign bank deposits or government bonds) denominated in foreign currency. For example, if the United States and Japan have an exchange rate of ¥120/$1, a $100 U.S. bank deposit costs ¥12,000. By treating the exchange rate as the price of one asset relative to the price of another, we can use the determinants of portfolio choice (introduced in Chapter 5) to show how exchange rates are determined in the short run.

Comparing Expected Returns on Domestic and Foreign Assets

Let's begin with an example of how exchange rate movements affect your comparison of interest rates on financial instruments in different countries. Suppose that you want to invest \$1000 for one year. You narrow your choices to a U.S. Treasury bill or a Japanese government bond. The U.S. instrument pays interest and principal in dollars with a nominal interest rate of 5% per year. The Japanese instrument pays interest and principal in yen and carries a nominal interest rate of 5% per year.

If the risk, liquidity, and information characteristics of the two instruments are comparable,[†] which one should you buy? The theory of portfolio allocation tells you that if both instruments are denominated in the same currency, you should invest in the one with the higher return. However, because the two assets are denominated in different currencies, you also have to estimate whether the exchange rate between the U.S. dollar and the Japanese yen will change during the year in predicting your return.

How can you allow for a change in exchange rates in making an investment decision? You need to measure the return on the two instruments, using dollars as a common yardstick. To do so, express expected returns on both securities in dollars. If you invest \$1000 in the U.S. Treasury bill, you will receive an interest return of \$50, so your investment will be worth \$1050 after one year.

For the Japanese bond, you first must convert your \$1000 into yen; a year from now, you must convert your principal and interest from yen back into dollars to compare the return with that from the U.S. bond. Suppose that the current nominal exchange rate is ¥100/\$1 and that you expect the exchange rate to rise by 5% during the coming year. The expected future exchange rate, EX^e, then, is (¥100)(1.05)/\$1 = ¥105/\$1. When you convert \$1000 into yen at the current exchange rate, you have ¥100,000 for investment. After receiving a 5% interest return, your investment is worth ¥105,000 after a year. You expect the exchange rate at that time to be ¥105/\$1, so the expected dollar value of your investment will be ¥105,000/105 = \$1000. Hence, even though the Japanese bond pays the same stated rate of interest as the U.S. Treasury bill, it carries a lower expected return: \$0 instead of \$50.[††]

From the example, we can write a general equation an investor can use to compare total returns from investing \$1 in a domestic or a foreign asset. Let i and i_f represent the interest rate for the domestic and the foreign security, respectively. Investing \$1 in the domestic security yields $\$(1 + i)$ after a year. Now let EX represent foreign-currency units per dollar; that is, \$1 will buy EX of the foreign security. At the end of a year, the amount invested yields a total

---

[†]Recall that the theory of portfolio allocation tells us that investors should compare expected returns on assets with similar risk, liquidity, and information characteristics. Comparing the expected return on a U.S. Treasury bond with that on a debt security for a high-risk Japanese firm, for example, would not be appropriate.

[††]This result is analogous to the difference between the current yield and total return for domestic assets, given the possibility of capital gains and losses, which we discussed in Chapter 4.

of $EX(1 + i_f)$ in the foreign-currency units. If we convert back to dollars, the total expected value of the investment after a year will be $EX(1 + i_f)/EX^e$, where EX^e is the expected future exchange rate.

Returning to the example of the one-year Japanese government bond, we have

$$\text{Value of \$1 investment after one year} = \frac{EX(1 + i_f)}{EX^e} = \frac{(¥100/1)(1.05)}{¥105/\$1} = \$1.00,$$

or $1000 for an investment of $1000, as we calculated previously.

For simplicity, we can approximate this expression with one that divides the return into two parts, interest and expected exchange rate change:

$$\text{Value of \$1 investment after one year} \cong \underbrace{1 + i_f}_{\text{Interest}} - \underbrace{\frac{\Delta EX^e}{EX}}_{\text{Expected exchange rate change}},$$

where $\Delta EX^e/EX$ represents the expected percentage change in the exchange rate for the year. In our example, $\Delta EX^e/EX = 5\%$, so

$$\text{Value of \$1 invested in a Japanese bond for 1 year} = 1 + 0.05 - (0.05) = \$1.00,$$

or the same zero return that we calculated before. When deciding between domestic and foreign investments, investors consider both the interest rate and the expected change in the exchange rate during the investment time horizon. The decision-making process is guided by the following reasoning: For each $1 you invest in a U.S. Treasury bill, you get back $1 plus 5¢ in interest, or

$$\$1 \xrightarrow{\text{Earns}} \underset{\text{Interest}}{i} \xrightarrow{\text{Yielding}} (1 + i).$$

Investing $1 in a Japanese bond requires more steps. First, you exchange your $1 for ¥100. That ¥100 earns interest of 5% for the year. At the end of the year, you must convert the principal and interest back to dollars at the exchange rate at that time (which you expect to be $1 = ¥105). Thus

$$\$1 \xrightarrow{\text{Exchanged for foreign currency}} EX \xrightarrow{\text{Earns}} \underset{\text{Interest}}{i_f} \xrightarrow{\text{Yielding}} EX(1 + i_f).$$

When you exchange $EX(1 + i_f)$ for domestic currency at the expected future exchange rate,

$$EX(1 + i_f) \xrightarrow{\text{Converts to}} \frac{EX(1 + i_f)}{EX^e} \xrightarrow{\text{Yielding approximately}} 1 + i_f - \frac{\Delta EX^e}{EX}.$$

Now you can compare these two investments in terms of dollars:

Proceeds from domestic asset	Proceeds from foreign asset
$1 + i$	$1 + i_f - \dfrac{\Delta EX^e}{EX}$

As was the case in the example, you would prefer to invest in U.S. Treasury bills if your return, $1 + i$, were greater than the return you would get from investing in Japanese bonds, $1 + i_f - \Delta EX^e/EX$. However, you would prefer to invest in Japanese bonds if your return, $1 + i_f - \Delta EX^e/EX$, were greater than the return, $1 + i$, you would get from investing in U.S. Treasury bills. If the returns on the U.S. and Japanese financial instruments were equal—that is, if $i = i_f - \Delta EX^e/EX$—you would be indifferent between investing in either. This result is analogous to the comparisons investors make between short-term and long-term debt instruments in the domestic market. In that case, when buying a long-term bond, investors consider both the current interest rate and the expected future interest rates.

Foreign-Exchange Market Equilibrium

Today's global economy is characterized by a high degree of **international capital mobility**—that is, the ability of investors to move funds among international markets easily. Hence investors can buy financial assets (with similar risk, liquidity, and information characteristics) denominated in many different currencies in many markets around the world.

Would a situation in which investors could earn a higher expected rate of return from buying Japanese rather than U.S. assets persist for a long time? To anticipate a bit, the answer is no. Let's assume that the U.S. and Japanese assets have identical risk, liquidity, and information characteristics. The theory of portfolio allocation suggests that investors should be indifferent between Japanese and U.S. assets. In other words, the expected returns on the two assets should be the same.

In reality, the opportunity for traders in the foreign-exchange market to make a profit ensures this result. If the Japanese asset has a higher expected rate of return than the U.S. asset, traders around the world recognize a chance to make a profit by selling U.S. Treasury bills to buy Japanese bonds. (Because the two assets are similar, investors and traders have no reason not to do so.) Now, what effect do these buying and selling transactions have on the expected returns? As investors and traders sell dollar-denominated assets (Treasury bills) and buy yen-denominated assets (Japanese bonds), they increase the demand for yen. This higher demand for yen pushes up the yen's value relative to the dollar to the point at which investors are indifferent between holding U.S. or Japanese assets.

What does international capital mobility imply about the relationship of expected returns from different international investment strategies? Let's look at how market forces equalize expected returns on domestic and foreign

Figure 8.3

Determining the Exchange Rate in Financial Markets

In the short run, financial markets determine the exchange rate. At the equilibrium exchange rate $EX^* = 100$, investors' expected rate of return on domestic assets, R, equals the expected rate of return on foreign assets, R_f.

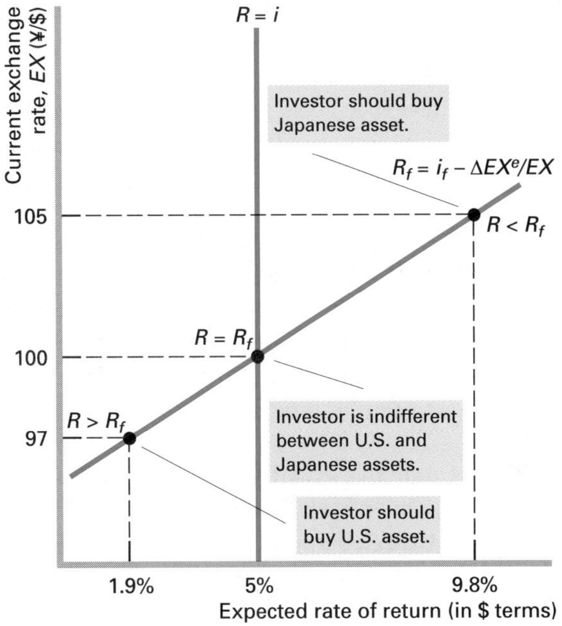

assets. We use a graph to illustrate the process for the U.S. versus Japanese investment example and to show, in general, how exchange rates are determined in the short run.

Figure 8.3 compares the expected returns on a U.S. bond and a Japanese bond with similar characteristics. The *y*-axis is the current exchange rate, or the number of yen per dollar. The *x*-axis is the expected rate of return, in dollar terms, from investing in a U.S. or Japanese asset. For U.S. assets, the expected rate of return R equals the U.S. interest rate i. The expected rate of return on foreign assets in dollar terms R_f equals $i_f - \Delta EX^e/EX$. Hence for Japanese assets, the expected rate of return R_f equals the Japanese interest rate i_f less the expected appreciation of the dollar.

A graph of R against the current yen/dollar exchange rate is simply a vertical line because the return on a U.S. asset in dollar terms is the same regardless of the exchange rate. (It is paid in dollars.) The diagram assumes a U.S. interest rate of 5%.

To graph R_f against the exchange rate, we must first specify the expected future yen/dollar exchange rate. We do this by calculating the dollar's expected rate of appreciation, a key component of R_f. Whenever the current yen/dollar exchange rate exceeds that expected future level, investors believe that the dollar is unusually strong and that it will eventually command fewer yen. That is, they expect the dollar to depreciate. Thus, for a given expected exchange rate, a graph of R_f against the current exchange rate slopes upward; as the yen/dollar exchange rate rises, the dollar's expected rate of appreciation falls, pushing up R_f.

For example, suppose that the future yen/dollar exchange rate is expected to be 100 and that Japanese interest rates are 5%. If the current exchange rate also is 100, no appreciation is expected, and R_f equals the 5% Japanese interest rate. If the current exchange rate is ¥105/$1 and the future exchange rate is expected to be ¥100 = $1, the dollar is expected to depreciate. In this case, investors predict that a dollar will bring only ¥100 in the future, not ¥105 as it does now. This expected 4.8% depreciation of the dollar (from ¥105/$1 to ¥100/$1) increases R_f to 9.8% (the 5% interest rate minus the −4.8% expected appreciation of the dollar). Alternatively, if the yen/dollar exchange rate falls to 97, the dollar is expected to appreciate 3.1% (from ¥97/$1 to ¥100/$1), and R_f falls to 1.9% (the 5% interest rate minus 3.1% expected appreciation). If we place these points on the graph and connect the three combinations of exchange rate and expected rate of return, we get the upward-sloping R_f line in Fig. 8.3.

Which exchange rate prevails in the market for foreign exchange? It is the rate that equates R and R_f. The intersection of R and R_f occurs at ¥100/$1, at which both R and R_f equal 5%. At any other current exchange rate, the expected appreciation or depreciation of the dollar causes R_f to differ from R.

What guarantees that the equilibrium current exchange rate is ¥100/$1? Suppose, for example, that the current yen/dollar exchange rate is 97. Hence the dollar is expected to appreciate by 3.1%. The expected rate of return on Japanese assets in dollar terms is 1.9% (the 5% interest rate minus 3.1% expected appreciation). Traders then will sell Japanese assets and buy U.S. assets because the U.S. interest rate is 5%. The increase in the demand for dollars puts upward pressure on the current yen/dollar exchange rate. Only when the current yen/dollar exchange rate rises to 100 will investors again be indifferent between Japanese and U.S. assets.

Now, suppose that the current yen/dollar exchange rate is ¥105/$1 and we expect the exchange rate to fall to ¥100 = $1. Hence the dollar is expected to depreciate by 4.8%. The expected rate of return on Japanese assets in dollar terms is 9.8% (the 5% interest rate minus the −4.8% expected appreciation). In this case, investors will sell U.S. assets and buy Japanese assets because the U.S. interest rate is only 5%. The increase in the demand for yen puts downward pressure on the current yen/dollar exchange rate. Only when the current yen/dollar exchange rate falls to 100 will investors again be indifferent between holding U.S. and Japanese assets.

Interest Rate Parity

The exchange rate market equilibrium we just described is called the **nominal interest rate parity condition:** When domestic and foreign assets have identical risk, liquidity, and information characteristics, their nominal returns (measured in the same currency) also must be identical. Thus any difference between the nominal interest rates on U.S. assets and those on Japanese assets reflects expected currency appreciation or depreciation. When the domestic interest rate is higher than the foreign interest rate, the domestic currency is expected to depreciate. When the domestic interest rate is lower than the foreign interest rate, the domestic currency is expected to appreciate. Using the expressions for domestic and foreign expected returns, we have the following:

$$\text{Expected return on domestic asset} = \text{Expected return on foreign asset}, \quad \text{or}$$

$$i = i_f - \frac{\Delta EX^e}{EX}. \tag{8.4}$$

The nominal interest rate parity condition does not imply that nominal interest rates are the same around the world. Rather, it says that expected nominal returns on comparable domestic and foreign assets are the same. If domestic and foreign assets are perfect substitutes, international investors are willing to hold outstanding domestic and foreign assets only when the expected returns on those assets are equivalent. Again, if we let R represent the expected rate of return on the domestic asset in dollar terms (equal to i) and R_f represent the expected rate of return on the foreign asset in dollar terms (equal to $i_f - \Delta EX^e/EX$), the nominal interest rate parity condition implies that

$$R = R_f. \tag{8.5}$$

We can also express interest rate parity in terms of the expected real interest rates in the domestic country, r, and that in the foreign country, r_f, and the current and expected values of the real exchange rate, EX_r and EX_r^e, respectively. The **real interest rate parity condition** states that expected real rates of interest measured in terms of the same group of goods are equal, or

$$\frac{\text{Expected gross real return}}{\text{on domestic investment}} = \frac{\text{Expected gross real return}}{\text{on foreign investment}}, \quad \text{or}$$

$$1 + r = (1 + r_f)\left(\frac{EX_r}{EX_r^e}\right). \tag{8.6}$$

The domestic real interest rate, r, and the foreign real interest rate, r_f, do not have to be equal to be consistent with real interest rate parity. Equation (8.6) requires that the two real interest rates be equal when measured in the same group of goods.†

CHECKPOINT

Suppose that the current euro/dollar exchange rate is 1.0 and that investors expect the dollar to appreciate to €1.1/$1 during the next year. If the current U.S. nominal interest rate is 7% per year, what should be the interest rate on a euro financial instrument with similar risk, liquidity, and information characteristics to maintain nominal interest rate parity? The nominal interest rate parity condition indicates that the U.S. interest rate

†If there were only one good, $EX_r = EX_r^e = 1$ and $r = r_f$. This corresponds to the world real interest rate discussed in the analysis of lending, borrowing, and interest rate determination in Chapter 6.

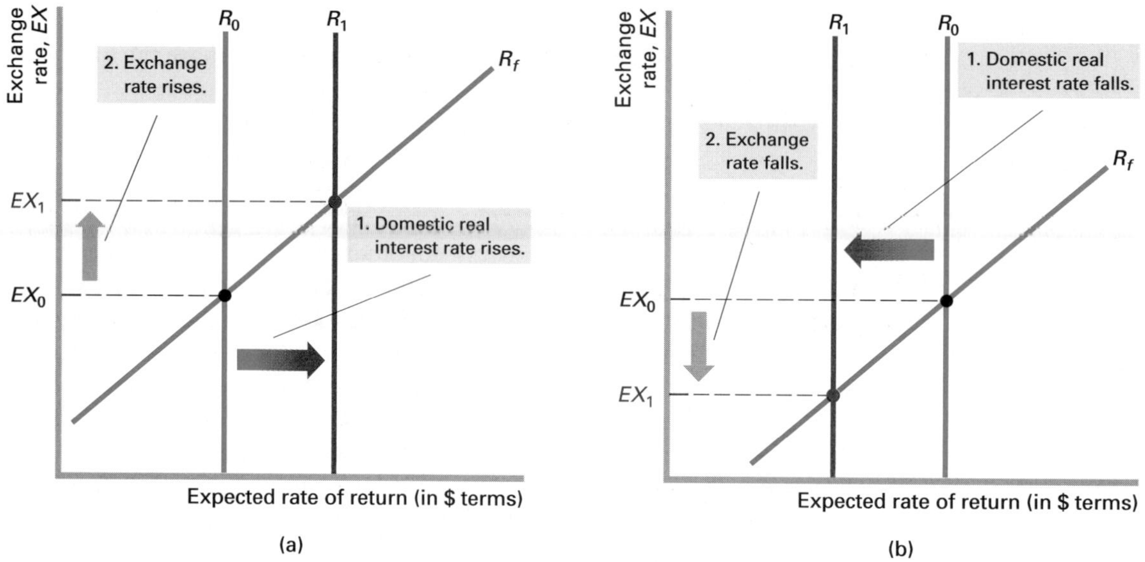

Figure 8.4

Effect of a Change in the Domestic Real Interest Rate on the Exchange Rate

The (a) portion of this graph shows the following:

1. An increase in the domestic real interest rate shifts R to the right from R_0 to R_1.
2. The domestic currency appreciates from EX_0 to EX_1; the exchange rate rises.

The (b) portion of this graph shows the following:

1. A decrease in the domestic real interest rate shifts R to the left from R_0 to R_1.
2. The domestic currency depreciates from EX_0 to EX_1; the exchange rate falls.

minus the expected appreciation of the euro equals the euro interest rate. The deutsche mark is expected to depreciate (1.1 − 1.0)/1.0, or 10%. With the U.S. interest rate at 7%, the euro interest rate would be 7% − (−10%), or 17%. o

EXCHANGE RATE FLUCTUATIONS

So far, we have explained the forces that determine what the exchange rate will be at a point in time, but we have not explained the exchange rate fluctuations that we observe in the short run. That explanation is our objective in this section. Exchange rate fluctuations can cause problems for households, businesses, and policymakers. For example, the soaring dollar in the early 1980s reduced the demand for U.S. exports, hurting U.S. exporters and workers.

We use the graph of the exchange rate and rates of return on domestic and foreign assets (Fig. 8.4) to identify the reasons why exchange rates fluctuate in the short run.

Changes in Domestic Real Interest Rates

The expected return on domestic bonds depends on the interest rate *i* on those instruments. That interest rate is the sum of the expected real rate of interest and

CASE STUDY

Should You Bank on International Investment?

Yields on government bonds in selected countries are reported in *The Wall Street Journal.* The top table of international bond data shows that yields in local currency terms vary significantly between countries. Should you move your savings into foreign bonds to take advantage of interest rate differences? Let's see.

Though not shown in the table, on December 21, 2000, a U.S. Treasury bond maturing in the year 2010 has a yield of 5.03% in U.S. dollar terms. The Japanese bond maturing in the year 2010 has a yield of 1.54% in yen terms, whereas the British bond maturing in 2009 has a yield of 4.97% in pound terms. If international investors and traders are indifferent between Japanese or British bonds, they must expect that the yen will appreciate against the pound. Using Eq. (8.4) we obtain:

$$1.54\% = 4.97\% - \text{Expected appreciation of yen,} \quad \text{or}$$

$$\text{Expected appreciation of the £/¥ exchange rate} = 4.97\% - 1.54\% = 3.43\%.$$

Comparing the two foreign bonds with the U.S. bond, we see that investors and traders expect the yen to appreciate against the dollar and the pound to depreciate against the dollar.

The bottom table shows that local currency and dollar total rates of return from international bonds over a time period differ substantially. Look at the "3 mos" column, which presents total rates of return measured in local currency terms and in dollars. Note, for example, that the total rate of return in yen from holding Japanese bonds in October–December 2000 was 2.37%, and the corresponding total rate of return in dollars was −2.99%. This difference indicates that payments in yen bought fewer dollars by the end of this period, meaning that the dollar appreciated against the yen.

To summarize, if you are thinking of putting some of your savings in assets denominated in a foreign currency, be sure to consider the consequences of exchange rate changes.

INTERNATIONAL GOVERNMENT BONDS

Prices in local currencies, from Telerate.

	COUPON	MATURITY (Mo./yr.)	PRICE	CHANGE	YIELD*
JAPAN (3 p.m. Tokyo)					
#129	4.80%	12/02	108.15	+ 0.03	0.51%
#156	4.50	12/04	115.82	+ 0.13	0.75
#202	1.80	12/10	102.29	+ 0.35	1.54
#39	2.50	12/20	105.41	+ 0.59	2.12
UNITED KINGDOM (5 p.m. London)					
	7.00%	11/01	101.33	+ 0.01	5.409%
	6.75	11/04	105.24	+ 0.01	5.255
	5.75	12/09	105.62	− 0.28	4.965
	6.00	12/28	125.52	− 0.54	4.404

*Equivalent to semi-annual compounded yields to maturity

Total Rates of Return on International Bonds

In percent, based on J.P. Morgan Government Bond Index, Dec. 31, 1987=100

— LOCAL CURRENCY TERMS —

	3 mos.
Japan	+ 2.37
Britain	+ 4.14
Germany	+ 3.38

— U.S. DOLLAR TERMS —

	3 mos.
Japan	− 2.99
Britain	+ 8.01
Germany	+ 10.79

Source: The Wall Street Journal, December 22, 2000. Republished by permission of Dow Jones, Inc. via Copyright Clearance Center, Inc. © 2000 Dow Jones and Company, Inc. All Rights Reserved Worldwide. (Quotes are from December 21, 2000.)

the expected rate of inflation. As Fig. 8.4(a) shows, if expected inflation is held constant, an increase in the domestic real interest rate increases the expected rate of return on domestic assets, shifting the R curve to the right from R_0 to R_1. Because of the higher return on domestic assets, investors increase their demand for dollars to buy domestic assets, resulting in an increase in the exchange rate from EX_0 to EX_1. But, as Fig. 8.4(b) shows, a decrease in the domestic real interest rate causes the expected real rate of return to shift to the left, from R_0 to R_1. The lower return on domestic assets increases investors' demand for foreign assets and thus for foreign currency. The higher demand for foreign currency exerts downward pressure on the current exchange rate, which falls from EX_0 to EX_1. To summarize, if nothing else changes, an increase in the domestic real interest rate causes the domestic currency to appreciate. A decrease in the domestic real interest rate causes the domestic currency to depreciate.

Changes in Domestic Expected Inflation

A change in the domestic nominal interest rate also can be caused by a change in expected inflation for any real rate of interest. In making our graphical analysis in Fig. 8.4 of the effect of changes in the domestic real interest rate on the current exchange rate, we assumed that the foreign expected rate of return, R_f, did not shift. However, when domestic expected inflation changes, the expected change in the exchange rate likely is affected. Why? An increase in domestic expected inflation erodes the currency's purchasing power, causing it to depreciate, or lose value against other currencies. Conversely, a decrease in domestic expected inflation raises the domestic currency's purchasing power, causing the domestic currency to appreciate.

Figure 8.5 shows that two effects are at work when the domestic interest rate increases because of an increase in expected inflation. First, the higher domestic nominal interest rate shifts the expected rate of return to the right from R_0 to R_1. Because returns on U.S. assets become more attractive relative to returns on foreign assets, investors increase their demand for dollars, and the current exchange rate rises. Second, an increase in expected inflation reduces expected appreciation of the domestic currency, so the expected foreign rate of return shifts to the right, from R_{f0} to R_{f1}, and foreign assets become more attractive for investors. Hence the demand for dollars decreases, and the current exchange rate falls. These two effects pull the current exchange rate in opposite directions.

Which effect dominates? Most analyses indicate that the decline in the anticipated appreciation of the domestic currency is greater than the increase in the domestic interest rate from the increase in expected inflation. Hence, for any current exchange rate, the expected return on domestic assets rises by less than the expected return on foreign assets.† As shown in Fig. 8.5, the shift from R_0 to the right to R_1 is smaller than the shift from R_{f0} to R_{f1}, causing the exchange rate to decline from EX_0 to EX_1. To summarize, an increase in the

†This effect is a feature of models of exchange rate determination in asset markets. See, for example, Rudiger Dornbusch, "Expectations and Exchange Rate Dynamics," *Journal of Political Economy,* 84:1061–1076, 1976.

Figure 8.5

Effect of an Increase in Domestic Expected Inflation on the Exchange Rate

1. For a constant domestic real interest rate, an increase in expected inflation raises the domestic nominal interest rate from R_0 to R_1.
2. At the same time, the higher domestic expected inflation reduces the expected appreciation of the domestic currency. The R_f curve shifts to the right from R_{f0} to R_{f1}.
3. Most empirical studies show that the second effect dominates the first, so the current exchange rate falls from EX_0 to EX_1.

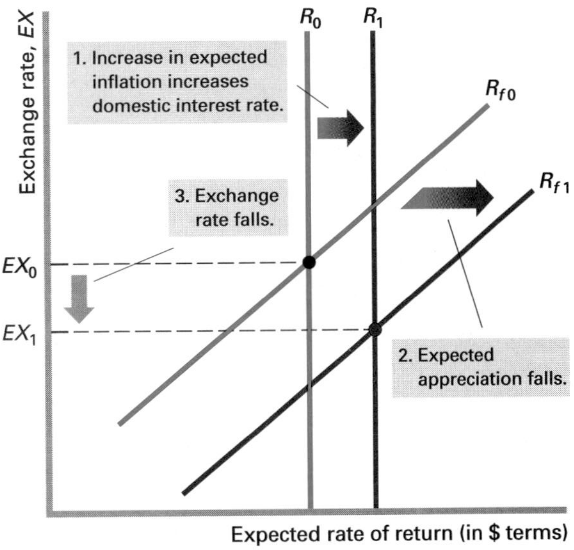

domestic interest rate in response to an increase in domestic expected inflation leads to depreciation of the domestic currency. A decrease in the domestic interest rate in response to a decrease in domestic expected inflation leads to appreciation of the domestic currency.

Changes in Foreign Interest Rates

In July 1993, when German short-term real interest rates rose relative to U.S. short-term real interest rates, domestic tourist industry groups expected that the dollar's value overseas would fall, raising the cost of foreign vacations. Indeed, the dollar's exchange value against the deutsche mark did drop. How could the tourist industry anticipate that this would happen?

To answer that question, let's explore the general case. The expected rate of return for foreign assets depends on both the foreign interest rate and the expected change in the exchange rate. Figure 8.6(a) shows that an increase in the foreign real interest rate shifts the foreign expected rate of return R_{f0} to the right to R_{f1} because, at any exchange rate, the foreign rate of return increases. As a result, the current exchange rate falls. Because the rate of return on foreign assets has gone up, investors and traders buy more foreign currency to buy foreign assets. The availability of a higher expected rate of return on foreign assets increases the demand for those assets relative to domestic assets, increasing the demand for foreign currency and decreasing the demand for domestic currency. As a result, the domestic currency depreciates.

If the foreign real interest rate declines instead, as Fig. 8.6(b) shows, the expected rate of return on foreign assets declines. That shifts the expected rate of return R_{f0} to the left to R_{f1} and increases the exchange rate, leading to an appreciation of the domestic currency. Investors and traders now buy more domestic currency to buy domestic assets because the rate of return on domestic assets has gone up.

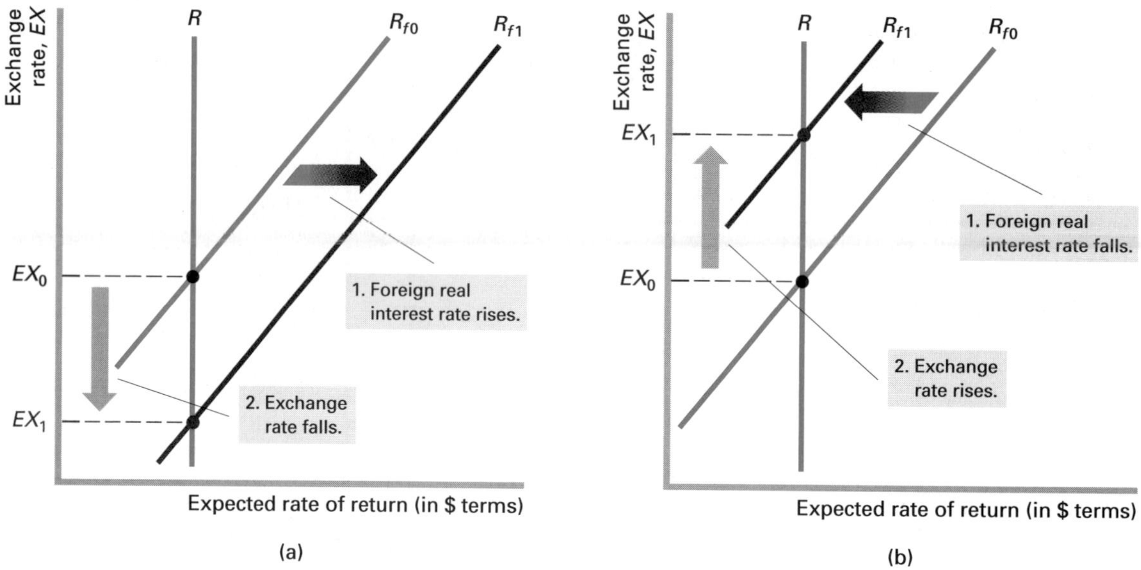

Figure 8.6

Effect of a Change in the Foreign Interest Rate on the Exchange Rate

The (a) portion of this graph shows the following:

1. An increase in the foreign real interest rate shifts R_f to the right from R_{f0} to R_{f1}.
2. The exchange rate falls; the domestic currency depreciates.

The (b) portion of this graph shows the following:

1. A decrease in the foreign real interest rate shifts R_f to the left from R_{f0} to R_{f1}.
2. The exchange rate rises; the domestic currency appreciates.

To summarize, a rise in the foreign real interest rate causes the domestic currency to depreciate. A fall in the foreign interest rate causes the domestic currency to appreciate.

Changes in the Expected Future Exchange Rate

As our analysis of the interest rate parity condition showed, the expected appreciation or depreciation of the domestic currency also affects the expected rate of return on foreign assets. Changes in the current exchange rate account for movements in the foreign rate of return, R_f. Changes in the expected future exchange rate can account for shifts in R_f. Let's examine how this process works by tracing the market forces. If the expected future exchange rate increases, expected appreciation of the domestic currency rises. Investors increase their demand for the domestic currency; all else being equal, the exchange rate rises, as Fig. 8.7(a) shows. Hence the expected rate of return on foreign assets falls, thereby shifting the expected rate of return from R_{f0} to the left to R_{f1} and increasing the exchange rate.

If instead the expected future exchange rate decreases, expected dollar appreciation declines, shifting the expected rate of return from R_{f0} to the right to R_{f1},

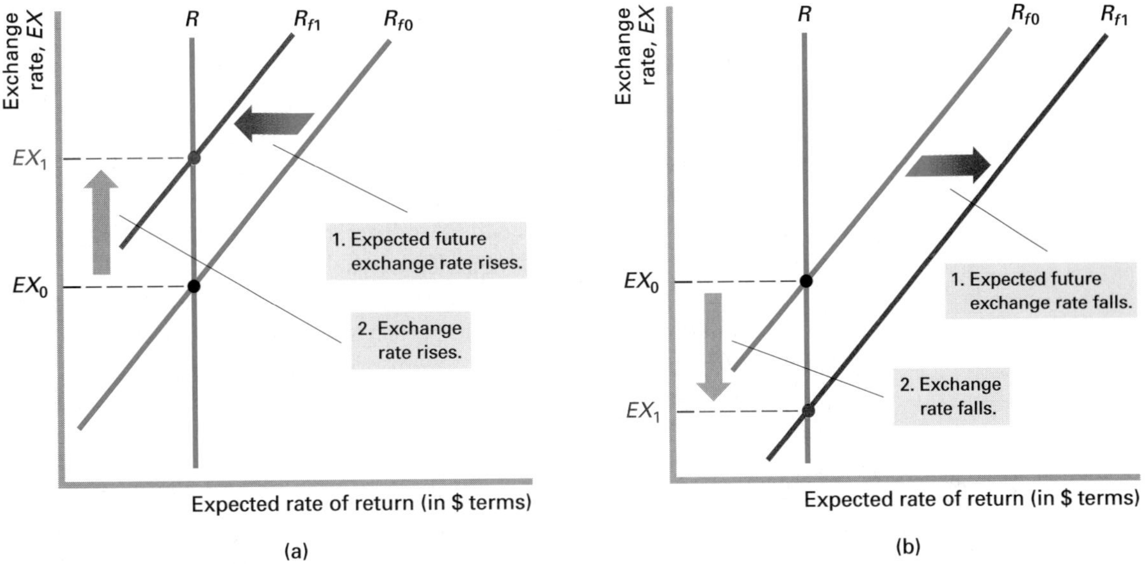

Figure 8.7

Effect of Changes in Exchange Rate Expectations on the Exchange Rate

The (a) portion of this graph shows the following:

1. An increase in the expected future exchange rate decreases the expected return on foreign assets, causing R_f to shift to the left from R_{f0} to R_{f1}.
2. The current exchange rate rises.

The (b) portion of this graph shows the following:

1. A decrease in the expected future exchange rate increases the expected return on foreign assets, causing R_f to shift to the right from R_{f0} to R_{f1}.
2. The current exchange rate falls.

as Fig. 8.7(b) shows. Investors now expect a higher return from investing in foreign assets, because they will be able to exchange foreign currency for more units of domestic currency. As foreign assets now have a higher expected rate of return, R_f shifts to the right in Fig. 8.7(b), and the exchange rate falls. In September 1992, for example, international investors' and foreign exchange traders' belief that the foreign exchange value of the British pound would soon fall pushed the current exchange rate down. The British government was forced to abandon its efforts to stabilize the value of the pound against other European currencies.

An increase or decrease in the expected future exchange rate reflects shifts in one or more of the underlying determinants of the exchange rate—differences in price levels, differences in productivity growth, shifts in preferences for domestic or foreign goods, and differences in trade barriers—as well as changes in expected future interest rates.

Factors that increase the expected future exchange rate shift the foreign expected rate of return to the left and cause the domestic currency to appreciate. Factors that decrease the expected future exchange rate shift the foreign expected rate of return to the right and cause the domestic currency to depreciate.

Currency Premiums in Foreign-Exchange Markets

The nominal interest rate parity condition in Eq. (8.4) is based on the assumption that domestic and foreign investments are perfect substitutes. This assumption is similar to the concept in the expectations theory of the term structure of interest rates (Chapter 7): If we hold default risk, liquidity, information costs, and taxation constant, assets of different maturities have perfect substitutability. That is, you should be indifferent between holding a 30-year Treasury bond and holding a sequence of three-month Treasury bills, one after the other. When we discussed the term structure, we pointed out that the preferred habitat theory allows for imperfect substitutability of assets so that differences in yield partially reflect a term premium. For example, investors might require a higher rate of return to induce them to hold long-term bonds.

We can modify the nominal interest rate parity condition by incorporating into it imperfect substitutability between domestic and foreign currency assets. We do this with a currency premium. The **currency premium** is a number that indicates investors' collective preference for financial instruments denominated in one currency relative to those denominated in another. That is,

$$i = i_f - \frac{\Delta EX^e}{EX} - h_{f,d}, \tag{8.7}$$

where $h_{f,d}$ is the currency premium.

For example, suppose that the one-year Treasury bill rate in the United States is 8% and the one-year government bond rate in Germany is 5%. Suppose also that investors expect the dollar to depreciate against the deutsche mark by 4% over the coming year. Using Eq. (8.7), we find that the one-year deutsche mark/dollar currency premium is

$$8\% = 5\% - (-4\%) - h_{f,d}, \quad \text{or} \quad h_{f,d} = 1\%.$$

That is, investors require a 1% higher expected rate of return on the German bond relative to the U.S. Treasury bond to make the two financial instruments equally attractive.

If $h_{f,d}$ is positive, the modified nominal interest rate parity condition, Eq. (8.7), implies that investors prefer the domestic-currency asset, assuming that nothing else changes. In other words, investors will not buy a foreign bond if the expected rate of return just equals that of a domestic bond. The foreign bond is less preferable, so investors must receive something extra—a currency premium—to offset their hesitancy. The size of the currency premium depends on investors' aversion to currency risks, differences in liquidity in markets, a lack of information about foreign investment opportunities, and investors' belief that one country is more stable or safer than another. These three factors contribute to currency risk and make investors prefer to hold domestic assets rather than foreign assets.

OTHER TIMES, OTHER PLACES . . .

Interest and Exchange Rates in the 1980s

Our analysis of the relationship between exchange rates and interest rates suggests that shifts in the real interest rate in the United States, relative to other countries, can affect the exchange rates. The accompanying figure shows the real interest rate and the exchange rate index, which is a trade-weighted exchange rate calculated by the Fed. As you can see in the figure, the real interest rate and the exchange rate both increased during the early 1980s. Both peaked in 1985 and fell for the next three years, rising somewhat again in 1989.

What events caused these fluctuations? The rise in the real interest rate reflects shifts in international lending and borrowing. In the early 1980s, a rising stock market, probusiness policies of the Reagan administration, and a cut in taxes on investment made the United States an attractive place in which to invest. In addition, many international investors were concerned that less developed countries (LDCs) had borrowed too much from the international capital market in the 1970s, and they wanted to shift funds from those countries. At the same time, large U.S. budget deficits increased government borrowing. This combination of events increased the real interest rate and demand for U.S. assets, raising the exchange rate. Thus the U.S. real interest rate exceeded foreign real interest rates in the early 1980s. The interest rate parity condition, Eq. (8.4), implies the dollar would appreciate. This did indeed happen.

In the second half of the 1980s, real interest rates in the United States were generally lower than in the first half and were not significantly greater than those in other industrial countries (in part because of an increase in investment demand abroad). With this change of events, the demand for dollar-denominated assets declined relative to assets denominated in other currencies. Using the interest rate parity condition, we would predict a decline in the exchange rate, which subsequently materialized.

These events in the international capital market teach us two lessons. First, understanding shifts in the underlying determinants of lending and borrowing is important for explaining changes in real interest rates around the world. Second, movements in interest rates and exchange rates are related and should be examined together.

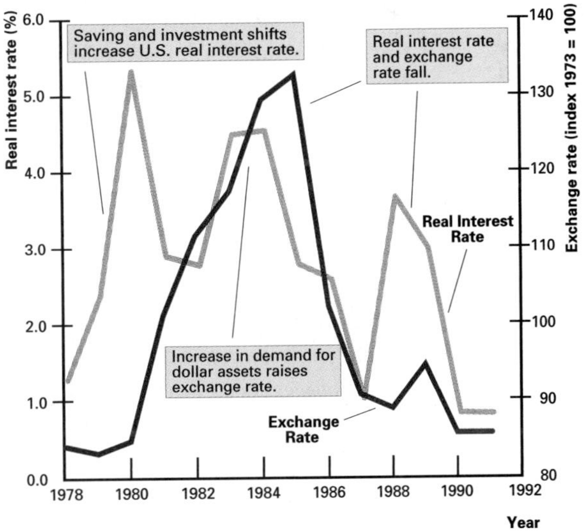

Shifts in currency risk premiums can lead to large gains and losses on investments. For example, Long Term Capital Management, a large U.S. hedge fund, had to be rescued in September 1998, when major increases in currency premiums in emerging markets led to large losses.

A (Big) New Kid on the Block: The Euro

Beginning in 1999, the European monetary union gave birth to the **euro**, a common currency for Austria, Belgium, Finland, France, Germany, Ireland, Italy, Luxembourg, the Netherlands, Portugal, and Spain. The British pound remains separate. Since January 4, 1999, exchange rates of these 11 countries have been fixed against one another and against the euro (worth about $0.89 at the beginning of 2001). By January 1, 2002, colorful new euro notes and coins will appear.

Will national currencies in Europe eventually disappear? In principle, yes. Until January 1, 2002, and for a maximum of six months thereafter, national currencies will continue to circulate (though with fixed exchange rates). By late 2002, however, national currencies are set to disappear, replaced simply by different denominations of the euro.

The new eurozone is a large market whose gross domestic product approaches that of the United States. The euro's debut makes life simpler for travelers, eliminating the need to change money and pay transaction fees at each border crossing. In financial markets, the U.S. dollar is the most important currency for foreign-exchange transactions, with the German mark a distant second. Many analysts believe that the euro has strong potential to compete with the U.S. dollar as the most widely traded currency.

Will the euro work? No one knows for sure. Since the meeting in Maastricht, the Netherlands, in December 1991, in which European Community leaders devised a plan for a single currency for Europe, the plan has experienced many ups and downs. The euro entered the currency stage on January 1, 1999, at an initial exchange rate of €1 = $1.18. While many European central banks hoped the euro would be a strong currency alternative to the U.S. dollar, its value actually declined by about 15% to $1.00 per euro by the beginning of 2000 and dropped further by the beginning of 2001.

We can use our economic analysis of exchange rates to show why the euro had such a rocky start against the U.S. dollar. In principle, relative real interest rates (United States versus Europe) or relative expected inflation (United States versus Europe) could be the culprit. The greater villain of the play is the difference between U.S. and European real interest rates. At the time of the euro's emergence, European economies were recovering very slowly from a recession, and real and nominal interest rates were falling. By contrast, the continuing economic boom in the United States caused U.S. real and nominal interest rates to exceed the corresponding European rates. Following Eq. (8.4), then, the higher U.S. interest rates relative to European interest rates led to an expected and actual depreciation of the euro.

How low can the euro go? Many commentators argue that as the recently inaugurated European Central Bank (a counterpart to the Federal Reserve in the United States) improves its credibility with financial markets, the euro's value will rise. Some skeptics maintain, however, that until European economic performance improves substantially relative to that in the United States, the euro will remain weak relative to the U.S. dollar.

KEY TERMS AND CONCEPTS

Appreciation
Currency premium
Depreciation
Euro
Exchange rate
- Nominal exchange rate
- Real exchange rate

Foreign-exchange markets
- Forward transactions
- Spot market transactions

International capital mobility
Law of one price
Nominal interest rate parity condition
Purchasing power parity (PPP) theory
Quotas
Real interest rate parity condition
Tariffs

SUMMARY

1. The exchange rate, or, more precisely, the nominal exchange rate, is the price of one currency in terms of another currency. The real exchange rate is the price of a group of goods in one country relative to the price of the same group of goods in another country. Changes in the nominal exchange rate reflect changes in the real exchange rate, domestic inflation, and foreign inflation.
2. In the long run, the exchange rate between two countries reflects relative price levels (purchasing power parity), relative productivity levels, preferences for domestic or foreign goods, and trade barriers.
3. In the short run, financial markets determine nominal exchange rates as investors and traders compare expected rates of return on domestic and foreign assets.
4. The theory of portfolio allocation suggests that the expected rates of return on domestic and foreign assets with similar default risk, liquidity, and information costs should be the same. The nominal interest rate parity condition states that the domestic nominal interest rate equals the foreign nominal interest rate minus the expected appreciation of the domestic currency. Hence any factor that shifts domestic or foreign interest rates will cause the exchange rate to change. When domestic and foreign assets are not perfect substitutes, the domestic expected rate of return equals the foreign expected rate of return minus a currency premium reflecting risk, liquidity, and information costs.

REVIEW QUESTIONS

1. What is the term for the idea that domestic nominal interest rates should equal foreign nominal interest rates minus the anticipated rate of change of the exchange rate?
2. What is the difference between the nominal exchange rate and the real exchange rate?
3. Why might a fall in the value of the yen be considered good news for Japanese businesses, but bad news for Japanese consumers?
4. If the U.S. dollar appreciates against the euro and the British pound but depreciates against the Japanese yen and the Canadian dollar, do the following exchange rates rise or fall? (a) euro/U.S. dollar; (b) U.S. dollar/pound; (c) yen/U.S. dollar; (d) U.S. dollar/Canadian dollar.
5. Suppose that the price in the United States of German BMWs rises from \$31,000 to \$33,000, the price of Japanese Nikon cameras falls from \$110 to \$105, the price of English shoes falls from \$205 to \$180, and the price of French truffles rises from \$35 to \$40 per box. Which currencies have appreciated against the dollar and which have depreciated?
6. The inflation rate is 3% in the United Kingdom, 1% in Japan, and 5% in the United States. The pound/dollar real exchange rate is rising at a 2%

MOVING FROM THEORY TO PRACTICE . . .

FINANCIAL TIMES DECEMBER 16–17, 2000

The Euro Recovers

The euro yesterday rose to its highest level since the world's main central banks intervened to halt its slide in late September, shrugging aside disappointing economic data.

Concern over faltering U.S. stocks following a profits warning from Microsoft helped the euro climb above the $0.90 level against the dollar.

Hopes that the long-suffering European currency was finally finding its feet were also kindled by a sharp rally against the yen above ¥101 to its highest level in four months. In London it closed at ¥100.9 and $0.898.

The move came despite further evidence of slowing growth in the euro-zone from the Ifo index of German business confidence, which fell for the sixth consecutive month in November to its lowest level of the year.

"Not long ago the euro was hypersensitive to bad news and would refuse to rise on good news," said Ray Attrill, director of research for economic consultancy 4Cast in London. "That the euro is coping well with negative news suggests confidence in the currency is finally recovering."

Expectations that **(a)** George W. Bush would emerge victorious in the race for the U.S. presidency had supported the dollar over recent sessions. Traders have assumed that a Republican administration would loosen the federal purse strings, providing a spur to the slowing U.S. economy and helping to stabilize the stock markets.

(b) But attention has shifted back to concerns over flagging consumer demand and slowing growth in corporate profits. . . .

Profit warnings have risen sharply compared with this time last year.

(c) The bad news has underlined that economic and corporate growth in the United States is slowing, making dollar assets less attractive relative to the eurozone.

Meanwhile, analysts pointed to signs that the exodus of direct investment funds from the eurozone—which has depressed the currency since its inception—may be slowing and even reversing. . . .

Y2K may not have ravaged the world's information technology systems, but the year 2000 was not a happy one for the euro. Introduced in 1999, the euro continued its slide against the U.S. dollar, falling to as low as \$0.83 on October 18, 2000. Some analysts blamed the sometimes-hard-to-understand monetary policy decisions of the European Central Bank; other economists pointed to generally weaker economic performance in Europe than in the United States. As 2000 drew to a close, however, the euro's foreign-exchange value improved somewhat, leading many economists and market participants to speculate about potential explanations for the euro's reversal of fortune.

a If the prevailing view among market participants were that the new Bush administration and the U.S. government would pursue an expansionary fiscal policy, the anticipated boom in the United States would, all else being equal, lift U.S. interest rates. Turning to the nominal interest rate parity condition (assuming that euro-denominated and dollar-denominated bonds are perfect substitutes):

$$i_{\$} = i_{euro} - (\Delta EX^{e}_{euro/\$}/EX_{euro/\$}).$$

If U.S. interest rates are expected to rise, either expected future appreciation of the dollar declines or the current exchange rate increases.

b With slower growth in the United States, U.S. yields should fall, all else being equal. With no changes in euro rates by the European Central Bank, then, the nominal interest rate parity condition predicts that the euro would rise in value against the dollar. Given the increase in the foreign-exchange value of the euro observed in the data, market participants may be placing more weight on a slower-growth scenario for the U.S. economy.

c What if bad news about the U.S. economy leads the Federal Reserve to reduce short-term interest rates in the United States? In this case, a decline in $i_{\$}$ would give the European Central Bank some breathing room to reduce i_{euro} while avoiding a depreciation of the euro against the U.S. dollar. That is, the European Central Bank could avoid the exchange rate changes against the dollar by matching interest rate cuts by the Fed.

For further thought . . .

Suppose that purchasing power parity relationships indicate that the euro is overvalued relative to the U.S. dollar. How would that factor affect the expected rate of return that you would require to invest in existing euro-denominated bonds?

Source: Excerpted from Christopher Swann and Andrew Hill, "Euro Recovers as Fears Grow Over the US Economy," *Financial Times*, December 16–17, 2000. Republished by permission.

rate, and the yen/dollar real exchange rate is falling at a 3% rate. Find the percentage change in the dollar's nominal exchange rate relative to the pound and the yen.

7. If a cow costs $500 in the United States, ¥150,000 in Japan, and €550 (550 euros) in France, and if the law of one price holds, what are the euro/dollar and yen/dollar exchange rates?
8. If inflation is 3% in both the United Kingdom and the United States, what does the purchasing power parity theory imply about whether the dollar will appreciate or depreciate against the pound? What assumption is vital to this theory?
9. U.S. goods have always been popular in Eastern Europe, but because of trade barriers, few imports of such goods were allowed. With the opening of Eastern European economies, what should happen to the value of the dollar?
10. European countries have focused public policies on investment and efficient production during the past decade. If the European program is successful (relative to other countries), what should happen to the euro exchange rate?
11. Suppose that real returns on investments in the United States rise relative to returns in other countries. What would you expect to happen to the value of the dollar?
12. Suppose that, owing to political uncertainty, the market places a currency premium on assets in the country of Panama. Now suppose that constitutional reform provides political stability. What should happen to the difference between U.S. and Panamanian interest rates?
13. What is the name of the new common European currency? Which large European country is not participating in the move to a common currency? Can you think of reasons why a country might not want to give up its domestic currency?

ANALYTICAL PROBLEMS

14. Suppose that the pound/yen exchange rate rises while the dollar/yen exchange rate falls. What should happen to the prices of imports into Japan from the United Kingdom and the United States?
15. If the dollar/pound exchange rate rises and the yen/dollar exchange rate falls, which of the two foreign currencies (if either) appreciates relative to the dollar? Which (if either) depreciates?
16. If $2 buys £1 and €2.2 buys £1, how many euros are required to buy $1?
17. In the spring of 1999, an investor wrote the following to the financial advice column of an on-line magazine: "It says in the papers that interest rates in Japan are under one percent. U.S. Treasury bills currently pay almost five percent. Why isn't everybody borrowing money in Japan and investing it in the United States? It seems like a sure thing." Is it a sure thing?
18. When the Federal Reserve moved to lower U.S. interest rates in the fall of 1998, some analysts argued that this would make it easier for countries like Brazil that wanted to maintain a fixed exchange rate with the U.S. to do so. Explain their reasoning.
19. Where would you invest (at home or abroad) if the domestic interest rate is 6%, the foreign interest rate is 4%, and the expected depreciation of the domestic currency is 1%?
20. If the expected real return on U.S. assets rises while real returns on foreign investments remain unchanged, what should happen to the exchange rate?
21. Suppose that the real interest rate in the United States is substantially higher than the real interest rate in Japan and exchange rates are fixed so as to avoid expected appreciation or depreciation of either currency. What should happen to investment flows into and out of each country?
22. If $1 buys €1, £1 buys €1.5, and £1 buys $2, can you trade these currencies to make a profit? If so, how much money can you make if the exchange rates remain fixed at these levels?
23. If a compact disc (CD) costs $16 in the United States, £6 in the United Kingdom, and ¥3500 in

Japan—and the exchange rates are \$2/£1 and ¥200/\$1—what are the real exchange rates in terms of CDs?

24. Suppose that you are a U.S. investor considering investment opportunities in the United States, Canada, and Mexico. You can earn nominal returns of 7% in the United States, 8% in Canada, and 15% in Mexico. Should you invest in Mexico? Why or why not?
25. Suppose that the current exchange rate is ¥250/\$1 and that the interest rate is 6% in Japan and 7% in the United States. According to the nominal interest rate parity condition, what is the expected future exchange rate?
26. If the current exchange rate is €1.5/£1 and is expected to fall to €1.35/£1 next year, and if the current nominal interest rate in the United Kingdom is 12%, what should be the interest rate in the eurozone (assume that there are no differences in risk, liquidity, or information characteristics), according to the nominal interest rate parity condition?
27. Compare the assumptions underlying the expectations theory of the term structure of interest rates with the assumptions underlying the nominal interest rate parity condition. Then compare the assumptions underlying the preferred habitat theory of the term structure with assumptions underlying currency premiums in foreign-exchange markets. Is a segmented market model of foreign-exchange markets consistent with international capital mobility? Why or why not?
28. Most economists believe that the attractiveness of investment in the United States increased relative to the attractiveness of investment in other countries during the early 1980s. Using a bond market diagram (Chapter 6), explain the consequences for the real rate of interest in the United States. Using the real interest rate parity condition, predict what would happen to the effective real exchange rate index.
29. Suppose that German bonds pay a lower nominal rate of interest than British bonds do but that both bonds have similar default risk, liquidity, and information costs. Describe circumstances under which portfolio investors would prefer to invest in German bonds.

DATA QUESTION

30. Locate the table of foreign exchange rates in a recent issue of the *Federal Reserve Bulletin* in your library. You should find average exchange rates for many foreign currencies relative to the U.S. dollar for the past few years. Against how many of the currencies listed did the dollar appreciate? Against how many did it depreciate? You should also find an index of the value of the dollar against a weighted average of leading industrial countries' currencies. Did the dollar rise or fall according to this index during the past two years?

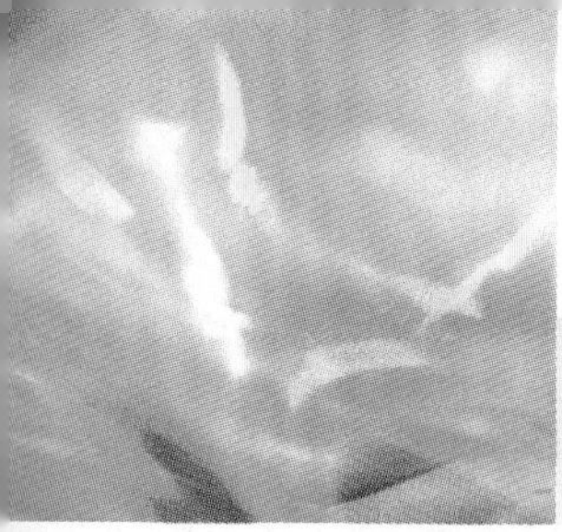

CHAPTER 9

Derivative Securities and Derivative Markets

Many commentators called it the year of the derivative. The period from spring 1994 through spring 1995 brought exotic financial instruments called derivatives to the front page of newspapers and to television screens all over the world. There were casualties: A prosperous California county sought bankruptcy protection. A distinguished British investment firm older than the United States of America failed. The chairman of the American Stock Exchange termed derivatives "the 11-letter four-letter-word." At the same time, many economists and market participants praised derivatives as financial instruments that allow investors to manage and transfer risk. What should an investor believe? Do derivatives offer investors a way to gamble with their funds, or can derivatives be used to reduce risk? As you learn more about derivative securities in this chapter, you will see that derivative markets offer investors risk-sharing, liquidity, and information services.

The derivative securities that we describe in this chapter—futures contracts and options contracts—derive their value from an underlying asset. These assets may be commodities, such as pork bellies or oil, or financial assets, such as stocks or bonds. To understand why investors include derivatives among their investments, we describe the situations in which derivatives benefit the parties in a transaction, the obligations and benefits of each type of derivative, and the strategies investors use in buying and selling derivatives. One reason for the popularity of futures and options is the existence of organized exchanges where they can be traded. These derivative markets generate liquidity and information and provide common arrangements for clearing and settling transactions. The appendix to the chapter describes the use of a third type of derivative: swaps.

FORWARD TRANSACTIONS AND DERIVATIVES

The financial markets described in earlier chapters matched borrowers and lenders through the trading of such financial instruments as stocks and bonds. An increasing amount of activity takes place in markets where the actual instruments for borrowing and lending are not traded. Rather, trading occurs in **derivative markets,** in which participants buy and sell securities that derive their economic value from underlying assets. Such assets, principally futures and options contracts, are called **derivative instruments.** Derivative securities offer benefits to borrowers, lenders, and traders that are not available in other types of securities.

Many lenders and borrowers want to lock in the rate of return or the interest costs on funds borrowed rather than risk the fluctuations that might occur over time. That is, they want to negotiate today their returns or their costs on trades to be executed in the future. For example, the financial manager of a corporation would like to know in advance how much the interest costs will be on funds needed to finance future capital projects.

In contrast to **spot transactions,** in which settlement is immediate, **forward transactions** give savers and borrowers the ability to conduct a transaction now and settle it in the future. Historically, forward transactions took place in agricultural and other commodity markets to reduce price fluctuation problems. Such fluctuations imposed significant risks on sellers, for whom the revenue from the sale of the commodity was their sole source of income.

Consider the situation facing a wheat farmer who planted wheat in the spring but received no payment for the crop until it was harvested. The farmer expected to receive $10,000 for the crop. But suppose that between planting time and harvest time, the price of wheat dropped to $7500 for the crop; the farmer would lose $2500 of the expected return. Similarly, suppose a miller needed wheat to grind into flour. If the price of wheat fluctuates, the miller faces uncertain input prices. Therefore the miller might agree to pay, at planting time, $10,000 for the farmer's wheat at harvest time. By engaging in a forward transaction, the farmer reduces the risk of a loss and the miller reduces the risk of a price fluctuation. In general, by agreeing on the price in advance, buyers and sellers use forward transactions to reduce risks associated with price fluctuations. But what happens if prices change between the time of the agreement and the time of settlement? Fluctuations in prices over the life of the forward transaction confer capital gains and losses on the contracting parties, much as movements in market interest rates affect the values of lenders' assets and borrowers' obligations over time.

Although forward transactions provide risk sharing, they have liquidity and information problems. Because forward contracts generally contain terms specific to the particular buyer and seller in the exchange, convincing other traders to take over the contract and accept the same terms may be difficult. Therefore the contracts are likely to be illiquid. In addition, forward contracts are subject to default risk, or the possibility that the buyer or seller may be unable or unwilling to fulfill the contractual obligation. As a result, buyers and sellers of the contract will incur information costs when analyzing the creditworthiness of potential trading partners. Derivative markets evolved to reduce both liquidity and information problems. To show how they do so, we first trace the development of two categories of derivative market instruments: futures and options.

FUTURES

Futures contracts evolved in markets for agricultural and mineral commodities to maintain the risk-sharing features of forward transactions while increasing liquidity and lowering information costs. A **futures contract** is an agreement that specifies the delivery of a commodity or financial instrument at an agreed-upon future date at a currently agreed-upon price. Most futures traded today are financial futures rather than commodity futures. That is, the underlying asset is not a crop or mineral, but a financial asset. You might, for example, buy a futures contract requiring you to buy a Treasury bill six months from now at a price you agree to today. Trading of futures contracts on agricultural and mineral commodities declined from 70% of total futures transactions in 1981 to less than one-third in the new century. Therefore we use financial futures as examples in this description of futures contracts and their use in risk sharing.

Futures contracts specify the rights and obligations of the buyer and seller with regard to the underlying asset. Buyers and sellers of futures contracts have symmetric rights. The *buyer* of a futures contract assumes the **long position,** or the right and obligation to receive the underlying financial instrument (say, Treasury bonds) at the specified future date. The *seller* assumes the **short position,** or the right and obligation to deliver the instrument at that time.

The principal financial futures contracts traded in the United States include those for interest rates (Eurodollars; Treasury bills, notes, and bonds; and the municipal bond index), stock indexes (S&P 500, NYSE Composite, and Value Line indexes), and currencies (such as U.S. dollars, Japanese yen, German marks, Canadian dollars, British pounds, and Australian dollars).

Futures trading traditionally has been dominated by markets in Chicago (the Chicago Board of Trade and the Chicago Mercantile Exchange), although markets in New York, London, Paris, Tokyo, Sydney, and Singapore have become strong competitors. Significant computer and telecommunications improvements have strengthened trading links among exchanges.

Financial futures contracts are regulated by exchange rules approved by the Commodity Futures Trading Commission (CFTC). The CFTC monitors potential price manipulation and conduct of exchanges. Since 1981, the National Futures Association has complemented the CFTC's efforts as a self-regulatory organization.

Futures Pricing

Unlike other obligations such as the amount of the commodity or financial asset and time horizon of the contract or delivery location, the **futures price** is not specified in the futures contract. Instead it is set by the futures market and reflects traders' expectations of the **spot price,** or the price of the underlying asset on the date of delivery. The spot price and the futures price are determined by supply and demand. If market participants expect bumper crops in the next harvest, they probably believe that agricultural commodity prices will fall. In this case, the futures price may be below the current spot price. As the

USING THE NEWS . . .

Reading Financial Futures Listings

The Wall Street Journal reports information on futures contracts each business day. An example of interest rate futures on U.S. Treasury securities appears here. The uppermost set of quotations refers to Treasury bond futures traded on the Chicago Board of Trade (CBT). The heading shows that the size of a contract is $100,000; individual quotations represent percentages of $100 of face value. Fractional values are reported in thirty-seconds of a percent.

The leftmost column states the contract month for delivery (from December 2000 to September 2001). The next four columns present price information from the previous trading day: the opening (Open) price, the high and low for the day, and the closing (Settle) price. The Chg column reports the change in the price of the futures contract from the previous day's closing price. The December 2000 contract closed at 104 15/32, down 3/32 from the previous day, so each contract's value fell by (3/32)($1000) = $93.75. The price calculations are based on an 8% coupon, 15-year Treasury bond. Note that the price of the December 2000 contract, 104 15/32, is higher than the face value of 100. Therefore the yield to maturity is less than the coupon rate of 8%. The next two columns tell you lifetime high and low prices for the contract. The last column, Open Interest, reports the volume of contracts outstanding: 32,899 for the December 2000 contract.

You can get free information from these quotes. The interest rate futures contracts tell you market participants' expectations of future interest rates. Note that futures prices are about the same from December 2000 to September 2001, telling you that futures market investors expected long-term Treasury interest rates to remain about the same.

Although not shown, you can also find interest rate futures quotations for Treasury notes and bills and foreign currencies. The financial futures page also gives you quotes on stock index futures, such as contracts on Standard & Poor's 500 stocks (known as the S&P 500). Investors use stock index futures to anticipate broad stock market movements.

FUTURES PRICES

INTEREST RATE

TREASURY BONDS (CBT)-$100,000; pts. 32nds of 100%

Closing price. (→ Settle)

	Open	High	Low	Settle	Chg	Lifetime High	Lifetime Low	Open Interest
Dec	104-15	104-15	104-01	104-15	−3	105-06	88-13	32,899
Mr01	104-19	104-24	104-02	104-16	−5	105-10	88-06	417,964
June	104-08	104-16	104-02	104-15	−5	105-06	96-21	1,569
Sept	...	...	...	104-12	−5	103-07	96-22	419

Est vol 218,000; vol Mon 166,775; open int 452,907, – 3,175.

Source: The Wall Street Journal, December 20, 2000. Republished by permission of Dow Jones, Inc. via Copyright Clearance Center, Inc. © 2000 Dow Jones and Company, Inc. All Rights Reserved Worldwide. (Quotes are for December 19, 2000.)

time to deliver approaches, the futures price comes closer to the spot price, eventually equaling the spot price on the date of delivery. Why? At the date of delivery, no investor or trader is willing to pay more or less for the underlying asset than its current market value, which is the spot price.

Suppose that you buy in March a $1 million futures contract in three-month U.S. Treasury bills (T-bills) to be delivered in June. T-bills are discount obligations. Hence the futures price, say $980,000, which represents the futures price you pay today for T-bills to be delivered in June, is less than the face amount of the T-bills.

The futures price of $980,000 implies an expected future three-month interest rate of just over 2%, or an annualized rate of 8.42%. If the current annual interest rate on T-bills is 10.4%, the *current spot price* of $1 million in T-bills (that is, for immediate delivery) will be $975,610. Of course, you don't know what the actual spot price of the three-month T-bills will be in June; it will depend on the market interest rate at that time. If that interest rate turns out to be 10.4% as well, you will have lost money on your long position and the seller will have gained on his or her short position.

In the futures market on any particular day, either the buyer or the seller may gain with respect to his or her initial position. Because buyer and seller trade with each other anonymously through an exchange, the exchange requires collateral from traders by mandating that gains and losses be settled each day.† This daily settlement of positions is called **marking to market** the accounts of the buyer and seller, whose account values are set at that day's market value. If the price of your $1 million, three-month T-bill contract rises from $975,610 to $985,610, the value of your long position has increased by $10,000, and the holder of the short position correspondingly loses. In this case, the exchange would collect $10,000 from the holder of the short position and transfer it to your account. Ultimately, the contract is settled in cash. (Even in the case of commodities, actual delivery rarely takes place and contracts are settled in cash.)

Using Futures to Manage Risks

Futures contracts offer risk-sharing and profit opportunities to participants in futures markets. By gaining the right to buy or sell an asset (say, a Treasury bond) at a known price, buyers or sellers can reduce their exposure to risk. The practice of using futures to reduce risk is called **hedging.** In contrast to hedgers, other futures traders may be **speculators.** They seek profits by anticipating price movements. Speculators play an important role in futures markets: By betting on anticipated price movements, they assume the other side of hedgers' positions and provide liquidity in markets for hedgers.

Hedgers taking either long or short positions in financial futures include lenders, borrowers, suppliers, or customers concerned about the risk of fluctuations in interest rates and firms and financial services companies exposed to fluctuations in the value of foreign currencies. Hedgers can benefit by participating in financial futures markets in three key ways. First, they can spread the risk of price fluctuations by locking in a future price today. Second, they can access liquid markets. Third, their information costs are reduced by the introduction of organized exchanges. At the same time, derivative markets offer buyers and sellers opportunities to profit from disagreements among traders about future prices of a commodity or financial instrument by speculation or from anticipating changes in prices.

Fluctuations in market interest rates can change the value of fixed-rate

†In a forward contract, movements in current and expected future prices do not require transfers among buyers and sellers. The transaction is settled at the agreed-upon date at the agreed-upon price.

financial instruments that have long maturities. As interest rates became more volatile in the 1980s, savers and borrowers seeking to hedge their investments dramatically expanded derivative markets. That growth has continued unabated in the 1990s and the new century.

How does hedging actually work? Suppose that Bigtime Financial Services wants to extend a \$10 million, two-year loan to Smokestack Industries. After analyzing the company's creditworthiness, Bigtime charges an interest rate of 10% per year for each of the two years. Bigtime can raise funds for the first year at a cost of 8%, but it will have to go to the market to raise the funds for the second year. Borrowing at an interest rate differential of two percentage points offers a comfortable profit margin for the first year. However, Bigtime is worried that market interest rates might rise for the second year, increasing its cost of funds and reducing (or even eliminating) the profitability of the loan.

One way for Bigtime to manage its risk and hedge the loss from possible interest rate increases in the second year is to sell Treasury bill futures contracts. Specifically, it could agree to sell 10 contracts for one-year, \$1 million T-bills when the second year begins. The price that Bigtime charges for the T-bills at that time will reflect the interest rate that is expected to prevail during the second year.

To examine this strategy, let's suppose that the market expects the rate on one-year, \$1 million T-bills to be 8% when the second year begins. The one-year futures price of a \$1 million contract will then be \$926,000 (rounding to the nearest \$1000). That is, Bigtime will pay \$926,000 and will receive \$1 million from its futures position, or a one-year yield to maturity of 8%. Therefore Bigtime will promise to sell 10 contracts at \$926,000 each at the start of the second year.

Who would buy such a contract? Perhaps a speculator who believes strongly that T-bill prices will rise, say, to \$930,000. Such a person would want to lock in Bigtime's price of \$926,000 per T-bill because the speculator expects to resell the T-bills immediately for \$930,000. Hence speculators' self-interest adds liquidity to the market, allowing lenders to hedge their interest rate risk.

Suppose now that interest rates rise to 12%, or four percentage points above the expected 8% and two percentage points above the rate that Bigtime charged Smokestack Industries. On the one hand, Bigtime is harmed, as it loses money on its loan to Smokestack in the second year. The \$10 million loan brings in 10%, or \$1 million, but the cost of funds is now 12%, or \$1,200,000. Thus, instead of earning a \$200,000 profit (\$1,000,000 – \$800,000 expected cost of funds), Bigtime incurs a second-year loss of \$200,000. Overall, then, the higher interest rate reduces Bigtime's earnings by \$400,000 (from a \$200,000 profit to a \$200,000 loss).

On the other hand, Bigtime is helped by the unexpected interest rate increase, which lowers the cost of T-bills. At a one-year interest rate of 12%, the market price of a \$1 million T-bill is \$1,000,000/1.12, or \$893,000 (rounding to the nearest \$1000). Therefore, to fulfill its futures contract, Bigtime will buy \$10 million worth of T-bills for \$8,930,000 (10 × \$893,000

TABLE 9.1 **BIGTIME FINANCIAL SERVICES' USE OF FUTURES TO MANAGE RISK**

	Profits with no futures hedge	Profits with futures hedge
Year 1 (Market interest rate expected to be 8% in year 2)	Interest income [$10,000,000 × 10%] – Cost of funds [$10,000,000 × 8%] Year 1 profit [$200,000]	At the end of year 1, Bigtime sells 10 $1,000,000 T-bill futures contracts for $9,260,000. Bigtime must buy them back in year 2.
Year 2 (Market interest rates rise from 8% to 12%)	Interest income [$10,000,000 × 10%] – Cost of funds [$10,000,000 × 12%] Year 2 profits [–$200,000]	Bigtime buys back futures contracts for $8,930,000.
	Relative to its expected return, Bigtime loses $400,000 ($200,000 – (–)$200,000).	Bigtime makes $330,000 ($9,260,000 – $8,930,000) on its futures position.
	With the futures hedge, Bigtime loses $70,000 instead of $400,000.	

each) and sell them to the speculator for the agreed-upon futures price of $9,260,000 (10 × $926,000). Bigtime thus receives a profit of $330,000.†

On balance, if the interest rate rises to 12%, Bigtime loses $400,000 on its loan and gains $330,000 on its futures contract: –$400,000 + $330,000 = –$70,000, a net loss. If Bigtime had not sold futures, its loss would have been the full $400,000. The futures markets thus allowed Bigtime to reduce its potential loss. Table 9.1 summarizes Bigtime's gains from using futures to hedge risks.

Of course, the hedging strategy allowed by financial futures cut both ways. Had interest rates fallen, Bigtime would have gained on the loan because the cost of funds would have fallen but would have lost on the futures contract because the price of T-bills would have risen. By limiting potential gains and losses, then, futures markets allow investors to limit the risks from unexpected interest rate changes.

Anticipated price movements. The futures hedge in the Bigtime example was successful because the movement in the T-bill yield was *unanticipated*. If market participants had *anticipated* the interest rate movement, the higher expected future rate likely would have been incorporated into the initial T-bill futures price. That price per contract would have been $893,000 ($1,000,000/1.12), rather than $926,000 ($1,000,000/1.08). The futures hedge is most valuable for protecting against unanticipated changes in the price of the underlying asset.

Costs of hedging: transactions costs and basis risk. Other costs of hedging are transactions costs and basis risk. Futures markets do not provide hedging

†The speculator, much to his chagrin, lost money. He must buy the T-bills for $926,000 each while the market price is $893,000.

services for free; buyers and sellers pay transactions costs on futures contracts. Such costs aren't likely to be significant, particularly for very large transactions. The Bigtime example also simplified the situation facing most hedges because the spread between the rate on the hedged instrument (cost of funds) and the rate on the instrument actually traded in the futures market (T-bills) remained constant. We assumed that both rose by four percentage points. However, correlation between the changes in the two rates isn't necessarily one to one. This imperfect correlation is known as **basis risk.** If the cost of funds moves imperfectly (that is, other than in a one-to-one manner) with the yield on T-bills, Bigtime will experience a significant net loss on the combination of its lending and futures positions. For instance, suppose that the T-bill rate rose only two percentage points, to 10%. The market price would be $909,000 (rounded to the nearest $1000), or $9,090,000 for $10 million of T-bills. Bigtime would buy the T-bills and sell them at the contract price of $9,260,000 for a gain of $170,000. However, when the $400,000 loss on the loan in the second year was subtracted, Bigtime's profit would fall by $230,000. That loss is considerably more than the $70,000 lost when T-bill rates changed point for point with Bigtime's cost of funds.

CHECKPOINT

Assuming no basis risk, what would happen to Bigtime's profits if interest rates fell to 6% during the second year? Instead of earning $200,000 on the loan, Bigtime would net $400,000 ($1,000,000 income minus $600,000 funding costs). However, Bigtime would lose money on the futures contract. At 6%, the market price of a one-year, $1 million T-bill is about $943,000 ($1,000,000/1.06). Thus Bigtime would have to spend $9,430,000 to obtain $10 million in T-bills but could sell them only for $9,260,000, losing $170,000. On balance, Bigtime gains $30,000 ($200,000 gain on the loan minus $170,000 lost in the futures contract). Had it not sold the futures contract, it would have gained the full $200,000.

OPTIONS

A second type of derivative instrument is the **options contract,** which confers the rights to buy or sell an asset at a predetermined price by a predetermined time. For example, you might purchase the option to buy 100 shares of Boomco for $50 per share sometime during the next six months.

In contrast to symmetric rights and obligations under futures contracts, the buyer and seller in an options contract have asymmetric rights. The seller has obligations, and the buyer has rights. Options represent the right to buy or sell an underlying asset—shares of a stock or a basket of stocks, for example. If an investor buys a **call option,** he or she acquires the *right to buy* the underlying asset. Sellers of call options have the *obligation to sell* the asset. Investors also may purchase a **put option,** or the *right to sell* the underlying asset. Sellers of put options have the *obligation to buy* the asset. The price at which the asset is bought or sold is called the **strike price,** or **exercise price.**

The period over which a call or put option exists is determined by its **expiration date,** the date at which the rights under the options contract end. Essentially, a person providing call or put options is extending rights to another person. Those rights (to buy or sell at a specified price) are potentially valuable and so are not simply given away. Instead, the seller of the option charges a fee, called the **option premium.**†

Options on individual stock issues have been traded in over-the-counter markets and exchanges for decades. Since the 1970s, traders have reduced the risk of fluctuations in security returns with option contracts traded on the Chicago Board Options Exchange, the New York Stock Exchange, and the American Stock Exchange. In addition, the popularity of options on futures such as Treasury or Eurodollar interest rate futures or foreign currency futures has grown. The principal options contracts traded in the United States include options on individual stocks, stock index options (S&P 500 or NYSE Composite indexes), options on stock index futures contracts (S&P 500 or NYSE Composite indexes), interest rate options on futures (Eurodollar rates, U.S. Treasury notes and bonds, and the Municipal Bond index) and currency options and currency futures options (Japanese yen, Swiss francs, Canadian dollars, British pounds, Mexican pesos, and Brazilian reals).

Options on securities (that is, stocks, stock indexes, bonds, and bills) and on foreign currencies trading on stock exchanges are regulated by the Securities and Exchange Commission (SEC). Options on futures contracts or on foreign currencies traded on commodity markets are regulated by the CFTC.

Options Pricing

The value of the option premium is different from that of the futures price because options have asymmetric rights and obligations. The size of the option premium reflects the chance that the option will be exercised, in the same way that a car insurance premium reflects the risk of an accident. Just as a driver with a history of car accidents pays higher insurance rates, anything that increases the chance of the option's being exercised increases the size of the option premium.

Four factors influence the size of the option premium for put and call options. First, greater volatility in the price of the underlying asset increases the premium because the asset price is more likely to rise above the strike price, increasing the value of the options contract.

Second, as the option nears its expiration date, the size of the premium approaches its intrinsic value. The **intrinsic value,** or the amount the option actually is worth if it is immediately exercised, is the current price of the asset less the strike price of the underlying asset. Suppose, for example, that you are considering investing in a call option to buy common stock in Consolidated

---

†Throughout this discussion, we describe American options, which may be exercised at any time until the expiration date. European options may be exercised only on the expiration date.

USING THE NEWS . . .

Reading Options Listings

Reported data on options contracts contain many of the same measures as futures listings. However, there are some differences for individual options, according to whether the underlying asset is a direct claim (for example, a bond or shares of stock) or a futures contract (for example, a stock index futures contract).

The quotations shown here for options contracts are for options on Treasury bond and note futures (such as those discussed earlier) traded on the Chicago Board of Trade. Again, the size of the underlying futures contract is $100,000, but the prices are given in percentage points per $100 of face value; fractional values are reported in 64ths of a percent.

Open interest in Treasury bond calls is 214,720 contracts, with a trading volume the previous day of 42,967 contracts. Open interest in the Treasury bond puts is 190,181 contracts, with a trading volume of 34,408 contracts. Because calls and puts are different types of options, the open interest for the two types of options need not be the same.

The first column conveys the strike price, which ranges from 102 in the first line to 107 in the last line. The second, third, and fourth columns list the closing (Settle) prices for call options expiring in February 2001, March 2001, and June 2001, respectively. The 102 calls with a February expiration date have a closing price of 2 46/64. Each percentage point of the $100,000 Treasury bond contract is worth $1000, so these calls cost 2 46/64 ($1000) = $2718.75. For some contracts (for example, the 103 calls with a June expiration date), no price is given because the contract did not trade that day. The last three columns give the closing price for put options with expiration dates of February 2001, March 2001, and June 2001, respectively.

As with futures price quotations, options price quotations tell you about expectations. Note that the price of 104 calls is higher in the June contract than in the March contract, indicating that traders and investors expected the option to buy the Treasury bond futures at 104 to be worth more in March. Thus investors expected the bond price to rise and the yield to fall. The closing prices for the 106 and 107 calls are low, indicating that investors believed that Treasury bond prices are unlikely to be so high or yields so low.

Although not shown, quotations for options on individual stocks contain information on the closing price of the option (the premium) and the closing price of the individual stock. Volume statistics (such as trading volume or open interest) are usually not reported.

FUTURES OPTIONS PRICES

INTEREST RATE

T-BONDS (CBT)

$100,000; points and 64ths of 100%

Entries under dates are the option price, or premium.

Strike Price	Calls – Settle Feb	Mar	Jun	Puts – Settle Feb	Mar	Jun
102	2-46	3-01	3-51	0-14	0-34	1-24
103	1-60	2-19	. . .	0-28	0-52	. . .
104	1-17	1-45	2-40	0-49	1-13	2-11
105	0-50	1-13	. . .	1-18	1-45	. . .
106	0-28	0-53	1-47	. . .	2-20	3-15
107	0-15	0-35	. . .	2-46	3-02	. . .

Est. vol. 40,000;
Mn vol. 42,967 calls 34,408 puts
Op. int. Mon 214,720 calls 190,181 puts

T-NOTES (CBT)

$100,000; points and 64ths of 100%

Strike Price	Calls – Settle Feb	Mar	Jun	Puts – Settle Feb	Mar	Jun
102	2-41	2-50	3-15	0-07	0-16	0-49
103	1-51	2-00	2-36	0-16	0-30	1-05
104	1-05	1-23	1-63	0-34	0-52	1-31
105	0-36	0-55	1-33	1-02	1-20	. . .
106	0-17	0-34	1-10	. . .	1-62	. . .
107	0-08	0-20	0-56	. . .	. . .	. . .

Est. vol. 67,000 Mn 37,404 calls 75,934 puts
Op. int. Mon 250,408 calls 264,592 puts

Source: The Wall Street Journal, December 20, 2000. Republished by permission of Dow Jones, Inc. via Copyright Clearance Center, Inc. © 2000 Dow Jones and Company, Inc. All Rights Reserved Worldwide. (Quotes are for December 19, 2000. "Mon" refers to Monday, December 18.)

instruments at \$60 per share in June; the current share price is 62⅛, and the option premium is 4½. A portion of that premium (2⅛ of the 4½) equals the intrinsic value of 2⅛ per share you would earn from exercising the option immediately (that is, from buying a share for 60 and selling it for 62⅛). That portion is said to be *in the money.* A put option is in the money when the market price of the underlying asset is less than the strike price.

Third, the fact that buyers of call options in effect are buying the underlying asset on credit also helps to determine the option premium. You pay the option premium today but do not pay the strike price until you exercise the option. A longer time until expiration increases the value of the right conferred by the call option and hence increases the option premium. For put options as well, the further from expiration, the higher the option premium.

Fourth, the default-risk-free interest rate affects the value of the option premium. A higher interest rate reduces the present value of the exercise price, increasing the value of a call option and decreasing the value of a put option.

Market participants try to estimate these effects not just qualitatively but as precisely as possible, using mathematical models. Indeed, Wall Street firms have lured mathematicians, physicists, engineers, and economists—"rocket scientists"—to develop models for pricing more complex derivatives. This influx of talent includes three pioneers in the pricing of options: the late Fischer Black, Robert Merton of Harvard University, and Myron Scholes of Stanford University. Empirical testing of theoretical pricing models has demonstrated their usefulness. Improving the models in search of greater precision (and profit!) is a topic of active research in academia and among financial practitioners.

Using Options to Manage Risk

As with futures, hedgers can use options to reduce the risk of adverse fluctuations in commodity or stock prices, interest rates, and foreign currency exchange rates. The extent to which an options hedge is satisfactory depends on basis risk—that is, how closely movements in the value of the asset underlying the option mirror those of the hedged asset. Unlike futures contracts, options allow hedgers to keep profits on their positions in the presence of favorable shifts in the price of the underlying asset.

An options contract is more like insurance (hence the use of the term *premium*) than is a futures contract. In a futures hedge, a hedger can *sell* Treasury futures at any time, reducing potential net losses should market interest rates increase. If rates decrease, however, the hedger cannot earn an additional net profit. With options, a hedger can *buy* Treasury puts to protect against an increase in rates while still earning an extra return if market rates fall. In the Bigtime Financial Services example earlier, Bigtime could buy put options on \$10 million of Treasury bills. The benefit to the options buyer must be measured against the cost of the option premium, however. If the option premium is high, the transactions costs of using options may well exceed those for futures. Hence the choice between futures and options reflects a trade-off

OTHER TIMES, OTHER PLACES . . .

Futures Trading, Index Arbitrage, and the Stock Market Crash of 1987

Some market analysts blame a form of trading known as *index arbitrage* for the stock market crash of October 19, 1987. Index arbitrage is the simultaneous trading in stock index futures and the underlying stocks to exploit price differences. Such price differences would arise if an investor could buy a portfolio of the stocks used in the S&P 500 index at a price that was slightly lower or higher (net of transactions costs) than the price of the index futures. Suppose, for example, that the futures index for delivery one year from now sells for $1.1 million, while the stocks are selling for $1 million and the interest rate on a one-year Treasury instrument is 8½%. Let's say that you buy the stocks now and sell the index futures at the same time. At the end of the futures contract, you sell the stocks to close your futures position. You have received $1.1 million for the stocks, so you earned $100,000, or 10%, on your $1 million investment, regardless of stock price fluctuations in the interim. That return is greater than the return on the default-risk-free Treasury instrument (8½%). Index arbitrage is facilitated by computer monitoring of price margins.

This activity can contribute to market efficiency by eliminating price differentials among markets. Why, then, the controversy? The reason is that large trading volume can be generated by index arbitrage, particularly on days on which index futures contracts expire. On October 19, 1987, large sell orders on the New York Stock Exchange were placed as a result of S&P 500 index arbitrage, which some claimed worsened stock price fluctuations. However, there is little formal evidence to support the claim. Indeed, the presidential commission that was appointed to assess the origins of the stock market crash did not place much blame on index arbitrage. By 1995, index arbitrage trading accounted for about 4% of overall trading volume on the New York Stock Exchange.

between the generally higher cost of using options and the extra insurance benefit that options provide. As an option buyer, you assume less risk than with a futures contract because the maximum loss is the option premium. The option seller bears the risk of unfavorable price movements in the underlying asset.†

BENEFITS OF DERIVATIVE MARKETS FOR THE FINANCIAL SYSTEM

Derivative markets generate important risk-sharing benefits for hedgers and information about expectations of future prices for all market participants. These markets also provide a means for speculation. As a group, speculators play important roles in derivative markets because their presence facilitates risk sharing with hedgers. Active market participation by speculators generates liquidity, thereby improving market efficiency and the information content of prices. This increased efficiency benefits not only the derivative

† In the conventional covered option, the seller owns the underlying asset. In a *naked option,* the seller does not have an interest in the underlying asset.

CASE STUDY

Citron Pressed— The Orange County Fiasco

In April 1995, former Orange County (California) Treasurer Robert L. Citron, who was responsible for the biggest municipal bankruptcy ever, pleaded guilty to six felony charges of misleading investors and misrepresenting interest earnings from the county's doomed investment fund. While Citron blamed hard-to-understand derivatives and bad advice from Merrill Lynch for the losses, Orange County taxpayers looked on in shock at losses of $2 billion. While the headlines focused on derivatives, the culprits in the Orange County disaster were more likely bad decisions and bad supervision. Let's see what happened.

The Orange County Investment Pool, a repository for local and county tax receipts, bought large amounts of "stepped inverse floaters," notes with derivative features whose value is linked to the level of short-term interest rates. If short-term rates fall, the floaters' rate does the inverse. This increase brings about above-market returns for the noteholders. On the other hand, if short-term rates rise, rates on the notes fall. At the same time, the market value of the notes falls because their rates are below other rates in the market.

Citron's assumption throughout the 1990s was that short-term rates would fall, thereby making investments in the somewhat exotic inverse floaters a good bet. Orange County—rather than using derivatives to hedge risks—became a major speculator. As short-term rates fell from 1991 through 1993, the Orange County pool earned returns significantly greater than those earned by bond mutual funds. Beginning in February 1994, however, the Federal Reserve pursued a strategy of steadily increasing short-term interest rates, producing huge losses for the Orange County fund. As losses mounted, Citron took riskier positions to try to break even. In November 1994, the Irvine Ranch Water District president became suspicious. His request to redeem $400 million would have taken almost all of the pool's cash. On December 6, 1994, the pool filed for bankruptcy protection.

What went wrong? Although derivatives were present in the Orange County investments, the losses were caused not by the instruments themselves but by the erroneous assumption that interest rates would continue to fall in 1994. This bad decision was matched by poor supervision. Citron averted a run on the fund during 1994 because California law required disclosure of the pool's positions only once each year. Many commentators (and taxpayers) were left wondering how a single individual with relatively little experience in managing sophisticated financial instruments was allowed to manage the multibillion-dollar pool with so little oversight. Another casualty was Orange County's broker, Merrill Lynch, which paid a settlement of $400 million in June 1998.

CASE STUDY

Barings Lost—The Queen's Banker Goes Bust

Peter Baring, chairman of Barings P.L.C., the investment firm his family founded in 1763, thought that February 24, 1995, would be a good day. After all, he would tell the firm's employees that the company's profits during 1994—and their bonuses—were high. At 7:00 A.M. in London, however, Baring discovered a disastrous loss of about $1 billion, enough to wipe out the firm. Indeed, two days later, the firm was placed in bankruptcy proceedings. On March 5, ING, a Dutch banking and insurance firm, purchased Barings for £1, and assumed its assets and liabilities.

In 1818, the Duc de Richelieu declared that "there are six great powers in Europe: England, France, Russia, Austria, Prussia, and the Baring brothers." In 1995, the firm was investment advisor to none other than Queen Elizabeth II. In the wake of its collapse, Barings blamed derivatives and the trading bets of 27-year-old Barings trader Nick Leeson. Other commentators pointed to the need for closer top management scrutiny.

Leeson's job at Barings was in principle a low-risk form of arbitrage, riskless trading that takes advantage of price differentials between markets (in his case, Japan and Singapore). He was supposed to buy a futures contract in one market and sell it for slightly more in the other, profiting from the difference. Leeson soon departed from arbitrage and risk management. Itchy for a higher profile, Leeson began engaging in a risky investment strategy known as a "straddle." His straddle was a bet that the Tokyo stock market would remain in a narrow trading range. To execute the strategy, Leeson sold an equal number of call options and put options. As long as stock prices did not get out of the trading range set by the calls and puts, Barings and Leeson would profit. However, if the market moved out of the trading range, Barings would quickly sustain large losses. Leeson's positions were in trouble after the earthquake in Kobe, Japan, in January 1995. Through the first three weeks of February, he bought futures contracts on the Nikkei 225 stock index, betting that Japanese stock prices would rise. They fell instead.

As investigators probed the details of the Barings collapse, it became clear that top management had paid insufficient attention to Leeson's trading activities—in part because of the high profits he seemed to be generating. In the summer of 1994, Barings P.L.C. rejected the idea of buying software that continuously tracks traders' positions to calculate potential risk. It seems that, at $50,000, the software was too expensive.

markets, but also the markets for underlying assets (Treasury instruments, stocks, foreign exchange, and so on), because price changes in the derivatives market provide information about the value of underlying assets. Hence derivative markets contribute positively to the three key services of risk sharing, liquidity, and information provided by the financial system.

Nonetheless, some observers are critical of derivative markets. The multibillion-dollar speculative losses in derivatives by Orange County, California, in 1994 and Barings P.L.C. in 1995 have led to further calls for regulatory review. During 1994 and 1995, the General Accounting Office, the Congress, and the futures industry itself suggested new regulations of market participants. While derivatives played a role in the spectacular collapse of Long Term Capital Management in 1998, most analysts blame the firm's risk management system, not derivatives per se.

Standardization and Liquidity

For financial markets in derivative instruments to be liquid, futures and options contracts must apply to standardized products. Here, **standardization** means that contracts contain exact specifications—for example, the weight, quality, and grade of a commodity. Standardization increases liquidity and results in increased trading volume for the market as a whole, because traders do not have to spend time and money to determine the exact specifications of the financial instrument or good being traded. The terms of a futures contract specify the type of financial instrument or commodity, the amount or value of the financial instrument or commodity, and the location and time of delivery.

The specifications of financial assets—particularly government debt, foreign exchange, and groups of stocks—can be standardized easily. In the case of financial futures, the assets underlying the contracts are specific instruments, such as Treasury bills or bonds, or the cash value of the S&P 500 stocks. Sponsoring exchanges specify the terms of futures contracts, and, as we noted earlier, trading practices in the United States are regulated by the CFTC. The National Futures Association also exercises self-regulation.

Standardization also is important for options. An options contract is defined with respect to an underlying asset, traditionally 100 shares of a particular stock. For index options, the underlying asset is a group of equities represented by the index, say, the S&P 500. For options on futures contracts, the underlying obligations are futures; the buyer receives a T-bill futures contract rather than the underlying T-bill itself.

Rules for standardizing options contracts are developed by the exchange on which they are traded. An options contract specifies different strike prices and expiration dates, as determined by the exchange. As with futures contracts, the intent of standardization is to interest the greatest possible number of potential traders in order to provide liquidity.

Anonymous Trading and Information

Derivative markets also promote risk sharing by reducing information costs for hedgers and speculators. Exchanges permit buyers and sellers of futures contracts to trade at arm's length through an exchange, instead of trading with each other personally. This approach overcomes certain information problems: The exchange provides a clearinghouse to clear the trades of

Figure 9.1

Derivative Markets Add Value in the Financial System

Derivative markets for financial futures and options provide valuable risk-sharing, liquidity, and information services for savers and borrowers.

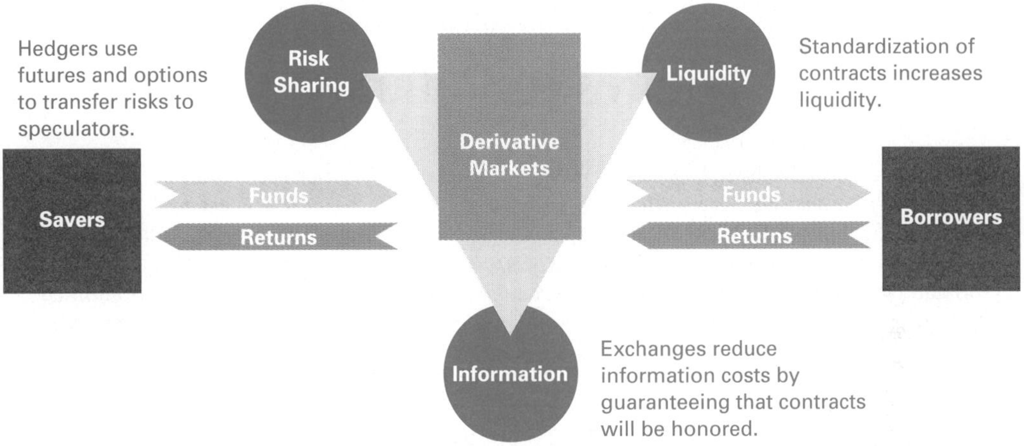

market participants. In so doing, the exchange, whose capital is provided by its members, guarantees that contracts will be honored. Thus trade can be anonymous; that is, buyers and sellers do not have to search for each other and do not have to assess the creditworthiness of trading partners. Organized exchanges match buyers and sellers as part of the exchange mechanism, through which prices are determined in an auction market by demand and supply. In the United States, only a commodity broker can trade futures on exchanges. Options contracts also are traded anonymously through exchanges by any broker who is registered to trade stocks.†

CHECKPOINT

Some futures and options contracts have failed after their introduction because there was insufficient demand for them. What factors do you think determine whether a particular futures or options contract will be demanded by hedgers or speculators? The underlying asset or commodity should exhibit significant price fluctuations to create a demand for hedging and speculation. In addition, the underlying asset should be standardized so that it can be easily traded on organized exchanges. o

Figure 9.1 summarizes the value that financial futures and options add in providing risk-sharing, liquidity, and information services in the financial system.

†Some options contracts are traded over the counter, but most are listed on an exchange (though, in the case of stock options, not necessarily on the same exchange as the underlying stocks). Just as exchanges do not set futures prices, exchanges do not contractually specify or regulate the prices of options contracts.

THE BANKER OCTOBER 9, 1999

Futures of Pollution

With global warming firmly on the international agenda, the Kyoto Summit examined three ways to reduce carbon dioxide emissions: taxation, regulation, and market mechanisms. The financial world is intrigued by the tradable pollution permit. But is it a nonstarter?

a

One of the more obscure business opportunities being explored by the financial services world is the trading of pollution permits. But is it a real business opportunity or just a fancy idea?

Last year's Kyoto Summit put global warming firmly on the international agenda by giving all the major industrial countries clear targets to reduce emissions of carbon dioxide by the end of the first decade of the new century. The agreement signed in Kyoto envisaged numerous ways of achieving the reductions: taxation, regulation, or market mechanisms. But so far as the financial world is concerned, only one is of interest—namely the tradable pollution permit.

b

The idea is that each country would issue a limited number of permits to industry, each of which entitles the holder to emit a given quantity of carbon dioxide over a given period. Were holders able to get their emissions down below that level, they could sell surplus permits to someone who was short of them. . . .

c

The beauty of the system is that it brings market forces to bear. The right to emit carbon dioxide would carry a clear price, and companies or countries would have an incentive to get their emissions as low as possible or be penalized.

The permit system also has the advantage over regulation and taxation that it can virtually guarantee to deliver a chosen target, because carbon dioxide could be emitted only up to the amount allowed by the number of permits in issue. . . .

In the United Kingdom, BP and Shell have launched internal schemes for trading permits among business units. Experimental trading has also been tried in Australia and Scandinavia.

The results are encouraging. They suggest that permit trading is much the cheapest and most efficient way of cutting back on greenhouse gases. This has prompted organized exchanges to design markets to trade the permits.

Chicago is already auctioning sulfur emission permits and the Sydney Futures Exchange has just announced that it will start trading "carbon sequestration credits" next year, with each credit representing a given amount invested in reforestation.

In London, the City Corporation asked the CSFI to explore the possibilities for creating a market in the City. Our conclusion was that there could, indeed, be a business opportunity for the City to act as the market not just for UK permits but for the proposed global market. The City has, after all, centuries of experience in trading unusual products, and it is already a large market for oil and gas, which would be the parallel products for pollution permits. . . .

Futures contracts evolve to provide risk-sharing, liquidity, and information services for investors in the financial system. As part of a market-oriented approach to reducing air pollution, the U.S. Clean Air Act of 1990 allowed polluters to buy and sell rights to sulfur dioxide. Economists argue that the price established in such a market will send important signals for investment. That is, a higher price for pollution rights will make firms more willing to invest in pollution abatement equipment or new technologies to control emissions. Speculators will provide the liquidity for the market in pollution rights. With some trading in emissions contracts in the United States, the question arises as to whether trading in pollution contracts could play a role in international coordination to reduce emissions.

(a) For emissions futures markets to be successful, market participants must agree on the emissions or pollutants to be traded, just as they must agree on the choice of copper, wheat, or Treasury bills. The standardization required for exchange trading will make the market more liquid.

(b) Who might participate in a futures market for emissions? Hedgers likely include businesses that produce emissions or use pollutants in their production processes; such firms could use futures contracts to mitigate the effects of fluctuating prices of emissions quotas on profits. Speculators would include investors who seek to profit from their belief that prices of emissions permits may rise or fall in the near future.

(c) The creation of a market for trading chemical emissions permits encourages the development of low-cost technologies for reducing pollution. A futures market aids planning by providing information on the expected future value of the permits. The liquidity provided by the futures market improves the information content of permit prices.

For further thought . . .

The Kyoto Protocol supports a substantial role for a global market for trading emissions permits. How might such a market be used to offer incentives to less developed countries to reduce their pollution?

Source: Excerpted from "Trading in Pollution," *The Banker*, October 9, 1999.

KEY TERMS AND CONCEPTS

Derivative instruments
Derivative markets
Forward transactions
Futures contract
- Basis risk
- Futures price
- Hedging
- Long position

Marking to market
Short position
Speculators
Spot price
Options contract
- Call option
- Exercise price
- Expiration date
- Intrinsic value
- Option premium
- Put option
- Strike price

Spot transactions
Standardization

SUMMARY

1. An increasingly significant amount of activity in financial markets takes place not in actual instruments for borrowing and lending, but in derivative instruments. A derivative instrument's economic value comes from the value of some underlying asset. Futures and options contracts, the two most widely used derivative instruments, facilitate risk sharing by bringing together individuals who want to reduce their exposure to fluctuations in the price of the underlying asset (hedgers) and individuals who hope to profit from anticipated fluctuations in the price of the underlying asset (speculators).
2. Derivative instruments specify rights and obligations regarding the underlying asset. The buyer of a futures contract, who assumes the long position, has both the right and the obligation to receive the underlying asset (say, Treasury bonds) at the agreed-upon future date. The seller, who assumes the short position, has the obligation to deliver the asset at that time. With an options contract, the seller has obligations, and the buyer has rights. Buyers of call options have the right to buy the underlying asset. Buyers of put options have the right to sell the underlying asset. Because of the asymmetry of rights and obligations between the buyer and seller, the buyer of a call or put option pays an option premium to the seller. The buyer of the option has the right to pay an agreed-upon price (called the strike, or exercise, price) by a certain time (the expiration date).
3. Costs of using futures contracts include transactions costs and basis risk (movements in the spread between the price of the hedged instrument and the instrument actually traded in the futures market). In addition, the hedging strategy cuts two ways. The hedger's potential losses are reduced by holding an offsetting futures position, but so are the gains if there is a favorable price movement in the underlying asset. With an options contract, a hedger is protected against adverse movements in the price of the underlying asset while benefiting from favorable price movements.
4. Speculation in derivative markets is beneficial for the financial system because it increases liquidity and helps to incorporate information into market prices. This increased efficiency benefits not only the derivative markets, but also the markets for underlying financial claims, which gain from the integration of price information.

REVIEW QUESTIONS

1. What is the difference between a spot transaction and a forward transaction? What advantages does a futures contract have over a forward transaction?
2. What is an options contract? What are the rights and obligations of buyer and seller? How does a call option differ from a put option?
3. What is the difference between using options to hedge and using options to speculate?

4. What are the main costs of using futures as a hedge?
5. What type of financial contract can be used like insurance to protect the value of other assets? How does the insurance aspect of this approach work?
6. Why is standardization important in futures and options markets?
7. What is important about anonymity in the trading of futures and options?
8. Why do the futures exchanges require marking to market every day?
9. Consider options on Bigmove Corporation stock. Suppose that there are call options with a strike price of \$75 and put options with a strike price of \$65. Which, if any, of the options are in the money if the current price of Bigmove's stock is (a) \$60, (b) \$70, and (c) \$80?
10. Why are option premiums generally greater than intrinsic value before the expiration date?
11. Suppose that a presidential candidate planned to include in her platform a plan to abolish options and futures markets, arguing that they are simply a "casino for the rich." As her economic advisor, would you agree with her position or try to change her mind?
12. If speculators were not present in derivatives markets, would these markets work more efficiently or less efficiently?
13. Suppose you become convinced that an Internet stock is greatly overvalued at its current stock price. How might you use the derivatives market to profit?
14. Explain index arbitrage (see the "Other times, other places . . ." box). How can you obtain a greater risk-free return by using index arbitrage than by buying Treasury bills?

ANALYTICAL PROBLEMS

15. In early 2000, the Dow Jones Industrial Average rose above the 11,000 level. If the Dow were to fall to 7000, who would gain the most: investors who had bought call options, investors who had sold call options, investors who had bought put options, or investors who had sold put options? Who would be hurt the most?
16. Suppose that a court decision will have a major impact on a firm's profits. If the court decision is favorable, you estimate that the firm's stock will be worth \$100 per share. If the court ruling is unfavorable, you estimate that the stock will be worth only \$60 per share. Currently, the price is \$80 per share, as half the market participants are betting on each possibility. Is there any way to use options contracts to profit from this situation?
17. In the fall of 1998, an article in *The Wall Street Journal* stated: "The risk of gyrating orange prices prompted some analysts to question PepsiCo's \$3.3 billion purchase of Tropicana [which is a brand of orange juice] from Seagram Co. when the deal was announced in July. Orange juice is a notoriously tough business that is subject to the vagaries of weather. . . . 'These are exactly some of the negative components that came up at the time of the acquisition—you're adding agricultural commodity risk to PepsiCo,' said Skip Carpenter, an analyst at Donaldson, Lufkin & Jenrette." Would Tropicana be better off if orange prices were high or if they were low? Explain how Tropicana might go about hedging the risk of an adverse price movement in oranges.
18. Suppose that a U.S. firm signs a contract to buy factory equipment from a Japanese firm at a cost of ¥250 million. The equipment is to be delivered to the United States and paid for in one year. The current exchange rate is ¥250/\$1. The current interest rate is 6% in the United States and 4% in Japan.
    a. If the U.S. firm trades dollars for yen today and invests the yen in Japan for one year, how many dollars does it need today?
    b. If the U.S. firm enters a futures contract, agreeing to buy ¥250 million in one year at an exchange rate of ¥245/\$1, how many dollars does it need today to invest at the U.S. interest rate of 6%?
    c. If the U.S. firm invests in the United States at 6% today, without entering into any other type of contract, does the firm know how many

dollars it needs today to fulfill its equipment contract in one year?

d. Which method(s) described in (a)–(c) provide(s) a hedge against exchange rate risk? Which do(es) not? Which method is the U.S. firm likely to prefer?

e. *Bonus:* What does the futures contract exchange rate have to be in (b) for the results in (a) and (b) to be equivalent?

19. Suppose that you own Treasury bonds with a face value of $1 million. You believe that the economy is growing strongly and that interest rates are about to rise. You want to protect the value of your assets without incurring the transactions costs of selling them. How could you use options to protect their value?

20. Suppose that you believe the fundamental value of Wal-Grey stock is about to rise from $50 to $100 because of its new management team. You have $20,000 that you can risk in the market, and you can think of four possible ways to profit: (a) use your $20,000 to buy shares of Wal-Grey; (b) borrow (at a 6% interest rate) an additional $20,000 on margin to buy a total of $40,000 worth of Wal-Grey stock; (c) enter into a futures contract to buy 400 shares of Wal-Grey in one year for $21,200 (you can invest safely for a year at a 6% interest rate); and (d) buy a call option (for every $1000 you spend on call options, you have the right to buy 100 shares of Wal-Grey at the current price of $50 per share). Calculate how much you earn or lose by each method if:

(i) Wal-Grey stock rises to $100 per share in one year.

(ii) Wal-Grey stock stays at $50.

21. Suppose that you manage a bank that has made many loans to people at a fixed interest rate. You are worried because you believe that inflation might rise and your bank will suffer a capital loss on its loans. How might you use options to protect your bank's portfolio, which includes many Treasury securities?

DATA QUESTION

22. In the library, look in the latest *Economic Report of the President* for annual data on the rise in the consumer price index (CPI). Suppose that options exist on the CPI. Call options on the CPI pay off whenever the CPI rises by 5% or more during the year. Put options pay off whenever the CPI rises by 2% or less during the year. In what years would CPI call options pay off? In what years would CPI put options pay off? How could a bank or other financial intermediary use these types of options to protect its portfolio? How expensive do you think these options were in the early 1960s? In the 1970s?

APPENDIX: Swaps

Although the standardization of futures and options contracts promotes liquidity, they often cannot be tailored to meet the needs of market participants. This problem has spurred the growth of *swap contracts* ("swaps"). A swap is an agreement between two or more parties (known as "counterparties") to exchange sets of cash flows over some future period. For example, Company A may consent to pay a fixed rate of interest on $10 million each year for five years to Bank B. Bank B, in return, may pay a floating rate of interest on $10 million each year for five years. The cash flows are generally related to the value of the underlying financial instruments, typically debt instruments or foreign currencies. Hence swaps are generally *interest rate swaps* or *currency swaps*. An industry of *swap facilitators* has emerged to identify and bring together prospective counterparties. Recent swap innovation has encompassed "credit derivatives," swaps in which credit risk can be separated from interest rate risk.

From a negligible presence in the early 1980s, the swap market has grown rapidly, with contract values exceeding $46 trillion in mid-2000. This growth in part reflects the flexibility of swaps, which, unlike exchange-traded derivatives, can be custom-tailored to meet the needs of the counterparties. In addition, swaps offer more privacy than exchange trading, and swaps are subject to almost no government regulation. However, unlike exchange-traded instruments, counterparties must be sure of the creditworthiness of their partners. This problem has led to the participation of large firms and financial institutions that can assess creditworthiness; these firms and institutions dominate the market.

In this appendix, we explain the execution of interest rate swaps and currency swaps (and introduce the recent development of credit derivatives). We discuss additional uses of interest rates swaps in Chapter 13 and of currency swaps in Chapter 16.

Interest Rate Swaps

In a basic (or "plain vanilla") interest rate swap, one counterparty has an initial position in a floating-rate obligation, while the other has an initial position in a fixed-rate obligation. The first counterparty can reduce its exposure to interest rate risk by swapping with the second counterparty. The second counterparty is exposed to more interest rate risk after the swap occurs and bears the risk in anticipation of a return.

Let's consider an example, in which the swap covers a five-year period and incorporates annual payments on a principal amount of $10 million. This principal is called a notional principal, because it is an amount used as a base for calculations but is not an amount actually transferred between the counterparties. Bigco agrees to pay a fixed interest rate of 10% to Bankco. Bankco in return agrees to pay to Bigco a floating rate equal to 3% above the London Interbank Offered Rate. This rate, known as LIBOR, is the rate at which large international banks lend to each other. Figure 9A.1 summarizes the payments in the swap transaction.

If LIBOR is 8% when the first payment is made, Bigco must pay $1 million (10% × 10 million) to Bankco; Bankco owes $1.1 million ((8 + 3)% × $10 million) to Bigco. Netting the two payments, Bankco pays $100,000 to Bigco. Generally, only the net payment is exchanged.

Why might firms and financial institutions participate in interest rate swaps? One motivation is to transfer interest rate risk to parties that are more willing to bear it. Second, one party may have better access to long-term fixed-rate capital markets than another. For example, in an early U.S. swap transaction in 1982, the Student Loan Marketing Association (Sallie Mae) and ITT Financial were counterparties. Sallie Mae had a portfolio consisting mostly of

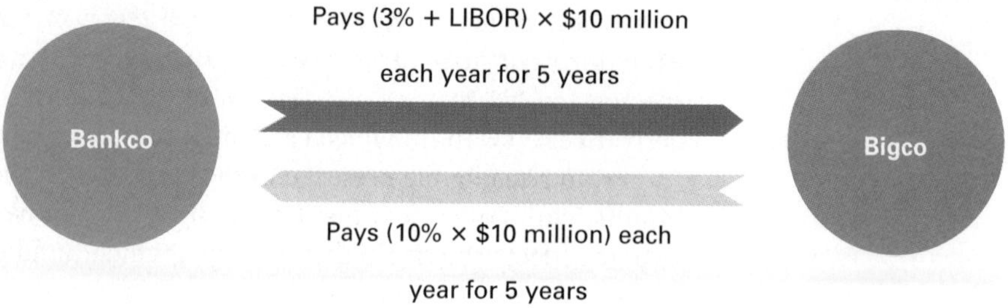

Figure 9A.1

Payments in a Swap Transaction

In a swap transaction, counterparties exchange fixed-rate and floating-rate payments on the notional principal in the transaction. On a notional principal of \$10 million, Bigco agrees to pay Bankco a fixed payment of \$1 million (10% × \$10 million) each year for five years. In return, Bankco agrees to pay Bigco a variable payment of (3% + LIBOR) × \$10 million each year for five years.

floating-rate assets, while ITT Financial had a portfolio consisting mostly of fixed-rate assets. Before the swap, Sallie Mae used its status to borrow in an intermediate-term fixed-rate debt market, while ITT Financial borrowed using commercial paper. After the swap, Sallie Mae paid ITT Financial's floating rate, while ITT Financial paid Sallie Mae's fixed rate. The swap gave both counterparties a better match with their assets.

Currency Swaps

In interest rate swaps, counterparties exchange payments on fixed-rate and floating-rate debt. In currency swaps, counterparties exchange principal amounts denominated in different currencies. For example, Le Taste Company might have French francs and want to swap the francs (or equivalent in euros) for U.S. dollars. Big Steel Company might have U.S. dollars and be willing to exchange those dollars for francs.

A basic ("plain vanilla") currency swap has three steps. First, the two parties exchange the principal amount in the two currencies. (Note the difference from the interest rate swap, in which the counterparties deal in the same currency and can pay only the net interest amount.) Second, the parties exchange periodic interest payments over the life of the agreement. Third, the parties exchange the principal amount again at the conclusion of the swap.

Suppose, for example, that the current spot exchange rate between French francs and U.S. dollars is 5 francs per dollar, or FF1 = \$0.20. Le Taste has FF50 million and would like to exchange the amount for dollars. In return, Big Steel would pay \$10 million to Le Taste at the beginning of the swap. Let's assume that the swap is for a five-year period and that the parties make annual interest payments. The U.S. interest rate is 8%, and the French interest rate is 10%. Hence Big Steel will pay 10% interest on the FF50 million it received, for an annual payment of FF5 million. Le Taste will pay 8% interest on the \$10 million it received, for an annual payment of \$800,000. (In practice, the two firms will make net payments.) At the end of five years, Le Taste and Big Steel again exchange principal amounts. Le Taste pays \$10 million, and Big Steel pays FF50 million, ending the swap.

Why might firms and financial institutions participate in currency swaps? One reason is that firms may have a comparative advantage in borrowing in their domestic currency. They can then swap the proceeds with a foreign counterparty to obtain foreign currency for, say, investment projects. In this way, both parties may be able to borrow more cheaply than if they had borrowed directly in the currency they needed.

Over the past decade, interest rate swaps and currency swaps have become more complex. On the one hand, this complexity serves the commercial and financial interests of transacting parties. On the other hand, many policymakers worry that defaults by some key participants could precipitate a crisis in swap markets.

Credit Derivatives

Swap contracts designed to transfer credit risk (as opposed to just interest rate risk or exchange rate risk) are a rapidly growing segment of derivative markets. In a *default swap,* two parties enter into a contract in which the hedger pays a periodic fee in return for a contingent payment by the speculator following a default or bankruptcy by a reference entity (such as a company that fails to pay its supplier). In a more complicated transaction known as a *total return swap,* the two parties transfer both interest rate risk and credit risk. This transaction exchanges the total economic performance of a specified asset for another cash flow. Although credit derivatives are increasingly used by a range of financial institutions—including banks, pension funds, insurance companies, and hedge funds (largely unregulated money managers for very wealthy individuals)—some analysts fear that not all market participants understand the risks involved.

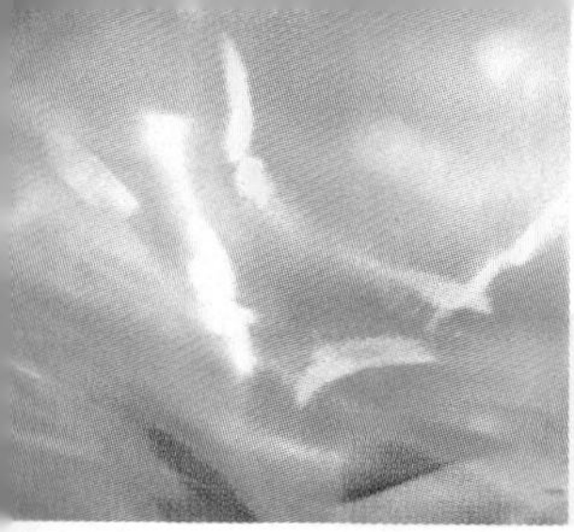

CHAPTER 10

Information and Financial Market Efficiency

The world waited to see what would happen. Collapsing stock markets in Asian economies in 1997 and 1998 made global equity investors nervous. Even in the United States, the stock market's down-then-up roller-coaster ride in the second half of 1998 left investors queasy. In Japan, economists worried that the drop in stock prices would erode confidence in the Japanese economy as households and firms reduced their spending—a typical reaction of participants in an economy to the bad news contained in a sharp decline in security prices. Economists are also aware that lenders and borrowers base financial decisions—about, say, portfolio allocation or building a plant—on information contained in financial assets.

Market participants use the information contained in market prices. Borrowers use financial market prices as a guide in their decisions to build new factories or to expand operations. Lenders make portfolio allocation decisions using prices of assets as an estimate of their value. In commodity markets, such as those for agricultural products, prices are signals to producers. An increase in wheat prices, for example, tells farmers that there are profits to be earned by planting more wheat. In the labor market, a drop in the price of machines relative to workers' wages tells business managers to devote resources to mechanizing their factories. Buyers and sellers use market prices to make spending and production decisions.

In this chapter, we focus on the information content of market prices for financial assets. We begin by looking at the way in which buyers and sellers in financial markets predict the future value of an asset and then act on their predictions. The expectations of borrowers and lenders determine how much they are willing to accept or pay for a financial claim. Information is an input to their decisions. Their knowledge of economic conditions, political events, consumer behavior, and conditions affecting individual industries or firms determines their estimates of the future value of financial assets. We then look at how this information is processed by financial markets. If the information is processed quickly and efficiently, then the prices in financial markets reflect the estimated value of the assets. We introduce an economic theory—the *efficient markets hypothesis*—that describes how the actions of buyers and sellers set market prices and how those prices in turn communicate information for financial and economic decisions.

RATIONAL EXPECTATIONS

Expectations of asset values by participants in financial markets determine market prices and changes in market prices. In this section, we analyze how financial market participants use information about financial assets to form expectations about prices. We will see that when market participants use all available information, market prices become signals for financial and economic decisions, and they convey information to market participants.

Expectations figured prominently in our previous discussion of financial decisions. Recall from Chapter 6 that expected wealth affects the demand for bonds. (If you get richer, you will increase your holdings of bonds.) And expected future profits influence bond supply by businesses. (A business owner who expects to make a lot of money from a new computer invention will want to borrow to invest in a factory to produce the equipment.) In addition, expectations of future inflation affect nominal interest rates and exchange rates. Finally, expected rates of return on alternative assets provide information for portfolio allocation decisions.

A few examples will illustrate how market participants' expectations of market value influence the asset's market price. If Middleroad, Inc., bonds yield 10% while U.S. Treasury bonds of the same price and maturity yield 7%, financial market participants have set the risk premium on Middleroad's bonds at 10% − 7% = 3%. The risk premium reflects lenders' expectations of default. Or, if the dollar is expected to appreciate against the Japanese yen during the next 60 days, the 60-day forward yen/dollar exchange rate should be higher than the current exchange rate. This expected increase in the yen price of dollar-denominated asset reflects the expected appreciation of the dollar. Finally, if Newfangleco discovers a cure for the common cold, the price of its shares should rise dramatically. The discovery leads investors to expect higher future returns and a higher share value. In each case, the current values of Middleroad's bonds, the yen/dollar exchange rate, and Newfangleco stock reflect the present value of expected future returns. When the market price of the financial instrument equals that present value, savers and borrowers can be sure that the price communicates information about market participants' expectations of value.

The market's valuation process is an ongoing activity. An investor does not assess a stock, make an investment decision, and consider that a complete task. The investor continues to monitor information that affects the security and adjusts the estimate of the security's value. The incorporation of new information into the analysis results in new estimates and new market prices. For example, if financial market participants expect that Slipperyslope Company may default on its bonds at some point during the next five years, investors, using this information, will require a higher return on Slipperyslope's bonds. Hence the interest rate that lenders will charge Slipperyslope on new debt will rise, and the price of its outstanding bonds will fall. This incorporation of new information into the price of the bonds tells lenders to require a higher expected rate of return on loans to Slipperyslope.

It also tells the managers of Slipperyslope that the cost of funds has gone up to reflect the investment risk associated with the firm. In the early 1990s, IBM witnessed a drop in market value due to the erosion of its mainframe business and competition from other makers of personal computers. Investors observing these conditions tended to reduce their assessment of the value of IBM stock, and the price fell. IBM responded by cutting costs and introducing new products.

How do market participants form expectations of prices of future returns? Early studies by economists of expectations focused on the use of information from the past. For example, expectations of the price of a company's stock would depend on the history of prices for the company's shares. This use of information is called *adaptive expectations*. When market participants have adaptive expectations, their expectations of changes in prices or returns change gradually over time as data on past prices or returns become available. That is, market participants only slowly adjust their expectations to news that could affect prices or returns.

When market participants have **rational expectations,** they use all information available to them. The information that they use includes not only past experiences, but also their expectations and predictions for the future. Therefore, in a market in which investors and traders have rational expectations, the market price of an asset equals the best guess of present value of expected future returns, or the asset's **fundamental value.** Market participants can then use the price as a measure of fundamental value.

Formally, economists define rational expectations to mean that expectations equal the optimal forecast (the best guess) of prices using all available information.[†] For any asset, the expectation of the asset's price, P^e, equals the optimal (best guess) price forecast, P^f; if market participants use all available information, $P^e = P^f$. For example, recall that the value of a bond today equals the present value of future interest and principal payments. If the price is greater than the value of the expected future returns, investors will sell the asset, forcing the price down to the current value. But if the asset's price is less than the present value of its expected future returns, investors will buy the asset, putting upward pressure on the price until it equals the current value.

Although investors and traders use rational expectations in their financial decisions, they cannot foretell the future. No one can predict exactly an asset's future price. When market participants have rational expectations, the deviation of the expected price from the actual future price is not predictable. Using all available information, investors and traders arrive at a forecast price for tomorrow (time $t + 1$). Let P_{t+1} represent the actual price of a share tomorrow and let P^e_{t+1} equal the expected price based on the information available at time t. When market participants have rational expectations, the difference

[†]John Muth, "Rational Expectations and the Theory of Price Movements," *Econometrica*, 29:315–335, 1961.

between the actual price and the expected price equals a random (unforecastable) error:[†]

$$P_{t+1} - P^e_{t+1} = (\text{Unforecastable error}_{t+1}). \tag{10.1}$$

In other words, if you use the same information that other market participants use in formulating their price forecast, you can't predict their mistakes.

THE EFFICIENT MARKETS HYPOTHESIS

Market participants acting rationally will estimate a value for any asset—but how does this behavior translate into the prices we observe in markets, and how can we be sure that a market price equals an asset's fundamental value? To answer these questions, let's begin with an analysis of the reasoning you might apply in deciding whether to purchase shares of stock in Consolidated Instruments. Using all the information available today (time *t*) regarding the prospects of the company, the industry, and the economy, you determine that Consolidated Instruments' shares are worth more than their market price. Although the stock is currently priced at \$20 per share, your forecast of the present value of future returns, based on information you received today, suggests that the stock price should be \$30 per share. This information prompts you (and other investors) to buy shares to realize the higher expected rate of return. In reaction to this surge of interest, the stock price rises until it reaches the higher price of \$30. By trading on the basis of your forecast, you profit from the ensuing increase in the price of shares in Consolidated Industries. Rational expectations provide the incentive to profit when market prices are higher or lower than the forecasted value. In this way, the self-interested actions of major, informed traders cause available information to be incorporated into market prices.

As long as the transactions costs of buying and selling financial instruments are low, the activities of traders and investors will tend to eliminate deviations from the price that available information predicts. Individual investors may profit from spotting prices higher or lower than forecasts of underlying values, and those who invest in gathering new information may also earn a profit from forecasting value. However, over a reasonable length of time, market participants should allow no unexploited profit opportunities. In this case, everyone can look to the market price as the best available signal of value.

The **efficient markets hypothesis** is a theory of market pricing behavior that applies rational expectations to the pricing of assets. According to the theory, when traders and investors use all available information in forming expectations of future rates of return and when the cost of trading is low, the equilibrium price of the asset equals the market's optimal forecast of fundamental value. The

[†] An implication of market efficiency is that prices of financial assets should approximately follow a random walk, meaning that the change in price from one trading period to the next is not predictable. The reason is that, because the current market price in an efficient market incorporates all available information, any change in market price from one period to the next reflects new information.

forecast of fundamental value in market prices, in turn, offers market participants guidance in financial and economic decisions. Figure 10.1 illustrates this flow of information in an efficient financial market.

For now, our assessment of the role that expectations play in determining market prices is based on the assumption that the same information is potentially available to all parties (borrowers, lenders, and traders). In Chapter 11, we identify problems arising from *asymmetric information*—for example, when a borrower has information about prospects or risks not shared by other market participants.

By summarizing information in market prices, financial markets provide signals for lending, borrowing, and portfolio allocation.

Determining an Asset's Expected Price

We know from the analysis of interest rate determination and the theory of portfolio allocation that the current market value of a financial instrument depends on its returns relative to returns on other investments with similar risk, liquidity, and information characteristics. Think of the income from a bond or shares of stock in two parts: a current return and the value of expected future returns. For a bond, your income comes from the coupon payments you receive while you hold the bond plus your expected future capital gain (or loss) when you redeem the bond. For shares of stock, your income comes from the dividends you receive while you hold the shares plus your expected future capital gain (or loss) when you sell the shares. Thus P_t, the price of an asset at time t, equals the sum of the expected return on the asset, D^e, next period, $t + 1$, plus the expected price, P^e, of the asset at $t + 1$. To account for the asset's risk, the expected return and the expected price must be discounted by

Figure 10.1

Flow of Information in an Efficient Financial Market

Efficient financial markets benefit both lenders and borrowers. When market prices reflect all available information, they guide decisions about lending, borrowing, and portfolio allocation.

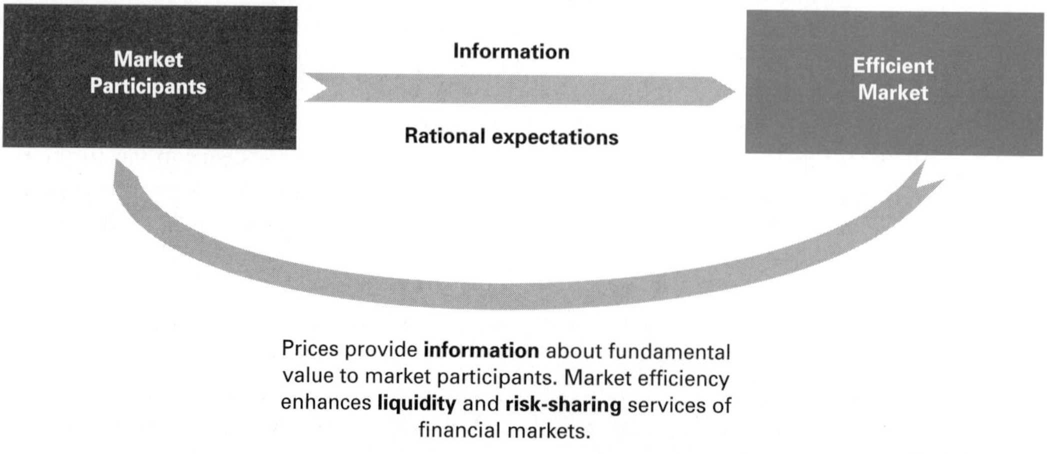

1 plus the interest rate adjusted for risk, so the asset's current price equals the present value of future returns from holding it, or

$$P_t = \frac{D^e_{t+1} + P^e_{t+1}}{1 + i}, \qquad (10.2)$$

where

P_t = price of financial assets at time t;

D^e_{t+1} = expected periodic return on the asset (coupon payment for a bond or a dividend for a share of stock) for time $t + 1$;

i = interest rate, adjusted for the asset's risk; and

P^e_{t+1} = expected price of the financial instrument at time $t + 1$.

In an efficient bond market, bonds with higher default risk have a lower price than default-risk-free bonds with the same returns. In an efficient stock market, a stock's price reflects the present value of expected future dividends. We can use Eq. (10.2) to determine whether a financial asset has a high price or a low price in an efficient market. A financial asset will have a high price today if (1) it is expected to have high returns (high D^e); (2) it is not very risky (low i); or (3) it is expected to rise in value in the future (an expected capital gain, or high P^e).

CHECKPOINT

In China, stock markets were nonexistent under communist rule until the 1990s. Can you imagine some likely problems in establishing stock markets there? The value of financial markets in channeling funds from savers to borrowers and in providing risk sharing for savers depends on market liquidity and the information content of market prices. Initially, new stock markets are likely to lack liquidity and efficient trading mechanisms for savers. Even more important, because little information about enterprises is available to market participants, market prices may not provide meaningful signals for saving and investment decisions. (Even if more information were available, individual savers might not know what to do with it.) **o**

Price Fluctuations

Although the efficient markets hypothesis says that the price of a financial instrument is based on all available information, the prices of financial assets such as stocks and bonds can change. Because their prices reflect information about fundamental value, they constantly change to reflect news about changes in fundamental value. The expression for the price of a financial instrument in Eq. (10.2) suggests that prices change in reaction to changes in expected future returns or in risk, liquidity, or information costs associated with the instrument. This reaction occurs whether the instrument is a bond, shares of stock, a foreign exchange contract, a futures contract, an options contract, or any other financial instrument.

One source of price fluctuations in an efficient market is shifts in interest rates. An increase in market interest rates reduces the present value of future interest and principal payments from a long-term bond. As a result, the price of a bond falls when yields rise. Similarly, an increase in expected future market interest rates raises long-term yields relative to short-term yields. Exchange rates also fluctuate in response to movements in interest rates at home and abroad. Finally, an increase in default risk increases the risk premium in a bond's interest rate and lowers the bond's price.

The financial news media tend to emphasize fluctuations in the stock market. One reason is that price fluctuations for individual stocks can be large. For example, in a single day, a share of stock might rise in price from \$10 to \$12, a 20% gain, or fall from \$10 to \$8, a 20% loss. Can such large fluctuations be consistent with an efficient financial market? The answer is yes. To find out why, let's examine a change in the price of a stock. Suppose that, using all currently available information, shareholders forecast dividends per share of Consolidated Industries (CI) stock to be \$2.00 this year, \$2.08 next year, and \$2.16 two years from now. On the basis of their assessment of prospects, market participants expect dividends to increase steadily at a rate of 4% per year. The value of a share today is the present value of future dividends. Thus, if i is the risk-adjusted interest rate appropriate for CI, the present value PV of expected future dividends is

$$\text{Present value} = \underbrace{\frac{2.08}{1+i}}_{\substack{PV\text{ of}\\ \text{year 1}\\ \text{dividend}}} + \underbrace{\frac{2.16}{(1+i)^2}}_{\substack{PV\text{ of}\\ \text{year 2}\\ \text{dividend}}} + \cdots.$$

According to the efficient markets hypothesis, if the CI share price is greater than this value, traders will sell shares, forcing the price down. Conversely, if the CI shares are undervalued, traders will buy shares, forcing the price to rise until the current value and the market price are equal.

Changes in expected dividends for just one period are unlikely to have much effect on share price, which represents the present value of all expected future dividends. Therefore, in principle, the efficient markets hypothesis allows for large movements in share prices. Let's find out why. Using our assumption that the CI dividend per share is expected to grow forever at a constant rate g (4% in this example), we can express the present value as

$$PV = (\$2.00)\left(\frac{1+g}{i-g}\right).$$

This equation restates the fundamental value, or price, of the share as the product of the current dividend per share (the first term on the right) and an expression including the risk-adjusted interest rate and the expected growth rate of dividends (the second term on the right). In other words, the equation says that a higher expected dividend growth rate increases value, whereas a higher risk-adjusted interest rate decreases the value of expected dividend returns.

If we expect a constant growth rate of $g = 0.04$ and a risk-adjusted interest rate $i = 0.10$, the fundamental value of Consolidated Industries shares (and price per share under the efficient markets hypothesis) is

$$PV = (\$2.00)\left(\frac{1.04}{0.10 - 0.04}\right) = \$34.67.$$

Suppose that bad news about the long-term growth prospects of CI's industry causes the expected growth rate of dividends g to fall to 2%. Then the share price falls to

$$PV = \$2.00\left(\frac{1.02}{0.10 - 0.02}\right) = \$25.50,$$

a decline in value of 26%. Hence, although news about short-term fluctuations in prospects affects prices only slightly under the efficient markets hypothesis, large swings in prices are possible in response to good or bad news about long-term prospects.

Investment Strategies

When prices of financial instruments summarize all information available to market participants, savers and borrowers obtain the information necessary to make decisions at low cost, as Table 10.1 shows. For example, higher stock prices tell businesses that investors expect profits to rise in the future

TABLE 10.1

SIGNALS FOR SAVERS AND BORROWERS IN AN EFFICIENT MARKET

An increase in . . .	Signals that . . .	Because of . . .
stock prices	businesses should invest more	greater investment opportunities
bond prices	savers should lower their required rate of return and borrowers should increase investment	lower default risk or lower overall level of interest rates
risk premiums	savers should increase their required rate of return and borrowers should decrease investment	greater default risk, lower liquidity, or higher information costs
the upward slope of the term structure	savers should require higher yields on long-term instruments relative to short-term instruments	higher expected future inflation or real interest rates
the difference between domestic and foreign real interest rates	savers should adjust their lending to domestic and foreign borrowers and exchange rates will shift	shifts in desired international lending and borrowing

and that the businesses should increase their spending on new plant and equipment. Higher bond prices indicate that market interest rates or risk premiums are falling, reducing returns to holding bonds and the cost of funds for borrowers. Recall that an upward-sloping yield curve informs borrowers of likely higher future real interest rates, or inflation. Widening differences between domestic and foreign real interest rates reveal shifts in desired international borrowing and lending and likely changes in exchange rates.

Understanding the efficient markets hypothesis allows you to formulate strategies for portfolio allocation, trading, assessing the value of financial analysis, and predicting changes in market prices of stocks, bonds, and other financial assets.

Portfolio allocation. As long as all market participants have the same information, the efficient markets hypothesis predicts that all above-normal profit opportunities will be exploited in the trading process. Hence you should not risk your savings in only one asset without information superior to that generally available (known as *insider information*) about a company's prospects. That is, investors should follow a strategy of holding a diversified portfolio.

Many individuals diversify their investments by purchasing mutual funds,

CONSIDER THIS . . .

Are Investors Really Rational?

Financial economists often use rational expectations to describe how investors process information about investments. The abstraction is not just a nicety—rational expectations are linked to market efficiency and its many benefits. But how realistic is the abstraction?

Working at the intersection of psychology and economics, some researchers have been developing *behavioral finance* theories of investor decision making. Behavioral finance specialists (including David Laibson of Harvard University and Richard Thaler of the University of Chicago) point to numerous gaps between observations about individuals' decision making and rational expectations. For instance, individuals often appear to separate their funds in "mental accounts," ignoring potential gains in mixing funds mentally allocated for short-term and long-term purposes. Other researchers note that individuals are "loss averse"—that is, their displeasure about a given loss is greater than the pleasure felt at a similar gain. Experiments also sometimes reveal individuals to be more myopic than rational expectations would require. Finally, individuals are often overconfident about their investment acumen.

Are these behavioral factors important? Potentially, yes and no. To the extent that many individual investors do not process information rationally, financial education for retirement planning and other investment decisions becomes very important. Whether the behaviorists' "irrational" investors are a big story for market outcomes is less clear, however. As long as the marginal investor (with the bulk of investments) has rational expectations, market efficiency may prevail. Nonetheless, behavioral finance is becoming an increasingly useful complement to conventional financial theory.

some of which invest in broad market portfolios or index funds, such as S&P 500 stocks. Hiring an investment firm to manage your funds actively would cost many times more than simply placing all your money in a mutual fund that holds a broad market portfolio. Large institutional investors are also placing larger portions of their equity investments in these index funds because actively managed funds often provide lower rates of return than broad market portfolio funds over long horizons.

Trading. Similarly, if prices reflect available information, buying and selling individual assets regularly is not a profitable strategy. Lacking superior information, an investor is ill advised to constantly move funds from one asset to another, or *churn*, a portfolio. Therefore you should buy and hold a market portfolio over a long time horizon.

Financial analysis and hot tips. The efficient markets hypothesis suggests that predicting an individual asset's price by focusing simply on past price data doesn't give the best possible forecast. Why? The reason is that these historical data do not reflect all available information. "Tips" published in leading commercial or financial publications are equally unlikely to lead you to profitable trades. The news will already be reflected in the market price by

OTHER TIMES, OTHER PLACES . . .

Charting the Civil War with the Gold Market

The efficient markets hypothesis explains how well financial markets communicate available information in prices of financial assets. In a sense, asset prices represent opinions of market participants about future asset returns, based on the information available to them. Kristen Willard of Columbia University, Timothy Guinnane of Yale University, and Harvey Rosen of Princeton University used this insight to ask how the market for "greenbacks" in the early 1860s reflected turning points in the American Civil War.†

To cover wartime expenses, the Union issued *greenbacks*, a legal tender currency that was not immediately convertible into gold. Because greenbacks could be exchanged for gold in the future (after the war's conclusion), markets watched war events to judge the cost of the war for the Union and the likelihood that the Union would prevail over the Confederacy. Events that increased costs to the Union decreased the chance that greenbacks would be fully redeemed with gold and therefore reduced the gold price of greenbacks.

Willard, Guinnane, and Rosen found that the gold market concurred with the later judgment by historians that the Battle of Gettysburg was a major turning point in the Civil War. They also found that some other events that are not emphasized by historians—such as Confederate General Early's retreat from Washington in 1864—were viewed as major events by gold traders. Using the logic of the efficient markets hypothesis, the authors stress that the "opinion poll" that is implicit in prices in financial markets can help us to understand how contemporaries viewed major historical events.

† Kristen L. Willard, Timothy W. Guinnane, and Harvey S. Rosen, "Turning Points in the Civil War: Views from the Greenback Market," *American Economic Review*, 86, September 1996.

informed traders who have learned about it before its publication. By chance, some analysts may appear to outperform broad-based market rates of return over an extended period of time. However, you should not expect to "beat the market" through forecasting gimmicks.

Do not conclude, however, that all financial analysis is worthless. The efficient markets hypothesis states that all *available* information is incorporated into the market price of a financial asset. If you can uncover new information that can change market prices, you may be able to profit.

Predicting price changes. Under the efficient markets hypothesis, today's price of an asset reflects all the information available today. But a price increase or decrease between today and tomorrow is unforecastable. Why? Today's market price is based on currently available information, and the only reason for a price change is tomorrow's "news."

Suppose that Microsoft announces that its earnings this year are 5% lower than last year's. Will the price of a share of Microsoft fall? Not necessarily. Analysts following Microsoft may have anticipated the decrease in earnings and incorporated that decrease into the share price. Only if the information of experts had differed from Microsoft's announcement would the price change. For example, if analysts studying Microsoft had forecast a decrease in earnings of 15%, that pessimistic expectation would have been incorporated previously into the price of Microsoft stock. Hence an earnings decrease of only 5% represents good news, and the share price may rise. Although the link between announcements and price movements may seem complex, the efficient markets hypothesis provides some simple guidance. Only the unexpected component of announcements (the true news) will affect the price.

CHECKPOINT

Your sister-in-law has told you that her specialized stock market fund has outperformed the total market for the last three years by constantly churning funds from one investment to another. Should you invest all your savings in her fund? No. The efficient markets hypothesis predicts that unless your sister-in-law has better information than other market participants have, you should invest in a broad market portfolio instead. o

ACTUAL EFFICIENCY IN FINANCIAL MARKETS

Many economists believe that highly liquid markets in which information costs are low (such as those for U.S. Treasury securities, foreign-exchange contracts, financial futures and options, some low-risk corporate bonds, mortgages, and commercial paper) are relatively efficient. Prices and returns determined in these markets appear to reflect available information about fundamental values. Early empirical work by Eugene Fama of the University of Chicago and others corroborated the prediction of the efficient markets hypothesis that changes in stock prices are not predictable.†

Other analysts—especially active traders and individuals giving investment advice—are more skeptical about whether the stock market is efficient. They point to three differences between the theoretical behavior of financial markets and the actual behavior that cause them to question the validity of the efficient markets hypothesis:

1. They cite pricing anomalies in the market that allow investors to earn consistently above-average profits. According to the efficient markets hypothesis, those profit opportunities should not exist—or at least should not exist very often or for very long.
2. They cite price changes that are predictable by using available information. According to the efficient markets hypothesis, investors should not be able to predict future price changes from past performance.
3. They cite price changes that appear larger than changes in fundamental value. According to the efficient markets hypothesis, prices should reflect the security's fundamental value.

Pricing Anomalies

The efficient markets hypothesis predicts that an investor will not be able to earn above-normal profits consistently from buying and selling individual stocks or groups of stocks. However, analysts have found strategies by which stock trading can result in above-normal returns. From the perspective of the efficient markets hypothesis, these trading opportunities are *anomalies*. Two such anomalies are the *small-firm effect* and the *January effect*.

Small-firm effect. Evidence from data collected since the mid-1920s indicates that savers could have earned above-normal profits by investing in the stocks of small firms—even after the greater risk associated with returns from those firms is taken into account. Although the small-firm effect was less pronounced during the 1980s, its long existence is inconsistent with the efficient markets hypothesis. However, some economists believe that the relatively low liquidity of markets for stocks of small firms and the relatively large information costs incurred by investors in evaluating those firms could explain why returns appear to be high.

---

†Three types of tests have been conducted for stock price data. The first uses only past stock price data as "available information" (test of *weak-form efficiency*). The second expands the information set to include all publicly available information (test of *semistrong-form efficiency*). The third type incorporates "insider information" known only to corporate managers in the information set (test of *strong-form efficiency*). Rejections of strong-form efficiency do not invalidate the intuition of the efficient markets hypothesis because the information is not available to traders and investors in financial markets. For a review of the early empirical work, see Eugene F. Fama, "Efficient Capital Markets: A Review of Theory and Empirical Work," *Journal of Finance,* 25:383–416, 1970.

January effect. For a long period of time, rates of return on stocks were abnormally high each January. Market participants often argue that the January effect results from investors seeking to minimize their tax liabilities: Investors sell stocks on which they have lost money at the end of the year to deduct the losses against capital gains realized on other assets during the year. In January of the new year, buying pressures emerge as investors rebalance their portfolios. Although this explanation seems logical, it is not consistent with the efficient markets hypothesis because institutional investors (such as private pension funds) are the largest market participants. These investors do not pay capital gains taxes and so should buy stock rather than sell stock in December if prices are abnormally low. In the 1980s and 1990s, economists found that the January effect diminished in importance except for shares of small firms.

Mean Reversion

Another prediction of the efficient markets hypothesis is that investors cannot relate changes in asset prices, and thus returns, to currently available information—only news can change prices and returns. The efficient markets hypothesis therefore is inconsistent with what is known as *mean reversion.* It is the tendency for stocks with high returns today to experience low returns in the future and for stocks with low returns today to experience high returns in the future. Some economists have found evidence consistent with mean reversion and against the efficient markets hypothesis. Other economists have noted that results supporting mean reversion are strongest for small-firm stocks and for data from the period before World War II.[†] These observations suggest that lower liquidity and higher information costs could be responsible for the apparent inefficiency. Hence, for most traders and investors, the notion that changes in stock prices are not predictable appears to be reasonable.

Excessive Volatility

The efficient markets hypothesis tells us that the price of an asset equals the market's best estimate of its fundamental value. Fluctuations in the actual market price therefore should be no greater than the fluctuations in the fundamental value. Robert Shiller of Yale University used actual data on dividends over a long period of time to calculate the fundamental value of the S&P 500 stocks.[††] He found that the actual market price fluctuated much more than his estimate of fluctuations in fundamental value, a rejection of the efficient markets hypothesis. Although some economists have criticized some of Shiller's

[†] A good summary of the evidence for and against mean reversion in stock prices can be found in Charles Engel and Charles S. Morris, "Challenges to Stock Market Efficiency: Evidence from Mean Reversion Studies," *Federal Reserve Bank of Kansas City Economic Review* (September–October):21–35, 1991.

[††] Robert J. Shiller, "Do Stock Prices Move Too Much to Be Justified by Subsequent Changes in Dividends?," *American Economic Review,* 71:463–486, 1981.

tests, many believe that those tests do cast some doubt on the validity of the efficient markets hypothesis as it applies to the stock market.

Statistical evidence from studies of financial markets generally confirms that stock prices reflect available information. However, examination of pricing anomalies, mean reversion, and excessive fluctuations in stock prices has generated controversy over whether the observed price fluctuations reflect only changes in fundamental value. Much of this debate centers on explanations for the tremendous volatility of stock prices in the late 1980s, particularly that surrounding the stock market crash of October 19, 1987.

Market Efficiency and the Crash of 1987

On Monday, October 19, 1987, the stock market crashed. The Dow Jones Industrial Average, the most often quoted stock index, fell by 508 points, losing nearly 23% of its value in a single day! Trading volume was a record 600 million shares. The decline in the market value of equities was significantly greater than occurred in the famous crash of October 28, 1929, when the Dow Jones Industrial Average fell by about 13%.

The 1980s had been a period of significant stock price increases—an unprecedentedly strong bull market. Soaring above 2500 in October 1987, the Dow Jones Industrial Average had been at 1500 as recently as 1985 and at only 1000 in 1982. Although stock prices had declined the week before the crash, the downturn on "Black Monday" was breathtaking.

This highly visible episode caused many economists and financial analysts to question the efficient markets hypothesis. There was no clearly identifiable bad news that day or during the previous weekend to suggest such a dramatic downward revaluation of the long-run profitability of U.S. business. Attempts to isolate particular bits of bad news—including congressional legislation that was thought to be harmful to equity markets and statements by policymakers in the United States and abroad—were unsuccessful. Economists then began trying to explain the crash on the basis of new approaches to asset pricing that did not rely on the efficient markets hypothesis.

Noise traders and fads. One explanation for the 1987 crash points to relatively uninformed traders called **noise traders,** who pursue trading strategies with no superior information. Noise traders often pursue **fads**—that is, overreaction to good or bad news about an issue or a class of assets (say, stocks or bonds in general). For example, noise traders may aggressively sell shares of stock or bonds of a company whose outlook is described unfavorably in a leading business publication. Of course, the efficient markets hypothesis holds that information that is available to market participants will have been reflected in the price long before the noise trader even removes the business publication from the mailbox! Nonetheless, the selling pressure from noise traders can force the share price down by more than the decrease suggested by the change in fundamental value.

Can't better-informed traders simply profit at the expense of noise traders? Not always. Albert Kyle of Duke University has shown that the presence of a significant fringe of noise traders creates additional risk in the market. An investor who believes in the efficient markets hypothesis has no assurance that a price will return to fundamental value after noise traders overreact.

Bubbles. Another explanation for the 1987 crash focuses on speculative episodes in the mid-1980s. When the price of an asset is more than its fundamental value, the price is said to contain a **bubble.** In those years of frantic stock market activity, some investors bought assets not to hold them but to resell them quickly at a profit, even though they knew that prices were greater than fundamental values.†

With a bubble, the "greater fool" theory comes into play: An investor is not a fool to buy the asset as long as there is a greater fool to buy it later for a still higher price. In other words, some investors might buy at inflated prices if they believe that they can sell to someone else for substantially more money. For example, suppose that you strongly suspect that the shares of Biogenetics, Inc., selling for $10, will never pay a dividend; that is, the stock has no fundamental value. However, knowing that the industry is "hot," you might still expect to find someone who will pay $12 per share next year. The stock will be a profitable investment for you as a buy-and-sell trader, as long as the risk-adjusted interest rate is less than 20%.

As long as the bubble grows at a slower pace than the economy as a whole, informed investors can profit by buying and selling the asset at prices greater than fundamental value. However, if the bubble grows at a faster rate than the economy as a whole, it will eventually absorb all the wealth in the market. Hence, at some point, the bubble must burst. Some observers believe that the prices in the Japanese stock market in the late 1980s, certain U.S. urban real estate markets in the late 1980s, and in high-technology stocks in the United States in 1999 and early 2000 all contained bubbles.

Trading mechanisms. Rather than disputing the efficient markets hypothesis, some economists instead have examined the role of trading mechanisms in fueling the downturn during the 1987 crash. Commissioned by President Reagan, this research was performed by a group chaired by Nicholas Brady, later Secretary of the Treasury. The Brady Task Force identified several weak links in the trading mechanism as explanations for the crash, rather than irrationality of market participants or fundamental imbalances in the economy as a whole.

First, the Task Force identified the way in which trades are executed on the New York Stock Exchange (NYSE) as one of the weak links. The large volume of sell orders early on October 19, 1987, overwhelmed the market makers known as *specialists*. Specialists have inventories of stock and will buy and sell the stock of companies in which they specialize to match buy and sell orders in individual stocks. On October 19, specialists' losses mounted, eroding their

†For an interesting discussion of financial bubbles in history and the present time, see Robert Shiller, *Irrational Exuberance,* Princeton, NJ: Princeton University Press, 2000.

CASE STUDY

What Goes Up . . .

Plunging stock prices in Japan in the 1990s caused many market analysts and economists to believe that a bubble in Japanese equities was bursting. As of December 2000, the Japanese Nikkei stock index had fallen by 67% from its all-time high at the end of 1989. If the collapse in Japanese stock prices was indeed a bubble bursting, historical episodes of bubbles suggest that the decline could reach 80% or more.

Bubbles are nothing new, as the accompanying table shows. The "tulipmania" in Holland in the seventeenth century is considered the original bubble, followed by a bubble in the price of shares in a firm developing French holdings in what is now the United States. Even Sir Isaac Newton discovered gravity in the bubble when he invested in the shares of South Sea Company in the early eighteenth century. In the twentieth century, U.S. markets experienced bubbles in stocks in the Roaring Twenties and in silver in the early 1980s. Stock markets in Mexico, Hong Kong, and Taiwan all suffered through the bursting of bubbles in recent years. The fear that Japanese stock prices had a bubble led many investors to sell their Japanese shares at a loss in the 1990s. Many economists believe that the boom, then bust, in NASDAQ-traded technology stocks in 1999 and 2000 shared elements of a bubble.

Booms and Busts

	% Rise bull phase	Length of up phase (months)	% Decline peak to trough	Length of down phase (months)
Tulips Holland (1634–37)	+5900%	36	−93%	10
Mississippi shares France (1719–21)	+6200%	13	−99%	13
South Sea shares Great Britain (1719–20)	+1000%	18	−84%	6
U.S. stocks United States (1921–32)	+497%	95	−87%	33
Mexican stocks Mexico (1978–81)	+785%	30	−73%	18
Silver United States (1979–82)	+710%	12	−88%	24
Hong Kong stocks Hong Kong (1970–74)	+1200%	28	−92%	20
Taiwan stocks Taiwan (1986–90)	+1168%	40	−80%	12
Japanese stocks Japan (1965–?)	+3720%	288	*	*

* −67% from December 29, 1989, peak to the October 1998 trough (a trough hit again in December 2000).

Source: "When Bears Run Wild," April 4, 1992, from *The Economist Newspaper.*

equity capital during the day, and their financial stability began to be questioned. If specialists lack the necessary capital to make the market in their stocks, they are unable to function, the liquidity of stocks is reduced, and the ability of market prices to communicate information is curtailed. In response to the Commission's findings, the NYSE increased the minimum equity capital required of specialists and the minimum level of inventory of shares they would be required to maintain. Even with these changes, the specialists may not be able to cope much better today during such events.

Second, the Task Force suggested ways to avoid failure of the market trading mechanism. It recommended **circuit breakers,** or interventions designed to restore orderly markets. When prices or order volumes reach certain levels, trading will be halted. Staff economists argued that halts based on large price movements might unnecessarily block the flow of information contained in market prices to participants. They did, however, endorse trading halts based on large imbalances between buy and sell orders. One proposal suggested that during a trading halt, specialists would open their order books to take nonbinding orders and announce what they believe to be the market-clearing price. After a few rounds of such open-order periods, the market could be reopened. The incentive to participate could be provided by executing first the orders of those traders who participated in the open-order period.

Following the publication of the Task Force report, the Working Group on Financial Markets (composed of officials from the Treasury Department, the Federal Reserve, the Commodity Futures Trading Commission, and the Securities and Exchange Commission) recommended trading halts after major declines in stock market indexes. The Working Group composed a report recommending open-order periods during a trading halt. These recommendations were adopted, and the circuit breakers are still in place (though the circuit breakers were made less restrictive in February 1998).

The effectiveness of these proposals was tested almost exactly two years after the 1987 crash, when the Dow Jones Industrial Average dropped 190 points on October 13, 1989. Trading was not halted on the New York Stock Exchange, but price-based circuit breakers were in place in futures and options markets. Problems in the trading mechanism between the markets caused concern, suggesting that, to be most effective, the use of circuit breakers should be coordinated among the markets.

A third factor identified by some observers as a reason for the 1987 crash is computer-based, or program, trading. In **program trading,** computer-generated orders to buy or sell many stocks at the same time cause rapid adjustments of institutional portfolios. The large volume of sell orders generated by program trading during the crash met with NYSE disapproval. However, no solid evidence links program trading to stock price volatility.

Value Investing versus Efficient Markets

Despite the efficient markets hypothesis' intuitive appeal, some very successful large investors (such as Warren Buffett) have earned enormous returns from *value investing*—buying stocks with low prices relative to earnings, dividends, historical prices, or other measures of value. Originally the subject of research by Columbia University professors Benjamin Graham and David Dodd in the 1930s, the strategies were studied with renewed vigor by economists in the 1980s and 1990s. In both the United States and Japan, it appears that stocks with low market values of equity relative to historical prices outperform the market.

Josef Lakonishok of the University of Illinois, Andrei Shleifer of Harvard University, and Robert Vishny of the University of Chicago considered the success of various investment strategies over the period from 1968 to 1990.[†] They found that value stocks outperformed glamour stocks (those with high past growth) over this period by more than 10% per year. The authors emphasized that many investors likely have shorter time horizons than those required to obtain a payoff from value investing. They argued that whether such returns were likely to continue depends on the extent to which institutional investors, such as mutual fund or pension fund managers, rely more in the future on quantitative investment strategies that are designed to identify value stocks.

The results of Lakonishok, Shleifer, and Vishny raise a question about whether the high returns from value investing represent greater risk being assumed by investors. This is an important ongoing topic of research on the extent to which the stock market is efficient.

COSTS OF INEFFICIENCY IN FINANCIAL MARKETS

The arguments for and against the efficient markets hypothesis are not merely academic disagreements. Market efficiency provides an information service to the financial system, and a lack of efficiency is a cost to the economy and society. In this section, we detail what those costs are and demonstrate how the economy benefits when those costs can be reduced. We focus on two potential costs to the economy from financial market inefficiency: (1) those arising from excessive fluctuations in asset prices and (2) those arising from inefficiency caused by high information costs.

Costs of Excessive Price Fluctuations

When changes in prices of financial assets, such as stocks and bonds, do not reflect shifts in fundamental value, market prices contain less information. As a result, financial markets fail to send the appropriate signals for lending, borrowing, and portfolio allocation decisions. In addition, if prices are more volatile than fundamental values, stock and bond markets are not effectively providing risk-sharing services. At the same time that financial assets become less useful for risk sharing, trading volume may decline, making financial assets less liquid. Although these costs exist, there is no reliable way to measure them.

[†] Josef Lakonishok, Andrei Shleifer, and Robert W. Vishny, "Contrarian Investment, Extrapolation, and Risk," *Journal of Finance,* 49:1541–1578, 1994.

More recently, financial analysts and policymakers have worried that excessive fluctuations in the stock market could cause excessively volatile economic activity. They focus on the links between the financial system and the economy through lending and borrowing. For example, would household consumption and business investment increase and decrease as stock prices fluctuate, even if those price movements were the result of a fad or bubble? Evidence from the U.S. economy after the stock market crash of 1987 suggests that household consumption and business investment didn't decline immediately, although segments of the securities industry were hit hard with sharply reduced profits and layoffs. Rather, research indicates that consumers and businesses pay more attention to long-run movements than to short-term shifts in asset prices.

Despite the lack of evidence linking volatility in the stock market with fluctuations in economic activity, some policymakers have proposed regulatory interventions. In addition to the circuit breakers suggested by the Brady Task Force, legislators have proposed transaction taxes and changes in margin requirements.

If conducting transactions costs very little, bubbles might stimulate too much trading, contributing to excessive volatility. One proposal for preventing this situation is to charge a *transaction tax* for each market transaction. This tax would effectively raise the cost of trading and decrease trading activity. The tax has appeal, but it also creates two problems. First, decreasing trading volume can reduce liquidity in the stock market. Second, if the tax raises trading costs in the United States, stock trading activities along with revenue and jobs in the securities industry might move overseas. These drawbacks have caused Germany, the United Kingdom, the Netherlands, and Sweden to reduce or eliminate transaction taxes.

In the United States, the Federal Reserve Board sets a *margin requirement,* which is the minimum proportion of the purchase price of shares that an investor must supply from nonborrowed funds. An investor can borrow from a broker only the amount of the purchase price above the margin requirement. Some analysts claim that buying shares on credit encourages speculation and generates greater swings in gains and losses. One proposed reform is to raise margin requirements to discourage speculation. There is no clear evidence, however, that stock price volatility declines when margin requirements are increased, or vice versa. Moreover, as with transaction taxes, an additional cost of raising margin requirements to reduce trading is that it might reduce liquidity.

To summarize, while excessive price fluctuations can be costly, arguments for government intervention to reduce stock price volatility outside of periods of market crisis are weak.

Information Costs

When financial markets are inefficient, savers and borrowers face higher information costs—and the economy suffers because scarce resources (investment dollars) aren't allocated efficiently. Some of these costs are offset by other participants in the financial system. If information is not readily available to participants, market prices may not represent fundamental value—even if the prices reflect all *publicly available information.* To obtain the missing information, savers and borrowers must incur research and monitoring costs. Such expenses are unnecessary for individual savers and borrowers when market prices represent the best estimate of fundamental value.

In practice, businesses raise most of their funds from current and accumulated profits, not from financial markets. Savers and borrowers reduce actual information costs by channeling funds through intermediaries (particularly banks, but also mutual funds, pension funds, and insurance companies) instead of through markets. In fact, the largest participants in markets for bonds, stocks, and other financial instruments in the United States and other industrialized countries are not individual savers and borrowers, but financial intermediaries (Chapter 3). As we will see in Part 4, intermediaries both reduce information costs for many savers and borrowers and contribute to liquidity and efficiency of financial markets. As a result, policymakers in many countries are more concerned about the stability of financial intermediaries than about volatility in financial markets.

KEY TERMS AND CONCEPTS

Bubble
Circuit breakers
Efficient markets hypothesis
Fads
Fundamental value
Noise traders
Program trading
Rational expectations

SUMMARY

1. Market prices for financial instruments contain important information for lending, borrowing, and portfolio allocation decisions. When traders and investors have rational expectations, they use all available information in forming their expectations of future returns. In this case, the equilibrium price of a financial instrument is equal to the optimal forecast of fundamental value.
2. Under the efficient markets hypothesis, changes in the price of a financial instrument reflect news about changes in fundamental value and are not forecastable. Security prices fluctuate in an efficient market as fundamental value increases or decreases.
3. Although statistical evidence suggests that prices of liquid assets traded in financial markets reflect available information about fundamental value, stock prices appear to be more volatile than the efficient markets hypothesis suggests. For example, no apparent "fundamental" factor can explain the precipitous drop in stock prices during the stock market crash of October 19, 1987.
4. Potential costs to the economy from inefficient financial markets arise from excessive fluctuations of asset prices relative to fundamental values and from high information costs. Most economists believe that information costs resulting from the lack of substantial amounts of information are especially severe. These costs help to explain the relative unimportance of financial markets in raising funds for businesses.

THE WALL STREET JOURNAL MARCH 17, 1999

So, Is the Stock Market Overvalued?

Almost exactly a year ago, with the Dow Jones Industrial Average at 8782, we published an article in this space headlined "Are Stocks Overvalued? Not a Chance." The piece drew criticism from a financial establishment that had been preaching imminent disaster, pointing to high price–earnings ratios and low dividend yields and predicting that stock prices would fall when this zany euphoria wore off. They were dead wrong. Yesterday the Dow broke 10,000 before closing at 9930. Including dividends, the 30 stocks of the industrial average have returned 15% since our piece appeared, while the stocks of the Standard & Poor's 500 have returned 21%.

Dire warnings from **b** professionals have accompanied nearly every step of the Dow's rise from 777 on August 12, 1982. Could it be that the model that Wall Street has been using to assess whether stocks are overvalued—a model based largely on historic price–earnings ratios—is deeply flawed? We think so. Investors are ignoring the old shibboleths and pricing companies like Gillette at a P/E of 64 or Microsoft at a P/E of 66. This reflects not their nuttiness but their sanity. **a**

Contrary to Alan Greenspan's famous warning—made on December 5, 1996, with the Dow at 6437—investors' today are *rationally* exuberant. . . . Our calculations show that with earnings growing in the long term at the same rate as the gross domestic product and Treasury bonds below 6%, a perfectly reasonable level for the Dow would be 36,000—tomorrow, not 10 or 20 years from now. . . .

Stocks and bonds should offer similar returns at the very least. But according to Ibbotson Associates, large-company stocks have since 1926 been producing average annual returns of 11%, while long-term Treasury bonds have returned just 5.2%.

Why do stocks return so much more? . . . [The] best answer is that investors are irrationally fearful of the volatility of stocks, and therefore demand an extra return to compensate for their fears. What has happened since 1982, and especially during the past four years, is that investors . . . are requiring a much smaller extra return, or "risk premium," from stocks to compensate for their fear. That premium, which has averaged about 7% in modern history, is now around 3%. We believe it is headed for its proper level: zero. That means stock prices should rise accordingly. . . .

Will stock prices rise forever? No, they'll rise until they reach a level where stock returns (the money stocks put in your pockets over a long period) equal bond returns. We are not there yet, but we're on the way—as four straight years of 20%-plus returns attest. . . . **c**

In short, investors' enthusiasm is well founded. The risks of stock investing—never so great as imagined—really have declined. In 1952, a New York Stock Exchange survey found that only 4% of Americans owned equities; today, the figure is nearing 50%. It is this broad ownership of stocks that is the most profound evidence that investors have become more rational and that Dow 10,000 is only the beginning.

The efficient markets hypothesis says that the prices of financial assets such as stocks reflect available information about expected returns. That information can provide valuable guidance to savers and borrowers. Although most analysts would not dispute the notion that available information works its way into asset prices, some commentators have expressed concern that U.S. stocks are overvalued. That is, at the end of the 1990s and continuing into the new century, a vigorous debate took place about whether current market prices of equities exceeded underlying fundamental value. Our description of valuation in an efficient market can be used to shed light on this debate.

a The statement builds in the simple valuation model presented on page 239, in which the fundamental value of a stock depends on its dividend, the growth rate of dividends and earnings, and the appropriate discount rate. Low interest rates (discount rates) and continued profitability (dividends and earnings growth) would clearly be good news for stock values.

b From the valuation expression we derived on page 239, the return on stocks can be thought of as the sum of the dividend–price ratio (dividend yield) and the expected growth rate of dividends. The authors note that this return on stocks has historically been much greater than the return on Treasury bonds. One source of difference is the risk of stocks relative to the risk of Treasury bonds.

If no "equity risk premium" existed for stock returns, stock prices should rise until the dividend–price ratio plus the growth rate of earnings equals the expected rate of return on bonds. As the authors note, such a price increase could be significant.

c Should you rush headlong into stocks? Not necessarily. As the authors note, analysts' bullishness about future earnings may be overly optimistic. More generally, an analysis of the vanishing equity premium (appealing to, perhaps, changing investor attitudes, investor composition, or transactions costs) is in order. A difficult task remains: in an efficient market, one needs an explanation of why the equity risk premium took so long to shrink.

For further thought . . .

How might reductions in transactions costs for equities relative to bonds affect the equity risk premium? What does your answer imply about the link between market liquidity and market efficiency?

Source: From James K. Glassman and Kevin Hassett, "Stock Prices Are Still Far Too Low," *The Wall Street Journal*, March 17, 1999. Republished by permission of Dow Jones, Inc. via Copyright Clearance Center, Inc.

REVIEW QUESTIONS

1. Define rational expectations. In a market in which investors and traders have rational expectations, what should the price of an asset equal?
2. Is there a connection between market liquidity and market efficiency? Why or why not?
3. Give a concise definition of the efficient markets hypothesis. What assumptions does it require about liquidity and information?
4. If you believe that the stock market is an efficient market, why would an investment strategy of "buy and hold" be a good idea?
5. Suppose that the price of a stock rises only because people believe that it will rise, not because the corporation is likely to earn higher profits. What is this situation called? What is likely to happen to the price sometime in the future? Has it ever happened to an entire market?
6. Suppose that you believe that General Motors' earnings will rise by 20% this year, compared to only 10% last year. Should you buy GM stock?
7. If you are an informed trader, would you be happy to see numerous noise traders in the market?
8. State whether each of the following statements is true or false and, using the efficient markets hypothesis, briefly explain why.
   a. Stock prices do not change.
   b. Stock prices go up with published good news and down with published bad news.
   c. Stock prices reflect true underlying (fundamental) value.
9. Why are fads inconsistent with the predictions of the efficient markets hypothesis?
10. What is program trading? Does it play a significant role in increasing market volatility?

ANALYTICAL PROBLEMS

11. "They make money the old-fashioned way. They churn it." Why might someone who believes in market efficiency make this statement?
12. Jeremy Siegel and Richard Thaler argue that if the equity premium just reflects the increased risk of equities, then equities should be attractive to investors who are less risk averse than the marginal investor. If the equity premium is too large to be justified by the increased risk of equities, then it may reflect, in part, investors' "mistakes and fears." Siegel and Thaler state that: "[M]ost economists we know have a high proportion of their retirement wealth invested in equities. . . ." If true, what would be the implications of this fact for economists' views of the workings of the stock market?
13. Suppose that in looking at data on stock market returns, you find that returns are higher than average in January but below average during the rest of the year. Is this consistent with market efficiency? Why or why not? What could an investor do to take advantage of this situation?
14. Suppose you find that, after accounting for differences in risk, liquidity, and information costs, some stocks are overpriced ($P_{t+1} = 1.1P^e_{t+1} + \text{Error}_{t+1}$) and others are underpriced ($P_{t+1} = 0.9P^e_{t+1} + \text{Error}_{t+1}$). Are the markets efficient? What should you do to make expected profits?
15. According to the efficient markets hypothesis, would you be better off paying someone 5% of your savings to pick stocks for you or picking your own stocks by throwing darts at the stock pages of the newspaper? Why?
16. Suppose that you are shopping and find a wonderful new product that you think will be a big seller. It should increase tremendously the profits of the company that sells it. Should you buy shares in that company? Why or why not?
17. Suppose that Bigbucks Company pays a dividend this year of $7 per share. You expect the dividend to grow by 2% per year, so you discount Bigbucks's dividends at 4%. What is the most you

would be willing to pay for a share of stock in Bigbucks? Suppose instead that you discount Bigbucks's dividends at 3%. Now how much would you be willing to pay per share? If Bigbucks's dividends grow only 1% per year instead of 2% (using 4% as the discount rate again), how much would you be willing to pay per share?

18. What do you think caused the stock market crash of October 19, 1987? Why? What do you think is wrong, if anything, with the other explanations presented in the text?

19. Suppose that people generally overreact to news. That is, when good news arrives, the prices of a company's stocks and bonds increase too much, and after bad news arrives, the prices decline too much. How can you profit from this knowledge?

DATA QUESTION

20. Find the most recent *Economic Report of the President* in your library. Table B-91 in the back of the report lists common stock prices and yields. The next-to-last column of the table reports the "dividend–price ratio," which is defined as the average ratio of dividends to price for the S&P 500 stocks. An increase in the dividend–price ratio over time implies that dividends are growing more rapidly than market prices. A decrease in the dividend–price ratio over time implies that dividends are growing more slowly than market prices. What happened to the dividend–price ratio over the decade of the 1980s? If you believe that the stock market is efficient, how would you explain this pattern?

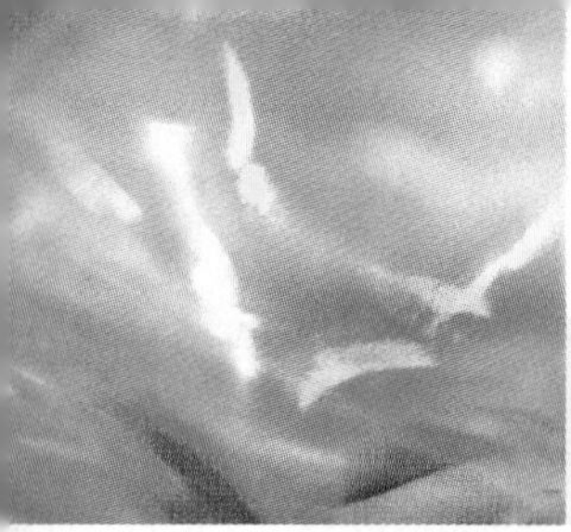

CHAPTER 11

Reducing Transactions Costs and Information Costs

The collapse of communist governments in the former Soviet Union and Eastern Europe in the early 1990s led to much rejoicing and hope for the emergence of individual freedom, political democracy, and market economies. As attention turned to getting private businesses started, financial analysts foresaw a daunting task. Savers seemed unwilling to lend their funds to local borrowers, preferring to invest in government bonds or foreign exchange. Borrowers found financial markets too poorly developed to be of much use. Hungary and Poland made strides in developing financial markets. Russia still struggled in the late 1990s and in the new century to do so. One prominent economist noted wearily that "hundreds of billions of dollars were being left on the table" because eager entrepreneurs were unable to fund new businesses while savers were unable to earn returns on their savings. Most financial experts suggested that efforts should focus on organizing financial intermediaries.

Financial markets in the United States and many other industrial economies perform the task of matching savers and borrowers more effectively than do those in newly emerging economies, but there are still obstacles to the efficient channeling of funds from savers to borrowers. In our discussions of financial markets, we assumed that borrowers were successful in raising funds in financial markets and that savers could use the information contained in market prices to make informed portfolio allocation decisions. Financial markets don't function quite as smoothly as we implied. In this chapter, we describe the obstacles that exist in financial markets—transactions costs and information costs—to see how they are mitigated in our financial system. Often, financial intermediaries such as banks reduce information costs more effectively than financial markets do, as we will explain here.

OBSTACLES TO MATCHING SAVERS AND BORROWERS

Suppose that you saved $3000 from working part-time and you want to invest it. Should you invest the money in stocks? A stockbroker will tell you that the commissions you must pay will be large relative to the size of your purchases because you are investing a small amount of money. This cost is particularly high if you are attempting to diversify by buying a few shares each of different stocks. Should you turn instead to the bond market to buy, say, a Treasury bill? Your broker will tell you, sorry, but the minimum face value is $10,000.

Undaunted, you decide to bypass financial markets. Conveniently, your roommate's brother-in-law needs $3000 to develop a potentially successful new Internet browser. But how do you know that he is the best person to write and market this computer application? Perhaps you should seek out other borrowers and evaluate their plans. If you decide to lend your money to the fledgling entrepreneur, your lawyer tells you that to draw up the contract describing the terms of your investment will cost $1500, or half the amount you have to invest. Hence you give up on the investment. The cost that you face and your decision not to invest also hurt the browser designer, who will have the same difficulty raising funds from other individual investors.

This example demonstrates **transactions costs,** the costs of buying or selling a financial instrument, such as a stock or a bond. **Information costs** are the costs that savers incur to determine the creditworthiness of borrowers and to monitor how borrowers use the acquired funds. These costs increase the cost of funds that borrowers must pay and lower the expected returns to savers, reducing the efficiency of financial markets. This inefficiency creates profit opportunities for individuals and institutions that can reduce transactions and information costs.

Transactions Costs

Brokerage commissions, minimum investment requirements, and lawyers' fees are all examples of transactions costs. There is obviously a need for a channel to match small savers and borrowers, and financial intermediaries have satisfied a need that financial markets are not filling. For example, mutual funds sell shares to many individual savers and, in turn, invest in a diversified portfolio of bonds or stocks. Banks accept deposits from individual savers and lend the funds to household and business borrowers. The economy also benefits from the growth generated by financial intermediaries, while the intermediaries earn a profit by charging savers and borrowers fees for reducing transactions costs.

Financial intermediaries reduce transactions costs by exploiting **economies of scale,** the reduction of costs per unit that accompanies an increase in volume. In the case of transactions costs, intermediaries' costs fall as the size of the funds raised increases. Transactions costs per dollar of investment decline as the size of transactions increases. For example, the transactions cost of buying $1,000,000 of Treasury bonds is not much greater than that of buying $10,000 of bonds. Individual investors can reduce transactions costs by combining their purchases through an intermediary. Thus 100 investors with $10,000 each to invest face lower costs per dollar if together they buy $1,000,000 of bonds than if they purchased the bonds individually.

There are other ways in which intermediaries benefit from economies of scale—for example, in drawing up legal contracts. Financial intermediaries spread legal costs among many individual savers so that each saver who wants to invest in an invention, the corner drugstore, or an IBM bond doesn't have to seek costly, customized legal advice. Financial intermediaries also take advantage of economies of scale to purchase sophisticated computer systems that provide financial services, such as automatic teller machine networks.

In Chapters 12 and 13, we examine in more detail how mutual funds, banks, and other financial intermediaries reduce transactions costs for savers and borrowers.

Asymmetric Information and Information Costs

In describing transactions in financial markets, we have assumed that savers and borrowers have the same information, or *symmetric information.* That is, individuals buying shares in or bonds of a company have the same information as the company's managers. This assumption does not mean that the parties will have perfect information; conditions may unfold differently from their initial expectations. For example, a change in consumers' tastes might mean that the borrower faces a more challenging market than expected and must default on bond payments. When the lender and borrower exchanged funds for a security, neither could perfectly anticipate market conditions or economic events, but both had the same information and could make informed decisions.

In the real world, borrowers may have private information. A company issuing bonds may be aware of a potential lawsuit or other unfavorable conditions, but the buyer of those bonds may be uninformed. **Asymmetric information** describes the situation in which one party in a transaction has better information than the other. Most typically, the borrower has better information than the lender. The existence of asymmetric information makes it costly for savers and borrowers to make exchanges in financial markets. In the next two sections, we describe two costs arising from asymmetric information:

Adverse selection: a lender's problem of distinguishing the good-risk applicants from the bad-risk applicants before making an investment.

Moral hazard: a lender's verification that borrowers are using their funds as intended.

In some cases, the cost of adverse selection and moral hazard can be so great that a lender will lend only to the government or other well-known borrowers. However, more generally there are practical solutions to these problems, in which the markets or financial intermediaries lower the cost of information needed to make investment decisions.

ADVERSE SELECTION

The used car market demonstrates the problems that adverse selection can pose for buyers and sellers in a market.[†] Suppose that your parents are trying

[†] This example of adverse selection was first described by George Akerlof of the University of California, Berkeley. George A. Akerlof, "The Market for 'Lemons': Quality Uncertainty and the Market Mechanism," *Quarterly Journal of Economics,* 84:488–500, 1970.

to sell their 2000 Chevrolet Caprice. Among all the 2000 Chevrolet Caprices in the newspaper ads, some are good cars and others are "lemons" (cars that are constantly in the repair shop). Sellers, such as your parents, know the quality of their cars, but uninformed readers of newspaper ads do not. Because these potential buyers can't distinguish good cars from lemons, they will offer the price of an *average-quality* 2000 Caprice to sellers of all 2000 Caprices. Your parents view this price as too low and consider their good Caprice to be *undervalued*. The price delights the Sunkists down the street, who own a lemon. Their Caprice is *overvalued* at the average price, and the Sunkists can hardly wait to unload it. As a result of this pricing process, owners of good Caprices may decide not to sell their cars. Therefore the available pool of used Caprices consists of cars of below-average quality, resulting in an adverse selection of potential used cars. In the used car market, buyers and sellers find trading among themselves costly.

To reduce the costs of adverse selection, car dealers act as intermediaries between buyers and sellers. To maintain their reputations with buyers, dealers are less willing to take advantage of their private information about the quality of the used cars that they are selling than are individual sellers. As a result, dealers sell both lemons and good cars for their true values. In addition, government regulations require that car dealers disclose information about the cars to consumers.

"Lemons Problems" in Financial Markets

Just as in the used car market, lemons problems make lending in financial markets more costly, and financial information disclosure regulations again come to the rescue. How does adverse selection affect the stock and bond markets' ability to channel funds from savers to borrowers? First, let's look at the stock market. Suppose that Hitechco is a new maker of computer chips. If the firm obtains capital, it will be able to finance an exciting new technological development in chip making. If Hitechco issues new shares of stock, it can pursue the chip-making project. If it doesn't, it loses the opportunity.

At the same time, Lemonco is seeking funds to develop a product similar to Hitechco's, but, unknown to the market, Lemonco's product is inferior. In fact, on the basis of available information, investors can't determine the quality of the firms' scientific expertise and their productive capabilities. When Hitechco tries to sell stock, then, the market will assign the same value to it as to Lemonco's stock, and Hitechco's shares will be undervalued. Hitechco's cost of funds is higher than it would be if potential shareholders had all the information the firm possessed.

Adverse selection is present in the bond market as well. Suppose that Hitechco and Lemonco know more about the risk of their projects than do investors in the bond market. If an increase in interest rates on default-risk-free Treasury bonds makes them a more attractive investment than Hitechco or Lemonco bonds, lenders raise the interest rate they require to hold Hitechco and Lemonco bonds. In this situation, as lenders generally raise their required returns on bonds, adverse selection occurs. The reason is that, at high interest rates, only very risky borrowers, such as Lemonco, will be likely to borrow funds: If their projects are successful, both lenders and borrowers win big; if (as is more likely) they aren't, the lenders suffer. Lenders are aware of this problem and may restrict the availability of credit rather than raise rates to the level at which the quantities of funds demanded and supplied are equal. This restricting of credit is known as **credit rationing.** When lenders ration credit, borrowed funds become more costly for unknown firms—both good and bad.

Adverse selection is costly for the economy. When good firms have difficulty communicating information to financial markets, their external financing costs rise. This situation forces firms to grow primarily through investment of internal funds, or investment by firm insiders and accumulated profits.† Because the firms that are most affected are usually in dynamic, emerging sectors of the economy, opportunities for growth of physical capital, employment, and production are likely to be restricted.

Reducing Information Costs

The costs to savers and borrowers of adverse selection make it difficult for good borrowers to raise money in financial markets and lower the returns obtained by savers. Similarly, good borrowers are willing to pay to communicate information about their prospects. Some financial market participants charge fees for their services—to savers who seek information about borrowers and to borrowers who wish to communicate information about their prospects to savers—but these fees are lower than the information costs of adverse selection. Other costs can be mitigated by regulation of financial markets. As we will see later, these costs can also be reduced by financial intermediaries who can provide savers with information about the quality of potential borrowers.

Direct disclosure of information. In most industrialized countries, government agencies set requirements for information disclosure for firms that desire to sell securities in financial markets. In the United States, government regulations promulgated by the Securities and Exchange Commission† require publicly owned companies to report their performance in financial statements prepared by using standard accounting methods. Such disclosure reduces the information costs of adverse selection, but it doesn't eliminate them, for two reasons. First, some good firms may be too young to have much information for potential investors to evaluate. Second, lemon firms will try to present the required information in the best possible light so that investors will overvalue their securities.

---

†If entrepreneurs have to avoid high information costs associated with external financing by investing most of their savings in their businesses, they lose risk-sharing benefits of diversification.

††The SEC also mandates firms' ongoing disclosure of material information to the investor community. In August 2000, the SEC went further by approving Regulation Fair Disclosure (FD), which required U.S. companies to release material information to the general public at the same time it is issued to Wall Street professionals. Many economists argue that the regulatory change will make information dissemination to the institutional investors and analysts more difficult, while proponents see the new rule as empowering individual investors.

Private firms have tried to reduce the costs of adverse selection by collecting information on individual borrowers and selling the information to savers. As long as the information-gathering firm does a good job, savers purchasing the information will be better able to judge the quality of borrowers, improving the efficiency of lending. Although savers must pay for the information, they can benefit from the information by earning higher returns. Companies specializing in information—including Moody's Investor Service, Standard & Poor's Corporation, Value Line, and Dun and Bradstreet—collect information from businesses' income statements, balance sheets, and investment decisions and sell it to subscribers. Buyers include individual investors, libraries, and financial intermediaries. You can find some of these publications in your college library or through on-line information services. Private information-gathering firms cannot eliminate adverse selection, but they can help to minimize its cost.

Although only subscribers pay for the information collected, others can benefit without paying for it. Individuals who gain access to the information without paying for it are **free riders.** That is, they obtain the same benefits but do not incur the costs. The *free-rider problem* hurts the information-gathering firm and lessens its effectiveness. Suppose that you subscribe to Infoperfect, a service that gives you the best possible information on the stocks and bonds of many companies. You are willing to pay a fee to subscribe to Infoperfect because it enables you to profit by buying undervalued stocks and bonds (using information that is better than other investors have). While you are reminding yourself of your cleverness and foresight, Freeda Frieryde and her colleagues decide to buy and sell particular stocks and bonds whenever you do. Because Freeda broadcasts your every move, others are sharing in your profits. As a result, you are willing to pay less to Infoperfect, as are other investors. Deprived of the additional revenue, Infoperfect is less willing to collect as much information to sell to savers.

When direct disclosure of information fails to provide enough information to reduce the likelihood of adverse selection, lenders can redesign financial contracts to reduce information costs by focusing on borrowers' collateral and net worth.

Roles of collateral and net worth. When borrowers invest little of their own money in their business, their loss is small if they default on their bonds. To make it more costly for borrowers to take advantage of their asymmetric information, lenders often require borrowers to pledge some of their own assets as **collateral,** which the lender claims if the borrower defaults. Suppose that Eleanor Riche wants to borrow $10,000 to start a home improvement business called Newvo Riche. If she owns a house worth $250,000, a lender might not hesitate to lend her the money. In the event that Eleanor defaults, a lender could claim the house or other assets that she might have pledged as collateral. Collateral reduces the likelihood of adverse selection—lemon borrowers are unlikely to pledge their own funds—and is widely used in debt contracts for individuals and businesses.

Net worth, the difference between assets and liabilities, satisfies the same assurance that collateral does. If lenders can make a claim against net worth if the borrower defaults on its loans, the firm will be more cautious about making risky investments. When a firm's net worth is high, the chance that it will default is low: Bondholders must be paid off—from the firm's net worth, if necessary—before funds can be distributed to shareholders. As a result, costs of adverse selection are less likely in lending to borrowers with high net worth.

Concluding remarks. Adverse selection increases the information costs of channeling funds from savers to borrowers in financial markets. Increased information costs in turn increase the demand for financing arrangements in which information about borrowers can be collected at a lower cost. These arrangements include direct information disclosure and collateral and net worth.

CHECKPOINT

As you read about the possibilities offered by the World Wide Web, you decide you want to invest some of your savings in an Internet service provider. You note that many small firms appear to be making a lot of money, but rating agencies haven't followed them closely. What information costs do you face if you go ahead with your investment plans? Because it is likely to be difficult to distinguish good and lemon Internet service providers, adverse selection may occur. Some of the firms rushing to sell shares may be lemons. You will incur costs of acquiring information about the firms as a result. o

MORAL HAZARD

Even though a lender might gather information about the borrower—when deciding to make an investment or a loan or structure a bond agreement that minimizes the effects of adverse selection—the lender's information problems haven't ended. There is always the chance that, after the borrower receives the funds, the funds will not be used as intended. This situation, known as moral hazard, is more likely to occur when the borrower has an incentive to conceal information or act in a way that does not reflect the lender's interests. Moral hazard arises because of asymmetric information: The borrower knows more than the lender does about how the borrowed funds will actually be used, and the resulting problems increase the lender's costs.

Moral Hazard in Equity Financing

Monitoring problems increase the information costs of raising funds through stock issues. For example, say that you buy stock in Bigdream, Inc. How do you know whether the firm is investing the funds in its research and development laboratory or in wood paneling for the new executive dining room? The investment in research and development is likely to increase Bigdream's profits and your returns; the wood paneling is not. To find out whether the firm is using funds in a way that will benefit you, you need to spend time and money monitoring its activities. When Bigdream's managers tell you that your $1000 investment earned no returns, how do you know whether the claims

CONSIDER THIS . . .

Are Stock Market Signals Affected by Adverse Selection?

In an efficient capital market, the value of a company's stock provides the best signal to managers about the profitability of new investments. Stock prices increase in response to good news, suggesting that more capital should be allocated to the firm's lines of business. Similarly, a decline in stock prices reflects news about market pessimism regarding the firm's prospects.

How does asymmetric information affect these relationships? In the case of adverse selection, or the lemons problem, for the stock market, share prices of a good firm can be too low, sending inaccurate signals about its prospects. In such a situation, management knows that the firm's prospects are better than the market price signals and will not turn to the market. Instead, the firm might choose to avoid the market altogether and use internal funds to finance future growth.

A study of some 300 manufacturing firms during the 1970s and 1980s found that firms that rely heavily on internal funds tend to be young, rapidly growing firms. Moreover, these firms' capital spending is closely tied to their internal funds. In contrast, capital spending by more mature firms that are capable of raising funds in financial markets is not. Hence adverse selection affects financing and investment decisions for many U.S. firms.

Source: Steven M. Fazzari, R. Glenn Hubbard, and Bruce C. Petersen, "Financing Constraints and Corporate Investment," *Brookings Papers on Economic Activity,* 1:143–195, 1988; and the review in R. Glenn Hubbard, "Capital-Market Imperfections and Investment," *Journal of Economic Literature,* 36:196–229, 1998.

are true? Once you have bought the stock, the firm has an incentive to understate profits and reduce your dividend payments. To police such underreporting, outside suppliers of funds must audit the firm's finances every time an earnings report is issued—and such audits are costly.

The federal government and the business community itself regulate reporting by firms to reduce the chance of fraud. In addition to regulating annual reports for the benefit of owners and potential investors, the Securities and Exchange Commission—a government agency—and the Financial Accounting Standards Board—a private agency—have set standard accounting principles for firms to use in reporting their earnings and overall financial condition. These accounting principles are designed to help investors understand the financial condition of the firms in which they have invested. In addition, federal laws have made misreporting or stealing profits belonging to shareholders a federal offense, punishable by large fines or prison terms, or both.

Another information problem results from the behavior of a firm's agents, who have different goals than the principals. The shareholders, who *own* the firm's net worth, are the **principals**, and the managers, who *control* the firm's assets, are the **agents.** Called the **principal-agent problem,** this type of moral hazard may arise when managers do not own much of the firm's equity and thus do not have the same incentive to maximize the firm's value as the owners do. Because a firm's shareholders have a residual claim on its earnings, improvements in profitability (and hence in the firm's stock price) accrue to them and not to the managers who are charged with controlling the firm's assets. In the United States, for example, the majority of private economic activity occurs in large public corporations, whose managers do not own a significant part of the firm. Indeed, the stake of top management in a firm's ownership usually is less than 5%. Because management stakes in large U.S. corporations are typically less than 5%, an increase in management stakes might benefit their shareholders, though evidence is mixed.†

An example will demonstrate the principal-agent problem in stock ownership. Suppose that your neighbor, Reed Moore, asks you to join him in his new business venture, a bookstore. He needs $50,000 to open the bookstore, but he has only $2500. He read in the newspaper that you won the lottery and knows that you could invest $47,500. After you make the investment, you own 95% of the bookstore, and Reed owns the other 5%. You're pleased with the investment. If Reed provides savvy tips on the best books and chats with the customers over coffee, the bookstore could make $50,000 each year after paying his salary. Your share would be $47,500, a 100% return; Reed's share would be $2500 (in addition to his salary). But maybe not. Reed might decide to buy mahogany bookcases and oriental rugs and chat with customers over champagne, leaving no profit. Although Reed would forgo the $2500 in profits, he would still receive a salary—and enjoy working in plush surroundings. Nothing would be left over for you.

The principal-agent problem exists in most equity contracts. Many uses of corporate funds by managers are highly visible (such as spending on large-scale investment projects), but many are hidden from view (such as expenses for research, maintenance, management, and organizational efficiency). Although not fraudulent, expenses such as corporate art collections, mahogany desks, limousines, and jets do not directly benefit shareholders. Managers often run firms to satisfy their personal goals, which might include accruing prestige and power. If managers aren't motivated to maximize a firm's value, nonmanagement shareholders may get shortchanged.

The shareholders own the firm, so why can't they just fire bad managers? To determine whether management is using corporate funds efficiently requires detailed and costly audits. No individual small shareholder has an incentive to pay these monitoring costs. Even if some individual shareholder offered to do so, others might take a free ride on his or her efforts, preferring to wait and see what the individual learns. As a result, most small investors lack the ability and motivation to evaluate managers.

Moral Hazard in Debt Financing

One way to decrease the information costs arising from moral hazard is to use debt rather than equity financing. For example, rather than investing $47,500

---

†For evidence in favor of the claim, see Randall Mørck, Andrei Shleifer, and Robert Vishny, "Management Ownership and Market Valuation," *Journal of Financial Economics,* 20:293–315, 1988. For a dissenting view, see Charles P. Himmelberg, R. Glenn Hubbard, and Darius Palia, "Understanding the Determinants of Managerial Ownership and the Link Between Ownership and Performance," *Journal of Financial Economics,* 53:353–384, 1999.

in equity in Reed Moore's bookstore and receiving 95% of the bookstore's profits, you could lend Reed $47,500 and require him to pay you a fixed interest rate of 10%. In this case, you would get $4750 each year. Because the debt promises a fixed payment, you (or your accountant) don't need to audit Reed's operation of the bookstore unless he fails to meet the interest and principal payments and defaults on the loan. As long as Reed keeps making debt payments to you, it doesn't matter to you whether the bookstore reports earnings of $10,000 or $100,000 each year. The lower costs of monitoring make debt more attractive than equity in many cases.[†]

Even though debt financing can reduce moral hazard problems relative to equity financing in many cases, it does not eliminate moral hazard. Because a debt contract allows the borrower to keep any profits that exceed the fixed amount of the debt payment, borrowers have an incentive to assume greater risk to earn these profits than is in the interest of the lender. To demonstrate, suppose that you think you are lending money to Reed to finance the purchase of bookcases and a computer system. However, once the money is in Reed's hands, he decides to invest the money in a machine that sends subliminal messages to shoppers, telling them to buy expensive books. If the machine works, the bookstore—and Reed—will make a fortune. In the more likely case that it doesn't work, he won't be able to repay you. Even with a debt contract, the risk of moral hazard is present. Financial markets use restrictive covenants in debt contracts to combat moral hazard in debt financing.

The basic problem caused by moral hazard that you encountered in making a loan to Reed was that he might use the proceeds for risky purposes. Even if he does not have $25,000 of net worth to commit to the venture, you may be able to reduce the likelihood of moral hazard by placing in the debt contract restrictions, known as **restrictive covenants,** on Reed's management activities. The most typical restrictive covenant in business lending is a limit on the borrower's risk taking. For example, the lender can restrict the borrower to buying only particular goods or prohibit the borrower from buying other businesses.

A second type of restrictive covenant requires that the borrower maintain a certain minimum level of net worth. For example, if you apply for a mortgage loan to buy a house, the bank may ask you to take out sufficient life insurance to pay off the loan in the event that you die before the mortgage is repaid. Businesses may be required to maintain a certain level of net worth, particularly in liquid assets, to reduce incentives to take on too much risk.

Financial markets often address moral hazard in debt contracts by insisting that entrepreneurs or managers of firms place their own funds at risk. In that case, taking on risky projects increases the chance that insiders like Reed

---

[†] Many analysts believe that the dramatic increase in corporate borrowing and the decrease in the use of equity finance by corporations in the 1980s reflected an attempt to reduce the costs of principal-agent problems for shareholder value.

CONSIDER THIS . . .

Can Falling Prices Raise Information Costs?

High levels of borrower net worth reduce information costs associated with adverse selection and moral hazard. However, sudden reductions in borrower net worth can increase information costs of lending, sometimes to levels that sharply reduce borrowers' ability to raise funds for new plant and equipment and job creation. The classic example of this link among net worth, financing, and the economy is *debt deflation*. In debt deflation, falling prices raise the real value of firms' outstanding debt, reducing their net worth. As a result, savers know that the likelihood of adverse selection and moral hazard increases, and they reduce their willingness to lend to all but the safest borrowers (for example, the government). Faced with severe credit declines, firms significantly cut their spending, reducing economic activity.

The best-known example of debt deflation came during the Great Depression of the early 1930s. Declining prices increased the real debt burdens of borrowers by nearly 40% between 1929 and 1933. The combined effect of declining output and deflation sharply reduced borrowers' net worth, constraining borrowers' ability to obtain credit and leading to a collapse in lending, investment, and employment. More recent episodes of debt deflation in particular sectors include the collapse in Midwest farmland values in the early 1980s, the fall in oil prices in the mid-1980s, and the sharp decline in commercial real estate prices in Boston and New York in the late 1980s and early 1990s. In each case, the collapse in borrower net worth initiated by debt deflation raised the cost of funds to borrowers because of the increased severity of adverse selection and moral hazard.

Moore will lose their own money if they make bad decisions, thereby reducing the incentive to use outside investors' funds in risky ways. Suppose that Reed invested \$25,000, rather than \$2500 of his own net worth (his assets less his liabilities) in the bookstore. He is likely to be much more cautious in making management decisions. Thus, in general, the greater the net worth (equity capital) contributed by a firm's managers, the less likely is a problem caused by moral hazard to occur, and thus the greater is the firm's ability to borrow. At quite low levels of invested net worth, problems arising from moral hazard may prevent borrowing altogether.

A third type of restrictive covenant, common in consumer lending, requires the borrower to maintain the value of any collateral offered to the lender. For example, if you take out a loan to buy a new car, you will have to carry a minimum amount of insurance against theft and collision, and you can't sell the car to a friend if you haven't paid off the loan. If you take out a mortgage loan to buy a house, you will have to carry insurance on the house, and you can't sell your house without first repaying your mortgage loan.

However, restrictive covenants complicate debt contracts and reduce their marketability in secondary markets for savers. The cost of monitoring whether firms actually are complying with restrictive covenants further hampers marketability and liquidity. Finally, restrictive covenants cannot protect a lender against every possible risky activity in which the borrower might engage.

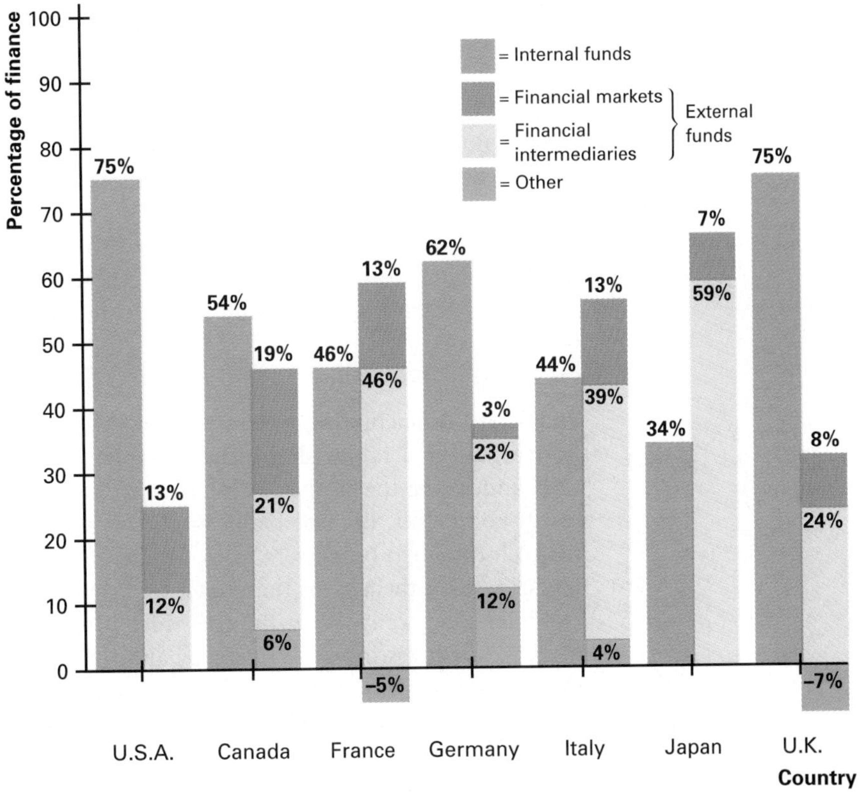

Figure 11.1

Sources of Finance for Business Firms

Business firms rely more heavily on financial intermediaries than on financial markets to raise external funds.

Source: U.S. data were averaged for the period 1946–1998 and are from Board of Governors of the Federal Reserve System, *Flow of Funds Accounts*, various issues. Data for other countries were averaged for the period 1970–1985 and are from Colin Mayer, "Financial Systems, Corporate Finance, and Economic Development," in R. Glenn Hubbard, ed., *Asymmetric Information, Finance, and Investment.* Chicago: University of Chicago Press, 1990, p. 312.

CHECKPOINT

Firms in cyclical industries—those whose profits rise and fall with economy-wide booms and busts—tend to borrow less than firms in noncyclical industries do. If monitoring costs are lower for debt financing than for equity financing, why don't all firms rely on debt? The strategy of using debt financing to reduce moral hazard problems is based on the assumption that fluctuations in the borrowing firm's profits reflect the efforts of its managers. If most of the profit swings reflect movements in economy-wide profitability, too much debt could cause a firm to go bankrupt when its profits slump and it cannot repay debtholders. As a result, the use of debt is concentrated in firms whose profitability depends less on economic movements. o

INFORMATION COSTS AND FINANCIAL INTERMEDIARIES

The presence of transactions costs and information costs increases the cost of funds that borrowers must pay and lowers the expected returns to lenders, reducing the efficiency of financial markets. We have examined the costs of adverse selection and moral hazard in equity and debt financing. In addition to responses by financial market participants to reduce those costs, financial intermediaries play key roles in the United States and most other industrial economies.

Recall that businesses raise most of their funds from current and accumulated profits, not from financial markets. As Fig. 11.1 shows, since World War II, nonfinancial corporations in the United States have raised more than two-thirds of the funds they needed internally. A similar pattern holds for other key industrialized countries. Figure 11.1 also shows that in none of the other industrialized countries listed do firms raise a substantial fraction of their financing from financial markets for stocks and bonds. Most external funds needed are raised through financial intermediaries such as banks.

Financial Intermediaries and Adverse Selection

Financial intermediaries, particularly banks, specialize in gathering information about the default risk of many borrowers. Banks raise funds from depositors and, using their superior information, lend them to borrowers that represent good risks. Because banks are better able than individual savers to distinguish qualified borrowers from lemons, banks earn a profit by charging a higher rate on their loans than the interest rate they pay to depositors.

Banks generally avoid the free-rider problem by holding the loans they make. Thus investors can't observe banks' activities and profit by mimicking them. By mainly holding loans that are not traded in financial markets, banks earn a profit on information collection.

Banks' information advantage in reducing costs of adverse selection accounts in large part for their role in providing external financing. Their specialization in evaluating borrowers to reduce the likelihood of adverse selection also explains why largely unknown small and medium-sized businesses depend on banks when they need a loan, whereas large, mature corporations have access to stock and bond markets.

CHECKPOINT

Why might the founder of a young firm in the growing biotechnology industry not raise funds by selling new shares in the firm, even to finance a very profitable investment opportunity? Adverse selection causes firms in emerging, growing industries to have the highest information costs. Faced with the high information costs of distinguishing between good firms and lemons, savers investing in financial markets require a higher return on investments in all firms in these industries to compensate them for the risk of investing in lemons. As a result, shares of good firms will be undervalued, and entrepreneurial firms will prefer to grow by using internal funds or loans from banks, which specialize in reducing problems of adverse selection. ●

Financial Intermediaries and Moral Hazard

Large investors often have more success than small investors in reducing the free-rider problem that arises in gathering information on the behavior of corporate managers. If a large investor, such as a financial intermediary, holds a large block of shares, the investor has an incentive to monitor closely how agents use their funds.

Some **venture capital firms,** which raise equity capital from investors and invest in emerging or growing entrepreneurial business ventures, use this method successfully. Venture capital firms insist on holding large equity stakes and sitting on the firm's board of directors to observe management's actions closely. In addition, when a venture capital firm acquires equity in a new firm, it holds the shares; that is, the shares are not marketable to other investors. As a result, the venture capital firm avoids the free-rider problem: Other investors are unable to take advantage of its monitoring efforts. The venture capital firm is then able to earn a profit from its monitoring activities, reducing the information costs of moral hazard and improving the allocation of funds from savers to borrowers.

Not all efforts by intermediaries to reduce the costs of principal-agent problems are directed at young firms. **Corporate restructuring firms** raise equity capital to acquire large blocks of the equity in mature firms to reduce free-rider problems (see the case study at www.awlonline.com/hubbard). The leaders of

OTHER TIMES, OTHER PLACES . . .

Investor Protection and Economic Growth

Recent research by economists using cross-country data has documented a link between financial development and economic growth. Robert King of the University of Virginia and Ross Levine of the World Bank, for example, presented the intriguing possibility that the institutional factors responsible for financial development were also important for the efficient accumulation and allocation of capital.[†] Their work raises an important question: Might cross-country differences in investor protection against adverse selection and moral hazard partly explain differences in economic performance?

In a series of papers, Rafael La Porta, Florencio Lopez-di-Silanes, and Andrei Shleifer of Harvard University and Robert Vishny of the University of Chicago document a wide variation across countries in protection of minority shareholders and creditors and in the efficiency of the judicial system in adjudicating disputes.[††] Those researchers show that in countries with weaker investor protection, such as France and Spain, firm insiders hold a much larger share of the firm's equity than do firm insiders in countries with stronger investor protection, such as the United Kingdom and the United States.

Do these cross-country differences matter for economic performance? Yes. Poor investor protection against adverse selection and moral hazard is associated with less well-developed financial markets, and entrepreneurs tend to hold poorly diversified portfolios in such economies, as they must hold more of their firm's shares. One recent study also concludes that the firms' cost of capital for investment and growth can be substantially higher in countries with weaker investor protection than in countries with stronger protection.[§] This link suggests important influences of policies to reduce information costs on economic growth.

[†] Robert G. King and Ross Levine, "Finance and Growth: Schumpeter Might Be Right," *Quarterly Journal of Economics,* 108:717–737, 1993.

[††] Rafael La Porta, Florencio Lopez-di-Silanes, Andrei Shleifer, and Robert W. Vishny, "Law and Finance," *Journal of Political Economy,* 106:1133–1155, 1998.

[§] Charles P. Himmelberg, R. Glenn Hubbard, and Inessa Love, "Investor Protection, Ownership, and Investment: Some Cross-Country Evidence," Working Paper, Columbia University, 2000.

many such firms (including Ivan Boesky, Carl Icahn, T. Boone Pickens, and Henry Kravis) became rich and famous (or notorious) in the 1980s.

Whenever monitoring is costly—as it is, for example, in debt financing when lenders must ensure that borrowers adhere to restrictive convenants—free-rider problems may occur. As an individual saver, you would find monitoring the activities of Reed Moore or General Motors (if you bought a GM bond) to be very expensive. Therefore you and others like you arc likely to try to seek a free ride on the monitoring efforts of others. Borrowers who are aware of the difficulties that you and others like you have in monitoring their efforts, and who believe that lenders will not incur monitoring costs, may be tempted to violate restrictive covenants.

Financial intermediaries, particularly banks, reduce this problem and earn a profit by acting as *delegated monitors* for many individual savers, who deposit their funds with the intermediary. (We examine this role for banks in Chapter 13.) When an intermediary such as a bank holds the loans it makes, other investors are unable to gain a free ride on the intermediary's monitoring efforts. As delegated monitors, financial intermediaries reduce the information costs of moral hazard and improve the channeling of funds from savers to borrowers. This result is a major reason that most lending takes place through financial intermediaries rather than through the direct issuance of marketable securities.

Figure 11.2 summarizes the remedies used to fight problems of moral hazard and adverse selection.

Figure 11.2

Remedies for Problems of Adverse Selection and Moral Hazard

When borrowers and savers have private information about their prospects or use of funds, information costs to savers arise. With adverse selection, savers can't tell good risks from bad risks; with moral hazard, savers can't monitor how funds are used. These problems impede the flow of funds to borrowers and returns to savers.

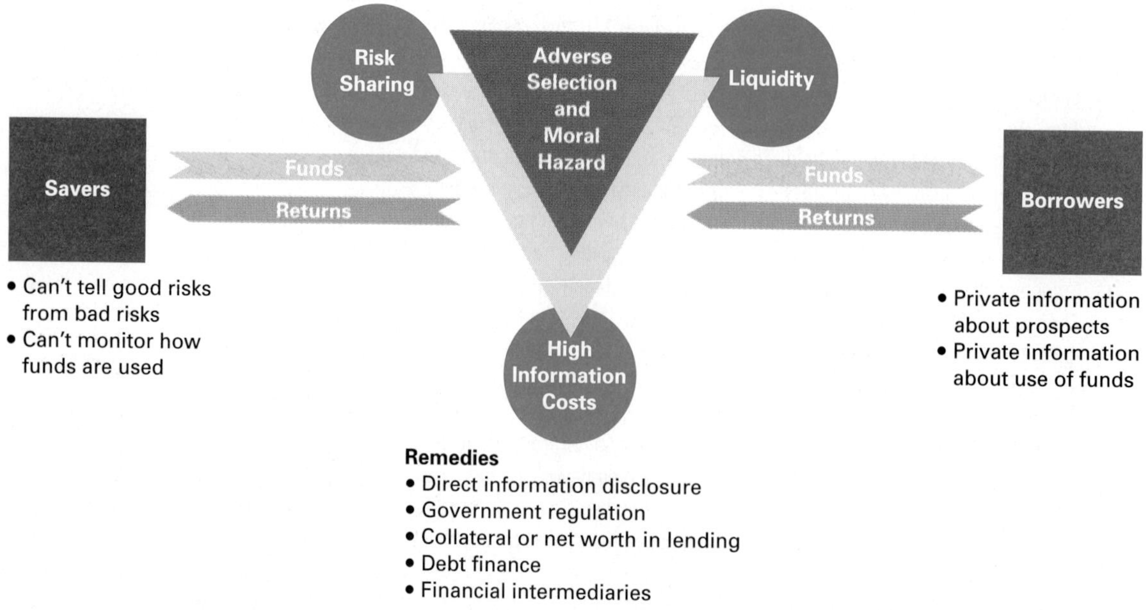

KEY TERMS AND CONCEPTS

Asymmetric information
- Adverse selection
- Moral hazard

Collateral

Corporate restructuring firms

Credit rationing

Economies of scale

Free riders

Information costs

Net worth

Principal-agent problem
- Agents
- Principals

Restrictive covenants

Transactions costs

Venture capital firms

SUMMARY

1. Financial markets do not efficiently match savers and borrowers when the transactions and information costs of lending are high.
2. Transactions costs make investing in debt and equity instruments in financial markets costly for small savers. Financial intermediaries take advantage of economies of scale by pooling savers' funds to lower transactions costs. As a result, individual savers are able to earn a higher return on their savings, and borrowers realize a lower cost of funds.
3. Information costs result from two problems of asymmetric information: adverse selection—difficulty in knowing the true prospects of the borrower before the transaction—and moral hazard—the need to monitor the borrower's use of funds after the transaction. Information costs arising from adverse selection and moral hazard reduce returns for savers and increase the cost of funds for borrowers.
4. Strategies to reduce costs of adverse selection in financial markets include direct disclosure of information and the use of collateral and net worth provisions in financial contracts.
5. The principal-agent problem, in which managers (agents) do not have the same incentive to maximize profits that shareholders (principals) have, illustrates moral hazard in equity financing. Solutions to the principal-agent problem include regulation of information disclosure and use of debt instead of equity financing.
6. Costs of moral hazard problems in debt financing are reduced by net worth requirements and use of restrictive covenants.
7. The important role played by financial intermediaries in channeling funds from savers to borrowers is explained by their relative success in lowering costs of adverse selection and moral hazard in financial markets.

REVIEW QUESTIONS

1. What advantages do financial intermediaries have over small savers in dealing with the transactions costs involved in making loans?
2. Distinguish symmetric information from asymmetric information, and state why the distinction is important for the financial system.
3. What is the difference between moral hazard and adverse selection? How does each contribute to making information asymmetric?
4. Explain why information collection in financial markets is subject to the free-rider problem. How do banks overcome the free-rider problem?
5. Explain what the "lemons problem" is. How does the lemons problem lead many firms to borrow from banks rather than from individual investors?
6. Why might the number of loans that aren't repaid to banks rise as interest rates rise? What might be a better strategy for banks than raising interest rates?

THE ECONOMIST JUNE 3, 2000

On the Cutting Edge of Corporate Control in China

With a capitalization of $350 billion, China's stock market is Asia's second biggest, behind Tokyo's. It is wildly popular with ordinary Chinese, . . . Yet it has serious flaws. Insider trading is rife; the rights of minority shareholders are brushed aside; private companies are discriminated against in favor of state enterprises, most of which perform atrociously; company accounts are opaque, though it is clear that most listed companies have high debts and low profits. The market . . . has recently been Asia's only raging bull. But foreigners are largely excluded, restricted to the moribund "B"-share market, denominated in foreign currencies. Since domestic investors are also not meant to buy "B" shares, these languish at a steep discount to the "A"-share market, denominated in yuan.

a

For years the supervisory watchdog, the China Securities Regulatory Commission (CSRC), seemed ineffectual. Then, early this year, Zhu Rongji, the prime minister, put Zhou Xiaochuan, a trusted ally and leading liberal, in charge. Sweeping change is in the air. The CSRC is hinting that it will be no slave to conservative ideology. Just like rich-world counterparts, it wants to set up a "second board" for unproven, high-tech, or fast-growing companies. It wants to break the dominance of the state companies, from which it plans to demand much greater accountability. It wants to develop derivatives—equity options and futures—that are currently frowned upon, but which institutional investors will need if they are to lay off risk. Above all, it wants to let foreign fund-managers and brokers into the domestic share market. . . .

b

The CSRC wants the expertise that foreigners can bring, particularly in the area of institutional fund-management, more than it wants their money. To that end, it hopes that foreign fund-managers will form joint ventures with local companies to launch open-ended funds with other forms of collective investment. Currently local managers offer a mere 10 closed-end investment trusts, each with no more than 2 billion yuan ($240 million) to invest. The next logical step is to allow foreign stockbrokers to form joint ventures. Undertakings China made to get into the World Trade Organization will allow foreigners to underwrite Chinese securities. But regulators acknowledge that this is a fat lot of good if they cannot distribute them, too. . . .

All these reformist noises have coincided with China's bid to join the WTO and with the American Congress's vote last week on permanent normal trading relations. . . . Private companies, the country's most vibrant, are starved of cash by both the stock market and the state banks. Ways have to be found to get capital to the deserving.

c

The other side of the coin is that the Chinese state faces a growing pension crisis, which in the long run can be solved only by developing the framework and the investment vehicles suitable for professional money management.

A major goal in shifting the Chinese economy from socialism to capitalism is privatization of state-owned enterprises. Citizens of China could be given the right to purchase vouchers to be used in bidding on previously state-owned enterprises. Once shares were distributed, owners could, in principle, be free to sell them to anyone else. Our analysis of information problems in financial markets predicts that diffuse ownership is not without its problems. While 49 million Chinese own shares, investor protection is in its infancy. The article considers issues being considered in China.

a Because individual entrepreneurs generally own, finance, and manage their own small businesses, privatization of these businesses can proceed relatively smoothly. However, larger enterprises that require external financing present important information problems. Because of the previous lack of private financial markets and institutions, investors will have a difficult time distinguishing good from bad firms. Moreover, for corporate control, new shareholders will incur significant monitoring costs. Numerous small shareholders will thus face adverse selection and moral hazard in the emerging financial market. Without new developments to reduce the information costs associated with these problems, the reconstituted enterprises will face high financing costs. In theory, "voucher funds," which pool the resources of individual shareholders, may be able to act as large shareholders, reducing problems of corporate control.

b In practice, the absence of disclosure rules (such as those enforced by the SEC) reduces the likelihood that all relevant information will be available to investors and traders. The China Securities Regulation Commission has been ineffective in this respect. Where there are information problems, financial markets respond because profits are to be made from developing new financing arrangements that benefit savers and borrowers. Voucher funds could hold large blocks of stock in a few firms to reduce moral hazard problems; investors would then hold shares in the mutual fund, rather than shares in the individual companies. This approach provides information benefits to savers, but it doesn't address savers' risk-sharing and liquidity needs.

c Well-defined property rights and legal systems are necessary for the development of markets. Market efficiency requires well-functioning secondary markets with low transactions and information costs. If liquid markets for the underlying shares do not develop, then as investors withdraw their investment fund balances, as they will to finance consumption, investment funds might have to liquidate their holdings at a loss. Hence one might expect that legal reform would lead to the development of exchanges.

For further thought . . .

Can you suggest a way in which the Chinese government might reduce the likelihood of the liquidity problem discussed in (c)? In other words, if privatized voucher funds hold relatively illiquid claims on borrowers while handling liquid claims to investors, how might the government avoid mass liquidation of underlying Chinese shares if mutual fund shareholders withdraw their funds?

Source: Excerpted from "Getting Their Skates On," *The Economist*, June 3, 2000.

7. Suppose that a bank makes a loan to a business and that the loan contract specifies that the business is not to engage in certain lines of business. What is this type of provision called? Why would the bank make such a provision?
8. What is the name of the main problem associated with the separation of ownership from management? What do managers do that owners don't like? What types of solutions are available?
9. Is a large firm with thousands of shareholders more or less likely to suffer a principal-agent problem than a small firm with just a few shareholders? Explain.
10. Describe opportunities for specialized investors or financial institutions in mitigating financing problems associated with adverse selection and moral hazard.

ANALYTICAL PROBLEMS

11. At a used car lot, a nearly new car with only 2000 miles on the odometer is selling for half the car's original price. The salesperson tells you that the car was "driven by a little old lady from Pasadena" who had it for two months and then decided that she "didn't like the color." The salesperson assures you that the car is in great shape and has had no major problems. What type of asymmetric information problem is present here? How can you get around this problem?
12. Why don't insurance companies sell income insurance? That is, if a person loses his or her job or doesn't get as big a raise as anticipated, that person would be compensated under his or her insurance coverage.
13. In which of the following situations is moral hazard likely to be less of a problem? Explain.
    (a) A manager is paid a flat salary of $150,000.
    (b) A manager is paid a salary of $75,000 plus 10% of the firm's profits.
14. A banker is thinking of making a loan to a small business. The owner of the business also owns a house and has a $40,000 investment in stocks and bonds. What kind of loan contract should the banker write to minimize costs of moral hazard?
15. Describe some of the information problems in financial markets that lead firms to rely more heavily on internal funds than external funds for investment. Do these problems necessarily imply that, as a result, too little good investment is being made? Why or why not?
16. Do you think that lemons problems are likely to be important in emerging stock and bond markets in Eastern Europe? Why or why not?
17. Suppose that you own some corporate bonds issued by the Buyusout Company. Would you be happy if the company underwent a leveraged buyout? Why or why not? Would you be happy if the company were taken over by a much larger firm, reducing its default risk? Why or why not?
18. In the early twentieth century J. P. Morgan placed representatives from his firm on the boards of directors of most of the companies in which his firm invested. He was often denounced for what some commentators saw as the excessive control he exercised in the business and financial world. Is it possible that, given the existence of asymmetric information problems, Morgan's policy of placing his men on many boards of directors may have improved the workings of the financial system?
19. On average, Japanese nonfinancial corporations have greater leverage than U.S. corporations do. Does that imply that Japanese firms are more financially fragile than U.S. firms? Why or why not?

DATA QUESTION

20. Suppose you believe that adverse selection problems are important in the stock market. If a firm announces that it will issue new shares, what pattern would you look for in data on the price of the firm's outstanding shares following the announcement? Explain.

PART 4

Financial Institutions

In Part 4 we focus on the roles played by financial institutions in the economy—in channeling funds between savers and borrowers and providing risk-sharing, liquidity, and information services—and how those roles evolve over time. We begin in Chapter 12 by introducing financial institutions: investment banks, brokerage firms, organized exchanges, mutual funds, finance companies, insurance companies, pension funds, commercial banks, savings institutions, credit unions, and government financial institutions. We discuss which competitive challenges each institution has faced, how institutions have adapted, and how they are likely to change in the future.

Much of our attention is on banks, which are the largest intermediaries and play a critical role in the payments system. Chapter 13 describes the activities of banking firms that contribute to their profits and analyzes the problems banks face in managing the risks of their deposit-taking and lending activities. In Chapter 14, we examine factors that shaped the development of the banking industry in the United States and other countries; many factors relate to government regulation. Chapter 15 studies the regulation of financial institutions as a pattern of crisis, regulation, response by the financial system, and response by regulators. In particular, we examine this pattern for regulations surrounding the lender of last resort, restrictions on competition, and deposit insurance. Chapter 16, the concluding chapter of Part 4, emphasizes new markets that international banks create and ways in which regulation shapes and responds to international banking services.

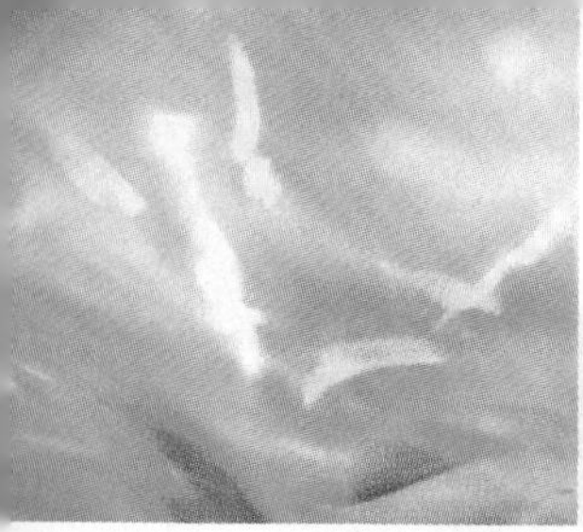

CHAPTER 12

What Financial Institutions Do

The late 1990s were challenging times for financial institutions. Competition, bad management, and poor decisions caused the failure of many savings institutions and banks in the early 1990s. Many surviving banks merged to increase their markets and to cut costs by exploiting economies of scale. The 1995 merger of banking giants Chase and Chemical formed the biggest bank in the United States—until 1998 mergers of Citicorp and Travelers, Bank America and NationsBank, and Deutsche Bank and Bankers Trust created still larger firms. New laws passed by Congress in 1994 and 1995 ushered in new competition between banks and other financial institutions. In 1994, Mellon Bank acquired Dreyfus, a leading mutual fund company; the 1998 Citicorp–Travelers merger created a financial supermarket. All of these changes blurred the distinctions among the types of financial institutions, creating new opportunities for financial institutions and offering new or improved services to savers and borrowers. Indeed, the three largest financial institutions in the world (by assets) in 2000—Deutsche Bank, Bank of Tokyo-Mitsubishi, and Citigroup—are active in most financial services.

In Part 4 of the text—and in this chapter—we examine the role of financial institutions in the financial system. To understand the changes that have taken place and that will continue to occur, we describe the traditional roles of the following organizations in the financial system:

1. *Securities market institutions:* investment banks, brokerage firms, and organized exchanges
2. *Investment institutions:* mutual funds and finance companies
3. *Contractual saving institutions:* insurance companies and pension funds
4. *Depository institutions:* commercial banks, savings institutions, and credit unions
5. *Government financial institutions*

Although securities market institutions are not financial intermediaries, we include them in our discussion of financial institutions because they help to match savers and borrowers in the financial system. Our focus in this chapter is on the risk-sharing, liquidity, and information functions of financial institutions and their role in matching savers and borrowers. We also describe the challenges each institution has faced and how institutions have adapted.

Financial intermediaries manage a sizable share of the assets in the financial system. Table 12.1 lists the share of each and the changes in assets each has held over approximately the past 40 years. These changes reflect competition, regulation, and financial innovation, as we will see. We can understand the changes and their impact only if we first know what the traditional roles for each organization are. This chapter will present that information and analyze major regulatory and competitive changes in the environment that have caused each institution to adapt—either by offering new products to savers and borrowers or by changing the way each does business.

SECURITIES MARKET INSTITUTIONS

Securities market institutions—in particular, investment banks, brokers and dealers, and organized exchanges—contribute to the efficiency of financial markets. These institutions reduce the costs of matching savers and borrowers and provide risk-sharing, liquidity, and information services that enable financial markets to function smoothly—and well-functioning markets, you'll recall, generate price information for market participants and help investors

TABLE 12.1 **FINANCIAL INTERMEDIARIES IN THE UNITED STATES†**

Class of institution	Assets ($ billions) 2000	% of total assets of intermediaries 1960	1970	1980	1990	2000
Mutual funds						
Money market mutual funds	1698	0.0	0.0	1.8	4.4	5.7
Other mutual funds	4988	2.9	3.5	1.6	5.7	16.6
Finance companies	1071	4.7	4.7	4.9	5.4	3.6
Insurance companies						
Life insurance companies	3199	19.4	14.8	11.0	12.1	10.7
Property and casualty companies	895	4.4	3.7	4.3	4.7	3.0
Pension funds						
Private pension funds	5129	6.3	8.1	12.0	14.4	17.1
State and local government retirement funds	3034	3.3	4.4	4.7	6.5	10.1
Depository institutions						
Commercial banks	6344	38.2	37.2	35.7	29.3	21.2
Savings institutions	1303	18.8	18.8	18.8	12.1	4.3
Credit unions	435	1.1	1.4	1.5	1.9	1.5
Government financial institutions	1883	1.0	3.4	4.2	3.7	6.3
	Total: $30.0 trillion					

† Data are as of September 30, 2000.

Source: Board of Governors of the Federal Reserve System, *Flow of Funds Accounts: Flows and Outstandings*, December 8, 2000.

make intelligent portfolio allocation decisions. Securities market institutions are not financial intermediaries, because they do not acquire funds from savers to invest in borrowers; they simply make it easier for investors to locate suitable borrowers and to reduce borrowers' costs in raising funds.

We discuss securities market institutions in two steps. First, we explain how investment banks gather information and help borrowers to raise funds in primary markets for debt and equity. Then we discuss the contributions of brokers, dealers, and organized exchanges in providing liquidity in secondary markets. Liquid secondary markets provide information to savers and borrowers as well as risk-sharing services for savers.

Information: Investment Banking

Underwriting. **Investment banks** assist businesses in raising new capital in primary markets, and advise them on the best way to do so: either by recommending a stock issue or by structuring debt contracts to attract investors. One way in which investment bankers earn income is by **underwriting** a firm's new stock or bond issue. Underwriters guarantee a price to the issuing firm, sell the issue at a higher price, and keep the profit, known as the *spread.* In exchange for this spread, the underwriting investment bank assumes the risk of not being able to resell the securities to investors.

In addition to underwriting, the investment bank might sell the issue under other conditions. For example, the investment bank might not guarantee prices of very risky new issues. The risk of price fluctuations may cause investment banks to be wary of making a fixed commitment to the issuing firm. Rather than guaranteeing the price, the investment bank will sell the issue on an *all-or-none* basis. In this case, the company issuing the securities receives nothing unless the investment bank sells the complete issue at the offering price. Another alternative, called *best efforts,* allows the investment bank to make no guarantee, requiring it to sell to investors only as much of the issue as it can.

Relatively small issues may be underwritten by a single investment banker, whereas large issues are sold by groups of underwriting investment banks called **syndicates.** In a syndicated sale, the lead investment bank acts as manager and keeps part of the spread. The remainder of the spread is split among the syndicate members buying the issue and to brokerage firms selling the issue to the public. Investment bankers market new issues to institutional investors (such as pension funds or insurance companies) or to individual savers through advertisements in *The Wall Street Journal.* Leading underwriting firms include major securities firms, such as Merrill Lynch, Goldman Sachs, and CS First Boston.

Underwriting lowers information costs between lenders and borrowers because investment banks put their reputations behind the firms they underwrite. Underwriters give investors confidence about a new issue. In addition, regulations require issuers of securities to disclose information about the stocks or bonds to inform investors of risks and to prevent fraud. Public issues in the United States must be registered with the Securities and Exchange Commission (SEC), a federal government regulatory body authorized by the Securities and Exchange Acts of 1933 and 1934 in response to disreputable underwriting practices in the 1920s. Firms issuing securities are required to file a prospectus with the SEC disclosing information on long-term issues of publicly traded securities.

During the 1980s, risks associated with underwriting bond issues rose because of the higher volatility of interest rates. At the same time, underwriting fees dropped. This occurred in large part because of SEC Rule 415, which allows a firm to register a new issue with the SEC and then wait as long as two years before selling it. During the waiting period, issuers can sell securities when underwriting fees are expected to be low, thus fostering competition. Another way in which Rule 415 increased competition among underwriters was by allowing issuers to choose an underwriter after registration, permitting the firm greater flexibility in bargaining with investment bankers. In the mid-1980s, bargaining led to reductions in fee income for underwriters, encouraging them to supplement their income by taking positions in bonds on their own account.

Recent trends. Investment banks during the 1980s also engineered corporate restructurings, mergers, and acquisitions in which substantial amounts of the firms' equity were bought with risky bonds. Financiers used investment banks to raise large amounts of risky debt through junk bonds, bonds with ratings of less than Baa (Moody's Investor Service) or BBB (Standard & Poor's). Michael Milken of Drexel Burnham Lambert helped to develop a liquid secondary market in these securities. Drexel Burnham, along with other major underwriters such as Merrill Lynch, Goldman Sachs, First Boston, and Lehman Brothers, helped financiers to raise large amounts of money through junk bonds. (Drexel Burnham filed for bankruptcy in 1990.) Also in the 1980s, investment banks engaged in *merchant banking*—that is, they placed their own funds at risk by investing in firms that were undergoing restructuring.

In the 1990s, investment banks became masters of *deleveraging,* helping firms to raise equity in public markets to reduce their debt burdens. Also, trading profits and fees from managing clients' funds and from advising are more important sources of investment banks' earnings. As investment banks' core business of underwriting became less profitable, their success in offering services to savers and borrowers allowed them to remain a force in matching savers with firms seeking external financing. The new century's growth areas for investment banking lie in part in Europe, where initial public offerings and restructurings are on the rise.

CHECKPOINT

Why do many issuers of bonds and stocks use underwriters? Successful underwriters are skilled in collecting financial market information and communicating it to their clients. Investment bankers collect information on issuing firms and put their reputations on the line in issues they underwrite. An investment bank's endorsement is particularly valuable for issuers that are less well known to small investors than to the major investment banking firms. **o**

Liquidity and Risk Sharing: Secondary Markets

The ability to buy and sell issues at low cost after their original issue increases the liquidity of stocks, bonds, and other financial instruments. For example, a saver might not want to buy stock in SolidState Corporation if she could not be certain of being able to sell the stock when she needed money. She might turn to other investments, such as bank deposits, that she would be able to convert to cash more easily. The existence of an arena in which securities can be converted easily to cash improves their liquidity. Secondary markets are this arena.

Brokers and dealers. Brokers and dealers facilitate the exchange of securities in financial markets by locating buyers when sellers want to convert securities to cash. The decrease in time and cost required to match buyers and sellers in secondary markets improves liquidity in those markets. **Brokers** earn commissions by matching ultimate buyers and sellers in a particular market. **Dealers** trade between ultimate buyers and sellers; they hold inventories of securities and sell them for a price higher than they paid for them, earning the spread between the bid and asked price. The largest firms in securities markets, such as Merrill Lynch, act as both brokers and dealers (and often as investment bankers as well). The fortunes of such "broker-dealers" rise and fall with stock and bond prices and trading opportunities. Their profits were very high in the mid-1980s, fell to zero by 1990, rebounded to high levels in most of the 1990s, and fell again in 2000.

To enhance the liquidity of services offered by brokers and dealers, the SEC strictly regulates brokers and dealers to ensure disclosure of information, prevent fraud, and restrict trading based on **insider information.** Insider information is available to individuals within an organization or to parties in a transaction (say, members of two firms engaged in a merger discussion) but unavailable to the general public. Historically—from the 1930s until 1975—the SEC also regulated brokerage commissions. As a result of increased competition since 1975, investors now pay significantly lower commissions—especially large institutional investors and individual investors using discount brokers; thus liquidity is improved in secondary markets. Discount brokers such as Charles Schwab offer lower commissions but fewer services (for example, no investment information libraries and minimal advice) than those offered by full-service firms such as Merrill Lynch. Trading volume expanded dramatically after commissions were lowered in 1975. Similarly, deregulation of commissions in England in 1986 (known as the "big bang"), as well as in Canada (1983), Australia (1984), France (1988), the Netherlands (1990), and Japan (beginning in 1998), generally expanded trading volume.

USING THE NEWS . . .

A Tombstone for Something New?

To learn about major financial offerings arranged by investment banks, you need only consult *The Wall Street Journal.* Advertisements for offerings—known as *tombstones*—state the size and price of the issue and the investment banks involved. In the tombstone shown here, CS First Boston and Merrill Lynch, respected investment banking firms, are managing the sale of 12,075,000 shares of stock in Garmin.

Some of the offering will be sold to foreign investors abroad through overseas affiliates of the investment banking firms. This underscores the importance of international borrowing and lending in today's financial system.

Garmin ad that appeared in *The Wall Street Journal,* December 20, 2000. Reprinted with permission.

New Issue December 8, 2000

12,075,000 Shares

GARMIN

Common Shares

Price $14 Per Share

The Nasdaq National Market symbol is GRMN

Joint Book-Running Managers

Credit Suisse First Boston **Merrill Lynch & Co.**

Copies of the Prospectus may be obtained in any State or jurisdiction in which this announcement is circulated from only such of the undersigned or other dealers or brokers as may lawfully offer these securities in such State or jurisdiction.

10,263,750 Shares

The above shares were underwritten by the following group of U.S. Underwriters.

Credit Suisse First Boston **Merrill Lynch & Co.**

Salomon Smith Barney

Banc of America Securities LLC **CIBC World Markets** **Goldman, Sachs & Co.** **ING Barings**

Invemed Associates, Inc. **Prudential VolpeTechnology Group** (A unit of Prudential Securities) **UBS Warburg LLC** **Wit SoundView**

Robert W. Baird & Co. **Edward D. Jones & Co., L.P.** **Legg Mason Wood Walker** (Incorporated) **McDonald Investments Inc.**

Sanders Morris Harris **C.E. Unterberg, Towbin** **Utendahl capital Partners, L.P.** **H.C. Wainwright & Co., Inc.**

1,811,250 Shares

The above shares were underwritten by the following international Managers.

Merrill Lynch International **Credit Suisse First Boston**

Salomon Smith Barney

Exchanges. Securities may be traded in one of two ways: through exchanges or in over-the-counter markets. An **exchange** is a physical location at which securities are traded. Essentially, an exchange is an institution providing an auction market for securities: assets are bought from the offerer of the lowest price and sold to the bidder of the highest price. Exchanges don't set prices but provide a way for buyers and sellers of financial assets to trade anonymously, lowering information costs for savers.

The best-known U.S. exchanges are the New York Stock Exchange (NYSE) and the American Stock Exchange (AMEX) in New York. There are also various regional exchanges. The exchanges themselves, together with the SEC, regulate trading practices and enforce prohibition of insider trading. Around the world, there are 142 exchanges. Among the oldest and best known are (with their dates of formal establishment) London (1773), Paris

(1802), Tokyo (1818), and Sydney (1872). As the euro arrived as a European currency in 1999, many analysts expected exchanges in Europe to consolidate, as the London and Frankfurt exchanges began to do in 1998. The controversial proposed merger of the London Stock Exchange and Frankfurt's Deutsche Borse to form iX had several twists and turns, with merger feelers from other exchanges during 2000. Separately, the Brussels, Paris, and Amsterdam stock exchanges announced their intention to merge in 2000.

The size of the issuing firm determines the exchange on which a stock is listed. The securities of the oldest and largest U.S. firms are listed on the NYSE; those of less well-known firms are listed on the AMEX; and those of the smallest and youngest business firms are generally traded in over-the-counter markets, which we discuss shortly.

In the New York Stock Exchange, buyers and sellers are matched on the floor of an exchange by a broker-dealer known as a **specialist,** who represents one or more stocks. For example, suppose that you place an order for 100 shares of General Motors stock. Your broker sends the order to a specialist in GM stock. Acting as a broker, the specialist puts together buy and sell orders at the same price. Then, acting as a dealer, the specialist uses inventory to match your buy order with someone else's sell order. The specialist system generally works well, but it can lead to a fragile market during a panic, as occurred during the stock market crash of October 19, 1987.

Over-the-counter trading. Broker-dealers also match buyers and sellers in **over-the-counter (OTC) markets,** in which trading takes place over the telephone and by computer. OTC trading has grown dramatically owing to advances in computer technology. Traders keep track of the market by examining the activity in individual issues on their computer screens. Under the Securities Amendment Act of 1975, the SEC fostered development of a consolidated arrangement for trading securities: the National Market System. Member broker-dealers regulate themselves through the National Association of Securities Dealers (NASD). The National Market System provides computerized quotes through the National Association of Securities Dealers' Automated Quotation (NASDAQ) system, developed in 1971. In November 1998, NASD and AMEX merged, yielding a firm with both auction market and over-the-counter capabilities. Outside the United States, Frankfurt's Neuer Markt exchange has been successful since its launch in 1997 in bringing younger German firms to market. NASDAQ, in turn, took a small stake in EASDAQ, a Brussels-based exchange founded in 1996 as a "NASDAQ for Europe."

Trading bonds. The markets for U.S. Treasury bonds and U.S. government agency securities is the most liquid market in the world, with small bid-asked spreads. However, the market for most individual bonds is relatively illiquid, though some issues for prominent companies (such as GM and IBM) have liquid markets. These firms' bonds are usually traded on organized exchanges, such as the NYSE. The vast majority of secondary market trading of corporate bonds is done in over-the-counter markets. Owing to their relative illiquidity, the bid-asked spreads for corporate bonds are higher than those for U.S. government securities. (The same is true in growing corporate bond markets in Europe and Japan.) For corporate bonds, the more highly rated bonds typically have lower bid-asked spreads than lower-rated bonds do.

Recent trends. The activities of brokers, dealers, and exchanges improve liquidity in secondary markets. Around the world, these organizations are being reshaped in response to the revolution in computing technology. Many brokers and dealers offer more opportunities for electronic communication among investors. Exchanges have also been affected by changes in technology. In 1971, the NYSE accounted for almost three-fourths of shares traded in U.S. exchanges; in 1991, it accounted for only about half of such trades.

Electronic auctions for large buyers and sellers in networks outside the NYSE improve liquidity by executing trades at lower cost. This competition from electronic trading reduced the value of seats on major exchanges in the late 1990s. Outside the United States, electronic trading has been introduced in exchanges in Toronto, Paris, London, Brussels, Madrid, Sydney, and Copenhagen. The latest source of competition for exchanges around the world has come from on-line *e-trading,* providing efficient service, low costs, and the comfort of trading from home.

Most analysts believe that electronic trading will eventually dominate traditional floor trading, diminishing the power of individual exchanges. Whereas traditional exchanges rely on a specialized class of liquidity suppliers effectively tied to the exchange, anyone with cash and a computer can supply liquidity in an electronic market. This phenomenon can be seen in the publicized actions of *day traders,* individuals trading electronically and eroding profit margins of traditional brokerage firms.

At the frontier of large-scale e-trading, *electronic communications networks* (ECNs) are redefining U.S. equity markets. ECNs are innovative stock-trading systems that rely on computer software to match buy and sell orders—typically with lower transactions costs than with traditional exchanges—generally for institutional investors. In early 2001, ECNs were largely NASDAQ players. Many analysts believe, however, that ECNs will become important executors of transactions of exchange-traded stocks in the near future.

INVESTMENT INSTITUTIONS

Investment institutions, which raise funds to invest in loans and securities, include mutual funds and finance companies.

Mutual Funds

Mutual funds are financial intermediaries that convert small individual claims into diversified portfolios of stocks, bonds, mortgages, and money market instruments by pooling the resources of many small savers.

Mutual funds obtain savers' money by selling shares in portfolios of financial assets and then using the funds of many savers to maintain and expand those portfolios. Mutual funds offer savers the advantage of reducing transactions costs. Rather than buying numerous stocks, bonds, or other financial instruments individually—each with its own transactions costs—a saver can buy into all the shares in the fund with one transaction. Mutual funds provide risk-sharing benefits by offering a diversified portfolio of assets and liquidity benefits by guaranteeing to quickly buy back a saver's shares. Moreover, the company managing the fund—the fund manager (say, Fidelity)—specializes in gathering information about different investments.

The mutual fund industry in the United States dates back to the organization of the Massachusetts Investors Trust (managed by Massachusetts Financial Services, Inc.) in March 1924. The fund's marketing stressed the usefulness of mutual funds for achieving a diversified portfolio for retirement savings. Later in 1924, the State Street Investment Corporation was organized; in 1925, Putnam Management Company introduced its Incorporated Investment Fund. These three investment managers are still major players in the mutual fund industry.

Types of funds. Mutual funds operate as either closed-end or open-end funds. In **closed-end mutual funds,** the mutual fund company issues a fixed number of nonredeemable shares, which investors may then trade in over-the-counter markets like common stock. The price of these shares fluctuates with the value of the underlying assets. Owing to differences in the quality of fund management or the liquidity of the shares, fund shares may sell at a discount or a premium relative to the market value of the underlying assets. More common are **open-end mutual funds,** which issue redeemable shares at a price tied to the underlying value of the assets.

Most mutual funds are called **no-load funds** because they earn income only from management fees (typically about 0.5% of assets), not from sales commissions. The alternative, **load funds,** charge commissions for purchases and sales.

The largest category of mutual funds, with assets of $4988 billion in 2000, consists of funds offering claims against portfolios of capital market instruments, such as stocks and bonds. Large mutual fund management companies, such as Fidelity, Vanguard, and Dreyfus, offer many alternative stock and bond funds. Some funds hold a wide range of stocks or bonds; others specialize in securities issued by a particular industry or sector; still others invest as an *index fund* in a fixed market basket of securities (say, shares of S&P 500 firms). Large mutual fund firms also often offer funds specializing in foreign securities, making it a convenient way for small investors to participate in foreign financial markets.

The greatest growth in mutual funds has been in **money market mutual funds,** which hold high-quality, short-term assets, such as Treasury bills, negotiable certificates of deposit, and commercial paper. Representing only about 8% of the total mutual fund market in 1975, these funds (generally offered by the same fund management companies that offer stock and bond funds) made up more than 25% of the market in 2000, with assets of $1698 billion. The underlying instruments in these funds have short maturities, so their asset values do not fluctuate much. Hence the funds provide savers with a liquid account that pays market interest rates. Most money market mutual funds allow savers to write checks above a specified minimum ($500, for example) against their accounts.

Regulation of the mutual fund industry. Heavy losses during the stock market crash of 1929 led investors to call for regulation of the mutual fund industry. With passage of the Securities Act of 1933, funds' shares had to be registered with the SEC prior to sale. The act also required disclosure to potential investors of information about portfolio holdings and investment policies and objectives. Mutual funds were prohibited from advertising anticipated returns, though they could state past returns. Congress and the SEC have amended the regulations governing mutual funds several times since 1933; more recent regulations also are generally intended to ensure disclosure of information and to prevent fraud. The Investment Company Act of 1940 assigned regulatory jurisdiction over mutual funds to the SEC. Subsequent regulation increased competition among mutual funds; amendments to the Investment Company Act in the 1970s reduced sales loads, and the Garn–St. Germain Act of 1982 allowed banks to offer money market deposit accounts.

In the early and mid-1990s, the SEC unveiled several regulatory proposals representing the most significant changes in mutual fund regulation in the United States since the 1940 Investment Company Act. One significant proposal is a requirement that the majority of the directors of any individual mutual fund be independent of the fund's sponsor, compared to 40% of the directors under existing law. (A company such as Fidelity or Vanguard offers several different funds and hence is the sponsor.) The idea is to limit the cost of administering the funds, particularly the increases in salaries that managers can vote for themselves when they sit on the board. The same proposal would amend the 1940 Act to set standards for maintaining liquidity of mutual funds and to require shareholder approval for any change in the fund's investment objectives. The SEC also proposed allowing foreign mutual funds to sell shares in the United States if the home-country regulation of those funds provides investor protection equivalent to that under U.S. law. These SEC proposals could expand significantly mutual funds' role as intermediaries.

Recent trends. Over the 1980s and 1990s, the role of mutual funds in capital markets has increased dramatically. Competition among hundreds of mutual funds firms gave investors thousands of funds from which to choose by 1998. Analysts predict major changes in the mutual fund industry in years to come. Expensive needed investments in technology to manage marketing and investor record keeping will give a significant advantage to large firms. The turn of the century will likely see fewer but very large mutual fund "families," along with smaller niche funds. The growth in self-directed retirement accounts (such as IRAs and 401(k) plans) will continue to propel the growth of mutual funds. Outside the United States, U.S. mutual fund firms began making significant inroads in Japan and Europe in the late 1990s and early 2000s.

Finance Companies

Finance companies are intermediaries that raise large amounts of money through the sale of commercial paper and securities. They then use these funds to make (generally) small loans to households and businesses. Finance companies had assets of about $1071 billion in 2000. Before making loans, finance companies must gather and monitor information about borrowers' default risks. Because finance companies do not issue deposits as banks do, however, federal and state governments generally have found little need for regulation beyond information disclosure to prospective borrowers and fraud prevention. However, some states regulate the terms of finance company loan contracts. The lower degree of regulation allows finance companies to provide loans tailored to match the particular needs of borrowers more closely than do the standard loans that other, more regulated institutions can provide.

Types of finance companies. The three main types of finance companies are consumer finance, business finance, and sales finance firms. Consumer finance companies make loans to enable consumers to buy cars, furniture, and appliances; to finance home improvements; and to refinance household debts. Finance company customers have higher default risk than good-quality bank customers do and so are charged higher interest rates.

Business finance companies engage in factoring—that is, the purchase of accounts receivable of small firms at a discount. The finance company holds the receivables until maturity to earn a profit. For example, Moneybags Finance Company might buy $100,000 of short-term accounts receivable of Axle Tire Company for $90,000—effectively lending Axle $90,000 and earning a $10,000 return when the accounts receivable are collected. Axle Tire is willing to sell its receivables to Moneybags because it needs the cash to pay for inventory and for labor costs, and it might have a cash-flow problem if it waited for all its customers to pay their bills. Another activity of business finance companies is to purchase expensive equipment (airplanes, for example) and then lease it to businesses over a fixed length of time. In this activity, finance companies specialize in gathering information about the value of collateral. Factoring loans are generally short-term, but leasing contracts can be for five years or more.

Sales finance companies are affiliated with companies that manufacture or sell big-ticket goods. Their purpose is to promote the business of the underlying manufacturer or retailer. For example, General Motors Acceptance Corporation (GMAC) offers financing to customers when they buy new GM cars. Department stores issue credit cards with which customers finance purchases at those stores (Sears or J.C. Penney, for example). This convenient credit is part of the selling effort of the manufacturer or retailer.

Recent trends. Over the 1980s, 1990s, and early in the new century, finance companies have increased their role in consumer and business lending. Many analysts think that finance companies have an advantage in monitoring the value of collateral, making them logical players in lending for consumer durables, inventories, and business equipment.

CONTRACTUAL SAVING: INSURANCE COMPANIES

Some events impose significant financial hardship when they occur, such as a medical emergency, a car accident, or the death of a spouse. **Contractual saving institutions** allow individuals (1) to pay money to transfer the risk of financial hardship to someone else or (2) to save in a disciplined manner for retirement. We discuss the first type of contractual saving institution—insurance companies—in this section. The second type—pension funds—is described in the next section.

Insurance companies are financial intermediaries that specialize in writing contracts to protect their policyholders from the risk of financial loss associated with particular events. Insurers obtain funds by issuing promises to pay under certain conditions and then lending the money to borrowers. The prospect of financial hardship leads many people to pay insurance companies fees, called *premiums,* so that the insurance company assumes risk. Consider an example: An individual may pay $1000 for a premium on life insurance, which the life insurance company will lend to a hotel chain.

In terms of premium income, U.S. insurance companies such as Allstate, Aetna, and Prudential are the largest insurers in the world, and U.S. premium income generally accounts for more than one-third of the global total. However, rapid growth in insurance coverage in the late 1990s came from Europe, Asia, and the emerging market economies of Eastern Europe.

The insurance industry has two segments. *Life insurance companies* sell policies to protect households against a loss of earnings from disability, retirement, or death of the insured person. *Property and casualty companies* sell policies to protect households and firms from the risks of illness, theft, fire, accidents, or natural disasters. Insurance companies' profitability depends in large part on their ability to reduce information costs of adverse selection and moral hazard. Hence, before we analyze these two types of insurance companies in greater detail, we need to discuss how insurance companies reduce information costs in providing insurance.

Principles of Insurance Management

In 2000, the U.S. insurance industry controlled assets of almost $4.1 trillion. Insurance companies make profits from the excess of premiums over claims payments and from investments in businesses. These institutions have long been important participants in the financial system, investing policyholders' premiums in capital markets, usually in stocks, bonds, mortgages, and direct loans to firms known as *private placements.* Insurance companies have fueled

U.S. industrial expansion for more than 150 years by holding capital market instruments as assets and issuing insurance policies as liabilities.

Risk pooling. Insurance companies can comfortably predict when and how much compensation savers will claim by taking advantage of the *law of large numbers*. This statistical concept states that although the death, illness, or injury risks of an individual cannot be predicted, the average occurrences of any such event for large numbers of people can generally be predicted. Thus, by issuing a sufficient number of policies, insurance companies take advantage of risk pooling and diversification to estimate the size of reserves needed for potential claims. Statisticians known as *actuaries* compile probability tables to help predict event risk in the population.

Insurance company problems. There is more to insurance management than simple risk pooling, however. An insurance company faces costs associated with asymmetric information because individuals or firms seeking insurance are likely to have information that the insurance company does not have. Insurers also face both adverse selection and moral hazard. For an insurance company, adverse selection occurs when the buyers who are most eager to purchase insurance are individuals whose probability of requiring an insurance payout over some period of time is highest. For example, if you learned that you had cancer, you probably would want to take out a generous health insurance policy. Moral hazard arises in insurance when individuals assume greater risk when covered by insurance than they would without it. With complete fire insurance on your business, for example, you might be tempted to save money by not buying fire extinguishers or flame-retardant office furniture. Insurance company procedures are aimed at reducing costs due to adverse selection and moral hazard.

Adverse selection and screening. Because adverse selection results from the policyholder's private information, insurance company managers gather information to screen out poor insurance risks. If you apply for health insurance on your own (that is, not through a group plan offered by your employer), you have to disclose information about your health history to the insurance company. Similarly, if you try to buy automobile insurance, you have to supply information about your driving record, including speeding tickets and accidents. When you buy life insurance—especially if you want to purchase a large policy—you have to answer detailed questions about your health history and personal habits (such as smoking and alcohol or drug use) and undergo urine and blood tests. These procedures may seem intrusive, but they allow insurance companies to reduce problems of adverse selection.

Risk-based premiums. A longstanding practice of insurance management to avoid adverse selection is to charge individuals **risk-based premiums,** premiums based on the probability of their collecting claims. Suppose that the Egalite Insurance Company charges drivers the same premium, based on the average risk in the population, while Varyem Insurance Company charges risk-based premiums. If Stanley Stolid applies for auto insurance with a record of no speeding tickets (he won't drive faster than 40 mph) and Gary Gunem applies to the same company with a record of 32 speeding tickets in the last 12 months, Gunem should pay a higher premium. Choosing between policies offered by Egalite and Varyem, Stanley would say "no thanks" to Egalite and buy insurance from Varyem. Gary would say "sure," leaving Egalite with a potential loss. This version of the lemons problem (Chapter 11) explains why private insurance companies vary premiums according to differences in risk.

Moral hazard complicates insurance company managers' decisions to offer policies to consumers. Recall that the financial system develops new financial arrangements to reduce information costs related to moral hazard. For insurance companies, these arrangements include such policy provisions as deductibles, coinsurance, and restrictive covenants.

Deductibles. One way to ensure that the policyholder exercises some care to prevent the insured event is to place some of the policyholder's own money at risk. Insurance companies do so by requiring a **deductible,** a specified amount to be deducted from the policyholder's loss when a claim is paid. A $500 deductible in your health insurance or automobile insurance policy, for example, holds you responsible for the first $500 of claimable expenses; the insurance company will pay the rest. The use of deductibles enables an insurance company to align policyholders' interests with its own. Because deductibles

CONSIDER THIS . . .

Can Investors Keep "Captives" at Bay?

Property and casualty insurance companies use economic principles of risk management to price risks. They also make a profit and offer a narrow set of insurance products—creating a combustible mix of possibilities for financial innovation.

Many large firms are taking a complete inventory of the risks they face and analyzing the risks as parts of a portfolio. Some companies hope to manage their risks with little or no outside insurance. Far-fetched? No. Companies in such diverse businesses as energy, telecommunications, and luxury goods are working with risk-management consulting firms to develop internal risk-management models for collections of risks. These models are then used by large firms that pool their risks internally in *captive insurance subsidiaries* instead of buying insurance from property and casualty insurers.

Will the captives carry the day? Likely, yes and no. Firms using a portfolio approach to defining risk may still be interested in transferring that risk. Even if companies do not want policies for individual risks (such as fire), they may want to cap the net risk of a portfolio of exposures—"portfolio insurance" of a sort.

Will commercial insurers seize the day? Perhaps. Insurers laughed in the 1960s at the notion of captive insurance subsidiaries (which now number more than 4000). In the early 1990s, they laughed at the packaging of risks into bonds traded in financial markets. Portfolio approaches to risk management . . . ?

reduce costs of moral hazard, insurance companies are able to lower the premiums that policyholders must pay.

Coinsurance. Although the policyholder is at risk for the amount of a deductible, the insurance company is still responsible for 100% of all allowable claims above that amount. To give the policyholder further incentive to hold down costs, insurance companies may offer **coinsurance** as an option. This option requires the policyholder to pay a certain percentage of the costs of a claim in addition to the deductible amount. For example, when you choose among the health insurance options that are available through your employer, some may offer you a lower premium in exchange for your agreeing to pay, say, 20% of insured expenses after you pay the deductible. Hence coinsurance aligns policyholders' interests with the interest of the company.

Restrictive covenants. To cope with moral hazard, insurers also sometimes use **restrictive covenants,** which limit risky activities by the insured if a subsequent claim is to be paid. For example, a fire insurance company may refuse to pay a business's claim if the business failed to install and maintain smoke alarms, fire extinguishers, or a sprinkler system in accordance with its contract. By forcing the policyholder to restrict risky activities so as to claim insured losses, restrictive covenants act as a valuable management tool in helping insurance companies to reduce moral hazard.

Other insurance policy provisions. Insurance companies use other practices to reduce moral hazard. First, most insurance policies include limits on individual claims paid, such as the lifetime claim limit imposed by health insurance companies. Second, insurance companies reserve the right to cancel policies if the policyholder engages in excessively risky behavior. Finally, insurance companies safeguard against fraud—as, for example, when policyholders seek reimbursement for theft or medical expenses that never took place—by hiring seasoned claims adjustors to investigate claims.

Having explored ways in which insurance companies reduce information costs in providing risk-sharing services, we are ready to look more closely at the services offered by life insurance companies and property and casualty insurance companies.

Life Insurance Companies

Life insurance companies provide insurance (and savings plans) to protect against financial hardship for the policyholder's survivors. In the United States in 2000, life insurance firms had assets totaling about $3.2 trillion. Two types of firms characterize this industry: (1) *mutual companies,* which are owned by the policyholders, and (2) *stock companies,* which are owned by the shareholders. The largest U.S. life insurance firms are generally mutual companies, which account for over half the industry's assets. However, these large companies represent only 10% of all life insurance companies; more than

90% are organized as stock companies. By the mid-1990s, some large mutual companies were contemplating a conversion to stock companies to strengthen their capital base by issuing stock in financial markets. Metropolitan Life announced in 1998 that it intended to go public, with other conversions expected in the near future.

Most policies issued are *whole life* or *term life*. For whole life insurance, the policyholder pays a constant premium over the life of the policy; cash value (the excess of the premium over the expected cost of payout) accrues in early periods and declines subsequently as the risk of death rises. Individuals can use whole life policies to save for the future. Policyholders can borrow against the cash value, and individuals can either withdraw the total *cash value* at retirement or turn that value into annual payments, known as *annuities*. Saving through whole life insurance receives favorable tax treatment in the United States: Accumulated returns from investing the premiums are not taxed. This favorable treatment has particularly encouraged the growth of saving through annuities provided by most insurance companies. In addition, they allow the saver to withdraw accumulated savings in a lump sum at retirement, thereby deferring taxes on the accumulated investment income.

Term life insurance, by contrast, pays off only at the death of the policyholder; the policies have no cash value. Hence premiums reflect only the probability of the policyholder's dying during the insured interval, or term. Financial innovations over the past decade have given households investment opportunities with higher returns than those on whole life investments. For this reason and because investors have questions about the financial condition of insurers, term life insurance has grown in popularity over whole life insurance.

Since the 1980s, life insurance companies have met the challenge of reduced demand for whole life policies by restructuring their business to manage assets for pension funds. Indeed, more than one-half of the assets under life insurance company management are for pension funds, not for insurance reserves. Table 12.1 shows the success of this strategy. While life insurance companies' market share of intermediated assets fell sharply from 1960 to 1980, their market share stabilized somewhat between 1980 and 2000. Figure 12.1 shows that life insurance companies invest most of their funds in stocks, bonds, and loans to policyholders.

Property and Casualty Insurance Companies

Property and casualty insurance companies in the United States, controlling assets of $895 billion in 2000, insure policyholders against events other than death. They also are organized as both stock and mutual companies. They sell insurance to cover losses from such risks as theft, illness, fire, earthquakes, and car accidents. The premiums that are charged correspond to the chance of the event occurring. For example, high-risk drivers who are more likely to have accidents pay more than low-risk drivers do for automobile insurance.

The asset portfolios of property and casualty insurance companies differ

Figure 12.1

Financial Assets of U.S. Insurance Companies

The differing mix of assets held by life insurance companies and property and casualty insurance companies reflects the difference in risk-sharing services they provide. (The data are as of September 30, 2000. Assets are listed by type and by percentage of total funds invested.)

Source: Federal Reserve, *Flow of Funds Accounts.*

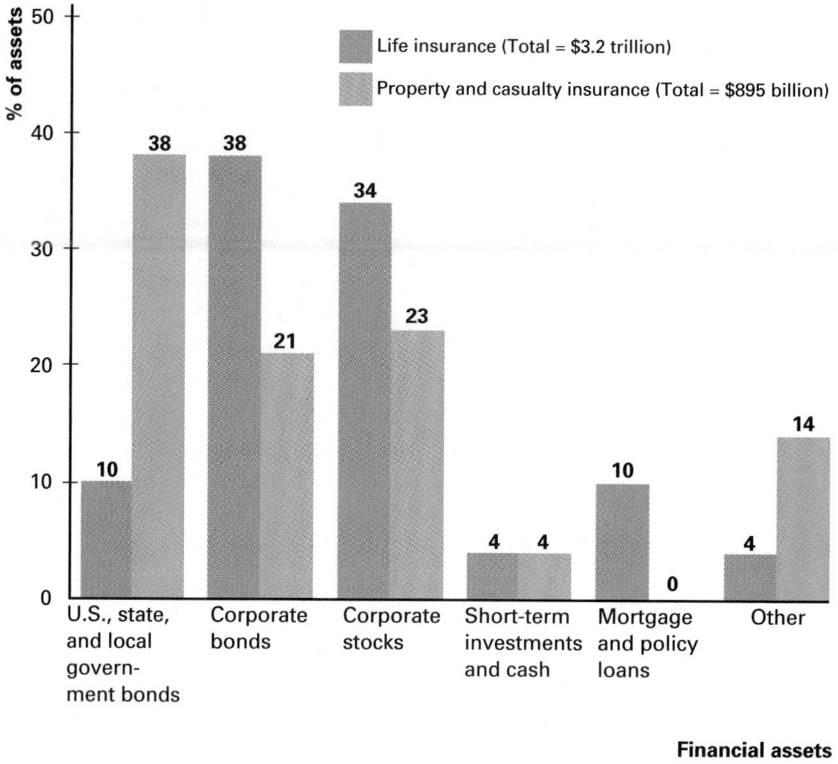

from those of life insurance companies. Because events such as fires and earthquakes are more difficult to predict statistically than are death rates in the population, the portfolios of property and casualty insurers largely contain liquid assets, such as short-term and long-term credit market instruments (see Fig. 12.1). In addition, property and casualty insurance companies differ from life insurance companies in the way they are taxed. Life insurance companies pay no tax on their income, whereas property and casualty insurers pay U.S. income tax on their net income but with allowances for tax-free reserves.†

A possible insurance crisis loomed in this segment of the insurance industry as claims and premiums rose dramatically during the 1980s and 1990s. Proposals for reform would limit the size of the awards in settling certain lawsuits—particularly for negligence or malpractice. The large claims against insurance companies may encourage them to acquire riskier assets or engage in activities to increase their current returns, practices that increase their financial fragility.

† Historically, these companies were allowed a deduction for funds set aside for future obligations, and much of their income was tax-exempt income in the form of interest on state and local government securities, for example. The U.S. Tax Reform Act of 1986 restricted these deductions, though property and casualty companies are still more lightly taxed than manufacturing companies are.

Regulation of Insurance Companies and Recent Trends

Most states establish insurance commissions to regulate insurance companies. Regulations typically require insurance companies to disclose the components of their portfolios (to reduce policyholders' information costs about the solvency of insurers), to submit to examinations to minimize fraud, to restrict holdings of risky assets, and to limit premiums.

The early and mid-1990s were turbulent times for both life insurance companies and property and casualty insurers. Some life insurance companies promised policyholders high returns on the saving component of whole life insurance in the mid-1980s when interest rates were relatively high. When interest rates fell in the 1990s, many of those promises led to losses for many insurers. For property and casualty companies, large losses from 1992's Hurricane Andrew caused policyholders to doubt insurers' ability to weather the next major disaster. These problems are prompting state insurance regulators and the Congress to review ways to ensure that insurance companies can honor their financial obligation to policyholders. In the meantime, financial markets are innovating ways for property and casualty companies to spread catastrophic risks. In 2000, some property and casualty insurers faced lawsuits stemming from "Y2K" information technology problems.

CHECKPOINT

Why are property and casualty companies more exposed to the risk of large unexpected insurance losses than life insurance companies are? Life insurance companies face relatively low risk in the aggregate, owing to the law of large numbers. In property and casualty insurance, a single event—Hurricane Andrew, for example—may lead to claims by a large number of policyholders at the same time. o

CONTRACTUAL SAVING: PENSION FUNDS

For many people, saving for retirement is the most important form of saving. People can accumulate retirement savings in two ways: through pension funds sponsored by employers or through personal savings accounts. **Pension funds** invest contributions of workers and firms in stocks, bonds, and mortgages to provide for pension benefit payments during workers' retirement. Representing about $8.2 trillion in assets in the United States in 2000, private and state and local government pension funds are the largest institutional participants in capital markets. Because retirements are predictable, pension funds can invest in long-term capital market instruments. Indeed, as Fig. 12.2 shows, private pension plans invest most of their assets in stocks, long-term bonds, and mortgages. With about 27% of all U.S. financial assets under their control, pension funds hold about 23% of the nation's publicly traded equities and about 12% of the value of corporate bonds.

Like insurance companies, pension funds are not deposit-taking intermediaries. An employee receives pension benefits from pension funds only if

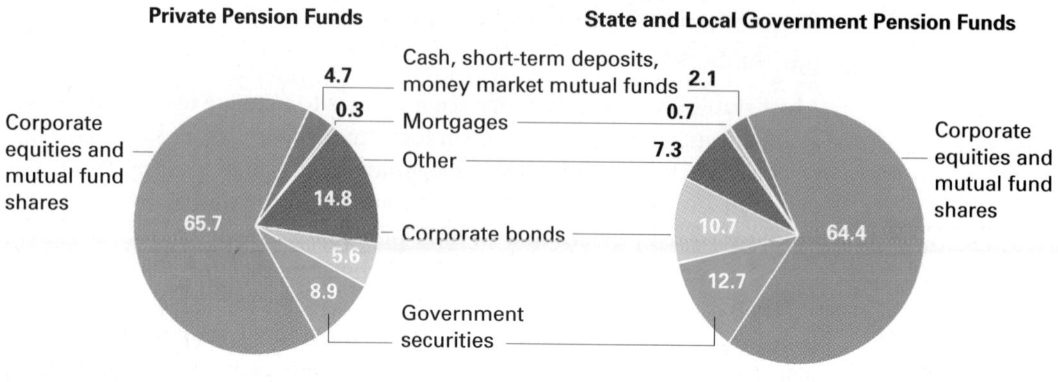

Figure 12.2

Assets of Pension Funds

Pension funds concentrate their investments in long-term capital market instruments. Data are as of September 30, 2000.

Source: Federal Reserve, *Flow of Funds Accounts.*

the employee is vested. *Vesting* is the length of service required before an employee is entitled to future benefits, and the required amount of time varies among plans.

Employees may prefer to save through pension plans provided by employers rather than through savings accounts for three reasons. First, pension funds may be able to manage a financial portfolio more efficiently, with lower transactions costs, than employees can. Second, pension funds may be able to provide benefits such as life annuities, which are costly for individual savers to obtain. Third, the special tax treatment of pensions can make pension benefits more valuable than cash wages to employees.†

Ownership of Pension Funds Assets

A key distinction among pension plans is whether they have *defined contributions* or *defined benefits.* In a **defined contribution plan,** contributions are invested for the employees, who own the value of the funds in the plan. If the pension plan's investments are profitable, pension income during retirement will be high; if the pension plan's investments are not profitable, retirement income will be low. The pension fund for most college professors is an example of a defined contribution plan. It invests pension contributions in stocks, bonds, mortgages, and money market instruments.

Pension assets in *employee stock ownership plans* (ESOPs) are invested primarily in employer securities. The value of pension assets depends on the performance of the firm, as measured by the value of employer securities.

† Your contribution to a pension fund can be excluded from your current income for tax purposes; your employer's matching contribution is tax-deductible for your employer. In addition, you can't be taxed on the investment earnings of a pension fund. Your taxation is deferred until you receive your pension benefits. You also have the option of transferring certain pension benefit payments into an individual retirement account (IRA) or other favorable distribution plan, which can reduce the tax you would otherwise owe on a lump-sum payment.

Such plans are designed to do more than help employees accumulate savings for retirement; they also may increase productivity by providing employees with a stake in company profitability.

Other types of defined contribution plans in which employers or employees contribute an amount based on earnings are more diversified. In some plans, contributions are invested in a pool that is similar to a mutual fund. In others, participants may choose to allocate their assets among a limited number of investment funds. For example, a plan might offer three investment choices: one that purchases U.S. Treasury securities, a second that purchases private bonds, and a third that purchases a portfolio of common stocks. Proposals to "privatize" Social Security, such as that announced by President George W. Bush in his 2000 campaign, generally would incorporate such a retirement pension option for households.

In a **defined benefit plan**—the more common type for most employees, particularly those in unions—the employee is promised an assigned benefit based on earnings and years of service. The benefit payments may or may not be indexed for inflation. If the funds in the pension plan exceed the amount promised, the excess accrues to the issuing firm or institution. If the funds in the pension plan are insufficient to pay the promised benefit, the issuing firm is liable for the difference.

Funding of Pension Plans

The principal difference between defined contribution and defined benefit plans is the method of **plan funding** that guarantees retirement benefits. For a defined contribution plan, funding is not an issue. By definition, these plans are *fully funded* by the employees who make the contributions and receive the returns on them. However, a defined benefit plan is fully funded only when the contributions, together with the projected future earnings, are sufficient to pay the projected assigned benefits. If the plan lacks these resources, it is underfunded. For a private firm, an underfunded defined benefit plan is a shareholder liability; an underfunded public plan is a taxpayer liability. As the efficient markets hypothesis would predict, the stock market lowers the value of the shares of firms with underfunded pension liabilities because those liabilities reduce the firms' value.

Regulation of Private Pension Plans

To reduce information costs for both defined contribution and defined benefit plans, pension funds disclose the composition of their portfolios. Regulations for defined contribution plans require information disclosure on the fund's portfolio of assets against fraud and mismanagement. Regulation of defined benefit plans is more complex because these pension funds may be underfunded, leaving workers without the retirement income they were promised. In response to difficulties in administering pension plans, Congress passed the Employee Retirement Income Security Act (ERISA) in 1974. This landmark legislation set national criteria for pension plan vesting and funding, restricted plans' ownership of certain types of risky investments, and enacted standards for information reporting and disclosure.

The act authorized creation of the Pension Benefit Guaranty Corporation (PBGC, or "Penny Benny") to insure pension benefits up to a limit if a company cannot meet its unfunded obligations (because of bankruptcy, for example). The PBGC charges companies a premium on pension liabilities and has an implicit line of credit from the U.S. Treasury. Many analysts are worried that, because the PBGC's premiums do not completely reflect differences in plan risk, government pension insurance may increase risk taking by firms' defined benefit pension plans. Because U.S. private pension plans collectively are underfunded by tens of billions of dollars, the PBGC must monitor carefully the health of the nation's pension plans. Some economists fear that a pension insurance disaster—like that which occurred for bank deposit insurance in the late 1980s—is on the horizon.

Public Pension Plans

Like private companies, governments provide pension plans for their employees. At the federal level, these include civil service and military plans. (Social Security is a general retirement benefit plan.) State and local governments also provide plans, which closely resemble private plans, for their employees. In the late 1980s, underfunding became an important problem in many states, resulting in downgrading of bond ratings for some states. The improving stock market and state finances in the 1990s mitigated the extent of underfunding.

Recent Trends

Fewer and fewer workers have the option of joining a traditional company pension plan, in which a retired worker collects a benefit based on earnings and years of service. While defined contribution plans have become more important, one segment of defined contribution plans is emerging as a major force in retirement saving: 401(k) plans. Named after the section of the Internal Revenue Code in which they are described, 401(k) plans are giving many employees a chance to be their own pension plan managers.

In a 401(k) plan, an employee can make tax-deductible contributions through regular payroll deductions (subject to an annual limit) and pay no tax on accumulated earnings until retirement. Employers can (and generally do) supplement employee contributions. Indeed, many employers match fully the employee contributions. Contributions to 401(k) plans have grown rapidly. Total contributions grew threefold in real terms over the decade after 1984; by the late 1990s, contributions equaled more than one-third of personal saving.

The employee can choose from a menu of options how funds are to be invested. These pension accounts are "portable"; you can take the funds with you as you change jobs. There is a risk: How much you have at retirement depends on how much you are willing to contribute when you are working and how well your investments have performed.

If you participate in a 401(k) plan, you may have to become your own pension manager. In this case, you can apply principles of investing and asset allocation discussed in Chapter 5. First, if your time horizon until retirement is a long one, you should invest your funds largely in stocks, which have generally higher returns than bonds or money market funds over long periods of time. Second, remember the advantages of diversification. Many 401(k) participants invest through mutual funds, which enable them to hold a large collection of assets at a modest cost.

CHECKPOINT

In the United States, direct ownership of equities supposedly is concentrated in the hands of the wealthiest individuals. One argument against this claim is that workers collectively own large amounts of stock through their companies' pension plans. Is this reasoning correct? Yes, for defined contribution plans, in which plan participants own the assets of the plan. However, more workers are covered by defined benefit plans. Because benefits are contractually specified, participants in these plans neither benefit from an increase in the market valuation of the pension plan's portfolio nor lose from a decrease in the market valuation. The shareholders of the firm benefit or lose, respectively. Hence participation in pension plans that own shares does not imply concentration of equity ownership in the hands of workers. o

DEPOSITORY INSTITUTIONS

Depository institutions are commercial banks, savings and loan associations, mutual savings banks, and credit unions. These institutions accept deposits and make loans, acting as intermediaries in matching lenders and borrowers. They are introduced briefly here. Their lines of business, regulation, and recent trends are explored in much greater detail in Chapters 13–16.

Commercial Banks

Commercial banks—the largest category of depository institutions—are financial intermediaries that accept deposits and make loans, offering risk-sharing, liquidity, and information services that benefit savers and borrowers. Savers obtain risk-sharing benefits from banks' diversified portfolios of loans; borrowers can obtain needed funds to finance the purchase of cars, inventories, or plants and equipment. Banks also provide liquidity services through checking accounts, in which savers' deposits are available on demand.

Banks have stiff competition from other financial institutions in the provision of risk-sharing and liquidity services. Today, savers can deposit their cash in a money market fund that invests, say, in Treasury bills, a transaction that was limited to large savers in the past. Savers can also purchase a diversified portfolio by buying shares in a mutual fund. However, many borrowers can't raise funds easily through bond or stock markets or other nonbank financial institutions. Commercial banks thus serve a special function in providing credit to particular types of borrowers by reducing the transactions and information costs of lending.

Transactions costs. One reason that borrowers with small or medium-sized credit needs do not rely on stock or bond markets is the high transactions cost of issuing such securities. Many transactions costs are fixed (for example, payments for SEC registration and investment bankers' services), so the average cost per dollar of funds raised may be too high to justify the effort. Averaging about 4% of funds raised for large issues of stock or bonds (say, more than $50 million), these costs can range from 13% to 20% for small issues (say, $500,000 or less).

Information costs. High information costs also restrict access to financial markets for households and small and medium-sized businesses. In fact, the most significant reason for the existence of commercial banks is their ability to reduce information costs. Recall that investors face high information costs in coping with adverse selection and moral hazard in financial markets. Banks, on the other hand, specialize in gathering information about borrowers' default risk, thereby reducing costs imposed by adverse selection. In the United States, bank loans are the dominant method of external financing for small and medium-sized firms but are much less important for large firms. This pattern holds for most industrialized countries. Banks reduce information costs associated with moral hazard by monitoring borrowers' activities. For the small saver to monitor borrowers' activities would be cumbersome and expensive. Banks act as delegated monitors for many individual savers and lenders who deposit their funds with the bank.

Savings Institutions

In the United States, **savings institutions** (savings and loan associations and mutual savings banks) originated as building and loan societies, in which individuals pooled money to be loaned to members to build homes. The modern savings and loan industry emerged in the 1930s as part of a general federal government policy of subsidizing home ownership. Savings institutions reduce problems of asymmetric information and default risk by requiring a down payment to make sure that the borrower maintains an economic interest in the value of the house. These savings institutions took on relatively short-term deposits to finance long-term home mortgages, thereby exposing themselves to risk in the event of market interest rate fluctuations. The mismatch of maturity assets and liabilities was a major factor in the deposit insurance crisis for U.S. savings institutions during the 1980s and early 1990s, which we address in Chapter 15. Over the 1980s and 1990s, savings institutions have declined significantly in importance relative to commercial banks.

Credit Unions

Consumer loans are subject to potentially severe private information problems and associated monitoring costs. One way for a lender to reduce information costs is to concentrate on making loans to groups about which the lender has good information. **Credit unions** are another specialized intermediary in consumer lending, taking deposits from and making loans to individuals who are well known to one another and who typically work at the same firm or in the same industry. Except for relatively small consumer loans, credit union assets are invested primarily in mortgage loans to members. The profits earned by credit unions are exempt from income taxes; this increases their attractiveness to savers in comparison with banks.

Table 12.2 on page 304 summarizes the risk-sharing, liquidity, and information services offered by private financial intermediaries.

CHECKPOINT

Why are mutual funds more likely to invest in stocks, bonds, or Treasury securities than in loans to households and small businesses, which is the business of banks? Most mutual funds issue very liquid claims to savers, so they invest in assets that can be bought and sold with low transactions costs. Because converting loans to households and small businesses into marketable securities is costly, investors in mutual funds would face the risk of having assets sold at a discount to meet withdrawal demands. o

GOVERNMENT FINANCIAL INSTITUTIONS

The U.S. government participates in financial intermediation both *directly*, through government-sponsored financial institutions, and *indirectly*, through guarantees of loans made by private financial intermediaries.

Direct Role: Federal Credit Agencies

Federal credit agencies are **government financial institutions** that make loans in the interest of public policy—most notably agricultural finance, housing finance, and student loans. In 2000, they held assets that were worth $1883 billion.

Government lending to farmers is the oldest form of U.S. government participation in financial intermediation. The Farm Credit System issues bonds and commercial paper in financial markets and uses the proceeds to make crop, equipment, and mortgage loans to farmers. Made up of a network of regional Banks for Cooperatives, Federal Land Banks, and Federal Intermediate Credit Banks, the Farm Credit System required a multibillion-dollar taxpayer bailout in 1987 as farm loan defaults soared.

Government intermediation for housing is the largest of the government lending activities. The Federal National Mortgage Association (FNMA, or "Fannie Mae"), the Federal Home Loan Mortgage Company (FHLMC, or "Freddie Mac"), and the Government National Mortgage Association (GNMA, or "Ginnie Mae") are government agencies that issue bonds in financial markets and use the proceeds to supply funds to the mortgage market. Only GNMA is a federal agency; the others are federally sponsored agencies. Although their debt is not explicitly guaranteed by the federal government, most market participants believe that the Treasury would not permit FNMA or

CASE STUDY

What Kind of Financial Institution Is a Hedge Fund?

Just a year after winning Nobel Prizes in economics, Robert Merton and Myron Scholes found themselves less pleasantly in the news—as high-profile partners in Long-Term Capital Management (LTCM), the "hedge fund" whose spectacular crash and rescue in the fall of 1998 captured headlines around the world. As a hedge fund, LTCM joined the ranks of a recently popular (if misunderstood) class of financial institutions. Mahaathir Mohamad, Malaysia's stormy prime minister, has called hedge fund managers "highwaymen of the global economy." Many journalists and policymakers share similar, if less colorfully stated, views. The LTCM case has the trappings of drama—Nobel Prize winners, multibillion-dollar losses, very rich investors, and a Federal Reserve-orchestrated rescue.

A *hedge fund* is a hybrid institution, a largely unregulated investment entity (generally organized as private partnerships) specializing in putting together short sales (borrowing a security and selling it in the hope of being able to repurchase it more cheaply before repaying the lender) and leverage (purchasing securities with borrowed funds) in a manner that mitigates risk. Such investment vehicles have been around in various forms since the 1950s. Hedge funds make profits from speculation, but they usually operate on both the "long" and "short" sides of the market at the same time (hence the name—from "hedging" their positions to prosper whichever way the market moves). This sort of activity can lead to significant leverage that can be magnified using derivatives.

LTCM used these funds to place some rather large bets. The firm specialized in detecting discrepancies among bond prices and predicting which way prices would move. As the Asian financial crisis emerged, LTCM decided to short U.S. Treasury securities (wagering that their prices would fall) and go long on risky U.S. corporate bonds and European government bonds (wagering that their prices would rise). The bet went badly, however. A classic "flight to quality" during the Asian crisis pushed up prices of U.S. Treasuries, ravaging risky corporate bond and European government bond markets and reducing those markets' liquidity. LTCM's large borrowings from banks and its central role in key bond markets led the Federal Reserve Bank of New York to bring LTCM's creditors together to rescue the firm in 1998.

Mutual funds also pool funds from individual investors to invest in securities, but hedge funds differ in important ways—from the small numbers of players to the $10 million minimum investment requirements to the lax disclosure requirements.[†] In addition, hedge fund managers tie up most of their own capital in the fund and earn 15% to 20% of the funds' profits over and above a management fee (which a mutual fund manager

† For a comparison of mutual fund and hedge fund regulation, see Franklin R. Edwards and R. Glenn Hubbard, "The Growth of Institutional Ownership: A Promise Unfulfilled," *Journal of Applied Corporate Finance*, 13:92–104, 2000.

would also receive). Hedge funds are smaller than mutual funds, with an estimated collective capital holding of $120 billion at the time of the LTCM debacle. These differences do not imply that hedge funds are a bad deal for wealthy households and institutional investors, which enjoyed very significant net returns from hedge fund investing in the 1990s. One lesson of mutual fund management—the importance of market liquidity for investment strategies—applies to hedge funds, though. As LTCM learned, trading is costly when markets become illiquid.

CASE STUDY

What Kind of Financial Institution Is a Venture Capital Fund?

Venture capital funds have played a starring role in America's new economy, financing large-scale new ventures and consolidating more mature firms. While wealthy individuals known as "angels" invest funds directly in new ventures, venture capital funds (VCs) act as intermediaries. They raise funds from institutional investors and very wealthy individuals (who commit funds as an illiquid investment for periods as long as 10 years), then invest those funds in portfolio companies. From a base of $3 billion in investments in VCs in 1990, investors pumped a record $56 billion into U.S. VCs in 1999. In addition, some large corporations invest funds in their own venture firms.

What accounts for VCs' popularity? Nothing succeeds like success. Annual returns on funds under management were very high in the middle and late 1990s, in part because of the boom in initial public offerings of VCs' portfolio companies (especially in the technology and telecommunications sectors). Will the good times continue to roll? Perhaps a bit less robustly in the near term. As the market for individual public offerings slowed in 2000 and in 2001, VCs found harvesting built-up gains more difficult.

The success of some venture capital funds reflects the special skill of their managers (called "general partners" in the typical VC organized as a partnership, with the outside investors being "limited partners"),† who specialize in reducing costs of adverse selection and moral hazard in entrepreneurial finance. Because screening and monitoring are time-consuming, VCs cannot profitably invest funds on as large a scale as do mutual funds, insurance companies, or pension funds.

What does the future hold? Although 2000 was a bad year for initial public offerings and many VCs, economists widely support the notion that the future of the venture capital industry is bright because of their role in the finance and governance of emerging companies.

† Venture firms are generally organized as partnerships because the Investment Company Act of 1940 imposes very stringent regulations on public firms that are essentially an investment portfolio.

TABLE 12.2 SERVICES PROVIDED BY PRIVATE FINANCIAL INTERMEDIARIES

Financial institution	Risk sharing	Liquidity	Information
Commercial banks	Offer claims on diversified portfolios of assets, reducing transactions costs for individual savers	Offer liquid claims on portfolios of assets as well as some less liquid saving methods	Offer lower transactions and information costs than financial markets for many savers and borrowers; specialize in resolution of information problems (adverse selection and moral hazard)
Savings institutions	Similar to banks	Similar to banks	—
Credit unions	Similar to banks	Similar to banks	Similar to banks
Investment banks	—	Participate in securities trading	Evaluate securities in the underwriting process and advise firms on external financing
Securities firms	Similar to banks, but with money market accounts	Participate in securities trading; offer liquid claims on portfolios of money and capital instruments	—
Mutual funds	Similar to banks, but with money market accounts	Offer liquid claims on portfolios of money and capital instruments	—
Finance companies	—	—	Collect information for credit analysis for borrowers (often similar to bank borrowers)
Insurance companies	Offer advantages of risk pooling against financial hardship from death or specified unforeseen events	—	Gather and monitor information on policyholders and on some of the less well-known firms to which they lend
Pension funds	Offer claims on (typically) diversified portfolio of assets for retirement saving	—	—

FHLMC to default on their obligations. These two agencies experienced very robust portfolio growth in the late 1990s, drawing substantial criticism from private-sector competitors.

To encourage lending to students for educational expenses, the government created a special charter for the Student Loan Market Association (SLMA, or "Sallie Mae") to purchase student loans made by private financial intermediaries under the auspices of the guaranteed Student Loan Program. In the late 1980s and early 1990s, SLMA experienced significant losses from loan defaults. In 1994, President Clinton signed a law directing the Department of Education to conduct a five-year test to determine whether the government could manage the student loan program more cheaply than the private sector. In 1995, the Congress rejected the expanded role for the government, and in 2001, the incoming Bush administration made review of the federal credit agencies a priority.

Indirect Role: Loan Guarantees

A second role for the federal government in intermediation is to guarantee loans made by private financial institutions. Such guarantees are analogous to insurance, because the lender (a private financial institution) is not harmed if the borrower defaults. As with direct intermediation, loan guarantees are administered by many agencies. The Farmers Home Administration (FmHA) guarantees certain loans to farmers; the Federal Housing Administration (FHA) and the Department of Veterans Affairs (VA) guarantee certain mortgage loans; and the Department of Education guarantees student loans.

Recent Trends

By the 1990s, many analysts questioned the advisability of maintaining or increasing the government's direct participation in financial intermediation. Private financial institutions have complained about the inroads of federally sponsored credit agencies into mortgage and other lending activities. Nonetheless, in the 1990s, proposals were being made in the Congress for new agencies to administer such activities as municipal road-building loans, mortgage insurance for veterans, and insurance for pollution control bonds.

The tenfold growth in loan guarantees during the past two decades and recent increases in defaults trouble many analysts and policymakers. The reason is that overly generous loan guarantees encourage moral hazard; private institutions will not be as careful in screening and monitoring borrowers in the presence of loan guarantees. These problems, in turn, cost taxpayers money. In the midst of the expensive bailout of federal deposit insurance in banking, the General Accounting Office (GAO) informed the Congress in 1990 that taxpayer losses from government loan guarantees may eventually exceed $100 billion. Since that time, losses have materialized from student loan guarantees and from defaults on the loan guarantees of the Department of Housing and Urban Development. Many analysts worry that, without reforms, taxpayer losses on guaranteed loans will be significant.

FINANCIAL INSTITUTIONS: BLURRING THE LINES

We have explained why various types of financial institutions—securities market institutions, investment institutions, contractual savings institutions, depository institutions, and government financial institutions—came into being and how they serve the needs of savers and borrowers. During the

1930s, laws and regulations built barriers that protected the services offered by each type of institution from competition. As deregulation of the financial services industry proceeded during the 1980s and 1990s, more providers of various services emerged.

The landmark *Gramm-Leach-Bliley Financial Services Modernization Act of 1999* removed many of the regulatory lines among financial institutions. Responding to competitive developments in markets for insurance, commercial banking, and securities, the act permits the acquisition of commercial banks by insurance companies and firms in the securities business and gives banks the right to conduct real estate activities and to underwrite insurance and securities. As a consequence, the services provided by different types of financial institutions now overlap greatly.

In the current environment, the provision of financial services is being organized more by function—delivery of risk-sharing, liquidity, and information services—than by the identity of the provider. The equivalent of checkable deposits can be maintained not only at commercial banks, but also at savings institutions, brokerage firms, and mutual funds, and nonbank alternatives often offer greater returns for depositors. Banks are using their relationships with depositors to compete head to head with insurance companies in selling life insurance (and vice versa, as in 1998, Metropolitan Life announced plans to acquire a bank). Finance companies are exploiting their ability at evaluating collateral and making inroads into banks' business lending activities. As regulations separating commercial and investment banking activities break down following the passage of the Gramm-Leach-Bliley Act, commercial banks are relying on their information collection strengths to compete aggressively with investment banks for underwriting business. Citigroup—formed from Citicorp and Travelers—worked in 1998 to create a financial supermarket. In 2000, securities giant Merrill Lynch and insurance powerhouse State Farm prepared to enter the banking business.

While most funds flowing between lenders and borrowers use the services of intermediaries, the market shares of individual intermediaries have changed significantly over the past few decades, as Table 12.1 shows. These changes in part reflect competition by function, as regulatory separation of institutions has been reduced. For example, the market shares (of intermediated assets) of commercial banks, savings institutions, and credit unions were stable over the period from 1960 to 1980 but fell sharply over the period from 1980 to 2000.

What accounts for this change? Depository institutions faced competition for checking account customers from more remunerative money market mutual funds, whose market share more than doubled. Households also switched funds out of bank savings accounts to stock and bond mutual funds. Banks also face strong competition for loans from finance companies, pension funds, and government financial institutions.

Common needs for the regulation of financial institutions and intermediaries emerge as competition induces distinctions among them to blur. As early as 1995, the White House, the Congress, and the Federal Reserve began urging the regulation of financial services by function. Under the Gramm-Leach-Bliley Act, regulatory oversight of multifunction financial institutions will be spread among the Treasury Department's Office of the Comptroller of the Currency (which has regulatory authority for bank subsidiaries engaged in securities underwriting), the SEC (which continues its regulatory oversight of securities activities), the Federal Reserve (which continues monitoring bank holding companies with insurance, real estate, and securities operations), and states (which maintain their regulatory authority over insurance businesses).

More generally, transmitting information is an important activity for all financial intermediaries. When information costs are relatively unimportant, regulations guaranteeing disclosure of asset portfolios, investment management practices, and supervision and examination are likely to be sufficient. However, for financial institutions and intermediaries that are involved in reducing information costs in financial markets, such regulations alone may be insufficient. Additional regulatory interventions focusing on the lending activities of banks and insurance firms, as well as the market-making activities of securities firms and exchanges, may be necessary.

KEY TERMS AND CONCEPTS

- Contractual saving institutions
  - Coinsurance
  - Deductible
  - Defined benefit plan
  - Defined contribution plan
  - Insurance companies
  - Life insurance companies
  - Pension funds
  - Plan funding
  - Property and casualty insurance companies
  - Restrictive covenants
  - Risk-based premiums
- Depository institutions
  - Commercial banks
  - Credit unions
  - Savings institutions
- Government financial institutions
- Insider information
- Investment institutions
  - Closed-end mutual funds
  - Finance companies
  - Load funds
  - Money market mutual funds
  - Mutual funds
  - No-load funds
  - Open-end mutual funds
- Securities market institutions
  - Brokers
  - Dealers
  - Exchange
  - Investment banks
  - Over-the-counter (OTC) markets
  - Specialist
  - Syndicates
  - Underwriting

SUMMARY

1. Investment banks assist firms in raising funds in primary financial markets by underwriting new issues of debt and equity. Brokers and dealers match buyers and sellers in secondary financial markets. Financial instruments such as stocks and bonds are traded in organized exchanges and over-the-counter markets.
2. Mutual funds convert small individual claims into diversified portfolios of money and capital market instruments. In addition to providing diversification, funds economize on costs associated with securities transactions.

THE WALL STREET JOURNAL JULY 14, 2000

Federal Credit Agencies: Is "Too Much" Lending Possible?

Camilla Douglas is proof it's easier to get a home in the United States than ever before. . . .

For that, Ms. Douglas can thank Fannie Mae and Freddie Mac, which provide the capital that keeps the housing market humming. Buying up mortgages, they keep banks flush with money for further home-lending, holding down mortgage rates in the meantime. They pioneered the 3%-down mortgage and a slew of other programs for lower-income borrowers.

a

Yet not everybody is happy with this picture. . . . Commercial banks and other competitors say Fannie Mae and Freddie Mac are unfairly moving onto their turf. Some academics and legislators think the companies are a potential savings-and-loan–style disaster in the making. . . .

Why is everybody so riled? On the surface, it looks like a matter of size: Fannie Mae and Freddie Mac, which are shareholder-owned but government-sponsored, have gotten bigger than anyone ever dreamed, squeezing out competitors in the process. . . . In all, they either own or guarantee about $2 trillion in mortgages.

. . . .Fannie and Freddie have been on a borrowing binge, and today their combined debt is roughly equivalent to the size of the entire U.S. Treasury. Last year alone, Fannie and Freddie issued $260 billion in long-term debt.

But beyond all that, many critics are also focusing on the *way* the companies have grown, and whether their behavior poses a significant risk to the economy and to taxpayers. . . .

So what is it, exactly, that's considered so risky? It boils down to two things: the companies' decision to buy large volumes of their own securities, and their expansion into new loan categories, both of which are made possible by the fact that Fannie and Freddie can often borrow more cheaply than competing banks.

Typically, Fannie and Freddie either hold the loans they buy as investments or pool them and sell them in the form of mortgage-backed securities. Despite being shareholder-owned, Fannie and Freddie operate under federal charters that exempt them from state and local corporate income taxes and give them a $2.25 billion line of credit with the Treasury. Investors interpret those and other ties as evidence the companies would be bailed out if they got into a jam. This implicit guarantee allows them in many cases to borrow more cheaply than other financial institutions, which competitors think is unfair.

b

Despite that advantage, Fannie and Freddie aren't allowed to expand beyond their core business of buying mortgages. . . . That means the companies have to find other ways to grow within the confines of their charters. . . .

So far, the most effective way has been to build up their portfolios by buying mortgage-backed securities, which the companies place on their books to play interest-rate spreads. It can be extremely lucrative.

But there is a danger. If interest rates move unexpectedly, the companies. . . could wind up losing billions of dollars if their portfolios were improperly hedged. . . .

c

Federal credit agencies, sometimes known as government-sponsored enterprises, are increasingly important financial intermediaries. This statement is particularly true in the case of housing finance. Fannie Mae and Freddie Mac purchase mortgages and sell packages of mortgages as securities, after guaranteeing payment of interest and principal.

a Private financial institutions develop to fill particular niches in matching savers and borrowers and to provide particular risk-sharing, liquidity, and information services to savers. Government financial institutions emerge to fill important niches not satisfied by private intermediaries or to advance public policy objectives, such as promoting home ownership. The activities of Fannie Mae and Freddie Mac have lowered mortgage costs for home buyers and generated significant profits for their shareholders.

b The implicit government guarantees leave taxpayers exposed to the risk of losses when the value of federal credit agencies' mortgages fall (when market interest rates rise, for example). This taxpayer risk is compounded by the fact that private lenders have found it more difficult to compete with federal credit agencies.

c Is this expanding intervention a win-win situation, raising profits and implementing the public purpose? Not likely. As we showed in this chapter and Chapter 11, one purpose of financial arrangements is to make sure that borrowers or insured individuals have appropriate incentives to perform. If investors in mortgage securities packaged by Fannie Mae and Freddie Mac believe that they are insured, they have no incentive to monitor managers of the federal credit agencies. How can taxpayers' interests be safeguarded? One option is to require shareholders in government-sponsored enterprises to place more of their own capital at risk, giving them an incentive to monitor the managers more closely.

For further thought . . .

If the federal government insured all mortgages, would the risk of fluctuating mortgage values be eliminated? Explain.

Source: Excerpted from Patrick Barta, "Loan Stars: Why Calls Are Rising to Clip Fannie Mae's, Freddie Mac's Wings." Reprinted by permission of *The Wall Street Journal*, July 14, 2000. Dow Jones & Co., Inc. All Rights Reserved Worldwide.

3. Finance companies make loans to consumers and firms with funds they raise in money and capital markets. Some such firms—sales finance companies—are tied to companies that manufacture or sell goods.
4. Life insurance companies and property and casualty insurance companies provide risk-sharing services to savers and are large investors in financial markets. Insurance companies reduce information costs of adverse selection and moral hazard by gathering and monitoring information about policyholders.
5. Private and public pension funds invest contributions of employees and firms to provide retirement benefits. The two broad categories of pension plans are defined benefit and defined contribution plans. In a defined benefit plan, employees receive a specified schedule of benefits, irrespective of the market performance of pension fund assets. In a defined contribution plan, participants receive the returns on their contributions, accepting the residual claim on fund earnings and the associated risk.
6. Depository institutions (commercial banks, savings institutions, and credit unions) accept deposits and make loans and investments. Like mutual funds, they issue liquid deposit claims against a portfolio of loans and investments. However, as borrowers may have private information about their prospects or their plans for using the borrowed funds, lenders at arm's length face high information costs. Bank lending requires an investment in gathering and monitoring information about the borrower.
7. The U.S. government participates in financial intermediation directly, through government-sponsored financial institutions known as federal credit agencies. It is also involved indirectly, through guarantees of loans made by private financial intermediaries.

REVIEW QUESTIONS

1. What are the five main groups of financial institutions? Which institutions belong in each group?
2. What role do underwriters play in bringing savers' funds to borrowers?
3. If you buy 100 shares of IBM stock on the New York Stock Exchange, does IBM get the money? Why or why not?
4. If you want to buy a $10,000 U.S. Treasury bond and a securities firm sells you one from its own holdings, is it acting as a broker or a dealer? If it arranges for you to buy one from someone else, is it acting as a broker or a dealer?
5. What is e-trading? What effect has it had on the value of seats on the major stock exchanges?
6. What are the different types of finance companies, and who uses them?
7. What is the moral hazard problem in insurance? How do insurance companies attempt to reduce the moral hazard problem?
8. How do insurance companies know how high their premiums should be for life and accident insurance? What kinds of problems do they face in assessing risks?
9. Why do property and casualty insurance companies invest more heavily in short-term assets than life insurance companies do?
10. What is the advantage of saving for retirement through a pension plan at work as opposed to saving on your own?
11. How do banks address adverse selection problems?
12. What types of depository institutions specialize in loans to consumers and homeowners? How are they different from commercial banks?
13. Describe how mutual funds provide services related to risk sharing and liquidity. Distinguish a mutual fund from a bank. What do the differences you highlighted imply about the need for regulation of mutual funds as opposed to banks?
14. Why do sales finance companies exist? Why might the General Motors Acceptance Corporation at certain times offer a lower interest rate on loans to buy GM cars than commercial banks would?

ANALYTICAL PROBLEMS

15. Explain how life insurance companies and private pension funds provide risk-sharing services for savers. Why do individuals not choose to self-insure—that is, insure their lives or retirement incomes on their own?

16. Suppose that a state has a number of low-income neighborhoods in its cities that have difficulty attracting businesses to locate there because the businesses find it problematic to secure fire insurance. Insurance companies say they are reluctant to write fire insurance policies in these neighborhoods because of the prevalence of arson fires. If the state legislature passes a law forbidding insurance companies from taking into account the arson experience of a neighborhood when deciding whether to offer fire insurance policies to businesses, predict the likely effect on the insurance market.

17. A country with restrictions on bank loan and deposit rates is more likely than other countries to develop significant markets in mutual funds for short-term claims. Would such mutual funds completely undo the interest rate regulations—that is, serve the same savers and borrowers equally well? Explain.

18. Is a compulsory government-sponsored Social Security retirement annuity system as subject to adverse selection as a private insurance company that offers individual annuity contracts? Explain.

19. If you believe the stock market is an efficient market, would you prefer to invest in an index mutual fund or in a mutual fund that is actively managed?

20. What type of financial institution would each of the following people be most likely to do business with?
    a. A person with $10,000 in savings who would like to earn a decent return at low risk and who does not know much about the stock and bond markets.
    b. A person with $350 who needs a checking account.
    c. A person who needs a $10,000 loan to open a pizza shop.
    d. A person who is recently married, is starting a family, and wants to make sure that his children are well taken care of in the future.
    e. The president of a small company who wants to list it on the stock exchange to obtain additional capital.
    f. Someone who has just received a large inheritance and wants to invest it in the stock market.
    g. A person with no credit history who is buying her first car.
    h. A family needing a mortgage loan to buy a house.
    i. A person who has declared bankruptcy in the past and is looking for a loan to pay off some past-due bills.

21. Suppose that you have a choice of one of three stock mutual funds. Fund One boasts an average return over the last five years of 8.33%, Fund Two has returned 8.10%, and Fund Three has earned 7.95%. You might think that Fund One is the best, but are there some reasons why Fund Two or even Fund Three might be better?

22. As an employee in a large firm, you are given the choice between a defined benefit pension plan and a defined contribution pension plan. What are the advantages and disadvantages of each?

23. The earnings on savings through whole life insurance policies are not taxed. The policy provides both insurance (it pays a benefit when the policyholder dies) and savings (policyholders can cash in the policy before death). If the investment earnings on policy contributions were taxed, what would happen to the relative demand for term life and whole life policies?

DATA QUESTION

24. In *The Wall Street Journal,* look at the listings of mutual funds. What types of funds are they, closed-end funds or open-end funds? How can you tell? Suppose that the price of a share in a mutual fund is less than the value of a share of the fund's portfolio. Should you buy into the fund?

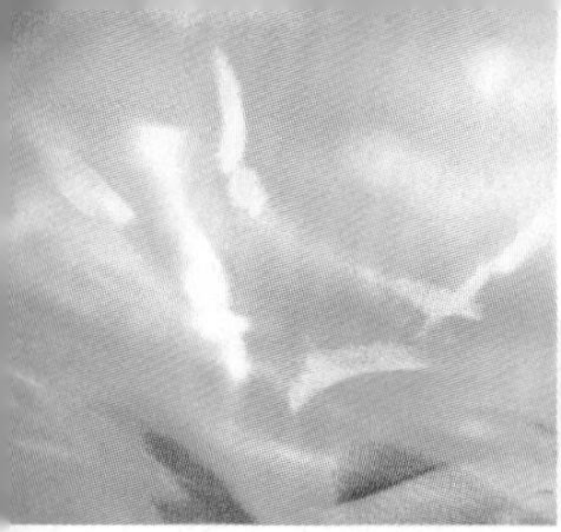

CHAPTER 13

The Business of Banking

Throughout the 1980s and early 1990s, Japanese banks dominated global banking. All ten of the world's largest banks were Japanese, and they controlled trillions of dollars in assets. In the mid- and late 1990s, however, heavy losses from bad debts and poor investments threatened the viability of Japanese banks, causing a crisis in the Japanese banking industry. According to many U.S. bankers, the Japanese faced the same problems in real estate lending and poor management that caused a U.S. banking crisis in the 1980s. Because of the size of these problems, the Japanese banking crisis caused some economists and financiers in 2000 to question the health of the Japanese economy and the international financial system.

How can such large and important financial institutions face problems that jeopardize their survival? In this chapter, we explain how banks do business and how they must operate to remain successful. From this investigation, you will see how large Japanese banks and U.S. banks can encounter the problems they have faced in recent decades.

Banking is a business; that is, banks fill a market need by providing a service and earn a profit by charging customers for that service. Banks earn profits by acquiring funds at a cost from savers and lending those funds to borrowers, adding value by providing risk-sharing, liquidity, and information services. Like any business, banks act to maximize their profits. The difference between the return that a bank earns from lending and the cost of obtaining the funds to lend—the spread—is the bank's profit. The objective of this chapter is to explain the business of banking. Our point of view is that of the bank as it acquires deposits and other funds and lends them to borrowers and provides other services.

Why should we study how banks conduct their business and earn profits? In addition to creating products and services, banks in the United States and in most developed economies are the leading financial intermediaries. In 2000, U.S.-chartered banks held more than $5.3 trillion in assets. U.S. households invest about 15% of their financial wealth in banks. Most payments in the U.S. economy are made by checks drawn on banks and then deposited in other banks. In this way, commercial banks play a key role in the economy's *payments system*, or the means of clearing and settling transactions. These transaction services promote the efficiency of the financial system and contribute to a healthy economy. Your understanding of the financial system would be incomplete without knowledge of how banks operate and remain strong.

After describing the activities of a bank that contribute to its profits, we look at the problems banks face in managing the risks of their deposit-taking and lending activities. In recent years, banks have faced competition from other financial institutions that could offer savers and borrowers similar services at a lower risk. We conclude the chapter with a description of activities that banks have adopted to challenge their competitors and remain prominent as financial intermediaries.

HOW BANKS EARN PROFITS

We begin our study of the business of banking by identifying a bank's sources and uses of funds, as summarized on its balance sheet. A **balance sheet** is simply a statement showing an individual's or firm's financial position at a particular point in time. It lists the uses of acquired funds, *assets;* the source of acquired funds, *liabilities;* and the difference between the two, *net worth*. The bank's net worth includes accumulated profits from doing business with savers and borrowers. Table 13.1 summarizes the consolidated balance sheet of all U.S. banks. By examining how banks attract funds and the loans they make with those funds, we can determine how a bank earns profits and maintains its role as a key intermediary in the financial system.

Bank Liabilities

Bank liabilities are the funds the bank acquires from savers. The bank uses the funds to make investments or loans to borrowers. To obtain funds, banks

TABLE 13.1

BALANCE SHEET OF U.S. COMMERCIAL BANKS, 2000†

Assets (uses of funds)		Liabilities (sources of funds) and net worth	
Reserves Cash items in process of collection Deposits at other banks	4.2%	Checkable deposits	11.3%
		Nontransaction deposits	
		Savings deposits and time deposits (CDs)	42.1
Securities	20.9	Large, negotiable time deposits (CDs)	10.2
U.S. government and agency	13.6	Borrowings (from the Federal Reserve, in the federal funds market, from subsidiaries and affiliates, and through repurchase agreements)	18.9
State and local government and other securities	7.3		
Loans	68.2		
Commercial and industrial	16.4	Miscellaneous liabilities	9.6
Mortgage	30.0	Equity capital (net worth)	7.9
Consumer	10.0		
Interbank	4.0		
Other loans	8.0		
Miscellaneous assets	6.7		

† Figures are expressed as a percentage of total assets for all domestically chartered commercial banking institutions in the United States as of September 2000.

Source: Federal Reserve Bulletin, December 2000, Table 1.26.

offer savers a range of deposit accounts that provide depositors with services (such as paying by check) or incentives (interest payments) that encourage savers to keep their funds on deposit at the bank. These accounts include checkable deposits and nontransaction deposits. In addition to these sources of funds, banks often borrow in money and capital markets. Checkable deposits, nontransaction deposits, and borrowings are liabilities for the bank.

Checkable deposits. Banks offer savers **checkable deposits,** accounts that grant a depositor the right to write checks to individuals, businesses, or the government. These accounts include non-interest-bearing demand deposits, interest-bearing negotiable order of withdrawal (NOW) accounts, and super-NOW accounts. A NOW account is available to individuals and allows the depositor to write checks while receiving interest; in super-NOW accounts, the depositor's NOW and savings account at a bank are linked. The interest rates the banks pay on NOW accounts are adjusted periodically to match changes in market interest rates. Taken together, checkable deposits account for about 11% of banks' funds in 2000, down from more than 60% in 1960. Changes in banking regulations and the development of new financial instruments caused this decline.

Banks must pay all checkable deposits on demand. In other words, the bank must exchange a depositor's check for cash immediately, provided that the depositor has at least the amount of the check on deposit. Savers use checkable accounts to settle transactions by exchanging checks for goods and services. These deposits provide a liquid asset for savers; because savers value liquidity, they accept lower interest rates on checkable deposits than on less liquid instruments. Why would savers accept a zero interest rate on demand deposits when NOW accounts pay interest? One reason is that U.S. banking regulations do not permit businesses to hold NOW accounts. In addition, depositors forgo the interest on demand deposits because banks charge no explicit fees for checking services, whereas they often do charge fees or higher penalties for NOW account services.

Nontransaction deposits. Savers use only some of their deposits for day-to-day transactions. To attract funds from depositors who want to earn interest on their funds, banks offer **nontransaction deposits.** These include savings accounts, *money market deposit accounts* (*MMDAs*), and time deposits (generally called *certificates of deposit,* or *CDs*). These liabilities accounted for about 52% of banks' funds in 2000 and were the largest source of their funds.

A generation ago, savings accounts (sometimes called *passbook accounts*) generated the nontransaction funds for banks. Technically, depositors must give the bank 30 days' notice for a withdrawal, but banks usually waive this requirement, making savings accounts, in practice, demandable. Banks use deposits in money market deposit accounts, the second category of nontransaction deposits, to purchase commercial paper and Treasury securities. The interest rate that is paid to savers changes frequently with short-term yields in money markets. These accounts also have limited checkwriting privileges.

Unlike savings deposits, *time deposits* have specified maturities that typically range from a few months to several years. Banks penalize savers who withdraw their funds prior to maturity by requiring the savers to forfeit part of the accrued interest. Banks offer *small-denomination time deposits,* time deposits for less than $100,000, which are not as liquid as savings accounts and so pay depositors a higher rate of interest. Banks also offer *large-denomination time deposits,* for more than $100,000. These are negotiable, and investors buy and sell them in secondary markets prior to maturity. Holders of large-denomination time deposits include financial institutions and nonfinancial corporations, which hold the negotiable CDs as an alternative to Treasury securities. Nonexistent in 1960, large-denomination CDs have become an important source of additional funds for banks.

Checkable and small-denomination time deposits together are the largest single source of funds for banks. One reason for their popularity is that in the United States, they are covered by **federal deposit insurance,** which provides government guarantees for account balances of currently up to $100,000. Deposit insurance gives banks an edge over other intermediaries in acquiring funds from small savers. Large-denomination negotiable certificates of deposit are not demandable and are riskier for savers because amounts over $100,000 are not covered by federal deposit insurance. In raising funds through such instruments, banks are competing with other borrowers in financial markets.

Borrowings. Banks often have more opportunities to make loans than they can finance with funds they attract from depositors. To take advantage of these opportunities, banks raise money by borrowing—and these borrowings are another liability for banks. However, if the interest rate the bank pays to borrow these funds is lower than the interest rate it earns by lending the funds to businesses and consumers, then the bank can profit by raising funds in this way. **Borrowings,** or nondeposit liabilities, include short-term loans in the federal funds market, loans from a bank's foreign branches or other subsidiaries or affiliates, repurchase agreements, and loans from the Federal Reserve System (known as *discount loans*). Transactions in the federal funds market and through repurchase agreements have become especially important to banks in managing liquidity. The *federal funds market* is the market for unsecured loans (often overnight) between banks. The interest rate on these interbank loans is called the *federal funds rate.* In *repurchase agreements* ("repos" or RPs), banks sell securities and agree to repurchase them, typically the next day. Banks use RPs to borrow funds from business firms or other banks, using the underlying securities as collateral. The corporation or other bank that buys the securities earns interest without any significant loss of liquidity. A negligible source of funds in 1960, borrowings accounted for about 19% of the funds raised by banks in 2000.

Bank Assets

Bank assets include cash items and funds used in securities investments, loans, and other asset holdings.

Cash items. The most liquid asset held by banks is **reserves,** which consist of **vault cash**—cash on hand in the bank or in deposits at other banks—and deposits with the Federal Reserve System. As part of its regulation of the banking system, the Fed requires that banks hold some of their deposits in non-interest-bearing accounts—as vault cash or in *reserve accounts* at a Federal Reserve bank. These **required reserves,** which are a percentage of the bank's checkable deposits, are a tax on bank intermediation because they bar a bank from lending all of its deposits. Banks also hold cash assets to provide them with the liquidity needed to meet normal outflows from demandable deposits.

A bank's claims on other banks for uncollected funds are assets. For example, suppose that your employer writes you a check drawn on another bank, which you deposit in your bank. Until the funds are collected, your bank holds the check as an asset, called a *cash item in process of collection.*

Small banks may maintain deposits at other banks to obtain foreign-exchange transactions, check collection, or other services. This function, called *correspondent banking,* has diminished in importance during the past 40 years.

Cash items—reserves, cash items in process of collection, and deposits at other banks—account for about 4% of banks' assets in 2000 (down from about 20% in 1960). Later in this chapter, we describe how and why banks were able to make this change—and profit from it.

Securities. **Marketable securities** are liquid assets that banks trade in securities markets. Banks are allowed to hold U.S. Treasury securities and limited amounts of municipal bonds—that is, obligations of state and local governments. Because of their liquidity, bank holdings of U.S. government securities are sometimes called *secondary reserves.* In the United States, commercial banks cannot invest checkable deposits in corporate bonds or common stock. Securities holdings totaled about 21% of bank assets in 2000.

Loans. The largest category of bank assets is **loans,** representing roughly 68% of the total in 2000. Banks in the United States are not allowed to make a loan to a single borrower of more than 15% of the bank's capital. Loans are illiquid relative to government securities and entail greater default risk and higher information costs. As a result, the interest rates on loans are higher than those on marketable securities. In addition to commercial and consumer loans, banks make overnight loans to each other through the federal funds market.

For commercial banks, the most important types of loans are commercial and industrial loans—called C&I loans—and real estate loans. Other commercial bank loans are made to consumers or overnight to other banks through the federal funds market. An important difference in the balance sheets of the principal types of depository institutions is evident in the *loans* category. Credit unions, for example, primarily make consumer loans, whereas mutual savings banks and savings and loan associations usually make home mortgage loans.

Other assets. This miscellaneous category covers banks' physical assets in equipment and buildings. It also includes collateral received from borrowers in default.

Bank Net Worth

Assets are things of value that a bank owns, whereas liabilities are things of value that a bank owes to others. The difference between the two—assets minus liabilities—equals the **bank net worth,** or equity capital. Net worth is the capital contributed by the bank's shareholders plus accumulated, retained profits. In other words, net worth (or equity capital) measures a bank's remaining value after it has met all its liabilities. Thus, as the values of a bank's assets or liabilities change in financial markets (say, because of new developments or information), a bank's net worth changes.

When savers deposit money in a bank, they expose themselves to the risk that, if the bank incurs losses from outside investments, they will lose some part of their deposits. Therefore a bank with a high net worth is appealing to savers because net worth provides a buffer against the risk of losses. This buffer is like that in other businesses, in which the owners' equity stakes are a cushion against potential losses.[†]

Bank net worth has been relatively stable during the past three decades at about 7% to 9% of total funds raised. The riskiness of bank assets has increased substantially, however, with banks holding more loans relative to cash and government securities. As a result, the effective equity cushion for depositors has declined. Banks have an incentive to reduce their equity to increase their expected rate of return, whereas depositors prefer a more substantial equity cushion. Not surprisingly, then, bank regulation focuses on appropriate levels of bank net worth.

Bank Failure

Like other firms, banks can become financially distressed and fail. A **bank failure** occurs when a bank cannot pay its depositors in full with enough reserves left to meet its reserve requirements. In practice, regulators can close a bank when they deem its net worth to be too low. The higher a bank's holdings of

[†] Of course, some savers want to own equity stakes in a bank because the bank profits from intermediation. Depositors still get their promised return, and the residual accrues to the saver, a shareholder.

reserves, marketable securities, or equity capital, the less likely is the bank to fail. This reality underscores the trade-off between bank safety and returns. Being too conservative lowers bank profitability.

Determining Bank Profits

If we observe changes in bank assets and liabilities as the bank accepts deposits and makes loans, we will see how a bank can operate profitably as it matches savers and borrowers. When a bank issues checkable deposits to finance business or consumer loans, it transforms a financial asset (a deposit) for a saver into a liability (a loan) for a borrower. Like other businesses, to profit and grow, banks take inputs, add value to them, and deliver outputs. To analyze the changes, we work with a simplified balance sheet that focuses only on the items that change in each transaction.

In particular, we use an accounting tool known as a **T-account,**[†] which lists changes in balance sheet items from an initial balance sheet position as they occur. Suppose, for example, that you decide to open a checking account at Megabank with $100 in cash. As a result, Megabank acquires $100 in vault cash, which it lists as an asset. Because you can go to the bank and withdraw your deposit at any time, Megabank must also list $100 of checkable deposits as a liability in the form of checkable deposits. The change in Megabank's balance sheet looks like this:

MEGABANK

Assets		Liabilities	
Vault cash	+$100	Checkable deposits	+$100

Recall that a bank's reserves consist of vault cash, deposits with other banks, and deposits with the Fed. Therefore, when you deposit $100, increasing Megabank's vault cash, you are increasing its reserves by $100.

If you open your account with a $100 check from your uncle rather than with $100 in cash, the change in the bank balance sheet is similar. The check represents a promise from the issuing bank to pay you $100. The balance sheet for Megabank reflects new assets, not in the form of vault cash but in the form of cash items in the process of collection, and lists $100 in checkable deposits as a liability:

MEGABANK

Assets		Liabilities	
Cash Items in the process of collection	+$100	Checkable deposits	+$100

[†] Strictly speaking, a T-account is used to identify changes in a given account, not to show the entire balance sheet. For simplicity of exposition, we combine changes in balance sheet items in a single "T-account."

CONSIDER THIS . . .

How Do Banks Account for Loan Losses?

Bankers understand that their loans entail default risk, or the risk that the borrower will not repay the loan in full, with interest. When a loan is not repaid, the bank's net worth—its equity capital—suffers. During the term of the loan, if the bank decides that the borrower is likely to default, the bank must *write off* the loan. In other words, the value of the loan is removed, entirely or in part, from the assets on the balance sheet. If an asset entry is reduced, a corresponding liability entry also must be reduced, so a loan loss reduces the bank's net worth.

In practice, a bank sets aside part of its net worth as a *loan loss reserve* to anticipate future loan losses. Using a loan loss reserve enables a bank to present a financially stable balance sheet. Each time the bank adds to its loan loss reserve, it reduces current profits. Hence, when a bad loan actually is written off, the bank's profits do not decline further. In a highly publicized example, Citibank added $4 billion to its loan loss reserve in 1987 to cover anticipated losses on its loans to some Latin American countries.

While measures of problem loans at banks fell over most of the 1990s, bank supervisors in late 2000 expressed concern that loan losses would soon rise at very large U.S. banks.

To collect the $100, Megabank will go to your uncle's bank, Midasbank. Megabank and Midasbank have accounts with the Fed, which settles transactions among banks by adjusting their reserve account deposits. The Fed will transfer $100 of reserves to Megabank's account from Midasbank's account. The balance sheets of the two banks reflect this movement:

MEGABANK

Assets		Liabilities	
Reserves	+$100	Checkable deposits	+$100

MIDASBANK

Assets		Liabilities	
Reserves	−$100	Checkable deposits	−$100

Note the predictable link between deposits and reserves for a bank: An increase in deposits increases reserves by the same amount. A decrease in deposits decreases reserves by the same amount.

What happens to the $100 that you deposited in Megabank? By answering this question, we can see how banks earn profits. In the preceding example, Megabank received an extra $100 in deposits. Suppose that banking regulations require Megabank to deposit 10% of its checkable deposits in a non-interest-bearing account with the Fed. Megabank cannot use these balances, which represent its required reserves. However, banks may lend or invest **excess reserves,** or total reserves less required reserves. To reflect the difference between required and excess reserves, we rewrite the balance held as reserves as follows:

MEGABANK

Assets		Liabilities	
Required reserves	+$10	Checkable deposits	+$100
Excess reserves	+$90		

Reserves that are kept in cash or in deposits at the Fed pay no interest. In addition, checkable deposits generate expenses for the bank: It must pay interest to depositors and pay the costs of maintaining checking accounts, including record keeping, check clearing, and so on. The bank therefore will want to use its excess reserves to generate operating income. One possibility is for the bank to lend its excess reserves. In doing so, it acquires claims on borrowers while providing savers with deposit claims.

To be successful, the bank must make prudent loans and investments so that it earns a high enough rate of interest to cover its costs and to profit. This plan sounds simple, but it hasn't been easy for banks to earn profits in the past decade. Recall from the introduction that nonperforming loans troubled Japanese banks in the mid- and late 1990s. In addition, over the same period, bank depositors were attracted to other investments that pay higher rates with relatively little risk (such as money market accounts). Thus the simple plan of attracting deposits and making loans is not as easy to implement as it might seem. In the next section, we describe in more detail the problems facing modern banks and explain how banks respond in their relationships with savers and borrowers to those changes.

THE RELATIONSHIP BETWEEN BANKS AND SAVERS

How do banks attract savers to deposit their funds in bank accounts? First, banks enable savers to hold claims against a diversified portfolio of loans, thereby obtaining risk-sharing benefits. In addition, bank deposits (particularly checkable deposits) meet savers' demands for liquidity. Finally, banks gather and monitor information about borrowers and collect information that is unavailable to individual savers. As delegated monitors, banks reduce information costs for individual savers. The role of banks in reducing information costs is particularly important, as savers could obtain risk-sharing and liquidity services from other financial intermediaries (which compete with banks for savers' funds). Savers also can structure their relationships with banks to ensure that bankers do not exploit private information to savers' detriment. Figure 13.1 illustrates banks' role as financial intermediaries.

To maximize profits in their relationship with savers, banks must deal with two problems: (1) managing moral hazard problems and (2) managing liquidity. In both cases, the bank must adopt practices that assure depositors that the bank is acting in their best interest.

Figure 13.1

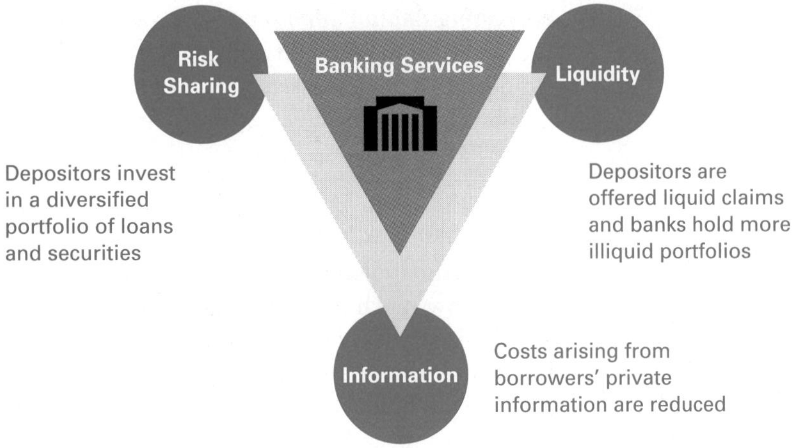

Bank Intermediary Services

The risk-sharing, liquidity, and information services that banks can provide give small savers and firms benefits that they could not otherwise afford.

Managing Moral Hazard

Although banks reduce information costs for savers, savers realize that banks have private information about the quality and risk of the bank's loan portfolio and that a bank might use this information in a way that jeopardizes savers' deposits. For example, if the bank makes loans that are very risky, uninsured depositors may be hurt. The asymmetry of information produces moral hazard. Banks can reduce the costs of moral hazard by issuing debt claims to savers and by using their own funds as well as those of depositors to make loans.

Debt and moral hazard. A short-term debt contract provides for both the liquidity needs of depositors and the discipline of bankers. Because checkable deposits are an important component of bank liabilities, the threat that savers will withdraw their funds on short notice ensures that bankers will not use their private information to their own advantage. Indeed, many economists have argued that this threat of fund withdrawal accounts for the longstanding importance of checkable deposits in financing bank lending.

Net worth and moral hazard. A second way for savers to prevent moral hazard is to insist that bankers and bank shareholders place their capital at risk when the bank makes loans. Bankers will act more responsibly when their own savings are at risk, so a rule requiring bankers and bank shareholders to invest their own funds increases incentives for responsible performance. In general, the greater the banker's stake in the bank, the less severe the moral hazard will be. Bankers engage in *capital adequacy management*—determining the amount of capital the bank should hold and obtaining the desired capital. This management centers on a trade-off between the benefit of capital in mitigating moral hazard and the cost of capital in reducing the profitability for bank shareholders. Government regulation and supervision have provided additional ways to reduce the cost of moral hazard to individual savers, as we relate in Chapters 14 and 15.

Managing capital adequacy. As owners, shareholders are concerned about the operating profitability of the bank and the amount of capital required to support the bank's assets. A straightforward measure of the bank's profitability is the net after-tax profit per dollar of assets, or **return on assets** (ROA):

$$\text{ROA} = \text{Net after-tax profit/Bank assets.}$$

This measure tells shareholders how well the bank is being managed, by conveying how much profit the bank earns per dollar of assets.

Bank shareholders do not, of course, "own" the bank's assets (largely loans and securities), but they do own the bank's capital. As owners, the bank's shareholders want to know the bank's return on their invested equity. A useful summary of this information is provided by the net after-tax profit per dollar of bank equity capital, or **return on equity** (ROE):

$$\text{ROE} = \text{Net after-tax profit/Bank equity capital.}$$

From the shareholders' perspective, an obvious link exists between the return on equity (how well they are doing on their invested capital in the bank) and the return on assets (how well the bank is managed). Note that

$$\underbrace{\frac{\text{Net after-tax profit}}{\text{Bank equity capital}}}_{\text{ROE}} = \underbrace{\frac{\text{Net after-tax profit}}{\text{Bank assets}}}_{\text{ROA}} \times \frac{\text{Bank assets}}{\text{Bank equity capital}}.$$

Hence, for a given ROA, the lower the amount of equity capital, the higher the bank's ROE. Holding capital is costly for the bank's shareholders.

As we saw earlier, however, bank capital has important benefits in reducing moral hazard. How, then, does a bank manager decide how much capital to hold? The benefit of capital in mitigating moral hazard is greatest when bank assets are very risky or when information about the quality of bank assets is difficult to obtain. Such situations also underlie government regulation of bank capital adequacy in most countries.

CHECKPOINT

Suppose that the government guaranteed all bank deposits without supervising banks' lending practices. What would you predict would happen to the riskiness of banks' loan portfolios? With a full guarantee of deposits, individual savers no longer would have an incentive to monitor banks. As a result, bankers would have an incentive to take greater risks unless large amounts of their own funds were at stake. Bankers would reap the profits from high interest rates charged to successful risky borrowers; the government would assume depositors' losses from risky loans to unsuccessful borrowers.

Managing Liquidity Risk

In their dealings with savers, banks face **liquidity risk,** or the possibility that depositors may collectively decide to withdraw more funds than the bank has immediately on hand. Such withdrawals would force the bank to liquidate relatively illiquid loans and probably receive less than the full value of those loans.

The challenge to banks in managing liquidity risk in their dealings with savers is to reduce risk exposure without sacrificing too much profitability. For example, a bank can easily minimize liquidity risk exposure by holding substantial reserves. However, such a strategy reduces profitability because the bank earns no interest on cash held as reserves. As we noted earlier, U.S. banks are required to maintain reserves with the Federal Reserve System. Even in the absence of this regulation, exposure to liquidity risk would lead banks to hold reserves, though probably not in the form of non-interest-bearing deposits with the Fed. Hence, banks use other strategies to reduce liquidity risk, which we classify as asset management and liability management practices.

Asset management by banks. One way to manage liquidity risk while earning interest is to lend money to other banks through the federal funds market, usually for one day at a time. Federal funds loans are liquid but have some, though small, default risk. A second option is to use repurchase agreements for government securities, lending securities to businesses and other banks overnight. However, these longer-maturity government securities have some risk that results from interest rate fluctuations. Most banks use a combination of the two techniques. This strategic mix reflects a trade-off between the lower expected return and default risk of the federal funds market and the higher expected return and risk of interest rate fluctuations in the government securities market.

Liability management by banks. To operate profitably, banks must keep on hand enough cash or assets that are easily convertible to cash to meet depositors' withdrawals without sacrificing too much operating income by holding cash instead of loans or securities. Many large banks (for example, Citibank in New York) have more loan opportunities than they have deposits, so they must decide how to borrow additional funds to make loans. Options include certificates of deposit, Eurodollars, federal funds, and RPs. These alternatives have different maturities and costs to the bank. However, banks must preserve their ability to borrow so as to use liability management, especially given that most borrowing will be unsecured and not covered by federal deposit insurance. Relying *only* on overnight loans (though possibly at a lower current cost) is, in general, unwise. Hence, banks also usually use longer-term borrowing with the attendant interest rate risk.

Asset and liability management example. Suppose that Megabank's balance sheet initially looks like this:

MEGABANK

Assets		Liabilities	
Reserves	$50 million	Deposits	$200 million
Marketable securities	$10 million	Net worth	$20 million
Loans	$160 million		

If the bank is required to keep 10% of its deposits in the form of non-interest-bearing reserves with the Fed, its $50 million of reserves includes $20 million of required reserves and $30 million of excess reserves. If a group of Megabank's large depositors withdrew $15 million, Megabank would lose $15 million of reserves (and deposits) but would not have to alter other entries in its balance sheet. In other words, with enough excess reserves, a bank does not need to manage liquidity risk actively.

Holding excess reserves is costly to Megabank because it is forgoing interest earnings on loans and securities. At the other extreme, suppose that Megabank's initial balance sheets were such that it held no excess reserves, making more loans to increase its profitability. In this case:

MEGABANK

Assets		Liabilities	
Reserves	$20 million	Deposits	$200 million
Marketable securities	$10 million	Net worth	$20 million
Loans	$190 million		

Once again, suppose that Megabank faces withdrawals of $15 million. Now:

MEGABANK

Assets		Liabilities	
Reserves	$5 million	Deposits	$185 million
Marketable securities	$10 million	Net worth	$20 million
Loans	$190 million		

To meet the Fed's reserve requirement, Megabank should have $18.5 million, or (0.10)($185 million), of reserves; it is short $13.5 million, or $18.5 million − $5 million.

To meet this shortfall, the bank could sell its marketable securities or reduce loans. In the first case, the bank would sell off U.S. Treasury or other securities and deposit the proceeds with the Fed. Because government securities are traded in liquid markets, the bank's transactions costs will be low. Hence, government securities are valuable as backup reserves. Alternatively, if Megabank has a large number of overlapping short-term loans, it could decide not to renew some of them. However, if the bank angered existing customers because it didn't renew their loans and lost those customers to another bank, it would have to pay information costs for new borrowers. In yet another solution, Megabank could simply sell off some loans to other banks. Private information again complicates the transaction. Because other banks do not know the quality of Megabank's loans, they might not be willing to pay Megabank the full value of the loans.

To increase liabilities, the bank can acquire reserves from other banks and corporations or from the Fed. Borrowing from other banks or corporations involves federal funds transactions and repurchase agreements. Borrowing from the Fed is accomplished through discount loans. If Megabank keeps its loan and securities holdings intact and meets its reserves shortage by borrowing equal amounts from these new sources, its balance sheet becomes:

MEGABANK

Assets		Liabilities	
Reserves	$18.5 million	Deposits	$185 million
Marketable securities	$10 million	Borrowings from other banks and corporations	$6.75 million
Loans	$190 million	Borrowings from the Fed	$6.75 million
		Net worth	$20 million

Megabank has managed its liquidity risk.

If Megabank is unable to manage its liquidity risk, it can fail. Suppose, for example, that rumors are circulating that $50 million of Megabank's loans were made to friends of J. P. Moregain, the bank's president, who have lost money in real estate speculation. Angry depositors withdraw $18.5 million immediately, leaving Megabank with $166.5 million in deposits, on which it should hold $16.65 million in reserves. But, as the balance sheet shows, its reserves have been wiped out:

MEGABANK

Assets		Liabilities	
Reserves	$0 million	Deposits	$166.5 million
Marketable securities	$10 million	Borrowings	$13.5 million
Loans	$190 million	Net worth	$20 million

When the bank reduces the value of loans on its books to $140 million, it has a *net worth* of −$30 million, or $150 million in assets and $180 million in liabilities. Unless the bank can convince other banks or the Fed to lend it funds, it will have to close its doors. In this case, the Federal Deposit Insurance Corporation (FDIC) will take control of the bank and decide whether to liquidate it or merge it with another bank.

THE RELATIONSHIP BETWEEN BANKS AND BORROWERS

Loans constitute the bulk of a bank's assets, so a key objective of a bank is to make good loans that earn higher rates than the rate the bank must pay on funds attracted from depositors and financial markets. Hence cultivating good loan customers and using credit-risk analysis to ensure that borrowers are creditworthy is central to a bank's long-term success. In addition, managing interest rate risk is important for the bank's profitability.

Managing Credit Risk

Banks profit from the spread between the interest rate they charge to borrowers and the interest rate they pay to depositors. To ensure reasonable profits, banks attempt to make loans that will be fully repaid with interest. As with lending in financial markets, the bank is concerned about **credit risk**—that is, the risk that borrowers might default on their loans. If banks do not manage credit risk effectively, they won't be profitable for their shareholders and won't be in business very long. Banks can reduce their exposure to credit risk on individual loans by investing in information gathering and monitoring. One basic management principle for banks, as for other financial intermediaries, is that diversification reduces the overall credit risk of the bank's portfolio. To manage credit risk of individual loans, banks use credit-risk analysis to examine borrowers and determine the appropriate interest rate to charge. In addition, bankers must cope with adverse selection and moral hazard in managing credit risks of individual loans.†

In loan markets, adverse selection occurs because applicants with risky projects are the most likely to apply for loans at a given interest rate: If their projects do well, they're big winners; but if their projects fare poorly, the bank is the big loser (the lemons problem again).

Moral hazard exists in bank loan markets because borrowers have an incentive, once they have obtained a loan, to use the proceeds for purposes that are detrimental to the bank. Banks use screening techniques, collateral requirements, credit rationing, monitoring, and restrictive covenants and develop long-term relationships with borrowers to help reduce costs of both adverse selection and moral hazard.

Diversification. The theory of portfolio allocation predicts that investors—individuals or financial institutions—can reduce exposure to the risk of price fluctuations by diversifying their holdings. This theory applies to banks as well; if banks lend too much to one borrower, to borrowers in one region, or to borrowers in one industry, they are exposed to risks from those loans. Although banks' skills in information collection and evaluation focus on particular borrowers, most economists argue that banks should diversify within their chosen niche and manage the risk of their exposure if they do not diversify.

Credit-risk analysis. In performing **credit-risk analysis,** the bank examines the borrower's likelihood of repayment and general business conditions that might influence the borrower's ability to repay the loan. Individuals and busi-

†The focus here is on banks' holdings of debt. Banks in the United States have been prohibited from investing deposits in significant equity holdings since passage of the National Banking Acts of 1863 and 1864. As a result, banks seldom hold equity stakes in firms.

CONSIDER THIS . . .

When Is Credit-Risk Analysis "Discrimination"?

How free should bankers be to ignore customers who seem unpromising? Under the Community Reinvestment Act of 1977 (CRA), banks are required not only to avoid discrimination but also to contribute to the availability of credit for their communities. Banks that are found to discriminate against members of minorities or that have not made sufficient efforts to lend to the credit-needy in their communities face fines and penalties. The challenge for policymakers is to identify measures that improve access to credit for minorities in a cost-effective way.

Among economists, home mortgage and other lending is the subject of ongoing controversial research. A 1992 study by the Federal Reserve Bank of Boston claimed evidence of extensive discrimination against African-American and Hispanic mortgage applicants, claims that stimulated the Clinton administration to seek sweeping measures to reform the CRA to combat discrimination. A 1995 study by the Federal Reserve Board challenged this result. That study examined whether minority borrowers defaulted more often than other borrowers. If discrimination occurs, default rates should be lower among minorities. In fact, the researchers found that minority borrowers defaulted more frequently. A second 1995 study by the Federal Reserve Bank of Chicago reexamined the applications used in the original Boston Fed study. It concluded that African-American and Hispanic applicants with good credit histories were about as likely as white applicants with comparable records to be approved. However, it also found that African-American and Hispanic applicants with poor credit histories were more likely to have their mortgage application declined than were similarly situated white applicants.

Whatever the ultimate answer on the existence of discrimination, many economists believe that the CRA is a costly device for increasing credit for minorities. A 2000 study of CRA loans by the Fed found that such loans were less profitable to banks than those made without government pressure. Given that the CRA raises the costs of operating a bank in urban areas, the response to the regulation may be less entry by banks into these communities over time. As a consequence, CRA regulation may backfire in its long-run effects on credit supply. An alternative approach would be to use explicit subsidies for certain kinds of lending instead of the penalties imposed only on banks.

nesses apply for loans to a *loan officer,* who manages the bank's relationship with the borrower, gathers information about the borrower and the purpose of the loan, and assesses the credit risk. To reduce the likelihood of adverse selection, loan officers screen applicants to eliminate potentially bad risks and to obtain a pool of creditworthy borrowers.

Individual borrowers usually must give the loan officer information about their employment, income, and net worth. Businesses supply information about their current and projected income and net worth. In addition, banks sometimes use *credit-scoring systems* to predict statistically whether an individual is likely to default. For example, individuals who change jobs often are more likely to default, statistically (all else being equal), than are those who stay with the same employer. Some analysts have challenged the use of credit-scoring systems as discriminating against particular groups, but other analysts see these methods as a valuable tool for credit-risk analysis.

Loan officers not only collect information before granting a loan, but they also monitor the borrower during the term of the loan. Loan officers monitor large commercial loans by reviewing financial statements, meeting occasionally with the borrower's management, and studying the industry's prospects. For loans to individuals, the loan officer makes sure that scheduled loan payments are made and that the borrower's financial condition hasn't changed for the worse.

A bank bases the interest rate it charges for loans on (1) the bank's cost of funds, (2) the default risk of the loan, and (3) the rates of return available to the bank from alternative investments. A bank can't make a profit by lending at an interest rate that is lower than what it pays for funds from deposit and nondeposit sources. In addition, to ensure that the bank is appropriately compensated for bearing risk, the spread between the interest rate charged by the bank for the loan and its cost of funds must reflect the default risk premium. Finally, the bank should not lend funds at an interest rate that is lower than what it could earn on other assets. For example, a bank would not lend $10,000 to a risky borrower at 6% interest if it could invest the same funds in a default-risk-free U.S. Treasury security yielding 8%. However, competition from other lenders limits the interest rate that a bank can charge. That is, if a bank charges too much, borrowers will seek alternative sources of credit from other financial institutions.

Historically, loan rates to businesses were based on (pegged to) the **prime rate,** which was the interest rate charged on six-month loans to borrowers with the lowest expected default risk, called high-quality borrowers. Other loans carried rates greater than the prime rate, according to the credit risk. However, by the 1990s, most large and medium-sized businesses were charged loan rates that reflected changing current market interest rates instead of the stated prime rate, which instead applied to smaller borrowers.

Collateral. To combat problems of adverse selection, banks also generally require that the borrower put up **collateral,** or assets pledged to the bank in the event that the borrower defaults. For example, if Phil Diamond wanted a loan from a bank to start a jewelry business, the bank likely would ask him to pledge some of his financial assets or his house as collateral. Collateral reduces the bank's losses in the event of default because the bank can seize the collateral. In addition, the bank might require Phil to maintain a **compensating balance,** a required minimum amount that the business taking out the loan must maintain in a checking account with the lending bank.

Credit rationing. In some circumstances, banks minimize the costs of adverse selection and moral hazard through **credit rationing.** In rationing credit, the bank either grants a borrower's loan application but limits the size of the loan or denies a borrower's loan application for any amount at the going interest rate.

The first type of credit rationing occurs in response to possible moral hazard. Limiting the size of bank loans reduces costs of moral hazard by increasing the chance that the borrower will repay the loan to maintain a sound credit rating. Your MasterCard or Visa card has a credit limit for the same reason. With a loan limit of $2500, you are likely to repay the bank so that you can borrow again in the future. If the bank were willing to give you a $2.5 million line of credit, you might be tempted to spend more money than you could repay. Hence, limiting the size of borrowers' loans to amounts less than borrowers demand at the going interest rate is both rational and profit-maximizing for banks.

The second type of credit rationing occurs in response to severe forms of adverse selection, when many borrowers have little or no collateral to offer to banks. What if a bank tries to raise the interest rate it charges to compensate itself for the presence of such high-risk borrowers? Low-risk borrowers then will tend to drop out, leaving the bank with even more potentially high-risk borrowers in its loan pool. Hence, keeping its interest at the lower level and denying loans altogether to some borrowers can be in the bank's best interest. This type of credit rationing is costly for the economy because some low-risk borrowers also are denied credit.

Monitoring and restrictive covenants. To reduce the costs of moral hazard, banks monitor borrowers to make sure that a borrower doesn't use the funds borrowed from the bank to pursue unauthorized, risky activities. As with insurance arrangements (Chapter 12), much of banks' efforts centers on determining whether the borrower is obeying *restrictive covenants*, or explicit provisions of the loan agreement that prohibit the borrower from engaging in certain activities.

Long-term relationships. One of the best ways for a bank to gather information about a borrower's prospects or to monitor a borrower's activities is for the bank to have a long-term relationship with the borrower. By observing the borrower over time—through checking account activity and loan repayments—the bank can significantly reduce problems of asymmetric information by reducing its information-gathering and monitoring costs. Borrowers also gain from long-term relationships with banks: The customer can obtain credit at a lower interest rate or with fewer restrictions because the bank avoids costly information-gathering tasks. Borrowers who value long-term relationships are less likely to default or violate restrictive covenants in loan agreements. Some analysts believe that the closer relationship between banks and nonfinancial businesses in other countries—notably Germany and Japan—improves the competitiveness of both. We explore the advantages and disadvantages of these financial ties in Chapter 14.

CHECKPOINT

Suppose that government intervention restricts the types of loans that a bank can make or the communities in which it can lend. What is likely to happen to the credit risk of the bank's portfolio? Such government restrictions would reduce the bank's ability to diversify its loan portfolios. As a result, even if the bank analyzed the credit risks of individual borrowers, the aggregate credit risk of its portfolio would increase. o

Managing Interest Rate Risk

The profits that banks earn from lending to borrowers are risky owing in part to changes in interest rates in financial markets. Banks experience **interest rate risk** if changes in market interest rates cause bank profits to fluctuate. The effect of a change in market interest rates on the value of a bank's assets and liabilities is similar to the effect of a change in interest rates on bond values. That is, a rise in the market interest rate lowers the present value of the outstanding amount of a loan even if there is little risk that the loan will not be paid off under the terms of the loan agreement. Banks are particularly affected by interest rate risk when they raise funds primarily through short-term deposits (such as checkable deposits or short-term time deposits) to finance loans or the purchase of securities with longer maturities.

Banks must first be able to compare the interest sensitivity of the values of different assets and liabilities. For example, suppose that Mightybank has the following balance sheet:

MIGHTYBANK

Assets		Liabilities	
Fixed-rate assets	$350 million	Fixed-rate liabilities	$230 million
Reserves		Checkable deposits	
Long-term marketable securities		Savings deposits	
Long-term loans		Long-term CDs	
Variable-rate assets	$150 million	Variable-rate liabilities	$230 million
Floating-rate loans		Short-term CDs	
Short-term securities		Money market deposit accounts	
		Federal funds	
		Net worth	$40 million
	$500 million		$500 million

Note that $150 million of Mightybank's $500 million in assets have variable interest rates that change at least once a year. Slightly less than half ($230 million out of $500 million) of Mightybank's total liabilities have variable interest rates. If interest rates go up, Mightybank will pay more for $230 million of its funds while increasing its interest earnings on only $150 million of its assets. Hence, Mightybank faces interest rate risk.

The significant increase in the volatility of market interest rates during the 1980s caused extensive interest rate risk for banks that had made fixed-rate loans using funds obtained from short-term, variable-rate deposits. An increase in market interest rates reduced the value of the banks' assets relative to their liabilities and contributed to the number of bank failures in the late 1980s.

To manage interest rate risk, banks begin by evaluating the vulnerability of their portfolios to the risk of fluctuations in market interest rates. One measure is the **duration** of a bank asset or liability, which is the responsiveness (of the percentage change in) the asset's or liability's market value to a percentage change in the market interest rate.† Duration is an example of an economic measure called an *elasticity*. (Because it is an elasticity, duration is scale-free and may be calculated for an asset or liability of any maturity.) On the liabilities side, checkable deposits have a short duration, whereas longer-term certificates of deposit have a long duration. On the assets side, loans to other banks in the federal funds market have a short duration, whereas commercial loans and marketable securities have a longer duration.

To assess the bank's exposure to interest rate risk, its managers calculate an average duration for bank assets and an average duration for bank liabilities. The difference between the two, known as the **duration gap**, measures the bank's vulnerability to fluctuations in interest rates. Bank managers use the information contained in the duration gap to guide their strategy. Reducing the size of the duration gap helps banks to minimize interest rate risk. To anticipate a fall in interest rates, a bank should arrange the maturity structure of its assets and liabilities to have a positive duration gap. To anticipate a rise in interest rates, a bank should arrange to have a negative duration gap.

The actual uses of asset and liability management to affect the duration gap vary from bank to bank. For example, small and medium-sized banks usually have less control over the duration of liabilities than do large banks. As a result, they focus on manipulating the duration of their assets. Large banks actively manage both assets and liabilities. For example, if Chase expected interest rates to go up, it might sell long-maturity instruments, such as negotiable certificates of deposit, and lend the money to other banks in overnight markets.

In addition to direct asset and liability management, banks cope with interest rate risk in other ways. Banks may issue floating-rate debt, or they may hedge by using interest rate swaps and financial futures and options to reduce the duration gap.

Floating-rate debt. One way banks reduce the risk of interest rate fluctuations is to use **floating-rate debt** by making the loan interest rate variable. With floating-rate debt, if market interest rates rise, the bank's interest income rises with its interest expense. Hence, its profit margin from lending is less responsive to interest rate movements than it would be if the loan interest rate were fixed. Floating-rate loans became much more popular in the United

---

†We present a more formal definition of duration in the appendix to this chapter.

States beginning in the early 1980s, when interest rates fluctuated widely. Most commercial loans have an interest rate that is equal to a benchmark rate plus some percentage set by the bank to reflect credit risk. The loan rate is adjusted as the benchmark rate changes. Typical benchmarks include commercial paper rates or the London Interbank Offering Rate (LIBOR), which measures rates that international banks charge on dollar-denominated loans. With adjustable-rate mortgages (ARMs), the mortgage interest rate rises and falls with market interest rates.

Floating-rate loans do not eliminate banks' exposure to risk, however. They reduce the bank's risk considerably, but the risk faced by the borrower goes up. If high market interest rates occur during periods of low earnings and economic stress for firms (as they sometimes do), borrowers' default risk rises. There is a trade-off between the bank's risk and the borrower's risk: Transferring interest rate risk to borrowers does not eliminate the risk; borrowers may not be able or willing to bear it.

Swaps. Introduced in 1981, swaps address banks' exposure to both interest rate and exchange rate risk. An **interest rate swap,** the most common form of swap, is an agreement to exchange the expected future returns on one financial instrument for the expected future returns on another. The outstanding amount of these widely used arrangements rose to tens of trillions of dollars in 2000.

Suppose, for example, that Megabank is about to make a long-term, fixed-rate loan to Big Steel, Inc. Because Megabank's sources of funds are relatively short-term, it pays a floating rate on its liabilities. The bank can use interest rate swaps to reduce its exposure to interest rate risk by exchanging Big Steel's fixed-rate payments for floating-rate payments from another bank or firm. The swap agreement relieves Megabank of much of the uncertainty of fluctuating interest rates. Conversely, the other bank or investor that has agreed to make the floating-rate payments in exchange for fixed-rate payments faces the possibility that a rise in interest rates would increase its payments. (It could use financial futures markets to reduce its exposure to risk.)

After making the loan to Big Steel, Megabank can sell swaps, eliminating its interest rate risk by transforming the fixed-rate payments from the loan into floating-rate payments. In addition to hedging, Megabank can use swaps to speculate on future interest rate movements. Suppose that Megabank has bought more swaps than it has sold. It promises to pay a floating rate in exchange for a fixed rate on the difference. If rates increase, Megabank takes a loss; if rates fall, it earns a profit.

Futures and options. Futures and options contracts also offer ways for banks to hedge their exposure to interest rate risk. Consider again Megabank's decision about making a long-term fixed-rate loan to Big Steel while raising funds through floating-rate liabilities. Megabank could sell Treasury bill futures contracts—promising to deliver T-bills at a future date. In that case, if market interest rates (and Megabank's cost of funds) rise, the value of Megabank's futures position rises; the higher interest rate reduces the value of the T-bills Megabank must deliver. If rates fall, Megabank's profit from the loan rises, but it loses on its futures position. Alternatively, Megabank can buy Treasury put options—giving it the right to sell T-bills in the future at a predetermined price. If rates rise, the value of the put option rises—thus protecting Megabank against an increase in rates while allowing it to earn an extra return if market rates fall.

Because financial futures and options are traded on exchanges, banks face lower transactions costs than are involved in using more customized interest rate swaps. However, precisely because financial futures and options contracts are standardized, banks may turn to swaps to find a contract fitting their needs. In practice, banks use both swaps and futures and options to deal with interest rate risk.

Table 13.2 summarizes the risks to which banks are exposed in their relationships with savers and borrowers.

CHECKPOINT

The efficient markets hypothesis states that stock market prices should be based on all available information. If banks are exposed to interest rate risk, what should investors expect with regard to the responsiveness of bank stock prices to changes in market interest rates? An increase in market interest rates reduces the value of banks' assets and the price of banks' shares, whereas a decrease in market interest rates raises the value of banks' assets and the price of banks' shares. Indeed, banks' share prices generally are much more responsive to interest rate movements than are shares of industrial companies' stock. o

EXPANDING THE BOUNDARIES OF BANKING

The business of banking seems simple: A bank takes in deposits and makes loans. As long as the spread between interest rates on loans (adjusted for expected loan losses) and interest rates on deposits is positive, the banker makes a profit. However, the activities of banks have changed dramatically during the past three decades.

TABLE 13.2 **EXPOSURE TO RISK IN BANKING CONTRACTS**

Interest rate risk	Liquidity risk	Credit risk
The market value of a bank's fixed-rate loans moves in the direction opposite to changing market interest rates.	Depositors demand to withdraw their funds, leaving the bank with insufficient reserves.	Borrowers may default on their loans.
Remedies:		
• Hedging risk with financial futures and options • Floating-rate loans • Interest rate swaps	• Holding substantial cash reserves • Asset management • Liability management	• Portfolio diversification • Credit-risk analysis • Monitoring and restrictive covenants • Long-term relationships

In 1960, banks obtained 61% of their funds from checkable deposits, most of the remainder coming from passbook accounts. These funds were invested largely in loans for businesses, mortgages, consumer credit, and other purposes (46% of bank assets). Securities of federal, state, and local governments accounted for 31% of bank assets, and cash assets accounted for 20%.

What a difference a generation makes! In the new century, U.S. banks raise far less of their funds from checkable deposits, relying more on time deposits and negotiable certificates of deposit. Another dramatic change between the 1960s and the early 2000s has been the significant increase in borrowings from the federal funds market and through repurchase agreements. An even bigger difference can be seen in banks' expansion into non-traditional lending activities.

Opportunities and Financial Innovation

Three changes account for major recent shifts in banks' sources and uses of funds. First, interest rates increased, becoming volatile during the 1980s. Banks began to manage their asset and liability holdings to earn higher interest returns and reduce their exposure to risks of interest rate fluctuations. Second, in 1960, U.S. banking regulations prohibited the payment of interest on checkable deposits. As these regulations were relaxed, allowing interest payments, depositors shifted from demand deposits to interest-bearing accounts. Finally, by the 1990s, the interest rates that banks could pay depositors were fully deregulated, and banks were free to compete in the financial marketplace.

As a result, banks in 2000 have increased the relative importance of loans in their asset portfolios. This step increased banks' exposure to credit risk as they obtained less liquid assets. The percentage of assets that are not held in marketable securities increased from 56% in 1960 to about 75% in 2000, while bank equity capital fell from 15% of those assets in 1960 to about 8% in 2000.

Financial innovations by banks and other financial institutions from the 1960s through the 1990s and into the new century increased competition among financial institutions. To maintain profitability as competition became intense for depositors and loan customers, banks had to find ways to capitalize on their greatest competitive advantage in relation to financial markets: their lower transactions and information costs in meeting the financial needs of many savers and borrowers. Banks have moved beyond traditional lending to accomplish that through off-balance-sheet activities, in which banks exploit their cost advantages without necessarily making traditional loans.

Off-Balance-Sheet Activities

Banks have increasingly turned to generating *fee income* in off-balance-sheet activities that exploit banks' competitive advantages in reducing transactions costs for bank customers and reducing information for borrowers in lending.

To generate fee income by reducing transactions costs, banks provide customized services to customers, such as servicing securities backed by mortgages (by collecting interest and principal payments from borrowers, then paying them to lenders, less a fee) and making foreign-exchange trades for customers. In addition, banks earn fees from trading in the multitrillion-dollar markets for financial futures and options and interest rate swaps. Although most bank trading in these markets provides services that are related to other bank businesses, banks sometimes speculate in these markets; speculation, of course, carries the risk of losing money. Finally, banks earn income from providing customized "private banking" services to high-net-worth households (those with financial assets exceeding $1 million), a group growing both in the United States and globally. These activities are "off-balance-sheet" in the sense that they do not require capital to support assets, as in traditional holdings of loans and securities.

When banks engage in **off-balance-sheet lending,** they do not hold as assets the loans they make. This category of arrangements includes three important innovations by banks: (1) standby letters of credit, (2) loan commitments, and (3) loan sales. These off-balance-sheet activities increase the default risk faced by the bank even when no loan is on the bank's books. Bank managers must take care, then, through capital adequacy management and credit risk management to guard against the heightened risk to the bank.

Standby letters of credit. Changes in the competitive environment led banks to exploit their skills at information gathering and monitoring. By doing so, banks regained some of the lending business they had lost to the market for commercial paper (short-term debt of corporations traded in financial markets) during the 1970s through a contractual innovation. Because commercial paper is short-term and generally rolled over (refinanced), borrowers want to ensure steady access to funds from lenders. Banks routinely sell to commercial paper borrowers a **standby letter of credit** (SLC), by which the bank promises to lend the borrower funds to pay off its maturing commercial paper if necessary. Historically, borrowers paid banks for this service by maintaining a compensating balance. In recent years, more often a fee (usually about 0.5%) is assessed.

The guarantee of creditworthiness symbolized by an SLC is particularly useful to less well-known borrowers. This approach splits credit provision into two parts: credit-risk analysis (information gathering) and actual funding. The SLC is a significant development because banks can provide credit-risk analysis efficiently, whereas a public market often can provide the actual funding more cheaply. Unlike conventional loans, SLCs do not appear on banks' balance sheets.

Growth in SLC issues has been phenomenal since the 1980s. The nation's biggest banks seized the largest share of this growth as part of their efforts to recapture their traditional corporate borrowers from the commercial paper market. Other lines of credit for which banks receive fees are those for bankers' acceptances and underwriting Euronotes.

Loan commitments. In a **loan commitment,** a bank agrees to provide a borrower with a stated amount of funds during some specified period of time. Borrowers then have the option of deciding when or if they want to take the loan. The ratio of loan commitments (used and unused) to total bank assets rose substantially in the 1980s and 1990s.

For a loan commitment, the participating bank earns a fee, which is usually split into two parts: an *upfront fee* when the commitment is written and a *nonusage fee* on the unused portion. For loans that are actually made, the interest rate charged in the usage fee is determined as a markup over a benchmark lending rate. Loan commitments fix the markup over the benchmark rate in advance, but not the interest rate. In addition, the bank's commitment to lend ceases if the borrower's financial condition deteriorates below some specified level.

Loan sales. During the 1980s, securitization in money and capital markets grew significantly. In securitization, financial intermediaries sell loans or securities directly to investors through markets instead of holding them. Intermediaries currently sell many types of bank loans, including mortgage loans, automobile loans, credit card receivables, and business loans, through markets. The process of securitization helps lenders to diversify and share risk because they can sell portions of the portfolio of loans that they originate. In addition, this process allows banks to focus on lowering information and transactions costs for many savers and borrowers without having to hold all their loans until maturity.

As part of the trend toward securitization during the 1980s, the market for bank loan sales in the United States grew from almost nothing to a substantial size. A **loan sale** is a financial contract by which a bank agrees to sell the expected future returns from an underlying bank loan to a third party. Loan sales are also called *secondary loan participations.* Formally, the loan contract is sold *without recourse;* that is, the bank provides no guarantee of the value of the loan sold and no insurance. Sales of C&I loans by banks surged in the 1980s, and the top-selling banks sold most of their C&I loan portfolios. The volume of loan sales declined during the early and mid-1990s, in part because banks had mispriced the loans of smaller firms with high debt levels. As the market picked up again in the late 1990s, many analysts predict that bank loan sales will continue to grow as capital requirements on banks provide banks with an incentive to sell off rather than hold loans.

Large banks sell loans primarily to domestic and foreign banks and nonbank financial institutions. Originally, they sold only short-term, high-quality loans with low information-gathering and monitoring costs. Increasingly, however, banks are selling lesser-quality and longer-term loans.

The existence of a flourishing loan sales market changes the role that banks play as intermediaries between savers and borrowers. For example, an active loan sales market effectively splits banking activities into deposit-taking and loan-making components, which raises a fundamental question: Does the growth of the market in loan sales imply that banks should disappear?

The answer is no. Loan sales represent an improvement in intermediation services. Such sales allow banks to achieve greater financial and geographic diversification by buying loans from and selling loans to other institutions while economizing on their equity capital. For example, banks could diversify loan portfolios across types of loans (say, by selling some car loans and buying some real estate loans) or across different regions of the country. This diversification lowers the exposure of the bank's portfolio to default risk on individual loans. Some economists believe that ensuring the performance of loan contracts no longer requires banks to risk their financial equity by holding loans until maturity. Thus banks can continue to provide their normal information-gathering and monitoring services while decreasing their exposure to credit risk and interest rate risk.

In selling loans, banks put their reputations on the line instead of their equity capital. A bank whose loans perform poorly is unlikely to remain a successful player in that market, and the big banks (the largest loan sellers) are greatly concerned about their reputation. Prices of loans sold contain a risk premium representing both the default risk of the underlying borrowers and the default risk of the selling bank to pay for the bank's implicit promise to stand behind the loan. One way in which banks can ensure the quality of the loan is to hold part of the loan to convince buyers of its commitment to monitoring the original borrower's activities.

Importance of off-balance-sheet activities. Off-balance-sheet activities have become increasingly important in generating banks' profits. Over the period from 1960 to 1980, U.S. banks' noninterest income from fee and trading income contributed about 19% of total bank income. That share climbed steadily through the 1980s and 1990s; by 2000, noninterest income contributed about 30% of total bank gross income (and as much as 40% for banks with assets exceeding $1 billion). This trend is not confined to the United States. Deregulation of Japanese financial markets during the 1980s and 1990s also forced Japanese banks to develop sources of income from off-balance-sheet activities. As European countries are moving toward more competitive banking markets, the relative importance of off-balance-sheet activities is increasing.

Trade-offs in off-balance-sheet activities. Banks generate fee income from trading financial instruments and from exploiting their transactions-cost and information-cost advantages on behalf of their customers. With this additional income comes a risk: Although an instrument that is guaranteed by the bank is not on its balance sheet, the bank is nonetheless exposed to default risk. The bank may have to make good on the obligation in the event of default. Likewise, in lines of credit, the bank may be required to lend funds when the borrower is a poor credit risk or when the bank's own liquidity is impaired. Finally, banks are exposed to risks in their participation in trading activities. Barings, a prominent U.K. bank, failed in 1995 because of excessive and unsupervised speculation in derivatives. In that same year, U.S.-based

CONSIDER THIS . . .

Grading Bank Derivatives: Extra Credit?

Traditional interest rate swaps, which entail minimal credit risks, have low margins for banks and other financial institutions. *Credit derivatives* offer banks and other institutions the opportunity to share default risk as well as interest rate or exchange rate risk. For example, in a *default swap*, a bank can transfer the risk of default to a speculator (such as a hedge fund) by paying a periodic fee in exchange for a contingent payment by the speculator in the event of default. Pitched as a means of improving a bank's risk exposure in the event of a borrower's default, the global credit derivatives market is projected to reach $1.6 trillion by 2002.

This growth notwithstanding, some analysts express concern that the market's development is held back by the lack of a uniform standard contract that would promote market liquidity. Questions about pricing and operational risk also remain. Banks can earn fee income by setting up credit derivative trades, but pricing such trades is a key determinant of ultimate profitability, as with loan origination. In addition, if a borrower's financial condition deteriorates over the life of a transaction, the bank could face a change in operational risk.

Credit derivatives bring together many types of financial institutions—including banks, insurance companies, pension funds, and hedge funds—as well as nonfinancial corporations. Despite the risks, participation in credit derivative markets is likely to become a more significant activity for banks over the next decade.

Bankers Trust faced lawsuits of more than $100 million from its customers in derivatives markets.

To assess their exposure to risk in off-balance-sheet activities, many banks are turning to sophisticated computer analysis. Large banks are pioneers in developing risk-assessment models. One popular method—known as the *value-at-risk (VAR) approach*—uses statistical models to estimate the maximum losses in a portfolio's value likely to be sustained over a particular time period, hence the "value at risk." Such techniques assist bank management in measuring and then reducing risk exposure. Many economists believe that banks' credit risk exposure through off-balance-sheet activities is not out of proportion to their other exposures to risk in their loan portfolios. Nevertheless, financial regulators around the world closely monitor risk exposures from banks' off-balance-sheet activities.

International expansion of off-balance-sheet activities. Since the mid-1980s, U.S.-style securitization has emerged in a number of other national markets. In general, financial institutions have promoted off-balance-sheet activities as ways to increase income without holding the additional capital that is required to support loans. The United Kingdom ranks second behind the United States in the development of off-balance-sheet securitization. Japanese banks have been more hesitant to remove loans from their balance sheets to avoid weakening their close relationships with nonfinancial firms, traditionally a distinguishing feature of the Japanese economy. The strong financial positions of German and Swiss banks have lessened pressure to initiate large-scale off-balance-sheet lending to bolster capital adequacy. Banks in France, Spain, and Italy are actively exploring off-balance-sheet securitization. The introduction of the euro in 1999 enhanced possibilities for securitization in Europe, in the view of many analysts.

CHECKPOINT

Suppose that changes in information-gathering methods significantly reduce the transactions and information costs of making small loans. What changes are likely to occur in banks' lending activities? If information costs are very low, banks can make the initial loans and sell them to investors in mutual funds, reducing the need to connect deposit taking and bank lending in bank intermediation. The growth in banks' off-balance-sheet lending reflects reductions in the transactions and information costs of certain types of lending. o

KEY TERMS AND CONCEPTS

- Balance sheet
- Bank assets
  - Loans
  - Marketable securities
  - Reserves
  - Vault cash
- Bank failure
- Bank liabilities
  - Borrowings
  - Checkable deposits
  - Nontransaction deposits
- Bank net worth
- Credit risk
  - Collateral
  - Compensating balance
  - Credit rationing
  - Credit-risk analysis
- Excess reserves
- Federal deposit insurance
- Interest rate risk
  - Duration
  - Duration gap
  - Floating-rate debt
  - Interest rate swap
- Liquidity risk
- Off-balance-sheet lending
  - Loan commitment
  - Loan sale
  - Standby letter of credit
- Prime rate
- Required reserves
- Return on assets (ROA)
- Return on equity (ROE)
- T-account

SUMMARY

1. Banks earn profits by providing transactions and intermediation services. They invest in gathering and monitoring information about borrowers.
2. The sources of funds for banks (liabilities) include checkable deposits, time deposits, and nondeposit sources (borrowings from other banks and businesses, borrowings from the Federal Reserve System, and equity capital). The uses of funds for banks (assets) include cash and reserves, loans, securities, deposits at other banks, and other assets. Banks' net worth equals the difference between assets and liabilities.

THE ECONOMIST NOVEMBER 11, 2000

Banking: "Clicks" or "Bricks"?

Until six months ago, no self-respecting financial consultant would travel without it: the bar chart showing that the marginal cost of Internet banking transactions was a tiny fraction of the cost of branch banking. It was the chart that launched dozens of stand-alone Internet banks. Unshackled from the cost of real property—and real people—Internet banks would, it was claimed, blow stuck-in-the-mud incumbents out of the water. However, as Roberta Arena, director in charge of the Internet for HSBC, a British banking giant, remarks wryly: "Easy to say; tough to do."

a

Now Internet banks around the world are faltering. Part of the reason is that their physical rivals have become wiser, launching their own integrated "clicks 'n bricks" strategies that offer customers electronic access as well as dark satanic branches. But they are not undisputed winners either. They are finding that the Internet is, at best, a zero-sum game.

b

The decline of the stand-alone Internet bank has been a global phenomenon. In America, Wingspan, one of the e-pioneers, announced in October 2000 that next year it will share information-technology facilities with its parent, Bank One, in order to save money. First-e, a Dublin-based Internet-only bank valued at €1.1 billion ($1.1 billion) when it was acquired by Spain's BBVA in March, has laid off staff and cut expensive television advertising. Marbles, an Internet credit card offered by Britain's HFC Bank, is also switching from TV advertising to cheaper direct mail; and SEB, a Swedish bank which has said that it sees the Internet as a means of expanding overseas, nonetheless acquired BFG in Germany because of its 170 physical branches. . . .

Why has the on-line "revolution" faded so fast? The biggest problem has been that, for all their talk of liberating customers from the yoke of traditional branches, Internet banks did not think clearly about what customers really wanted. For a start, they like to know that their money is secure. And whether it is fair or not, customers fret about the security of on-line transactions. . . . Traditional banks are still thought to be more secure, even though, as Barclays showed this summer, they too can bungle software upgrades and give one customer's details to another. . . .

Customer resistance to Internet-only banking has slowed revenue growth. This is of crucial importance to e-banks that were relying on that consultant's chart. Marginal costs for Internet transactions may be negligible, but fixed costs are anything but. . . .

Many Internet-only banks based their business plans on the assumption of rapid customer recruitment. But new Internet-only banks start with no customers at all. To get them, they had to spend real money—in Marbles's case, for example, some £25m to date—to build consumer awareness.

c

The bricks 'n mortar banks may have been slow on the uptake, but most now allow customers to do all their banking on-line. The result is that on-line banking is actually still growing, but mostly among traditional banks. . . .

For most of us, long lines to see bank tellers—to make a deposit, withdraw cash, or check account balances—are a thing of the past. Most of us use automated teller machines (ATMs) for our routine transactions. Some large banks are pushing the next frontier—on-line banking. Citibank (now part of Citigroup), for example, introduced a World Wide Web–based system in 1997. In late 1998, the bank unveiled its updated system, which would create a broad new retail banking and investment service on the Internet, combining banking, brokerage, and financial information.

Beyond Citi's effort, Internet-only banks were launched by Wingspan, First-e, and Egg. By late 2000, many banking analysts expressed concern that Internet-only banks were not likely to live up to recent expectations. Optimism in the late 1990s was fueled by demographics, increases in Internet usage, and high margins in e-commerce transactions. The late 1990s' question of "clicks or bricks?" soon turned into "How can clicks and bricks work together?"

a Bank managers try to maximize shareholders' return on equity. To the extent that Internet banking could reduce physical and staffing requirements associated with traditional branches, costs of providing banking services would fall. Hence the early promise of e-banking—higher profits for banks. Such a plan raises questions about competition among banks and about whether Internet banks have a sufficient "brand" image to attract customers.

b Why might Internet-only banking be a "zero-sum game"? If entry barriers into Internet-only banking are relatively low, the lure of high margins would attract many competitors. In this case, Internet offerings for banking services would be plentiful for household and business customers, but profits for Internet bank shareholders would be slim. Moreover, to the extent that Internet banking services are valued by customers, traditional banks are likely to provide those services, further depressing the hope for quick profits by Internet banks.

c To the extent that bank relationships with savers and borrowers are an important element of a bank's value, one might expect physical banks (or other financial institutions) to expand their "brand" value in e-commerce. As the article notes, in 2000 several leading financial institutions around the world used this strategy. Whether this development will boost bank profits in the short run remains to be seen, however. On the one hand, prominent physical banks have low costs of acquiring customers because of their large base of current customers. On the other hand, to the extent that physical banks as a group believe that they must invest in "clicks" as well as "bricks" to retain customers, costs rise. Ultimately, banks most successful in pursuing a "clicks and bricks" strategy will be those most efficient in reducing integrated costs of physical and electronic banking.

For further thought . . .

Based on banks' competitive advantages in reducing some transactions and information costs, can you think of profit opportunities for banks in e-commerce beyond those envisioned by early Internet banking advocates? Explain.

Source: Excerpted from "The Hollow Promise of Internet Banking," *The Economist*, November 11, 2000.

3. The problem of moral hazard arises in banking because bankers have access to private information that is unknown to depositors and other investors. Bankers may be tempted to make a more risky investment with others' funds than they would with their own. Having bankers maintain a cushion of net worth, or equity capital, aligns bankers' incentives with those of their suppliers of funds and reduces the risk of moral hazard.
4. The relative reliance on alternative liabilities and assets has changed dramatically during the past 30 years. In terms of liabilities, checkable deposits were a less significant source of funds in the 1990s. There is greater reliance by banks on such sources as negotiable certificates of deposit and overnight borrowing. In terms of assets, loans have grown in importance relative to the holding of marketable securities by banks.
5. Typically, bank loans are less liquid than are bank liabilities, posing a problem of liquidity risk. To avoid having to sell loans at a loss to pay unexpectedly heavy withdrawals by depositors, banks hold reserves in the form of cash, short-term marketable securities, or both. Although holding reserves is an easy strategy, it is not profitable. Hence banks use various techniques of asset and liability management.
6. Banks face credit risk, or the risk that borrowers might not be able to repay the loan principal plus interest. When a borrower defaults, the bank suffers a loss. Banks deal with credit-risk problems by gathering information, monitoring borrowers, and diversifying their loan portfolios.
7. Interest rate risk is the risk of changes in banks' net worth arising from fluctuations in market interest rates. The concept of duration gives financial institutions a way to compare the interest sensitivity of the value of different types of assets and liabilities. Strategies for reducing interest rate risk include using floating-rate debt, financial futures, options, and swaps.
8. In addition to their traditional activities of accepting deposits and making loans, banks have increasingly turned to off-balance-sheet activities. They generate fee income from trading financial instruments and from exploiting their transactions-cost and information-cost advantages on behalf of their customers.

REVIEW QUESTIONS

1. Why are a bank's liabilities said to be its sources of funds? Why are a bank's assets said to be its uses of funds?
2. As financial intermediaries, what services do banks provide to savers and borrowers?
3. What key advantage do banks have over other intermediaries in acquiring funds from small savers?
4. What are borrowings? Why do banks engage in borrowings?
5. How does the federal funds market work? How does a loan in this market differ from a repurchase agreement?
6. Why would government regulators and taxpayers like banks to have high net worth?
7. Describe the three types of risk that banks face.
8. How do banks try to reduce credit risk?
9. How do banks determine interest rates on loans?
10. What do banks do when some of their borrowers look as though they might default? What do they do when the borrowers actually default?
11. What are the goals of asset management and liability management? What can a bank do to meet these goals?
12. What are floating-rate loans? How do they help to reduce the interest rate risk for banks?
13. What are the main types of off-balance-sheet activities in which banks engage? Why have banks been involved in more of these activities recently and less in traditional banking?

ANALYTICAL PROBLEMS

14. If commercial banks were allowed to purchase significant equity positions in the companies to which they make loans, would this increase or decrease the degree of moral hazard in the financial system?

15. Suppose that all borrowers could raise funds through securities markets—for example, through stocks or bonds. Would there be a special economic function for banks? Explain.

16. In developing countries that have no active markets for short-term financial instruments, savers tend to allocate more of their funds to bank deposits than do savers in countries with more active financial markets. Explain.

17. Suppose that a bank uses checkable deposits to finance illiquid loans. If the bank has no private information about borrowers, can the bank fail because of *liquidity risk?* Why or why not? What if the bank has significant private information about the quality of its asset portfolio?

18. Suppose that banks collectively have not managed their exposure to interest rate risk well and that market interest rates increase and become more volatile. What do you predict will happen to the value of the equity capital in the banking industry? To the number of bank failures?

19. Why would banks usually welcome a reduction in reserve requirements? Would a reduction in reserve requirements matter to a bank that voluntarily held reserves for clearing purposes that were higher than required reserves?

20. Suppose that Bank A sells $10 million in securities to Bank B. Show the effect of this transaction on the balance sheets of both banks.

21. Suppose that Ann, who has an account at First Bank, writes a check for $1000 to Bill, who has an account at Melon Bank. When the check clears, how have the balance sheets of First and Melon been affected?

22. Suppose that First Bank has $34 million in checkable deposits, Second Bank has $47 million in checkable deposits, and the reserve requirement for checkable deposits is 10%. If First Bank currently has $4 million in reserves and Second Bank has $5 million in reserves, how much excess reserves does each bank have? Now suppose that a customer of First Bank writes a check for $1 million to a real estate broker who deposits it at Second Bank. After the check clears, how much excess reserves does each bank have?

23. Suppose that you are considering investing (or making a large deposit) in a bank that is making higher profits than other banks. You learn that profits are high because the bank has little equity capital and has nearly 100% of its assets in the form of loans and required reserves. Would you become an investor or depositor in such a bank?

24. In the early 1970s, savings institutions had mostly long-term mortgage loans as assets and had many checkable deposits and time deposits with short maturities as liabilities. What do you think happened to the value of these institutions when interest rates rose dramatically in the mid- and late 1970s? In answering this question, use the concept that measures the interest sensitivity of assets and liabilities.

25. Prepare the balance sheet of a bank that has $20 million in reserves, $40 million in securities, $140 million in loans, $150 million in deposits, and $50 million in equity capital. What are the bank's excess reserves if the reserve requirement is 10% of deposits? Suppose that checks drawn on the bank's accounts withdraw $10 million. Show what the revised balance sheet looks like. What are the bank's excess reserves? How much does the bank need to borrow? Suppose that the bank borrows half of its reserve deficiency in the federal funds market and the other half from the Fed. Now what does its balance sheet look like?

26. If you were a banker who believed that interest rates were about to rise, what would you try to do with your bank's portfolio?

Questions 27 and 28 relate to the chapter appendix:

27. Calculate the duration of an asset that makes nominal payments of $1100 one year from now, $1210

two years from now, and \$1331 three years from now. The interest rate is 10%. About how much will the market value of the asset change if the interest rate rises from 10% to 12%?

28. Calculate the duration gap for a bank that has assets of \$100 million with a duration of 13 and liabilities of \$93 million with a duration of 7.

DATA QUESTIONS

29. The *Federal Reserve Bulletin* contains a table called Bank Debits and Deposit Turnover that reports some interesting data about banks. Look at the data comparing the amount of money that flows through demand deposits and the turnover of demand deposits in major New York City banks and in other banks. What important conclusions about the U.S. payments system can you draw from these data? Why do you think that deposit turnover is so high in New York?

30. In the *Federal Reserve Bulletin,* find the table that reports Assets and Liabilities of Commercial Banks. What is the largest category of loans that banks make? What is the largest source of deposits? Add the total reserves of the banks (reserves with Federal Reserve Banks plus vault cash) and total investment securities. How does this amount compare to the total of funds in transaction accounts?

APPENDIX: Measuring the Duration of Bank Assets and Liabilities

To measure banks' exposure to interest rate risk, we must compare the interest sensitivity of the value of different assets and liabilities. Financial economists use a measure known as *duration* for this purpose. Duration measures the elasticity of the asset's (or liability's) market value with respect to a change in the interest rate.

Duration is the weighted sum of the maturities of the payments in the financial instrument, where the weights are equal to the present value of the payment divided by the present value of the asset or liability. If we denote the present value of a payment at time t by PV_t, then the market value MV of a T-period instrument is

$$MV = \sum_{t=1}^{T} PV_t,$$

and the duration d is

$$d = \sum_{t=1}^{T} t\left(\frac{PV_t}{MV}\right). \quad (13A.1)$$

One more step makes clear why the concept of duration is widely used to measure the responsiveness of the values of assets and liabilities to changes in market interest rates. The change in the market value of an asset or a liability is

$$\frac{\Delta MV}{MV} \cong -d\left(\frac{\Delta i}{1+i}\right), \tag{13A.2}$$

where i is the market interest rate and the relationship between the interest rate and the market value is negative. The duration d indicates the magnitude of this effect. For instruments with a long duration—that is, with greater cash flows in the distant future than in the present—the effect of interest rate changes on market value will be greater than for instruments with a shorter duration.

We can now determine the effects of interest rate changes on a bank's net worth. Because net worth NW is simply the difference between bank assets A and liabilities L, we have

$$\begin{aligned} \Delta NW &= \Delta A - \Delta L \\ &= \left(\frac{\Delta A}{A}\right)(A) - \left(\frac{\Delta L}{L}\right)(L). \end{aligned}$$

If we substitute assets and liabilities for market value in Eq. (13A.2), we get

$$\frac{\Delta A}{A} \cong -d_A\left(\frac{\Delta i}{1+i}\right) \tag{13A.3}$$

and

$$\frac{\Delta L}{L} \cong -d_L\left(\frac{\Delta i}{1+i}\right), \tag{13A.4}$$

where d_A and d_L represent duration measures for assets and liabilities, respectively. Hence

$$\Delta NW \cong -(d_A A - d_L L)\left(\frac{\Delta i}{1+i}\right). \tag{13A.5}$$

The terms in the first set of parentheses (scaled by assets A) represent the *duration gap* faced by the institution; that is,

$$Gap = d_A - d_L\left(\frac{L}{A}\right). \tag{13A.6}$$

Strategies for using the duration gap to guide bank management were discussed in this chapter.

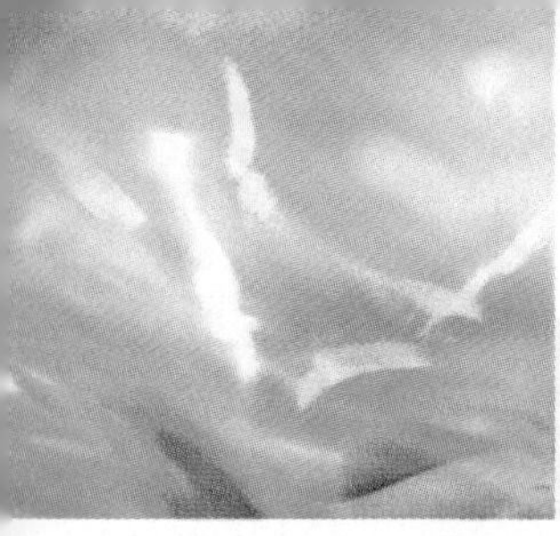

CHAPTER 14

The Banking Industry

If we compare the size of U.S. banks, number of U.S. banking firms, and concentration of assets held by U.S. banks with banks in other large economies, we develop a profile of the U.S. banking industry. Although the United States has the world's largest economy, U.S. banks are not as large by international standards. Indeed, as recently as 1995, only one of the top 30 banks in the world (ranked by assets) was a U.S. bank (then Citicorp). Between 1995 and 2000, mergers propelled two U.S. banks into the ranks of the top ten—Citigroup and BankAmerica. In 1998, U.S.-based Bankers Trust was also acquired by the German giant Deutsche Bank.

Another difference between the U.S. banking industry and those in most other countries is that the U.S. banking industry has an enormous number of banking firms. In 2000, there were about 8500 commercial banking firms in the United States (down from 14,404 in 1980). Currently, the United States has about 30 banks per million people, significantly more than in other industrial economies such as Japan and Canada. Many U.S. banks are also small by international standards: 61% have less than $100 million in assets.

Third, the U.S. banking industry traditionally has been much less concentrated as that in other countries: The share of U.S. deposits held by the five largest banks has been far less than that held by its counterparts in Japan, Canada, and Germany, which hold much higher percentages of their countries' deposits. However, these figures do not mean that U.S. households and businesses receive more *banking services* than their counterparts in other countries do. The United States does not have more bank offices, including branches, per capita—only more separately owned *banking firms* per capita.

The decade of the 1990s saw a major structural change in the U.S. banking industry. The industry consolidated significantly, with the number of domestically chartered commercial banks falling by about one-third, even as industry assets rose by about one-third. Over the 1990s, the 10 largest banking firms almost doubled their share of domestic deposits and total assets. By 2000, banks with more than $10 billion of assets (0.9% of banks) held approximately 68% of total bank assets and 65% of bank equity capital, whereas small banks with less than $100 million of assets (60% of banks) held just 4% of assets and 5% of equity capital.

Government regulation and regulatory changes are the primary reason for the differences in the U.S. banking industry and the changes in the U.S. banking structure and activities over the past decade. In this chapter, we describe the reasoning behind those regulations, the government agencies that monitor banks, and the tools the government uses to regulate bank activities. Recent trends in the banking industry have encouraged mergers and changed the services that banks provide for their customers. Regulations have been changing as well—in response to competition among different bank and nonbank financial intermediaries in providing financial services—stimulating consolidation in the industry. The business of banking is no longer the staid enterprise it once was, and we describe the changes that occurred in the past decade that will continue to shape the banking industry in the United States and in other industrial economies in the future.

ORIGINS OF TODAY'S U.S. BANKING INDUSTRY

We can trace the role of banks in the financial system to the cultural and political views held by many leaders and citizens in the early decades of the United States. Many people, particularly those in rural areas, feared big-city banking interests, particularly those in New York City. In 1791, Treasury Secretary Alexander Hamilton tried to establish a nationwide banking system, with the Bank of the United States in Philadelphia as the leading bank, to provide the nation with an efficient system of intermediation. Although the bank's 20-year charter was renewed (after a five-year hiatus) as the Second Bank of the United States in 1816, its survival was threatened by legislators from agricultural states. After his election, President Andrew Jackson, a populist hero, allowed the charter of the Second Bank to expire in 1836.

Although the establishment of a national banking system was doomed, states were given the right to control banks within their borders after 1836. This was the start of the Free Banking Period, during which banking was conducted with little government intervention. Some contemporary observers believe that the free banks were relatively successful intermediaries in matching savers and borrowers. The Free Banking Period lasted until passage of the National Banking Act during the Civil War.

The National Banking Act of 1863 established the current **dual banking system** in the United States, in which banks are chartered by either the federal government or a state government. Federally chartered banks, known as **national banks,** are supervised by the Office of the Comptroller of the Currency (OCC) in the U.S. Treasury Department and originally were allowed to issue bank notes as currency. To eliminate the ability of state-chartered banks, known as **state banks,** to issue bank notes as currency, Congress imposed a prohibitive tax on state bank notes in the National Banking Act of 1863. Congress intended to eliminate competition for national banks by drying up state-chartered banks' source of funds. However, state banks came up with a close substitute for currency—a **demand deposit,** or an account against which checks convertible to currency can be written. National banks adopted this innovation, and as a result, the two types of banks coexist today.

OTHER TIMES, OTHER PLACES . . .

Lessons from the Free Banking Period

Banking was not really "free" during the Free Banking Period. To obtain a state banking charter, banks typically had to agree to (1) pay gold to depositors on demand, (2) accept double liability for bank shareholders (that is, they would be responsible for twice the value of their contributed capital), and (3) deposit designated bonds (usually state bonds) with the state banking authority.

Historians often use the term "wildcat banking" to describe the Free Banking Period. They allege that banks frequently failed despite regulatory attempts to protect them, causing substantial losses to users of bank currency. Much of the subsequent debate in the United States about the instability of free market banking came from the experience of this period.

Arthur Rolnick and Warren Weber, economists at the Federal Reserve Bank of Minneapolis, have vigorously challenged this view in their study of banking during that period in Indiana, Minnesota, New York, and Wisconsin.† They found that about half the free banks closed but that fewer than one-third of those ultimately failed to redeem bank notes at face value. In general, losses on notes were small—on average, about one cent per dollar. The wave of bank failures during that period can be attributed to default on the bonds backing the bank notes rather than to loss of consumer confidence in banks.

Two lessons emerge from that period. First, regulations are necessary to provide information to the public about the quality of the bank assets that back bank notes. Second, given the public's knowledge of problems in assets backing the notes of a bank, bank failures are rational and reflect large swings in the value of banks' assets. Government intervention in the banking industry may be needed to help it adjust to such large variations in asset values.

† See Arthur J. Rolnick and Warren E. Weber, "The Free Banking Era: New Evidence on Laissez-Faire Banking," *American Economic Review*, 73:1080–1091, 1983.

Legislation affecting banking did not end with the National Banking Act of 1863. Economic crises resulting from waves of bank failures, in which savers lost their deposits and borrowers found it difficult to raise funds, led to the creation of the Federal Reserve System in 1913. The severe banking crisis of the 1930s prompted the introduction of federal deposit insurance, through which most depositors' funds are guaranteed. Other regulations beginning in the 1930s shaped the competitive landscape of banking. As we will see, regulation of the banking industry is being hotly debated. We describe these regulations, explain why they exist, and describe the agencies that charter and examine banks in the next section.

WHO REGULATES BANKS

The banking industry is highly regulated in the United States, as it is in most countries. Regulators are responsible for chartering banks and examining their operations. We first describe what this regulation entails and then describe the agencies that are responsible for regulating commercial banks, savings institutions, and credit unions. As a result of the dual banking system, bank regulation is enforced by many regulators with overlapping authority for these institutions.

Chartering and Examination

How does someone establish a bank? Individuals who want to start a bank must file an application for a federal charter with the Office of the Comptroller of the Currency. For a state charter, the would-be bankers must file an application with the appropriate state banking authority. When the federal or state regulatory agency evaluates the application, it considers the amount of equity capital supplied by the owners, the qualifications of the bank's proposed managers, and the bank's prospects for making profits. Before the late 1970s, the federal or state chartering authority also investigated whether the proposed bank's community "needed" a new bank. Often, an authority refused to grant the charter because it thought that the profits of existing banks would be harmed significantly, potentially causing them to fail. Since the 1980s, chartering authorities generally have not turned down applications on anticompetitive grounds.

A chartered bank must file quarterly reports of its earnings, assets and liabilities, and operations (called *Call Reports*); it also is subject to periodic examination of its financial condition by regulators. The FDIC examines banks at least every three years and generally more often. The Fed conducts examinations about every 18 months. Large national banks may be examined several times each year by the Office of the Comptroller of the Currency. These regulatory bodies often cooperate and accept each other's examination reports.

Examiners also make unexpected visits to banks to ensure that the banks are complying with all applicable laws and regulations. Examiners have fairly wide latitude to force a bank to sell risky investments or to write off the value of a worthless loan. An examiner who finds problems with excessive risk taking or low net worth may classify the bank as a "problem bank" and subject it to more frequent examinations. Although examiners help to control risky or dishonest bank management practices, some analysts believe that allowing examiners too much discretion forces banks to be too conservative in their lending practices. Regulators generally try to strike a balance.

In current practice, regulators use examinations to monitor compliance with capital standards and restrictions on permissible activities. After examination, a bank receives a grade in the form of a C (capital adequacy), A (asset quality), M (management), E (earnings), L (liquidity), and S (sensitivity to market risk) score. A sufficiently low *CAMELS rating* can lead to "cease and desist" orders to change behavior, a means of restraining moral hazard. Such a system mimics the way private markets approach moral hazard by inserting restrictive covenants in financial contracts.

Regulating Commercial Banks

As of 2000, the Office of the Comptroller of the Currency supervised the national banks that are members of the Federal Reserve System. These banks hold most of the assets in the U.S. commercial banking system. The state banks that are members of the Federal Reserve System are jointly supervised by the Fed and state banking regulators. The Fed also has supervisory responsibility for **bank holding companies,** which are companies that own more than one bank. Most of the remaining (smaller) banks are state banks that are not members of the Federal Reserve System but are covered by FDIC insurance; these are supervised by the FDIC. Some very small state banks with no FDIC insurance are supervised solely by state banking regulators.

This network of commercial bank regulatory authorities occasionally results in duplication of effort. Some analysts believe that regulation by more than one agency decreases the chance of lapses in supervision. They also believe that individual regulatory agencies may serve the banking industry better than they serve the interests of savers and borrowers. Since 1999, regulation of banking firms' activities in banking, securities, and insurance has been divided among federal and state banking, securities, and insurance regulators, as described later.

Regulating Savings Institutions

Savings institutions, comprising savings and loan associations and mutual savings banks, also are supervised by multiple regulatory agencies. Savings and loan associations (S&Ls) can be chartered by federal or state authorities. The majority of S&Ls are members of the Federal Home Loan Bank System (FHLBS), which was founded in 1932 as a "Federal Reserve" for S&Ls. The Office of Thrift Supervision, which is similar to the OCC, supervises the 12 district Federal Home Loan Banks of the FHLBS. It also charters and supervises federally chartered S&Ls. The FDIC provides federal deposit insurance to S&Ls through its Savings Association Insurance Fund (SAIF). [Before 1989, savings institutions were insured by the Federal Savings and Loan Insurance Corporation (FSLIC).]

About half the mutual savings banks are chartered by the states, and about half are chartered by the federal government. The primary regulators of mutual savings banks are state banking authorities. However, those with FDIC insurance must follow the FDIC's rules for state-chartered banks. The remainder of mutual savings banks generally have deposits insured by state deposit insurance funds.

Regulating Credit Unions

Unlike commercial banks and savings institutions, both of which take deposits from any saver and make loans to any borrower, U.S. credit unions are cooperative lending associations for a particular group, usually employees of a particular firm or governmental unit. As a result, most credit unions are small, although shareholders of a credit union may live in many states (or even in many countries, as in the case of the Navy Federal Credit Union). Both federal and state charters are available, but most credit unions are chartered and regulated by the federal government's National Credit Union Administration (NCUA). Federal deposit insurance is provided by the National Credit Union Share Insurance Fund (NCUSIF), a subsidiary of the NCUA.

The federal and state laws that created multiple regulatory authorities have shaped the U.S. banking industry in terms of the risks to which banks are exposed and their activities as financial intermediaries. Table 14.1 summarizes

TABLE 14.1 **REGULATION AND SUPERVISION OF U.S. DEPOSITORY INSTITUTIONS†**

<table>
<tr><th>Type of institution</th><th>Chartered by . . .</th><th>Supervised by . . .</th><th>Examined by . . .</th><th>Insured by . . .</th></tr>
<tr><td colspan="5">Commercial Banks</td></tr>
<tr><td>National banks</td><td colspan="3">Comptroller of the Currency</td><td>FDIC</td></tr>
<tr><td>State-chartered banks (members of the Federal Reserve System)</td><td>State authorities</td><td colspan="2">The Fed</td><td>FDIC</td></tr>
<tr><td>State-chartered banks (not members of the Federal Reserve System)</td><td>State authorities</td><td colspan="2">FDIC</td><td>FDIC</td></tr>
<tr><td>State-chartered banks (not insured by FDIC)</td><td colspan="4">State authorities</td></tr>
<tr><td colspan="5">Savings Institutions</td></tr>
<tr><td>Federal associations (insured)</td><td colspan="3">Office of Thrift Supervision (OTS)</td><td>FDIC</td></tr>
<tr><td>State savings associations (insured)</td><td>State authorities</td><td colspan="2">OTS and state authorities</td><td>FDIC</td></tr>
<tr><td>State savings associations (not federally insured)</td><td colspan="4">State authorities</td></tr>
<tr><td colspan="5">Credit Unions</td></tr>
<tr><td>Federal credit unions (insured)</td><td colspan="3">National Credit Union Administration (NCUA)</td><td>National Credit Union Share Insurance Fund (NCUSIF)</td></tr>
<tr><td>State credit unions (not federally insured)</td><td colspan="3">State authorities</td><td>NCUSIF or state authorities</td></tr>
</table>

† Regulatory authority as of January 2001. Securities activities of commercial banks are regulated by federal and state securities regulators, and insurance activities are regulated by state insurance regulators.

the chartering and supervisory responsibilities for banking activities of U.S. depository institutions.

CHECKPOINT

Mutual funds with short-term money market assets don't require much ongoing supervision as long as the funds truthfully disclose to savers the contents of their portfolio of assets. By this reasoning, can we say that if banks disclose the identity of loans in their asset portfolios, ongoing supervision won't be needed? The answer is no. Ongoing supervision is necessary because bankers use private information in making loans that cannot be evaluated well by outsiders. In contrast, mutual funds own more well-known assets. ○

WHY THE BANKING INDUSTRY IS REGULATED

Why is the banking industry in the United States and other countries subject to so much regulation relative to other financial intermediaries and markets?

One possibility is that banks assume special risks in their activities as intermediaries. We know that a difference in the maturities of banks' assets and liabilities can expose banks to interest rate risk, the chance that banks' net worth will decline if market interest rates rise. By itself, however, interest rate risk isn't currently much of a problem for banks. They can use instruments traded in financial markets to reduce their exposure to it. Even if deposit insurance didn't exist, banks could compensate depositors for the risk that the bank might fail because of interest rate risk by paying depositors a risk premium on their deposits.

Instead, the government's concern for the health of banking institutions has focused on *information problems* and *liquidity risk* associated with unanticipated withdrawals of deposits. Banks hold reserves as a cushion against anticipated and unanticipated withdrawals by savers. Savers, however, cannot know the true health of the bank because the bank has private information about its loan portfolio. Because banks have private information, depositors may lose confidence in even financially healthy banks. When enough savers lose confidence in a bank's portfolio of assets, a bank run can occur.

Bank Runs

Depositors begin to lose confidence in a bank when they question the value of the bank's underlying assets. Often, the reason for a loss of confidence is bad news, whether true or false. Suppose that the major loans of Anytown Bank are likely to default. The assistant bank manager discovers the problem and tells two friends, who tell everyone they know. Fearing that the bank probably will not be able to repay them in full, many (if not all) of the depositors rush to the bank to get their money back. Because it must pay on demand, Anytown Bank will pay depositors in full on a first-come, first-serve basis until its liquid funds are exhausted. This sequence of events is known as a **bank run.** In this case, the bad news is true, and a run forces the bank to close its doors.

Moreover, bad news about one bank can snowball and affect other banks. Suppose that State Bank of Anytown has no insolvency problem. Its loans are likely to be repaid in full and on time. However, as rumors spread that Anytown Bank will run out of funds and be unable to repay depositors, many of State Bank's depositors do not want to take any chances. They begin demanding *their* money back. If State Bank's assets are largely illiquid, it will be forced to liquidate its loans at deep discounts to raise money quickly as its reserves run out. As a result, it cannot repay its depositors in full and is forced to close its doors also. In this case, the bad news about State Bank is false, but the rumors made the news seem true and led to a second bank failure.

The Cost of a Bank Run

This spreading of bad news about one bank to include other banks is known as **contagion.** Even if the rumors are unfounded, solvent banks such as State Bank of Anytown can fail during a bank run because of the costs associated with a forced liquidation of their assets. A bank run feeds on a self-fulfilling perception: If depositors *believe* that the bank is in trouble, it *is* in trouble.

The underlying problem in bank runs and contagion lies in the private information about banks' loan portfolios. The private information makes it difficult for depositors to determine which banks are strong and which are weak. This situation is similar to adverse selection in financial markets, in which lenders cannot distinguish good from bad loan prospects. Because of the private information that banks obtain when acquiring assets, savers have little basis for assessing the quality of their banks' portfolios and distinguishing solvent from insolvent banks. Hence bad news about one bank can raise fears about the financial health of others. Figure 14.1 shows the anatomy of a bank run.

Policymakers wish to maintain the health of the banking industry because of banks' importance in reducing information costs in the financial system. The failure of financially healthy banks hurts the ability of less well-known borrowers (households and small and medium-sized businesses) to obtain loans, thereby reducing the efficiency with which savers and borrowers are matched. In financial markets, government intervention focuses on reducing information costs through disclosure of information and prevention of fraud. For financial institutions—banks in particular—government intervention is intended to maintain the financial health of the lender.

Figure 14.1

Bank Runs and Bank Failures

Bank runs can cause good banks to fail as well as bad banks. Bank failures are costly because they reduce credit availability for households and small firms.

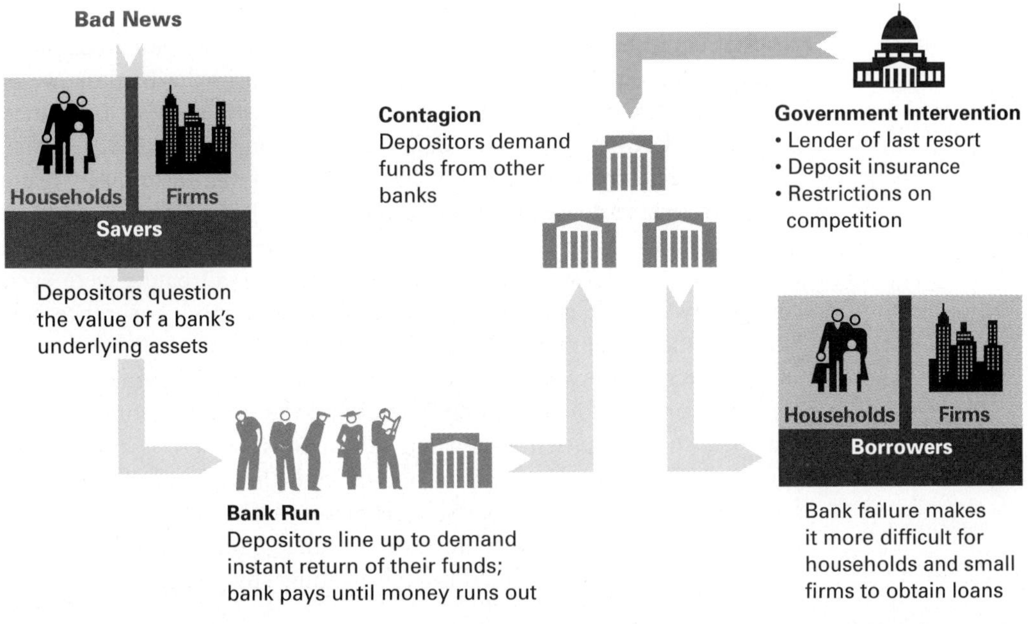

CHECKPOINT

How does asymmetric information contribute to bank runs? Would runs be as likely to occur if banks held only marketable securities? Banks acquire private information while evaluating and monitoring borrowers. As a result, uninformed depositors may be unable to determine the quality of a strong bank's assets and a weak bank's assets, and their withdrawals could force the liquidation of the bank's loan portfolio at a loss. If banks held only marketable securities, the value of their assets would be known. Depositors would not make a run on an institution they knew to be solvent. **o**

GOVERNMENT INTERVENTION IN THE BANKING INDUSTRY

The government has intervened in the banking system to ensure that banks serve savers and borrowers and to promote the efficiency of the financial system. Three regulatory interventions after the National Banking Act shaped the modern U.S. banking industry. In 1913, Congress created the **Federal Reserve System** (the Fed) to promote stability in the banking industry—by serving as a lender of last resort during banking crises. The Fed was given a monopoly in issuing currency, now known as Federal Reserve Notes. All national banks were required to join the system and obey its regulations. State banks were allowed to choose whether they wanted to belong to the Federal Reserve System; most chose not to, owing to the costs of complying with the Fed's regulations.

The second major intervention came during the Great Depression in the form of **federal deposit insurance,** a federal government guarantee of certain types of bank deposits. Thousands of bank failures had destroyed the savings of many depositors and eroded their confidence in the banking system. In 1934, Congress responded by creating the Federal Deposit Insurance Corporation (FDIC) to guarantee deposits at commercial banks. [At the same time, Congress created the Federal Savings and Loan Insurance Corporation (FSLIC) to insure deposits at savings institutions.] The act required banks that were members of the Federal Reserve System to purchase deposit insurance. Nonmember banks were given a choice. Virtually all banks were eventually covered by deposit insurance. The purchase of deposit insurance subjected banks to additional regulation by the FDIC.

Another significant government intervention in the banking industry is restrictions on bank competition, to stabilize the banks' profitability. The first such measures imposed **branching restrictions,** geographic limitations on banks' ability to open more than one office or branch. (Such restrictions are no longer a feature of U.S. banking regulation.) The National Banking Act of 1863 gave states the authority to restrict branch banking within their borders. Indeed, some states prohibited branch banking. By giving banks a monopoly over certain activities and limiting bank competition in local markets, the law sought to ensure a low cost of funds to banks and to stabilize the banking system. A second branching restriction, the McFadden Act of 1927, prohibited national banks from operating branches outside their home states. The act further required national banks to abide by state branching restrictions, thus placing them on an equal footing with state-chartered banks. These regulations led to a larger number of banking firms in the United States than would have existed otherwise. Anticompetitive restrictions also prevented banks from competing with investment banks, brokers, and dealers in the securities industry.

Lender of Last Resort

Bank runs and collapses of commercial credit were unavoidable, often devastating events in the U.S. financial system during the nineteenth and early twentieth centuries. During the National Banking Period (from 1863 to 1913), at least five major **banking panics,** or waves of severe bank runs, reduced the availability of credit to borrowers. The panics culminated in several deep business recessions. Simultaneously, stock and bond market prices fell, further spurring depositors to question the net worth of business borrowers and their ability to repay bank loans. Banking panics raised information costs for uninformed savers, leading them to withdraw funds from banks to invest in gold or high-quality bonds.

What the banking industry was missing during this period was a "banker's bank," or **lender of last resort,** to serve as an ultimate source of credit to which banks could turn during a panic. Many small banks that were particularly vulnerable during a panic exacerbated the problem. The lender of last resort advances credit to solvent banks using a bank's good, but illiquid, loans as collateral. Insolvent banks are allowed to fail.

Prominent private bankers such as J. P. Morgan and George F. Baker understood the severity of the problems of bank runs and contagion and the need for a lender of last resort. In the late nineteenth century, they and several other New York City bankers used the New York Clearing House to attack the problem of contagion. Member banks agreed to lend funds to banks that were threatened with a run during a panic. To provide cash to satisfy the public's demand for currency instead of bank deposits, the clearing house issued *loan certificates,* which could be used to settle transactions among member banks without using currency. To reduce the chance of a run on individual banks, the clearing house reported information about its balance sheet as a group, rather than for member banks separately. In theory, if the bad news hit all members of the clearing house at the same time, the members would have to break their promise of full convertibility of bank deposits into cash and issue certificates that would be usable at other member banks to supplement their cash reserves.

Despite their significant advantages over individual banks in dealing with panics, private arrangements such as the New York Clearing House cannot easily cope in practice with *common shocks*—that is, shocks to the members as a whole. Hence the clearing house could not make a credible promise to lend during a common downturn. The severe panic of 1907 and associated business recession led President Woodrow Wilson and the Congress to create the Federal Reserve System. The Fed was designed to be a lender of last resort to prevent general banking panics. Member banks were compelled to keep reserve deposits at the Fed and could borrow from the Fed through discount loans. The Fed's resources, including gold, member bank reserves, and the statement of "full faith and credit of the U.S. government," enable it to deal with disturbances to the banking system better than private arrangements can. With the exception of its weak performance during the banking panics of the early 1930s, the Federal Reserve System's credible record as lender of last resort financially stabilized the banking industry. The Fed's role as lender of last resort has expanded over the years to include ensuring general financial stability. For example, the Fed's lending to banks during the stock market crash of October 1987 helped to forestall the failure of securities firms. In 1998, the Fed brought together creditors of Long-Term Capital Management, a large and financially troubled hedge fund, to avoid contagion.

Federal Deposit Insurance

The basic idea behind deposit insurance is to guarantee the value of savers' deposits—to promise that if a bank fails, the insuring authority will reimburse the saver for funds lost. As with the lender of last resort, federal deposit insurance reduces the information costs incurred by savers in evaluating a bank's assets. To be credible, the guarantee must be backed by sufficient funds to calm the fears of bank depositors during a panic.

Numerous bank failures during the 1920s and early 1930s led to the creation of the Federal Deposit Insurance Corporation (FDIC) in 1934. During the financial crisis from 1930 to 1933, more than one-third of all U.S. banks failed (about 2000 each year). These failures meant delays in receiving funds and, in many cases, outright losses for depositors. Following the establishment of the FDIC, calmer days resulted for the banking industry, with failure rates averaging fewer than 10 per year between 1934 and 1981.

The FDIC initially insured deposits up to \$2500; it now insures deposits up to \$100,000. Thus the FDIC protects any depositor with less than \$100,000 in a bank account from loss in the event of bank failure. As a result, most depositors have little incentive to withdraw their money and cause the bank to fail if there are questions about the bank's strength. Although about 99% of all depositors are fully insured, the remaining 1% account for more than one-fourth of all deposits. Hence savers with more than \$100,000 in deposits still have reason to question a bank's financial condition and demand their funds when they are in doubt about it. For example, if Cindy Croesus holds a \$1 million negotiable CD at Doubtful Bank, \$900,000 of her investment is at risk, and she will understandably withdraw her funds at a moment's notice if she is worried about her bank's financial health.

The FDIC participated in the resolution of a number of bank failures during the 1980s. Bank failures accelerated in the 1980s, climbing from 10 in 1981 to 79 in 1984, when the giant Continental Illinois National Bank, one of the 10 largest U.S. banks at the time, failed. The rate of failures increased later in the 1980s, peaking in 1989 at 206. Whereas 168 banks failed in 1990, only 13 banks failed in 1994, and only one bank failed in 1997.

How the FDIC deals with bank failure. The FDIC generally handles bank failures in one of two ways: It pays off depositors, or it purchases and assumes control of the bank.

In some cases of bank failure, the FDIC closes the bank and pays off the insured depositors immediately. To recover its funds, the FDIC draws payments from the bank's remaining funds and net worth, including the sale of the bank's assets. If those funds are insufficient, the FDIC makes up the difference from its insurance reserves. After compensating insured depositors, any remaining funds are paid to uninsured depositors. Although the FDIC doesn't use this method often, it did so occasionally during the 1980s. For example, when the FDIC closed the Penn Square Bank of Oklahoma, uninsured depositors lost, on average, only about 20% of their deposits.

The FDIC prefers to keep a failed bank running by purchasing the bank and assuming control over it. The FDIC then tries to find a financial institution that is willing to take over the bank to gain entry into new geographic markets and access to the failed bank's goodwill (its network of customer relationships). Banks became especially interested in acquiring other banks after the Banking Act of 1982 permitted acquisition of failed banking institutions across state lines. When the FDIC purchases and assumes control of a failed bank, the transition typically costs the FDIC money. Generally, it tries to find an acquiring bank to take on *all* of the failed bank's deposits. In that case, the FDIC subsidizes the assumption by providing loans at low rates of interest or buying problem loans in the failed bank's portfolio.

The FDIC must assess the relative costs of the two methods of dealing with a failed bank. Paying off depositors has the advantage of low cost to the deposit insurance fund because only insured depositors are compensated. As long as the perceived value of the insolvent bank's goodwill is less than the value of uninsured depositors' claims, the FDIC saves money by compensating depositors. However, because banks have a special role in the intermediation process, forcing all failed banks to close their doors may not be in the best interests of borrowers or the economy. Although keeping banks open by purchasing them and assuming their assets may be costly, some economists argue that this policy may actually be cheaper for the FDIC in the short run. Its reserves do not have to shrink, and regulators do not have to report operating losses. (We return to this point in Chapter 15 when we analyze the 1980s crisis in federal deposit insurance, in which insolvent institutions continued to operate, losing even more money, with regulators' approval—a process that foreshadowed events in Japan in the 1990s and early in the new century.)

Stability of the bank insurance fund. The FDIC earns income through the insurance premiums paid by insured banks and investment earnings (since 1996, assessments have been minimal for banks, with funds coming principally from investment earnings, though savings institutions still pay premiums). It receives no regular appropriation from Congress. At the end of the 1980s, however, the FDIC was unable to make good on its guarantee of commercial bank deposits without significant regulatory reforms or a cash infusion from the Treasury. In 1988, the FDIC's outflows exceeded inflows from bank insurance premiums for the first time in its history. The FDIC's Bank Insurance Fund held $13.2 billion at the end of 1990, or about 0.7% of total insured bank deposits. The FDIC paid out more than $9 billion in 1990, bringing reserves down to about 0.2% of insured deposits. It then paid out $11 billion in 1991, making its net worth a *negative* $7 billion at the end of 1991, or about –0.4% of total insured bank deposits. In November 1991, Congress approved the Treasury Department's emergency request for an infusion of $70 billion into the fund, including a $30 billion line of credit. As a result of a fall in the number of bank failures and an increase in deposit insurance premiums in the early 1990s, the Bank Insurance Fund restored its funding level required by the Congress. Indeed, in November 1995, the FDIC voted to eliminate remaining premiums for most banks (92%, accounting for 95% of U.S. insured deposits), replacing them with a $2000 annual fee. Premiums for the weakest banks fell to $0.27 per $100 of insured deposits from $0.31. In 2000, a proposal by the FDIC to increase coverage to $200,000 was greeted skeptically by most economists, who feared that the large resulting increase in insured deposits would increase the likelihood of another deposit insurance crisis.

Should these ups and downs of the Bank Insurance Fund cause you to withdraw all your money from the bank? The answer is no, because the size of the FDIC's insurance fund is not what maintains public confidence in it. The true deposit insurance is the implicit guarantee of the U.S. Treasury and the Federal Reserve System. In addition to the Treasury's recent rescue of the FDIC, the Fed on numerous occasions has lent large sums of money to troubled banks (including $5 billion in one transaction in the rescue of Continental Illinois).

Monitoring banks, capital requirements, and evaluating risk. In Chapter 13, we noted that, because bankers have private information about the quality of their loan portfolios, savers should monitor bankers. However, the introduction of federal deposit insurance reduces the need for savers with large deposits to monitor banks and eliminates it for savers with small deposits. As a result, legislation and regulations have had to provide ways to monitor banks, primarily reducing costs of moral hazard.

Insured banks have an incentive to make risky loans and investments. Therefore banking laws and regulations limit this behavior by restricting the types of assets that banks can hold. For example, banks are not allowed to invest deposits in common stocks. To ensure that bank examiners are doing their job, the *Federal Deposit Insurance Corporation Improvement Act of*

1991 (FDICIA) requires the FDIC, as insurer, to monitor the supervisory evaluation of the bank's federal or state examiner. In addition, the FDIC considers other information that is appropriate for evaluating risk, including results of statistical monitoring systems. Bank examiners for the FDIC may instruct bankers to sell risky assets to remove them from their portfolios.

Banking laws and regulations also require banks to maintain a minimum level of net worth, or equity capital. The bank's equity capital is its cushion against losses on loans and investments. Banks want to hold as little capital as necessary, to increase the return on their equity. For example, if a bank with $250 million in assets and $20 million in capital earns $2 million, it achieves a 10% return on equity. But if it could earn $2 million with only $10 million in capital, the return would jump to 20%. In the absence of federal deposit insurance, to reduce the costs of moral hazard, savers would insist that bankers place their own net worth at risk. With deposit insurance, individual savers are less concerned about the value and quality of a bank's assets, giving banks an incentive to hold less equity capital. FDICIA strengthened capital requirements for U.S. banks. However, even with a minimum level of capital requirement, capital–asset ratios for commercial banks are only about half their 1930 level (before the introduction of federal deposit insurance).

During most of the FDIC's existence, minimum capital requirements were stated as a fixed percentage of a bank's assets. However, as bank failures increased in the mid-1980s, regulators discovered that the requirements did not reflect differences in banks' risk taking, especially the risk of their off-balance-sheet activities, such as trading in financial futures and options and interest rate swaps. In 1988, regulators from many countries worked under the auspices of the Bank for International Settlements (BIS) in Basle, Switzerland, and agreed to design more stringent, default-risk-based capital requirements.† Since that time, the BIS has proposed that banks develop their own systems to assess their exposure to interest rate risk.

FDICIA legislated a new supervisory framework connecting enforcement actions to the bank's level of capital. This approach, known as "prompt corrective action," attempts to link the extent of supervisory intervention to the extent of capital inadequacy. Under FDICIA, federal banking agencies assign a bank to one of five categories: well capitalized, adequately capitalized, undercapitalized, significantly undercapitalized, and critically undercapitalized. Banks that fall into one of the last three categories face mandatory enforcement actions.

To assign banks to capital categories, regulators consider ratios of capital to risk-weighted assets (*risk-based capital requirement*) and capital to total average assets (*leverage* ratio). Banking agencies use two definitions of capital. Tier 1 capital includes the most permanent types of capital (common

†International coordination is important. Otherwise, banks in a country that has a high capital requirement may be put at a short-term competitive disadvantage against banks in a country that has a low capital requirement.

stockholders' equity) to absorb losses. Tier 2 capital components offer some protection against loss but have a limited life and may carry an interest obligation (including subordinated debt and intermediate-term preferred stock). For an institution to be considered well capitalized, it must have total capital of at least 10% of risk-weighted assets and Tier 1 capital of at least 6% of risk-weighted assets.† To avoid prompt corrective action, total capital must exceed 6% of total risk-weighted assets, and Tier 1 capital must exceed 3% of total risk-weighted assets. The leverage ratio must exceed 5% for the bank to be considered well capitalized and must be at least 4% to avoid prompt corrective action. Although capital standards are an important discipline against moral hazard, economists argue that such standards have limitations in dealing with the complex activities of banks in the new century.

While bank examinations and capital standards have figured prominently in bank regulation in recent years, regulators in the United States and other industrial countries have increasingly focused their attention on assessments of banks' internal risk management. Judging a bank's risk position by examining its current balance sheet ignores the fact that, in today's financial system, given the many new financial instruments, taking very large bets quickly is relatively easy. In this setting, an institution judged to be healthy from a capital adequacy standpoint can assume large risks and fail quickly if outcomes are adverse, as was the case in Barings' spectacular failure in 1995 (discussed in Chapter 9).

Accordingly, regulators now emphasize the quality of the bank's internal models for evaluating and controlling exposure to risk. In the United States, the Fed and the Comptroller of the Currency feed risk management process ratings into the CAMELS system. In addition, banks are required to consider interest-rate risk exposure in deciding capital requirements. They must establish limits on internal risks and designate personnel to monitor and manage the risks.

Finally, as we saw for analyses of financial markets in Chapter 11, disclosure requirements can play a valuable role in producing information on bank risk, which can in turn improve the ability of bank depositors, shareholders, and regulators to evaluate bank performance. In 1994, the Eurocurrency Standing Committee of the G-10 central banks recommended that financial risk assessments produced by banks' risk management models be included in public disclosures.

---

†Two other types of capital requirements have been used in recent practice. First, minimum capital standards must be connected to the bank's exposure to risks in off-balance-sheet activities, including trading positions in derivatives and interest rate swaps. Under the auspices of the Bank for International Settlements, industrial countries coordinate their capital requirements for "risk-weighted" assets. Second, because large U.S. banks are also engaged in substantial trading activities, the Federal Reserve requires that banks develop internal risk analysis models to forecast the largest trading loss they could sustain over a 10-day period. Banks must hold incremental equity capital amounting to at least three times this potential loss, and the capital may be held in standard equity capital or Tier 3 capital—that is, short-term securities that cannot be converted to cash upon maturity should the bank be judged to be undercapitalized relative to the new requirement.

Restrictions on Banking Industry Competition

The final category of government intervention in the banking industry is restrictions on competition. In the United States, these restrictions have taken two forms: (1) geographic branching restrictions and (2) restrictions on permissible activities of banks. Both restrictions have been loosened significantly in recent years.

Branching restrictions. Branching restrictions figured prominently in federal and state banking regulation until recently. To promote competition among banks, the McFadden Act prohibited national banks from establishing branches across state lines. In addition, it compelled national banks to comply with the branching restrictions in the states in which they are located. State branching regulations traditionally assumed one of three forms: restricting banks to a single bank (unit banking), to branches within a narrow geographic area (limited branching), or to branches within a single state (statewide branching). As early as 1995, no state still enforced unit banking, and 45 states plus the District of Columbia allowed statewide branching.

The combination of state branching restrictions and the McFadden Act protected small banks by limiting the ability of large banks to expand outside their regions or states. Branching restrictions for savings institutions and credit unions are more lenient. Almost all states allow branching for savings and loan associations and mutual savings banks. Since 1980, federally chartered S&Ls have been permitted to establish branches statewide in all 50 states. Since 1981, mergers of financially troubled S&Ls have been allowed across state lines.

Geographic restrictions may push banks toward local lending, lowering the costs of providing risk-sharing, liquidity, and information services to individuals and businesses in a region. However, geographic restrictions also reduce banks' ability to diversify assets, raising their exposure to credit risk. For example, a bank in an agricultural state may make most of its loans to farmers. If farm prices are low, then the bank faces the prospect of default on many of its loans. The effects of recessions are also often regional. If all firms in a region face adverse conditions, then loans to those firms lack diversification and raise credit risk.

In addition, because the fixed costs of funding a bank (for example, computer systems, regulatory reporting, and so on) are high, branching restrictions may reduce banks' profitability. Indeed, in the debate over branching restrictions in the early 1990s, California-based Bank of America estimated that elimination of branching restrictions alone would save it $50 million per year in duplicated overhead costs. (In 1998, Bank of America merged with NationsBank.) Thus limited competition may lead to bank inefficiency and lower rates of return for investors, with significant costs to the economy.

Advocates of limited branching argued that the large number of U.S. banks benefits the banking system because it promotes competition. In fact, the opposite is true. When a bank's territory is protected by regulation, it may operate inefficiently yet still compete successfully against more efficient banks.

CONSIDER THIS . . .

Is Bank Consolidation Good for Business?

Consolidation of the U.S. banking industry is occurring rapidly, fueled in part by regulatory changes permitting nationwide banking. Advocates of consolidation point to improved diversification of bank assets and lower overhead costs as benefits of this trend. For example, California, which has allowed statewide branching in a geographically large and economically diverse state since 1909, avoided the banking crises related to agriculture that other states experienced in the mid-1980s. There are many fewer banks per capita in California as well. Some critics of consolidation argue, however, that the emergence of fewer and much larger banks will dampen competition and reduce lending to small business borrowers.

Most economists side with the advocates of consolidation. Competition is generally enhanced by nationwide banking, because banks formerly protected from out-of-state competition now must provide better service and lower costs to stay in business.

While larger banks will emerge, banking economists suggest that there will be at least 10 banks with assets exceeding a threshold of $100 billion. Small community banks are unlikely to be driven out of business where knowledge of local markets is important. California and New York, for example, have a number of community banks even though small and large banks have competed within the states for a long time. These smaller banks plus focused lending departments of larger banks lead most economists to be skeptical of the notion that small-business lending will suffer greatly as a result of consolidation, although some decline may well occur.

Analysts await news of how stronger diversification in nationwide banks will fare in a downturn. In a more expansionary setting, some commentators worry that rapid expansion of banks across geographic boundaries may increase risk taking and make bank failures more likely.

Why has this anticompetitive inefficiency persisted so long? The answer lies in the politics of U.S. finance mentioned at the beginning of the chapter. Americans have long and continually distrusted large, big-city banks. Indeed, the states with the strongest populist, anti-big-bank sentiment in the nineteenth century—usually agricultural states in the Midwest and South—were more likely to have restrictive branching regulations after that time. The large number of relatively small commercial banks reflects in large part the legacy of those political struggles.

Competitive forces in the banking industry are difficult to restrain. Innovations by financial institutions, including bank holding companies, nonbank banks, and automated teller machines, steadily eroded restrictions on geographic competition.

As early as the 1950s, banks began to get around branching restrictions by forming *bank holding companies (BHCs)*. A bank holding company is a large firm with many different banks as subsidiaries. Congress relaxed branching restrictions in the Bank Holding Company Act of 1956, permitting bank holding companies to provide nonbank financial services on an interstate basis. The act directed the Fed to regulate the new activities of *multibank* holding companies, so a loophole existed for expansion into nonbanking activities by *one-bank* holding companies. Congress closed this loophole in the 1970 Amendment to the Bank Holding Company Act, but the period since 1970 has been one of significant expansion by bank holding companies. Virtually all large banks are owned by bank holding companies, and banks in holding companies hold more than 90% of commercial bank deposits.

For many years, financial institutions circumvented branching restrictions through BHCs. The Bank Holding Company Act of 1956 defined a bank as a financial institution that accepts demand deposits and makes commercial loans. Financial institutions got around the regulation by splitting these two functions: They created **nonbank offices,** which did not take demand deposits but made loans, and **nonbank banks,** which took demand deposits but did not make loans. The regulatory response to this activity was the Competitive Equality Banking Act of 1987, which forbade opening additional nonbank banks, although it allowed additional nonbank offices to be opened.

During the 1980s, banks further broke branching restrictions by expanding the use of **automated teller machines** (ATMs), which spread rapidly in the 1980s and 1990s. The development of ATMs was made possible by the combination of falling computer costs and regulatory opportunity. Because ATMs technically are not bank branches, they are not subject to branching restrictions. These facilities can be located some distance from the main bank and actually function as bank branches, accepting deposits, processing withdrawals, making loans through credit cards, and conducting various other transactions. Many ATMs are linked through electronic banking networks such as NYCE or CIRRUS.

After the mid-1970s, limits imposed by branching restrictions faded significantly before their eventual repeal—both within states (as noted above) and across states. In 1975, Maine became the first state to allow complete interstate banking. In 1982, Massachusetts and other New England states entered into a regional compact to permit growth of larger banking organizations in New England. Such regional arrangements in New England and elsewhere spawned *superregional banks.* Indeed, some superregional banks approach *money center banks* (large, established national banks in major cities) in size and profitability. By 1995, 49 states and the District of Columbia allowed some degree of interstate banking; 37 had legislated nationwide entry.

The **Riegle-Neal Interstate Banking and Branching Efficiency Act of 1994** provided a consistent nationwide standard for interstate expansion after September 1995. As of that time, states could permit interstate mergers within their own borders, and bank holding companies could begin acquiring banks in other states. As of July 1997, banks could begin merging with institutions in any state that has not declined to participate in interstate branching. The 1998 merger of NationsBank and Bank of America produced the first bank with branches on both coasts.

Bankers and bank analysts cheer the favorable climate for nationwide branching. First, interstate branching will permit many banks to create single institutions, instead of series of state-by-state affiliates, saving money through new efficiencies and reducing their regulatory burdens. Second, the shares of some regional banking groups will likely rise in response to newly permitted acquisitions. The 1990s witnessed a significant decline in the number of banks.† This decline was driven largely by consolidation, with bank failures playing a secondary role. From 1985 to 1992—a tough time for the U.S. banking industry—the number of banks fell by about 3000 (more than twice the number of failures that occurred during the same period). In the healthier period for the industry from 1992 to 2000, the number of U.S. commercial banks declined by slightly more than 3500, with fewer than 5% being accounted for by failures. Consolidation within and across regions has driven the decline in the number of banking firms. Many analysts predict that the changed regulatory climate will continue to reduce the number of banks.

Restrictions on the scope of bank activities. Before 1933, commercial banks were securities market financial institutions as well as depository institutions. In particular, some banks underwrote corporate securities, selling good-quality issues to the public and placing poor-quality issues in trust accounts for individuals or pensions in its care. As a result, banks earned investment banking fees for risky activities, the risk being borne in part by their depositors.††

The wave of bank failures during the 1930s and the public outcry over abusive banking practices led Congress to reduce conflicts of interest by limiting the scope of permissible activities for commercial banks. The Banking Act of 1933 (known as the Glass-Steagall Act) prohibited commercial banks from participating in underwriting corporate securities and broker-dealer activities, although banks were allowed to continue selling new issues of government securities (see Fig. 14.2). In addition, banks could hold only those debt securities that were approved by regulatory agencies. Thus the Glass-Steagall Act erected a wall between commercial banking and investment banking, forcing a wave of divestitures by financial institutions. Figure 14.3 illustrates how the wall has broken down over time. For example, J. P. Morgan, then a commercial bank, spun off Morgan Stanley, an investment bank, and First National Bank of Boston spun off First Boston Corporation.

The Glass-Steagall Act separated ownership of financial institutions and nonfinancial firms to limit the concentration of power—that is, to prevent financiers from being able to monopolize major industries and reward affiliates while starving their competitors' credit needs. Some policymakers justified their fear of such activity by pointing to J. P. Morgan and other financiers, who used their financial power to create monopolies in the late nineteenth and

† Allen Berger of the Federal Reserve Board, Anil Kashyap of the University of Chicago, and Joseph Scalise of the Federal Reserve Board estimated in 1995 that the number of independent U.S. banking firms would fall to between 3500 and 5000 in the next decade. Allen N. Berger, Anil K. Kashyap, and Joseph M. Scalise, "The Transformation of the U.S. Banking Industry: What a Long, Strange Trip It's Been," *Brookings Papers on Economic Activity,* 2:55–218, 1995.

†† Economists have generally been skeptical about the conflict-of-interest argument for separating commercial and investment banking, as under Glass-Steagall. See, for example, the review in Randall Kroszner, "Rethinking Bank Regulation: A Review of the Historical Evidence," *Journal of Applied Corporate Finance,* 11:48–58, 1998.

Figure 14.2

The Glass-Steagall Wall

The Glass-Steagall Act of 1933 sought to reduce conflicts of interest by creating a wall separating the permissible activities of commercial banking and investment banking.

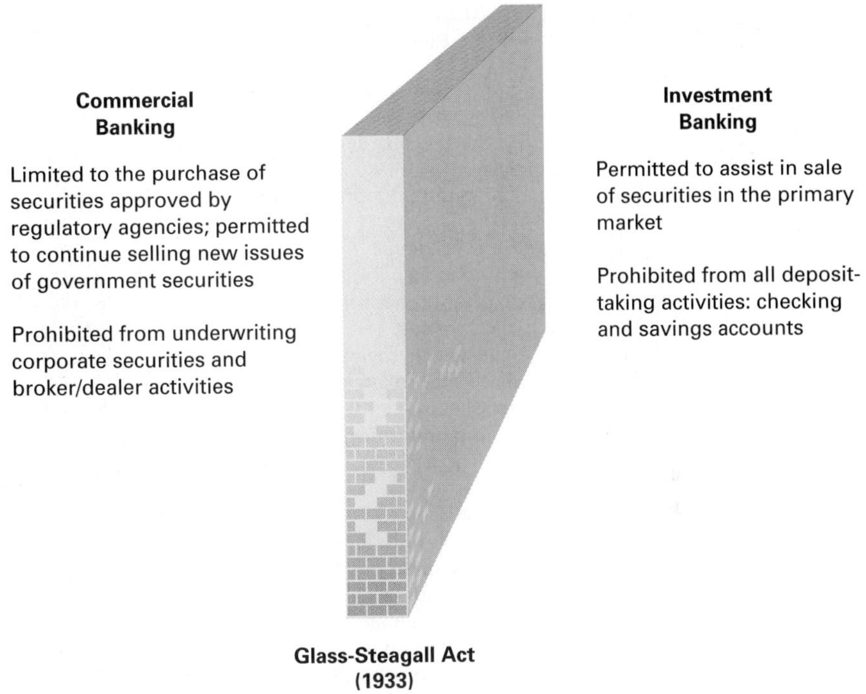

early twentieth centuries. However, such activities are much less likely today because of greater competition in finance and industry.

The debate over retaining these restrictions. In today's regulatory environment, many analysts believe that the fears of the early 1930s about abusive banking practices are unwarranted. They argue that the SEC and federal banking regulatory agencies—and banks' concern for their reputations—limit the potential for problems. In principle, the Glass-Steagall Act was designed to protect depositors of commercial banks from risky investment activities by the banks. In practice, however, it has protected the investment banking industry from competition, enabling it to earn higher profits than the commercial banking industry. As a result, borrowers pay more for issuing new securities than they would if competition from banks were allowed.

Opponents of breaking down the wall between commercial and investment banking point out that commercial banks have a cost advantage in obtaining funds because bank deposits are generally insured by the FDIC. Securities firms have no such insurance and pay a higher cost for funds, usually in the form of loans from banks themselves. Allowing commercial banks to participate in risky broker-dealer and investment banking activities exposes the FDIC—and, through it, taxpayers' funds—to additional risk. Some compromises are possible. They include charging risk-based premiums for bank deposit insurance or increasing net worth requirements for banks that engage in securities market activities.

Figure 14.3

Breaking Down the Glass-Steagall Wall

Beginning in the 1970s, commercial banks and investment banks introduced innovations that allowed them to offer competing services. These innovations continue to steadily erode the wall created by the Glass-Steagall Act. Over time, this financial innovation has been ratified by changes in regulation, culminating in the Gramm-Leach-Bliley Financial Services Modernization Act of 1999.

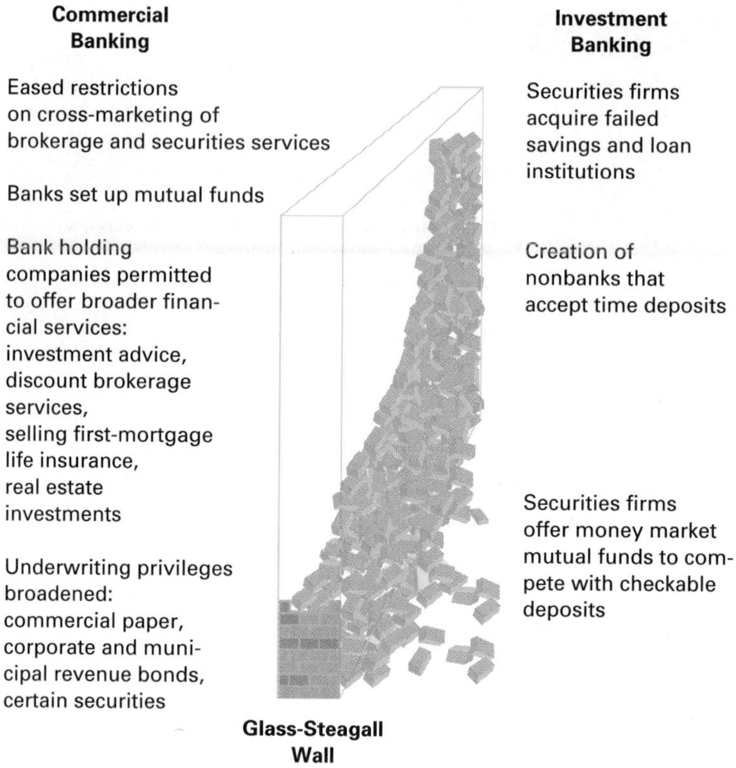

Regulation still prohibits banking firms from entering the markets of nonfinancial firms. Allowing banks to participate in nonfinancial activities is called **universal banking.** Although not permitted in the United States, full universal banking exists in other countries (notably Germany). Where banks own shares of companies to which they grant loans and may influence the management of those firms, advocates of universal banking argue that creating a role for commercial banks in corporate finance improves information gathering and monitoring, thereby reducing problems of adverse selection and moral hazard. If a bank holds shares in a nonfinancial firm and is represented on its board of directors, the information gap shrinks, and monitoring the firm's activities becomes easier and more efficient. One problem with integrating financial and commercial activities in the United States is the safety net afforded banks by deposit insurance; risky activities by banks could generate large taxpayer losses through deposit insurance. Further debate over whether expanding risk taking by banks is a good idea and whether U.S. banks are big enough to compete in the world banking is taking place after the passage of comprehensive banking industry reform legislation.

During the past two decades, commercial banks to a large degree have overcome the restrictions that kept them from offering investment services, as shown in Fig. 14.3. Because the role of banking in finance is to generate information, investment banking and raising long-term capital for corporations are logical extensions of banking. Hence banks have been major players in underwriting commercial paper. Because the Glass-Steagall Act was passed before international banking networks became firmly established, it does not regulate the overseas activities of banks. Therefore Eurobonds could always be written by U.S. banks. In June 1988, the Supreme Court allowed the Federal Reserve System to authorize bank affiliates to underwrite commercial paper, municipal revenue bonds, and mortgage-backed and consumer-debt-backed securities. Revenue from underwriting is restricted to 5% of the affiliate's gross revenue. In June 1989, the Fed gave some commercial banks limited power to underwrite corporate bonds, allowing them to compete with investment bankers. These activities were required to be conducted in separate subsidiaries within a bank holding company, with no access to insured bank deposits.

Banks also offered investment advice and brokerage services. In 1983, the Fed permitted bank holding companies to provide discount brokerage services. In 1987, the Office of the Comptroller of the Currency approved full-service brokerage powers for national banks. In 1987 and 1988, the Fed extended these powers to bank holding companies. Finally, in 1992, the Fed relaxed existing barriers between banks and their securities affiliates by lifting restrictions on the cross-marketing of banking and securities services. This action enables customers to deal with one institution whether discussing a bank loan or raising funds by selling commercial paper or issuing stock. Hence, from the banking side, the line between the banking and the securities industries is thin indeed.

By the early 1990s, banks had begun to compete with securities firms in setting up proprietary mutual funds, in which they act as investment advisors and in selling funds managed by other financial services companies. In addition to their significant role in managing money market mutual funds, banks participate increasingly in managing stock and bond mutual funds.

The clamor to eliminate Glass-Steagall restrictions was heard from the other direction as well. Securities firms, such as Fidelity and Merrill Lynch, have long been active sellers of money market mutual funds, which provide a close substitute for bank deposits. Merrill Lynch and others have purchased banks and turned them into nonbanks. Regulators halted this activity in 1987, but securities firms have continued to establish nonbanks by acquiring failing savings institutions.

The separation of finance from commerce also is breaking down. Nonfinancial firms already engage in significant financial sector activities. For example, General Motors, Ford, and Chrysler have long offered financial services by providing credit to customers to purchase automobiles, and each owns insurance companies. Through its GE Capital arm, GE has become a leader in financial services.

While financial innovation and regulatory response served to erode the effects of Glass-Steagall restrictions on banks, full-scale repeal came in 1999. Virtually every session of Congress during the 1990s witnessed a legislative attempt to tear down the Glass-Steagall wall between banking and other financial services. The megamerger of Citicorp and Travelers in 1998 brought the pressure to the boiling point, and Glass-Steagall abolition came soon thereafter.

The landmark **Gramm-Leach-Bliley Financial Services Modernization Act of 1999** repealed Glass-Steagall by allowing ownership of banks by securities and insurance firms and allowed banks to participate in securities, insurance, and real estate activities.[†] The Gramm-Leach-Bliley Act pursues a "functional" approach to regulation: Federal and state banking regulators regulate banking activities; federal and state securities regulators regulate securities activities; and state insurance regulators regulate insurance activities.

Did the Gramm-Leach-Bliley Act go far enough in liberating banks from restrictions on the scope of activities? Perhaps not. On the one hand, the act made U.S. banking laws conform more closely to the banking laws of other industrial countries. On the other hand, it still allows fewer activities for banks and their subsidiaries than for financial holding companies, and generally separates banking and commerce. Most other countries also permit banks greater discretion in choosing the organizational form in which they conduct securities activities. Recent research suggests that countries with greater restrictions on banks' participation in securities activities and commerce have less efficient banks and a greater likelihood of a banking crisis, all else being equal.[††]

CHECKPOINT

Suppose that commercial banks are allowed to enter all investment banking and securities activities. What do you predict would happen to profit margins in underwriting services and to the salaries and bonuses of investment bankers? Full-scale entry by banks into investment banking and securities businesses likely would reduce the profitability of underwriting and related investment banking businesses, reducing investment bankers' compensation. **o**

THE BANKING INDUSTRY IN OTHER COUNTRIES

Outside the United States, banks perform different services in the economy, in large part because of differences in regulations. However, the worldwide trends of competition among financial intermediaries and financial deregulation are shaping the banking industry in other industrial economies in ways that are similar to those in the United States.

The role of banks in lowering costs of matching savers and borrowers suggests that several beneficial links can be developed between banking and industry: (1) financing growth opportunities in sectors with information problems,

[†]For excellent overviews of the act and its likely consequences, see James R. Barth, R. Dan Brumbaugh, Jr., and James A. Wilcox, "The Repeal of Glass-Steagall and the Advent of Broad Banking," *Journal of Economic Perspectives,* 14:191–204, 2000; and Edward G. Boehne, "Financial Modernization: Vastly Different or Fundamentally the Same?," Federal Reserve Bank of Philadelphia *Business Review,* 3–14, July–August 2000.

[††]See James R. Barth, Gerald Caprio, and Ross Levine, "Banking Systems Around the Globe: Does Regulation Affect Performance and Stability?" Paper presented at National Bureau of Economic Research Conference on Prudential Supervision, January 2000.

CASE STUDY

Is Banking a Declining Industry?

As we noted in Chapter 12, banks lost ground to other intermediaries in the share of assets under their control during the 1980s and 1990s. Indeed, the rapid growth of nonbank sources of credit and the increase in bank failures during the 1980s led many analysts to conclude that banking is a declining industry. Regulatory burdens and increasing competition have *changed* the business of banking over the past two decades. But is the banking industry in decline?

On the one hand, banks' assets made up about 25% of all assets held by private financial institutions in 1998, down from 50% as recently as 1974. On the other hand, the ratio of bank assets to gross domestic product remained at about the same level in 1974 and 1994; these data do not suggest a decline in banking relative to the overall level of economic activity.

Another way to assess whether banking is a declining industry is to examine the trend in lending to nonfinancial businesses, the traditional activity of banks. Allen Berger of the Federal Reserve Board, Anil Kashyap of the University of Chicago, and Joseph Scalise of the Federal Reserve Board note that over the period from 1979 to 1995, U.S. banks' share of real lending to nonfarm, nonfinancial corporate business fell by one quarter from 20% to 15%, with most of the decline occurring in the 1989–1992 period.[†] However, more than offsetting this fall in U.S. bank lending over the period was an increase in lending to U.S. corporations by foreign banks. Hence, taken together, U.S. and foreign banks' share of corporate lending shows no significant decline.

Banks experienced strong competition in both their lending and deposit-taking activities in the 1980s and 1990s, owing to four key innovations. On the lending side, the growth of the commercial paper market has made it possible for large, high-quality corporate borrowers to raise more funds outside of bank loans. In addition, finance companies can tap the commercial paper market for funds, then lend the proceeds to businesses and households. The expansion of the junk bond market during the 1980s also enabled many lower-quality corporate borrowers to raise funds outside of bank loans. On the deposit side, banks face aggressive competition from money market mutual funds, which allow savers to write checks and pay higher rates of return than those typically offered on bank checking accounts.

Finally, *securitization*—the transformation of traditional illiquid financial assets (such as loans and residential mortgages) into marketable securities for trade on capital markets—has emerged because of declines in transactions costs and information costs. Banks can bundle portfolios of loans into standardized amounts to diversify risk and earn a return from servicing the loans (that is, collecting interest and principal payments from borrowers and paying them to lenders). Beginning with mortgages, securitized transactions

[†] See Allen N. Berger, Anil K. Kashyap, and Joseph M. Scalise, "The Transformation of the U.S. Banking Industry: What a Long, Strange Trip It's Been," *Brookings Papers on Economic Activity*, 2:55–218, 1995.

cover certain leases, credit card receivables, and car loans. Securitization makes traditional banking with on-balance-sheet loans and capital to support them less attractive.

In addition, when markets dry up, even very large firms turn to banks seeking liquidity. In the second half of 1998, for example, when risk spreads increased and volume fell sharply in the commercial paper market as a result of adverse events in international securities markets, large firms drew down funds from backup bank lines of credit. When market liquidity became too expensive, banks came through as a reliable source of liquidity for nonfinancial companies.

Focusing just on traditional lending and deposit-taking activities probably understates banks' importance relative to nonbank competitors. The growth of off-balance-sheet activities—the biggest change in banks' business in the past two decades—has helped banks to unbundle information and monitoring services from lending activities. Likewise, banks' provision of derivative instruments, notably interest rate swaps, increases bank involvement in information and risk management.

How important are these new activities? Between 1980 and 2000, banks' noninterest income (that from off-balance-sheet activities) doubled. Hence, while banks' direct lending role (measured by interest income) declined relative to other financial institutions, their indirect role expanded.

John Boyd of the Federal Reserve Bank of Minneapolis and Mark Gertler of New York University constructed a revised measure of total bank assets that adjusted for off-balance-sheet activities.† Their adjustments remove about half of the unadjusted decline noted earlier in banks' share of total assets since 1974. Indeed, they note that, viewed from the period since the 1950s, banks' share of intermediated assets has been fairly stable. They concluded that banking—broadly defined—is not in decline.

Nevertheless, traditional banking—that is, making loans funded with demand and time deposits—is no longer so prominent in the financial system. The reason is that the relatively healthy profitability of banks since 1992 reflects the increased importance of profitable off-balance-sheet activities. Because the overall profitability of banks has not increased in recent years, the increase in earnings from off-balance-sheet activities must be matched by a decline in the profitability of traditional deposit-taking and lending activities of banks.

The factors behind the financial innovations described above are the culprits in the decline of traditional banking. Shifts in regulation, improvements in information technology, and the rise of alternative assets to be required and traded in capital markets have all reduced the competitive advantages of banking.

How will banks respond? To maintain the profit levels required to give shareholders a reasonable return on equity, banks must either change those lines of business or increase their willingness to take risk. In fact, banks have done a bit of both. As we saw in Chapter 13, banks have developed new off-balance-sheet lines of business. In addition, the overall risk of bank loan portfolios has increased, with a greater fraction of lending taking place in commercial real estate loans, telecommunications loans, and loans for corporate restructurings. Such loans are typically riskier than traditional business loans.

---

†See John H. Boyd and Mark Gertler, "Are Banks Dead? Or, Are the Reports Greatly Exaggerated?" Federal Reserve Bank of Minneapolis *Quarterly Review,* Summer 1994.

Is this quest for new lines of business healthy? From one standpoint, yes. Competition has transformed banks, enabling them to exploit their competitive advantage in reducing transactions costs and information costs without depending on less profitable lines of business. These changes are not without concerns, however. Increased risk taking in banking requires regulators—who must worry about the integrity of the financial system and costs of deposit insurance—to monitor banks' new activities.

The patterns we have noted for the United States are also occurring around the world, as deregulation, financial innovation, and the rise of securities markets have exposed banks to greater competitive pressure. Indeed, banks in Europe and Japan experienced low levels of returns on assets and returns on equity in the late 1990s and in 2000, leading to consolidation and, in some cases, government bailouts.

The U.S. case also makes clear the importance of political and regulatory support for financial consolidation. To the extent that the American experience is instructive, Europe may receive similar benefits and costs from consolidation, although many analysts argued even in 2001 that European consolidation may be limited by structural differences among regulations, capital markets, and tax policies of European nations. Likewise, in Japan, with some exceptions, political forces have attempted to resist market pressures for consolidation.

(2) making sure that managers of large-scale enterprises are working to maximize the long-run value of those firms, and (3) reducing costs of financial distress for firms that are having difficulty meeting their current obligations to banks and other creditors. These activities lower transactions and information costs.

The rapid growth of the Japanese and German economies since World War II can be traced in part to the close cooperation of banks and commercial and industrial firms. After World War II, many new firms and industries in Japan and Germany entered new markets, creating problems of asymmetric information and a demand for bank financing. The banks in those countries took advantage of the opportunities presented for intermediation. We now evaluate how Japanese and German banks filled industry's needs following World War II and then briefly examine the prospects for the integration of banking in Europe.

Japanese Banking

Government regulation in Japan of capital markets and financial institutions historically made it easier for firms to obtain financing from banks. In addition, the cooperative organizational structure of Japanese industry influences the role of Japanese banks.

Regulation. For much of the post–World War II period, government regulation kept Japanese firms from issuing securities internationally or issuing risky debt instruments in domestic financial markets. Hence firms turned to banks for financing, making Japanese nonfinancial corporations largely dependent on bank loans. Government authorities—in particular, the (then) Ministry for

Trade and Industry (MITI) and the Ministry of Finance (MOF)—greatly influenced the channeling of funds to industries by banks. Short-term banking was the province of city and regional banks. Long-term credit banks were the only institutions allowed to make long-term loans (usually three- to five-year unsecured loans), but they could not make short-term loans. Finally, small mutual banks, known as *sogos,* were created to ensure that local small firms had access to credit.

Structure. The structure of Japanese industry differs significantly from that of U.S. industry. Many large Japanese firms have been affiliated with industrial groups, or *keiretsu.* The six major keiretsu—Mitsubishi, Mitsui, Sumitomo, Fuyo, Daiichi Kangyo, and Sanwa—were established during the 1950s, but some trace their origins to the prewar period. These large groups are diversified and vertically integrated. In the early 1980s, such group firms accounted for about half of Japanese sales in the natural resources, primary metals, industrial machinery, chemicals, and cement industries. Moreover, group firms traded much more with other group members than with nongroup firms.

Two organizing principles of group finance are of interest. First, the extensive trading relationships are reinforced by cross-shareholding within the group; that is, firms with close ties often hold large equity stakes in each other. Second, each group has a **main bank** that (1) owns some equity in the member firms, (2) is a primary source of credit for group firms, (3) monitors the activities of member firms, in some instances even placing key bank personnel in managerial positions in the firms, and (4) helps member firms recover from financial distress, taking the lead in organizing financial restructurings (other banks defer to the main bank's leadership in this respect). In sum, the main banks' relationships with borrowers are structured to reduce costs of adverse selection and moral hazard.

Benefits and costs. Economists have studied the value to savers and borrowers of this relationship between industry and banking. They found convincing evidence that group firms with access to main bank credit invest more and grow faster than their often credit-rationed, nongroup counterparts do. In addition, group firms that are in financial distress recover faster in terms of investment and sales growth than do similarly situated nongroup firms. This success is attributed to the role of main banks, which provide supplementary credit and write down the value of their loans without a bankruptcy proceeding. Because the main banks actively monitor the firms, the main banks have good information about the firms' prospects for long-term recovery and growth.

However, these relationships also have costs: Interest rates on loans are often higher than market interest rates on bonds, and banks may restrict some of the firms' activities. Owing to these costs, Japanese firms pressed for and received relief from the government in the form of the Foreign Exchange Law Reform of 1980. It allowed firms to issue bonds abroad without government permission. Then, in January 1983, deregulation permitted firms to issue bonds without collateral. Many firms subsequently went outside their main bank relationships to obtain funds from securities markets in Japan and abroad. The share of external funds raised by bank borrowing fell from 80% in 1980 to about 50% in 1985 and has continued to decline.

Current status. Recent trends in Japanese banking resemble trends in the U.S. banking industry. As a consequence of financial deregulation, Japanese banks have lost many of their large-firm customers to financial markets. The large Japanese city banks—among the world's largest in terms of assets—earned low returns on assets relative to many large U.S. banks in the 1990s. In the mid- and late 1990s, many large Japanese banks were financially weak, owing to rising default rates and the collapsing stock market. Indeed, since 1998, the Japanese government has taken on a major commitment to shore up the troubled industry. Japanese banks' strategy in the 1990s was to move into the securities business while remaining close enough to Japanese industry to lend money and provide advice. In that sense, Japanese banks are becoming more like their U.S. counterparts. In a law patterned after the Glass-Steagall Act, Japan officially separated commercial and investment banking. Nonetheless, Japanese banks have expanded into foreign securities operations. Japanese banks also consolidated assets, as with the merger of the Bank of Tokyo and Mitsubishi.

German Banking

Germany is one of only a few countries that allow full universal banking; others are France, Luxembourg, and the Netherlands. (British-style universal banking, found in the United Kingdom, Canada, and now the United States, allows bank participation in securities, but significant bank holdings of common stocks are less common.) Recall that universal banking allows banks to carry out banking and many nonbanking activities within a single firm. In Germany, for example, Deutsche Bank owns a significant stake in Daimler-Benz, a large automobile manufacturer (now Daimler-Chrysler). German universal banking requires that bank participation in nonfinancial firms include direct voting rights for bank-owned shares. The significant reinforcement of proxy votes for shares held by the bank as custodian for its clients is also required.

Banking and industry developed together in Germany, with establishment of the first joint-stock bank in 1848. Initially, banks relied on their own capital to make long-term loans. Later, Deutsche Bank became the first major bank to seek deposits, although at that time, it invested deposits only in safe and liquid short-term loans to merchants. Large national banks emerged in the late nineteenth century. Because of the strong role of banks for most of this century, securities markets are less well developed in Germany than in the United Kingdom or the United States.

Benefits and costs. Many observers have concluded that the close alliance between banking and industry helped to accelerate industrialization and growth in post–World War II Germany. They contend that universal banking benefits German industry by extending to it the information-related strengths of commercial banking arrangements. However, other experts suggested potential problems of conflict of interest and unfair loan pricing. Recall that the fear of conflict of interest prompted the separation of commercial and investment banking by the Glass-Steagall Act in the United States. However, strict supervision, coupled with vigorous competition in financial and product markets, can counterbalance this problem. A second and more important problem regards the pricing of bank loans in Germany. Without aggressive competition from securities markets, banks may charge higher interest rates to firms than they could in the face of competition. A final significant reservation is that the relationship between industry and banks under universal banking might require a wider role for the new European Central Bank in a financial crisis: If deposits in financial institutions are insured to protect depositors from losses when banks fail, commercial or industrial firms that own financial institutions also may need to be covered by insurance.

Current status. Complementing the few very large banks in Germany—such as Deutsche Bank—are numerous smaller banks. Current developments in German banking resemble those in the United States, Japan, and elsewhere. Increasing volatility of interest rates and exchange rates has generated a trend toward securitization. In addition, investment banking is emerging as an important activity within commercial banks, and German banks are facing strong competition from other European banks and from U.S. banks. In 1998, Deutsche Bank acquired U.S.-based Bankers Trust.

Integration of European Banking

In the past, only very restricted bank branching across national borders has been allowed in Europe. The European Community (EC) began removing national barriers to trade in goods and financial markets in 1992. It is also gradually shifting to a banking industry that resembles interstate banking in the United States. The goal is a uniform charter for banking operations. Hence, as with relaxed U.S. branching restrictions, substantial bank consolidation is occurring. Indeed, the Second Banking Directive would have a long-run effect similar to that of financial modernization in the United States à la the Riegle-Neal and Gramm-Leach-Bliley Acts.

What predictions can we make as to the effect of European integration on the banking industry? Integration should promote risk sharing and lead to greater diversification. In addition, activities of banks, securities firms, and insurance firms are likely to become more interconnected. In Europe, as in the United States, banks have successfully ventured into broader securities and investment activities. As capital markets develop further in Europe, the information-gathering and monitoring skills of banks, as well as their branch networks, make them formidable competitors in Europe's increasingly important securities and insurance markets. As in the United States, European financial regulators must monitor banks closely as banking markets become more competitive.

KEY TERMS AND CONCEPTS

Automated teller machines
Bank holding companies
Bank run
Banking panics
Branching restrictions
Contagion
Demand deposit
Dual banking system
National banks
State banks
Federal deposit insurance
Federal Reserve System
Gramm-Leach-Bliley Financial Services Modernization Act of 1999
Lender of last resort
Main bank
Nonbank banks
Nonbank offices
Riegle-Neal Interstate Banking and Branching Efficiency Act of 1994
Universal banking

SUMMARY

1. The United States has a dual banking system: Commercial banks are chartered and examined both by the federal government and by states. Regulatory agencies that are responsible for commercial bank regulation include the Federal Deposit Insurance Corporation (FDIC), the Office of the Comptroller of the Currency, the Federal Reserve System, and state banking authorities. Savings and loan associations generally are insured by the FDIC and regulated by the Office of Thrift Supervision. Mutual savings banks are also insured by the FDIC but regulated by state authorities. Credit unions generally are insured by the National Credit Union Share Insurance Fund and regulated by the National Credit Union Administration.
2. Loss of confidence by depositors in a bank can lead to a bank run, in which the bank is forced to liquidate its assets to pay depositors and close its doors. Because of private information in banking, bank runs can cause solvent banks as well as insolvent banks to fail. If sound banks fail after a run, the economy suffers because banks lose their effectiveness as financial intermediaries.
3. To promote stability, government has intervened in the banking industry by (a) creating a lender of last resort, (b) introducing federal deposit insurance, and (c) restricting permissible bank activities.
4. Federal deposit insurance was introduced in the United States in the 1930s to guarantee bank deposits and guard against bank runs. Until the early 1980s, it was very successful in reducing bank failures. In response to the greater number of bank failures in the 1980s and early 1990s, the FDIC and other regulatory agencies now require banks to hold greater minimum amounts of net worth, or equity capital, than before and to refrain from participation in risky activities.
5. Because of the McFadden Act, which prohibits branching across state lines, and state branching restrictions, the United States has traditionally had a large number of relatively small commercial banks. In recent years, banks have circumvented branching restrictions by forming bank holding companies, creating nonbank offices and nonbank banks, and introducing automated teller machines. In addition, states have relaxed their branching restrictions, and federal legislation has been passed to permit nationwide banking.
6. The Glass-Steagall Act separated commercial banking from investment banking and brokerage businesses. The act's restrictions on banks' activities were circumvented by bank holding companies that can now underwrite many types of securities and engage in brokerage activities. Conversely, securities firms competed with banks for deposits. The Glass-Steagall Act was finally repealed by the Gramm-Leach-Bliley Financial Services Modernization Act of 1999. Although some nonfinancial firms have entered the financial services industry, the separation of banking and commerce in the United States remains relatively strong.

THE ECONOMIST OCTOBER 28, 2000

The Bigger They Come . . .

"They may have invented a better mousetrap," muses David Gibbons, "but I doubt it." Mr. Gibbons is the man responsible for looking at American banks' credit risk . . . at America's Office of the Comptroller of the Currency (OCC). For all that the banks he oversees seem to have found a way of generating huge profits fairly safely, Mr. Gibbons thinks that they have been underestimating their risks. . . .

The biggest, most sophisticated banks claim that they are now well managed and understand their risks better, and investors seem to believe them. . . . But . . . [t]here have been too many banking crises in recent years to put much faith in banks. Just think back to the Latin American debacle of the 1980s; the savings-and-loan trouble in America in the early 1990s. . . .

There are now signs—tentative for the moment, but worrying enough already—that big banks are messing up again. Three problems stand out. The first is that problem loans in America are increasing, even though the economy is still bowling along at a fair rate. The second is that recent turmoil in the capital markets may well have caused difficulties for some of the commercial banks that have been rapidly expanding their investment-banking businesses in recent years. And one reason for this is the third problem: the banks' huge lending exposures to telecoms firms.

(a) Take the last one first. The worries here involve mainly . . . the risk that banks have too many eggs in one basket, and if the telecoms basket breaks, so will the banks. Most, though not all, of these worries are in Europe. . . .

American banks are better capitalized, bigger, more diversified, more profitable and more sophisticated about risk management than ever before. . . .

Mr. Gibbons, for one, is unconvinced. In particular, he worries about American banks' phenomenal profitability. . . . (b) How have they managed it? By taking ever more risk, thinks Mr. Gibbons. And for that, thank some of the recent changes in financial markets.

The first is deregulation. In many ways, this has been a good thing. . . . Thanks to a loosening of the division between commercial and investment banking dictated by the Glass-Steagall Act, commercial banks have also been able to get into the investment-banking business. . . .

But there is a downside to deregulation. . . . Banks have opened their coffers and lent as if there were no tomorrow. . . .

Banks have started to take more private-equity stakes in companies. . . .

Mortgages are another difficult area. Many banks have transferred credit-card loans to home-equity loans, which are tax-deductible for the borrower and offer collateral for the lender. (c) But, as with car loans, their attraction depends on property prices holding up and the economy continuing to thrive. If they do not, things might turn ugly. "Big banks seizing homes is not a pretty sight," says Mr. Mayo. . . .

Moreover, some of the biggest lenders to telecoms companies in Europe are those American banks that have taken lots of risk back home. . . .

The banking industry is highly regulated in the United States and most other countries. Just as gradual deregulation and increased competition have shaped developments in the contemporary U.S. banking industry, so a strong link exists between deregulation and changes in the banking industry in Europe, where the industry—facing increased competition and new opportunities—is on the cusp of consolidation and change.

As the year 2000 drew to a close, some banking industry commentators worried that competition and consolidation in the United States and Europe were prompting banks to take on additional risk to maintain their profitability. Assuming greater risk could leave bank loan portfolios—and taxpayer-financed deposit insurance—worse off in the event of an unexpected downturn. With many economists forecasting a slowdown in economic growth in 2001, the quality of banks' loans became a topic of frequent discussion in the business and financial press.

a Bank consolidation in the United States and Europe focused attention on the investment decisions of the largest banks, which had recently increased their importance in the banking sector. One way in which banks as a group could increase risk taking is by concentrating their lending in high-risk/high-expected-reward industries such as telecommunications (a hot industry in 1999 and part of 2000). Bank connections to the telecom sector could come through direct lending, merger and acquisition activity, and participation in derivative contracts. Such moves reduce the diversification of loan portfolios, thereby increasing banks' exposure to a downturn in the currently favored sector.

b Banks are special institutions only to the extent that they have a competitive advantage in the provision of some bundle of risk-sharing, liquidity, and information services. In particular, knowledge of local borrowers is likely to be important in commercial lending, suggesting an ongoing role for banklike institutions. In late 2000, however, many banking industry analysts feared that newly consolidated megabanks—particularly in the United States—were earning high returns from investments for which they lacked a competitive advantage. Deregulation permitted banks to enter currently profitable, though riskier, financial market activities.

c Traditional bank lending involves careful analysis of the borrower's collateral values and bank capital required to support loans. Securitizing credit card and mortgage loans offers banks fee income but doesn't take bankers off the hook. The profitability of securitization depends on the borrower's collateral values remaining high. (After nine years of expansion, consumer credit quality deteriorated significantly during 2000.) In addition, to the extent that currently high returns in equity from securitization reflect too little capital being committed to the activity, regulatory changes in capital requirements may reduce this source of profits.

For further thought . . .

Because bankers have private information about the assets in their loan portfolio, failures of individual banks might be contagious, creating a role for a lender of last resort. How might the consolidation of banks within Europe affect the design of lender-of-last-resort mechanisms within Europe?

Source: Excerpted from "The Bigger They Are," *The Economist*, October 28, 2000.

7. The banking industry differs by country in response to differences in bank regulation. Banks in Japan and Germany are permitted to have closer relationships with borrowers than are U.S. banks; some analysts argue that these relationships contributed to the rapid growth of investment and output in these countries since World War II. Nonetheless, as domestic financial systems become more integrated internationally, banking industries in various countries appear to be becoming more similar.

REVIEW QUESTIONS

1. What is the dual banking system? Why does it persist?
2. What is the main function of federal deposit insurance?
3. Why does the United States have so many banks?
4. What is meant by contagion? What problems does it pose for the stability of the banking system?
5. If bank runs closed only insolvent banks, should anyone care? Why might bank runs create a need for regulation?
6. How did the establishment of the Federal Reserve System reduce the chance of banking panics?
7. What are the advantages and disadvantages of the payoff method compared to the purchase-and-assumption method of dealing with failed banks?
8. How do risk-based capital requirements work?
9. Which government regulations restrict bank competition? How did they come about? Are they likely to continue into the future?
10. What are the costs to banks of geographic restrictions on bank competition? To savers? To borrowers? In a banking system with banks of different sizes, which banks stand to gain from geographic restrictions? To lose?
11. How have banks tried to get around restrictions on branching? What was the regulatory response to these attempts?
12. What is the difference between a nonbank office and a nonbank bank?
13. Which law forced the separation of commercial banking from investment banking in the United States? Why was it enacted? Is it still in force? Explain.
14. How does the U.S. experience of separating commerce from banking compare to that of countries having universal banking?
15. What can banks do to link banking and industry more beneficially?
16. How does universal banking work in Germany? What concerns might taxpayers have if universal banking were tried in the United States and banks were still covered by FDIC insurance?

ANALYTICAL PROBLEMS

17. How did private bankers attempt to deal with the problems of bank runs and contagion during the National Banking Period? Under which circumstances were these private attempts to deal with these problems likely to be successful and under which circumstances were they likely to be unsuccessful?
18. Evaluate this statement: "The recent wave of bank mergers has eliminated many smaller banks. This is bad news for small businesses, because they receive most of their loans from small banks."
19. Why was the Fed concerned about the possible failure of Long-Term Capital Management? What negative consequences may result from the Fed's actions in this situation?
20. Evaluate the following statement: The United States has about 8900 banks, whereas Canada has only a few, so the U.S. banking industry must be more competitive.
21. The ceiling on the size of an account covered by federal deposit insurance is $100,000. If you heard

that your bank might be in trouble, what would you do if you had $10,000 in the bank? If you had $200,000 in the bank? Does deposit insurance fulfill its role in reducing failures if a bank has many large depositors? Why or why not?

22. Suppose that banks, preparing for increased international competition, are trying to improve their capital by making fewer loans, buying more securities, and holding more cash. Suddenly, bank funding for several large (and solvent) corporations is in jeopardy. What would you do if you were the Chairman of the Federal Reserve Board?

23. By the 1980s, the level of bank net worth (equity capital) relative to bank assets had declined significantly from pre-1934 levels. All other things being equal, could the introduction of federal deposit insurance in 1934 account for this change? Explain.

24. Evaluate the following statement: A banking system with deposit insurance needs more supervision from third-party examiners than does a banking system without guarantees for depositors.

DATA QUESTION

25. Find the most recent issue of the *World Almanac* in your library and locate historical data on the number of U.S. bank failures each year. In the four decades following the introduction of federal deposit insurance (by the Banking Act of 1933), what happened to the number of bank failures relative to the number in the decade before the introduction of deposit insurance? On the basis of this information, can you conclude that deposit insurance made financial intermediaries healthier? Explain.

CHAPTER 15

Banking Regulation: Crisis and Response

The economy recovered after the Great Depression, and it prospered during and after World War II. Thanks to the banking regulations enacted in the Depression's aftermath—expansion of the Fed's role as lender of last resort, restrictions on competition for banking services, and federal deposit insurance—which attempted to reduce the chance of a future banking crisis, the environment for banking became very comfortable. During this period, bank managers were said to follow a "3-6-3" rule: Borrow at 3%, lend at 6%, and be on the golf course at 3:00.

But this nirvana didn't last long. Other participants in the financial system saw opportunities to serve savers and borrowers in ways that regulated banks could not; the economic forces of the business cycle and episodes of inflation and high market interest rates turned restrictions on the interest that banks could pay into a millstone; deposit insurance gave banks an incentive to act imprudently. The regulations that were designed to keep the banking system healthy contributed in part to problems that began in the 1960s and 1970s, which in turn led to opportunities for innovation. Banking regulators found themselves more like the scientists who attempt to develop a flu vaccine each year than the researchers who were able to prevent smallpox or whooping cough with a single shot. Like the influenza virus, which can mutate each year, the ills that regulations tried to fix occurred with sufficient variety that no single regulation could ensure the profitability of the banking industry. Indeed, bank regulators were aiming at a moving target.

In this chapter we describe the recent history of banking regulation, looking specifically at the crises that fostered the regulation, the effect of the regulations, and the challenges that regulators faced in trying to maintain the banking industry as a conduit of funds from savers to borrowers. As you look at each type of regulation—lender of last resort, restrictions on competition, and deposit insurance—you will notice that a four-stage pattern emerges: (1) crisis, (2) regulation, (3) response by the financial system, and (4) response by regulators. Once you become comfortable with this process of evaluating the regulation of financial institutions, you can use it to interpret future developments in the banking industry and in other financial institutions in the United States and abroad.

THE PATTERN OF REGULATION

The first stage in the regulatory pattern is a *crisis* in the banking industry. For example, if savers lost confidence in banks' ability to use their funds wisely, a bank run would result as savers tried to withdraw their funds. When savers lose confidence in them, banks are unable to fulfill their role as intermediaries for many borrowers. Adverse selection and moral hazard can create instability, leading to crises in the banking system.

The second stage occurs when government steps in to end the crisis through *regulation*. The government generally intervenes when it perceives instability in financial institutions and when political pressures make intervention advisable. For example, government regulation in the United States and other countries has responded to banking panics by attempting to maintain banks' profitability or reducing monitoring costs for savers.

The third stage is *response by the financial system*. A major regulatory intervention—deposit insurance, for example—leads to changes and innovation in the activities of financial institutions (borrowing, lending, and provision of risk-sharing, liquidity, and information services). As in manufacturing companies or other service businesses, *innovation* (the development of new products or lines of business to serve consumers) gives one company an edge over its competitors. The motivation for financial innovation is the same as that in other businesses: profit.

The fourth stage occurs with *regulatory response*. Regulators observe the impact of regulation on changes in the way that financial institutions do business. In particular, when financial innovations circumvent regulatory restrictions, regulators must adapt their policies or seek new authority as a regulatory response.

LENDER OF LAST RESORT

Congress created the Federal Reserve System as the lender of last resort to provide liquidity to banks during banking panics. Essentially, creation of the Fed was a regulatory response to the crisis of bank failures and contractions in bank lending during the late nineteenth and early twentieth centuries. As we will see, however, for a lender of last resort to be effective, its promise to lend to banks during a crisis must be credible and carried out swiftly. The evolution of the Fed's activities illustrates how regulation introduced in response to one crisis can be adapted to respond to future crises.

The Great Depression

The first crucial test for the Federal Reserve System's effectiveness in reducing the costs of financial instability followed the stock market crash of October 1929. In responding to the crash, the Fed performed its role as lender of last resort quickly and decisively by extending credit to the New York banks that made loans to stockbrokers and speculators.

The Fed soon faced a more serious problem: The banking panics that began in late 1930, as a wave of bank failures hit the U.S. economy, caused savers to lose confidence in the banking system. Demand deposits shrank sharply as the public converted them to currency because they perceived bank deposits to be risky. Banks liquidated loans and raised their reserve holdings to 22% of deposits in 1932 (up from 15% of deposits in 1930), but bank intermediation had broken down. In March 1933, President Roosevelt declared a *bank holiday,* forcing all banks to close for a time.

The economic collapse during the early 1930s—the Great Depression—was the most severe financial setback in U.S. history. Many economists consider the bank failures to be a key reason the downturn lasted so long. When banks failed, many borrowers, unable to find substitutes for bank loans (through sales of bonds or shares), couldn't obtain credit. Many small and medium-sized businesses and farms failed as a result. Disruption in the banking system demonstrates how crucial banks are in reducing the information costs of savers in finding creditworthy borrowers. The large number of small, poorly diversified banks—particularly those that held agricultural loans during a period of falling commodity prices—compounded the banking crisis.

During the banking panics, the Fed failed to act decisively as the lender of last resort; it did not lend aggressively enough to struggling banks. Moreover, the Fed actually *raised* the interest rate it charged on loans to member banks in 1931. It is easy to look back and see how the Fed should have acted, but at the time, the Fed shared the view of many economists who believed that the Great Depression would work itself out with no central bank intervention. In addition, the Fed's charter allowed it to lend only to banks that pledged good-quality commercial loans as collateral. The Fed also faced problems because its policy to maintain a fixed exchange rate under the gold standard limited its ability to act. In 1931, when England suspended convertibility of the pound into gold, participants in international financial markets thought that the United States might abandon its fixed exchange rate promise and gold convertibility as well. As a result, foreign investors rushed to convert dollars into gold. To maintain the exchange rate and protect its gold reserves, the Fed increased the interest rate it charged on loans to banks. This increased the exchange rate of the dollar versus other currencies and restored the relative attractiveness of the United States as a place to keep funds. However, higher interest rates made it difficult for struggling banks to borrow from the Fed.

Congressional action after 1932 attempted to solve the problems that had prolonged the banking crisis. Congress amended the Fed's charter to limit convertibility of the U.S. dollar into gold and broadened the definition of permissible collateral for loans from the Fed. Decision making within the Fed was centralized to improve its ability to respond quickly during a crisis. Nonetheless, the financial community remained uncertain as to whether the

Fed could be an effective lender of last resort for the banking industry. The Fed's weakness during the calamitous early 1930s motivated the introduction of federal deposit insurance in 1934.

CHECKPOINT

Suppose that banks used checkable deposits to finance commercial loans that could be traded on secondary markets. Would there be a role for a lender of last resort? If banks' loan portfolios were very liquid and sufficient information on their quality were available so that they could be traded, liquidity risk and information costs would be greatly reduced. As a result, there would be less need for a lender of last resort. However, if liquidity and information costs were extremely low, there also would be less need for traditional banking firms. o

Success in Recent Years

Despite its shaky start as a lender of last resort during the Great Depression, the Federal Reserve System has performed well since World War II. The following four episodes show how the Fed can intervene successfully to prevent financial crises.

The Penn Central Railroad crisis. When the Penn Central Railroad, once one of the largest corporations in the United States, filed for bankruptcy in 1970, it defaulted on $200 million of commercial paper. Investors became doubtful about the quality of commercial paper issued by other large companies and wary of supplying funds to that market. Without any intervention by the Fed, raising money in the commercial paper market would become costly because investors would require a large premium to compensate them for the perceived risk. The Fed increased the availability of credit to commercial banks to encourage them to extend short-term credit to make available the amount of funds that firms would ordinarily borrow in the commercial paper market. It also provided loans to these banks to make the extra lending possible. These actions averted a crisis in the banking system and financial markets.

The Franklin National Bank crisis. When the Franklin National Bank collapsed in 1974, it had issued a large amount of negotiable certificates of deposit. These time deposits could be bought and sold by individuals and institutions with a penalty for early withdrawal but weren't guaranteed by federal deposit insurance. In this instance, investors questioned the quality of other banks' negotiable CDs and cut back their holdings of such deposits. The decline in demand for negotiable CDs worried bankers because they are a significant source of funds to banks. To avert a panic in the negotiable CD market, the Fed reduced investors' information costs by providing discount loans to banks. This action eased investors' fears about the general quality of negotiable CDs.

CONSIDER THIS . . .

How Does a Lender of Last Resort Protect the Payments System?

Although Congress created it to act as the lender of last resort for the banking system, the Fed today also engages in a variety of lending activities to maintain the soundness of financial trading mechanisms. One important trading mechanism is the *payments system,* or the means for clearing transactions in the economy by check. The New York-based Clearing House for Interbank Payments and Settlements (CHIPS) settles dollar-denominated transfers among both domestic and foreign-owned banks. If a market participant in CHIPS fails during a business day, all its payments are canceled. These cancellations in turn affect all other participants with which the failed bank was dealing. Hence the failure of a large bank could trigger failures of other institutions. The Fed must wrestle with difficult decisions about how to react, particularly when a crisis develops as the result of failure of a foreign-owned bank.

Another important clearing mechanism is the *Fedwire* system, which is used in clearing securities transactions. Positions are not closed during the day, so if a bank can't settle an overdraft by the end of the day, the Fed effectively must convert it to a (possibly involuntary) discount loan. The role of lender of last resort in maintaining the health of the payments system gets murky when we consider the blurring of distinctions between commercial and investment banking and, in some instances, between finance and commerce. If commercial firms were allowed to conduct banking activities, a crisis in banking could force the Fed to make unsecured, interest-free loans to investment banking firms or even to manufacturing firms.

The Hunt brothers' silver speculation crisis. In the 1980s, Herbert Hunt and Nelson Bunker Hunt, heirs of legendary oil baron H. L. Hunt, used their sizable fortunes and borrowed funds to corner the silver market. Their scheme worked for a while, but the price of silver ultimately tumbled. The collapse of this speculative scheme caused woes not just for the brothers but also for large brokerage houses, including industry giant Merrill Lynch, to which they owed money. The amounts at stake were large enough to threaten the financial stability of the exchange on which the futures contracts were traded. Such a failure would have been costly to savers and borrowers who depended on the exchange to provide information services that are essential to trading in and liquidity of futures contracts. In this case, the Fed worked with a group of banks to provide loans to exchange members, thereby avoiding a rise in information costs and a market panic.

The stock market crash of 1987. The stock market crash on October 19, 1987, raised fears of a repetition of the events that followed the 1929 crash. In particular, investors feared credit squeezes on broker-dealers in the securities industry. Before the stock market opened for trading the following day, Federal Reserve Chairman Alan Greenspan announced to the news media the Fed's readiness to provide liquidity in support of the economic and financial system. At the same time, the Fed, acting as lender of last resort, encouraged banks to lend to securities firms and extended discount credit to banks. This action by the Fed reduced information costs and allowed financial markets to provide risk-sharing and liquidity services to market participants. In addition, the action ensured the soundness of the payments system.

Concluding Remarks

A lender of last resort can help to stabilize the banking system during a crisis. In the United States, the Federal Reserve System has generally performed this role successfully. Indeed, in late 1998, the Fed averted a possible panic from the financial woes of Long-Term Capital Management, a large U.S. hedge fund, by simply using its influence to bring the firm's creditors together. Figure 15.1 summarizes the evolution of the Fed's role in the cycle of financial crisis, regulation, financial system response, and regulatory response.

ANTICOMPETITIVE BANK REGULATION

A second way in which the federal government sought to maintain banking stability was to limit competition among banks and between banks and other financial institutions. Such intervention was intended to (1) reduce the likelihood of bank runs and (2) reduce the chance of moral hazard in banks' behavior. The argument for limiting competition is that it increases a bank's value, thereby reducing bankers' willingness to make excessively risky investments.

Anticompetitive regulations do not promote banking stability in the long run. Instead, they create an incentive for unregulated financial institutions and markets to compete with banks by offering close substitutes for bank deposits and loans. A dramatic example of how anticompetitive regulation led to competition, financial innovation, and regulatory response occurred in the fight over limits on the interest that banks could pay depositors. The battle began with the Banking Act of 1933, which authorized **Regulation Q.** It placed ceilings on allowable interest rates for time and savings deposits and prohibited the payment of interest on demand deposits (then the only form of checkable deposits). Regulation Q was intended to maintain banks' profitability by limiting competition for funds among banks and guaranteeing a reasonable spread between interest rates on loans and interest rates paid to depositors. In fact, it forced banks to innovate to survive.

The market for short-term credit exists in large part to accommodate firms' demand for working capital, the funds firms use to pay for materials, labor, and inventories before the sale of products can generate revenue. Households and firms hold short-term liquid assets as a buffer against changes in income or spending. Historically, commercial banks dominated the short-term credit market. They specialize in reducing information costs by forming long-term relationships with borrowers and continually reauthorizing short-term loans. Also, by lending through such banks, savers obtain risk-sharing and liquidity benefits.

Setting a ceiling on interest rates that banks could pay depositors was supposed to give banks a competitive advantage in the market for loans. The low cost of funds as a result of interest rate ceilings made banks the leading lenders

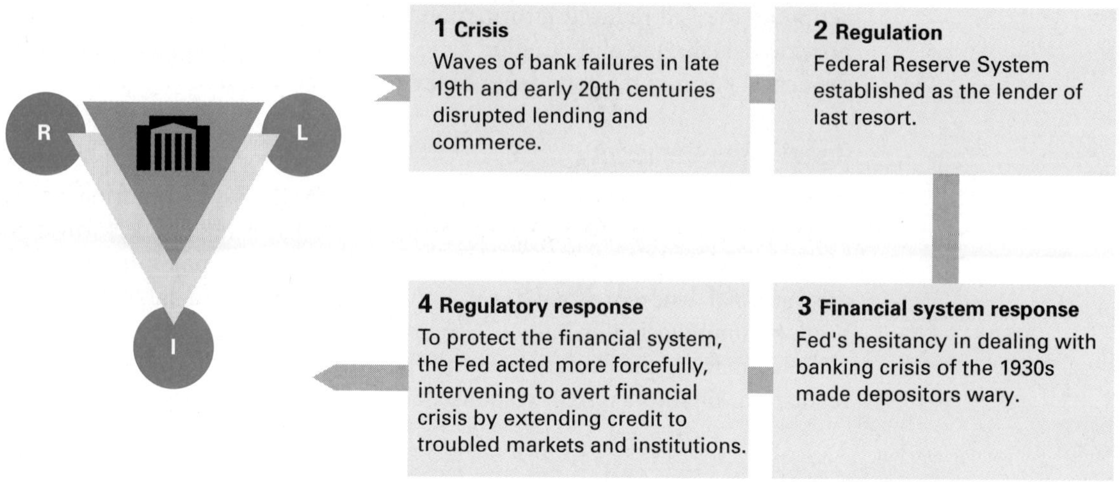

Figure 15.1

Lender of Last Resort: Crisis, Regulation, Financial System Response, and Regulatory Response
Instability in the banking system reduced the liquidity of bank deposits and raised information costs, leading to a collapse in bank lending and a call for a lender of last resort. After the Fed's early failures to act as a lender of last resort, its powers were broadened, and additional bank regulation was developed.

to households and businesses. But whenever market interest rates rose above that ceiling, large and small savers seeking the highest rates of return had a strong incentive to search for alternatives in the marketplace. This is exactly what happened during the 1960s—and increasingly in the 1970s and 1980s. Large corporations and wealthy households substituted such short-term investments as Treasury bills, commercial paper, and repurchase agreements in place of short-term deposits at banks. The benefits of greater rates of returns from these securities justify the transactions costs of hiring a cash management team or paying brokerage fees to find and manage alternative investments when market interest rates are high.

The financial system responded by introducing money market mutual funds in 1971 as an alternative to bank deposits. This innovation enabled depositors whose bank deposits were paying below-market interest rates (because of Regulation Q) to hold portfolios of government securities and commercial paper. Money market mutual funds gave small and medium-sized depositors an opportunity to earn market rates of return with low transactions costs. They ensured both liquidity and diversification, services that were formerly provided only by banks. These funds grew in popularity in 1978, when market interest rates climbed above the 5.25% ceiling on interest rates for savings accounts and time deposits. Their assets rose from $4 billion in 1977 to $230 billion in 1982 to more than $1160 billion in 2000. The evolution of money market mutual funds in response to regulation is not unique to the United States.

Development of the money market mutual fund market also provided *borrowers* with a new source of funds. Large, well-established firms could raise short-term funds in the commercial paper market, where savers sought higher rates of return than returns on bank deposits and low information costs. This alternative to bank borrowing created new competition between commercial and investment banks and significant loss of loan business for commercial banks. By 2000, total lending in the commercial paper market accounted for about one-third of short-term business financing, compared to 10% in 1980, 7% in 1970, and 2% in 1960. The loss of business that banks suffered was even more damaging than the statistics imply because, as our analysis of the costs of adverse selection predicts, only high-quality borrowers had access to commercial paper, leaving banks with low-quality borrowers.

The exit of savers and borrowers from banks to financial markets is known as **disintermediation,** which costs banks lost revenue from not having savers' funds to loan. In some cases, it also costs borrowers and the economy: Although high-quality, established borrowers are able to raise funds in markets such as the commercial paper market, households and less well-established business firms aren't able to do so. As a result, banks aren't able to provide more efficient intermediation than financial markets even when the transactions and information costs of market alternatives are high. Let's look at how the costs of disintermediation can affect the economy.

The Credit Crunch of 1966

In 1966, deposits in commercial banks, savings banks, and savings and loan associations (S&Ls) were subject to interest rate ceilings under Regulation Q. Rising market interest rates caused depositors to shift funds from commercial banks and S&Ls to financial markets. Large commercial banks redirected their investment strategies to raise funds through unregulated sources, such as Eurodollar deposits. Smaller banks and S&Ls had fewer alternative sources of funds and were forced to curtail lending. In the first half of 1966, primarily mutual savings banks and S&Ls were affected by disintermediation, because households' savings deposits were their primary source of funds and their mortgage lending fell dramatically. Commercial banks felt the pinch in the second half of the year when the Fed lowered the interest rate ceiling on bank time deposits, forcing them to cut back on interest paid to depositors.

The blow to mortgage lending and the housing industry caused a **credit crunch,** or a reduction in borrowers' ability to obtain credit at prevailing interest rates. A credit crunch affects small firms the most. In fact, smaller creditworthy firms had to cut back disproportionately on investment because they normally depend on bank loans for external financing.

Banks' Response

As savers and borrowers were lured from banks to financial institutions that offered more attractive interest rates, banks actively countered with their own innovations. To reestablish their ties to borrowers, banks used their information-cost and transactions-cost advantages to enter the commercial paper market through the back door by offering standby letters of credit (Chapter 13). That innovation enabled banks to minimize the damage from anticompetitive regulation by earning fees that compensated them for their information services.

To circumvent the interest rate regulation, banks also developed new financial instruments for savers. Citibank introduced the **negotiable certificate of deposit** (or negotiable CD) as a time deposit with a fixed maturity of, say, six months, to compete with commercial paper. CDs differ from demand deposits in that depositors are penalized with early withdrawal; this feature makes CDs relatively illiquid for the cash management needs of large firms. *Negotiable* CDs circumvent this limitation because they can be sold to someone else even though they cannot be redeemed prior to maturity without penalty. When Citibank created them, negotiable CDs of at least $100,000 were exempt from Regulation Q. Negotiable CDs are now an important source of funds for commercial banks, with a typical denomination of $1 million.

In addition, banks came up with ways to pay interest on depositors' funds. A break for small depositors came when a Massachusetts mutual savings bank created a substitute for checking accounts that was not governed by Regulation Q. Called a **negotiable order of withdrawal (NOW) account,** it required only the introduction of a "withdrawal slip" that the depositor could sign over to someone else. This withdrawal slip functioned like a check; a NOW account is like a checking account. Technically, however, it isn't a demand deposit, so interest can be paid on it. Following a favorable Massachusetts court decision in 1972, NOW accounts spread throughout New England, New Jersey, and New York, effectively offering checking accounts paying 5.25% interest at the time, in contrast to the 0% on traditional demand deposits. (NOW accounts today offer varying interest rates linked to short-term market interest rates.) Small savers holding checking accounts and passbook savings accounts transferred their funds to NOW accounts. In an additional development in 1974, credit unions began issuing share drafts, or checkable deposits paying interest on minimum account balances.

For large depositors, banks used repurchase agreements (RPs), overnight Eurodollars, and automatic transfer system (ATS) accounts. Under a repurchase agreement, the bank regularly converts the balance of a demand deposit into overnight RPs. Recall that in an RP, a corporation purchases Treasury bills from a bank, and the bank commits to repurchase them the next day for a slightly higher price, thereby paying interest to the depositor. In overnight Eurodollar transactions, a customer's demand deposit is automatically withdrawn and deposited in a foreign branch that pays interest. Finally, ATS accounts effectively pay interest on checking accounts by "sweeping" a customer's checking account balance at the end of the day into overnight RPs.

CHECKPOINT

You are an intelligent banker, always looking for ways to increase your bank's profits. You notice that when someone moves money from a demand deposit into a savings account, interest is earned for that day as long as the transfer occurs before midnight. However, there is a law against paying interest on demand deposits. What can you think of to get around this law?

You could automatically transfer balances from demand deposits to savings accounts and back by computer each night at midnight. In this way, the demand deposits, in effect, would earn interest, even though technically you are allowed to pay interest only on savings accounts. ●

Regulatory Response

The breakdown of interest rate regulation in banking came about because of pressure on regulators from small and medium-sized banks. These banks, like large banks, lost deposits to money market mutual funds. Unlike large banks, however, they had limited access to innovations that were not subject to regulation. In response to financial system's circumvention of Regulation Q, Congress enacted two pieces of legislation: the Depository Institutions Deregulation and Monetary Control Act of 1980 (DIDMCA) and the Garn–St. Germain Act of 1982.

DIDMCA. With passage of the **Depository Institutions Deregulation and Monetary Control Act of 1980,** Congress eased the anticompetitive burden on banks and helped to provide fairness in the financial services industry. The act eliminated interest rate ceilings (known as *usury ceilings*) on mortgage loans and certain types of commercial loans. It also provided for uniform reserve requirements and access to Federal Reserve System services (such as discount loans and check clearing) for all depository institutions. In addition, DIDMCA permitted banks throughout the United States to offer NOW and ATS accounts, thereby allowing banks to compete with money market mutual funds. The effect of this change was dramatic: NOW and ATS deposits rose almost fourfold—from \$27 billion to \$101 billion—between 1980 and 1982. Also, DIDMCA phased out Regulation Q gradually from 1980 to 1986. As a result, DIDMCA was popular both with banks that were eager to compete and with depositors who were eager to earn interest on deposits.

Other depository institutions received benefits, too (in return for their political support of the legislation). The act allowed S&Ls and mutual savings banks to broaden their lending beyond mortgages. Savings and loan associations were allowed to invest as much as 20% of their assets in corporate bonds, commercial paper, and consumer loans; they also were allowed to expand into credit card lending and trust services. Mutual savings banks were permitted to compete with commercial banks by making commercial loans (for up to 5% of their assets) and accepting checkable deposits in connection with their loans.

However, the DIDMCA phaseout of interest rate ceilings was not a cure-all for financial institutions. Because Regulation Q was eliminated only gradually, money market mutual funds continued to expand at the expense of S&Ls and mutual savings banks; by post–World War II standards, an unprecedented number of S&Ls and mutual savings banks failed (250 in 1982 alone). Regulatory change to address this problem soon followed.

Garn–St. Germain Act. Congress passed the **Garn–St. Germain Act of 1982** to combat problems caused by the gradual demise of Regulation Q under

DIDMCA. To give them a more potent weapon against money market mutual funds, the act permitted depository institutions to offer savers federally insured **money market deposit accounts** (MMDAs), which provide services similar to those of money market mutual funds. These accounts were subject neither to reserve requirements nor to Regulation Q ceilings. The combination of market interest rates and the safety and familiarity of banks made the new accounts an instant success.

To solve the special problems facing savings institutions, the Garn–St. Germain Act broadened the ability of federally chartered savings institutions to invest in areas other than mortgages (as much as 30% of their assets in consumer loans and 10% in commercial loans by 1984). Because these changes made savings institutions comparable to banks, the act required that (as of 1984) Regulation Q ceilings be applied uniformly to all depository institutions until the ceilings expired in 1986.

Concluding Remarks

The landmark DIDMCA and Garn–St. Germain legislation placed the banking industry on a more equal footing with its competitors. However, the Garn–St. Germain Act moved savings institutions from the usually calm waters of mortgage lending into the choppy waters of bank lending. Figure 15.2 summarizes the process of financial crisis, regulation, financial system response, and regulatory response as it applies to interest rate ceilings. Liberalization of deposit

Figure 15.2 **Interest Rate Ceilings: Crisis, Regulation, Financial System Response, and Regulatory Response**

Regulation Q imposed interest rate ceilings on bank deposits. Beginning in the late 1960s, nonbank financial firms created innovations that enabled savers to earn higher returns. These innovations allowed nonbanks to gain a competitive advantage in providing liquidity services and lending. Financial innovation by banks and regulatory changes allowed banks to compete more effectively against nonbanks.

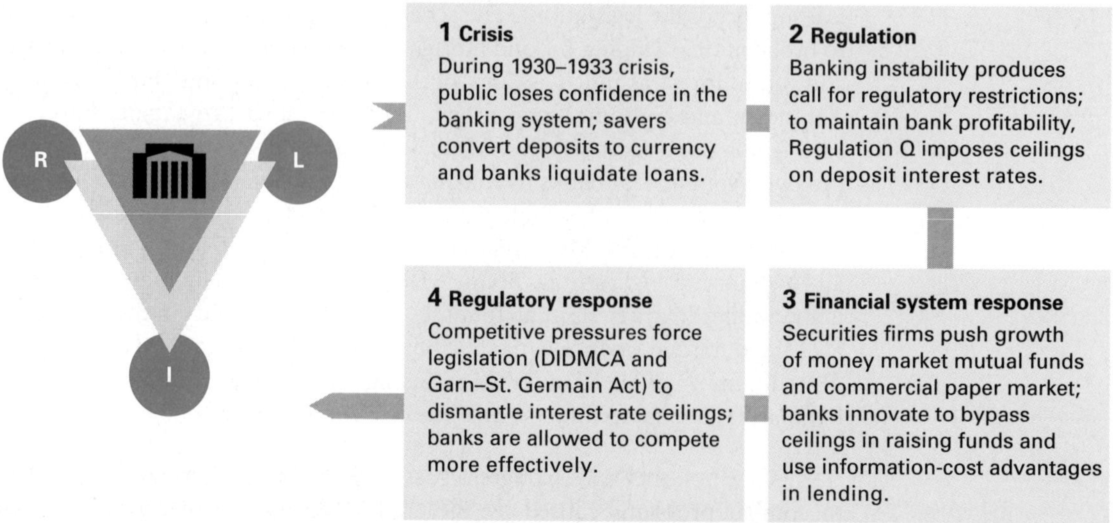

interest rate ceilings in European countries and Japan also illustrates the interplay between financial innovation and financial regulation.

THE U.S. DEPOSIT INSURANCE CRISIS OF THE 1980S

Introduced in response to the banking crises of the 1930s, federal deposit insurance functioned smoothly from its inception in 1934 until the early 1980s. Economists and politicians hoped that bank runs could be consigned to the history books and that the economic costs of a collapsing banking system could be avoided. However, beginning in the 1970s, unnoticed problems were building. The first of the depository institutions to exhibit signs of trouble were S&Ls; next were banks. The lessons of these episodes are currently shaping the activities and regulation of virtually all financial institutions, banks and nonbanks alike.

Beginning of the Crisis: Worsening Conditions in S&Ls

While the origins of federal deposit insurance lie in the 1930s, the stages of crisis and response that we study begin much later. In particular, the story unfolds in two parts. One relates to the outmoded structure of S&Ls (also called *thrifts*), and the other relates to the financial innovation and regulatory changes in the 1970s and early 1980s (discussed in the preceding section).

To promote mortgage lending, banking regulation created S&Ls in the 1930s from the remnants of building and loan societies (many of which had failed). These institutions held long-term, fixed-rate mortgages and financed them with short-term time deposits. As long as interest rates were stable and regulation limited interest payments to depositors (the situation from the 1930s through much of the 1960s), little went wrong. However, the mismatch between the maturities of S&Ls' assets and those of their liabilities created the potential for interest rate risk.

Some episodes of rising market interest rates worried S&Ls in the 1960s and 1970s. However, the real trouble began as U.S. interest rates rose dramatically in late 1979. As a result, the cost of funds for S&Ls escalated, the present value of their existing mortgage assets plummeted, and their net worth declined precipitously. At about the same time, the 1981–1982 recession raised default rates on mortgages, particularly for S&Ls that were located in farm or energy-producing states (such as Texas), where conditions were especially bad. About half the S&Ls had a negative net worth by the end of 1982. Our analysis of moral hazard suggests that this condition should have sounded a warning for deposit insurance. Because savers' deposits (to a regulated amount) were guaranteed by the Federal Savings and Loan Insurance Corporation (FSLIC), managers of S&Ls were strongly tempted to engage in riskier investments.

Financial System Response

Recall, however, that in the early 1980s, Congress tried to help S&Ls by relaxing restrictions on their asset holdings. In making these regulatory changes,

Congress intended to allow S&Ls to diversify and combat exposure to interest rate risk by making available new assets, including direct real estate investments, commercial mortgages, and junk bonds. Many S&Ls took advantage of these opportunities. By the early 1990s, S&Ls (originally created to bolster mortgage lending) accounted for fewer than half of U.S. mortgage loans.

In 1980, DIDMCA raised the federal deposit insurance ceiling from $40,000 per account to $100,000 per account, even as the phaseout of Regulation Q increased S&Ls' costs of funds. Now S&Ls could issue insured CDs in larger amounts at high interest rates, with the proceeds invested in risky assets. Our analysis of the costs of adverse selection cautions the *uninsured* saver to be wary of the promise of higher yields (as it brings with it greater risks). Insured depositors flocked to the higher yields because the government guaranteed their deposits. To make matters worse, financial innovators effectively raised the deposit insurance limit many times over by creating **brokered deposits.** In a brokered deposit, a depositor with $1 million goes to a broker, who buys ten $100,000 CDs in ten different banks, giving the depositor ten different bank accounts with insurance on the entire $1 million. Federal authorities banned brokered deposits in 1984, but a federal court decision later reversed the ban.

Moreover, many S&Ls did not manage their assets and liabilities to reduce their exposure to interest rate risk. In principle, savings institutions could have lessened interest rate risk by using variable-rate mortgages, known as *adjustable-rate mortgages* (ARMs). The lender adjusts the mortgage interest rate when market interest rates rise or fall, thereby cushioning the effects of interest rate changes on the institution's net worth. Although ARMs now are popular in mortgage lending, they haven't been a cure-all for at least two reasons. First, the indexes on which they are based are imperfect, and rate adjustment is normally subject to both annual and mortgage term caps. Second, an ARM may increase credit risk. Significant increases in monthly payments may increase the risk of borrower default. That is, payments being held constant, the loan balance could balloon to more than the collateral value of the loan. During the 1980s, S&Ls also made little use of other risk-sharing devices that were available to them. This circumstance isn't really surprising: Moral hazard problems suggest that depository institutions with low net worth have an incentive to increase risky behavior rather than decrease exposure to interest rate risk.

Finally, many analysts blame lax regulatory supervision during the 1980s for encouraging fraud and prolonging the crisis. Some S&L executives used savers' deposits to fund lavish lifestyles or simply embezzled funds. For example, the First Network Savings Bank, whose failure in 1990 cost federal deposit insurance agencies 25 cents on each dollar of deposits, used deposits to build the world's largest "museum of magic" at its headquarters. In another notorious case, S&L entrepreneur Don Dixon was convicted of embezzling bank funds, which he spent on prostitutes, hot tubs, and designer shotguns. Dixon went to jail, but taxpayers paid for the 96% of his S&L's loans that had defaulted.

To avoid bankrupting its reserves, the Federal Home Loan Bank Board (FHLBB) and its deposit insurance subsidiary, the FSLIC, allowed insolvent S&Ls to continue to operate. The cost of closing insolvent S&Ls quickly escalated in the late 1980s and early 1990s. Economists have estimated that the costs to the FSLIC of closing the insolvent S&Ls in 1982 would have been about $20 billion. Although this number is small relative to the costs of the crisis by the 1990s (hundreds of billions of dollars), it was greater than the reserves the FSLIC had built up since 1934. Even so, the FSLIC could have made a credible deposit insurance guarantee based on the implicit backing of the Treasury and the Fed.

To understand the escalation of costs, let's consider how insolvent institutions avoided closure. In the process of evaluating nonfinancial businesses, analysts gauge net worth. To avoid classifying S&Ls as insolvent and depleting deposit insurance funds to reimburse depositors, regulators changed the accounting rules. Instead of estimating economic net worth, they used regulatory accounting principles to allow S&Ls to carry on their books at face value many assets whose value actually had declined because of rising interest rates. In addition, regulators gave S&Ls an inflated value for goodwill, the intangible value of the institution as a going concern. In 1982, total industry net worth was reported at 3.7% of assets under regulatory accounting principles. Had the assets been measured at market value, the industry's net worth would have been –12%. As a result of such calculations, many insolvent or nearly insolvent S&Ls continued to operate, rather than being closed by the FSLIC.

Although deposit insurance reduces the need for individual depositors to monitor banks, the principal-agent problem doesn't disappear. Bank regulators act as agents for the taxpayers who are the principals; taxpayers collectively bear the costs of deposit insurance bailouts. However, as studies by Edward Kane of Boston College have stressed, regulators' incentives differ from those of taxpayers. Regulators hold their positions for relatively short periods of time, so they have an incentive to loosen capital requirements and supervision at the first sign of trouble. They don't want troubled institutions to fail under their supervision. Regulators also have an incentive to pay more attention to elected lawmakers who can influence their careers than to taxpayers.

A good example of the principal-agent problem is the "Keating Five" scandal in 1990. Charles Keating, an S&L entrepreneur, contributed about $1.3 million to the campaigns of five U.S. Senators in return for their assistance in getting FHLBB Chairman Edwin Gray to deal lightly with the problems of Keating's Lincoln Savings and Loan in 1987. Lincoln operated with severe financial problems until its failure in 1989, costing taxpayers about $2.5 billion. The Senators who should have acted on behalf of the taxpayers instead accepted contributions from Keating. Keating and his son were convicted in 1992 on numerous counts of fraud and betrayal of fiduciary trust by both state and federal courts.

Regulatory Response: The S&L Bailout

By the end of 1986, losses in the S&L industry had wiped out the FSLIC's reserves. President Reagan requested $15 billion for FSLIC, an amount that analysts decried as inadequate. In the Competitive Equality Banking Act of 1987, Congress gave the administration even less than its request. Deprived of funds to resolve the situation, the FHLBB allowed insolvent institutions to continue operating, paying high interest rates to attract more funds guaranteed by deposit insurance.

Lack of decisive action brought disaster, with actual thrift losses approaching $20 billion by 1989. In January 1989, the FSLIC reported to Congress that 350 federally insured S&Ls were insolvent. Initial estimates of the costs of meeting obligations to insured depositors exceeded $90 billion. Because these estimates referred to costs net of recoveries from asset sales, the initial outlays needed to close insolvent institutions would be much greater. At the same time, William Seidman, then chairman of the FDIC, estimated that ultimately, more than 700 FSLIC-insured S&Ls with combined assets of $400 billion would have to be reorganized or liquidated.

The incoming Bush administration and Congress mandated reform in the **Financial Institutions Reform, Recovery, and Enforcement Act of 1989** (FIRREA), the most comprehensive legislation for the S&L industry since the 1930s. The act eliminated the FSLIC, the separate deposit insurance authority for S&Ls, and formed the Resolution Trust Corporation (RTC) to handle thrift insolvencies and to sell off the more than $456 billion of real estate owned by failed S&Ls. The RTC Oversight Board—made up of the Secretary of the Treasury (as chairperson), the Chairman of the Board of Governors of the Federal Reserve System, the Secretary of Housing and Urban Development, and two other appointees—supervised the RTC; the FDIC managed the RTC. On December 31, 1995, the RTC ceased operations—one year ahead of schedule—having liquidated the assets of failed institutions. The total cost of the thrift cleanup was $145 billion.

The act also created the Resolution Funding Corporation and authorized it to borrow funds to cover insolvencies. The FDIC organized a new deposit insurance fund, the Savings Association Insurance Fund (SAIF), for the S&L industry. Finally, FIRREA mandated uniform capital requirements and accounting and disclosure standards for commercial banks and savings institutions. S&Ls are now supervised and examined by the Office of Thrift Supervision (OTS), an arm of the Treasury Department. Its responsibilities are similar to those the Treasury's Office of the Comptroller of the Currency has for national banks.

To restore SAIF reserves, the FDIC raised the deposit insurance premiums of S&Ls from 20.8 cents per $100 of deposits to 23 cents and then to 32.5 cents. It raised bank deposit insurance premiums from 8.3 cents to 15 cents per $100 of deposits, with an additional increase to 23 cents in 1991 and, depending on bank riskiness, to as high as 31 cents (with an average of 25.4 cents) in 1993; in the summer of 1995, bank premiums were cut to as low as 4 cents per $100 of deposits. In November 1995, bank deposit insurance premiums were replaced for most banks with a flat $2000 annual fee, though savings institutions continued to pay 23 cents per $100 of deposits.

The 1989 legislation also reregulated investment activities of S&Ls, which had been deregulated under DIDMCA in 1980 and the Garn–St. Germain Act in 1982. It mandated that junk bond holdings be sold off by 1994 and tightened rules for other lending activities. It limited loans for commercial real estate to four times the institution's equity capital rather than to 40% of assets (which applied most severely to institutions with capital equal to less than 10% of assets). The act required that housing-related investments be at least 70% (instead of at least 60%) of total assets. Because low net worth was one reason for the onset of the S&L crisis, FIRREA raised capital requirements for S&Ls from 3% to 8% of assets, eventually conforming to risk-based capital standards mandated for commercial banks. Finally, it gave regulators broader authority to issue cease-and-desist orders, impose civil penalties, and fire managers. At the same time, it allocated an extra $75 million each year for three years to the Justice Department to aid regulators and law enforcement officials in investigating and prosecuting fraud.

On the one hand, FIRREA dealt successfully with the S&L crisis by providing substantial resources to close insolvent institutions. On the other hand, many analysts believe that the act imposed severe restrictions on depository institutions without satisfactorily addressing adverse selection and moral hazard arising from federal deposit insurance.

The Congressional Budget Office estimated in the early 1990s that the present value of the cost of the S&L debacle through the year 2000 could be as much as $200 billion in 1992 dollars. The vast sums spent in resolving this crisis are transfers from taxpayers to depositors and not a loss of current output for the economy. However, they have caused inefficiency in the economy by diverting the nation's savings in the 1980s from productive investment financed from uninsured sources to less productive investment funded by insured deposits. This large-scale financial inefficiency raises the question: Can the same thing happen in the commercial banking industry?

The Widening Crisis: Commercial Banks

Like S&Ls, commercial banks in the United States prospered greatly between the Great Depression and the mid-1970s. Regulation protected bank profitability. Branching restrictions limited competition faced by local bankers. Regulation Q granted protection against competition by limiting payments to depositors and guaranteed a healthy margin between loan and deposit rates. Thus, owing to regulation, banks were earning above-normal profits, and their markets were protected from entry. The potential for interest rate risk was low.

As in the S&L industry, recall that the pace of financial innovation in commercial banking accelerated in the 1960s and 1970s, owing in large part to the desire to circumvent protective regulation. Increased competition resulting from financial innovation outside the banking industry reduced the value of a key part of banks' net worth: the market power associated with the value of bank charters.

As interest rates rose in the 1970s and early 1980s and the cost of funds to banks climbed, asset portfolios had to earn more income to maintain profitability. The quest for profitability forced banks to accept riskier loans in energy production, real estate, debt issued by developing countries, and agriculture. The two recessions of the early 1980s caused a substantial number of defaults and business failures. Lack of diversification left many groups of banks particularly susceptible (lenders to energy producers in the Southwest and lenders to agriculture and import-sensitive manufacturing in the Midwest, for example). When oil and agricultural commodity prices fell in the 1980s, loans in these sectors declined in value.

Volatile interest rates and exchange rates also took their toll on banks' net worth. Because interest rate risk and exchange rate risk had been small in the past, banks had made few preparations for greater risk. Some bank failures in the 1970s resulted from these risks, however. For example, the Franklin National Bank had tried to increase net worth by speculating in foreign currencies and lengthening the maturity of its assets. Collapse of the dollar and a significant increase in interest rates caused the bank's failure in 1974.

During the late 1980s and early 1990s, banks found themselves exposed to risk through their investment in *highly leveraged transactions* (HLTs), in which banks financed buyouts of firms by their managers or other investors. Some large banks lost heavily on HLT loans to financiers such as Robert Campeau and Donald Trump who ran into financial trouble. The fall in commercial real estate prices in New York, Boston, and other large cities bankrupted some prominent real estate developers, leaving banks with overvalued, empty office buildings and property in the midst of the recession.

During the 1980s, FDIC policy was not too successful in dealing with large-bank insolvencies. Tough with small banks, the FDIC relied primarily on the purchase-and-assumption method to make sure that no depositors and creditors lost money when large banks became insolvent.† Examples include the \$1.7 billion bailout of Continental Illinois in 1984 and the \$3 billion bailout of the First Republic Bank of Dallas in 1988. Many analysts expressed concern that FDIC protection of all deposits at large banks created a belief within large banks that the FDIC considered them *too big to fail*. This belief may have led to increased risk taking by large banks. We return to this problem later.

During the 1980s, branching restrictions limited diversification, which

† Since 1970, only about 25% of bank failures have been resolved by using the payoff method. The banks involved have generally been small, the largest being Penn Square Bank in Oklahoma, which failed in 1982. Between 1985 and 1990—the period with the greatest number of bank failures since the 1930s—full protection by deposit insurance was extended to more than 99% of *uninsured* deposits.

exposed banks to greater credit risk in their loan portfolios. For example, during the oil boom in the 1970s, Texas commercial banks grew significantly and were among the most profitable in the United States. Texas's branching restrictions limited banks to a single full-service location. With limited ability to diversify beyond local energy-related loans, Texas banks suffered greatly when the price of oil plummeted in the 1980s. By 1990, nine of the top ten banks in Texas at the beginning of the decade had gone out of business or had been acquired.

Bank failures remained a problem for the FDIC in the early 1990s as the FDIC, the Treasury Department, and Congress grappled with finding a solution. Although the number of bank failures fell from 205 in 1989 to 104 in 1991, the assets of failed banks in 1991 were $46.7 billion, or 50% more than the figure for 1989. By 1994, bank and thrift failures had become much rarer (only 48 banks from 1994 through 2000), although some analysts worried about banks' ability to cope with increasing competition from nonbank financial institutions.

The United States isn't the only country facing deposit insurance problems. The Japanese banking industry experienced turmoil in the 1990s and early in the new century as well, as several large credit unions failed. In France, taxpayers rescued the state-owned Crédit Lyonnais, whose aggressive lending and weak capital resembled those of the U.S. S&Ls of the 1980s.

Options for Regulatory Reform

The principles of insurance management (Chapter 12) suggest several options for banking industry regulatory reform. The options include changes in insurance coverage, insurance pricing, the scope of bank activities, regulatory supervision, and capital requirements.

Insurance coverage. One proposal for reform is to reduce the level of deposit insurance coverage. The lower the amount of deposits covered, the greater is the incentive for depositors to monitor banks. However, the economic rationale for deposit insurance is aimed as much at protecting the economy from the cost of banking panics as at protecting small or large depositors. Indeed, the speed with which uninsured depositors can now move their funds increases the likelihood of a bank run at the first hint of bad news.

This connection between insurance coverage and the likelihood of a run explains the FDIC's handling of large-bank insolvencies. For example, when Continental Illinois became insolvent in 1984, the FDIC guaranteed all deposits—insured and uninsured—and even made sure that no Continental bondholder lost money. Afterward, the Comptroller of the Currency informed Congress that the FDIC maintained a list of banks that it deemed "too big to fail." In these cases, the FDIC would ensure that no depositor or creditor lost money.

The too-big-to-fail policy weakens the desire of large depositors to incur the costs of monitoring a bank. For example, if large deposits were uninsured and large depositors thought that the FDIC would use the payoff method to deal with insolvent banks (closing the bank, paying off insured depositors, and using any remaining funds to pay uninsured depositors), they would monitor banks' lending practices closely. As a result, banks would be less likely to engage in very risky activities. Hence reducing insurance coverage provides a check on bank risk taking.

Moreover, the too-big-to-fail policy is unfair, because it treats small and large banks differently. When the FDIC closed the minority-owned Harlem's Freedom National Bank in 1990 (with less than $100 million of deposits), its large depositors—including such charitable organizations as the United Negro College Fund and the Urban League—received only about 50 cents per dollar of uninsured deposits. Only a few months later, in January 1991, the much larger Bank of New England failed as a result of a collapse in the value of its real estate portfolio. Its large depositors were fully protected by the FDIC, costing taxpayers about $2.3 billion.

FDICIA narrowed significantly the too-big-to-fail distinction to cases in which a failure would generate "serious adverse effects on economic conditions or financial stability." In such a case, two-thirds of the FDIC's directors and the Board of Governors of the Federal Reserve System, joined by the Secretary of the Treasury, would have to approve. The Fed would also be called on to share losses incurred by the FDIC if the Fed's lending to a bank magnified the FDIC's losses.

This improvement notwithstanding, bank regulators are not likely to allow a very large bank to fail; to do so might lead to a banking panic. Regulatory authorities also have been cool to the use of coinsurance, in which depositors have only partial insurance coverage (Chapter 12). Although coinsurance (say, paying off depositors at 85 cents per dollar) would encourage depositors to monitor banks, the problem of bank runs remains. In the early and mid-1990s, regulators instead stressed the need for better ongoing supervision of banks' activities, along with the authority to force banks to stop engaging in certain activities.

Narrow banking. In the late 1980s, some economists proposed **narrow banking**—that is, insuring only deposits in safe assets such as T-bills or high-quality commercial paper, as a method of deposit insurance reform. (Because of the low risk that is inherent in such assets, deposit insurance would be redundant but could promote public confidence.) Banks would make loans from bank equity and raise funds through risky securities. These funds would not be insured, and fewer limits would be placed on the scope of bank activities, sharply reducing moral hazard. However, these proposals would severely curtail the information-gathering and monitoring activities that are essential to bank lending. Because some borrowers have few alternatives to bank deposits, narrow banking could reduce these borrowers' access to the financial system. For a bank to make new loans, old loans would have to be sold or new funds would have to be attracted.

Private deposit insurance. Several economists have suggested that deposit insurance be provided by private insurance companies, at least for deposits greater than the $100,000 ceiling covered by the FDIC. This option would provide an incentive for the private insurer to monitor the banks whose deposits are insured. However, a private insurer probably wouldn't be able to pay off depositors during a general banking crisis. As a result, the problems of bank runs and banking panics remain. Although private insurance alone cannot substitute for federal deposit insurance, economists and policymakers increasingly are offering suggestions that combine private insurance arrangements with a lender-of-last-resort role by the Fed to reduce the chance of a financial crisis.

Risk-based pricing of deposit insurance. Another option for reform is to make deposit insurance premiums reflect risk, as they do in automobile or fire insurance, so that banks would bear more of the risk associated with their lending decisions. A safe bank would pay a low premium, and a risky bank would pay a high premium. However, evaluating risk isn't easy. Assigning market values to some bank loans can be quite difficult. Moreover, risk can be assessed easily after the fact by examining operating income or losses, but risk-based pricing of deposit insurance must be forward-looking to be useful—a much more difficult task.

Risk-based pricing of deposit insurance was mandated in the **Federal Deposit Insurance Corporation Improvement Act of 1991** (FDICIA), which established risk groups according to how well capitalized the bank is. In September 1992, the FDIC voted to implement risk-based premiums for the first time in the history of deposit insurance. These premiums became effective in January 1993, ranging from 23 cents per $100 for well-capitalized banks with no supervisory problems to 31 cents per $100 of deposits for less than adequately capitalized institutions with substantial supervisory problems. Most banks paid the lowest rate, although some large banks (including Citibank) initially paid higher premiums under the new system. Premiums were reduced substantially for all risk classes in late 1995.

Supervision. Passage of FIRREA gave the FDIC more supervisory responsibility. The act requires the FDIC as insurer to monitor the evaluation of a depository institution's federal or state supervisor. It broadens the authority of regulators to intervene in bank management, especially at poorly capitalized banks. New regulatory powers include the ability to set dividend payments and executive pay at poorly capitalized banks and to hire and fire managers in some cases. Proponents say that the new procedures will encourage better management because well-capitalized banks are exempt from the most severe restrictions. Opponents argue that the fear of regulatory intrusion will discourage banks from making commercial loans and encourage them to invest deposits in Treasury securities, thereby diminishing banks' role as intermediaries. How banks, which—after 1999—could participate in a broader range of activities, adjust to the regulations will continue to shape the banking industry during the beginning decade of the new century.

Capital requirements. Moral hazard occurs when banks seek to use their equity capital in risky ventures in an attempt to increase their return on equity. Setting higher minimum capital requirements reduces the potential for moral hazard and the cost to the FDIC of bank failures. As we noted earlier, FIRREA has moved toward reducing moral hazard for S&Ls.

A bank's equity capital is its cushion for paying depositors if its assets decline in value. Minimum capital requirements reduce the likelihood that banks will engage in risky activities. These requirements are set by using *historical cost,* or *book-value,* measures. When assets are valued by using historical cost, changes in the market values of a bank's assets and liabilities (owing to changes in, say, default risk or market interest rates) don't affect the calculation by regulatory authorities of a bank's net worth. This measurement difference is significant because changes in market values of assets and liabilities are precisely what tell depositors and investors when shifts occur in the true value of banks' equity capital. The shifts in market value also set the incentives for moral hazard.

Many economists support the use of *market-value accounting* in calculating minimum capital requirements. Periodically (say, once each quarter), regulators could determine the market value of a bank's assets and liabilities and whether its market-value capital (the difference between the market values of its assets and its liabilities) meets minimum capital requirements. If not, the FDIC would be informed, and the bank would be closed before its market-value net worth became negative. This action would prevent both a loss to the FDIC and excessive risk taking by the bank. Although only an approximation, market-value assessments can highlight a bank's financial condition to bank regulators—and to shareholders and creditors. The push toward more market-value accounting for measuring banks' equity capital has continued during the 1990s, and economists are researching practical ways of implementing market-value accounting.

Another goal of regulators is to assess accurately the risk to which banks are exposed. The 1988 Basle capital standards (Chapter 14) used credit risk to classify bank assets and off-balance-sheet activities. The bank's risk-weighted assets equal the sum of its risk-weighted components. Banks' capital requirements are defined relative to risk-weighted assets. FDICIA authorized the FDIC to use capital-adequacy categories to limit banks' participation in certain activities.

These risk-based capital standards assess only credit risk and ignore interest rate risk. For example, if banks reduced their investments in short-term commercial and industrial loans and increased their investments in long-term Treasury securities, they would substitute interest rate risk for credit risk. On April 30, 1993, banking supervisors from industrialized countries agreed in Basle to propose internationally coordinated capital requirements linked to interest rate risk and exchange rate risk. Responding to the fast pace of market developments, in April 1995, that group of supervisors proposed that financial institutions develop their own risk-assessment procedures subject to regulatory review (see also Chapter 14). Further modifications of the Basle risk-based capital requirements were proposed in January 2001.

FDICIA implemented a "prompt corrective action" rule, which mandated that the FDIC and other regulators take action if a bank's capital falls below the required level. For example, regulations require closure or conservatorship within 90 days for the weakest institutions. By directing the FDIC to shut down institutions when their net worth is less than 2% of assets rather than delaying until net worth becomes negative, this requirement decreases potential FDIC (taxpayer) losses and limits the scope for moral hazard. Although the requirement reduces the likelihood of the long delays that were experienced in closing weak institutions in the S&L crisis, regulators must still confront the problem that book-value measures of bank capital do not accurately measure market-value net worth.

Current Issues in Regulatory Reform

In February 1991, the U.S. Treasury Department suggested numerous regulatory reforms for the banking system. These proposals addressed many of the regulations that we have discussed, including anticompetitive restrictions, deposit insurance coverage, and supervision. The department also suggested that banking regulation be more closely linked to bank capital, a proposal that was adopted in part in FDICIA. Many economists believe that the steps taken in FDICIA need to be extended to decrease further the chance of another deposit insurance crisis.

Two major changes in other banking regulations are likely to mitigate future problems in deposit insurance. First, regulations that relax branching restrictions will encourage banks to diversify their assets and reduce the likelihood of a banking crisis. Bank failures during the 1980s were concentrated in states with branching restrictions and in banks that concentrated their loans in particular industries, such as oil (Texas) or agriculture (Kansas). States' liberalization of branching laws and the passage of the federal Riegle-Neal Interstate Banking and Branching Efficiency Act of 1994 have made nationwide banking possible.

Second, some analysts view regulatory overlap as a problem because regulations are complex and regulators duplicate one another's efforts. Currently, four federal agencies share bank supervision. These agencies are the Office of the Comptroller of the Currency, the Federal Reserve, the FDIC, and the Office of Thrift Supervision. In 1994, the Clinton administration unveiled a proposal to create a banking superregulation, combining the supervisory responsibilities of the four federal regulatory agencies. The Fed strongly opposed the proposal, and Fed Chairman Greenspan outlined an alternative: reduce the present four supervisory agencies to two (merge OCC and OTS, and strip the FDIC of all but insurance responsibilities), and expand the Fed's role. The Fed offered a sensible criticism of the Clinton plan: Divorced from collecting information from banks, the Fed would find it harder to forestall and address financial crises. As of early 2001, the Fed, the Treasury, and the Congress were still debating the course of regulatory consolidation in the aftermath of the Gramm-Leach-Bliley Act of 1999.

Concluding Remarks

The deposit insurance crisis and its aftermath illustrate the stages of financial crisis, regulation, financial system response, and regulatory response, as depicted in Fig. 15.3. Recent reforms in deposit insurance and likely reforms in other areas of banking regulation generally allow banks to maintain their intermediary role in matching savers and borrowers. The government would permit regulatory intervention when a crisis threatened the entire banking system. Future comprehensive reform of U.S. banking regulation likely will increase the power of the Fed as the lender of last resort and of bank regulators as monitors.

The United States is not unique in relying on its central bank to manage banking crises and in insuring savers' deposits. Although most industrialized countries (and several developing countries) now have deposit insurance systems, deposit insurance authorities resolve bank failures differently. In the United States, the FDIC assumes the lead in handling financially distressed banks. In most other countries, private banks bear more of the costs of

Figure 15.3

Deposit Insurance: Crisis, Regulation, Financial System Response, and Regulatory Response

Federal deposit insurance was introduced in response to bank runs in the early 1930s. Information problems led to a crisis in deposit insurance in the 1980s, which in turn led to regulatory reform.

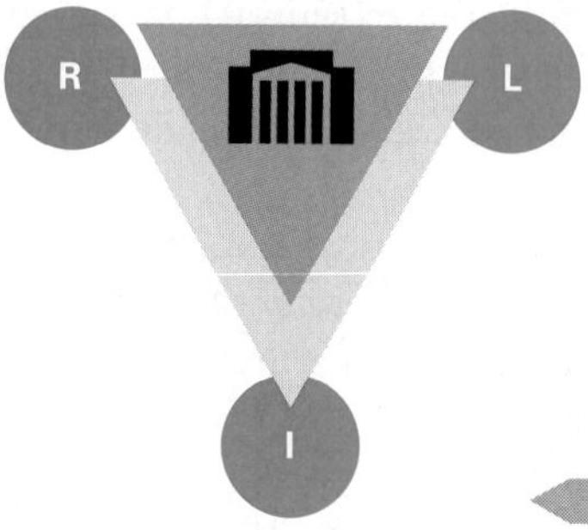

1 Crisis
In the 1960s and 1970s, rising interest rates threaten S&Ls and banks with interest rate risk; the 1981–1982 recession causes high default rates on mortgages.

2 Regulation
Congress relaxes restrictions on the type of assets S&Ls and banks can own, and it raises the federal deposit insurance ceiling.

3 Financial system response
S&Ls and banks increase risk taking, including real estate investments, commercial mortgages, and junk bonds; savers use brokered deposits to ensure deposit protection.

4 Regulatory response
Lack of decisive action on failing thrifts increases the amount of money needed to pay insured depositors: Deposit insurance reform in FIRREA and FDICIA brought more stringent capital requirements, closer supervision, and reform of regulatory authorities.

OTHER TIMES, OTHER PLACES . . .

The Cycle of Crisis and Response: Russia and Japan

We can use the framework of crisis and response to explain the aftermath of financial crises in other countries, such as Russia and Japan. (Regulatory liberalization and inadequate financial supervision also played a role in the Asian financial crisis of 1997, as we will see in Chapter 22.)

Russia. Prior to the fall of communism in the Soviet Union, banks were owned by the government. When the Russian economy jettisoned communist controls, banks had little experience in addressing adverse selection and moral hazard in private lending markets, and Russian authorities had little expertise in monitoring market-oriented lenders. The seeds of a banking crisis were thus sown. The crisis arrived with full force on August 24, 1995, when fears over banks' solvency led to a collapse of the interbank loan market and government intervention. Three years later, the government restricted repayment of foreign debt to husband resources in the troubled banking sector. By the turn of the century, the Russian central bank noted that a large bailout would be required to compensate stakeholders of the almost half of all banks that were deemed likely to fail. This bailout would be accompanied by substantial regulatory intervention. Whether this intervention heads off the next banking crisis depends on bankers' and investors' incentives to reduce costs of adverse selection and moral hazard.

Japan. In the case of Japan, post–World War II regulations led to a segmented financial system that placed strict limits on activities of banks and securities firms. Financial deregulation in the 1980s, along with lax regulatory oversight, precipitated a boom in risky loans in real estate. The collapse of the Japanese property market in the early 1990s left banks with large loan losses and weak capital positions. The second half of the 1990s witnessed the first bank failures in Japan since World War II, with failures of Cosmo Credit Corporation, Kizu Credit Cooperative, Hanwa Bank, and Hokkaido Takushoku Bank. The megamerger of the Bank of Tokyo and Mitsubishi Bank was designed to shore up the profitability of those institutions.

The regulatory response in Japan largely resembled that of the United States in the 1980s. While capital adequacy standards were nominally in place, Ministry of Finance regulations permitted banks to inflate the value of their assets (by carrying them at historical cost as opposed to current market value) to meet capital standards. Allowing weak banks to continue operating engendered a financial system response of further increases in risk taking.

By 1998, the Japanese government was forced to intervene, and supervisory authority over banks was awarded to the Financial Supervisory Agency (FSA), which reported to the Prime Minister rather than the Ministry of Finance. This change was accompanied by a bailout package of ¥60 trillion (about $500 billion). The jury is still out on future financial system responses, however, because the closure of insolvent banks is not necessarily required. Nonetheless, the government's seizure in late 1998 of the large Long-Term Credit Bank of Japan, which was subsequently sold to a group of U.S. investors, was a promising sign of reform. Financial regulation reforms announced in 2001 were viewed as less promising signs.

resolving failures but are backed by the central bank as the lender of last resort in the event of a general banking crisis. Some analysts believe that the relatively small number of banks in other countries allows private banks in those countries to monitor one another more closely in private insurance arrangements.

LESSONS FROM BANKING REGULATION FOR OTHER INSTITUTIONS

Our analysis of financial crisis, regulation, financial system response, and regulatory response in the banking industry offers lessons that can be extended to other financial institutions. Let's now consider current and likely future developments in the regulation of insurance companies and private pension funds, both of which face problems similar to those of banks.

Insurance Regulation

The distinction between banks and insurance companies for regulatory purposes may be outdated. Like banks, insurance companies are financial institutions that accept funds from individuals in return for promises to repay. Just as banks are connected through interbank money markets and loan sales, insurers are linked through risk-sharing arrangements known as reinsurance. One important difference between banks and insurance companies is that no federal program corresponding to deposit insurance is available to the insurance industry.

Developments in the insurance industry have paralleled those in the banking industry. Property and casualty companies experienced a crisis in the late 1800s by underpricing policies and then going broke after several major disasters occurred. Life insurance companies were protected from price competition by restrictions imposed by state regulation in New York (the headquarters of many large insurance companies). In the 1930s and after World War II, Congress attempted to provide stability in the insurance industry. Most notable was the McCarran-Ferguson Act of 1945, which explicitly protected insurers from prosecution under federal antitrust laws. Rapidly rising interest rates in the late 1970s made savers and investors more aware of nonbank opportunities, and financial deregulation broadened their options. Life insurance firms offered higher-yield investment options than banks, but the high yields paid to investors reduced profits significantly. Property and casualty firms competed for premium revenue to invest at record returns, only to discover that even those returns were not enough when record claims came flooding in.

The insurance industry in the 1990s is undergoing change like that in banking. In the aftermath of the catastrophic Executive Life Insurance Company failure early in the decade, which nearly led to a life insurance run, government regulators imposed risk-based capital requirements. The requirements, effective in 1994, were created by the National Association of Insurance Commissioners, a group of state insurance commissioners that designs uniform standards for the industry. The higher the calculated risk levels, the more capital an insurer must have on its balance sheet to support the risks.

In addition, the insurance industry and the federal government have discussed the consolidation of state "guarantee funds," which are similar to deposit insurance to protect policyholders. The funds do not cover all insurers or products. Nationwide, they would amount to only a few billion dollars per year, a small amount compared to the dollars that were needed to bail out ailing S&Ls.

In the aftermath of the multibillion-dollar losses resulting from Hurricane Andrew during September 1992, many analysts questioned the industry's ability to withstand further crises. Some observers believe that any self-regulation should be augmented by a standing national guarantee fund financed by insurance companies or by federal minimum standards for state insurance funds. While the debate over regulation takes place, financial markets are developing new ways to spread catastrophic risks through tradeable securities.

Pension Fund Regulation

Problems arising from deposit insurance protection also apply to pension funds. The Employee Retirement Income Security Act of 1974 (ERISA) created the Pension Benefit Guaranty Corporation (PBGC) to insure defined benefit pensions when companies go bankrupt. (No such need arises for defined contribution plans, which, by definition, are fully funded.) The PBGC is troubled by the hundreds of large underfunded plans that loom as liabilities if the companies offering them fail. In 1992, following the bankruptcies of Eastern Airlines and Pan American Airlines, the PBGC had a deficit of more than $2 billion. The mid-1990s produced better news, as the PBGC estimated that unfunded, government-guaranteed liabilities fell from $71 billion to $31 billion in 1995. Plan funding improved following the passage of the Retirement Protection Act of 1994.

As in the case of deposit insurance, pension fund managers have incentives to take risks if large profits from such risks accrue to the shareholders of the firm (the residual claimants of the plan) and any losses accrue to the PBGC. As the FDIC did in banking, the PBGC proposed reforms to tie insurance premiums to the riskiness of each pension plan. First, the PBGC increased premiums in 1990 and has proposed additional increases. Second, underfunded plans now pay much higher premiums relative to funded plans than they did under earlier law. Third, the PBGC argued that if a company declares bankruptcy, the PBGC should have a higher-priority claim than other creditors to ensure that participants in pension plans get the benefits promised to them. Some economists have even questioned whether the government's PBGC is preferable to private insurance, which could simply adjust rates to reflect the cost of moral hazard in companies' underfunding of pension liabilities.

CHECKPOINT

Suppose that a financially distressed steel manufacturer with large underfunded pension liabilities is insured by the PBGC, which charges premiums that don't reflect differences in risk. The firm's CEO learns about a new steel-making technology that offers a 10% chance of huge profits and a 90% chance of failure. The investment has a negative present value and would bankrupt the firm if it were unsuccessful. Should the company undertake the project? The prospect might be tempting. If the investment pays off, the CEO and other shareholders profit because they are residual claimants of the company's defined benefit plan. If the investment fails, the PBGC must fulfill the pension promises that the company made to its workers. o

MOVING FROM THEORY TO PRACTICE . . .

THE WALL STREET JOURNAL DECEMBER 11, 2000

Crisis and Response in Japan

In a skyscraper overlooking Japan's government district, the commission charged with rescuing this nation's creaky banking system is ready to call it quits.

The Financial Reconstruction Commission, a small emergency agency set up in 1998, poured $80 billion of public money into capital-strapped lenders and forced a wave of bank mergers. It beat back the worst financial panic here in a half-century. . . .

The problem is, Japan's banking crisis won't be anywhere near solved. . . .

Failing to fix it means the world's second-largest economy is vulnerable to a destabilizing crisis, like a wave of financial-institution collapses here that had U.S. leaders sweating bullets two years ago. But even without a collapse, the undercapitalized banks are cutting back on credit to promising young businesses while keeping their weakest borrowers alive with new loans, to avoid taking even-deeper write-offs. This avoids short-term pain but cripples Japan as a whole, by allocating capital where it is least productive. . . .

(a) Why can't Japan end its banking nightmare? For an answer, peer inside the smoke-filled rooms of the nation's parliament, where old-guard politicians opposed to bank reform have killed much of the momentum for change that built up two years ago. At that time, with banks failing and the economy verging on depression, the government launched the Financial Reconstruction Commission with a no-nonsense leader. But he was out in less than a year, followed by a parade of less-resolute chairmen. . . .

Then politicians turned to matters closer to their hearts: the tribal infighting within the LDP [Liberal Democratic Party] that determines which faction holds sway. Prime Minister Keizo Obuchi, in a cabinet shuffle to preserve the delicate balance keeping his faction in power, changed the bank agency's leadership. Bank shares tumbled.

The new man, Michio Ochi, was a fleshy-faced former bureaucrat known mainly for being the son-in-law of a noted former prime minister, a large photo of whom hangs in his office. Still, the 71-year-old didn't sound like a pushover. "We have to complete Japan's financial revival by March 2001," he said upon taking over. "By that deadline, we have to finish the cleanup, and banks are to dispose of their bad loans."

Yet behind the scenes, he was making moves that would slow the cleanup. His predecessor had pushed even small banks to meet global capital standards; Mr. Ochi let drop that a less-strict requirement seemed fine. His predecessor had prodded banks to merge; Mr. Ochi said the state shouldn't force mergers. . . . (b)

As Mr. Ochi sees it, "People have histories, banks have histories. You have to make decisions based on those histories. . . . To decide whether some bank is going to live or die based on a number like the capital-adequacy ratio is, in my opinion, a little rough.". . . . (c)

In the late 1990s and into the new century, Japan's financial institutions endured a financial crisis much as U.S. thrifts did during the 1980s. Deflation and a weak economy caused housing values to fall and reduced the net worth of many housing lenders and some very large banks. Many institutions responded to relatively lax supervision by assuming greater risks and losses. By late 1995, the Ministry of Finance had dealt with the developments in the financial system by instituting sweeping new regulations. A planned bailout of several housing loan companies received a political setback in early January 1996 because the public blamed bankers for the financial crisis. The large bailout announced in October 1998 raised similar concerns. By late 2000, Japan's earlier commitment to switch to a tougher, contemporary U.S.-style deposit insurance regime was mired in politics.

a Lax supervision creates an environment in which banks take excessive risks and may even act fraudulently. (In a celebrated financial scandal of 1995, Daiwa Bank revealed that a bond trader had concealed losses of $1.1 billion over a number of years. Daiwa failed to notify U.S. authorities for weeks. The Federal Reserve eventually suspended Daiwa's license to do business in the United States.) Our economic analysis suggests that the Bank of Japan and the Ministry of Finance should increase both communication with banks and supervision to mitigate the costs of excessive risk taking.

b Recall that in the United States, much of the debate over deposit insurance reform stressed the importance of workable capital requirements. The requirement that banks develop more adequate internal controls for risk management mimics regulatory response in the United States. To be effective, however, internal controls must be assessed periodically by regulators, and penalties for inadequate control must be imposed.

c In the United States, FDICIA emphasized "prompt corrective action." To achieve the goal of balance-sheet restructuring without rewarding past mistakes, Japanese regulators must attempt to apply different standards and supervision to banks according to their net worth and risk exposure. U.S. experience suggests that the success of this approach depends on regulators' ability to penalize banks that are not in compliance.

For further thought . . .

Many foreign investors complain that the Japanese reforms do not emphasize sufficiently the need for full disclosure by banks. If banks fully disclosed their net worth and risk exposure, do you think that the Japanese banking crisis would have been as severe as it was? Explain.

Source: Excerpted from Bill Spindle and Phred Dvorak, "Japanese Bank Reform, Vital to the Economy, Snags on Political Reef," *The Wall Street Journal*, December 11, 2000.

KEY TERMS AND CONCEPTS

Brokered deposits

Credit crunch

Depository Institutions Deregulation and Monetary Control Act of 1980

Disintermediation

Federal Deposit Insurance Corporation Improvement Act of 1991

Financial Institutions Reform, Recovery, and Enforcement Act of 1989

Garn–St. Germain Act of 1982

Money market deposit accounts

Narrow banking

Negotiable certificate of deposit

Negotiable order of withdrawal (NOW) account

Regulation Q

SUMMARY

1. Bank regulation follows a pattern of financial crisis, regulation, financial system response, and regulatory response. In response to a reduction in banks' ability to provide risk-sharing, liquidity, and information services during banking panics, government has intervened to promote bank stability. Major interventions in the United States include those to (a) create a lender of last resort, (b) restrict competition, and (c) reduce savers' risks through federal deposit insurance. In each case, both regulation and the banking industry were shaped by unintended consequences of intervention.
2. After its failures during the banking collapse in the early 1930s, the Fed emerged as a stabilizing lender of last resort. On many occasions, it has provided emergency liquidity to temporarily weak institutions in the financial system, averting financial crises.
3. Regulation Q restricted interest rates paid on deposits, creating inefficiencies in bank intermediation. To escape the interest rate ceilings, financial institutions introduced alternatives to bank intermediation, including money market mutual funds and the commercial paper market. Two pieces of legislation, the Depository Institutions Deregulation and Monetary Control Act of 1980 and the Garn–St. Germain Act of 1982, effectively removed interest rate ceilings and reduced the likelihood of disintermediation.
4. Federal deposit insurance was introduced in response to the wave of bank failures in the early 1930s. The deposit insurance crisis in the savings and loan industry began in the late 1970s and early 1980s. Deposit insurance provided a valuable source of financial stability, but moral hazard arose as insolvent S&Ls took on substantial risks and incurred large losses. Reforms have centered on changes in deposit insurance pricing and coverage, equity capital requirements, and regulatory supervision.
5. Problems faced by a lender of last resort or deposit insurance authority underscore the need for careful supervision of bank activities. The problems encountered by banking regulatory authorities during the past decade likely will surface in the regulation of insurance companies and pension funds. Federal regulators continue to debate how to safeguard savers' funds without creating unwise incentives for intermediaries.

REVIEW QUESTIONS

1. At the turn of the century, the New York Clearing House performed relatively well in coming to the rescue of individual member banks but did less well in paying off depositors when all its members were in trouble. On the basis of your understanding of that experience, can you suggest guidelines for creating a lender of last resort for banks?

2. What significant errors by the Fed worsened the Great Depression?
3. Some recent lender-of-last-resort actions by the Fed assisted nonbank segments of the financial system (in particular, the commercial paper market and securities exchanges). Suggest some potential information problems in those markets that might justify intervention by the lender of last resort.
4. What are the major costs of disintermediation?
5. What types of innovations did banks develop to get around ceilings on deposit interest rates?
6. How does deposit insurance encourage banks to take too much risk?
7. What initially caused the S&L crisis of the 1980s? What subsequent events caused S&Ls to lose even more money?
8. Why didn't regulators close all the insolvent S&Ls in the early 1980s?
9. Why was the Financial Institutions Reform, Recovery, and Enforcement Act of 1989 passed? What were its key provisions?
10. Why did so many commercial banks fail in the 1980s?
11. What is narrow banking? How would the existence of narrow banks eliminate the need for deposit insurance?
12. How could a run on an insurance company occur? Is there a need for a government guarantee program for the insurance industry similar to that for banking? Why or why not?
13. What is the main problem with underfunded pension plans? Why is this potentially a serious political issue?

ANALYTICAL PROBLEMS

14. Explain the difference between a bank that is illiquid and one that is insolvent. Explain the role this difference played in the Fed's response to the banking panics of the early 1930s.
15. How did the Fed's conflicting responsibilities with respect to maintaining the gold standard and maintaining the health of the banking system explain some of the actions it took in the early 1930s?
16. Describe what happened as interest rates rose above the fixed interest rate ceilings when Regulation Q was in effect.
17. Suppose that, as an innovative banker, you are thinking of ways to increase profits. You note that your bank is required to hold 10% in reserves on deposits held in the United States but that there are no reserve requirements on deposits held outside the country. What innovation does this knowledge suggest?
18. As a smart banker, you are thinking of ways to increase profits. You recognize the time difference between the operating hours of your bank's branches in the United States and Europe. You also note that you can receive interest on loans made for a fraction of a day and that money left in U.S. accounts over a weekend earns nothing. What innovation does this knowledge suggest?
19. Suppose that you manage a small S&L that has a net worth of –\$50 million. You fear that within two years, regulators will discover that your firm is insolvent and will shut you down. You have two possible investment strategies: (a) continue to operate as you have been, offering market interest rates on CDs to finance mortgage loans, or (b) offer higher than market interest rates on CDs and use the increased funds to speculate in junk bonds and real estate. Your analysis tells you that strategy (a) has a 10% chance of losing \$10 million and a 90% chance of gaining \$20 million, with an expected return of \$17 million. Strategy (b) has an 80% chance of losing \$50 million and a 20% chance of gaining \$75 million, with an expected return of –\$25 million. What strategy should you follow? Why? What are the consequences of your choice? What should a regulator do in this situation?

20. Suppose that one of the largest banks in the United States defaults on its sales of securitized mortgages, throwing the market into shock. No one wants to buy securitized mortgage loans until they can reevaluate their riskiness, so banks all over the country stop making mortgage loans. As Chairman of the Federal Reserve Board, what could you do?

21. Suppose that terrorists blew up the computers that run the CHIPS system, disrupting all payments nationwide. As a top official of the Federal Reserve System, what would you do?

22. In the late 1990s the Securities and Exchange Commission became concerned that some banks might be maintaining excessive loan loss reserves (an account that represents banks' best estimates of losses likely on their loan portfolios). The SEC believed some banks were planning to draw down their loan loss reserves to keep their reported earnings high during periods when their reported earnings would otherwise be low. Banks must operate under accounting rules that do not allow this practice. Some banks complained that at the same time that the SEC was investigating whether their loan loss reserves were too high, the Federal Reserve and the Office of Comptroller of the Currency were urging banks to make sure their loan loss reserves were not too low. Discuss how the different responsibilities of the SEC, on the one hand, and the Federal Reserve and the Office of Comptroller of the Currency, on the other, might lead them to send different messages to banks with respect to loan loss reserves.

23. On the basis of what you know about the history of the U.S. banking system, what deposit insurance program and set of regulations do you think would be ideal? What should be the limit on the size of accounts covered by deposit insurance? How can you minimize moral hazard problems? How can you encourage banks to diversify? Should different types of financial institutions exist, each with a different regulator, or should they all be the same? Should narrow banks exist? (*Hint:* There is no single correct answer.)

DATA QUESTION

24. In each issue of the *Federal Reserve Bulletin,* you can find consolidated balance sheet information for U.S. commercial banks. Using issues of the *Federal Reserve Bulletin,* calculate the fractions of banks' assets at the end of 1994, 1995, 1996, 1997, 1998, 1999, and 2000 held in the form of (a) U.S. government securities and (b) commercial and industrial loans. Do relative changes in these holdings suggest that banks reduced their exposure to credit risk over this period? Explain. Do these changes indicate that banks may have increased their exposure to other types of risk? Explain. Does your analysis suggest any steps for improving the design of bank capital requirements?

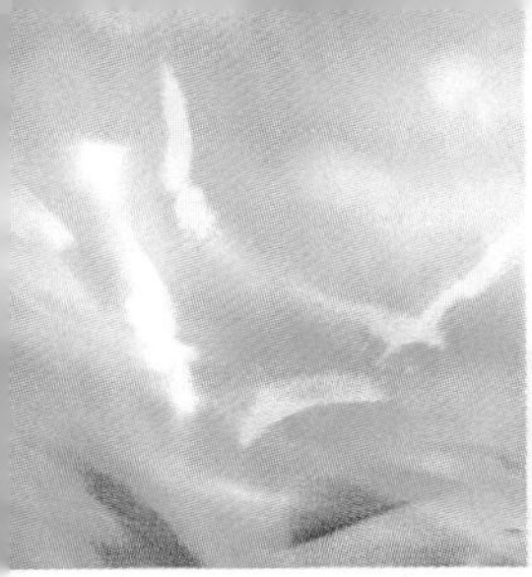

CHAPTER 16

Banking in the International Economy

What would it take to throw the world into a financial upheaval? Imagine . . . Young whiz-kid traders in New York, London, and Hong Kong have never seen anything like it. In the weeks following Russia's default, investors and lenders fled emerging markets. International banks feared a domino effect summed up in the words of a leading banker: "The entire market is, in effect, closed." Fiction? No—events during the fall of 1998. Savers, borrowers, banks, and regulators are learning that globalization brings new complexities to the management of financial institutions.

International banking hasn't always been important for U.S. banks, savers, and borrowers. Before World War II, the U.S. economy was basically a closed economy. In closed economies, capital flows between the United States and other countries were restricted by regulation, and the volume of international trade was small relative to the level of domestic economic activity. In addition, before the development of computer-based information systems, cross-border communication costs were relatively high. The high cost of providing the risk-sharing, liquidity, and information services that are central to banking discouraged the expansion of financial institutions across national boundaries.

The tremendous growth in international trade and capital mobility after World War II led to rapid expansion of international banking. By the 1960s, advances in data processing and telecommunications had decreased the costs of providing banking services and fueled the expansion of international banking and competition among banks in deposit taking and lending. These activities grew rapidly in the 1980s: International bank lending in the United States, Western Europe, and Japan rose from $324 billion in 1980 to several trillion dollars by 2000. By 2000, more than 160 U.S. banks had offices in other countries. Foreign banks have become active in the United States as well, accounting for a significant share of total U.S. banking activities. Sometimes unregulated by either U.S. or foreign authorities, these banks have deposits and loans in the trillions of dollars.

In this chapter, we focus on the activities of international banks. Banks provide the same services to savers and borrowers on a global scale as they do for domestic individuals and businesses. To demonstrate what these services are, we first describe new risk-sharing, liquidity, and information services to support international trade. With an understanding of these services, we examine new markets that international banks create. Finally, we analyze how regulation shapes and responds to international banking services.

ORGANIZATION OF INTERNATIONAL BANKS

International banks provide risk-sharing, liquidity, and information services to firms and individuals engaged in international trade and finance. For example, Sears may use an international bank to provide credit for its purchase of shoes from an Italian firm. Royal Dutch Shell Oil Company may use an international bank to help it manage daily fluctuations in the values of the currencies in which it deals. As they do for their customers domestically, U.S. banks operate internationally to gather information for credit-risk analysis and to help their customers with transactions. International banking activities performed by U.S. banks parallel those performed domestically. Foreign banks operate in the United States (and in other countries outside their domestic markets) for much the same reasons.

There are three similarities between domestic and international banking. First, like domestic banks, international banks accept deposits from savers and lend to borrowers. Second, international banks lower transactions costs—facilitating risk sharing and liquidity in financial markets—and lower information costs for many individual borrowers and lenders. Finally, international financial regulation can lead to innovation in banking products and markets outside a country's borders, just as domestic regulations can stimulate innovation within those borders.

International banking takes place in many countries around the world, although it is concentrated in the United States, Japan, Europe, and the Caribbean—because many businesses in the United States, Japan, and Europe are engaged in global trade and because New York, Tokyo, and London are financial centers. About half of all foreign liabilities and assets are held (in order of size) by banks in the United Kingdom, Japan, the United States, and Switzerland. The United Kingdom and Switzerland have the longest history of international banking; participation in international banking by U.S. banks has increased to match the growth of foreign trade by U.S. businesses.

In the 1980s, when financial restrictions were relaxed—particularly those regulations that prevented banks' industrial customers from obtaining financing in foreign capital markets—Japanese banks expanded their role in international banking. At the same time, deregulation of deposit rates (similar to the elimination of Regulation Q in the United States) reduced profits in domestic Japanese banking, giving Japanese banks an incentive to borrow and lend abroad. Although they held only 4% of international bank loans in 1980, Japanese banks held 40% by the end of the decade. Indeed, by the early 1990s, most of the largest banks in the world (by assets) were Japanese, and

Japanese banks surpassed U.S. banks as leaders in international banking. By the late 1990s, the share of international bank loans held by Japanese banks had fallen substantially, as Japanese banks looked inward during a domestic banking crisis.

Some important international financial centers are located in unregulated **offshore markets**—markets that have little or no regulation and tax bank profits at very low rates. The leading offshore markets are in the Caribbean (especially the Bahamas and the Cayman Islands), Hong Kong, and Singapore.

Overseas Organization of U.S. Banks

Many U.S. banks have subsidiaries or branches abroad, with more than $500 billion of assets. To organize their foreign activities, U.S. banks can use (1) branches, (2) Edge Act corporations, (3) interests in foreign financial firms, or (4) international banking facilities.

Branches. Some U.S. banks operate wholly owned **branches** around the world to accept deposits and make loans. Because they are additional offices of U.S. banks, these foreign branches are supported directly by a U.S. bank's capital and resources. Branches in London control the most assets, owing to London's preeminence as a global financial center. However, U.S. bank branches in the Far East and Latin America have grown as U.S. trade with local firms in these regions has expanded. Finally, many U.S. banks operate branches in the tax-haven countries of the Caribbean. These branches largely act as shell operations that exist primarily to transfer funds around the world. With some exceptions, foreign branches of U.S. banks offer a full line of banking services, though foreign laws may limit these services.

Edge Act corporations. Special subsidiaries of U.S. banks and sometimes of foreign banks are called **Edge Act corporations.** Created by the Edge Act of 1919, these subsidiaries serve customers that are active in international commerce. They also enjoy privileges that are not given to domestic banks, such as exemption from interstate branching restrictions. Edge Act corporations may accept deposits from foreign residents and domestic residents (as long as the bank uses the deposits in international trade transactions). An Edge Act corporation can perform only international banking services: It may make loans to finance overseas trade and deal in foreign exchange, but it cannot accept general deposits from U.S. residents or extend domestic commercial loans to U.S. residents. Before the 1990s, many banks formed Edge Act corporations to circumvent limitations on other forms of entry across major banking markets in the United States. Approval for the formation of an Edge Act corporation must be granted by the Federal Reserve System, subject to statutory capital requirements.

Interests in foreign financial services firms. A domestic bank holding company can own a controlling interest in foreign financial services companies such as banks or finance companies. Rules imposed by the Fed (which regulates the international banking activities of member banks, their bank holding companies, and their Edge Act corporations) require that U.S. banks' interest in foreign financial services firms be "closely related to banking." These activities are governed by Federal Reserve Regulation K.

International banking facilities. Created in 1981 by the Federal Reserve Board, **international banking facilities** (IBFs) are U.S. institutions that aren't allowed to conduct domestic banking business. IBFs accept time deposits from and make loans to foreign households and firms. The IBF cannot conduct business inside the United States except with its parent bank or with other IBFs. IBFs have been desirable to banks because they are exempt from reserve requirements, federal restrictions on interest payments to depositors, and (in some states) state and local taxation. In practice, an IBF is just a room or office inside a conventional bank. Effectively, IBFs are regulated in the same manner as foreign branches of U.S. banks. The Fed has successfully encouraged both U.S. and non-U.S. banks to conduct a large share of their banking business in the United States through IBFs.

Organization of Foreign Banks in the United States

The same international forces that increased the presence of U.S. banks abroad led foreign banks to open offices in the United States. As of 2000, foreign banks hold about $600 billion of assets in the United States, or about 12% of total bank assets in this country. Such extensive holdings have generated fears of foreign control of U.S. banking (particularly in states such as California where foreign bank influence is strong). Some analysts worry that foreign bankers will lend their U.S. deposits abroad, denying credit to worthy domestic borrowers. However, experts studying the lending patterns of Japanese and other foreign-owned banks in the United States found little evidence of this practice.

When operating in the United States, a foreign bank can organize its activities as (1) an agency office, (2) a branch of the foreign bank, or (3) a subsidiary of a U.S. bank. An **agency office** cannot take deposits from U.S. residents, although it can transfer funds from abroad to the United States and make loans in the United States. The prohibition on accepting deposits limits the activities of agency offices, but they benefit from not being subject to regulations for deposit-taking financial intermediaries (such as branching restrictions or requirements for FDIC insurance). A **foreign bank branch,** on the other hand, is a full-service institution, accepting deposits, making loans, and bearing the name of the foreign bank. The Riegle-Neal Interstate Banking and Branching Efficiency Act of 1994 allowed foreign banks to operate branches in any state outside of its home state as long as domestically owned banks could branch under the same circumstances. A **subsidiary U.S. bank** is treated like a domestic bank; that is, it is subject to domestic bank regulations and need not have the same name as its foreign parent. A subsidiary U.S. bank also may establish Edge Act corporations or international banking facilities.

Most foreign bank branches in the United States and other countries are primarily *wholesale* operations, meaning that they serve other banks that in turn serve the small retail accounts of individuals and firms. However, many foreign banks are entering the retail banking market by buying interests in U.S. banks.

Before passage of the International Banking Act of 1978, foreign banks operating in the United States enjoyed cost advantages over U.S. banks because they were exempt from limits on branching across state lines and from reserve requirements. However, since 1978, foreign banks basically have been subject to the same rules as those governing U.S. banks. In particular, they may establish additional full-service branches only in a home state or in states that permit nationwide entry (although they may keep any full-service branches that were established before passage of the International Banking Act).

After scandals relating to the failure of the Bank of Credit and Commerce International (BCCI) in 1991, Congress passed the Foreign Bank Supervision Enhancement Act of 1991 to strengthen oversight of foreign banks. Under the new law, foreign banks come under the scrutiny of the Federal Reserve, in addition to the Office of the Comptroller of the Currency or state banking regulators. When approving establishment of a new U.S. branch of a foreign bank, the Fed must be satisfied that the foreign bank's worldwide activities are adequately supervised by regulators in its home country. The law's intent is to equalize operating standards for domestic and foreign banks. The new scrutiny should reduce the likelihood of a repetition of the BCCI scandal.

Leaders in Global Banking

International banking has blossomed significantly outside the United States, with major growth in Europe and the Asian Pacific region. As early as 1997, ten major non-U.S. banks held more than 50% of their assets abroad (a U.S. bank, Citicorp, now Citigroup, was a bit ahead with 60% of its assets abroad). The leaders include British, Swiss, and French banks and increasingly the Bank of China. The growing prominence of the Bank of China results from growth in China's foreign trade as well as the bank's expansion (in Russia, Germany, and Canada). Japanese banks withdrew somewhat from global banking as the banks repaired their positions in the battered Japanese economy.

MANAGING EXCHANGE RATE RISK

In addition to the risks borne by domestic banks, international banks are exposed to exchange rate risk in their foreign transactions. Because exchange rate fluctuations can affect the bank's profits, a successful international bank must manage its exchange rate risk when accepting deposits and making loans. Recall that banks participating in domestic transactions must develop ways to manage interest rate risk so that their profit from lending exceeds the interest they pay depositors. Similarly, international banks must manage

CONSIDER THIS . . .

Why Did Closing BCCI Take So Long?

The difficulty of enforcing international banking regulation became apparent when the Bank of Credit and Commerce International (BCCI), incorporated in Luxembourg and the Cayman Islands, failed in July 1991. With the sheik of Abu Dhabi as a prominent investor, BCCI did business in 70 countries. When large loan losses caused it to fail, supervisors in the United Kingdom, the United States, and other countries found evidence of fraudulent behavior for several preceding years. In the United States, BCCI had hidden behind First American Bankshares and its well-connected leaders, Clark Clifford, an advisor to several presidents, and Robert Altman. The prosecution of Clifford and Altman collapsed in early 1993 with Clifford's failing health and Altman's acquittal. The main problem was that nearly all of the crucial records and witnesses were in Abu Dhabi. Not until January 1994 did the Emirate make a financial settlement with U.S. authorities and extradite Swaleh Naqvi, BCCI's former boss, to the United States. In 1995, a Luxembourg court approved a $1.8 billion compensation scheme from the government of Abu Dhabi, but some disgruntled BCCI depositors were suing the Bank of England for not intervening sooner in the BCCI crisis.

Although banking has become international, supervision has not. Central banks may agree about which country should take the lead in regulation and supervision, but cooperation is largely voluntary. The BCCI scandal increased pressure for greater international coordination of bank regulation. However, important challenges include (1) lack of regulation in some developing countries, (2) coordinating the coverage of deposit insurance across national borders, and (3) disagreement over which authority should dispose of a bank's branch assets in an international bankruptcy. These key issues for international bank regulation will be debated for many years.

As the BCCI affair drew to a close, central banks—particularly the Bank of England—received blame for their slow discovery of the scandal. In July 1992, the Basle Committee proposed further standardization of the regulation of international banks. Under this standardization, a home-country regulator has supervisory responsibility and the authority to obtain information about a bank's activities. In host countries, regulators may limit a foreign bank's activities if they become concerned about the oversight in the home country. Although these regulatory improvements are significant, some analysts worry that a scandal like BCCI could once again occur.

exchange rate risk, to minimize fluctuations in banks' net worth that accompany increases or decreases in exchange rates. Like interest rate risk, exchange rate risk can affect the value of bank assets and liabilities and hence net worth.

For example, suppose that a U.S. bank makes a loan in Japanese yen for ¥1500 million but it has only ¥1000 million in deposits; it funds the loan by exchanging other currencies. The exchange rate at the time the loan is made is $1 = ¥100. Now suppose that the value of the yen falls against the dollar, say to $1 = ¥150. Hence the value of the bank's asset, the loan, in dollar terms falls from $15 million (¥1500 million/100) to $10 million (¥1500 million/150), a decline of $5 million. The value of the bank's liability, its deposits, measured in dollars also falls, from $10 million (¥1000 million/100) to $6.7 million (¥1000 million/150), a reduction of $3.3 million. Thus the bank's net worth, computed by subtracting the values of its liabilities from the values of its assets, falls by $1.7 million, even though there is no change in the loan's repayment or default risk.

As in the case of interest rate risk, the bank can avoid exchange rate risk entirely by matching the currency denomination of assets and liabilities. However, banks may want to speculate deliberately against exchange rate movements. Because large banks can readily sell deposits in any major currency, currency-mismatching problems are easy to manage.

One strategy that banks use to hedge against exchange rate fluctuations is financial futures or options (Chapter 9). For example, if a U.S. bank makes a loan abroad in yen when it holds yen deposits of less than the loan value, it can use futures contracts to hedge against the possibility that the value of the yen will fall relative to that of the dollar. Recall, however, that there are transactions costs in hedging and that no hedge is perfect (Chapter 9).

SERVICES PROVIDED BY INTERNATIONAL BANKS

Like domestic banking, international banking provides risk-sharing, liquidity, and information services. And like domestic banks, international banks develop new ways to manage risk in banking contracts. They also reduce transactions and information costs for savers and certain borrowers. Let's explore some significant examples of each type of service.

Reducing Transactions Costs

Bank trading improves the liquidity of foreign-exchange markets and helps to maintain efficient capital markets for international lending and borrowing.

International banks engage in foreign-exchange trading (buying and selling currencies on spot, forward, and futures markets) to reduce transactions costs for their customers in addition to reducing their own exchange rate risk. As a result, foreign-exchange trading is an important international banking activity, with a daily volume of more than $1 trillion. Most of banks' foreign-exchange trading volume is with other banks to facilitate cross-border investments and financial transactions. Foreign-exchange trading by banks during the 1980s and 1990s grew more rapidly than the value of world trade in goods.

The skills that a bank acquires in managing its own exchange rate risk can be extended to firms doing business abroad, reducing their transactions costs. Banks often arrange a **currency swap,** or an exchange of expected future returns on debt instruments denominated in different currencies. This form of hedge works in much the same way as interest rate swaps do in domestic banking. Currency swaps allow parties in a transaction to share or transfer exchange rate risk. Commercial banks are (as with interest rate swaps) instrumental in maintaining the market. To demonstrate how a currency swap works, consider the exchange between two multinational firms, Big Steel in the United States and Le Taste in France. Big Steel wants to build a steel-making plant in France, and Le Taste wants to manufacture men's suits in the United States. To make its investments, each firm needs local currency—euros for Big

Steel and U.S. dollars for Le Taste. Because a multinational corporation often is better known in its home country, borrowing in that country's currency in domestic capital markets often is cheaper for such firms.

Both Le Taste and Big Steel sell bonds, in France and the United States, respectively. They then swap the proceeds and pay off each other's obligations. For example, Le Taste's revenues and costs are both denominated in dollars after the swap. The swap matches currencies for financing needs while maintaining lower borrowing costs. The intermediary banks assisting the companies perform normal banking functions: assessing and sometimes bearing credit risk.

For banks, swaps provide a convenient way to take deposits or make loans in as many countries as they choose. Swaps can greatly reduce currency mismatch and the resulting exchange rate risk. In this way, a U.S. bank can keep its balance sheet entirely in U.S. dollars, irrespective of the large number of non-U.S. transactions in which it participates. As the swap market has become more competitive, reducing the profitability of simple transactions to banks, banks have come up with more imaginative—and risky—swaps, requiring more elaborate hedging strategies in managing risk.

Providing Information Services

One of the difficulties of international transactions is changes in currency values. Suppose that Luxury Stores in Chicago wants to import men's suits from Le Taste in Lyons, France. Luxury Stores will have to pay Le Taste in euros. If Luxury Stores has agreed to pay Le Taste in euros on delivery, it has to worry about euro–dollar exchange rate movements that might occur after it has placed the order and before it receives the suits. International banks act as dealers in foreign exchange, helping firms move funds from country to country. A bank can assist by providing Luxury Stores with an interest-bearing account at its branch in Lyons so that Luxury will have a local euro-denominated account to use in its dealings with Le Taste. Or the bank can help Luxury to hedge its risk with financial futures, options, or other strategies.

Credit risk also arises as a normal part of international commerce just as it does in domestic commerce. Exporters and importers enter into agreements in which the importer agrees to pay at some future date for goods delivered now. The credit risk that is inherent in such a transaction is magnified because the exporter often has limited information about the importer. If the exporter cannot assess the importer's creditworthiness, the exporter might not make the transaction, decreasing the volume of trade. International banks solve this type of information problem by substituting their own creditworthiness for that of the importer.

One banking service that is aimed at reducing credit risk is the sale of bankers' acceptances. A **banker's acceptance** is a time draft—that is, an order to pay a specified amount of money to the holder of the acceptance on a specified date. Acceptances are a form of the bills of exchange that have been used to finance international trade since the thirteenth century. The Federal Reserve Act of 1913 authorized U.S. banks to use these instruments for short-term financing of their customers' foreign and domestic trade. By the end of the 1920s, outstanding bankers' acceptances in the United States totaled $1.7 billion. Just after World War II, only $104 million were outstanding. By 1987, the amount had grown to $71 billion, but by 2000, it had declined to less than $10 billion. The global volume of bankers' acceptances mirrors the importance of international trade to the world economy; U.S. banks lost market share during the 1990s.

How does a banker's acceptance work? A bank provides a guarantee to the importer to pay the exporter for its goods. The bank does this by *accepting* an order to pay funds drawn on the bank by the exporter. The importer pays the bank a fee (averaging about 0.5% of the amount of the transaction) for this service, based on the importer's creditworthiness. The bank then either holds the acceptance in its own portfolio as an investment or sells it at a discount in a secondary market. Regardless of the bank's strategy, it pays the exporter immediately. The importer repays the bank when the acceptance matures; if the bank has sold the acceptance, the bank then repays the holder of the acceptance.

Let's return to the example of Luxury Stores' importing men's suits from Le Taste, shown in Fig. 16.1. To obtain the necessary financing, Luxury

Figure 16.1 **Information and the Banker's Acceptance**

To avoid the high information costs required for an exporter to assess an importer's creditworthiness (for future repayment), the importer goes to a bank to obtain a letter of credit. With the bank's assurance of payment, the transaction can be completed. Bankers' acceptances are an example of the information services for international trade and finance that banks can provide.

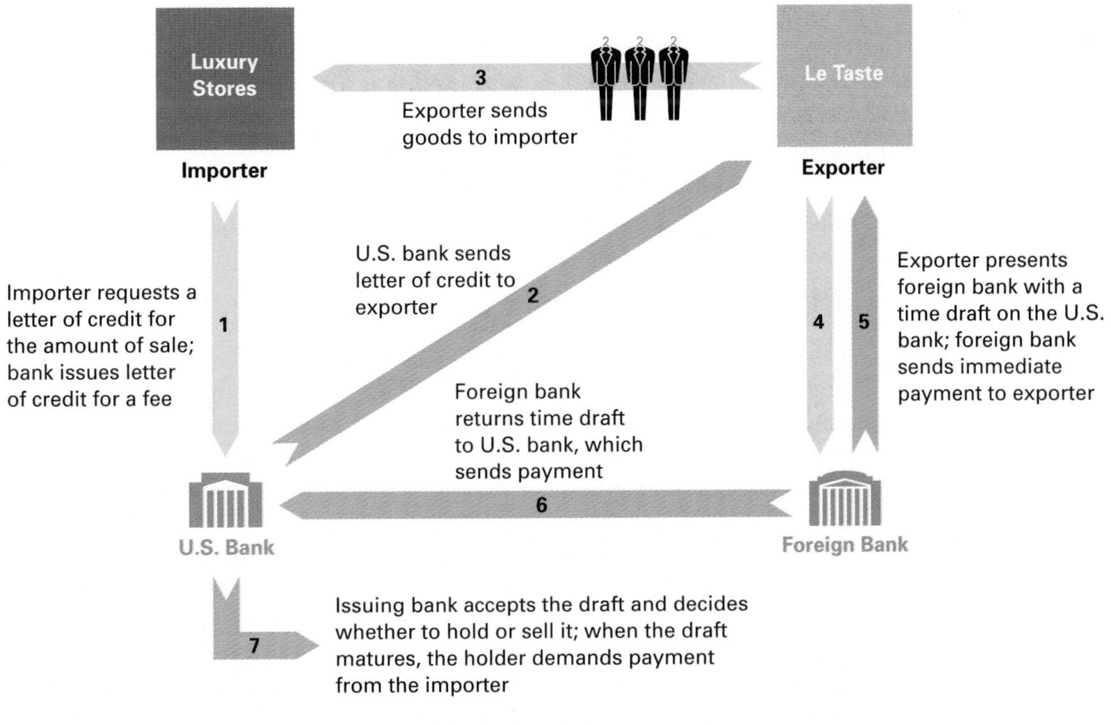

Stores asks its bank to issue a letter of credit for the amount of the sale. The bank does so and sends the letter of credit to Le Taste. When Le Taste ships the suits, it uses the letter of credit to draw a time draft on Luxury Stores' U.S. bank and presents the draft to its local bank in Lyons to obtain immediate payment. Next, Le Taste's French bank sends the time draft back to Luxury Stores' U.S. bank. When that bank accepts the draft, it pays Le Taste's bank. Finally, when the time draft matures, Luxury Stores is responsible for paying the accepting bank the face amount of the draft. Figure 16.1 summarizes this process, which works in reverse when a U.S. exporting firm wants to sell goods to a foreign importer. Bankers' acceptances generally have low default risk because both the importer and the bank sign it. (Note the similarity to U.S. banks' provision of standby letters of credit in the domestic commercial paper market.)

Like domestic banks, international banks are centers of information gathering. Banks need considerable specialized knowledge to create bankers' acceptances. As a result, bankers' acceptances are issued only by banks that have domestic and foreign departments staffed by personnel who are knowledgeable about the markets in which these instruments are used and traded.

CHECKPOINT

Because bankers' acceptances allow banks to exploit their information role in financial markets, which banks would you predict are most active in the banker's acceptance market? In a banker's acceptance transaction, the bank reduces information costs by substituting its creditworthiness for the borrower's. For a banker's acceptance to be useful in international markets, the bank's creditworthiness must be easily ascertained. As a result, large, well-known banks dominate the banker's acceptance market. o

International banks expand on domestic banks' provision of risk-sharing, liquidity, and information services, as summarized in Fig. 16.2.

THE RISE OF EUROMARKETS

Before World War II, London was the leading global financial and commercial center. The British pound largely served as the **international transaction currency,** the currency of choice in settling international transactions. After World War II, the United States became the dominant financial and industrial nation. Thus the U.S. dollar became the international transaction currency, even in exchanges in which neither the buyer nor the seller was a U.S. firm. In certain markets, such as the world oil market, trades are still made in dollars. During the years following World War II, the former Soviet Union and Eastern Bloc countries accumulated dollar reserves for international trade. For political reasons, they did not want to keep these reserves in banks inside the United States. Instead, they deposited their U.S. dollar reserves in European banks. Rather

Figure 16.2

International Banking Services

In international banking, banks specialize in providing risk-sharing, liquidity, and information services. They do so by acting as intermediaries in currency swaps, foreign-exchange trading, and credit transactions.

than converting them into European currencies, they kept them denominated in dollars, and these accounts became known as **Eurodollars.**

A new Eurodollar deposit is created each time a deposit in a U.S. bank account is transferred to a bank outside the United States while being kept in dollars. For example, if Royal Dutch Shell draws $10 million from an account in a U.S. bank and deposits the same amount in its London bank account in dollars, it has created $10 million in Eurodollars. Royal Dutch Shell and other multinational corporations maintain dollar deposits outside the United States because of the dollar's wide use as a currency in international trade.

British banks, seeking to circumvent the Bank of England's restrictions on the use of British pounds in making loans outside the country, created a market for Eurodollars. By using Eurodollars, British banks could set competitive interest rates to attract deposits while making external loans in dollars. The emergence of Eurodollars illustrates how the shift in demand to U.S. dollars led to innovations in international financial institutions and markets.

Interestingly, domestic interest rate regulations and reserve requirements gave U.S. banks a further reason to participate in the growing Eurodollar market. When regulatory ceilings imposed by Regulation Q limited the interest banks could pay depositors and market interest rates were high, U.S. commercial banks were hard put to attract new domestic deposits. However, Eurodollar deposits at European branches of U.S. banks were not subject to interest rate ceilings and reserve requirements. Therefore U.S. banks began to acquire Eurodollar deposits in their European branches. The branch banks then transferred the deposits to the U.S. parent banks to buy securities or make loans. By 1970, when the rate ceilings on negotiable certificates of deposit under Regulation Q were dropped, U.S. banks already had a substantial interest in the Eurodollar market. This financial innovation in response to regulation is similar to development of negotiable CDs. Recall that negotiable CDs were created in response to disintermediation and the growth of money market mutual funds and the commercial paper market in the United States.

Since 1960, the Eurodollar market has grown from negligible size to trillions of dollars in gross assets. From 1973 to 2000, the market grew at a compound annual rate of about 20%.

Much of current international banking business is conducted in relatively unregulated banking centers known as **Euromarkets.** These are markets for **Eurocurrency deposits,** or time deposits denominated in a currency other than that of the issuing domestic financial center (for instance, dollar deposits at a French bank), as well as Euroloans, Eurobonds, and Eurocommercial paper (loans, bonds, and commercial paper denominated in a currency other than that of the issuing financial center). More than half of Eurocurrency deposits are in negotiable certificates of deposit with maturities of at least 30 days. Eurocurrency deposits account for the overwhelming majority of banks' foreign-owned deposits; within Eurocurrency deposits, the largest category are Eurodollars.

The U.S. dollar remains the dominant currency in the Euromarkets. Before the mid-1980s, roughly 80% of Eurocurrency deposits were denominated in U.S. dollars. The U.S. dollar's share of the market fell during the late 1980s and 1990s, reaching about 60% by the end of the 1990s.

As it is now used, the term *Eurodollar market* encompasses more than just Europe. It refers broadly to the international demand for dollar-denominated loans and deposits. The Eurodollar market is valued because of the usefulness of the dollar denomination and because international banking operations are less regulated than domestic banking operations. For example, by the mid-1980s, foreign branches of U.S. banks in countries (such as the Bahamas and the Cayman Islands) that have low taxes on financial services firms owned large amounts of Eurodollars because of fewer regulatory requirements.

Since 1981, international banking facilities have been authorized to provide Eurodollar banking in the United States. Called *booking sites,* these facilities, which may be within an office of a U.S. bank, weren't subject to interest rate ceilings when they existed. Booking sites don't have to meet reserve requirements and aren't covered by deposit insurance. However, they aren't allowed to conduct business in the United States.

Euromarket Customers

Euromarket customers have changed in response to shifts in international lending and borrowing patterns. Through the early 1970s, loans were made primarily to governments or state-owned enterprises in industrial countries. Deposits were drawn from multinational corporations and U.S. banks. After the oil shocks of the 1970s, the huge dollar surpluses of the nations belonging to the Organization of Petroleum Exporting Countries (OPEC) were the largest source of deposits. Euroloans were made to developing nations, which needed the funds to pay higher import bills and for new investment. In the late 1980s, oil prices and OPEC deposits declined. Today, the countries with large trade surpluses to deposit in Eurodollar accounts are Japan and South Korea; borrowers include multinational corporations in the United States and abroad. In many cases, large Euroloans have been used to finance mergers and acquisitions in both Europe and the United States.

Loans in Euromarkets

The typical Euroloan is a floating-rate obligation of relatively long maturity—say, five to ten years. Banks charge interest rates based on a markup over the London Interbank Offered Rate (LIBOR). Analogous to the federal funds rate in the United States, LIBOR is the interest rate at which the Eurodollar banks conventionally lend to one another, reflecting the perceived credit risk of the loans. This pattern is changing as markets evolve following the 1999 introduction of the euro. Germany, France, and other continental European countries support the Euro Interbank Offered Rate (EURIBOR), which is the formal successor to the set of national rates.

Euroloans usually are quite large—often for billions of dollars—and therefore would result in lack of diversification for a single commercial bank lender. In a **loan syndication,** individual banks hold fractions of a loan. The loan is arranged and managed by a lead bank, which earns a fee for arranging the loan and its syndication. The primary motivation for syndication is risk sharing. Major money-center banks as well as regional banks participate

CONSIDER THIS . . .

Will Europe Kill the Eurobond?

U.S. tax policy provided a stimulus to the Eurobond market in the 1960s when the United States imposed a tax on interest payments. Seizing the day (or at least the profit opportunity), bond issuers moved to Europe and, in particular, to London. In contrast to domestic bonds in Europe, Eurobonds pay interest without reducing tax, and the market flourishes.

In late 1998, the European Commission issued a draft directive that would require European Union (EU) countries to impose a withholding tax of at least 20% on interest paid on Eurobonds held by EU citizens. The U.K. government objected strongly, arguing that investors would refocus attention on non-EU jurisdictions such as Switzerland. Uncertainty about the tax made many market participants nervous.

The European Commission and the German finance ministry stood solidly behind the proposal as a further step toward "harmonizing" taxes in Europe. Many analysts, pointing up the link between regulation and financial innovation, remained fearful that failure to exempt the Eurobond market from the withholding tax would "harmonize" the market—by moving it out of the EU.

in loan syndication. These arrangements do not substitute for credit-risk management, however. Significant defaults on large syndicated loans to less developed countries during the 1970s and 1980s caused several medium-sized banks to stop participating, and the volume of newly syndicated loans declined. Since the mid-1980s, the growth in syndicated lending has resumed, as loans to private firms in industrialized countries have increased.

Eurobonds account for the vast majority of new issues in the international bond market. The value of new issues in the Eurobond market now exceeds that in the domestic corporate bond market in the United States. London has been the traditional center for Eurobond issues, but competition is emerging from other European financial centers and from Japan. Another development in the 1980s was the partial shift away from bank borrowing toward Eurocommercial paper and Eurobonds. The Glass-Steagall Act's historical separation of commercial banking and securities activities (the separation was repealed in 1999) never applied to overseas branches handling foreign accounts, so U.S. banks have eagerly entered these new markets.

CHECKPOINT

Why might a regional bank in Nebraska be more likely to invest in syndicated Euroloans than to lend directly to European borrowers? The bank obtains the benefit of diversification with low information costs, paying the lead bank a small fee for assessing borrowers' creditworthiness and arranging syndication. o

FINANCIAL REGULATION IN INTERNATIONAL BANKING

Recall that government regulation of domestic financial institutions spurs banks to create new services that are then subject to competition and government regulation. A similar pattern of change occurs in international banking. As technology lessens the cost of gathering and communicating information internationally, the cost of using overseas markets also declines. These low costs allow domestic banks to conduct financial activities outside their domestically regulated jurisdictions, as the rise of Eurocurrency and Eurobond markets in the 1960s and 1970s demonstrated. Innovation by banks triggers regulatory response, but a country's domestic regulators must consider the impact of domestic regulation on banks' international competitiveness. For example, if one country restricts its banks' ability to perform a financial activity, banks in countries with a more favorable regulatory climate will step in to perform the service. Thus, as financial systems become more globally integrated, the activities of financial institutions in various countries are becoming increasingly similar.

In the 1980s, several governments in developing nations threatened to default on their Euroloans. Central banks in the United States, Europe, and Japan were forced to face the possibility of a global banking crisis. To avoid

OTHER TIMES, OTHER PLACES . . .

Do Sovereigns Default?

Banks incur greater credit risk when lending money to foreign governments than they do when lending to private individuals or companies. The banks have no way to prevent the borrower from defaulting on the loan, and incentives for foreign countries to maintain debt payments are weaker than those for domestic units of government. Countries that default may lose access to foreign credit markets for a time, and banks cannot seize easily a country's property within its own borders. During the 1980s, more than 40 developing countries restructured bank loans of about $300 billion.

From 1970 until the early 1980s, rising commodity prices and low real interest rates enhanced the creditworthiness of many developing nations. These conditions encouraged borrowing for investment and development and to finance government budget deficits. In the early 1980s, rising real interest rates and falling oil prices caused several Latin American countries to halt interest payments. In August 1982, Mexico was unable to roll over its obligations. Along with other countries, it began to renegotiate interest rates or repayment terms with private commercial banks in the United States, Europe, and Japan.

Citicorp, BankAmerica, Chase Manhattan, J. P. Morgan, Bankers Trust, Chemical, and First Chicago sustained large losses from defaults on loans to foreign governments. At the onset of the crisis in 1982 and 1983, many analysts worried that the foreign-debt problems of these banks could create a banking crisis. However, by adding funds to loan loss reserves to cover foreign-debt losses, the banking system managed to avoid a crisis. However, U.S. banks lost $10 billion in the second quarter of 1987, their worst performance since the Great Depression. Large banks' loan loss reserves now total more than half their exposure to developing-nation debt. In the late 1980s and early 1990s, large U.S. banks increased their equity capital from a low of about 4% of assets in 1981 to more than 7%. The foreign-debt problems didn't cause the international banking system to collapse, but it made international banks more conservative in their credit-risk analysis of foreign government as borrowers.

such crises, central banks of the leading industrialized nations recommended three types of regulation: (1) minimum levels of net worth (capital requirements), (2) deposit insurance, and (3) central bank intervention.

Capital Requirements

One way to reduce the chance that risky international banking activities will induce a global banking crisis is to increase the amount of money that banks can lose by raising capital requirements. Efforts to coordinate capital standards for commercial banks began in December 1987, when 12 countries, including the United States, met in Basle (Chapter 14). Implementing the Basle agreement has not been easy because of differences in regulation and accounting requirements, as well as difficulties in standardizing the definition of capital. The Basle agreement left loopholes in that definition and in the method of accounting for off-balance-sheet items, such as interest rate swaps, in risk weighting. In 1993, the Bank for International Settlements (BIS) and the International Organization of Securities Commissions (IOSCO) issued common capital standards for banks and brokers engaging in swaps and the use of financial futures and options. Although some questions remain to be resolved, most observers believe that the international coordination of minimum capital requirements has reduced the exposure of central banks to the risk of an international banking crisis.

In 1995, the Basle Committee on Banking Supervision, operating under the auspices of the BIS, proposed that banks develop their own risk-assessment procedures subject to regulatory review. Under this new approach, banks could use internal risk-management models to determine their exposure to interest rate risk and exchange rate risk. If a bank's internal model is revealed to be inaccurate over time, regulators may increase the bank's capital requirement. This alternative has the advantage of providing banks with incentives to improve their risk-management systems. A new challenge arises for regulators, however: Evaluating banks' models requires that regulators become proficient in often sophisticated modeling techniques. Ultimately, the approach is only as effective as regulators' ability to assess the validity of banks' risk-management models. In the aftermath of the rescue of Long-Term Capital Management, a large U.S. hedge fund, in late 1998, regulators around the world urged renewed attention to models of risk management.

Deposit Insurance

In the late 1990s, leaders of central banks and finance ministries continued to push for coordination of and restrictions on deposit insurance. Deposit insurance coverage outside the United States typically is less generous than that in the United States, and programs have not experienced the large losses that have been incurred recently in the United States.

Until international standards for insurance premiums are set and implemented, most U.S. banks will pay more modest premiums than, say, German and Japanese banks do. Coordination could mean higher costs for U.S. banks. Currently, to the extent that these banks pay premiums beyond a fixed fee, they pay premiums only on domestic and repatriated Eurodollar deposits; if coordinated international deposit insurance is included in an agreement, large U.S. international banks could face a significant increase in the cost of insurance. Also facing higher costs would be banks in countries such as France and the Netherlands, because, under their current national regulations, they pay deposit insurance premiums only after payouts are made.

Coordination among European countries is under way. In April 1992, the European Community voted on the first step of coordinating deposit insurance, focusing on the development of a unified system for monitoring banks' activities. In May 1994, a new directive established a minimum amount close to the current average amount guaranteed in individual countries to be guaranteed by all member countries' programs. According to the directive, membership should be mandatory everywhere, and intervention will not be limited to bankruptcy.

Despite current efforts at international coordination, deposit insurance in many European countries lacks two provisions important in the U.S. system. First, monitoring agencies generally lack the power of the FDIC. Second, European systems are mainly financed by member banks, and only in three countries (the Netherlands, Spain, and the United Kingdom) must the government or central bank participate to fund extraordinary needs.

Central Bank Intervention

After the debt crisis in developing nations began in the early 1980s, central banks met on several occasions at the Bank for International Settlements to discuss their roles as lenders of last resort during a banking crisis. They concluded that each central bank would concentrate on ensuring the financial stability of its own domestic banks. However, the increasing international linkages among banks, especially in their off-balance-sheet activities, has led to continuing discussions among central banks about how to intervene in an international banking crisis.

In the 1980s and 1990s, central banks also met to discuss the coordination of bank regulation and supervision. Regulatory differences are apt to diminish in the competitive global financial system of the new century. Regulation by function likely will emerge, and regulation by institutions likely will decline. Besides deposit insurance, regulation of commercial banks with respect to geographic extent and scope of permissible activities is likely to have two characteristics. First, in addition to owning banks, bank holding companies would be free to provide a broad range of financial services, including securities and insurance, with regulation and supervision of those lines of business. Second, the extent to which bank holding companies would be allowed to participate directly in nonfinancial business would depend on local legal tradition. Restrictions will probably be most stringent in the United States and less stringent in Europe and Japan.

International Coordination

It is difficult to allocate supervisory responsibility and tasks in international banking because international regulators must coordinate the activities of lenders of last resort and deposit insurance authorities as well as regulatory restrictions on bank activities. Economists and policymakers are debating various proposals, but some common themes have emerged. Branches and subsidiaries of foreign banks generally should be treated as the equivalent of domestic banks by the lender of last resort (if those banks abide by host-country supervisory rules and information-disclosure regulations). Cross-border transactions of domestic banks should be monitored by the home-country lender of last resort. Likewise, deposit insurance should follow host-country rules for branches and subsidiaries and home-country rules for cross-border transactions of domestic banks. Finally, restrictions on bank activities should be determined by home-country rules for cross-border transactions by domestic banks and by internationally coordinated rules for foreign branches and subsidiaries. How such coordination can be achieved was a subject of continuing debate in the late 1990s. In October 1998, the Bank for International Settlements released reports on the international financial architecture stressing regulatory transparency, strong domestic financial systems, and coordinated management of international financial crises.

THE FINANCIAL TIMES JANUARY 17, 2001

New Basle Committee Proposals

Financially sound companies in emerging markets should be able to borrow money more easily under new proposals to strengthen the solvency of the world's banking system.

(a) The new framework issued by the Basle committee on banking supervision yesterday would mean banks holding less capital when lending to such companies. However, banks would have to raise the amount of capital they hold for loans to less financially sound companies.

The long-awaited proposals—set to come into effect in 2004—would also allow big banks with sophisticated risk management systems to hold less capital and therefore strengthen their competitive position.

Others would have to hold more to reflect a wider range of risks than under the old rules established in 1988 and in force in more than 100 countries.

Overall, the banking system would not have to hold more capital as a result of the proposals, said Bill McDonough, president of the Federal Reserve Bank of New York, who chairs the committee.

As with the first Basle accord, banks would have to hold capital of at least 8% of their risk-adjusted assets—a percentage of the value of their loans—to meet potential credit problems. (b) But the exact amount required would be more finely tuned, with more grades of loans.

Companies and banks in emerging markets could now be given better risk grades than their home countries.

Securitized loans would need more capital set aside unless the risk is completely transferred out of the bank. However, there would be greater allowance for factors that reduce risk, such as collateral or guarantees.

One other change from 1988 is that credit risk would depend on not only the borrower, but also how exposed the bank is to a single borrower or sector.

(c) For the first time there will be a requirement to hold capital to cover operating risk—losses from inadequate staff, systems or unexpected events.

Enforcing the new rules—which are out for comment until the end of May—will need much greater intervention by regulators. Banks would also be expected to disclose much more information about risk strategies and capital requirements, in a bid to increase market pressures on them to pursue prudent lending.

The committee said it will work with regulators to ensure they are able to do the job. "We acknowledge that implementation might create resource problems, quantitatively and qualitatively," said Claes Norgren, director-general of the Financial Supervisory Authority and a committee member.

For international banks, 2000 still recalled memories of the Asian financial crisis, Russia's woes, volatile financial markets, and hedge fund troubles. Regulators struggled to keep up with events—and to recall and apply lessons from the recent past. The BCCI scandal taught international banking regulators at least two lessons. First, international banks doing business in many countries require careful supervision. Second, such supervision is easier when bank accounting and capital standards are coordinated across countries. The difficulties of foreign bank supervision became apparent to U.S. regulators again in 1995, when Japan's Daiwa Bank concealed information from the Federal Reserve about spectacular losses that one of its traders had incurred in the U.S. bond market over more than a decade.

In January 2001, the Basle Committee on Banking Supervision issued new proposals for capital requirements. Reacting to the proposals, many analysts praised the new developments but argued that regulators around the world have more lessons to learn.

a The international financial regulatory agencies represented in the Basle Committee on Banking Supervision argue that the use of risk management systems and collateral requirements should permit banks to lower the amount of equity capital they hold to support loans and other risky activities. Such a development would, however, place additional pressure on regulators of international banking to evaluate and monitor the new risk management systems. Because the proposed rules would broaden the definitions of risks to be measured, some institutions may wind up having to hold *more* capital.

b The new rules support the idea that overemphasis on macroeconomic conditions obscures the important roles played by financial institutions in providing risk-sharing, liquidity, and information services. In particular, inadequate supervision and regulation of financial institutions can create moral hazard, excessive risk taking, and financial crisis. "Micro" incentives for institutions are important in addition to "macro" conditions.

c There is certainly nothing wrong with risk taking per se, provided that risks are fairly priced and there is no implicit public subsidy for assuming risks. Some activities, such as trading and hedge fund commitments, are very risky. Two problems potentially emerge for regulators of financial institutions in this case: (1) the lack of transparency in risks, and (2) the possibility of public subsidies to banks through deposit insurance or implicit bailout promises. These problems suggest that, absent supervision, excessive risk taking is possible. The new bank solvency proposals are designed to force banks to internalize better the costs of the risks they assume.

For further thought . . .

Risk management is complex. In 1998, two Nobel Prize winners in economics were among the casualties of financial crises. What might regulators do to monitor risk taking by financial institutions?

Source: Excerpted from John Willman, "Basle Committee Unveils Bank Solvency Proposals," *Financial Times*, January 17, 2001.

KEY TERMS AND CONCEPTS

Agency office
Banker's acceptance
Branches
Currency swap
Edge Act corporations
Euromarkets
- Eurocurrency deposits
- Eurodollars
- Loan syndication

Exchange rate risk
Foreign bank branch
International banking facilities
International banks
International transaction currency
Offshore markets
Subsidiary U.S. bank

SUMMARY

1. The growth of international banking is a result of the explosion in international trade and the increasing integration of financial markets during the past 30 years. International banks primarily supply intermediation and transaction services.
2. International banks earn profits by providing risk-sharing, liquidity, and information services. For example, as with interest rate risk in domestic banking, international banks manage their exposure to exchange rate risk by using financial futures, options, and swaps; they also assist their customers in managing exchange rate risk. Banks promote liquidity by reducing customers' transactions costs in buying and selling foreign exchange and deposits denominated in foreign currencies. Through bankers' acceptances, banks provide information services to customers involved in international trade.
3. The Eurodollar market developed after World War II as a market for dollar-denominated deposits and loans. In recent years, currencies other than the U.S. dollar have been included in the market. Deposits in the Eurodollar market are short-term time deposits. Loans are of longer maturity (typically, five to ten years) and are made with a floating interest rate, determined as a spread over the London Interbank Offer Rate. To share risk, many large Euroloans are syndicated, with participation by many banks.

REVIEW QUESTIONS

1. Why does the international banking market exist?
2. Why has international banking grown so rapidly during the past two decades?
3. What are the most important international banking centers?
4. Do you expect that Edge Act corporations will become more or less important in the future?
5. What are international banking facilities? What can they do that regular U.S. banks cannot do?
6. What is the major type of risk that international banks must manage? What techniques do they use?
7. What is a currency swap? What benefits have made it so popular?
8. Why did foreign-exchange trading by banks grow so much during the 1980s and 1990s?
9. What is the fundamental problem that leads to credit risk in international trade? What financial instrument do banks use to avoid this problem?
10. What are Euromarkets? What brought them into existence? Who are their customers? What currencies do they use?
11. What is a loan syndication? Why is it often used with Euroloans?
12. How did U.S. banks get involved in Euromarkets?
13. Relate the problem of exchange rate risk in international banking to interest rate risk in domestic banking. On the basis of your understanding of interest rate risk, suggest strategies for managing exchange rate risk in international banking.

14. What is the purpose of capital requirements in international banking?
15. Describe how domestic financial regulation in the United States and elsewhere contributed to the development of Euromarkets. How does the growth of such markets complicate the responsibilities of a lender of last resort?

ANALYTICAL PROBLEMS

16. Suppose that your bank made a loan of ¥1 billion but has no yen deposits. Describe a financial futures contract that would provide a hedge against exchange rate risk.
17. Would it surprise you to learn that a banker's acceptance written on a U.S. firm and given to a firm in Japan ultimately is cashed by a firm in the United States? Explain.
18. During 1998 in Japan deposit rates paid by foreign-owned banks were lower than those paid by domestic banks. Can you think of reasons why this was the case?
19. Suppose that a U.S. firm, Big Ball, plans to sell 100,000 baseballs to a Japanese importer, Ichi-ball. Describe how Ichi-ball's bank in Japan could initiate a banker's acceptance to finance the transaction.
20. Evaluate: Credit risk is less important in international banking than in domestic banking.

DATA QUESTION

21. Find the most recent edition of the *Statistical Abstract of the United States* (published by the Department of Commerce) in your library. In the section called "Banking, Finance, and Insurance," you should be able to find a table reporting summary statistics on the location of the 500 largest banks in the world. Has the relative importance of U.S. banks (measured in this way) increased or decreased since 1970? On the basis of our analysis of financial institutions in Part 4, can you explain this trend? Does this trend tell you whether the profitability of U.S. banks is likely to rise or fall relative to that of banks in other countries? Explain.

PART

5

The Money Supply Process and Monetary Policy

In Part 5, we turn our attention to the money supply process and monetary policy. Chapter 17 and 18 provide a nuts-and-bolts analysis of the determination of the money supply and the monetary base.

To see *why* certain decisions are made and implemented, in Chapter 19, we study the Fed's organization and structure and its role as an economic policy-making body. We follow this analysis in Chapter 20 by describing the implementation of the Fed's monetary policy tools and seeing how they can be used to affect short-term interest rates.

In Chapter 21, we analyze how the Fed conducts monetary policy to achieve goals that promote economic well-being. We also identify difficulties in designing effective monetary policies and describe how the Fed can enact policies that achieve those goals. Chapter 22 broadens the analysis of monetary policy to include international considerations, such as monitoring exchange rate fluctuations. After describing consequences of central bank interventions in the foreign-exchange market, we evaluate successes and failures of central banks' exchange rate agreements.

Two themes guide our analysis in Part 5. First, to understand the money supply process and monetary policy, we need to understand the behavior of the actors that are involved—central banks, banks, and the public—at home and abroad. Second, we use this understanding of behavior to evaluate current policies and predict consequences of future policies.

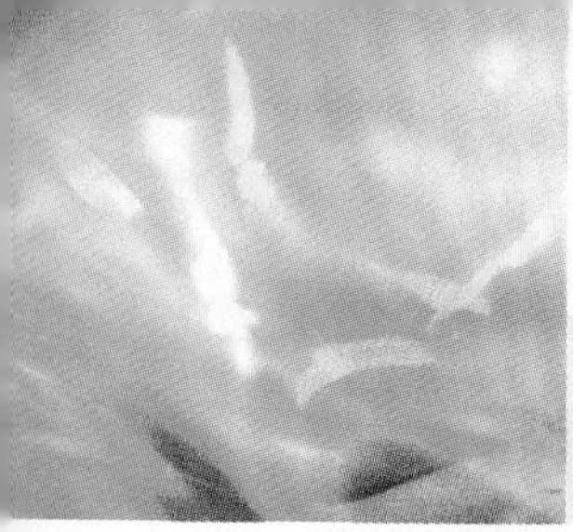

CHAPTER 17

The Money Supply Process

In the fall of 1998, Edward Boehne, a Federal Reserve executive, knew the Fed had goofed. When he checked into a hotel in a small town in Pennsylvania, the clerk looked at his title and said, "You didn't do enough." By mid-November 1998, the Fed had intervened three times to expand the money supply. After the third time, investors reacted to the good news of the expansionary policy by buying stock, causing the U.S. stock market to rise. Business executives celebrated falling interest rates, which could stimulate spending for plant and equipment.

The money supply is an economic variable that has an impact on interest rates, exchange rates, inflation, and an economy's output of goods and services. Fluctuations in the money supply can affect returns on investments, the prices of goods and services, and general economic well-being. As a result, the central bank—whether it is the European Central Bank, the Fed in the United States, the Bank of Japan, or the Bank of England—attempts to manage the money supply. How does a central bank like the European Central Bank or the Fed do this? To answer this question, you must know what influences the money supply and how a central bank can increase or decrease the amount of money in circulation. Our goal in this chapter is to construct a model that explains the size and variation in the money supply. Specifically, we look at the **money supply process** in the United States.

We organize our investigation of the money supply process by first describing the monetary base and then identifying the factors that convert the monetary base to the money supply. Then we combine these variables to determine the money supply. Our model includes the behavior of three actors in the money supply process: the Fed, the banks in the banking system, and the nonbank public. The Fed plays the largest role in determining both the monetary base and the money multiplier—but the Fed doesn't have complete control over the money supply. The behavior of banks and the nonbank public is crucial to the quantity of money that circulates in the economy. Figure 17.1 represents the money supply process, the actions that determine the quantity of money in the economy. This figure also shows which actors in the economy primarily influence each variable. In a nutshell, this diagram shows the components of the model and is the backbone of our analysis in this chapter.

In building the model of the money supply process, we work with a very limited definition of money. "Money" is limited to assets that are used as a

Figure 17.1

The Money Supply Process
Three actors determine the money supply: the central bank (the Fed), the nonbank public, and the banking system.

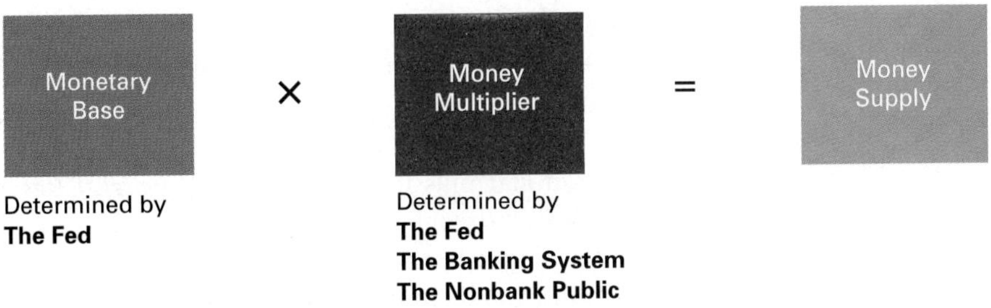

medium of exchange, specifically currency and checkable deposits in financial institutions. This monetary aggregate, *M1,* is the Fed's narrowest measure of money. The chapter appendix describes the money supply process for the next broadest measure of the money supply, *M2*.

THE FED AND THE MONETARY BASE

In addition to acting as a banker's bank, regulating the banking industry, and operating a network to clear checks, the Fed has another function. The Fed is the institution that is responsible for managing the nation's money supply. One way it does that is to control the monetary base. The **monetary base** comprises all currency in circulation and reserves held by banks.

We start our investigation of the monetary base—the first variable in the money supply process—by identifying the assets and liabilities on the Fed's balance sheet that measure components of the monetary base. Then we look at actions of the Fed that cause these assets and liabilities to change, thereby increasing or decreasing the monetary base.

To observe how the Fed manages the monetary base, we work with a simplified balance sheet. Although the Fed's actual balance sheet is more complex than the one we introduce here, the four entries shown in the following balance sheet matter the most in identifying the Fed's actions to increase or decrease the monetary base.

BALANCE SHEET OF THE FEDERAL RESERVE SYSTEM

Assets	Liabilities
U.S. government securities	Currency in circulation
Discount loans to banks	Reserves

The Fed's Liabilities

The Fed's principal liabilities are currency in circulation and reserves (deposits by banks with the Fed and cash held by banks). The sum of these two liabilities, together with the monetary liabilities of the U.S. Treasury (primarily coins in circulation, called *Treasury currency in circulation*), equals the monetary base. We consider the monetary base to be the sum of the Fed's currency in circulation and reserves, because the monetary liabilities of the Treasury are so small:

$$\text{Monetary base} = \text{Currency in circulation} + \text{Reserves}.$$

The dollar bills in your wallet are *Federal Reserve Notes.* They are part of the Fed's currency outstanding, which includes currency in circulation and vault cash. Specifically, **currency in circulation** is the currency held by the nonbank public, and **vault cash** is the currency held by depository financial institutions. Vault cash is still a liability of the Fed, but it is counted as reserves:

$$\text{Currency in circulation} = \text{Currency outstanding} - \text{Vault cash}.$$

At the end of September 2000, currency in circulation equaled $523.9 billion.

Reserves. The second largest liability of the Fed is **bank reserves,** or vault cash in banks and deposits by commercial banks and savings institutions with the Fed. Reserve deposits are assets for financial institutions. They are liabilities for the Fed because the Fed must redeem banks' requests for repayment on demand in Federal Reserve Notes. The total reserves of the banking system are the sum of banks' deposit accounts with the Fed ($6.8 billion as of September 2000) and vault cash ($39.3 billion as of September 2000). Thus

$$\text{Reserves} = \text{Deposits with the Fed by depository institutions} + \text{Vault cash}.$$

We can also view reserves from the banks' perspective. Total reserves are made up of amounts that the Fed compels depository institutions to hold, called **required reserves,** and extra amounts that depository institutions elect to hold, called **excess reserves:**

$$\text{Reserves} = \text{Required reserves} + \text{Excess reserves}.$$

The Fed specifies a percentage of deposits that banks must hold as reserves, which is known as the **required reserve ratio.** For example, if the required reserve ratio is 10%, a bank would have to set aside 10% of its checkable deposits—combinations of vault cash and deposits with the Fed—as reserves with the Fed. As of September 2000, of the $39.3 billion of bank reserves, only about $1.1 billion was excess reserves. Because the Fed doesn't pay interest on reserves, depository institutions prefer not to hold all their liquid balances as reserves. Instead, they hold some of their balances in marketable securities, on which they can earn interest.

The Fed's Assets

The two principal Fed assets are government securities and discount loans. The levels of these assets held by the Fed are determinants of the monetary base. In addition, the Fed earns income on its portfolio of government securities and interest on its discount loans. The Fed does not pay interest on currency or reserves. Most of the Fed's earnings of about \$34 billion are returned to the Treasury.

Government securities. The Fed's portfolio of government securities consists principally of holdings of U.S. Treasury obligations: Treasury bills, notes, and bonds. As of September 2000, the Fed held about \$511 billion in Treasury securities.

Discount loans. By extending loans to depository institutions to help banks handle liquidity problems, the Fed can increase the level of reserves. It earns a market interest rate on the U.S. government securities that it holds as assets. When the Fed lends to depository institutions, the loans are called **discount loans.** In making such loans, the Fed specifies an interest rate on the loans known as the **discount rate.** As of September 2000, the Fed's outstanding discount loans totaled about \$372 million. The discount rate at the same date was 6%.

How the Fed Changes the Monetary Base

The Fed increases or decreases the monetary base by manipulating the levels of its assets—that is, the Fed changes the monetary base by buying and selling Treasury securities or by making discount loans to banks. We describe the execution of these transactions in Chapter 20. In the description of the transactions that follows, we show how each changes the monetary base.

Open market operations. The most direct method the Fed uses to change the monetary base is **open market operations**—that is, buying or selling securities, generally U.S. government securities. In an **open market purchase,** which raises the monetary base, the Fed buys government securities. To execute such a transaction (for example, to buy \$1 million in government securities), the Fed draws checks totaling \$1 million on the Federal Reserve Bank of New York and uses them to buy the securities through banks or from the nonbank public. Commercial banks can redeem these checks for currency or, more likely, the banks can deposit the funds with the Fed as reserves. In either case, an open market purchase raises the monetary base, B, because the base is the sum of currency in circulation, C, and bank reserves, R. This relationship is expressed as

$$B = C + R. \tag{17.1}$$

When bank reserves, R, increase, the monetary base, B, increases. The following transactions will illustrate how this change in B takes place.

Suppose that the Fed buys \$1 million in T-bills from Megabank and pays for them with a check for \$1 million. Megabank can either deposit the funds in its account with the Fed or hold them as vault cash. Either action increases the reserves in the banking system by \$1 million. The banking system's balance sheet shows a decrease in security holdings of $1 million and an increase in reserves of the same amount:

BANKING SYSTEM

Assets		Liabilities	
Securities	−$1 million		
Reserves	+$1 million		

The changes in the Fed's balance sheet show an increase in securities (an asset) and an increase in reserves (a liability) by $1 million:

FEDERAL RESERVE

Assets		Liabilities	
Securities	+$1 million	Reserves	+$1 million

The open market purchase from depository institutions increases reserves and thus the monetary base by $1 million.

If the Fed purchases government securities from the nonbank public, sellers have two options: (1) to hold the proceeds as checkable deposits or (2) to hold the proceeds as currency. If the sellers deposit checks drawn on the Fed in the banking system, checkable deposits increase by $1 million. When banks deposit the Fed's checks in their account with the Fed, reserves also rise by $1 million:

NONBANK PUBLIC

Assets		Liabilities	
Securities	−$1 million		
Checkable deposits	+$1 million		

BANKING SYSTEM

Assets		Liabilities	
Reserves	+$1 million	Checkable deposits	+$1 million

As a result of the open market purchase, the Fed's portfolio of securities rises by $1 million, and bank reserves rise by the same amount:

FEDERAL RESERVE

Assets		Liabilities	
Securites	+$1 million	Reserves	+$1 million

As in the case of an open market purchase from depository institutions, this open market purchase from the nonbank public increases bank reserves by $1 million, thereby increasing the monetary base by $1 million.

If households and businesses decide to cash the Fed's checks and hold the proceeds as currency, the nonbank public decreases its holdings of securities by $1 million and increases its currency holdings by the same amount. The Fed increases currency in circulation by $1 million to acquire the $1 million of securities in the open market purchase:

NONBANK PUBLIC

Assets		Liabilities	
Securities	−$1 million		
Currency	+$1 million		

FEDERAL RESERVE

Assets		Liabilities	
Securites	+$1 million	Currency in circulation	+$1 million

While the proceeds from the sale of securities to the Fed are held as currency, the monetary base (the sum of currency in circulation and bank reserves) increases by the amount of the open market purchase, or $1 million.

To summarize, an open market purchase increases the monetary base by the amount of the purchase in all cases. The effect of the open market purchase on bank reserves depends on whether the nonbank public chooses to hold some of the proceeds as currency.

Similarly, the Fed can *reduce* the monetary base by an **open market sale** of government securities. Whether the securities are purchased with currency or with checkable deposits, an open market sale decreases the monetary base by the amount of the sale.

For example, suppose the Fed sells $1 million of securities to depository institutions or the nonbank public. If payments to the Fed are entirely in the form of checkable deposits, the Fed receives in payment $1 million in checks drawn on commercial banks. In this case, bank reserves with the Fed (a Fed liability) fall by $1 million, the Fed's securities holdings (an asset for the Fed) also fall by $1 million, and the monetary base falls by $1 million:

BANKING SYSTEM

Assets		Liabilities	
Securities	+$1 million		
Reserves	−$1 million		

FEDERAL RESERVE

Assets		Liabilities	
Securites	−$1 million	Reserves	−$1 million

Thus, if payments to the Fed are entirely in checkable deposits, reserves (and the monetary base) decline by the amount of the open market sale.

However, if payments to the Fed are entirely in currency, the open market sale won't affect reserves:

NONBANK PUBLIC

Assets		Liabilities	
Securities	+$1 million		
Currency	−$1 million		

FEDERAL RESERVE

Assets		Liabilities	
Securites	−$1 million	Currency in circulation	−$1 million

However, the monetary base (currency in circulation plus reserves) falls by $1 million.

The effects of open market operations on reserves and the monetary base are summarized in Fig. 17.2.

Discount loans. Although the Fed uses open market operations most often in managing the monetary base, it can also increase or decrease reserves by making discount loans to depository institutions. This change in bank reserves changes the monetary base.

Figure 17.2

Effect of Open Market Operations on Reserves and the Monetary Base

One method that the Fed uses to increase the monetary base is open market purchases of securities from the nonbank public or banks. The nonbank public holds the proceeds of the sale as currency (increasing currency in circulation) or deposits the proceeds in banks. Banks may choose to hold the proceeds as vault cash or deposit the proceeds in a Fed account, increasing reserves in either case. Because increases in currency in circulation or in reserves raise the monetary base, open market purchases increase the monetary base. The process of reducing the monetary base (not shown here) works in reverse.

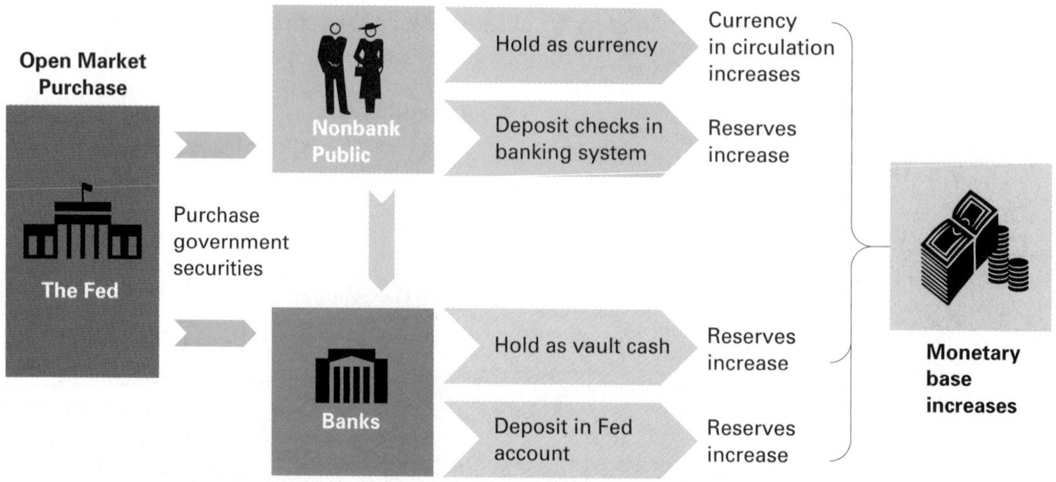

Let's examine the balance sheets for both the banks and the Fed to see how the monetary base changes if banks obtain \$1 million in discount loans from the Fed. For the Fed, assets rise by \$1 million from the addition to discount loans, and liabilities rise by \$1 million from the addition to bank reserves. Thus the discount loan affects both sides of the Fed's balance sheet:

FEDERAL RESERVE

Assets		Liabilities	
Discount loans	+\$1 million	Reserves	+\$1 million

Both sides of the banking system's balance sheet are also affected. Banks acquire \$1 million of assets in the form of reserves and \$1 million of liabilities in the form of discount loans payable to the Fed:

BANKING SYSTEM

Assets		Liabilities	
Reserves	+\$1 million	Discount loans	+\$1 million

As a result of the Fed's making \$1 million of discount loans, bank reserves and the monetary base increase by \$1 million.

However, if banks repay \$1 million in discount loans to the Fed, the preceding transactions are reversed. Reserves fall by \$1 million, as do the Fed's discount loans (assets) and the banking system's discount loans (liabilities):

FEDERAL RESERVE

Assets		Liabilities	
Discount loans	−\$1 million	Reserves	−\$1 million

BANKING SYSTEM

Assets		Liabilities	
Reserves	−\$1 million	Discount loans	−\$1 million

The effects of discount loans on reserves and the monetary base are summarized in Fig. 17.3.

Comparing Open Market Operations and Discount Loans

Although open market operations and discount loans both change the monetary base, the Fed has greater control over open market operations than over discount loans. The Fed completely controls the volume of open market operations because it initiates purchases or sales of securities by placing orders with dealers in the government securities markets. Of course, if the Fed wants to sell

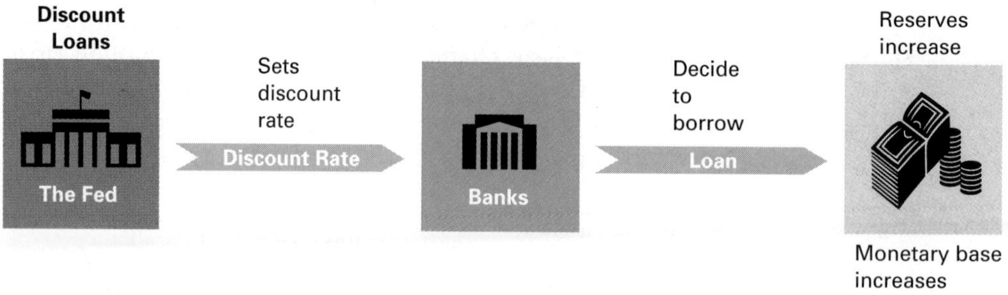

Figure 17.3

Effect of Discount Loans on Reserves and the Monetary Base

A second method for the Fed to increase the monetary base is through discount loans. The Fed does not control completely the volume of discount loans; it can reduce the discount rate, but banks must decide whether to borrow from the Fed. If banks choose to borrow from the Fed, reserves increase, increasing the monetary base. The process of reducing the monetary base using discount loans (not shown here) works in reverse.

a T-bill, someone must buy it or there is no open market operation. The Fed can sell securities at whatever price it takes to accomplish its goal, however.

The Fed's control over discount lending is much less complete than its control over open market operations because banks decide whether to borrow from the Fed. The Fed has some control over discount loans because it sets the discount rate. In fact, the discount rate differs from most interest rates because it is set by the Fed, whereas most interest rates are determined by market forces. An increase in the discount rate makes borrowing from the Fed more expensive for banks. If nothing else changes, banks then decrease their discount borrowing, which in turn reduces the monetary base. Hence decisions by both banks and the Fed determine the volume of discount loans.

The discount rate typically is lower than other short-term market interest rates, such as the federal funds rate or the rate on three-month T-bills. (The federal funds rate is the rate that banks charge each other on overnight loans.) Thus banks have a profit opportunity in that they can borrow from the Fed at the discount rate and lend the funds at higher rates. However, the Fed discourages banks from borrowing from it too often. Instead, banks borrow more frequently in the federal funds market from other banks that have extra reserves; they are willing to pay a higher interest rate than the discount rate for doing so.

As a result of the difference in the Fed's control over open market operations and discount loans, we think of the monetary base as having two components: the *nonborrowed monetary base*, B_{non}, and *borrowed reserves*, BR, or discount loans. We can express the monetary base, B, as

$$B = B_{non} + BR. \tag{17.2}$$

Although decisions by both the Fed and depository institutions determine the volume of discount loans, the Fed has greater control over the nonborrowed monetary base. In Chapter 18, we discuss in more detail the components of the monetary base and the Fed's ability to control each component.

CHECKPOINT

Which has a greater impact on the monetary base: an open market purchase of $10 million or a discount loan of $10 million? How do bank reserves change in each case? In each case, the monetary base rises by $10 million. The effect on bank reserves of an open market operation depends on how much currency the public chooses to hold. In the case of a discount loan, reserves rise by the amount of the loan. **o**

THE SIMPLE DEPOSIT MULTIPLIER

We now turn to the money multiplier in our quest to determine the factors that contribute to the money supply. The analysis proceeds in three steps because the money multiplier is determined not only by the Fed, but also by the actions of the nonbank public and banks in the banking system. The first step, which we describe in this section, shows how the money supply can be increased or decreased through multiple deposit creation. In this part of the analysis, we determine the simple deposit multiplier—a factor that converts the monetary base into a portion of the money supply. The second step adds the actions of the nonbank public on the money multiplier, and the third includes the actions of banks. In the sections that follow, we describe those steps and refine the simple deposit multiplier to find the money multiplier.

Multiple Deposit Expansion

What happens when the Fed increases bank reserves through open market operations or discount loans? To answer this question, we trace the changes that occur in a single bank and in the banking system.

How a bank responds to an increase in reserves. Suppose that the Fed purchases $100,000 in T-bills from Megabank, increasing Megabank's reserves by $100,000. After this transaction, Megabank's balance sheet changes to reflect these transactions:

MEGABANK

Assets		Liabilities
Securities	−$100,000	
Reserves	+$100,000	

The Fed's purchase of Megabank's T-bills increases Megabank's excess reserves, not its required reserves. The reason is that required reserves are determined as a percentage of the bank's checkable deposits. Because this transaction has no effect on Megabank's checkable deposits, it doesn't change the amount of reserves that Megabank is required to hold. Megabank earns no interest on the additional reserves obtained from the T-bill sale and will therefore try to use them to earn a return.

Suppose that Megabank loans $100,000 to Amalgamated Industries, there-by acquiring an asset on which it earns interest. Megabank extends the loan by creating a checking account for Amalgamated and depositing the loan proceeds in it. Both the asset and liability sides of Megabank's balance sheet increase by $100,000:

MEGABANK

Assets		Liabilities	
Securities	−$100,000	Checkable deposits	+$100,000
Reserves	+$100,000		
Loans	+$100,000		

Recall that the money supply equals currency in circulation plus checkable deposits (the definition of *M1*). By lending money to Amalgamated, Megabank creates checkable deposits. As a result of Megabank's actions, the money supply increases because checkable deposits have increased. Money is created because something that becomes money—namely, funds in the hands of the borrower—is exchanged for something that is not money—namely, a loan note in the hands of the lender.

Suppose that the required reserve ratio established by the Fed is 10%. That is, 10% of Megabank's checkable deposits must be held in cash reserves either at the Fed or as vault cash. Because Megabank increased its reserves by $100,000 and its deposits by $100,000, it must hold ($100,000)(0.10) = $10,000 as reserves. It now has additional excess reserves of $100,000 − (0.10)(100,000) = $90,000. However, the bank can't lend this amount because Amalgamated will be withdrawing its loan proceeds to buy goods and services supplied by other businesses and individuals. When Amalgamated has withdrawn the entire proceeds of the loan, Megabank will have lost $100,000 of reserves and checkable deposits:

MEGABANK

Assets		Liabilities	
Securities	−$100,000	Checkable deposits	$0
Loans	+$100,000		
Reserves	$0		

How the banking system responds to an increase in reserves. When Amalgamated writes checks to other businesses and individuals, these recipients deposit the proceeds in other banks—and those banks, in turn, make new loans. Thus the $100,000 increase in reserves from the Fed's purchase of securities from a single bank has expanded the volume of checkable deposits in the banking system. This process is called **multiple deposit expansion.** How much can other banks lend from an increase in their reserves? Because borrowers are likely to withdraw loan proceeds, banks cannot lend a greater amount than their total excess reserves. Nevertheless, multiple deposit expansion extends

CONSIDER THIS . . .

What Are the Origins of Multiple Deposit Expansion?

Multiple deposit expansion increased the money supply long before the founding of the Federal Reserve System. Indeed, we trace the safekeeping of money (say, gold or silver) using a deposit contract to Greek and Roman times. However, the earliest banks served only as warehouses for funds; that is, bankers did not make loans from deposits.

By the thirteenth and fourteenth centuries, deposit banking was well established in Italy and Spain, countries that were heavily engaged in trade and commerce. Merchant bankers there loaned money to businesses and maintained reserves to cover depositors' withdrawals. In Barcelona, for example, banks typically held reserves in gold of less than 30% of deposits. This system of banking, known as *fractional reserve banking,* was a significant step toward a more sophisticated financial system.

Although the Roman Catholic Church objected to charging interest on loans financed by deposits, a practice it called *usury,* the importance of deposit banking for commerce overcame those objections. Indeed, "a banker's social standing in thirteenth-century Florence was probably at least as good as in twentieth-century New York."† Deposit expansion, then and now, enables a greater volume of loans and deposits to be supported by a given level of bank reserves.

† Sidney Homer and Richard Sylla, *A History of Interest Rates.* New Brunswick, N.J.: Rutgers University Press, 1991, pp. 76–77.

the monetary base and increases the money supply, as we describe in the following examples.

Suppose that Amalgamated uses the $100,000 it borrowed from Megabank to buy $100,000 of equipment from Toolco. Toolco deposits the $100,000 in its bank, Onebank. After this transaction, Onebank's balance sheet changes as follows:

ONEBANK

Assets		Liabilities	
Reserves	+$100,000	Checkable deposits	+$100,000

Onebank's reserves have increased by $100,000. If the required reserve ratio is 10%, Onebank now has additional excess reserves of $90,000. Because Onebank can safely lend only this amount of excess reserves, it makes a $90,000 loan to Midtown Hardware to purchase new office equipment. Initially, Onebank's assets (loans) and liabilities (checkable deposits) rise by $90,000; but when Midtown spends the loan proceeds, Onebank's balance sheet changes as follows:

ONEBANK

Assets		Liabilities	
Reserves	+$10,000	Checkable deposits	+$100,000
Loans	+$90,000		

Midtown Hardware withdraws \$90,000 to buy office equipment from Computer Universe. Computer Universe deposits the \$90,000 in its bank, Twobank:

TWOBANK

Assets		Liabilities	
Reserves	+\$90,000	Checkable deposits	+\$90,000

Now, checkable deposits in the banking system have risen by another \$90,000. In total, the volume of deposits has risen by \$100,000 at Onebank and \$90,000 at Twobank, for a total of \$190,000.

Twobank faces the same decisions that confronted Megabank and Onebank. It wants to use the increase in reserves to expand its loans, but it can prudently lend only the increase in excess reserves. With a required reserve ratio of 10%, Twobank must add (\$90,000)(0.10) = \$9000 to its required reserves and can lend only \$81,000. Twobank lends the \$81,000 to Howard's Barber Shop for remodeling. Initially, Twobank's assets (loans) and liabilities (checkable deposits) rise by \$81,000; but when Howard's spends the loan proceeds, Twobank's balance sheet changes as follows:

TWOBANK

Assets		Liabilities	
Reserves	+\$9,000	Checkable deposits	+\$90,000
Loans	+\$81,000		

If the proceeds of the loan to Howard's Barber Shop are deposited in another bank, checkable deposits in the banking system will have risen by another \$81,000. The \$100,000 increase in reserves supplied by the Fed has increased the level of checkable deposits by \$100,000 + \$90,000 + \$81,000 = \$271,000. The money supply is growing with each loan. The initial increase of the monetary base changes the money supply by a multiple of that amount.

The process still isn't complete. The recipient of the \$81,000 check from Howard's Barber Shop will redeposit it, and checkable deposits at other banks expand. The process continues to ripple through the banking system and the economy, as Table 17.1 shows. Note that new checkable deposits continue to be created each time money is redeposited and loaned but that the increment gets smaller each time. The reason is that part of the money at each step cannot be lent; banks must hold it as reserves. As long as each bank lends the full amount of its excess reserves, we can calculate the amount of money created by the Fed's initial \$100,000 purchase of securities. The change in deposits, ΔD, is related to the initial change in reserves, ΔR, as follows:

$$\text{Change in deposits} = \text{Loan to Amalgamated} + \text{Loan to Midtown} + \text{Loan to Howard's} + \cdots$$

TABLE 17.1 **MULTIPLE DEPOSIT EXPANSION FOR THE FED'S PURCHASE OF $100,000 IN GOVERNMENT SECURITIES FROM MEGABANK AND A REQUIRED RESERVE RATIO OF 10%**

Bank	Increase in deposits	Increase in loans	Increase in reserves
Onebank	$ 100,000	$ 90,000	$ 10,000
Twobank	90,000	81,000	9,000
Nextbank3	81,000	72,900	8,100
Nextbank4	72,900	65,610	7,290
Nextbank5	65,610	59,049	6,561
.	.	.	.
.	.	.	.
.	.	.	.
	$1,000,000	$900,000	$100,000

or

$$\begin{aligned}\Delta D &= \Delta R + \Delta R[1 - (\overline{R/D})] + \Delta R[1 - (\overline{R/D})]^2 + \cdots \\ &= \$100{,}000 + \$100{,}000(1 - 0.10) + \$100{,}000(1 - 0.10)^2 + \cdots\end{aligned}$$

where

$$\begin{aligned}D &= \text{deposits} \\ R &= \text{reserves, and} \\ \overline{R/D} &= \text{the required reserve ratio.}\end{aligned}$$

We can restate the relationship between the change in the level of checkable deposits and the change in the level of reserves by simplifying the preceding equation. The change in checkable deposits equals the change in reserves multiplied by the **simple deposit multiplier,** which is the reciprocal of the required reserve ratio:

$$\Delta D = \Delta R\left\{\frac{1}{1 - [1 - (\overline{R/D})]}\right\} = \Delta R\left(\frac{1}{\overline{R/D}}\right), \tag{17.3}$$

or, in our example,

$$\Delta D = 100{,}000\left(\frac{1}{0.10}\right) = \$1{,}000{,}000.$$

Eventually, the increase in reserves of $100,000 leads to a tenfold expansion of checkable deposits. Thus the volume of checkable deposits expands by a factor equal to the reciprocal of the required reserve ratio, in this case 1/0.10 = 10.

If a depository institution decides to invest all or some of its excess reserves in marketable securities, deposit expansion still results in the same relationship between the change in reserves and the change in deposits. Suppose that Onebank had decided to purchase $90,000 worth of Treasury bills instead of extending the $90,000 loan to Midtown. Onebank would write a check to the owner of the securities in the amount of $90,000, which the seller would deposit in the banking system, and so on. Thus the effect on multiple deposit expansion is the same whether banks use excess reserves to make loans or buy securities.

At first you might think that individual banks are creating money. However, an individual bank can lend only the amount of its reserves that exceeds the amount it wants (or is required) to maintain. Deposits are expanded or created when borrowers do not hold the proceeds of loans as currency. If funds are redeposited, money flows back into the banking system as reserves. If banks do not want to hold excess reserves, the multiple deposit expansion process ends only when all excess reserves have been eliminated. Multiple deposit expansion refers to the banking system as a whole, not to the action of an individual bank.

CHECKPOINT

Suppose that, in Nationia, bank reserves equal $10 million and the required reserve ratio is 10%. If citizens of Nationia do not hold currency, how large is the stock of checkable deposits (if banks hold no excess reserves)?

$$D = \frac{R}{R/D}$$

$$= \frac{\$10 \text{ million}}{0.10} = \$100 \text{ million.}$$

What will happen to the level of checkable deposits if the central bank of Nationia increases the level of bank reserves by $500,000?

$$\Delta D = \Delta R\left(\frac{1}{R/D}\right)$$

$$= \frac{\$500{,}000}{0.10} = \$5 \text{ million.}$$

The level of checkable deposits rises by $5 million. **o**

Multiple Deposit Contraction

The Fed expands the volume of checkable deposits in the banking system by increasing reserves. Similarly, it can *contract* the volume of such deposits in the banking system by reducing reserves. The Fed does so by selling government securities in an open market operation. This action has a ripple effect that is similar to deposit expansion in the banking system, but in the opposite direction. The result of the open market sale is **multiple deposit contraction.**

Suppose that the Fed sells \$100,000 in Treasury securities to Megabank, thereby reducing Megabank's reserves by \$100,000. If Megabank has not maintained any excess reserves, it cannot now meet its reserve requirement. Megabank continually makes loans, and loans continually come due. Megabank can, if it has to, call some loans—that is, not renew them. By doing so, Megabank replenishes its reserves and can thus meet withdrawals. To raise reserves, then, Megabank could demand repayment of \$100,000 of loans but could also sell \$100,000 of securities. In either case, Megabank gains the needed \$100,000 of reserves. In the process, however, another bank loses reserves and checkable deposits. For example, if a depositor at Onebank buys \$100,000 of securities from Megabank, Onebank's reserves and checkable deposits fall by \$100,000.

When it loses \$100,000 in checkable deposits to Megabank (with a required reserve ratio of 10%), Onebank's required reserves decline by \$10,000. Hence it must increase its reserves by \$100,000 − \$10,000 = \$90,000. Onebank now faces the problem that Megabank experienced. If it has no excess reserves, it will have \$90,000 less reserves than it needs to satisfy the reserve requirement. As a result, Onebank must sell securities or demand repayment of loans to raise its reserves by \$90,000.

ONEBANK

Assets		Liabilities	
Reserves	−\$10,000	Checkable deposits	−\$100,000
Securities, Loans	−\$90,000		

Onebank's contraction will ripple through the banking system to other banks. Suppose that the \$90,000 that Onebank receives for its securities (or from loan repayments) is a check drawn on Twobank. Remember that Onebank faced a required reserves shortfall as a result of the loss of reserves to Megabank. The same problem now confronts Twobank. Twobank's required reserves are insufficient by \$90,000 − (0.10)(\$90,000), or \$81,000.

Our examination of multiple deposit expansion showed that an increase in reserves is multiplied in the banking system. Similarly, a decrease in reserves is multiplied in the banking system, resulting in multiple deposit contraction. If we assume that banks hold only required reserves, the reduction in deposits in the banking system because of the decrease in reserves is equal to the change in reserves multiplied by the reciprocal of the required reserve ratio:

$$\Delta D = \Delta R\left(\frac{1}{R/D}\right)$$

This is the same formula that we developed for multiple deposit expansion.

Multiple deposit expansion and multiple deposit contraction result from the actions of many banks in the banking system, not from the actions of one bank. As you can see from the examples, banks are a link between the Fed and the nonbank public, taking the increase in reserves from the central bank and funneling them to the nonbank public—and, in the process, increasing the money supply.

THE MONEY MULTIPLIER AND DECISIONS OF THE NONBANK PUBLIC

The simple deposit multiplier illustrates how a change in the monetary base results in a change in the money supply—but it is not the complete story. In deriving the simple deposit multiplier, we made an assumption that individuals and businesses held all their money as checkable deposits and that all excess reserves are loaned out. But everyone holds some money in cash, and banks do not always lend out their excess reserves. The behavior of individuals, the nonbank public, and banks changes the prediction of how the monetary base is multiplied to become the money supply. In this section, we look at the decisions that the nonbank public make that influence the money multiplier; in the next section, we look at the decisions of banks. You may read in the financial press that "the Fed controls the money supply." This statement is not quite correct, as you will soon see. The Fed acts to set the monetary base, but the behavior of the nonbank public and banks also influences the money supply.

The money supply equals currency in circulation and checkable deposits, which we represent by the now familiar equation:

$$M = C + D.$$

The amounts held as checkable deposits, D, are subject to multiple deposit creation; the amounts held as currency, C, are not. Therefore the money supply is likely to expand at a greater rate if the nonbank public has large holdings of D relative to C. We can express the proportion of cash to checkable deposits in a measure called the **currency–deposit ratio** (C/D). However, before demonstrating that a low value of the currency–deposit ratio increases the money supply, we examine how and why the currency–deposit ratio has changed over time. The ratio generally declined from the late nineteenth century through the mid-1960s, except during World War I, the early 1930s, and World War II. Beginning in the late 1960s, C/D began to rise steadily.

Determinants of Portfolio Choice

The decision the nonbank public makes on how to allocate liquid deposits between currency and checkable deposits is an example of portfolio allocation. As in our analysis in Chapter 5, we can predict how individuals make this decision according to their wealth as well as characteristics of each asset.

Wealth. One decision that the nonbank public makes is how much of its wealth to hold in the form of currency. Currency is a *necessity* asset. The proportion of wealth held in currency doesn't increase as a person gets richer. In other words, a typical wealthy individual will hold more currency than a not-so-wealthy individual will, but the wealthy person will not hold proportionately more. The reason is that checkable deposits are safer and more efficient for payment than holding larger amounts of currency. Hence an individual's currency–deposit ratio declines with increases in income and wealth. Moreover, for the economy as a whole, as the economy grows and national wealth increases, the currency–deposit ratio, C/D, declines. This change in national wealth explains the pattern of declining C/D before World War I, between the two world wars (except for the early 1930s), and after World War II until the early 1960s. These were periods of relatively steady economic growth, and therefore C/D decreased.

Expected returns. In choosing to hold currency or checkable deposits, the nonbank public compares the expected returns on these assets. The demand for an asset (in this case, currency or checkable deposits) depends on its expected return relative to expected returns on assets with similar risk, liquidity, and information characteristics. Because holding currency yields no interest, an increase in the interest paid on checkable deposits decreases the demand for currency relative to checkable deposits, decreasing C/D. A decrease in interest rates paid on checkable deposits increases C/D. Between 1933 and 1980, banking regulations prohibited banks from paying interest on checkable deposits; since 1980, regulations have allowed interest-bearing checkable deposits. As a result, the nonbank public is more likely to hold checkable deposits than cash.

Risk. Most often, there is little difference in the default risk of holding currency and checkable deposits. During a banking panic, however, there is a difference in the risk of currency versus checkable deposits. The return from holding currency is 0% in nominal terms, whereas holding checkable deposits in a failed bank can lead to a negative return. Therefore in times of crisis in the banking industry, we would expect to find an increased currency–deposit ratio. Indeed, in the early 1930s, when the public lost confidence in the banking system, depositors converted checkable deposits into currency, increasing C/D. Since the 1930s, most bank deposits have been covered (within limits) by federal deposit insurance. Reassured that their checkable deposits are safe, the nonbank public is less likely to include default risk in comparing currency with checkable deposits.

Liquidity. Currency is the most liquid asset possible because Federal Reserve Notes are definitive money in the United States. Checkable deposits by definition are convertible on demand into currency. Therefore the nonbank public doesn't generally consider liquidity differences when allocating how much currency to hold relative to checkable deposits.

Information cost. At first, the costs of obtaining information about currency and checkable deposits might seem to be identical. After all, no information is required to assess the value of currency, and with federal deposit insurance and bank supervision, individual depositors need little information to assess the value of checkable deposits. Nevertheless, there is an important difference between the two assets: Currency holdings are anonymous, whereas checkable deposits aren't. In other words, when you hold your money as checkable deposits, you leave a trail of information, but how much currency you hold would be very difficult for someone to discover. Currency thus carries an *anonymity premium,* meaning that it has a higher value than checkable deposits for its usefulness in illegal activities, such as drug transactions, black-market sales, and tax avoidance. The anonymity premium can help to explain two patterns observed during the twentieth century. First, the increase in *C/D* during wars, such as World Wars I and II, reflects the use of currency in black-market activities and high income tax rates during the war years. Second, from the late 1960s until the present, there has been a steady increase in *C/D*. Economists point to high marginal income tax rates during the 1960s—providing an incentive for individuals to accept untaxed cash—and the apparent increase in illegal activity in the drug trade during the 1980s and 1990s as reasons for this reversal. Analysts refer to economic activity and income earned but not reported to taxing authorities as *the underground economy.*

There is good reason to estimate a sizable underground economy in the United States because the amount of currency outstanding for every person in the country is more than $1000. Few individuals hold that much cash at any time, so it seems plausible that large amounts of cash are circulating in the underground economy to finance illicit activities or to avoid taxes. In fact, some experts estimate that the underground economy may account for more than 10% of total U.S. economic activity. In a $10 trillion U.S. economy, this amount would be more than $1 trillion. Collecting tax revenue from underground economic activity would sharply reduce the federal budget deficit. Significant amounts of U.S. currency also circulate as low-information-cost assets abroad—in Russia, for example.

If the underground economy, by definition, isn't measured, how can we estimate its size? Using what we know about the determinants of currency holdings by the nonbank public, we can trace movements in *C/D* to the underground economy. For example, an increase in marginal tax rates or the imposition of rationing (as in wartime) would increase the anonymity value of currency and hence *C/D*. Conversely, legalization of drugs, prostitution, or gambling would decrease the need for currency for underground transactions, reducing *C/D*.

Concluding Remarks

Table 17.2 summarizes the decisions the nonbank public makes in choosing currency over checkable deposits, and it shows the impact of these decisions on the currency–deposit ratio. The currency–deposit ratio represents a

TABLE 17.2 **DETERMINANTS OF THE CURRENCY–DEPOSIT RATIO**

An increase in . . .	Causes *C/D* to . . .	Because . . .
wealth	fall	in general, *C/D* decreases with rising income and wealth in the economy.
expected returns on deposits	fall	an increase in interest rates offered on checkable deposits increases the public's demand for those deposits relative to currency and decreases *C/D*.
riskiness of deposits	rise	under normal circumstances, default risk does not affect *C/D*. During banking panics, an increase in the perceived riskiness of deposits increases *C/D*.
liquidity of deposits	no change	under normal circumstances, there is little difference in the liquidity of currency and checkable deposits and thus little or no effect on *C/D*.
information or anonymity value of cash	rise	an increase in the demand for anonymity, owing to black-market, tax evasion, other illegal activities, or desirability abroad increases *C/D*.

portfolio allocation decision by the nonbank public. Currency holdings relative to checkable deposits are influenced by the determinants of portfolio choice: wealth and expected returns adjusted for risk, liquidity, and information-cost characteristics.

CHECKPOINT

In each of the following cases, what would you expect to happen to the currency–deposit ratio?

(a) Interest rates on checkable deposits rise.

(b) Higher tax rates prompt increased underground activity.

(c) A tremendous wave of counterfeit bills hits the United States.

Answers:

(a) Expected return on deposits rises, so *C/D* falls.

(b) Increased underground activity raises demand for currency, so *C/D* rises.

(c) Increased risk of currency reduces demand for currency, so *C/D* falls. o

BANK BEHAVIOR: EXCESS RESERVES AND DISCOUNT LOANS

In addition to assuming that the nonbank public holds all its currency in checkable deposits when constructing the simple deposit multiplier, we assumed that banks held no excess reserves. (Excess reserves, you will recall, are reserves greater than those required by the Fed.) But banks sometimes hold excess reserves in vault cash or deposits with the Fed. When banks hold reserves, the size of the money multiplier is less than the simple deposit multiplier would suggest. Like the nonbank public, banks make portfolio allocation decisions that determine whether they will hold excess reserves or use them to make loans or investments. In addition, banks must decide whether to borrow from the Fed, and their decisions to incur discount loans also affect the amount of the monetary base that the Fed controls.

Excess Reserves

How do banks determine how much excess reserves to hold relative to their deposits? The principal determinant is the expected return from holding excess reserves as compared to the return on alternative uses of the funds. Because reserves deposited with the Fed pay no interest, the opportunity cost of holding excess reserves is the market interest rate—the rate that the bank could obtain by lending or investing its funds.

Figure 17.4 shows that banks hold generally small levels of excess reserves, but the amount of excess reserves fluctuates over time. In the early 1980s, when market interest rates were high, banks decreased their excess reserves. An increase in market interest rates, all else being equal, decreases excess reserves; a decrease in the market interest rate increases excess reserves. In other words, holdings of excess reserves by banks are inversely related to the market interest rate.

The reason banks hold excess reserves despite the opportunity cost has to do with Fed–bank relationships. The Fed stipulates certain reserve requirements,

Figure 17.4

Excess Reserves and Discount Loans (1959–2000)

Banks hold some reserves in excess of their required reserves. Discount loans represent reserves borrowed by banks from the Fed.

Source: Federal Reserve Bulletin, various issues.

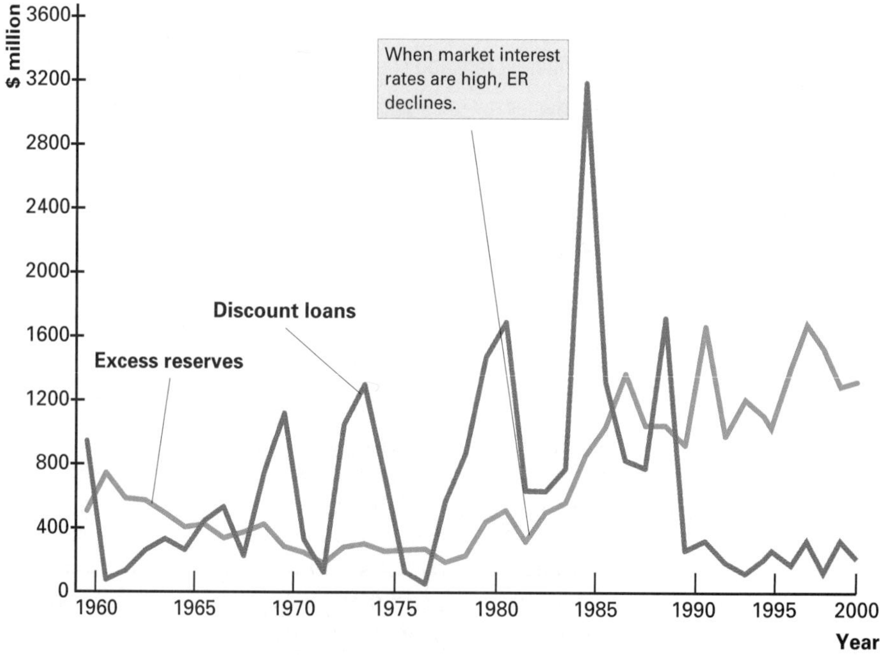

but it discourages banks from frequent borrowing at the discount rate to satisfy reserve requirements. When a bank's reserve holdings are insufficient, the Fed may impose penalties. Such penalties include a penalty rate on discount loans needed to satisfy the reserve requirement and a "stern discussion." To avoid relying on discount borrowing to satisfy reserve requirements, banks hold small amounts of excess reserves. In addition, when banks overestimate withdrawals expected from depositors, they end up with reserves in excess of those required.

An even more important reason for banks to hold excess reserves is that they serve as a cushion against high expected deposit outflows or significant variability in deposit outflows. Without this cushion, if deposit withdrawals exceeded reserves, a bank would be forced to bear the costs in one of three ways: (1) by selling securities, (2) by calling in loans, or (3) by borrowing from the Fed or in the open market. In extreme cases, the bank could fail. Hence the benefit of excess reserves as a cushion against deposit outflows can outweigh the opportunity cost of other uses of those funds. As an example, banks maintained high excess reserve holdings during the early 1930s to ensure that they could satisfy future deposit withdrawals. The theory of portfolio allocation predicts that an increase in the expected level or variability of deposit outflows increases excess reserves. Conversely, a decrease in the expected level or variability of deposit outflows decreases excess reserves. Thus the level of excess reserves in the banking system is positively related to the expected level or variability of deposit outflows.

Discount Loans

The Fed makes discount loans available to banks, but the level of loans is determined by the banks themselves. Banks are more inclined to borrow from the Fed when the market interest rate they can earn on their loans and investments is greater than the discount rate. Banks are less likely to borrow from the Fed when the spread between the market interest rate and the discount rate is small. Hence discount borrowing by banks is positively related to the market interest rate and negatively related to the discount rate. When market interest rates are high relative to discount rates, as in the early 1980s in Fig. 17.4, banks have an incentive to seek discount loans.

Economists have documented that when the spread between the rates on three-month T-bills and discount loans increases, so does the volume of discount lending. In addition, the Fed's willingness to lend to banks influences the volume of discount loans made to banks. The Fed generally discourages routine discount borrowing, but on occasion it has strongly encouraged banks to borrow from it. For example, it did so during the October 1987 stock market crash.

Table 17.3 summarizes the determinants of banks' decisions regarding excess reserves and discount loans. Banks' portfolio allocation decisions about excess reserves and discount loans—decisions based on expected returns—influence the money multiplier and the money supply.

TABLE 17.3 **DETERMINANTS OF EXCESS RESERVES AND DISCOUNT LOANS**

An increase in . . .	Causes . . .	Because . . .
market interest rates	excess reserves to fall	the opportunity cost of holding excess reserves rises.
average level or variability of deposit outflows	excess reserves to rise	banks require a greater cushion against outflows.
market interest rates relative to the discount rate	discount loans to rise	banks' profits from discount borrowing increase.

Before going on to the conclusion of the money supply process, it is worth reflecting on the Fed's actions and the behavior of banks and the nonbank public. We now have all the pieces we need to calculate an accurate **money multiplier**—an expression that converts the monetary base to the money supply. This expression is a modification of the simple deposit multiplier that includes the nonbank public's decisions on holding currency versus checkable deposits and banks' decisions on holding reserves and taking discount loans. You also can see why we say that the Fed doesn't "control" the money supply. Although it influences the amount of checkable deposits in the economy by determining in large part the monetary base, it cannot completely control the actions of other players in the economy. Therefore it is more accurate to say that the Fed manages the money supply or guides monetary policy—but it does not wave a magic wand and establish a particular amount of money in the economy.

DERIVING THE MONEY MULTIPLIER AND THE MONEY SUPPLY

We can synthesize the information presented about the monetary base and the modification of the simple deposit multiplier into an equation that predicts what the money supply will be. The conclusion of our efforts requires two steps: First, we must calculate the money multiplier; then we can use this expression to find the money supply.

We build on our analysis of decisions by the Fed, the nonbank public, and banks to derive the money multiplier. In particular, we take into account (1) the effects of Fed decisions on the level of reserves; (2) the effects of portfolio allocation decisions by the nonbank public, assuming that the ratio of currency to checkable deposits, C/D, is constant; and (3) the effects of decisions by banks about excess reserves, ER, assuming that banks hold a constant proportion of deposits as excess reserves, ER/D.

Let's begin by considering how the Fed affects the money multiplier m by setting the required reserve ratio. Total reserves, R, equal the sum of required reserves, RR, and excess reserves, ER:

$$R = RR + ER. \tag{17.4}$$

The Fed sets the level of required reserves by requiring banks to hold a certain percentage of checkable deposits as reserves. Thus required reserves equal the required reserve ratio, R/D, multiplied by the level of checkable deposits, D:

$$RR = \left(\overline{R/D}\right)\left(D\right). \tag{17.5}$$

Substituting this expression for required reserves into Eq. (17.4) for total reserves, we get

$$R = \left(\overline{R/D}\right)\left(D\right) + ER. \tag{17.6}$$

Recall that we started our discussion of the money supply process by noting that the money supply can be thought of as the product of the monetary base and the money multiplier. Hence we need to move from reserves to the monetary base. The monetary base, B, equals the sum of currency, C, and reserves, R, so we use Eq. (17.6) to obtain

$$\begin{aligned} B &= C + R \\ &= C + \left(\overline{R/D}\right)\left(D\right) + ER. \end{aligned} \tag{17.7}$$

Suppose, for example, that checkable deposits total \$1 billion and that currency totals \$300 million. Suppose also that the Fed requires banks to hold 10% of their checkable deposits as reserves and that banks hold no excess reserves. How large is the monetary base? It is the sum of currency (\$300 million) and reserves (the required reserve ratio, 0.10, times the level of deposits, \$1 billion):

$$B = \$300 \text{ million} + (0.10)(\$1 \text{ billion}) = \$400 \text{ million}.$$

Now we incorporate the nonbank public's and banks' portfolio allocation decisions into the equation for the monetary base. If currency holdings by the nonbank public are a constant fraction of checkable deposits, then

$$C = (C/D)(D).$$

If banks' holdings of excess reserves are a constant fraction of checkable deposits, then

$$ER = (ER/D)(D).$$

Substituting these two expressions into Eq. (17.7), we obtain the following equation for the monetary base:

$$B = (C/D)(D) + (\overline{R/D})(D) + (ER/D)(D)$$
$$= [(C/D) + (\overline{R/D}) + (ER/D)](D). \tag{17.8}$$

If we divide both sides of Eq. (17.8) by the term in the brackets and rearrange, we can express the relationship of checkable deposits to the monetary base as

$$D = \left[\frac{1}{(C/D) + (\overline{R/D}) + (ER/D)}\right](B). \tag{17.9}$$

Returning to our example, we can verify that checkable deposits are equal to $1 billion. The monetary base is $400 million; banks hold no excess reserves, so $ER/D = 0$; and the required reserve ratio is 0.10. The currency–deposit ratio is $300 million/$1 billion, or 0.30. Hence

$$D = \left(\frac{1}{0.30 + 0.10 + 0}\right)(\$400 \text{ million}) = \$1 \text{ billion.}$$

Finally, we are ready to complete the process by moving from deposits to the money supply, M, which is equal to currency, C, plus deposits, D. Then, substituting $(C/D)(D)$ for C, we get

$$M = C + D$$
$$= [(C/D)D] + D$$
$$= D[1 + (C/D)].$$

Substituting for D and using Eq. (17.9) gives an expression relating the money supply, M, to the monetary base, B:

Money supply = (Money multiplier) (Monetary base),

or

$$M = \left[\frac{1 + (C/D)}{(C/D) + (\overline{R/D}) + (ER/D)}\right](B). \tag{17.10}$$

The expression in brackets in Eq. (17.10) is equal to the money multiplier, m. The money supply equals the monetary base times the money multiplier. The money multiplier conveys by how much the money supply responds to a given change in the monetary base.

OTHER TIMES, OTHER PLACES . . .

The Money Multiplier and Money Supply During the Early 1930s

During the depths of the Great Depression in the United States (1930–1933), the money multiplier was extremely unstable. Why did this happen? What insights can we gain from that experience for predicting the multiplier in the future?

The most severe banking crisis in U.S. history occurred in the early 1930s. Problems originated in the late 1920s, as falling farm prices caused farmers to default on agricultural bank loans. Other sources of the crisis were the failures of some prominent U.S. and European financial institutions in 1930 and 1931 and Britain's abandonment of the gold standard in September 1931, which led international investors to question whether the dollar would continue to be tied to gold. By 1933, more than one-third of the commercial banks in the United States had failed or had been taken over by other banks.

The banking crisis significantly changed the money multiplier by affecting the portfolio allocation decisions of the nonbank public and banks. First, because of the perceived increase in riskiness of bank loan portfolios, wary depositors converted (or tried to convert) deposits into currency. The currency–deposit ratio, *C/D*, increased steadily after 1931 and dramatically in early 1933, more than doubling. Currency holdings by the public represent a leakage from the deposit creation process, so the multiplier and money supply fell while the monetary base was relatively stable.

Because of the wave of bank runs, by 1932 banks had to anticipate greater deposit outflows and increased their holdings of excess reserves. As a result, the ratio of excess reserves to deposits, *ER/D*, increased, further reducing the money multiplier.

The Fed did not aggressively increase its discount lending during the banking panic of 1931–1933, worsening the problems of the banking system and prompting the public to convert checkable deposits to currency and banks to convert loans to reserves. As a result of these portfolio allocation decisions by banks and the nonbank public, the money multiplier fell from 3.8 in March 1930 to 2.3 in March 1933. Although the monetary base *increased* by about 20% over the same period, the money supply actually *fell* by 28%.

Note: Figures are based on data from Milton Friedman and Anna J. Schwartz, *A Monetary History of the United States, 1867–1960.* Princeton, N.J.: Princeton University Press, 1963, pp. 299–419.

For example, suppose that Nationia's monetary base is \$10 billion, the required reserve ratio is 0.15, the currency–deposit ratio is 0.35, and banks hold no excess reserves. How large is the stock of checkable deposits? How large is the total money supply? The money multiplier in this case is

$$m = \frac{1 + (C/D)}{(C/D) + (\overline{R/D})} = \frac{1.35}{0.35 + 0.15} = 2.7.$$

The money supply is equal to the money multiplier times the monetary base, so

$$\text{Money supply} = 2.75(\$10 \text{ billion}) = \$27 \text{ billion}.$$

Checkable deposits, D, are

$$D = M - C = M - (C/D)(D),$$

so

$$D = \frac{M}{1 + (C/D)} = \frac{\$27 \text{ billion}}{1.35} = \$20 \text{ billion.}$$

We now have a complete description of the money supply process:

1. The money supply equals the monetary base times the money multiplier.
2. The monetary base comprises the nonborrowed base, determined primarily by the Fed through open market operations, and discount loans, determined jointly by the banks and the Fed.
3. The money multiplier depends on the required reserve ratio (determined by the Fed), excess reserves relative to deposits (determined by banks), and the currency–deposit ratio (determined by the nonbank public).

Table 17.4 summarizes the variables determining the money supply. As we show below, understanding these variables helps us to account for actions of the Fed, banks, and the public in the short run and in the long run.

TABLE 17.4 VARIABLES IN THE MONEY SUPPLY PROCESS

An increase in the . . .	Based on the actions of . . .	Causes the money supply to . . .	Because . . .
nonborrowed base, B_{non}	the Fed (open market operations)	rise	the monetary base rises, and more reserves are available for deposit expansion.
reserve requirements, $\overline{R/D}$	the Fed (reserve requirements)	fall	fewer reserves can be lent out, and the money multiplier falls.
discount rate	the Fed (discount policy)	fall	discount loans become more expensive, reducing borrowed reserves and the monetary base.
currency–deposit ratio, C/D	the nonbank public (portfolio decisions)	fall	the money multiplier falls, reducing deposit expansion.
excess reserves relative to deposits, ER/D	banks (portfolio decisions)	fall	the money multiplier falls, reducing deposit expansion.
expected deposit outflows	the nonbank public (transactions considerations)	fall	excess reserves rise relative to deposits, reducing the money multiplier and deposit expansion.
variability of deposit outflows	the nonbank public (transactions and portfolio considerations)	fall	excess reserves rise relative to deposits, reducing the money multiplier and deposit expansion.

CASE STUDY

Using the Money Supply Equation to Predict Money Growth

The money supply equation allows us to forecast growth of the money supply. We analyze the determinants of changes in the money supply, *M* (measured by *M1*), first by examining changes in the money multiplier, *m,* and then by examining changes in the monetary base, *B.* Recall that the monetary base, *B,* equals the sum of the nonborrowed base, B_{non}, and borrowed reserves, *BR* (discount loans). Thus we can express the money supply as

$$M = m(B_{non} + BR).$$

The money multiplier, *m,* depends on the required reserve ratio, the currency–deposit ratio, and the ratio of excess reserves to checkable deposits.

To focus on growth rates of the money supply, we need an expression for the percentage change in *M:* $\%\Delta M$. The percentage change in *M* is approximately equal to the sum of the percentage change in the money multiplier, $\%\Delta m$, and the percentage change in the monetary base, $\%\Delta(B_{non} + BR)$:

$$\%\Delta M \cong \%\Delta m + \%\Delta(B_{non} + BR).$$

Let's begin with a simple example and assume that the money multiplier is constant so that $\%\Delta m = 0$. We can then express the percentage change in the money supply as $\%\Delta M = \%\Delta(B_{non} + BR)$. To forecast the growth rate of the money supply, we need to predict the growth rate of the monetary base. To do so, we study Fed decisions about open market operations that affected the nonborrowed base, B_{non}, and bank and Fed decisions about discount loans, *BR.* As we noted earlier, *BR* is small relative to B_{non}, so, not surprisingly, most analysts studying the money supply are Fed watchers, or careful observers of the Fed's actions and intentions. As long as the percentage change in the money multiplier is zero or very small, careful forecasting of changes in discount loans and especially in the nonborrowed base will produce a good prediction of the growth of the money supply.

We can use some actual data to translate changes in the money supply into changes in the monetary base and the money multiplier. Figure 17.5 presents data on percentage changes in the money supply, the monetary base, and the money multiplier from 1979 through 2000. During this period, the money supply grew at an average annual rate of about 5.3%. This growth was fueled mainly by increases in the monetary base, which averaged 6.6% overall. From beginning to end, the money multiplier declined. Figure 17.5 shows that virtually all the average annual rate of growth in the money supply (7.3%) from 1980 through 1984 can be explained by growth in the monetary base (7.2%); the money multiplier grew by only 0.1% per year. Virtually all the growth in the monetary base represented growth in the nonborrowed base from the Federal Reserve System's open market operations. The only significant exception during the 1980s and early 1990s came in 1984,

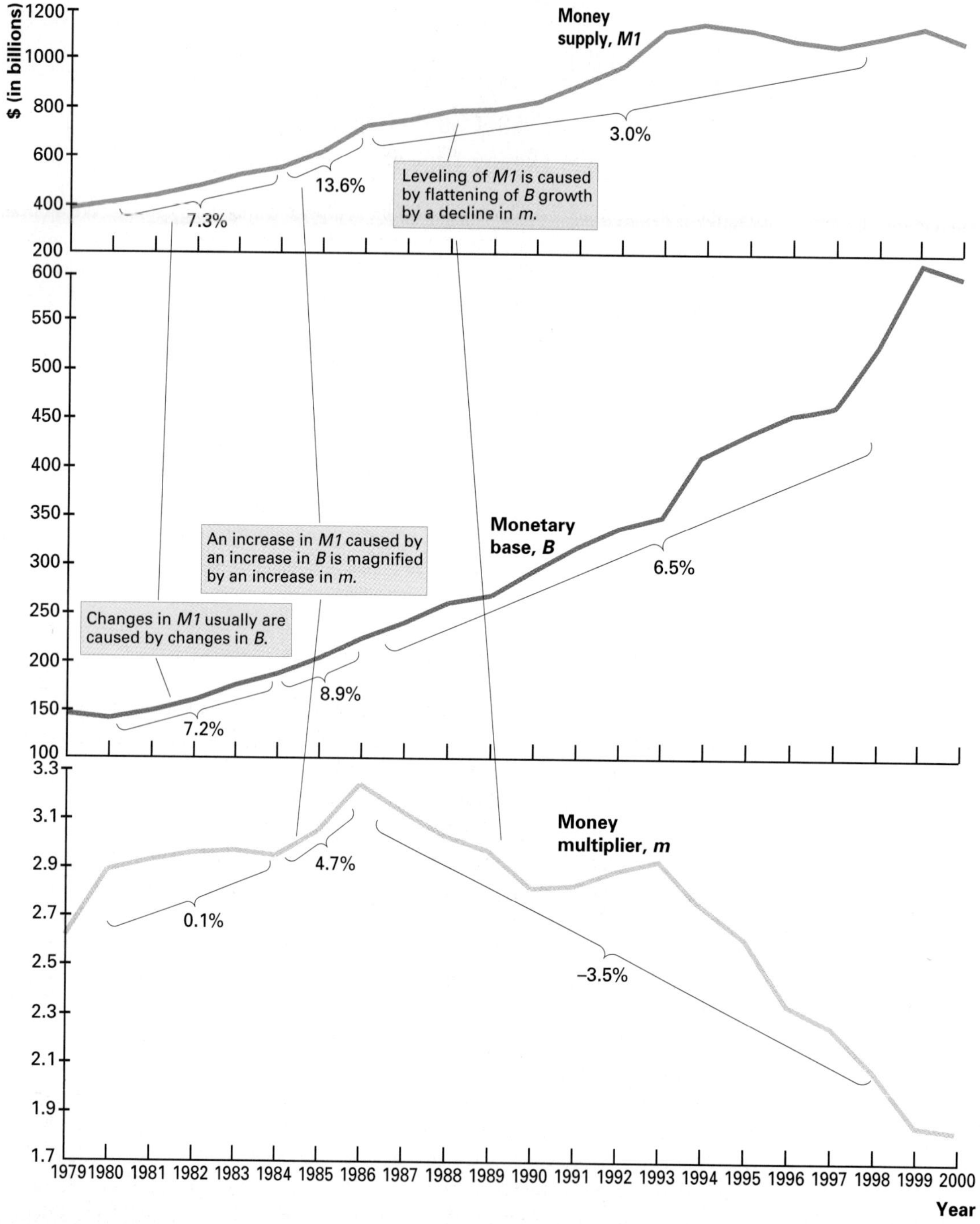

Figure 17.5 **Accounting for Changes in the Money Supply (*M1*)**

Over long periods of time, fluctuations in the monetary base primarily determine changes in the money supply. Over short periods of time, fluctuations in the money multiplier magnify or dampen the effects of changes in the monetary base on the money supply.

Source: Federal Reserve Bulletin.

when the Fed provided discount loans of about $5 billion to the distressed Continental Illinois Bank. Over periods of several years, the primary determinant of changes in the money supply is changes in the nonborrowed portion of the monetary base, B_{non}, which is controlled by the Federal Reserve System through open market operations.

Many forecasters in the financial community try to predict *short-term* movements in the money supply. Over short periods of time, however, the correlation between the Fed's actions to change the monetary base and actual changes in the money supply are much less precise. Short-run disturbances in the components of the money multiplier disrupt the relationship, as the second and third periods in Fig. 17.5 indicate.

Note that over short periods of time, the money multiplier may change significantly. For example, in 1985 and 1986, the money multiplier grew at a rate of 4.7% per year. Over the same period, the monetary base grew by 8.9% per year, and the *M1* money supply grew by 4.7% + 8.9% = 13.6% per year. To account for the change in the money multiplier, we must analyze changes in its components. The culprit turned out to be the currency–deposit ratio, *C/D*. Not shown in Fig. 17.5, *C/D* declined by about 17% over these two years, increasing the money multiplier. This effect was reversed after 1986, and since then, the declining money multiplier has generally reflected an increase in the currency–deposit ratio.

Our analysis of this description of changes in the money supply during the 1980s and 1990s shows that changes in the money multiplier may lead to a significant change in the money supply in a short period of time. Nonetheless, over long periods of time, in periods in which households' demand for money is stable, the majority of changes in the money supply can be explained by changes in the monetary base. By far the most important determinant of changes in the monetary base is the Fed's actions to change the nonborrowed base through open market operations.

KEY TERMS AND CONCEPTS

Bank reserves
- Excess reserves
- Required reserve ratio
- Required reserves

Currency–deposit ratio
Currency in circulation
Discount loans
Discount rate
Money supply process
- Monetary base
- Money multiplier

Multiple deposit contraction
Multiple deposit expansion
Open market operations
- Open market purchase
- Open market sale

Simple deposit multiplier
Vault cash

SUMMARY

1. The basic measure of the money supply we model is *M1*, the sum of currency in the hands of the nonbank public and checkable deposits at depository institutions. The three participants in the money supply process are the Federal Reserve System, depository institutions (banks), and the nonbank public.
2. The money supply process has two parts. First, actions by the Fed largely determine the monetary base. Then the money multiplier measures the amount by which the money supply changes in response to a change in the monetary base.

THE NEW YORK TIMES JANUARY 4, 2001

The Fed and the Monetary Base: Thwarting a Slowdown

Confronted with increased evidence that the economy is stalling, the Federal Reserve slashed its benchmark interest rate by half a percentage point yesterday, stunning investors and sending a powerful signal that the Fed is worried about the prospects for keeping the decade-long expansion alive.

a Acting between scheduled meetings, and with barely disguised haste, the central bank cut its federal funds target rate on overnight loans between banks to 6% from 6.5%. In a statement, it then signaled that it was likely to cut rates further in coming weeks and months.

"There's a simple message," Bruce Steinberg, chief economist at Merrill Lynch, said. "The Fed will do whatever it takes to keep the U.S. economy from going down the tubes."

The action, announced just after 1 P.M., caught most investors flat-footed. It set off a strong rally on Wall Street, where lower rates are seen as a powerful antidote to the months-long tumble in stock prices. . . .

It was the first rate reduction since November 1998, the first half-point rate cut since 1992, and the first time the central bank has changed policy between meetings since October 1998, a time when the global financial crisis was threatening the United States. . . .

The hastiness of the decision to cut rates was underscored by the way the Fed handled the other interest rate it controls, the discount rate on loans to banks by the Federal Reserve system. Although the discount rate is usually kept below the federal funds target rate, the Fed often moves the two rates up and down more or less in tandem.

b But while the central bank cut the federal funds rate by half a point yesterday, it only cut the discount rate by a quarter of a percentage point, to 5.75%. It did so because, under the central bank's procedures, changes in the discount rate are prompted by requests from the Federal Reserve banks—and no bank had thought to ask, before yesterday, for more than a quarter-point reduction in the discount rate. As a result, the Fed said it would act soon to cut the discount rate again by another quarter point, once it got a formal request from one or more of the banks to do so.

The Fed made clear that yesterday's action was likely to be the first step in a series of rate cuts intended to prolong an expansion that became the longest on record last February. . . .

In its statement yesterday, the Fed signaled that the central bankers believed that further rate cuts would probably be necessary. . . .

Even as it took strong action to head off a recession, the Fed offered a few reassuring words. It noted that there is almost no inflation, and it suggested that Mr. Greenspan's faith in the economy's long-term potential was unshaken, noting that "there is little evidence to suggest that longer-term advances in technology and associated gains in productivity are abating."

In January 2001, the Federal Reserve cut short-term interest rates by one-half of a percentage point, from 6.5% to 6%. To accomplish this, the Fed used open market purchases of short-term Treasury securities to increase bank reserves and the monetary base. The open market purchases put upward pressure on the prices of Treasury securities and downward pressure on yields—the Fed's great goal—as the monetary base expanded.

a During 2000, the growth rate of *M1*, the Fed's measure of money in the form of currency and checkable deposits, slowed significantly, becoming negative over the year; *M2* growth also slowed. Some economists and policymakers worried that the reduction in money growth increased the chance that the U.S. economy would slip into a recession during 2001. This worry was not lost on Fed officials, who remembered accusations that low rates of growth in the money supply in 1990, 1991, and 1992 prolonged the most recent U.S. recession and delayed the economic recovery from it.

The slowdown in money growth reflects some combination of a slowdown in the growth rate of the monetary base or a fall in the money multiplier. While *M1* fell during 2000, the monetary base grew modestly. While monetary base growth slowed, the money multiplier (influenced by decisions of the nonbank public and banks) fell as well. The required reserve ratio (*R/D*) did not change during the year, and the ratio of excess reserves to checkable deposits (*ER/D*) fell during 2000. An important culprit for the decline in *M1* was a fall in the money multiplier that was traced to a jump in the currency–deposit ratio (*C/D*). (Many economists explained this shift by a large increase in demand for U.S. currency abroad.)

b The Fed's reduction in the discount rate made it more attractive for banks to borrow from the Fed. The monetary base is composed of nonborrowed reserves (supplied by the Fed through open market operations) and borrowed reserves (supplied by the Fed through discount lending). Most of the Fed's intended changes in the monetary base are accomplished through open market operations. The article considers the change in the discount rate to be largely symbolic both because the volume of discount borrowing is relatively small and because banks must decide whether to seek discount loans.

For further thought . . .

During 2000, some financial practitioners suspected that the decline in *M1* was due to banks' practice of "sweeping" funds from interest-bearing checking accounts (a component of *M1*) into savings accounts (not in *M1*, but a component of *M2*). How would you evaluate the merits of this explanation?

Source: Richard W. Stevenson and Louis Uchitelle, "Federal Reserve, Reacting to Signals of a Slowdown, Cuts Key Rate Half a Point," *The New York Times*, January 4, 2001.

3. The Fed influences the monetary base primarily by buying and selling government securities (open market operations). Purchases of securities by the Fed increase the monetary base. Sales of securities by the Fed decrease the monetary base. The Fed also can change the monetary base by making discount loans to banks. An increase in discount lending increases the monetary base; a decrease in discount lending decreases the monetary base.
4. The process by which an increase in bank reserves increases the level of checkable deposits is called multiple deposit expansion. The Fed can add to reserves in the banking system by buying government securities or making discount loans. The increase in reserves allows banks to make additional loans, which lead to additional deposits in banks. As a result, the money supply increases. In the simplest case—in which currency holdings do not change and banks do not hold excess reserves—multiple deposit expansion is limited only by the Fed's reserve requirements. An increase in the level of bank reserves raises the level of checkable deposits by a multiple of the change in the reserves. This multiple, the simple deposit multiplier, is equal to the reciprocal of the required reserve ratio.
5. The money multiplier represents the link between the monetary base and the money supply. If the multiplier is constant, the change in the money supply equals the multiplier times the change in the monetary base. An increase in currency or reserve holdings relative to checkable deposits reduces the money multiplier.
6. Despite the Fed's important role in the money supply process through open market operations, discount lending, and reserve requirements, the Fed doesn't completely control the money supply. Portfolio allocation decisions by banks and the nonbank public also affect the monetary base and the money multiplier. The nonbank public decides how to allocate its holdings between checkable deposits and currency. An increase in the nonbank public's demand for currency relative to deposits increases the currency–deposit ratio, reducing the money multiplier. Banks must decide what proportion of checkable deposits to hold as excess reserves (above those required by regulation). Holdings of excess reserves raise the ratio of effective reserves to deposits and reduce the money multiplier. These portfolio allocation decisions by the nonbank public and banks are determined by the principal factors governing asset demand: wealth, expected returns, risk, liquidity, and information. Finally, the Fed doesn't control discount lending. The Fed sets the discount rate (the interest rate charged on discount loans), but the decision to borrow is made by banks.
7. Putting it all together, the money supply process involves important roles for the Fed, banks, and the nonbank public. We can express the money supply (represented by *M1*, the sum of currency and checkable deposits) as

   Money supply = (Money multiplier) × (Nonborrowed base + Discount loans).

REVIEW QUESTIONS

1. What are the major assets and liabilities of the Federal Reserve System? Describe each briefly.
2. What are the components of the monetary base? Why is the monetary base a useful concept?
3. What is the difference between currency in circulation and currency outstanding? Which is added to reserves to get the monetary base?
4. What are excess reserves and how are they calculated? What determines the amount of required reserves?
5. If the Fed wants to increase the money supply, should it make an open market purchase or sale? Should it make more discount loans or fewer? If the Fed wants to decrease the money supply, what should it do?
6. If a bank has $10,000 in excess reserves, what is the most new lending that it should do? Why shouldn't it do more than that amount?
7. A student remarks, "If any one bank can safely loan only an amount equal to its excess reserves, I don't understand how the banking system as a whole can loan out an amount equal to several times the initial excess reserves in the system." Resolve the seeming paradox.

8. If the discount rate is usually below the federal funds rate, why don't banks borrow from the Fed at the discount rate and lend the money out at the federal funds rate to profit from the difference in the interest rates?

9. Wealth in the United States has grown steadily. If wealth were the only factor affecting currency demand, what do you expect would have happened to the currency–deposit ratio over time?

10. What happens to the simple deposit multiplier when the Fed makes more discount loans?

11. Suppose that the Fed wanted to increase the money supply (*M1*) by 10% next year. It predicts that the money multiplier will increase by 2%. How much should it increase the monetary base?

12. What happened to the value of the money multiplier between 1979 and 1986? What has happened to its value since 1986? What may have caused these movements in the size of the money multiplier? What consequences do these movements have for forecasters in the financial community who attempt to predict short-term movements in the money supply?

ANALYTICAL PROBLEMS

13. Suppose that Bank Five lends $100,000 to the Monkey Wrench Company. Using T-accounts, show how this transaction is recorded on the bank's balance sheet. If Monkey Wrench spends the money to buy materials from Scrap Steel, Inc., which does its banking at Wonder Bank, show the effect on Bank Five's balance sheet. What is the total change in Bank Five's assets and liabilities?

14. Suppose that a bank currently has assets of $24,000 in reserves and $176,000 in loans and liabilities of $200,000 in deposits. If the required reserve ratio is 10%, what are the bank's required and excess reserves? What is the bank likely to do?

Questions 15 and 16 require the use of the following bank balance sheet (amounts are in millions of dollars).

Assets		Liabilities	
Reserves	48	Checkable deposits	300
Loans	280	Time deposits	200
Securities	182	Net worth	10
	510		510

15. Calculate the bank's excess reserves when the required reserve ratio on checkable deposits is 14% and the required reserve ratio on time deposits is 3%. Now suppose that the required reserve ratios are changed to 16% on checkable deposits and 0% on time deposits. Again, calculate the bank's excess reserves.

16. Suppose that the bank sells $3 million in securities on the open market. Calculate the change in the bank's excess reserves when the required reserve ratio on checkable deposits is 14%.

17. Explain why you agree or disagree with the following observation: "If deposit insurance were eliminated, the Fed's control over the money supply would be reduced."

18. Consider the following data (all values are in billions of dollars):

	June 1930	June 1931	June 1932
Currency	$3.681	$3.995	$4.959
Checkable deposits	21.612	19.888	15.490
Bank reserves	3.227	3.307	2.829

Calculate the values for each period for the currency–deposit ratio, the ratio of total reserves to deposits, the monetary base, the money multiplier, and the *M1* money supply. Can you explain why the currency–deposit ratio and the ratio of total reserves to deposits moved as they did between 1930 and 1932?

19. In the following bank balance sheet, amounts are in millions of dollars. The required reserve ratio is 3% on the first $30 million of checkable deposits and 12% on any checkable deposits over $30 million.

Assets		Liabilities	
Reserves	18.9	Checkable deposits	180.0
Loans	150.0	Net worth	20.0
Securities	31.1		200.0
	200.0		

a. Calculate the bank's excess reserves.

b. Suppose that the bank sells $5 million in securities to get new cash. Show the bank's balance sheet after this transaction. What are the bank's new excess reserves?

c. Suppose that the bank loans its excess reserves in part (b) to a business. Show the bank's balance sheet after the loan has been made but before the business has spent the proceeds of the loan. Now what are the bank's excess reserves?

d. Suppose that the business spends the proceeds of the loan. Revise the bank's balance sheet and calculate its excess reserves.

20. If the required reserve ratio is 25%, banks hold no excess reserves, and the public holds currency equal to 25% of deposits, what is the value of the *M1* money multiplier?

21. Suppose that the statistics for the economy as a whole (in billions of dollars) are as follows:

Currency held by the public	100
Reserves held by banks	200
Checkable deposits held at banks	800
Time deposits held at banks	1200
Excess reserves held by banks	40

If the required reserve ratio on checkable deposits is 20%, what is the value of the *M1* money multiplier?

22. What would the money multiplier be if banks held no excess reserves, the currency–deposit ratio was 1, and the reserve requirement for checkable deposits was 100%?

23. Analysts have noted that at times, a substantial increase in demand for U.S. currency corresponds to a crisis in some foreign country. Is this a coincidence? Explain.

24. Suppose that First Bank discovered that its computer had been programmed incorrectly and that it suddenly was short of reserves by $100 million. What would you expect to happen to the federal funds rate, the number of discount loans made by the Fed, and the amount of excess reserves held by other banks?

25. Suppose that banks were so risk-averse that they would gladly sell securities so as to hold excess reserves. In other words, if the Fed engaged in open market purchases, banks would hold the entire amount of the increase in the monetary base in the form of excess reserves. What would be the money multiplier in such a case? Could the Fed increase the money supply if it wanted to?

Questions 26 and 27 pertain to the chapter appendix.

26. What would happen to *M1* and *M2* if the public decided to hold less currency and more time deposits, so *C/D* fell by 1% and *N/D* rose by 1% (assuming that the ratio of reserves to deposits is less than 100%)?

27. Consider Bank A's balance sheet (all amounts are in millions of dollars).

Assets		Liabilities	
Reserves, *R*	48	Checkable deposits, *D*	300
Loans, *L*	280	Time deposits, *N*	200
Securities, *S*	182	Net worth, *NW*	10
	510		510

For the economy as a whole, the initial level of checkable deposits, *D*, is $2 trillion. Relevant ratios are as follows:

Currency–deposit ratio, *C/D*	0.2
Time deposit–checkable deposit ratio, *N/D*	1.5
Money market account–deposit ratio, *MM/D*	0.5
Excess reserve–deposit ratio, *ER/D*	0.06
Required reserve ratio, $\overline{R/D}$	0.14

a. Calculate the monetary base *B*, *M1* (= C + D), and *M2* (= *M1* + N + *MM*). Does Bank A have any excess reserves? Are there any excess reserves in the economy as a whole?

b. Calculate the multipliers (the respective *m* values) for *M1* and *M2*.

c. Suppose that the Fed changes the required reserve ratio to 16%, or 0.16. In response, banks as a whole reduce their excess reserves to zero. What happens to Bank A's balance sheet? Calculate its required reserves. What are Bank A's excess reserves? Calculate the new *M1* and *M2* multipliers.

d. Suppose that, instead of taking the actions in part (c), the Fed buys $88.888 billion in securities on the open market, including $1.5 million from Bank A. What happens to Bank A's balance sheet? Calculate its required and excess reserves. Calculate the new size of the monetary base.

DATA QUESTION

28. Look up the following data in the latest issue of the *Federal Reserve Bulletin* in your library: currency holdings, C; checkable deposits, D; required reserves, RR; excess reserves, ER; and the $M1$ money supply. From these data, calculate the ratios C/D, ER/D, and $\overline{R/D}$. Calculate the $M1$ money multiplier using the multiplier formula. Alternatively, calculate the $M1$ money multiplier using the equation $M1 = (m)(B)$. Compare these multipliers. How do they compare with the simple deposit multiplier, $1/(\overline{R/D})$?

APPENDIX: The Money Supply Process for *M2*

In the aftermath of financial innovation during the 1980s (much of which we discussed in Chapter 15), many analysts and policymakers became concerned that $M1$ no longer adequately represented assets functioning as the medium of exchange. As a result, they focused more attention on $M2$. It is a broader monetary aggregate than $M1$, including not only currency, C, and checkable deposits, D, but also the nontransaction accounts. These accounts consist of savings and small-time deposits, N, and certain money market accounts, MM. Money market items in $M2$ include money market deposit accounts at commercial banks, general-purpose and broker-dealer money market mutual funds, overnight repurchase agreements issued by banks, and overnight Eurodollars issued to U.S. residents by foreign branches of U.S. banks. As a sum of its components, $M2$ is

$$M2 = C + D + N + MM. \tag{17A.1}$$

The $M2$ measure of the money supply is less sensitive than $M1$ to shifts in the nonbank public's portfolio preferences. Suppose that, because of financial innovation, the nonbank public wants to switch from checkable and nontransaction deposits to money market–type accounts. In that case, D and N would fall, and MM would rise by the same amount, leaving $M2$ *unchanged*. However, $M1$, the sum of currency and checkable deposits, would fall.

If we make assumptions similar to those used in deriving the $M1$ multiplier, namely, that C/D, N/D, and MM/D are constant, we can express $M2$ as

$$\text{Broader money supply} = (M2 \text{ multiplier})(\text{Base}),$$

or

$$M2 = \left[\frac{1 + (C/D) + (N/D) + (MM/D)}{(C/D) + (\overline{R/D}) + (ER/D)}\right](B). \tag{17A.2}$$

The $M2$ multiplier is significantly larger than the $M1$ multiplier. The reason is that the terms N/D and MM/D are added to the numerator. Because the volume of both nontransaction accounts and money market–type accounts is greater than the volume of checkable deposits, *N/D* and *MM/D* are greater than 1. With no reserve requirements for these measures, *M2* money expansion from a change in the monetary base is greater than that for *M1*. Indeed, the *M2* multiplier has been more stable than the *M1* multiplier during the 1980s and 1990s.

Components of the *M2* multiplier affect the size of the multiplier in a manner similar to that for *M1*. Increases in the required reserve ratio and the currency–deposit ratio reduce the extent of deposit expansion, thereby reducing the multiplier. However, an increase in the nonbank public's preference for nontransaction or money market–type accounts relative to checkable deposits increases the multiplier.

Fed watchers predict the growth of *M2* in much the same way as they do for *M1*. They forecast changes in the monetary base—particularly in the nonborrowed base—and in the components of the *M2* multiplier.

CHAPTER 18

Changes in the Monetary Base

"The devil lies in the details," commented a frenzied trader at the government securities trading desk of the Federal Reserve Bank of New York. She was trying to implement the Fed's instructions for changing the monetary base. The trader and her colleagues had just finished a week of hectic buying and selling of securities on the Fed's behalf. None of the transactions was carried out to implement a planned change in the monetary base by the Fed. Instead, each of the trades was designed to offset some disturbance to the monetary base beyond the Fed's direct control. Each disturbance created the need for offsetting transactions by the Fed's traders—a vast amount of detailed work for them.

What caused the problems for this trader? In Chapter 17, we described the Fed's ability to manage the size of the monetary base primarily by buying and selling Treasury securities in open market transactions. In the real world, however, the situation facing the Fed is not quite so simple. The monetary base fluctuates, particularly over short horizons, for many reasons. For the Fed to control the size of the monetary base and the money supply, it must offset these changes. This task can be daunting, as is illustrated by the problems facing the traders at the Fed's securities trading desk. In this chapter, we describe reasons why the monetary base fluctuates. We also examine the connection between the government budget deficit and changes in the monetary base, an important policy topic in the United States and other countries.

BALANCE SHEET OF THE FEDERAL RESERVE SYSTEM

We opened our discussion of the monetary base in Chapter 17 by looking at the Fed's balance sheet. To build our model of the money supply process, we focused on two assets—government securities and discount loans—and two liabilities—currency in circulation and reserves—to simplify our analysis. Although changes in the Fed's securities holdings and discount loans are the major sources of variation in the monetary base, there are other sources of variation as well. To identify these sources, we start once again with the Fed's balance sheet, but this time we include all of the assets and liabilities of the Fed. Table 18.1 shows the Fed's balance sheet for September 30, 2000. As you

TABLE 18.1 **THE FEDERAL RESERVE'S BALANCE SHEET ($ BILLIONS)**

Assets		Liabilities	
Securities (U.S. Treasury, government agency, and bankers' acceptances)	528.9	Currency outstanding	538.8
		U.S. Treasury deposits	8.5
Discount loans	0.4	Foreign and other deposits	0.3
Items in the process of collection	5.4	Deferred availability credit items	5.2
Other Federal Reserve assets	35.9	Other Federal Reserve liabilities and capital accounts	15.2
Gold and SDR certificate accounts	14.2	Deposits by depository institutions	17.6
Coin	0.8		
	$585.6		$585.6

Source: Data are for September 30, 2000, and are taken from *Federal Reserve Bulletin,* December 2000, p. A10.

read the description of each item, note its relative size to the other assets and liabilities listed.

The Fed's Assets

The Fed's largest asset is its holdings of securities, which it acquires in open market operations. In addition, in its role as a banker's bank, the Fed holds discount loans (claims on banks that have borrowed funds from it) and other assets, including cash items in the process of collection, other Federal Reserve assets, gold and special drawing right certificate accounts, and Treasury currency outstanding.

Securities. Most of the Fed's portfolio of securities consists of U.S. Treasury securities, with smaller amounts of U.S. government agency securities and bankers' acceptances. The Fed controls the amount of securities it holds through open market operations. An open market purchase increases the Fed's holdings of securities; an open market sale decreases the Fed's holdings of securities.

Discount loans. The Fed makes discount loans to banks, generally to assist them in overcoming short-term liquidity problems. Although the Fed doesn't completely control the amount of discount loans, it influences the amount by setting the discount rate, the interest rate that it charges on discount loans to banks.

Items in the process of collection. These assets are holdings from the Fed's check-clearing role in the payments system. They include funds that the Fed has not yet collected from banks against which checks have been drawn. If a bank presents a check to the Fed for clearing, several days may elapse before the bank receives its funds. The funds that are on deposit with the Fed prior to the check's being cleared are an asset and are recorded as an item in the process of collection.

Other Federal Reserve assets. These assets include the Fed's foreign-exchange reserves—deposits and bonds denominated in foreign currencies—as well as buildings, equipment, and other physical goods owned by the Fed.

Gold and SDR certificate accounts. Gold used to be the official medium of exchange in international financial transactions. Currently, special drawing rights (SDRs), issued by the International Monetary Fund, are exchanged by parties that are engaged in international financial transactions. When the U.S. Treasury acquires SDRs or gold in its international transactions, it issues SDR or gold certificates (claims on the SDRs or gold) to the Fed. The Fed then credits the Treasury with deposit balances. Hence the gold and SDR accounts consist of gold and SDR certificates issued to the Fed by the Treasury.

Coin. This small item in the Fed's balance sheet includes U.S. Treasury currency held by the Fed. It is mostly in the form of coins.

The Fed's Liabilities

The Fed's principal liability is currency outstanding. Other Fed liabilities include U.S. Treasury deposits, foreign and other deposits, deferred availability cash items, other Federal Reserve liabilities and capital accounts, and deposits by depository institutions.

Currency outstanding. Currency issued by the Fed in the form of Federal Reserve Notes is a liability for the Fed.

U.S. Treasury deposits. The Treasury typically deposits receipts from taxes, fees, and sales of securities in accounts in commercial banks. When the Treasury needs the funds to pay for expenditures, it transfers the funds to its accounts at the Fed.†

Foreign and other deposits. These deposits include those made at the Fed by international agencies (such as the United Nations), foreign central banks and governments, and U.S. government agencies (such as the FDIC).

Deferred availability cash items. These liabilities arise from the Fed's role in the check-clearing process. When a bank presents a check to the Fed to be

†We don't consider Treasury deposits with the Fed to be part of the monetary base because they aren't assets of either the nonbank public or banks, which, along with the Fed, are the principal participants in the money supply process.

cleared, the Fed promises to credit the bank within a certain period of time (never more than two days). Analogous to cash items in the process of collection on the assets side of the Fed's balance sheet, these promises to pay are liabilities of the Fed.

Other Federal Reserve liabilities and capital accounts. This catch-all account includes liabilities that are not contained in other categories of the balance sheet. It also includes shares of stock in the Federal Reserve System purchased by the Fed's member banks.

Deposits by depository institutions. These deposits at the Fed are assets to banks and liabilities for the Fed. They are part of bank reserves, which also include vault cash held in banks.

DETERMINING THE MONETARY BASE

In this section, we extend our simple expression for the monetary base, $B = C + R$, to include the effect of all assets and liabilities contained on the Fed's balance sheet. Our objective is to develop a complete equation for the monetary base that allows us to see how all components of the monetary base determine its size.

We start by using the components of the Fed's balance sheet to refine our interpretation of C and R. Currency in circulation, C, is the total of Federal Reserve Notes and Treasury currency not held at the Fed (Treasury currency outstanding minus Coin) less banks' vault cash.† Reserves, R, consist of deposits at the Fed by depositing institutions and Federal Reserve Notes held as vault cash. Hence

$$\begin{aligned} B &= C + R \\ &= \text{Federal Reserve Notes} + \text{Reserve deposits by depository institutions} \\ &\quad + \text{Treasury currency outstanding} - \text{Coin}. \end{aligned} \tag{18.1}$$

The terms on the right-hand side of Eq. (18.1) represent uses of the monetary base—that is, how the base is allocated among Federal Reserve currency held by the nonbank public and banks, bank reserves held at the Fed, and Treasury currency outstanding. Equation (18.1) doesn't reveal all the potential sources of change in monetary base. To identify them, we return to the Fed's balance sheet. Both Federal Reserve Notes and deposits by depository institutions are Fed liabilities. Because assets must equal liabilities, we use information from the balance sheet to equate the sum of Federal Reserve Notes and deposits by depository institutions with the other entries. Specifically, the sum

†Federal Reserve Notes constitute about 90% of the nation's currency. The balance consists principally of coins issued by the U.S. Treasury, but some $300 million in U.S. Treasury Notes, called "greenbacks," dating back to Civil War issues, are still outstanding.

of Federal Reserve Notes and deposits by depository institutions equals the total of all Fed assets minus the total of the other liabilities:[†]

Federal Reserve Notes + Reserve deposits by depository institutions
= Securities + Discount loans + Cash items in the process of collection
+ Other Federal Reserve assets
+ Gold and SDR certificates
+ Coin
– U.S. Treasury deposits – Foreign and other deposits
– Deferred availability cash items
– Other Federal Reserve liabilities and capital accounts. (18.2)

We can simplify Eq. (18.2) by taking the difference between the two items that relate to check clearing (cash items in the process of collection and deferred availability cash items) and calling it **Federal Reserve float.**[††] Simplifying in this way and substituting the elements on the right-hand side of Eq. (18.2) for the sum of currency in circulation and deposits by depository institutions in Eq. (18.1) yield the complete expression for the monetary base, B:

B = Securities + Discount loans + Federal Reserve float
+ Other Federal Reserve assets + Gold and SDR certificates
+ Treasury currency outstanding
– U.S. Treasury deposits – Foreign and other deposits
– Other Federal Reserve liabilities and capital accounts. (18.3)

CHANGES IN THE MONETARY BASE

Equation (18.3) contains the nine sources of change in the monetary base. Increases in the six items added on the right-hand side of Eq. (18.3) increase the monetary base, and decreases in those items decrease the monetary base. Increases in the three items subtracted on the right-hand side of Eq. (18.3) decrease the monetary base, and decreases in those items increase the monetary base. Increases and decreases in each of the factors in the equation cause the monetary base to fluctuate. It was the variation in these sources that caused the problems faced by the trader described at the opening of the chapter. It is relatively easy to juggle two balls and keep them in the air; but as you add more and more objects, juggling becomes more difficult. Because there are nine items that can fluctuate, the problem of maintaining the monetary base can be daunting for the traders at the Fed's securities desk. In this section, we describe the effect on the monetary base caused by each component of Eq. (18.3). We summarize the effects of an increase in each component in Table 18.2.

[†] Not all bank deposits at the Fed are included in reserves because some are service-related deposits. Technically, these deposits must be subtracted from the right-hand side of Eq. (18.2) to define the monetary base precisely.

[††] When the Fed reports its balance sheet in the *Federal Reserve Bulletin,* the total of Federal Reserve float, securities, and bank borrowing is called "Federal Reserve credit."

TABLE 18.2 **SOURCES OF CHANGE IN THE MONETARY BASE**

An increase in . . .	Causes the monetary base to . . .	Because . . .
securities	rise	reserves rise.
discount loans	rise	reserves rise.
Federal Reserve float	rise	cash items in the process of collection rise relative to deferred availability cash items, increasing reserves.
other Federal Reserve assets	rise	an increase is like an open market purchase, increasing reserves.
Treasury currency outstanding	rise	bank vault cash or currency in circulation rises, increasing reserves.
gold and SDR certificate accounts	rise	an increase is like an open market purchase, increasing reserves.
U.S. Treasury deposits at the Fed	fall	reserves and/or currency in circulation falls.
foreign and other deposits at the Fed	fall	reserves fall.
other Federal Reserve liabilities and capital accounts	fall	contributions to capital accounts reduce reserves.

Determinants That Increase the Monetary Base

Securities and discount loans. In Chapter 17, we traced the effects of the Fed's open market operations and discount loans on the monetary base. An increase in the Fed's holdings of securities acquired through open market purchases or an increase in the volume of discount loans increases the monetary base dollar for dollar.

Federal Reserve float. Federal Reserve float occurs during the check-clearing process when the Fed doesn't credit a bank with payment at the same time that it debits the bank on which the check is drawn. Suppose that Bigco receives a check for $1 million from Engulf, drawn on Engulf's bank, Megabank in New York. Bigco deposits the $1 million check in Onebank in Chicago. The clearing process works as follows: Onebank sends the check to the Federal Reserve Bank of Chicago, which sends it to the Federal Reserve Bank of New York, which presents it to Megabank.

The Fed promises to credit the payee bank (Onebank) within two business days, even if the Fed takes longer to present the check to the payor bank (Megabank). The difference in timing between the crediting of Onebank and debiting of Megabank causes float. Let's see how the float resulting from this transaction affects the Fed's balance sheet. When the Federal Reserve Bank of Chicago gets the check, its assets rise by $1 million with an entry under cash

USING THE NEWS . . .

Federal Reserve Data and Change in the Monetary Base

Each week (on Friday or Monday), *The Wall Street Journal* publishes Federal Reserve data on bank reserve changes. The Member Bank Reserve Changes data provide information on sources of change in the monetary base. For example, for the week ending January 31, 2001, the predominant source of change in the monetary base came from the Fed's purchases of U.S. government securities ($516.8 billion). Other sources are also listed, including discount loans (adjustment credit, seasonal borrowing, and extended credit), which totaled $43 million. Note that the Fed's holdings of securities increased from the previous year (increasing the monetary base) but that discount loans fell (decreasing the monetary base). The predominant use of the monetary base was currency in circulation, at about $578 billion on this date.

The Reserve Aggregates data present information on various measures of reserves and the monetary base. For instance, the average value of the monetary base was about $591.5 billion for the week ending on January 24, 2001.

FEDERAL RESERVE DATA

MEMBER BANK RESERVE CHANGES

Changes in weekly averages of reserves and related items during the week and year ended January 31, 2001 were as follows (in millions of dollars)

	Jan. 31 2001	Chg fm Jan. 24 2001	wk end Feb. 2 2000
Reserve bank credit:			
U.S. Gov't securities:			
Bought outright	516,799	– 189	+ 16,296
Held under repurch agreemt	....	....	....
Federal agency issues:			
Bought outright	130	....	– 45
Held under repurch agreemt	....	....	....
Acceptances			
Borrowings from Fed:			
Adjustment credit	12	– 67	– 70
Seasonal borrowings	31	+ 8	+ 7
Extended credit	....	....	....
Float	686	– 492	– 290
Other Federal Reserve Assets	37,068	+ 338	+ 1,634
Total Reserve Bank Credit	573,712	– 3,843	+ 15,342
Gold Stock	11,046	....	– 2
SDR certificates	2,200	....	– 4,000
Treasury currency outstanding	31,513	+ 14	+ 3,231
Total	618,471	– 3,828	+ 14,570
Currency in circulation	578,111	+ 2,128	+ 11,294
Treasury cash holdings	455	+ 10	+ 329
Treasury dpts with F.R. Bnks	8,903	+ 1,825	+ 2,772
Foreign dpts with F.R. Bnks	110	+ 25	– 36
Other dpts with F.R. Bnks	277	+ 10	+ 29
Service related balances, adj	6,585	– 362	– 643
Other F.R. liabilities & capital	18,198	– 50	– 146
Total	612,640	– 669	+ 13,600

RESERVE AGGREGATES

(daily average in millions)

	Two weeks ended: Jan. 24	Jan. 10
Total Reserves (sa)	39,038	38,553
Nonborrowed Reserves (sa)	38,972	38,443
Required Reserves (sa)	37,932	37,052
Excess Reserves (nsa)	1,105	1,501
Borrowings from Fed (nsa)-a	66	110
Free Reserves (nsa)	1,039	1,391
Monetary Base (sa)	591,506	587,817

a-Excluding extended credit. nsa-Not seasonally adjusted. sa-Seasonally adjusted.

Source: The Wall Street Journal, February 2, 2001. Republished by permission of Dow Jones, Inc. via Copyright Clearance Center, Inc.,

items in the process of collection. The Fed's liabilities also rise by $1 million because there is an offsetting deferred availability cash items entry:

FEDERAL RESERVE

Assets		Liabilities	
Cash items in the process of collection	+$1 million	Deferred availability cash items	+$1 million

After two days, the Fed credits Onebank with $1 million, even if the check has not yet cleared. At this stage of the transaction, Onebank has gained $1 million of reserves, even though Megabank hasn't yet lost reserves. Total reserves in the banking system, then, have increased by $1 million:

FEDERAL RESERVE

Assets		Liabilities	
Cash items in the process of collection	+$1 million	Deferred availability cash items (Onebank)	+$1 million
		Deposits by Onebank	+$1 million
		Deferred availability cash items (Onebank)	−$1 million

When the check finally is presented to and accepted by Megabank, its account balance with the Fed is reduced by $1 million:

FEDERAL RESERVE

Assets		Liabilities	
Cash items in the process of collection	0	Reserves	
		Deposits by Onebank	+$1 million
		Deposits by Megabank	−$1 million

After this transaction, the banking system's reserves return to the level that existed before the Bigco and Engulf transaction.

In reality, checks continually flow through the Fed's clearing system, so the amount of cash items in the process of collection exceeds the amount of deferred availability cash items. This Federal Reserve float is a source of increases in the monetary base. It fluctuates daily and is beyond the Fed's direct control. Over long periods of time, however, float is not a significant source of change in the monetary base. An increase in Federal Reserve float causes a dollar-for-dollar increase in the monetary base.

Gold and SDR certificate accounts. The acquisition of gold or SDRs by the Fed expands the monetary base just as an open market purchase of securities does. An increase in the Fed's gold or SDR certificate accounts leads to a dollar-for-dollar increase in the monetary base.

Other Federal Reserve assets. An increase in the Fed's holdings of other assets—say, a deposit or bond denominated in a foreign currency—works like an open market purchase of securities, increasing reserves and the monetary base. Hence intervention by the Fed in the foreign-exchange market affects the other Federal Reserve assets balance. An increase in other Federal Reserve assets raises the monetary base dollar for dollar.

Treasury currency outstanding. Treasury currency outstanding is not an item on the Fed's balance sheet, but it does affect the monetary base. When the amount of Treasury currency held in bank vaults (where it becomes part of vault cash and reserves) or by the nonbank public (where it becomes currency in circulation) increases, the monetary base rises. An increase in Treasury currency outstanding leads to a dollar-for-dollar increase in the monetary base.†

Determinants That Decrease the Monetary Base

Increases in any of the remaining three sources of change in the monetary base in Table 18.2 reduce the monetary base.

U.S. Treasury deposits at the Fed. Whenever the federal government makes a payment—for highway construction, the salary of a staff economist, or a retiree's Social Security benefits—the Treasury writes a check drawn on its account at the Fed. This Treasury account at the Fed is known as the **General Account.**

Suppose that the government buys \$1000 worth of small tools from Toolco, which deposits the \$1000 check in its bank, Megabank. Megabank then sends the check to the Fed, which increases Megabank's balance and reduces the Treasury's General Account balance. As a result of the purchase from Toolco, Megabank's reserves—and the banking system's reserves—rise by \$1000, the amount of the payment:

FEDERAL RESERVE

Assets	Liabilities	
	Deposits	
	Megabank	+\$1000
	U.S. Treasury	−\$1000

Bank reserves and the monetary base rise whenever the federal government makes a payment. Likewise, bank reserves and the monetary base fall whenever the federal government receives a payment.

The flow of payments out of and into the General Account is extremely large. The U.S. government spends more than \$1.8 trillion each year, or about \$7 billion each business day. Because government receipts and expenditures differ significantly over short periods of time, the Treasury's balance would fluctuate significantly if it deposited all its receipts with the Fed.

To reduce the impact of its transactions on the monetary base, the Treasury first deposits most of its receipts (income tax withheld from a worker's paycheck, for example) into **Treasury tax and loan accounts** in banks. The Treasury keeps these accounts at most local banks. When the Treasury moves funds from its tax and loan accounts to the General Account, it times these transfers to match its payments from the General Account. In this way, the

†In practice, increases in Treasury currency are generally met with offsetting changes in other entries on the Fed's balance sheet. For example, if the Treasury mints more coins and sends them to the Fed, the Fed credits the Treasury's deposits. The monetary base is unaffected because coin (a Fed asset) and Treasury deposits (a Fed liability) rise by the same amount.

Treasury reduces the effects of its receipts and payments on bank reserves. An increase in U.S. Treasury deposits with the Fed reduces reserves and the monetary base dollar for dollar.

Before 1978, Treasury tax and loan accounts were an interest-free source of funds for banks. Since then, banks have had to pay interest on these deposits after one day at an interest rate equal to 0.25% below the average federal funds rate for the week.

Foreign and other deposits at the Fed. The Fed acts as the U.S. banker for foreign central banks and international agencies. Increases or decreases in the amount of these deposits affect bank reserves and the monetary base in a manner similar to the effect of fluctuations in the Treasury's General Account. However, these fluctuations are much smaller than those of Treasury deposits. An increase in foreign and other deposits at the Fed reduces reserves and the monetary base dollar for dollar.

Other liabilities and capital accounts. If a bank joins the Federal Reserve System and purchases the required amount of stock in the Fed, the Fed's capital accounts increase. The bank's deposits with the Fed fall by the same amount. As a result, bank reserves and the monetary base fall. An increase in other liabilities and capital leads to a dollar-for-dollar reduction in the monetary base.

Concluding Remarks

The most important source of change in the monetary base is the Federal Reserve System's holdings of securities, which it controls through open market operations. Some determinants that are not under the Fed's control (such as U.S. Treasury deposits with the Fed and Federal Reserve float) can lead to significant fluctuations in the monetary base over a day or a week. However, these fluctuations are usually predictable, so Fed traders can reverse them with open market operations. Although some components of the monetary base fluctuate over short periods of time, those fluctuations do not significantly reduce the Fed's ability to control the monetary base.

CHECKPOINT

What is the effect of each of the following events on the monetary base?

(a) The Treasury withdraws $9 billion from its tax and loan account and deposits the funds in the General Account.

(b) The Fed buys $1 billion of gold.

(c) The Fed sells $100 million worth of bonds denominated in deutsche marks.

Answers:

(a) The increase in Treasury deposits with the Fed decreases the monetary base by $9 billion.

(b) The Fed's gold purchase, like an open market purchase, raises the monetary base by $1 billion.
(c) The sale reduces other Federal Reserve assets and the monetary base by $100 million. o

THE FEDERAL BUDGET DEFICIT AND THE MONETARY BASE

The federal budget deficit was a major topic of political debate and controversy in the 1980s and 1990s. Some businesspeople and policymakers complained about the large deficits of the 1980s and early 1990s—the excesses of government spending over tax revenue—because they were afraid that it would increase the monetary base and, ultimately, the money supply. (The United States reported budget surpluses at the end of the 1990s, forecasted to continue for the first decade of the new century.) Behind this concern was the fear that persistent increases in the money supply would lead to inflation. (We explore the relationship between the money supply and inflation in Part 6.)

Is there a connection between the federal budget deficit and change in the monetary base? To answer this question, we begin with some simple government budget accounting. The government can finance a deficit by raising taxes, borrowing money (selling bonds), or creating money to finance part of its spending for goods and services and payments to individuals.

In the United States, the President and Congress determine federal government expenditures and tax rates, and they define the types of income and expenditures that are subject to taxation. A budget deficit results when government expenditures exceed tax revenue. To finance this deficit, the Treasury sells securities and uses the proceeds to pay the costs of government. This type of transaction (except possibly for short-term lags between receipts and expenditures) doesn't alter the monetary base. In terms of budget arithmetic,

$$\text{Government expenditures} - \text{Tax revenue} = \text{Federal budget deficit} = \text{Sales of securites by the Treasury.} \quad (18.4)$$

The President and Congress set spending and tax policies, but the Fed's actions most directly affect the monetary base. When the Treasury issues securities, the monetary base changes only to the extent that the Fed buys those securities.

Because the Fed, banks, and the nonbank public purchase Treasury securities in the market,

$$\text{Sales of securities by the Treasury} = \text{Change in Treasury securities held by banks and the nonbank public} + \text{Fed purchases of Treasury securities.} \quad (18.5)$$

Recall that a purchase of securities by the Fed leads to an equivalent increase in reserves and expansion of the monetary base. Hence combining Eqs. (18.4) and (18.5) yields

Federal budget deficit = Change in Treasury securities held by banks and the nonbank public + Fed purchases of Treasury securities
= Change in Treasury securities held by banks and the nonbank public + increase in monetary base. (18.6)

Equation (18.6) shows the relationship among federal spending and tax decisions, sales of securities by the Treasury, and changes in the monetary base. Economists call it the **government budget constraint** because it shows the trade-offs facing the government when it runs a deficit. Thus a federal budget deficit must be financed by a combination of an increase in Treasury securities held by banks and the nonbank public and an increase in the monetary base. The media sometimes refer to the latter strategy as "printing money."

OTHER TIMES, OTHER PLACES . . .

Dealing with the Debt: The Treasury–Federal Reserve Accord

Government budget deficits increase the monetary base only when the Fed purchases Treasury bonds issued to finance the deficit. The Fed is independent of the Treasury Department, and at times there have been conflicts between the Fed and the Treasury over the extent to which the Fed should finance the federal budget deficit.

One noteworthy conflict raged after World War II. In 1942, the Fed had agreed to peg the interest rate on short-term Treasury securities at 3/8% per year. In other words, to assist the Treasury's efforts to finance the war, the Fed agreed to buy quantities of securities sufficient to maintain that interest rate. Immediately after the war, no problem emerged because the federal government had budget surpluses in 1947–1949. The Fed didn't have to continue purchasing Treasury securities on the open market to maintain the agreed-upon yield. In fact, the Fed sold Treasury securities to maintain the interest rate at the pegged level.

The advent of the Korean War in 1950 significantly increased government spending and borrowing. To keep its promise, the Fed bought large quantities of Treasury securities, expanding the monetary base and fueling inflation. Fed officials publicly questioned the wisdom of effectively placing control of changes in the monetary base in the hands of the Treasury. On March 3, 1951, the Treasury and the Fed reached a compromise: the Treasury–Federal Reserve Accord. The Fed stopped buying bonds and increasing the monetary base to keep yields on Treasury securities low. (The Treasury's delegate was William McChesney Martin, who later became Chairman of the Board of Governors of the Federal Reserve System.) President Truman nonetheless encouraged the Fed to buy bonds if interest rates rose sufficiently. It wasn't until President Eisenhower took office that the Fed finally ceased intervening to maintain the interest rate at or below a specified level.

Although some countries allow their Treasury departments to determine the volume of currency, the United States does not. Here, currency must be issued by the Federal Reserve System. In fact, the Fed is not literally printing money but is purchasing Treasury securities in the market for its own account. When the Fed purchases Treasury securities to finance budget deficits, we say that it is **monetizing the debt.**

Alternative Strategies

We can use T-accounts to illustrate the effects on the monetary base of alternative strategies to finance government spending. Suppose that the President and Congress agree to embark on a new $2 billion program to repair interstate highways. This program could be paid for by raising taxes, selling bonds to the public, and selling bonds to the Fed.

Raising taxes. Suppose that the President and Congress agree to raise the tax on gasoline to obtain the $2 billion. The nonbank public then collectively writes checks to the Treasury totaling $2 billion, which are first deposited in the Treasury's tax and loan accounts and then redeposited in the Treasury's General Account at the Fed. In the process, deposits in the banking system fall by $2 billion, reducing reserves by the same amount. The Treasury's deposits at the Fed rise by $2 billion. In the end, the T-accounts for the nonbank public, the Treasury, the banking system, and the Federal Reserve System show the following entries:

NONBANK PUBLIC

Assets		Liabilities	
Deposits	−$2 billion	Taxes due	−$2 billion

TREASURY

Assets		Liabilities	
Deposits at the Fed	+$2 billion		
Taxes due	−$2 billion		

BANKING SYSTEM

Assets		Liabilities	
Reserves	−$2 billion	Deposits	−$2 billion

FEDERAL RESERVE

Assets		Liabilities	
		Reserves	−$2 billion
		U.S. Treasury deposits	+$2 billion

When the Treasury pays contractors the $2 billion by check for the highway projects, the funds flow back into the banking system and have no net effect on reserves and monetary base:†

BANKING SYSTEM

Assets		Liabilities	
Reserves	0	Deposits	0

FEDERAL RESERVE

Assets		Liabilities	
		Reserves	0
		U.S. Treasury deposits	0

Thus, in general, financing government spending by raising taxes doesn't affect the monetary base.

Selling bonds to the public. Suppose that to finance highway repair, the Treasury sells $2 billion of bonds to the nonbank public, which pays by check. In this case, the Treasury's deposits increase by $2 billion, while the nonbank public loses $2 billion of deposits:

NONBANK PUBLIC

Assets		Liabilities	
Deposits	−$2 billion		
Securities	+$2 billion		

TREASURY

Assets		Liabilities	
Deposits	+$2 billion	Securities	+$2 billion

BANKING SYSTEM

Assets		Liabilities	
Reserves	−$2 billion	Deposits	−$2 billion

FEDERAL RESERVE

Assets		Liabilities	
		Reserves	−$2 billion
		U.S. Treasury deposits	+$2 billion

† If the transactions took place in currency (which is not very likely), the monetary base would also be unaffected.

When the Treasury pays the highway contractors by check, the funds flow back into the banking system and have no effect on reserves and the monetary base:

BANKING SYSTEM

Assets		Liabilities	
Reserves	0	Deposits	0

FEDERAL RESERVE

Assets		Liabilities	
		Reserves	0
		U.S. Treasury deposits	0

As we noted earlier, financing government spending by selling bonds to the nonbank public doesn't affect the monetary base.

Selling bonds to the Fed. Although the U.S. Treasury cannot directly finance government spending by creating money, selling bonds to the Fed has the same effect. Two steps are involved. First, as in the preceding case of bond financing, the Treasury sells \$2 billion of bonds to the nonbank public to finance the highway repairs; as was noted, this transaction doesn't change the monetary base. In the second step, however, the Fed buys the \$2 billion of bonds from the nonbank public. This open market purchase increases the monetary base by the same amount. Financing government spending by selling bonds that the Fed ultimately acquires leads to an increase in the monetary base.

The Government Budget Constraint and the Monetary Base

Although useful for connecting the elements of government finance, the government budget constraint can be misinterpreted. In the United States, no one participant makes all of the government's budget and financing decisions: Authority is divided among the President, Congress, and the Federal Reserve. The Fed's decisions regarding changes in the monetary base reflect its own monetary policy objectives; the influence of federal budget deficits on those decisions is indirect (though the Fed monitors the effect of interest rates on the economy). The Fed has not monetized the large federal deficits of the 1980s and early 1990s to any great extent. Even during the 1980s, the monetary base increased by less than \$15 billion per year, while the federal budget deficit averaged about \$155 billion per year. Hence, even in the presence of these large budget deficits, the Fed monetized less than 10% of the annual deficit. There is no direct relationship between government deficits and the monetary base. The monetary base rises when the government runs a deficit only when the Fed acquires government bonds that are used to finance the deficit.

Over long periods of time, changes in the money supply primarily reflect changes in the monetary base rather than changes in the money multiplier.

The Treasury doesn't control the Fed and therefore can't force the central bank to monetize government deficits. In other countries, the degree of central bank independence varies. Our analysis of the government budget constraint might lead you to suspect that the less independent the central bank is, the more likely it is to monetize government budget deficits and increase the money supply. In a study of monetary policy in 17 countries during the 1970s and 1980s, Alberto Alesina of Harvard University analyzed the independence of central banks.[†] The measure that he used incorporated information on the formal relationships between the central bank and the government, including the presence of government officials on the bank's board and the existence of rules forcing the central bank to monetize portions of budget deficits. Countries in which the central bank had the least independence (such as Italy) experienced the most rapid growth of the money supply. Countries with relatively independent central banks (such as the United States and Japan) had slower rates of growth of the money supply. The Maastricht Treaty gave the European Central Bank independence to pursue its goal of price stability.

[†] Alberto Alesina, "Politics and Business Cycles in Industrial Democracies," *Economic Policy,* no. 8, April 1989.

KEY TERMS AND CONCEPTS

Federal Reserve float

General Account

Government budget constraint

Monetizing the debt

Treasury tax and loan accounts

SUMMARY

1. Changes in the monetary base can be explained by fluctuations in nine determinants. Increases in the Fed's holdings of securities, discount loans, Federal Reserve float, other Federal Reserve assets, Treasury currency outstanding, and gold and SDR accounts lead to an equal increase in the monetary base. Increases in U.S. Treasury deposits with the Fed, foreign and other deposits with the Fed, and other Federal Reserve liabilities and capital accounts lead to an equal decrease in the monetary base.
2. The most important determinant of change in the monetary base is the Federal Reserve's holdings of securities. The Fed controls the amount of its holdings through open market operations. Some determinants that are not under the Fed's control (such as U.S. Treasury deposits with the Fed and Federal Reserve float) can lead to significant fluctuations in the monetary base over a day or a week. However, these fluctuations are predictable and can be reversed by open market operations.
3. A given government budget deficit can be financed by selling government securities to banks and the nonbank public or to the Fed. Financing a deficit by selling bonds to banks and the nonbank public doesn't affect the monetary base. Financing a deficit by selling bonds to the Fed leads to an equivalent expansion of the monetary base.

REVIEW QUESTIONS

1. What are the sources and uses of the monetary base?
2. What is the government budget constraint? Does it imply that budget deficits increase the monetary base? Explain.
3. State whether each of the following is an asset or a liability of the Fed:
   a. Holdings of securities
   b. U.S. Treasury deposits
   c. Cash items in the process of collection
   d. Deposits by depository institutions
   e. Coins
   f. Deferred availability cash items
   g. Foreign deposits
   h. Federal Reserve Notes outstanding
   i. Discount loans
   j. Gold and SDR certificate accounts
4. Explain whether an increase in each of the following items from the Fed's balance sheet will cause the monetary base to increase or decrease:
   a. U.S. Treasury deposits
   b. Federal Reserve float
   c. Discount loans
   d. Foreign and other deposits
5. What is the Fed's biggest asset? What is its biggest liability?
6. Define "Federal Reserve float." Do increases in float cause the monetary base to rise or fall?
7. Why does the relationship between a government's budget deficits and the inflation rate depend on how independent the central bank is from the government?
8. What is the Treasury's General Account? Does the Treasury keep all its money there?
9. Why did the beginning of the Korean War increase the desire of Fed officials to be relieved of the commitment to peg the interest rate on Treasury securities?
10. *Evaluate:* The Fed controls all determinants of change in the monetary base, and therefore the Fed controls the monetary base.

ANALYTICAL PROBLEMS

11. Suppose that the following changes take place in the Fed's balance sheet:

Securities	–	\$1 billion
Discount loans	+	\$250 million
SDR certificates	+	\$500 million
Cash items in the process of collection	+	\$2 billion
Deferred availability cash items	+	\$1 billion
General Account	–	\$2 billion
Deposits by depository institutions	+	\$1 billion

    What are the changes in Federal Reserve float? In the monetary base?

12. Suppose that the federal government's annual budget deficit is \$250 billion and that the Fed's holdings of government securities increase by \$10 billion over the year. How much of the deficit was monetized?
13. Suppose that an erroneous report that Congress has abolished the FDIC is widely believed and banks start to experience withdrawals of deposits. What will be the impact on the monetary base? What actions might the Fed take to help banks deal with the withdrawals? What would the impact of those actions be on the monetary base? Would the Fed be likely to take action to offset this impact?
14. Suppose that the Treasury decides to move its principal checking account from the Fed to the Chase Bank. Discuss the implications for the stability of the monetary base over time.
15. Suppose that the President and Congress sign a budget agreement that eliminates the federal budget

THE FINANCIAL TIMES MARCH 18, 1999

ECB Warns on Budget Deficits

(a) The European Central Bank yesterday warned European governments they could be at risk of being fined for running excessive budget deficits.

In its monthly report for March, the ECB produced its most detailed and coherent critique yet of fiscal policy by national governments in the eurozone.

While the ECB did not mention any specific countries, the comments signaled renewed confidence by the central bankers after last week's resignation of Oskar Lafontaine as Germany's finance minister. He had been a staunch critic of the ECB's monetary policy.

In its report, the ECB said yesterday: "In the event of a severe or prolonged growth slowdown, government deficits could easily approach the 3% deficit limit because current fiscal plans do not incorporate sufficient safety margins."

The deficit limit is a main provision in the stability and growth pact, agreed by European Union leaders at the 1997 European summit in Amsterdam. (b) The pact calls on governments to run balanced budgets over the economic cycle, and sets out a tough regime of penalties for countries whose budget deficits exceed 3% of gross domestic product.

(c) None of the 11 eurozone members is in danger of breaching this ceiling in the 1999 fiscal year, although only a few are on target to achieve balanced budgets in the next few years.

The ECB said in its report that governments should set aside money to pay for necessary structural reforms to deal with aging populations and heath care reforms.

Since the launch of the euro in January, European economic policy has been deadlocked as finance ministers have called on the ECB to cut interest rates, while central bankers are demanding tougher action on budgets. Neither side has given ground so far.

Today, the ECB's executive council will meet for its regular fortnightly meeting, amid some expectations that the ECB would cut rates, now that Mr. Lafontaine has gone.

In its third report since the start of the euro, the ECB defended the present policy stance. "The current stance of monetary policy is appropriate not only to maintain price stability, but also to support economic growth and employment."

The report noted in particular the risk of a further slowdown in economic growth and the continued decline in producer prices. But the central bank also warned that high wage settlements and the weakness of the euro could put prices under pressure.

The government budget constraint tells us that a budget deficit can be financed by a combination of selling bonds to banks and the nonbank public and money creation (increases in the monetary base). Persistent rapid growth in the money supply leads to inflation. (We examine this process in Part 6.) If the money multiplier is stable over the long run, persistent growth in the money supply can be traced to persistent growth in the monetary base from central bank decisions. As many European countries were coming together in preparation for a common monetary policy under the European Central Bank (ECB), government budget deficits had to be held to agreed-upon limits. To the extent that rapid monetary base growth financed government budget deficits, a country's inflation could exceed the ECB's target, a major public policy concern.

a The ECB's concern was that excesses of government spending over tax revenue might ultimately be financed by increases in the monetary base by the central bank, thereby fueling inflation. Outside the eurozone, for example, the Russian central bank, which is not independent of the government, increased the monetary base in the early 1990s through open market purchases of bonds issued by state-owned enterprises. Later in the 1990s, the government's budget deficit was brought more under control, reducing the need for inflationary finance.

b In the long run, if the public will not continue to increase its holdings of government bonds to finance deficits caused by structural imbalances in social programs, money creation will have to make up the difference. If a central bank monetizes the government's debt, the monetary base will grow even faster. Continued growth of the monetary base exerts upward pressure on the inflation rate. This outcome would be inconsistent with a common monetary policy under the ECB.

c Would you expect future budget deficits to increase inflation? This result seems likely because economic reform remained shaky in some European countries in the late 1990s. Many analysts were concerned that, because of political pressure, governments might cut taxes and delay spending reductions.

For further thought . . .

Why might reducing budget deficits help a country stabilize its exchange rate with the U.S. dollar? Explain.

Source: From Wolfgang Munchau, "ECB Warns on Budget Deficits," *Financial Times*, March 18, 1999. Reprinted by permission.

deficit. Does this agreement mean that the monetary base will grow by less than it would otherwise? Explain.

16. Explain the effect on the monetary base of each of the following:
    a. $25 billion is withheld from payrolls as withholding taxes and paid to the U.S. Treasury through tax and loan accounts.
    b. A financial crisis erupts, and the Fed makes $2.5 billion of discount loans to the distressed Bigbank.
    c. The World Bank deposits $10 million in its account at the Fed.
    d. An electricity blackout knocks out banks' computers in New York for two days.
    e. The Treasury decides to buy $1 billion of earth-moving equipment for use in a new public highway construction program and puts the funds in the General Account.
    f. The Fed buys $1 billion of U.S. Treasury securities.
    g. The regional Federal Reserve banks decide to put expensive new marble shells around their buildings.
17. For cash items in the process of collection, the Fed's balance sheet shows $10 billion, while deferred availability cash items are $8 billion. What is the size of the Federal Reserve float? Why do you think the Fed tries to keep the float as small as possible?
18. Suppose the Fed buys $150 million of Japanese yen with Federal Reserve Notes. What is the net effect on the monetary base? How has the Fed's balance sheet been affected?
19. Suppose the Fed buys $100 million of British pounds with Federal Reserve Notes and, at the same time, sells $100 million of U.S. government securities for cash in a domestic open market operation. What is the net effect on the monetary base? How has the Fed's balance sheet been affected?
20. Suppose the Sacagawea dollar coin suddenly becomes popular, and people stop using as many dollar bills as they once did. What happens to the monetary base?
21. Economic theory tells us that (under reasonable assumptions) a rise in the government budget deficit raises interest rates. Show how the debt is monetized if the Fed tries to maintain stable interest rates when the government budget deficit rises.
22. Suppose the government of a country substantially increases its spending. What are the main ways in which this additional funding might be financed? What factors will determine which way is chosen?

DATA QUESTIONS

23. Obtain a copy of the latest *Economic Report of the President* from your library. Find the U.S. budget deficit for 1999, and the change in the monetary base in 1999. Do you think the Fed is actively monetizing federal budget deficits? Why or why not?
24. Look at the assets and liabilities of the Fed over the past six months as listed in the latest *Federal Reserve Bulletin*. Which items seem to fluctuate greatly from month to month? Which items are fairly stable? Which seem to grow at a constant rate?

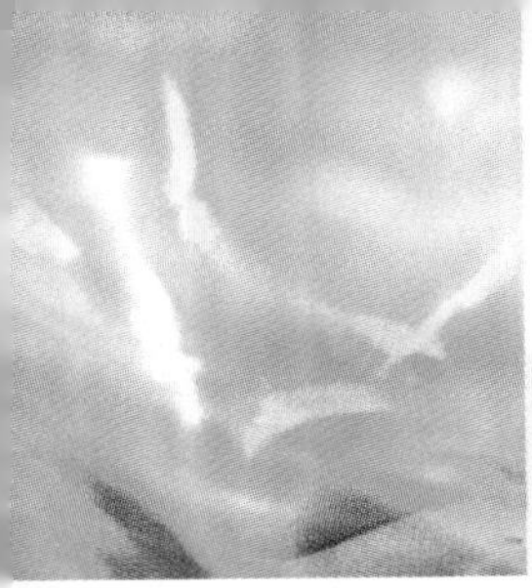

CHAPTER 19

Organization of Central Banks

Will he or won't he? In early 1996, analysts speculated about whether President Clinton would nominate Alan Greenspan for a third term as Chairman of the Board of Governors of the Federal Reserve System, the "CEO" of the U.S. central bank. Some rumors suggested that the President delayed the Fed chairman's reappointment to obtain a more expansionary monetary policy from the Fed. Financial markets were worried that the failure to reappoint Greenspan would deprive the central bank of the services of a well-respected leader. Greenspan was reappointed in 1996, but internal and external pressure on the Fed led to a tug-of-war over the course of monetary policy. In 1998, a similar tug-of-war took place around the world, as Chairman Greenspan, Bank of Japan Governor Masaru Hayami, and European Central Bank President Wim Duisenberg struggled to balance monetary policy objectives and political pressures.

Why should the choice of a central bank chairman be the subject of political controversy and an event that can trouble financial markets? You know from earlier chapters that the Fed plays an active role in the money supply process. But in learning about the money supply process, we viewed the Fed as a "black box." That is, we observed the results of the Fed's actions in managing the monetary base, setting reserve requirements, and making discount loans, but we didn't look inside the Fed to see *why* those decisions were made and implemented. That is our mission in this chapter and the next two chapters. In this chapter, we begin our study of the way the Fed conducts monetary policy by looking at the structure of the Fed. The Federal Reserve chairman has often been called the second most important person in the nation. The reason is that the Fed is in control of monetary policy—a set of decisions that affect the well-being of individuals and firms during economic downturns and upturns. It is little wonder, then, that speculation on Greenspan's appointment caused some jitters on Wall Street.

Our specific objectives in this chapter are to learn about the Fed's organization and structure and its role as an economic policymaking body. We also describe the political arena in which the Fed operates and the debate over the independence of the central bank. We then examine the organization and independence of central banks outside the United States, including the new European Central Bank.

POWER SHARING IN THE FEDERAL RESERVE SYSTEM

Few countries have as complex a structure for their central bank as the United States has in its Federal Reserve System. The Fed's organization was shaped by the same political struggle that gave the United States a fragmented banking system: advocates of strong economic institutions versus those who feared large, powerful economic interests. To understand why the Fed is organized as it is, we need to look back in history at the nation's earlier attempts to create a central bank.

Creation of the System

Not long after the United States won its independence, Treasury Secretary Alexander Hamilton organized the Bank of the United States, which was meant to function as a central bank but had both government and private shareholders. Distrust of the Bank of the United States by Southern and Western agrarian and small-business interests resulted in the bank's demise in 1811. In 1816, the Second Bank of the United States was formed, but populist President Andrew Jackson did not renew its national charter when it expired in 1836. (The bank survived for a time as a state-chartered bank in Pennsylvania.)

Abolition of the Second Bank of the United States left the nation without an official lender of last resort for banks. The void was filled by private institutions such as the New York Clearing House, but severe nationwide financial panics in 1873, 1884, 1893, and 1907—and accompanying economic downturns—raised fears in Congress that the U.S. financial system was unstable. After the 1907 panic and economic recession, Congress considered options for government intervention. Many officials worried that bankers such as New York financier J. P. Morgan, who had served as a de facto lender of last resort, would be unable to manage future crises. Congress appointed a National Monetary Commission to begin formal studies leading to the design of a central bank. With the support of President Woodrow Wilson, the Federal Reserve Act became law in 1913.

The Federal Reserve Act of 1913 created a central bank for the United States, the **Federal Reserve System.** The act provided for checks and balances that were designed to diffuse economic power in three ways: among bankers and business interests, among states and regions, and between government and the private sector. The act and subsequent legislation created four groups within the system, each empowered in theory to perform separate duties: the Federal Reserve banks, member banks, the Board of Governors, and the Federal Open Market Committee (FOMC). The responsibilities that were assigned to each reflected the original intent of the 1913 act to give the central bank control over the amount of currency outstanding and the volume of discount loans to member banks (the lender-of-last-resort function). In theory, the President and Congress didn't envision that the Fed would control monetary policy, broadly defined. In practice, however, over time, the Fed has assumed the lead role in making monetary policy. In the rest of this section, we describe the roles of the principal groups within the Federal Reserve System in conducting open market operations, setting reserve requirements, and making discount loans.

Federal Reserve Banks

The Federal Reserve Act divided the United States into 12 Federal Reserve districts, each of which has a **Federal Reserve bank** in one city (and, in most cases, additional branches in other cities in the district) to conduct discount lending. Figure 19.1 shows the Federal Reserve districts and locations of the Federal Reserve banks. The map may appear strange at first glance: No state (not even California or New York) is a single Federal Reserve district. Some states are split by district boundaries, and economically dissimilar states are grouped in the same district. Most Federal Reserve districts contain a mixture of urban and rural areas, as well as manufacturing, agriculture, and service business interests. This arrangement is intentional, to prevent any one interest group or one state from obtaining preferential treatment from the district Federal Reserve bank. Nor can a district easily have its way at the expense of other districts, owing to supervision by the Board of Governors and the Federal Open Market Committee. If one district is suffering from a recession, it cannot singlehandedly alter Fed money and credit policies to meet its needs. Some cities (New York, Chicago, and San Francisco) clearly

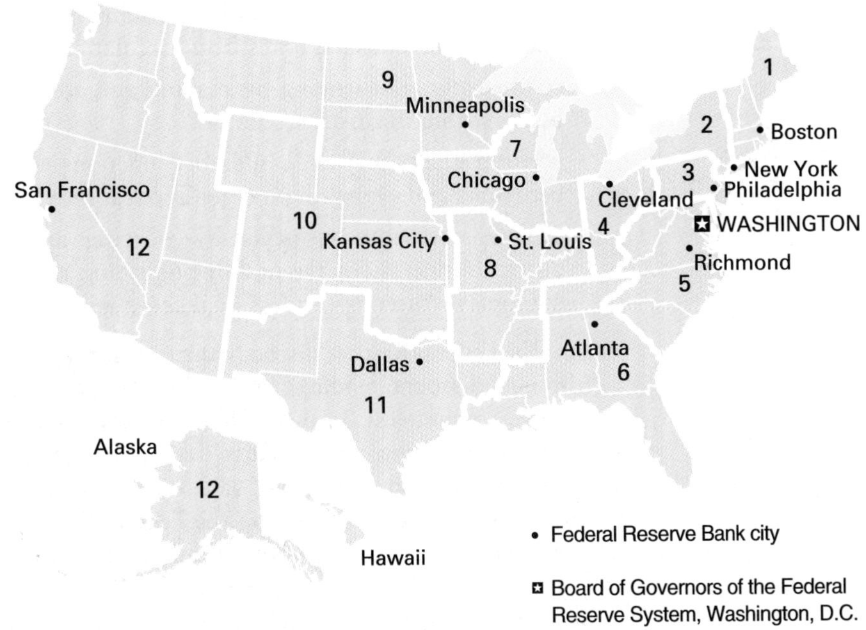

Figure 19.1

Federal Reserve Districts and Banks

The division of the 50 states into 12 Federal Reserve districts was designed so that each district contained a mixture of urban and rural areas and manufacturing, agriculture, and service business interests.

Source: Federal Reserve Bulletin, December 2000, p. A74.

were population centers in 1914 and so were chosen as locations for Federal Reserve banks. Other cities were chosen because of political pressure during the debate over the Federal Reserve Act. (For example, Richmond, Virginia, was the home of Carter Glass, one of the legislative architects of the Federal Reserve System.)

Who owns the Federal Reserve banks? In principle, the private commercial banks in each district that are members of the Federal Reserve System own the district bank. In fact, each Federal Reserve bank is a private–government joint venture. Member banks receive dividends (limited to 6%) on the shares of stock they own in the district bank.

A guiding principle of the 1913 Federal Reserve Act was that one constituency (for example, finance, industry, commerce, or agriculture) would not be able to exploit the central bank's economic power at the expense of another constituency. Therefore Congress restricted the composition of the boards of directors of the Federal Reserve banks. The directors represent the interests of three groups: banks, businesses, and the general public. Member banks elect three bankers (*Class A directors*) and three leaders in industry, commerce, and agriculture (*Class B directors*). The Fed's Board of Governors appoints three public interest directors (*Class C directors*). Subject to the Board's approval, the nine directors of a Federal Reserve bank elect the president of that bank.

The 12 Federal Reserve banks carry out duties related to the Fed's roles in the payments system, monetary control, and financial regulation. Specifically, the district banks

- manage check clearing in the payments system;
- manage currency in circulation by issuing new Federal Reserve Notes and withdrawing damaged notes from circulation;
- conduct discount lending by making and administering discount loans to banks within the district;
- perform supervisory and regulatory functions such as examining state member banks and evaluating merger applications; and
- provide services to businesses by collecting and making available data on district business activities and by publishing articles on monetary and banking topics written by professional economists employed by the banks.

The Federal Reserve district banks engage in monetary policy both directly (through discount lending) and indirectly (through membership in Federal Reserve committees). In theory, Federal Reserve banks establish the discount rate and determine the amounts that individual (member and nonmember) banks are allowed to borrow.[†] The district banks indirectly influence policy through their representatives on the Federal Open Market Committee, which sets guidelines for open market operations (purchases and sales of securities by

---

[†]In practice, the discount rate is reviewed and approved for each Federal Reserve district by the Board of Governors in Washington, D.C.

the Fed to affect the monetary base), and the Federal Advisory Council, a consultative body composed of district bankers.

Member Banks

The Federal Reserve Act required all national banks to become **member banks** of the Federal Reserve System. State banks may elect to become members; currently, only about one in seven state banks is a member. Some 40% of all banks in the United States now belong to the Federal Reserve System. These member banks hold almost three-fourths of all bank deposits.

Historically, one reason for the low voluntary membership rate was the cost. The Fed's reserve requirements compel banks to keep part of their deposits as idle funds, effectively imposing a tax on bank intermediation. In contrast, when banks are chartered by states rather than the federal government, their reserves can earn interest. As nominal interest rates rose during the 1960s and 1970s, the opportunity cost of Fed membership increased, and fewer state banks elected to become or remain members.

During the 1970s, the Fed argued that the so-called reserve tax on member banks placed them at a competitive disadvantage relative to nonmember banks. It claimed that declining bank membership eroded its ability to influence the money supply and urged Congress to compel all commercial banks to join the Federal Reserve System. Although Congress has not yet legislated such a requirement, the Depository Institutions Deregulation and Monetary Control Act (DIDMCA) of 1980 required that all banks (by 1987) maintain reserve deposits with the Fed on the same terms. This legislation gave member and nonmember banks equivalent access to discount loans and to payments system (check-clearing) services. It effectively blurred the distinction between member and nonmember banks and halted the decline in Fed membership. Today, about 3000 banks are Federal Reserve System members.

CHECKPOINT

Suppose that City National Bank pays a 7% annual interest rate on checkable deposits, subject to a reserve requirement of 10%. What is City National's effective cost of funds? Against \$100 of deposits, City National must hold \$10 in reserves (in vault cash or deposits with the Fed), leaving \$90 to invest. The bank must pay depositors (0.07)(\$100) = \$7 to obtain \$90 in funds to invest in loans or securities, so its effective cost of funds is not 7%, but 7/90 = 7.8%. Thus reserve requirements impose a tax on bank intermediation, raising City National's cost of funds from 7% to 7.8%. o

Board of Governors

The **Board of Governors** is headquartered in Washington, D.C. Its seven members are appointed by the President of the United States and confirmed by the U.S. Senate. To provide for central bank independence, the terms of board members were set so that one U.S. President generally cannot appoint a full

Board of Governors. Governors serve a nonrenewable term of 14 years; their terms are staggered so that one term expires every other January.† Geographical restrictions ensure that no one Federal Reserve district is overrepresented.

Currently, many board members are professional economists from business, government, or academia. Chairmen of the Board of Governors since World War II have come from various backgrounds, including Wall Street (William McChesney Martin), academia (Arthur Burns), business (G. William Miller), public service (Paul Volcker), and economic forecasting (Alan Greenspan). The chairman serves a four-year term and may be reappointed or serve out the balance of a 14-year member's term.

The Board of Governors administers monetary policy to influence the nation's money supply through open market operations, reserve requirements, and discount lending. Since 1935, it has had the authority to determine reserve requirements within limits set by Congress. The Board of Governors also effectively sets the discount rate (which is in principle established by the Federal Reserve banks) through its review and determination procedure. It holds seven of the 12 seats on the Federal Open Market Committee and therefore influences the setting of guidelines for open market operations. In addition to its formal responsibilities relating to monetary control, it informally influences national and international economic policy decisions. The chairman of the Board of Governors advises the President and testifies before Congress on economic matters.

The Board of Governors has certain responsibilities relating to financial regulation. Before the elimination of Regulation Q in 1986, the board administered interest rate regulations. It also sets *margin requirements,* or the proportion of the purchase price of securities that an investor must pay in cash rather than buying on credit. In addition, it determines permissible activities for bank holding companies and approves bank mergers. Finally, it exercises certain administrative controls over individual Federal Reserve banks, reviewing their budgets and setting the salaries of their presidents and officers.

Federal Open Market Committee

The 12-member **Federal Open Market Committee** (FOMC) gives direction to the Fed's open market operations. Members of the FOMC are the chairman of the Board of Governors, the other Fed governors, the president of the Federal Reserve Bank of New York, and the presidents of four of the other 11 Federal Reserve Banks (who serve on a rotating basis). Only five Federal Reserve bank presidents are voting members of the FOMC, but all 12 attend meetings and participate in discussions. The committee meets eight times each year.

The Fed influences the monetary base primarily through open market operations. Therefore, in practice, the FOMC is the centerpiece of Fed policymaking. The FOMC doesn't literally buy or sell securities for the Fed's account. Instead, it summarizes its views in a *directive* issued to the Fed's

†Technically, a governor could resign before the term expired and then be reappointed, thereby lengthening the term. Since 1970, this practice has been rare.

trading desk at the Federal Reserve Bank of New York. There, the manager for domestic open market operations communicates each day with members of the FOMC (and their staffs) about execution of the directive.

Power and Authority Within the Fed

Because Congress configured the Federal Reserve System with many formal checks and balances to ensure that no one group could effectively control it, central (or national) control of the system was virtually nonexistent during the Fed's first 20 years. After the severe banking crisis of the early 1930s, many analysts concluded that the decentralized district bank system could not adequately respond to national economic and financial disturbances. The Banking Acts of 1933 and 1935 gave the Board of Governors authority to set reserve requirements and the FOMC the authority to direct open market operations. The Banking Act of 1935 also centralized the Fed's participation in the money supply process, giving the Board of Governors a majority (seven of 12) of seats on the FOMC and thereby great influence in implementing monetary policy.

The Board of Governors and the FOMC exert most of the Fed's formal influence on monetary policy. However, many Fed watchers believe that the informal authority of the chairman, the staff of the Board, and the FOMC predominates. The informal authority of Fed Chairman Greenspan led to conflict with President Clinton, who urged the Fed to pursue an expansionary monetary policy during 1996. In other words, the informal power structure within the Fed may be more concentrated and influential than the formal power structure. Because the Federal Reserve Bank of New York always occupies a seat on the FOMC, the president of that bank also can be quite influential. Figure 19.2 shows the organizational and power-sharing arrangements within the Fed, both in theory and in practice.

Member banks, the nominal owners of Federal Reserve banks, have little actual influence within the system. The distinction between *ownership* and *control* within the Federal Reserve System is clear. Member banks own shares of stock in the Federal Reserve banks, but shareholding confers none of the rights that are typically granted to shareholders of private corporations. Member banks receive at most a 6% annual dividend, regardless of the Fed's earnings, and so do not have the residual claim that is normally granted to equity. Moreover, member banks have virtually no control over how their stakes in the system are used because the Board of Governors in Washington formulates policy directives. Although member banks elect the six Class A and Class B directors, there is generally only one candidate per position, whom the Federal Reserve bank or Board of Governors suggests.

Although there is no direct evidence as to who actually holds power in the Fed, the impressions of experienced insiders are revealing. On the basis of his personal experience as a Fed official, economist Sherman Maisel estimated the relative influence of groups within the Fed in setting monetary policy: the chairman of the Board of Governors, 45%; the staff of the Board and the FOMC, 25%; and other governors and the Federal Reserve banks,

Figure 19.2 **Organization and Authority of the Federal Reserve System**

The Federal Reserve Act of 1913 established the Federal Reserve System but incorporated a series of checks and balances into the system. Part (a) shows that in theory, its economic power is diffuse. Part (b) shows that informal power within the Fed is more concentrated in the hands of the chairman of the Board of Governors than the formal structure suggests.

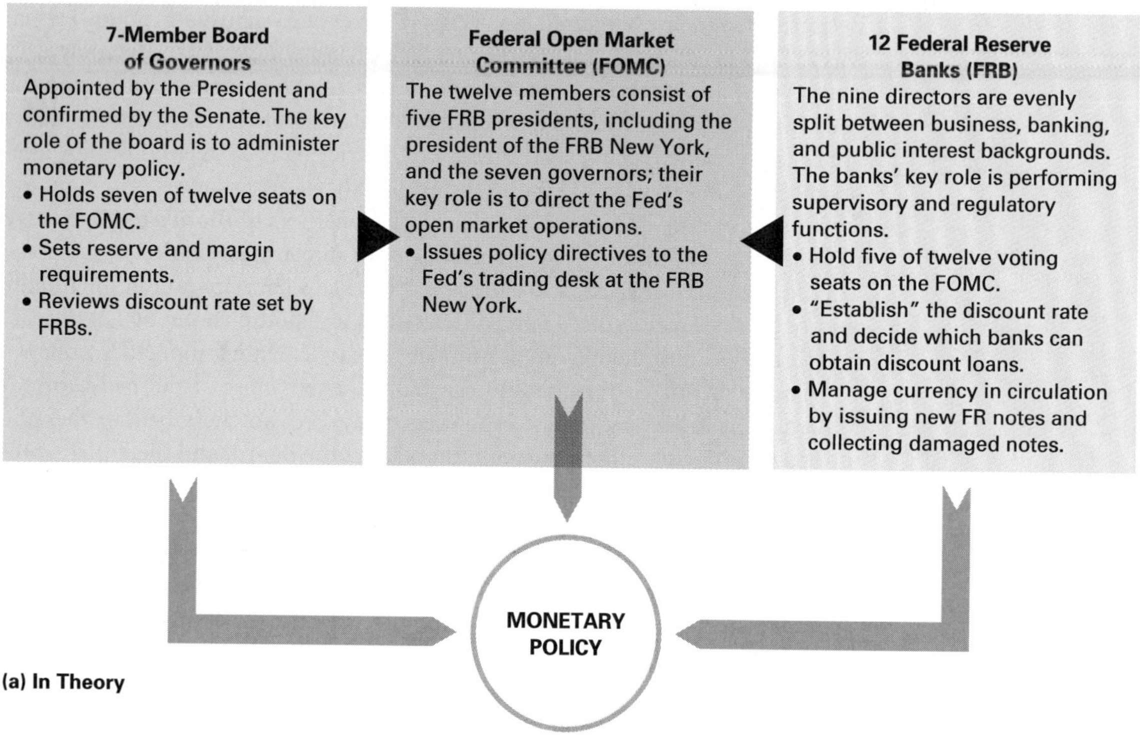

(a) In Theory

not particularly powerful.† Those impressions were recorded in the 1970s, but current actions support them. Some board members and district bank presidents on the FOMC may challenge the chairman's agenda, but the chairman's influence still dominates.

HOW THE FED OPERATES

The government created the Fed to manage the banking system and the money supply. Lacking a constitutional mandate, the Fed operates in a political arena, and it is subject to pressure by legislators and officials. The central bank also exerts power in economic policymaking because of its role in the money supply process. In this section we describe how the Fed operates in the political environment, and we discuss the debate over the independence of the central bank.

†Sherman J. Maisel, *Managing the Dollar.* New York: W. W. Norton, 1973.

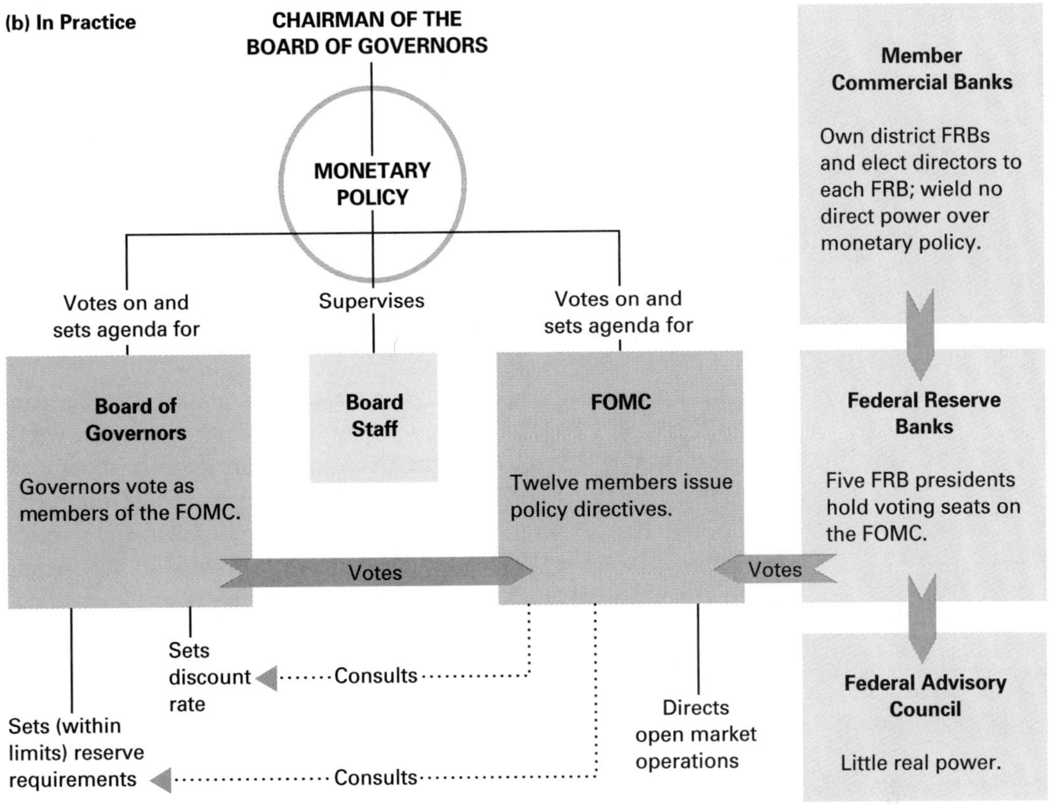

Handling External Pressure

Congress intended the Federal Reserve System generally to operate independently of external pressures (for example, from the President, Congress, the banking industry, or business groups). Board members are appointed for long, nonrenewable terms of office, reducing any one President's influence on the Board's composition and the temptation for governors to take actions merely to please the President and Congress.

The Fed's financial independence allows it to combat external pressure. Generally, federal agencies are subject to the annual appropriations process, during which Congress scrutinizes budgetary requests, authorizes funds, and then appropriates the funds. Not only is the Fed exempt from this process, but it is also a profitable organization, contributing funds to the Treasury rather than receiving funds from it. Most of the Fed's earnings come from interest on the securities it holds; smaller amounts come from interest on discount loans and fees that are received from financial institutions for check-clearing and other services. In recent years, the Fed's net income has exceeded $25 billion annually—substantial profits when compared even to the largest U.S. corporations.

Despite the attempt to give the Fed independence, it isn't completely insulated from external pressure. First, the President can exercise control over the membership of the Board of Governors. Often, governors do not serve their full 14-year terms, because they can earn higher incomes in private business. Therefore a President who serves two terms in office may be able to appoint several governors. Additionally, the President may appoint a new chairman every four years—an appointment that can sometimes make or break his presidency. A chairman who is not reappointed may serve the remainder of his or her term as a governor but traditionally resigns, thereby giving the President another vacancy to fill.

Second, although the Fed's significant net income exempts it from the appropriations process (Congress's "power of the purse"), the Fed remains a creation of Congress. The U.S. Constitution does not specifically mandate a central bank, so Congress can amend the Fed's charter and powers or even abolish it entirely. Members of Congress usually are not shy about reminding the Fed of this fact. Nor is Congressional oversight merely rhetoric. In the middle and late 1970s, Congress forced the Fed to explain its goals and procedures. Passed in 1975, House Concurrent Resolution 133 requires the Fed to announce targets for the growth of monetary aggregates. In addition, the Humphrey-Hawkins Act (officially the Full Employment and Balanced Growth Act of 1978) requires the Fed to explain how these targets are consistent with the President's economic objectives. Nevertheless, in practice, the Congress has not often successfully challenged the Fed's policies.

Examples of Treasury–Fed Conflict

Elected officials lack formal control of monetary policy, and this lack of control at times has resulted in conflicts between the Fed and the President, who is often represented by the Secretary of the Treasury. During World War II, the administration increased its control over the Fed. To help finance wartime budget deficits, the Fed agreed to hold interest rates on Treasury securities at low levels. It could do so by buying bonds that were not purchased by private investors, thereby predetermining (pegging) the rates. After the war, the Treasury wanted to continue this policy, but the Fed didn't agree. The Fed's concern was inflation: Larger purchases of Treasury securities by the Fed increased the monetary base, potentially increasing the money supply growth rate and inflation. Price controls that had restrained inflation during the war were lifted after the war ended.

Chairman of the Board of Governors Marriner Eccles particularly objected to the rate-fixing policy. His opposition to the desires of the Truman administration cost him the Fed chairmanship in 1948, although he continued to fight for Fed independence during the remainder of his term as a governor. On March 4, 1951, the wartime policy of fixing the interest rates on Treasury securities was formally abandoned with the Treasury–Federal Reserve Accord.

Conflicts between the Treasury and the Fed didn't end with that accord, however. For example, President Ronald Reagan and Federal Reserve Chairman Paul Volcker argued over who was at fault for the severe business recession of the early 1980s. Reagan blamed the Fed's contractionary monetary policy. Volcker held that the Fed could not expand money supply growth until the budget deficit—which results from policy actions of the President and Congress—was reduced.

Early in the George H. W. Bush administration, the conflict was less severe, even though the Treasury typically argued for a more expansionary monetary policy than the Fed wanted. During the debate in 1991 over reforms of U.S. banking regulations, the Treasury and the Fed argued over which would have greater responsibility in overseeing the banking system. Finally, in late 1991 and early 1992, the Treasury pressured the Fed to reduce short-term interest rates. Although the Fed did reduce the discount rate, there is no way of knowing whether Treasury pressure influenced its decision. In early 1993, the Clinton Treasury argued that the Fed should not raise short-term interest rates in the face of the administration's budget package; and in 1994, the administration challenged the Fed's repeated increases in the federal funds rate. In 1996, some members of Congress questioned whether the Fed was sufficiently stringent in its operating budget in light of cutbacks in government budgets. As the George W. Bush administration took shape in early 2001, some commentators worried about a conflict between the Treasury and the Fed over the administration's tax policy.

Factors That Motivate the Fed

We have shown that the Fed has considerable power over monetary policy. Let's now examine alternative explanations of how the Fed decides to use its

CONSIDER THIS . . .

Importance of Selecting a Fed Chairman

In the summer of 1979, President Jimmy Carter perceived the failure of his economic policies to roll back inflation as a huge stumbling block in his quest for reelection. Inflation was accelerating, and the value of the dollar was declining sharply on foreign-exchange markets. To try to turn the economy around before the election, Carter sought to replace Federal Reserve Chairman G. William Miller (who was leaving to become Secretary of the Treasury) with a champion of price stability. On July 24, 1979, Carter offered the Fed chairmanship to Paul Volcker, the president of the Federal Reserve Bank of New York and former undersecretary of the Treasury for monetary affairs. Volcker's views on Fed policies were well known. Earlier in 1979, he had argued for a contractionary monetary policy, with a significant increase in the federal funds rate, to fight inflation. The inflation challenge led Volcker to accept the new post (despite having to take a pay cut from $116,000 to $57,500).

In October 1979, the Volcker Fed began a restrictive policy of significantly lower money supply growth that resulted in a dramatic increase in the federal funds rate. High interest rates and a sagging economy were major factors in President Carter's campaign woes. By 1982, the rate of inflation had declined significantly, but the decline came too late for Jimmy Carter. Carter had appointed Federal Reserve Chairman Volcker, but the short-term effects of his policies had helped to hand the 1980 presidential election to Republican Ronald Reagan.

power. We consider two views of Fed motivation: the public interest view and the principal-agent view.

The public interest view. The usual starting point for explaining the motivation of business managers is that they act in the interest of the constituency they serve: the shareholders. The **public interest view** of Fed motivation holds that the Fed, too, acts in the interest of its primary constituency (the general public) and that it seeks to achieve economic goals that are in the public interest. Examples of such goals are price and employment stability and economic growth.

Does the evidence support the public interest view? It doesn't appear to with regard to price stability. The record of persistent inflation since World War II undercuts the claim that the Fed has emphasized price stability. Similarly, some economists dispute the Fed's contributions to the stability of other economic indicators.

The principal-agent view. Many economists view organizations as having conflicting goals. Although they are created to serve the public and perform a public service, government organizations also have internal goals that might not match their stated mission. In effect, public organizations face the agency problem just as private corporations do. In this section, we describe goals other than those outlined in the Federal Reserve Act that might influence the Fed's decisions and the way in which it exerts its economic power.

Recall that when managers (agents) have little stake in their businesses, their incentives to maximize the value of shareholders' (principals') claims may be weak; in that situation, the agents don't always act in the interest of the principals. James Buchanan and Gordon Tullock of George Mason University formulated a **principal-agent view** of motivation in bureaucratic organizations such as the Fed. They contend that bureaucrats' objective is to maximize their personal well-being—power, influence, and prestige—rather than the well-being of the general public. Hence the principal-agent view of Fed motivation predicts that the Fed acts to increase its power, influence, and prestige as an organization, subject to constraints placed on it by principals such as the President and Congress.

How can we determine whether the principal-agent view accurately explains the Fed's motivation? If it does, we might conclude that the Fed would fight to maintain its autonomy. Unquestionably, it does so; the Fed has resisted congressional attempts to control its budget many times. In fact, the Fed is one of the most successful bureaucratic organizations in mobilizing constituents (such as bankers and business executives) in its own defense.

Proponents of the principal-agent view also think that the Fed would avoid conflicts with groups that could limit its power, influence, and prestige. For example, the Fed could manage monetary policy to assist the reelection efforts of presidential incumbents who are unlikely to limit its power. The result would be a **political business cycle,** in which the Fed would try to lower interest rates to stimulate credit demand and economic activity before an election to make the Fed look good. After the election, the economy would pay the piper when the Fed contracted economic activity to reduce the inflationary pressure caused by its earlier expansion—but, by then, the President who was sympathetic to the Fed would have been reelected. The facts don't completely support the political business cycle theory, however. For example, expansion of money supply growth preceded President Nixon's reelection in 1972, but contraction of money supply growth preceded President Carter's and President Bush's unsuccessful bids for reelection in 1980 and 1992, respectively.

Nevertheless, the President's desires may subtly influence Fed policy. One study of the influence of politics on changes in monetary policy from 1979 through 1984 measured the number of signals of desired policy from the administration in articles appearing in *The Wall Street Journal*. The author found a close correlation between changes in monetary policy and the number of administration signals.[†]

One criticism of the principal-agent view addresses the need to separate the Fed's intentions from external pressure: The Fed itself might want to act in one way, whereas Congress and the President might try to get the Fed to pursue other goals. The principal-agent view also fails to explain why Congress allows the Fed to be relatively independent through self-financing. Some economists suggest that the Fed may provide Congress with long-run benefits through self-financing. If self-financing gives the Fed an incentive to conduct more open market purchases, thereby expanding the money supply, more residual revenue will accrue to the Treasury for appropriation by Congress.

Fed Independence

Usually, the political issue of Fed independence arises not because of academic disagreement over monetary policy or even the role of the Fed in managing monetary policy, but because of the public's negative reaction to Fed policy. For example, legislation introduced in Congress in 1982 to decrease the Fed's autonomy stemmed from public reaction to high interest rates. We now analyze the arguments for and against Fed independence.

Arguments for independence. The main argument for Fed independence is that monetary policy—which affects inflation, interest rates, exchange rates, and economic growth—is too important and technical to be determined by politicians. Because of the frequency of elections, politicians may be myopic, concerned with short-term benefits without regard to potential long-term costs. Short-term and long-term interests often clash after inflation. Supporters argue that monetary policy tends to be too expansionary if it is left to policymakers with short horizons, leading to inflation. Therefore the Fed cannot assume that politicians' objectives reflect public sentiment. The public may well prefer that the experts at the Fed, rather than politicians, make monetary policy decisions.

Another argument for Fed independence is that complete control of the

[†]Thomas Havrilesky, "Monetary Policy Signaling from the Administration to the Federal Reserve," *Journal of Money, Credit, and Banking*, 20:83–101, February 1988.

OTHER TIMES, OTHER PLACES . . .

Conflicts Between the Treasury and the Central Bank in Japan over Independence

The United States isn't the only country in which tensions between the Treasury and the central bank influence monetary policy. Japanese monetary policy during the late 1980s and early 1990s provides another good example. During the mid-1980s, Bank of Japan Governor Satoshi Sumita conducted an expansionary monetary policy. Mr. Sumita, a former vice minister of finance (the Ministry of Finance is akin to the U.S. Treasury), favored low interest rates. Yasushi Mieno, appointed to head the Bank of Japan in 1989, pursued a more contractionary policy. *The Wall Street Journal* reported that "Mr. Mieno took away the *sake* bowl just as the party started getting rambunctious."† That is, Japanese money growth would be reduced, leading to concerns that the runup in Japanese stock prices would end.

During 1990, increases in the Bank of Japan's discount rate sent Japanese stock market prices plunging and threatened some highly leveraged firms with financial distress. The surprise decision by the Bank of Japan to reduce its discount rate from 6% to 5.5% on July 1, 1991, caused Japanese central bank watchers to worry that Mieno was currying favor with Finance Minister Ryutaro Hashimoto. The finance minister was a strong candidate to be the Japanese prime minister, and Mieno's actions seemed to create a political business cycle.

Like Federal Reserve actions in the United States, the Bank of Japan's actions can be viewed as reflecting responsible, independent behavior: The bank may have tried to ease the likelihood of a financial crisis in Japan induced by high interest rates, even though it could attempt relatively contractionary policies over the medium term.

† Marcus W. Brauchli and Clay Chandler, "Financial Shift: In a Major Reversal, the Bank of Japan Cuts Its Key Interest Rate," *The Wall Street Journal*, July 2, 1991.

Fed by elected officials increases the likelihood of political business cycle fluctuations in the money supply. For example, those officials might pressure the Fed to assist the Treasury's borrowing efforts by buying government bonds, increasing the money supply and fueling inflation.

Arguments against independence. The importance of monetary policy for the economy is also the main argument against central bank independence. Supporters claim that in a democracy, elected officials should make public policy. Because the public holds elected officials responsible for perceived monetary policy problems, some analysts advocate giving the President and Congress more control over monetary policy. The counterargument to the view that monetary policy is too technical for elected officials is that national security and foreign policy also require sophisticated analysis and a long-term horizon, and these functions are entrusted to elected officials. In addition, critics of Fed independence argue that placing the central bank under the control of elected officials could confer benefits by coordinating and integrating monetary policy with government taxing and spending policies.

Those who argue for greater congressional control make the case that the Fed has not always used its independence well. For example, some critics note that the Fed, because of its deflationary bias, failed to assist the banking system during the economic contraction of the early 1930s. Another example that many economists cite is that Fed policies were too inflationary in the 1960s and 1970s. Finally, some analysts believe that the Fed acted too slowly in addressing credit problems during the recession of the early 1990s.

Concluding remarks. Economists and politicians don't universally agree on the merits of Fed independence. Under the present system, however, the Fed's independence is not absolute, and so it sometimes satisfies one or the other group of critics. In practice, debates center on proposals to limit Fed independence in some respects, not to eliminate its formal independence. Some recent proposals include shortening the term of office of governors, making the chairman's term coincide more closely with that of the President, and placing the Secretary of the Treasury on the FOMC. Enacting any of these proposals would tend to make the Fed's economic policies more consistent with the President's.

CENTRAL BANK INDEPENDENCE IN OTHER COUNTRIES

The degree of central bank independence varies greatly from country to country. When we compare the structure of the Fed with that of central banks in Canada, Europe, and Japan, four patterns emerge. First, in countries where central bank board members serve fixed terms of office, none is as long as the 14-year term for Federal Reserve governors, implying nominally greater independence for the Fed. Second, in those countries, the head of the central bank has a longer term of office than the four-year term of office of the chairman of the Board of Governors in the United States. Third, of these countries, only Germany has had a federal structure for the central bank (we discuss the European Central Bank below).

Finally, the overall degree of independence of the central bank varies. An independent central bank is free to pursue its goals without direct interference from other government officials and legislators. Most economists believe that an independent central bank can more freely focus on keeping inflation low (we discuss this goal in more detail in Chapter 21). The European Central Bank is, in principle, extremely independent, whereas the central banks of Japan and the United Kingdom traditionally have been less independent, though by 1998, both had become more independent and more focused on price stability. The updated Bank of Japan Law, in force since April 1998, gives the nine-member policy board more autonomy to pursue price stability. The Ministry of Finance retains control over much of the Bank of Japan's budget, however.

The push for central bank independence to pursue a goal of low inflation has increased in recent years. Indeed, in most of the industrialized world, central bank independence from the political process is gaining ground as the way to organize monetary authorities. In practice, the degree of actual independence in the conduct of monetary policy varies across countries. What conclusions should we draw from differences in central bank structure? Many analysts believe that an independent central bank improves the economy's performance by lowering inflation without raising output or employment fluctuations. Calculations by Alberto Alesina and Lawrence Summers of Harvard University indicate that the countries that have the most independent central banks (Germany and Switzerland) had the lowest average rates of inflation during the 1970s and 1980s. New Zealand, Italy, and Spain, with much less independent central banks, had significantly higher rates of inflation.

What constitutes meaningful central bank independence? Economists emphasize that declarations of independence are insufficient. The central bank must be able to conduct policy without direct interference from the government. The central bank also must be able to set nonconflicting goals for which it can be held accountable. The leading example of such a goal is a target for inflation. Central banks in Canada, Finland, New Zealand, Sweden, and the United Kingdom have official inflation targets. A number of European countries, including France and Germany, had informal inflation targets (prior to the emergence of the European Central Bank). Many economists urge that the U.S. Fed adopt an inflation target.

ORGANIZATION AND INDEPENDENCE OF THE EUROPEAN CENTRAL BANK

As part of the move toward economic integration in Europe, the *European Central Bank* (ECB) is charged with conducting monetary policy for Europe (that is, for the 11 countries participating in European Monetary Union). Representatives of many European nations signed an important agreement in Maastricht, the Netherlands, in December 1991. This agreement detailed a gradual approach to monetary union to be completed between 1994 and 1999. Although the monetary union became effective only on January 1, 1999, groundwork for the ECB had been laid in advance. Indeed, European nations coordinated an expansionary monetary policy in late 1998.

The ECB's organization is in some respects similar to that of the U.S. Fed. The ECB's executive board, chaired initially by Wim Duisenberg (a former Dutch finance minister), has six members who work exclusively for the bank. Board members (a Vice President, initially Christian Noyer of France, and four others) are appointed by the heads of state and government, based on the recommendation of the Council of Ministers of Economics and Finance, after consulting the European Parliament and the Governing Council of the ECB. Executive board members serve nonrenewable eight-year terms (although Executive Board President Duisenberg tentatively agreed to step aside after four years). Also participating in the governance of the ECB are the Governors of each of the 11 member national central banks, each of whom will have a term of at least five years. The long terms of office are designed to increase the political independence of the ECB.

In principle, the ECB has a high degree of overall independence, with a clear mandate to emphasize price stability, following the lead of the

Bundesbank (Germany's central bank). Whether legal independence will translate into actual independence is difficult to say, however. Such a translation requires observing the new institution for a period of time.

Based on the historical experience of the Federal Reserve, there may be cause for concern. The decentralized central banking system envisioned in the original Federal Reserve Act of 1913 led to power struggles within the system and offered no mechanism to achieve consensus during the financial crisis of the early 1930s. National central banks have considerable power in the ECB. The Governors of the European System of Central Banks (ESCB) hold a majority of votes in the ECB's governing council, 11 votes against the six held by the Executive Board. Although the ECB began with only about 500 staff members, national central banks had more than 60,000 employees in 1999.

Where might conflict arise? While the ECB statute emphasizes price stability, countries have argued—and likely will continue to argue—over the merits of expansionary or contractionary monetary policy. Also, no consensus has been reached on the way the ECB will function as the lender of last resort in dealing with domestic financial crises. Optimists believe that the united ECB and monetary union forces Europe to confront key structural economic weaknesses, such as an oversized public sector and inflexible labor markets. Pessimists argue that monetary unions generally require a broader political union (the case for the Fed, but not for the ECB) to be successful. One thing is clear—all eyes are on the ECB.

KEY TERMS AND CONCEPTS

Federal Reserve System
- Board of Governors
- Federal Open Market Committee
- Federal Reserve bank
- Member banks

Political business cycle

Principal-agent view

Public interest view

SUMMARY

1. The Federal Reserve Act of 1913 created the U.S. Federal Reserve System (the Fed). Its three principal components are the Federal Reserve banks, the Board of Governors, and the Federal Open Market Committee (FOMC).
2. The Fed's formal activities are conducting open market operations, setting reserve requirements, and making discount loans. The FOMC issues guidelines for open market operations. The Board of Governors sets reserve requirements. Depository institutions obtain discount loans through district Federal Reserve banks, although the Board of Governors essentially determines the discount rate (the interest rate charged on discount loans).
3. In practice, power within the Federal Reserve System is more centralized than is apparent from the official structure. The Board of Governors, especially its chairman, typically dominates monetary policy decisions.

THE ECONOMIST JANUARY 6, 2001

The ECB's Terrible Twos

You might think that life was at last getting easier for the infant European Central Bank. The twin threats that have hung over its goal of price stability, high oil prices and the weakness of the euro, are both subsiding. The euro's sharp recovery has stifled the gripes of Europe's politicians about both the ECB's policies and its President, Wim Duisenberg. Even the recent slowdown in most of the euro area's economies may prove to be good news, since most economists now expect
a the next move in interest rates to be downward, following a climb of two-and-a-quarter percentage points between November 1999 and October 2000.

This week marked another seminal moment besides the currency's climb . . . On January 1 Greece became the euro's twelfth member, shedding Europe's oldest currency, the drachma. . . . Its arrival somewhat makes up for the disappointment of the Danish vote against entry in a referendum held in September. The odds against either of the two other EU non-euro members, Britain and Sweden, joining soon have risen since the Danish vote. . . .

[T]he ECB faces several daunting challenges over its next two years. Its monetary-policy task is likely to prove especially hard, as uncertainty over the path of the world economy grows. So far, it has operated in a largely benign global climate in which any talk of recession was far-fetched. But it may this year have to act more vigorously to sustain growth and fend off deflation—especially if the euro keeps on rising. . . .

Next January will see the introduction of euro notes and coins, a logistical and marketing operation of immense proportions. And Mr. Duisenberg has promised to "retire" sometime in 2002, to be replaced by the urbane governor of the Bank of France, Jean-Claude Trichet. This was the compromise agreed at the time of Mr. Duisenberg's appointment in May 1998; but it has no legal force, and a judicial investigation into Mr. Trichet's handling of Crédit Lyonnais, a French bank, may preclude his appointment to the ECB presidency in any case.

As if all this were not enough, there are . . . other difficulties that, sooner or later, will have to be resolved, either by the ECB itself or by the European Union's politicians. [One] is that the ECB has not yet learned how to communicate the way it executes monetary policy to financial markets and the media; or, put another way, outside commentators have not yet learned to "read" the ECB as clearly as they can America's Federal Reserve. . . . b

Unable to rely on a strong individual, the ECB has set out a monetary-policy strategy with two "pillars" . . . The first pillar is the money supply, reflecting the fact that inflation in the long run is a monetary phenomenon. The second consists of other, short-run influences on the price level. . . . The problem is that it is not clear to ECB-watchers. . . . whether the governing council is using this framework in a consistent way. . . .

The doubts about the presidency of the ECB will also continue to cast a cloud. Mr. Duisenberg is still expected to stick to his bargain and quit next year. c

Although the European Central Bank (like the U.S. Federal Reserve System) has considerable independence from national governments, a strong central bank leader is necessary to realize independence in practice. While Wim Duisenberg, the first President of the ECB, is well respected, his ability to communicate the goals of the ECB and resist political pressure must be judged over time.

a Many critics of the Fed and the ECB have suggested that policymaking affecting the economy—including monetary policy—should be in the hands of elected officials. If the public interest view of central bank behavior is correct, the central bank's monetary policy focus on low inflation—the goal it set for itself—was appropriate even if government officials favored more expansionary policies. In terms of the principal-agent view, the ECB's constituency would have been anti-inflation bond markets, which normally favor slow rates of growth of the money supply. Analysts disagreed at the time over which view of the central bank's motivation was most believable.

b Even if low inflation is the ECB's goal, most analysts gauged the ECB to be faring poorly relative to the Fed in communicating its policy stance and the "balance of risks" in the economy seen by policymakers. In additon, some European politicians worried that Mr. Duisenberg could be too open—as with ill-timed remarks on currency intervention that sent the euro to its all-time low against the dollar in the fall of 2000.

c The battle over Mr. Duisenberg's tenure suggests that political pressure on the ECB may not be far from the sidelines. The ECB President may be fearful of the costs of a political business cycle, in which expansionary policy could assist a government's reelection efforts but also necessitate a future monetary contraction to combat inflation.

For further thought . . .

Suppose that the ECB decides to cut short-term interest rates. At the same time, senior officials in European governments argue publicly that more rapid money growth is needed to stimulate the economy. Under the public interest view, would the ECB be more or less likely to proceed with its intentions? Why?

Source: Excerpted from "The Terrible Twos Begin," *The Economist*, January 6, 2001. www.economist.com

4. The Fed is relatively independent of the political process, owing to the long-term appointments of members of the Board of Governors and to the Fed's financial independence. However, because the Federal Reserve System was created by legislation, not by the Constitution, Congress could enact legislation to reduce its power (or even to eliminate it).
5. The public interest view of Fed motivation argues that the Fed pursues monetary policies and financial regulation in the broad national interest. Alternatively, the principal-agent view stresses that the Fed is more interested in enhancing its own well-being as an organization than in the national interest.
6. Should the Fed be independent? Some argue that it should because its longer time horizon (relative to those of elected officials) enables it to pursue monetary policies in the long-term interest of the nation. Critics of central bank independence note that monetary policy is an important part of the national policy agenda and hence should be controlled by elected officials.
7. The degree of independence from the political process and the general procedures for appointing governors vary for central banks of other industrialized countries. Countries having relatively independent central banks generally have lower inflation rates than do countries having less independent central banks.

REVIEW QUESTIONS

1. Why did Congress pass the Federal Reserve Act in 1913 when the United States had gotten along without a central bank since 1836?
2. What are the Board of Governors' duties and responsibilities with regard to monetary policy?
3. Who are the voting members of the Federal Open Market Committee?
4. Where does most of the Fed's income come from?
5. What features of the Fed help to make it independent of political pressure? How does the U.S. Constitution protect the Fed?
6. How many district Federal Reserve banks are there? Where are they located?
7. Who guides the open market operations of the Fed?
8. Why do Federal Reserve districts cut across some state lines, and why do the directors of the district banks represent business, banking, and the general public?
9. Is speculation in shares of stock of the Federal Reserve banks possible? Why or why not?
10. What are the duties of Federal Reserve banks?
11. "It is impossible to know where the true power and authority in an organization lie just from examining the formal structure of the organization." Does this observation apply to the Federal Reserve System? Explain.
12. *Evaluate:* The Federal Reserve System is independent of the political process in the United States.
13. *Evaluate:* To conduct monetary policy in the national interest, the Federal Reserve System should be independent of the political process in the United States.
14. *Evaluate:* The Fed's independence from the government's appropriations process necessarily rules out the principal-agent view of Fed motivation.

ANALYTICAL PROBLEMS

15. Is it easier for a central bank to be independent in a modern, industrial country or in a less developed country? What implications does your answer have for what the average inflation rate is likely to be in modern, industrial countries as opposed to less developed countries?
16. Suppose that you are the president of the country Moolah and that you are writing a new constitution for it. Would you give monetary policymakers complete independence from your government? Why or why not?
17. Research shows that 9 to 18 months after the Fed eases monetary policy, the economy shows increased real growth. Suppose that 18 months before a presi-

dential election, the Fed announces a reduction of the discount rate by 1 percentage point. What would you conclude about the Fed's motivation? Would your conclusion change if, six months earlier, real output growth had been forecast to be 3% but the economy weakened and real output grew by only 1%?

18. Why might the President not want to appoint a tough-minded, independent chairman of the Federal Reserve Board of Governors but prefer someone with whom he or she had previous political ties?

19. Are the high rates of inflation that the United States experienced during the 1970s consistent with the public interest view of the Fed's motivation?

20. Is the principal-agent view of the Fed's motivation believable if Fed policymakers routinely turn down jobs on Wall Street that would double or triple their salaries?

21. A recent proposal would remove the presidents of the Federal Reserve banks from the FOMC and add the Secretary of the Treasury and the chairperson of the President's Council of Economic Advisers to the FOMC. What would such a proposal do to the Fed's independence? Would it make the Fed more accountable for its actions? How would regional concerns and information be communicated to the Fed?

22. Suppose that economic conditions worsen and the Fed considers easing monetary policy. But before the Fed can act, the President's chief economic advisor holds a press conference and states that the Fed should ease its policy to stimulate the economy. Does this statement make easing the policy less or more difficult for the Fed? Why?

23. According to an article in *The Wall Street Journal*, early in 1999: "Germany's determined finance minister, Oskar Lafontaine, urged the new European Central Bank to cut interest rates to boost corporate profits and, most important of all, create jobs." What impact do you believe the fact that the European Central Bank had been newly created would have on the likelihood of its accepting the advice of the German finance minister?

24. In Japan, the central bank is not formally independent. Yet Japan's inflation rate is much lower than that of the United States. Does this condition suggest that low inflation doesn't really depend on central bank independence? Why or why not?

25. *Evaluate:* The Fed's occasional mobilization of banking interests to defend itself against legislative attacks is inconsistent with the public interest view of Fed motivation.

26. During the debate in 1991 over reform of U.S. banking regulations, the Treasury advocated the removal of barriers between banking and commerce (for example, allowing nonfinancial firms to own depository institutions), but the Fed opposed such a move. Offer an explanation of the Fed's response in terms of (a) the public interest view of Fed motivation and (b) the principal-agent view of Fed motivation.

DATA QUESTIONS

27. In the *Federal Reserve Bulletin,* the Federal Reserve Open Market Transactions table lists the changes in the Fed's holdings of U.S. government and other securities in the System Open Market Account. Determine how much its holdings have changed during the past three years. In which year was monetary policy the "easiest"? In which year was it the "tightest"?

28. In the latest *Annual Report of the Board of Governors of the Federal Reserve System,* look up the table that reports historical data on "Income and Expenses" of Federal Reserve banks. Find the column that lists payments to the U.S. Treasury—the Fed's profits that are returned to the government. What is the total amount of the Fed's profits for the past three years? Now determine the total amount of U.S. federal government revenue for the past three years from the *Economic Report of the President.* What proportion of the government's total revenue was the Fed's income?

29. Look for articles in *The Wall Street Journal* in which the President or the Treasury Department (or another arm of the administration) delivers strong policy suggestions to the Fed, and then watch for the Fed's response.

CHAPTER 20

Monetary Policy Tools

In 1998, the Federal Reserve made headlines again and again. Fearing for the health of the U.S. economic expansion in the wake of the Asian financial crisis, the Fed used its policy tools to reduce short-term interest rates three times that fall. The Fed reacts to the economic environment in setting monetary policy, and changes in monetary policy (implemented with open market operations, discount lending, or setting reserve requirements) affect interest rates, output, and inflation.

In this chapter, we describe the implementation of the Fed's monetary policy tools and see how they can be used to affect short-term interest rates. This chapter extends our study of monetary policy tools from Chapters 17 and 18, in which we described how those tools could change the monetary base and the money supply. As you might expect, the Fed's actions and uses of its policy tools are not without their critics. We also include some of the controversy about the Fed's use of monetary policy tools and alternatives that economists have proposed to improve monetary decisions.

Another theme of this chapter is *Fed watching:* Many individuals and organizations scrutinize the actions of the Fed to forecast changes in interest rates and to predict economic changes. Leading banks and Wall Street firms rely on in-house analysis of the Fed's intentions and actions in guiding lending and investment decisions. Individuals watch the Fed's moves to guide decisions about buying a home or making investments. As you will see, understanding how the Fed uses its policy tools is an important component of Fed watching.

OPEN MARKET OPERATIONS

Open market operations, the purchases and sales of securities in financial markets by the Fed, are the dominant means by which the Fed changes the monetary base. Recall from Chapter 17 that an open market purchase increases the monetary base (generally by increasing bank reserves) and that an open market sale decreases the monetary base. If the money multiplier is relatively stable, the Fed can use open market operations to regulate the money supply by changing the monetary base.

The original Federal Reserve Act didn't specifically mention open market operations, because they weren't well understood in financial markets at that time. The Fed began to use open market purchases as a policy tool during the 1920s when it acquired World War I Liberty Bonds from banks, enabling banks to finance more business loans. Before 1935, district Federal Reserve banks conducted limited open market operations in securities markets, but these transactions lacked central coordination to achieve a monetary policy goal. The lack of concerted intervention by the Fed during the banking crisis of the early 1930s led Congress to establish the Federal Open Market Committee (FOMC) to guide open market operations.

The Fed generally conducts open market operations in liquid Treasury securities markets, affecting interest rates in those markets. An open market purchase of Treasury securities increases their price, all else being equal, thereby decreasing their yield and expanding the money supply. An open market sale decreases the price of Treasury securities, thereby increasing their yield and contracting the money supply. Open market purchases tend to reduce interest rates and so are viewed as *expansionary;* open market sales tend to increase interest rates and so are viewed as *contractionary.*

The Fed's actions influence interest rates on other securities. Although the differences in yields on different assets depend on their risk, liquidity, and information costs, the change in the interest rate on Treasury securities has an immediate impact on their yield and return. When the news media say that the Fed sets interest rates, they are implicitly summarizing this process.

We now turn to actions that the FOMC takes to carry out open market transactions.

Implementing Open Market Operations

How does the FOMC guide open market operations? It meets eight times per year (roughly every six weeks) and issues a **general directive** stating its overall objectives for monetary aggregates and interest rates. The directive also describes instructions for open market operations. These directives are less precise than reserve requirement and discount rate policies. Lacking perfect foresight, the FOMC can't determine in advance the exact actions that are needed to achieve its objectives for changes in interest rates and monetary aggregates.

The Federal Reserve System's account manager (a vice president of the Federal Reserve Bank of New York) is responsible for carrying out open market operations that fulfill the FOMC's objectives. The **Open Market Trading Desk,** a group of traders at the Federal Reserve Bank of New York, trades government securities over the counter electronically with primary dealers. Primary dealers are private securities firms selected by the Fed that trade government securities and are permitted to trade directly with the Fed. Before making transactions, the trading desk notifies all the dealers at the same time, asks them to submit offers, and gives them a deadline. The Fed's account manager goes over the list, accepts the best offers, and then has the trading desk buy or sell the securities until the volume of reserves reaches the Fed's desired goal. These securities are either added to or subtracted from the portfolios of the various Federal Reserve banks according to their shares of total assets in the system.

How does the account manager know what to do? The manager interprets the FOMC's most recent directive, holds daily conferences with two members of the FOMC, and personally analyzes financial market conditions. Then the manager compares the level of reserves in the banking system with the desired level recommended by the directive. If the level that the directive suggests is greater than actual bank reserves, the account manager purchases securities to raise the level of bank reserves toward the desired level. If the level that the directive suggests is less than actual reserves, the account manager sells securities to lower reserves toward the desired level.

One way the account manager conducts open market operations is through **outright purchases and sales** of Treasury securities of various maturities by the trading desk—that is, by buying from or selling to dealers. More commonly, the manager uses **Federal Reserve repurchase agreements** (analogous to commercial bank repos, discussed in Chapter 13). Through these agreements, the Fed buys securities from a dealer in the government securities market, and the dealer agrees to buy them back at a given price at a specified future date, usually within one week. In effect, the government securities serve as collateral for a short-term loan. For open market sales, the trading desk often engages in **matched sale-purchase transactions** (sometimes called *reverse repos*), in which the Fed sells securities to dealers in the government securities market and the dealers agree to sell them back to the Fed in the near future.

In conducting the Fed's open market operations, the trading desk makes both dynamic and defensive transactions. Open market operations that are intended to change monetary policy as desired by the FOMC are known as **dynamic transactions.** A much greater volume of open market transactions are **defensive transactions,** which the Fed's traders use to offset fluctuations in the monetary base arising from portfolio allocation preferences of banks and the nonbank public, financial markets, and the economy. In other words, the Fed uses defensive transactions to offset the effects of disturbances to the monetary base, not to change monetary policy.

Defensive open market operations may be used to compensate for either predictable or unexpected events that change the monetary base. For example, the nonbank public predictably increases its demand for currency before Christmas and other holidays and in response to seasonal preferences for travel. The Fed can also predict certain types of borrowing: Borrowing within the banking system occurs periodically to satisfy reserve requirements; and the U.S. Treasury, foreign governments, and large corporations often sell or buy blocks of securities at announced intervals. Other, less predictable, disturbances come from the Treasury or the Fed. Although the Treasury attempts to synchronize withdrawals from its bank accounts with its bill paying (to avoid large shifts in the currency or reserves), it doesn't always succeed. Disruptions in the Fed's own balance sheet caused by Federal Reserve float or changes in discount loans, the amount of Treasury coins outstanding, or the Treasury's holdings of Federal Reserve Notes also produce short-term fluctuations in the monetary base. Fluctuations in Treasury deposits with the Fed and in Federal Reserve float are the most important of the unexpected disturbances to the monetary base.

There are other reasons for defensive transactions besides those needed to correct fluctuations in the monetary base. Even if the monetary base remains constant, movements of currency between the nonbank public and bank reserves affect the volume of bank deposits. Multiple deposit expansion or contraction then causes fluctuations in monetary base. Economic disturbances, such as major strikes or natural disasters, also cause unexpected fluctuations in the demand for currency and bank reserves. The Fed's account manager must respond to unintended increases or decreases in the monetary base and sell or buy securities to maintain the monetary policy indicated by the FOMC's guidelines.

CONSIDER THIS . . .

A Day's Work at the Open Market Trading Desk

9:00 A.M.

The account manager begins informal discussions with market participants to assess conditions in the government securities market. From these discussions and from data supplied by the staff of the FOMC, the account manager estimates how the prices of government securities will change during the trading day.

10:00 A.M.

The account manager's staff compares forecasts on Treasury deposits and information on the timing of future Treasury sales of securities with the staff of the Office of Government Finance in the Treasury Department.

10:15 A.M.

The account manager reads staff reports on forecasted shifts in the monetary base arising from temporary portfolio shifts, fluctuations in financial markets or the economy, or weather-related disturbances (for example, events that might extend the time for checks to clear).

11:15 A.M.

After reviewing the information from the various staffs, the account manager studies the FOMC's directive. This directive identifies the ranges for growth rates of the monetary aggregates and the level of the federal funds rate desired. The account manager must design *dynamic* open market operations to implement changes requested by the FOMC and *defensive* open market operations to offset temporary disturbances in the monetary base predicted by the staff. The account manager places the daily conference call to at least two members of the FOMC to discuss trading strategy.

11:30 A.M.

On approval of the trading strategy, the traders at the Federal Reserve Bank of New York notify the primary dealers in the government securities market of the Fed's desired transactions. If traders plan to make open market purchases, they request quotations for asked prices. If traders plan to make open market sales, they request quotations for bid prices. (Recall that government securities are traded over the counter.) The traders select the lowest prices offered when making purchases and accept the highest bids when making sales.

12:30 P.M.

Soliciting quotes and trading take about 45 minutes, so by about 12:30 P.M., the trading room at the Federal Reserve Bank of New York is less hectic. No three-martini lunch for the account manager and staff, though; they spend the afternoon monitoring conditions in the federal funds market and the level of bank reserves to get ready for the next day of trading.

Open Market Operations versus Other Policy Tools

Open market operations have several benefits that other policy tools lack: control, flexibility, and ease of implementation.

Control. Because the Fed initiates open market purchases and sales, it completely controls their volume. Discount loans also increase or decrease the monetary base, but discount loans enable the Fed to influence the direction of the change in the monetary base rather than to control the volume of reserves added to or taken from the monetary base.

Flexibility. The Fed can make both large and small open market operations. Often, dynamic transactions require large purchases or sales, whereas defensive transactions call for small securities purchases or sales. Other policy tools lack this flexibility. Reversing open market operations is simple for the Fed. For example, if it decides that its open market sales have made the money supply grow too slowly, it can quickly authorize open market purchases. Discount loans and reserve requirement changes are more difficult to reverse quickly.

Ease of implementation. The Fed can implement its securities transactions rapidly, with no administrative delays. All that is required is for the trading desk to place buy and sell orders with dealers in the government securities markets. Changing the discount rate or reserve requirements requires lengthier deliberation.

Fed Watching and FOMC Directives

Merely observing the Fed's trading activity doesn't necessarily provide reliable information regarding the Fed's *intentions* for monetary policy. For example, the Fed could acquire securities one day and dispose of securities the next day while pursuing the same overall monetary policy. To discern the Fed's intentions, Fed watchers read carefully the directives issued by the Fed.

Fed watchers disagree over the Fed's practice of issuing vaguely worded directives expressing its objectives for monetary aggregates. Indeed, the Fed has sometimes been criticized for not being more precise in stating its policy objectives. One explanation for the vagueness of these policy statements and FOMC directives is an example of the principal-agent problem: To avoid being accountable for errors, the Fed states monetary policy objectives in vague terms so that virtually any outcome can be termed a success. Advocates of this view point to both the delay in the Fed's release of minutes of FOMC meetings and the practice of reporting targets only for multiple monetary aggregates whose growth corresponds most closely to the Fed's target ranges.

Vagueness notwithstanding, Fed watchers can and do with some effort interpret the meaning of each word in the Fed's statements. They do this to try to discern the Fed's policy goals. As of February 1994, the Fed began announcing policy changes made by the FOMC at the time they are made; analysts still read directives carefully for clues about the likely future course of monetary

CONSIDER THIS . . .

How Do You Decode FOMC Statements?

Since February 2000, the essence of the FOMC's policy decisions has been expressed in its statement issued at the end of each meeting. Prior to this time, substantive statements were released only in the event of a policy action or to clarify the FOMC's view about prospective developments in the economy. Under the earlier procedures, the Fed's statements and its domestic policy directive described a "policy bias" toward increasing or decreasing the federal funds rate. The new procedures are designed to make more transparent the Fed's communication with the public.

Under the new procedures, the statement will point out the FOMC's view of the "balance of risks," described in the context of the Fed's goals as follows:

> Against the background of its long-run goals of price stability and sustainable economic growth and of the information currently available, the Committee believes that the risks are [balanced with respect to prospects for both goals] [weighted mainly toward conditions that may generate heightened inflation pressures] [weighted mainly toward conditions that may generate economic weakness] in the foreseeable future.

The shift in FOMC policy in late 2000 and early 2001 can be seen in the statements released after the meetings on November 15, 2000, December 19, 2000, and January 3, 2001:

> November 15: "The Committee. . . continues to see a risk of heightened inflation pressures. . . . [T]he risks continue to be weighted mainly toward conditions that may generate heightened inflation pressures in the foreseeable future."

> December 19: "While some inflation risks persist, they are diminished by the more moderate pace of economic activity. . . . [T]he risks are weighted mainly toward conditions that may generate economic weakness in the foreseeable future."

> January 3: "Inflation pressures remain contained. . . . [T]he risks are weighted mainly toward conditions that may generate economic weakness in the foreseeable future."

Over that two-month period, the Fed sent strong signals that the balance of risks favored a shift toward an easing of monetary policy with cuts in the federal funds rate at the January 3 meeting and again at the January 31 meeting.

policy. In February 2000, the Fed began to discuss the future "balance of risks" in its FOMC statement, giving its opinion about the relative risk toward economic weakness or higher inflation.

Open Market Operations in Other Countries

Although the Fed relies most heavily on open market operations to change the money supply, central banks in some other countries favor different policy tools. Often, the choice of policy tools depends on the organization of a country's financial markets and institutions. The Fed uses open market operations because the markets for U.S. government securities are highly liquid.

In contrast, historically, the Bank of Japan did not rely on open market operations because a market for government securities didn't exist until the mid-1980s. Japan issued its first six-month treasury bills in 1986 and its first three-month treasury bills in 1989. Until then, the Japanese central bank had used interest rate controls and direct discount lending to banks to influence the money supply in the *Gensaki* market. The Bank of Japan conducts transactions for repurchase agreements in that market; the market is open to financial institutions and nonfinancial corporations and has been free of interest rate regulations since its inception in 1949. Nevertheless, the government treasury bill market in Japan is smaller than that in the United States. Economists studying the Japanese financial system predict that the market for short-term government securities will continue to grow in the new century, providing a better environment for open market operations by the Bank of Japan.

While the European Central Bank commenced operation only in January 1999, analysts expect it to continue to conduct open market operations principally through fixed-term, fixed-frequency securities repurchase operations, the regular money market tenders through which European central banks have injected liquidity into the financial system. Outright transactions and foreign-exchange repurchase agreements are also likely to be used.

DISCOUNT POLICY

Discount policy, which includes setting the discount rate and terms of discount lending, is the oldest of the Federal Reserve's principal tools for regulating the money supply. Discount policy affects the money supply by influencing the volume of discount loans, which are part of the monetary base. An increase in the volume of discount loans raises the monetary base and the money supply, whereas a decrease in the volume of discount loans reduces the monetary base and the money supply. The discount rate at which the Fed lends funds to depository institutions and its general attitude toward discount lending depend on the effects it wants to have on the money supply. The **discount window** is the means by which the Fed makes discount loans to banks, serving as a channel to meet the liquidity needs of banks.

Before 1980 (except for a brief period during 1966), the Fed made discount loans only to banks that were members of the Federal Reserve System. Indeed, banks perceived the ability to borrow from the Fed through the discount window as an advantage of membership that partially offset the cost of maintaining reserve requirements. Since 1980, all depository institutions have had access to the discount window. Each Federal Reserve bank maintains its own discount window.

Using the Discount Window

The Fed influences the volume of discount loans in two ways: It sets the price of loans (the discount rate) and the terms of its loans.

We can describe the *price effect* on discount loans of a change in the discount rate as follows. Suppose that the Fed increases the discount rate. Banks react to the higher discount rate by reducing their borrowing at the discount window. Hence an increase in the discount rate decreases the volume of discount loans, reducing the monetary base and the money supply. The higher discount rate also exerts upward pressure on other short-term interest rates. As a result, banks find it more expensive to raise funds from other sources, such as by borrowing in the federal funds market or by issuing certificates of deposit. A decrease in the discount rate has the opposite effect: The volume of discount loans rises, increasing the monetary base and the money supply. However, the Fed cannot be sure that banks will borrow from the discount window when the discount rate declines. If profitable lending and investment opportunities aren't available, banks might not increase their discount borrowing.

In addition to setting the discount rate, the Fed sets the conditions for the availability of loans. The Fed uses the discount window to make one of three types of loans: adjustment credit, seasonal credit, and extended credit. Temporary, short-term **adjustment credit** loans to depository institutions help them to avoid more costly means of liquidity management. Temporary, short-term **seasonal credit** loans satisfy seasonal liquidity requirements of smaller depository institutions in geographical areas where agriculture or tourism is important. These loans reduce banks' costs of maintaining excess cash or seasonally liquidating loans and investments. The Fed makes longer-term **extended credit** loans to a financial institution under exceptional circumstances to alleviate severe liquidity problems and restore the bank to financial health. An example is the more than $5 billion in discount loans that was extended to Continental Illinois Bank in 1984 before its takeover by the FDIC.

Policing the Discount Window

Although the Fed allows banks to borrow from the discount window, it discourages banks from heavy use of discount loans. Figure 20.1 shows that the discount rate in the United States generally falls below short-term market interest rates, such as the federal funds rate. As a result, the discount window is a tempting source of funds for banks that have profitable loan opportunities. Recall that if banks could obtain discount loans freely through the discount window, they could earn a profit from the spread between the discount rate and market interest rates. Because the Fed would be subsidizing banks' returns on lending, banks would have an incentive to borrow more, thus increasing the monetary base. So as not to stimulate too much discount borrowing, the Fed uses public criticism, fines, and financial audits. Making discount borrowing public decreases requests for discount loans because banks fear that their investors and depositors will perceive their borrowing as a sign of poor financial health. What constitutes "too much borrowing"? The answer isn't always precise, though sometimes the Fed's behavior suggests a rule of thumb. (For example, the Fed may censure a bank that borrows in more than half the weeks during a certain period.)

Over the years, many economists have suggested that the discount rate be set higher than short-term market rates, effectively making it a penalty rate. Borrowing would not offer profit opportunities, so banks would borrow only if they truly needed the liquidity. The Bank of England follows this strategy and

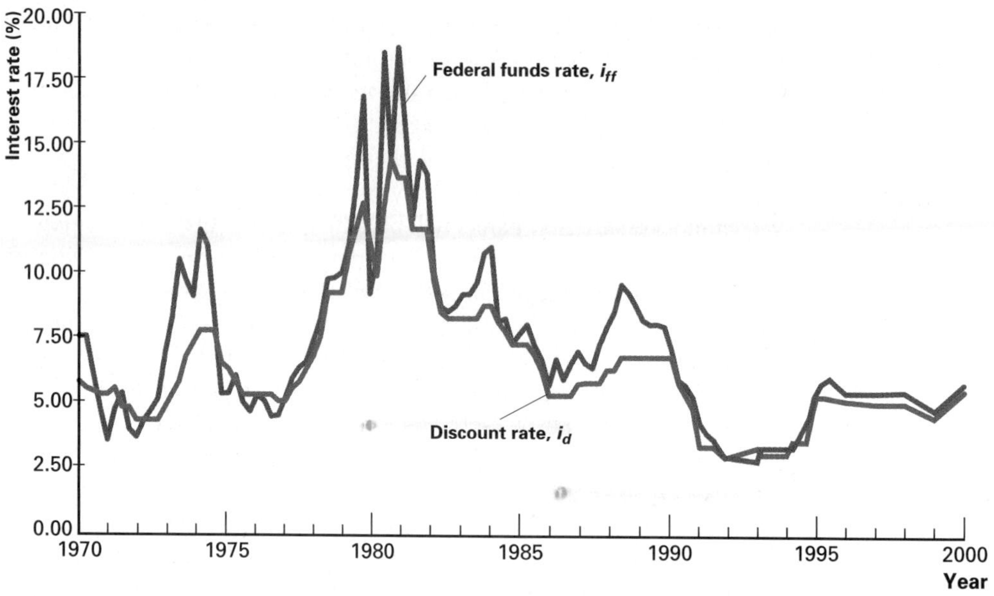

Figure 20.1

The Discount Rate and the Federal Funds Rate, 1970–2000

The discount rate set by the Fed generally is less than the market-determined federal funds rate. This gap gives banks an incentive to borrow from the Fed.

Source: Federal Reserve Bulletin.

sets its discount rate higher than the market interest rate on short-term government securities. Since the late 1970s, the Fed has sometimes adjusted its discount rate in response to changes in short-term market rates. When market interest rates fall, the Fed decreases the discount rate to aid bank borrowing to meet liquidity needs; when market interest rates rise, the Fed increases the discount rate to limit profit opportunities from discount borrowing. Discount borrowing increases when market interest rates rise relative to the discount rate. Nonetheless, because the volume of discount loans is small even when the federal funds rate significantly exceeds the discount rate, most economists conclude that the Fed generally polices the discount window successfully.

Benefits of Discount Policy

Discount policy offers the Fed certain advantages that the other policy tools do not have. We describe two of these below: (1) contributing to the Fed's role as lender of last resort and (2) signaling the Fed's policy intentions. We then discuss drawbacks of discount policy as a monetary policy tool.

Averting financial crises: lender of last resort. The discount window provides the most direct way for the Fed to act as a lender of last resort to the banking system. Open market operations can change the level of bank reserves and affect short-term interest rates (such as the federal funds rate), but they can't address well the illiquidity problems of individual banks. Hence the Fed relies more on discount lending in its role as lender of last resort. The Fed's successes in handling the Penn Central crisis in the commercial paper market in 1970 and the stock market crash of 1987 suggest that decisive discount policy can reduce the costs of financial disturbances to the economy.

The Fed extends discount loans at its discretion, and economists continue to debate the merits of this practice. Some analysts believe that an overly generous discount policy during financial crises encourages too much risk taking by banks and the nonfinancial corporations that borrow from them. The reason is that banks, knowing that the Fed provides discount loans at favorable terms during business downturns, enforce credit standards less strictly, as happened during the 1980s.

Other analysts praise the Fed's discount window interventions, such as those that took place during the Penn Central crisis of 1970, the Franklin National Bank crisis of 1974, the Hunt brothers' silver manipulation efforts in 1980, the Continental Illinois Bank collapse in 1984, and the stock market crash of October 1987. They conclude that these cases demonstrate the need for the Fed to continue its use of the discount window to extend credit, case by case, as a lender of last resort during financial crises.

Signaling Fed policy: the announcement effect. Because the Fed changes the discount rate infrequently relative to the continuous movement in market interest rates, Fed watchers pay close attention to announcements of such changes, which may indicate major policy changes. Changes in the volume of discount loans themselves do not significantly affect the money supply, so Fed watchers look to discount rate changes for signals of the Fed's intentions. For example, if market interest rates rise and the Fed doesn't then increase the discount rate, analysts might interpret the Fed's inaction either as a belief that the increase will be temporary or as an indication that it will make open market purchases to decrease short-term rates. Similarly, an increase in market rates followed by an increase in the discount rate might be interpreted as a commitment by the Fed to higher interest rates and more restrictive credit conditions. Fed watchers' guesses when market interest rates fall and the Fed does or doesn't decrease the discount rate also are easy to imagine. Fed watchers must look for *clues* of the Fed's intentions because the Fed makes its policy decisions known only after a six-week delay.

This interpretation of Fed intentions, called the **announcement effect,** illustrates how new information influences security prices and returns. According to the efficient markets hypothesis (Chapter 10), all available information is incorporated into market prices. In an efficient market, the announcement of a change in the discount rate contains new information about future Fed policy and causes short-term market interest rates to change.

In late December 1991, for example, the Fed cut the discount rate by a full percentage point to 3.5% (and additional smaller cuts followed in 1992). Because the Fed had been reducing the discount rate gradually since the economy entered a recession in 1990, the big change signaled that the Fed was interested in expansion. The signals materialized in other interest rates. Within 90 minutes of the Fed's announcement, Morgan Guaranty Trust Company in New York cut its prime lending rate by a full percentage point, and many other major banks followed Morgan's lead. At the same time, long-term interest rates fell to levels that had not been experienced for four years.

Drawbacks of Discount Policy as a Monetary Policy Tool

Few economists advocate the use of discount policy as a tool of *monetary control.* Fluctuations in the spread between the federal funds rate and the discount rate set by the Fed can cause unintended increases or decreases in the monetary base and the money supply. Moreover, the Fed doesn't control discount policy as completely as it controls open market operations, and changing discount policy is much more difficult than changing open market operations (because banks must decide whether to accept discount loans). Hence the Fed doesn't use discount policy as its principal tool for influencing the money supply.

Discount Policy in Other Countries

Outside the United States, central banks generally use discount lending as a monetary policy tool and as a means of mitigating financial crises. In Japan, for example, the Bank of Japan quotes the *official discount rate* as the cost of its loans to private financial institutions that have accounts at the bank. Changes in the official discount rate are interpreted by financial market participants as reflecting changes in the Bank's basic stance on monetary policy. The European Central Bank uses standing discount facilities to provide and absorb overnight liquidity and signal the stance of monetary policy. As is the case in the United States (where discount loans are made by regional Federal Reserve Banks), the standing facilities are administered in a decentralized manner by national central banks.

CHECKPOINT

When reading *The Wall Street Journal,* you notice that short-term market interest rates (such as the federal funds rate or the yields on three-month Treasury bills) have been declining but that the Fed hasn't reduced its discount rate. Are the Fed's intentions for monetary policy expansionary or contractionary? The Fed may be trying to signal to financial markets that it wants short-term rates to rise. In that case, the Fed would be signaling a contractionary policy. **o**

RESERVE REQUIREMENTS

The Fed mandates that banks hold a certain fraction of their deposits in cash or deposits with the Fed. These **reserve requirements** are the last of the Fed's three principal monetary tools that we examine. In Chapter 17, we showed that the required reserve ratio is a determinant of the money multiplier in the money supply process. Recall that an increase in the required reserve ratio reduces the money multiplier and the money supply, whereas a reduction in the required reserve ratio increases the money multiplier and the money supply. Reserves can be stored as vault cash in banks or as deposits with the Federal Reserve. About 90% of banks meet their reserve requirements with vault cash. The other 10% comprise larger banks whose deposits at Federal Reserve banks account for most of those deposits.

The Board of Governors sets reserve requirements within congressional limits, an authority that was granted by Congress in the Banking Act of 1935. Historically, reserve requirements varied geographically, with member banks in large cities being required to hold more reserves relative to deposits than were banks in smaller cities and towns. This difference dates back to 1864, following the passage of the National Banking Act of 1863, and is another instance of the political compromises between rural and urban interests. Representatives of agricultural states feared abuse by large Eastern banks. To garner these representatives' support for the National Banking Act (1863) and later the Federal Reserve Act (1913), Congress authorized low reserve requirements for rural banks. Between 1966 and 1972, the Fed altered reserve requirements to reflect the size as well as location of depository institutions. In 1980, the Depository Institutions Deregulation and Monetary Control Act established uniform reserve requirements for all depository institutions, regardless of location.

Changes in Reserve Requirements

The Fed changes reserve requirements much more rarely than it conducts open market operations or changes the discount rate. Therefore Fed watchers view the announcement of a change in reserve requirements as a major shift in monetary policy. Because changes in reserve requirements require significant alterations in banks' portfolios, frequent changes would be disruptive. As a result, in the 30 years between 1950 and 1980, the Fed adjusted required reserve ratios gradually (about once a year) and followed changes by open market operations or discount lending to help banks adjust.

During the 1980s, the only changes in reserve requirements were shifts that were mandated by the Depository Institutions Deregulation and Monetary Control Act. Examples were a reduction (from November 1980 through October 1983) in the maturity of nonpersonal time deposits subject to a 3% reserve requirement (from four years to 18 months) and the automatic adjustment of the level of checkable deposits subject to the 3% requirement. In 1990, the Fed lowered reserve requirements on certain other time deposits to zero. In 1992, it reduced the reserve requirement on checkable deposits to 3% on the first \$46.8 million and 10% on those in excess of \$46.8 million. In 2001, the reserve requirement on checkable deposits was 3% on the first \$42.8 million and 10% on those in excess of \$42.8 million. Eurocurrency liabilities and nonpersonal time deposits currently have no reserve requirement. Over the past several years, lower reserve requirements and the introduction of sweep accounts at banks (which move customer deposits each day from liabilities against which reserves are required to liabilities with no reserve requirement) have reduced required reserve balances.

Measurement and Compliance

Every two weeks, the Fed monitors compliance with its reserve requirements by checking a bank's daily deposits. These two-week *maintenance periods* begin on a Thursday and end on a Wednesday. For each period, the Fed measures the bank's daily deposits with Federal Reserve banks. It calculates the average daily balances in the bank's transactions accounts over a two-week period ending the previous Monday. The Fed also checks the bank's vault cash over a two-week period ending the Monday three days before the maintenance period begins. These built-in accounting lags give the Fed time to analyze the reserve–deposit ratio and give the bank time to adjust its portfolio.

If a bank can't meet its reserve requirements, it can carry up to 4% or $50,000, whichever is greater, of its required reserves to the next two-week maintenance period. If this carryover proves inadequate and the bank still is deficient, the Fed charges interest on the deficit at a rate 2% above the discount rate. This higher rate gives banks an incentive to satisfy reserve requirements. (Similarly, a bank can carry forward up to 4% surplus of required reserves in anticipation of future deficits.) A bank that has inadequate reserves also may borrow funds in the federal funds market or from the Fed through the discount window. The federal funds market can be very active on Wednesdays, when maintenance periods end, as banks try to meet their reserve requirements.

Criticism of Reserve Requirements

Economists and policymakers continue to debate what the Fed's role in setting reserve requirements should be. In the following discussion, we present arguments for and against reserve requirements as a monetary policy tool.

Reserve requirements are costly as a monetary policy tool. Reserves earn no interest, so the use of reserve requirements to control the money supply process effectively places a tax on bank intermediation. In other words, by not being able to lend reserves, banks face a higher cost on funds that they obtain from depositors. For example, suppose that banks pay depositors 5% on deposits and that the required reserve ratio is 10%. On a deposit of $100, the bank must keep $10 in reserves and may loan the remaining $90. It must pay depositors $5 in interest, so its cost of funds to lend $90 is ($5/$90)(100) = 5.6%, rather than 5%.

Large increases in reserve requirements can adversely affect the economy. Increasing the tax on bank intermediation reduces bank lending, which decreases credit availability and the money supply.

Because reserve requirements are a tax on bank deposits and because unwise changes in reserve requirements may have bad economic consequences, economists and policymakers often debate whether the Fed *should* set reserve requirements. Over the years, they have offered two arguments in support of reserve requirements: the liquidity argument and the monetary control argument. To analyze whether the Fed should set reserve requirements, we need to find out how well each argument stands up to close scrutiny.

Liquidity argument. When banks convert liquid deposits to illiquid loans, they incur liquidity risk. As a result, some analysts argue that reserve requirements create a liquid pool of funds to assist illiquid, but solvent, banks during a banking panic. One problem with this view is that, although reserve requirements do produce a pool of liquid funds for the banking system as a whole, they have a limited effect on the liquidity of an individual bank. The decision to hold liquid assets is a portfolio allocation decision that is made by a bank. Reserve requirements limit the funds that a bank has available to invest in loans or securities, but they don't eliminate the need to maintain some portion of these funds in liquid assets. Individual banks still need to hold some of their portfolios in marketable securities as a cushion against unexpected deposit outflows.

Another problem with the liquidity argument is that the likelihood of a liquidity crisis depends not only on the volatility of withdrawals from banks, but also on the volatility of the value of bank assets and the availability to banks of funds from nondeposit sources. However, improvements in markets for loan sales and the growing number of nondeposit sources of funds make liquidity crises less likely, regardless of the volatility of depositors' withdrawals. Moreover, the Fed's ability to intervene directly in a liquidity crisis by making discount loans lessens the danger of such a crisis.

Monetary control argument. A second argument for reserve requirements is that they increase the central bank's control over the money supply process. Recall that the percentage of deposits that are held as reserves is one determinant of the money multiplier and hence of the responsiveness of the money supply to a change in the monetary base. Fed control of the reserve–deposit ratio through reserve requirements makes the money multiplier more stable and the money supply more controllable.

There are two problems with this argument. First, banks would hold reserves even if there were no reserve requirements. Hence reserve requirements need not greatly increase monetary control. Second, there is little evidence that reserve requirements actually improve the stability of the money multiplier.

Nobel laureate Milton Friedman proposed an extreme example of the monetary control argument: Banks should hold 100% reserves. Under such a system, bank reserves would equal deposits, and the monetary base (the sum of bank reserves and currency in the hands of the nonbank public) would equal the sum of currency and bank deposits, or the *M1* money supply. With 100% reserves, multiple deposit expansion would cease, giving the Fed complete control over currency plus deposits but not over the composition of deposits.

Would complete control of currency and bank deposits translate into control of the *effective* money supply? Probably not. Under a 100% reserve system, banks could not originate or hold loans. Alternative financial intermediaries

OTHER TIMES, OTHER PLACES . . .

An Early Mistake in Setting Reserve Requirements

During the banking crisis of the early 1930s, commercial banks cut back on lending and accumulated excess reserves of about $800 million by the end of 1933. Excess reserves were greater than 40% of required reserves, compared to less than 1% today. By the end of 1935, the level of excess reserves reached more than $3 billion, or about 115% of required reserves. The newly created Federal Open Market Committee worried that significant levels of excess reserves would eliminate its ability to dominate the money supply process. For example, an economic upturn could lead banks to reduce their excess reserves, thereby expanding the money supply.

The Fed needed to find a way to reduce the level of reserves. Large-scale open market sales of securities weren't possible; at about $2.5 billion, the Fed's portfolio of government securities wasn't large enough to eliminate banks' excess reserves. As a result, after it obtained control over the setting of reserve requirements in 1935, the Fed's first significant change was a series of increases in required reserve ratios between August 1936 and May 1937. These effectively doubled the level of required reserves relative to deposits.

This strategy was unsuccessful because bank holdings of excess reserves reflected deliberate portfolio allocation decisions. Hence when the Fed increased reserve requirements, banks maintained their high excess reserves by cutting back on loans. This decline in bank lending made credit unavailable for many borrowers. Many economists blame the large reduction in the growth of the money supply and in the supply of bank credit as important causes of the business recession in 1937 and 1938. As bank lending declined, the Fed was pressured to reduce reserve requirements, which it did.

would emerge to fill this lending vacuum. Because banks have special information advantages in certain types of lending, this shift in financial intermediation could be costly for the economy. Therefore high reserve requirements are not likely to improve monetary control or promote financial intermediaries' role in matching savers and borrowers.

Coping with reserve requirements. One incentive to form bank holding companies (BHCs) was the exemption of such companies' debt from reserve requirements. The Fed responded in 1970 to the growth in this alternative source of funds by imposing a 5% reserve requirement on commercial paper issued by BHCs. In October 1979, in an attempt to increase its control over the money supply, the Fed announced reserve requirements of 8% for several nondeposit sources of bank funds, including repurchase agreements, federal funds borrowing, and asset sales to foreign banks. Since passage of the Depository Institutions Deregulation and Monetary Control Act of 1980, the Fed has applied reserve requirements only to checkable deposits, Eurocurrency accounts, and nonpersonal time deposits with a maturity of less than 18 months. (And since 1992, reserve requirements apply only to checkable deposits.) Hence banks (particularly large banks) can effectively avoid the tax on intermediation as they acquire funds.

Reserve Requirements in Other Countries

Although the reserve requirements imposed by the Bank of Japan do not allow for the payment of interest (consistent with U.S. practice), not all countries follow this practice. In late 1998, for example, the European Central Bank (ECB) inaugurated a system of interest-bearing minimum reserves as a monetary policy tool for the 11 members of European economic and monetary union. The ECB's required reserve ratio varies between 1.5% and 2.5%, and reserve balances are credited with interest at the prevailing repo rate, the ECB's key short-term interest rate.

Around the world there has been a general trend toward lower reserve requirements. Such requirements were eliminated entirely in the 1990s in Canada, Australia, New Zealand, and Switzerland, for example. One reason for this trend is the acknowledgment of central banks that reserve requirements effectively tax banking and financial intermediation. Such a tax raises the cost of funds and can make banks less competitive in the global financial marketplace. When the Fed announced lower reserve requirements in the United States in 1992, it specifically cited the "tax cut" argument to justify its action.

CHECKPOINT

Suppose the Fed reduces the reserve requirement on checkable deposits. How does your bank benefit? Do you and other depositors benefit? In the short run, your bank's profits increase; it can invest the freed funds and earn additional income from loans and investments (reserves pay no interest). In the long run, returns to depositors increase, as the bank becomes willing to pay more to attract deposits. o

FED WATCHING: ANALYZING THE POLICY TOOLS

All three of the Fed's principal monetary policy tools influence the monetary base primarily through changes in the demand for or supply of reserves. Hence to develop your skills as a Fed watcher, you need to study carefully the market for reserves, also known as the federal funds market. This section demonstrates how you can predict the outcome of changes in Fed policy on the level of bank reserves, R, and the federal funds rate, i_{ff}. The change in the federal funds rate will be mirrored by other short-term interest rates. Thus being able to predict how the fed funds rate will change will help you to make more informed investment decisions.

The Federal Funds Market

To analyze the determinants of the federal funds rate, we need to examine the banking system's demand for and the Fed's supply of reserves. We use a graphical analysis of the demand for and supply of reserves to see how the Fed uses its policy tools to influence the federal funds rate and the money supply.

Demand. Reserve demand reflects banks' demand for required and excess reserves. The demand function for federal funds, *D*, shown in Fig. 20.2, includes both required reserves, *RR*, and excess reserves, *ER*, for constant reserve requirements and market interest rates other than the federal funds rate. As the federal funds rate, i_{ff}, increases, banks prefer to hold a lower level of reserves; a higher federal funds rate increases the "reserve tax," so required reserves arc negatively related to market interest rates. Banks' demand for excess reserves is also sensitive to interest rate changes; at a lower federal funds rate, the opportunity cost of holding excess reserves falls and the quantity of excess reserves demanded rises. Hence the total quantity demanded of reserves is negatively related to the federal funds rate.

Supply. The supply function for reserves, *S*, also shown in Fig. 20.2, represents the supply by the Fed of borrowed reserves (discount loans) and nonborrowed reserves (supplied by open market operations). Note that the supply curve is not a straight line: The vertical portion represents nonborrowed reserves, *NBR*, supplied by the Fed; that is, regardless of the federal funds rate, reserves equal to *NBR* are available. The change in the slope of the supply curve occurs at the discount rate, i_d: As the federal funds rate falls below the discount rate, borrowing from the Fed is zero because banks can borrow more cheaply from other banks. Hence, in this case, reserves equal nonborrowed reserves. As the federal funds rate moves above the discount rate, borrowing increases. The slope of the supply curve represents the sensitivity of borrowing to movements of the federal funds rate above the discount rate. A relatively flat slope tells you that even a small increase in the federal funds rate relative to the discount rate leads to substantial discount borrowing. A steep slope tells you that discount borrowing is less sensitive to the difference between the federal funds rate and the discount rate.

Equilibrium. The equilibrium federal funds rate and level of reserves occur at the intersection of the demand and supply curves in Fig. 20.2. Equilibrium reserves equal R^*, the equilibrium federal funds rate equals i^*_{ff}, and the discount rate is i_d.

Open Market Operations

Suppose that the Fed decides to purchase $1 billion of Treasury securities. If nothing else changes, an open market purchase of securities by the Fed shifts the reserve supply curve to the right, from S_0 to S_1, as in Fig. 20.3(a), increasing bank reserves and decreasing the federal funds rate. As a result of the open market purchase, the volume of bank reserves increases from R^*_0 to R^*_1, and the federal funds rate declines from i^*_{ff0} to i^*_{ff1}. Similarly, an open market sale of securities by the Fed shifts the reserve supply curve to the left, from S_0 to S_1, in Fig. 20.3(b), decreasing the level of bank reserves from R^*_0 to R^*_1 and increasing the federal funds rate from i^*_{ff0} to i^*_{ff1}. An open market purchase of securities by the Fed decreases the federal funds rate. An open market sale of securities increases the federal funds rate.

Figure 20.2

Equilibrium in the Federal Funds Market

Equilibrium in the market for reserves is at the intersection of the demand (D) and supply (S) curves. Given nonborrowed reserves, NBR, and the discount rate, i_d, equilibrium reserves equal R^*, and the equilibrium federal funds rate is i^*_{ff}.

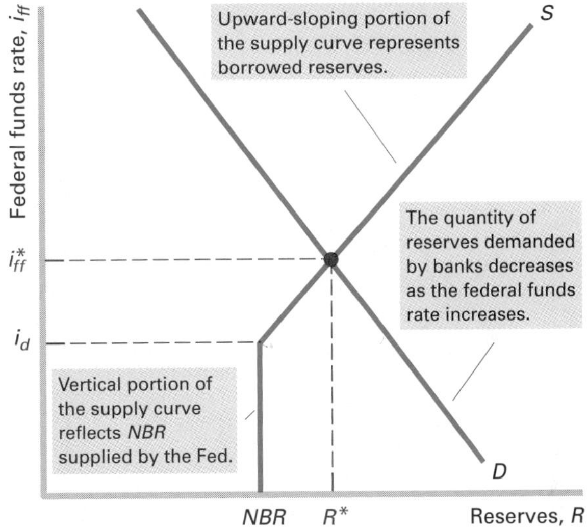

Changes in the Discount Rate

Now let's examine the effects of a change in the discount rate on the level of reserves and the federal funds rate. Suppose that the Fed decides to raise the discount rate. An increase in the discount rate means that banks will find borrowing to be less attractive at any federal funds rate. Figure 20.4(a) shows that an increase in the discount rate from i_{d0} to i_{d1} lengthens the vertical part of the supply curve to the new, higher discount rate, shifting the supply curve from S_0 to S_1. The slope of the supply curve doesn't change, as a higher discount rate doesn't increase banks' sensitivity to changes in the federal funds rate. Less borrowing occurs at each federal funds rate because the spread between the federal funds rate and the (now higher) discount rate is smaller than before. The equilibrium level of reserves falls from R^*_0 to R^*_1, and the federal funds rate rises from i^*_{ff0} to i^*_{ff1}.

Suppose that the Fed decides to cut the discount rate. In this case, banks now find borrowing more attractive at any federal funds rate. Figure 20.4(b) shows that a decrease in the discount rate from i_{d0} to i_{d1} shortens the vertical portion of the supply curve to the new, lower discount rate, shifting the supply curve from S_0 to S_1. More borrowing occurs at each federal funds rate because the spread between the federal funds rate and the (now lower) discount rate is greater than before. The equilibrium level of reserves rises from R^*_0 to R^*_1, and the federal funds rate falls from i^*_{ff0} to i^*_{ff1}.

If nothing else changes, an increase in the discount rate by the Fed leads to an increase in the federal funds rate and a fall in reserves. A decrease in the discount rate leads to a decrease in the federal funds rate and an increase in reserves.

Changes in Reserve Requirements

Finally, suppose that the Fed decides to raise the required reserve ratio. If the other factors underlying the demand and supply curves for reserves are held

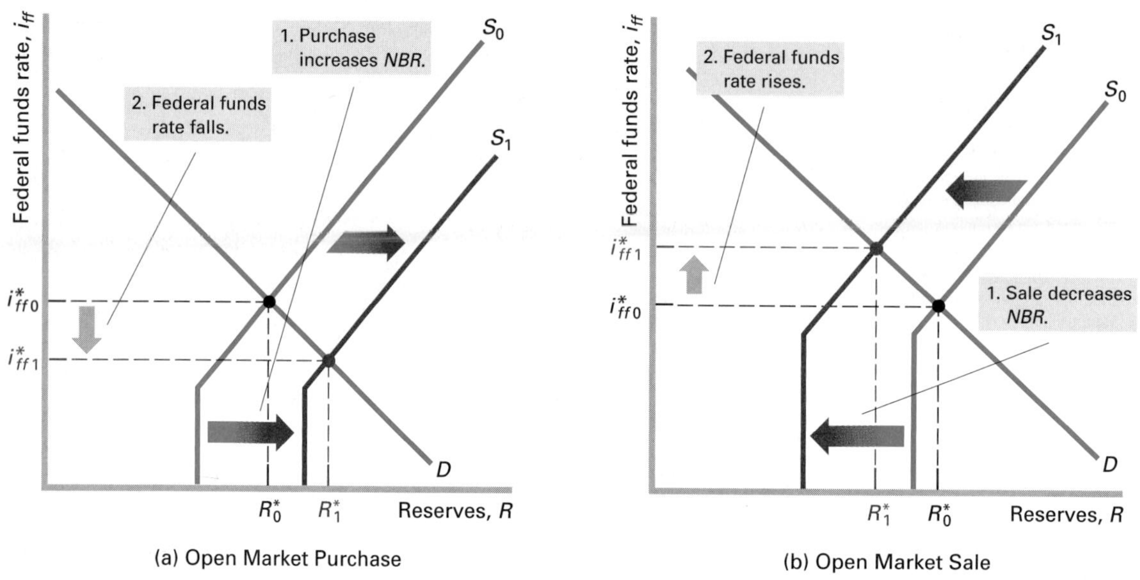

Figure 20.3 **Effects of Open Market Operations on the Federal Funds Market**

As shown in (a):

1. An open market purchase of securities by the Fed increases nonborrowed reserves, shifting the supply curve to the right from S_0 to S_1.
2. Reserves increase from R^*_0 to R^*_1, while the federal funds rate falls from i^*_{ff0} to i^*_{ff1}.

As shown in (b):

1. An open market sale of securities by the Fed reduces nonborrowed reserves, shifting the supply curve to the left from S_0 to S_1.
2. Reserves decrease from R^*_0 to R^*_1, while the federal funds rate rises from i^*_{ff0} to i^*_{ff1}.

constant, an increase in the required reserve ratio shifts the demand curve to the right (from D_0 to D_1) because banks have to hold more reserves, as in Fig. 20.5(a). As a result, the level of bank reserves increases (from R^*_0 to R^*_1) and the federal funds rate increases (from i^*_{ff0} to i^*_{ff1}). However, a reduction in the required reserve ratio, as shown in Fig. 20.5(b), shifts the demand curve to the left (from D_0 to D_1) because banks demand a smaller amount of reserves, decreasing bank reserves (from R^*_0 to R^*_1) and the federal funds rate (from i^*_{ff0} to i^*_{ff1}). If nothing else changes, an increase in reserve requirements increases the federal funds rate. A decrease in reserve requirements decreases the federal funds rate. Generally, however, the Fed does not use changes in reserve requirements to affect the federal funds rate; instead, the Fed uses changes in nonborrowed reserves to offset effects on the federal funds rate of a change in reserve requirements.

Other Disturbances of the Monetary Base

You can use graphs to analyze other disturbances of the monetary base that might lead the Fed to conduct defensive open market operations. For example, an increase in Federal Reserve float increases nonborrowed reserves

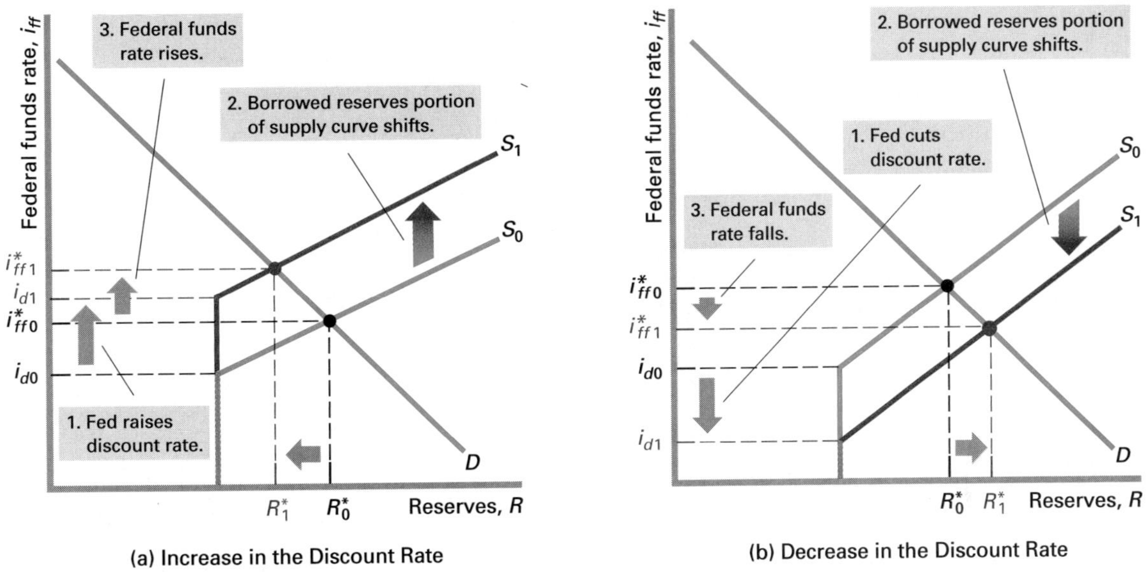

Figure 20.4 Effects of Changes in the Discount Rate on the Federal Funds Market

As shown in (a):

1. The Fed raises the discount rate from i_{d0} to i_{d1}.
2. The vertical portion of the supply curve lengthens; the new supply curve is S_1.
3. The level of reserves falls from R^*_0 to R^*_1, and the federal funds rate rises from i^*_{ff0} to i^*_{ff1}.

As shown in (b):

1. The Fed cuts the discount rate from i_{d0} to i_{d1}.
2. The vertical portion of the supply curve shortens; the new supply curve is S_1.
3. The level of reserves rises from R^*_0 to R^*_1, and the federal funds rate falls from i^*_{ff0} to i^*_{ff1}.

(Chapter 18). Hence the supply curve for reserves shifts to the right, leading to higher reserves and a lower federal funds rate than otherwise would occur. As we noted in discussing defensive transactions earlier in this chapter, the Fed can shift the supply curve for reserves back to the left (by reducing nonborrowed reserves) with an open market sale of securities.

As another example, a large increase in U.S. Treasury deposits with the Fed causes bank deposits to fall. As a result, reserves fall, the supply curve for reserves shifts to the left, and the federal funds rate rises. The Open Market Trading Desk, being in contact with the Treasury, knows about the Treasury action and therefore offsets it with another defensive open market purchase of securities. This action shifts the supply curve back to the right and restores the level of reserves and the federal funds rate to their initial levels.

The Federal Funds Rate and Monetary Policy

Many economists and financial market analysts use changes in the federal funds rate as a summary measure of the Fed's intentions for monetary policy. The reason is that the Fed's substantial control of the level of bank reserves gives it great influence over the level of the federal funds rate. An increase in

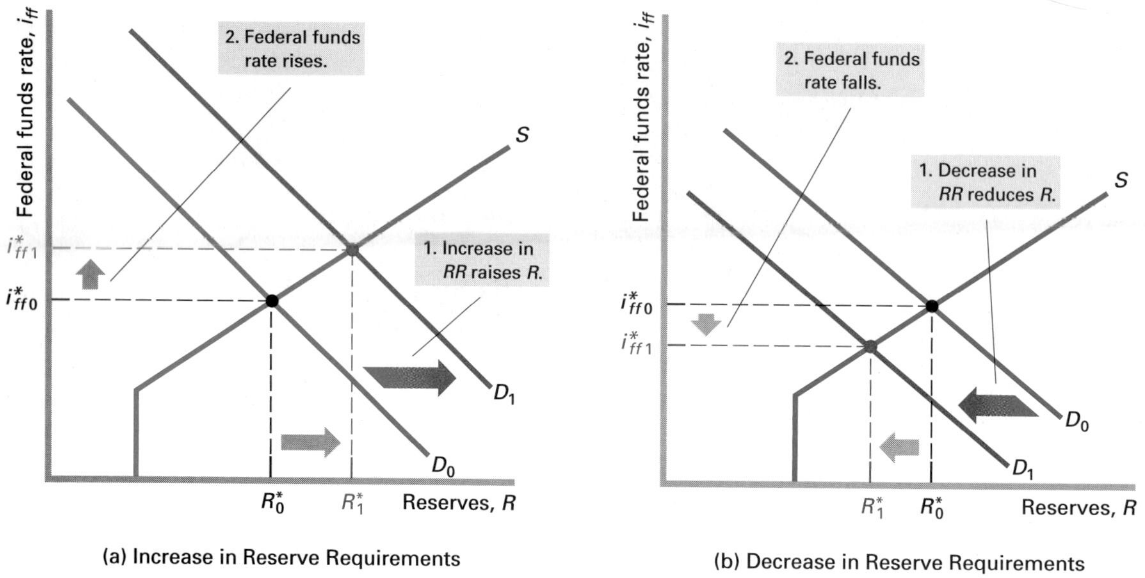

Figure 20.5 **Effects of Changes in Required Reserves on the Federal Funds Market**

As shown in (a):

1. An increase in reserve requirements by the Fed increases required reserves, shifting the demand curve from D_0 to D_1 and raising reserves from R^*_0 to R^*_1.
2. The federal funds rate rises from i^*_{ff0} to i^*_{ff1}.

As shown in (b):

1. A decrease in reserve requirements by the Fed decreases required reserves, shifting the demand curve from D_0 to D_1 and reducing reserves from R^*_0 to R^*_1.
2. The federal funds rate falls from i^*_{ff0} to i^*_{ff1}.

the federal funds rate relative to other interest rates is interpreted as contractionary, signaling the Fed's intention to raise interest rates and discourage spending in the economy. Conversely, a decrease in the federal funds rate relative to other interest rates is interpreted as expansionary, signaling the Fed's intention to reduce interest rates and encourage spending. The use of short-term interest rates to signal shifts in monetary policy is also common in countries in the European Monetary Union, the United Kingdom, and Japan.

Our graphical analysis confirms this view and shows how analysts can predict consequences of the Fed's actions for the level of reserves and the federal funds rate. Thus, if nothing else changes, an open market purchase of securities by the Fed reduces the federal funds rate. Purchases are expansionary because they increase the supply of reserves that banks use either to purchase securities or to make loans. As a result, the larger reserves in the banking system lead to lower short-term interest rates. Sales are contractionary because they reduce reserves and increase short-term interest rates. An increase in the discount rate is contractionary when it signals that the Fed wants to raise short-term interest rates. A reduction in the discount rate is expansionary when it signals that the Fed wants to reduce short-term interest rates. If nothing else changes, an increase in reserve requirements with no offsetting changes in the supply of reserves is contractionary and raises the federal funds rate. A decrease in reserve requirements is expansionary and lowers the federal funds rate.

Predicting the outcome of a change in the Fed funds rate. On January 3, 2001, the Federal Open Market Committee voted to lower its federal funds rate target from 6.5% to 6%. How does this action affect the federal funds rate? It is a market-determined interest rate, not literally set by the Fed. We can illustrate what happens using the reserves market diagram. As in Fig. 20.3(a), the Fed fulfills its intention to reduce the federal funds rate by increasing the supply of reserves. It conducts open market purchases to increase nonborrowed reserves. This action shifts the supply curve from S_0 to S_1, increasing reserves from R_0^* to R_1^* and lowering the federal funds rate from i_{ff0}^* to i_{ff1}^*.

Also on January 3, the Fed reduced the discount rate from 6% to 5.75%. Many policymakers and analysts praised the Fed's symbolic gesture as indicating its commitment to safeguard the economy's expansion. They reasoned that, as shown in Fig. 20.4(b), the fall in the discount rate from i_{d0} (6%) to i_{d1} (5.75%) would shift the reserves supply curve from S_0 to S_1. As a result, reserves would rise from R_0^* to R_1^*, and the federal funds rate would fall from i_{ff0}^* to i_{ff1}^*.

The falling cost of funds to lenders leads to lower interest rates charged to private borrowers, as indicated by the decrease in loan rates to household and business borrowers. This decrease in loan rates increases demand for business investment and consumer durables.

Concluding Remarks

Fed watchers try to predict the Fed's actions regarding open market operations, discount policy, and reserve requirements so as to forecast changes in the federal funds rate. (Recently, analysts have also begun to consider the role played by uncertainty in bank reserve balances in determining the federal funds rate; for example, on busier days, banks may desire to hold a larger cushion of reserves to protect against penalties for overnight overdrafts.) Predicting Fed changes is the first step toward predicting the effects of monetary policy on other interest rates. However, the Fed's significant control over the federal funds rate does not imply that it can control other interest rates. Recall, for example, that the expectations theory of the term structure of interest rates states that longer-term interest rates reflect, in part, expectations of *future* short-term rates. Therefore *expected future Fed actions,* not just current Fed policy, are important.

CHECKPOINT

Suppose that you read in *The Wall Street Journal* that the Fed raised its target for the federal funds rate by one-half of a percentage point. How would you expect the Fed to achieve its objective? Using the graphical analysis of the federal funds market, you would expect the Fed to use open market sales to reduce nonborrowed reserves, shifting the *NBR* curve to the left and raising the federal funds rate. o

THE WALL STREET JOURNAL FEBRUARY 1, 2001

Fed Rate Cut Combats a Contagion

a With yesterday's half-point interest rate cut, Federal Reserve Board Chairman Alan Greenspan is hoping to lift the nation's economic spirits before they pull the economy into recession.

Together with another half-point cut earlier this year, the Fed's actions mark the central bank's most aggressive easing move since 1982. But there's a key difference between now and 19 years ago. Back then, the central bank was struggling to revive an economy that had fallen into deep recession, with unemployment rates near the double digits. This time around, Mr. Greenspan is administering medicine to a patient who's still showing remarkable health, including a jobless rate that, at 4%, is near a 30-year low.

More than usual, the Fed chief appears to be engaged in a game of psychology, struggling less to revive a moribund economy than to restore a sense of confidence to the nation's consumers and businesses. He remains convinced that the New Economy is for real, and that it promises above-average economic growth . . . But recent surveys show that many consumers and businesses have lost that faith. . . .

b Many economists, including William Dudley, head of U.S. economic research at Goldman Sachs in New York, think Mr. Greenspan's rapid action now means a recession is less than a 50% probability. The January 3 surprise cut—which came between meetings of the FOMC, instead of at one of the committee's regularly scheduled gatherings—helped stocks and corporate bonds turn in a healthy January performance. That makes it easier for companies to issue securities to fund new investment, and it makes holders of the securities feel wealthier and more inclined to spend.

"You don't want [confidence] to break," says Mr. Dudley. "But the financial markets suggest we're not at that breaking point." Mr. Dudley argues that maintaining confidence is the key to keeping a temporary slowdown from snowballing into a more serious recession. Since World War II, the unemployment rate has never gone up more than 0.33 percentage point during any period of economic growth, except during one strike-affected period, he notes. But in a recession, it has never gone up less than 1.9 percentage points. Once unemployment starts rising, it can be hard to stop.

For all the talk of consumer confidence, business confidence may be just as critical at this juncture, and it is eroding even faster. When the key decision makers at the nation's largest corporations are feeling pessimistic, outlays by businesses for new equipment—once a major driver of growth—suffer. . . .

Yesterday, the Fed also cut the largely symbolic discount rate by half a point to 5%, for a total reduction of one percentage point since the start of the year. In its statement, the Fed said that "the risks are weighted mainly toward conditions that may generate economic weakness in the foreseeable future," which means rates are more likely to fall soon than to rise. Some analysts think the next cut could happen before the FOMC meets again March 20. . . . c

Analysts first look for effects of the Fed's use of open market operations and discount policy in the federal funds market, the market through which banks lend to each other overnight. Actions by the Federal Reserve to push the federal funds rate down are interpreted as expansionary monetary policy, since interest rates that are charged to households and businesses will also fall, encouraging spending.

a On January 31, 2001, the Federal Open Market Committee voted to lower its federal funds rate target from 6% to 5.5%, the lowest rate in nearly three years. How does this action affect the federal funds rate? It is a market-determined interest rate, not literally set by the Fed. We can illustrate what happens using the reserves market diagram. In part (a) of the figure, the Fed fulfills its intention to reduce the federal funds rate by increasing the supply of reserves. It conducts open market purchases to increase nonborrowed reserves. This action shifts the supply curve from S_0 to S_1, increasing reserves from R_0^* to R_1^* and reducing the federal funds rate from i_{ff0}^* to i_{ff1}^*.

b Short-term interest rates are closely linked to the federal funds rate. The falling cost of funds to lenders leads to lower interest rates charged to private borrowers, as indicated by the decrease in loan rates to household and business borrowers. This decrease in loan rates raises demand for business investment and consumer durables, lessening the likelihood of an economic downturn.

c Also on January 31, the Fed reduced the discount rate by a half point from 5.5% to 5%. Many policymakers and analysts praised the Fed's symbolic gesture as indicating its commitment to reinvigorating the economy while continuing to hold the line on inflation. As shown in part (b) of the figure, they reasoned that the cut in the discount rate from i_{d0} (5.5%) to i_{d1} (5%) would shift the reserves supply curve from S_0 to S_1. As a result, reserves would rise from R_0^* to R_1^*, and the federal funds rate would fall from i_{ff0}^* to i_{ff1}^*. To achieve a particular federal funds rate target, the Fed also can decrease nonborrowed reserves, as in part (a) of the figure.

For further thought . . .

What would be the effect of an increase in the discount rate on the yield on three-month Treasury bills? On longer-term bonds?

Source: Excerpted from Greg Ip and Nicholas Kulish, "Psychology Test: Latest Fed Rate Cut Combats a Contagion of Low Confidence," *The Wall Street Journal*, February 1, 2001.

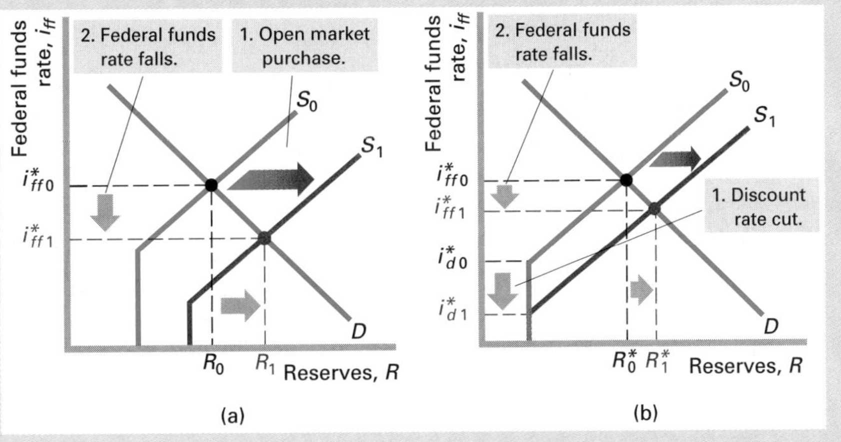

KEY TERMS AND CONCEPTS

Discount policy
- Adjustment credit
- Announcement effect
- Discount window
- Extended credit
- Seasonal credit

Open market operations
- Defensive transactions
- Dynamic transactions
- Federal Reserve repurchase agreements
- General directive
- Matched sale-purchase transactions
- Open Market Trading Desk
- Outright purchases and sales

Reserve requirements

SUMMARY

1. Open market operations (purchases and sales of securities in financial markets) are the most widely used of the Fed's principal monetary policy tools. The Federal Open Market Committee (FOMC) issues guidelines for open market operations as general directives. Some transactions are dynamic—that is, designed to implement changes in the monetary base suggested by the FOMC. Most transactions are defensive—that is, designed to offset unintended disturbances in the monetary base.
2. The Fed's discount policy sets the discount rate and the terms of discount lending. The Fed fulfills its role as the lender of last resort by providing adjustment, seasonal, and extended credit.
3. Reserve requirements are a potent but drastic way to control the monetary base. Increases in reserve requirements decrease the money multiplier; decreases in reserve requirements increase the money multiplier. Because large changes in reserve requirements can cause costly reallocations of banks' portfolios, the Fed generally avoids them.
4. The federal funds rate is one indicator of monetary policy. A decrease in the federal funds rate relative to other market interest rates is usually associated with an expansionary monetary policy. An increase in the federal funds rate relative to other market interest rates is usually associated with a contractionary monetary policy.

REVIEW QUESTIONS

1. If open market operations are considered the Fed's most important monetary policy tool, why were they not mentioned in the original Federal Reserve Act?
2. Since the 1930s, what has been the Fed's most important tool for monetary policy? What part of the Federal Reserve System determines how this tool is used?
3. What advantages do open market operations have over the other monetary policy tools available to the Fed?
4. *Evaluate*: The Fed was originally established to use discount loans to help put an end to banking panics. Deposit insurance has effectively put an end to banking panics; therefore, we no longer need the Fed. If we allow the Fed to continue to operate we ought, at the very least, to eliminate its ability to grant discount loans.
5. Why do borrowed reserves tend to rise when the federal funds rate rises?
6. What causes changes in the discount rate?
7. *Evaluate:* The Fed changes the reserve requirement frequently because it is such a powerful tool.
8. What is the maintenance period for bank reserves? How does the Fed calculate a bank's required reserves?
9. If a bank is required to hold reserves of $150 million but held only $149 million of reserves over the maintenance period, will the Fed penalize it? Why or why not?
10. What is wrong with the liquidity argument for reserve requirements?

11. Why must the Fed police the discount window? Would it need to do so if the discount rate were a penalty rate?
12. What type of credit (adjustment, seasonal, or extended) does each of the following discount loans represent?
    a. Bigbank borrows from the Fed because of liquidity problems when one of its major depositors suddenly switches its accounts to another bank.
    b. Fear that Megabank will fail prompts large depositors to withdraw their funds, forcing Megabank to borrow several billion dollars from the Fed for the next year.
    c. First Bank borrows $5 million so that it can make loans to farmers for planting, as it does every April.
13. What is a Fed watcher?
14. *Evaluate:* The efficient markets hypothesis implies that the market fully anticipates changes in the Fed's discount rate so that there is no announcement effect.
15. What are the two views as to why the Fed's policy statements are often vague? Could political pressure also explain the Fed's unwillingness to be precise? Why or why not?
16. In daily trading by the Open Market Trading Desk at the Federal Reserve Bank of New York, why does the account manager consult with market participants? With the Treasury Department? With two or more members of the FOMC?
17. What are the differences between dynamic and defensive open market operations?

ANALYTICAL PROBLEMS

18. What interest rate is most directly affected by open market operations? What happens to this interest rate and the money supply when the Fed engages in open market purchases? When the Fed engages in open market sales?
19. If the money multiplier is 8, how large a change in the money supply will result from the sale of $1 billion of bonds by the Fed on the open market? Will the money supply increase or decrease?
20. How could the Fed use its three principal monetary policy tools to decrease the money supply by $100 million if the money multiplier is 10 and the monetary base is $500 million?
21. What is the Fed likely to do near the Christmas holiday season, when the public uses more currency?
22. Which of the following open market operations are defensive and which are dynamic?
    a. The Treasury makes a large payment, which the Fed offsets with an open market purchase.
    b. The economy strengthens unexpectedly, to which the Fed responds with open market sales.
    c. Bad weather prevents checks from being cleared as quickly as usual, allowing float to increase in the banking system; the Fed responds with open market sales.
    d. The dollar's foreign exchange value declines, prompting the Fed to respond with open market sales.
23. Suppose that, owing to an oil price shock, inflation in the economy is increasing, causing interest rates to rise. The Fed announces an increase in the discount rate. Does this signal a tightening of monetary policy? Why or why not?
24. The following list contains parts of two different directives to the Open Market Trading Desk from the FOMC. Which is expansionary and which is contractionary?
    a. . . . risks are weighted mainly toward conditions that may generate economic weakness in the foreseeable future . . .
    b. . . . risks are weighted mainly toward conditions that may generate inflationary pressures in the near future . . .
25. Suppose that the Fed were no longer allowed to grant discount loans. Show the effects on the reserves market diagram. Under these circumstances would an open market purchase have a smaller or a larger effect on the equilibrium federal funds rate? Use a reserves market diagram to illustrate your answer.

26. On the reserves market diagram, show how the Fed can use open market operations to offset an increased demand for reserves by holding the federal funds rate constant.

27. On the reserves market diagram, show how the Fed can use discount policy to reduce the federal funds rate. First, show what would happen if the Fed reduced the discount rate (the point on the supply curve at which the slope changes moved lower). Second, show what would happen if the Fed allowed more borrowing at a fixed discount rate (the sloping section of the supply curve became flatter).

28. For (a)–(d), use the graphical analysis of equilibrium in the reserves market to predict changes in nonborrowed reserves, borrowed reserves, and the federal funds rate.
    a. The Fed conducts open market sales of securities.
    b. The Fed more strongly discourages banks' use of the discount window.
    c. Banks and the nonbank public become concerned that a banking crisis is imminent and that depositors will prefer to invest in securities in financial markets.
    d. The Fed lowers the discount rate and conducts open market purchases of securities.

DATA QUESTION

29. Banks complain that reserve requirements hurt their profits because they pay interest to depositors but don't earn anything on their reserves. In the latest *Federal Reserve Bulletin,* find the table that lists reserve requirements. Suppose that a bank has $1 billion in transaction accounts. Calculate the bank's required reserves. In the same publication, look at the average federal funds rate for the past year. Multiply the federal funds rate times the amount of required reserves to determine the cost to the bank of complying with reserve requirements. However, the bank would have held reserves for transaction purposes, even if no reserves were required. Suppose that the bank would hold 5% of its deposits in reserve even if reserves were not required. How much does this holding of nonrequired reserves reduce the bank's profits? What, then, is the true cost of reserve requirements?

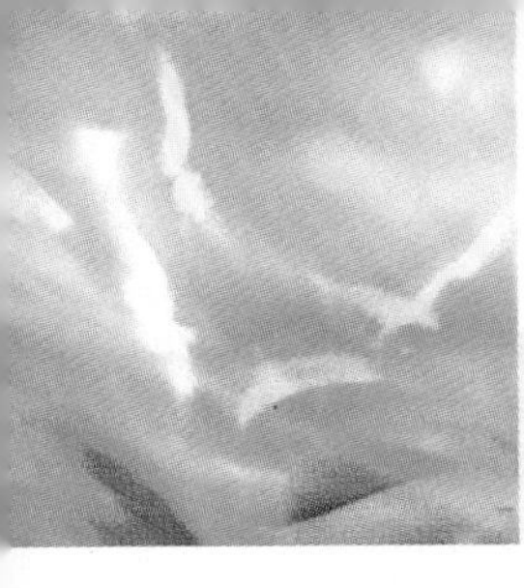

CHAPTER 21

The Conduct of Monetary Policy

The 1990s witnessed a bull market for central banks as well as for stocks. In the United States, the Fed's influence has grown, and its image in the public's eye has improved. In 1982, a Tennessee construction journal had as its cover a "wanted" poster of then-Fed Chairman Paul Volcker, accusing him of "premeditated and cold-blooded murder of millions of small businesses." By the end of the 1990s, Mr. Volcker's successor, Alan Greenspan, was revered by most investors and citizens. In 1999, investors had high hopes for the success of the newly inaugurated European Central Bank. The ways in which central banks conduct monetary policy remains the stuff of headlines.

The Fed uses its monetary policy tools—open market operations, discount policy, and reserve requirements—to change the money supply and short-term interest rates and, ultimately, to achieve its goals for economic performance. In this chapter, we describe how the Fed conducts monetary policy to achieve goals that promote economic well-being. Although it is easy to identify the goals of monetary policy, which we present in the first section, it is not always so simple to enact policies that achieve those goals. In the second section of the chapter, we identify the difficulties in designing effective monetary policies and describe how the Fed can set targets that help it achieve its goals. But as the journal cover of Chairman Volcker demonstrated, the Fed must make choices in selecting its targets. In addition, the outcome of the Fed's policies might not have precisely the economic impact that the theory predicts. We conclude the chapter with an evaluation of the Fed's conduct of monetary policy in achieving its policy goals, and we consider the outlook for future monetary policy in the United States and other industrialized nations.

GOALS OF MONETARY POLICY

Most economists and policymakers agree that the overall aim of monetary policy is to advance the economic well-being of the country's citizens. What is *economic well-being?* There are many ways to assess economic well-being, but typically, it is determined by the quantity and quality of goods and services that members of the economy can enjoy. If an economy functions optimally, then citizens allocate limited resources to provide maximum benefits to all. Economic well-being, then, also applies to the efficient employment of labor and capital and to the steady growth in output that arises from the productive use of these factors of production. In addition, stable economic conditions—minimal fluctuations in the business cycle, steady interest rates, and smoothly functioning financial markets—are qualities that enhance economic well-being. The Fed has set six **monetary policy goals** that are intended to promote a well-functioning economy: (1) price stability, (2) high employment, (3) economic growth, (4) financial market and institution stability, (5) interest rate stability, and (6) foreign-exchange market stability. The Fed tries to set monetary policy to achieve these goals, as do most other central banks.

Price Stability

Inflation, or persistently rising prices, erodes the value of money as a medium of exchange and a unit of account. Especially since inflation rose dramatically and unexpectedly during the 1970s, policymakers have set **price stability** as a policy goal. In a market economy, in which prices communicate information about costs and about demand for goods and services to households and businesses, inflation makes prices less useful as signals for resource allocation. When the overall price level changes, families have trouble deciding how much to save for their children's education or for retirement, and businesses facing uncertain future prices hesitate to enter into long-term contracts with suppliers or customers. Severe inflation causes even greater economic costs. Rates of inflation in the hundreds or thousands of percent per year—known as *hyperinflation*—can severely damage an economy's productive capacity. In extreme cases, money changes value so quickly that it no longer functions as a store of value or medium of exchange. Citizens take cash in wheelbarrows to purchase groceries. During the hyperinflation of the 1920s in Germany, economic activity contracted sharply. The resulting economic instability paved the way for Hitler's fascist regime. The range of problems caused by inflation—from economic uncertainty to devastation—make price stability a desirable monetary policy goal.

High Employment

High employment, or a low rate of unemployment, is another monetary policy goal. Unemployed workers and underused factories and machines lower output (gross domestic product, GDP). Unemployment causes financial distress and decreases self-esteem for workers who lack jobs. Beyond the Fed, branches of the government reinforce the goal of high employment. For example, Congress enacted the Employment Act of 1946 and the Full Employment and Balanced Growth Act of 1978 (the Humphrey-Hawkins Act) to promote high employment and price stability.

Although the Fed is committed to high employment, it does not seek a zero percent rate of unemployment. Even under the best economic conditions, some workers move into or out of the job market or are between jobs. Workers sometimes leave one job to pursue another and might be unemployed in the meantime. Individuals also leave the labor force to obtain more education and training or to raise a family, and reentry may take time. This type of *frictional unemployment* enables workers to search for positions that maximize their well-being.

Although some unemployment always exists, the level of unemployment is determined by the normal working of a healthy economy. When all workers who want jobs have them and the demand for and supply of labor are in equilibrium, economists say that unemployment is at its *natural rate*. In the 1960s, economists thought that the natural rate was 4%, but changes in the economy as a result of technological advances and demographic shifts have increased the natural rate somewhat. The unemployment that is caused by changes in the structure of the economy (such as shifts in manufacturing techniques, increased use of computers and electronic machines, and increases in the production of services instead of goods) is called *structural unemployment*.

Economic Growth

Policymakers also seek steady **economic growth,** increases in the economy's output of goods and services over time, which raises household incomes and thereby increases government revenues. Economic growth depends on high employment. With high employment, businesses are likely to grow by investing in new plant and equipment that raise profits, productivity, and workers' incomes. With high unemployment, businesses have unused productive capacity and are much less likely to invest in capital improvements. Economic growth policies can provide incentives for saving to ensure a large pool of investment funds and direct incentives for business investment. Policymakers attempt to encourage *stable* economic growth, because a stable business environment allows firms and households to plan accurately and encourages the long-term investment that is needed to sustain growth.

Financial Market and Institution Stability

When financial markets and institutions are not efficient in matching savers and borrowers, resources are lost. Firms with the potential to produce high-quality products and services cannot obtain the financing they need to design, develop, and market these products and services. Savers waste resources looking for satisfactory investments. **Financial market and institution stability—** maintaining the viability of financial markets and institutions to channel funds from savers to borrowers—makes possible the efficient matching of savers and borrowers.

The Fed was created after financial panics in the late 1800s and early 1900s. During the past two decades, the Fed's response to problems in the commercial paper, stock, and commodity markets averted financial panics. Of course, the policy goal of financial market and institution stability doesn't guarantee that the Fed's intervention will eliminate panics. For example, federal deposit insurance reduced the severity of banking panics, but the existence of this insurance might have been one cause of the crisis in financial institutions during the late 1980s and early 1990s.

Interest Rate Stability

Like fluctuations in price levels, fluctuations in interest rates make planning and investment decisions difficult for households and businesses. Increases and decreases in interest rates make it hard for businesses to plan investments in plant and equipment and make households more hesitant about long-term investments in houses. Because people often blame the Fed for increases in interest rates, the Fed's goal of **interest rate stability,** or limited fluctuations in interest rates on bonds, is motivated by political pressure as well as by a desire for a stable saving and investment environment.

Foreign-Exchange Market Stability

In the global economy, **foreign-exchange market stability,** or limited fluctuations in the foreign-exchange value of the dollar, is an important monetary policy goal of the Fed. A stable dollar makes planning for commercial and financial transactions simpler. In addition, fluctuations in the dollar's value change the international competitiveness of U.S. industry: A rising dollar makes U.S. goods more expensive abroad, reducing exports; a falling dollar makes foreign goods more expensive in the United States.

Can the Fed achieve these monetary policy goals with its policy tools? We next turn to the problems that the Fed faces and the techniques it uses to tackle those problems.

PROBLEMS IN ACHIEVING MONETARY POLICY GOALS

The Fed's objective in setting monetary policy is to use its policy tools to achieve monetary policy goals. The Fed may be successful in pursuing related goals. It might spur both high employment and economic growth because steady economic growth contributes to high employment. Similarly, actions that encourage stability in financial markets and institutions can also promote interest rate stability. But the Fed is not so lucky in achieving all its goals. It faces trade-offs in attempting to reach other goals, particularly high economic growth and low inflation. To demonstrate the problem, suppose the Fed, intending to reduce inflation, uses open market sales to reduce money supply growth. Recall from Chapter 20 that open market sales increase interest rates. Higher interest rates typically reduce consumer and business spending in the short run. Thus a policy that is intended to achieve one monetary policy goal (lower inflation) has an adverse effect on another (economic growth). In 1995, many members of Congress supported a bill that was introduced by then-Senator Connie Mack of Florida that would force the Fed to focus almost entirely on achieving price stability, and many economists support such a focus.

The Fed faces another problem in reaching its monetary policy goals. Although it hopes to encourage economic growth and price stability, it has no direct control over real output or the price level. Interactions among households and businesses determine real output and the price level. The Fed's changes in the money supply have an indirect influence on the behavior of other economic variables. The Fed can influence the price level or output only by using its monetary policy tools—open market operations, discount policy, and reserve requirements. These tools don't permit the Fed to achieve its monetary policy goals directly.

The Fed also faces timing difficulties in using its monetary policy tools. The first obstacle preventing the Fed from acting quickly is *information lag*. This is the Fed's inability to observe instantaneously changes in GDP, inflation, or other economic variables.[†] If the Fed lacks timely information, it can set policy that doesn't match actual economic conditions, and its actions can actually worsen the problems it is trying to correct. A second timing problem is *impact lag*. This is the time that is required for monetary policy changes to affect output, employment, or inflation. Changes in the monetary base affect the economy over time, not immediately. Because of this lag, the Fed's actions may affect the economy at the wrong time, and the Fed might not be able to recognize its mistakes soon enough to correct them.

The Fed attempts to solve these problems by using targets to meet its goals. Targets partially solve the Fed's inability to control directly the variables that determine economic performance, and they reduce the timing lags in observing and reacting to economic fluctuations. In the remainder of this section, we describe targets, their benefits and drawbacks, and their use in setting monetary policy. This analysis provides the theoretical background for a review of actual Fed policies in the next section. There we describe the actual success and failure the Fed has experienced in its monetary policy measures in the post–World War II era.

Using Targets to Meet Goals

Targets are variables that the Fed can influence directly and that help achieve monetary policy goals. The Fed relies on two types of targets: intermediate targets and operating targets.

Intermediate targets. **Intermediate targets** are financial variables (such as the money supply or short-term interest rates) that the Fed believes will directly help it to achieve its goals. To understand how intermediate targets work in achieving a goal, imagine the situation facing an archer who is trying to hit a

[†]The problem is not limited to monetary policy. One famous instance of information lag in fiscal policy occurred in June 1930, when President Hoover told a group of business leaders that their call for an economic stimulus package was unnecessary: "Gentlemen," he said, "you have come sixty days too late. The depression is over." (Quoted in Arthur M. Schlesinger, Jr., *The Crisis of the Old Order*, Boston: Houghton Mifflin, 1957, p. 331.)

bull's-eye (the goal) that is out of sight on the other side of a hill. The archer would have to guess where the bull's-eye was before shooting. To improve the archer's chance of hitting the bull's-eye, imagine that a ring could be positioned at the top of the hill, in the archer's line of sight, so that going through this intermediate target would make it easier for the arrow to come somewhere near the bull's-eye on the other side of the hill. If the archer makes it through the intermediate target, she knows at once that she has a good chance of hitting the bull's-eye. This target gives immediate feedback and increases the chances of hitting the goal. Intermediate monetary policy targets are like the archery ring at the top of the hill.

When the Fed uses an intermediate target—say, the monetary aggregate *M1*—it has a better chance of reaching a goal such as price stability or full employment, which is not directly under its control, than it would if it focused solely on the goal. It also knows relatively quickly whether its policy actions are consistent with achieving the goal. From statistical studies, the Fed might estimate that a 3% increase in *M1* would achieve the level of employment and degree of price stability it desired. If the money supply actually grew by 4%, the Fed would know immediately that it was stimulating the economy too much, setting the stage for future inflation. The Fed could then use its monetary policy tools (most likely open market operations) to slow *M1* growth to the target of 3%. Hitting the *M1* intermediate target has no value in and of itself. It simply helps the Fed to achieve its stated goals.

Operating targets. In fact, the Fed controls intermediate target variables, such as interest rates and monetary aggregates, only *indirectly* because private-sector decisions also influence these variables. The Fed seeks targets that are better links between its policy tools, intermediate targets, and goals. These new targets, called **operating targets**, are variables that the Fed controls directly with monetary policy tools and that are closely related to intermediate targets. Examples of operating targets include the federal funds rate and nonborrowed reserves. The federal funds rate is a commonly used interest rate operating target because the market for bank reserves, which the Fed influences heavily, determines the rate.

As Fig. 21.1 shows, the Fed selects goals but ultimately controls only policy tools. To sum up our discussions of intermediate and operating targets, the Fed uses targets to achieve its monetary goals in a two-step process. First, it sets an intermediate target (such as money supply growth) to help achieve goals. Second, it sets an operating target (such as nonborrowed reserves growth) to help it to achieve the intermediate target. An advantage of this two-step targeting procedure is that the Fed can quickly monitor changes in operating targets and determine whether its intervention is having the desired effect. Operating targets provide feedback, enabling the Fed to gauge the effectiveness of its policies and to adjust them rather than waiting to evaluate the ultimate success or failure of efforts to achieve its goals. If this two-step process is to be successful, the Fed must select the appropriate targets with care. We now turn to the types of variables that are candidates for the Fed's targets.

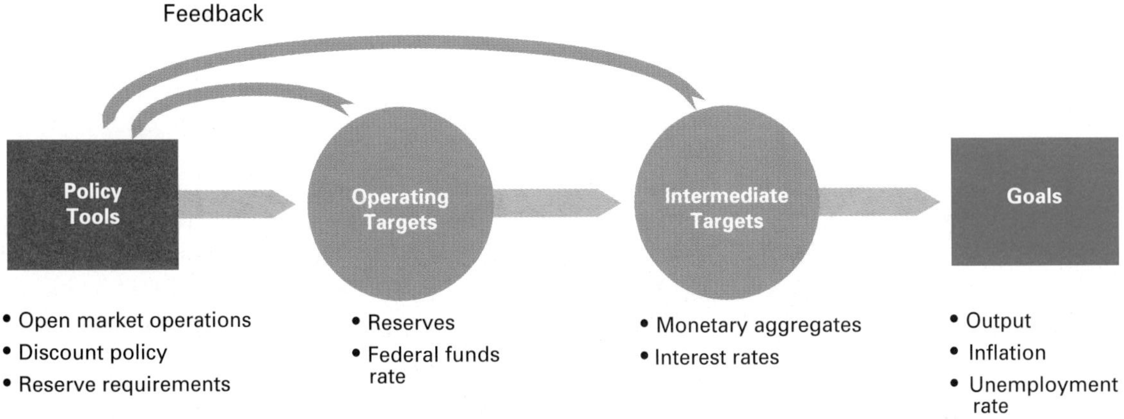

Figure 21.1

Achieving Monetary Policy Goals

The Federal Reserve establishes goals for such economic variables as output, inflation, and the rate of unemployment. The Fed controls directly only its policy tools. It also uses targets—intermediate targets and operating targets—which are variables that the Fed can influence that help achieve monetary policy goals. To be successful, targets must be measurable and controllable and must have a predictable relationship with the Fed's goals. Targets also provide the Fed with feedback on how well it is achieving its goals.

Monetary Aggregates and Interest Rates as Targets

Recall that the Fed cannot generally achieve all of its goals at the same time. Trade-offs among goals force the Fed to select one type of target over another and to favor one goal over another in its policy.

In principle, the Fed has a range of intermediate and operating targets from which to choose, including monetary aggregates (or measures of credit outstanding) and interest rates. The Fed uses either money supply growth targets or interest rate targets. Which should it choose? That is a complicated question, which we will examine shortly. First, however, you need to understand that the Fed can use either money supply growth targets or interest rate targets, but not both. Ultimately, then, the Fed *must* choose.

To understand why, let's turn to a graphical analysis of the demand and supply of money (*M1*). In Fig. 21.2, we plot the quantity of money M_d that households and businesses hold depending on the interest rate. We know that currency held pays no interest and that checkable deposits pay less than open market interest rates. Hence the opportunity cost of holding *M1* balances rises with the market interest rate. And as Fig. 21.2 shows, in the money market, the demand for *M1* and the market interest rate are negatively related.

Suppose that the Fed decides to use *M1*, the money supply, as an intermediate target, setting it equal to M^*, as in Fig. 21.2(a). For the money demand curve M_{d0}, the equilibrium market interest rate equals i^*_0. Any shifts in households' and businesses' demand for currency and bank deposits translate into interest rate movements. In other words, if the demand for money to use in transactions increases at any specific interest rate, the money demand curve shifts to the right from M_{d0} to M_{d1}. With the Fed holding the money

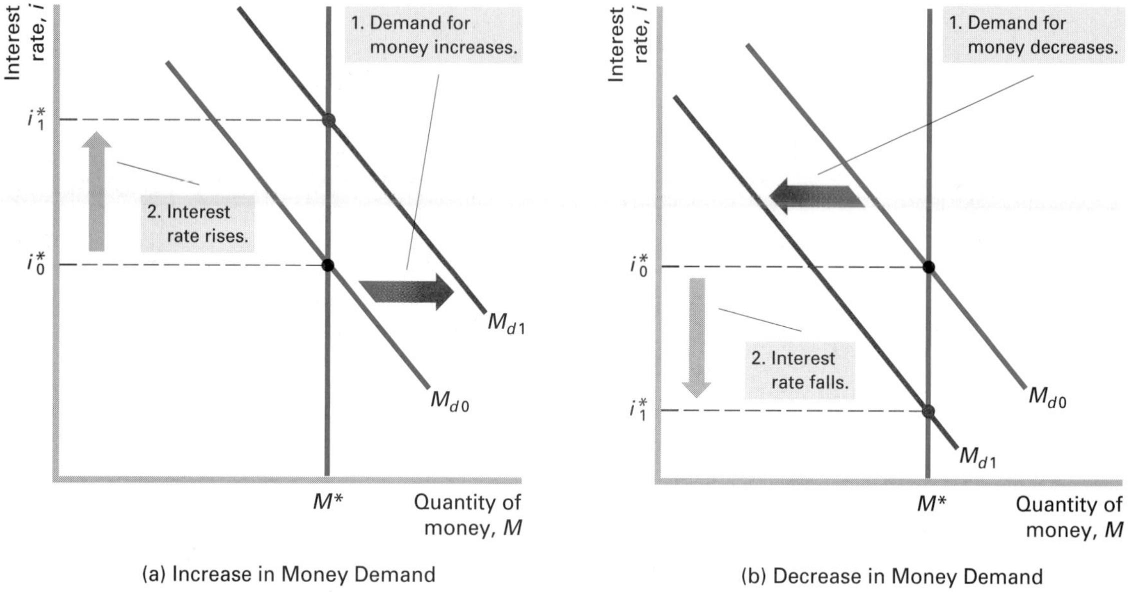

Figure 21.2 **Money Supply Targeting and Interest Rate Fluctuations**

Setting an intermediate target in terms of a monetary aggregate causes interest rates to fluctuate.

As shown in (a):
1. An increase in money demand from M_{d0} to M_{d1} raises the interest rate from i^*_0 to i^*_1.

As shown in (b):
1. A decrease in money demand from M_{d0} to M_{d1} lowers the interest rate from i^*_0 to i^*_1.

supply constant at M^*, the equilibrium market interest rate rises from i^*_0 to i^*_1. Suppose instead that the demand for money declines from M_{d0} to M_{d1} at any specific interest rate (Fig. 21.2b). In this case, if the money supply remains constant at M^*, the equilibrium market interest rate falls from i^*_0 to i^*_1. Using a monetary aggregate for an intermediate target causes interest rates to fluctuate in response to changes in money demand.

Now let's see what happens if the Fed chooses an interest rate as the intermediate target. Let's assume, as in Fig. 21.3(a), that the initial money demand and supply curves are M_{d0} and M^*_0, respectively, and that the Fed sets an interest rate target at the equilibrium interest rate, i^*_0. In this case, when the demand for money increases from M_{d0} to M_{d1} at any specific interest rate, the interest rate rises from i^*_0 to i^*_1. According to Fig. 21.3(a), if the Fed wants to maintain an interest rate of i^*_0, it will have to increase the money supply from M^*_0 to M^*_1. Let's suppose instead that the demand for money declines from M_{d0} to M_{d1} at any specific interest rate (Fig. 21.3b). In this case, the interest rate falls from i^*_0 to i^*_1. If the Fed wants to maintain an interest rate of i^*_0, it will have to reduce the money supply from M^*_0 to M^*_1. Note that the money supply curve is, effectively, now horizontal at the targeted interest rate. Setting an intermediate target in terms of the interest rate causes the quantity of money to fluctuate in response to changes in money demand.

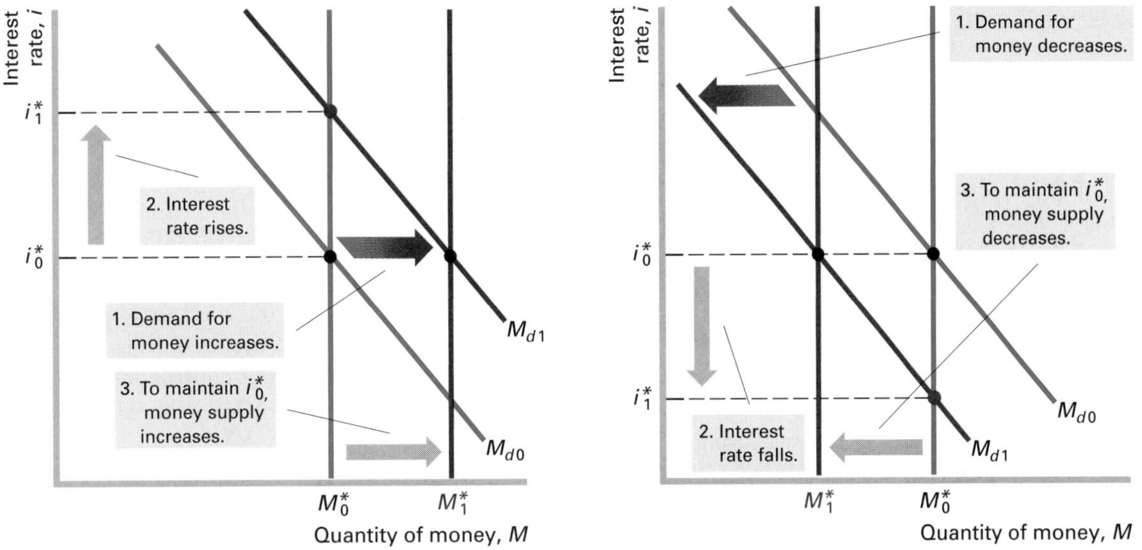

(a) Increase in Money Demand

(b) Decrease in Money Demand

Figure 21.3

Interest Rate Targeting and Money Supply Fluctuations

Setting an intermediate target in terms of an interest rate causes the quantity of money to fluctuate in response to changes in money demand.

As shown in (a):
1. An increase in money demand from M_{d0} to M_{d1} requires the Fed to increase the money supply from M^*_0 to M^*_1 to maintain an interest rate of i^*_0.

As shown in (b):
1. A decrease in money demand from M^*_{d0} to M^*_{d1} requires the Fed to reduce the money supply from M^*_0 to M^*_1 to maintain an interest rate of i^*_0.

This analysis demonstrates the trade-off that the Fed faces in setting targets. The Fed cannot set intermediate targets in terms of both monetary aggregates and interest rates. How, then, does the Fed select targets?

CHECKPOINT

Suppose that households increase their demand for checkable deposits (and hence *M1* rises). Will using *M1* as an intermediate target permit the Fed to accommodate this portfolio allocation shift without affecting interest rates? If the Fed targets the money supply, an increase in the demand for money will, all else being equal, tend to increase short-term interest rates. If the Fed wanted to accommodate the portfolio allocation shift without affecting interest rates, it would conduct open market purchases to increase nonborrowed reserves and the money supply. **o**

Selecting Intermediate Targets

In addition to deciding whether an intermediate target should be a monetary aggregate or an interest rate, the Fed must evaluate the measurability, controllability, and predictability of the variable that is chosen to be the intermediate target. We describe these choices for intermediate targets next and then turn to specific decisions for choosing operating targets.

Measurability. The first criterion for a good target variable is that it must be measurable in a short time frame to overcome information lags. The Fed must be able to measure the target over a short period of time to assess quickly whether its intermediate target is likely to be met. For example, the government compiles data quarterly on a goal variable such as nominal GDP and releases the data after a one-month delay. As potential intermediate targets, both interest rates and monetary aggregates are quickly observable and measurable. With computers, analysts can track interest rates continuously. Money measures are not quite as accessible, although they are reported with at most a two-week lag.

The instantaneous measurability of market interest rates doesn't necessarily make them better intermediate targets than monetary aggregates. The *nominal* interest rate can be measured easily, but assessing the *real* interest rate is more troublesome, owing to the difficulty of measuring market expectations of inflation. Hence, as with monetary aggregates, the Fed can't perfectly measure the relevant interest rates over a short period of time.

Controllability. After identifying the potential targets that are measurable, the Fed must determine whether it can control them to overcome impact lags. An effective intermediate target must be responsive to the Fed's attempts to shift course. For example, during the 1980s, many economists suggested that the Fed select a broader variable than conventional monetary aggregates, such as the stock of nonfinancial credit outstanding (loans to and bonds issued by nonfinancial corporations) or even nominal GDP. However, the Fed cannot control such variables sufficiently with its policy tools. The Fed's influence over monetary aggregates and short-term interest rates is much greater, and so it prefers to use them as intermediate targets.

By using its monetary policy tools (primarily open market operations), the Fed exerts significant control over the money supply but not complete control. The decisions of banks and the nonbank public also influence the money supply. The Fed can also affect interest rates because open market operations help to determine the supply of bonds. Once again, however, absolute control is impossible, because the Fed cannot control expectations of inflation and hence the real interest rate.

Predictability. We don't observe a preferred type of variable for intermediate targets based on measurability or controllability. The Fed also needs targets that have a predictable impact on the policy goals. How do monetary aggregates and interest rates stack up according to this criterion?

The case for interest rate targets rests on the observation that interest rates influence lending, borrowing, and portfolio allocation decisions. Hence the Fed could increase economic activity by reducing real interest rates to stimulate consumer and business spending. If the Fed wanted to cool off the economy instead, it could discourage consumer and business spending by attempting to increase real interest rates.

There are two problems with interest rates as intermediate targets. First, the Fed's influence over real interest rates is weaker than its influence over nominal interest rates. Second, a Fed policy to stabilize interest rates may be inconsistent with the Fed's goal of maintaining steady economic growth. Suppose businesses and consumers increase their spending because they are optimistic about future economic conditions. As a result, consumers spend more and save less, and businesses increase their investment in plant and equipment. These actions increase interest rates. If the Fed is trying to stabilize interest rates, it will make open market purchases to try to lower interest rates. This fall in interest rates encourages consumers and businesses to spend even more. As a result, the policy of holding interest rates constant is like pouring gasoline on a fire.

The same problem occurs during an economic downturn. A loss of consumer and business optimism reduces spending and depresses interest rates. If the Fed didn't step in, lower interest rates would eventually encourage consumer and business spending, cushioning the downturn and putting the economy back on track. If the Fed were targeting interest rates, it would use open market sales to raise interest rates in the face of the downturn, worsening the economy's problems. In either case, if swings in consumer and business optimism are the major determinants of fluctuations in the economy's output of goods and services, a policy of stabilizing interest rates destabilizes economic growth.

What if the Fed selects a monetary aggregate as an intermediate target instead of an interest rate? In the case of economic expansion, the rising demand for money (to fund a higher level of transactions) increases interest rates, as was shown in Fig. 21.2. Higher interest rates help to keep the economy from overheating by reducing consumer and business spending. In the case of an economic downturn, the falling demand for money leads to lower interest rates, as shown in Fig. 21.2. The fall in interest rates cushions the downturn.

Do the problems that are encountered with interest rate targets when consumer and business spending fluctuate imply that the Fed should always target monetary aggregates? Not necessarily. As Fig. 21.2 shows, a money supply target means that shifts in the demand for money at any interest rate translate into interest rate changes. An increase in interest rates depresses the level of consumer and business spending, whereas a decrease in interest rates stimulates spending. Hence, if shifts in the money demand relationship occur frequently, money supply targets likely will produce interest rate fluctuations that destabilize the economy.

This analysis demonstrates that no single variable can act as an intermediate target having all the qualities the Fed desires. How, then, does the Fed choose an intermediate target? The answer depends on sources of fluctuations in economic conditions and in the money supply. If the relationship between consumer and business spending and investment decisions and the interest rate is stable, interest rate targets offer the Fed a more predictable way to stabilize economic fluctuations (even though the Fed can't completely control the real interest rate, which is relevant to consumer and business decisions). However, if the relationship between the demand for money and other assets and the interest rate is stable, targeting monetary aggregates offers the Fed a more predictable connection with its goals. The Fed doesn't have the luxury of complete real or financial stability and must cope with disturbances to both sides of the economy.

Selecting Operating Targets

After the Fed selects an appropriate intermediate target, it must decide on the operating target that will best influence the intermediate target. The Fed uses similar criteria when comparing variables for operating targets: The variables should be measurable, controllable, and predictable. In addition, the operating target should be consistent with the intermediate target. The Fed largely controls both reserve aggregates and the federal funds rate and accurately measures them quickly. Hence, if the Fed selects a monetary aggregate as the desired intermediate target, it will select a reserve aggregate (such as the monetary base or nonborrowed reserves) as the operating target because reserve aggregates have a predictable influence on monetary aggregates. But if it picks a market interest rate as the intermediate target, the Fed will select an interest rate such as the federal funds rate as an operating target because the federal funds rate has a predictable impact on market interest rates. Whether the Fed selects a reserve aggregate or the federal funds rate, it uses its three monetary policy tools (principally open market operations) to influence that operating target.

THE MONETARY POLICY RECORD

Much of the theory that we have described so far about the conduct of monetary policy to achieve economic goals evolved as the Fed designed, implemented, and evaluated economic policy since World War II. In this section, we describe how the Fed has conducted monetary policy—which goals it favored, which targets it used, and whether it was successful in improving economic well-being. Not all of the Fed's efforts have been successful. Using monetary policy tools to control the money supply or interest rates was a new task for the Fed, and it learned what worked and what did not as it attempted to select targets. As part of this learning, the Fed encountered the problem that we identified earlier: constraints imposed by trade-offs among goals and selecting variables that could be evaluated in a timely fashion while still influencing variables that directly affect output, employment, and inflation. In particular, in the postwar period, the Fed has emphasized, at various times, goals of stabilizing economic growth and price stability. Its intermediate and operating targets have at various times included monetary aggregates and short-term interest rates.

Early Interest in Targets: 1951–1970

The Fed's interest in targets began in the early 1950s from its struggle with the U.S. Treasury over the control of monetary policy. During World War II, the Fed agreed to peg interest rates on government securities at their prewar levels (approximately 3/8% on Treasury bills and 2½% on long-term Treasury bonds) to help the Treasury finance the war effort. The Fed did so by purchasing securities whenever their market prices fell below levels that reflected the pegged rates. The onset of the Korean War in 1950 led to higher levels of government borrowing, causing market interest rates to rise. To maintain its interest rate target, the Fed purchased even larger amounts of government securities. These open market purchases expanded the monetary base, eliminating the Fed's control of the money supply process and causing inflation to rise to 8% by early 1951. The Fed formally abandoned the policy under the Federal Reserve–Treasury Accord in March 1951.

That accord freed the Fed to pursue an independent monetary policy. Believing that fluctuations in consumer and business spending were being managed by government tax and expenditure policy (fiscal policy), the Fed attempted to stabilize fluctuations in the money supply. Under the leadership of Chairman William McChesney Martin, the Fed began to implement a strategy targeted to respond to conditions in the money market. Policies to achieve financial stability set monetary aggregates as intermediate targets. In particular, Fed policy used as intermediate targets short-term interest rates and the level of **free reserves,** or the difference between excess reserves, *ER,* and borrowed reserves, *BR* (discount loans), in the banking system.

The Fed believed that free reserves represented slack in the banking system because banks could freely lend (nonborrowed) excess reserves, expanding the money supply through the deposit expansion process. Hence the Fed considered free reserves an indicator of money market conditions. In contrast to a target—which the Fed attempts to control—an **indicator** is a financial variable whose movements reveal information about present or prospective conditions in financial markets or the economy. An increase in free reserves indicates an easing of money market conditions, whereas a decrease in free reserves indicates a tightening of money market conditions. However, during this period, the Fed used free reserves not just as an indicator, but also as an intermediate target, selling securities as free reserves rose and buying securities as free reserves fell.

Interest rates fluctuate during the business cycle. An increase in economic activity during a boom period causes market interest rates to rise. Higher rates increase the opportunity cost of holding excess reserves, so excess reserves decline. At the same time, higher market interest rates raise the incentive for banks to borrow at the discount window (assuming that the discount rate is unchanged), so borrowed reserves (discount loans) increase. These changes cause free reserves to decline. Could the Fed maintain stable interest rates by using free reserves as an intermediate target? Because the Fed is targeting free reserves, the Fed responds with open market purchases that are sufficient to reduce interest rates to a level consistent with previous positions in excess and borrowed reserves—and hence in free reserves.

The process works in reverse during an economic downturn. A decline in national income reduces market interest rates. Hence excess reserves increase and borrowed reserves decrease, so free reserves increase. The Fed responds to the increase in free reserves with open market sales of securities to restore the existing level of free reserves.

Targeting free reserves reduces the Fed's control over the money supply. During a boom, when the demand for money rises, the Fed's actions expand the money supply; in a downturn, when the demand for money falls, the Fed's actions contract the money supply. Hence targeting free reserves also gives the Fed little control over the money supply. In effect, the Fed responds passively to conditions in the economy. Financial economists describe such actions as **procyclical monetary policy,** meaning that the Fed's policy *amplifies* rather than dampens economic fluctuations.

What about the argument that shifts in consumer and business spending could be ignored in favor of a focus on stable interest rates? In fact, government tax and spending policy did not completely stabilize the economy. Rather, the increases in government spending for the Great Society programs and the Vietnam War in the mid- and late 1960s overheated the economy. Procyclical monetary policy failed to promote stable economic growth. *Monetarists*, economists who believe that money supply targets are the best way to conduct monetary policy, were vocal critics of the Fed's targeting procedures.

Similar problems exist with the Fed's use of short-term interest rates as the intermediate target. In this situation, the Fed meets increases in market interest rates during an expansion by making open market purchases, thereby expanding the monetary base and the money supply and loosening interest rates. During an economic downturn, a decline in market interest rates induces the Fed to sell securities, reducing the monetary base and the money supply. Hence interest rate targets fail to promote stable economic growth. This strategy, too, results in procyclical monetary policy.

Because of the experience with procyclical monetary policy during the 1950s and 1960s, increased criticism of its targeting procedures by academic and business economists led the Fed to search for new targets in the late 1960s.

Experimenting with Monetary Targets: 1970–1979

Monetarist critics of the Fed's procyclical monetary policy during the 1950s and 1960s initially welcomed the appointment of Arthur Burns as chairman of the Board of Governors in 1970. Burns stated his belief that the Fed should commit itself to the use of monetary aggregates as targets. However, the Fed's monetary policy during Burns's tenure in the 1970s was as procyclical as the policy during the previous two decades.

Why did the Fed's attempt at monetary targeting fail? Most critics attribute the failure to the Fed's using the federal funds rate as an operating target while using *M1* and *M2* as intermediate targets. The target range for the federal funds rate was narrow; ranges for the monetary aggregates were broad. The Federal Open Market Committee (FOMC) instructed the Open Market Trading Desk to implement policy that would achieve *both* targets. However, as we noted earlier, the Fed can't attain both interest rate and monetary aggregate targets simultaneously. The FOMC gave the federal funds rate top priority, countering departures from the narrow target range with open market purchases or sales, which significantly reduced monetary aggregates. This priority for interest rate targeting made sense if, as the Fed believed, fluctuations in economic growth had been stabilized.

However, fiscal policy did not stabilize fluctuations in economic growth, and procyclical monetary policy reemerged. To counter the increase in the federal funds rate, the Fed made open market purchases, causing faster growth of the monetary base and *M1* than the Fed intended. To solve this problem, the FOMC attempted to put money growth back on course by widening the target range for the federal funds rate. When the economy expanded further, the federal funds rate increased again, bringing additional open market purchases and faster money growth. As a result, both the federal funds rate and the money supply exceeded their target ranges, accompanied by significant inflationary pressures. From late 1972 to early 1973, the federal funds rate virtually doubled from 4½% to 8½%, and *M1* growth exceeded its target level by a wide margin.

The FOMC effectively used the federal funds rate as an operating target for monetary policy. Just as this policy contributes to inflationary pressures during an economic expansion, however, it also reinforces economic contraction. By the end of 1974, the U.S. economy had fallen into its most serious recession since the 1930s. As a result, decreasing credit demand led to a substantial decline in the federal funds rate. The rate was then at the bottom of the target range, so the Trading Desk used open market sales to keep it from falling further. As a result, money supply growth fell. By early 1975, *M1* actually contracted, reinforcing the economic downturn.

The Fed's procyclical monetary policy continued through the 1970s. Burns and his successor, G. William Miller, publicly announced money supply targets while privately targeting the federal funds rate. As long as growth fluctuated, the Fed's desire to control short-term interest rates simply was not consistent with controlling monetary aggregates with an eye toward price stability.

The Congress often puts pressure on the Fed to alter the way it conducts monetary policy. The procyclical monetary policy during Burns's tenure angered Congress, which moved to curb the Fed's powers. It passed a concurrent resolution calling for the Fed to be more accountable to Congress. It then passed the Humphrey-Hawkins Act in 1978, which codified those ideas, including the requirement that money and credit targets be set.

De-emphasizing Interest Rates: 1979–1982

In July 1979, President Jimmy Carter appointed Paul Volcker as chairman of the Board of Governors of the Federal Reserve System. Volcker was committed to crushing inflation and chose monetary aggregates as intermediate targets. Under Volcker, the Fed shifted its policy to emphasize nonborrowed reserves as an operating target. The FOMC reversed the practice of the previous decade by paying less attention to the federal funds rate, expanding its target range more than fivefold. As Fig. 21.4 illustrates, the federal funds rate became much more volatile. At the same time, the Fed didn't tighten its control over money growth. Note that fluctuations in the growth rate of *M1* in 1979–1982 were *greater* than fluctuations under Burns and Miller. The actual growth rate of *M1* exceeded the target range in 1980 and 1982 and fell below the range in 1981.

Why did the Fed's shift in targeting in October 1979 fail to produce greater control of monetary aggregates to promote price stability? Many economists believe that the fluctuations in GDP and financial markets added too much uncertainty to make money growth targets attainable. Much of this instability resulted from deregulation of the banking industry. Financial innovation led to new substitutes for conventional demand deposits so that monetary aggregates had to be redefined. In addition, business recessions occurred in 1980 and again in 1981–1982. Finally, the Fed implemented credit controls (controls on bank lending) from March until July 1980.†

Many economists believe that the Fed's intention in 1979 was not to gain control over monetary aggregates, but to reduce the high rate of inflation, which was widely viewed by policymakers and the electorate as unacceptable. These economists speculate that the Fed announced monetary targets to disguise its agenda of using high interest rates to combat inflation. As evidence, they point to the significant increase in the federal funds rate that the Fed tolerated in late 1979 and again in late 1980 and 1981 while inflation remained stubbornly high. Indeed, with the decline in inflation during the 1981–1982 recession, the FOMC permitted the federal funds rate to fall. The volatility of the federal funds rate and the growth rates of monetary aggregates from 1979 to 1982 may say more about the Fed's concern with inflation than about monetary control.

Policy After 1982: Back to Interest Rates

In October 1982, the Fed began to pay more attention to the federal funds rate, emphasizing less the targets for monetary aggregates and ranges of acceptable fluctuations in the money supply. Borrowed reserves became the stated operating target for monetary policy. Rising market interest rates during the boom following the 1981–1982 recession induced the Fed to use borrowed reserves, putting upward pressure on the federal funds rate. To ease this pressure, the Fed purchased securities and increased nonborrowed reserves, which slowed the rise in interest rates and borrowed reserves. As a result, the

---

†Reserve requirements added a further complication during this period. Until 1983, required reserves for a given week were based on the deposits that had been made two weeks earlier; this made the nonborrowed reserves target difficult to implement. Since 1984, the Fed has required contemporaneous reserve requirement accounting.

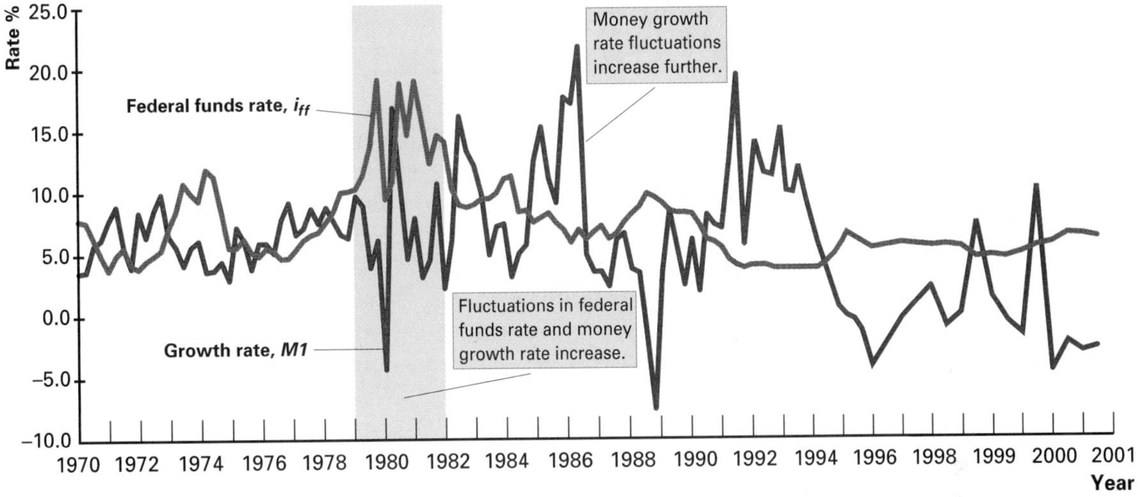

Figure 21.4

Federal Funds Rate and Money Supply Growth Rate, 1970–2000

The Fed's emphasis on controlling monetary aggregates from October 1979 to October 1982 led to large fluctuations in the federal funds rate, as our graphical analysis suggests. Note, however, that the *M1* growth rate was actually *less* stable during 1979–1982 than during 1975–1979. The Fed's targeting procedure focused on controlling nonborrowed reserves, but major shifts in the *demand* for money as a result of deregulation and financial innovation made money growth erratic. After October 1982, the Fed's renewed interest in stabilizing the federal funds rate further destabilized money supply growth.

Source: Federal Reserve Bulletin, various issues.

monetary base increased, in effect returning the Fed to a procyclical monetary policy. Under this approach, in an economic downturn, falling interest rates would slow discount borrowing, leading the Fed to sell securities to offset the drop in borrowed reserves. As a result, the monetary base and the money supply would decline.

Return to Fig. 21.4 and note the smaller fluctuations in the federal funds rate after 1982. Since February 1987, the Fed hasn't announced targets for *M1*. Fed officials justify this decision by reasoning that deregulation and financial innovation during the 1980s made *M1* less relevant as a measure of the medium of exchange. During this period, the Fed increased its reliance on targets for *M2*, a broader monetary aggregate with a more stable historical relationship with economic growth. Even this relationship broke down in the early 1990s. By that time, the Fed paid little attention to growth in monetary aggregates in comparison to the attention paid to the federal funds rate. Indeed, in July 1993, Fed Chairman Alan Greenspan informed the Congress that the Fed would cease its emphasis on using *M1* or *M2* targets to guide the conduct of monetary policy. The Fed has correspondingly increased its reliance on interest rate targets.

In the early 1990s, the Fed became concerned that a *bank credit crunch,* or a severe contraction of the volume of bank lending, was reducing economic growth. In addition to targeting the money supply, the Fed used its monetary policy tools

OTHER TIMES, OTHER PLACES . . .

Does the Conduct of Monetary Policy Respond to Political Pressure?

Politics may influence the Fed's practices. As the 1980 primary election approached, politicians believed that the high U.S. inflation rate and the low value of the dollar were unacceptable to voters. In part reflecting these pressures, the Fed adopted a strategy of targeting nonborrowed reserves to reduce the growth rate of the money supply and thereby stem inflation. Knowing that this anti-inflation strategy would increase interest rates and wanting to avoid being blamed for the resulting increase, the Fed did not publicly state its objective. Instead, it stated in technical terms its intention to focus on monetary aggregates to deflect political criticism of high interest rates during its battle against inflation.

The intersection of economic policies and political desires appeared again in 1982. Three years after the Fed announced its "policy" of targeting monetary aggregates, Congress criticized the Fed for the volatility of monetary aggregates and the economic downturn in 1981 and 1982. This criticism put the Fed in a bind: If it openly widened target ranges for monetary aggregates to make interest rates less volatile, it would have to admit that it was to some extent using the federal funds rate as an operating target, which it had said before that it wouldn't do. Instead, the Fed chose to claim that it used borrowed reserves as the operating target. By this method of announcing one policy while following another, the Fed tried to balance its economic interest in fighting inflation with its political interest in not being blamed for high interest rates.

to influence the level of bank lending, including reducing reserve requirements in December 1990 and February 1992.

Increasing International Concerns: The 1980s and 1990s

Just as the rising importance of international trade changed financial markets and banking, exchange rate movements in international financial markets shaped Fed policymaking more during the 1980s and 1990s than ever before. Foreign-exchange market developments came to the forefront in 1985, when the foreign-exchange value of the dollar rose so high that U.S. businesses faced competitive losses in international markets. The FOMC indicated in its directives that bringing the dollar down would be appropriate. The Fed used an expansionary monetary policy to decrease the value of the dollar in foreign-exchange markets and to reduce short-term interest rates. To decrease the value of the dollar on foreign-exchange markets, the Fed tried to reduce the demand for dollars. By increasing money growth, it tried to lower short-term rates, making investment in dollar-denominated assets less attractive than investment in assets outside the United States, which paid higher interest rates. As investors sold dollars to buy non-U.S. assets, the dollar's value against other currencies declined. Later in the 1980s, the Fed promoted an increase in short-term rates to raise the value of the dollar. The Fed's actions were joined by coordinated efforts of other central banks through the Plaza Accord (September 1985) and the Louvre Accord (February 1987). In May and June 1994 and on several occasions during 1995, the Fed joined the Treasury in an intervention to support the dollar's value against the Japanese yen; interventions to influence the yen–dollar exchange rate continued later in the 1990s.

In the fall of 1998, Fed concerns about the stability of the international financial system after the Russian financial collapse and continued economic weakness in Asia led it to reduce the federal funds rate by 0.75 percentage points.

Concluding Remarks

The Fed's practices since World War II have not produced very successful intermediate targets. During the 1990s, the Fed emphasized a goal of low inflation and used all the tools at its disposal to achieve that goal. The Fed's recent experience suggests that no single target is appropriate. The economy and the financial system experience many different types of disturbances, the relative significance of which changes over time. Hence the Fed's current strategy is a practical one, however imperfect.

REEVALUATING FED TARGETING POLICY

The underlying assumption behind the use of intermediate targets is that financial variables that the Fed can directly measure and control may influence variables that the Fed can't directly control but that are affected by the target variables in a predictable way. Our discussion of post–World War II monetary policy in the United States illustrates why many economists question the merits of financial variables as *targets* rather than *indicators*. Relationships between measures of money and economic activity appeared to be stable during the 1970s, when many economists and policymakers urged the Fed to use monetary aggregates as intermediate targets. However, the relationship between money and nominal GDP weakened greatly during the 1980s. Critics conclude that, although no measure of money is a perfect intermediate target, owing to short-term instability (and even longer-term drift) in the relationship of the target to goals, other variables might be more useful as indicators.

Alternative Intermediate Targets

Target variables that have recently been suggested to the Fed include nominal GDP, commodity prices, the yield curve, and the foreign-exchange value of the dollar. Let's consider them and then analyze the Fed's current strategy.

Nominal GDP. The collapse in the previously stable relationships between money (or the stock of nonfinancial credit outstanding) and nominal GDP caused some economists in the 1980s to suggest that the Fed use the rate of growth of nominal GDP as a target variable. They reasoned that if real GDP growth is independent of monetary policy in the long run, the use of a nominal GDP target focuses attention on long-run price stability—and the unit-of-account function of money. Critics countered that the Fed's tools don't give it enough control over nominal GDP to achieve accurately any selected target. They proposed that the Fed adjust interest rate operating targets to influence nominal GDP. However, many Fed officials doubted that such a procedure could succeed.

Economists suggested three other variables to the Fed during the 1980s and 1990s: commodity prices, the Treasury yield curve, and the foreign-exchange value of the dollar. They argued that the markets for these assets are *efficient*. In other words, their prices reflect available economic information, including information for the Fed about the current and expected future economic outlook.

Commodity prices. The Fed could influence commodity prices through open market operations in commodity markets. Alternatively, if commodity prices provide advance information about future changes in inflation, the Fed could use price data as a signal of the need to adjust reserve aggregates or the federal funds rate. However, studies of this link show that commodity prices do not predict general inflation well. Hence commodity prices are not likely to be an effective indicator.

Yield curve. Under the expectations theory of the term structure of interest rates, the nominal interest rate on long-term securities indicates the market's expectations of future short-term nominal interest rates. If real interest rates were constant, the yield curve would indicate inflationary expectations, since expected inflation is the difference between the nominal and real interest rates. However, real interest rates aren't constant, so interpreting the slope of the yield curve requires guesses about the relative importance of expected shifts in real rates and inflation. Nevertheless, the slope of the yield curve contains statistically significant predictive power for both real output and inflation, and the Fed and other central banks examine the yield curve when evaluating changes in monetary policy.

Foreign-exchange value of the dollar. Increasing sensitivity of the U.S. economy to international events prompted interest in the information content of changes in the foreign-exchange value of the dollar. Most economists don't advocate the usefulness of exchange rates as targets. However, some evidence suggests that exchange rate movements to a degree do predict future real output and inflation. In spite of this information benefit, analysts generally conclude that exchange rate movements are useful as indicators only in conjunction with such conventional indicators as domestic interest rates.

The Taylor Rule

While the Fed relies on federal funds rate targeting in the context of U.S. monetary policy, the central bank still needs a way to choose the target level of interest rates. Actual Fed deliberations are complex and incorporate many factors about the economy. John Taylor of Stanford University has synthesized these factors in the **Taylor rule** for federal funds rate targeting.† The Taylor rule states

†John B. Taylor, "Discretion Versus Policy Rules in Practice," *Carnegie-Rochester Conference Series on Public Policy* 39:195–214, 1993.

that the current federal funds rate target should be the sum of the inflation rate, the equilibrium real federal funds rate (defined as the federal funds rate consistent with long-run full employment), and two additional terms. The first of these terms is the "inflation gap"—the difference between current inflation and a target rate; the second is the "output gap"—the percentage difference of real GDP from its estimated full-employment level. That is, the Taylor rule states that

$$\text{Federal funds rate target} = \text{Inflation} + \text{Real equilibrium fed funds rate} \\ + (1/2)\ \text{Inflation gap} + (1/2)\ \text{Output gap}.$$

In calibrating this rule, Taylor assumed that the equilibrium real fed funds rate is 2% and the target rate of inflation is 2%. Implementing the Taylor rule in practice requires estimating the inflation gap and the output gap. Taylor's incorporation of the inflation gap and the output gap into his monetary policy rule reflects the oft-stated concerns of Fed Governors and economists about both inflation and real output fluctuations. If, for example, inflation were 4%—so that the inflation gap is 4% − 2% = 2%—and real GDP were 2% greater than full-employment potential GDP, the Taylor rule recommends a federal funds rate target of 4% inflation + 2% equilibrium real federal funds rate + (1/2) (2% inflation gap) + (1/2) (2% output gap) = 8%.

The Taylor rule also offers a way to analyze the conduct of monetary policy by comparing the federal funds rate target predicted by the rule with the actual federal funds rate target. Under Federal Reserve Chairman Arthur Burns (1970–1979), the federal funds rate target was lower than that recommended by the Taylor rule, offering an explanation for the steady rise in inflation during Burns's oversight. Going the opposite direction, the Fed under Chairman Paul Volcker kept the federal funds rate higher than the Taylor rule level to reduce inflation. During the Greenspan era, the federal funds rate has been much closer to the Taylor rule predictions, consistent with the view that the Fed's conduct of monetary policy has been successful in the 1990s and in the new century. Although the Taylor rule remains silent about changes in the inflation target or the equilibrium interest rate, many economists view the "rule" as a convenient way to analyze the federal funds target.

The Future of Targeting

Fed policymaking must strike a balance in its use of intermediate targets: Suitable intermediate targets can improve the chances of achieving goals, but evidence from the 1980s and 1990s suggests that suitable variables (those that the Fed can measure and control and that have a predictable impact on goal achievement) are not easy to find. As we pointed out, the Fed deals with this trade-off by compromising. Although it specifies targets for money aggregates, the Fed often defines these targets vaguely and as broad ranges in the FOMC directives. As a result, intermediate targets are less connected to day-to-day or month-to-month operating decisions than the theory of targeting suggests.

The Fed has done a substantial amount of research on the role of intermediate targets in the conduct of monetary policy, and ongoing analysis is likely. However, the practical importance of intermediate targets in the future

CASE STUDY

Is Inflation Targeting a Good Idea?

Over the past decade, many economists and central bankers have expressed significant interest in using *inflation targeting* as a framework for carrying out monetary policy. While the debate over inflation targeting remained at a relatively early stage in the United States in the late 1990s, several countries have adopted formal inflation targets. For policymakers in the Fed and the Congress, key elements of the debate over inflation targeting center on how such a policy would work in practice and whether arguments in favor of inflation targeting dominate arguments against such a system.

Economists generally define inflation targeting as a framework for monetary policy in which the central bank commits to conduct policy to satisfy a publicly announced inflation target within a given time frame.† In principle, inflation targeting need not impose an inflexible rule for the central bank; monetary policy could still use discretion in addressing special situations. Nevertheless, monetary policy objectives and operation would focus on inflation and inflation forecasts. If the Fed were to focus explicitly on low inflation, it would have to decide how to reconcile this objective with other objectives—say, output stabilization. For example, an inflation targeting system could accommodate an output stabilization objective by permitting wide inflation target bonds and long inflation target horizons. The central bank must then balance the flexibility of this accommodation with the possibility that financial market participants may question its commitment to price stability.

Arguments in favor of inflation targets focus on four points. First, announcing explicit targets for inflation would draw the public's attention to what the Fed can achieve in practice; most economists believe that over the long run, monetary policy has a greater effect on inflation than the growth of real output. Second, the establishment of transparent inflation targets for the United States would provide an anchor for inflationary expectations. Third, announced inflation targets would help institutionalize good U.S. monetary policy. Finally, inflation targets would promote accountability for the Fed by providing a yardstick against which performance could be measured.

Opponents of inflation targets also make four points. First, rigid numerical targets for inflation diminish the flexibility of monetary policy to address other policy goals. Second, because monetary policy influences inflation with a lag, inflation targeting requires that the Fed depend on forecasts of future inflation, uncertainty about which can create problems for the conduct of policy. Third, holding the Fed accountable only for a goal of low inflation may make it more difficult for elected officials to monitor the Fed's support for good economic policy overall. Finally, uncertainty about future levels of output and employment can impede economic decision making in the presence of an inflation target;

† For broad overviews of issues surrounding inflation targeting, see Guy Debelle, Paul Masson, Miguel Savastano, and Sunil Sharma, *Inflation Targeting as a Framework for Monetary Policy*, Washington, D.C.: International Monetary Fund, 1998; and George A. Kahn and Klara Parrish, "Conducting Monetary Policy with Inflation Targets," *Federal Reserve Bank of Kansas City, Economic Review* (Third Quarter 1998): 5–30.

that is, inflation targets may obscure this uncertainty by adjusting the amount of time over which deviations from the inflation target are permitted.

Should the Fed adopt inflation targets? On the question of whether inflation targets improve economic policy, the jury is still out. New Zealand, the country with the oldest inflation-targeting regime, had only a decade of experience by 2000. Many economists and central bankers have suggested that gains from transparency and accountability can be achieved without explicit inflation targets, and credibility of monetary policy is better established through experience.[†]

[†] See, for example, the interview study of central bank credibility conducted by Alan Blinder of Princeton University. Alan S. Blinder, "Central Bank Credibility: Why Do We Care? How Do We Build It?," Mimeograph, December 1998.

conduct of monetary policy depends largely on whether controllability and predictability criteria for these targets can be satisfied.

The Fed's targeting efforts for monetary control since World War II haven't been as successful as those of some other countries. Fed watchers believe that the most important reason for continuing to use targets for monetary policy is that a commitment to meeting those targets keeps the money supply process under control. Most economists support the idea that the Fed can significantly control the monetary base and, to the extent that money multipliers remain stable over the long run, can influence the money supply greatly. By the mid-1990s, the Fed began to examine the desirability of **inflation targets,** and announced intentions for inflation to be pursued using the Fed's policy tools.

In practice, several countries have adopted inflation targeting, including New Zealand (1990), Canada (1991), the United Kingdom (1992), Finland (1993), Sweden (1993), Australia (1994), and Spain (1994). More limited forms of inflation targets have been adopted in Brazil, Chile, and Israel. Generally speaking, the move to inflation targeting has been accompanied by lower inflation (albeit sometimes at the cost of higher unemployment). The question of whether the reductions in inflation are traceable to inflation targeting per se or to the better communication of the central bank's ongoing objectives continues to foster debate.

Federal Reserve performance in the 1980s, 1990s, and the new century has been excellent, even without a formal inflation target. The 1990s, for example, witnessed low inflation and a substantial economic expansion. The Fed's implicit strategy has been to keep inflation low and steady in the long run. Such a strategy leads Fed policymakers to examine a range of data offering information on future inflationary trends. In addition, the Fed in recent years has acted preemptively when inflation fears have arisen.

The Fed's strategy of an implicit "nominal anchor" has much to recommend it. First, its communication about the importance of low inflation for overall U.S. macroeconomic performance builds public support for the policy. Second, given long and variable lags in the effects of monetary policy on the economy, the Fed's preemptive attacks on incipient inflation are likely to be more successful than waiting to act until actual inflation is rising. This strategy is not without risks, however. The central bank's prestige derives largely from public trust in the anti-inflation statements of Fed officials, particularly Chairman Alan Greenspan. The fact that Fed leadership will eventually change (though in the 2000 presidential campaign, Arizona Senator John McCain stated that if Chairman Greenspan died, he would prop him in his chair and go on) highlights the need for increasingly formal communication with the public and its elected officials about both the desirability of low inflation and the steps the Fed will take to combat incipient inflation.

INTERNATIONAL COMPARISON OF MONETARY POLICY CONDUCT

Although there are institutional differences in the ways in which central banks conduct monetary policy, there are two important similarities in recent practices. First, most central banks in industrial countries have increasingly used short-term interest rates (such as the fsederal funds rate in the United States) as the operating target through which goals are pursued. Second, many central banks are focusing more on ultimate goals such as low inflation than on particular intermediate targets. We discuss these practices and institutional settings in the conduct of monetary policy in Canada, Germany, Japan, the United Kingdom, and the European Union.

As in the United States, in *Canada,* the Bank of Canada became increasingly concerned about inflation during the 1970s, and it announced in 1975 a policy of gradually reducing the growth rate of *M1*. By the late 1970s, policy shifted toward an exchange rate target; by late 1982, *M1* targets were no longer used. However, in 1988, the then governor of the Bank of Canada, John Crow, announced the Bank's commitment to price stability. In this regime, a series of declining inflation targets are announced. Consistent with the inflation targets, the Bank of Canada sets explicit operational target bands for the overnight rate (analogous to the federal funds rate).

The *German* central bank, the Bundesbank, began experimenting with monetary targets in the late 1970s to combat inflation. The aggregate that it selected, *central bank money,* or *M3,* is defined as a (weighted) sum of currency, checkable deposits, and time and savings deposits. The Bundesbank believed that movements in central bank money had a predictable impact on nominal GDP and that this monetary aggregate was significantly controllable by using central bank tools. Target ranges were set each year during the late 1970s and through the 1980s, during which the Bundesbank lowered its targets for money growth. For the first half of the 1980s, the central bank successfully achieved its targets. Discretionary departures from its targets became more common from 1986 through 1988, as officials wanted to decrease the value of the (then) West German mark relative to the U.S. dollar. To do so, the Bundesbank increased money growth faster than its announced targets.

The reunification of Germany in 1991 posed problems for the Bundesbank's commitment to its announced targets. Two pressures were particularly significant: First, the exchange of West German currency for less valuable East German currency brought inflationary pressures. Second, political objectives for economic growth after reunification raised fears of a weakening of the resolve to keep inflation low. These pressures on the Bundesbank's operating procedures yielded a more flexible indicator approach, similar to that used by the Fed.

Germany, which has had an informal inflation target since 1975, had an inflation goal of 2% per year prior to the inauguration of the European Central Bank in 1999. The Bundesbank believes that adherence to *M3* targeting will keep inflation in check. The central bank uses changes in the *lombard rate* (a short-term repurchase agreement rate) to achieve its *M3* target. Some analysts are concerned, however, that financial innovation in Germany has made *M3* demand more difficult to predict.

The apparent German success in the conduct of monetary policy may be traceable to factors beyond monetary targeting per se. Many analysts note that the Bundesbank has permitted substantial deviation from monetary targets for significant periods of time. The success of German monetary policy may lie more in the clear communication of the central bank's focus on controlling inflation than in a strict emphasis on monetary targeting.

In the aftermath of the first OPEC oil shock in 1973, *Japan* experienced an inflation rate in excess of 20%, stimulating a reorientation by the Bank of Japan on money growth targets. In particular, beginning in 1978, the Bank of Japan announced targets for an aggregate corresponding to *M2 + CD*. Following the 1979 oil price shock, the central bank reduced money growth. The gradual decline in money growth over the period from 1978 through 1987 that the Bank of Japan announced and implemented was associated with a faster decline in inflation than that in the U.S. experience. The consistency with which the Bank fulfilled its promises bolstered the public's belief in the Bank's commitment to lower money growth and lower inflation. During this period, the Bank of Japan used a short-term interest rate (in the Japanese interbank market, analogous to the U.S. federal funds market) as its operating target.

Like those in the United States, Japanese banks and financial markets experienced a wave of deregulation and financial innovation during the 1980s. As a consequence, the Bank of Japan began to rely less on the *M2 + CD* aggregate in the conduct of monetary policy. After 1987, the Bank's concern over the foreign-exchange value of the yen—which had risen significantly against the U.S. dollar—dominated monetary policy until 1989. The rapid rate of money growth during this period led to a boom in Japanese asset prices (particularly in land and stocks). In an attempt to reduce speculation in asset markets during the boom, the Bank of Japan adopted a contractionary monetary policy, which led to a decline in asset prices and ultimately to a drop in Japanese economic growth. Despite the success of the Bank of Japan's fight against inflation during the 1978–1987 period, it has not adopted formal inflation targets (though the Bank emphasizes price stability as an objective).

As an operating policy instrument, the central bank uses short-term interest rates and its discount rate. Excessively tight Japanese monetary policy in 1999 and 2000 is viewed by many financial market commentators to be a significant factor in the continuing weakness of Japanese economic performance.

In the *United Kingdom*, the Bank of England announced money supply targets in late 1973 in response to inflationary pressures. As was the case in the United States, money targets—in this case a broad aggregate, *M3*—were not pursued aggressively. In response to accelerating inflation in the late 1970s, the Thatcher government formally introduced in 1980 a strategy for gradual deceleration of *M3* growth. Just as achieving the *M1* targets in the United States was made more complicated by financial innovation, the Bank of England had difficulty achieving *M3* targets. Beginning in 1983, it shifted its emphasis toward targeting growth in the monetary base (again with an eye toward a gradual reduction in the rate of growth of the money supply). In 1992, the United Kingdom adopted inflation targets. Consistent with those targets, short-term interest rates have been the primary instrument of monetary policy. Since early 1984, interest rate decisions have been made at monthly meetings between the Governor of the Bank of England and the Chancellor of the Exchequer. When interest rates are changed, a detailed explanation is offered to emphasize that decisions reflect monetary policy's emphasis on inflation goals.

In the *European Union*, following the signing of the Maastricht Treaty, the European System of Central Banks (ESCB), consisting of the European Central Bank (ECB) and the national central banks of all member states of the European Union, commenced operation in January 1999. Modeled on the law governing the German Bundesbank, the primary objective of the ESCB is to maintain price stability. As a secondary objective, the ESCB also has to support the general economic policies in the European Union. The ECB attaches a significant role to monetary aggregates—in particular, the growth rate of the *M3* aggregate. In addition, however, the ECB has emphasized a goal of price stability, defined as an inflation range of 0% to 2%. In practice, the ECB's strategy has not always been clear, as it has not committed to either a monetary targeting approach or an inflation targeting approach.

KEY TERMS AND CONCEPTS

Free reserves
Indicator
Inflation targets
Monetary policy goals
- Economic growth
- Financial market and institution stability
- Foreign-exchange market stability
- High employment
- Interest rate stability
- Price stability

Procyclical monetary policy
Targets
- Intermediate targets
- Operating targets

Taylor rule

SUMMARY

1. The Fed's broad monetary policy goals are price stability, high employment, economic growth, financial market and institution stability, interest rate stability, and foreign-exchange market stability. These goals are not generally attainable at the same time and, in fact, may conflict at times. Therefore the Fed must make trade-offs among them.
2. The Fed cannot directly control its goals with its tools of monetary policy, so it selects intermediate targets (financial variables that have a predictable impact on the goals). The Fed uses its monetary policy tools to influence operating targets (financial variables that are more directly under its control) that have a predictable impact on intermediate targets.
3. Because financial markets determine interest rates and monetary aggregates together, the Fed must choose between them as intermediate targets. To do so, it uses the criteria of predictability, controllability, and measurability.
4. Since World War II, the Fed's use of targets in the conduct of U.S. monetary policy hasn't led to its control of the money supply. During the 1980s, deregulation and financial innovation made money supply targets more difficult to achieve. Since the mid-1980s, the Fed's policy has responded to direct information about changing conditions in the economy and financial markets.
5. Most economists believe that, as a technical matter, the Fed largely controls the money supply over the long run. Open market operations are a primary determinant of the monetary base. With an appropriately defined monetary aggregate (predictably affected by the monetary base through the money multiplier), monetary control should be possible.

REVIEW QUESTIONS

1. What are the Fed's monetary policy goals?
2. Construct a hypothetical scenario under which the Fed's goals of high employment and foreign-exchange market stability might conflict. In the case of such a conflict, which goal is the Fed likely to emphasize?
3. Suppose that the demand for money becomes less stable (that is, on the money demand–money supply diagram it shifts more frequently). Would this make selecting a monetary aggregate as an intermediate target more or less desirable? Explain.
4. What factors determine the variables that are selected as intermediate targets for monetary policy?
5. What is the difference between a target and an indicator? Is it possible for the Fed to use an indicator as a target?
6. Why is price stability a goal of monetary policy?
7. Should a goal of monetary policy be to reduce the unemployment rate to zero? Why or why not?
8. Why should policymakers care about fluctuations in interest rates or exchange rates?
9. Why do policymakers use a two-step targeting procedure, with both operating and intermediate targets, instead of single-step targeting?
10. Why can't the Fed target both the money supply and interest rates simultaneously?
11. Why was the Fed's pegging of interest rates before 1951 potentially inflationary?
12. Why was using free reserves as an intermediate target in the 1950s a procyclical monetary policy?
13. Why did the federal funds rate become more volatile in 1979? Did the Fed achieve greater monetary control? Why or why not?
14. If the Fed wants to decrease the value of the dollar on foreign-exchange markets, what should it do? What should it do if it wants to increase the foreign-exchange value of the dollar?
15. Why wouldn't commodity prices be useful intermediate targets for monetary policy?
16. How does political pressure influence the Fed's choice of targets? What did the Fed do in 1982 to accommodate these pressures somewhat?
17. Why is the choice of intermediate targets for monetary policy important for the selection of operating targets?

THE WALL STREET JOURNAL FEBRUARY 14, 2001

The Chairman's Upbeat View

Federal Reserve Chairman Alan Greenspan sounded more upbeat about the economy than he did three weeks ago, but that didn't change expectations that the Fed (a) will cut interest rates again at its March 20 policy-setting meeting.

Mr. Greenspan told the Senate Banking Committee that Fed policy makers still believe—as they did when they cut rates January 31—that "for the period ahead, downside risks predominate."

Although "at the moment, we are not" in a recession, he said in response to a senator's question, a recession is a serious enough event that "we should take whatever actions we can to reduce the probability that it will occur."

Mr. Greenspan lowered the Fed's forecast of growth for this year's fourth quarter to between 2% and 2.5% from a year earlier—similar to what private economists expect. The Fed, he said, now expects the economy to strengthen after the "current rebalancing" is over. The previous forecast, made last July, was for growth between 3.25% and 3.75%.

The Fed's inflation forecast for the fourth quar- (b) ter also fell to between 1.75% and 2.25% from between 2% and 2.5%, indicating there is room to cut rates in spite of two half-point interest-rate cuts in January that lowered the target for the federal-funds rate (the rate on overnight loans between banks) to 5.5%.

He was generally more chipper about the economy than he was in testimony three weeks ago before the Senate Budget Committee. The "exceptional weakness so evident . . . toward the end of last year," perhaps due to bad weather, "apparently did not continue in January," he said. Though consumer confidence has fallen, "it remains at a level that in the past was consistent with economic growth." . . .

On a technical issue, Mr. Greenspan said that as the supply of Treasury secu- (c) rities diminishes, the Fed is examining whether to accept state- and foreign-government debt securities as collateral in "repurchase agreements." These are open-market operations aimed at influencing interest rates.

Mr. Greenspan listed factors that had pulled the economy down late last year, and noted that some are improving.

"The recent decline in energy prices and further declines anticipated by futures markets, should they occur, would tend to boost purchasing power" and aid a recovery, he said. . . .

Mr. Greenspan remained optimistic that the acceleration in productivity growth of the late 1990s, which enables the economy to produce more goods and services with an hour of labor, remains intact. Indeed, the Fed projects a rise in the unemployment rate this year to about 4.5% from its current 4.2% despite continued growth precisely because it thinks the economy will not need as many additional workers to achieve that growth—one drawback of an otherwise positive development.

Since the passage of the Humphrey-Hawkins Act in 1978, the chairman of the Board of Governors is required to testify before Congress twice each year on the Fed's conduct of monetary policy. This testimony covers the Fed's goals and the ways in which it intends to use monetary policy to achieve those goals. The central bank almost always faces conflicting goals. In the background of Chairman Greenspan's testimony was a tension between the goals of long-term price stability and the economy's recovery. Lower short-term interest rates might help the sputtering economy, but the Fed would also look out for signs of inflation.

a Chairman Greenspan's lack of discussion about money supply measures indicates that monetary aggregates per se are not intermediate targets for the Fed. Indeed, the Fed hasn't used a strict intermediate target–operating target approach to achieve its goals. Instead, it works with interest rate targets that are consistent with the goal of low inflation while using information on a number of financial variables to monitor its progress.

b The weakening economy put downward pressure on inflation in the short run. The chairman's testimony also included discussion of the Fed's goal of price stability. To maximize the effectiveness of this focus, the Fed should clearly articulate its goals for inflation. If, for example, market participants believe that the Fed's actions reflect an acceptance of the current level of inflation or one that is slightly higher, then long-term rates may rise. To make sure its intentions are clear to the market, the Fed should communicate what rates of inflation it believes are unacceptable and what policy actions it believes are consistent with acceptable rates and then implement those actions.

c One consequence of the very large projected federal budget surpluses is that the supply of U.S. government debt is expected to be reduced substantially—by some estimates to close to zero—over the period from 2001 to 2006. The Federal Reserve has traditionally conducted open market operations by buying and selling U.S. Treasury securities. If the supply of Treasury securities were too small, the Fed could still conduct open market operations, but it would have to purchase other debt instruments—in particular securities issued by state governments or foreign governments.

For further thought . . .

Most analysts believe that current monetary aggregates are not useful intermediate targets because their relationships with output growth or inflation are not stable. Does this belief imply that monetary aggregates generally are uninformative for the central bank? Explain.

Source: Excerpted from Greg Ip, "Greenspan Presents a More Upbeat View," *The Wall Street Journal*, February 14, 2001. Republished by permission of Dow Jones, Inc. via Copyright Clearance Center.

ANALYTICAL PROBLEMS

18. *Evaluate:* If the Fed uses the federal funds rate as an operating target, increases (decreases) in the demand for money increase (decrease) the money supply.
19. State whether each of the following variables is most likely to be a goal, an intermediate target, an operating target, or a monetary policy tool.
    a. *M2*
    b. Monetary base
    c. Unemployment rate
    d. Open market purchases
    e. Federal funds rate
    f. Nonborrowed reserves
    g. *M1*
    h. Real GDP growth
    i. Discount rate
20. A recent proposal suggested that the Fed use the monetary base as its operating target to achieve a specified nominal GDP range as its intermediate target. What are the pros and cons of this suggestion?
21. How does using interest rates as an operating or intermediate target lead to procyclical monetary policy? How could policymakers use interest rates in the policy process and avoid procyclical policy?
22. Design a mechanism for monetary policy control of the economy, assuming that the Fed had a good model of the economy that provided accurate forecasts. Why would such a procedure be less useful with less accurate forecasts?
23. When would a simple rule for monetary policy, such as one that makes *M2* rise at a steady rate of 3% each year, be valid? When would problems with such a rule occur?
24. Outline a procedure for Fed control of the federal funds rate. Is this procedure consistent with control of the money supply process? Why or why not?
25. *Evaluate:* If the Fed uses nonborrowed reserves as its operating target, increases (decreases) in the demand for money increase (decrease) the money supply.
26. *Evaluate:* The money supply is inherently procyclical, rising during (and amplifying) economic expansions and declining during (and amplifying) economic contractions.
27. Does it matter for the Fed's conduct of monetary policy whether the federal government's budget is balanced, in surplus, or in deficit? Choose a particular time period in the years since 1945 to illustrate your answer.

Use graphical analysis of the money market to answer Questions 28 and 29.

28. Does using the federal funds rate as an operating target imply that the money supply curve is horizontal? Why or why not?
29. Do interest rate targets help the Fed to soften the impact of economic downturns? Why or why not?

DATA QUESTION

30. Look through past issues of the *Federal Reserve Bulletin* to find when the chairman of the Fed's Board of Governors last testified before Congress as required by law under the Humphrey-Hawkins Act. The chairman testifies twice each year, in February and July. Read through the chairman's testimony and identify the variables that the Fed is using as operating targets and intermediate targets. What other variables does the chairman mention as important indicators for the economy? Can you identify the Fed's goals?

CHAPTER 22

The International Financial System and Monetary Policy

Foreign-exchange traders were caught offguard. Currency traders expected the foreign-exchange value of the dollar to continue to rise against the euro. In a powerful show of force, the Federal Reserve, the European Central Bank, and the Bank of Japan bought billions of U.S. dollars worth of euros in the foreign-exchange market on September 22, 2000, and sent the value of the yen soaring against the dollar. The Fed, the U.S. Treasury, and the European Central Bank were trying to break the euro's downward spiral against other leading currencies.

This example demonstrates that central banks participate in international currency markets. In our discussion of the Fed's role in the money supply process, we limited our investigation to the domestic economy. But the Fed and central banks in other countries also attempt to manage the exchange rates of their currencies. In August 1995, the Fed acted aggressively to increase the dollar's foreign-exchange value; in the episode described above, the Fed bid down the value of the dollar against another currency. A central bank's role in the international financial system also influences its ability to conduct domestic monetary policy.

In this chapter we focus on the central bank's participation in the foreign-exchange market. We begin by showing how the Fed's and other central banks' actions influence the monetary base and then describe the effect of these transactions on the exchange rate. We then shift our focus to the interaction of the Fed with other central banks in the international financial system. After describing the Fed's transactions in the international financial system, we explain the relationship between the Fed's transactions and other flows of capital and goods in international markets by analyzing the balance-of-payments accounts. Political forces as well as economic forces influence the Fed's international transactions and monetary policy. In particular, the exchange rate system determines how a central bank must act in influencing the foreign-exchange value of its currency. In the fourth section of the chapter, we describe different exchange rate systems and their effect on domestic monetary policy. As we did for domestic monetary policy in Chapter 21, we also examine the successes and failures of different exchange rate systems.

FOREIGN-EXCHANGE INTERVENTION AND THE MONEY SUPPLY

In our analysis of the money supply process, we described the actions of three participants: the central bank, the banking system, and the nonbank public. However, because international financial markets are linked, *foreign* central banks, banks, and savers and borrowers also can affect the domestic money supply. In particular, international financial transactions affect the money supply when central banks or governments try to influence the foreign-exchange values of their currencies. As a result, such intervention may cause domestic and international monetary policy goals to conflict.

The Federal Reserve and other central banks participate in international markets to control the foreign-exchange value of their currency. The term **foreign-exchange market intervention** describes deliberate actions by a central bank to influence the exchange rate. Foreign-exchange market interventions alter a central bank's holdings of **international reserves**, assets that are denominated in a foreign currency and used in international transactions.

If the Fed wants to increase the value of the dollar, it will sell foreign securities and buy dollars in international currency markets. If the Fed wants to reduce the value of the dollar, it will sell dollars and buy foreign assets. Such transactions affect the domestic monetary base, as you can easily observe by noting the changes in the Fed's balance sheet.

Suppose, for example, that in an effort to reduce the foreign-exchange value of the dollar, the Fed buys foreign assets, say, short-term securities issued by foreign governments, worth a dollar value of $1 billion. This transaction increases the Fed's international reserves by $1 billion—hence the Fed's foreign assets rise by $1 billion. If the Fed pays for the foreign assets by writing a check for $1 billion, it adds $1 billion to banks' deposits at the Fed. Reserves of the banking system, a Fed liability, also rise by $1 billion. We can summarize the effect of this transaction on the Fed's balance sheet as follows:

FEDERAL RESERVE

Assets		Liabilities	
Foreign assets (international reserves)	+$1 billion	Bank deposits at Fed (reserves)	+$1 billion

Alternatively, the Fed could pay for the foreign assets with $1 billion of currency. Because currency in circulation also is a liability for the Fed, its liabilities still rise by $1 billion:

FEDERAL RESERVE

Assets		Liabilities	
Foreign assets (international reserves)	+$1 billion	Currency in circulation	+$1 billion

Because the monetary base equals the sum of currency in circulation and banking system reserves, either transaction causes the monetary base to rise by the amount of the foreign assets (international reserves) acquired. In other words, a purchase of foreign assets by a central bank has the same effect on the monetary base as an open market purchase of government bonds. When a central bank buys foreign assets, its international reserves and the monetary base increase by the amount of foreign assets acquired.

Similarly, if a central bank sells foreign assets to purchase its domestic-currency-denominated assets, its holdings of international reserves and the monetary base fall. Suppose that the Fed sells $1 billion of foreign assets to buy $1 billion of domestic assets. The Fed loses international reserves, causing its foreign assets to fall by $1 billion. At the same time, if the purchasers of the foreign assets sold by the Fed pay with checks drawn on domestic banks, banks' reserves at the Fed, a Fed liability, fall by $1 billion. The transaction affects the Fed's balance sheet as follows:

FEDERAL RESERVE

Assets		Liabilities	
Foreign assets (international reserves)	−$1 billion	Bank deposits at Fed (reserves)	−$1 billion

If the Fed had instead purchased domestic currency with the proceeds of its sale of foreign assets, currency in circulation (another Fed liability) would have fallen by the amount of foreign assets sold. Because the monetary base is the sum of currency in circulation and reserves, it falls by the amount of foreign assets (international reserves) sold, regardless of whether the Fed buys domestic bank deposits or currency with the proceeds.

In other words, a sale of foreign assets by a central bank has the same effect on the monetary base as an open market sale of government bonds. Purchases of domestic currency by a central bank financed by sales of foreign assets reduce international reserves and the monetary base by the amount of foreign assets sold.

When a central bank allows the monetary base to respond to the sale or purchase of domestic currency in the foreign-exchange market, the transaction is called an **unsterilized foreign-exchange intervention.** Alternatively, the central bank could use domestic open market operations to offset the change in the monetary base caused by a foreign-exchange intervention. To demonstrate, consider a Fed sale of $1 billion of foreign assets. In the absence of any offsetting interventions, the monetary base falls by $1 billion. At the same time, however, the Fed could conduct an open market purchase of $1 billion of government bonds to eliminate the decrease in the monetary base arising from the foreign-exchange intervention. In this case, the Fed's assets fall by $1 billion when it sells foreign assets. As we showed earlier, the monetary base falls by $1 billion if the Fed does nothing else. However, a Fed purchase of $1 billion of securities on the open market would restore the monetary base to its level prior to the foreign-exchange intervention. The following example illustrates these transactions:

FEDERAL RESERVE

Assets		Liabilities	
Foreign assets (international reserves)	−\$1 billion	Monetary base (currency in circulation and reserves)	+\$0 billion
Securities	+\$1 billion		

A foreign-exchange intervention that is accompanied by offsetting domestic open market operations that leave the monetary base unchanged is called a **sterilized foreign-exchange intervention.**

CHECKPOINT

What is the effect on the Japanese monetary base if the Bank of Japan purchases \$5 billion in the foreign-exchange market? The Bank of Japan's holdings of international reserves rise by \$5 billion, and the Japanese monetary base increases by the yen equivalent of \$5 billion. **o**

FOREIGN-EXCHANGE INTERVENTION AND THE EXCHANGE RATE

If foreign-exchange interventions affect the domestic money supply, why do central banks intervene? Central banks and governments seek to minimize changes in exchange rates. A depreciating domestic currency raises the cost of foreign goods and may lead to inflation. Central banks attempt to reduce depreciation by buying their own currencies in the foreign-exchange market. Conversely, an appreciating domestic currency can make a country's goods uncompetitive in world markets. Central banks attempt to reduce appreciation by selling their own currencies in the foreign-exchange market.

In this section, we examine the effects of unsterilized and sterilized foreign-exchange market interventions on the exchange rate, using the graphical analysis of exchange rate determination developed in Chapter 8. Recall from that analysis that traders and investors—individuals, businesses, governments, and central banks—in asset markets determine the exchange rate in the short run. At the equilibrium exchange rate, expected returns on domestic and foreign assets (expressed in domestic currency terms) are equal. Hence at that exchange rate, investors are indifferent between holding domestic and foreign assets.

Unsterilized Intervention

Let's begin with unsterilized intervention. Figure 22.1 shows interventions to increase and decrease the exchange rate. The exchange rate, *EX*, is expressed in

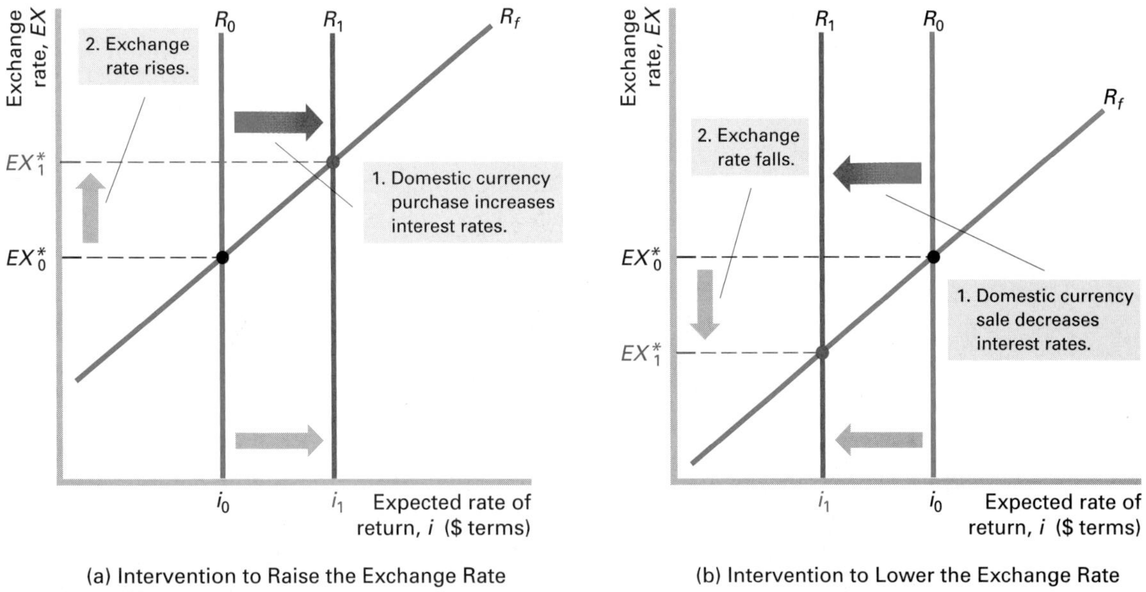

Figure 22.1 **Unsterilized Foreign-Exchange Market Interventions and the Exchange Rate**

As shown in (a):

1. To raise the exchange rate, the central bank must buy domestic currency, losing international reserves and decreasing the monetary base.
2. Domestic short-term interest rates increase from i_0 to i_1, so the expected rate of return on domestic assets rises from R_0 to R_1. That causes the exchange rate to rise from EX_0^* to EX_1^*.

As shown in (b):

1. To lower the exchange rate, the central bank must sell domestic currency, gaining international reserves and increasing the monetary base.
2. Domestic short-term interest rates decrease from i_0 to i_1, so the expected rate of return on domestic assets falls from R_0 to R_1. This causes the exchange rate to fall from EX_0^* to EX_1^*.

foreign currency per unit of domestic currency. The curve representing the expected rate of return on domestic deposits, R, is vertical (at the domestic interest rate, i). The curve representing the expected rate of return on foreign deposits, R_f, slopes upward to the right. Recall from Chapter 8 that $R_f = i_f - \Delta EX^e/EX$, where i_f is the foreign interest rate and ΔEX^e is the expected appreciation of the domestic currency. Thus, if savers' expectations of the future exchange rate cause EX to rise, the foreign currency is expected to appreciate, which in turn increases R_f. When capital and foreign-exchange markets are in equilibrium, the expected rate of return on domestic assets equals the expected rate of return on foreign assets ($R_0 = R_f$); the equilibrium exchange rate is EX_0^*.

Suppose that the central bank wants to increase the exchange rate from EX_0^* to EX_1^*, as in Fig. 22.1(a). To raise the foreign-exchange value of its currency, the central bank must buy domestic currency (or domestic deposits) from foreigners and sell foreign assets. The transaction resembles a domestic open market sale of securities because the foreign-exchange intervention reduces the monetary base. If nothing else changes, the intervention increases the domestic short-term interest rate from i_0 to i_1. As a result, the domestic expected rate of return shifts to the right from R_0 to R_1. Because the expected rate of return on domestic assets has increased relative to the expected rate of return on foreign assets, investors will increase their demand for domestic assets and domestic currency. The exchange rate then rises from EX_0^* to EX_1^*.[†] Thus, if nothing else changes, an unsterilized intervention in which the central bank sells foreign assets to purchase domestic currency leads to a decrease in international reserves and in the money supply and an appreciation of the domestic currency.

Conversely, suppose that the central bank wants to lower the exchange rate with unsterilized foreign-exchange intervention, as represented in Fig. 22.1(b). The central bank buys foreign assets, increasing the monetary base and reducing the short-term interest rate from i_0 to i_1. The domestic expected rate of return shifts from R_0 to R_1. The expected rate of return on domestic assets has declined relative to the expected rate of return of foreign assets, so investors will reduce their demand for domestic assets and domestic currency. The exchange rate falls from EX_0^* to EX_1^*. Thus, if nothing else changes, an unsterilized intervention in which the central bank buys foreign assets and sells domestic currency leads to an increase in international reserves and the money supply and depreciation of the domestic currency.

CHECKPOINT

Suppose that the Fed pursues a contractionary monetary policy to increase the short-term interest rate in the United States. What would you predict the consequences for the exchange rate to be? All else being equal, the higher expected rate of return on dollar assets increases the demand for U.S. assets relative to foreign assets, causing the dollar to appreciate. o

Sterilized Intervention

In analyzing the effects of an unsterilized foreign-exchange intervention, we assumed that domestic and foreign assets are perfect substitutes. This assumption means that the expected rates of return on domestic and foreign assets are equal in equilibrium. Because a sterilized foreign-exchange intervention doesn't affect the money supply, it will not affect domestic interest rates or expected appreciation of the domestic currency. Hence the domestic expected rate of return, R, and foreign expected rate of return, R_f, do not shift. Thus a sterilized intervention does not affect the exchange rate.

---

†The decline in the domestic money supply may increase expected appreciation of the domestic currency, causing R_f to shift to the left, further raising the exchange rate. For simplicity, we ignore this effect here.

When domestic and foreign assets are not perfect substitutes, an increase in the supply of domestic assets implies greater exchange rate risk, raising the risk premium for the domestic expected rate of return and reducing the exchange rate.† In theory, with a currency risk premium, an increase in the domestic money supply from a sterilized intervention leads to depreciation of the domestic currency, as in the case of an unsterilized intervention. However, most studies by economists have concluded that a sterilized intervention has virtually no effect on the exchange rate. Hence effective central bank interventions that are intended to affect the exchange rate are generally unsterilized.

The currency premium $h_{f,d}$ can be negative; domestic investors may require a higher expected return on foreign assets than on domestic assets. Many economists believe that domestic and foreign assets are imperfect substitutes because investors face difficulties in gathering information about foreign assets or because foreign assets may be exposed to risks of seizure by foreign governments.

Capital Controls

If domestic and foreign assets are not perfect substitutes—that is, if they don't have similar risk, liquidity, and information characteristics—a sterilized intervention can affect the exchange rate. In the past, **capital controls,** or government-imposed barriers to foreign savers investing in domestic assets or to domestic savers investing in foreign assets, caused foreign assets to be less liquid than domestic assets. (Explicit capital controls are now relatively rare in most industrialized countries, though in response to the Asian financial crisis some emerging economies imposed them in 1998.) Capital controls also limit domestic investors' ability to diversify their portfolios internationally, leading those investors to require a higher expected return on domestic assets than on foreign assets.

The major currency crises of the 1990s in Mexico and East Asia were fueled in part by significant changes in capital inflows and capital outflows, leading some economists and politicians to advocate restrictions on capital mobility in emerging market countries. Although capital outflows were, indeed, an element of the financial crises—leading some political leaders such as Malaysian Prime Minister Mahathir to limit capital outflows—most economists remain skeptical about the effectiveness of such controls. In principle,

---

†In this case, the nominal interest rate parity condition in the foreign-exchange market reflects a currency risk premium $h_{f,d}$ [introduced in Chapter 8, Eq. (8.7)]:

$$i = i_f - \frac{\Delta EX^e}{EX} + h_{f,d}.$$

With the addition of a risk premium, a sterilized foreign-exchange market intervention can affect the exchange rate; that is, if a sterilized sale of the domestic currency increases $h_{f,d}$, then, if nothing else changes, EX must fall to satisfy the interest rate parity condition.

controls can further weaken confidence in the government and the domestic financial system. In practice, they can precipitate evasion by and corruption of public officials.

Capital inflow restrictions receive more support from economists, in part because such inflows often lead to domestic lending booms and increased risk taking by domestic banks. Other economists point out that this problem could be made less severe by improving bank regulation and supervision in emerging market countries. In this way, capital inflows could still serve as important financial mechanisms for channeling foreign investment to countries with promising investment opportunities.

Recent Fed Interventions

Since the early 1970s, the foreign-exchange value of the dollar has been determined in currency markets. Nonetheless, the Fed and the Treasury have intervened in the foreign-exchange market on several occasions to increase or decrease the exchange rate. U.S. officials carry out intervention through the Exchange Stabilization Fund at the Treasury. The Treasury is the senior authority in organizing foreign-exchange interventions, although it trades through the Federal Reserve Bank of New York. The FOMC has independent authority to conduct foreign-exchange interventions, but in practice, the Treasury and the Fed coordinate their efforts.

During the 1980s, the Reagan administration and the Fed pursued interventions at alternative times to raise or lower the foreign-exchange rate of the dollar. In 1981, the incoming administration announced that it would not intervene in the foreign-exchange market, even though the dollar was appreciating because of high domestic real interest rates. After the dollar's value had almost doubled relative to other major currencies between early 1981 and September 1985, Treasury Secretary James Baker and Federal Reserve Chairman Paul Volcker met with their counterparts from France, Germany, Japan, and the United Kingdom in New York to achieve an agreement to bring down the foreign-exchange value of the dollar. These countries agreed, in the so-called Plaza Accord, to a joint effort to reduce the dollar's value and stabilize the values of the other four currencies against the dollar. Another round of interventions followed in February 1987, the so-called Louvre Accord, which established unofficial trading ranges for currencies. In January 1988, major central banks intervened to halt the dollar's slide and stabilize exchange rates for a time. In the late 1980s and the 1990s, the Treasury and Fed continued to intervene in foreign-exchange markets. In September 2000, the Fed joined the European Central Bank and other central banks to support the euro. Most analysts believe that it is increasingly difficult for governments and central banks to affect the exchange rate by intervening in today's vast foreign-exchange market, in which more than $1 trillion changes hands daily. In early 2001, Treasury Secretary Paul O'Neill announced that the Bush administration would not intervene in the foreign-exchange market to affect the value of the dollar.

BALANCE OF PAYMENTS

In describing the foreign-exchange market interventions that the Fed undertakes to manage the exchange rate, we simply noted the increase or decrease in international reserves on the Fed's balance sheet without any mention of why the central bank holds the reserves or what factors account for the size of reserve holdings. Transactions in international reserves are one of several capital flows between the United States and other countries. To understand how

CASE STUDY

Do Sterilized Interventions Affect the Exchange Rate?

Beginning in the mid-1980s, the G7 countries—the United States, Japan, Germany, Canada, Italy, France, and the United Kingdom—have occasionally pursued coordinated sterilized interventions to influence the dollar's value in world currency markets. According to our theory, sterilized interventions are unlikely to change the exchange rate, but some empirical studies have claimed that concerted interventions by major central banks affect the exchange rate by signaling future changes in monetary policy. In one study, Pietro Catte, Giampoalo Galli, and Salvatore Rebecchini found that all 19 interventions between 1985 and 1991 were successful to some degree.[†] Critics of such studies note that central banks may not intervene at all unless they perceive that they can influence currency markets at that time.

In a later study, Maurice Obstfeld of the University of California, Berkeley, analyzed the ability of interventions between 1993 and 1995 to affect the yen–dollar exchange rate.[††] He found little evidence to support the claim that interventions per se can slow down foreign-exchange market trends and no evidence that they can reverse market trends. The one exception was the intervention of August 14, 1993, which pushed up the dollar's value against the yen. Obstfeld noted, however, that the intervention coincided with a statement by then U.S. Treasury Department Undersecretary Lawrence Summers that the United States did not intend to use dollar depreciation as a means of gaining access to Japanese markets.

To summarize, although coordinated changes in monetary policy are likely to affect the exchange rate, sterilized interventions by themselves are unlikely to have a long-term effect on the exchange rate.

[†] Pietro Catte, Giampoalo Galli, and Salvatore Rebecchini, "Concerted Interventions and the Dollar: An Analysis of Daily Data," in Peter B. Kenen, Francesco Papadia, and Fabrizio Saccomani, eds., *The International Monetary System*. Cambridge, UK: Cambridge University Press, 1995.

[††] Maurice Obstfeld, "International Currency Experience: New Lessons and Lessons Relearned," *Brookings Papers on Economic Activity* 1:119–220, 1995.

USING THE NEWS . . .

The U.S. Balance of Payments

Information on the balance of payments is widely reported in newspapers. The trade balance receives special attention when it is reported near the end of each month. The U.S. Department of Commerce publishes the complete balance-of-payments accounts quarterly in the *Survey of Current Business.* Forecasters, traders, and financial institutions use them to predict changes in exchange rates and interest rates.

Source: Survey of Current Business.

	Transactions, 1999	$ billion
Trade balance (2) + (6) = −$345.5 billion	1. Exports of goods, services, and income (2 + 3 + 4)	1232.4
	2. Goods	684.4
	3. Services	271.9
	4. Income receipts on investments	276.2
Current account balance (1) + (5) + (9) = −$331.5 billion	5. Imports of goods, services, and income (6 + 7 + 8)	−1515.9
	6. Goods	−1029.9
	7. Services	−191.3
	8. Income payments on investments	−294.6
	9. Unilateral transfers	−48.0
Official settlements balance (12) + (16) = $51.6 billion	10. Capital account transactions, net	−3.5
	11. U.S. assets abroad, net [increase of capital outflows (−)] (12 + 13 + 14)	−430.2
	12. U.S. official reserve assets	−8.7
	13. U.S. government assets (other than ORA), net	2.8
Capital account balance (10) + (11) + (15) = $319.9 billion	14. U.S. private assets, net	−441.7
	15. Foreign assets in the U.S., net [increase of capital inflow (+)] (16 + 17)	753.6
	16. Foreign official assets, net	42.9
	17. Other foreign assets, net	710.7
	18. Allocations of Special Drawing Rights	0.0
	19. Statistical discrepancy	−11.6

the Fed amasses international reserves and how much it has available for foreign-exchange market interventions, we must look at the broader flow of funds between the United States and foreign countries. The simplest way to describe these international capital flows is by studying the balance-of-payments accounts. The **balance-of-payments accounts** measure all flows of private and government funds between a domestic economy (in this case, the United States) and all foreign countries.

The balance of payments for the United States is a bookkeeping procedure similar to one that households or businesses might use to record receipts and payments. In the balance of payments, inflows of funds from foreigners to the United States are *receipts,* which are recorded as positive numbers. Receipts include inflows of funds for purchases of U.S.-produced goods and services (U.S. exports), for acquisition of U.S. assets (capital inflows), and as gifts to U.S. citizens (unilateral transfers).

Outflows of funds from the United States to foreigners are *payments,* which are recorded with a minus sign. Payments include purchases of foreign goods and services (imports), money spent on purchases of foreign assets by U.S. households and businesses (capital outflows), and gifts to foreigners, including foreign aid (unilateral transfers). The principal components of the balance-of-payments accounts summarize transactions for purchases and sales of goods and services (the current account balance, which includes the trade balance) and flows of funds for international lending or borrowing (the capital account balance, which includes the official settlements balance). In exploring which cash flows belong to each component, you will see how the flows of funds generated from international transactions influence the economy and the Fed's source of international reserves that are needed to conduct international monetary policy.

Each international transaction represents an exchange of goods, services, or assets among households, businesses, or governments. Therefore the two sides of the exchange must always balance. In other words, the payments and receipts of the balance-of-payments accounts must equal zero, or

$$\text{Current account balance} + \text{Capital account balance} = 0. \qquad (22.1)$$

The Current Account

The **current account** summarizes transactions between a country and its foreign trading partners for purchases and sales of currently produced goods and services. To begin, the **trade balance** is the difference between goods exports and imports (line 2 plus line 6 in the table above, because imports are entered with a minus sign). The U.S. trade balance in 1999 was a deficit of $345.5 billion, with imports of $1029.9 billion exceeding exports of $684.4 billion. When exports exceed imports, the trade balance is a surplus.

The three other components of the current account are exports and imports of services (lines 3 and 7), net investment income (lines 4 and 8), and unilateral transfers (line 9). In 1999, the United States had a surplus in the sale of services, selling $80.6 billion more of services to foreigners than U.S. residents purchased abroad. Net investment income was negative for the United States in 1999 by $18.4 billion. That is, U.S. residents paid out less investment income to foreign investors than they received from foreign investments. Finally, the United States contributed, on balance, $48.0 billion in unilateral transfers. The **current account balance** equals the sum of the trade balance, services balance, net investment income, and unilateral transfers. There was a *deficit* of $331.5 billion in 1999.

If there is a current account surplus (a positive number), United States citizens have funds to lend to foreigners. If there is a negative balance, or deficit, as there was in 1999, the United States must borrow the difference to pay for goods and services purchased abroad. In particular, policymakers have been concerned about U.S. current account deficits in the 1980s, 1990s, and early 2000s because those deficits require the United States to borrow funds from foreign savers to finance the deficits. As in the case of households and businesses, governments' current account surpluses or deficits require offsetting financial transactions. A current account surplus or deficit in the balance of payments must be balanced by international lending or borrowing or by changes in official reserve transactions. Hence the large U.S. current account deficits in the 1980s, 1990s, and early 2000s caused the United States to rely heavily on savings from abroad—international borrowing—to finance domestic consumption, investment, and the federal budget deficit.

The current account balance also provides information about anticipated movements in exchange rates. If there is a current account deficit, U.S. citizens have a greater demand for foreign goods and services than foreigners have for U.S. goods and services. Therefore U.S. citizens must increase their demand for foreign currencies to buy these foreign goods and services, causing the dollar to decline in value against foreign currencies. Also international lending or borrowing to achieve a balance of payments of zero involves shifts in demand for domestic and foreign assets that can affect domestic and foreign interest rates and the exchange rate (Chapter 8).

Although the balance of payments is a set of accounting relationships, the model of lending and borrowing decisions that was introduced in Chapter 6 helps to explain what factors determine international lending and borrowing. For a large open economy such as that of the United States, factors that tend to increase national saving or international lending lead to a capital outflow and a current account surplus. Factors that tend to decrease national saving or increase international borrowing lead to a capital inflow and a current account deficit.

The Capital Account

The **capital account** measures trade in existing financial or real assets among countries. When someone in a country sells an asset (a skyscraper, a bond, or shares of stock, for example) to a foreign investor, the transaction is recorded in the balance-of-payments accounts as a **capital inflow** because funds flow into the country to buy the asset. When someone in a country buys an asset abroad, the transaction is recorded in the balance-of-payments accounts as a **capital outflow** because funds flow from the country to buy the asset. Thus, when a wealthy British investor buys a penthouse apartment in New York's Trump Tower, the transaction is recorded as a capital outflow for the United Kingdom and a capital inflow for the United States.

The **capital account balance** is the amount of capital inflows (line 15) minus capital outflows (line 11)—plus the net capital account transactions (line 10), which consist mainly of debt forgiveness and transfers of financial assets by migrants when they enter the United States. The capital account balance is a surplus if the citizens of the country sell more assets to foreigners than they buy from foreigners. The capital account balance is a deficit if the citizens of the country buy more assets from foreigners than they sell to foreigners. In 1999, the United States had capital inflows of $753.6 billion and capital outflows of $430.2 billion—plus net capital account transactions of −$3.5 billion—for a net capital account balance (an increase in U.S. assets held by foreigners) of $319.9 billion.

The Official Settlements Balance

Not all capital flows among countries represent transactions by households and businesses; changes in asset holdings by governments and central banks supplement private capital flows. **Official reserve assets** are assets held by central banks that can be used in making international payments to settle the balance of payments and conduct international monetary policy. Historically, gold was the leading official reserve asset. Official reserves now are primarily government securities of the United States and other industrialized countries, foreign bank deposits, and special assets called Special Drawing Rights created by the International Monetary Fund (an international agency, which we discuss later in this chapter).

The **official settlements balance** equals the net increase (domestic holdings minus foreign holdings) in a country's official reserve assets. Line 12 shows that the Fed decreased its holdings of official reserve assets by \$8.7 billion. (Because an increase is represented by a minus sign in the accounts—as it is a capital outflow—the positive value here indicates a decrease in holdings.) Line 16 shows that foreign central banks increased their holdings of U.S. dollar-denominated reserve assets by \$42.9 billion. This official capital inflow reflects intervention by other central banks to support the foreign-exchange value of the dollar, as well as accumulation of international reserves by emerging economies in Asia. In 1999, then, the United States had an official settlements balance of −\$8.7 billion minus \$42.9 billion, or −\$51.6 billion.

The official settlements balance is often called the *balance-of-payments surplus or deficit*. In 1999, the United States had a balance-of-payments deficit of \$51.6 billion. When a country has a balance-of-payments surplus, it gains international reserves because its receipts exceed its payments—foreign central banks provide the country's central bank with international reserves. When a country experiences an official settlements balance deficit, or a balance-of-payments deficit, it loses international reserves. Because U.S. dollars and dollar-denominated assets serve as the largest component of international reserves, a U.S. balance-of-payments deficit can be financed by a reduction in U.S. international reserves and an increase in dollar assets held by foreign central banks. Similarly, a combination of an increase in U.S. international reserves and a decrease in dollar assets held by foreign central banks can offset a U.S. balance-of-payments surplus.

Relationships Among the Accounts

Recall that, in principle, the current account balance and capital account balance sum to zero. In reality, measurement problems keep this relationship from holding exactly. An adjustment for measurement errors, the **statistical discrepancy** (line 19) is reported in the capital account portion of the balance-of-payments accounts. In 1999, it equaled \$11.6 billion (a capital inflow). Many analysts believe that large statistical discrepancies in countries' balance-of-payments accounts reflect hidden capital flows (related to illegal activity, tax evasion, or capital flight because of political risk).

To summarize, international goods and financial transactions affect both the current account and the capital account in the balance of payments. To close out a country's international transactions for balance of payments, its central bank and foreign central banks engage in official reserve transactions, which can affect the monetary base.

CHECKPOINT

Using the balance-of-payments accounts, explain what factors determined the shift for the United States from being a net creditor to being a net debtor during the 1980s. Large U.S. trade deficits (a minus sign in the balance of payments) mean that the United States is borrowing from abroad. In the balance of payments, this shows up as an inflow of foreign capital (a plus sign in the balance of payments). Hence large trade deficits are associated with the country's becoming a net debtor to foreign savers. **o**

EXCHANGE RATE REGIMES AND THE INTERNATIONAL FINANCIAL SYSTEM

The Fed and other central banks engage in foreign-exchange market interventions to maintain the foreign-exchange value of their nations' currencies. Political agreements influence the size and timing of each central bank's purchases and sales of international reserves. Specifically, nations agree to participate in a particular **exchange rate regime**, or system of adjusting exchange rates and flows of goods and capital among countries. At times, countries have agreed to fix exchange rates among their national currencies, and this agreement committed the central banks to act to maintain these exchange rates. At other times, exchange rates have been allowed to fluctuate, but central banks still often acted to limit exchange rate fluctuations. In this section, we describe those exchange rate regimes and their impact on central banks' conduct of monetary policy. In particular, we analyze exchange rate regimes in terms of (1) how the promise holds the system together, (2) how exchange rates adjust to maintain the promise, and (3) how central banks act to maintain equilibrium in the international monetary and financial system. We also evaluate successes and failures of each system.

Fixed Exchange Rates and the Gold Standard

In the past, most exchange rate regimes were **fixed exchange rate systems,** in which exchange rates were set at levels that were determined and maintained by governments. The classical gold standard that supported the international monetary and financial system before World War I illustrates the successes and failures of a fixed exchange rate system. Under a **gold standard,** currencies of participating countries are convertible into an agreed-upon amount of gold. The exchange rates between any two countries' currencies are fixed by their relative gold weights.

For example, if \$1 could be exchanged for $1/20$ of an ounce of gold while FF1 (French franc) could be exchanged for $1/80$ of an ounce of gold, \$1 = FF4 and \$0.25 = FF1. Let's consider an example of trade and capital flows between France and the United States to illustrate the effect of this system of fixed exchange rates. Under a fixed exchange rate system based on a gold standard, a U.S. importer could buy goods from a French exporter by either (1) exchanging dollars for French francs in France and buying goods or (2) exchanging dollars for gold in the United States and shipping gold to France to buy francs and French goods.

Suppose that the demand for French goods rises relative to the demand for U.S. goods, leading to a rising demand for francs and a falling demand for dollars. Hence there is pressure for the exchange rate in francs per dollar to fall in the foreign-exchange market—say, from $1 = FF4 to $1 = FF3. In this situation, U.S. importers could make a profit from shipping gold to France to buy francs, as long as the United States and France continue to exchange currencies for gold at the agreed-upon rate.

Therefore, if Sally Sharp, a cloth importer in Philadelphia, wants to buy FF5000 worth of cloth from Deluxe of Paris, she can use either of the two strategies described. First, if she tries to sell dollars for francs in the foreign-exchange market, she will find that she must pay 5000/3 = $1666.67 for the cloth. Alternatively, she can exchange $1250 for gold, ship the gold bars to France, and demand that the Bank of France exchange the gold for francs at the fixed exchange rate. At the official exchange rate of $1 = FF4, she will get FF5000 for her gold, enough to buy the cloth. The second strategy provides the cheaper solution for Sally. Sally's saving on this transaction, $416.67, makes it the best way to buy the cloth, as long as the cost of shipping the gold from Philadelphia to France does not exceed $416.67.

What happens in France as U.S. importers like Sally Sharp ship their gold to Paris? Gold flows into France, expanding that country's international reserves because gold is eventually exchanged for francs. The United States loses an equivalent amount of international reserves because dollars are given to the government in exchange for gold. An increase in a country's international reserves increases its monetary base, whereas a decrease in its international reserves lowers its monetary base. Hence the monetary base rises in France and falls in the United States, putting upward pressure on the price level in France and downward pressure on the price level in the United States. French goods become more expensive relative to U.S. goods. Therefore the relative demand for French goods falls, restoring the trade balance and causing the exchange rate to rise toward the official rate of $1 = FF4.

However, if the relative demand for U.S. goods rises, market forces put upward pressure on the exchange rate. Gold then flows from France to the United States, reducing the French monetary base and increasing the U.S. monetary base. In this case, the accompanying increase in the U.S. price level relative to the French price level makes French goods more attractive, restoring the trade balance. The exchange rate moves back toward the fixed rate of $1 = FF4.

One problem with the economic adjustment process under the gold standard was that countries with trade deficits and gold outflows experienced declines in price levels, or deflation. Periods of unexpected and pronounced deflation caused recessions. During the 1870s, 1880s, and 1890s, several deflation-induced recessions occurred in the United States. A falling price level raised the real value of households' and firms' nominal debt burdens, leading to financial distress for many sectors of the economy.

Another consequence of fixed exchange rates under the gold standard was that countries had little control over their domestic monetary policies. The reason was that gold flows caused changes in the monetary base. As a result, countries faced unexpected inflation or deflation from international trade or financial disturbances. Moreover, gold discoveries and production strongly influenced changes in the world money supply, making the situation worse. For example, in the 1870s and 1880s, few gold discoveries and rapid economic growth contributed to falling prices. In the 1890s, on the other hand, the gold rushes in Alaska and what is now South Africa increased price levels around the world.

In theory, the gold standard required that all countries maintain their promise to convert currencies freely into gold at fixed exchange rates. In practice, England made the exchange rate regime's promise credible. The strength of the British economy, its frequent trade surpluses, and its large gold reserves made England the anchor of the international monetary and financial system.

During World War I, the collapse of the international trading system led countries to abandon their promises to convert currency into gold. The gold standard had a brief revival during the period between the two world wars, but economists generally believe that it deepened the worldwide depression of the early 1930s. The Federal Reserve System's attempts to reduce gold outflows in 1930 and 1931, by increasing the discount rate, contributed to the U.S. financial crisis. Subsequently, the United States suspended the general public's right to convert dollars into gold. Ben Bernanke and Harold James of Princeton University found that countries that tried to defend the gold standard in the early 1930s suffered more severe deflation and depression than did countries that abandoned the gold standard.[†]

Adapting Fixed Exchange Rates: The Bretton Woods System

Despite the gold standard's demise, many countries remained interested in the concept of fixed exchange rates. As World War II drew to a close, representatives of the Allied governments gathered at Bretton Woods, New Hampshire, to design a new international monetary and financial system. The resulting agreement, known as the **Bretton Woods system,** lasted from 1945 until 1971. Its framers intended to reinstate a system of fixed exchange rates but to permit smoother short-term economic adjustment than was possible under the gold standard. The promise that was to hold the system together was that

[†] Ben Bernanke and Harold James, "The Gold Standard, Deflation, and Financial Crisis in the Great Depression: An International Comparison," in R. Glenn Hubbard, ed., *Financial Markets and Financial Crises.* Chicago: University of Chicago Press, 1991.

foreign central banks would be able to convert U.S. dollars into gold at a price of $35.00 per ounce. Hence agreed-upon exchange rates defined foreign currencies in dollar terms, and dollars were convertible to gold by the United States at the official price of $35.00 per ounce. The United States held this special role because of its dominant position in the global economy at that time and the fact that it held much of the world's gold. Because central banks used dollar assets and gold as international reserves, the dollar was known as the *international reserve currency.*

Under the Bretton Woods system, exchange rates were supposed to adjust only when a country experienced fundamental disequilibrium—that is, persistent deficits or surpluses in its balance of payments at the fixed exchange rate. To help countries make short-run economic adjustment to a balance-of-payments deficit or surplus while maintaining a fixed exchange rate, the Bretton Woods agreement created the **International Monetary Fund** (IMF). Headquartered in Washington, D.C., this multinational organization grew from 30 member countries to more than 150 by 1999. In principle, the IMF was to be a lender of last resort to prevent the short-term economic dislocations that threatened the stability of the gold standard. In practice, the IMF also encourages domestic economic policies that are consistent with exchange rate stability and gathers and standardizes international economic and financial data to use in monitoring member countries.

Not directly related to its establishment of the international monetary system, the Bretton Woods agreement created the **World Bank,** or International Bank for Reconstruction and Development, to make long-term loans to developing countries. These loans were designed to build infrastructure (highways and bridges, power generation and distribution, and water supply, for example) to aid economic development. The World Bank raises funds to lend by selling bonds in the international capital market. Continuation of the traditional roles of both the IMF and the World Bank is currently being debated.

Although the IMF no longer attempts to foster fixed exchange rates (its core Bretton Woods system function), its activities as an international lender of last resort have grown. During the developing world debt crises of the 1980s, the IMF provided credit to such countries to help them repay their loans. IMF lending during the Mexican financial crisis (1994–1995) and the East Asian financial crisis (1997–1998) inspired major controversy over its role in the international financial system.

Advocates of IMF intervention point to the absence of a lender of last resort in emerging market financial crises. Critics of the IMF raise two counterarguments. The first is that the IMF encourages moral hazard in the form of excessive risk taking by bailing out foreign lenders. According to this view, the IMF's bailout of foreign lenders in the Mexican crisis encouraged risky lending to East Asian countries, precipitating that crisis. The second argument is that, in contrast to the IMF's treatment of foreign lenders, the institution's "austerity" programs in developing countries focus on tight macroeconomic policies, leading to unemployment and political risk.

CONSIDER THIS . . .

Are the IMF and the World Bank Obsolete?

Some analysts argue for rethinking the purposes of the IMF and the World Bank. These multilateral lending institutions have outlived the Bretton Woods system that created them. In the 1940s and 1950s, the international capital market was small; in the 1990s, the international capital market is the conduit for billions of dollars each day. These analysts ask, Why not let the international market make loans to governments?

Proponents of continuing the present system give two arguments. First, the IMF and the World Bank play an important role in gathering and maintaining information and expertise on the economies of many nations, particularly those of developing countries. A loan from one of these institutions can be a better indicator to private lenders of creditworthiness than can a privately rendered credit rating. Second, the IMF and the World Bank can subsidize lending by obtaining funds at a lower cost than the borrower. These reasons, they say, support the conclusion that the IMF and the World Bank should not become obsolete.

During the early 1990s, countries in Eastern Europe, the Commonwealth of Independent States, and Africa placed great demands on the IMF and the World Bank. Some critics have proposed a merger of the two institutions as an intermediate solution for an international monetary and financial system to meet existing demands.

The IMF came under widespread criticism for its handling of the Asian financial crisis and its effects on other emerging economies (particularly Brazil) in 1997 and 1998. The principal concern was that IMF policies led to hardship for many citizens of Thailand, Indonesia, and Malaysia, while not sufficiently punishing speculators with losses, giving rise to moral hazard. While the Clinton administration and the U.S. Congress battled over whether the IMF should receive additional funding, many economists urged wholesale reform of the IMF. In particular, four principles have been urged in the reform discussion: (1) deal expeditiously with insolvent institutions; (2) adopt and enforce capital standards; (3) encourage market discipline; and (4) maintain free flows of capital. The current debate over the IMF affords an opportunity to implement reforms that can curtail the moral hazard associated with international bailouts.

In 2001, the incoming Bush administration assumed a tougher stance on IMF bailouts, urging a greater focus on providing short-term liquidity assistance.

In 1999, a U.S. congressional commission (the International Financial Institutions Advisory Commission), chaired by Allan Meltzer of Carnegie Mellon University, criticized IMF lending operations and argued for more transparency and a greater reliance on microeconomic policies to reform financial regulation. In the aftermath of the Meltzer Commission's report, the IMF remains at the center of controversy both in Washington and in emerging market economies.

The fixed exchange rate system. Central bank interventions in the foreign-exchange market to buy and sell dollar assets maintained the fixed exchange rates of the Bretton Woods system. Exchange rates could vary by 1% above or below the fixed rate before countries were required to intervene to stabilize them. If a foreign currency appreciated relative to the dollar, the central bank of that country would sell its own currency for dollars, thereby driving the exchange rate back to the fixed rate. If a foreign currency depreciated relative to the dollar, the central bank would sell dollar assets from its international reserves and buy its own currency to push the exchange rate back toward the fixed rate.

A central bank can maintain the exchange rate within the acceptable level as long as it is able and willing to buy and sell the amounts of its own currency that are necessary for exchange rate stabilization. When a foreign central bank buys its own currency, it sells dollars (international reserves); when it sells its own currency, it buys dollars. Hence there is an important asymmetry in central banks' adjustments in response to market pressures on the exchange rate. A country with a balance-of-payments surplus has no constraint on its ability to sell its own currency to buy dollars to maintain the exchange rate, although it may be unwilling to do so. However, the ability to buy its own currency (to raise its value relative to the dollar) is limited by the country's stock of international reserves.

As a result, reserve outflows caused by balance-of-payments deficits created problems for central banks that were bound by the Bretton Woods system. When a country's stock of international reserves was exhausted, the central bank and the government would have to implement restrictive economic policies to reduce imports and the trade deficit or abandon the policy of stabilizing the exchange rate against the dollar.

Maintaining the exchange rate: devaluations and revaluations. As an alternative to defending the fixed exchange rate by buying or selling reserves or changing domestic economic policies, a country can change the exchange rate. When its currency is overvalued relative to the dollar, the country can **devalue** its currency—that is, lower the official value of its currency relative to the dollar, thereby resetting the exchange rate. A country whose currency is undervalued relative to the dollar can **revalue** its currency—that is, raise the official value of its currency relative to the dollar.†

In practice, countries didn't often pursue devaluations or revaluations. Governments preferred to postpone devaluations rather than face political charges that their monetary policies were flawed. Revaluations also were not a popular choice. Domestic producers and their workers complained vigorously when the currency was allowed to rise against the dollar because domestic goods became less competitive in world markets, reducing profits and employment. The political pressures against devaluations and revaluations usually limited government changes in the exchange rate to responses to foreign-exchange market pressures.

Speculative attack. When market participants believe that the government is unable or unwilling to maintain the exchange rate, they may sell a weak

†Remember, in a flexible exchange rate system, a falling value of the exchange rate is known as *depreciation*, and a rising value of the exchange rate is known as *appreciation*.

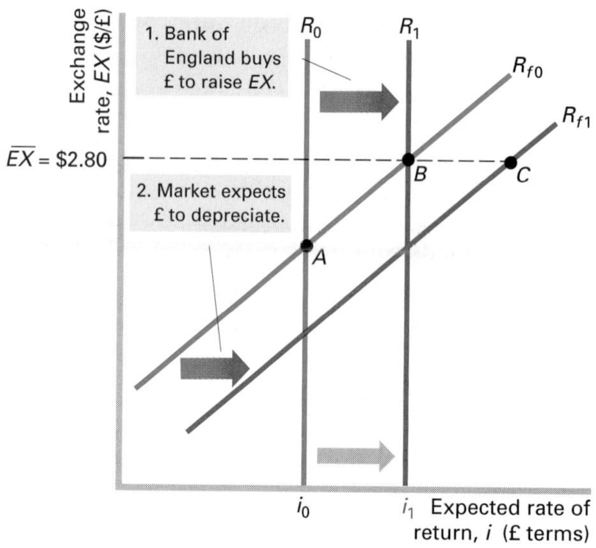

Figure 22.2

Speculative Attack on the Bretton Woods System: The British Pound, 1967

1. At A, the pound is overvalued at the official exchange rate, $\overline{EX}$. The Bank of England sells dollars to buy pounds, increasing short-term interest rates from i_0 to i_1. The domestic expected return shifts from R_0 to R_1, and the exchange rate returns to the fixed rate $\overline{EX}$ of £1 = \$2.80 at B.

2. Market participants expect the Bank of England to run out of dollars, and the R_f curve shifts from R_{f0} to R_{f1}. A significant increase in i would be required to restore an equilibrium exchange rate of $\overline{EX}$ at C. The Bank of England was forced to devalue the pound.

currency or purchase a strong currency. These actions, known as a **speculative attack**, force a devaluation or revaluation of the currency. Speculative attacks sometimes produce international financial crises. That happened in 1967, when the British pound was overvalued relative to the dollar. To explain the situation, let's use the method of exchange rate determination shown in Fig. 22.2. The intersection of the domestic expected rate of return, R_0, and the foreign expected rate of return, R_f, at point A gives an exchange rate (in \$/£) that is lower than the fixed exchange rate $\overline{EX}$ of £1 = \$2.80. To defend the overvalued exchange rate, the Bank of England had to sell dollars from its international reserves to buy pounds. The resulting decrease in the money supply increased short-term interest rates from i_0 to i_1, shifting the expected rate of return from R_0 to R_1 and momentarily restoring the exchange rate $\overline{EX}$ of £1 = \$2.80 at point B.

As the Bank of England's international reserves shrank, currency traders knew that, at some point, it would have to abandon its stabilization efforts. Speculators responded by selling pounds to the Bank of England (for \$2.80/£1), expecting the pound to fall in value against the dollar. When the pound fell, the speculators used dollars to buy back even more pounds, thus earning a substantial profit. In terms of our graphical analysis, market participants expected the exchange rate (defined from the British perspective in \$/£) to fall, thereby increasing the expected rate of return on non-British assets, R_f, relative to the British expected return R. Figure 22.2 shows the effect of this change in expectations in the shift from R_{f0} to R_{f1}. The overvaluation of the pound is even greater at the new intersection of R and R_f. This difference between the fixed and market exchange rates forced the Bank of England to buy even more pounds until it ran out of dollars. To defend the exchange rate $\overline{EX}$, the Bank of England would have had to increase short-term interest rates by an amount sufficient to maintain $\overline{EX}$ at point C. On November 17, 1967, the Bank of England lost more than \$1 billion of international reserves (on top of earlier losses of several billion dollars). On November 18, it devalued the pound by 14%.

Devaluations are forced by speculative attacks when central banks are *unable* to defend the exchange rate, as in England's 1967 crisis. Revaluations, on the other hand, can be forced by speculative attacks when a central bank is *unwilling* to defend the exchange rate. A speculative attack on the undervalued deutsche mark in 1971 forced a revaluation of the mark against the dollar and hastened the demise of the Bretton Woods system.

By 1970, the U.S. balance-of-payments deficit had grown significantly. By the first quarter of 1971, the large balance-of-payments surpluses outside the United States were causing fear in international financial markets because many currencies were undervalued relative to the dollar. Worries were greatest in Germany as the Bundesbank (the German central bank) pursued policies to maintain a low inflation rate. The Bundesbank faced a dilemma. If it defended the fixed exchange rate, it would have to sell marks in the foreign-exchange market. By doing so, it would acquire international reserves, increasing the German money supply and putting upward pressure on German prices. If it revalued the mark, it would avoid inflationary pressures but would be breaking its promise under the Bretton Woods system.

This dilemma set the stage for a speculative attack on the mark. In this case, speculators bought marks with dollars, expecting the mark to rise in value against the dollar. When the mark did rise, the speculators used the marks to buy back even more dollars, thus earning a profit.

As Fig. 22.3 shows, the intersection of the R_0 and R_f curves at point A in early 1971 yielded an exchange rate (from Germany's perspective in \$/DM) that was higher than the fixed rate of \$0.27/DM1. To defend the exchange rate, the Bundesbank had to sell marks. The resulting increase in the money supply lowered short-term interest rates in Germany, shifting the R curve from R_0 to R_1 and momentarily restoring the established exchange rate $\overline{EX}$ of DM1 = \$0.27 at point B. Because foreign-exchange market participants expected the Bundesbank to revalue the mark to avoid inflationary pressures, they also expected the mark to appreciate. These expectations decreased the expected rate of return on non-German assets relative to German assets, shifting the R_f curve to the left from R_{f0} to R_{f1}. This shift left the mark even more undervalued, and the Bundesbank had to increase its foreign-exchange intervention to maintain the fixed exchange rate. To defend the exchange rate $\overline{EX}$, the Bundesbank would have had to decrease short-term interest rates by an amount sufficient to maintain $\overline{EX}$ at point C. Having purchased more than 1 billion U.S. dollars early on May 5, 1971 (expanding its monetary base by the same amount), the Bundesbank halted its intervention later that day. The mark, along with the currencies that were tied to it, began to float against the dollar.

United States abandons Bretton Woods. One problem with the Bretton Woods system was that, even though individual currencies could be devalued or revalued against the dollar, changing the *dollar's* value required a coordinated realignment of all other currencies. This requirement was difficult to

Figure 22.3

Speculative Attack on the Bretton Woods System: The Deutsche Mark, 1971

1. At *A*, the mark is undervalued at the official exchange rate, $\overline{EX}$. The Bundesbank sells marks to buy dollars, decreasing short-term interest rates from i_0 to i_1. The domestic expected return shifts from R_0 to R_1, and the exchange rate returns to the fixed rate $\overline{EX}$ of DM1 = \$0.27 at *B*.

2. Market participants expect the Bundesbank to resist the money supply increases required to reduce the value of the mark. The expected appreciation shifts the R_f curve from R_{f0} to R_{f1}. A significant increase in the German money supply (to decrease *i*) would be required to restore an equilibrium with an exchange rate of $\overline{EX}$ at *C*. The Bundesbank revalued the mark.

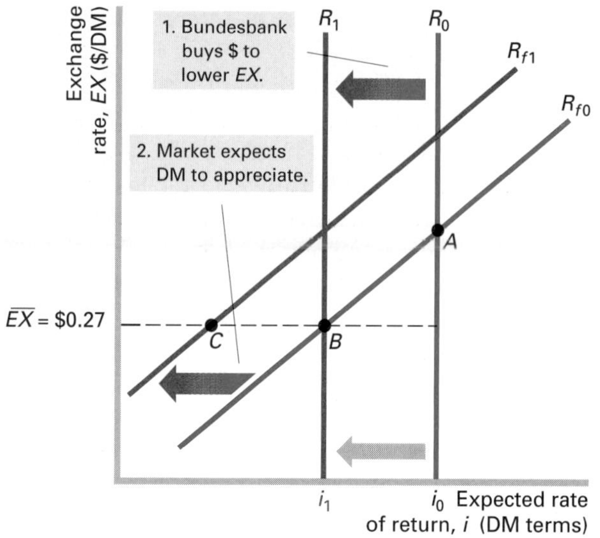

achieve in practice. As U.S. inflation increased and balance-of-payments deficits mounted in the late 1960s, foreign central banks acquired large amounts of dollar-denominated assets. Recall that the Bretton Woods system was held together by the U.S. promise to exchange foreign central banks' dollars for gold at \$35 per ounce. By 1971, however, the dollar assets that were owned by foreign central banks totaled more than three times the official U.S. gold holdings at the \$35 per ounce of gold rate. Moreover, U.S. tax policies to encourage exports and discourage imports to reduce its balance-of-payments deficit hadn't worked, and the Fed was unwilling to pursue a contractionary monetary policy. Nor would IMF intervention have worked; the IMF could not force countries such as Germany to pursue expansionary policies, and the United States, as the linchpin of the Bretton Woods system, could ignore the IMF.

On August 15, 1971, the Nixon administration attempted to force revaluations of other currencies against the dollar. The United States suspended the convertibility of dollars into gold and imposed supplementary tariffs on imports that would be reduced only if a country revalued its exchange rate. This process of revaluations against the dollar was completed at the Smithsonian Conference in December 1971. Following the revised agreement, the Fed resumed control of its own domestic monetary policy rather than being guided by pressures under the Bretton Woods system.

The exchange rate conditions that were agreed to at the Smithsonian Conference were not stable in the face of world events. The oil price shocks of 1973 and 1974 had uneven effects on economies. For example, the inflationary effect of these price increases was greater for Japan than for the United States, creating market pressures for depreciation of the yen. Such pressures spread unevenly to other countries because of the global recession of

1974–1975. In practice, many currencies began to float, although central banks intervened to prevent large fluctuations in exchange rates. At its January 1976 conference in Jamaica, the IMF formally agreed to allow currencies to float. At that conference, IMF members also agreed to eliminate gold's official role in the international monetary system.

Even before formal abandonment of the Bretton Woods system, the IMF had begun issuing (in 1970) a paper substitute for gold. The IMF creates these international reserves, known as **Special Drawing Rights** (SDRs), in its role as lender of last resort. The price of gold is now determined by the forces of demand and supply in the market.

To summarize, the Bretton Woods system was a fixed exchange rate system with a lender of last resort to smooth out short-term economic adjustments in response to balance-of-payments deficits. The lack of commitment of the United States to price stability led to strong market pressures on fixed exchange rates, ultimately causing the market to collapse. Table 22.1 compares the classical gold standard and the Bretton Woods system for fixing exchange rates.

Central Bank Intervention After Bretton Woods

Since the demise of the Bretton Woods system, the United States officially has followed a **flexible exchange rate system** in which the foreign-exchange value of the dollar is determined in currency markets. Moreover, since 1976, many countries' exchange rates have floated, being determined by demand and supply. However, the Fed and central banks abroad haven't surrendered their right to intervene in the foreign-exchange market to encourage appreciation or depreciation of the domestic currency. Nonetheless, international efforts to maintain exchange rates continue to affect domestic monetary policy.

TABLE 22.1 **COMPARISON OF EXCHANGE RATE REGIMES**

	Classical Gold Standard	Bretton Woods System
Promise anchoring the system	Currencies convertible into gold at fixed rates.	Currencies convertible into U.S. dollars at fixed rates; dollars convertible into gold at fixed rate.
Exchange rate adjustments	Not permitted.	Devaluation or revaluation permitted in response to fundamental disequilibrium.
Adjustment of economies	Money supply adjustments create inflation or deflation until the fixed exchange rate is restored.	IMF lending could smooth adjustment to short-term overvaluation of exchange rates.
Principal problems	Balance-of-payments deficits lead to deflation and recessions, with no gradual adjustment for short-term problems. Countries with balance-of-payments deficits have an incentive to abandon the promise of convertibility.	Difficult to devalue the U.S. dollar in response to U.S. balance-of-payments deficits.

Policy trade-offs. Central banks generally lose some control over the domestic money supply when they intervene in the foreign-exchange market. To raise the exchange rate (if nothing else changes), a central bank must sell international reserves and buy the domestic currency, thereby reducing the domestic monetary base and money supply. To lower the exchange rate (if nothing else changes), a central bank must buy international reserves and sell the domestic currency, thereby increasing the domestic monetary base and money supply. Hence a central bank often must decide between actions to achieve its goal for the domestic money supply and actions to achieve its goal for the exchange rate.

The case of the U.S. dollar. Because of the traditional role of the dollar as an international reserve currency, U.S. monetary policy hasn't been severely hampered by foreign-exchange market transactions. After the Bretton Woods system collapsed, the dollar retained its role as a reserve currency in the international monetary and financial system. However, during the 1980s, the Japanese yen and the German mark (as well as SDRs) became more important as additional reserve currencies. In 1990, the U.S. dollar accounted for about 60% of international reserves, with 9% and 19% accounted for by the Japanese yen and the German mark, respectively.[†] By 2000, the dollar still accounted for about 60% of international reserves. Most economists believe that the U.S. dollar isn't likely to lose its position as the dominant reserve currency in the early 2000s.

Many industrial economies have high standards of living without the privilege of their currency being the reserve currency. Nonetheless, because the dollar was less important as a reserve currency in 2001 than it was in 1951 or even 1981, many analysts believe that the United States has something to lose if the dollar is toppled from its reserve currency pedestal.

Why? First, U.S. households and businesses might lose the advantage of being able to trade and borrow around the world in U.S. currency. This advantage translates into lower transactions costs and reduced exposure to exchange rate risk. Second, foreigners' willingness to hold U.S. dollar bills confers a windfall on U.S. citizens because foreigners are essentially providing an interest-free loan. Also, the dollar's reserve currency status makes foreign investors more willing to hold U.S. government bonds, lowering the government's borrowing costs. Finally, New York's leading international role as a financial capital might be jeopardized if the dollar ceased to be the reserve currency.

During the 1980s and 1990s, some business leaders and policymakers pressured the Fed to abandon domestic monetary policy goals and either decrease or increase the value of the exchange rate. The soaring exchange rate in the early 1980s significantly hurt U.S. exports and raised criticism of the Fed for not pursuing a more expansionary monetary policy to cause the dollar to

[†] See Paul Volcker and Toyoo Ghoten, *Changing Fortunes*, New York: Times Books, 1992, p. 305.

depreciate. The Fed responded by increasing money supply growth and agreed to intervene to reduce the dollar's value after the Plaza Accord in September 1985. By February 1987, the dollar had fallen significantly from its 1985 high, and the United States and other industrialized countries met in Paris to consider interventions to halt the dollar's slide. In April and May 1991, the Fed intervened to halt the dollar's appreciation in response to political tensions in Eastern Europe and strains among the republics of the former Soviet Union. On 18 occasions between April 1993 and August 1995, the Fed sold Japanese yen and bought dollars in an attempt to halt the dollar's plunge against the yen; in June 1998, the Fed intervened again, this time to support the dollar's value against the yen. In September 2000, the Fed joined other central banks in an attempt to raise the foreign-exchange value of the euro.

Fixed Exchange Rates in Europe

One benefit of fixed exchange rates is that they reduce the costs of uncertainty about exchange rates in international commercial and financial transactions. Because of the large volume of commercial and financial trading among European countries, the governments of many European nations have sought to reduce costs of exchange rate fluctuations.

The exchange rate mechanism and European monetary union. European Economic Community member countries formed the **European Monetary System** in 1979. Eight European countries also agreed at that time to participate in an **exchange rate mechanism** (ERM) to limit fluctuations in the value of their currencies against each other. Specifically, the member countries promised to maintain the values of their currencies within a fixed range set in terms of the *ecu*, the composite European currency unit. They agreed to maintain exchange rates within these limits while allowing these rates to fluctuate jointly against the U.S. dollar and other currencies. The anchor currency of the ERM has been the German mark.

As part of the 1992 single European market initiative, European Community countries drafted plans for **European monetary union,** in which exchange rates would be fixed by using a common currency. Although these plans place severe restrictions on domestic monetary policy for the participants, a monetary union would have important economic benefits for member countries. With a single currency, for example, transactions costs of currency conversion and bearing or hedging exchange rate risks would be eliminated. In addition, the removal of high transactions costs in cross-border trades would increase production efficiency by offering the advantages of economies of scale.

Three conditions are necessary to ensure that monetary union will work in Europe, however. First, there must be either a single currency within the union or multiple currencies with immutable (absolutely unchanging) fixed exchange rates (as is the case for the euro). Second, there must be a single exchange rate (and hence a single exchange rate policy) between the union's currency and other currencies. Third, central banks of member nations must surrender domestic autonomy in conducting open market operations, setting reserve requirements, making discount loans, enforcing capital controls, and intervening in foreign-exchange markets.

Will the European monetary union be successful? If it is, it must overcome several major problems. Within Europe, there is no centralized organization for stabilizing adjustments to balance-of-payments fluctuations by individual countries. As a result, member countries of a monetary union would face greater fluctuations in income and employment from regional shocks to demand, because they wouldn't be able to adjust their exchange rates. Some economists believe that much of the political turmoil over monetary union in Europe arises from controversy about the costs of being unable to conduct independent monetary policy under a fixed exchange rate regime.

Prospects for European monetary union in practice. In 1989, a report issued by the EC recommended a common central bank, the **European Central Bank** (ECB), to conduct monetary policy and, eventually, to control a single currency. The European Monetary Institute (EMI), set up in Frankfurt on January 1, 1994, was the forerunner of the ECB. In anticipation of monetary union, the EMI coordinated the monetary policies of member countries and monitored the functioning of the ERM. The ECB, which formally commenced operation in January 1999, is structured along the lines of the Federal Reserve System in the United States, with an Executive Board (similar to the Board of Governors) appointed by the European Council and governors from the individual countries in the union (comparable to Federal Reserve Bank presidents). Like the Fed, the ECB is independent of member governments; Executive Board members are to be appointed for nonrenewable eight-year terms to increase their political independence. The ECB's charter states that the ECB's main objective is price stability.

Some analysts believe that the European Central Bank is less likely to be politically independent in practice. Member countries may well argue the merits of expansionary or contractionary monetary policies. A dominant country—such as Germany—may well prevail in a debate over monetary policy, and some members of the union will be forced to adopt policies that are inconsistent with their domestic goals. And there are differing views about domestic discretion in lender-of-last-resort roles in dealing with crises in domestic financial markets or institutions.

At Maastricht, the Netherlands, in December 1991, member countries agreed on a gradual approach to monetary union, with a goal of convergent monetary policies by the mid-1990s and completion of monetary union in Europe by January 1, 1999. To have a single currency and monetary policy required more convergence of domestic inflation rates and budget deficits than existed in the mid-1990s. By the time monetary union began in 1999, 11 countries met the conditions for participation (with respect to inflation rates, interest rates, and budget deficits). The United Kingdom, Denmark, and Sweden declined to participate, and Greece aspired to membership.

In the late 1990s, some economists suggested that the foreign-exchange

OTHER TIMES, OTHER PLACES . . .

Speculative Attack: 1990s Style

In 1991, the German government's budget deficit grew as it financed the unification of East and West Germany. To reduce inflationary pressures from the vast public expenditures that were required, the Bundesbank raised short-term interest rates. As German interest rates rose above those of England, Italy, France, and other European countries, speculators questioned whether those countries would be willing to raise their interest rates or instead would devalue their currencies against the mark. (Sweden, for example, briefly raised short-term interest rates to 500% to deter a speculative attack.)

England was the first test case. As shown in the figure, from point *A*, the Bank of England sold its foreign-exchange reserves of marks to buy large quantities of pounds to support its exchange rate against the mark under the ERM. The purchase shrank the money supply and shifted short-term interest rates from i_0 to i_1. The British domestic expected return shifted from R_0 to R_1, and the exchange rate returned to $\overline{EX}$ at point *B*. In this unstable situation, speculators used pounds to buy marks from the Bank of England, believing that the pound's imminent devaluation would enable them to use the marks to buy back more pounds. The R_f curve shifted from R_{f0} to R_{f1}.

To maintain the fixed exchange rate would require a significant increase in the British exchange rate to restore equilibrium at *C*.

Because England was suffering a recession, few analysts believed that it would be willing to tolerate high short-term interest rates to deflect a devaluation of the currency. They were right; after a week, the British government withdrew the pound from the ERM. After the British devaluation, Italy withdrew the lira and Spain devalued the peseta. As the graph shows, this episode is reminiscent of the British devaluation of the pound against the dollar in 1967. However, not all currencies were devalued.

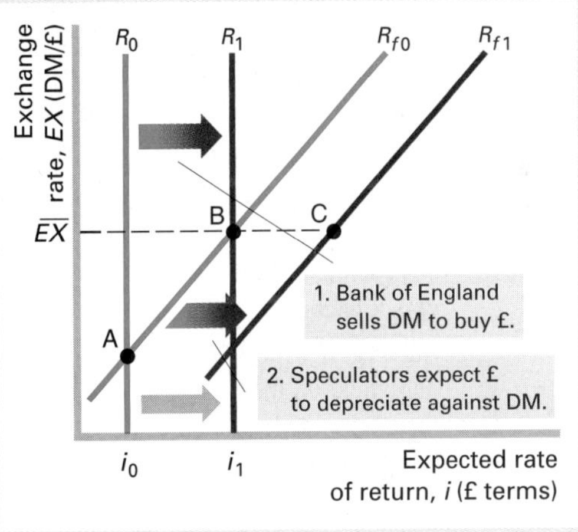

market might undermine fixed exchange rates in a speculative attack. The foreign-exchange market handles more than $1 trillion worth of dollar, yen, euro, and other currency transactions each day, as hedgers transfer risks to speculators betting on the direction of currency markets. Events of September 1992 showed that a market of this size can overwhelm the foreign-exchange market interventions of central banks and finance ministers, even when governments act in concert. During that month, speculators launched attacks on several currencies as monetary unification was being debated in Europe. Following these speculative attacks, the United Kingdom and Italy withdrew from the ERM.

CASE STUDY

Financial Collapse in Mexico

Less than three weeks after the inauguration of President Ernesto Zedillo in 1994, Mexico abandoned its acclaimed seven-year official connection between the peso and the dollar. In January 1995, the Clinton administration began putting together a financial rescue package of about $40 billion, which was subsequently implemented with a U.S. contribution of about $20 billion. What went wrong?

Though the institutional setting and history are different, the Mexican crisis has parallels to speculative attacks on European countries. In those speculative attacks, currency market participants perceived the lack of a credible commitment to an exchange rate target and forced a realignment of the exchange rate. In Mexico, the lack of a credible commitment figured prominently as well.

Mexico began pegging the peso to the dollar in December 1987; after January 1989, the peso was allowed to depreciate against the dollar, though at a very small rate, given Mexican inflation rates during the 1980s. In 1991, the Mexican government introduced a band within which the exchange rate could fluctuate. These steps were part of an effort by Mexico to demonstrate its commitment to low inflation. Accompanying these monetary policy changes were other economic reforms, including privatization of many state-owned firms, deregulation of capital markets, and a cut in public sector borrowing.

During 1994, financial markets began to doubt Mexico's resolve to defend the peso-dollar exchange rate. After the ruling party's presidential candidate, Luis Donaldo Colosio, was assassinated in March 1994, interest rates on *cetes* (one-year peso-dominated liabilities) rose relative to those on *tesobonos* (the government's three-month dollar-linked bond). This widening differential signaled expectations of a possible devaluation. Feeding this concern was inflationary pressure from a more expansionary Mexican monetary policy during 1994. Indeed, the real appreciation of the peso during 1994 outstripped increases that were plausibly based on fundamentals (such as deregulation and the passage of the North American Free Trade Agreement). With the overvalued peso, Mexico's current account deficit rose to nearly 8% of GDP in 1994, a level of foreign borrowing that was almost impossible to explain.

Investors' fears drained the central bank's foreign-exchange reserves, particularly after Zedillo's inauguration on December 1, 1994. In response to the ensuing speculative attack on the peso, the Mexican government devalued the peso by 15% against the dollar on December 20. Speculative attacks continued, and the sharp drop in the peso's value in currency markets led the government to retreat to a floating rate. A domestic financial crisis followed.

Before the peso's collapse, the Mexican central bank faced a dilemma. The real appreciation of the peso and high nominal interest rates weakened Mexico's economic performance. The adverse consequences for economic performance could be remedied by devaluation, but a devaluation would likely signal a lack of commitment to a low rate of inflation. If Mexican monetary policy had been credibly anti-inflationary, the exchange rate collapse and financial crisis might have been avoided. Financial markets' expectation that short-run domestic concerns would carry the day led to the speculative attacks, just as it did in the European attacks.

CASE STUDY

Financial Collapse in Asia

The dizzying pace of currency devaluations and debt defaults that spread from Thailand through Asia to Russia and the emerging economies in Latin America in 1997 and 1998 left everyone from currency speculators to home buyers wondering what went wrong. When Thailand devalued the *baht* in July 1997, a small stone set off an avalanche of devaluations and shrinking output in Thailand, Indonesia, South Korea, and Malaysia—with the shock waves being felt in Japan and China. Russia's debt default in 1998 triggered another round of capital flight from emerging economies and contributed to the spectacular collapse of Long-Term Capital Management, a large U.S. hedge fund. Malaysia responded to the crisis by blaming currency speculators and imposing capital controls, leading many economists to fear a downward spiral of capital controls and trade restrictions in emerging economies.

What went wrong? Prior to the Asian financial crisis, private short-term capital flows swelled the coffers of Asian countries, stimulating substantial domestic borrowing (often in foreign-currency-denominated debt). Indeed, the swing in net private capital flows to Thailand, South Korea, Malaysia, Indonesia, and the Philippines between 1996 and 1998 was about 11% of pre-crisis GDP. In one view, subsequent shifts in market expectations and confidence were the main cause of the initial crisis—a crisis made worse by the harsh policy response of the IMF and the international financial community.

According to another view, the Asian economies entered 1997 with weak economic and financial fundamentals. In these economies, weak banks with lax supervision and poor risk management provided a recipe for moral hazard—excessive risk taking and lending to unprofitable investment projects. The international dimension of the moral hazard problem required moral hazard by international banks, which prior to the crisis loaned large sums to the region's domestic financial intermediaries. (The debt accumulated in this way consisted mainly of foreign-currency-denominated liabilities.) Weaknesses in the undercapitalized financial system led to a buildup of nonperforming loans, a problem exacerbated by the rapid pace of current account liberalization and financial market deregulation in the region, which increased the supply of funds from abroad.

Why did international banks participate? In this view, international lenders assumed that the short-term interbank cross-border loans would be guaranteed by explicit government intervention to bail out debtors or by an indirect bailout by the IMF. Several leading economists, including Paul Krugman, then of M.I.T., argued that anticipation of a future bailout gave international investors a strong incentive to take on excessive risk in lending to Asian economies.

Which explanation is correct? In all likelihood, both sets of factors played a role. Weak fundamentals in the economies and financial systems of Asia have spawned efforts at reform in countries ranging from Thailand to Japan. While most economists argue against policies to discriminate capital flows, criticisms of the IMF's role have been harsh. In particular, many economists encourage the IMF to conform its international lending to central banking principles—by being a lender of last resort and insisting on strong buffers for domestic banking systems to make a financial crisis less likely.

CONSIDER THIS . . .

Back to the (Currency) Drawing Board

In some emerging markets, the perception that the central bank is not committed to an exchange rate target may lead the central bank to strengthen its commitment by adopting a *currency board*—that is, by completely backing the currency with reserves of a strong foreign currency (say, U.S. dollars). Under a currency board, the central bank signals its commitment to the exchange rate target by being willing to exchange domestic currency for the foreign currency.

Such a policy offers advantages in terms of both transparency and commitment. The central bank's hands are tied so that it cannot exercise discretion to produce an inflationary monetary policy. That loss of flexibility, however, implies that the central bank will be unable to act as a lender of last resort by creating money during a financial crisis. Concern over the health of the domestic economy can also lead citizens to convert their assets to foreign currencies, contracting the domestic money supply and leading to an economic downturn.

While currency boards have been established in several countries in recent years—Hong Kong (1983), Argentina (1991), Estonia (1992), Lithuania (1994), Bulgaria (1997), and Bosnia (1998)—the Argentine experience is perhaps most illustrative of the strengths and weaknesses. To reduce inflation from stratospheric levels, Argentina implemented a currency board, fixing the exchange rate of the Argentine peso to the U.S. dollar at a one-for-one ratio. Following the introduction of a currency board, annual inflation fell to less than 5% by late 1994, and economic growth was substantial over that period. The Mexican peso crisis led to speculation about the ill health of the Argentine banking system, leading to significant conversions to dollars. The resulting sharp decline in the Argentine money supply was associated with a decline in real GDP of 5% in 1995. Assistance from the IMF and the World Bank in 1995 was required for the currency board's survival. In March 2001, the Argentine government renewed its commitment to the currency board.

An additional fear with a currency board is the risk that participants might abandon it. Some economists argue that a still stronger solution of literally using the foreign currency as the domestic currency—*dollarization*—is the better way to go. Ecuador, for example, adopted dollarization in March 2000 to reduce the chance of a speculative attack. This more extreme version of a currency board suffers from the same drawback as a currency board, plus an additional cost. When a country gives up its currency, it loses *seignorage*, the revenue received because governments do not have to pay interest on currency (which they can invest in bonds). As a result, other taxes must be raised or public spending must be reduced.

Under the exchange rate mechanism of the European Monetary System, the German mark serves as an anchor because few analysts expect it to be devalued. Therefore monetary unification is likely to give Germany, whose central bank has a strong anti-inflation reputation, the greatest power over unified monetary policy.

In the aftermath of the 1992 speculative attacks, the French ratified the Maastricht Treaty in a close vote. The treaty had been rejected by popular vote in Denmark earlier in the year, though the Danes subsequently ratified the treaty in May 1993. Though treaty ratification is now complete, a speculative attack on the French franc in July 1993 and changes in the ERM raised doubts about the viability of monetary union. Nonetheless, even in the aftermath of the Asian financial crisis, the European monetary union made its debut in 1999.

While the prospect of speculative attacks worries European policymakers, speculative attacks are by no means confined to Europe, as the case studies of Mexico and Asia show.

How Successful Are Fixed Exchange Rates Likely to Be in the Long Run?

Many countries have indicated a desire to stabilize or fix exchange rates. Going forward, how likely are fixed exchange rate arrangements to be successful in the long run? Available evidence does not indicate much hope for success for agreements among major economies.

Many small economies have successfully pegged their exchange rate against the dollar for at least a decade, though these economies generally rely on oil exports (such as Bahrain and the United Arab Emirates) or tourism (such as the Bahamas and Barbados). Other small economies have pegged their currencies to nondollar currencies (such as Monaco against the French franc and Vatican City against the Italian lira).

Postwar evidence suggests that prospects for success among large economies may be slim, however. Among larger economies, historical problems with the stability of the European Monetary System cause some analysts to doubt the ability of European countries to maintain virtually fixed exchange rates for the foreseeable future. Even Hong Kong's commitment, with foreign-exchange reserves in excess of its monetary base, may be questioned. While Hong Kong defended itself during the Asian crisis in 1997 and 1998, some economists have speculated that China, which absorbed Hong Kong on July 1, 1997, might not want to continue to use badly needed foreign-exchange reserves to battle speculators. Nevertheless, some economists in 1998 urged Indonesia, Malaysia, and Thailand to adopt a *currency board*, backing their currency with foreign-exchange reserves to bolster domestic monetary credibility.

KEY TERMS AND CONCEPTS

- Balance-of-payments accounts
  - Capital account
  - Capital account balance
  - Capital inflow
  - Capital outflow
  - Current account
  - Current account balance
  - Official reserve assets
  - Official settlements balance
  - Statistical discrepancy
  - Trade balance
- European Central Bank
- Exchange rate regime
  - Bretton Woods system
  - Devaluation
  - European Monetary System
  - European monetary union
  - Exchange rate mechanism
  - Fixed exchange rate systems
  - Flexible exchange rate system
  - Gold standard
  - Revaluation
- Foreign-exchange market intervention
  - Capital controls
  - Sterilized foreign-exchange intervention
  - Unsterilized foreign-exchange intervention
- International Monetary Fund
- International reserves
- Special Drawing Rights
- Speculative attack
- World Bank

THE WALL STREET JOURNAL SEPTEMBER 25, 2000

Central Banks Boost the Euro

The United States finally joined Europe in attempting to rescue the beleaguered euro, but Treasury Secretary Lawrence Summers wants everyone to know that doesn't mean he is abandoning the strong-dollar policy that has been a mainstay of the Clinton administration economic policy for the past five years.

a In the first U.S.-supported intervention in currency markets since Mr. Summers became secretary, the United States, Europe, Japan, Britain, and Canada bought between $3 billion and $5 billion of euros on Friday, according to foreign-exchange traders. The coordinated action stopped—at least for one day—the euro's 21-month-long decline.

The 11-nation common currency had fallen to 85.73 U.S. cents Friday morning, and was already rising when the Group of Seven major industrialized nations and the European Central Bank intervened, pushing the euro up to 90.40 cents. By late trading in New York, it had slipped a bit, to 87.84 cents.

The move came 15 years to the day after G-7 economic officials met at the Plaza Hotel in New York and agreed, successfully, to push down the U.S. dollar. But U.S. officials prefer parallels to the June 1998 U.S. intervention to help Japan boost the yen, which left the dollar in a strong position against the currencies of other major trading partners. . . .

The G-7 said it acted out of "shared concern about the potential implications of recent movements in the euro for the world economy." But Mr. Summers and Federal Reserve Chairman Alan Greenspan made sure b the Europeans agreed that their announcement would say that the action took place "at the initiative of the European Central Bank"—a loud hint that the United States is willing to help, but doesn't want to undermine the strong-dollar stance. . . .

The big test of whether the central banks succeeded comes when markets reopen this morning. Wim Duisenberg, president of the ECB, talked of an "orderly reversal" of the euro's movements, while other G-7 officials were more vague about what constitutes victory, stressing the importance of signaling investors that government won't stand aside indefinitely.

The Europeans began talking about intervention September 9 at a gathering in Versailles, France, and then started courting Washington a week ago. U.S. officials launched a series of conference calls among themselves to figure out whether it made sense to join in, should the Europeans ask. On the line were Mr. Summers; Mr. Greenspan; Peter Fisher of the Federal Reserve Bank of New York; Timothy Geithner, undersecretary of the treasury for international affairs; and Assistant Treasury Secretary Ted Truman. c One thing that made them especially cautious about risking intervention was uncertainty about why the euro was falling so quickly and therefore whether intervention would work. . . .

Mr. Greenspan then took a call from Mr. Duisenberg, who said the ECB wanted to intervene the next day and to secure U.S. support. Mr. Greenspan laid out the U.S. conditions, and Mr. Duisenberg assented. . . .

As we noted in the introduction to the chapter, the Fed intervened in foreign-exchange markets in September 2000 to bolster the value of the euro.

a The U.S. Treasury and the Fed worried about the impact of the weakening euro on European economies and on the outlook for U.S. multinational firms doing business in Europe. Within Europe, the euro's sharp drop in 1999 and 2000 fueled inflation in Europe by making imports—notably, dollar-priced oil imports—more expensive. The European Central Bank (ECB) then faced a choice between attacking incipient inflation with higher short-term interest rates—weakening European economies—or accommodating higher-than-target inflation. For the United States, weaker European economies would not be welcome news, given concerns over the duration of the U.S. expansion.

b Although the foreign-exchange market interventions cost billions of dollars, they are not likely to be effective in the long run in a market with daily foreign-exchange trading in excess of $1 trillion. Alternatively, the ECB could attempt to raise the euro's value by increasing short-term interest rates in Europe. In Fig. 22.1(a) on page [573], let R represent the euro expected return curve, and let R_f represent the U.S. expected return curve. An increase in eurozone interest rates shifts R to the right from R_0 to R_1, leading to an increase in the euro–dollar exchange rate from EX_0^* to EX_1^*. The greater the expected future depreciation of the euro against the dollar, the larger the increase in the eurozone short-term interest rate required to accomplish the decrease in the value of the current exchange rate.

The ECB maintains a number of policy goals, including a low rate of inflation and foreign-exchange market stability. On the one hand, by increasing short-term interest rates, the ECB may avert a further decline in the euro's value. On the other hand, the higher interest rate may lead to recessionary pressures in Europe. This discrepancy represents a basic tension between "foreign" and "domestic" objectives for monetary policy.

c Most economists believe that the key to fixing the European Union's currency is structural reform of European economies and their fiscal policies. Credible reform would reduce fears of future declines in the euro–dollar exchange rate. According to the nominal interest rate parity condition, a decrease in expected future appreciation of the dollar increases the current exchange rate. As the figure shows for the €/$ rate, a decrease in expected dollar appreciation shifts the R_{US} curve to the left from R_{US0} to R_{US1}, leading to an increase in the current exchange rate (measured as dollars per euro) from EX_0^* to EX_1^*.

For further thought . . .

Suppose that you are a currency trader and believe that domestic political concerns in the United States will lead the Fed to reduce U.S. short-term rates significantly. How would you react?

Source: Michael M. Phillips and G. Thomas Sims, "U.S. Joins in Action to Boost Euro," *The Wall Street Journal*, September 25, 2000. Republished by permission of Dow Jones, Inc., via Copyright Clearance Center, Inc. 2000, Dow Jones and Company, Inc.

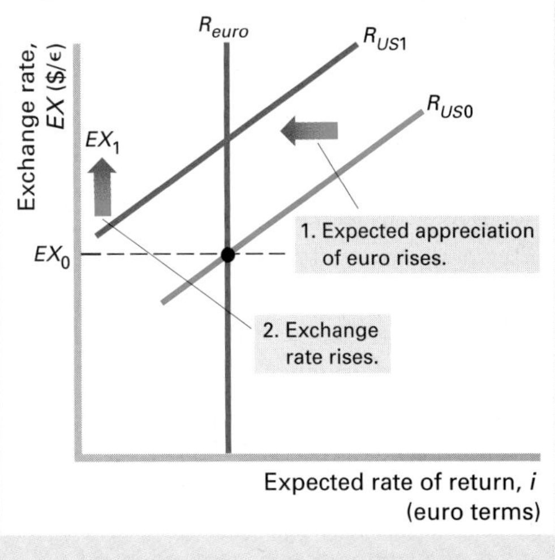

SUMMARY

1. A central bank's interventions in the foreign-exchange market affect its holdings of international reserves and the domestic monetary base. If nothing else changes, when a central bank buys foreign assets, its international reserves and monetary base increase by the amount of foreign assets acquired. When a central bank sells foreign assets, its international reserves and monetary base fall by the amount of foreign assets sold.
2. The depreciation or appreciation of a country's currency affects the domestic economy. A depreciating domestic currency raises the cost of foreign goods and may lead to inflation. Central banks hope to lessen these problems by buying their own countries' currencies. An appreciating currency may make domestic goods uncompetitive in world markets. Central banks attempt to counter this problem by selling their own countries' currencies in the foreign-exchange market.
3. The balance of payments is an accounting system for keeping track of flows of private and government funds between a country and other countries. The balance-of-payments accounts have two principal parts: the current account and the capital account. The official settlements balance in the capital account represents the net flows of international reserves that must move between countries to finance a balance-of-payments surplus or deficit.
4. Countries have entered into several international agreements to stabilize exchange rates. Before World War I, many countries agreed to convert their currencies into gold at fixed exchange rates. A second major exchange rate system, the Bretton Woods system, was established after World War II. Under the Bretton Woods system, the U.S. dollar was convertible into gold and other currencies were convertible into dollars at fixed exchange rates. Because devaluing the dollar was difficult, despite persistent U.S. balance-of-payments deficits, the Bretton Woods system collapsed in 1971. The present international financial system is best described as one in which exchange rates fluctuate with market forces but central banks intervene in the foreign-exchange market. In Europe, analysts are now observing how successful the fixed exchange rate system through European monetary union will be in practice.

REVIEW QUESTIONS

1. If the Fed buys $3 billion worth of foreign assets with dollars, what happens to U.S. international reserves? What happens to the monetary base? Is this a *sterilized* or an *unsterilized* foreign-exchange intervention?
2. Suppose that the Fed sells $1 billion worth of foreign assets in exchange for dollars; at the same time, the Fed engages in a $1 billion open market purchase. What happens to the monetary base? Is this a *sterilized* or an *unsterilized* foreign-exchange intervention?
3. Using the exchange rate diagram, show how an unsterilized intervention by Japan can be used to reduce the value of the yen relative to the dollar. Also show how an unsterilized intervention by the United States can be used to reduce the value of the yen relative to the dollar.
4. Under what key assumption does a sterilized intervention have no effect on the exchange rate? If this assumption isn't met, what is the effect on the dollar when the Fed buys foreign assets with dollars in a sterilized intervention? What do the data suggest about this assumption?
5. What are the problems with allowing a currency to appreciate relative to other currencies? What are the problems with allowing it to depreciate?
6. What is the difference between flexible and fixed exchange rate systems?
7. What is the purpose of the U.S. balance-of-payments system?
8. The following appears in a column of business commentary in a newspaper: "In recent years the newly industrializing countries have experienced very large capital inflows as multinational corporations headquartered in Japan, Western Europe, and North America have begun relocating their manufacturing facilities to these countries. With the help

of the cutting-edge technology embodied in these factories and the low wages paid to local workers, these newly industrializing countries have been able to run large current account surpluses (exporting more goods and services than they import)." An economist comments on this as follows: "This assertion can be true only if the rules of accounting and arithmetic have been repealed." Discuss.

9. If Japan has a trade surplus, which is larger, its exports or its imports?
10. Why don't countries have control of their money supplies under a gold standard?
11. Why did the United States abandon the Bretton Woods system in 1971?
12. What are the purposes of the IMF and the World Bank?
13. Under a fixed exchange rate system, why do governments often put off devaluation or revaluation? What do markets often do that forces them to devalue or revalue?
14. Why did Europe seek a monetary union in the early 1990s?
15. *Evaluate:* Because the U.S. dollar is the dominant reserve currency, the United States can experience large balance-of-payments deficits indefinitely.
16. *Evaluate:* If exchange rates are flexible, outcomes in the foreign-exchange market have no effect on domestic monetary policy.
17. Compare IMF assistance to halt a speculative attack on an overvalued currency in the Bretton Woods system to the Fed's lender-of-last-resort role for banks.

ANALYTICAL PROBLEMS

18. Suppose that new data show that the United Kingdom is about to head into a recession. Futures contracts on the pound indicate that it is expected to depreciate relative to the mark, yen, and dollar. What do you think financial markets expect the Bank of England to do in the future?
19. If you compared the sum of exports out of every country with the sum of imports into every country, what should be the world's current account balance?
20. If the U.S. current account surplus is \$105 billion and the statistical discrepancy is −\$25 billion, what is the capital account balance? Does this represent a capital outflow or inflow?
21. Under a gold standard, what happens to gold flows if a country runs persistent balance-of-payments deficits?
22. Suppose that a less developed country is running a large government budget deficit and that its central bank is not independent. What problems might this country face in pegging the value of its currency to the dollar?
23. During the fall of 1998 Brazil was attempting to peg the value of its currency against the dollar. In October an article in *The Wall Street Journal* stated: "Brazil will outline today a much-anticipated package of tax increases and budget cuts for 1999, President Fernando Henrique Cardoso said, in a move that should clear the way for the release of emergency funds from the International Monetary Fund." Why would the IMF care whether Brazil balances its budget? Why does Brazil need funds from the IMF?
24. In the spring of 1999 an article in *The Wall Street Journal* stated: "Romania's central bank vowed to intervene to defend the country's currency, the leu. . . . But traders said authorities will have to work quickly to maintain confidence in the currency. . . . With reserves at just \$1.59 billion at the end of February, the central bank's arsenal for staving off further speculation is limited." Is it likely that the Romanian central bank was trying to defend an exchange rate that was greater than or less than the exchange rate that would have prevailed in the absence of intervention? Draw a diagram to illustrate your answer. Briefly explain what traders would have to gain by speculating against the leu and what the Romanian central bank's dollar reserves have to do with its ability to defend the Romanian currency.

25. Suppose that the United Kingdom is attempting to maintain its exchange rate with Japan. But you note that Japanese real interest rates are higher than U.K. real interest rates and that inflation is lower in Japan than in the United Kingdom. What is your prediction about the future change in the ¥/£ exchange rate? What actions might you take to try to profit from your knowledge? What would happen if many other people joined you, especially if the United Kingdom had few international reserve assets?
26. If the United States, Japan, and the United Kingdom agree to try to lower the value of the dollar relative to both the yen and the pound while raising the value of the yen relative to the pound, what type of unsterilized interventions should take place?
27. Suppose that the United States has a trade deficit of $45 billion but a current account balance of $20 billion. What is the balance of net services plus investment income plus unilateral transfers?
28. Suppose that a U.S. import company buys 10 Toyota autos from Japan at $20,000 each, and the Japanese company uses the money to buy a $200,000 U.S. Treasury bond at the Treasury auction. How are these two transactions recorded in the balance-of-payments accounts for the United States?
29. Suppose that a Japanese firm donates $1 million of art to a U.S. art center. How is this transaction recorded in the balance-of-payments accounts for the United States? What is the change in the current account balance?
30. Suppose that the U.S. government sells old warships worth $300 million to Japan, and Japan's government pays for them with its official holdings of dollar assets. How is this transaction recorded in the U.S. balance-of-payments accounts?

DATA QUESTIONS

31. Look up exchange rate data in the latest *Economic Report of the President*. In 1991, the Fed increased money supply growth, reducing short-term interest rates. What happened to the value of the dollar compared to the German mark? Compared to the Japanese yen? Compared to the currencies of other countries? Are these results consistent with our theory about what happens to the exchange rate with expansionary monetary policy?
32. Describe, in general terms, the movements of the dollar against an index of the currencies of other industrial countries during the past 30 years.

PART 6

The Financial System and the Macroeconomy

The final part of the book focuses on the macroeconomy: how output and the price level are determined, and links among money, financial markets and institutions, and the economy. Chapter 23 begins this analysis by examining behavior in the money market, which is determined by money supply (Part 5) and money demand. Here we use models of money demand to explain why individuals and households hold money balances.

Chapters 24 and 25 are the key analytical chapters, offering alternative approaches to modeling and evaluating relationships between the financial system and the economy. Chapter 24 develops the *IS-LM-FE* model to explain links between interest rate determination in asset markets and output determination in the market for goods and services. In Chapter 25, we develop the *AD-AS* model, focusing on understanding, evaluating, and predicting effects of changes in aggregate demand and aggregate supply on output and the price level.

Chapters 26–28 examine ways in which monetary policy affects output and inflation. Chapter 26 studies models and evidence of links between the money supply and output and offers applications to recent policy episodes. Chapter 27 investigates how information costs in the financial system affect the way monetary policy influences the economy. In Chapter 28, we examine the causes and consequences of inflation, and we explain the link between money supply growth and inflation, costs of inflation to households and businesses, and ways in which monetary policy can reduce inflation.

CHAPTER 23

The Demand for Money

We begin our study of monetary economics and the macroeconomy by looking at behavior in the money market, which is determined by money supply and money demand. In Part 5, we studied determinants of the money supply. In this chapter, we turn to money demand. We use models of money demand to explain why individuals and businesses hold money balances—that is, cash, checkable deposits, and their close substitutes. We then use the models of money demand to show how the behavior of individuals and businesses causes the level of money balances in the economy to increase or decrease.

Our knowledge of the determinants of money demand comes from the work that economists have performed over the past century. The first model that we introduce was developed by Irving Fisher, who was interested in the effect of income on the amount of money that an individual would hold. Subsequent economists added other determinants—such as interest rates and financial innovation—to the model of money demand, and we add their interpretation to Fisher's model to conclude with a model that explains the change in money balances in today's economy.

We use the behavior of individuals and businesses in deciding on the level of money balances they wish to hold to organize our investigation of money demand. After defining the appropriate measure of money balances, we discuss *transactions motives* and build a model that shows that money demand is related to the money balances that people need to make purchases. Then we turn to *portfolio allocation motives* and demonstrate how people compare the benefits of holding money with the return they can earn on other assets. From these simpler models, we create the more detailed model that includes all of the determinants of money demand. Finally, we show that the theoretical model can explain relatively well actual changes observed in money demand. The demand for money is a key variable in the models that we build in subsequent chapters to explain links among money, the financial system, output, and prices.

TRANSACTIONS MOTIVES

Money, you will recall, serves many functions. It is a medium of exchange, a store of value, a unit of account, and a means of deferred payment. In developing early theories about money demand, economists limited their view of money to its function as a medium of exchange and proposed that the most obvious reason that households and businesses demand money (currency, checkable deposits, and other close substitutes) is for use in making transactions. This is the premise of the model that we introduce in this section: the quantity theory of money demand.

We start our analysis of this money demand model by reviving a term that measures money demand accurately: real money balances. Then we analyze the quantity theory of money demand to see how it explains changes in real money balances. Although it was a step in the right direction, the basic quantity theory of money demand failed to explain completely actual changes in real money balances. We describe problems with the theory and extend it to incorporate other motives of households and businesses for holding real money balances.

Real Money Balances

To develop an equation that accurately represents money demand, we need a term that represents money—or more precisely, the money balances that people hold to make transactions. The term that we use in all money demand models is **real money balances**, and the following example demonstrates why this is a valid measure.

In our example, we look at the decisions that two individuals make about how much cash or checkable deposits to hold. We are more interested in the benefits of cash balances to each individual than in the number of dollars or other currency they hold. Therefore, to eliminate the reliance on a specific currency, we will consider the behavior of two consumers in different countries: Theodore Cleaver, an American, and Gundal Haskell, a German. Gundal's cash balances are measured in euros, and Theodore's are measured in dollars.

Suppose also that it takes 1.1 euros to equal $1 in purchasing power. That is, prices of goods measured in euros are lower (by 1.1 times) than prices of goods measured in dollars. If Theodore and Gundal have the same money balances, the number of euros held by Gundal will be 1.1 times as large as the number of dollars held by Theodore. In other words, Gundal's nominal money balances are 1.1 times as large as Theodore's. Hence the demand for money for transactions is proportional to the price level.

We can extend this argument to money demand over time in an economy. In 1965, the price level in the United States was less than one-fourth of what it is today. No doubt your parents have told you how inexpensive eating out or going to the movies was years go. In fact, to conduct the same level of real transactions today as in 1965, you would need more than $4.00 for each 1965 dollar: Your nominal money balances would have to be more than four times as high. As was the case for Theodore and Gundal, if nothing else changes, a higher price level leads to a proportionately higher nominal demand for money.

Because changes in nominal money holdings are proportional to changes in the price level, we cannot use an expression in an equation for money demand that represents nominal cash balances because the value of that measure varies as the price level changes. Instead, we must use *real money balances*, the value of money balances adjusted for changes in purchasing power. If we let M represent the money supply and let P represent the price level in the economy (that is, the dollar price of a selected group of goods), real money balances are equal to the money supply divided by the price level, or

$$\text{Real money balances} = \frac{M}{P}.$$

The economy's real money balances represent the purchasing power of money holdings.

Velocity and the Demand for Real Balances

In the early 1900s, classical economist Irving Fisher of Yale University analyzed the relationship between real money balances and transactions. He developed a model of money demand that contained a variable called the **velocity of money**. This variable represents the average number of times a dollar is spent in the economy each year on a purchase of goods and services.[†] In our version of the velocity of money equation, we use Y, which measures aggregate output or aggregate income, to represent the volume of real transactions. In the equation for velocity, we represent total spending on goods and services by $P \times Y$, where P is the price level. M represents the quantity of money. Combining the variables for total spending and the quantity of money, Fisher defined the velocity of money as

$$V = \frac{PY}{M}. \tag{23.1}$$

If the quantity of money is \$3 trillion and nominal GDP is \$9 trillion, velocity equals 3: On average, a dollar is spent three times each year to purchase goods and services in the economy.

Multiplying both sides of Eq. (23.1) by M, we get

$$MV = PY. \tag{23.2}$$

Equation (23.2), known as the **equation of exchange,** states that the quantity of money times the velocity of money equals nominal spending in the economy. Note that the equation of exchange is an identity and therefore always holds.

[†] See Irving Fisher, *The Purchasing Power of Money*. New York: Macmillan, 1911. Fisher actually described velocity using transactions, rather than income or output. Output measures such as gross domestic product (GDP) are imperfect proxies for the volume of transactions. Purchases of assets, such as bonds, houses, or cars, require monetary transactions, but the purchases are not included in production or GDP. The annual volume of transactions is much higher than GDP, so transactions velocity is greater than velocity calculated by dividing GDP by the money stock.

This is because of the way we define velocity in Eq. (23.1); rather than observing velocity, we divide total spending by money balances to produce velocity.

To convert Eq. (23.2) into a theory of money demand that shows how the behavior of individuals and businesses in making transactions influences the quantity of real balances, *M/P*, we rewrite Eq. (23.2) as

$$\frac{M}{P} = \left(\frac{1}{V}\right)Y. \tag{23.3}$$

Fisher assumed that velocity, *V*, was a constant, and he proposed that the demand for real balances was proportional to the level of transactions.† Thus Fisher converted Eq. (23.2) into a **money demand function,** which relates the demand for real money balances to its underlying determinants. Fisher attributed the demand for real money balances to income (as the determinant of transactions). He called his explanation of money demand the **quantity theory of money demand.**

Using income as a determinant of the demand for money makes sense. To conduct everyday transactions, households and businesses increase their nominal money holdings as prices rise. What about the demand for real money balances? As the real incomes of households and businesses increase, they typically conduct more real transactions. In other words, the value of high-income households' purchases will be greater than the value of low-income households' purchases. Similarly, a large department store with sales of $10 million per year will have a greater volume of transactions with suppliers, employers, and customers than will the corner general store with annual sales of $100,000. We can generalize from this observation that the public's demand for money rises with real income. The effect on real money balances is that (if nothing else changes) the quantity of real money balances rises with real incomes.

Changes in Velocity over Time

A key assumption of Fisher's theory was that the velocity of money is constant. In Fisher's time, economic data were not measured as precisely as they are now, and so his assumption about velocity wasn't testable; today, it is. Economists generally use nominal income (GDP) to study the volume of transactions. We can obtain data on money holdings and nominal income from sources such as the *Federal Reserve Bulletin* and the Council of Economic Advisers' *Economic Report of the President* and use them to calculate velocity. Figure 23.1 illustrates the year-to-year percentage change in the velocity of money (measured using *M1* and *M2*) for each year since the founding of the Federal Reserve System in 1914. Note that velocity isn't constant, even for short periods of time. Before the late 1940s, the velocity of both *M1* and *M2* fluctuated significantly, increasing in some periods and decreasing in others.

† Fisher actually allowed for a uniform rate of growth over time in velocity, reflecting changes in means of making payments. Changes in velocity must be *predictable* to ensure the usefulness of the money demand function in Eq. (23.3).

CONSIDER THIS . . .

The Money Growth Slowdown in the Early 1990s: Was Velocity the Culprit?

Why do economists and policymakers view velocity fluctuations as a problem? The Fed uses money supply and interest rate targets to influence its goals to restrain inflation and encourage real output growth. Unpredictable changes in velocity make it more difficult for the Fed to use targets for the money supply to achieve its goals. The significant instability of *M1*'s velocity during the 1980s led the Fed to drop its targets for *M1* after 1987. Since that time, it has relied on indicators of inflation and, to a lesser extent, on *M2*.

During the early 1990s, the Fed was unsuccessful in achieving its *M2* growth targets. The Fed's 1992 annual target range for *M2* growth was 2.5–6.5%. However, the Fed achieved only about 1.5% growth. Therefore 1992 was the third year in a row for which the Fed failed to achieve much above the lower end of its target growth rate range. Many analysts and policymakers blamed the Fed's failure to hit its money growth targets for the economy's slow recovery from recession.

The Fed focused on *M2* because of its predictable relationship with the level of nominal GDP. From 1959 to 1989, the *M2* velocity—nominal GDP divided by *M2*—was stable. In the early 1990s, the relationship between *M2* and nominal GDP broke down. From 1989 through 1992, yields on Treasury bills and other short-term securities declined much faster than deposit rates on *M2* assets, thus lowering the opportunity cost of holding *M2*. This reduction in opportunity cost should have increased money demand and reduced velocity, but velocity stayed roughly constant.

What happened? Most of the collapse in *M2* growth can be explained by the drop in the amount of small time deposits, which resulted in part from the closing of weak savings and loan institutions. In addition, time deposits at commercial banks fell because banks tend to adjust yields on small time deposits much more rapidly than they adjust yields on checking and saving accounts. As a result, a change in the opportunity cost of holding checkable deposits (one component of *M2*) wasn't the same as a change in the opportunity cost of holding small time deposits (another component of *M2*), so velocity was unstable.

During the period from early 1994 to early 1995, a surge in velocity also led to slower-than-predicted growth in *M2*. By the end of the 1990s, the Fed, taking into account uncertainty about the behavior of velocity, did not place a high priority on bringing the growth of *M2* to within the targeted range. Nevertheless, Fed economists continue to search for ways to modify *M2* to improve its ability to achieve its money growth targets and policy goals.

For example, velocity declined during economic downturns in the early 1920s and 1930s and during World War II. From the late 1940s to about 1980, the velocity of *M1* declined infrequently, but its growth wasn't always even. During the 1970s, some economists suggested that as long as a trend in velocity was allowed for, the quantity theory could still accurately characterize the relationship between nominal GDP and money.

However, as Fig. 23.1 shows, the velocity of *M1* declined significantly during the 1980s. Economists propose two reasons for changes in velocity or in demand for real balances: financial innovation and movements in interest rates. The inclusion in *M1* of interest-bearing substitutes for conventional checkable deposits in the early 1980s increased the demand for *M1* at each

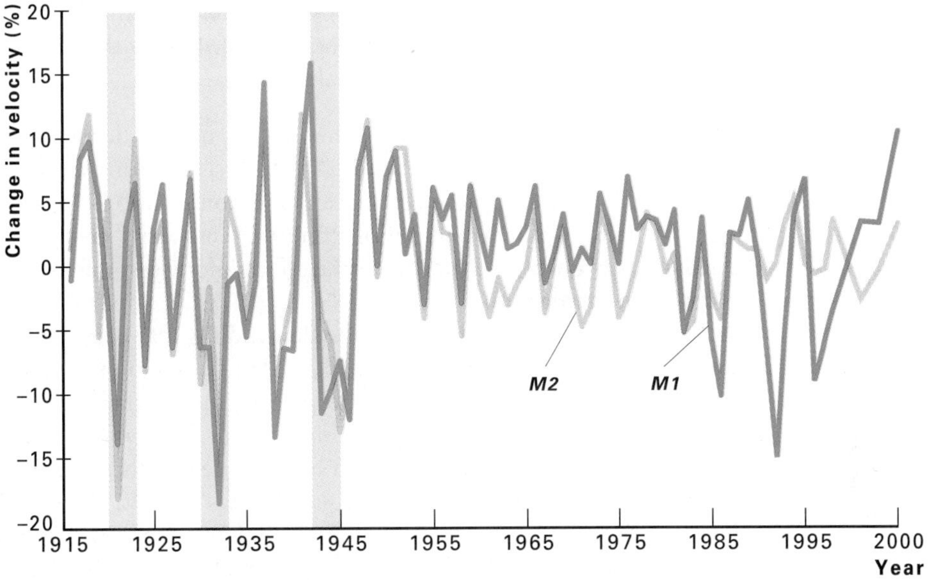

Figure 23.1

Changes in Velocity of *M1* and *M2* in the United States (Percentage Change from Previous Year), 1915–2000

The velocity of money measures depicted equal (1) nominal GDP divided by *M1*, and (2) nominal GDP divided by *M2*. Velocity is not constant, even over short periods of time.

Sources: Federal Reserve Bulletin and Council of Economic Advisers, *Economic Report of the President*, various issues.

level of nominal GDP, thereby decreasing velocity. The fall in interest rates on nonmoney assets in the early 1980s also likely increased the demand for money relative to other assets, implying a decline in velocity. The velocity of *M2* was generally more stable after the early 1950s, though the stable relationship between *M2* and nominal GDP began to deteriorate in the early 1990s.

How do fluctuations in velocity alter the predictions of the Fisher model? There must be other factors besides income that influence the real money balances that individuals and firms will hold. Payments system factors, interest rate changes, and portfolio allocation decisions are the most important.

Payments system factors. Velocity is determined in part by the ways in which individuals conduct transactions. If substitutes for money in transactions, called **payments system factors**, can be used to purchase goods and services, they will alter the demand for money. As an example, people who use credit cards or automated teller machines need less currency and checkable deposits for current spending. As the number of payments system factors increases, *M1* velocity, PY/M, will increase. Alternatively, if money becomes more convenient for carrying out transactions, the public will demand more money to finance current spending. For example, if credit card companies started imposing a $1 charge for processing each purchase, you would probably pay for fewer transactions with charge cards and carry more cash. Money balances would rise, and the velocity of money would fall. Payments system factors change in response to the same factors that determine financial innovation: shifts in the demand for, costs of providing, and regulation of financial services.

Interest rate changes. The early theories of money demand, such as the quantity theory, didn't include interest rates as a factor in the demand for money needed for transactions. In separate contributions to the theory of money demand, William Baumol of Princeton University and James Tobin of Yale University developed models of the effects of interest rates on the demand for real money balances.†

To see how interest rates affect the demand for real balances, assume that Stanley Suffolk receives a paycheck of \$2500 once each month and spends that amount at a constant rate during the month (the balances are held only to make transactions). One solution for him is to draw down his account evenly over (say) 30 days of the month so that his average monthly balance is \$2500/2 = \$1250. At the end of the month, Stanley has \$0 left. When he gets paid again, the process continues. The annual velocity of money for Stanley is his nominal income, \$30,000, divided by his average monthly balance, \$1250, or 24. Assuming that money pays a zero interest return, however, he forgoes earning interest on his money.

To earn interest instead of letting his funds lie idle, Stanley could invest part of his paycheck of \$2500, say, \$1250, in Treasury bonds, adding interest income to his spendable resources. If Stanley invests \$1250, his money balance will be zero halfway through each month rather than at the end of the month. If the interest rate on Treasury bonds is 0.75% per month, he earns an additional \$4.69 [(0.5)(0.0075)(\$1250)] per month, or \$56.25 per year. Stanley cannot spend Treasury bonds directly, though he can convert them to money. This strategy does have costs: the costs of converting other assets into money. Hence Stanley trades off the benefits of holding money with the opportunity cost measured by the market interest rate he could earn by holding bonds. Figure 23.2 illustrates this trade-off.

Baumol and Tobin noted that this trade-off indicates that the transactions motive for holding money depends on interest rates. An increase in the market interest rate increases the opportunity cost of holding real money balances for transactions purposes. As a result, individuals hold smaller money balances, and velocity increases. A decrease in money market interest rates reduces the cost of holding money; individuals will hold larger money balances, and velocity will decline. Hence the demand for money is negatively related to market

---

†The original Baumol and Tobin papers appeared in 1952 and 1956, respectively. Many years later, David Romer of Harvard University expanded the Baumol–Tobin approach to address effects of shifts between money and nonmoney assets on the economy. William J. Baumol, "The Transactions Demand for Cash: An Inventory-Theoretic Approach," *Quarterly Journal of Economics*, 66:545–556, 1952. James Tobin, "The Interest-Elasticity of the Transactions Demand for Cash," *Review of Economics and Statistics*, 38:241–247, 1956. David Romer, "A Simple General Equilibrium Version of the Baumol–Tobin Model," *Quarterly Journal of Economics*, 101:663–686, 1986.

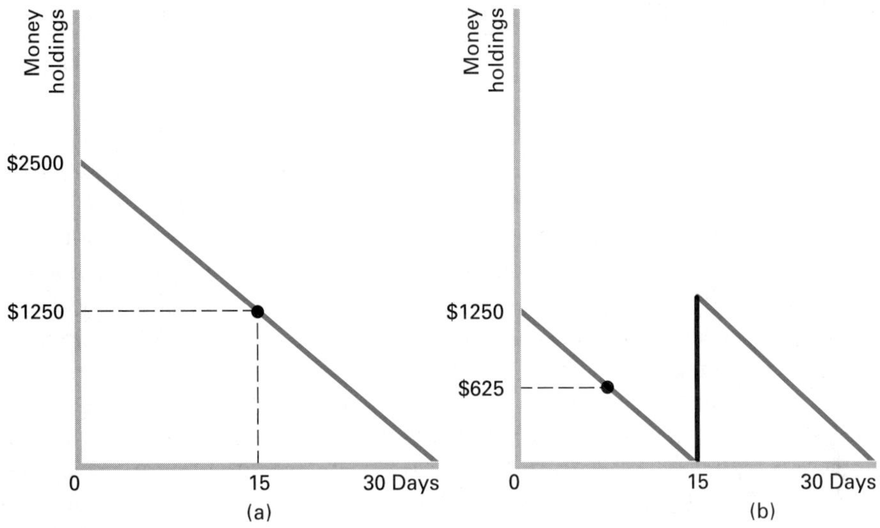

Figure 23.2

Interest Rates and Money Demand in the Baumol–Tobin Model

In (a), Stanley holds his $2500 monthly income entirely in money balances at the beginning of the month. Each day, he spends 1/30 of his balance, which goes to zero at the end of 30 days. Stanley's average money balance is $2500/2 = $1250.

In (b), Stanley holds half of his monthly income in money balances at the beginning of the month; he invests the other half in Treasury bonds. Each day, he spends 1/30 of his income—or 1/15 of his balance, which goes to zero at the end of 15 days, at which time Stanley sells his bonds and holds the proceeds as money balances. He exhausts these balances at the end of 30 days.

interest rates, whereas the velocity of money balances held to conduct transactions is positively related to market interest rates. The Baumol–Tobin theory is another application of the economic concept of opportunity cost. The interest rate is a measure of the opportunity cost of holding real money balances, and interest rates do influence the demand for real money balances that individuals hold to make transactions.

Portfolio allocation decisions. Velocity also changes over time in response to portfolio allocation decisions. Because money is an asset as well as the medium of exchange, changes in expected returns on money or in risk, liquidity, or information costs associated with it will change households' and businesses' demand for cash balances.

CHECKPOINT

What are the effects of the following on the demand for real money balances and the velocity of *M1*? (a) Financial institutions offer cash management services to firms. (b) Bank credit cards become less widely used. (a) Cash management allows more of investment portfolios to be in nonmoney assets, the demand for *M/P* falls, and *V* rises because people have less need to hold money. (b) Because more cash is used in transactions, the demand for *M/P* rises and *V* falls. **o**

PORTFOLIO ALLOCATION MOTIVES

Models of the demand for real balances that rely solely on transactions motives do not completely explain observed movements in real money balances. To develop more accurate models, many economists working after Fisher included other reasons for holding money in their models of money demand. In addition to money being a medium of exchange, its function as a store of value is the basis for individuals' decisions to hold money balances. But in serving this function, money competes with other assets as a store of value. Individuals and businesses will decide whether to hold money or other assets on the basis of the advantages and drawbacks of money compared to other assets. This decision-making process should seem familiar by now; it is another application of the theory of portfolio allocation.

In this section, we introduce two models of the demand for real balances that include portfolio allocation decisions along with transaction motives to predict the level of real money balances that individuals and businesses will hold. We start by reviewing the determinants of portfolio choice that influence holdings of real money balances, and then we describe and compare the theories of economists John Maynard Keynes and Milton Friedman.

Income and wealth. Real money balances held in currency and checkable deposits are necessity assets. Therefore households and businesses with greater income and wealth won't hold the same proportion of their assets in zero- or low-yielding money balances as households and firms with low incomes will. Individuals with high income may maintain higher-yielding accounts that they can easily transfer to checkable deposits; large firms may do the same. In addition, businesses may have a line of credit with banks, which permits them to conduct transactions with low cash or checkable deposit balances. Higher-income households can use bank credit cards (Visa or MasterCard) similarly. The demand for real balances increases with real income, but it does so less than proportionately.

Expected returns. When assessing the return on money assets, households and businesses must take into account not only the interest that is paid on money balances, but also money's *convenience yield*. This is the amount of interest that households or businesses are willing to sacrifice in return for the low risk associated with holding money, the ease with which they can use money to make transactions, and the low information costs of money's value. If nothing else changes, an increase in the interest paid on money balances or in the convenience yield on money will lead households and businesses to increase their money balances and the quantity of money demanded. A decrease in the interest paid on money balances or in the convenience yield will lead households and businesses to decrease their money balances and the quantity of money demanded. Thus households and businesses compare the expected returns on nonmoney assets with the expected returns on money (from interest and convenience yield) in deciding how much money to hold.

Risk, liquidity, and information. When allocating how much of their assets to hold as money, individuals and firms also consider the risk, liquidity, and information benefits of holding money. If returns on alternative assets (such as commercial paper, bonds, or stocks) become more risky, savers may switch their holdings into money, increasing money demand. Innovations that allow easy movements of funds from less liquid forms to more liquid forms, such as from bonds or stocks to a checking account or from home equity to a line of credit, reduce the value that is placed on money's liquidity. The more liquid other assets become, the more savers focus on money's explicit interest return—the interest that is paid on money balances. Finally, some individuals place a high value on holding currency because it gives them anonymity. People who are involved in the drug trade, tax evasion, and other illegal activities may value currency because cash transactions are difficult to trace. Hence the demand for money may be affected by changes in the volume of illegal activity or the tax code.

CHECKPOINT

Suppose that, of a total wealth of $25,000, Ms. Smart allocates $20,000 to Treasury bills yielding 5% and places $5000 in a NOW account yielding 3%. What value does Ms. Smart place on her checkable deposits? What if the yield on T-bills rises to 10%? Implicitly, Ms. Smart values the liquidity services of her checkable deposits at least as much as (0.02)($5000), or $100 per year, the interest forgone. If the yield on T-bills rises to 10%, however, Ms. Smart may decide that the liquidity benefits of checkable deposits are too expensive (with $350 per year of forgone interest) and may reduce her money holdings to, say, $4000. o

Motives for Holding Money: Keynes's Liquidity Preference Theory

In his celebrated 1936 book, *The General Theory of Employment, Interest, and Money*, John Maynard Keynes built a model of money demand that included portfolio allocation motives. Although he believed that transactions motives contributed to the change in the demand for real balances, his **liquidity preference theory** emphasized the sensitivity of money demand to changes in interest rates.

Keynes proposed that individuals and businesses adopt a *speculative motive* in comparing nonmoney assets with money. This behavior is an example of a simplified portfolio allocation decision. Keynes hypothesized that individuals allocated their wealth between two assets: money and "bonds" (representing all other financial assets), assuming that the expected return on bonds is determined by the interest rate on bonds adjusted for expectations of capital gains or losses. For money, defined as the sum of currency and checkable deposits (*M1*), Keynes assumed that the return is zero. (At the time of his writing, the interest rate on currency was zero, and checkable deposits paid no interest.)

Suppose that you speculate that interest rates on bonds will fall, and therefore you expect a capital gain from holding bonds. Accordingly, you want to hold less of your wealth in money and more of it in bonds. But if you expect interest rates to rise (and hence expect a capital loss on bonds), the zero return on money may outweigh the potentially negative total return on bonds. Then you will hold more money and less wealth in bonds. Hence the demand for money balances is negatively related to the interest rate on nonmoney assets.†

In addition to the speculative motive for holding real money balances, Keynes cited two other reasons that individuals will demand money: the *transactions motive* and the *precautionary motive*. The transactions motive is the same behavior that Keynes's predecessors stressed in their models: the use of money to carry out ordinary transactions. Keynes also theorized that individuals would hold money to pay for unexpected transactions, which he called the *precautionary motive*.

Incorporating this behavior into his liquidity preference model, Keynes proposed that money holdings depended on real income, Y, as well as the interest rate on nonmoney assets. Expressed symbolically, he showed that the demand for real money balances, M/P, is a function, L (for liquidity preference), of real income, Y, and the interest rate, i:

$$\frac{M}{P} = L(Y, i). \tag{23.4}$$

Because the quantity of real balances demanded rises with income and transactions, an increase in Y leads to an increase in M/P—a positive relationship. Because a higher interest rate raises the opportunity cost of holding money and reduces the quantity of money demanded, an increase in i leads to a decrease in M/P—a negative relationship.

The negative relationship between real money balances and interest rates in the Keynesian liquidity preference theory allows us to explain fluctuations in velocity. To demonstrate the changes in velocity, we have to rewrite Eq. (23.4) as

$$\frac{P}{M} = \frac{1}{L(Y, i)}.$$

If we multiply both sides of this equation by Y, we get

$$\frac{PY}{M} = \frac{Y}{L(Y, i)}.$$

But PY/M equals velocity, V [from Eq. (23.1)], so

$$V = \frac{Y}{L(Y, i)}. \tag{23.5}$$

†Keynes recognized expectations by assuming that investors expect interest rates to return to some "normal" level. If interest rates are above that normal value, individuals expect falling rates and capital gains on bonds (and the opposite if interest rates are less than the normal value). Evidence shows that the assumption of a normal value for nominal interest rates is much less plausible today than it was in the 1930s.

From this equation, you can see that velocity varies if aggregate income changes or if interest rates fluctuate.

Suppose that the interest rate on bonds, i, rises but that aggregate income, Y, doesn't change. Because the opportunity cost of holding money has gone up, you would use some of your money holdings to buy bonds, reducing your demand for real money balances. Hence the denominator of the right-hand side of Eq. (23.5) would fall, raising velocity. More generally, fluctuations in interest rates cause fluctuations in the velocity of money.

Broader Portfolio Factors: Friedman's Money Demand Model

Milton Friedman proposed another explanation of money demand in 1956.† He didn't attempt to separate money demand into components, or motives, as Keynes had done. Instead, he relied more generally on the determinants of asset demand.

In trying to explain the public's demand for money, Friedman examined *M2*, a broader measure of money than *M1*. On the basis of the determinants of portfolio choice, he reasoned, money holdings depend on an individual's expected average income over a lifetime, Y^*. He called Y^* *permanent income* and assumed that it is proportional to wealth. Wealth influences portfolio allocation, and it also influences an individual's demand for real money balances when we add portfolio allocation motives to our model. To compare expected returns on money and nonmoney assets, Friedman theorized that the demand for money should depend negatively on two measures of the opportunity cost of holding money: (1) the difference between the expected return on financial assets, i, and the return on money, i_M, and (2) the difference between the expected return on durable goods measured by expected inflation, π^e, and the return on money. That is, Friedman's model for the demand for real money balances can be expressed as

$$\frac{M}{P} = L(Y^*, i - i_M, \pi^e - i_M). \tag{23.6}$$

In Friedman's model, the demand for real money balances increases with increases in permanent income, Y^*—a positive relationship—and falls with increases in the opportunity cost of holding money, $i - i_M$ and $\pi^e - i_M$—both negative relationships.

Comparing the Two Models: Keynes versus Friedman

Both Keynes and Friedman incorporated portfolio allocation motives in their theories of money demand, but there are differences in their models. In Friedman's theory, money demand depends on households' permanent income; hence money demand responds only slightly to short-run fluctuations in income

†Milton Friedman, "The Quantity Theory of Money: A Restatement," in Milton Friedman, ed., *Studies in the Quantity Theory of Money*, Chicago: University of Chicago Press, 1956.

or wealth. In addition, whereas Keynes considered only money and all other financial assets (lumped together as bonds), Friedman allowed for portfolio substitution among money, bonds, equities, and durable goods. His "expected inflation" term includes the return on durable goods, which varies as their nominal values appreciate with inflation. Therefore, according to Friedman, if households expect a high rate of inflation (and a low return on money as a result), they will invest more of their wealth in housing and consumer durable goods as inflation hedges. In this case, real money balances will fall. Finally, Keynes assumed the rate of return on money to be zero. In Friedman's model, the return on money consists of both explicit interest payments on money and the services provided by financial institutions, such as check clearing and bill paying. In Friedman's model, the differences between the return on various nonmoney assets and the return on money influences the public's demand for real money balances. Friedman believed that such differences would be small, offering little hope that changes in interest rates would affect the demand for money.

EXPLAINING MONEY DEMAND

We can now synthesize our analyses of transactions and portfolio allocation motives for holding money to formulate a model of the public's demand for real money balances that includes transactions motives and portfolio allocation motives. Our model contains the following relationships:

1. The demand for real money balances depends positively on the level of transactions, which we represent with real income, Y. If you expect to make more purchases next year than this year, you will generally hold more money balances.
2. The demand for real balances depends negatively on payments system factors, S, that provide alternatives to money for making payments. The widespread use of bank credit cards generally reduces money demand.
3. Because there are many alternatives to money as a financial asset, the expected return on each (adjusted for differences in risk, liquidity, and information costs) in principle also influences the demand for money.

Hence we can use the nominal interest rate, i, to represent expected returns on nonmoney assets. Consistent with the theory of portfolio allocation, if nothing else changes, the demand for real money balances depends negatively on the difference between the expected return on alternative assets, i, and the yield on money (including the convenience yield), i_M.† Therefore, if Treasury bill yields rise relative to yields on money balances, savers will reduce their holdings of money to buy T-bills. The quantity of money demanded declines because wealth will be reallocated to the now higher-yielding alternatives.

†Note that we could have discussed *real* expected returns, subtracting expected inflation from i and i_M. The difference, $i - i_M$, would be unaffected, however.

The Money Demand Function

We combine these factors in a liquidity preference model that we can use to predict the demand for money in the United States and other countries. The demand for real money balances is the demand for nominal money balances, M_d, divided by the price level, P:

$$\frac{M_d}{P} = L(Y, S, i - i_M) \tag{23.7}$$

The liquidity function, represented by L in Eq. (23.7), describes the demand for real balances as a function of real income, Y; payments system factors, S; and expected returns on nonmoney assets and money, $i - i_M$. Therefore

- an increase in real income raises the real quantity of money demanded;
- an increase in the availability of money substitutes as means of payments reduces the real quantity of money demanded;
- increases in the opportunity cost of holding real money balances decrease the real quantity of money demanded (and the opportunity cost of holding money rises when market interest rates rise relative to the return on money); and
- an increase in expected inflation leads to an increase in the opportunity cost of holding money, and hence to a decline in money demand, if market interest rates rise more than the interest paid on money balances as expected inflation rises.

The demand for money expressed by Eq. (23.7) provides potentially useful information about movements in real money balances over time in response to shifts in real income and expected returns on money and nonmoney assets. Table 23.1 summarizes these determinants of money demand.

Measuring Money Demand

How well does the demand-for-money equation work in measuring actual changes in real balances? To connect the money demand expression, Eq. (23.7), to actual money holdings, we need to be able to measure money. The Fed tries to solve this problem by grouping liquid financial assets into *monetary aggregates*. The narrowest aggregate, *M1*, reflects money's function as the medium of exchange and comprises currency and checkable deposits. Broader monetary aggregates, such as *M2* and *M3*, include the assets in *M1* plus other assets with less liquidity. Attempts to estimate money demand relationships, such as that expressed in Eq. (23.7), use alternative definitions of money drawn from the monetary aggregates.

Grouping liquid assets into monetary aggregates is only a partial solution to the problem of measuring money. An aggregate is defined as the sum of the amounts of various assets outstanding, with each asset having the same weight. Shifts in regulation and financial innovation affect the liquidity of certain financial assets. These shifts imply that accurate measures of money may

TABLE 23.1 **DETERMINANTS OF THE DEMAND FOR MONEY**

An Increase in ...	Causes Money Demand to ...	Because of ...
price level, P	increase proportionally	*transactions motives:* A doubling of the price level doubles the number of dollars needed for transactions.
real income, Y	increase less than proportionally	*transactions motives:* Increases in income raise the amount of transactions and the demand for liquid assets.
availability of money substitutes, S, as means of payment	decrease	*transactions motives:* More money substitutes cause households and businesses to economize on money holdings.
interest rate on nonmoney assets, i	decrease	*transactions and portfolio allocation motives:* A greater return on alternative assets leads households and businesses to switch from holding money.
return on money, i_M	increase	*portfolio allocation motives:* A greater return on money makes households and businesses more willing to hold money.

be hybrids of the Fed's official measures. Recently, economists have developed *weighted aggregates*, sometimes called *Divisia aggregates*, which index assets by their liquidity. For example, a dollar that is held in currency or checkable deposits might be given more weight in a revised aggregate than a dollar that is held in time or savings deposits. These measures, which are used by many academic economists and the Fed, have led to money demand models that fit the data better.

Even if economists could measure money demand perfectly, a second problem remains: the closeness with which the demand for real balances can be related to its determinants in Eq. (23.7). Financial economists usually estimate money demand functions such as Eq. (23.7), using *M1* or *M2* and price level, real income, interest rate, and expected inflation data. In so doing, they can isolate the partial effect of individual determinants of money demand on real money balances, all other determinants being held constant. In 1973, Stephen Goldfeld of Princeton University showed that the simple money demand function fit the data at that time very well.

Problems with the validity of this model began to surface after 1973. During the 1970s, high nominal interest rates created a demand for liquid alternatives to money. The financial system responded by producing such innovations as liquid, interest-bearing substitutes for checkable deposits (which at the time paid no interest) for households and overnight repurchase agreements for businesses. With these interest-bearing instruments in place, the demand for money, measured as *M1*, declined.

OTHER TIMES, OTHER PLACES . . .

The Case of the Missing Money

In 1973, Stephen Goldfeld of Princeton University attempted to measure the strength of each variable in the model of the demand for *M1* in Eq. (23.7), and he found that the model explained the data reasonably well. The trouble started soon after Goldfeld's 1973 paper was published. Between late 1974 and the beginning of 1976, Goldfeld's money demand equation [based on Eq. (23.7)] substantially overpredicted the actual demand for currency and checkable deposits in the United States. In other words, for the changes in the price level, real income, and interest rates during that period—and the relationship Goldfeld had estimated before 1973—the actual demand for money was too low.† Goldfeld referred to this episode as "the case of the missing money." After this episode, the money demand function performed much better for the rest of the 1970s. However, in the 1980s, the money demand function underpredicted money demand on several occasions (notably in 1982 and 1985).

How should we interpret this failure of the simple money demand function? In theory, the model described by Eq. (23.7) captures the key factors affecting money demand. But in using the model, analysts had to make practical concessions. Specifically, variables representing changes in the payments system are hard to construct and hence were usually omitted. At times, however, such changes are important. When they are, the simple money demand functions will yield inaccurate predictions.

† See Stephen Goldfeld, "The Case of the Missing Money," *Brookings Papers on Economic Activity*, 3:683–734, 1976.

During the early 1980s, many financial innovations increased the velocity of *M1*. As interest-bearing checkable deposits, such as negotiated order of withdrawal (NOW) accounts and automatic transfer service (ATS), were incorporated into the definition of *M1*, the demand for *M1* balances increased substantially. Later in the 1980s, monetary policymakers focused more on demand for *M2* balances as households began to hold more of their transactions balances in money market mutual funds, which are included in *M2* but not in *M1*.

Economists and policymakers have learned that, although explaining shifts in the simple money demand function is straightforward (at least after the fact), such factors often are hard to quantify. The financial system changes over time in response to shifts in the cost of providing, the demand for, and the regulation of financial services. Effects of these changes on the demand for money make forecasting it a difficult task. Similar challenges confront the people who make money demand forecasts in other countries.

KEY TERMS AND CONCEPTS

Equation of exchange
Liquidity preference theory
Money demand function
Payments system factors
Quantity theory of money demand
Real money balances
Velocity of money

THE NEW YORK TIMES JANUARY 30, 2001

A Legal Tender of One's Own

Later this year Europe will begin distributing the coins and bills of its new currency, the euro. But [Guardiagrele, a] hilltop hamlet of 10,000, huddled beneath snow-dusted peaks and in sight of the Adriatic Sea, is a step ahead.

Last summer, a restless retired law professor whose family has been among the local notables for centuries, Giacinto Auriti, realized a decades-old dream of deposing the Italian central bank from its money-printing monopoly by printing and distributing a local currency called the simec. . . .

Though his final goal is for the simec to become a global currency, supplanting monies around the world including the euro, for the moment his simec is the coin of a narrow realm. In that sense, it is like the local currencies that have been introduced in about 60 communities in the United States since an environmentalist, Paul Glover, introduced "Ithaca Hours" in upstate New York in 1993 to bolster local business and keep wealth in local hands.

(a) To be sure, the simec, an Italian abbreviation for "econometric symbol," ignited a frenzy of shopping here when it was issued last year, cheering local officials who were casting about for ways to supplement traditional businesses like shoemaking and wrought iron. But it also divided local merchants and provoked a raid by the Italian financial police, who impounded boxloads of simecs until a court ordered them returned. It also made some people wonder if Professor Auriti were not some kind of monetary Pied Piper leading the locals astray. . . .

Franco Caramanico, a former engineer who has been mayor since 1997, is an unabashed admirer of Professor Auriti. "He's a person who believes in his ideals, and not only believes, but puts his fortune behind it," Mr. Caramanico said in his office in a disused Franciscan monastery. . . .

The danger, of course, as with every currency, is inflation, and that could become acute if Professor Auriti carries out two other corollaries of his theory. (b) One is that cash should be distributed freely, and not lent through the banking system at interest, as nefarious central bankers do, so he wants to begin doling out regular payments of simecs to families. . . .

For Mayor Caramanico, confidence in the simec is at risk. Professor Auriti is not legally bound to redeem simecs for lire and, if there were a run and the simec could not be redeemed for lire, some in Guardiagrele could get burned, he fears. "The basis of it all is trust," he said. "If there is trust and the simec is accepted—fine. If not, there are risks." (c)

Substituting money-based transactions for barter transactions economizes on resources. One important benefit of a useful money is the ability to generate "prices" to allocate labor, capital, and other resources. To understand the demand for money, we must be able to evaluate the usefulness of money in transactions and as an asset. While we often think of "money" as the official money, unofficial monies can arise for transactions for goods and assets. The basic question remains: Will consumers and firms find the "money" candidate useful in trading with one another?

a To serve as a medium of exchange, money must be accepted in payment for goods and services purchased by households and businesses. It is the confidence of the public that produces a useful money.

b Equation (23.7) reminds us that households and businesses compare expected returns on assets in deciding how much to hold in real money balances. Inflation (in simec terms) would decrease the Italian community's willingness to hold simec money balances. In this case, the public might convert simec balances into the money Professor Auriti despises—Italian lire supplied by the Italian central bank. Auriti may avoid such a conversion with his fixed exchange rate with the Italian lira.

c Or can he? Confidence is, indeed, the glue that binds the community together in its acceptance of a "money." Expected inflation in simecs could lead the public to question Professor Auriti's promise to exchange simecs for lire at the promised rate of one simec for two lire. The failure of the system might jeopardize public willingness to accept the new money. Were it not for the existence of the lira, the loss of confidence in simec money could exert a tax on the public, which would have to turn to less efficient means of conducting transactions.

For further thought . . .

Suppose that the Italian central bank supplies a fixed quantity of real money balances and that the demand for real money balances is described by Eq. (23.7). If the central bank does not change the real money supply, but public confidence in the lira rises significantly, what do you think will happen to the returns on money and nonmoney assets? Explain.

Source: Excerpted from John Tagliabue, "A Legal Tender of One's Own," *The New York Times*, January 30, 2001.

SUMMARY

1. Households' and firms' desires to hold money assets represent the demand for money. The demand for money is a demand for real money balances; that is, the demand for nominal money balances is proportional to the price level.
2. The principal determinants of the demand for real money balances are real income and the opportunity cost of holding money. Higher levels of real income increase the volume of transactions and hence the demand for money as a medium of exchange. Increases in the returns on nonmoney assets relative to the return on money decrease the demand for money, holding constant risk, liquidity, and information characteristics of money and nonmoney assets.
3. Early researchers, notably Irving Fisher, proposed a theory of the demand for money in which velocity, the average number of times that a dollar is spent each year in buying goods and services, is constant. The resulting quantity theory of money demand indicated that the demand for real money balances depended only on real income. Data for the United States do not support the hypothesis that velocity is constant. Subsequent researchers developed theories in which interest rates affect velocity and money demand. Particularly noteworthy in this research was the liquidity preference theory of John Maynard Keynes, which provided a foundation for contemporary models of the demand for money. Milton Friedman proposed a theory that emphasized a stable demand for a broad measure of money, a theory that provides another foundation for contemporary models of the demand for money.
4. The relationship among money demand, real income, and the opportunity cost of holding money also depends on payments system factors: substitutes for money as a means for making and receiving payments. Changes in these factors can cause the demand for real money balances to shift relative to its historical relationship to real income and the opportunity cost of holding money.
5. Financial economists have estimated the effects of real income, interest rates, and other variables on the demand for money using data from the United States and other economies. Such relationships were stable in the United States through the early 1970s. They shifted during the 1970s and 1980s, reflecting (among other things) changes in payments system factors, increases in the liquidity of nonmoney assets as a result of financial deregulation, and increases in the interest return on money assets. As money demand shifted, so did velocity—the ratio of nominal income to money.

REVIEW QUESTIONS

1. How do *real* money balances differ from *nominal* money balances?
2. Who is likely to have greater money balances: someone with an income of $50,000 per year or someone with an income of $25,000 per year? Explain.
3. Why is the equation of exchange considered to be an identity? What key assumption did Irving Fisher make to turn the quantity exchange into a theory of money demand?
4. Has velocity been constant over time in the United States? Explain.
5. Is it surprising that velocity varies greatly from one country to another? Why or why not?
6. Define *payments system factors*. Why are they important for money demand?
7. What is the key difference between the Fisher and the Baumol–Tobin approaches to the demand for money?
8. What happens to money demand if
   a. the risk of nonmoney assets rises?
   b. the liquidity of nonmoney assets rises?
   c. the information costs of nonmoney assets rises?
9. In the Baumol–Tobin approach, which opportunity cost affects money demand?
10. If your income doubles, is your demand for money balances likely to double? Explain.

11. According to Keynes's liquidity preference theory, what happens to money demand if interest rates are expected to fall?
12. According to the liquidity preference theory, what happens to money demand in a recession? In an expansion? What happens to velocity in a recession? In an expansion?
13. What income concept is important in Friedman's approach to money demand? How is this income concept defined? Why does this concept make estimating money demand empirically more difficult?
14. Why does higher expected inflation reduce money demand if the yield on money does not change? If the yield on money rises but expected inflation doesn't change, what happens to money demand?
15. What is a *weighted monetary aggregate*? Why might its use be superior to simple sum aggregates such as *M1* and *M2*?

ANALYTICAL PROBLEMS

16. You have been asked to model the demand for *M1* and *M2* measures of money in the United States. Discuss effects on the demand for these monetary aggregates in response to
    a. a decrease in expected inflation
    b. an increase in enforcement of laws against drug sales and tax evasion
    c. an expectation by investors that the stock market values will collapse in the near future
17. Suppose real income in the economy is \$6 trillion, the price level is 1.0, and velocity is constant at 3.0.
    a. What are the quantities demanded of nominal and real money balances?
    b. Suppose that the central bank sets the nominal money supply at \$2.5 trillion. What happens to the price level? Why?
18. If nominal GDP is \$6 trillion and the *M1* measure of the money supply is \$1.2 trillion, what is velocity?
19. Given what you know of economic events during the early 1930s, explain why velocity may have declined particularly sharply during those years.
20. Between 1970 and 1980, the nominal demand for money doubled, but the real demand for money didn't change. What happened to the price level during this period?
21. If nominal money demand is proportional to nominal income, by how much will real money demand increase if real income rises 10%?
22. Suppose that on average a dollar is spent four times per year to purchase final goods and services. How big is the money supply if nominal GDP is \$6 trillion?
23. If the Fed had based monetary policy in the 1980s on the assumption that velocity would be constant, would inflation have been higher or lower than it actually was? Why?
24. Is velocity more likely to be stable if Keynes's view of the demand for money is correct or if Friedman's view is correct? Explain.
25. Suppose that you have a checking account that pays interest of 3%; you maintain at least \$1000 in the account at all times so that you can avoid paying service charges. If you wanted to, you could put the \$1000 in a money market fund earning 8%. How much in service charges must you avoid for this deal to be profitable for you?
26. Why is money demand high in southern Florida and near the Mexican border?
27. Suppose that velocity rises but incomes haven't changed. What do you think happened to interest rates, according to the Keynesian liquidity preference theory? Why?
28. Suppose that expected inflation rises by 3%, the yield on money rises by 3%, and the yield on nonmoney assets rises by 3%. What is the effect on real money demand? What if expected inflation rose by only 2%? What if the yield on nonmoney assets rose by 4%?
29. Suppose that computer technology became so cheap that there was no need ever to use cash or to have money in a non-interest-bearing checking account. Computers make it possible to keep any money that you have in the bank in an investment fund, to maximize your return. This system effectively makes bank deposits a nonmoney asset.

What do you think is likely to happen to the ability of money demand functions to track money demand when such an innovation occurs? How might the definition of money change if such an innovation occurs?

30. In Nationia, no explicit interest is paid on money balances, and households and businesses receive a constant convenience yield from holding money. The demand for real balances is

$$\frac{M_d}{P} = 1000 + 0.25Y - 1000i.$$

   a. In Nationia, $Y = 2000$, $P = 100$, and $i = 0.10$. Solve for (i) nominal and real money balances and (ii) velocity.
   b. Using the values for Y, P, and i in (a) as initial conditions, how is velocity affected by an increase in the interest rate? In real income?

31. Discuss at least one problem in estimating the demand for money using the approach derived in this chapter. Suggest an approach that would reduce the effect of this problem on forecasts of money demand.

DATA QUESTION

32. In the latest issue of the *Economic Report of the President,* find data on nominal GDP and the *M1* and *M2* measures of the money supply for the last three years. Calculate velocity for both *M1* and *M2* for each year. Do you see any trend in velocity? If so, what is it?

CHAPTER 24

Linking the Financial System and the Economy: The *IS-LM-FE* Model

Beginning in late 1991, the Fed cut short-term interest rates to stimulate the economy's recovery from the 1990–1991 recession. In particular, the Fed hoped to encourage businesses to invest in new plant and equipment by making it cheaper to finance spending on capital assets. As output increased and the economy recovered, the Fed increased interest rates in 1994 and 1995 to keep output on a steady growth path and to dampen inflationary pressures. In late 1998, the Fed cut short-term interest rates, fearful of the consequences of the Asian financial crisis for the U.S. economic expansion. In early 2001, the central bank lowered short-term rates to reduce the likelihood of a recession.

How does the Fed know that interest rates will have an effect on output? What is the link between the actions of participants in the financial system—the central bank, firms participating in financial markets to raise funds, and savers seeking financial assets—and the performance of the economy?

We begin to answer these questions in this chapter by building a model—the *IS-LM-FE* model—that links interest rate determination in asset markets to output determination in the market for goods and services. Like many models, the *IS-LM-FE* model makes many simplifications about the economy. Nonetheless, its predictions about the effect of interest rates on output—and output on interest rates—gives monetary policymakers insights about how the economy will respond to policy changes.

We start the chapter with a description of the assumptions that we use to build the model and the simplifications that the model makes about the financial system and the economy. In addition to building the model, we observe how the model allows us to predict changes over time in interest rates, output, and other variables that measure economic performance.

A MODEL FOR GOODS AND ASSET MARKETS: ASSUMPTIONS

The *IS-LM-FE* model is a model of behavior in the market for goods and services and in the market for financial assets. These markets in developed economies such as the United States are complex. Thousands of goods and services are traded, and an array of financial assets changes hands each day. Suppliers in the goods market decide how much to produce, and buyers decide how much to purchase. Suppliers of securities in financial markets decide how much to borrow, and buyers of those securities decide how much to lend and how to allocate their wealth. In any specific market—for apples or autos or T-bills—the price adjusts to equate the quantities demanded and supplied by market participants.

We begin with a simplification: We focus on the equilibrium of goods and financial markets at a point in time. Taking into account the interactions among markets, economists refer to a **general equilibrium** as an outcome in which all the markets in the economy are in equilibrium at the same time.

Another simplification that we make in our model is to group all the individual markets for goods and services into three broad categories: (1) goods, (2) money, and (3) nonmoney assets. The **goods market** includes trade in all goods and services that the economy produces at a particular point in time. We group all trades of assets used as the medium of exchange in the **money market**. These assets are currency, checkable deposits, and other close substitutes for cash. The third market, the **nonmoney asset market**, includes trades of assets other than money that are stores of value. Purchases and sales of stocks, bonds, houses, and other nonmoney financial assets fall into this group. Separating markets into these three categories allows us to describe simply and graph the effects of changes in the economy or of government policy on prices in markets for goods and services and for financial assets.

We build the *IS-LM-FE* model using graphs and equations, and we use two variables to summarize equilibrium in the markets for goods, money, and nonmoney assets. We represent current output of goods and services by Y. This variable typically represents gross domestic product (GDP), and it is a measure of economic activity.[†] The second key variable in our model is the expected real interest rate, r, which measures the return to savers and the cost of funds to borrowers.

We build the *IS-LM-FE* model in three steps that coordinate with our grouping of market and our interest in the behavior of participants in the goods market and in the financial markets:

1. We investigate the demand for current output and construct the IS curve.
2. We then examine firms' willingness to supply current output and construct the FE line.

[†] Y, you will recall, has other meanings as well. It can represent aggregate income. We also used Y in Chapter 23 to represent the volume of transactions. In this chapter, our analysis is eased by viewing Y as output.

3. Finally, we determine the willingness of individuals to hold money and nonmoney assets and construct the LM curve.

When we combine these curves, we have a model that illustrates the economy's equilibrium and allows us to observe the factors that change it. Working with the *IS-LM-FE* model, we can predict the effect of changes in monetary policy on output and on other economic variables.

The *IS* Curve

We begin our investigation of the market for goods and services by describing the behavior of individuals and firms. In examining the decisions that individuals make in determining how much to consume or to save and the decisions that firms make in determining how much to invest in capital equipment, we can construct a relationship between interest rates and output called the *IS* curve.

Saving, Investment, and Aggregate Demand

We start with an equation that represents the goods market for a closed economy when it is in equilibrium. We will relax the assumption of a closed economy later on and extend our analysis to an economy that engages in foreign trade and investment. When the goods market is in equilibrium, the quantity of goods demanded equals the quantity of goods supplied. We represent the quantity of goods supplied by current output Y. In a closed economy, the quantity of goods demanded, or *aggregate demand*, is equal to the sum of:

National consumption, C: The quantity of goods and services that households want to consume (C is a measure of household spending on goods and services);

National investment, I: The quantity of capital goods demanded by businesses for investment (I is a measure of business spending on capital goods); and

Government purchases, G: The quantity of goods and services purchased by the government (G is a measure of government spending on goods and services).

The goods market is in equilibrium when current output supplied equals aggregate demand:

$$Y = C + I + G. \tag{24.1}$$

We return to the supply of current output later. Subtracting C and G from both sides of Eq. (24.1), we get

$$Y - C - G = I.$$

Investment represents the increase in capital investment by businesses. The left-hand side, $Y - C - G$, represents output not consumed in the current period by households or the government—that is, *national saving,* S. Therefore $Y - C - G = S$. When the goods market is in equilibrium, national saving and investment are equal, or

$$S = I. \tag{24.2}$$

Our next task is to identify the behavior that causes individuals and governments to save and businesses to invest in capital assets. This analysis will allow us to predict levels of saving and investment in the economy that accompany changes in output. This information will help us to construct our model of behavior in the goods markets, but it is also useful for policymakers who may want to encourage saving or investment. Saving and investment contribute to the future well-being of the economy. If policymakers know the incentives that individuals and businesses have to save or invest, they can design programs to increase the amounts saved or invested.

Determinants of National Saving

The determinants of national saving are current output, household consumption, spending, and government purchases. Therefore we need to consider both household and government spending and saving decisions to determine the level of national saving. Let's begin with households.

Households care not only about current consumption, but also about *future* consumption spending. For example, you may save to pay for your education, to raise a family, to buy a house, or to fund your retirement. The three key factors determining household saving are current income, expected future income, and the expected real rate of interest.

Current income. What would you do if your current income went up—say, you won $5000 in the lottery—but your future prospects didn't change? You would probably spend part of the income on consumption goods that you have been wanting, such as a new CD player. Because you care about future consumption, too, you would probably save part of the extra income. Hence both your consumption and saving likely will increase when your current income increases. If your current income falls, the process works in reverse: Both current consumption and saving fall. This argument can be extended to the economy as a whole, suggesting that when total output changes, current consumption also changes, but to a lesser degree than the change in total output. Hence the level of national saving, $Y - C - G$, increases when current output rises and decreases when current output falls.

Expected future income. Suppose your company sponsors your training in graduate school, making you eligible for a higher-paying position when the training is complete. Because you anticipate a higher income, you will probably increase your spending today. Similarly, if you expect that your company will pay you less beginning next year, you may reduce your consumption today to build a cushion for the future. For the economy as a whole, an expected future increase in income raises consumption, so if current output doesn't change, national saving, $Y - C - G$, falls. An expected future decrease in income lowers consumption, so if current output doesn't change, national saving rises.

Expected real interest rate. The expected real interest rate represents the return that savers expect to earn from lending their funds to borrowers in the financial system. An increase in the real interest rate increases your reward for saving for future consumption while also allowing you to save less to pay for future consumption. A decline in the real interest rate decreases your reward for saving but requires that you save more to meet a given goal for future consumption. Available empirical evidence suggests that household saving increases with the interest rate, although the effect probably isn't large.

Government purchases. Government purchases, G, for goods and services such as military equipment, highways, education, and public employees' salaries also influence national saving. If we hold current output constant, an increase in government purchases reduces national saving as long as household consumption falls less than one for one in response. Evidence suggests that consumers do not reduce their spending dollar for dollar in response to more government purchases. That is, if nothing else changes, an increase in government purchases lowers national saving.

Determinants of National Investment

Businesses invest in capital assets to increase future profits. The two principal determinants of the size of national investment are the expected future profitability of capital invested and the expected real interest rate.

Expected future profitability of capital. An increase in expected future profitability of capital (from, say, a new technology or discovery) enhances businesses' willingness to invest (as we described in Chapter 6). Corporate taxes also influence expected future profitability. An increase in taxes on business income or a decrease in tax incentives for new investment will reduce businesses' willingness to invest at any level of expected future pretax profitability. Similarly, a decrease in business income taxes or an increase in tax incentives for new investment stimulates businesses' willingness to invest at any level of expected future pretax profitability.

Expected real interest rate. When businesses evaluate investment alternatives, they must weigh other possible uses for their funds, including purchasing financial assets. The expected real interest rate represents the cost of funds for investment. Hence an increase in the expected real interest rate lowers the demand for investment, as businesses could hold funds more profitably in other assets. Conversely, a drop in the expected real interest rate raises investment demand.

CHECKPOINT

You and other investors have just formed Biopil, a pharmaceutical corporation. If *The Wall Street Journal* reports that the federal government has initiated a tax break for new investment, how does that news affect your investment decision? If the expected future pretax profitability of your investment doesn't change, the tax break reduces your cost of funds. You should expand Biopil's capital investment. o

Constructing the *IS* Curve

Using the information about the effect of interest rates on investment and saving, we can construct a curve that shows how aggregate demand for current output responds to changes in interest rates. The resulting curve, the ***IS* curve**, summarizes the equilibrium in the market for goods and services, and it is the first part of our model linking the financial system with the goods market.

To construct the *IS* curve, we start with a relationship between investment and saving and the interest rate. In the diagram shown in Fig. 24.1(a), the horizontal axis represents national saving and investment, and the vertical axis represents the real interest rate. (For simplicity, we assume that the expected and actual real interest rates are equal.) We hold the other determinants of saving and investment constant. The saving curve slopes up; an increase in the real interest rate raises the level of saving, all else being equal. The investment curve slopes down; an increase in the real interest rate reduces the level of investment, all else being equal.

Figure 24.1(a) shows saving and investment curves for two values of current output *Y*: \$10,000 billion and \$11,000 billion. When current output increases, saving also increases. Therefore each current output level is associated with a different saving curve. An increase in current output from \$10,000 billion to \$11,000 billion shifts the saving curve to the right from S_0 to S_1, thereby changing the equilibrium in the goods market from E_0 to E_1 and reducing the real interest rate from 4% to 3%.

The two equilibrium points in Fig. 24.1(a) are plotted in Fig. 24.1(b) as two possible current output–real interest rate combinations that equilibrate saving and investment. In Fig. 24.1(b), the *IS* curve depicts the general relationship between aggregate demand for current output and the real interest rate. At each point on the *IS* curve, desired saving equals desired investment; that is, the *IS* curve presents combinations of current output and the real interest rate for which the quantities of goods demanded and supplied are equal. The *IS* curve slopes downward and to the right because, at higher levels of current output, current saving rises and the real interest rate falls to restore equilibrium in the goods market.

Points that are not on the *IS* curve represent unequal levels of saving and investment; the goods market is not in equilibrium for the corresponding real interest rates. Consider the example shown in Fig. 24.2(a). At a real interest rate of 5% and an output of \$10,000 billion, saving exceeds investment, creating an excess supply of goods, indicated at point 1. To restore equilibrium

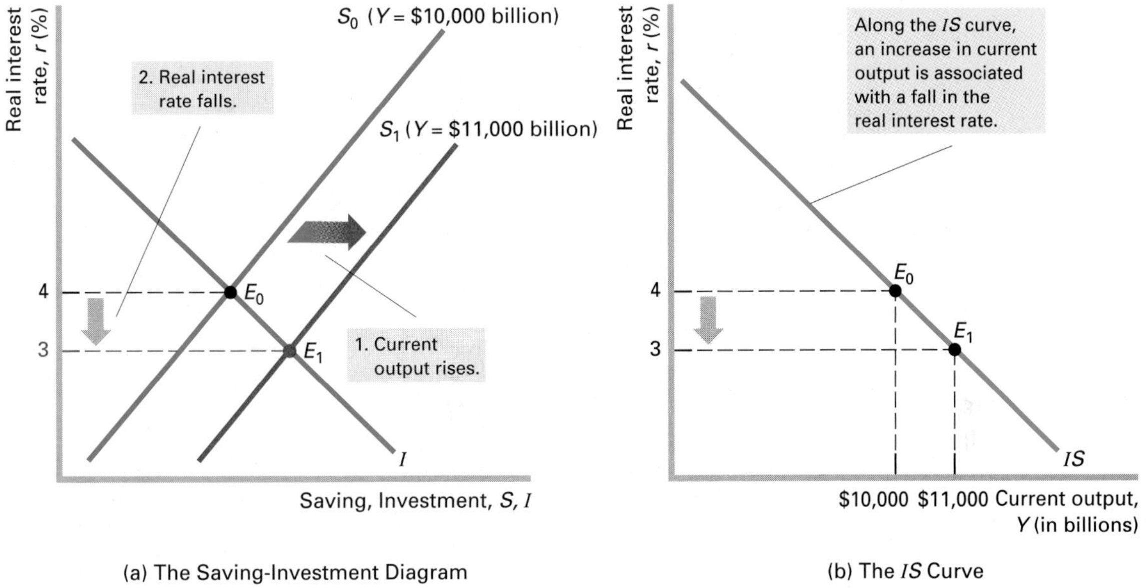

Figure 24.1 **The *IS* Curve**

As shown in (a):
1. An increase in current output from $10,000 to $11,000 billion increases current saving, shifting the *S* curve to the right from S_0 to S_1.
2. The increase in saving reduces the real interest rate *r* from 4% to 3%.

As shown in (b):
The *IS* curve slopes downward, maintaining equality of saving and investment; higher levels of current output are associated with lower values of the real interest rate.

in the goods market, the real interest rate must fall to 4%, at point 3. At a real interest rate of 3% and output of $10,000 billion, investment exceeds saving, creating an excess demand for goods, indicated at point 2. To restore equilibrium in the goods market, the real interest rate must rise to 4%, at point 3.

The curve shown in Fig. 24.2(b) reflects this pattern. At point 3, the goods market is in equilibrium; therefore point 3 lies on the *IS* curve. Points such as 1 that lie above the *IS* curve represent an excess supply of goods. Point 1 represents the same level of current output supplied as at point 3 but at a higher real interest rate. Recall that an increase in the real interest rate reduces desired consumption, increasing desired saving and decreasing desired investment. The level of goods demanded at a real interest rate of 5% is less than the current output of goods; that is, there is an excess supply of goods at point 1.

Points such as 2 that lie below the *IS* curve represent an excess demand for goods. Point 2 represents the same level of current output as at point 3 but at a lower real rate of interest. Then consumption increases, decreasing saving and increasing investment. The quantity of goods demanded exceeds the current output of goods.

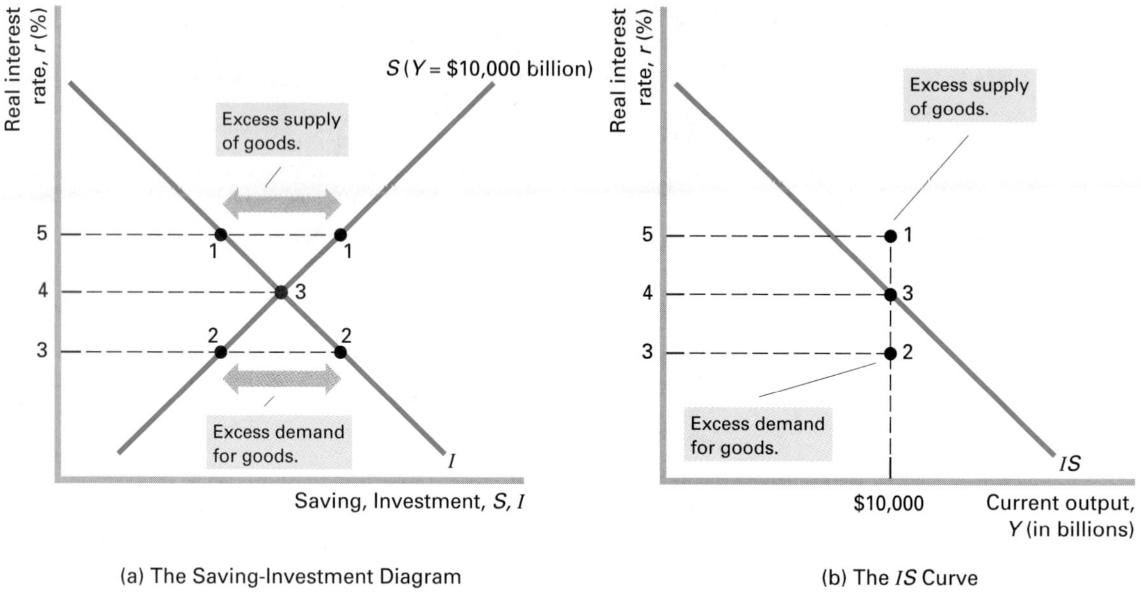

Figure 24.2 **Excess Demand and Supply in the Goods Market**

As shown in (a):
When desired saving exceeds desired investment (as at 1), there is an excess supply of goods. When desired saving is less than desired investment (as at 2), there is an excess demand for goods. Desired saving equals desired investment at point 3.

As shown in (b):
When there is an excess supply of goods (as at 1), the real interest rate is above its equilibrium level. When there is an excess demand for goods (as at 2), the real interest rate is below its equilibrium level. Only points on the *IS* curve (as at 3) represent equilibrium combinations of the real interest rate and the quantity of output demanded.

The *IS* Curve for an Open Economy

So far, we have assumed that demand and supply in the goods market are limited to *domestic* saving and investment. When savings can be channeled internationally in an open economy, the goods market is in equilibrium when desired international lending (or borrowing) by a country equals desired international borrowing (or lending) by other countries.

To understand how international capital mobility affects the *IS* curve in a *large open economy* such as that of the United States, Japan, or Germany, note that domestic saving (sources of funds from within the economy) need not equal domestic investment (demand for funds within the economy). Because capital is mobile internationally in an open economy, an increase in domestic saving can finance either domestic or foreign investment.

Recall that an increase in domestic saving in a large open economy causes the domestic real interest rate to fall (Chapter 6). However, greater domestic saving finances investment at home and abroad, so the real interest rate doesn't have to fall by as much as it would in a closed economy to absorb the greater quantity of domestic saving. Likewise, an increase in investment in the domestic economy can be financed by savings from abroad as well as from home. Hence the real interest rate won't have to rise by as much as it would in a closed economy to restore equilibrium in the goods market. In a large open economy, in contrast to a closed economy, any change in the demand for current output requires a smaller change in the domestic real interest rate. As a result, the *IS* curve for a large open economy is flatter than that for a large closed economy. (We analyze this difference in the appendix to this chapter.)

The flatter *IS* curve for the large open economy illustrates the important effects of financial market integration on the economy. Figure 24.1 showed that when current output increases, desired saving increases, and that the supply of goods exceeds demand at the initial real rate of interest. To restore equilibrium in the goods market, the domestic real interest rate must fall to raise the quantity of goods demanded to the quantity of goods supplied. The same events occur in an open economy, but the integration of the goods market and asset market modifies them. As for the closed economy, the domestic real interest rate falls as desired domestic saving increases. However, the decline in the interest rate (which also is felt abroad in integrated capital markets) increases both the foreign and domestic demand for domestic goods. As a result, investment increases in the foreign country and foreign saving decreases. Foreigners increase their international borrowing, so some of the increased domestic saving flows abroad.

The flow of goods matches exactly this movement of savings in an open economy. The domestic economy lends funds to foreigners, and its *current account balance*—the difference between exports and imports, or net exports—increases as foreigners increase their demand for domestically produced goods. The foreign economy borrows funds from the domestic economy, and its own current account balance decreases as foreigners demand more goods from the domestic economy. In a large open economy, the real interest rate doesn't have to fall by as much to restore equilibrium in the goods markets in response to an increase in current domestic output. Similarly, the real interest rate doesn't have to increase by as much to restore equilibrium in response to a decrease in current domestic output.

Our analysis of implications for the slope of the *IS* curve of international integration of goods and financial markets is relevant for the large open economies such as the United States, Germany, and Japan. Goods and financial markets in a *small open economy* are integrated with those of the rest of the world. However, flows of goods and capital to and from a small open economy are too small to affect the world interest rate. As a result, the *IS* curve for a small open economy is simply horizontal at the world real rate of interest r_W. A small open economy therefore can lend or borrow in international capital markets at that real rate of interest. Any value of output in the small open economy is consistent with the equilibrium real interest rate. In our graphical analysis of the economy's equilibrium, we use the *IS* curve for a large open economy.

CONSIDER THIS . . .

Are Savings Internationally Mobile?

Our discussion of the *IS* curve for a large open economy implies that if saving were completely mobile among countries, domestic saving wouldn't have to equal domestic investment. Savings would flow to the economies that offered the highest expected return, and expected returns would equalize around the world (adjusting for differences in the risk, liquidity, and information characteristics of the financial instruments). As a result, if saving increased in a country, rather than reducing the domestic real interest rate below worldwide levels (thereby increasing investment at home), some of the additional funds would flow abroad.

Using data from the 1960s and 1970s, Martin Feldstein and Charles Horioka examined relationships between domestic saving and investment relative to aggregate output in the United States, Japan, and many European countries.† They estimated that a $1.00 change in domestic saving led to an approximately equal change in domestic investment, casting doubt on international capital mobility. However, Feldstein and Philippe Bacchetta later found that during the 1980s, changes in domestic saving and investment were not as highly correlated.††

Hence the most recent evidence suggests that the economies of the United States, Japan, and many European nations are large open economies and that international borrowing and lending are significant in financial markets.

† Martin Feldstein and Charles Horioka, "Domestic Saving and International Capital Flows," *Economic Journal,* 90:314–329, 1980.

†† Martin Feldstein and Philippe Bacchetta, "National Saving and International Investment," in B. Douglas Bernheim and John B. Shoven, eds., *National Saving and Economic Performance,* Chicago: University of Chicago Press, 1991.

CHECKPOINT

Suppose that the real interest rate in Massachusetts is very low—say, 0.5%—but the real interest rate in California is very high—say, 10%. What would you do if you were a Massachusetts saver? You probably would invest part of your savings in California to take advantage of the higher expected return. As financial markets have become more global, savings can flow abroad in search of higher returns. o

Shifts of the *IS* Curve

Increases or decreases in the demand for goods change the equilibrium real interest rate for each level of current output and cause the *IS* curve to shift. These increases or decreases in the real interest rate may be the result of an increase or decrease in one of the determinants of desired saving and investment: current and expected future income, government purchases, or the expected future profitability of capital. An increase in one of these factors shifts the *IS* curve up and to the right by increasing the real interest rate that is required to reach equilibrium in the goods market for any given level of current output. For example, a military buildup, an increase in the overseas popularity of U.S. cars, a decline in households' willingness to save, or development of a major new technology that produces an environmentally safe substitute for plastics causes such a shift. A reduction in one of the determinants shifts the *IS* curve down and to the left by decreasing the real interest rate that is required to reach equilibrium in the goods market for any given level of current output. Table 24.1 summarizes the factors that account for shifts in the *IS* curve.

DETERMINING OUTPUT: THE FULL EMPLOYMENT LINE

The *IS* curve illustrates combinations of the level of current output and the real interest rate for which the goods market is in equilibrium. Each point on the *IS* curve represents equilibrium in the goods market, but we cannot use the *IS* curve alone to find the level of current output that actually prevails in the market for goods and services. We need another piece of information: the level of output that firms are willing to supply in the goods market. The supply of **current output,** or the level of output that firms produce at any particular time, is determined by (1) the existing capital stock and (2) the use of variable production factors, such as labor. The capital stock reflects the accumulated

TABLE 24.1 **ACCOUNTING FOR SHIFTS OF THE *IS* CURVE**

An Increase in . . .	Shifts the *IS* Curve . . .	Because . . .
government purchases	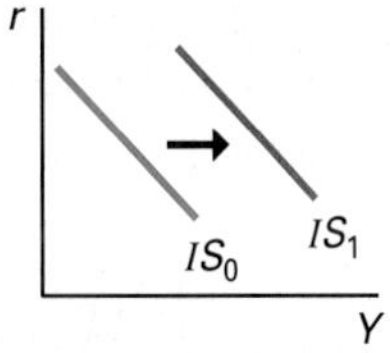	an increase in government purchases increases the demand for current output, decreasing saving and increasing the real interest rate required to restore equilibrium in the goods market.
foreign demand for domestically produced goods	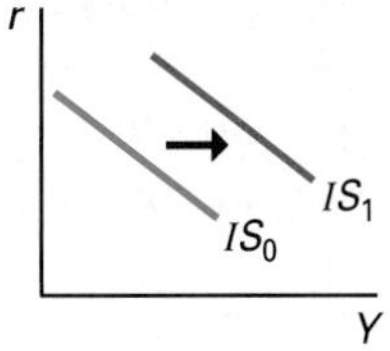	an increase in foreign demand increases the demand for current output, increasing the real interest rate required to restore equilibrium in the goods market.
households' willingness to save	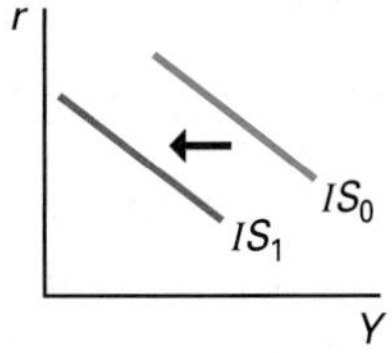	an increase in saving decreases the demand for current output, reducing the real interest rate required to restore equilibrium in the goods market.
expected future profitability of capital	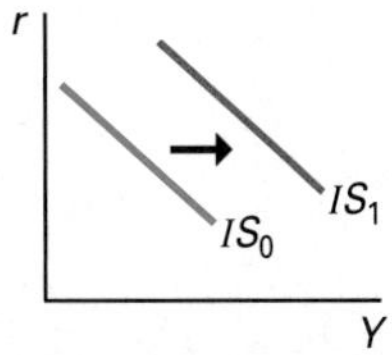	with higher expected future profitability of capital, firms want to invest more, raising the demand for current output and the real interest rate required to clear the goods market.

investment of previous years. We therefore assume that it is fixed, with new investment being incorporated as capital stock for use in the future. For simplicity, we also assume that the supply of variable factors is fixed. (Later, we will examine output in the long run when firms can adjust all factors in production.) Hence **full employment output** in the economy in the current period is the production level that is achieved by the use of all available production factors, regardless of the real rate of interest. Therefore it is constant at Y^* in Fig. 24.3, and the resulting vertical line is called the **full employment (*FE*) line.**

The intersection of the *IS* curve and the *FE* line represents goods market equilibrium. For example, suppose that (as shown in Fig. 24.3) the equilibrium in the goods market is described by the combination of current output of $10,000 billion and a real interest rate of 4%. When output equals $10,000 billion, a real interest rate of 4% ensures that desired saving equals desired investment because the point ($Y =$ $10,000 billion, $r = 4\%$) is on the *IS* curve.

OTHER TIMES, OTHER PLACES . . .

The Gulf War and "Confidence"

The determinants of saving and business investment are based on expectations of the future, which can be interpreted in part as a reflection of consumer confidence or optimism about the future. Iraq's invasion of Kuwait in August 1990 and the ensuing Gulf War in early 1991 adversely affected U.S. consumer and business confidence. Consumers worried about the effects of possible increases in oil prices on the purchasing power of their incomes. In fact, a University of Michigan survey measured consumer confidence dropping by 28% in the last half of 1990 and rebounding after the war's conclusion. Business confidence also dropped, and firms cut back on inventory investment and, to a lesser extent, on capital investment. At the same time, the U.S. government increased its expenditures to finance the war. How did these changes in spending affect aggregate demand?

Researchers at the Federal Reserve Bank of San Francisco found that reductions in consumption and investment due to falling consumer confidence shifted the *IS* curve down to the left from IS_0 to IS_1. This effect dominated the higher U.S. government purchases, which shifted the *IS* curve up to the right from IS_0 to IS_2, as shown in the accompanying diagram. Analysts believe that the net result of the two movements was a shift down to the left, because the military principally used its stock of existing weapons rather than spending money on new weapons.

Source: "The Gulf War and the U.S. Economy," Federal Reserve Bank of San Francisco *Weekly Letter,* September 13, 1991.

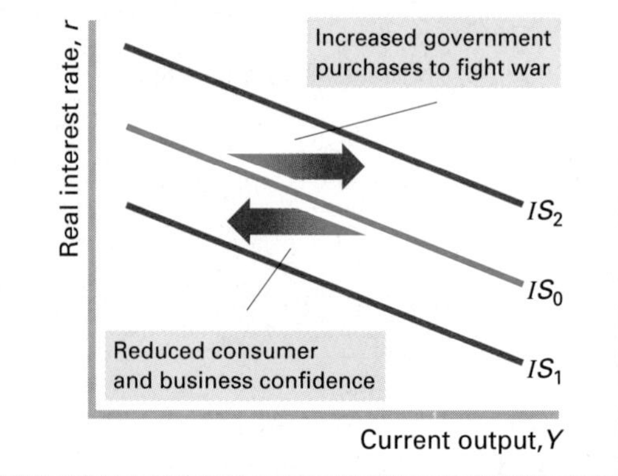

Figure 24.3

Determining Current Output in the Goods Market

Equilibrium output in the goods market is Y^*, given by full utilization of all existing production factors. The equilibrium real interest rate, r^*, brings saving and investment into equilibrium at that level of output.

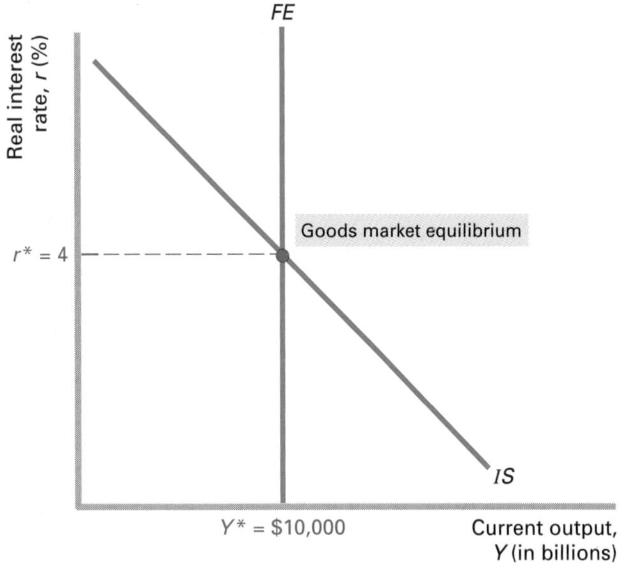

Current output is influenced by the efficiency of existing production factors. An increase in the current productivity of either capital or labor shifts the *FE* line to the right. For example, if everyone decided to work harder each hour this year, current productivity would rise, shifting the *FE* line to the right. By contrast, an unexpected oil price increase reduces the productivity of energy-using machines, shifting the *FE* line to the left. Although changes in expected future productivity affect investment and the *IS* curve, they don't affect current output. Only the productivity of factors that are already in place affect current output. Table 24.2 summarizes the factors that account for shifts in the *FE* line.

CHECKPOINT

Suppose that you manage a tool factory in northern Michigan. What would happen to your company's ability to use its plant and equipment to generate output if a series of snowstorms idled the factory for several weeks? What effect would the storms have on the *FE* line? If workers were unable to get to work, current output would fall, shifting your factory's *FE* line to the left. Weather fluctuations, strikes, and trade disruptions act as productivity shocks, shifting the economy's *FE* line. o

THE *LM* CURVE

We now turn to the third step in building a model that shows the relationship between the financial system and the economy. In this section, we construct the *LM* curve, a graphical relationship between the interest rate and output that exists when asset markets are in equilibrium.

We simplify our view of asset markets by dividing them into money and nonmoney markets. The money market is in equilibrium only when the non-

TABLE 24.2 **ACCOUNTING FOR SHIFTS OF THE *FE* LINE**

A(n) . . .	Shifts the *FE* Line . . .	Because . . .
increase in current productivity of capital or labor	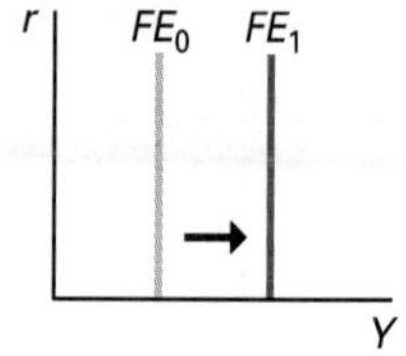	an increase in productivity implies that more output can be produced from the existing amount of factors.
decrease in current productivity of capital or labor	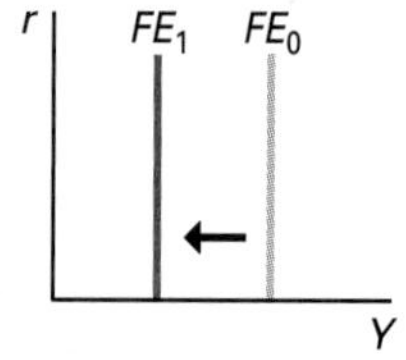	a decrease in productivity implies that less output can be produced from a given amount of factors in place.

money asset market also is in equilibrium. We first establish the link between the equilibrium in the money market and equilibrium in the nonmoney asset market. Then we examine the conditions in which the money market is in equilibrium.

Asset Market Equilibrium

Money assets and nonmoney assets (such as stocks and bonds) offer savers alternative ways to allocate their wealth. For example, Jane Rich must decide how to allocate her wealth, w, between money and nonmoney assets. Her demand for money balances, m_d, added to her demand for nonmoney assets, n_d, equals her total wealth, w, or

$$m_d + n_d = w.$$

Each household and business faces this portfolio allocation decision. The markets for money and nonmoney assets are in equilibrium when the total quantities demanded equal the total quantities supplied. Therefore, for the economy as a whole, the total demand for money balances, M_d, and nonmoney assets, N_d, equals total wealth, W, or

$$M_d + N_d = W. \tag{24.3}$$

On the supply side, total wealth W equals the sum of the total quantity of money supplied, M_s, and the total quantity of nonmoney assets supplied, N_s, or

$$M_s + N_s = W. \tag{24.4}$$

Because the market mechanism ensures that in equilibrium, the quantity of an asset supplied equals the quantity demanded, we can equate Eq. (24.3) and

Eq. (24.4). Doing so gives us a relation between the equilibrium in the two asset markets:

$$(M_d - M_s) + (N_d - N_s) = 0, \text{ or}$$
$$M_d - M_s = N_s - N_d. \tag{24.5}$$

When the total quantity of money demanded exceeds the quantity supplied, that is, $M_d > M_s$, the expression on the left-hand side of Eq. (24.5) is positive, representing an excess demand for money. When $N_s > N_d$, the total quantity of nonmoney assets supplied exceeds the quantity demanded, creating an excess supply of nonmoney assets. Thus Eq. (24.5) states that the *excess demand* for one of the two assets (money or nonmoney) equals the *excess supply* of the other. In equilibrium, asset prices adjust so that there is no excess demand or supply in the money market; in other words, the left-hand side of Eq. (24.5) equals zero. Hence the right-hand side of Eq. (24.5) must also equal zero. Therefore the money market is in equilibrium only if the nonmoney market is in equilibrium. Knowing that the equilibrium in one of the two asset markets is related to the equilibrium in the other, we can make an important simplification: Any combination of current output and the real interest rate for which the money market is in equilibrium will imply that the nonmoney asset market is in equilibrium, and vice versa. We use this simplification to confine our attention to determinants of equilibrium in the money market.

CHECKPOINT

If Jane Rich is satisfied with the proportion of her wealth that is held in money, is she also satisfied with her nonmoney asset holdings of savings in bonds and stocks? Yes. Jane's demand for real money balances depends on the expected returns that are available on nonmoney assets. Her satisfaction with her wealth allocation implies that she has compared her returns from holding money with expected returns on other assets (adjusted for differences in risk, liquidity, and information costs).

Constructing the *LM* Curve

On the supply side, the quantity of real money balances supplied equals the aggregate money supply M_s divided by the general price level P: $(M/P)_s$, or *MS*. The demand for real money balances is $(M/P)_d$, or *MD*. But money demand depends on real income (or output) Y, the interest rate on nonmoney assets i, the return on money i_M, and other factors, so we can replace $(M/P)_d$ with the function $L(Y, I, i_M)$. Equilibrium is reached when the quantity of real money supplied equals the quantity of real money demanded:

$$\left(\frac{M}{P}\right)_s = \left(\frac{M}{P}\right)_d = L(Y, i, i_M, \ldots),$$

where L is the liquidity preference relation linking the demand for real money balances to its determinants.

Let's examine those determinants more closely. The variable i represents the nominal market interest rate on nonmoney assets and is the sum of the underlying real interest rate, r (assumed to be the expected real rate of interest), and expected inflation, π^e:

$$i = r + \pi^e.$$

Substituting this expression for the nominal interest rate i into the preceding expression, we get

$$\frac{M}{P} = L(Y, r + \pi^e, i_M, \ldots). \tag{24.6}$$

Equation (24.6) contains too many variables for our analysis of r and Y. If we hold constant the other factors in Eq. (24.6)—the nominal money supply M, price level P, expected rate of inflation π^e, and nominal return on money i_M—we can describe combinations of current output Y and real interest rate r for which the money market (and hence the nonmoney asset market) generally is in equilibrium.

Suppose that households and businesses are satisfied with their real money balances M/P when output in the economy is \$10,000 billion and the real rate of interest is 4%, indicated by E_0 in Fig. 24.4(a); that is, the money market is in equilibrium at that point. If real output increases to \$11,000 billion, Eq. (24.6) indicates that the quantity of real money demanded, $(M/P)_d$, increases; the money demand curve shifts from MD_0 to MD_1. With all the other factors held constant, the real interest rate r must increase from 4% to 5% to reduce the quantity of real money demanded, as shown by E_1 in Fig. 24.4(a).

Figure 24.4(b) illustrates the combinations of current output and the real interest rate for which the money market is in equilibrium, a set of points called the ***LM* curve.** It is a graph of the relationship in Eq. (24.6), in which the quantity of real money demanded (the liquidity preference function L) equals the quantity of money supplied. Because a higher real interest rate is associated with a higher level of output in a money market equilibrium, the LM curve slopes upward to the right. The size of the increase in the real interest rate that is required to restore equilibrium in the money market depends on how responsive money demand is to the interest rate. Therefore the slope of the LM curve depends on the sensitivity of the demand for real money balances to the nominal interest rate i.

When the interest sensitivity of the demand for real money balances is low, interest rates must change a lot for the money market to remain in equilibrium if output changes. Since large interest rate changes are associated with a given output change, the LM schedule will be steeply sloped. If the demand for real balances were completely insensitive to the opportunity cost of holding money, the LM curve would be vertical. Conversely, if the demand for real money balances were sensitive to the interest rate, then whenever money demand changed in response to an increase in output, a much smaller increase in the real interest rate would be required to restore equilibrium in the money

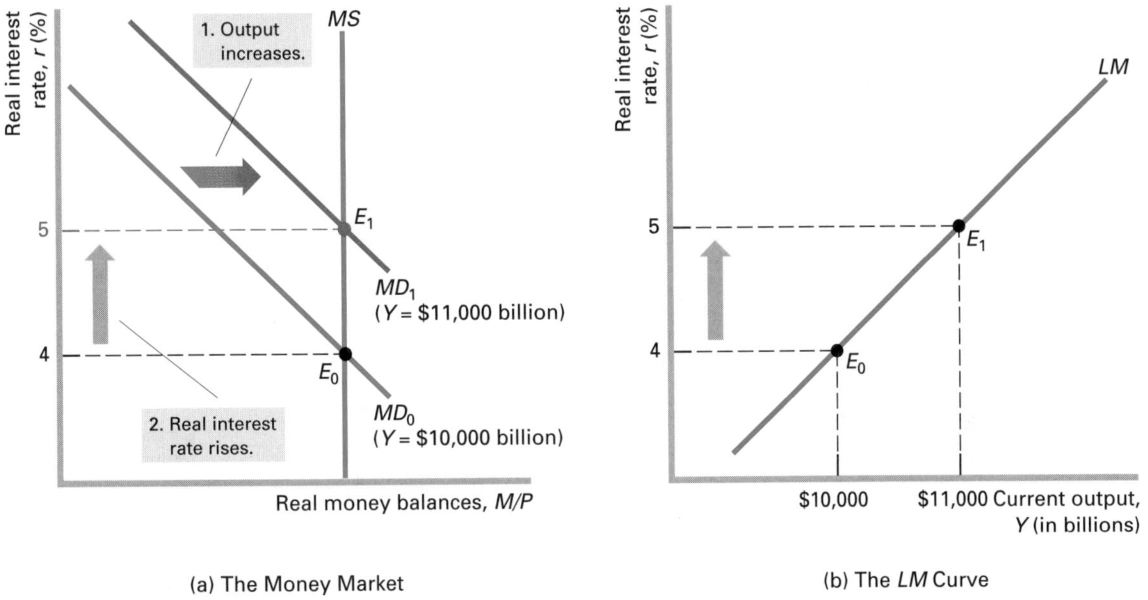

Figure 24.4 **The *LM* Curve**

As shown in (a):

1. When current output increases, real money demand increases.
2. If real money balances supplied are held constant, an increase in current output raises the real interest rate.

As shown in (b):

The *LM* curve slopes upward. To maintain equilibrium in the money market, higher levels of current output result in higher values of the real interest rate.

market. In this case, the *LM* curve would be relatively flat. If the demand for real balances were infinitely sensitive to the interest rate, the *LM* curve would be horizontal.

To summarize, the slope of the *LM* curve depends on the interest sensitivity of the demand for money. If the demand for money is sensitive to the interest rate, the *LM* curve is relatively flat; if the demand for money is insensitive to the interest rate, the *LM* curve is relatively steep.

At any point along the *LM* curve, the quantity of money demanded equals the quantity supplied. However, as was the case for the *IS* curve, only points on the *LM* curve represent an equilibrium in the asset markets. To understand why, consider Fig. 24.5(a). When current output is $10,000 billion and the real interest rate is 5%, there is an excess supply of money, indicated by point 1. Households and businesses use some of this excess money to buy nonmoney assets, causing their prices to rise and the interest rate to fall until the real interest rate equals 4%, at point 3. Conversely, when output equals $10,000 billion and the real interest rate is 3%, there is an excess demand for money, indicated by point 2. Households and firms sell nonmoney assets for money, causing their price to fall and the interest rate to rise until the real interest rate equals 4%, at point 3.

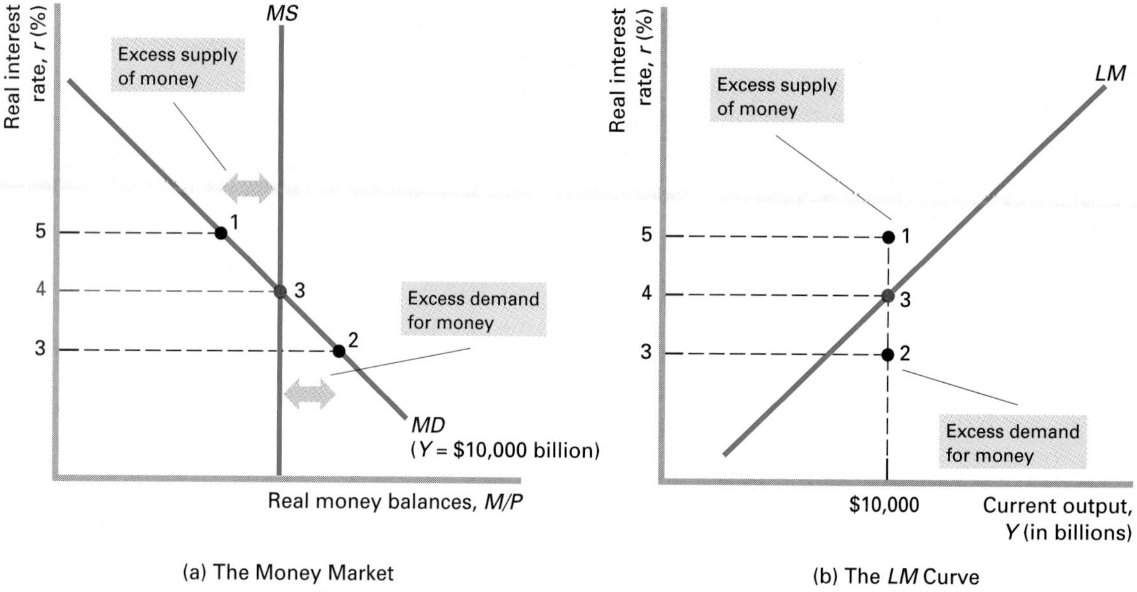

Figure 24.5

Points Off the *LM* Curve

As shown in (a):

When real money balances supplied exceed the quantity demanded (as at 1), there is an excess supply of money. When the quantity of money demanded exceeds the quantity supplied (as at 2), there is an excess demand for money. The money market is in equilibrium at point 3, where the quantities demanded and supplied of real balances are equal.

As shown in (b):

When there is an excess supply of money (as at 1), the real interest rate is above its equilibrium level. When there is an excess demand for money (as at 2), the real interest rate is below its equilibrium level. Only points on the *LM* curve (as at 3) represent equilibrium combinations of the real interest rate and output consistent with asset market equilibrium.

Figure 24.5(b) illustrates this process with the *LM* curve. Point 1 and others that are above the *LM* curve represent an excess supply of money and an excess demand for nonmoney assets. Point 2 and others that are below the *LM* curve represent an excess demand for money and an excess supply of nonmoney assets. Again, money demand and supply are in equilibrium at point 3.

CHECKPOINT

Suppose that the Fed wanted to induce you to hold no more than $1000 of your assets in currency and non-interest-bearing checkable deposits. If you wanted to hold more than $1000 because your income and volume of transactions are rising, how could the Fed convince you not to hold more currency in your wallet or checking account? If the Fed could raise the real rate of return on other financial assets, you would want to increase your holdings of financial assets. How much the real rate would have to rise depends on how sensitive to interest rate changes your portfolio decisions are. Along your *LM* curve, then, an increase in *Y* (income) is associated with an increase in *r*. **o**

Shifts of the *LM* Curve

When we analyzed the *IS* curve, we saw that changes in variables other than current output or the real interest rate could shift the curve. The same is true for the *LM* curve. The variables that are responsible for shifts of the *LM* curve are those in Eq. (24.6): the nominal money supply M, the price level P, the nominal return on money i_M, and the expected rate of inflation π^e.

Changes in real money balances supplied. The level of real money balances—the nominal money supply divided by the price level—is taken as a given in the derivation of the *LM* curve. What happens to the money market equilibrium when the quantity supplied of real balances increases as occurs, for example, when the Fed pursues an expansionary monetary policy? To restore equilibrium in asset markets, the quantity of money demanded must be increased in one of two ways. For a constant output level, a drop in the real interest rate makes the option of holding money more attractive and thus increases the quantity of money demanded. In other words, if expected inflation is held constant, the nominal interest rate falls to reduce the opportunity cost of holding money instead of nonmoney assets. Or if the real interest rate is held constant, an increase in the equilibrium level of output increases the quantity of real balances demanded. In either case, the *LM* curve shifts down and to the right.

When the quantity supplied of real money balances declines, as in the case of a contractionary monetary policy, equilibrium is restored by reducing the quantity of money demanded. For a constant current output level, an increase in the real rate of interest restores equilibrium in the money market by lowering the quantity of real balances demanded. For a constant real interest rate, a decline in current output restores money market equilibrium. A decrease in the nominal money supply, M, for a constant price level, shifts the *LM* curve up and to the left.

These possibilities illustrate shifts of the *LM* curve that are caused by changes in the nominal money supply (for a constant price level). Similarly, we can examine the effects on the *LM* curve of a change in the price level by holding the nominal money supply constant. For example, a decline in the price level because of a drop in energy prices increases real money balances, causing the *LM* curve to shift down and to the right. An increase in the price level because of a rise in energy prices reduces real money balances so that the *LM* curve shifts up and to the left.

Changes in the nominal return on money. Increases or decreases in the nominal return from holding money change the demand for money and cause the *LM* curve to shift. Recall that households and businesses compare returns on money and nonmoney assets when deciding how much wealth to hold as money balances. Although not all components of money (currency, for example) pay interest, some (such as interest-bearing checkable deposits) do. What is the effect on the *LM* curve of an increase in the nominal return on money—say, as the result of deregulation of the interest paid on checkable deposits?

If we assume that the other determinants of money demand do not change, an increase in i_M (the nominal return on money) makes money balances more attractive to investors relative to nonmoney assets. As a result, the quantity of real money balances demanded increases. A higher real interest rate, then, is required to restore equilibrium in the money market. As the real interest rate on nonmoney assets increases, the nominal interest rate on those assets rises relative to the nominal return on money, making them more attractive to investors than money, thereby reducing the quantity of money demanded. Asset market equilibrium is restored by increasing the real interest rate for any level of output. A decrease in the nominal return on real money balances makes nonmoney assets more attractive to investors than money. As a result, the quantity of money demanded declines. To restore equilibrium in the money market, the nominal interest rate must fall. Asset market equilibrium is restored by increasing the quantity of money demanded.

Therefore, if nothing else changes, an increase in the nominal return on money shifts the *LM* curve up and to the left. A decrease in the nominal return on money shifts the *LM* curve down and to the right.

Changes in expected inflation. Recall that the nominal rate of interest equals the sum of the expected real rate of interest r and the expected rate of inflation π^e. Increases or decreases in the expected rate of inflation affect asset market equilibrium by changing the nominal rate of interest associated with any real rate of interest.

What if expected inflation rises because of the public's expectation that the Fed is pursuing a policy that will spur inflation? If the *real* interest rate were to remain unchanged, the *nominal* interest rate would rise. For a constant nominal return on money, nonmoney assets would be relatively more attractive to savers, reducing the demand for real money balances. To restore equilibrium in the money market, the real interest rate must fall at any level of output to preserve asset market equilibrium.

An increase in expected inflation causes the *LM* curve to shift down by the amount by which the expected rate of inflation increases. Similarly, a drop in expected inflation causes the *LM* curve to shift up by the amount of decline in the expected rate of inflation. Table 24.3 summarizes the factors that affect the *LM* curve.

CHECKPOINT

Suppose that widespread use of bank debit cards and credit cards reduces the demand for money at any particular level of income and interest rates. How does the *LM* curve respond if the money supply doesn't change? Because the demand for money has fallen, the real interest rate at any particular income level would have to be lower to encourage the public to hold the quantity of money supplied. The *LM* curve shifts down and to the right. o

TABLE 24.3 FACTORS SHIFTING THE *LM* CURVE

An Increase in . . .	Shifts the *LM* Curve . . .	Because . . .
the supply of nominal money balances, M_s	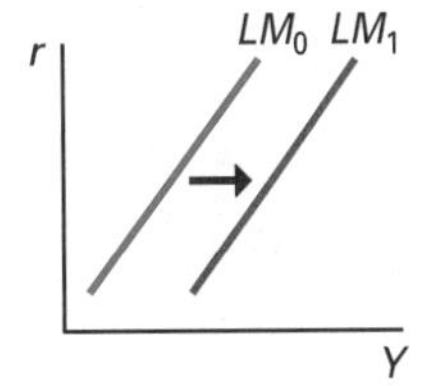	the real interest rate falls, increasing demand for money at any output level.
aggregate price level, P	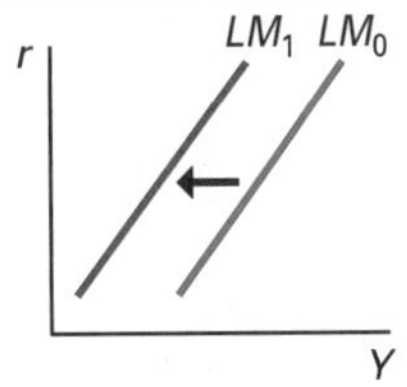	the real interest rate rises, reducing demand for money at any output level.
nominal return on money, i_M	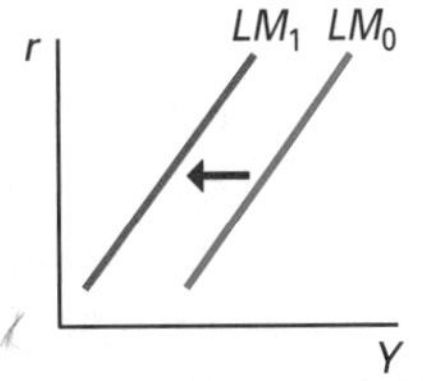	the real interest rate rises, reducing demand for money at any output level.
expected rate of inflation, π^e	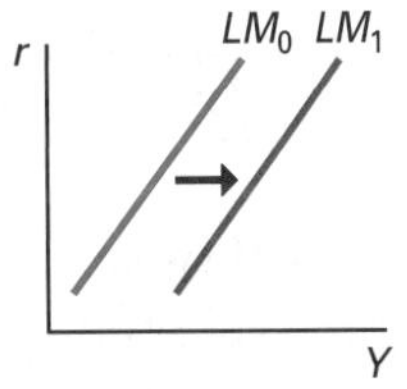	the real interest rate falls, increasing demand for money at any output level.

THE FINANCIAL SYSTEM AND THE ECONOMY: THE *IS-LM-FE* MODEL

Each curve in the *IS-LM-FE* model represents a portion of the behavior that we are trying to explain: effects of changes in interest rates on output, effects of output on interest rates, and the supply of current output. Changes in interest rates affect output through the *IS* curve, and changes in output affect interest rates through the *LM* curve. The *FE* line represents the amount of current output that can be produced by full employment of the economy's resources. At the intersection of the *IS* curve and the *LM* curve, the economy's real interest rate equates saving and investment, and households and businesses are satisfied with their allocation of assets between money and nonmoney assets. At the intersection of the *IS* curve and the *FE* line, current output is consistent with full employment of the economy's resources.

Figure 24.6

The Economy and Financial System in Long-Run Equilibrium

Long-run equilibrium in the economy occurs when a combination of the real rate of interest, r^*, and the level of current output, Y^*, causes the *IS* curve, *LM* curve, and *FE* line to intersect.

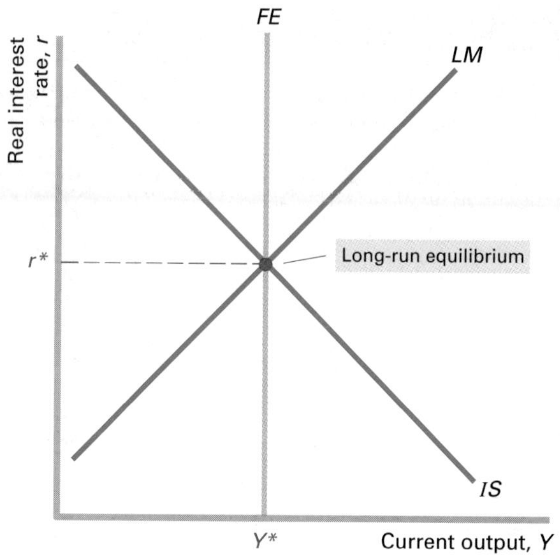

The financial system and the goods market are both in equilibrium when the *IS* curve, *FE* line, and *LM* curve all intersect at the same point, as Fig. 24.6 shows. This equilibrium point establishes the level of current output and the real interest rate. Thus equilibrium occurs at the real interest rate at which the current output supplied is equal to the current output demanded. We now analyze how this equilibrium changes in response to factors that shift the *IS* curve, *FE* line, and *LM* curve.

Using the Model to Explain the Economy's Equilibrium

Shifts in the *IS* curve, *FE* line, or *LM* curve cause changes in the equilibrium of the financial system and the economy. We describe examples of each type of shift; we then examine how policymakers use the model to analyze how the financial system and the economy return to equilibrium.

Shifts in the *IS* curve. Changes in government purchases of goods and services shift the *IS* curve. Suppose that the President and Congress decide that the United States should undertake a large-scale military buildup, as occurred in the early 1980s. Starting from equilibrium at E_0 in Fig. 24.7(a), an increase in government purchases shifts the *IS* curve up and to the right, from IS_0 to IS_1. Note that the IS_1 curve intersects the *FE* line at E_1, representing the same level of output as E_0 but at a higher real interest rate. However, if we hold expected inflation and the nominal return on money constant, the asset markets are no longer in equilibrium; the intersection of the *IS* curve and *FE* line is not on the *LM* curve, and there is an excess supply of money. Moreover, the intersection of the *IS* and *LM* curves at E_2 is not on the *FE* line, since the implied current output level is greater than the current output level indicated by the *FE* line. Hence, if we hold the

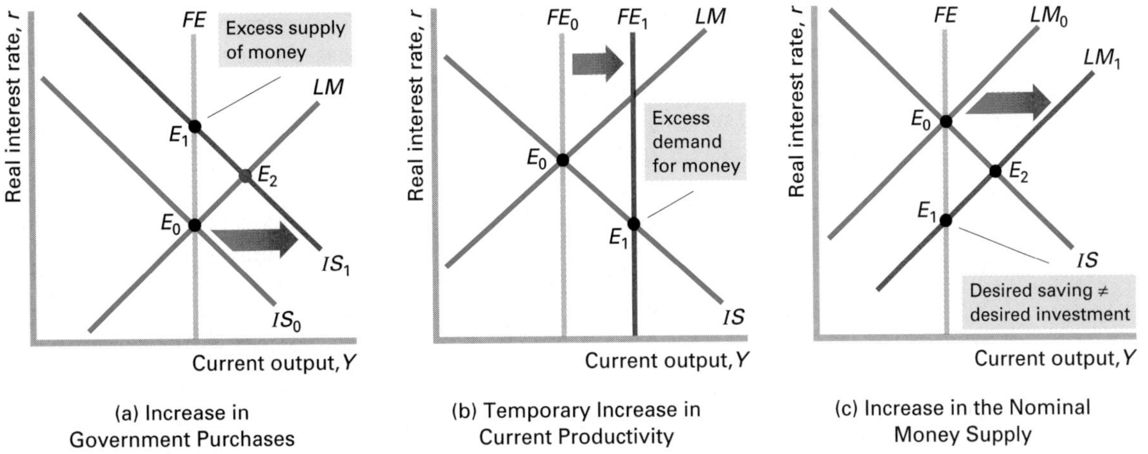

Figure 24.7

Changing the Equilibrium

As shown in (a):

At point E_0, the economy and the financial system are in equilibrium. The increase in government purchases shifts the *IS* curve from IS_0 to IS_1. The *IS* curve and *FE* line intersect at E_1, but the asset markets aren't in equilibrium. There is an excess supply of money.

As shown in (b):

At point E_0, the economy and the financial system are in equilibrium. The boost in current productivity shifts the *FE* line from FE_0 to FE_1. The new goods market equilibrium lies at point E_1, but the asset markets aren't in equilibrium. There is an excess demand for money.

As shown in (c):

At point E_0, the economy and the financial system are in equilibrium. When the Fed increases the nominal money supply, the *LM* curve shifts from LM_0 to LM_1. It intersects the *IS* curve at E_2, but that point isn't on the *FE* line. The *LM* curve and *FE* line intersect at E_1, but desired saving and investment are not equal.

determinants of the three curves constant, there is no combination of current output and real interest rate for which all markets in the economy and the financial system are in equilibrium.

Shifts in the *FE* line. Suppose that the economy is at equilibrium initially at E_0 in Fig. 24.7(b) and that a decline in energy prices leads to a temporary increase in productivity, as occurred in the middle and the late 1980s. The increase in productivity shifts the *FE* line to the right from FE_0 to FE_1, while the positions of the *IS* and *LM* curves remain unchanged. As a result, the *IS* curve and FE_1 now intersect at E_1, at which the asset markets are no longer in equilibrium. At E_1, the real rate of interest is too low to maintain asset market equilibrium at current levels of output, prices, expected inflation, and nominal return on money. The excess demand for real money balances throws the asset markets out of equilibrium. At the intersection of the *IS* and *LM* curves at E_0, the output level is less than that at FE_1.

Shifts in the *LM* curve. What happens to the equilibrium of the financial system and the economy if the Fed significantly increases the money supply, as occurred in the late 1970s? Suppose that the goods market and asset markets are in equilibrium at E_0 in Fig. 24.7(c). An increase in the nominal money supply shifts the LM curve down and to the right from LM_0 to LM_1.

As a result, E_0—where the *IS* curve and *FE* line intersect—no longer denotes an asset market equilibrium. Because E_0 lies above the new LM curve, it represents an excess supply of money. At E_1, the new LM curve intersects the *FE* line, but the goods market is no longer in equilibrium. Because E_1 lies below the *IS* curve, there is an excess demand for goods at that point. Note that at E_2—where the *IS* and LM curves intersect—desired saving and investment are not equal, and the implied value of current output is greater than actual current output (represented by the *FE* line). Hence, if we hold the determinants of the three curves constant, there is no combination of current output and real interest rate for which all markets in the economy and the financial system are in equilibrium.

Restoring Equilibrium: Price-Level Adjustment

How can the economy and financial system achieve equilibrium when one of the three curves shifts? Some variable will have to change in response to the changes that we analyzed. Let's assume that the price level *P* is flexible and can adjust freely in response to such changes. Is this assumption realistic? The answer depends on the definition of the period over which prices adjust. If the period is a week, the assumption of flexible prices may not be realistic. If the period is three years, the assumption may be more accurate. In Chapter 25, we examine reasons why prices may not be flexible in the short run and show how sticky prices affect short-run equilibrium. For now, however, let's assume that prices are flexible in the long run and return to the shifts in the *IS* curve, *FE* line, and LM curve that we analyzed earlier.

Shifts in the *IS* curve. Recall that the shift in the *IS* curve resulting from a military buildup left the asset markets out of equilibrium, with a higher real interest rate than at initial equilibrium. With the increased opportunity cost of money, households and businesses try to use their higher than desired real money balances to buy goods, putting upward pressure on prices. As Fig. 24.8(a) shows, the higher price level reduces the supply of real money balances, causing the LM curve to shift from LM_0 to LM_1, where it intersects the *IS* curve and the *FE* line at E_1.

Hence, if nothing else changes, an increase in government purchases has no effect on output in the long run when prices are flexible. However, both the real rate of interest and the price level increase, so the quantity of real money balances demanded equals the quantity supplied. For any expected rate of inflation, the higher real rate of interest implies a higher nominal rate of interest and a decline in the quantity of real money balances demanded.

The higher real rate of interest in the economy increases private saving and decreases current consumption and investment. The reduction in private

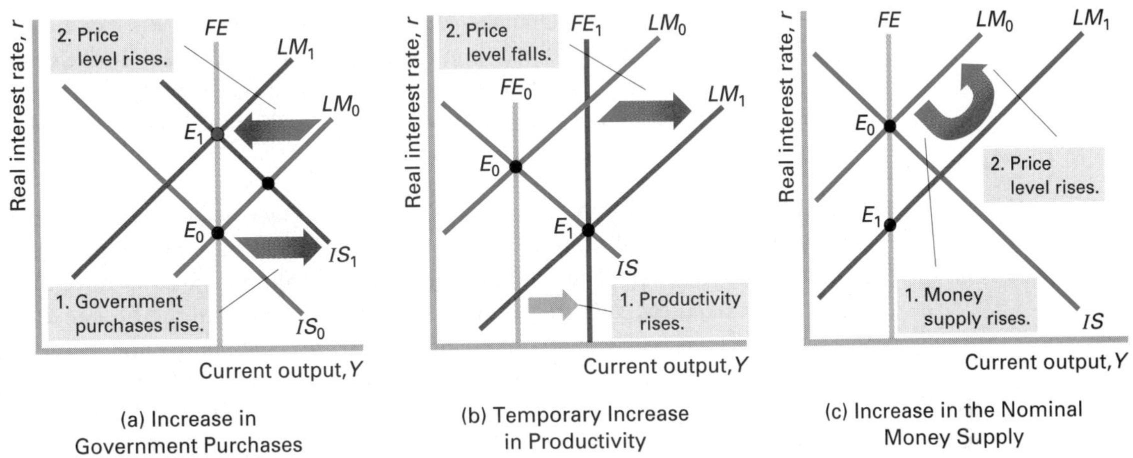

Figure 24.8 **Price-Level Adjustment to Restore the Economy's Equilibrium**

As shown in (a):
1. From an initial equilibrium at E_0, higher government purchases shift the *IS* curve from IS_0 to IS_1.
2. The price level rises, shifting the *LM* curve from LM_0 to LM_1 to restore equilibrium at E_1.

As shown in (b):
1. From an initial equilibrium at E_0, increased productivity shifts the full employment line from FE_0 to FE_1.
2. A fall in the price level shifts the *LM* curve from LM_0 to LM_1 and restores equilibrium at E_1.

As shown in (c):
1. From an initial equilibrium at E_0, an increase in the nominal money supply shifts the *LM* curve from LM_0 to LM_1.
2. The price level increases, shifting the *LM* curve back from LM_1 to LM_0 and restoring equilibrium at E_0.

consumption and investment that accompanies an increase in government purchases in a closed economy is known as *crowding out.*†

Shifts in the *FE* line. In Fig. 24.8(b), starting from equilibrium at E_0, an increase in the full employment level of current output generates an excess demand for real money balances. At levels of the real interest rate and current output that lead to equilibrium in the goods market, households prefer to hold larger money balances. The excess supply of goods pushes prices down. Lower prices, in turn, increase the demand for goods and increase households' real money balances. The *LM* curve shifts from LM_0 to LM_1 to intersect the *IS* curve and *FE* line at E_1, and the asset markets return to equilibrium, but at a lower real interest rate and a higher level of current output.

†In a large open economy, such as the U.S. economy, an increase in the real rate of interest increases desired international lending by foreign investors, resulting in capital flows from abroad into the domestic economy. Consequently, the current account balance of the domestic economy deteriorates. In other words, an increase in government purchases results in a decrease in net exports.

Hence, if nothing else changes, an increase in productivity in the current period raises output while decreasing the price level and the real interest rate. For a given expected inflation, the lower real interest rate increases the quantity of real money balances demanded. The lower price level raises the real value of money balances.†

Shifts in the *LM* curve. Finally, recall the situation in which the Fed increased the nominal money supply, shifting the *LM* curve down and to the right. In that case, at E_0 in Fig. 24.8(c), households and businesses have more real money balances than they desire. At E_1, where LM_1 and the *FE* line intersect, there is excess demand for goods and services. What would happen if households and businesses tried to spend their excess real money balances to purchase additional goods and services in the goods market? If the aggregate output of goods is fixed in the short run (represented by the *FE* line), higher spending by households and businesses will not raise output but will raise the price level.

As the price level rises, real money balances fall because they equal nominal money balances divided by the price level. The reduction in real money balances causes the *LM* curve to shift up and to the left (from LM_1 back to LM_0). To restore equilibrium in all markets, the price level must rise by the amount by which the nominal money supply initially increased. The economy and the financial system return to equilibrium at E_0.

Money, Output, and Prices in the Long Run

Our conclusions about the effects of changes in the money supply on equilibrium strongly suggest that any percentage increase in the nominal money supply leads to an equal percentage increase in the price level, leaving real money balances unchanged. This constancy of money's effect on the economy in the long run is known as the **neutrality of money.** Monetary neutrality implies that a one-time change in the nominal money supply affects only nominal variables, such as nominal output or the price level. Real output and the real interest rate remain unaffected by a one-time increase or decrease in the nominal money supply.

The concept of monetary neutrality depends on the assumption that prices are flexible. Recall that the way in which neutrality is achieved in response to an increase in the money supply is for the price level to rise. Over short periods of time, the assumption of price flexibility isn't realistic. Many economists believe that changes in the money supply do affect the real economy *in the short run* (as we will demonstrate in Chapter 26). However, economists generally accept the *long-run* neutrality of money.

Earlier in the chapter, we described the big changes in fiscal policy,

† In a large open economy, such as the U.S. economy, a drop in the real interest rate reduces desired international lending from abroad to the domestic economy, and the current account balance increases.

monetary policy, and productivity growth that took place in the 1980s and 1990s. We can use the *IS-LM-FE* model to analyze these events. We can represent the large increases in the federal budget deficit in the early 1980s by an expansionary, outward shift of the *IS* curve, creating short-run pressures for higher output and interest rates. By the late 1990s, an emerging federal budget surplus put downward pressure on interest rates. Two major monetary policies dominated the period. The major monetary contraction beginning in late 1979 can be represented by a contractionary upward shift of the *LM* curve, putting upward pressure on interest rates and downward pressure on output in the short run. In the late 1980s and 1990s, the increase in the credibility of the Federal Reserve's anti-inflation stance reduced the public's expectation of inflation. The decline in expected inflation can be represented by a downward shift of the *LM* curve, putting downward pressure on interest rates and upward pressure on output in the short run. Finally, growth in productivity in the economy can be represented by an outward shift of the *FE* line, increasing output. The rise in energy prices in the early 1980s reduced productivity in the short run, shifting the *FE* line to the left, reducing output.

KEY TERMS AND CONCEPTS

Current output
Full employment (*FE*) line
Full employment output
General equilibrium
Goods market
IS curve
LM curve
Money market
Neutrality of money
Nonmoney asset market

SUMMARY

1. Combinations of current output and the real rate of interest for which the goods market is in equilibrium make up the *IS* curve. The *IS* curve slopes downward: Higher current output requires a lower real interest rate to equate desired saving and investment and achieve equilibrium.
2. The *IS* curve shifts in response to changes in variables that change the equilibrium real interest rate associated with a specific level of current output. These variables include government purchases, foreign demand for domestic goods, households' willingness to save, and the expected future profitability of capital.
3. The full employment (*FE*) line represents current output supplied by full employment of existing factors of production. It is assumed to be independent of the real rate of interest. The intersection of the *IS* curve and *FE* line shows the interest rate and output in the goods market.
4. Asset market equilibrium refers to equilibrium in the markets for money and nonmoney assets. When one of the two asset markets is in equilibrium, the other also is in equilibrium. Plotting combinations of the real interest rate and current output for which the money market is in equilibrium yields the *LM* curve.
5. The *LM* curve slopes upward because money demand depends positively on current output and negatively on the real interest rate. The more sensitive the demand for money is to the interest rate, the flatter the *LM* curve is.

THE WALL STREET JOURNAL FEBRUARY 15, 2001

Productivity: The Magic Elixir

The stock market is down. Layoffs are up. Recession warning flags are flying. Pundits are drafting obits for the New Economy.

a And the next five or 10 years are still likely to be among the best for American workers and consumers since George W. Bush was a 25-year-old hellion in Texas and Richard Nixon was in the White House.

The key is how much of the late-1990s spurt in productivity growth persists and how much was a fluke. How much was driven by an accelerating decline in computer-chip prices, which might not last? How much by strong business spending on information technology, which is weakening? And how much by human ingenuity in using computers and communications gear to work smarter throughout the economy?

Productivity, the goods and services produced from each hour of work, is the magic elixir of economic progress. It's why we live better than our grandparents did without working longer days. Productivity grew at about 2.7% a year for the quarter-century after World War II. Around 1973, it slowed mysteriously to about 1.5% a year, and then perked up around 1995. For the past couple of years, productivity has been growing at better than 3% a year.

Academic economists, very few of whom foresaw the productivity revival, are dissecting data for the late 1990s to explain the past and guess at the future. They agree that something big happened, and that it has to do with information technology; they disagree on details. b Robert Gordon at Northwestern University, who doubts that the Internet is as important an invention as air conditioning, is among the least optimistic. He figures that 0.4 or 0.5 percentage points of the recent increase in annual productivity growth is lasting. Many of his prominent peers, including those at the Federal Reserve, say it's likely to be at least twice that. . . .

But will productivity growth hold up? Federal Reserve Chairman Alan Greenspan, the one economist whose opinions actually count, remains an optimist. One reason, he said this week, is that productivity growth stayed strong when the economy weakened late last year, an unusual and heartening development.

The big issue isn't what computers and the chips embedded in everything from microwaves to mobile phones have done so far. It's how much more existing technology—not counting the stuff still to be invented—can do if businesses, workers, and consumers are willing to change their ways. The answer: a lot. . . .

Treasury Secretary Paul O'Neill, fresh from his perch atop Alcoa Inc., says, "The potential for productivity gains in the U.S. economy is higher than we realize. If you look at the penetration of good ideas, . . . we're still at the 20% to 30% level of what's possible." . . . c

Buying computers and software is easy; rethinking and redesigning the way we work to take full advantage of them is not. Technology changes rapidly; people do not. But they are beginning to.

The 2000 U.S. presidential campaign featured a heated debate over what the federal government should do with anticipated budget surpluses, predicted to be several trillion dollars over the next 10 years. To many seasoned observers, the debate seemed strange, as the previous two decades featured extensive discussion of what to do about persistent federal budget deficits. Some of this shift could be explained by changes in federal tax and spending policy in the 1990s. An additional reason for the change, in the view of many economists, is an acceleration of *productivity growth.*

a An increase in productivity increases the economy's full employment level of output. As shown in the figure, the productivity boom shifts the *FE* line to the right, from FE_0 to FE_1, increasing the economy's full employment level of output from Y_0 to Y_1. If nothing else happened, eventually the economy's equilibrium would be restored with a lower price level and real interest rate and a higher current output [as in the movement described in Fig. 24.8(b)]—definitely good news. This productivity-led economic expansion would have the opposite effects on the economy as did the adverse oil supply shocks of the 1970s.

b What if the increase in productivity growth is small or short-lived? The salutary effects of the rightward shift of the *FE* line described above would be attenuated. To the extent that monetary policy had been set based on the assumption of more significant productivity growth, inflationary pressure could materialize.

c Improvements in the way people use existing technology can increase the productivity of information technology capital and other capital. These productivity improvements reinforce the favorable shift in the economy's full employment output depicted in the figure.

For further thought . . .

Assuming the validity of the efficient markets hypothesis, how should stock prices react to an increase in the expected rate of productivity growth?

Source: David Wessel, "The Magic Elixir of Productivity," *The Wall Street Journal,* February 15, 2001. Republished by permission of Dow Jones, Inc., via Copyright Clearance Center.

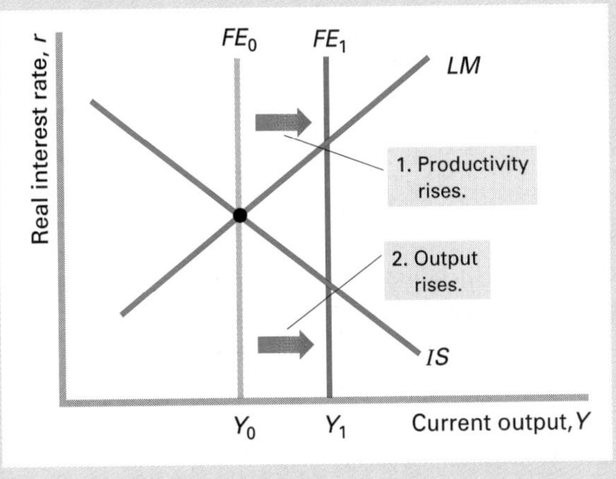

6. Factors that change the supply of or demand for real money balances shift the *LM* curve. They include the nominal money supply, price level, nominal interest rate on money, and expected rate of inflation.
7. When the financial system and the economy are in equilibrium, the *IS* curve, *LM* curve, and *FE* line intersect at the same real interest rate and level of current output. The financial system and the economy are in general equilibrium when the goods and asset markets are in equilibrium simultaneously. When the curves do not intersect simultaneously, the price level adjusts, causing the *LM* curve to shift to maintain equilibrium.
8. In long-run equilibrium, one-time changes in the nominal money supply affect only the price level, not real output or the real interest rate. Hence, as long as the price level in the economy is flexible, money is neutral.

REVIEW QUESTIONS

1. How does an increase in the nominal money supply affect the *IS* and *LM* curves and *FE* line?
2. Suppose that the quantity of money balances supplied equals the quantity of money balances demanded. Can the demand for nonmoney assets exceed the supply of nonmoney assets? Why or why not?
3. Of the *IS* curve, *LM* curve, or *FE* line, which is shifted directly by a change in fiscal policy in a closed economy? In which direction does it shift if government expenditures increase?
4. The *LM* curve shows points of equilibrium in the money market for what two variables?
5. What is general equilibrium? In the *IS-LM-FE* model, what happens to the *IS* and *LM* curves and *FE* line at general equilibrium?
6. What are the three components of aggregate demand in a closed economy? What is the relationship of national saving and investment in a closed economy at equilibrium?
7. What are the two principal determinants of investment?
8. Why does the *IS* curve slope downward?
9. Suppose that data showed no relationship between the levels of saving and investment in various countries. What would that suggest about whether the countries have closed or open economies? Suppose that, instead, the data showed saving and investment to be highly correlated. What would that imply?
10. Why does the *LM* curve slope upward?
11. Why is the *FE* line vertical? What determines the location of the *FE* line?
12. What does "money is neutral" mean? If money is neutral, what effect does a 10% increase in the nominal money supply have on current output? On the real interest rate? On real money demand? On the price level?
13. Why do many economists believe that changes in the money supply affect the economy in the short run but not in the long run?

ANALYTICAL PROBLEMS

14. Suppose the demand for investment spending does not depend on the expected real interest rate. Draw the resulting *IS* curve. In these circumstances, what will be the effect on equilibrium output of an increase in the nominal money supply?
15. Suppose that firms become nervous about the future because of increased uncertainty; as a result, they reduce their investment spending. Of the *IS* curve, *LM* curve, or *FE* line, which would be shifted by this reduction? In what direction would it shift?
16. What effect does each of the following events have on national saving, and what happens to the *IS* curve as a result?
    a. The government cuts defense spending by 10%.
    b. The Alaskan oil fields actually are much smaller than was earlier believed, cutting expected future income by 3%.

c. Barriers to international trade are lowered, allowing gains from specialization and increasing expected future income by 5%.

d. The government expands its health care coverage, increasing government purchases by 15%.

17. Suppose that during a particular year the full employment level of output increases by 5%, when policymakers in Washington had expected it to increase by 2%. What is likely to happen to the actual inflation relative to the expected inflation rate?

18. Suppose that a large open economy is initially at equilibrium with domestic saving equal to domestic investment so that the current account balance is zero. Now suppose that current domestic output decreases. What happens to the real interest rate, domestic saving, domestic investment, and the current account balance?

19. Suppose that a country that has a small open economy passes a law taxing investment heavily. What effect would the tax have on desired investment? What happens to the real interest rate? What happens to the country's current account balance?

20. What effect does each of the following events have on real money demand and real money supply? What happens to the *LM* curve as a result?

a. Expected inflation rises because of an oil price increase.

b. Increased bank regulation forces banks to reduce the nominal interest rate they pay on checking accounts.

c. A drop in the exchange rate causes an increase in the price level.

d. The Fed makes open market purchases.

21. Consider a small open economy that is in general equilibrium. What effect on the real interest rate and output level does each of the following events have after equilibrium is restored?

a. An increase in expected future productivity of investment.

b. A decrease in government purchases.

c. An increase in expected inflation.

d. A decrease in foreign demand for domestically produced goods.

e. An increase in the nominal interest rate on money assets.

f. An increase in households' willingness to save.

g. A decrease in nominal money balances.

h. A decrease in the price level.

22. Suppose that a closed economy is in general equilibrium when new antipollution laws go into effect, reducing current productivity. What happens to the real interest rate, current output, the price level, saving, investment, and real money demand?

23. What happens to the price level to restore equilibrium in each of the following cases for a closed economy?

a. The *IS* curve shifts up and to the right.

b. The *IS* curve shifts down and to the left.

c. The *FE* line shifts to the right.

d. The *FE* line shifts to the left.

e. The *LM* curve shifts down to the right.

24. Use an *IS-LM-FE* diagram to show the effect of the Asian financial crisis of 1997–1998 on the U.S. economy. On the same diagram show the Fed's policy response to the crisis (as discussed at the beginning of this chapter).

25. What happens if Europeans reduce their demand for U.S.-made automobiles? Which curve or line shifts in response? Does the price level rise or fall to restore equilibrium? What happens to the real interest rate and the level of current output? What happens to saving, investment, real money demand, nominal money supply, and the current account, if we assume that the United States is a large open economy?

26. In the *IS-LM-FE* model, what happens when expected inflation declines? Which curve or line shifts initially? What happens to restore equilibrium? What are the ultimate effects on the real interest rate and current output?

27. In a small open economy, what happens to the price level if the world real interest rate falls?

28. What happens to the *IS* curve of a large open economy in which capital controls are enforced to prevent international borrowing or lending?

29. Suppose that new computer technology greatly enhances the ability of doctors to diagnose and treat diseases, sharply reducing the amount of time that workers spend on sick leave. What effect does this have initially on the *IS-LM-FE* model? How does the price level change to restore equilibrium? What is the ultimate effect on the real interest rate and the level of current output?

30. Suppose that widespread use of bank debit cards and credit cards reduces the demand for money at any particular level of income and interest rates. What would be the effect on long-run equilibrium in the *IS-LM-FE* model? (In long-run equilibrium, prices are flexible.)

31. In the early 1980s, the U.S. government cut income taxes without reducing spending, significantly increasing the government's budget deficit (the difference between government purchases and taxes, net of transfers). Suppose that private saving didn't increase to offset the decrease in government saving.

    a. What are the effects on the price level and real interest rate, assuming that nothing else changes and that the United States has a closed economy?

    b. Now suppose that the United States and its principal trading partners (such as Germany) are large open economies. What is the effect of the U.S. tax cut on the real interest rate and price level in Germany?

    c. What could Germany or the United States do to offset the effects of U.S. budget deficits on the price levels in the two countries?

The following question pertains to the discussion in the appendix to this chapter.

32. A closed economy has the following characteristics:

    Consumption: $C = 0.75(Y - T) - 120r + 450$.
    Investment: $I = 600 - 180r$.
    Government purchases: $G = 300$.
    Taxes, net of transfers: $T = 225$.
    Demand for real money balances:
    $L = 0.15Y - 120i + 87.75$.
    Nominal money supply: $M_s = 600$.
    Expected rate of inflation $\pi^e = 0.05$.

    The goods market equilibrium is represented by the *IS* curve.

    a. What is the equation of the *IS* curve?

    b. Plot the *IS* curve.

    Asset market equilibrium is described by the *LM* curve.

    c. Suppose that the price level is 3. What is the equation of the *LM* curve?

    d. For the assumption in (c), draw the *LM* curve.

    Current output supplied is represented by the *FE* line.

    e. Suppose that full employment current output $Y^* = 4665$. What are the equilibrium values of the price level and the real interest rate in the economy?

    Suppose that the nominal money supply increases from 600 to 660.

    f. What happens to the price leve!, the real interest rate, and output in the new long-run equilibrium?

DATA QUESTION

33. Olivier Blanchard of M.I.T. and Lawrence Summers of Harvard University, calculated the annual real interest rate on medium-term U.S. Treasury bonds for each year from 1980 through the first quarter of 1984 to be 1.0%, 2.2%, 6.9%, 4.3%, and 6.5%. Find a recent issue of the *Economic Report of the President* on the World Wide Web or in your library and calculate the percentage change in aggregate output in each year (from Table B-2). Using the *IS-LM-FE* diagram, offer an explanation for the observed pattern in real interest rates and output growth during this period.

APPENDIX: Derivation of the *IS* Curve

By making simple assumptions about the relationship between national saving and investment, we can derive the *IS* curve algebraically. We do so here for a closed economy, a large open economy, and a small open economy.

Closed Economy

As discussed in the chapter, we determine equilibrium in the goods market by equating national saving, S, and investment, I, or

$$S = I. \tag{24A.1}$$

In a closed economy, the financial system matches domestic saving and investment, so national saving consists of domestic private saving, S_P, and government saving, S_G.

Private saving equals income, Y, minus taxes (net of transfer payments), T, less current consumption, C.[†] Government saving equals taxes (net of transfer payments), T, minus government purchases, G. Substituting these variables into Eq. (24A.1) we have

$$\underbrace{\underbrace{(Y-T-C)}_{S_P}+\underbrace{(T-G)}_{S_G}}_{S}=I. \tag{24A.2}$$

Note that equating saving and investment in Eq. (24A.2) yields an expression for *aggregate demand* for current output in the closed economy:

$$Y = C + I + G. \tag{24A.3}$$

Equation (24A.3) shows that total output is the sum of current consumption, investment, and government spending on goods and services.

Equation (24A.3) is an accounting identity, not a model of economic decisions. *Current consumption* C depends positively on *current disposable income* (total current income Y minus taxes, net of transfers, T) and negatively on the real interest rate r (which measures the opportunity cost of trading current for future consumption). Hence

$$C = c_1(Y - T) - c_2 r + C_0, \tag{24A.4}$$

where C_0 represents other potential determinants of consumption (for example, wealth, consumer confidence, or households' preference for current

[†]We do not consider business saving separately here. In the economy, households own businesses and business savings.

consumption relative to expected future consumption). The coefficient on income after taxes, net of transfers, c_1, represents the *marginal propensity to consume:* When the real interest rate and other determinants of consumption are held constant, an increase in $(Y - T)$ by \$1.00 raises C by c_1, which has a value between 0 and 1.

Investment I depends positively on the profitability of investment opportunities I_0 and negatively on the real interest rate r, or

$$I = -ar + I_0. \tag{24A.5}$$

An increase in the profitability of investment opportunities increases I_0. John Maynard Keynes, whose work in the 1930s led to development of the *IS-LM* model, thought that shifts in the investment schedule were driven by businesses' confidence about the future, which he called *animal spirits.*

For simplicity, let's take government spending on goods and services and taxes, net of transfers, as a given at levels G and T, respectively. We can now equate domestic saving and investment in the economy:

$$\underbrace{\underbrace{[Y - T - (c_1(Y - T) - (c_2 r + C_0)]}_{S_P} + \underbrace{(T - G)}_{S_G}}_{S} = \underbrace{-ar + I_0}_{I}. \tag{24A.6}$$

Collecting terms, we express Eq. (24A.6) as a relationship between aggregate demand for current output and the real interest rate:

$$Y = \frac{C_0 + I_0 + G - c_1 T}{1 - c_1} - \left(\frac{c_2 + a}{1 - c_1}\right) r. \tag{24A.7}$$

Current output increases in response to an increase in C_0, I_0, and G. Increases in T and r decrease current output. The first term in Eq. (24A.7) consists of variables whose values are *exogenous*—that is, given outside the model. We know that r and Y are *endogenous* variables, the equilibrium values of which we are trying to determine.

By how much does output increase in response to an increase in these variables? From Eq. (24A.7) and for a constant r, a \$1.00 increase in C_0, I_0, or G raises the demand for current output by $\$1/(1 - c_1)$. If the marginal propensity to consume c_1 were 0.8, a \$1.00 increase in C_0, I_0, or G would raise Y by \$1.00/(1 − 0.8), or \$5.00.†

†Note that the coefficient of G in Eq. (24A.7) is $1/(1 - c_1)$, whereas the coefficient of T is $-c_1/(1 - c_1)$. Hence raising both G and T by \$1.00 (a "balanced budget" change) raises aggregate demand by

$$\frac{1}{1 - c_1} - \frac{c_1}{1 - c_1} = 1.$$

An equal increase in government purchases and taxes, net of transfers, raises aggregate demand by the amount of the increase in G and T in this approach.

Large Open Economy

We derive the *IS* curve for a large open economy by extending our closed economy model to include net saving supplied by foreigners S_F. The equality of saving and investment then becomes

$$S_P + S_G + S_F = I. \tag{24A.8}$$

When $S_F > 0$, foreign saving flows into the domestic economy. This capital inflow finances greater domestic consumption and investment. As a result, the current account balance *NX*, the difference between exports and imports, falls. Hence, as we showed in Chapter 22,

$$S_F = -NX.$$

The national income accounting identity for an open economy is

$$Y = C + I + G + NX. \tag{24A.9}$$

To convert Eq. (24A.9) into an equation for the *IS* curve, we first let

$$NX = NX_0 - dr.$$

The NX_0 term allows for shifts in demand for domestic versus foreign goods. An increase in the domestic real interest rate r increases the flow of foreign savings into the domestic economy, thereby decreasing the current account balance. Substituting for the elements of the right-hand side of Eq. (24A.9) gives us the equation for the *IS* curve:

$$Y = \underbrace{[C_0 + c_1(Y - T) - c_2 r]}_{C} + \underbrace{(I_0 - ar)}_{I} + \underbrace{G}_{G} + \underbrace{(NX_0 - dr)}_{NX}.$$

Rearranging terms, we get

$$Y = \frac{(C_0 + I_0 + G + NX_0) - c_1 T - (c_2 + a + d)r}{1 - c_1},$$

or

$$r = -\left(\frac{1 - c_1}{c_2 + a + d}\right)Y + \left(\frac{1}{c_2 + a + d}\right)(C_0 + I_0 + G - c_1 T + NX_0). \tag{24A.10}$$

The *IS* curve is flatter (that is, $\Delta r/\Delta Y$ is smaller in absolute value) than the closed economy *IS* curve derived in the text.

Small Open Economy

In a small open economy, the rate of interest for the *IS* curve is the world real rate of interest, or $r = r_w$. Unlike a large open economy, a small open economy cannot affect the world real rate of interest by increasing or decreasing its desired national saving or investment.

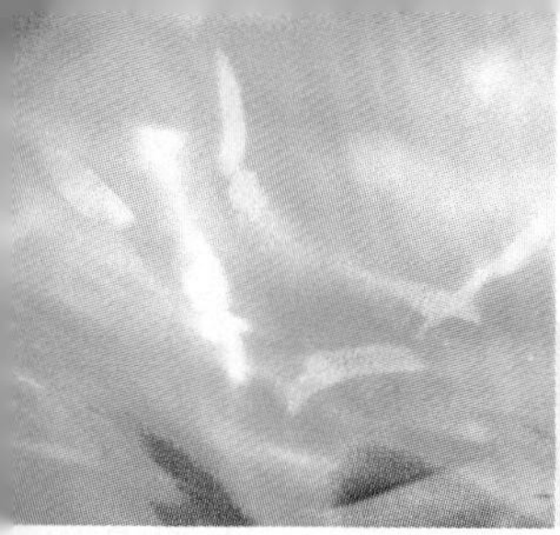

CHAPTER 25

Aggregate Demand and Aggregate Supply

In addition to damaging the nation's psyche, America's participation in the Vietnam conflict left scars on the economy. Economists blamed the persistent increases in the price level that began the late 1960s on the government's decision not to raise taxes to finance the war. After the war, the oil supply shocks that occurred between 1973 and 1975 made matters worse. The term "stagflation"—falling output and rising prices—entered the economic lexicon. Stagflation was a double blow to workers who lost jobs and faced higher prices. These events transformed the way economists, businesspeople, and policymakers thought about how the financial system and the economy interact and about what factors determine the economy's output and price levels.

Fluctuations in output and the price level, such as those in the 1970s, cause problems for individuals and businesses. As a result, many of them pressured policymakers to develop programs to maintain steady output growth and a stable price level. But to design these policies, they need to know what factors cause changes in output and in the price level. We study these determinants in this chapter by building a model that relates output to price level: the *AD-AS* model. Once we build the model, we use it to explain events such as the inflationary consequences of the Vietnam War, the stagflation of the 1970s, and the recession of the early 1990s. We also use it in subsequent chapters to assess the impact of monetary policies that are designed to promote price stability and steady economic growth.

THE AGGREGATE DEMAND CURVE

To begin, we seek a relationship for the demand for goods and services that we can use to determine how price level changes affect output. We start with an expression for aggregate demand that we can use in our model. **Aggregate demand** for the economy's output equals the sum of demands for (1) goods and services for consumption, *C;* (2) investment in business plant and equipment, inventories, and housing, *I;* (3) government purchases of goods and services (not including transfer payments to individuals), *G;* and (4) net exports (domestic sales of goods and services to foreigners minus domestic purchases of goods and services from foreigners), NX. Hence aggregate demand for current output, Y_d, is

$$Y_d = C + I + G + NX. \tag{25.1}$$

The **aggregate demand (AD) curve** illustrates the relationship between the aggregate demand for goods and services (the goods market) and the aggregate price level.

Deriving the Aggregate Demand Curve

The shape and position of the AD curve are important in determining the values of output and the price level that exist when the economy is in equilibrium. In the remainder of this section, we describe why the AD curve is downward-sloping; then we describe the factors that change its position—that is, cause the AD curve to shift.

The AD curve is downward-sloping because an increase in the price level reduces the aggregate demand for goods and services if nothing else changes. Although the aggregate demand curve and the demand curves for individual goods and services are all downward-sloping, there are differences between these two types of curves. For example, the quantity of wheat that is demanded depends negatively on the price of wheat, but the demand curve for wheat relates the quantity of wheat that is demanded to the price of wheat relative to prices of substitutes. An increase in the price of wheat relative to the price of corn reduces the quantity of wheat that is demanded. In contrast, the aggregate demand curve relates the aggregate quantity of output demanded, Y_d, to the aggregate price level, P. Therefore, if prices of all goods rise by 5%, the aggregate price level P rises by 5%, but relative prices do not change. Nonetheless, the increase in the price level, P, reduces the aggregate quantity of output demanded, Y_d.

An increase in the price level reduces real money balances, changing the equilibrium in the money market. This, in turn, affects aggregate demand. To demonstrate how this happens, we trace the steps that occur when the price level rises:

1. When the price level, P, rises, for any nominal money supply, M, the supply of real money balances, (M/P), falls.

2. For the public to be willing to hold a smaller quantity of real money balances and a larger quantity of nonmoney assets, the real interest rate must rise. A higher real interest rate on nonmoney assets increases the opportunity cost of holding money, so the public is willing to hold the lower level of real money balances.

3. The rise in real interest rates makes firms less willing to invest in plant and equipment, and it gives consumers an incentive to save rather than spend. If we include this behavior in our expression for Y_d, then C and I fall, and Y_d declines as P increases.

4. There is also a change in net exports because of the effect of rising real interest rates on the exchange rate. A higher domestic real interest rate makes returns on domestic financial assets more attractive relative to those on foreign assets, raising the exchange rate. The rise in the exchange rate increases imports and reduces exports, thereby reducing *NX* and Y_d in Eq. (25.1).

Conversely, a decrease in the price level increases real money balances, leading to a drop in the real interest rate in the money market. The lower real interest rate reduces saving (thereby increasing consumption) and raises investment and net exports. Hence from Eq. (25.1), the quantity of aggregate output demanded rises.

Figure 25.1 shows the *AD* curve, which slopes down and to the right, giving it a shape like any demand curve. But as you can see from our analysis, the reason for the *AD* curve's shape is quite different from that of an individual demand curve. Points along the aggregate demand curve represent combinations of the price level and current output for which the goods market and the asset markets are in equilibrium at the same time. Within asset markets, the money market is in equilibrium because the quantity of real money balances equals the available supply. The nonmoney asset market is in equilibrium because households and businesses are satisfied with their holdings of nonmoney assets. The goods market is in equilibrium because saving equals investment. The simultaneous equilibrium of all three markets that constitute the financial system and the economy is called *general equilibrium*. Each point on the *AD* curve represents a potential equilibrium output and the price level. Which equilibrium point prevails depends on the supply of output, which we discuss later.

Shifts of the Aggregate Demand Curve

In addition to knowing the pattern or shape of the *AD* curve, the placement of the *AD* curve on the graph is crucial to our understanding of the effects of

Figure 25.1

The Aggregate Demand Curve

The aggregate demand curve *AD* illustrates the negative relationship between the price level and the aggregate quantity of output demanded. The aggregate demand curve slopes downward. Increases in the price level reduce real money balances, raising the real interest rate and reducing the quantity of output demanded.

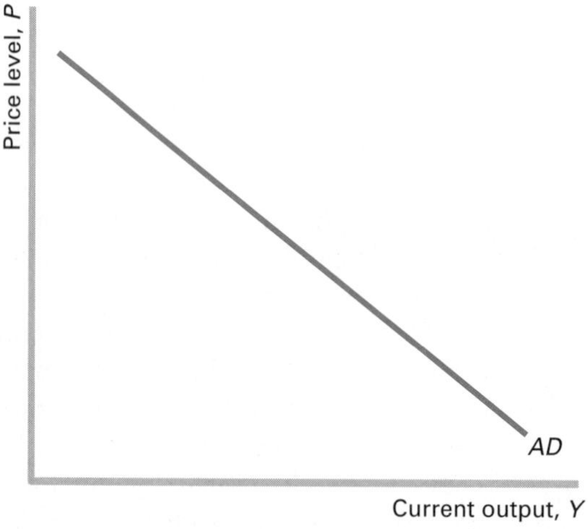

policy measures. Shifts of the aggregate demand curve occur when aggregate demand for the economy's current output increases or decreases at a particular price level. A shift of the aggregate demand curve to the right is *expansionary* because the price level is associated with a higher level of aggregate demand for current output. Expansionary shifts in aggregate demand can be traced to the asset markets or the goods market. A shift of the aggregate demand curve to the left is *contractionary* because the price level is associated with a lower level of aggregate demand for current output. Like expansionary shifts, contractionary shifts in aggregate demand can originate either in the asset markets or in the goods market.

Shifts originating in the asset markets. If the Fed increases the nominal money supply and prices are sticky in the short run, real money balances rise. The real interest rate then falls in the asset markets. To maintain equilibrium in the goods market at the lower interest rate, saving must fall (raising consumption, C), and investment, I, must rise. As a result, aggregate demand rises, shifting the aggregate demand curve to the right.

Another cause of expansionary shifts originating in the asset markets is a decline in money demand. It can be the result of a drop in the interest paid on money relative to that on other assets or of a change in the payments system that makes money less desirable for use in transactions. At any level of real money supply, the decline in money demand reduces the real interest rate. As in the case of an increase in the nominal money supply, the drop in the real interest rate raises aggregate demand in the goods market and shifts the AD curve to the right.

In the asset markets, contractionary shifts result from a decline in the nominal money supply or a rise in money demand at each level of output. If the Fed restricts the nominal money supply, real money balances fall in the short run; the real interest rate rises to restore equilibrium in the asset markets. To maintain equilibrium in the goods market at the higher interest rate, saving must rise (reducing consumption, C), and investment, I, must fall. As a result, aggregate demand falls. A rise in money demand means that at any level of money supply, the real interest rate must rise to restore equilibrium in the money market. The increase in the real interest rate reduces aggregate demand.

Shifts originating in the goods market. Expansionary shifts also can originate in the goods market owing to changes in saving and investment, in government purchases, or in net exports. A decline in saving or an increase in investment at any real interest rate raises aggregate demand. A decline in saving might occur if consumers expect an increase in expected future income or if they feel confident about the future conditions—raising consumption, C. Taxes may also play a role in the behavior of consumers and affect aggregate demand. Some, though not all, economists also believe that increases in current income from tax cuts reduce desired saving and increase consumption. Firms increase investment, I, if they expect the future profitability of capital

CONSIDER THIS . . .

Do Tax Cuts Stimulate Aggregate Demand?

Economists and policymakers have debated vigorously whether reductions in current taxes—holding government spending constant—increase aggregate demand. Those who believe that tax cuts increase aggregate demand reason that consumers spend some of the additional income from the tax cut, raising consumption and thereby increasing aggregate demand. Those who believe that tax cuts don't increase aggregate demand argue that a tax cut today increases the budget deficit. They propose that the public understands that the government's borrowing must eventually be repaid (with interest). In this view—known as the *Ricardian equivalence proposition*†—the reduction in taxes doesn't improve consumers' well-being: The increase in current income from a tax cut is offset by higher taxes in the future to pay off the debt.

Economists who hold the view that tax cuts raise aggregate demand make two arguments. The first is that a tax cut gives consumers who may face restrictions on the amount that they can borrow the opportunity to increase their consumption, thereby raising aggregate demand. The second is that consumers may not understand that government borrowing must be repaid by themselves as taxpayers. Therefore they will then try to increase current consumption—and aggregate demand—even though they are no better off.

Which school of thought is correct? Indirect evidence indicates that part of the population faces borrowing constraints on consumption. More directly, consumption rose in the United States following the large deficit-financed tax cuts legislated in 1981. In other cases, however, tax cuts have not significantly increased consumption.

† The Ricardian equivalence proposition traces its origin to David Ricardo, an eighteenth-century economist. Robert Barro has argued the proposition most persuasively; see Robert Barro, "The Ricardian Approach to Budget Deficits," *Journal of Economic Perspectives*, 2:37–54, 1989.

to rise or business taxes to fall. An increase in government purchases, G, directly adds to aggregate demand. An increase in foreign demand for U.S.-produced goods raises the demand for current output and net exports, NX. Each change in C, I, G, or NX increases aggregate demand in the goods market and shifts the AD curve to the right.

In the goods market, contractionary shifts reflect a decline in desired consumption or investment, in government purchases, or in net exports. A decline in consumption reflects a decrease in expected future income or less confidence about future economic conditions. Firms reduce investment if they expect the future profitability of capital to decline or business taxes to rise. A drop in government purchases directly reduces aggregate demand, as does a decline in foreign demand for U.S.-produced goods. Table 25.1 summarizes factors that shift the aggregate demand curve.

CHECKPOINT

Many businesspeople and policymakers argue that an investment tax credit—giving firms the right to subtract part of the purchase price of new factories and equipment from their income tax bill—is an effective way to stimulate aggregate demand. Why? An investment tax credit reduces the cost of investing, raising the after-tax profitability of building a new factory or installing new equipment. As a result, desired investment rises, shifting the *AD* curve to the right. **o**

TABLE 25.1

DETERMINANTS OF SHIFTS IN THE AGGREGATE DEMAND CURVE

An Increase in . . .	Shifts the *AD* Curve . . .	Because . . .
the nominal money supply	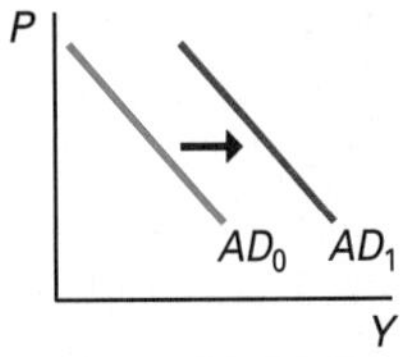	real money balances rise and the real interest rate falls.
the interest rate on money balances	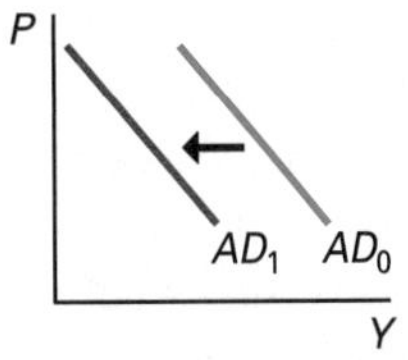	money demand rises and the real interest rate rises.
expected future output	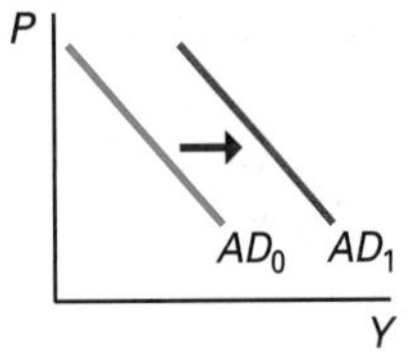	consumption rises.
government purchases	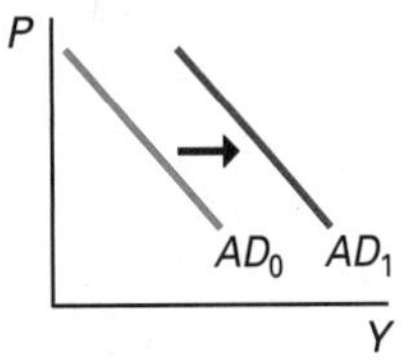	aggregate demand increases directly.
the expected future profitability of capital	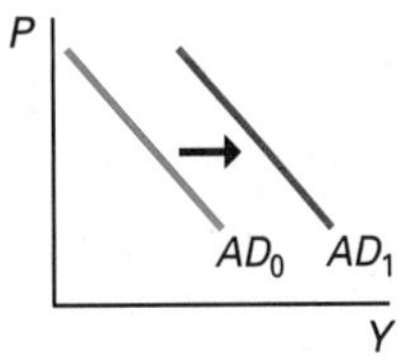	investment rises.
business taxes	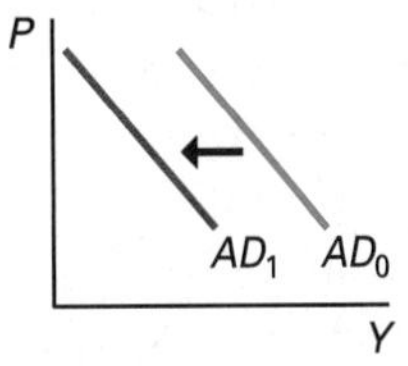	investment declines.

THE AGGREGATE SUPPLY CURVE

We now proceed to the second step in building the *AD-AS* model. Here we explain **aggregate supply**, the total quantity of output that producers are willing to sell at various price levels. Our goal is to construct an **aggregate supply (*AS*) curve**, which represents levels of output that producers are willing to supply at each price level.

We are interested in the shape and position of the aggregate supply curve, but our analysis is not as simple as it was for aggregate demand. Firms differ in their reaction to changes in the price level in the short run and the long run. For example, firms may adjust factors of production to minimize labor costs or to take advantage of improved technology, but such changes take time to incorporate into the production process. Therefore we divide our analysis of aggregate supply according to the time horizon that firms face. We start by examining the short-run aggregate supply curve and then turn to the long-run aggregate supply curve. In addition, economists are not in complete agreement about the behavior of firms, particularly in the short run. Although most economists believe that the aggregate quantity of output that is supplied in the short run increases as the price level rises and that, in the long run, changes in the price level have no effect on the aggregate quantity of output supplied, they attribute these patterns to different causes. We therefore describe the views of two different schools of thought: the new classical economists and the new Keynesian economists. These interpretations of firms' behavior will allow us to construct short-run and long-run aggregate supply curves. As we discuss in Chapter 26, the two views offer somewhat different answers to the question of whether public policy should be used to stabilize economic fluctuations.

Although the aggregate supply curve (particularly the short-run aggregate supply curve) may look like the supply curve facing an individual firm, it represents different behavior. The quantity of output that an individual firm is willing to supply depends on the price of its output relative to the prices of other goods and services. In contrast, the aggregate supply curve relates the aggregate quantity of output supplied to the price level. The new classical and new Keynesian views offer different explanations of this relationship.

Short-Run Aggregate Supply Curve

Most economists believe that short-run aggregate supply is positively related to the general price level. Therefore the **short-run aggregate supply (*SRAS*) curve** slopes upward.

New classical view and misperception. The **new classical view** of aggregate supply in the short run builds on research by Nobel laureate Robert E. Lucas, Jr., of the University of Chicago. He studied the effects on aggregate supply of the imperfect information that firms possess. Because Lucas described firms' misperceptions, his explanation is also known as the **misperception theory**. To understand how it works, let's begin with an example.

Consider the supply decisions of Bigplay, a toy manufacturer. Bigplay maximizes profits by increasing the volume of toys it produces when the relative price of toys is high and decreasing production when the relative price of toys is low. Bigplay's managers face an information problem: They care about *relative* prices, so they need to know the price of toys *and* the general price level. Although they know a lot about toy prices, their knowledge of the general price level is not complete because they lack continuous information on all prices outside the toy market.

Suppose that the price of toys increases by 15%. If the general price level doesn't change at the same time, the relative price of toys has increased, and Bigplay should supply more toys. But if all prices in the economy are 15% higher, the relative price of toys is unchanged, and Bigplay would have no incentive to manufacture more toys. Bigplay's managers should separate an observed change in the price of toys into a change in the general price level and a change in the relative price of toys. Lacking complete information about the general price level, Bigplay guesses that a 15% increase in the price of toys reflects an increase in the general price level of 10% and an increase in the relative price of toys of 5%. Because of the increase in the relative price, Bigplay will increase the quantity of toys it produces.

Bigplay is only one producer. Generalizing to include all producers in the economy, we discover why the misperception theory suggests a relationship between aggregate output and the price level. Suppose that all prices in the economy rise by 15% but that relative prices don't change. If individual producers fail to recognize the situation, aggregate output increases. This change in output occurs because producers think that some of the increase in prices represents increases in their products' relative prices, and they increase the quantity of their products supplied.

How do producers distinguish between general and relative price increases? Suppose that, before they observe any price changes, some producers forecast that the general price level will rise by 10%. If those producers observe an increase of 15% in the prices of their goods, they will assume that the relative prices of their products have increased by 5% and will increase the quantities supplied of their goods. That assumption may be incorrect.

According to the new classical view, suppliers that have perfect information about price changes would react in the following way. They would raise the quantity of toys supplied when prices of toys increased only if that increase differed from the expected increase in the general price level in the economy. If all producers expect the price level to increase by 10%, and Bigplay sees the price of toys increase by only 5%, the toy manufacturer will *cut* toy production. If all prices actually increase by only 5%, producers (having expected a 10% increase in the price level) will collectively cut production.

From this ideal behavior, we can write an equation for aggregate output supplied. The new classical view suggests a positive relationship between the aggregate supply of goods and the difference between the actual and expected price level. If P is the actual price level and P^e is the expected price level, the relationship between aggregate output and the price level, according to the new classical view, is

$$Y = Y^* + a(P - P^e), \tag{25.2}$$

where Y is aggregate output, Y^* is **full employment output,** or the output produced by full employment of existing factors of production, and a is a positive number that indicates by how much output responds when the actual price level is greater than the expected price level.

Equation (25.2) states that output supplied, Y, equals full employment output, Y^*, when the actual price level and the expected price level are equal. When the actual price level is greater than the expected price level, firms increase output. When the actual price level is less than the expected price level, output falls. As a result, output can be higher or lower than the full employment level in the short term until firms can distinguish changes in relative prices from changes in the general price level. Thus, in the short run, for an expected price level, an increase in the actual price level raises the aggregate quantity of output supplied. Hence the aggregate supply curve slopes upward.

CHECKPOINT

Chair Lair—your custom-made furniture store—is experiencing its best year ever. Sales are up 25%, and you raise the prices on your popular models. How can you determine whether to increase production or just raise prices? If the increased sales are the result of increased customer demand for your chairs relative to other goods, you should increase your production. If the higher sales are the result of rising prices generally, you should increase prices without changing production. You can check aggregate economic statistics on inflation and sales of goods generally. You can gather information on your prices and sales (and those of other businesses in the furniture industry) based on your own experience more quickly than reliable data for the economy are published. This information allows you to estimate, on average, how much of a given price change reflects general price movements and how much reflects changes in relative prices. o

New Keynesian view and sticky prices. John Maynard Keynes and his followers believed that prices failed to adjust in the short run in response to changes in aggregate demand. That is, prices are sticky in the short run. In the most extreme view of price stickiness, we would observe a horizontal *AS* curve; prices would not adjust to increases or decreases in aggregate demand. Contemporary economists who follow Keynes's view of price stickiness have sought reasons for the failure of prices to adjust in the short run. Their work has modified Keynes's view that prices fail to adjust in favor of a slow or gradual adjustment. Economists who embrace the **new Keynesian view** use characteristics of many real-world markets—rigidity of long-term contracts and imperfect competition—to explain price behavior.

One form of rigidity arises from long-term nominal contracts for wages (between firms and workers) or prices (between firms and their suppliers or customers). Under a long-term nominal contract, a wage rate or price is set in advance for several to many periods in nominal terms.[†] Suppose, for example, that *all* workers agreed to a fixed wage for the next three years. Then, on the basis of this labor cost and other components of expected total production costs, all firms set prices that would remain fixed for the next three years. In this case, firms would not be able to change prices easily in response to changes in demand because their costs of production are fixed.

Although many such long-term arrangements exist in the economy, not all contracts come up for renewal during a particular period; that is, contracts are overlapping or staggered. Hence only some wages and prices can be adjusted in the current period. Contracts ultimately will be adjusted to changes in expected money growth, but they can't all adjust immediately. For example, businesses that expect high current money growth to lead to a rise in the price level in the future can negotiate price changes for the future but not for the period under contract. New Keynesians reject the notion that all prices are flexible in the short run; they believe that the price level adjusts slowly to changes in the nominal money supply.

New Keynesians also attribute price stickiness to differences in market structure and the price-setting decisions that take place in different types of markets. In markets for wheat or stocks or Treasury bills, the product is standardized, many traders interact, and prices adjust freely and quickly to shifts in demand and supply. In such competitive markets, the purchases and sales of individual traders are small relative to the total market volume. For example, a few wheat farmers can't raise their prices above those of other wheat farmers; in the competitive wheat market, no one would buy their wheat. Individual traders are *price takers*; that is, they take the market price (as reported on the floor of an exchange or in the newspaper) as a given.

However, many markets in the economy—such as the markets for high-fashion clothing, art, and medical care—don't resemble the continuously adjusting price-taking markets of exchanges because their products are not standardized. When products have individual characteristics and there are few sellers of each product, monopolistic competition results. A seller who raises prices might see the quantity demanded fall, but not to zero. In monopolistically competitive markets, sellers do not take prices as a given because they are price setters. New Keynesian economists argue that prices will adjust only gradually in monopolistically competitive markets.

To understand why, consider the market for high-fashion clothing. Firms in this market might have a central meeting place where buyers submit bids

---

[†] If wages or prices in a long-term contract were fully indexed to, say, changes in the general price level, wages or prices could still adjust to aggregate nominal disturbances. An example is *cost of living adjustments* (COLAs) in many wage contracts. Evidence for the United States suggests that such contracts generally are only partially indexed.

and sellers quote asking prices (much as buying and selling in the market for Treasury securities is conducted). If a designer gets favorable reviews, demand increases and the product's price rises, whereas unfavorable reviews by critics reduce the product's price. Individual high-fashion clothing stores do not continuously adjust prices. Instead, they set the price of clothes in nominal terms for periods of time and meet the demand at that price. They may, however, change prices from time to time in response to major changes in demand or costs of production.

New Keynesian economists contend that this pricing behavior can be in firms' interests as long as markets are monopolistically competitive and there are costs to changing prices. The costs of changing prices—informing current and potential customers, remarking prices, and so on—may not seem that large. Why then do new Keynesians think they are so important?

To return to our example of a perfectly competitive market, when a seller of goods or assets traded on exchanges charges a price that is just a bit high, that seller will sell nothing at all. However, a monopolistically competitive firm (such as a clothing boutique) won't lose many of its customers if its prices deviate slightly from the market price. If potential profits are small relative to the cost of changing prices, the firm won't change its price.

Why is a firm willing to meet demand by selling more at the posted price? For a monopolistically competitive firm, the product price is higher than the marginal cost—that is, the cost of producing an extra unit. Hence the firm is happy to sell extra output. As a result of satisfying the level of demand, the firm's output will rise and fall, depending on aggregate demand.

Let's translate this description of price-setting behavior into an equation that will show how changes in the price level affect output. Because new Keynesians show that the behavior of firms with flexible prices differs from that of firms with sticky prices, we must start with an expression that shows the decisions each firm faces in setting its prices. Firms with flexible prices can change their prices freely and continually. The price, p, that an individual firm in this category charges is related to the aggregate price level, P, and output, Y, relative to full employment output, Y^*. An increase in the price level means that the firm's costs are higher and that the firm would like to charge more for its output. An increase in aggregate output implies that higher incomes in the economy are likely to raise the demand for the firm's product. As the marginal cost of producing output tends to rise at higher levels of production (because of, for example, the need to pay overtime wages to workers), the firm's desired price rises with the level of demand. That is,

$$p = P + b(Y - Y^*), \tag{25.3}$$

where b is a parameter with a value greater than zero. Equation (25.3) reveals that a price-setting firm's desired price depends on the price level, P, and the level of aggregate output relative to full employment output, $(Y - Y^*)$.

Firms with sticky prices set their prices in advance on the basis of their expectation of output. If we let the superscript e denote expectation, we can rewrite Eq. (25.3) for price-setting firms as

$$p = P^e + b(Y^e - Y^{*e}),$$

To keep the analysis simple, let's further assume that firms expect output to be at the full employment level. In this case, $b(Y^e - Y^{*e})$ is zero, and

$$p = P^e.$$

Price-setting firms base their prices on their expectations of other firms' prices, as reflected in the expected aggregate price level.

We combine our analysis of pricing decisions by the two types of firms to develop the new Keynesian aggregate supply curve. The aggregate price level, P, is the weighted average of the prices that are charged by the flexible-price and sticky-price firms. If c represents the fraction of firms with sticky prices and $(1 - c)$ represents the fraction of firms with flexible prices, the aggregate price level is

$$P = cP^e + (1 - c)[P + b(Y - Y^*)].$$

Subtracting $(1 - c)P$ from both sides of the equation and dividing both sides by c give the general price level:

$$P = P^e + b\left(\frac{1 - c}{c}\right)(Y - Y^*). \tag{25.4}$$

This expression for the aggregate price level is a reminder that (1) an increase in the expected price level raises expected costs and leads firms to raise prices, and (2) an increase in current output raises the demand for an individual firm's products, so flexible-price firms raise their prices.[†]

The short-run aggregate supply curve that is implied by the new Keynesian view slopes upward: An increase in current output leads to an increase in the price level in the short run. The larger the proportion of firms in the economy with sticky prices, the flatter the *SRAS* curve will be. Indeed, if all firms had sticky prices in the short run, the *SRAS* curve would be horizontal.

CHECKPOINT

Amalgamated Industries has two major divisions: one grows fruit in California, and the other manufactures and sells designer sweaters in New York. If aggregate demand rises, which price should rise first? Agricultural products are sold largely in competitive markets with flexible prices. An increase in aggregate demand will raise the price

[†]Note that we can rearrange the terms in Eq. (25.4) to yield an expression that is similar to Eq. (25.2):

$$Y = Y^* + \left[\frac{c}{b(1 - c)}\right](P - P^e).$$

of Amalgamated Industries' fruit because the quantity supplied can't increase in the short run. In the designer sweater market, markups of price over cost are much higher, and Amalgamated's stores are less likely to change the price tags in the short run. Its sweater stores will meet the greater demand at the unchanged price in the short run. **o**

Long-Run Aggregate Supply Curve

The short-run aggregate supply curve, *SRAS*, slopes upward in both the new classical and new Keynesian explanations of aggregate supply, but this relationship doesn't hold in the long run. In the new classical view, firms eventually realize that the price level is changing in response to a change in current output. They adjust their estimates of the expected price level until the actual and expected price level are equal—that is, until $P = P^e$. This relationship shows that current output Y equals full employment output Y^*, so the **long-run aggregate supply (*LRAS*) curve** is vertical at Y^*. In the new Keynesian view, both firms with flexible prices and firms with sticky prices adjust their prices in response to a change in demand in the long run. As with the new classical view, the *LRAS* curve is vertical at the full employment level of output $Y = Y^*$.

Figure 25.2 summarizes the short-run and long-run aggregate supply relationships between price level and current output.

Shifts in the Short-Run Aggregate Supply Curve

Changes in aggregate supply can explain changes in output in the short run. In both the new classical and new Keynesian explanations of short-run aggregate supply, the factors that shift the short-run aggregate supply curve also affect the costs of producing output. These factors are (1) changes in labor costs, (2) changes in other input costs, and (3) changes in the expected price level.

Figure 25.2

The Short-Run and Long-Run Aggregate Supply Curves

The *SRAS* curve slopes upward: When the price level P exceeds the expected price level P^e, the quantity of output supplied rises. In the long run, the actual and expected price levels come together: The *LRAS* curve is vertical at the full employment level of output, Y^*.

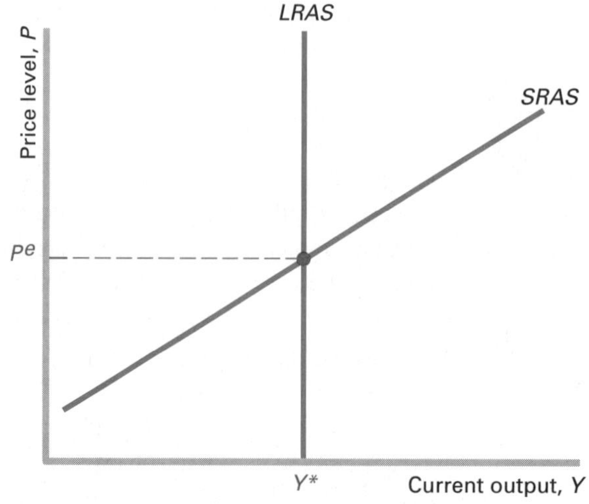

Changes in labor costs. Labor typically accounts for most of the costs of producing output. When output, Y, exceeds the full employment level, Y^*, the high volume of output produced raises the demand for labor. The higher labor demand, in turn, bids up wages, increasing firms' labor costs. As a result, the short-run aggregate supply curve shifts up and to the left. When output falls below the full employment level, workers' wages decline. The resulting drop in production costs shifts the short-run aggregate supply curve down and to the right.

Changes in other input costs. Shifts in the price or availability of raw materials or in production technologies affect production costs and the aggregate supply curve. Such changes are commonly called **supply shocks**. Supply shocks include changes in technology, weather, or the prices of oil and other inputs of energy and materials. Positive supply shocks, such as the development of labor-saving technologies or lower food prices owing to good growing seasons, shift the aggregate supply curve down and to the right. Negative supply shocks, such as an increase in the price of oil, shift the aggregate supply curve up and to the left.

Changes in the expected price level. When workers bargain for wages, they compare their wages to the costs of goods and services that they buy. When workers expect the price level to rise, they will demand higher nominal wages to preserve their real wages. Similarly, firms make decisions about how much output to supply by comparing the price of their output to the expected prices of other goods and services. When the expected price level rises, firms raise prices to cover higher labor and other costs. An increase in the expected price level shifts the short-run aggregate supply curve up and to the left. A decline in the expected price level shifts the short-run aggregate supply curve down and to the right. This occurs because firms reduce prices as nominal wages and other costs fall.

Shifts in the Long-Run Aggregate Supply Curve

The long-run aggregate supply curve, *LRAS*, indicates the full employment level of output in the economy at a specific time. The *LRAS* curve shifts over time to reflect growth in the full employment level of output. Sources of this economic growth include (1) increases in capital and labor inputs and (2) increases in productivity growth (output produced per unit of input).

Increases in inputs raise the economy's productive capacity. When firms invest in new plant and equipment (excluding replacement of old plant and equipment), they increase the capital stock. Labor inputs increase when the population grows or more people participate in the labor force. Studies of output growth in the United States and other countries show that over long periods of time, the pace of output growth also is influenced significantly by productivity growth. Productivity growth is the improvement in the efficiency with which capital and labor inputs produce output.

OTHER TIMES, OTHER PLACES . . .

Shock Therapy and Aggregate Supply in Poland

The close of 1992 brought holiday cheer to the beleaguered Polish economy after three years of shock therapy prescribed by Western economic advisers. Although factory output dropped by nearly 40% in 1990 and 1991 from the levels that had been produced during the communist regime, output was growing and inflation was beginning to decline.

Like other former communist countries in Eastern Europe, Poland had tried to transform its centrally planned economy and remove price controls by pursuing radical economic reforms—but much more rapidly than most of the other countries. Lifting price controls (which had fixed the price level) increased the expected price level, shifting the *SRAS* curve up and to the left. Because reductions in the growth rate of the nominal money supply and elimination of many subsidies decreased aggregate demand, the shift in the *SRAS* curve led to a severe decline in output in the short run.

The immediate result of the shock therapy was a rise in the price level (a result of the shift in the *SRAS* curve) as well as a decline in output. By 1992, falling economic activity in Poland placed downward pressure on inflation.

Polish policymakers were more interested in long-run prospects for economic growth than in the short-run changes in output. Long periods of price control and government allocation had reduced the efficiency with which the Polish economy produced and distributed goods and services. Hence the big question was whether the reforms would improve the outlook for long-run aggregate supply.

While experts maintained that the end of price controls and government allocation would lead to more efficient and competitive firms, it was clear that many individuals would be worse off in the short run. The gamble in Poland was that these short-term costs would be rewarded handsomely in long-term gains in production and consumption possibilities for Polish citizens.

Many economists, notably Jeffrey Sachs of Harvard University, argued that the rebound of the Polish economy in 1992 was the beginning of favorable shifts in long-run aggregate supply in Poland. The removal of central planning and improvements in factory productivity shift the *LRAS* curve to the right, increasing output and dampening inflationary pressures. These long-run developments hold the key to the future growth of Poland's economy, which saw generally strong economic growth and falling inflation between 1992 and 1999.

The principal sources of change in productivity growth are energy prices, technological advances, worker training and education, and regulation of production. The huge increases in oil prices in 1973 reduced productivity in heavy energy-using industries and (in the view of many analysts) led to a worldwide slowdown in productivity growth. Technological advances, as in communications technology and computers, raise productivity. Many economists believe that environmental, health, and safety regulations reduce productivity growth, because capital and labor inputs are devoted to these activities instead of to producing goods and services. However, such consequences of regulation do not necessarily mean that they are not in society's interest. For example, society must weigh the benefits of cleaner air or increased workplace safety against the potential costs of reduced productivity.

Table 25.2 summarizes factors that shift the short-run and long-run aggregate supply curves.

EQUILIBRIUM IN AGGREGATE DEMAND AND AGGREGATE SUPPLY

We now have a model that shows us what level of output is likely to prevail in the economy at a given price level. The relationships for aggregate demand and short-run and long-run aggregate supply are the components of a model that we can use to determine the level of output and the price level in the economy.

TABLE 25.2 **DETERMINANTS OF SHIFTS IN THE AGGREGATE SUPPLY CURVE**

An Increase in . . .	Shifts the *SRAS* Curve . . .	Because . . .
labor costs	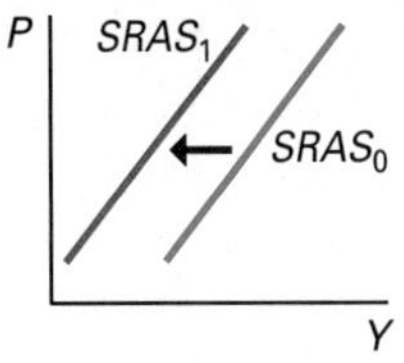	costs of production rise.
other input costs	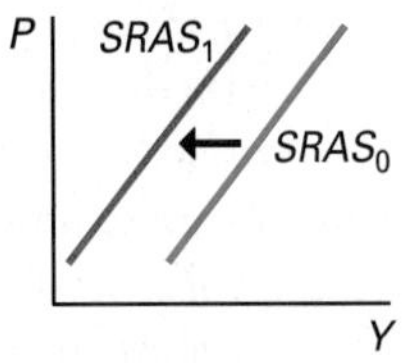	costs of production rise.
expected price level	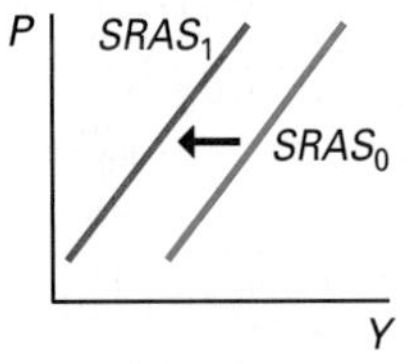	wages and other costs of production rise.
An Increase in . . .	**Shifts the *LRAS* Curve . . .**	**Because . . .**
capital and labor inputs	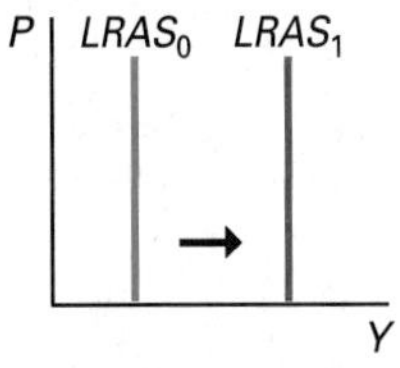	productive capacity rises.
productivity	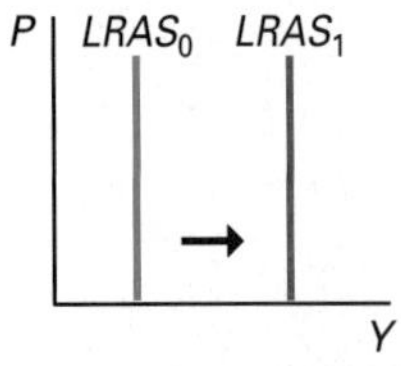	efficiency of factors used to produce output rises.

At that equilibrium, the aggregate demand curve and aggregate supply curve intersect. Because there is a difference in the behavior of firms in supplying output in the short run and the long run, we have two equilibrium values for output and the price level: short-run equilibrium and long-run equilibrium.

Short-Run Equilibrium

To determine output and the price level in the short run, we combine the aggregate demand curve, *AD*, and the short-run aggregate supply curve, *SRAS*. Figure 25.3 shows these two curves.

The economy's short-run equilibrium occurs at the intersection, E_0, of the *AD* and *SRAS* curves. No other point represents equilibrium. For example, E_1 is an equilibrium level of aggregate demand, but at price level P_1, firms would supply more output than households and businesses would demand. The price level would fall to restore equilibrium at E_0. Point E_2 lies on the *SRAS* curve. However, at price level P_2, households and businesses would demand more output than firms would be willing to produce. The price level would rise to equate the quantity of output demanded and the quantity of output supplied.

CHECKPOINT

Does a rising price level indicate good news or bad news about the economy? It depends. If the price level rises because of a shift in the *AD* curve, output rises in the short run. For example, a tax cut to spur business investment increases aggregate demand for current output and the price level. However, if the price level rises because of a shift in the *SRAS* curve, output falls in the short run. For example, a harsh winter during which workers often can't get to their jobs reduces the quantity of output supplied and increases the price level. o

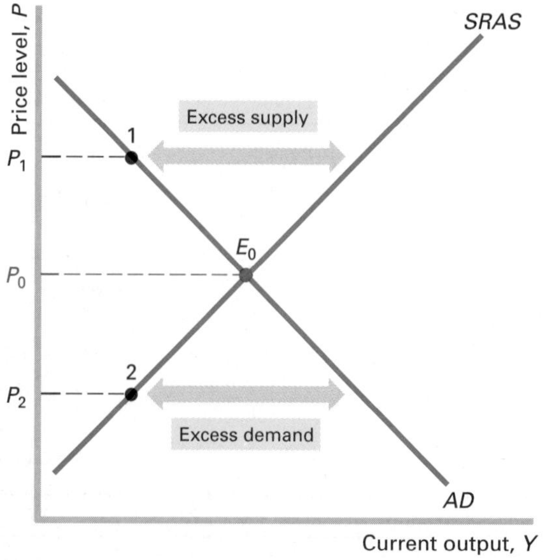

Figure 25.3

Short-Run Equilibrium
The economy's short-run equilibrium is represented by the intersection of the *AD* and *SRAS* curves at E_0. The equilibrium price level is P_0. Higher price levels are associated with an excess supply of output (at point 1, for example), and lower price levels are associated with excess demand for output (at point 2, for example).

CONSIDER THIS . . .

Can Shifts in Aggregate Demand Affect Output in the Long Run?

In general, increases or decreases in aggregate demand have no effect on the full employment level of output. That is, the *LRAS* curve does not shift in response to a shift in the *AD* curve. Some economists believe that large negative shifts in aggregate demand actually reduce the full employment level of output. In that situation, known as *hysteresis*, unemployment rates can be higher than those associated with the full employment level of output for extended periods of time.

Some economists believe that hysteresis is a source of persistent unemployment. If unemployment rates rise, more individuals lose their skills (or are viewed by employers as lacking current skills) and therefore have difficulty being rehired. Furthermore, workers who are unemployed for long periods may become discouraged and drop out of the labor force permanently. Obstacles to locating new jobs extend an individual's job search process and reduce the full employment level of output. Some economists argue that the persistently high unemployment rates in many European countries (particularly in the United Kingdom) in the early 1980s resulted from hysteresis. The government of Prime Minister Margaret Thatcher pursued a contractionary monetary policy in the early 1980s, but effects on output and unemployment lasted for several years. Economists who attribute this decline in full employment to hysteresis believe that expansionary monetary or fiscal policies were needed to restore the economy's initial level of output and employment.

Not all economists accept the proposition that expansionary shifts in aggregate demand are necessary to restore higher output and employment. They note, for example, that generous unemployment insurance systems (that pay workers benefits when they are unemployed) in many European countries might account for persistent unemployment. Evidence for hysteresis is inconclusive. The phenomenon remains a topic of ongoing research because it suggests that economic downturns that are caused by a decline in aggregate demand can impose costs on the economy for long periods of time.

Long-Run Equilibrium

Our analysis of the economy's equilibrium in the short run suggests many possible combinations of output and the price level, depending on where the aggregate demand curve and the short-run aggregate supply curve intersect. However, in the long run, the price level adjusts to bring markets for goods and assets into equilibrium at full employment output, Y^*. In Fig. 25.4, the aggregate demand curve AD_0 and the short-run aggregate supply curve $SRAS_0$ intersect at this level of output, with a price level of P_0.

Now suppose that aggregate demand expands unexpectedly, shifting the aggregate demand curve to the right from AD_0 to AD_1. Output and the price level increase in the short run. The new short-run equilibrium, $E_{1'}$, lies at the intersection of the AD_1 and $SRAS_0$ curves. Over time, as firms learn that the general price level has risen, the *SRAS* curve shifts to the left from $SRAS_0$ to $SRAS_1$ because at the new price level, firms are willing to supply less output. In the long run, the *SRAS* curve will have to shift far enough to intersect with AD_1 at Y^*. The long-run equilibrium is at point E_1, with a price level P_1 and full employment output Y^*.

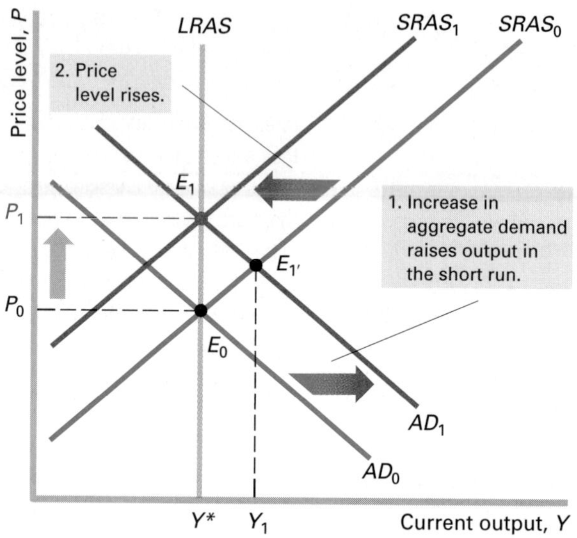

Figure 25.4

Adjustment to Long-Run Equilibrium

1. From initial equilibrium at E_0, an increase in aggregate demand shifts the *AD* curve from AD_0 to AD_1, increasing output from Y^* to Y_1.
2. Because $Y_1 > Y^*$, prices rise, shifting the *SRAS* curve from $SRAS_0$ to $SRAS_1$. The economy's new equilibrium is at E_1. Output has returned to Y^*, but the price level has risen to P_1.

The *LRAS* curve is vertical at Y^*, the full employment level of output. Shifts in the *AD* curve affect the level of output only in the short run. This outcome holds in both the new classical and new Keynesian views, although price adjustment is more rapid in the new classical view.

If aggregate demand contracted unexpectedly, so that the *AD* curve shifted to the left, the process would be reversed. Initially, output and the price level will decline. Over time, as firms learn that the price level has fallen, the *SRAS* curve will shift to the right. This process of adjustment is more gradual (owing to sticky prices for many firms) in the new Keynesian view than in the new classical view. At the new long-run equilibrium, output equals Y^*, and the price level is lower than P_0.

In the long run, the *LRAS* curve is vertical at Y^*, the full employment output level. The economy will produce Y^*, and the price level will adjust to shifts in aggregate demand to ensure that all markets for goods and assets are in equilibrium.

Because the *LRAS* curve is vertical, economists generally agree that changes in aggregate demand affect the price level but not the output level in the long run. This link between shifts in *AD* and the price level is called **monetary neutrality**. It means that money has no effect on output in the long run, because an increase in the nominal money supply raises the price level in the long run but doesn't change equilibrium output. Conversely, a decline in the nominal money supply lowers the price level in the long run but has no effect on output.

The Real Business Cycle View

Although most economists believe that shifts in aggregate demand affect output and the price level, some economists who hold another view believe that changes in aggregate demand have no effect on output, even in the short run. In other words, not only is the long-run aggregate supply curve vertical, but the short-run aggregate supply curve also is vertical. Unlike the new classical view, the alternative **real business cycle view** assumes perfect information. Unlike the new Keynesian explanation of sticky prices, it assumes perfectly flexible prices. The real business cycle model explains short-term changes in output primarily as temporary shocks to productivity. These shocks include changes in the availability of raw materials (food, energy, and minerals, for example), regulatory restrictions on production or markets, and innovations that make the economy more productive.

Shocks to productivity result in increases or decreases in current productivity, which in turn affect the *SRAS* curve, as Fig. 25.5 shows. During the Gulf War, for example, the crisis in the Middle East reduced the supply of oil in world markets, increasing somewhat the price of oil. In this case, starting from an initial equilibrium at E_0 in Fig. 25.5, the productivity of energy-using producers decreases, and the *SRAS* curve shifts to the left from $SRAS_0$ to $SRAS_1$. If the productivity shock is expected to be temporary, lasting only for the current period, future productivity is unaffected and the *AD* curve doesn't shift. Because the *AD* curve doesn't shift, the new short-run equilibrium lies at the intersection of the *AD* curve and the $SRAS_1$ curve—at E_1 in Fig. 25.5. At that point, output is lower and the price level is higher than at the economy's initial equilibrium, E_0.

Ongoing research on the real business cycle model focuses on the significance of temporary disturbances to productivity in explaining output fluctuations. As we discuss next (and in Chapter 26), however, evidence from many episodes suggests that increases or decreases in aggregate demand affect output in the short run.

ECONOMIC FLUCTUATIONS IN THE UNITED STATES

We can use economic models to explain past events and to predict future economic developments. Fluctuations in current output can be explained by shifts in the aggregate demand curve or the aggregate supply curve. We now use *AD-AS* analysis to help explain three episodes of economic fluctuations in the

Figure 25.5

Productivity and Short-Run Fluctuations in the Real Business Cycle Model

In the real business cycle model, short-run movements in output are explained by shocks to productivity.

1. From an initial equilibrium at E_0, an increase in the price of oil reduces productivity, shifting the *SRAS* curve from $SRAS_0$ to $SRAS_1$. Output falls from Y_0 to Y_1.
2. The price level rises from P_0 to P_1.

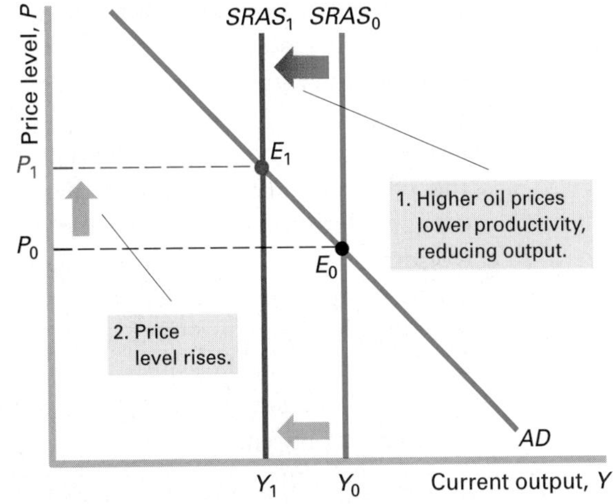

United States: (1) shocks to aggregate demand, 1964–1969; (2) supply shocks, 1973–1975 and 1995–2000; and (3) a credit crunch shock to aggregate demand, 1990–1991. Then we use *AD-AS* analysis to predict consequences for output and prices of pro-investment tax reform. In Chapter 26, we apply the *AD-AS* model to predict the outcome of monetary policies on output and the price level.

Shocks to Aggregate Demand, 1964–1969

By 1964, U.S. participation in the conflict in Vietnam had grown to a major war effort, and real government purchases—principally for military equipment and personnel—had expanded by about 9% since 1960. Those expenditures would expand by another 21% from 1964 through 1969. The Fed was alarmed by the prospect of rising interest rates. (If nothing else changed, the rise in aggregate demand from government purchases would increase money demand and the interest rate.) As a result, the Fed pursued an expansionary monetary policy: The annual growth rate of *M1* rose from 3.7% in 1963 to 7.7% in 1964.

The combination of fiscal and monetary expansions led to a series of shifts to the right of the aggregate demand curve. Rising aggregate demand caused output to exceed the full employment level in the mid-1960s, putting upward pressure on production costs and the price level. As we demonstrated in the analysis of short-run and long-run equilibrium with the *AD-AS* diagram, the *SRAS* curve shifts up and to the left, restoring the economy's full employment equilibrium at a higher price level. Because fiscal and monetary expansion continued for several years, the *AD-AS* analysis indicates that output growth and inflation (the rate of change in the price level) should have risen from 1964 through 1969. The demand expansion panel in Fig. 25.6 shows that is generally what happened.

Supply Shocks, 1973–1975 and 1995–2000

By the early 1970s, many economists and policymakers believed that output growth and inflation went hand in hand—a sensible conclusion when changes in the economy's equilibrium output and price level are driven by changes in aggregate demand. The United States (and other industrialized countries) experienced negative supply shocks in 1973 and 1974. In 1973, the Organization of Petroleum Exporting Countries (OPEC) sharply reduced the supply of oil in the world oil market in an attempt to punish the United States and other countries for supporting Israel in the 1973 Arab–Israeli conflict. Along with the quadrupling of world oil prices, poor crop harvests around the world caused food prices to rise significantly. In the United States, these two negative supply shocks were reinforced by the lifting of wage and price controls that had been in effect since 1971, which caused a round of catch-up wage and price increases.

In *AD-AS* analysis, this set of negative supply shocks shifts the short-run aggregate supply curve up to the left, raising the price level and reducing output. As Fig. 25.6 shows, output growth fell in 1974 and 1975 while inflation rose.

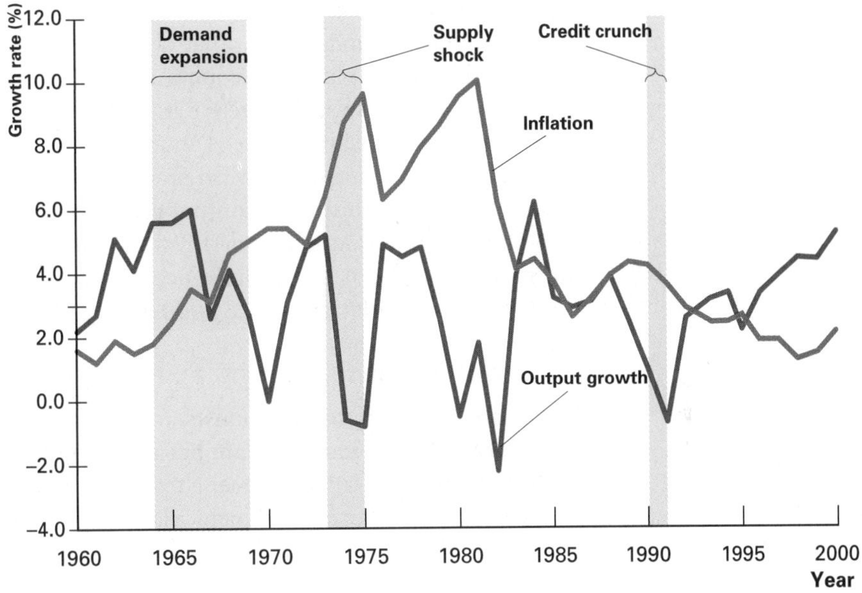

Figure 25.6

Output Growth and Inflation, 1960–2000

The short-run changes in output growth and inflation observable between 1960 and 2000 can be explained by shifts in aggregate demand or aggregate supply that caused output to exceed or fall short of the full employment level.

Source: Council of Economic Advisers, *Economic Report of the President.*

This type of inflation causes the economy to stagnate, a result that is known as *stagflation.* The falling output and rising prices indicated that aggregate supply shocks, as well as aggregate demand shocks, could change the economy's short-run equilibrium. A similar pattern occurred in response to adverse oil supply shocks in the 1978–1980 period.

We can also examine favorable supply shocks, such as those experienced in the U.S. economy in the late 1990s. In the background, the Federal Reserve had begun to increase interest rates in February 1994 to counteract what it saw as inflationary pressures. The economic boom continued, with high output growth and a decline in inflation toward 2%. This favorable supply shock can be illustrated using *AD-AS* analysis.

Many economists highlight the role of productivity growth stemming from information-technology-related investments—partially in the "new economy." As a consequence, the aggregate supply curve shifted to the right, increasing output and reducing inflation.

Credit Crunch and Aggregate Demand, 1990–1991

Many analysts believe that a reduction in banks' ability or willingness to lend, called a *credit crunch*, deepened the 1990–1991 recession. The Gulf War provided a negative supply shock early in the recession. Recall that financial institutions such as banks are likely to be important suppliers of funds to borrowers that have few alternative sources of finance from nonmoney markets. Two events may have led to a credit crunch during this recession. First, more stringent bank regulation reduced banks' ability to lend. Second, declines in real estate values and the large debt burdens of many corporations reduced banks' willingness to lend to borrowers at any expected real interest rate. Because households and small and medium-sized businesses weren't able to replace bank credit with funds from other sources, spending for consumer durable goods and business plant and equipment fell.

In *AD-AS* analysis, the decline in spending translates into a reduction in aggregate demand, shifting the *AD* curve to the left. Over time, the drop in aggregate demand puts downward pressure on prices, shifting the *SRAS* curve down. Figure 25.6 shows that output growth fell during the 1990–1991 recession and that inflation fell from 4.3% in 1989 to 2.9% in 1992. Some economists worried about the reemergence of such a credit crunch pattern in output growth and inflation in late 2000 and early 2001.

Are Investment Incentives Inflationary?

In the late 1990s, many economists and policymakers urged consideration of tax reforms that would stimulate business investment. Such reforms included the introduction of an investment tax credit—in which the government directly subsidizes the cost of new plant and equipment—or expensing—in which businesses write off the purchase of new plant and equipment all at once, rather than gradually. Many economists argued that such reforms would significantly increase business investment demand and output of capital goods. Would they also increase inflation?

In *AD-AS* analysis, the stimulus in investment translates into an increase in aggregate demand, shifting the *AD* curve to the right. However, as the new plant and equipment are installed, the economy's capacity to produce increases, and the *AS* curve shifts to the right, reducing the inflationary pressure from pro-investment tax reform. Recent evidence suggests that the supply response is potent and investment incentives are unlikely to be inflationary.

KEY TERMS AND CONCEPTS

Aggregate demand
Aggregate demand (*AD*) curve
Aggregate supply
Aggregate supply (*AS*) curve
Long-run aggregate supply (*LRAS*) curve
Short-run aggregate supply (*SRAS*) curve
Full employment output
Misperception theory
Monetary neutrality
New classical view
New Keynesian view
Real business cycle view
Supply shocks

SUMMARY

1. Aggregate demand represents the level of current output that households and firms are willing to purchase at a particular price level. Aggregate supply represents the amount of output that producers in the economy are willing to sell at a particular price level.

2. The aggregate demand (*AD*) curve illustrates the quantity of current output that is demanded at each price level. The price level and the aggregate quantity of output demanded are negatively related. Each point along the *AD* curve represents a combination

of price level and aggregate output for which the goods and asset markets are in equilibrium. Factors that shift the *AD* curve include increases or decreases in the nominal money supply, money demand, determinants of desired saving, and determinants of desired investment.

3. The aggregate supply (*AS*) curve represents the quantity of output supplied at each price level. The long-run aggregate supply (*LRAS*) curve is vertical at the full employment level of output. Increases or decreases in the current productivity of factors of production shift the *LRAS* curve. The short-run aggregate supply (*SRAS*) curve slopes upward. In the new classical view, an unexpected increase in the aggregate price level increases the quantity of output that firms are willing to supply in the short run. In the new Keynesian view, the *SRAS* curve slopes upward because many firms have sticky prices and are willing to meet the demand for their output over a range from an initially stated price. In both new classical and new Keynesian views, shifts in the *SRAS* curve reflect shifts in the expected price level or costs of production.
4. The economy's short-run equilibrium output and price level occur at the intersection of the *AD* curve and the *SRAS* curve. The economy's long-run equilibrium occurs at the intersection of the *AD* curve and the *LRAS* curve.
5. Changes in the equilibrium price level and output can be explained by shifts in the aggregate demand curve, the aggregate supply curve, or both.

REVIEW QUESTIONS

1. Why is there a negative relationship between the price level and aggregate output along the *AD* curve?
2. Which of the following will shift the *AD* curve to the right?
   a. The Fed carries out an open market sale.
   b. The interest rate on checkable deposits falls.
   c. The federal government launches a massive program to rebuild the nation's highways.
   d. The federal government cuts the corporate profits tax.
3. Why does a rise in the price level increase aggregate output supplied in the short run, according to the new classical view?
4. What is meant by the term *price stickiness* in the new Keynesian view? What elements of the economy lead to price stickiness?
5. What is the slope of the long-run aggregate supply curve? Why does it have this slope?
6. What predictions do the new classical and new Keynesian views yield about monetary neutrality in the long run?
7. According to the new Keynesian view, what is the effect on output in the short run of an increase in government defense purchases?
8. What is a real business cycle? If a winter storm temporarily reduces agricultural output, which curves shift in the *AD-AS* diagram?

ANALYTICAL PROBLEMS

9. The derivation of the *AD* curve presented in the chapter depends on (for an increase in the price level) the impact of a rising real interest rate on the demand for real money balances. Suppose you believe Irving Fisher's formulation of the quantity theory of money and you do not believe that the real interest rate affects the demand for real money balances. Is it possible for you to give another rationale for a downward-sloping *AD* curve?
10. Using the new classical view and the *AD-AS* diagram, describe the effects on the price level and current output of an increase in the price of oil. How would your answer differ if the Fed increased the money supply to stimulate aggregate demand?
11. Suppose that the economy is initially in equilibrium at full employment. Then the government unexpectedly increases income taxes. What are the effects on

THE FINANCIAL TIMES FEBRUARY 7, 2000

Memo to Tokyo: Print Money

The Japanese government yesterday said the country's gross domestic product was likely to have contracted . . . —indicating that the world's second largest economy could be heading back into recession.

Taichi Sakaiya, head of the Economic Planning Agency, said Japan's GDP was likely to have suffered a sharp fall during the quarter after a 1% fall in the third quarter. The technical definition of recession is two consecutive quarters of negative GDP growth.

a Mr. Sakaiya blamed a drop in private consumption and in big-ticket information technology purchases stemming from fears about the millennium bug.

But he said the economy should achieve the 0.6% growth target he had set for the year to March. Japan achieved 1.5% growth in the first quarter of 1999, and 1% in the second quarter.

A recession would be a blow to the election prospects of Keizo Obuchi, Japan's prime minister, who must call lower house elections before October. And it would underline the dependence of an economy—which has contracted in seven of the last nine quarters—on massive injections of government cash.

Economists said fourth quarter figures were expected to have suffered from a sizable drop in private consumption, which had been hit by substantial declines in year-end bonus payments and a sharp fall in the number of people in full-time employment. Consumer spending makes up 60% of GDP.

Private sector capital spending, public works spending, housing investment, and net exports might also have been a drag on GDP growth, while inventory stockpiling due to Y2K fears was unlikely to have been high enough to offset the overall decline.

The economists added that forecasting Japan's GDP figure was notoriously difficult because of poor statistics. Revisions to the data for the quarter to September are expected on Wednesday, but are not expected to show the economy expanded during that period. The data for the three months to December must be released before March 17.

b Nonetheless, some economists said there were signs that Japan remained on a path to recovery. "Evidence of normal positive cyclical dynamics has become overwhelming in the past six months," said Richard Jerram at ING Baring in Tokyo.

c "Only an external shock such as a rapid strengthening of the yen or a major policy mistake such as large-scale fiscal tightening is likely to derail the recovery," added Peter Morgan at HSBC Securities in Tokyo.

Analyzing the News . . .

For most of the post–World War II period, the Japanese economy has been a growth miracle. By the early 1990s, slowing growth of aggregate demand and rising production costs worried many analysts and policymakers in Japan. Indeed, real GDP growth fell from 4% per annum in 1991 to anemic and even negative levels throughout much of the late 1990s and 2000. At the same time, inflation fell, and Japan actually experienced modest deflation in the late 1990s. We can use *AD-AS* analysis to explain the developments discussed in the article.

a Are Japan's woes due to weak aggregate demand or to the adverse consequences of supply shocks on output? Over the mid- and late 1990s, output growth and inflation both declined markedly in Japan. This positive association between output changes and price changes suggests that *AD* shifts were more important. As part (b) of the figure shows, all else being equal, a drop in aggregate demand shifts the *AD* curve to the left—from AD_0 to AD_1—reducing output (from Y_0 to Y_1) and the price level (from P_0 to P_1).

b As part of a path to recovery, many economists argued that the Bank of Japan should expand the Japanese money supply. As we observed in our analysis of aggregate demand, a monetary expansion reduces the real interest rate in the short run, increasing aggregate demand and shifting the *AD* curve to the right. All else being equal, this policy change would raise output and prices. As part (a) of the figure shows, the monetary policy stimulus shifts the *AD* curve to the right, from AD_0 to AD_1, increasing output from Y_0 to Y_1. The price level rises from P_0 to P_1. Some economists argue that aggregate demand is so weak in Japan—in part because of recent declines in asset prices and increases in bank failures—that some demand-enhancing policy is necessary.

c Are aggregate supply disturbances unimportant? Not necessarily. The aging of Japan's workforce and decline in working hours imply a slower growth of aggregate supply. These trends shift the *LRAS* curve to the left, reducing output growth and increasing inflation. In the medium to long run, Japan's problems may center more on improving productivity and the growth of aggregate supply.

For further thought . . .

Suppose that the Japanese government's policies are unsuccessful in raising aggregate demand. Discuss the implications for short-run equilibrium output in the United States.

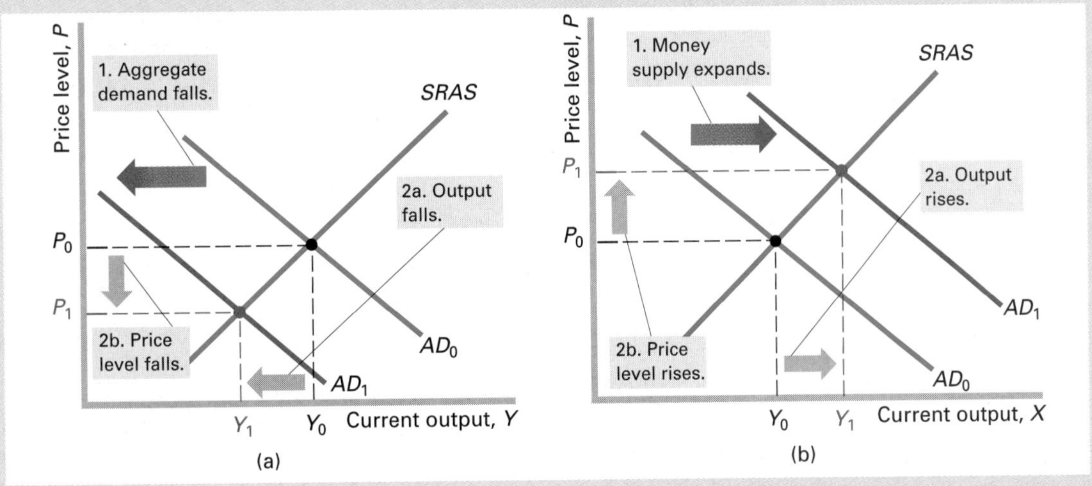

output and the price level in the short run and the long run, according to the new Keynesian view?

12. The Fed today is often said to see price stability as its most important goal. Back in the 1964–1969 period the Fed increased the rate of growth of the money supply even though federal expenditures were rising rapidly and GDP was already near its full employment level. Why do you believe the Fed acted as it did during the late 1960s? If confronted with the same circumstances today, would the Fed be likely to react in the same way?

13. The chapter describes the aggregate demand shocks of 1964–1969 and the aggregate supply shocks of 1973–1975 and 1995–2000. Draw an *AD-AS* diagram to illustrate what happened during these years.

14. In the mid-1970s and again in the late 1970s, OPEC raised oil prices sharply. The higher cost of oil reduced the productivity of energy-using industries. Show what would happen to output and the price level in the short run according to the new Keynesian view.

15. One way in which misperception of the aggregate price level is thought to affect the economy is through the labor market. Suppose that the unemployment rate u is related to the rate of inflation π and the expected rate of inflation π^e, as follows:

$$\pi = 0.08 - 2u + \pi^e.$$

a. If there is no misperception of inflation (so $\pi = \pi^e$), what is the unemployment rate (in percent)?

b. If expected inflation is 8% and actual inflation is 4%, what is the unemployment rate?

c. If expected inflation is 4% and actual inflation is 8%, what is the unemployment rate?

16. John Maynard Keynes stressed the role played by *animal spirits*—changes in the confidence or optimism of entrepreneurs and managers—in economic fluctuations. Suppose that a wave of optimism hits the U.S. business community. Describe the effects of aggregate demand and the price level in terms of the new Keynesian view.

17. Suppose that as a result of a vigorous "thrift campaign" by U.S. policymakers, the public increases its saving rate. In other words, at any particular combination of income and real interest rate, the public saves more income. Describe the short-run and long-run effects on output in terms of the new Keynesian view.

18. Because of an increase in the expected future productivity of capital, the stock market rises. Describe the effects on investment, current output, and future output in terms of the new classical view.

19. Many economists and policymakers worry that increased government purchases are not expansionary because they crowd out private investment spending. Using the derivation of the *AD* curve, explain the logic of this argument.

20. Suppose that Congress passes a law allowing all taxpayers to subtract $500 from their tax bill while government spending remains unchanged. Assuming that the Ricardian equivalence proposition holds, describe the effect of this policy on aggregate demand.

21. Suppose that the President and Congress agree on an infrastructure program to raise federal spending on highways, bridges, and airports. Proponents of the program argue that it will increase productivity in the long run. Opponents of the program argue that it will reduce private investment in the short run. Using the *AD-AS* diagram, illustrate these positions.

22. The Fed can use expansionary or contractionary policy to shift the *AD* curve. Using the *AD-AS* diagram, illustrate how monetary policy should be used to return output to its full employment level when

a. the *AD* curve intersects the *SRAS* curve to the left of the full employment level of output

b. the *AD* curve intersects the *SRAS* curve to the right of the full employment level of output

23. Throughout the 1980s, the interest rate that banks' customers received on their deposits increased, owing in large part to improvements in computer and communications technologies. What effect did this development have on the *AD* curve? If it is not offset by other factors, what effect did this development have on the price level, assuming a vertical *LRAS* curve?

DATA QUESTIONS

24. Find the latest volume of the *Economic Report of the President* in your library and calculate the annual percentage change in the gross domestic product (in constant dollars) and in the price deflator for the gross domestic product. Using these two series, identify episodes in which shifts in aggregate demand are more important in explaining changes in output as well as episodes in which shifts in aggregate supply are more important.

25. Using data in the *Economic Report of the President,* calculate the growth rate of output per worker in the nonfarm business sector for three time periods: 1960–1969, 1973–1979, and 1985–1990. Evaluate the implications of the patterns of growth in output per worker for shifts in the *LRAS* curve during the three periods.

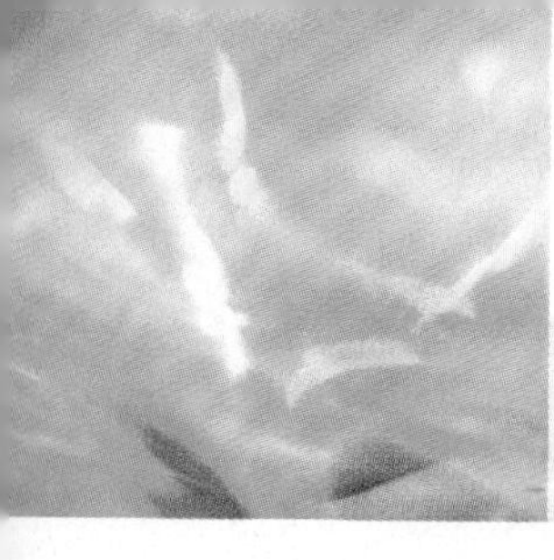

CHAPTER 26

Money and Output in the Short Run

A group of business executives gathered for a dinner in 1992 at New York's Waldorf-Astoria Hotel to hear a speech entitled "Monetary Policy and the New World Order" given by a respected member of the Fed's Board of Governors. The speech followed major changes in monetary policy in the 1980s and early 1990s, and the question and answer period was lively: "You can talk about long-run adjustments," an angry CEO whose firm had suffered losses and layoffs in the recession said to the speaker, "but answer this: Why does a fall in the money supply put people out of work?"

During recessions, output declines. As firms experience a decrease in demand, they may lay off workers, increasing unemployment. Recessions are troublesome to both individuals and businesses. Unemployed individuals experience economic hardship, loss of self-esteem, and erosion of their skills. During a downturn, businesses lose profits and may fail. Could the Fed intervene to reduce the severity of downturns? Should it?

In this chapter, we examine changes over time in the money supply and output to find out whether there is a link between these two variables. In the first section, we present the evidence that economists study to determine whether there is a link between the money supply and output. Economists differ in their interpretations of the evidence, and as a result, they propose different explanations for the reasons that output may (or may not) vary with changes in the money supply. We then describe the explanations for the patterns proposed by three groups of economists: real business cycle economists, new classical economists, and new Keynesian economists. On the basis of these explanations, we describe how monetary policy might alleviate the severity of economic downturns. We conclude with an analysis of policy enacted during the 1980s and 1990s.

TRACKING MONEY AND OUTPUT MOVEMENTS IN THE SHORT RUN

Although the money supply and output have grown steadily over long periods of time, both of these economic variables fluctuate over the short run as the economy moves through the business cycle. During the **business cycle,** output grows during an expansion or a boom until it reaches a peak. Then it declines as the economy moves into a contraction or recession until it reaches a trough. This pattern varies from several months to several years, and expansions and recessions vary in intensity. Business cycles have existed since the Industrial Revolution and have been analyzed by economists since the nineteenth century. Figure 26.1 shows periods of contraction—*recessions*—from 1950 to the present.

The growth of the money supply also varies over the business cycle, as Fig. 26.1 shows. Movements in the growth rate of the money supply are *procyclical*; that is, the growth rate generally increases during expansions and decreases during recessions. In studying data such as those presented in Fig. 26.1, economists have found that changes in the nominal money supply often precede the fluctuations in output that occur during the business cycle; that is, monetary expansions precede business cycle peaks, and monetary contractions precede business cycle troughs.

How do economists interpret this pattern of changes in the money supply with output? There is no single answer because these changes can be explained differently. For example, some economists contend that changes in the money supply are responsible for subsequent changes in output, whereas others believe that changes in the money supply reflect, rather than cause, changes in output. In the next three sections, we use the aggregate demand–aggregate supply model that we built in Chapter 25 to study the explanations of the pattern shown in Fig. 26.1. Specifically, we look at the views of real business cycle economists, new classical economists, and new Keynesian economists. We then turn to the policy recommendations of each to see how and whether the Fed might try to reduce the severity of declines in output during recessions.

Figure 26.1

Money Supply Growth and the Business Cycle, 1950–2000

Data are for *M1* growth at an annual percentage rate. The shaded areas represent recessions designated by the National Bureau of Economic Research, a private economic research organization responsible for dating U.S. business cycles.

Source: Federal Reserve Bulletin.

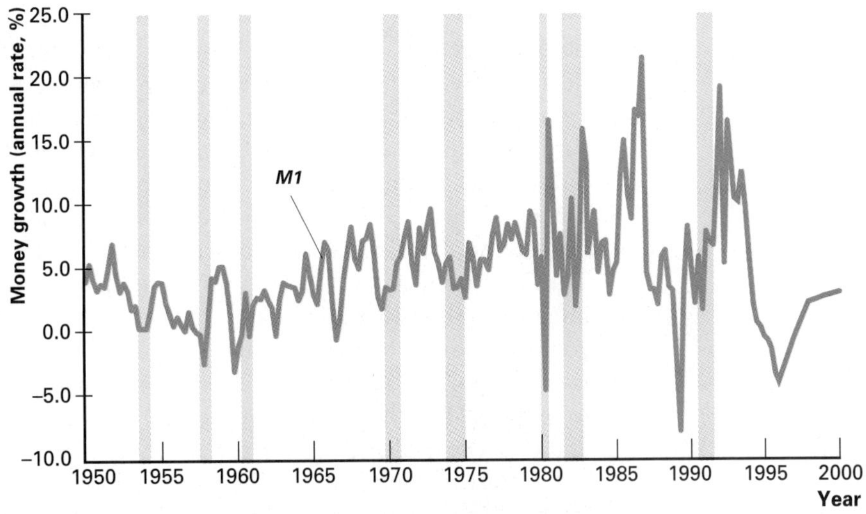

THE REAL BUSINESS CYCLE MODEL

In the long run, prices are flexible; that is, firms adjust their prices to match changes in cost or demand. When prices are flexible, the nominal money supply has no impact on the level of economic activity; therefore *money is neutral*. One-time increases or decreases in the nominal money supply affect the price level but not real output.

The real business cycle model holds that prices are flexible even in the short run and that output is at the full employment level in the economy's short-run equilibrium. Hence the economy's short-run aggregate supply curve, *SRAS*, is vertical. But actual output fluctuates over time. The real business cycle model says that the observed fluctuations in output in the short run primarily are caused by temporary shocks to productivity. These shocks include shifts in the availability of key raw materials (food, energy, and minerals, for example), regulatory restrictions on production or markets, and innovations that make the economy more productive.

The real business cycle model also holds that increases or decreases in the money supply have no effect on economic activity, even in the short run. In Fig. 26.1, it appears that the money supply grows more rapidly before and during expansions than it does during contractions. Does this pattern necessarily contradict the assumption that money is neutral? Proponents of the real business cycle model answer *no*, arguing that even though the money supply and output move together, changes in the money supply don't necessarily *cause* changes in output. Specifically, proponents of the real business cycle model offer two arguments against a causal relationship between the money supply and output. First, they suggest that some other variable might be responsible for the shifts in money supply and output. Second, they propose that changes in output might cause changes in the money supply. This second argument is an example of a type of reasoning called *reverse causation*.

The second argument is used more often than the first by the real business cycle economists, who argue that current and anticipated future changes in output affect the *demand for money* rather than the *supply of money*. To demonstrate, suppose that the economy experiences a boom brought on by a favorable productivity shock, such as a temporary decline in oil prices. Anticipating a future increase in income, households and businesses demand more currency and checkable deposits because of greater demand for money for transactions. The increase in demand for money resulting from the rise in output and the boom causes the Fed passively to increase the money supply. Thus real business cycle advocates argue that changes in output increase the money supply, rather than that a change in the money supply affects output—a classic example of reverse causation. These economists present a view that is at one pole of our analysis: There is no causal link from the money supply to output. The other schools of thought do believe that there is a causal link, and they cite evidence against reverse causation.

To test the link between the money supply and output, Milton Friedman (then of the University of Chicago, now at Stanford University) and Anna

Schwartz (of the National Bureau of Economic Research) examined the historical pattern between these two variables. They found that the money supply growth rate fell before each decline in output.† This pattern held for every recession for the period studied, almost 100 years. Friedman and Schwartz documented that the peak in the nominal money supply growth rate precedes the peak in output on average by 16 months. This time period was not constant for all business cycles; it ranged from a few months to more than two years. On the basis of their examination of many business cycles in the period between the Civil War and 1960, Friedman and Schwartz concluded that *changes in money growth cause output fluctuations*. They also concluded, however, that money's effects on output appeared only after long and variable lags.

The test of Friedman and Schwartz's assertion is whether the changes in the money supply that they identified were "independent." An independent change in the money supply is one that is not influenced by a change in output or by some third factor that influenced both money and output.

Independent events can also be Fed policies that are designed to achieve objectives other than increases in output. By tracing the impact of an independent change, we can draw conclusions about how changes in the money supply affect output in the short run. Friedman and Schwartz studied specific historical episodes that fit the description of independent events: the banking panics prior to the founding of the Federal Reserve System, the wave of bank failures during the early 1930s, and the increases in reserve requirements in 1936 and 1937. They associated the decline in the money supply during banking panics, such as the panic of 1907, when the public converted bank deposits into currency, with the subsequent decline in economic activity caused by deposit contraction and reduction of money growth. The wave of bank failures during the early 1930s significantly reduced the money supply, and Friedman and Schwartz blamed the loss of output during the early 1930s on this "Great Contraction." They also traced the pronounced recession of 1937–1938 to the monetary contraction resulting from the Fed's increase in the required reserve ratio, which reduced the money supply. The change in reserve requirements was independent because it was associated with the Fed's desire to increase its control over the money supply, not with a policy to influence the current level of economic activity. All these episodes show linkage from a change in money supply growth to a change in the level of output. In this spirit, Christina Romer and David Romer of the University of California, Berkeley, identified six independent monetary policy shifts after 1960 in which the FOMC announced a contractionary monetary policy to fight inflation.†† Each episode was followed by a decline in output. They maintain that because the monetary contractions were intended to reduce inflation, they are independent of current output conditions.

---

† Milton Friedman and Anna J. Schwartz, *A Monetary History of the United States*. Princeton, N.J.: Princeton University Press, 1963.

†† Christina Romer and David Romer, "Does Monetary Policy Matter?: A New Test in the Spirit of Friedman and Schwartz," in O. J. Blanchard and S. Fischer, eds., *NBER Macroeconomics Annual*. Cambridge, Mass.: MIT Press, 1989, pp. 121–170.

Another way to explore whether changes in money growth cause changes in output is to study more continuous measures of the extent to which monetary policy is likely to increase or decrease output. By means of statistical tests, Ben Bernanke and Alan Blinder of Princeton University documented that increases in the federal funds rate cause output to fall.† They argue that changes in the federal funds rate are independent since they are determined largely by actions of the Fed. These findings confirm that the money supply declines almost immediately in response to a contractionary policy by the Fed and that output declines with a lag of between six months and one year. Therefore the evidence on money and output movements doesn't support the basic real business cycle model; in the short run, money appears not to be neutral.

Although the real business cycle model provides an accurate view of the long run, in which prices are flexible and money is neutral, its predictions for the short run are not consistent with historical evidence. Two other schools of thought—the new classical school and the new Keynesian school—develop the idea that money and output are related. They offer different explanations for the link, as described next.

CHECKPOINT

During the fourth quarter of each year, especially in the month of December, measures of money and retail sales are higher than they are during the rest of the year. Do these temporary changes mean that the increase in the money supply caused the change in output? Real business cycle economists note that a more likely explanation is that the demand for goods rises for the holiday season, increasing the public's demand for currency and checkable deposits. The Fed smooths the surge in money demand by increasing the money supply to satisfy the demands of households and businesses. o

MONEY AND OUTPUT: THE NEW CLASSICAL MODEL

New classical economists attribute the link between the money supply and output to imperfect information. Specifically, they believe that firms do not completely adjust their prices and workers do not adjust their wages in the short run because business managers and workers have imperfect information about changes in the price level. Inflexible prices prevent money from being neutral in the short run. In the new classical view, output increases when the price level is higher than expected. Households and businesses incorporate expectations of changes in the money supply into their forecasts of the aggregate price level. Expected increases in the money supply raise

†Ben S. Bernanke and Alan S. Blinder, "The Federal Funds Rate and the Channels of Monetary Transmission," *American Economic Review,* 82:901–921, 1992.

households' and firms' expected value of the price level, and expected decreases in the money supply reduce the expected value of the price level. According to new classical economists, the impact of changes in the nominal money supply on output in the short run depends on whether those changes are expected or unexpected.

Expected changes in the money supply. To understand the distinction between expected and unexpected changes in the nominal money supply, suppose that the economy is in equilibrium and that the Fed announces a 10% increase in the nominal money supply. This announcement becomes part of the information that households and businesses use in forecasting the aggregate price level. We illustrate the impact on output using the *AD-AS* diagram. Starting from the economy's equilibrium at E_0 in Fig. 26.2(a), a one-time expected increase in the nominal money supply shifts the aggregate demand curve from AD_0 to AD_1 and increases the expected price level, thereby shifting the short-run aggregate supply curve up from $SRAS_0$ to $SRAS_1$. The economy's new short-run equilibrium has a higher price level, P_1, but output doesn't change. In this case, households and businesses expect the price level to increase because of the expected increase in the money supply. Hence they are not surprised when the price level does increase, and so real output is not affected. Therefore new classical economists conclude that a perfectly anticipated change in the money supply has no effect on real output, and changes in the money supply are neutral.

Unexpected changes in the money supply. What if an increase in the money supply is *unexpected*? For example, suppose that the Fed surprises households and businesses by suddenly increasing the money supply by 10%. In Fig. 26.2(b), from an initial equilibrium at E_0, the monetary expansion shifts the aggregate demand curve to the right from AD_0 to AD_1. The expected price level doesn't change, so the short-run aggregate supply curve remains at $SRAS_0$. At the new equilibrium, E_1, output has risen from Y_0 to Y_1, and the actual price level has risen from P_0 to P_1. Because the actual price level exceeds the expected price level, firms are fooled into thinking that the relative prices of their products have increased. Therefore they increase their output. An unanticipated change in the money supply is not neutral because output increases in response to an unexpected increase in the nominal money supply and decreases in response to an unexpected decrease.

New classical economists have examined whether unexpected and expected changes in the money supply have different effects on output or prices. They haven't arrived at a consensus, but the available evidence suggests that *both* expected and unexpected changes in the nominal money supply affect current output. This evidence is inconsistent with the new classical view. New Keynesian economists have tried to explain this evidence while retaining the sensible assumption of the new classical approach that households and businesses use available information in forming their expectation of money growth or the price level.

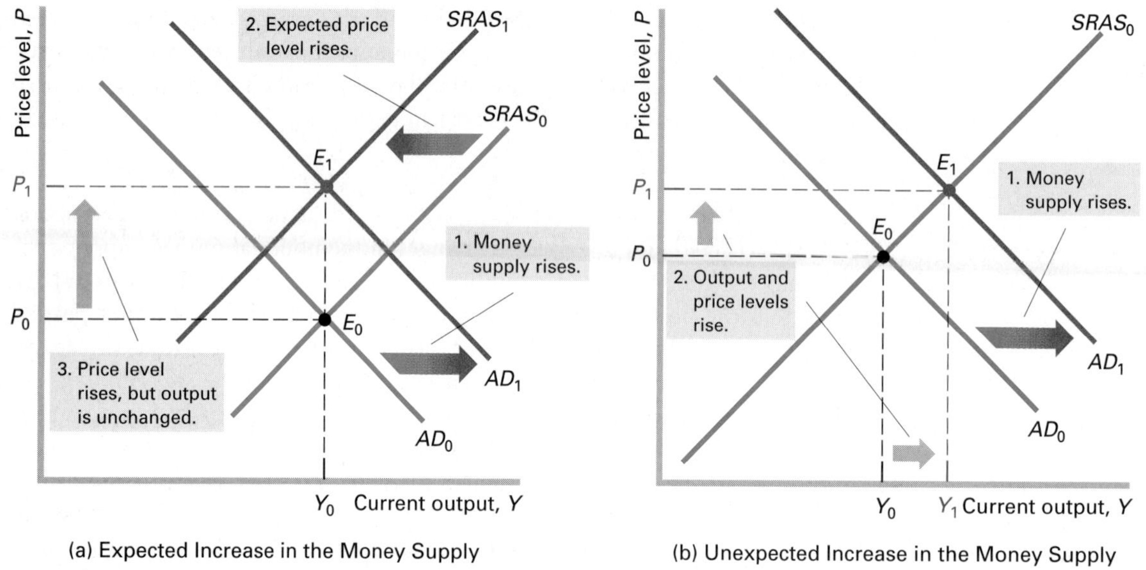

Figure 26.2

Money and Output Changes in the New Classical Model

In the new classical model, only unexpected changes in the money supply affect output in the short run.

As shown in (a):

1. From an initial equilibrium at E_0, an expected increase in the nominal money supply shifts the *AD* curve from AD_0 to AD_1.
2. The expected price level increases, shifting the *SRAS* curve from $SRAS_0$ to $SRAS_1$.
3. At the new equilibrium, E_1, the price level rises to P_1, and output remains unchanged at Y_0.

As shown in (b):

1. From an initial equilibrium at E_0, an unexpected increase in the nominal money supply shifts the *AD* curve from AD_0 to AD_1.
2. At the new equilibrium, E_1, the price level rises to P_1, and output rises to Y_1.

CHECKPOINT

Suppose that you knew that the aggregate price level was closely correlated with the size of the money supply and that you could observe the size of the money supply continuously. Would the misperception theory be useful in explaining the business cycle? Why or why not? No. Because you can observe the money supply continuously, there would be no misperception. o

MONEY AND OUTPUT: THE NEW KEYNESIAN MODEL

New Keynesian economists link output movements to changes in the money supply by arguing that prices are not completely flexible. The new Keynesians propose two reasons for price stickiness in the short run: long-term contracts and imperfect competition among sellers in the goods market.

According to new Keynesians, neither expected nor unexpected changes in the nominal money supply are neutral in the short run. Figure 26.3(a) illustrates the effect of an unexpected decline in the money supply. Suppose that

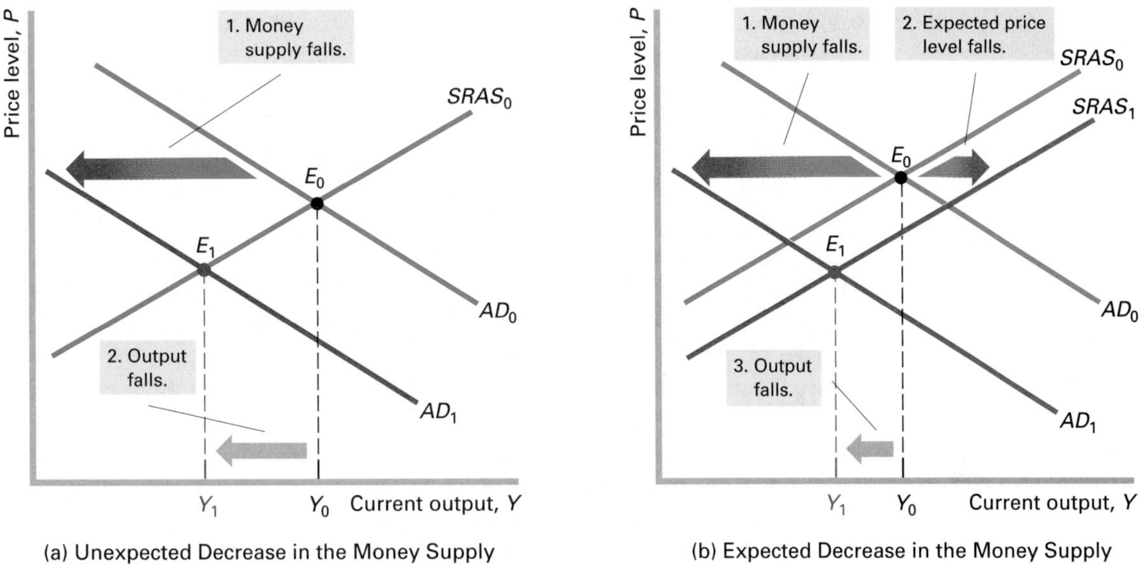

Figure 26.3

Money and Output in the New Keynesian Model

Money is not neutral in the short run in the new Keynesian view.

As shown in (a):

1. From an initial equilibrium E_0, a monetary contraction shifts the *AD* curve from AD_0 to AD_1.
2. Because the decline in the money supply is unexpected, the *SRAS* curve remains at $SRAS_0$. At the new equilibrium E_1, output has fallen from Y_0 to Y_1.

As shown in (b):

1. From an initial equilibrium E_0, a monetary contraction shifts the *AD* curve from AD_0 to AD_1.
2. Because the decline in the money supply is expected, the expected price level falls, and some but not all prices fall. The *SRAS* curve shifts from $SRAS_0$ to $SRAS_1$.
3. At the new equilibrium, E_1, output has fallen from Y_0 to Y_1, which is greater than Y_1 in (a).

the Fed announces a reduction of the money supply that was not anticipated by households and firms. From an initial equilibrium at E_0, the monetary contraction shifts the AD curve to the left from AD_0 to AD_1. The contraction was unexpected, so prices do not adjust downward, and the $SRAS$ curve remains at $SRAS_0$. The new equilibrium lies at E_1, the intersection of the AD_1 and $SRAS_0$ curves. Because aggregate supply doesn't adjust in the short run, output falls from Y_0 to Y_1. This pattern closely resembles that proposed by the new classical economists.

Now let's consider the case of an expected monetary contraction. New Keynesians believe that households and businesses use all available information to forecast demand and the price level. Hence, when the money supply is expected to fall, the expected price level also should fall. Firms with flexible prices—prices that can be changed in the current period—lower their prices, as in the new classical explanation. However, many prices do not adjust in the current period, so the aggregate price level falls slowly in response to the expected decline in the nominal money supply. Similarly, if firms are monopolistically competitive and prices are costly to adjust, prices will adjust only gradually in response to an anticipated change in the money supply.

Figure 26.3(b) illustrates the effect on output of an expected decrease in the money supply. Starting from the economy's equilibrium at E_0, the drop in the money supply shifts the aggregate demand curve to the left from AD_0 to AD_1. In this case, some prices can and do adjust by falling in the short run. The short-run aggregate supply curve shifts downward from $SRAS_0$ to $SRAS_1$. At the new equilibrium E_1, however, output is lower than at E_0, so the price level hasn't completely adjusted. This drop in output isn't as large as that in the case of an unexpected decrease in the money supply, depicted in Fig. 26.3(a). In the new Keynesian model, even expected changes in the nominal money supply can have real effects in the short run, although those effects are smaller than the effects of an unexpected change.

New Keynesians believe that the money supply affects output by influencing the determinants of aggregate demand through changes in interest rates. Because the price level adjusts gradually to a change in the money supply, an increase in the nominal money supply raises real money balances in the short run. To induce households and firms to hold greater real money balances, the market-clearing real interest rate falls. A drop in the nominal money supply reduces real money balances in the short run. To restore equilibrium,

CONSIDER THIS . . .

Can One Size Fit All in Europe?

The sensitivity of key components of aggregate demand to interest rates figures prominently in new Keynesian analyses of effects of monetary policy on the economy. Since January 1, 1999, the 11 countries participating in the European monetary union have shared a common short-term interest rate. But do they share a common sensitivity of aggregate demand to interest rates?

As of 2001, the answer was no. Economists at the International Monetary Fund have concluded that, within the European Monetary Union, in Austria, Belgium, Finland, Germany, and the Netherlands, the effect of a rise in rates of output takes twice as long to happen as in France, Italy, and Spain. The initial effect, however, is twice as large in the latter group of countries.

Why the differences? Higher interest rates influence economies by raising the cost of borrowing for investment, increasing debt-service burdens (and reducing spending), and pushing up the exchange rate (depressing exports). As a result, countries with greater reliance on short-term borrowing, weaker household and business balance sheets, and more important trade sectors are the most exposed to interest rate changes in the short run. Hence, when the European Central Bank tightens monetary policy, the pain will be distributed unevenly across the 11 countries.

Over time, these differences should become less important. With a common currency (the euro), for example, a Europe-wide market for consumer credit could both boost competition and force banks to pass on changes in interest rates more rapidly. This convergence will not happen immediately, so that the European Central Bank's task of judging the impact of monetary policy is likely to be a difficult one.

CASE STUDY

How Does Money Affect Aggregate Demand in the New Keynesian View?

Suppose that the Fed increases the nominal money supply and that the price level adjusts gradually as the new Keynesians predict. The real interest rate falls in the short run, affecting the cost of funds for investment, stock prices, and exchange rates.

Interest Rates and Investment. A lower real interest rate reduces the opportunity cost of business investment. Investment rises, increasing aggregate demand. Lower real interest rates also reduce the cost to firms of carrying additional inventories, and firms therefore increase their inventory investment. Thus, in the new Keynesian model, lower real interest rates lead to higher levels of current output by lowering the cost of funds for business investment. Lower interest rates also reduce borrowing costs and the opportunity cost of housing and consumer durable goods relative to owning financial assets, leading to greater household investment in durable goods.

Stock Prices. Increases in the money supply cause investors to shift their portfolios, leading to higher stock prices. There are two reasons for the rise in stock prices. The first is that higher money balances encourage households and businesses to spend some of these balances on goods and assets, including stocks. The higher demand for stocks raises their price. Second, all else being equal, interest rates fall in response to an increase in the money supply. As interest rates decline, stocks become a more attractive investment relative to bonds. Thus, again, the increase in demand for stocks raises their price. In either case, higher stock prices raise the market value of firms. Changes in stock prices affect both consumer and business spending. An increase in stock prices raises financial wealth (part of lifetime resources) and therefore consumer spending. For business, higher stock prices signal improved profitability prospects. Firms often issue new shares, using the proceeds to buy new plant and equipment and thereby increasing capital investment. When stock market valuation of firms is low, firms reduce investment in new plant and equipment.

Exchange Rates. If the price level adjusts gradually in response to a monetary expansion, the real interest rate that is available on domestic assets falls relative to rates on foreign assets. As a result, global investors rebalance their portfolios to allocate more of their holdings to foreign assets and less to domestic assets. The demand for U.S. dollars declines, so the value of the dollar relative to other currencies—the exchange rate—declines. The less valuable dollar makes U.S.-produced goods cheaper relative to foreign goods, stimulating exports from the United States and reducing imports to the United States. The rise in net exports increases aggregate demand.

the real interest rate must rise. These interest rate movements affect aggregate demand by influencing investment, consumption, and net exports, as the case study explains.

CHECKPOINT

You are a new Keynesian and chairman of the Federal Reserve Board. Your staff tells you that a decline in business optimism has reduced desired investment and aggregate demand. How could you use monetary policy to restore the level of aggregate demand? The decline in business optimism shifts the *AD* curve to the left. If you did not want to wait for the process of gradual price adjustment to restore the economy's equilibrium, you could use open market purchases to increase the nominal money supply. Because the price level adjusts gradually, this change would increase real money balances supplied, reducing the real interest rate and raising aggregate demand (shifting the *AD* curve to the right). o

SHOULD PUBLIC POLICY STABILIZE ECONOMIC FLUCTUATIONS?

When the economy moves into the contractionary phase of the business cycle, output declines and unemployment increases. These problems, as we have stated, cause hardship for individuals and businesses. We have also observed in the models that new classical economists and new Keynesian economists have proposed that increases in the money supply can increase output. It may be possible, then, to develop monetary policies that could reduce the severity of recessions and smooth short-run fluctuations in output. Such policies, known as **stabilization policies**, attempt to shift the *AD* curve by changing the nominal money supply (monetary policy) or the level of government purchases or taxes (fiscal policy).

In this section, we extend our analysis of the link between the money supply and output to investigate whether we can use this relationship to improve economic conditions in the short run. Once again, economists have differing views on the role of monetary policies that are designed to change the money supply. They debate whether monetary policy is effective as stabilization policy because they differ in their opinion of the effect of changes in the money supply on output and interest rates. On another level, they disagree as to whether monetary policy should be used to stabilize fluctuations. In this section, we consider the views of each school of thought and their policy recommendations.

The Real Business Cycle and New Classical Views

The real business cycle model places no value on policies that are intended to stabilize economic fluctuations because it assumes that productivity disturbances cause fluctuations. Prices adjust quickly to these disturbances, so changes in the nominal money supply have no effect on current output or the real interest rate. Therefore economists who favor the real business cycle model see no reason to implement stabilization policy.

New classical economists also are critical of stabilization policy. They stress that only unexpected changes in policy have real effects. Their view is that the only way public policy could smooth economic fluctuations is by confronting households and businesses with surprise moves. In practice, they argue, such surprises are likely to introduce substantial uncertainty in households' and businesses' decisions, leading to random output fluctuations.

New classical economists assume that the public uses *rational expectations* in interpreting the effects of changes in economic variables such as the price level or changes in the money supply. The rational expectations assumption does not mean that households and businesses can tell the future, only that people use all available information in evaluating variables.† But they can make mistakes in their predictions. If households and businesses form rational expectations about the price level, the actual price level will be close to the expected price level on average. On average, the actual and expected price levels are close, so the Fed gains little by using unexpected changes in the money supply to stabilize output fluctuations. As a result, new classical economists recommend against stabilization policy.

The New Keynesian View

According to new Keynesian economists, upturns and downturns in economic activity may represent times when the economy is not at its long-run equilibrium. These departures are particularly serious when output is below the full employment level because recessions bring unemployment. The new Keynesians believe that shifts in aggregate demand cause movements in current output. Therefore there may be a role for stabilization policy in reducing output fluctuations and especially recessions.

New Keynesians believe that expected and unexpected changes in monetary policy affect current output and the real interest rate in the short run.†† Because of sticky prices, this link between the money supply and output exists even when the public uses rational expectations to estimate the expected price level. Hence monetary policy could smooth output fluctuations. Let's see how it might be done. Suppose that from an initial full employment equilibrium at E_0 in Fig. 26.4(a), a decline in business confidence shifts the *AD* curve to the left from AD_0 to AD_1. As a result, at E_1, the economy is in a recession. Output falls from Y^* to Y_1. With no policy intervention, the economy will eventually correct itself. In other words, with output less than full employment at E_1, prices will fall over time, shifting the *SRAS* curve down from $SRAS_0$ to $SRAS_1$,

† In Chapter 10, we stated that the *efficient markets hypothesis* holds that asset prices increase or decrease in response to the arrival of new information. For example, when analysts predict an increase in the price of a share of Bigco, that information is incorporated into the share price because of rational expectations. When the firm's earnings are greater than is predicted by analysts, the price of the stock rises. Hence only deviations from expectations change the price. This utilization of information and the reaction of prices to new information are features of an efficient market. The efficient markets hypothesis is another application of rational expectations.

†† Fiscal policy (changes in taxes or government purchases) also affects output in the short run in the new Keynesian view. Here we analyze only monetary policy.

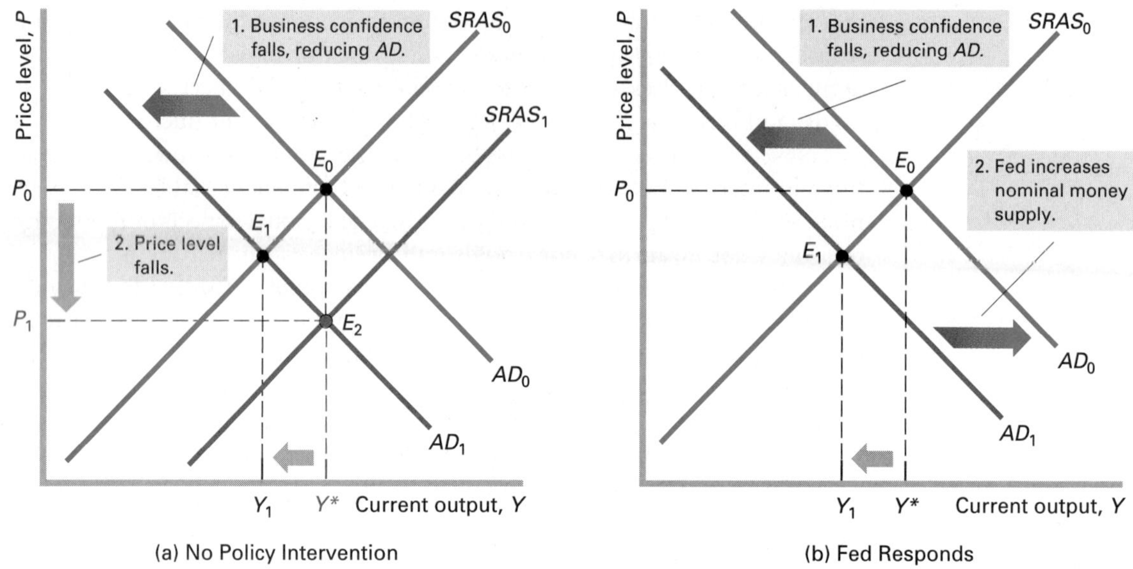

Figure 26.4 **Effects of Activist Policy in the New Keynesian Model**

As shown in (a):

1. From an initial full employment equilibrium at E_0, a decline in business confidence shifts the *AD* curve from AD_0 to AD_1, and output falls from Y^* to Y_1. At E_1, the economy is in a recession.
2. Over time, the price level adjusts downward, restoring the economy's full employment equilibrium at E_2.

As shown in (b):

1. From an initial full employment equilibrium at E_0, a decline in business confidence shifts the *AD* curve from AD_0 to AD_1. At E_1, the economy is in a recession.
2. The Fed speeds recovery by increasing the nominal money supply, which shifts the *AD* curve back from AD_1 to AD_0. Relative to the nonintervention case, the economy recovers more quickly (to E_0) but with a higher long-run price level.

and restoring the initial level of output at the economy's equilibrium at E_2. Economic activity eventually rebounds, but the possibly long period of gradual price adjustment brings lost output and unemployment.

Alternatively, as Fig. 26.4(b) shows, the Fed could try to speed recovery by increasing the nominal money supply, shifting the *AD* curve back to the right from AD_1 to AD_0. Because prices adjust only gradually, the expansionary policy moves the economy from recession at E_1 to its initial full employment equilibrium at E_0 more quickly than the "do nothing" alternative does. Stabilization policy, however, has a side effect: It leads to a higher price level than would exist if no action were taken.

During the 1960s, many economists encouraged the use of monetary and fiscal policies to smooth fluctuations in the economy. However, others warned that there may be long and variable **lags in the policymaking and implementation process** that make it difficult to fine-tune the economy. One such lag that is caused by the time needed to gather data on economic variables is called a *data lag*. Gross domestic product (GDP) data for a quarter are not published until several months later, although data on related variables (say, retail sales)

OTHER TIMES, OTHER PLACES . . .

Yasushi Mieno and the Stabilization Policy Debate in Japan

In early 1992, Yasushi Mieno, then the Governor of the Bank of Japan, was feeling pressure. The Japanese stock market had declined significantly, and the economy was heading into its worst slowdown in almost 20 years. The Bank of Japan had reduced the discount rate from 6% in the summer of 1991 to 4.5% six months later, but business leaders lobbied Mieno to pursue a more expansionary policy. Some leading politicians even advised Prime Minister Miyazawa to dismiss the governor of the central bank.

Mieno essentially was pushed to conduct stabilization policy. Why did he resist? Mieno and the Bank of Japan believed that the Japanese economy had overheated in the late 1980s and early 1990s and that the stock market decline was just reversing an inflationary bubble. Using the *AD-AS* diagram, we can trace this reasoning. Mieno believed that the Japanese economy was proceeding from a short-run equilibrium at E_0, at which output Y_0 was greater than long-run full employment output Y^*, toward E_1. The declining stock market and falling business confidence shifted the *AD* curve to the left from AD_0 to AD_1.

If the Bank of Japan pursued an expansionary policy in an attempt to maintain output at Y_0, in the short run, the *AD* curve would shift to the right from AD_1 to AD_0. However, to achieve the economy's long-run equilibrium—the intersection of the AD_0 and *LRAS* curves at E_3—the price level must rise. Mieno's strategy was to await downward adjustment of the price level as the *SRAS* curve shifted from $SRAS_0$ to $SRAS_1$. With that strategy, the long-run equilibrium at E_2 has full employment output but a lower price level than at E_3. Mieno believed that the *SRAS* adjustment would be rapid, so he sought to avoid implementing a stabilization policy. Deflationary pressures still slowed the economy in the remainder of the 1990s and the early 2000s, however, contributing to slow economic growth.

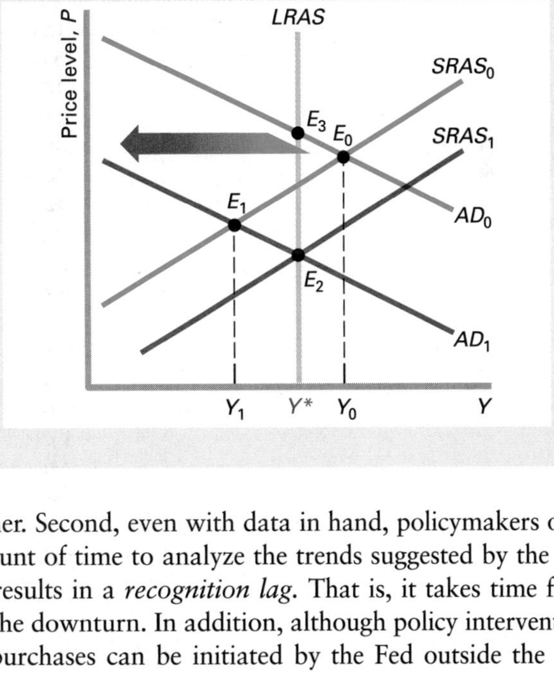

are available sooner. Second, even with data in hand, policymakers often need a substantial amount of time to analyze the trends suggested by the economic variables, which results in a *recognition lag*. That is, it takes time for policymakers to detect the downturn. In addition, although policy interventions such as open market purchases can be initiated by the Fed outside the legislative process, fiscal policies (such as tax or spending changes) require legislative action. This is often a time-consuming process, resulting in a *legislative lag*. Putting tax and expenditure policy into effect typically requires even more time, called an *implementation lag*. Even after a policy is finally implemented, its effect on the economy isn't immediate, creating an *impact lag*. Because of these lags, policy interventions can't begin to counterbalance every economic fluctuation. Therefore economists generally advocate that policymakers focus on long-run objectives such as low inflation or steady economic growth.

Lags in the policymaking and implementation process haven't convinced most new Keynesian economists that stabilization policy lacks value. However, most economists concur that policymakers shouldn't attempt to fine-tune the economy, trying to smooth every minor disturbance in aggregate demand. Instead, they argue, policymakers should restrict the use of activist policy to fighting major downturns in the economy.

Table 26.1 summarizes the money–output relationship and the desirability of stabilization policy according to the real business cycle, new classical, and new Keynesian models.

EXPLAINING EVENTS OF THE 1980s AND 1990s

We are now ready to use new classical and new Keynesian analysis to analyze changes in policy and to interpret the effects of these changes on output. Both the new classical and new Keynesian views offer explanations for the short-run non-neutrality of money, and both are consistent with rational decisions by households and businesses. But are they consistent with actual economic events? We can find out by using these models to interpret macroeconomic effects of policy shifts in the early 1980s and the early 1990s. Although the

TABLE 26.1 **SUMMARY OF MONETARY POLICY AND OUTPUT: THREE ALTERNATIVES**

Alternative	Is Current Output Affected by an . . . Unexpected Change in the Money Supply?	Expected Change in the Money Supply?	Is Activist Policy Desirable?
Real business cycle model	No	No	No
	Prices are perfectly flexible, so monetary policy cannot affect real money balances or output in the short run.		
New classical model	Yes	No	No
	Only unexpected changes in the money supply affect output.		Monetary policy affects output and the real interest rate only by "fooling" households and firms.
New Keynesian model	Yes	Yes	Rarely
	Both unexpected and expected changes in the money supply affect output, although effects of unexpected changes are greater.		Frequent changes in monetary policy can reduce the credibility of the monetary authority.

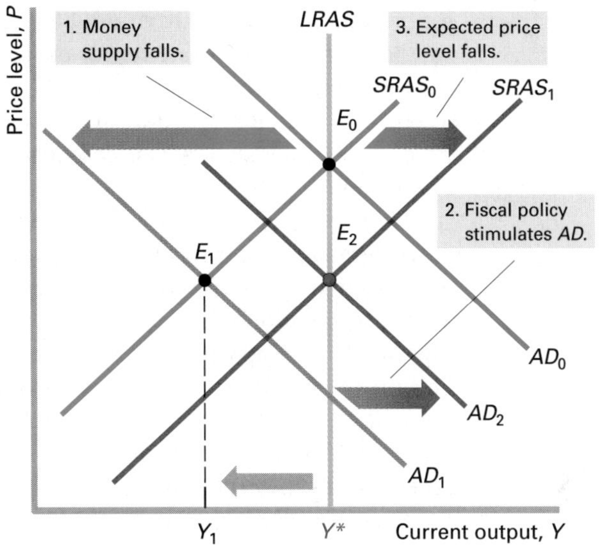

Figure 26.5

Policy Mix in the Early 1980s

The economy's adjustment to aggregate demand shock in the early 1980s is consistent with the new Keynesian view.

1. From an initial equilibrium at E_0, a monetary contraction shifts the *AD* curve from AD_0 to AD_1, and output falls from Y^* to Y_1. At E_1, the economy is in a recession.
2. The fiscal stimulus from tax cuts and increases in government purchases shifts the *AD* curve from AD_1 to AD_2.
3. Over time, the net contraction in output places downward pressure on inflation, shifting the *SRAS* curve down from $SRAS_0$ to $SRAS_1$, restoring full employment output at E_2.

different models may produce varying predictions about the responses of output and interest rates to policy changes, they share an emphasis on the importance of policy credibility for shaping those responses. That is, announced changes in policy will influence households' and businesses' decisions only to the extent that announcements are *believed.*

Effects of Policy Shifts in the Early 1980s

The early 1980s witnessed major shifts in both monetary and fiscal policies. Changes in monetary policy had already begun in October 1979 when the Fed, under Chairman Paul Volcker, announced that it would target monetary aggregates (instead of the federal funds rate) and that it would reduce the rate of money supply growth. Monetary restraint continued more or less through 1981. In 1981, Congress and President Reagan agreed to the Economic Recovery Tax Act, which cut income tax rates significantly. At the same time, government purchases of military equipment rose. Therefore monetary policy was contractionary, but fiscal policy was expansionary.

We can use the *AD-AS* diagram and the new Keynesian analysis to trace the effects of these policy changes. In 1979, the economy was essentially at full employment, at E_0, in Fig. 26.5. The monetary contraction shifted the aggregate demand curve to the left from AD_0 to AD_1, shifting the economy's equilibrium to E_1. In response to the tax cut and the military buildup, the *AD* curve shifted to the right from AD_1 to AD_2.

According to the new Keynesians, the effect on output of the policies of the early 1980s is ambiguous because the two shifts in aggregate demand were in opposite directions. Because the monetary contraction preceded the fiscal expansion by more than a year, output should have fallen first—from Y^* to Y_1—which the actual drop in output in two recessions during 1980–1982 confirmed. Inflation fell from double-digit levels to about 4% by 1983, shifting the short-run aggregate supply curve from $SRAS_0$ to $SRAS_1$. However, this occurred only after the economy endured the recession, a process that is consistent with gradual price adjustment described by the new Keynesians. When the price level adjustment was completed, the economy returned to a long-run equilibrium at E_2.

How would new classical economists interpret these events? The Fed stated on many occasions that its shifts in monetary policy were intended to combat inflation. According to new classical economists, an announced policy to reduce inflation could lead to a combination of falling prices and lower expected inflation, which would soften the leftward shift of the *AD* curve. This process of adjustment—the shift of the short-run aggregate supply curve from $SRAS_0$ to $SRAS_1$—would be quicker than in the new Keynesian analysis. Hence, at first glance, the new classical prediction is inconsistent with the experience of the economy during that period.

However, both the new Keynesian and new classical economists stress the importance of policy announcement *credibility.* Although Federal Reserve Chairmen Arthur Burns and G. William Miller said that they wanted to reduce inflation in the 1970s, actual Fed policy was inflationary. New classical and new Keynesian economists would predict that a lack of credibility about the Fed's anti-inflation stance would fail to lower prices or expectations of future inflation. Long-term interest rates *increased* from late 1979 through late 1981 (with the exception of the second quarter of 1980). Under the expectations theory of the term structure of interest rates, the long-term rate is an average of expected future rates, so financial market participants probably didn't expect inflation to abate.

New classical economists believe that the Fed should try to reduce inflation in a major one-shot policy shift, *as long as that shift is announced and is credible.* With the gradual adjustment of prices in the new Keynesian view, gradual reduction in money growth could reduce inflation with smaller costs from reduced output—again as long as the reductions are announced and are credible.

Effects of Policy Shifts in the Early 1990s

At the beginning of the 1990s, the U.S. economy was at full employment equilibrium at E_0 in Fig. 26.6. Monetary and fiscal policy shifts in the early 1990s moved in opposite directions from the policy shifts of the early 1980s. After substantial negotiation, President George H. W. Bush and the Congress compromised on a deficit-reduction bill in October 1990 that increased taxes and reduced federal government spending, shifting the *AD* curve to the left from AD_0 to AD_1. Fed Chairman Alan Greenspan, who had often expressed concern about the pressure on interest rates from the federal budget deficit, indicated to Congress that the Fed would ease monetary policy if a deficit-reduction measure were adopted. The Fed followed through (but not fast enough in the minds of some economists and policymakers), increasing the money supply growth rate. This shifted the aggregate demand curve to the right from AD_1 to AD_2.

The economy suffered a recession, reducing output from Y^* to Y_1 in 1990

Figure 26.6

Policy Mix in the Early 1990s

The economy's adjustment to aggregate demand shock in the early 1990s is consistent with the new Keynesian view.

1. From an initial equilibrium at E_0, a fiscal contraction shifts the *AD* curve from AD_0 to AD_1. Output falls from Y^* to Y_1. The economy's equilibrium shifts to E_1.

2. A monetary stimulus shifts the *AD* curve from AD_1 to AD_2.

3. Over time, the contraction in output places downward pressure on inflation, shifting the *SRAS* curve from $SRAS_0$ to $SRAS_1$ and restoring full employment output at E_2.

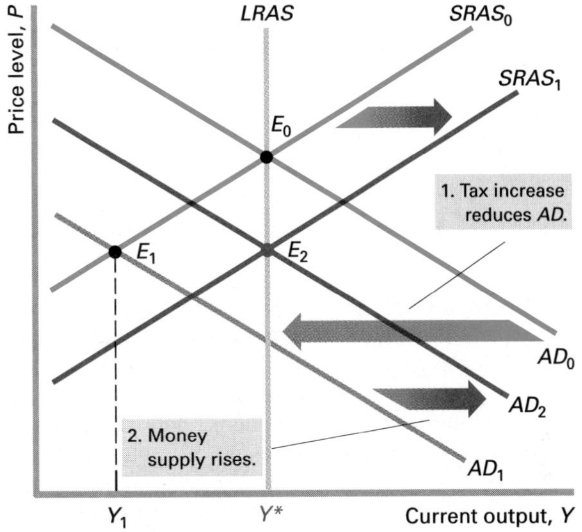

and 1991 and suggesting that the monetary stimulus may not have been sufficiently strong at the time.† Over time, the weak economy put downward pressure on inflation, shifting the *SRAS* curve down from $SRAS_0$ to $SRAS_1$. The short-term real interest rate fell, consistent with the new Keynesian predictions. The recession and gradual price adjustment don't support the new classical prediction that expected policy changes should have no effect on unemployment. The move toward a new equilibrium at E_2 in 1993 reflects full employment output, with lower inflation than at E_0.

Although the credibility of U.S. monetary policy announcements may well have been higher in the early 1990s than in the early 1980s, long-term interest rates did not decline by as much as short-term rates during 1990–1992. This resistance suggests that the public didn't believe that inflation would be low in the long run (recall that the long-term interest rate is the sum of the real interest rate and expected inflation). Both the new Keynesian and new classical views suggest that a lack of credibility could weaken the ability of monetary or fiscal policies to stimulate the economy.

Concluding Remarks

Evidence of effects on output of monetary and fiscal policies during the early 1980s and early 1990s supports the new Keynesian view. In particular, even expected changes in monetary policy can affect output and the real interest rate, with prices and inflation adjusting only gradually. Also important is the implication of both the new Keynesian and the new classical views that policy credibility is an important determinant of the effect of policy shifts on the economy.

† In addition, during the early 1980s and early 1990s, there were adverse supply shocks from significant increases in oil prices.

THE FINANCIAL TIMES FEBRUARY 5, 2001

Will the Fed Step on the Gas?

"Expansions don't die in their beds of old age," Rudiger Dornbusch, the eminent economist, once said. "They are murdered by the Federal Reserve, bludgeoned to death by high interest rates. . . ." (a)

As U.S. economic growth suddenly slows, Professor Dornbusch's detective-novel allusion has taken on a new resonance. In recent weeks, the Fed has moved to cut interest rates by a whole percentage point, the largest reduction in short-term rates in a single month since 1984. But a growing number of critics are investigating not the central bank's efforts to avert recession, but the role it might have played in killing the country's longest postwar expansion in the first place.

Did Alan Greenspan, the Fed chairman, and his colleagues, in an effort to vanquish the illusory threat of higher inflation, stifle the economy with overly aggressive increases in interest rates in 1999 and 2000? Or is the dramatic slowdown the result of factors—oil prices, a collapsing technology stock bubble, financial distress—beyond the Fed's control? . . .

"It looks like we are already in a mild recession," says Brian Westbury, chief economist at Griffin, Kubik, Stephens and Thompson, investment consultants in Chicago. "The number one cause of the problems we're seeing was misguided Federal Reserve policy." The present downturn, he believes, fits the pattern of past Fed-induced recessions, from financial stresses to manufacturing weakness to consumer retrenchment.

The case against the Fed is a simple one. Since June 1999, the central bank raised the Fed funds rate, its main interest rate instrument, by 1.75 percentage points to 6.5%, the highest in nine years. But it did so with scant evidence of overheating; the core rate of consumer price inflation hovered between 2% and 2.5% throughout. . . .

(b) But there are some serious objections to this argument. All but a handful of economists shared the Fed's diagnosis; growth was above 5%, the unemployment rate at 30-year lows, and the stock market had soared to unheard-of valuations. And although consumer price inflation was muted, there was clear evidence of rising wage costs and commodity prices. . . .

There are other critics of the Fed's policy in the last few years. Some argue that it should have restrained growth much earlier when the economy began accelerating on a wave of euphoria about the productivity miracle. But, then there was also plenty of evidence that something important really had changed and the only suggestion of overheating was the clearly exuberant stock market. . . . (c)

And, of course, it is still quite possible that recession will be avoided. If the Fed's aggressive action last month to revive the economy proves successful, the slowdown will prove mild and mercifully short. The world's most powerful central bankers could then rest easy, safe in the knowledge that they will be identified once again not as culprits but as heroes.

During early 2001, policy statements by the new George W. Bush administration and the new Congress were not the only source of political debate in Washington, D.C. Euphoria over the economy during the 2000 election campaign gave way to fears of an impending U.S. recession. With this economic chill in mind, Fed Chairman Alan Greenspan grappled with whether to pursue a more expansionary monetary policy. Some policymakers and business leaders complained that the Fed's single-minded focus on low inflation reined in the U.S. economy's growth to an unacceptably low level and made the economy vulnerable to recession. The Fed cut the federal funds rate twice in early 2001, and the European Central Bank discussed a reduction of short-term interest rates in Europe, but remained fearful of inflation.

a Critics of Mr. Greenspan's position argue that the policy keeps the U.S. economy's output at a level, *Y*, that is less than its full employment level, Y^*. Under the new Keynesian view (which is consistent with recent evidence linking money and output changes), a switch to a more expansionary policy shifts the *AD* curve to the right, from AD_0 to AD_1 in part (a) of the figure, raising output from Y_0 to Y^*. While the policy change also puts upward pressure on inflation, the gains in output benefit many households and businesses.

b The argument of some economists within the Fed that a more expansionary monetary policy by the Fed would increase inflation with little or no gain in output begins with a different assumption. Suppose, as in part (b) of the figure, output in the economy's equilibrium is already at Y^*, the full employment level. In this case, a more expansionary policy shifts the *AD* curve to the right. The short-run gain in output (from Y^* to Y_1) is ultimately met with higher inflation (the price level rises from P_0 to P_1) if the long-run aggregate supply curve is vertical at Y^*.

c In the long term, greater output growth depends on growth in productivity, or output per worker. In analysis, this requires a rightward shift of the *LRAS* curve, making possible higher output without higher prices. Virtually no economist would argue that the Fed can influence the position of the *LRAS* curve.

For further thought . . .

The extent to which aggregate demand shifts raise prices in the short run depends on the slope of the *SRAS* curve. How would you advise the Fed to investigate the slope of the *SRAS* curve?

Source: Excerpted from Gerard Baker, "The Accused," *The Financial Times*, February 5, 2001.

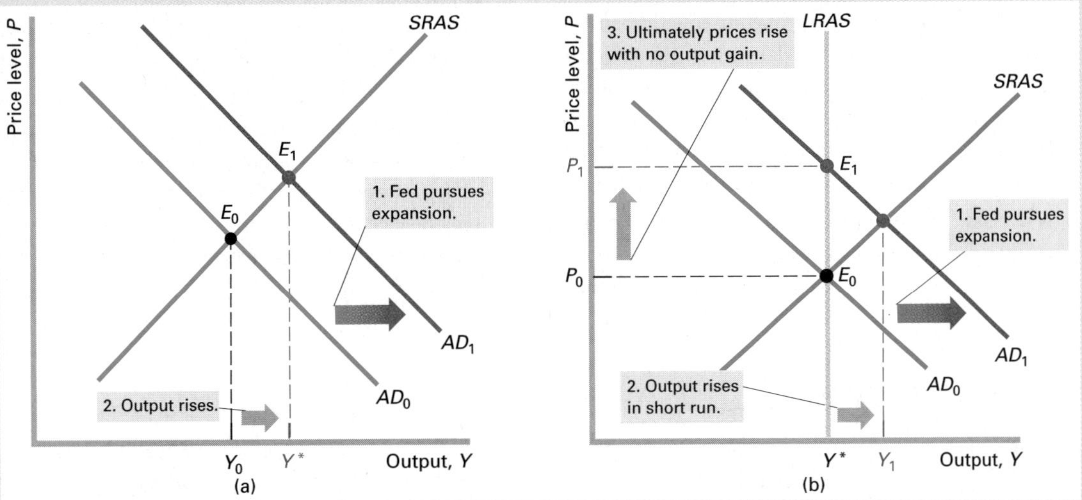

KEY TERMS AND CONCEPTS

Business cycle

Lags in the policymaking and implementation process

Stabilization policies

SUMMARY

1. Economists generally agree that money is neutral in the long run, but many disagree about whether changes in the nominal money supply lead to changes in output in the short run. Determining whether changes in the money supply cause changes in output requires looking at independent increases or decreases in the money supply. Historical evidence suggests that independent reductions in the rate of growth of the nominal money supply have preceded declines in output. To interpret whether this relationship is causal, economists describe the ways in which money affects the economy.
2. Money is neutral in the long run because prices are flexible. In the real business cycle model, prices are flexible even in the short run. The intersection of the *AD* curve and the *SRAS* curve, which is vertical at the full employment level of output, represents the economy's equilibrium. Fluctuations in output are the result of shifts in productivity. Changes in the nominal money supply have no effect on output, even in the short run. Instead, movements of money and output together in the short run represent reverse causation: the effect of output on money demand, not the effect of the money supply on output. However, historical evidence for the United States is not consistent with the view that money is neutral in the short run.
3. New classical economists advance a different explanation of the relation of money and output. The misperception theory suggests a positive relationship between output and unexpected changes in the price level, based on the assumption that people have rational expectations. Expected changes in the nominal money supply are neutral. Unexpected increases in the nominal money supply increase real output. Evidence suggests that both expected and unexpected changes in the nominal money supply affect real output in the short run, implying that the new classical view may be incomplete.
4. New Keynesian economists use sticky prices to explain short-run non-neutrality of money. Prices are slow to adjust, either because of long-term nominal contracts or because of the combination of monopolistic competition and costs of adjusting prices. Both expected and unexpected changes in the nominal money supply affect output in the short run, but unexpected changes have a greater effect.
5. Efforts to smooth short-run fluctuations in output are known as stabilization policies. Real business cycle proponents believe that stabilization policy is completely ineffective. Unexpected policy changes can affect output in the new classical view, but they do so only by fooling households and firms; policy credibility is enhanced by not fine-tuning short-run economic fluctuations. Similarly, although new Keynesian economists argue that monetary policy can affect output and real interest rates in the short run, they believe that long-run policy goals are likely to be inconsistent with numerous short-term interventions.

REVIEW QUESTIONS

1. Define the term "business cycle." Why do economists care about business cycles?
2. *Evaluate:* Price flexibility necessarily implies that money is neutral.
3. Why might money be non-neutral when prices are set by monopolistically competitive firms? Why might money be non-neutral when long-term nominal contracts are important?

4. Why is it important to identify whether changes in the money supply are independent of changes in output?
5. Why is money neutral in the short run in the real business cycle model? If money is neutral, what causes business cycles in the real business cycle model?
6. How can money be neutral in the long run but not in the short run in the new Keynesian model? What is the primary difference between the real business cycle model and the new Keynesian model?
7. What are the major differences between the new classical and new Keynesian models? What role does the idea of rational expectations play in these two approaches?
8. What is meant by stabilization policy? In theory, how can stabilization policy be used during the business cycle?
9. If new classical economists believe changes in the money supply can have an effect on real output, why are they opposed to stabilization policy?
10. Milton Friedman and Anna Schwartz argue that bank failures in the early 1930s and the Fed's decision to raise reserve requirements in 1937 led to declines in the money supply. Why do bank failures and increases in reserve requirements reduce the money supply? Although Friedman and Schwartz have documented instances of the effect of independent movements in the money supply on real output, they are skeptical of the usefulness of stabilization policy. Why do you suppose they hold this position?
11. Define the following lags in the policymaking and implementation process:
    a. data lag;
    b. recognition lag;
    c. legislative lag;
    d. implementation lag; and
    e. impact lag.
12. Why does a monetary contraction put people out of work? Use the *AD-AS* diagram for the new Keynesian model to explain your answer.
13. If money is neutral, why is money growth correlated with output growth in the real business cycle model?

ANALYTICAL PROBLEMS

14. Suppose that you observed a substantial decline in the money growth rate six months before the start of every recession. Would that be enough to convince you that money affects output? Why or why not?
15. You are the Chairman of the Board of Governors of the Federal Reserve System and have just learned that the federal government is going to reduce expenditures sharply. This shock shifts the *AD* curve to the left. How would you respond to keep the economy at full employment equilibrium if
    a. you use the new classical model?
    b. you use the new Keynesian model?

    In each case, show the *AD-AS* diagram associated with your answer.
16. After years of spending more than their incomes, people decide to reduce their debt, thus increasing saving. What effect does this action have on the *AD* curve? If you are a new Keynesian economist in charge of monetary policy, what should you do?
17. Suppose that for the last several years output has been at its full employment level and has not been growing, and that the money supply has not been growing. Suppose the Federal Reserve chairman announces that he intends to increase the money supply 5% to expand output. Explain how successful this policy will be from the point of view of the new classical model and from the point of view of the new Keynesian model. Illustrate your discussion with an *AD-AS* diagram.
18. Suppose that for a long period of time, the Fed maintained that it would not change monetary policy in response to recessions, but, in fact, it expanded the money supply each time the economy was in a recession. How would this pattern affect the Fed's credibility? Suggest implications for the responses of interest rates on Treasury bills and 30-year Treasury bonds to the Fed's interventions.

19. Suppose that the federal government seriously tried to balance its budget by raising business taxes. According to the new classical view, what effect would this action have on output and the price level? How could monetary policy be used to offset this effect?

20. Fed officials, who can use expansionary or contractionary monetary policy to shift the *AD* curve, sometimes say that they "can't do everything." Using *AD-AS* diagrams, illustrate how monetary policy can be used to offset the effects of both *AD* and *AS* shocks on output. How does the equilibrium price level change in the two cases? Suppose that monetary policy was used to stabilize the price level instead. Draw *AD-AS* diagrams to show the effects of both aggregate demand and aggregate supply shocks on output. How does the equilibrium output level differ in the two cases?

21. The increasing power of personal computers has greatly increased the economy's expected future productivity, increasing expected future output. What is the likely effect of this development on aggregate demand today? How might monetary policy be used to offset this effect?

22. According to the new classical view, how should the Fed use monetary policy to stabilize output in the short run if the expected price level increases, shifting the *SRAS* curve up? What would the Fed need to do in the long run to restore the initial price level? How would your answer differ if you applied the new Keynesian model?

23. (Difficult problem) Suppose that the economy is in either a *good* state or a *bad* state and that monetary policy is either *contractionary* or *expansionary*. Suppose further that the state of the economy and the condition of monetary policy tell you all you need to know to determine the unemployment rate and the inflation rate. Finally, suppose that people care most about the sum of the unemployment rate, u, and the inflation rate, π, which is called the *misery index*, or $m = u + \pi$. The respective factors and their values are as follows:

Monetary Policy	Factor	Economy: Good	Economy: Bad
Contractionary	u	5%	10%
	π	5	3
	m	10	13
Expansionary	u	4	8
	π	10	4
	m	14	12

If the economy is in a good state, a contractionary monetary policy to prevent inflation is best. But if the economy is in a bad state, an expansionary monetary policy to help the economy recover is best. For example, with a contractionary monetary policy in a bad state, the unemployment rate rises to 10% with only 3% inflation; with an expansionary monetary policy, the unemployment rate is lower at 8%, with inflation only slightly higher at 4%.

a. If the Fed knows exactly when the state of the economy changes and it changes policy to minimize the misery index, what is its monetary policy and the misery index when the economy is good? When the economy is bad?

b. Now suppose that there are some lags in the process. Suppose further that the Fed doesn't know the current state of the economy, but knows only what it was six months ago (that is, there may be both recognition and data lags). Then suppose that if the economy was in a good state six months ago, the probability is 90% that it is still in a good state today and 10% that it is now in a bad state; if the economy was in a bad state six months ago, the probability is 75% that it is now in a good state and 25% that it is now in a bad state. If the Fed wants to minimize the misery index on average, what should its policy be if the economy was in a good state six months ago? If it was in a bad state six months ago?

c. Suppose that in addition to the data and recognition lags, there is also an effectiveness lag of six months. What should policy be today if the economy was in a good state six months ago? If it was in a bad state six months ago?

d. What do your answers to (a)–(c) suggest about the ability of policymakers to use stabilization policies?

24. The text states that "most economists concur that policymakers shouldn't attempt to fine-tune the economy, trying to smooth every disturbance in aggregate demand. Instead, they argue, policymakers should restrict the use of activist policy to fighting major downturns in the economy." Evaluate Fed policy in the late 1990s in the light of these observations.

DATA QUESTIONS

25. Find monthly or quarterly data on the (civilian) unemployment rate from 1946 to the present in a source such as *Business Statistics* or *Employment and Earnings* (for more recent data, see the *Survey of Current Business* or the *Economic Report of the President*). Looking just at the unemployment rate data, try to guess when all the recessions since 1946 began and when they ended. Compare your answers to the information in Fig. 26.1 on page 691.

26. Find some measure of the inflation rate (consumer price index, producer price index, GDP deflator) in a major data source, such as the *Economic Report of the President,* for each year since 1946. Cover the inflation rates shown for 1960 to the present with a piece of paper. Now, on the basis of the historical inflation rates for 1946 to 1959, estimate the inflation rate for 1960. Then, looking only at the data for 1946 to 1964, estimate the inflation rate for 1965. Repeat for 1970, 1975, 1980, 1985, 1990, 1995, and 2000. Now compare your estimates to the actual inflation rates. How close were you? Were your estimates of inflation based on rational expectations? What other information besides past inflation rates would you find useful when forecasting inflation?

CHAPTER 27

Information Problems and Channels for Monetary Policy

In the fall of 1991, the economy was recovering from a recession that began in 1990. The Gulf War had gone well earlier in the year, and President George H. W. Bush's prospects for reelection seemed excellent. Nevertheless, the weak economy loomed as an obstacle to a second term. President Bush and his economic advisors believed that the economy was suffering from a *credit crunch*—an inadequate supply of bank loans. The supply of bank loans was believed to be too low because banks were nervous about the economy and regulators were eager to avoid a repeat of the savings and loan crisis. In addition, many economists believed that businesses and households faced weak balance sheet positions. That is, their liabilities were high in proportion to their assets, and their low net worth would dampen spending and prolong the recession. In this environment, the President's advisors argued for a more expansionary monetary policy. In fact, the Fed cut interest rates aggressively to stimulate more lending only after the economy began to contract. (In late 1998 and again in early 2001, the Fed acted more quickly when signs of a credit crunch appeared.)

The model that we've used to analyze monetary policy might not give us accurate predictions about the situation facing President Bush and Fed Chairman Greenspan. To analyze monetary policy, we made many simplifications about the financial system. We assumed that all financial assets were close substitutes for one another and that savers and borrowers could choose freely among financial assets. But the actual financial system is more complex than the one represented in our model. In particular, banks perform information services that are not matched by financial markets, and households and businesses don't always have equal access to funds that they need to finance the purchase of durable goods or to invest in plant and equipment.

Our objective in this chapter is to make our model of the macroeconomy and the role of the financial system within the economy more realistic and to use the revised model to make more accurate predictions about the outcome of monetary policy. In the first section, we include our revised view of the financial system in our model and use it to predict the short-run effects of monetary policy on output. We start by describing ways in which information costs affect the behavior of banks, households, and businesses. We modify our predictions in the model of Chapter 26 even when there are no efforts by the central bank to alter the money supply. At the conclusion of the first section, we discuss two episodes that support our revised view of the financial system.

In the second section of the chapter, we study the transmission mechanisms for monetary policy. Assuming that information costs may alter the availability of funds for households and businesses, we describe how monetary policy affects output. We use the *AD-AS* model to trace the impact of the change in the money supply on the economy. Our base case is the monetary transmission mechanism posed by the new Keynesians and presented in Chapter 26: With sticky prices in the short run, a change in the money supply affects the real interest rate. Changes in the real interest rate in turn affect household consumption, business investment, and aggregate demand. Here we refer to this transmission mechanism—or channel—as the *money channel.* We then explore two alternative channels in which information costs magnify the effects of monetary policy on output. In the *bank lending channel*, a change in the supply of bank loans affects funds available to bank-dependent borrowers, changing their spending and aggregate demand. In the *balance sheet channel*, a change in interest rates accompanying a shift in monetary policy changes the net worth of borrowers, affecting their spending and aggregate demand.

MACROECONOMIC COSTS OF INFORMATION PROBLEMS

In this section, we describe how information problems in lending can create obstacles for borrowers who need external financing. For households, this may mean that they cannot obtain loans to buy homes, automobiles, or other consumer durables. For businesses, this may mean that they cannot obtain financing to expand their operations.

In building our model of the macroeconomy, we made no distinction between sources of financing. In effect, we assumed that all sources of financing were perfect substitutes. A business, for example, would have equally good chances of raising funds in the bond market and obtaining a bank loan. In reality, information problems make alternative forms of financing imperfect substitutes. If a business is denied a bank loan, it may have to forgo its investment projects because the only other options are to issue bonds or shares of stock. For small firms, the cost of a stock or bond issue is prohibitive. Individual borrowers face similar constraints. An individual who cannot obtain a mortgage probably cannot buy a house.

We now describe the macroeconomic impacts of these information problems and their effect on our modeling of financial markets and output determination. We then illustrate graphically how they might change the levels of output and interest rate predicted by our model of the macroeconomy.

Information Problems in Lending: Role of Financial Intermediaries

Asymmetric information in financial markets, as we described in Chapter 11, makes it difficult and costly to match savers and borrowers. Savers have to devote resources to assessing a borrower's creditworthiness, and acceptable borrowers may have to accept high costs of funds or may even find that funds are unavailable to them. In either case, borrowers' spending is less than what it would be in the absence of asymmetric information.

Although financial markets offer some information services to improve the matching of savers and borrowers, they are not effective for households and small and medium-sized businesses. Banks step into this role by specializing in reducing information costs of lending, enabling savers to channel their funds to borrowers more efficiently. As a result, a majority of lending occurs through financial intermediaries rather than direct stock and bond issues.

Because banks reduce costs of asymmetric information in lending, bank credit is the most likely source of funds for small firms. Large businesses also may borrow from banks, but such firms alternatively may turn to the stock and bond markets for investment funds. Nevertheless, problems of asymmetric information can affect capital investment decisions, even in large companies.

To summarize, the ability and willingness of financial intermediaries to make loans can affect the supply of external financing that is available to borrowers and may change the level of aggregate demand and output in the short run as predicted by our macroeconomic model.

Information Problems in Lending: Role of Net Worth

Businesses have two sources of funds: internal funds and external funds. Internal funds are available to a firm from its current and past profits. External funds are obtained from outside investors or creditors. Economists have found that internal funds are a cheaper source of financing than external funds—at times even for large firms with higher net worth and more internal funds available. Outside investors have less information about firms' investment plans and opportunities than do inside managers or large shareholders. Therefore they require a premium to compensate them for having to obtain information about firms. This premium—or higher costs of funds—makes external financing more expensive than internal financing. These asymmetric information problems for large firms suggest that, all else being equal, increases in firms' net worth will increase investment. Economists studying investment have also found that the greater is a borrower's net worth compared to the borrower's desired level of capital investment, the smaller is the gap between the cost of external and internal financing. Hence, when the borrower's net worth is high, information costs are less likely to constrain capital investment spending.

Asymmetric information may magnify short-run fluctuations in output. Suppose that an adverse shock to the oil supply plunges the economy into a recession. Because of the recession, firms earn smaller profits, reducing their internal funds, and investment spending falls (even if true future investment opportunities do not change). The drop in output is magnified by the decline in capital investment and by cutbacks in consumer spending by workers who lose their jobs, worsening the recession. Conversely, a favorable current productivity disturbance may raise investment and output by increasing firms' internal funds. Recent evidence shows that fluctuations in the amount of internal funds have important effects on investment in plant and equipment for young, rapidly growing firms and smaller effects on more mature firms. These differential effects reflect the greater severity of asymmetric information problems facing outside investors in young firms.

Consequences of a Drop in Bank Lending

We use the *AD-AS* model to demonstrate the effect of a drop in bank lending on the economy as a whole. Suppose, for example, that the federal government issued a regulation restricting bank lending. Such a restriction isn't likely to affect all borrowers equally. Some borrowers—particularly households and small and medium-sized businesses—probably can't replace bank credit with other forms of financing. As a result, spending on consumer durables or business plant and equipment by these bank-dependent borrowers falls. We show the impact of this regulation in Fig. 27.1.

Figure 27.1(a) shows that the initial short-run equilibrium lies at E_0, with a price level P_0 and output Y_0. The decline in bank lending reduces the availability of credit to bank-dependent borrowers, reducing consumer and business spending and shifting the *AD* curve to the left from AD_0 to AD_1; at the new equilibrium, E_1, output falls in the short run from Y_0 to Y_1, and the price level falls from P_0 to P_1.

Figure 27.1(b) depicts the market for money. The public's demand for real money balances depends positively on the level of income or output (Chapter 23). Because we are not yet considering Fed policy, we hold the money supply curve, *MS*, unchanged. Hence, as output falls in response to the decline in bank lending, the money demand curve in Fig. 27.1(b) shifts to the left from MD_0 to MD_1, and the equilibrium real interest rate in the money market (the open market interest rate) falls from r_0 to r_1.

The effect of less lending on output and the real interest rate is different from the effect of the Fed's reducing the nominal money supply, which we analyzed in Chapter 26. In the case of a restriction on lending, banks can't lend to households and businesses as easily, so the banks prefer instead to hold Treasury bills. The nominal money supply doesn't change, because securities dealers will deposit the proceeds of the sale of T-bills in bank accounts. The drop in the open market real interest rate from r_0 to r_1 is a feedback effect (the decline in money demand) from the decline in aggregate demand resulting from the regulation.

We can generalize the responses illustrated in Fig. 27.1. As long as bank loans are imperfect substitutes for other sources of funds for many borrowers, a decline in banks' ability or willingness to lend reduces output in the short run. In addition, the real interest rate falls.

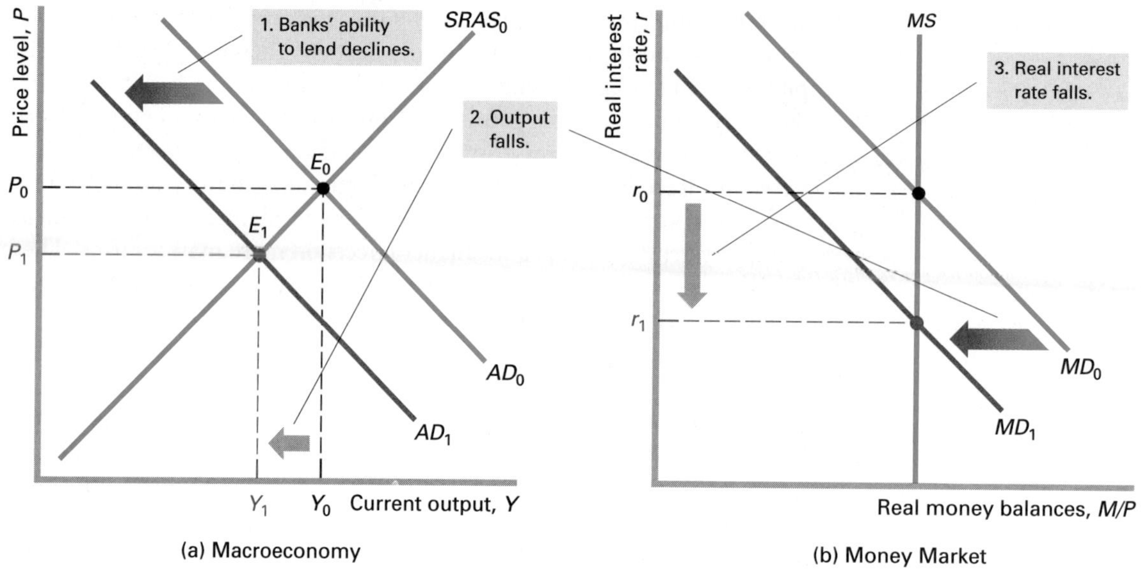

Figure 27.1

Effects of a Restriction on Bank Lending

As shown in (a):

1. The restriction on bank lending reduces the availability of credit to bank-dependent borrowers, shifting the *AD* curve from AD_0 to AD_1.
2. Output falls.

As shown in (b):

3. In the money market, the fall in output reduces the demand for money. Open market interest rates fall because of the decline in money demand from MD_0 to MD_1. A decline in bank lending reduces output and the real interest rate, if nothing else changes.

CHECKPOINT

The managers of Toolco want to expand their small chain of four hardware stores. They believe that the economy is about to turn around and that spending on home improvement will rise. Mainbank, Toolco's banker for 10 years, acknowledges Toolco's reputation but won't grant the loan. What are Toolco's financing alternatives? Unless the managers have personal resources to invest, Toolco has few alternatives. The transactions costs of a commercial paper or bond offering are too great to justify the expense. For businesses like Toolco, current and past profits and bank loans provide most of the financing for growth. o

Consequences of a Fall in Borrowers' Net Worth

We can analyze the consequences of a fall in net worth using the *AD-AS* model. Figure 27.2 shows that the economy's initial short-run equilibrium lies at E_0, with a price level P_0 and output Y_0. The decline in borrower net worth raises information costs and reduces the ability of households and firms to borrow at any given interest rate. As a result, consumer and business investment spending falls. The *AD* curve shifts to the left from AD_0 to AD_1; at the new equilibrium, E_1, output falls in the short run from Y_0 to Y_1, and the price

Figure 27.2

Effects of a Decline in Borrowers' Net Worth

1. The decline in borrowers' net worth raises information costs and reduces borrowers' ability to obtain funds at any given interest rate, shifting the *AD* curve from AD_0 to AD_1.
2. Output falls.

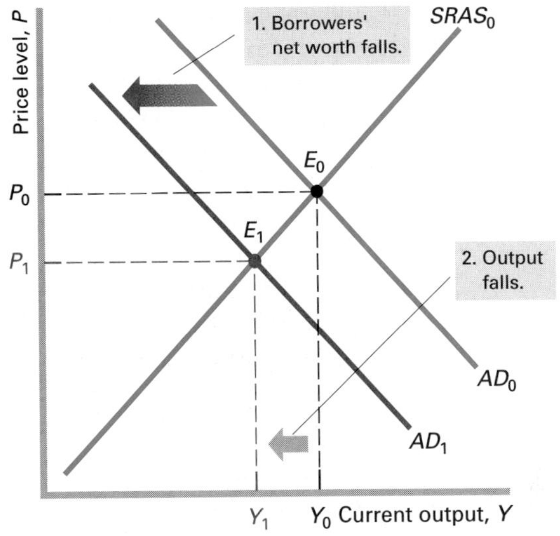

level falls from P_0 to P_1. Though not shown in Fig. 27.2, the decline in output reduces the public's demand for real money balances and the equilibrium real interest rate, just as it did in Fig. 27.1(b).

We can generalize the response illustrated in Fig. 27.2. As long as internal funds and external funds are imperfect substitutes, a decline in borrowers' net worth, all else being equal, reduces output and the real interest rate in the short run.

Information costs in the financial system and regulatory restrictions on lending have created situations that have caused banks to curtail lending and borrowers to experience losses of net worth, forcing them to reduce spending. We describe two such situations next.

Financial Panics

During the late nineteenth and early twentieth centuries, the United States experienced several **financial panics**—periods characterized by violent fluctuations in asset prices in financial markets, bank runs, and bankruptcies of many firms. In the financial panics, bad news about a particular firm or bank sent interest rates up and stock prices down in financial markets. In addition, depositors, fearful of bank failures, withdrew deposits that had been available for bank lending, decreasing the money supply. The crisis in financial markets and institutions raised lenders' information costs in evaluating borrowers. Because of the decline in the money supply (of which bank deposits are an important component) and its effects on bank-dependent borrowers, the decline in bank lending magnified reductions in aggregate demand. In some financial panics, an unanticipated drop in the price level raised the real value of firms' debt obligations, reducing firms' net worth. The collapse in net worth raised information costs in lending and led to declining investment and output. Hence a financial panic causes the *AD* curve to shift to the left (as depicted in Fig. 27.1a), resulting in less output.

Ben Bernanke of Princeton University has stressed that the wave of bank failures in the early 1930s led to a financial panic and increased the severity of the Great Depression. Depositors withdrew funds that banks could have used to make loans and held currency and U.S. government securities instead. Banks sharply reduced their willingness to lend to risky borrowers, preferring to hold only high-quality marketable securities. The increase in the demand for safe securities decreased yields significantly. The spread in interest rates on so-called safe and risky securities widened to levels that have not been seen again since that time. Consumer and investment spending by households, farms, and small and medium-sized businesses (all heavily dependent on bank financing) declined substantially.

Credit Controls and Credit Crunches

Full-scale financial panics are rare nowadays in the United States because of legislation that created a lender of last resort (the Fed) and federal deposit insurance. A more recent cause of a drop in bank lending on the economy is the imposition of **credit controls**, or regulatory restrictions on bank lending. Because of the importance of bank lending to many borrowers, a reduction in the supply of bank credit should contract the spending of bank-dependent borrowers and reduce open market interest rates.

In March 1980, President Carter attempted to reduce aggregate demand and inflation by authorizing the Fed to impose direct credit controls on consumer lending by banks, department stores, and certain other firms. The Fed imposed a voluntary Special Credit Restraint Program for the banking system, which requested that banks reduce their acquisition of funds from nondeposit sources. The Fed also placed a surcharge of 3% on some discount borrowing by large banks and a special reserve requirement of 15% on new money market mutual fund assets, and it increased reserve requirements on certain large-denomination certificates of deposit. Households and many small businesses dramatically cut back on borrowing. As in Fig. 27.1, the reduction in bank credit availability shifted the *AD* curve to the left, reducing output. Indeed, real GDP and industrial production declined in the spring and summer to produce a short but relatively sharp recession. The reduction in output led to a drop in money demand, causing the real open market interest rate to fall. At the same time, the yield on three-month T-bills dropped from 15% to about 7% (the drop in the federal funds rate was still more dramatic); long-term rates also declined. Spending by households contracted significantly, and there was a smaller, though still important, reduction in business spending. The effect of the credit controls on the economy was so severe that the controls were removed by July 1980. As soon as the controls were lifted, interest rates and aggregate demand increased. This episode verifies our predictions in Fig. 27.1, which showed that a reduction in bank loans would reduce output and interest rates.

In addition to credit controls, credit crunches can reduce output in the short run. A **credit crunch** is a decline in either the ability or the willingness of

OTHER TIMES, OTHER PLACES . . .

The Global Banking Crisis and the Great Depression

The Great Depression of the 1930s was not confined to the United States. The worldwide deflation of the early 1930s weakened borrowers' net worth and exacerbated the economic downturn in many countries. Adding to this, the banking crisis in the United States during the early 1930s spurred the decline in economic activity by reducing credit to many types of borrowers. Outside the United States, major banking panics occurred in 1931 in Austria, Germany, and many Eastern European, South American, and Middle Eastern countries, where the banking systems were fragile. Some countries, notably Canada and the United Kingdom, had stable systems with a few large, well-diversified national banks. These countries were less vulnerable to banking panics than were countries with small, undiversified local banks, such as France and the United States.

Ben Bernanke and Harold James of Princeton University examined data from 24 countries and grouped them according to whether they experienced a banking crisis during the Depression:

Banking Crisis	No Banking Crisis
Austria	Australia
Belgium	Canada
Estonia	Czechoslovakia
France	Denmark
Germany	Finland
Hungary	Greece
Italy	Japan
Latvia	The Netherlands
Poland	Norway
Romania	New Zealand
United States	Spain
	Sweden
	United Kingdom

Bernanke and James found that the countries that suffered a banking crisis experienced greater subsequent declines in output and employment than did countries that did not experience a banking crisis. The divergence was greatest in 1932, the year following the main banking crises, when declines in industrial production averaged 16% and 2%, respectively, in the two groups of countries.

Source: Ben Bernanke and Harold James, "The Gold Standard, Deflation, and Financial Crisis in the Great Depression: An International Comparison," in R. Glenn Hubbard, ed., *Financial Markets and Financial Crises.* Chicago: University of Chicago Press, 1991.

banks to lend at any particular interest rate. An example of a regulation-induced credit crunch reducing banks' *ability* to lend occurred in the period prior to the early 1980s, with Regulation Q's limitation on the interest rates that banks could pay on deposits. When open market interest rates on T-bills and other financial instruments rose above the Regulation Q ceiling, depositors shifted funds from bank deposits to those higher-interest alternatives. The withdrawal of funds from the banking system is called *disintermediation.* As a result of disintermediation, banks were not able to lend as much. Spending in sectors that depend on bank financing (particularly housing and small business investment) declined significantly, contributing to downturns in spending and output.

A credit crunch also may occur because of a decline in banks' *willingness* to lend. The reason is weakness on the part of either banks (because of low levels of bank capital, for example) or borrowers (because evaluating and monitoring financially distressed borrowers entails greater transactions and information costs for banks). In a credit crunch, banks decide to hold much smaller portions of their portfolios in loans, thereby decreasing the volume of bank loans and increasing the effective bank loan rate. For borrowers, the transactions and information costs of nonbank financing are high, so a reduction in bank lending decreases spending.

At the beginning of the 1990–1991 recession, the U.S. economy probably experienced a credit crunch. The decline in bank lending occurred because banks questioned the strength of borrowers' balance sheets—that is, banks believed that borrowers might be unable to carry out long-term projects. The borrowers that were most severely affected were real estate developers and firms with high debt burdens. The volume of lending declined dramatically in the fall of 1990, and surveys of small businesses revealed that credit had become more difficult to obtain, even for firms with a good credit history. In the fall of 1998, many economists suspected a credit crunch when banks curtailed lending to risky borrowers in the wake of the Asian financial crisis and the collapse of Long-Term Capital Management, a large U.S. "hedge fund." When the Federal Reserve reduced short-term U.S. interest rates in early 2001, it cited weak balance sheets and the potential for a credit crunch as a motivation for its action.

EXPANDED CHANNELS FOR MONETARY POLICY

In this section, we combine what we now know about banks' ability and willingness to lend and borrowers' net worth to explain how monetary policy works. We investigate how this behavior might change the predictions of how an increase or decrease in the money supply affects aggregate demand and output.

In Chapter 26, we described several transmission mechanisms for monetary policy. New classical economists assumed that only unexpected changes in the money supply would change output. New Keynesians assumed that changes in the money supply altered the real interest rate, which then influenced consumer spending, investment spending, and net exports. The change in aggregate demand caused output to increase or decrease. Building on this discussion of links between money and output, we are now ready to describe channels of monetary policy—the precise links through which monetary policy affects aggregate demand and output.

The simplest channel through which changes in the money supply affect aggregate demand and output is described by the new Keynesian view, which stresses the effects of monetary policy on aggregate demand through interest rates. We begin by observing the role of banks in that explanation of how monetary policy works. We then contrast this with other interpretations of the monetary transmission mechanism.

The Money Channel: Monetary Policy and Interest Rates

In our discussion of monetary policy and economic activity in Chapter 26, we assumed that borrowers are indifferent to how or from whom they raise funds and regard alternative sources of funds as close substitutes. This assumption allows us to focus on the market for money. In the market for money, the supply of money (influenced strongly by actions of the Fed) and the public's demand for money determine open market interest rates, which affect spending decisions by households and businesses.

These assumptions underlie the **money channel**, in which changes in the money supply affect output in the short run through changes in interest-sensitive components of aggregate demand. In this channel, the real interest rate changes in response to changes in the money supply, and aggregate demand responds to the change in the interest rate. The effect of changes in the money supply on interest rates arises from the public's portfolio decisions about allocating wealth between money and nonmoney assets. Financial institutions (banks) meet the public's demand for money by supplying deposits. This analysis is consistent with the predictions of the new Keynesian view described in Chapter 26.

Consider a monetary expansion, in which the Fed supplies additional reserves to the banking system. Banks use these resources to purchase securities on the open market or to make loans to households and businesses. When a bank buys securities in financial markets, it offers deposits to securities sellers. When a bank makes loans, it makes deposits available to borrowers in exchange for a promise to repay with interest. (Banks earn profits on these activities, because the interest the bank earns on marketable securities or on loans is greater than the interest that banks pay to depositors.) Let's consider how either action by banks affects interest rates and output. To increase the level of deposits at current interest rates, banks can buy securities in financial markets. The resulting price increases of securities reduce yields on those securities and encourage households and firms to allocate more of their portfolios to bank deposits than to securities. If bank deposits and securities are close substitutes in the eyes of the public, interest rates in general will fall. Banks can also increase the level of deposits by reducing interest rates on loans. The lower rates encourage households and firms to borrow additional funds, thereby increasing deposits. Banks can reduce the level of deposits desired at current interest rates either by selling securities in their portfolios (to encourage the public to accept them instead of deposits) or by decreasing the demand for deposits by raising interest rates on loans. Either method changes deposits by affecting interest rates.

Loans by financial institutions play no special role in the money supply process in the money channel. If the Fed wants to increase spending and output, it can increase the level of bank reserves, causing banks either to increase deposits by buying securities or to make more loans at lower interest rates. Either way, the public accepts the increase in money because of lower interest rates. The lower interest rates that result from the increase in the money supply expand the economy by increasing business investment and consumer spending on durable goods and housing.

The money channel provides a simple framework for analyzing the effects of monetary policy on economic activity resulting from changes in interest rates. However, it ignores the importance of financial intermediaries in reducing information costs of borrowing and lending.

The Bank Lending Channel: Monetary Policy and Banks

Some economists argue that some borrowers depend on banks for external financing and that this dependence affects outcomes of monetary policy. These economists focus on the **bank lending channel**, emphasizing the behavior of bank-dependent borrowers. For these borrowers, bank loans are special because these borrowers have few or no alternative sources of funds. In the bank lending channel, a change in banks' ability or willingness to lend affects bank-dependent borrowers' ability to finance their spending plans. The bank lending channel's focus on bank loans also suggests a modified view of how monetary policy affects the economy. In this channel, a monetary expansion increases banks' ability to lend; increases in loans to bank-dependent borrowers increase their spending. A monetary contraction decreases banks' ability to lend; decreases in loans to bank-dependent borrowers reduce their spending.

Money Channel and Bank Channel Predictions

We now compare the change in output that would occur in response to a change in the money supply as described by the money channel and the bank lending channel. In the money channel, changes in the nominal money supply affect output by influencing the open market interest rate in the money market. Figure 27.3 illustrates this process graphically with the *AD-AS* model. For simplicity, let's assume an extreme characterization of the new Keynesian view: that all firms have sticky prices in the short run, so the *SRAS* curve is horizontal. Consider a monetary expansion, in which the Fed increases the level of bank reserves through open market operations, raising the nominal money supply. As a result, the real money supply curve in Fig. 27.3(a) shifts to the right from MS_0 to MS_1. With the higher level of reserves, banks try to increase deposits by buying securities in financial markets, making loans, or both. When they buy securities, security prices rise and yields fall. Interest rates on bank loans decline. The increase in the money supply leads to a decline in the real interest rate from r_0 to r_1 in the short run. In Fig. 27.3(b), the increase in the money supply shifts the *AD* curve to the right from AD_0 to AD_1. At the new equilibrium, E_1, output rises to Y_1. The higher level of current output raises money demand from MD_0 to MD_1 in Fig. 27.3(a). Therefore the real interest rate rises from r_1 to $r_{1'}$. When the shifts in the money and goods markets are complete, output rises and the real interest rate falls in the short run in response to monetary expansion.

Hence, in the money channel, an increase in the nominal money supply decreases the real interest rate and increases output in the short run. This expansion occurs because, if nothing else changes, open market interest rates fall in the short run to induce households and firms to hold a greater quantity of money.

The predictions of the bank lending channel are similar to those of the money channel in one respect: When banks expand deposits by making loans, the increase in bank reserves leads to lower loan interest rates. Many borrowers can choose between bank loans and borrowing from nonbank sources, so lower bank loan rates lead to lower interest rates in financial markets.

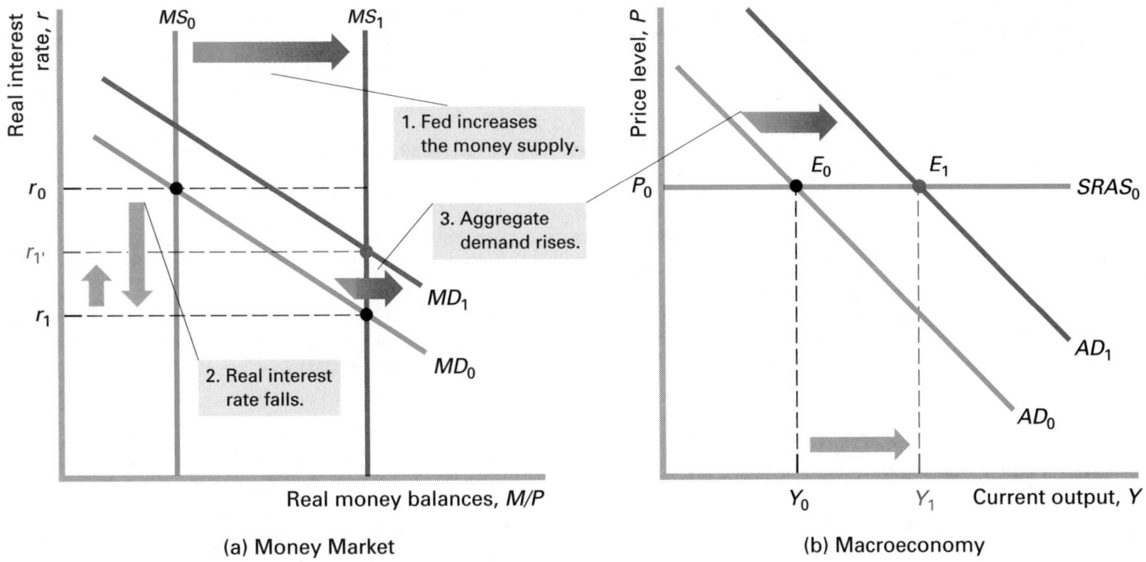

Figure 27.3

Monetary Expansion Effects in the Money Channel

In the money channel, monetary expansion reduces the real interest rate and raises output in the short run.

As shown in (a):
1. The Fed increases the nominal money supply, raising the real money supply in the short run from MS_0 to MS_1.
2. The real open market interest rate falls from r_0 to r_1, bringing the money market back into equilibrium.

As shown in (b):
3. From an initial equilibrium, E_0, the drop in the real interest rate causes the aggregate demand curve to shift from AD_0 to AD_1, increasing output in the new equilibrium, E_1, from Y_0 to Y_1.

In part (a), we see that:
Money demand rises from MD_0 to MD_1, so the interest rate rises to $r_{1'}$. On balance, the real interest rate declines, from r_0 to r_1, as a result of the monetary expansion.

The bank lending channel holds further, however, that monetary policy affects the economy through the volume of bank lending to and spending by bank-dependent borrowers. To see this, let's return to the case of an expansionary monetary policy by the Fed. In the bank lending channel, the initial effect in the money market is the same as that in the money channel: As Fig. 27.4(a) shows, the increase in the money supply from MS_0 to MS_1 reduces the open market real interest rate from r_0 to r_1. In the bank lending view, the *AD* curve shifts to the right for two reasons: (1) the increase in households' and firms' spending from the drop in the interest rate and (2) the increased availability of bank loans. In other words, if banks expand deposits by lowering interest rates on loans, the amounts that bank-dependent borrowers can borrow and spend increases at any real interest rate in financial markets. From an initial equilibrium at E_0, the shift of the *AD* curve from AD_0 to AD_1 in Fig. 27.4(b) is greater than in the money channel. That is, at the new equilibrium, E_1, the increase in output—from Y_0 to Y_1—is greater than that shown in Fig. 27.3(b).

Because of the greater spending at any particular interest rate, the money demand curve in Fig. 27.4(a) shifts up and to the right from MD_0 to MD_1. As

Figure 27.4

Monetary Expansion Effects in the Bank Lending Channel

In the bank lending channel, monetary expansion raises output in the short run, but the effect on the real interest rate is ambiguous.

As shown in (a):

1. The Fed increases the money supply, raising the real money supply in the short run from MS_0 to MS_1.
2. The real open market interest rate falls initially from r_0 to r_1.

As shown in (b):

3. From an initial equilibrium, E_0, aggregate demand rises because of an increase in interest-sensitive spending and in spending by bank-dependent borrowers. At the new equilibrium, E_1, these effects raise money demand from MD_0 to MD_1.

In part (a), we see that:

4. In the new equilibrium, the real interest rate actually rises from r_0 to $r_{1'}$; that is, the larger feedback effect in the credit view can cause the real interest rate to rise during monetary expansion.

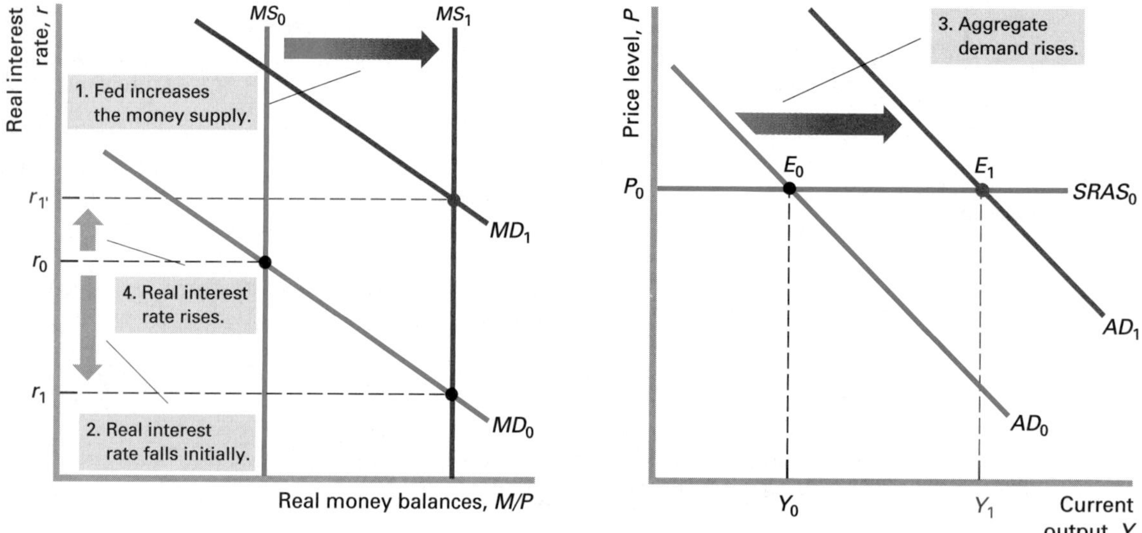

(a) Money Market

(b) Macroeconomy

a result, the short-run effect of the monetary expansion on the open market real interest rate is ambiguous. The case depicted in Fig. 27.4(a), with the new equilibrium real interest rate at $r_{1'}$, is one in which the effect on the interest rate of the increase in money demand is greater than the effect of the increase in money supply.

In both channels, expansionary monetary policy by the Fed initially decreases the level of interest rates, increasing aggregate demand and output in the short run. Similarly, contractionary monetary policy increases interest rates, decreasing aggregate demand and output in the short run.† The bank

†A monetary contraction by the Fed reduces the level of bank reserves and deposits. Hence the bank lending channel assumes that banks find nondeposit sources of funds (say, certificates of deposit) to fund loans to be more costly than deposits at the margin. See the discussion in R. Glenn Hubbard, "Is There a 'Credit Channel' for Monetary Policy?" *Federal Reserve Bank of St. Louis Review* 77 (June 1995):63–77.

lending channel includes behavior that the money channel does not: Banks' portfolio decisions about lending cause bank-dependent sectors of the economy to change their spending. Because many borrowers are bank-dependent and have few substitutes for bank loans, changes in banks' ability or willingness to lend may significantly affect the volume of loans and output.

The Balance Sheet Channel: Monetary Policy and Net Worth

Another way in which monetary policy may affect the economy is through the effects of monetary policy on firms' balance sheet positions. Analysts have attempted to model this channel by describing effects of monetary policy on the value of firms' assets and liabilities and on the liquidity of balance sheet positions—that is, the quantity of liquid assets that households and firms hold relative to their liabilities. According to these analysts, the liquidity of balance sheet positions is a determinant of spending on business investment, housing, and consumer durable goods. The **balance sheet channel** describes ways in which interest rate changes from monetary policy affect borrowers' net worth. We know that when information costs of lending are great, high levels of net worth and liquidity help borrowers to carry out their planned spending.

How does monetary policy affect borrowers' balance sheets? Recall that information problems increase the gap between the cost of external and internal funds as a borrower's net worth falls. That is, a decline in a borrower's net worth increases the cost of raising funds for capital investment. Increases in interest rates in response to a monetary contraction increase borrowers' debt-service burdens for borrowers with floating-rate loans and reduce the value of borrowers' net worth (by reducing the present value of their assets). This fall in net worth raises the cost of external financing by more than the increase that is implied by higher interest rates and reduces firms' ability to invest in plant and equipment. This is the effect that is emphasized by the balance sheet channel. Even if monetary policy has no effect on banks' ability to lend, the decline in borrowers' net worth following a monetary contraction reduces aggregate demand and output. Moreover, the balance sheet channel implies that spending by low-net-worth firms particularly is likely to fall following a monetary contraction.

We illustrate outcomes in the balance sheet channel for a monetary expansion in Fig. 27.5. As Fig. 27.5(a) shows, the increase in the money supply from MS_0 to MS_1 reduces the open market real interest rate from r_0 to r_1. In the balance sheet view, the AD curve shifts to the right for two reasons: (1) the response of households' and firms' spending to the decline in the interest rate and (2) the increased ability of borrowers to obtain funds because of higher net worth and liquidity. From an initial equilibrium at E_0, the shift of the AD curve from AD_0 to AD_1 in Fig. 27.5(b) is greater than in the money channel. As a result, at the new equilibrium, E_1, the increase in output—from Y_0 to Y_1—is larger than in Fig. 27.3(b). As we saw in analyzing the bank lending channel, the money demand curve in Fig. 27.5(a) shifts up and to the right from MD_0 to MD_1. The short-run effect of the monetary expansion on the real interest rate is ambiguous; the case illustrated in Fig. 27.5(b) shows a higher equilibrium real interest rate.

The balance sheet channel shares with the money channel and the bank lending channel the idea that expansionary policy initially decreases interest rates, increasing output, while contractionary policy initially increases interest rates, reducing output. The balance sheet channel emphasizes the link between households' and businesses' net worth and liquidity and businesses' spending. In the presence of information costs, changes in net worth and liquidity may significantly affect the volume of lending and economic activity.

In the balance sheet channel, holdings of liquid assets also reduce the likelihood of **financial distress,** which arises when households or businesses have to sell illiquid assets, possibly at a loss, to meet current obligations. As a result of financial distress, household and business spending would fall for any particular level of market interest rates.

For both households and businesses, the likelihood of experiencing financial distress decreases when they have substantial liquid financial assets (or

Figure 27.5

Monetary Expansion Effects in the Balance Sheet Channel

In the balance sheet channel, monetary expansion raises output in the short run, but the effect on the real interest rate is ambiguous.

As shown in (a):

1. The Fed increases the money supply, raising the real money supply in the short run from MS_0 to MS_1.
2. The real open market interest rate falls initially from r_0 to r_1.

As shown in (b):

3. From an initial equilibrium, E_0, aggregate demand rises because of an increase in interest-sensitive spending and because of the rise in net worth. In the new equilibrium, E_1, these effects raise money demand from MD_0 to MD_1.

In part (a), we see that:

4. In the new equilibrium, the real interest rate rises from r_0 to $r_{1'}$.

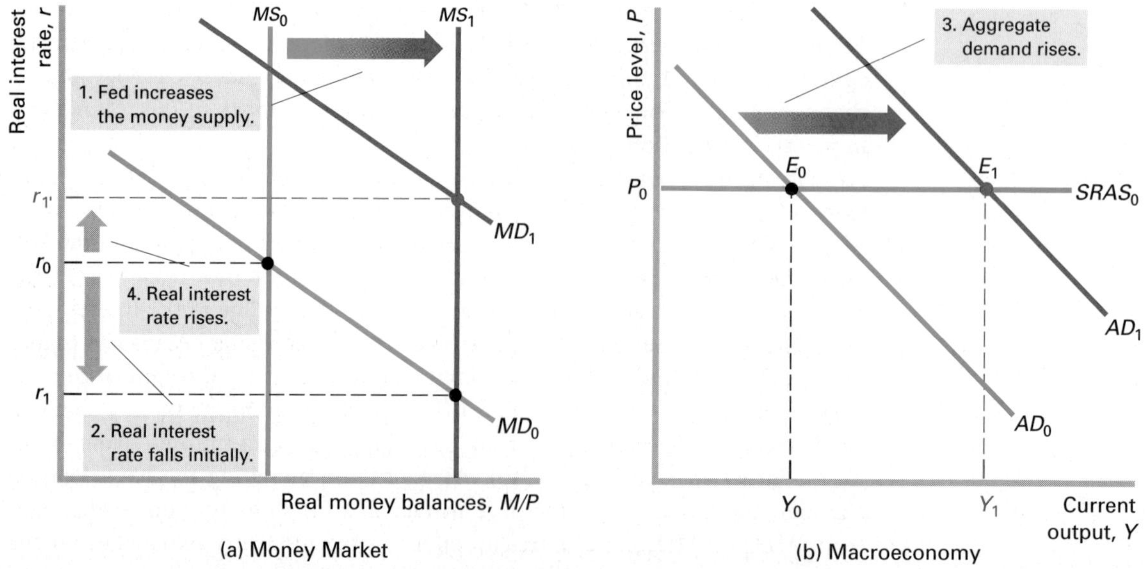

access to credit from financial institutions) relative to their liabilities. When households have high levels of liquid assets relative to their liabilities, they are more willing to invest in consumer durable goods or housing because they estimate the likelihood of financial distress to be low. Similarly, when firms' liquid asset holdings are high relative to their liabilities, they are more willing to invest in new plant and equipment, all else being equal.

During some significant episodes, declining liquidity of household and business balance sheets reduced spending on consumer durable goods, housing, and business plant and equipment. After the stock market crash of 1929, the number of households and businesses experiencing financial distress grew. This situation was caused by the reduction in the value of financial assets combined with the increase in the real value of outstanding debt obligations (because of the decline in the price level). From 1929 to 1933, expenditures on business fixed investment (in constant dollars) fell by 73%, and expenditures on consumer durable goods and housing declined by 50% and 80%, respectively. Many economists suggest that deteriorating balance sheet positions also accounted in part for the severity of the recessions of 1974–1975, 1981–1982, and 1990–1991.

Monetary policy can affect the likelihood of financial distress. Recall that independent increases in the money supply lower interest rates and raise stock prices, thereby raising the value of liquid financial assets. When the value of households' or firms' financial assets is relatively greater than the value of their financial liabilities, the probability of financial distress diminishes. The increase in the value of financial assets encourages spending on consumer durable goods and investment. In addition, short-term declines in interest rates can reduce the cost of servicing outstanding debt obligations, thereby increasing liquidity for households and firms.

Validity of the Bank Lending and Balance Sheet Channels

How valid are the changes in demand and output that occur as a result of the bank lending channel and balance sheet channel? In this section, we work (1) with the bank lending and balance sheet channels to determine whether monetary policy has a different impact on different groups of borrowers, and (2) with the bank lending channel to see whether shifts in bank loan supply are independent of shifts in bank loan demand.

Effects of monetary policy on borrowers. Unlike the money channel, the bank lending and balance sheet channels acknowledge differences among borrowers in the financial system. In the bank lending channel, transactions costs of bank and nonbank financing, particularly those costs related to information, are higher for households and small and medium-sized firms than for large, well-known firms. If the bank lending channel is correct, a credit crunch in bank lending should be felt disproportionately by the borrowers for which transactions and information costs of nonbank finance are the highest. We noted earlier the significant effect on households during the Carter credit controls episode. In the balance sheet channel, differences in borrowers' net worth affect their sensitivity to monetary policy. Economists have documented the importance of credit supply effects on small firms relative to large firms. For example, Mark Gertler of New York University and Simon Gilchrist of Boston University examined the effect of contractionary monetary policies enacted since World War II on the output of manufacturing firms.[†] They found that changes in the *M2* money supply and in the federal funds rate had a greater impact on the availability of bank loans and on output for small, low-net-worth firms than for large, high-net-worth firms. These pronounced differences in the output of manufacturing firms in response to monetary policy suggest that both the bank lending and balance sheet channels explain part of the link between money and output in the modern U.S. economy.

Distinguishing changes in supply and demand for credit. When analyzing real-world data, we need to determine whether shifts in *bank loan supply* are independent of shifts in *bank loan demand*. For example, a decline in bank lending during a recession doesn't necessarily indicate a credit crunch. Rather, it might be explained by a reduction in the demand by households and firms for credit of all types.

Some episodes clearly support a role for independent shifts in bank loan supply. The decline in output and interest rates during the monetary contraction associated with the Carter credit controls is inconsistent with the money channel. Moreover, because the credit controls were unexpected and imposed by the government, the decline in economic activity as a result of the controls clearly caused the decline in money demand and the fall in interest rates.

An additional example comes from the banking collapse of the 1930s. In their explanation of monetary factors as causing the Great Depression, Milton Friedman and Anna Schwartz blamed the drop in the money supply accompanying the contraction of the banking system. Bank lending channel advocates see two problems with this conclusion as a complete explanation for the severe economic decline from 1930 to 1933. First, it doesn't explain why the decline was so protracted. Second, the decline in the *real money supply* (which affects the *AD* curve) wasn't nearly as great as the drop in the nominal money supply because the aggregate price level declined significantly as well.

More generally, one way to learn whether less bank lending reflects a shift in banks' ability or willingness to lend is to examine the behavior of borrowers that have some access to nonbank sources of finance. Do these borrowers seek funds elsewhere, such as the commercial paper market? Anil Kashyap of the University of Chicago, Jeremy Stein of Harvard University, and David Wilcox of the Federal Reserve Board studied bank lending and the issuing of commercial paper to learn what happens to the mix of borrowing from banks

---

[†] Mark Gertler and Simon Gilchrist, "Monetary Policy, Business Cycles, and the Behavior of Small Manufacturing Firms," *Quarterly Journal of Economics*, 109:309–340, May 1994.

and the commercial paper market when the Fed contracts the level of bank reserves.† They found that commercial paper issues increased significantly but that bank lending remained flat or declined. The fact that commercial and bank loans did not move together in those episodes strongly suggests that changes in overall credit demand are not responsible for the pattern. Kashyap, Stein, and Wilcox found that changes in the mix of short-term financing (away from bank loans and toward commercial paper) accompanying contractionary monetary policy reduced business inventories (for which bank credit is an important source of finance). They also had a smaller effect on business equipment investment.

The evidence broadly supports the idea that lending by financial intermediaries plays an important role in determining output and interest rates. Indeed, some analysts and policymakers blamed a credit crunch for worsening the 1990–1991 recession. Other analysts stressed the role that weak household and corporate net worth played in exacerbating the recession.

The bank lending channel suggests that financial institution strength is necessary for the financial system and the economy to function smoothly. Adverse shocks to banks' ability or willingness to lend (as in a credit crunch) may have severe economic effects. Monetary policy can work by affecting the public's portfolio allocation decisions regarding money and nonmoney assets or by affecting banks' portfolio allocation decisions regarding loans and securities. A general unwillingness of banks to lend does not imply that monetary policy is ineffectual, even in the bank lending channel. An increase in bank reserves through open market purchases will still raise the volume of bank deposits as a result of banks' greater holdings of marketable securities. Likewise, in the balance sheet channel, a change in interest rates following a change in monetary policy triggers balance sheet effects on borrowers. Accepting the bank lending or balance sheet channel, then, does not require rejecting the money channel's implication that monetary policy works through interest rates. Instead, these bank lending and balance sheet channels offer additional methods by which the financial system and monetary policy can affect the economy.

The chapter opened by describing the downturn during 1990 and 1991. It is likely that both the bank lending and balance sheet channels can help us to explain economic events during that period.†† Banks responded to a fall in their net worth during the late 1980s and to the imposition of tougher capital adequacy standards by reducing their lending to households and businesses. Bank-dependent borrowers found credit harder to obtain at any given interest rate and reduced their spending. At the same time, many corporate and

† Anil Kashyap, Jeremy Stein, and David Wilcox, "Monetary Policy and Credit Conditions: Evidence from the Composition of External Finance," *American Economic Review*, 83:78–98, January 1993.

†† For suggestive empirical evidence along these lines, see R. Glenn Hubbard, Kenneth N. Kuttner, and Darius Palra, "Are There 'Bank Effects' in Borrowers' Costs of Funds," *Journal of Business*, in press.

CONSIDER THIS . . .

Was There a Credit Crunch During the 1990–1991 Recession?

The National Bureau of Economic Research determined that the economy entered a recession in July 1990. In the spring of 1990, the media reported that banks were cutting back on lending, with adverse consequences. Members of President Bush's cabinet argued in June that the credit crunch would harm the economy unless the Federal Reserve intervened.

Some economists claim that a credit crunch deepened the recession. The banking system was under close scrutiny by regulatory authorities because of large losses and the ongoing deposit insurance crisis, which may have contributed to the decline in bank lending in 1990. New bank lending declined significantly. As the accompanying chart shows, bank loans to businesses *declined* in the fall of 1990 while commercial paper issues *increased*, a pattern that often indicates a credit crunch in the bank lending channel. In addition, small manufacturing firms grew more slowly than large ones in 1990. Hence many economists argue that a credit crunch exacerbated the downturn during the recession. Later in the recession, the demand for all forms of credit fell, suggesting the weakening of a credit crunch.

Source: The Federal Reserve Bank of St. Louis, *U.S. Financial Data,* October 31, 1991.

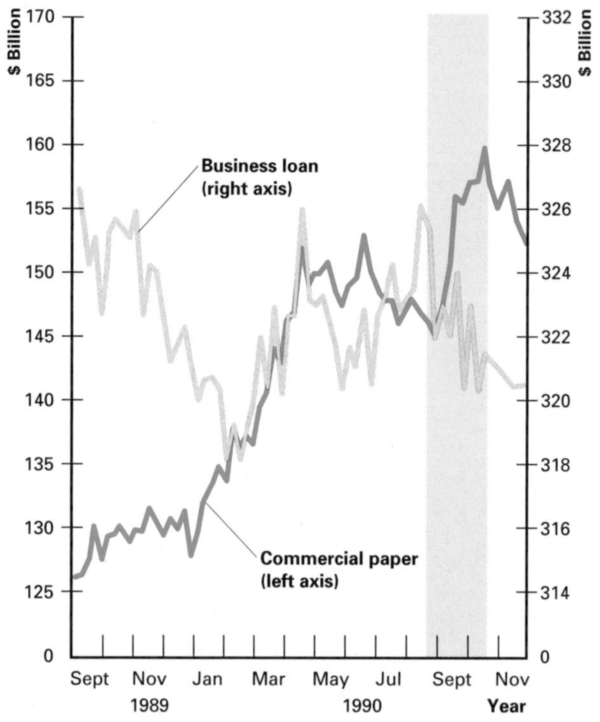

household borrowers emerged from the 1980s with substantial debt burdens and low net worth, making them vulnerable to any downturn. Low borrower net worth made it harder for businesses and households to borrow, slowing down the economic recovery.

CHECKPOINT

Bigmart, a major discount retailer, wants to expand the number of its stores but is concerned about the implications of a recent decline in bank lending in the economy. The CEO of Bigmart believes that the drop in bank lending is the result of a credit crunch, which will be reversed soon by policy actions to loosen regulations on bank lending. Bigmart's treasurer warns against expansion, saying that the decline in bank lending is the result of weak loan demand and reflects a sluggish economy. To support one of the two positions, what information should you assemble? A credit crunch implies greater declines in lending to and investment by bank-dependent borrowers. Therefore you could compare data on borrowing by households and small businesses with data on borrowing by large businesses. In addition, you could compare recent trends in bank lending with other short-term financing, say, in commercial paper markets. If bank lending and commercial paper issues are both declining, the credit crunch explanation is less convincing. o

Implications for Public Policy

When the Fed is developing monetary policy, it attempts to predict the influence of the policy on aggregate demand and output. The Fed's assessment should include the information costs that borrowers and lenders experience. Such an assessment should also analyze the financial health of banks and borrowers. For example, during the debate over the reform of federal deposit insurance, most commentators agreed that some form of government intervention—a lender-of-last-resort role for the Fed or a modified form of deposit insurance—has to be retained to avoid negative effects on the economy due to troubles in the banking system. There are other implications for financial regulation. In the past, some financial regulation caused credit crunches in the United States. In particular, binding ceilings on interest rates paid to depositors formerly caused contractions in mortgage lending, consumer financing, and small-business loans. In addition, because bank lending often is localized, credit crunches often have regional or industry dimensions. Removing regulatory restrictions on diversification of bank portfolios would reduce the likelihood of such credit crunches. The balance sheet channel emphasizes that the Fed should evaluate firms' and households' net worth and liquidity in deciding the course for monetary policy. Particularly since 1991, the Federal Open Market Committee has monitored private sector net worth in charting policy actions.

In the bank lending and balance sheet channels, long-term policy directions for developing economies and emerging market economies center on the need for strong private financial institutions and strong financial markets. The growth of healthy banking institutions specializing in reducing transactions and information costs for small savers and borrowers can help to reduce the effective cost of financing for households and young, growing enterprises. As a result, fostering a sound banking system in an economy that previously relied on incomplete, informal, or nonmarket mechanisms for allocating funds can stimulate economic activity toward the full employment level. Indeed, recent empirical evidence suggests a strong link in such economies between the size of the private intermediary sector and economic growth and the rate of capital accumulation.†

†See Robert G. King and Ross Levine, "Finance and Growth: Schumpeter Might Be Right," *Quarterly Journal of Economics*, 108:717–737, August 1993.

THE FINANCIAL TIMES DECEMBER 22, 2000

A New Credit Crunch for Japan?

Concerns are growing about the health of the Japanese banking sector after the Nikkei 225 index dropped another 3.5% yesterday, taking its losses for the year to about 30%.

a The fall in share prices has created a double-edged problem for the country's banks because of their large share portfolios and high levels of nonperforming loans.

Two years after Japanese banks were hit by a financial crisis that forced the government to nationalize two banks and led to consolidation in the industry, some observers are concerned that Japan could suffer another financial crisis under the pressure of the banks' problem loans.

Some economists warn that Japan's economy cannot achieve a full recovery unless the bad-loan issue is unraveled and that new bad debts are piling up before old ones have been resolved.

b The optimists argue that the injection of public funds into the banks makes a financial crisis less likely. "The banks have a larger capital base because of public funds than they did at the time of the financial crisis two years ago," said Hideyasu Ban, analyst at Morgan Stanley Dean Witter. . . .

The plunge in the stock market and the weakening economic outlook put the banks under increased pressure to diversify their sources of income.

But analysts do not expect new income streams, such as asset management, to make a meaningful contribution to profits for two or three years.

The banks use their share portfolios as part of their calculations toward working out adequate reserves to back problem loans.

c Declining share prices slash the banks' problem-loan reserves, creating a need for the reserves to be topped up. This need, in turn, means the banks may be forced to sell their share portfolios.

James Fiorello, banks analyst at ING Barings, the investment bank, says that while problem loans in the sector were down 5% year-on-year to ¥17,200 billion, problem loans to bankrupt companies—the most dangerous category—had risen 13%. He added that according to his analysis, there were further hidden problem loans of ¥17,600 billion on banks' balance sheets.

He said the combination of declining share prices, the need to bolster reserves and no real declines in bad debts levels could mean banks have no choice but to offload their share portfolios.

"Should the banks begin to engage in desperate stock selling in order to raise one-time profits, it could have a sudden negative impact on the overall market, and return to haunt them," Mr. Fiorello added.

In the fall of 1998, many economists and policymakers praised the Federal Reserve's commitment to low inflation while cutting interest rates to ward off effects of the Asian crisis. At the same time, the Bank of Japan received suggestions that it pursue expansionary policy, stimulating aggregate demand in Japan.

a Deflation—falling prices—in Japan in the mid-1990s eroded the net worth of borrowers, and higher loan defaults and falling asset values reduced the net worth of banks. As part (a) of the figure shows, the decline in borrowers' and banks' net worth reduced aggregate demand. That is, at any open market interest rate, borrowers could obtain less financing for consumption or investment, shifting the *AD* curve to the left from AD_0 to AD_1. Output fell from Y_0 to Y_1.

b The injection of taxpayer funds and a 1998 expansionary policy by the Bank of Japan provided a double stimulus to the Japanese economy. In the money channel, the monetary expansion reduces real interest rates, raising interest-sensitive spending and aggregate demand. As part (b) of the figure shows, from the initial equilibrium at E_0, the *AD* curve shifts to the right from AD_0 to AD_1. At E_1, output rises from Y_0 to Y_1. Through the bank lending and balance sheet channels, the monetary expansion further increases aggregate demand by bolstering borrowers' ability to obtain financing at any open market interest rates. As a result, the *AD* curve shifts to the right from AD_1 to $AD_{1'}$, and, at the new equilibrium at $E_{1'}$, output rises from Y_1 to $Y_{1'}$. Many analysts feared that, absent future intervention by the Japanese government and the Bank of Japan, a credit crunch could reemerge.

c The author of this article implicitly argues that policy analysts and commentators should keep in mind the different circumstances underlying monetary policy's effects on the economy through the money channel, the bank lending channel, and the balance sheet channel. Examining the relative strength of each channel offers guidelines for policy design and effectiveness. As some experts note, however, the Japanese government must take care to avoid exacerbating moral hazard by its involvement.

For further thought . . .

Does a low interest rate on Japanese bonds necessarily imply that the Bank of Japan is pursuing an expansionary policy? Why or why not?

Source: Excerpted from David Ibison and Bayan Rahman, "Problem Loans Could Come Back to Haunt Japan's Banks as Nikkei Decline Continues," *The Financial Times*, December 22, 2000.

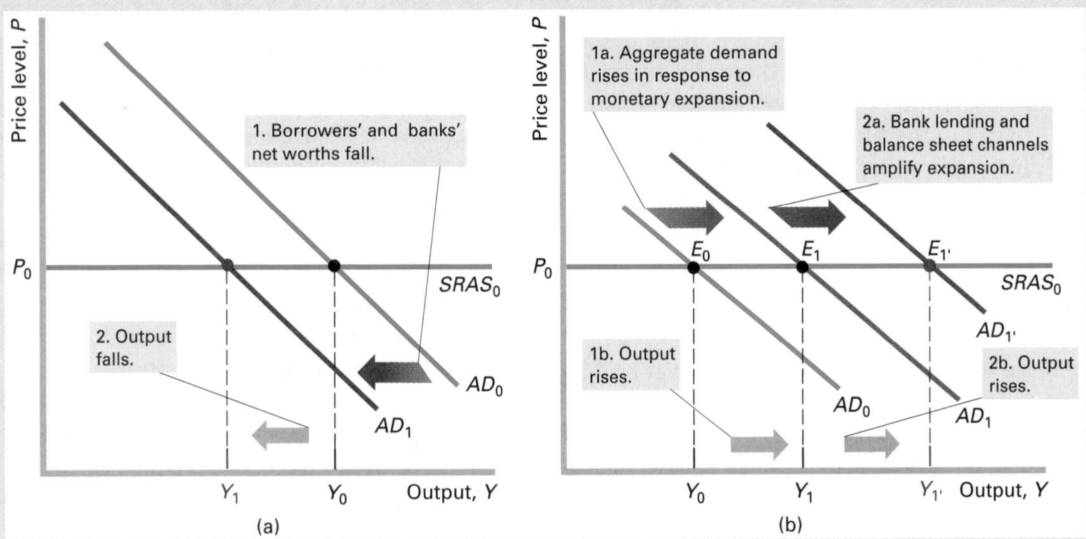

KEY TERMS AND CONCEPTS

Balance sheet channel
Bank lending channel
Credit controls
Credit crunch
Financial distress
Financial panics
Money channel

SUMMARY

1. Asymmetric information in financial markets makes internal funds a cheaper source of financing for firms than external funds. Information costs are greater the lower is the borrower's net worth, all else being equal. A fall in borrowers' net worth raises information costs in lending and decreases borrowers' ability to raise funds at any given market interest rate, shifting the *AD* curve to the left. An increase in borrowers' net worth reduces information costs in lending, shifting the *AD* curve to the right.

2. Transactions costs related to asymmetric information may be high for some borrowers, particularly households and small and medium-sized businesses. As a result, obtaining financing from lenders other than banks is expensive for such borrowers. Nonbank financing is an imperfect substitute for bank loans for many borrowers. Thus shifts in the ability or willingness of banks to make loans can have a significant impact on aggregate demand and output. An increase in banks' ability or willingness to lend shifts the *AD* curve to the right. An independent decrease in bank lending shifts the *AD* curve to the left. Studies of financial panics, credit crunches, and credit controls have documented the link between economic activity and financial institutions' ability or willingness to extend credit. In these episodes, reductions in bank lending lead to lower output and a lower real interest rate.

3. Effects of monetary policy or output can be analyzed in terms of the money channel, the bank lending channel, or the balance sheet channel. In the money channel, based on the new Keynesian view of the macroeconomy, an expansionary policy by the Fed to increase the nominal money supply shifts the *AD* curve to the right, increasing current output and decreasing the real interest rate. In the bank lending channel, monetary policy can also shift the *AD* curve in another way: If banks increase deposits in a monetary expansion by increasing their willingness to make loans, the amount that bank-dependent borrowers can borrow and spend increases at any level of the open market real interest rate. The result is a shift of the *AD* curve to the right. In the balance sheet channel, the fall in interest rates accompanying a monetary expansion increases borrowers' net worth and liquidity, reducing information costs and the cost of external financing. The *AD* curve shifts to the right.

4. Economists have documented differential effects of monetary policy on small and large firms. The spending of households and small firms is more sensitive to changes in monetary policy than is the spending of large firms. Because smaller firms are likely to be both bank-dependent and relatively low-net-worth borrowers, this observation is consistent with both the bank lending and balance sheet channels of how monetary policy affects the economy.

5. Because asymmetric information problems are important, policies that promote efficient financial intermediation should improve economic performance. Healthy financial institutions can reduce transactions and information costs for small savers and borrowers. This lowers the effective cost of external financing for households and young, growing enterprises.

REVIEW QUESTIONS

1. Why does a majority of lending take place through financial intermediaries rather than through direct stock and bond issues?
2. What impact does a firm's net worth have on the gap between the cost of external and internal financing?
3. Why are internal funds a cheaper source of financing for many firms than external funds?
4. Suppose that your research shows that the rate at which firms generate internal funds is closely related to the amount of their new investment spending if they are growing rapidly but not if they are growing slowly. What economic theory does this result support?
5. What is a financial panic? What happens to bank lending in such a situation?
6. In a financial panic, what would you expect to happen to the difference in interest rates on commercial paper and T-bills? Why?
7. How effective were the Carter administration's credit controls in reducing credit expansion?
8. How did Regulation Q lead to credit crunches before 1980? In answering this question, define the term "disintermediation."
9. Compare and contrast the money channel and the bank lending channel.
10. What is financial distress?
11. How does the liquidity of balance sheet positions affect the likelihood of financial distress?
12. How does expansionary monetary policy help to reduce financial distress?
13. Which view is supported by actual economic data: the money channel or the bank lending channel? What are the main pieces of evidence?
14. How did the Carter credit controls cause a recession?
15. You have been assigned to determine whether the economy is experiencing a credit crunch. What patterns in movements in the federal funds rate, the volume of bank lending, and the volume of short-term lending in financial markets will you look for? Why?
16. *Evaluate:* The money, bank lending, and balance sheet channel explanations of how monetary policy affects the economy are necessarily inconsistent.
17. *Evaluate:* The money channel stresses portfolio allocation decisions of the public, whereas the bank lending channel stresses portfolio allocation decisions of banks.

ANALYTICAL PROBLEMS

18. Suppose that new tax laws increase the tax rate on retained earnings—that is, the profits of firms that are not distributed to shareholders. How is this change likely to affect the economy?
19. Why is a credit crunch more likely to occur in a recession?
20. If Congress were to tax banks 100% on any "excess profits" (that is, profits above some level), what effect would this tax have?
21. *Evaluate:* Low real interest rates represent expansionary monetary policy, whereas high real interest rates represent contractionary monetary policy.
22. Suppose that new developments in information technology reduce significantly the information-gathering advantage of banks. Discuss the implications for the bank lending channel.
23. In the early 1990s, the banking system in the United States went through a period of restructuring in which banks moved their portfolios into safer assets (T-bills), and bank regulations became more restrictive. According to the bank lending channel, what effect should these changes have had on the macroeconomy?

24. Suppose that the economy goes through a recession in which many people are unable to repay their credit card debts. Banks lose a lot of money and decide to curtail credit card issuance sharply. Is this action likely to be expansionary or contractionary? Why?

25. Suppose that the Fed reduces the nominal money supply. Will the open market real interest rate rise more in the money channel or the bank lending channel? Illustrate your answer by using the *AD-AS* diagram for the new Keynesian model. (For simplicity, you can assume that the *SRAS* curve is horizontal.)

26. Does a reduction in bank lending during a recession necessarily imply that the economy is experiencing a credit crunch? Why or why not? What data would you examine to determine whether there is a credit crunch?

27. Contrast the policy of the Fed at the beginning of the 1990s with its policy in late 1998. What might account for the difference between how the Fed acted during the two periods?

28. At the beginning of the Great Depression, some economists argued that falling prices would help to bring the economy back to full employment. Between 1929 and 1933, consumer prices fell by 25% and producer prices fell by 30% without seeming measurably to aid recovery. Is it possible that falling prices may have had a destabilizing impact on the U.S. economy during those years?

DATA QUESTION

29. Look in the *Federal Reserve Bulletin* for data on the amount of bank loans and the amount of commercial paper for the latest six months for which data are available. Is the amount of bank lending rising, falling, or steady? Is the amount of commercial paper issued rising, falling, or steady? Is the economy in a credit crunch? Why or why not?

CHAPTER 28

Inflation: Causes and Consequences

Inflation—the scourge of the U.S. economy in the late 1970s and early 1980s—fell during the late 1980s and early 1990s, virtually vanishing by some measures by the beginning of the twenty-first century. This change brought praise for the Federal Reserve and Fed Chairmen Paul Volcker and Alan Greenspan. Worry over inflation declined more slowly, as most economists still urged central banks to focus their energy on low inflation. Worry over the costs of fighting inflation also declined slowly. Indeed, during 1996, many policymakers debated whether the Fed's anti-inflation stance was too tough, compromising jobs and growth to appease financial markets. Against this backdrop, most economists praised Greenspan and the Fed for gradually reducing the U.S. inflation rate in the 1980s and 1990s.

To understand why the Fed is at center stage in the debate over inflation, we need to connect changes in the money supply to inflation. Nobel laureate Milton Friedman once remarked that "inflation is always and everywhere a monetary phenomenon." In the first section of this chapter, we show why this is true. A number of factors can lead to changes in the price level, but sustained increases in the price level—inflation—can be traced to sustained monetary expansion. To explain the widespread opposition to inflation, we then investigate the costs of inflation to households and businesses. Even with opposition to inflation, inflationary episodes occur; we analyze pressures on policymakers to permit inflation. Finally, we describe and estimate costs of reducing inflation and discuss the link between the credibility of monetary policy and those costs. The Federal Reserve's efforts since the 1980s to put forth a credible low-inflation policy make the Fed wary of allowing increases in inflation.

EXPLAINING PRICE LEVEL CHANGES

The federal government tracks the price level and reports its value. When official statistics report that inflation is 3%, it means that a measure of the general price level has risen by 3% over some period. Three commonly used measures of changes in the price level are the consumer price index (CPI), the producer price index (PPI), and the implicit price deflator for the gross domestic product. To get the most up-to-date information on them, you can consult

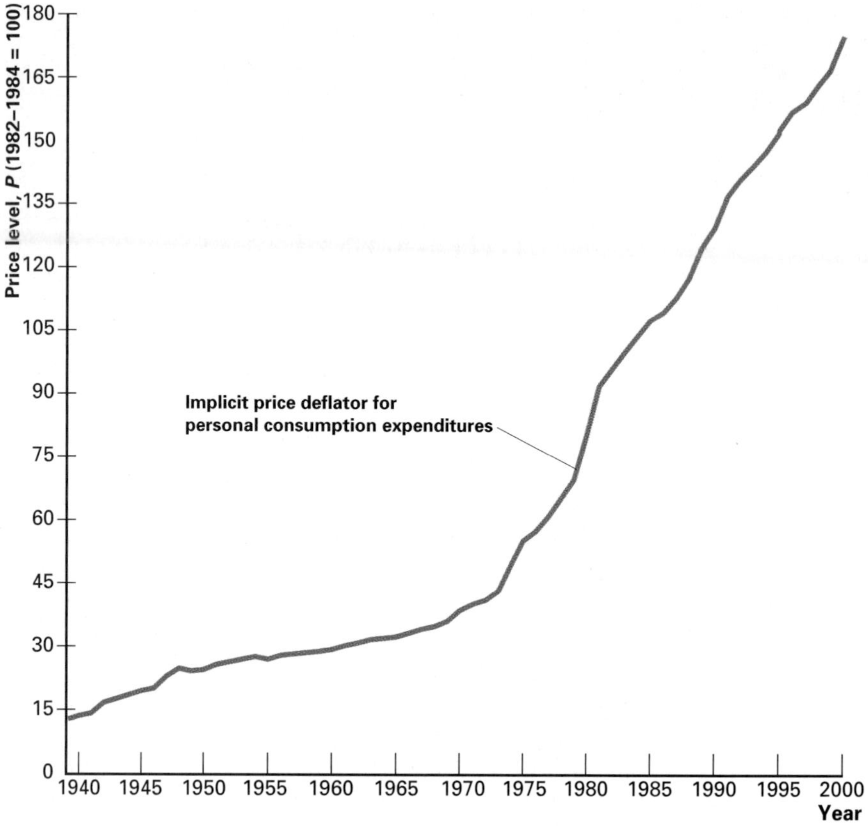

Figure 28.1

Consumer Price Level in the United States, 1939–2000

Throughout U.S. history, the price level has increased and decreased at various times. During the past several decades, the price level has increased, although at an uneven rate. The graphed data represent the implicit price deflator for personal consumption expenditures.

Source: Council of Economic Advisers, *Economic Report of the President,* various issues.

U.S. government publications such as the Bureau of Labor Statistics' *Monthly Labor Review* or the Council of Economic Advisers' *Economic Indicators*.

Figure 28.1 shows that consumer prices rose by more than 950% from 1939 through 2000. In other words, at the end of 2000, you would have needed \$1.00 to make a purchase that would have cost less than \$0.10 in 1939. Since World War II, increases in the price level have been ever present but uneven. The price level increased rapidly in the 1960s and 1970s and more slowly in the 1980s and 1990s. A steady rise in the price level isn't normal by historical standards. Indeed, throughout U.S. history, prices have fallen in more years than they have risen. In this section, we extend the aggregate demand–aggregate supply model of the financial system and the economy that we developed in Chapter 25 to study the causes of changes in the price level and inflation.

Causes of Price Level Changes

To identify the reasons the price level changes, we return to the equation of exchange that we presented in Chapter 23. This equation expresses the relationship among the nominal money supply, M, the price level, P, and output, Y:

$$MV = PY.$$

V is the velocity of money. Recall that V is defined as PY/M because the equation of exchange is an identity.

To move from price level changes to inflation, we have to change the equation of exchange somewhat. We are interested in the *rate of change* in prices rather than the price level itself. Therefore we change the equation to percentage change form. The percentage change in the nominal money supply, $\dot{m}$, the percentage change in velocity, $\dot{v}$, the percentage change in the price level, π, and the percentage change in output, $\dot{y}$, can be expressed as

$$\dot{m} + \dot{v} = \pi + \dot{y}.$$

Rearranging terms to isolate determinants of price level changes gives

$$\pi = \dot{m} + \dot{v} - \dot{y}. \tag{28.1}$$

When prices are rising, π represents inflation. Equation (28.1) shows us that inflation, π, equals the rate of growth of the nominal money supply, $\dot{m}$, plus the rate of growth of velocity, $\dot{v}$, less the rate of growth of real output, $\dot{y}$. To link the variables in this equation with the *AD-AS* model, we can use $\dot{y}$ to represent the growth rate of aggregate supply (the economy's growth in output), and we can use $\dot{m} + \dot{v}$ to represent the growth rate of nominal aggregate demand. We use these relationships in the following graphs to observe what happens when there is a one-time change in the price level and more sustained changes in the price level.

Causes of Price Level Fluctuations

To assess potential causes of short-term inflation, we must determine whether the growth rate of nominal aggregate demand can exceed the growth rate of aggregate supply over short periods of time. Equation (28.1) identifies three causes of short-term inflation: (1) Nominal aggregate demand could rise in response to an increase in the nominal money supply. (2) Nominal aggregate demand could rise because of short-run increases in velocity owing to increases in government spending, consumer spending, or investment spending. (3) Even if nominal aggregate demand does not change, the growth rate of aggregate supply could fall.

Response to monetary policy. A one-time increase in the money supply ultimately leads to an increase in the price level, all else being equal. To see this, recall that new classical and new Keynesian economists believe that the aggregate supply curve slopes upward in the short run, as Fig. 28.2 shows. In the new classical view, unexpected changes in the price level may cause producers to change their output. Hence the actual level of output can be less than or greater than the level that is consistent with long-run full employment. In the long run, the aggregate supply curve is vertical at the full employment level of output.

What is the effect of an *unexpected* increase in the money supply on the price level? An unexpected increase in the money supply shifts the *AD* curve

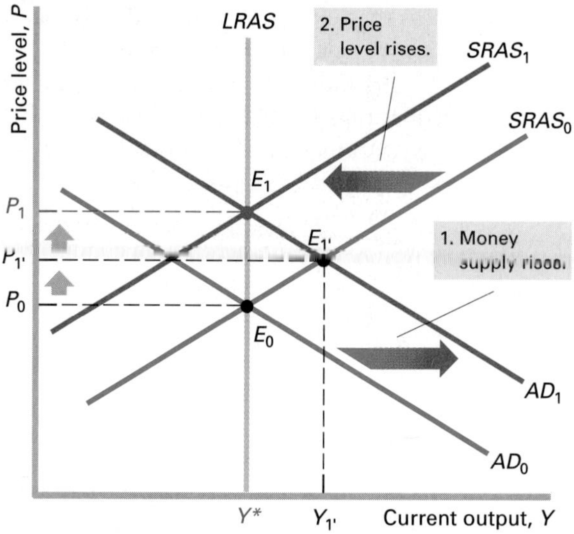

Figure 28.2

Price Level Increase Resulting from an Increase in the Money Supply

1. In both the new classical and new Keynesian views, an unexpected increase in the nominal money supply shifts the *AD* curve from AD_0 to AD_1, moving the equilibrium from E_0 to $E_{1'}$.

2. In the short run, actual output, $Y_{1'}$, exceeds full employment output, Y^*. As a result, upward pressure on prices pushes the *SRAS* curve from $SRAS_0$ to $SRAS_1$ to intersect the AD_1 curve at E_1. A one-time increase in the money supply causes the price level to rise from P_0 to $P_{1'}$. In the long run, only the price level is affected, rising to P_1.

to the right, from AD_0 to AD_1 in Fig. 28.2. As a result, the economy moves from initial equilibrium at E_0 to a new short-run equilibrium at $E_{1'}$, representing both a higher price level and increased output. In other words, new classical economists predict that the short-run reaction to an unexpected increase in aggregate demand is an increase in both output and the price level.

In the long run, however, the gap between the full employment and actual levels of output puts upward pressure on the price level, shifting the *SRAS* curve to the left from $SRAS_0$ to $SRAS_1$. Because firms recognize the true price level over time, the economy's long-run equilibrium lies at the intersection of the AD_1 and *LRAS* curves at E_1. Money is neutral in the long run; only the price level, not the level of output, is affected.

Although some prices are sticky in the short run in the new Keynesian view, the process of price adjustment to an output change is similar to that predicted by new classical economists. However, the adjustment is slower. From a full employment equilibrium at E_0, an unexpected increase in the nominal money supply shifts the *AD* curve to the right from AD_0 to AD_1. In the short run, output increases to $Y_{1'}$ at $E_{1'}$. However, the higher aggregate demand puts upward pressure on wages and prices, shifting the *SRAS* curve gradually upward from $SRAS_0$ to $SRAS_1$. The economy returns to full employment equilibrium at E_1, with output Y^* and a higher price level $P_1 > P_0$. Hence, in the new Keynesian explanation of price level changes, as in the new classical view, an unexpected increase in aggregate demand causes the price level and output to increase in the short run.

Response to other changes in aggregate demand. The aggregate demand curve represents the combinations of the price level and output at which the goods and asset markets are in equilibrium. How do changes in government spending, consumer spending, or investment spending affect the price level?

Let's consider a one-time increase in government spending on roads and bridges, for example. (Shifts in consumer or investment spending have similar effects.) As was the case for a one-time increase in the money supply, in the short run, the *AD* curve shifts to the right, as it did in Fig. 28.2. This shift increases both output and the price level. New classical and new Keynesian economists predict that the price level rises in the short run and that the excess of actual output over full employment output puts upward pressure only on prices in the long run. Hence increases in government spending (and consumer spending or investment spending) raise output and the price level in the short run. Such changes increase only the price level in the long run, leaving output unchanged.

Response to supply shocks. Shifts in the short-run aggregate supply curve due to supply shocks, such as changes in raw materials' prices or workers' wage demands, can cause changes in the price level. As Fig. 28.3 shows, an adverse supply shock, such as a one-time increase in the price of oil, raises input prices and shifts the short-run aggregate supply curve from $SRAS_0$ to $SRAS_1$. If the money supply and government taxes and spending don't change, the aggregate demand curve remains at AD_0. As a result, the economy's equilibrium shifts from E_0 to E_1. The price level has risen from P_0 to P_1, resulting in an increase in the price level in the short run.

At E_1, however, output Y_1 is below the full employment level of output, Y^*. Over time, prices fall, and the *SRAS* curve shifts back down from $SRAS_1$ to $SRAS_0$. The economy eventually returns to equilibrium at E_0. Thus supply shocks can affect the price level in the short run, but they do not cause sustained changes in the price level—inflation.

Figure 28.3

Price Level Increase from an Oil Price Increase

1. An increase in the price of oil shifts the short-run aggregate supply curve from $SRAS_0$ to $SRAS_1$.

2. The price level rises from P_0 to P_1, causing inflation in the short run.

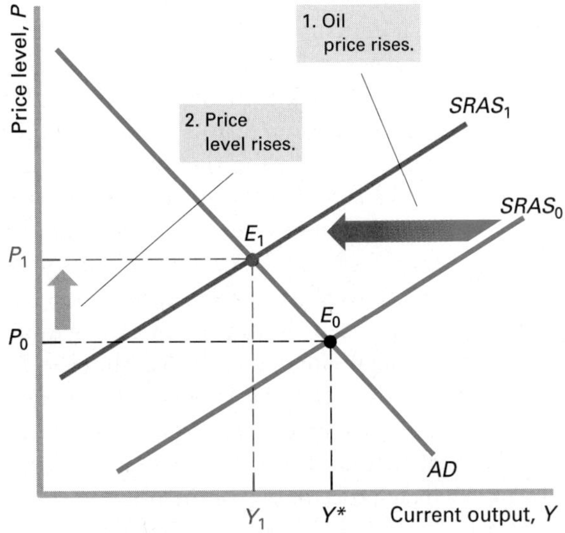

Sustained Changes in the Price Level: Inflation

One-time increases in the money supply, other short-run increases in nominal aggregate demand, or supply shocks can increase the price level. Sustained rates of change in the price level constitute **inflation**. We can use Eq. (28.1) to determine sources of inflation. Inflation arises whenever the growth rate of nominal aggregate demand exceeds the growth rate of aggregate supply over sustained periods of time.

One-time changes in government spending or taxes cannot by themselves produce inflation, as just defined. This is because such inflation would have to result from persistent increases in government spending or decreases in taxes. Government spending and the size of government are limited by both the obvious consideration that government spending cannot exceed the economy's total production (GDP) and limitations on spending imposed by the political process. These same constraints apply to tax changes. If the money supply is unchanged, expansionary fiscal policy alone cannot produce inflation for a long period of time. Similarly, while one-time adverse supply shocks can increase the price level in the short run, a one-time supply shock alone can't lead to prolonged inflation.

Returning to Milton Friedman's prediction from the chapter introduction, economists attribute persistent inflation to sustained growth in the nominal money supply at a rate faster than the growth rate of velocity and the growth rate of output. Figure 28.4 illustrates how money supply growth could cause inflation. Suppose that households and businesses expect the growth rates of velocity and output to be 0% and the money supply to increase steadily by 5% each year.

Let's begin with the new classical explanation for inflation. From initial equilibrium at E_0, the AD curve shifts to the right from AD_0 to AD_1 as the nominal money supply increases. The money supply growth leads individuals and firms to change their expectations of the price level from P_0 to P_1. (Recall that anticipated changes in the money supply lead households and businesses to expect a higher price level.) The $SRAS$ curve shifts upward from $SRAS_0$ to $SRAS_1$ (quickly, in the new classical approach), and the economy's equilibrium shifts from E_0 to E_1. As the nominal money supply increases again, the AD curve shifts to the right from AD_1 to AD_2. The process then repeats as the $SRAS$ curve shifts upward from $SRAS_1$ to $SRAS_2$ to reflect the rise in the expected price level. At the economy's new equilibrium, E_2, the price level has risen to P_2. Thus sustained increases in the price level over the long run can be traced to persistent increases in the nominal money supply.

In the new Keynesian explanation of inflation, sustained increases in the nominal money supply also shift the aggregate demand curve to the right from AD_0 to AD_1. The $SRAS$ curve shifts upward gradually from $SRAS_0$ to $SRAS_1$. Output initially rises from Y^* to Y' and the price level rises from P_0 to $P_{1'}$ as at $E_{1'}$ until the $SRAS$ curve is at $SRAS_1$, as households and businesses change their expectations of the price level. At the new equilibrium E_1, the price level

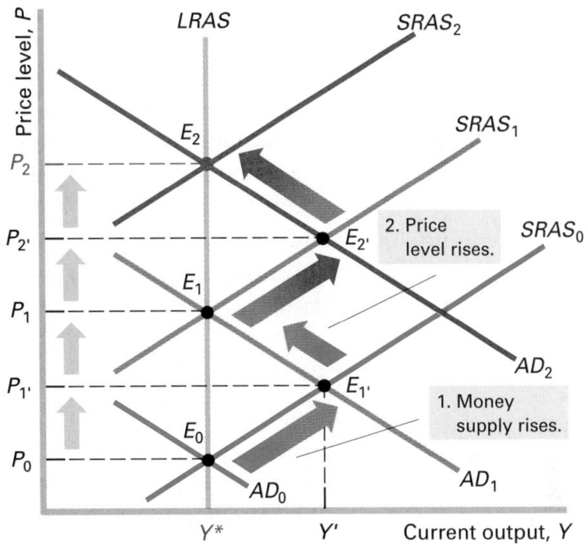

Figure 28.4

Persistent Money Supply Growth and Inflation

Money is neutral in the long run. Persistent growth of the money supply leads to inflation with no long-term increase in real output.

1. Increases in the nominal money supply shift the aggregate demand curve from AD_0 to AD_1 and then from AD_1 to AD_2.
2. Increases in the expected price level as a result of the increase in the money supply shift the *SRAS* curve upward. In both the new classical and new Keynesian views, the shift is from $SRAS_0$ to $SRAS_1$ (as the expected price level increases from P_0 to P_1) and then from $SRAS_1$ to $SRAS_2$ (as the expected price level increases from P_1 to P_2).

has risen to P_1, but output remains at its initial level, Y^*. As the money supply increases again, the *AD* curve shifts farther to the right, from AD_1 to AD_2. Before prices adjust, output rises from Y^* to Y' and the price level rises from P_1 to $P_{2'}$ as at $E_{2'}$. As the expected price level rises from P_1 to P_2, the *SRAS* curve shifts upward from $SRAS_1$ to $SRAS_2$. At the new equilibrium E_2, output is Y^* and the price level is P_2.

Hence, in both the new classical and new Keynesian views, sustained growth in the money supply doesn't affect real output in the long run but does lead to inflation. As Fig. 28.1 shows, the U.S. economy has experienced long-term inflation since World War II. The reason is that, as our analysis of inflation over the long term reveals, the rate of growth of the nominal money supply has been "too fast" relative to the rates of growth of velocity and output. The observation that long-term inflation is principally a monetary phenomenon also is consistent with evidence from other countries. During the 1980s, countries with high average rates of inflation (such as Argentina and Israel) experienced rapid average rates of growth of the nominal money supply. Countries with low average rates of inflation experienced slow average rates of growth of the nominal money supply.

CHECKPOINT

Do government budget deficits cause inflation? In the short run, government budget deficits can raise aggregate demand and thus [according to Eq. (28.1)] lead to short-term inflation. For government budget deficits to be inflationary in the long run, the Fed must be expanding the monetary base to acquire government bonds. More rapid growth of the monetary base raises the growth rate of nominal money supply, leading to inflation if nothing else changes. o

COSTS OF INFLATION

Since the early 1980s, Fed policymakers have made low inflation a major goal to avoid the rapid and sustained price increases that occurred during the 1970s. They reacted to complaints by households and businesses that such inflation placed undue burdens on them. In this section, we examine what those costs are. We divide our analysis into an investigation of (1) *expected inflation*, which households and businesses take into account when conducting financial transactions, and (2) *unexpected inflation*, which causes households and businesses to redistribute funds.

Expected Inflation

Expected inflation can affect the allocation of the economy's resources. First, inflation causes money to lose value. Specifically, it places a tax on real money balances when those balances pay less than the market rate of interest. This tax is a loss in purchasing power. For example, if you held \$100 in currency in 1996 when the rate of inflation was about 3%, you lost \$3.00 of purchasing power over the year. By imposing a tax on real money balances, inflation reduces the public's demand for real money balances. One cost of this tax, known as **shoe leather costs,** is the cost to consumers and businesses of making more trips to the bank to avoid holding significant amounts of currency or of shifting funds from interest-bearing assets into money. When the public's shoe leather costs exceed the government's revenue gain from the inflation tax, inflation generates an excess burden, or social loss. Stanley Fischer of the World Bank has estimated that the annual excess burden in the United States of a modest inflation rate of 5% is approximately 0.3% of GDP, or about \$30 billion in 2001 dollars.†

Inflation distorts the taxes that individuals and firms pay on their income. Income tax rates usually apply to nominal income, and income tax rates are progressive. Under a progressive tax system, tax rates increase as income increases. If tax brackets are not indexed for inflation, as income rises with inflation, individuals are subject to higher tax rates, even though they might not gain purchasing power from the increase in income. This problem, called *bracket creep,* was particularly severe in the 1970s, when income brackets were not indexed and the individual income tax was more progressive than it was in the early 2000s. The tax code also fails to adjust values of inventories and the value of depreciation allowances for inflation, raising the corporate tax burden during periods of high inflation.

Expected inflation also can distort financial decisions because lenders pay taxes on nominal rather than real returns. Suppose that expected inflation is 4% and that an individual faces a tax rate of 30%. On an investment with a nominal interest rate of 8%, an individual realizes a real after-tax return of

† See Stanley Fischer, "Towards an Understanding of the Costs of Inflation: II," in K. Brunner and A. Meltzer, eds., *Carnegie Rochester Conference Series on Public Policy*, 15, 1981.

$(1 - 0.30)(8\%) - 4\% = 1.6\%$. Suppose that the expected inflation rate rises to 8% and that the nominal interest rate rises by the same amount to 12%. The investor's real after-tax return falls to $(1 - 0.30)(12\%) - 8\% = 0.4\%$. Hence nominal interest rates would have to increase by more than the change in inflation (8% – 4%) to maintain the real return of 1.6%. But there are winners as well as losers during a period of high inflation. Borrowers such as corporations and individual home buyers benefit from expected inflation, because borrowers deduct nominal interest payments (*not* real interest payments) in calculating their income tax liabilities. Changes in expected inflation can change the real after-tax cost of borrowing. For example, with high expected inflation, corporations find debt financing more attractive, because nominal interest payments are deductible. Households find housing investment more attractive relative to stocks, because home mortgage interest is deductible for tax purposes.

Another cost of expected inflation according to the new Keynesians arises from so-called **menu costs,** or costs to firms of changing prices (reprinting price lists, informing customers, and so on). Faced with different menu costs, not all firms change prices at the same time; that is, price changes that are brought on by inflation are not synchronized throughout the economy. Even so, expected inflation can change relative prices in the short run and make the allocation of the economy's resources less efficient.

Unexpected Inflation

Many labor contracts that arise from collective bargaining agreements specify wage payments in nominal amounts for an agreed-upon time period. Similarly, prices in contracts for goods and financial assets are sometimes set in nominal amounts and are valid for a specific number of months or years. Although many of these contracts have provisions for expected inflation, unexpected inflation, or the difference between actual and expected inflation, redistributes wealth. For example, suppose that a borrower and a lender expect no inflation and agree to a one-year, $1000 loan at 4% interest. Regardless of the inflation rate for the year, the lender receives ($1000)(1.04) = $1040 from the borrower at the end of the year. If the actual rate of inflation is 7%, the lender's real return (the return in terms of purchasing power) is –3%. Conversely, the borrower's real interest rate is –3%. The unexpected inflation of 7% (7% – 0%) effectively transferred $70 of real purchasing power from the lender to the borrower. Another example of this redistribution occurs when unexpected inflation reduces real wages for employees who have nominal wage contracts.

The effects of unexpected inflation are more difficult to gauge than those of expected inflation for the macroeconomy. *Losses* to some parties are matched by *gains* to others. Nonetheless, that redistribution of resources can generate costs. For example, amounts that businesses or households spend on forecasting inflation to protect themselves against unfavorable redistributions represent a cost of unexpected inflation.

CHECKPOINT

Consider the actions of four people: Ms. A borrowed money at a fixed nominal interest rate; Mr. B lent money at a fixed nominal interest rate; Ms. C borrowed money at a variable interest rate (indexed for inflation); and Mr. D lent money at a variable interest rate. If inflation rises, who loses the most in real terms? Who gains the most? Lenders and borrowers incorporate expected inflation into the agreed-upon interest rate. When the interest rate is fixed, additional (unexpected) inflation redistributes purchasing power from lenders to borrowers: Mr. B loses the most, and Ms. A gains the most. **o**

Inflation Uncertainty

Uncertainty about the rate of inflation causes the most serious cost of inflation: distortion of information provided by prices. In a market economy, households and businesses view prices of goods and assets as signals for resource allocation. For example, an increase in the price of beef relative to the price of chicken encourages farmers to produce more beef and individuals to consume more chicken. An increase in stock market prices relative to the general level of prices is a signal that businesses' prospects are good and that there are opportunities for profitable investment. *Relative prices*, not individual prices, provide these signals. When inflation fluctuates significantly, relative prices may change in response to general price-level changes, distorting the valuable signals provided by prices. Variations of relative prices because of uncertain inflation cause households and businesses to waste resources investigating price differences.

An extreme case of uncertain inflation occurs in a **hyperinflation,** in which the rate of inflation is hundreds or thousands or more percentage points per year for a significant period of time. The costs of hyperinflation are extremely high. Households and businesses must minimize currency holdings, and firms must pay employees frequently. Employees must spend money quickly or convert it to more stable foreign currencies before prices increase further.

A classic example of hyperinflation occurred in Germany after World War I. A burst of money creation by the government ignited inflation, increasing the price level by a factor of more than 10 billion between August 1922 and November 1923. For example, if a candy bar cost the equivalent of 5 cents in August 1922, this increase in the price level would have raised its cost to more than $500,000,000 by November 1923. Our analysis of money demand tells us that in such an extreme case, the demand for real money balances should plummet. In Germany, that proved to be the case: By October 1923, real money balances had shrunk to only about 3% of their August 1922 value. The German hyperinflation ended suddenly in late 1923, with a strong government commitment to stop the money printing presses. With a significant decline in growth of the money supply, hyperinflation ended.

Confusing signals from prices are particularly problematic during hyperinflation. With overall prices rising very rapidly, merchants change prices as often as possible. Prices therefore quickly fail to indicate value or direct resource allocation. The government's tax-collecting ability diminishes significantly during hyperinflation. Because tax bills typically are fixed in nominal terms, households and businesses have a major incentive to delay their payments to reduce their real tax burdens.

INFLATION AND MONETARY POLICY

Although inflation imposes economic costs, governments sometimes pursue inflationary monetary policies to achieve other goals, particularly full employment of the economy's resources. Low inflation may be desirable, but it may bring hardship in terms of lost output and jobs when the economy isn't operating at or near capacity. Angry voters pressure elected officials to do something when recessions idle factories and swell unemployment. In fact, movements in current output can greatly influence the outcome of elections, creating a temptation to increase aggregate demand in the short run and to increase inflation. Ray Fair of Yale University has noted that significant GDP growth and a falling unemployment rate increased the reelection chances of the incumbent President and other candidates of the same party.

The Full Employment Act of 1946 and the Humphrey-Hawkins Act of 1978 committed the federal government to promoting full employment and a stable price level. Particularly during the 1960s and 1970s, U.S. policymakers often pressed for full employment even at the expense of inflation. Two types of inflationary pressures resulted: **cost-push inflation**, which results from workers' pressure for higher wages, and **demand-pull inflation**, which results from policymakers' attempts to increase aggregate demand for current output above the full employment level.

Cost-Push Inflation

Cost-push inflationary pressures begin when workers push for higher wages either to raise their real wages (wages adjusted for changes in purchasing power) or to "catch up" to current or expected future inflation. As Fig. 28.5 shows, when the economy starts at full employment at E_0, an increase in wages raises production costs and the expected price level, shifting the $SRAS$ curve upward from $SRAS_0$ to $SRAS_1$. With no change in monetary policy, short-run equilibrium occurs at the intersection of the AD_0 and $SRAS_1$ curves, at $E_{1'}$, with a drop in output from Y^* to Y' (and more unemployment) and a rise in the price level from P_0 to $P_{1'}$. Without any other government action over time, wages and prices would fall in response to the slack economy, and the economy's equilibrium would return to E_0.

However, if policymakers were committed to maintaining the full employment level of output even in the short run, expansionary policy would follow wage increases. This effect would be to push the aggregate demand curve to the right from AD_0 to AD_1, with the short-run equilibrium at E_1 and a higher price level at P_1 rather than at $P_{1'}$. If this process continues (that is, if workers again push for higher wages and policymakers increase the money supply),

Figure 28.5

Cost-Push Inflation

If policymakers expand the money supply to accommodate workers' demands for higher wages for a significant period of time, cost-push inflation will result.

1. Cost-push inflation can occur in the short run if workers push for higher wages so that the *SRAS* curve shifts from $SRAS_0$ to $SRAS_1$. In the short run, output falls from Y^* to Y'.

2. In the long run, cost-push inflation can occur only if the Fed pursues an inflationary policy (shifting the aggregate demand curve to the right from AD_0 to AD_1) to avoid output and job losses. These effects occur in both the new classical and new Keynesian views.

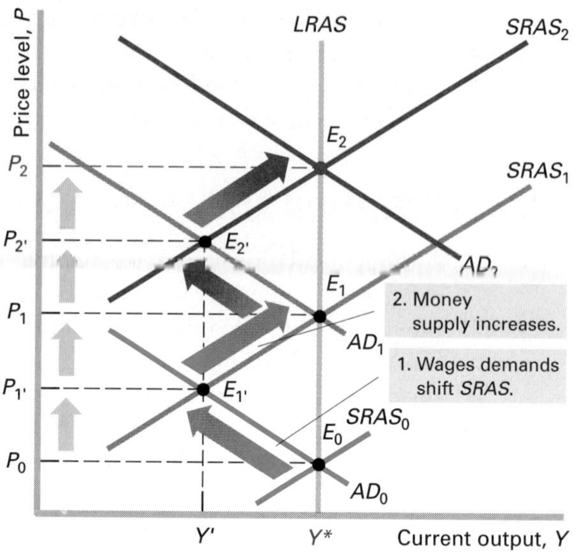

inflation can occur. Hence, if a second wage push shifts the *SRAS* curve to the left from $SRAS_1$ to $SRAS_2$ and policymakers' actions shift the *AD* curve from AD_1 to AD_2, the price level eventually rises from P_1 to P_2 (which is higher than $P_{2'}$ at $E_{2'}$) although output remains at Y^*. At each point, higher wages lead to lost output and jobs; policymakers then pursue an *accommodating policy*, stimulating aggregate demand to restore output and jobs but at the cost of greater inflation. A sustained cost-push inflation is a monetary phenomenon. Without inflationary responses via expansionary monetary policy actions, cost-push inflation could not persist in the long run.

Demand-Pull Inflation

Another type of inflation results from policymakers' attempts to keep the economy operating at a level greater than its long-run full employment level.† In this instance, employment is above the full employment level. Full employment does not mean that there is 0% unemployment. Even at the full employment level of output, some people who want jobs might not have them. Unemployment may exist because there is a mismatch between the skills or location of workers and job requirements (*structural unemployment*) or because workers who have quit jobs, have been laid off, or are new to the workforce are searching for suitable jobs (*frictional unemployment*). The **natural rate of unemployment** is simply the level that exists when the economy produces the full employment level of output. Let's see what happens when policymakers try to reduce the unemployment rate below the natural rate of unemployment for a sustained period of time.

†The appendix to this chapter extends the analysis to consider a possible policy trade-off between inflation and the unemployment rate.

Figure 28.6

Demand-Pull Inflation

If policymakers attempt to increase current output above the full employment level Y^* for a significant period of time, demand-pull inflation will result.

1. When expansionary monetary policy shifts the aggregate demand curve from AD_0 to AD_1, output is temporarily above the full employment level at Y'.

2. The higher expected price level shifts the *SRAS* curve upward so that in the long run, only the price level—and not the output level—is affected. The longer policymakers attempt to increase output above the full employment level (or, equivalently, to reduce the unemployment rate below the natural rate), the greater the cumulative inflation.

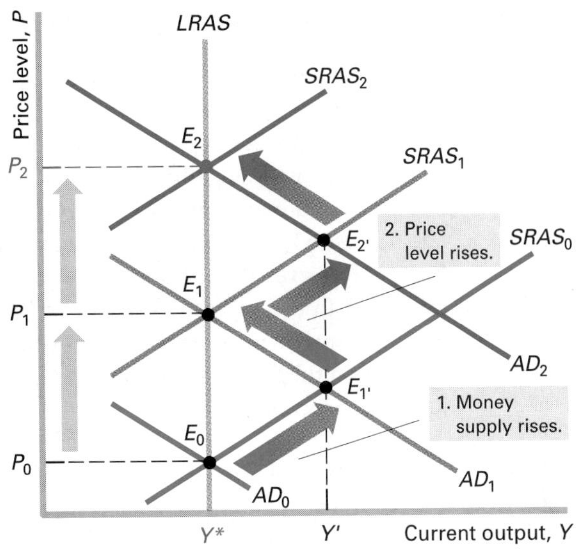

Suppose, as in Fig. 28.6, that the economy starts at full employment equilibrium, E_0. To increase output above the full employment level to Y', policymakers unexpectedly expand the money supply to shift the aggregate demand curve to the right from AD_0 to AD_1. As a result, as both the new classical and new Keynesian economists predict, output rises in the short run, and the economy's equilibrium shifts from E_0 to $E_{1'}$. As prices adjust, however, the *SRAS* curve shifts upward from $SRAS_0$ to $SRAS_1$, and output returns to the full employment level, Y^*, with the price level increasing from P_0 to P_1. The new equilibrium occurs at the intersection of the AD_1 and $SRAS_1$ curves, at E_1. The expansion of output above the full employment level lasts longer according to the new Keynesian economists than to new classical economists because the price adjustment is gradual.

If the process continues, the *AD* curve shifts to the right from AD_1 to AD_2, raising output to Y' in the short run (at $E_{2'}$). Over time, the *SRAS* curve shifts upward from $SRAS_1$ to $SRAS_2$, placing the economy at full employment equilibrium E_2, with a higher price level at P_2. Because the long-run aggregate supply curve is vertical, policymakers cannot permanently maintain the unemployment rate below the natural rate or, equivalently, permanently maintain a level of output greater than the full employment level.

Both cost-push inflation and demand-pull inflation cause sustained increases in the price level. In cost-push inflation, there are periodic episodes in which unemployment is higher than the natural rate (caused by attempts to keep real wages "too high"). In demand-pull inflation, there are attempts to keep the unemployment rate below the natural rate. Recognizing these differences in the real world can nonetheless be difficult. Economists do not agree on how to measure the natural rate of unemployment. In addition, cost-push inflation can occur as a catch-up response to demand-pull inflation.

COSTS OF REDUCING INFLATION

When policymakers pursue high levels of output and employment growth at the expense of maintaining a low inflation rate, they may exert an inflationary bias on monetary policy.† Eventually, households, businesses, and policymakers become less willing to bear high inflation than to maintain high levels of output and employment growth. One such shift in opinion occurred in the late 1970s, when President Carter appointed Paul Volcker as chairman of the Federal Reserve. What options do policymakers and the Fed have in reducing inflation? In this section, we describe **disinflation**, a decline in long-run inflation. The predictions and recommendations of the new classical economists differ from those of the new Keynesians, and we describe each view of the disinflation process.

New Classical Disinflation: Reducing Inflation Cold Turkey

A hallmark of the new classical view of the macroeconomy is that wages and prices adjust quickly to changes in expectations. Hence the new classical recommendation, illustrated in Fig. 28.7, for reducing the rate of inflation is to lower expectations about future money growth and inflation **cold turkey**—that is, all at once.

For example, suppose that because of long-term inflation, the public expects Fed actions to shift the *AD* curve from AD_0 to AD_1. As the expected price level increases, the short-run aggregate supply curve shifts from $SRAS_0$ to $SRAS_1$. Hence, with a built-in expected rate of inflation, the economy's equilibrium moves from E_0 to E_1.

Figure 28.7 shows that in cold turkey disinflation, when the Fed announces that it will reduce the rate of money supply growth to eliminate inflation, the *SRAS* curve does not shift from $SRAS_0$ to $SRAS_1$. Because money supply growth doesn't continue, the *AD* curve shifts back to AD_0. Hence, because the policy shift is expected, the economy's equilibrium lies at E_0. Wages and prices adjust rapidly in the new classical view, so inflation falls with little or no loss in output. Accordingly, the costs of cold turkey disinflation in terms of lost output and jobs are small.

Thomas Sargent of Stanford University has stressed the importance of changing expectations to reduce inflation while keeping costs low in terms of lost output and jobs.†† He studied hyperinflation in four European countries during the period between World War I and World War II, including Germany, which we discussed earlier. Financing rising government budget deficits with money creation ignited rapid inflation. In each case, announcements of budget reforms and cessation of inflationary increases in the domestic money

† Another possibility (not considered here) is that the Fed may incorrectly estimate the growth rate of velocity over long periods of time, allowing an inflationary money supply growth.

†† Thomas J. Sargent, "The Ends of Four Big Inflations," in R. E. Hall, ed., *Inflation: Causes and Effects*. Chicago: University of Chicago Press, 1981.

Figure 28.7

New Classical Suggestion: Cold Turkey Disinflation

When the public expects inflation, the economy's equilibrium moves from E_0 to E_1.

1. In a cold turkey disinflation, the Fed announces that it will reduce the rate of money growth to eliminate inflation; the *AD* curve does not shift from AD_0 to AD_1.

2. The price level adjusts rapidly to this policy change, so that the *SRAS* curve does not shift from $SRAS_0$ to $SRAS_1$. Equilibrium remains at E_0, and disinflation occurs with no loss in output.

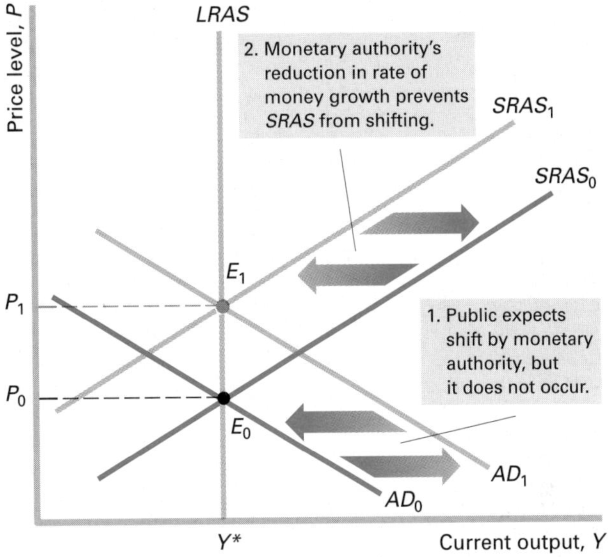

supply reduced inflation dramatically. In those cases, output losses were small, lending support to the new classical view that the costs of disinflation will be significantly less for expected reductions in money growth than for unexpected reductions.

New Keynesian Disinflation: Reducing Inflation Gradually

The cold turkey disinflation that the new classical economists recommend works best for countries that are experiencing hyperinflation because contracts in those economies tend to be indexed to changes in the price level. But can the gains of cold turkey disinflation be applied to reducing inflation in economies that have moderate inflation rates, such as the United States, Japan, and the European nations? The new Keynesians do not think so. They believe that there is always some nominal price stickiness. New Keynesian economists argue that long-term nominal contracts and the costs of changing prices slow the adjustment of the price level to changes in expectations. Even when households and businesses have rational expectations, not all prices adjust immediately to changes in expectations about future inflation.

The new Keynesians propose a different process for disinflation. Let's reconsider cold turkey disinflation in the new Keynesian view. Suppose that the economy is at full employment, with the inflation rate and growth rate of the nominal money supply at 10%. In Fig. 28.8, from initial equilibrium at E_0, the aggregate demand curve is expected to shift from AD_0 to AD_1, with the *SRAS* curve shifting from $SRAS_0$ to $SRAS_1$. Hence the public expects the new equilibrium to lie at E_1, with output Y^* and a higher price level P_1. Now suppose that the Fed decides that the rate of inflation is too high and announces that it will reduce money growth to zero to reduce the long-run inflation rate to zero. (For simplicity, we assume that long-run rates of output and velocity

Figure 28.8

New Keynesian Suggestion: Gradual Disinflation

With a built-in expected rate of inflation, the economy's equilibrium will shift from E_0 to E_1.

1. In cold turkey disinflation, the Fed announces that the growth rate of the nominal money supply will be reduced to lower inflation; the *AD* curve does not shift from AD_0 to AD_1.
2. The price level falls gradually in the short run from $SRAS_1$ to $SRAS_{1'}$.
3. Instead of shifting to E_1, the economy shifts to $E_{1'}$, with a significant output loss. Only gradually will the economy return to full employment at E_0 with a lower rate of inflation.

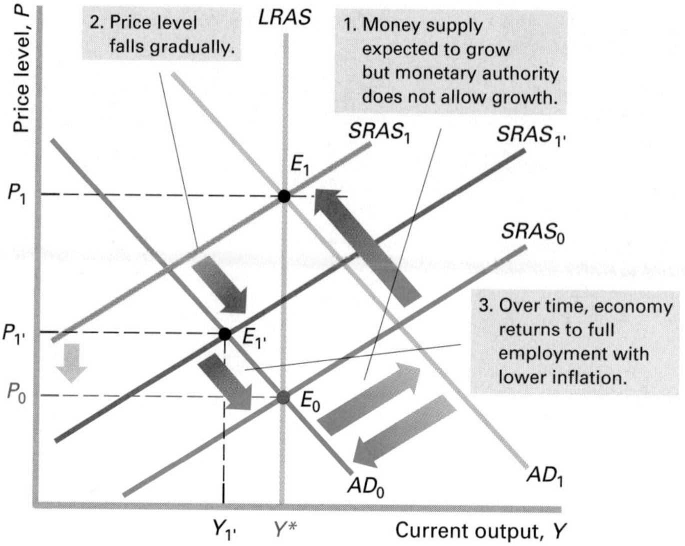

growth are zero.) As a result, instead of the aggregate demand curve shifting to AD_1, consistent with expected money growth of 10% per year, it remains at AD_0. In the short run, the *SRAS* curve shifts to $SRAS_{1'}$ because in the new Keynesian view, not all prices can change instantly. As a result, at $E_{1'}$, output falls to $Y_{1'}$. Disinflation (the price level is $P_{1'}$, lower than P_1) is accompanied by a loss of current output and jobs. Only over time does the economy return to full employment equilibrium at E_0.

Because of these costs, new Keynesian economists support a policy of **gradualism,** or slowly and steadily reducing the rate of growth of the money supply so that the inflation rate can adjust slowly, with smaller losses of output and jobs. These economists concede that gradual disinflation is slower than the cold turkey disinflation but maintain that overall costs to the economy are smaller.

CENTRAL BANK CREDIBILITY

We have shown that to achieve disinflation at a low cost, the public's expectation of the inflation rate must be reduced. This will shift the *SRAS* curve down so that lower inflation is not "paid for" by lost output and jobs. However, merely announcing a disinflationary policy might not be enough to change the public's expectations. An additional, crucial factor is **central bank credibility:** For households and businesses to respond to an announced commitment to reducing inflation, the public must believe that the central bank will, in fact, carry out its disinflationary promises. The public might not believe the central bank because disinflation entails economic costs—lost output and jobs—that are likely to be politically unpopular. If the public believes that policymakers will back off from the stated objective to reduce inflation, inflationary expectations will change very slowly until the central bank convinces the public of its credibility.

Strategies for Building Credibility

In this section, we demonstrate why a central bank that follows a credible policy can pursue a less costly strategy in reducing inflation than can a central bank that does not back up its inflation-fighting goals. We compare the actions of the Fed and the public to determine which behavior gives them the greatest possible benefits, and we consider how the Fed and the public respond to each other's actions.

We use Fig. 28.9 and assume that the economy is at full employment equilibrium at E_0, that the growth rate of real output is 0%, and that the nominal money supply and the price level are both growing at 5% each year. Accordingly, the AD curve shifts from AD_0 to AD_1 and the $SRAS$ curve shifts from $SRAS_0$ to $SRAS_1$; the public expects the economy's equilibrium to be at E_1 next year.

The Federal Reserve Board chairman wants a 0% inflation rate but doesn't want output to fall. Accordingly, in an interview with *The Wall Street Journal*, the chairman offers a bargain to firms, the gist of which is

OTHER TIMES, OTHER PLACES . . .

Central Bank Credibility in the United States and Japan

Since World War II, the U.S. Federal Reserve System has frequently stated an anti-inflation policy. During the second half of the 1970s, when inflation rose steadily, the credibility of the Fed's promise to fight inflation eroded. In October 1979, the Fed announced that it would focus on targets for the growth rates of monetary aggregates and that target ranges would be reduced significantly to reduce inflation.

The Fed experienced difficulty in achieving its targets, owing in part to deregulation and the wave of financial innovation in the early 1980s. The Fed's announced intention to combat inflation indeed succeeded over time. Inflation fell from double-digit levels in 1979 to about 4% per year by 1982 and has remained relatively low since then. In part because of the Fed's lack of credibility at that time, disinflation was not without cost, however. In response to the contractionary monetary policy that was initiated in late 1979, output and employment declined and real interest rates increased. The economy experienced a severe recession in 1981 and 1982.

Because Japan relied wholly on imported oil, the oil shocks of 1973 and 1974 led to wholesale price inflation of more than 30% by 1974. In 1975, the Bank of Japan (the Japanese central bank) announced that it would target the growth rate of the Japanese *M2* to reduce inflation. The consistency with which the Bank of Japan fulfilled its promises quickly bolstered its credibility. The central bank did in eed succeed in reducing inflation in the 1980s and did so without large losses in output and employment.

What do these episodes tell us? The experiences of the United States and Japan illustrate that a prolonged effort by the central bank to reduce the rate of growth of the nominal money supply will reduce inflation. The importance of credibility in determining the costs of disinflation is striking. On the one hand, the U.S. Federal Reserve System, with low initial credibility and a poor performance in hitting its announced money growth targets, achieved disinflation only after a recession and significant unemployment. On the other hand, the highly credible Bank of Japan managed to reduce inflation with little direct output loss. Alan Blinder of Princeton University found in a survey of economists and central bankers that credibility is believed to be the key factor in a central bank's success in achieving its goals.

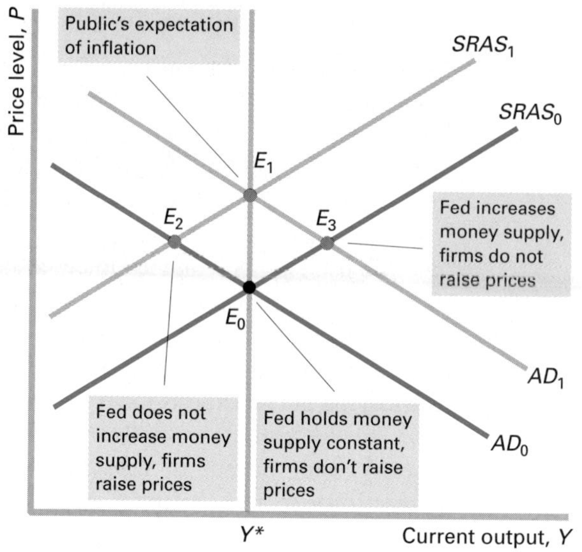

Figure 28.9

Strategies for Changing the Economy's Equilibrium

From initial full employment equilibrium at E_0, the public expects that money supply growth and the resulting increase in inflation will lead to a new equilibrium at E_1. If the Fed agrees to hold the nominal money supply constant and firms agree not to raise prices, the economy can remain at E_0, with full employment and no additional inflation. If the Fed doesn't increase the money supply but firms raise prices, output falls, as at E_2. If the Fed unexpectedly increases the nominal money supply and firms do not raise prices, output rises, as at E_3.

"You business executives don't like inflation, and the Fed doesn't either. If you don't raise prices this year, the Fed won't increase the money supply." This proposition offers some attractive benefits: If neither the nominal money supply, M, nor the price level, P, shifts, the aggregate demand curve won't shift. By announcing the proposed agreement in *The Wall Street Journal*, the Fed hopes that the short-run aggregate supply curve will not shift either. The economy will remain in equilibrium at E_0, and the Fed and businesses will avoid inflation with no loss of output.

To obtain cooperation from firms, the Fed chairman adds a threat to the offer: "If your firms increase prices anyway, the Fed will stick by its promise of no money supply growth." That would be unattractive to the public. If the nominal money supply didn't increase but prices did, the economy would come to equilibrium at E_2, making everyone worse off. Inflation would result, firms would lose output and profits, and workers would lose jobs. The public doesn't like inflation, and firms don't like output losses. Although the Fed's anti-inflation stance is clear, political pressures may be exerted on the Fed if its actions are perceived to have caused a recession.

Let's examine the payoffs for the economy from alternative actions of the Fed and firms. For simplicity, each side has two strategies: Firms can raise prices or not raise prices; the Fed can increase the nominal money supply or not increase the nominal money supply. Figure 28.10(a) represents the payoffs for the economy in each case (the equilibrium points refer to those in Fig. 28.9). The top left square represents the initial situation, with the economy at full employment and the nominal money supply and the price level expected to grow at a rate of 5% per year. If the Fed and firms accept the bargain not to raise the money supply and prices (bottom right square), the economy remains at full employment and inflation falls to zero. If firms increase prices and the Fed follows through on its threat to leave the nominal money supply unchanged (bot-

Fed \ Firms	Raise prices	Don't raise prices
Increase the money supply	$Y = Y^*$ (E_1) Inflation = 5%	$Y > Y^*$ (E_3) Inflation $<$ 5%
Don't increase the money supply	$Y < Y^*$ (E_2) Inflation $<$ 5%	$Y = Y^*$ (E_0) Inflation = 0%

(a) Payoffs for the Economy

Fed \ Firms	Raise prices		Don't raise prices	
	E_1		E_3	
	Fed	Firms	Fed	Firms
Increase the money supply	Status quo	Status quo	Better than status quo	Worse than status quo
	E_2		E_0	
	Fed	Firms	Fed	Firms
Don't increase the money supply	Worse than status quo	Worse than status quo	Better than status quo	Better than status quo

(b) Payoffs to Players

Figure 28.10

Payoffs from Alternative Actions

(The equilibrium points refer to those in Fig. 28.9.)

a. The Fed and firms would like the economy to achieve equilibrium at E_0.

b. Payoffs for the economy are the greatest at E_0. Economic equilibrium can remain at E_0 (the status quo) if firms believe that the Fed's concern with unemployment is much greater than its concern with inflation.

tom left square), inflation (though less than 5%) results, but the economy enters a recession. If firms keep their promise not to raise prices but the Fed increases the money supply anyway (top right square), short-term expansion results.

These four outcomes are the potential payoffs for the economy, but recall our assumption that the Fed and firms pursue the strategy that will give each the greatest payoff. Therefore we must consider the payoffs presented in Fig. 28.10(b). The top left square represents the status quo at which current output is at full employment.

Let's first consider the Fed's view, as indicated in the left-hand portion of each square. Because the Fed dislikes inflation, it wants firms to keep their promise not to raise prices; the "Don't raise prices" squares at the top and bottom right represent an improvement over the status quo from the Fed's perspective. Both result in full or greater than full employment and inflation that is lower than 5%. If political pressures associated with rising unemployment prevail, the top right-hand square (short-term expansion) is a good outcome from the Fed's point of view; the bottom left-hand square (a recession) is a situation to be avoided.

Now let's consider firms' decisions. Suppose that they believe that the Fed is more likely to favor a strategy to minimize the chance of a recession (even though it says that it is firmly committed to reducing inflation). In this case, firms believe that the Fed will increase the money supply. Firms then will raise prices (their best move for the Fed's expected action). As Fig. 28.10(a) shows, the result is an inflationary equilibrium.

To achieve disinflation without the costs depicted in the lower right-hand corner, the Fed's promise must be credible. If firms believe that the Fed will not increase the money supply, they will not raise prices. Central bank credibility is essential to achieving disinflation at low cost to the economy.

New classical economists believe that cold turkey disinflation not only works, but enhances the central bank's credibility. When the public observes that money growth has been sharply reduced, inflationary expectations fall quickly. However, new Keynesian economists question the credibility of the cold turkey disinflation in the real world. Whereas a cold turkey reduction in money growth will make headlines, it also will reduce output and employment substantially in the short run. As a result, political objections could force the central bank to back off. New Keynesian economists stress that a gradualist policy, by being more feasible politically, may be a more credible way to reduce inflation than the cold turkey reduction.

Appointing a "tough" central banker, then, is likely to increase the public's willingness to believe anti-inflation statements by the central bank.† A tough central banker openly dislikes inflation and is believed to be willing to tolerate higher unemployment if necessary to bring inflation down. An example is Paul Volcker, who was appointed by President Jimmy Carter in 1979. President Carter wanted to convince the public about his anti-inflation resolve by appointing Volcker. While the Volcker Fed's policies indeed reduced inflation, the economy experienced significant losses in output and employment. Hence his appointment alone did not completely relieve credibility suspicions.

Rules versus Discretion

Many economists and policymakers believe that the key to central bank credibility is the adoption of and adherence to rules. A **rules strategy** for monetary policy suggests that the central bank follow specific and publicly announced guidelines for policy. When the central bank chooses a rule, this strategy requires that it follow the rule, whatever the state of the economy. One example of a monetary policy rule is a commitment by the Fed to expand the monetary base by 5% each year, regardless of disturbances in money and financial markets or the economy. The main criterion for formulating rules, advocates suggest, is that rules should apply to variables that are significantly controllable by the Fed. An instruction to "maintain the growth rate of real GDP at 4%" is not a useful rule because the Fed has no direct control over GDP.

Economists and policymakers who oppose the rules approach support a **discretion strategy** for monetary policy, which means that the central bank should adjust monetary policy as it sees fit to achieve goals for economic growth, inflation, and other economic and financial variables. This approach

†The idea that a tough central banker may enhance central bank credibility was put forth by Kenneth Rogoff, "The Optimal Degree of Commitment to an Intermediate Monetary Target," *Quarterly Journal of Economics* 99:1169–1189, November 1985.

CONSIDER THIS . . .

Can Credibility Enhance Central Bank Flexibility?

Achieving credibility in the conduct of monetary policy brings benefits in terms of future flexibility. Once a central bank establishes a credible reputation for carrying out its promises, inflexible rules may no longer be required. The successful track record of the Bundesbank, the German central bank, in fighting inflation convinced participants in international financial markets that price stability is the Bundesbank's dominant goal. This credibility has given the bank some flexibility in responding to short-term changes such as those caused by German reunification in the early 1990s. In 1999, analysts awaited news of whether the new European Central Bank would achieve the same credibility as the Bundesbank in pursuing low inflation.

A case in which a central bank's lack of credibility led to economic problems is the Reserve Bank of New Zealand's announcement in 1989 of a policy to reduce inflation nearly to zero by 1993. To provide an incentive for success, the salary of the governor of the central bank was actually tied to the central bank's success in reducing inflation. However, the Reserve Bank of New Zealand lacked credibility because of its past behavior. Although the central bank exceeded its targets in 1991 and 1992 in bringing down inflation, the early lack of credibility gave the central bank little room to react to the decline in economic activity that began in 1990. In fact, the Reserve Bank had to pursue a contractionary monetary policy (worsening the recession) to convince the public of its commitment to lower inflation. Many economists argue that an inflation target per se is not a good substitute for central bank flexibility.

differs from the rules strategy in that it allows the Fed to change its policy to adjust to changes in the economy.

Proponents of the rules strategy argue that the central bank must commit to rules that limit its ability to adjust monetary policy to achieve short-term objectives. However, inflexible rules may be needlessly rigid and have unforeseen consequences. For example, if a rule specifying a constant rate of growth of *M1* had been in effect in the early 1980s (when deregulation and financial innovation increased the demand for money), monetary policy would have led to more contraction than the Fed intended.

Many economists believe that a middle course is desirable. They argue that rules can allow policymakers to make adjustments in policy as long as those adjustments are stated as part of the rules. For example, the Fed could decide to maintain the growth of *M2*, not at a constant rate but at a rate that would be adjusted in a predetermined manner for movements in inflation. The problem with this strategy is that it limits a central bank's discretion over monetary policy. If rules are not binding and central banks can modify their policies, the rules will not be successful. The central bank will be tempted to abandon the announced policy in favor of short-term objectives. Hence establishing a credible commitment to a rule is more important than stating a precise form of the rule (such as a specified growth rate for *M2*).

Even a modified rule isn't foolproof. The same lack of flexibility that can make a rule credible can limit the central bank's ability to respond during a financial crisis. Both new classical and new Keynesian economists agree that if the central bank avoids the temptation to intervene regularly to fine-tune the economy, its ability to respond effectively during a crisis will be enhanced. Most economists believe that the best way to achieve commitment to rules is to remove political pressures on the central bank. The idea is that when the central bank is free of political pressures, the public is more likely to believe the central bank's announcements.

Price Controls and Credibility

Political constraints may limit the central bank's willingness to follow a disinflationary policy, raising an interesting question: Wouldn't **price controls**, or official government restrictions on price changes, stop inflation?

Binding and enforced price controls can reduce increases in the price level but might not stop inflation, for two reasons. First, the mechanics of demand and supply tell us that if the price of a product is prevented from rising to equate the quantity demanded and the quantity supplied, shortages and long lines will develop. Second, and more important, if the public expects the price controls to be removed sometime in the future, inflation is suppressed, only to burst forth when controls are lifted. Price controls combined with a credible disinflationary monetary policy are more likely to reduce inflationary expectations than are price controls alone.

The U.S. experience with price controls in the early 1970s during the Nixon administration (August 1971–April 1974) bears out this conclusion. The Nixon administration and the Fed (under Chairman Arthur Burns) pursued expansionary policies during the period in which price controls were in effect. As a result, the controls reduced inflation only during that period. Robert J. Gordon of Northwestern University found that the burst of inflation between April 1974 and mid-1975 was so great that the price level was even higher than it probably would have been without the controls.[†]

[†]See Robert J. Gordon, "The Impact of Aggregate Demand on Prices," *Brookings Papers on Economic Activity*, 3:613–685, 1975.

KEY TERMS AND CONCEPTS

Cost-push inflation
Demand-pull inflation
Discretion strategy
Disinflation
  Central bank credibility
  Cold turkey
  Gradualism
  Price controls

Hyperinflation
Inflation
Menu costs
Natural rate of unemployment
Rules strategy
Shoe leather costs

Appendix
Okun's law
Phillips curve
  Expectations-augmented Phillips curve
  Simple Phillips curve

SUMMARY

1. Price level changes result from the interaction of shifts in aggregate demand and aggregate supply. Increases in the price level can be explained by factors that shift the *AD* curve or the *SRAS* curve. In particular, increases in the money supply, other increases in nominal aggregate demand, or supply shocks may lead to an increase in the price level.
2. Inflation is a sustained rate of increase in the price level. Inflation is primarily a monetary phenomenon: In both the new classical and new Keynesian views, sustained increases in the nominal money supply cause sustained inflation.
3. Both expected and unexpected inflation have economic costs. By imposing a tax on money holdings, expected inflation reduces the public's demand for real money balances. Costs of expected inflation include shoe leather costs and distortions to saving and investment that arise because the U.S. tax system is defined in nominal terms. Unexpected inflation redistributes economic resources, forcing households and businesses to spend resources on forecasting inflation. It also distorts the relative price signals for resource allocation that markets provide.
4. Monetary policy can have an inflationary bias (despite the costs of inflation) if policymakers perceive that growth in output and jobs can be achieved with higher inflation. In the long run, policymakers cannot maintain output above the full employment level without high and rising inflation.
5. Disinflation is a decrease in the economy's long-run rate of inflation. In the new classical view, disinflation can be achieved with only small losses in output if money growth is cut drastically and immediately—cold turkey disinflation. New Keynesian economists argue that prices adjust only gradually in response even to expected changes in money growth. Accordingly, they suggest a strategy of gradualism for disinflation: By reducing the rate of growth of the money supply gradually, the price level can adjust slowly, with smaller losses of output and jobs.
6. Another factor influencing the costs of disinflation is the credibility of the central bank. If the public believes that policymakers will not carry through on their disinflationary promises, inflationary expectations will change very slowly—until the central bank convinces the public of its credibility. New classical economists believe that cold turkey disinflation enhances the central bank's credibility. New Keynesian economists believe that a gradualist policy is a more credible way than the cold turkey approach to reduce inflation.

REVIEW QUESTIONS

1. How does inflation hurt people? Who gets hurt?
2. The President proposes spending an additional $100 billion on a large telescope to look for life in other galaxies. Opponents of the plan argue that this spending would be inflationary. As a presidential adviser, what would you tell the President about this argument?
3. What is the principal cause of long-term inflation?
4. According to the new classical approach, what will be the effect on the economy of an increase in the money supply that people fully anticipate?
5. What does "inflation is a tax on money balances" mean?
6. According to the new classical view, what is different about each short-run aggregate supply curve?
7. Why would you never expect the unemployment rate to be zero?
8. What are people likely to do (financially) in a hyperinflation?
9. Why did the price level increase by a factor of more than 10 billion in Germany between August 1922 and November 1923? What happened to the demand for real money balances? What brought the hyperinflation to an end?
10. How does the tax system distort financial decisions in its interaction with inflation?

THE NEW YORK TIMES JANUARY 30, 2000

Growth or Inflation?

In the summer of 1992, a pervasive gloom cast a shadow over the American economy. The unemployment rate rose to 7.8%, the worst in years. . . . And the federal budget deficit rose to its highest level ever.

A best-selling book by a prominent economist, Lester Thurow, reflected a widely held view that the United States would continue to stumble behind a vigorous Japanese economy and a unified Europe. Even President Bush, who would soon lose his job over the dismal economy, acknowledged that something was wrong.

What almost no one divined was that the American economy had already embarked on a historic expansion, one that took three more years to really bloom. And how rich that bloom now is. The expansion—an uninterrupted rise in the value of the goods and services that the nation produces—becomes the longest in history next month. . . .

What accounts for the durability of the expansion? The Internet and the spread of personal computers are high on the list, because they raise productivity. . . .

Still, new technology is by no means the only reason for the booming economy. Another is that strong profits and low-cost financing, mainly through the stock market, have resulted in record levels of corporate investment in all kinds of machinery, not just computers, and so in increased production. (a) Moreover, Asia and Latin America have become growing sources of manufactured goods, a new supply line that was particularly noticeable during the Asian financial crisis. . . .

However the expansion is finally explained, an old set of rules, deeply ingrained in economic forecasting and college textbooks, is losing its punch. . . .

That idea of the economy's limits gained an iron grip on academic theory and government policy. Unemployment could not fall below 6%, the rules had it, or labor shortages would drive up wages, then prices. In the 70s and 80s, that happened just often enough to demonstrate the theory's accuracy. Industry could no longer operate flat out, risking inflationary shortages, which also occurred often enough to be disconcerting.

So the Fed sought to slow the economy whenever it seemed to be expanding by more than 2.25% a year or so. That was considered the outer limit, an inflationary trigger point, all right for a few months or even a year, but beyond what the nation could sustain for a significant period. . . . (b)

The view of Treasury Secretary Lawrence H. Summers reflects the new consensus. "Three to 3.5%," he said in an interview, "is probably not an implausible number right now as a sustainable growth rate for the economy."

The difference may seem small, but the amount of money it represents is considerable in the giant American economy, which produces more than $9 trillion a year in goods and services. Increasing that output by Mr. Summers's new rate means an additional $345 annually for each person in the United States. That has been happening, and then some, since 1996.

Though Alan Greenspan was confirmed by the U.S. Senate for a fourth term as Chairman of the Federal Reserve Board in 2000, some legislators and businesspeople believed that the Fed under Mr. Greenspan's leadership focused too much on its goals for restraining inflation, rather than encouraging short-run economic growth. (This tension came to a head in late 2000, as some analysts warned of recessionary pressures in the U.S. economy.)

To economists, financial market participants, central bankers, and politicians, one watchword in 1999 and 2000 was "inflation"—not *actual* inflation so much; there had been no burst in wage inflation. The fear was over *expected* inflation—that an expanding U.S. economy would stimulate future inflation, leaving the Federal Reserve with the unpleasant choice between accommodating inflation on the one hand and aborting the economy's expansion on the other. To sidestep this choice, the central bank tried to be vigilant in watching for incipient signs of inflation.

a Business leaders argue implicitly that global competition makes the economy's *SRAS* curve flatter than conventionally thought, so increases in demand generate higher output with little inflationary consequences. Many economists believe that this claim is overstated. In addition, persistent expansion of demand runs the risk of the inflationary spiral and contractionary policy response described in (b).

Is there a way out of the growth versus inflation choice? Yes. Rising productivity shifts the *LRAS* curve to the left, raising full employment output and providing the opportunity for noninflationary wage increases.

b What might the Fed's logic have been in pursuing policies to hold back additional growth in demand in 1999 and 2000? Suppose the Chairman believes that the economy is roughly at full employment. Consider the *AD-AS* diagram, in which the economy starts at a full employment equilibrium at E_0, the intersection of the AD_0, $SRAS_0$, and *LRAS* curves. Now a boom in demand shifts the economy's aggregate demand curve to the right from AD_0 to AD_1, leading to a short-run increase in output from Y^* to $Y_{1'}$, and upward pressure on prices. The economy's long-run equilibrium lies at E_1, with output, Y^*, and a higher price level, P_1. In that sense, the overheating economy can be a warning of inflation to come.

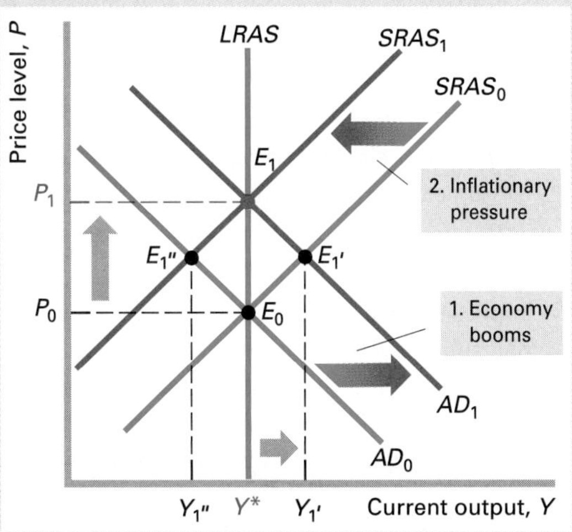

Once an inflationary spiral has begun, fairly drastic action by the Fed may be required to regain credibility with the public and financial markets. In the context of the *AD-AS* diagram, once the Fed finds itself at $E_{1'}$, it may have to pursue a contractionary monetary policy that shifts the aggregate demand curve from AD_1 to AD_0. If inflationary expectations lead to the *SRAS* curve's remaining at $SRAS_1$ instead of $SRAS_0$ following the contraction, the economy winds up at $E_{1''}$, and output, $Y_{1''}$, is less than Y^*. Only gradually, as inflation subsides, does the economy return to the full employment equilibrium E_0.

For further thought . . .

Why might the Fed be unwilling to accommodate incipient inflation even if the *SRAS* curve is relatively flat (so that some short-run gain in output is possible)?

Source: Excerpted from Louis Uchitelle, "107 Months and Counting," *The New York Times*, January 30, 2000. Copyright © 2000, by the New York Times Co. Reprinted by permission.

11. According to the new classical view, what actions should policymakers take to reduce inflation?

12. How might menu costs affect the allocation of resources in the economy when there is inflation? For what types of firms might menu costs be important?

13. Why don't new Keynesians believe in cold turkey disinflation? What do they suggest instead?

14. Why don't economists find price controls an attractive way to reduce inflation?

15. *Evaluate:* Inflation isn't necessarily a monetary phenomenon. Workers can push up wages in cost-push inflation. Increases in government spending can lead to demand-pull inflation.

16. *Evaluate:* An announced monetary contraction can reduce inflation with no loss in output in the new classical approach.

17. Why is it important to policymakers that people believe them when they say that they are going to reduce the inflation rate?

ANALYTICAL PROBLEMS

18. In a 1998 publication of the Federal Reserve Bank of St. Louis, William Dewald argued that *M2* velocity had settled down to a value of about 2. He observed that the trend growth rate of output had been about 2.5% and inflation was currently about 1.5%. He concluded: "[I]f *M2* growth continues to range from 5 to 7 percent and *M2* velocity [stays around 2], the inflation trend would accelerate by 1 to 3 percentage points. . . . It is such arithmetic that has some economists worried about inflation rising again." Explain the author's arithmetic. Be as specific as possible in explaining why he believes inflation may accelerate by 1 to 3 percentage points.

19. Some economic historians have argued that one source of discontent among farmers in the United States during the late nineteenth century was that they were debtors at a time of falling prices. Other economic historians have argued that deflation should not have been a problem for farmers, because it went on for several decades. Evaluate these views, being sure to discuss under what circumstances debtors are hurt by deflation.

20. Describe what happens in both the short and long run in the new Keynesian view when the Fed reduces the money supply unexpectedly.

21. If the Fed wanted to reduce the inflation rate, why might a coordinated fiscal policy move to reduce the federal budget deficit help to reduce the costs of disinflation? How would the credibility of such a move be aided by such coordination between fiscal and monetary policies?

22. Suppose that the economy initially is in equilibrium at full employment. Then the government unexpectedly increases income taxes. What are the effects on output and the price level in the short and long run, according to the new classical view?

23. Suppose that the economy initially is at a point at which output exceeds the full employment level of output. In the new Keynesian view, what could the Fed do to restore equilibrium at the full employment level of output? (Use the aggregate demand–aggregate supply diagram.) What would happen in the long run if the Fed didn't do anything?

24. Suppose that Ms. A is in the 50% tax bracket. When inflation is zero, she earns a nominal return (before taxes) of 4%. Suppose that inflation rises to 10% and that the nominal return (before taxes) rises to 14%. What is Ms. A's after-tax real return when inflation is zero? When inflation is 10%?

25. In the new classical view, can optimism among consumers be self-fulfilling? Use the aggregate demand–aggregate supply model to show why or why not.

26. Suppose that monetary policymakers take actions that shift the *AD* curve so that it intersects both the *SRAS* curve and the *LRAS* curve to maintain full employment. What would happen to the economy if the true *LRAS* curve were to the left of where the policymakers perceived it to be?

27. What should money growth be if real output grows 3% per year, velocity grows 2% per year, and the

Fed wants inflation to be 4% per year? What should it be if the Fed targets zero inflation?

28. Would it be a good idea to pass a law that requires the Fed to keep money supply growth below 5% each year? Why or why not?

29. Suppose that the nominal interest rate is 8% and that expected inflation is 5%. What is the expected real rate of return? Calculate the actual real rate of return for each of the following cases, and state whether lenders or borrowers are better off than they expected to be.
    a. Actual inflation is 10%.
    b. Actual inflation is 0%.
    c. Actual inflation is 5%.

30. The Federal Reserve Board chairman announces a policy of keeping short-term interest rates low. The financial press criticizes the policy as inflationary. Why?

31. Is it possible for policymakers to trade off more inflation for higher output in the short run? In the long run? In your answer, explain the differences in the new classical and new Keynesian views.

32. At a meeting with his cabinet, the President decides that the country's inflation rate of 15% is too high. The central bank is independent of the administration and announces that it will maintain the rate of money growth at current levels. The President imposes price controls, outlawing all increases in wages or prices.
    a. Using the new Keynesian view, illustrate the effects of the price controls on output and the price level. (Assume that firms have a maximum capacity for production; that is, output can't exceed production capacity.)
    b. Having kept inflation at bay for two years, the President hands out "Inflation: Rest in Peace" buttons and removes the controls. Use the aggregate demand–aggregate supply analysis to illustrate the effects on the economy. Do these effects necessarily accompany the removal of price controls? Why or why not?

33. Suppose that the Fed gets new information suggesting that the aggregate demand curve has shifted to the left but that the public doesn't have this information. Using the new classical view, what will happen to output and inflation if the Fed does nothing? What will happen to the price level if it uses expansionary policy to offset the shock and stabilize output?

34. Milton Friedman argued in 1968 that there was no permanent trade-off between unemployment and inflation. Demonstrate what would happen in both the new classical and new Keynesian views if the Fed continuously attempted to keep output above its full employment level.

35. Suppose that the Fed believes that the new classical view is correct and tries cold turkey disinflation to reduce inflation from 10% to 0%. What happens to the economy (output, unemployment rate, and inflation rate) if, in fact, the new Keynesian view is the correct one?

36. Germany experienced a hyperinflation during the early 1920s. In early 1971 under the Bretton Woods system West Germany was committed to maintaining a fixed exchange rate between the mark and the dollar. Many speculators believed that this exchange rate left the mark undervalued versus the dollar and they believed that Germany's inflation history made it unlikely that the West German central bank would be willing to defend the fixed exchange rate indefinitely. Explain the reasoning of these speculators.

DATA QUESTIONS

37. In the latest *Economic Report of the President*, look up data on the consumer price index for the past 11 years. Calculate the inflation rate for the past 10 years from the index levels. Has the inflation rate been declining or rising? What do you think have been the major factors causing this movement in the inflation rate?

38. Look in the latest *Economic Report of the President* for data on the percentage change in the consumer price index and producer price index from December of any one year to December of the following year, and compare these two measures of the inflation rate. Could you use one to predict the other? Why or why not?

APPENDIX: Inflation versus Unemployment: The Phillips Curve

If there are costs to inflation, why is it tolerated? Virtually everyone feels the pinch of rising prices, so policymakers have reason to worry about inflation: It is a real economic problem, and it angers voters. However, another issue concerns voters: unemployment. Workers fear losing a job and the income that it represents. News stories sometimes cite the *misery index*, the sum of the inflation rate and the unemployment rate, as a measure of economic distress.

Inflation and Unemployment

Why should we think about inflation and unemployment *together*? In an influential article, A. W. Phillips analyzed data on British inflation and unemployment rates from 1861 to 1957 and reported a statistical regularity, which quickly was dubbed the **Phillips curve**. The unemployment rate tended to be high when the inflation rate was low, and vice versa.† This finding raised a tantalizing possibility: Could a policymaker choose between inflation and unemployment (depending on the relative social concern over the two problems), tolerating a higher value of one to obtain a lower value of the other? Exploiting this trade-off, U.S. economic policy in the 1960s favored a steadily declining unemployment rate accompanied by a gradually increasing inflation rate. Events of the 1970s and since fundamentally changed this relationship.

To analyze whether there is a trade-off between inflation and unemployment, we need to examine the relationships between (1) output changes and the unemployment rate and (2) price adjustment and output changes. As we consider these relationships, note that analysis of an inflation-unemployment trade-off follows closely the development of the aggregate demand–aggregate supply model.

Output Changes and the Unemployment Rate

How responsive is the unemployment rate to changes in output? **Okun's law,** a statistical relationship between changes in output, Y, and the unemployment rate, u, provides a widely cited answer.

We begin our explanation of Okun's law by defining the natural rate of unemployment, u^*, as the rate of unemployment that exists when the economy produces the full employment level of output, Y^*. This unemployment rate is not zero. (Recall that even at the full employment output level, unemployment exists because of structural or frictional unemployment.) The late Arthur Okun, chairman of the Council of Economic Advisers under President Lyndon

† A. W. Phillips, "The Relationship Between Unemployment and the Rate of Change of Money Wage Rates in the United Kingdom, 1861–1957," *Economica*, 283–299, 1958. Phillips's study focused specifically on *wage* inflation.

Johnson, found that the unemployment rate increased whenever actual output is less than full employment output, or

$$\frac{Y - Y^*}{Y^*} = 2.5(u - u^*).$$

In other words, the gap between actual and full employment output rises by 2.5 percentage points for each percentage-point increase in the unemployment rate. Okun's law enables us to discuss changes in the unemployment rate in terms of particular changes in actual output.†

We can now trace the potential relationship between unemployment and inflation depicted in Fig. 28A.1. When the unemployment rate equals the natural rate, actual output and full employment output are equal. When the unemployment rate is above the natural rate, actual current output is below full employment output. When the unemployment rate is below the natural rate (the portion of the Phillips curve above the line for 0% inflation), actual current output exceeds the full employment level.

In this chapter, we showed that output changes and inflation are connected by the process of price adjustment. When actual and full employment output are equal, there is no pressure for inflation to change. When actual output exceeds full employment output, the inflation rate increases; and when actual output is less than the full employment level, the inflation rate declines.

Linking Okun's law and the process of price adjustment yields a negative relationship between inflation, π, and the unemployment rate, u:

$$\pi = -h(u - u^*), \tag{28A.1}$$

where $h > 0$ indicates the extent to which the inflation rate is associated with the deviation of the actual unemployment rate from the natural rate of unemployment. The relationship in Eq. (28A.1) is known as the **simple Phillips curve**, where inflation is positive when $u < u^*$ and negative when $u > u^*$, as plotted in Fig. 28A.1.

The well-defined, negatively sloped simple Phillips curve disappeared in the 1970s. This result had been anticipated in the late 1960s when various economists stressed the importance of distinguishing between expected and unexpected inflation in assessing a trade-off between output and inflation. Whether monetary policy can exploit such a trade-off between inflation and unemployment rates as is suggested by the simple Phillips curve depends on whether money supply changes are expected or unexpected. Nobel laureate Milton Friedman now of Stanford University and Edmund Phelps of Columbia

†Okun actually estimated that each percentage-point increase in the unemployment rate raised the output gap by 3.0 percentage points, but more recent research suggests that the coefficient is closer to 2.5. See Arthur M. Okun, "Potential GNP: Its Measurement and Significance," reprinted in Arthur M. Okun, *The Political Economy of Prosperity.* Washington, D.C.: The Brookings Institution, 1970, pp. 132–145.

Figure 28A.1

The Simple Phillips Curve

The simple Phillips curve shows the relationship between unemployment and inflation for a constant natural rate of unemployment. When the unemployment rate equals the natural rate, u^*, the rate of inflation, π, equals zero.

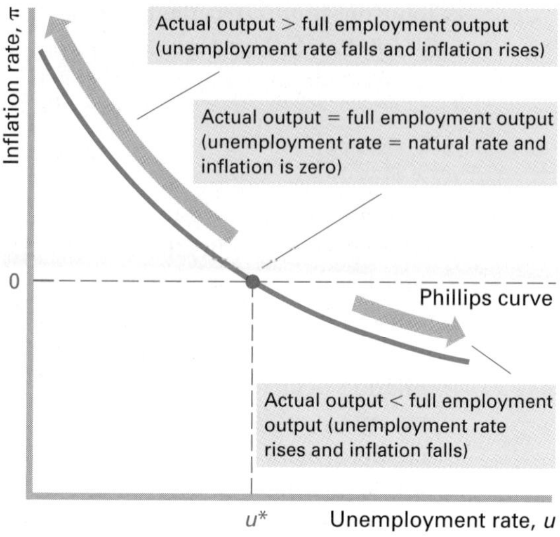

University argued that only the portion of inflation that is *unexpected* (and not the total rate of inflation) could affect output. The essence of the Friedman–Phelps argument is that there is no long-run trade-off between output and inflation.

We use the new classical view to determine whether there is a trade-off between output and expected inflation. (Results from the new Keynesian view are qualitatively similar.) Suppose that the economy is at full employment (with no growth in output) but with an ongoing expected rate of inflation and money growth of 5% each year; that is, the aggregate demand curve shifts upward each year, as Fig. 28A.2 shows.

The long-run aggregate supply curve for any year is represented by the full employment level of output. What about the short-run aggregate supply curve? Because households and businesses expect the money supply growth, they expect the price level to increase each year. Hence the short-run aggregate supply curve shifts to the left and the economy's full employment equilibrium shifts from E_0 to E_1 in any year. Output doesn't change, but the price level increases in response to the expected increase in the money supply.

Now suppose that the rate of the money supply increases unexpectedly. Instead of growing at 5% per year, the money supply unexpectedly grows by 10%. Because a 5% rate of money growth and inflation had been expected, the aggregate demand and short-run aggregate supply curves should have shifted from AD_0 and $SRAS_0$ to AD_1 and $SRAS_1$, respectively. In that case, the price level rises from P_0 to P_1, and the economy is in equilibrium at E_1. However, because money growth was higher than expected, the economy's equilibrium lies at the intersection of $SRAS_1$ (conditional on an expected rate of inflation of 5%) and AD_2 (representing an increase in money growth of 10%), at point $E_{1'}$. Output is higher than the full employment level ($Y_1 > Y^*$), and the price level

Figure 28A.2

Expected and Unexpected Inflation and Output Changes

1. At E_0, the economy is at full employment. The public expects an inflation rate of 5% because it expects the Fed to increase the money supply by 5%, thereby shifting the *AD* curve from AD_0 to AD_1. The increase in the expected price level shifts the *SRAS* curve from $SRAS_0$ to $SRAS_1$. As a result, the economy is expected to achieve equilibrium at E_1, at full employment but at a higher price level, P_1.

2. With unexpected money growth, the *AD* curve shifts to AD_2. The *SRAS* curve remains at $SRAS_1$, as expected inflation was only 5%. As a result, output increases in the short run; the short-run equilibrium lies at $E_{1'}$.

3. Over time, the price level increases so that the long-run equilibrium lies at E_2. The unexpected increases in the money supply and inflation have no effect on output in the long run.

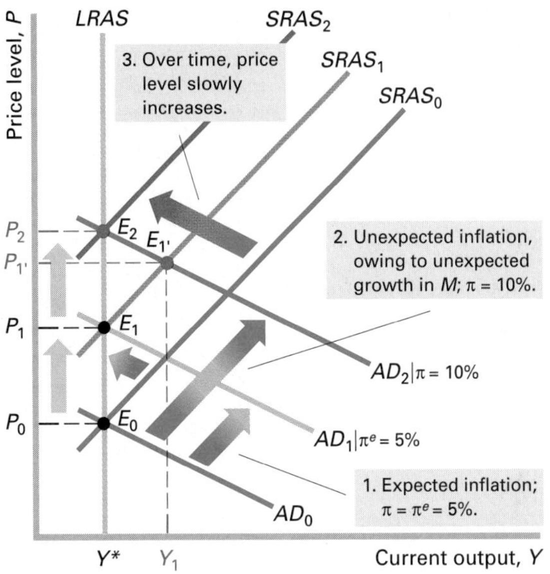

rises by more than 5% (at $P_{1'}$) but less than 10% (at P_2) in the short run. In the long run, as producers realize that the equilibrium aggregate price level is higher, prices rise and the economy's equilibrium is characterized by full employment output and a higher price level (reflecting inflation of 10%), at E_2.

Therefore output increases in response only to *unexpected* inflation. If we connect output and the unemployment rate through the relationships of Okun's law, we obtain a revised relationship between the inflation and unemployment rates:

$$\pi = \pi^e - h(u - u^*), \tag{28A.2}$$

where π^e is the expected rate of inflation. The fundamental contribution of Friedman and Phelps yields an **expectations-augmented Phillips curve,** in which the simple Phillips curve is combined with expected inflation. If the expected rate of inflation were zero, the expectations-augmented Phillips curve and the simple Phillips curve would be identical.

For any expected rate of inflation, a Phillips curve (a relationship between inflation and unemployment rates) exists. However, if expected inflation changes over time, as it did in the 1970s and 1980s, the simple Phillips curve relationship isn't stable.

The expectations-augmented Phillips curve suggests an important difference between short-term and long-term trade-offs between inflation and unemployment rates. The *short-run Phillips curve* describes the relationship between the inflation and unemployment rates, as Fig. 28A.3 shows. The short-run Phillips curve suggests a trade-off only between the unemployment rate and *unexpected* inflation.

Figure 28A.3

Output, Unemployment, and Inflation in the Expectations-Augmented Phillips Curve

For any expected inflation rate, the short-run expectations-augmented Phillips curve slopes downward. An increase in expected inflation shifts the short-run Phillips curve upward. A decrease in expected inflation shifts the short-run Phillips curve downward.

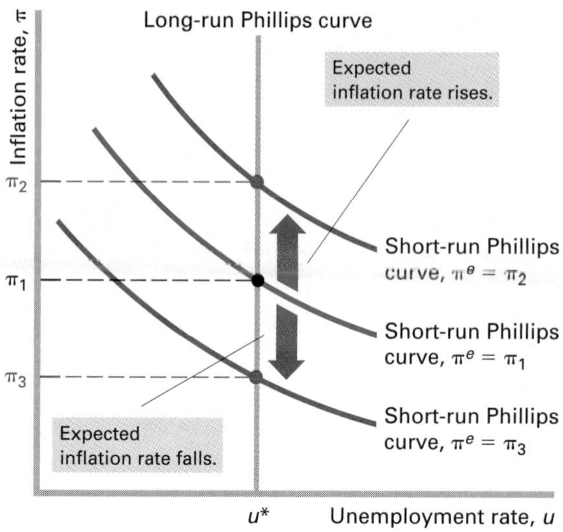

If expected inflation changes, the short-run Phillips curve shifts. An increase in expected inflation from π_1 to π_2 shifts the short-run Phillips curve upward. A decrease in expected inflation from π_1 to π_3 shifts the short-run Phillips curve downward. Hence the point that is raised by Friedman and Phelps is that any observed relationship between the unemployment rate and the actual inflation rate will change over time as the expected inflation rate changes. As a result, actual inflation can be high even when the unemployment rate is higher than the natural rate.

The Long-Run Phillips Curve

Both new classical and new Keynesian economists agree that policymakers cannot maintain an unemployment rate that is below the natural rate without permanently maintaining a high rate of inflation. Over time, rational expectations of the inflation rate will equal the actual rate, on average. That is, expected inflation π^e equals actual inflation π. Hence, for the expressions represented by the expectations-augmented Phillips curve, u must equal u^* in the long run. Then, as Fig. 28A.3 shows, the long-run Phillips curve is vertical.

With a vertical long-run Phillips curve, changes in the nominal money supply cannot affect output or the unemployment rate in the long run. In other words, money is neutral in the long run, as we demonstrated in the aggregate demand–aggregate supply analysis. This proposition is common to both the new classical and new Keynesian models.

Trade-off Exploitation in the Short Run

Both new classical and new Keynesian economists stress that the long-run Phillips curve is vertical: There is no trade-off between inflation and unemployment rates in the long run. New classical economists also question whether policymakers can exploit a trade-off between inflation and unemployment rates even in the short run. In the new classical view, households and businesses have rational expectations. They learn over time about the behavior of the Fed, the President, and Congress—and they will anticipate changes in policy in reaction to economic events. As long as the public expects changes in policy, those changes will have no real effects (on output or the unemployment rate). Expectations of policy shifts will be correct on average, so unexpected inflation will be zero on average. Because unexpected inflation cannot be created repeatedly, the Phillips curve doesn't offer a short-run trade-off for policymakers in the new classical view.

New Keynesian economists agree that rational expectations on the part of the public limit the short-run trade-off offered by the Phillips curve. However, in the new Keynesian view, the expected inflation is the forecast made at the time sticky prices are set. If actual inflation exceeds expected inflation, inflationary expectations adjust gradually in the aggregate. As a result, the unemployment rate can exceed the natural rate for a period of time. Nevertheless, many new Keynesian economists believe that policymakers should limit their attempts to exploit a short-run trade-off between inflation and unemployment rates to enhance the long-run credibility of policy.

If the new classical and new Keynesian views do not suggest important reductions in unemployment from unexpected inflation, why might policymakers be tempted to allow inflation? One possibility in the new Keynesian view is that exploiting a short-run trade-off can have political payoffs for policymakers, as we discussed in the chapter.

Glossary

Accommodating policy Actions to stimulate aggregate demand to restore output and jobs, but at the cost of greater inflation. (28)

Adverse selection The problem of distinguishing good-risk applicants from bad-risk applicants before making a loan or providing insurance. (11, 12)

Agency office A foreign bank office in the United States that cannot take deposits from U.S. residents, although it can transfer funds from abroad to the United States and make loans in the United States. (16)

Agents Managers who control (but do not own) the assets of a firm or organization. (11)

Aggregate demand The sum of demands for an economy's goods and services for consumption, investment, government purchases (not including transfer payments), and net exports. (25)

Aggregate demand (*AD*) curve The graph of the relationship between the aggregate demand for goods and services and the aggregate price level. (25)

Aggregate supply The total amount of output that producers in the economy are willing to supply and sell at a given price level. (25)

Aggregate supply (*AS*) curve The graph of the relationship between the aggregate output that firms in the economy are willing to supply and the aggregate price level. (25)

Announcement effect A signal to financial markets by the Fed of its policy intentions through changes in the discount rate. (20)

Appreciation An increase in the value of a currency against another currency. (8, 22)

Asset A thing of value that can be owned; a use of funds and a claim on a borrower's income. (2, 3)

Asymmetric information A condition that occurs when borrowers have some information about their opportunities or activities that they do not disclose to lenders, creditors, or insurers. (3, 11)

Auction market A secondary financial market in which prices are set by competitive bidding by a large number of traders acting on behalf of individual buyers and sellers. (3)

Automated teller machines Electronic devices for performing banking transactions. (2, 13)

Balance-of-payments accounts An accounting device for measuring private and government flows of funds between a country and foreign countries. (22)

Balance sheet A statement showing an individual's or firm's financial position at a point in time. It lists assets, liabilities, and net worth. (13)

Balance sheet channel A description of ways in which interest rate changes from monetary policy affect borrowers' net worth and spending decisions. (27)

Bank A financial institution that accepts deposits from savers and makes loans to borrowers. (12, 13)

Bank assets Cash items and funds used in securities investments, loans, and other asset holdings by the bank. (13)

Bank failure A situation in which a bank cannot pay its depositors in full and still have enough reserves to meet its reserve requirements. (13)

Bank holding company A large firm that holds many different banks as subsidiaries. It was originally used by banks to get around branching restrictions. (14)

Bank lending channel A description of ways in which monetary policy influences spending decisions of bank-dependent borrowers. (27)

Bank liabilities Funds acquired by the bank from savers. (13)

Bank net worth The excess of the value of bank assets over the value of bank liabilities. (13)

Bank reserves The sum of an institution's vault cash and deposits with the central bank. (13)

Bank run A sequence of events in which depositors lose confidence in a bank, for real or imagined reasons, and make withdrawals, exhausting the bank's liquid funds. (14)

Bankers' acceptances Time drafts that establish credit between parties who do not know each other, facilitating international trade. (3, 16)

Banking panics Waves of severe bank runs that cause contractions in credit availability, often culminating in business recessions. (14)

Barter The exchange of goods and services by trading output directly with one another. (2)

Basis risk The imperfect correlation of changes in the

price of a hedged instrument and changes in the price of the instrument actually traded in the futures market. (9)

Beta A measure of the response of a security's expected return to changes in the value of the market portfolio. (5)

Board of Governors The Board of the Federal Reserve System, made up of seven members, appointed by the President, who administer monetary policy and set the discount rate. (19)

Bond rating A single statistic summarizing the assessment of a firm's net worth, cash flow, and prospects—in short, its likely ability to meet its debt obligations. (7)

Borrowed reserves (*BR*, discount loans) A component of the monetary base consisting of reserves borrowed from the central bank. (17)

Borrowers Demanders of funds for consumer durables, houses, and business plant and equipment. (3)

Borrowings Nondeposit liabilities of a bank, including short-term loans in the federal funds market, loans from the bank's affiliates, and discount loans. (13)

Branches Individual banking offices in different locations owned by the same banking firm. (13, 14)

Branching restrictions Geographical limitations on banking firms' ability to open more than one office, or branch. (14)

Bretton Woods system A fixed exchange rate system that permitted smoother short-term economic adjustments than were possible under the gold standard, based on the convertibility of U.S. dollars into gold at a price of $35.00 per ounce. (22)

Brokered deposits A financial innovation in which a depositor with an amount to invest over the deposit insurance limit goes to a broker who buys certificates of deposit in different banks, giving the depositor insurance on the entire amount. (15)

Brokers Individuals who earn commissions by matching buyers and sellers in a particular market. (12)

Bubble A situation in which the price of an asset is more than its fundamental value. (10)

Budget deficit The excess of government spending over tax revenue. (5, 18)

Business cycle The periodic fluctuations in aggregate output, consisting of expansion (a boom) followed by contraction (a recession). (1, 26)

Call option The right to buy an underlying asset, which is obtained by the buyer of the call option. Sellers have an obligation to sell. (10)

Call report Periodic report filed by a U.S. bank with regulatory authorities, describing its earnings, assets and liabilities, and operations. (14)

CAMELS rating system Bank examination grade in the United States in the form of C (capital adequacy), A (asset quality), M (management), E (earnings), L (liquidity), and S (sensitivity to market risk). (14)

Capital account The balance-of-payments account that measures trade in existing assets among countries. (22)

Capital account balance A country's capital inflows minus its capital outflows. (22)

Capital controls Government-imposed barriers to foreign savers' investing in domestic assets or to domestic savers' investing in foreign assets. (22)

Capital inflow The flow of funds into a country to buy domestic assets. (22)

Capital markets Financial markets for trading debt instruments with a maturity greater than one year and equity instruments. (3)

Capital outflow The flow of funds from a country to buy foreign assets. (22)

Cash markets Markets in which actual claims are bought and sold with immediate settlement. (3)

Central bank A special governmental or quasi-governmental institution within the financial system that regulates the medium of exchange. (2)

Central bank credibility The belief by the public that central bank announcements reflect its true policy intentions. (28)

Certificate of deposit (CD) A fixed-maturity instrument, sold by a bank to depositors, that pays principal and interest at maturity, with a penalty for early withdrawal. (3)

Checkable deposits Accounts that grant a depositor the right to write checks to individuals, firms, or the government. (13)

Checks Promises to pay definitive money on demand; checks are drawn on funds deposited with a financial institution. (2)

Circuit breakers Interventions that are designed to restore orderly securities markets. (10)

Closed economy An economy of a country that neither borrows from nor lends to foreign countries. (5)

Closed-end mutual fund A fund that sells a fixed number of nonredeemable shares, which are then traded over-the-counter like common stock. The price fluctuates with the value of the underlying assets. (12)

Coinsurance An insurance option that requires the policyholder to pay a certain fraction of the costs of a claim, in addition to the deductible. (12)

Cold turkey Reducing inflation all at once, rather than gradually. (28)

Collateral Assets that are pledged to pay for a loan in the event of default on the loan. (11, 13)

Commercial bank(s) The largest group of depository institutions, which offer risk-sharing, liquidity (checking accounts), and information services that benefit savers and borrowers. (3, 12, 13)

Commercial bank loan A loan to businesses or consumers that is made by banks and financial companies. (3)

Commercial paper A liquid, short-term investment for savers that is used by high-quality, well-known firms and financial institutions to raise funds. (3, 13)

Commodity money Physical goods (particularly precious metals) that are used as the medium of exchange. (2)

Compensating balance A required minimum amount in a checking account that is used as a form of collateral in commercial loans. (13)

Compounding Earning interest on interest as savings are accumulated over a period of time. (4)

Consol A (perpetual) coupon bond with an infinite maturity; its price is based on the present value of the coupon payments. (4)

Consumer price index (CPI) An index of prices of a marketbasket of goods purchased by urban consumers. It is a commonly used measure of inflation. (2, 28)

Contagion The spreading of bad news about one bank to other banks. (14)

Contractual saving institutions Financial institutions (insurance companies and pension funds) that allow individuals to transfer risk of financial hardship and accumulate funds for retirement. (12)

Corporate bonds Intermediate and long-term obligations issued by large, high-quality corporations to finance plant and equipment spending. (3, 7)

Corporate control A contest for ownership and control of a firm that pits shareholders against managers in an effort to direct the firm's resources to their highest-valued use. (11)

Corporate restructuring firms Investors that raise equity capital to acquire shares in other firms to reduce free-rider problems and moral hazard. (11)

Cost-push inflation Price increases resulting from workers' pressure for higher wages. (28)

Coupon bond A credit market instrument that requires multiple payments of interest on a regular basis, such as semiannually or annually, and a payment of the face value at maturity. (4)

Coupon rate An interest rate equal to the yearly coupon payment divided by the face value. (4)

Credit controls Regulatory restrictions on bank lending. (27)

Credit crunch A decline in either the ability or the willingness of banks to lend at any given interest rate. (14, 26, 27)

Credit derivative Swap contract allowing the user to exchange credit risk without having to exchange the underlying asset. (9)

Credit market instruments Methods of financing debt, including simple loans, discount bonds, coupon bonds, and fixed payment loans. (4)

Credit rationing The restricting of credit by lenders such that borrowers cannot obtain the funds they desire at the given interest rate. (11, 13)

Credit risk (default risk) The probability that a borrower will not pay in full promised interest, principal, or both. This characteristic of a credit market instrument influences its interest rate. (7, 13)

Credit-risk analysis The examination of a borrower's likelihood of repayment and general business conditions that might influence the borrower's ability to repay the loan. (13)

Credit union A financial intermediary that takes deposits from and makes loans to individuals who work at the same firm or in the same industry. (12)

Crowding out The reduction in private consumption and investment that accompanies an increase in government purchases in a closed economy. (24)

Currency A type of money, such as dollar bills and coins. (2)

Currency in circulation Federal Reserve Notes (official currency) held by the nonbank public. (17)

Currency–deposit ratio The relationship of currency, C, held by the nonbank public to checkable deposits, D. (17)

Currency premium A number that indicates investors' collective preference for financial instruments denominated in one currency relative to those denominated in another. (8, 22)

Currency swap An exchange of expected future returns on debt instruments denominated in different currencies. (16)

Current account A balance-of-payment account that summarizes transactions among countries for purchases and sales of currently produced goods and services. (22)

Current account balance The sum for a country of the trade balance, services balance, net investment income, and unilateral transfers. (22)

Current output The output of goods and services produced in the economy in the immediate period. (24)

Current yield The coupon payment divided by the current price of a bond. (4)

Day traders Individuals trading stocks on-line. (12)

Dealers Individuals who hold inventories of securities and sell them for a price higher than they paid for them, earning the spread between the bid and the asked price. (12)

Debt A claim that requires a borrower to repay the amount borrowed (the principal) plus a rental fee (interest). (3)

Debt deflation A decrease in prices that raises the real value of households' and firms' outstanding debt, reducing their net worth and their ability to finance desired spending. (11, 27)

Deductible A specified amount to be subtracted from a policyholder's loss when a claim is paid by the insurance company. (12)

Default The inability to repay all or part of an obligation. (3)

Default risk (credit risk) The probability that a borrower will not pay in full promised interest, principal, or both. This characteristic of a credit market instrument influences its interest rate. (7)

Default-risk-free instruments Securities that guarantee that principal and interest will be repaid in nominal terms. For example, U.S. Treasury securities are default-risk-free. (7)

Default swap Bilateral contract in which the hedger pays a periodic fee in return for a contingent payment by a speculator following a credit event, which could be triggered by a bankruptcy or default by a reference entity. (9)

Defensive transactions Open market transactions used by the Fed to offset fluctuations in the monetary base arising from disturbances in portfolio preferences of banks and the nonbank public, financial markets, and the economy. (20)

Defined benefit pension plan A common pension plan in which the employee is promised an assigned benefit based on earnings and years of service, and payments may or may not be indexed for inflation. (12)

Defined contribution pension plan A pension plan in which contributions are invested for employees, who own the value of the funds in the plan. (12)

Definitive money Money that does not have to be converted into a more basic medium of exchange, such as gold or silver. (2)

Deflation A condition in which falling prices cause a given amount of money to purchase more goods and services. (2)

Demand deposit An account against which checks convertible to currency can be written. (13)

Demand for money A decision by the public concerning how much of its wealth to hold in money balances, which is affected by current and anticipated future changes in output. (23, 26)

Demand-pull inflation Price increases resulting from policymakers' attempts to increase aggregate demand for current output above the full employment level. (28)

Depository institutions Commercial banks, savings and loan institutions, mutual savings banks, and credit unions that accept deposits and make loans, acting as intermediaries in the saving-investment process. (3, 12)

Depository Institutions Deregulation and Monetary Control Act of 1980 (DIDMCA) Regulatory reform eliminating interest rate ceilings, providing for uniform reserve requirements, and broadening the scope of permissible activities by S&Ls. (15)

Depreciation A decrease in a currency's value against another currency. (8, 22)

Derivative instrument An asset, such as a futures or option contract, that derives its economic value from an underlying asset such as a stock or bond. (9)

Derivative market Markets in which such claims as futures or option contracts—that derive their economic value from an underlying asset such as a stock or bond—are traded. (9)

Determinants of portfolio choice The key factors affecting a saver's portfolio allocation of assets. They are a saver's wealth, expectations of return on assets, degree of risk of assets, liquidity of assets, and the cost of acquiring information about assets. (5)

Devaluation The lowering of the official value of a country's currency relative to other currencies, thereby resetting the exchange rate. (22)

Direct finance A form of financing wherein an individual saver holds financial claims issued directly by an individual borrower. (3)

Discount bond A credit market instrument in which the borrower repays the amount of the loan in a single payment at maturity but receives less than the face value initially. (4)

Discount loan A loan made by the Federal Reserve System (central bank) to a member bank. (14, 17)

Discount policy The oldest of the Federal Reserve's principal tools for regulating the money supply. It includes setting the discount rate and terms of discount lending. (20)

Discount rate The interest rate specified by the Fed for loans to depository institutions. (17)

Discount window The means by which the Fed makes discount loans to banks, serving as a channel for meeting the liquidity needs of banks. (20)

Discretion strategy An attempt by the central bank to adjust monetary policy as it sees fit to achieve its goals. (28)

Disinflation A policy-induced decline in long-run inflation. (28)

Disintermediation An exit of savers and borrowers from banks to financial markets. (15)

Diversification Splitting wealth among many different assets to reduce risk. (3, 5)

Dividends Periodic payments (usually once each quarter) that owners of equities generally receive from the firm. (3)

Dual banking system The system in the United States in which banks are chartered by either the federal government or a state government. (14)

Duration For an asset or liability, the responsiveness of the percentage change in the asset's or liability's market value to a percentage change in the market interest rate. (13)

Duration gap A bank's exposure to fluctuations in interest rates, measured as the difference between the average duration for bank assets and the average duration for bank liabilities. (13)

Dynamic transactions Open market operations aimed at achieving desired changes in monetary policy indicated by the Federal Open Market Committee. (20)

Economic growth A goal of monetary policy, seeking increases in the economy's output of goods and services over time. (21)

Economies of scale A fall in the transactions costs per dollar of investment as the size of the transactions increases. (11)

Edge Act corporations Special subsidiaries of U.S. banks that conduct only international banking services, as provided in the Edge Act of 1919. (16)

Efficient financial market A market in which all information that is available to market participants is reflected in market prices. (10)

Efficient markets hypothesis A proposition that applies rational expectations to the pricing of assets. It says that when traders and investors use all available information in forming expectations of future rates of return and the cost of trading is low, the equilibrium price of the security is equal to the optimal forecast of fundamental value based on the available information. (10)

Electronic cash (e-cash) Digital cash employed to buy goods and services on the Internet. (2)

Electronic communications network (ECN) An automated trading system that disseminates orders to third parties and dealers and can execute such orders within the network itself. (12)

Electronic funds transfer systems Computerized payment clearing devices, such as debit cards and automated teller machines. (2)

Electronic money (e-money) Money stored electronically on cards or computer accounts. (2)

Equation of exchange An equation stating that the quantity of money times the velocity of money equals nominal spending in the economy. (23)

Equilibrium real interest rate The interest rate at which desired lending and desired borrowing are equal. It is determined by the intersection of the demand curve and the supply curve for loanable funds in a closed economy. (6)

Equity A claim to a share in the profits and assets of a firm. (3)

E-trading Trading financial instruments via computerized systems as opposed to using the floor of an exchange. (12)

Eurobonds Obligations that are denominated in a currency other than that of the country where they are sold, usually in U.S. dollars. (3)

Eurocurrency deposits Time deposits that are denominated in a currency other than that of the issuing domestic financial center (for instance, dollar deposits at a French bank). (16)

Eurodollars A deposit denominated in dollars in a bank or bank branch outside the United States. (3, 16)

Euromarkets Relatively unregulated banking centers in which funds are raised in a currency other than that of the issuing domestic financial center. (16)

European Central Bank A European-wide monetary institution that has been proposed to conduct monetary policy and control a single currency. (22)

European Monetary System A monetary agreement by a number of EC nations to limit exchange rate fluctuations. (22)

European monetary union A plan drafted as part of the 1992 single European market initiative, in which exchange rates are fixed (as of 1999), ultimately by using a common currency. (22)

Excess reserves Reserves that depository institutions elect to hold that are greater than the reserves required by the Fed. (13, 17)

Exchange rate The price of one country's currency in terms of another, such as yen per dollar or francs per pound. (1, 8)

Exchange rate mechanism A device used by a group of EU nations to limit fluctuations in the values of their currencies relative to one another. (22)

Exchange rate regime A system of adjusting currency values and flows of goods and capital among countries. (22)

Exchange rate risk The potential fluctuations in an asset's value because of increases or decreases in exchange rates. (16)

Exchanges Auction markets at which buyers and sellers of securities trade, such as the New York and American Stock Exchanges. (3, 12)

Expectations-augmented Phillips curve An expanded Phillips curve relationship in which the Phillips curve shifts with changes in expected inflation. (28)

Expectations theory of the term structure of interest rates The proposition that investors view assets of all maturities as perfect substitutes, given the same levels of default risk, liquidity, information costs, and taxation. (7)

Expected real interest rate The nominal interest rate minus the expected rate of inflation. (4)

Extended credit Longer-term discount loans extended to a bank by the Fed under exceptional circumstances to alleviate severe liquidity problems. (20)

Fads Overreaction to good or bad news about an issue or a class of assets. (10)

Federal deposit insurance A federal government guarantee of certain types of bank deposits for account balances of up to $100,000. (13, 14, 15)

Federal Deposit Insurance Corporation Improvement Act of 1991 (FDICIA) Regulatory reform in which the bank supervisory framework connected enforcement actions to the bank's level of capital. (14)

Federal funds instruments ("Fed funds") Overnight loans between banks of their deposits with the Fed. (3)

Federal funds rate The interest rate charged on the overnight loans among banks. (3, 13, 20)

Federal Open Market Committee (FOMC) The Federal Reserve System committee, with 12 members, that gives directions for open market operations. Members include the Board of Governors, the president of the Federal Reserve Bank in New York, and the presidents of four other Federal Reserve banks. (19)

Federal Reserve bank A district bank of the Federal Reserve System that, among other things, conducts discount lending. (19)

Federal Reserve float The difference between cash items in the process of collection and deferred availability cash items reported in the Fed's balance sheet. (18)

Federal Reserve System (the Fed) The central bank in the United States, which promotes price stability in the banking industry and issues currency. (1, 14, 17, 19, 20, 21)

Fiat money Money authorized by central banks as the definitive money, which does not have to be exchanged by the central bank for gold or some other commodity money. (2)

Finance company Intermediaries that raise funds in large amounts through the sale of commercial paper and securities to make (generally smaller) loans to households and businesses. (12)

Financial distress A situation in which households or firms must sell illiquid assets, possibly at a loss, to meet current obligations. (27)

Financial futures (contracts) Claims that imply settlement of a purchase of a financial instrument at a specified future date, though price is determined at the outset. (3, 9)

Financial innovation Alterations in the operation of financial markets and institutions caused by changes in costs of providing risk-sharing, liquidity, or information services, or changes in demand for these services. (3, 15)

Financial institutions Go-betweens for savers and borrowers, such as banks or insurance companies. (1, 3, 12)

Financial Institutions Reform, Recovery, and Enforcement Act of 1989 (FIRREA) The regulatory reform that eliminated the FSLIC and formed the Resolution Trust Corporation to clean up the thrift crisis. (15)

Financial instruments IOU notes created by financial institutions, which are assets for savers and liabilities for (claims on) borrowers. (1, 3)

Financial integration The way in which financial markets are tied together geographically—domestically and internationally. (3)

Financial intermediaries Institutions such as commercial banks, credit unions, savings and loan associations, mutual savings banks, mutual funds, finance companies, insurance companies, and pension funds that borrow funds from savers and lend them to borrowers. (1, 3)

Financial intermediation Indirect finance through institutions that raise funds from savers and invest in debt or equity claims of borrowers. (3)

Financial markets Places or channels for buying and selling newly issued or existing bonds, stocks, foreign exchange contracts, and other financial instruments. (1, 3)

Financial panics Periods characterized by violent fluctuations in financial markets, bank runs, and bankruptcies of many firms. (14, 27)

Financial structure The mix of finance between equity and debt, as well as the source of funds (direct finance through financial markets or indirect finance through financial intermediaries). (11)

Financial system A network of markets and institutions to transfer funds from individuals and groups who have saved money to individuals and groups who want to borrow money. (1, 3)

Fisher hypothesis A proposition stating that the nominal interest rate rises or falls point-for-point with expected inflation. (4)

Fixed exchange rate system A system in which exchange rates are set at levels determined and maintained by governments. (22)

Fixed payment loan A credit market instrument that requires the borrower to make a regular periodic payment (monthly, quarterly, or annually) of principal and interest to the lender. (4)

Flexible exchange rate system An agreement among nations in which currency values are allowed to fluctuate freely. (22)

Floating-rate debt Loans whose interest payments vary with market interest rates. (13)

Foreign bank branch A full-service affiliate of a foreign financial institution, bearing its name, accepting deposits, and making loans. (16)

Foreign-exchange market intervention Deliberate action by the central bank to influence the exchange rate. (22)

Foreign-exchange market stability A goal of monetary policy to limit fluctuations in the foreign-exchange value of the currency. (21)

Forward transactions Agreements to exchange currencies, bank deposits, or securities at a set date in the future. They provide savers and borrowers the ability to conduct a transaction now and settle it in the future. (8, 9)

Free cash flow Funds that represent the difference between the firm's cash receipts and cash disbursements, including payments to equityholders and debtholders. (11)

Free reserves The difference between excess reserves and borrowed reserves (discount loans) in the banking system. (21)

Free-rider problem A situation in which individuals obtain and use information that others have paid for. (11)

Frictional unemployment Unemployment caused by searches by workers and firms for suitable matches of workers to jobs. (28)

Full employment (*FE*) line A vertical line depicting the economy's production level achieved by the use of all available production factors, regardless of the real rate of interest. (24)

Full employment output The production level achieved by using all available factors of production in place in the economy in the current period, irrespective of the real rate of interest. (24, 25, 28)

Fully funded pension plan A pension plan in which the contributions, together with the projected future earnings, are sufficient to pay the projected assigned benefits. (12)

Fundamental value The present value of an asset's expected future returns, which equals the market price of the asset in an efficient financial market. (10)

Futures contract An agreement that specifies the delivery of a specific underlying commodity or financial instrument at a given future date at a currently agreed-upon price. (10)

Garn-St. Germain Act of 1982 Regulatory reform authorizing banks to issue money market deposit accounts and broadening the permissible activities of S&Ls. (15)

GDP deflator An index of prices of all goods and services included in the gross domestic product, which is the final value of all goods and services produced in the economy. (2)

General Account The U.S. Treasury's deposit account with the Federal Reserve. (18)

General directive A summary of the Federal Open Market Committee's overall objectives for monetary aggregates and/or interest rates. (20)

General equilibrium Outcome in which all markets in the economy are in equilibrium at the same time. (24)

Gold standard A fixed exchange rate system in which the currencies of participating countries are convertible into an agreed-upon amount of gold. (22)

Goods market The market for trade in all goods and services that the economy produces at a particular point in time. (24)

Government allocation Distribution of goods and services by which a central authority collects the output of producers and distributes it to others according to some plan. (2)

Government budget constraint An equation depicting the relationships among federal spending and tax decisions, sales of securities by the Treasury, and changes in the monetary base. (18)

Gradualism A policy, recommended by new Keynesian economists, in which the rate of growth of the money supply is slowly reduced so that the inflation rate can adjust slowly, with smaller losses of output and jobs. (28)

Gramm-Leach-Bliley Financial Services Modernization Act of 1999 U.S. regulatory change that repealed the Glass-Steagall Act and removed the separation of the banking and securities industries. (14)

Hedge fund A largely unregulated speculative investment vehicle for high-net-worth individuals and institutional investors. (12)

Hedging Reducing one's exposure to risk by receiving the right to sell or buy an asset at a known price on a specified future date. (9)

High employment A goal of monetary policy emphasizing a low rate of unemployment. (21)

Hyperinflation Rapid inflation in excess of hundreds or thousands of percentage points per year for a significant period of time. (2, 28)

Hysteresis A situation in which unemployment rates can be higher than those associated with full employment for extended periods of time. (25)

Idiosyncratic risk (unsystematic risk) A unique risk that assets carry that does not affect the market as a whole. For example, the price of an individual stock is influenced by factors affecting the company's profitability, such as a strike or the discovery of a new product. (5)

Income The flow of earnings over a period of time. (2)

Indexed bond A bond whose payments of principal and interest are adjusted for changes in the price level. (4)

Indicator A financial variable whose movements reveal information to the central bank about present or prospective conditions in financial markets or the economy. (21)

Inflation A condition in the economy in which rising prices cause a given amount of money to purchase fewer goods and services, thus decreasing the purchasing power of money. (2, 28)

Inflation target A goal for inflation announced by the central bank and pursued by using its policy tools. (21)

Information Facts about borrowers and about expectations of returns on financial assets. (3)

Information costs The costs that savers incur in finding out the creditworthiness of borrowers and monitoring how borrowers use the funds acquired. (3, 11)

Information lag A condition that makes it impossible for the Fed to observe instantaneously movements in GDP, inflation, or other goal variables. (21)

Insider information Facts that are known to a firm's management but are not available to other investors or prospective investors in the firm. (10)

Insurance company Financial intermediaries that specialize in writing contracts to protect their policyholders from the risk of financial loss associated with particular events. (12)

Interest A rental fee for using borrowed funds. (4)

Interest rate The cost of borrowing funds, usually expressed as a percentage of the amount borrowed. (1, 4)

Interest rate risk The risk that the value of financial assets and liabilities will fluctuate in response to changes in market interest rates. (13)

Interest rate stability A goal of monetary policy focusing on reducing fluctuations in interest rates. (21)

Interest rate swap An agreement to sell the expected future returns on one financial instrument for the expected future returns on another. (9, 13)

Intermediaries See *Financial intermediaries.*

Intermediate targets Objectives for financial variables—such as the money supply or short-term interest rates—that the Fed believes will directly help it to achieve its ultimate goals. (21)

Intermediate-term debt A debt instrument that has a maturity between 1 and 10 years. (3)

International banking facilities (IBFs) Institutions within the United States that cannot conduct domestic banking business but can take time deposits from and make loans to foreign households and firms. They are exempt from reserve requirements, federal restrictions on interest payments to depositors, and, in some states, state and local taxation. (16)

International banks Financial institutions that provide risk-sharing, liquidity, and information services to firms and individuals engaged in international trade and finance. (16)

International capital market The market for lending and borrowing across national boundaries. (1, 5)

International capital mobility The ability of investors to move funds among international markets. (8)

International Monetary Fund (IMF) The multinational lender of last resort, created by the Bretton Woods agreement to help countries make short-run economic adjustments to a balance-of-payments deficit or surplus while maintaining a fixed exchange rate. (22)

International reserves A central bank's assets that are denominated in a foreign currency and used in international transactions. (22)

International transactions currency The currency of choice in settling international commercial and financial transactions. (16)

Investment banks Securities market institutions that assist businesses in raising new capital and advise them on the best means of doing it (issuing shares or structuring debt instruments). (12)

Investment institutions Financial institutions (mutual funds and finance companies) that raise funds to invest in loans and securities. (12)

***IS* curve** The negative relationship between the real interest rate and the level of income, all else being equal, that arises in the market for goods and services. (24)

Junk bonds Corporate bonds issued by lower-quality and thus riskier firms. (3, 7)

Lags in policymaking and implementation process Delays in deciding upon and carrying out monetary policy. (26)

Large open economy The economy of a country whose domestic saving and investment shifts are large enough to affect the real interest rate in the international capital market. The United States, Japan, and Germany are examples of countries with large open economies. (5)

Law of one price A theory stating that if two countries produce an identical good, profit opportunities should ensure that the price of the good is the same around the world, no matter which country produces the good. This law assumes that the goods are tradeable and allows differences that reflect transportation costs. (8)

Legal tender The requirement that a particular currency be acceptable in the settlement of commercial and financial transactions. (2)

Lemons problem An adverse selection problem in which individuals do not know the quality of asset choices (for example, of used cars), so they average quality, overvaluing some assets and undervaluing others. At the average price, owners of the undervalued assets are less likely to sell, but owners of the overvalued assets are more likely to sell. (11)

Lender of last resort The ultimate source of credit to which banks can turn during a panic. (14)

Leveraged buyout (LBO) A type of restructuring in which external equity is replaced by debt. (11)

Liabilities Sources of funds and claims on future income of borrowers. (3)

Life insurance company A firm that sells policies to protect households against a loss of earnings from disability, retirement, or death of the insured person. (12)

Liquidity The ease with which one can exchange assets for cash, other assets, or goods and services. (1, 3, 7)

Liquidity of balance sheet positions The quantity of liquid assets that households and firms hold relative to their liabilities, which is a determinant of spending on business investment, housing, and consumer durables. (27)

Liquidity preference theory A proposition, developed by John Maynard Keynes, that emphasizes the sensitivity of money demand to changes in interest rates. (23)

Liquidity risk The possibility that depositors may collectively decide to withdraw more funds than the bank has on hand. (13)

***LM* curve** The positive relationship between the real interest rate and the level of income, all else being equal, that arises in the market for real money balances. (24)

Load fund A mutual fund that charges commissions for purchases and/or sales. (12)

Loan A transaction in which the borrower receives funds from a lender and the borrower agrees to repay funds with interest. (4)

Loan commitment An agreement by a bank to provide a borrower with a stated amount of funds during some specified period of time. (13)

Loan sale A financial contract in which a bank agrees to sell the expected future returns from an underlying bank loan to a third party. (13)

Loan syndicate An arrangement in which a loan is arranged and managed by a lead bank; other banks hold fractions of the loan. (16)

Long-run aggregate supply curve (*LRAS*) The graph of the relationship of firms' output to price level in the long run. It is vertical at the full employment output. (25)

Long-term debt A debt instrument that has a maturity of 10 years or more. (3)

Luxury asset An asset for which the wealth elasticity of demand exceeds unity. (6)

M1 The narrowest monetary aggregate, which measures money as the traditional medium of exchange, including currency, traveler's checks, and checkable deposits. (2)

M2 A monetary aggregate that includes the components of *M1* plus short-term investment accounts that could be converted to definitive money, but not as easily as the components of *M1*. *M2* now includes money market deposit accounts, noninstitutional money market mutual fund shares, and other very liquid assets of firms such as overnight repurchase agreements and overnight Eurodollars. (2)

M3 A monetary aggregate that includes *M2* plus some less liquid assets, including large-denomination time deposits, institutional money market mutual fund balances, term repurchase agreements, and term Eurodollars. (2)

Main bank In Japan, a large bank within a finance group that owns some equity in member firms, is a major source of credit for group firms, and monitors activities of member firms. (14)

Management buyout (MBO) A form of restructuring in which a firm's managers acquire a greater stake in the firm by buying back shares from other shareholders. (11)

Market risk (systematic risk) A risk that is common to all assets of a certain type, such as potential general fluctuations in economic conditions that can increase or decrease returns on stocks collectively. (5)

Marketable securities Liquid assets that banks hold and can trade in secondary markets. (13)

Matched sale-purchase transactions (reverse repos) Agreements that are often used by the Fed Trading Desk for open market sales, in which the Fed sells securities to dealers in the government securities market and the dealers agree to sell them back to the Fed in the very near future. (20)

Maturity The length of time before a debt instrument expires. The maturity can be a very short period of time (30 days or even overnight) or a long period of time (30 years or more). (3)

Medium of exchange A term that economists use to describe money. (2)

Member banks Banks that are members of the Federal Reserve System. (19)

Menu costs Costs to firms that are caused by changing prices because of inflation (reprinting price lists, informing customers, and so on). (28)

Misperception theory Propositions about the effects of imperfect information on the part of firms on aggregate supply. (See also *New classical view*.) (25)

Monetary aggregates Measures of the quantity of money that are broader than currency. They include *M1*, *M2*, and *M3*. (2, 23)

Monetary base All reserves held by banks as well as all currency in circulation. (17)

Monetary neutrality The proposition that money has no effect on output in the long run because an increase (decrease) in the nominal money supply raises (lowers) the price level in the long run but does not change equilibrium output. (25)

Monetary policy The management of the money supply and its links to prices, interest rates, and other economic variables. (1, 21, 26)

Monetary policy goals Objectives set by the central bank in carrying out monetary and regulatory policy. (21)

Monetary theory The area of study concerning the relationships linking changes in the money supply to changes in economic activity and prices in the economy. (1)

Monetizing the debt The Fed's purchasing of Treasury securities to finance budget deficits. (18)

Money Anything that is generally accepted as payment for goods and services or in the settlement of debts. Money acts as a medium of exchange, is a unit of account and a store of value, and offers a standard of deferred payment. (1, 2)

Money center banks Large, established national banks. (14)

Money channel The path through which monetary policy affects output through effects on interest-sensitive spending. (27)

Money demand function A function relating the demand for real money balances to its underlying determinants. (23)

Money market deposit account (MMDA) Federally insured bank deposit accounts that provide services similar to those of money market mutual funds. (15)

Money market mutual funds Funds that issue shares to savers backed by holdings of high-quality short-term assets. (12)

Money markets Financial markets that trade assets used as the medium of exchange, such as currency or shorter-term instruments with a maturity of less than one year. (3, 12)

Money multiplier The number that indicates how much the money supply changes in response to a given change in the monetary base. (17)

Money supply The stock of the medium of exchange supplied by the central bank. (17)

Money supply process The means by which actions of the central bank, the banking system, and the nonbank public determine the money supply. (17)

Moral hazard The lender's difficulty in monitoring borrowers' activities once the loan is made. (11)

Mortgages Loans, usually long-term, to households or firms to purchase buildings or land. The underlying asset—house or factory or piece of land—serves as collateral. (3)

Multiple deposit contraction The process by which a decrease in bank reserves reduces the volume of checkable deposits in the banking system. (17)

Multiple deposit expansion Part of the money supply process in which funds are deposited and redeposited in banks. Banks serve as a link between the central bank and the nonbank public, taking increases in reserves from the central bank and funneling them to the nonbank public by making loans. (17)

Municipal bonds Obligations of state and local governments that are exempt from federal, state, and local income taxes. (7)

Mutual funds Financial intermediaries that raise funds by selling shares to individual savers and investing them in diversified portfolios of stocks, bonds, mortgages, and money market instruments. (3, 12)

Narrow banking Deposit insurance reform in which only deposits in safe assets would be insured. (15)

National banks Federally chartered banks supervised by the Office of the Comptroller of the Currency, a department of the U.S. Treasury. Originally, national banks were allowed to issue bank notes as currency. (14)

Natural rate of unemployment The rate of unemployment that exists when the economy produces the full employment level of output. (28)

Negotiable certificate of deposit A large-denomination fixed-maturity instrument that is sold by a bank to investors and can be traded in a secondary market. (3, 13)

Negotiated Order of Withdrawal (NOW) Effectively, a bank checking account that pays interest. (15)

Net worth (equity capital) The difference between a firm's current and expected future holdings (assets) and its debts (liabilities). (11, 13)

Neutrality of money The absence of an effect of change in the nominal money supply on output and the real interest rate. (24, 26)

New classical view A theory stating that for short-run aggregate supply, there is a positive relation between aggregate supply and the difference between the actual and the expected price level. (25)

New Keynesian view Economic explanations for price stickiness in the short run, based on features of many real-world markets: the rigidity of long-term contracts and imperfect competition among sellers in the goods market. (25)

No-load funds Funds that earn income only from management fees (typically about 0.5% of assets), not from sales commissions. (12)

Noise traders Relatively uninformed traders who pursue trading strategies with no superior information and who may overreact. (10)

Nominal exchange rate The value of one currency in terms of another currency. (8)

Nominal interest rate An interest rate that is unadjusted for changes in purchasing power. (4)

Nominal interest rate parity condition The market equilibrium condition in which domestic and foreign assets have identical risk, liquidity, and information characteristics, so their nominal returns—measured in the same currency—also must be identical. (8)

Nonbank banks Financial institutions that take demand deposits but do not make loans. (14)

Nonbank office Affiliates of bank holding companies that do not accept demand deposits but do make loans. (14)

Nonmoney asset market A market that handles trading in assets that are stores of value, including stocks, bonds, and houses. (24)

Nontransaction deposit Claims on banks including savings deposits and time deposits. (13)

Off-balance-sheet lending Bank lending activities in which the bank does not necessarily hold as assets the loans that it makes, including standby letters of credit, loan commitments, and loan sales. (13)

Official reserve assets Assets held by central banks that can be used in making international payments to settle the balance of payments. (22)

Official settlements balance The net increase in a country's official reserve assets. (22)

Offshore markets International financial centers that are located in unregulated areas with low tax rates on banks—for example, in the Caribbean (the Bahamas and Cayman Islands) and in Hong Kong and Singapore. (16)

Okun's law A statistical relationship identified by Arthur Okun between changes in output and the unemployment rate. (28)

Open economy An economy in which borrowing and lending take place in the international capital market. (5)

Open-end mutual funds Mutual funds that issue redeemable shares at a price tied to the underlying value of the assets. (12)

Open market operations The purchase and sale of securities in financial markets by the Federal Reserve System. Open market operations are its most direct route for changing the monetary base. (17, 20)

Open market purchase The buying of government securities by the Fed, with the intent of raising the monetary base. (17)

Open market sale The sale of government securities by the Fed, with the intent of reducing the monetary base. (17)

Open Market Trading Desk A group of traders at the Federal Reserve Bank of New York who buy and sell securities for the Fed's account. (20)

Operating targets Variables directly under the Fed's control that are closely related to the intermediate targets of monetary policy. Operating targets include the federal funds rate and nonborrowed reserves. (21)

Options contract A right (option) conferred upon a trader to buy or sell a particular asset (shares of stock, a bond, or unit of foreign currency, for example) within a predetermined time and at a predetermined price. (3, 9)

Outright purchase or sale The Fed's buying securities from or selling securities to dealers. (20)

Over-the-counter (OTC) markets Secondary financial markets for broker-dealers that are organized via telephone and computer, with no centralized place for auction trading. (3, 12)

Payments system A mechanism for conducting transactions in the economy. Commercial banks play a key role in this system by clearing and settling transactions in the economy. (2, 13)

Payments system factors Substitutes for money in transactions that affect the demand for money. (23)

Pension fund A financial institution that invests contributions of workers and firms in financial assets to provide retirement benefits for workers. (12)

Phillips curve A relationship, found by A. W. Phillips, in which high unemployment was associated with a low rate of wage inflation, and vice versa. (28)

Plan funding A method by which pension assets accrue to finance retirement benefits. (12)

Political business cycle model The theory that the policymakers will urge the Fed to try to lower interest rates to stimulate credit demand and economic activity prior to an election. (19)

Portfolio A collection of assets. (3, 5)

Preferred habitat theory of the term structure of interest rates Proposition that investors care about both expected returns and maturity, viewing instruments with different maturities as substitutes, but not perfect ones. (7)

Present value (*PV*, present discounted value) A concept that is used to evaluate credit market instruments by placing all payments in terms of today's dollars so that they can be added together. (4)

Price controls Official government restrictions on price changes. (28)

Price index A summary statistic that incorporates changes in the price of a set of goods relative to the price in some base year. (2)

Price level The average price of a market basket of goods and services in the economy. (1)

Price stability A goal of monetary policy to stabilize the purchasing power of the currency. (21)

Primary markets Financial markets in which newly issued debt or equity claims are sold to initial buyers by private borrowers to raise funds for durable-goods purchases or new ventures and by governments to finance budget deficits. (3)

Prime rate Traditionally, the interest rate charged on six-month loans to high-quality borrowers. (13)

Principal-agent problem The type of moral hazard that may arise when managers (agents) who control a firm's assets do not own very much of the firm's equity and therefore do not have the same incentive to maximize the firm's value as the owners (principals) do. (11)

Principal-agent view A theory of central bank decision making implying that officials maximize their personal well-being rather than that of the general public. (19)

Principals Owners (but not direct managers) of a firm or organization. (11)

Producer price index (PPI) An index of the prices that firms pay in wholesale markets for crude materials, intermediate goods, and finished goods. It is a commonly used measure to calculate inflation. (2, 28)

Productivity growth A measure of the growth of output in a country relative to the growth of inputs. (8)

Program trading Using computer-generated orders to buy or sell many stocks at the same time, causing rapid adjustments of institutional portfolios. (10)

Property and casualty insurance company A firm that sells policies to protect households and firms from risks of illness, theft, accident, or natural disasters. (12)

Public interest view A theory of central bank decision making implying that officials act in the interest of citizens' well-being. (19)

Purchasing power The ability of money to be used to acquire goods and services. (2)

Purchasing power parity (PPP) theory of exchange rate determination The proposition that changes in the nominal exchange rate between two currencies are accounted for by differences in inflation rates in the two countries. This theory assumes that real exchange rates are constant. (8)

Put option The right to sell an underlying asset, which is obtained by buying the put option. Sellers of put options have an obligation to buy the asset. (10)

Quantity theory of money demand A theory, developed by Irving Fisher and others, that states that the determinant of the demand for real balances is the real volume of transactions. (23)

Quota A common trade barrier that limits the volume of foreign goods that can be brought into the country. (8)

Rate of capital gains The percentage change in the price of a financial asset. (4)

Rational expectations The assumption in the model of an efficient market that participants will use all available information in estimating the expected price level or change in the money supply so that the market price equals the present value of expected future returns. (10, 26)

Real business cycle view The theory that changes in aggregate demand have no effect on output, even in the short run, assuming perfect information and perfectly flexible prices. Short-term changes to output are primarily temporary shocks to productivity, such as changes in the availability of raw materials. (25)

Real exchange rate The purchasing power of a currency relative to the purchasing power of other currencies. (8)

Real interest rate An interest rate that is adjusted for changes in purchasing power caused by inflation. (4)

Real money balances The value of money balances adjusted for changes in purchasing power. (23)

Recession A contraction in current output in the business cycle. (26)

Regulation Q The regulation, authorized by the Banking Act of 1933, that placed ceilings on allowable interest rates on time and savings deposits and prohibited the payment of interest on demand deposits (then the only form of checkable deposits). (15)

Repurchase agreements (repos or RPs) Very short-term loans that are used for cash management by large corporations. Maturities are typically less than two weeks and often the next day. (3, 13)

Required reserve ratio The percentage of deposits that banks must hold as reserves, as specified by the Fed. (17)

Required reserves The minimum amount that depository institutions are compelled to hold as reserves by the Federal Reserve System. (13, 17)

Reserve requirement The requirement that banks hold a fraction of checkable deposits as vault cash or deposits with the central bank. (17)

Reserves A bank asset consisting of vault cash (cash on hand in the bank) plus deposits with the Federal Reserve. (13)

Restrictive covenants Limits on the actions of a borrower or insured person made by a lender or insurer. For example, a lender may restrict risk-taking activities of the borrower, require the borrower to maintain a certain level of net worth, or require the borrower to maintain the value of collateral offered to the lender. (11, 12)

Restructuring Rearranging the financial structure of a firm to shift control over the resources of the firm and to provide incentives for managers to maximize the firm's value. (11)

Return on assets (ROA) A measure of a bank's operating performance (net after-tax profit/bank assets). (13)

Return on equity (ROE) A measure of banks' shareholders' returns (net after-tax profit/bank equity capital). (13)

Revaluation Raising the official value of a country's currency relative to other currencies, thereby resetting the exchange rate. (22)

Riegle-Neal Interstate Banking and Branching Efficiency Act of 1994 Act providing a consistent nationwide standard for interstate bank expansion, eliminating the significance of prior state branching restrictions. (14)

Risk The degree of uncertainty of an asset's return. (1)

Risk-averse Characteristic of savers who desire to minimize variability in return on savings. (5)

Risk-based premium A fee for insurance that is based on the probability of the insured individual's collecting a claim. (12)

Risk-loving Characteristic of savers who actually prefer to gamble by holding a risky asset with the possibility of maximizing returns. (5)

Risk-neutral Characteristic of savers who judge assets only on their expected returns. (5)

Risk premium The difference between the yield on a financial instrument and the yield on a default-risk-free instrument of comparable maturity. It measures the additional yield a saver requires to be willing to hold a risky instrument. (7)

Risk sharing Services provided by the financial system wherein savers and borrowers spread and transfer risk. (3)

Risk structure of interest rates The differences in risk, liquidity, information costs, and taxation that result in differences in interest rates and yields across credit market instruments of the same maturity. (7)

Rules strategy An attempt by the central bank to follow specific and publicly announced guidelines for policy. (28)

Savers Suppliers of funds, providing funds to borrowers in the anticipation of repayment of more funds in the future. (3)

Saving curve A graph that illustrates the relationship between aggregate saving and the expected real rate of interest. (5)

Saving-investment diagram A graph that shows the relationship between the saving and investment curves. It is used to determine the equilibrium real interest rate. (24)

Savings institution A category of banking firms including S&Ls and mutual savings banks. (12)

Seasonal credit Discount lending to satisfy geographically specific seasonal liquidity requirements. (20)

Secondary markets Financial markets in which claims that have already been issued are sold by one investor to another. (3)

Securities market institutions Financial institutions (investment banks, brokers and dealers, and organized exchanges) that reduce costs of matching savers and borrowers. (12)

Segmented markets theory The proposition that yields on each financial instrument are determined in a separate market, with separate market-specific demand and supply considerations. (7)

Shoe leather costs The cost to consumers and businesses of minimizing currency holdings due to inflation. (28)

Short-run aggregate supply (*SRAS*) curve A plot of the relationship between aggregate output supplied and the price level. (25)

Short-term debt A debt instrument that has a maturity of less than one year. (3)

Simple deposit multiplier The reciprocal of the required reserve ratio. (17)

Simple loan A credit transaction in which the borrower receives from the lender an amount of funds called principal and agrees to repay the lender principal plus an additional amount called interest (as a fee for using the funds) on a given date (maturity). (4)

Simple Phillips curve The statistical relationship between inflation and the difference between unemployment and the natural rate of unemployment. (28)

Small open economy An economy in which total saving is too small to affect the world real interest rate, so the economy takes the world interest rate as a given. (6)

Special Drawing Rights (SDRs) Paper substitute for gold, issued as international reserves by the International Monetary Fund in its role as lender of last resort. (22)

Specialist A broker-dealer on the floor of the exchange who makes a market in one or more stocks and matches buyers and sellers. (12)

Specialization A system in which individuals produce the goods or services for which they have relatively the best ability. (2)

Speculation The attempt to profit from disagreements among traders about future prices of a commodity or financial instrument by anticipating changes in prices. (10)

Speculative attack The sale of weak currencies or purchase of strong currencies by market participants who believe a government will be unable or unwilling to maintain the exchange rate, in an attempt to force a devaluation or revaluation of the currency. (22)

Spot transactions Transactions in which trade and settlement occur at the same time. (9)

Stabilization policies (activist policies) Public policies designed to smooth short-run fluctuations in output involving shifts of the *AD* curve by changes in government purchases or taxes or by changes in the nominal money supply. (26)

Standard of deferred payment The feature of money by which it facilitates exchange over time in credit. (2)

Standby letter of credit (SLC) A promise that a bank will lend the borrower funds to pay off its maturing commercial paper if necessary. (13)

State and local government bonds (municipal bonds) Intermediate- and long-term bonds issued by municipalities and state governments that are exempt from federal income taxation and allow governmental units to borrow the funds to build schools, roads, and other large capital projects. (3)

State banks Banks that are chartered by a state government. (14)

Statistical discrepancy An adjustment to the capital account in the balance-of-payments accounts to reflect measurement errors and omissions. (22)

Sterilized foreign-exchange intervention A transaction in which a foreign-exchange intervention is accompanied by offsetting domestic open market operations to leave the monetary base unchanged. (22)

Stock market A market in which owners of firms buy and sell their claims. (1)

Stocks Equity claims issued by corporations. They represent the largest single category of capital market assets. (3)

Store of value A function of money; the accumulation of value by holding dollars or other assets that can be used to buy goods and services in the future. (2)

Subsidiary U.S. bank Affiliate of a foreign bank that is subject to domestic banking regulations and need not bear the name of its foreign parent. (16)

Supply shocks Shifts in the price or availability of raw materials or in production technologies that affect production costs and the aggregate supply curve. (25)

Syndicate See *Loan syndicate*. (16)

T-account A simplified accounting tool that lists changes in balance sheet items as they occur. (13)

Takeover A struggle for corporate control in which a group of current or new shareholders buys a controlling interest in a firm, reshapes the board of directors, and even replaces managers. (11)

Targets Variables that a central bank can influence directly and that help to achieve monetary policy goals. (21)

Tariff A common trade barrier consisting of a tax on goods purchased from other countries. (8)

Taylor rule Monetary policy guideline for the federal funds rate target developed by economist John Taylor. (21)

Term premium The additional yield that investors require for investing in a less preferred maturity. (7)

Term structure of interest rates The variation in yields for related instruments differing in maturity. (7)

Theory of portfolio allocation A statement that predicts how savers allocate their assets on the basis of their consideration of their wealth, expected return on the assets, degree of risk, liquidity of the assets, and the cost of acquiring information about assets. (5)

Time deposits Accounts with a specified maturity, which could range from a few months to several years. (13)

Total rate of return The sum of the current yield of a credit market instrument and the rate of capital gain or loss on it. (4)

Total return swap Bilateral contract transferring interest rate risk and credit risk by exchanging the total economic performance of a specified asset for another cash flow. (9)

Trade balance The component of the current account that equals the difference between merchandise exports and imports. (22)

Transactions costs The cost of trade or exchange; for example, the brokerage commission charged for buying or selling a financial claim like a bond or a share of stock. (3, 11)

Treasury tax and loan accounts U.S. Treasury's deposit accounts with commercial banks. (18)

Underfunded A term used to describe a defined benefit plan when contributions, together with the projected future earnings, are not sufficient to pay off projected defined benefits. (12)

Underground economy Economic activity that is not measured in formal government statistics. (17)

Underwriting A way in which investment banks earn income; in the simplest form, they guarantee a price to an issuing firm that needs capital, sell the issue at a higher price, and keep the profit, known as the "spread." (12)

Unit of account A function of money; the provision of a way of measuring the value of goods and services in the economy in terms of money. (2)

Universal banking Allowing banks to be involved in many nonbanking activities with no geographic restrictions. (14)

Unsterilized foreign-exchange intervention A transaction in which the central bank allows the monetary base to respond to the sale or purchase of domestic currency. (22)

U.S. government agency securities Intermediate- or long-term bonds issued by the federal government or government-sponsored agencies. (3)

U.S. Treasury bills (T-bills) Debt obligations of the U.S. government that have a maturity of less than one year. (3)

U.S. Treasury bonds Securities issued by the federal government to finance budget deficits. (3)

U.S. Treasury securities Debt obligations issued by the federal government to finance budget deficits. (3)

Value-at-risk (VAR) approach Use of statistical models to estimate the maximum loss in a portfolio's value likely to be sustained over a particular time period. (13)

Vault cash The cash on hand in the bank. (13, 17)

Velocity of money The average number of times a unit of currency is spent each year on a purchase of goods and services in the economy. (23)

Venture capital firm A firm that raises equity capital from investors to invest in emerging or growing entrepreneurial business ventures. (11)

Venture capital funds (VCs) Intermediaries raising funds from institutional investors and wealthy individuals to invest in portfolio companies. (12)

Wealth The sum of the value of assets. (2)

Wealth elasticity of demand The relationship of the percentage change in quantity demanded of an asset to the percentage change in wealth. (5)

World Bank (International Bank for Reconstruction and Development) The bank created by the Bretton Woods agreement to grant long-term loans to developing countries for their economic development. (22)

World real interest rate The real interest rate determined in the international capital market. (6)

Yield curve A graph showing yields to maturity on different default-risk-free instruments as a function of maturity. (7)

Yield to maturity The interest rate measure at which the present value of an asset's returns is equal to its value today. (4)

Selected Answers to Questions and Problems

CHAPTER 1

Review Questions

1. No, the funds would not generally be allocated to most valued uses; financial markets and institutions work better.
3. The financial system provides three key services to savers and borrowers: risk sharing (people can share and transfer risk), liquidity (people can exchange their assets for other assets at low cost), and information (financial markets communicate information, and financial institutions specialize in gathering and using information about borrowers, so they can lend more efficiently).

Analytical Problems

7. The local bank provides you risk-sharing, liquidity, and information services.
9. In a global economy, their exports to the United States would decline, possibly leading to an economic downturn.

CHAPTER 2

Review Questions

1. To serve as money, they must generally be accepted as means of payment. Your acceptance of dollar bills and checks as money is based on your belief that others will accept them.
3. In a barter system, there are too many prices, and nonstandard goods complicate pricing. Trade requires a double coincidence of wants.
5. Commodity money has real uses (e.g., gold, silver); fiat money has no intrinsic value.
7. A payments system is a mechanism for conducting transactions. If the payments system became less efficient, the costs to the economy would be fewer and more costly transactions, that is, losing gains from specialization.
9. No. Houses, bonds, and stocks are also stores of value. There is an advantage to money's being a store of value, because after trading for it, it can be held; otherwise, something else is likely to become money that is also a store of value.
11. The definitions of the money supply range from narrow, *M1*, to broad, *L*. The definitions of the money supply can be used for different purposes and have varied over time in their usefulness for predicting future movements in prices and output.

Analytical Problems

13. Whether caused by inflation or deflation, changes in the purchasing power of money affect money's usefulness as a store of value and as a standard of deferred payment.
15. The reason is convenience; one avoids transactions costs of running to the bank all the time.
17. Not necessarily; if prices rose more than 10%, your real income has fallen.
19. In Friedmania, bad money drives out good; people will spend the new crowns and hoard the old crowns.
21. Liquidity indicates the ease with which an asset can be converted to definitive money. Ranking from most to least liquid: dollar bill, checking account, money market mutual fund, passbook savings account, corporate stock, gold, house.

CHAPTER 3

Review Questions

1. Savers have more resources than they want to spend currently; borrowers have fewer resources than they currently want to spend. Risk sharing allows diversification and transfer of risk; liquidity allows flexibility in asset holdings; and information is efficiently gathered by financial intermediaries who specialize

in doing so. Taken together, the three services reduce the costs of financial transactions.

3. There tend to be more buyers and sellers of money market assets than there are buyers and sellers of capital market assets. Hence, money market assets tend to be more liquid than capital market assets. Because the assets of banks are primarily capital market assets, banks sometimes have difficulty converting their assets into cash.
5. "Integration" represents the extent to which financial markets are tied together geographically. Increased integration tends to equalize returns across geographic boundaries (raising costs and returns for some and lowering them for others), likely reducing borrowing costs by allowing for geographical diversification.
7. The transaction (a) takes place through a financial intermediary, (b) is in a primary market, and (c) is in a capital market.
9. The transaction (a) takes place in a financial market, (b) is in a primary market, and (c) is in a capital market.
11. The transaction (a) takes place through a financial intermediary, (b) is in a primary market, and (c) is in a money market.

Analytical Problems

13. Asset A yields 6% after taxes; asset B yields 6%; asset C offers the highest return, yielding 6.5%.
15. *Insider trading* refers to trading by managers who own large amounts of a firm's stock or by others who have privileged information. Legalizing insider trading might reduce the confidence of investors in the fairness of financial markets, thereby reducing their participation in them.
17. Investors want to eliminate unnecessary risk in their returns; they may trade off additional risk for additional return.
19. Leading candidates include government regulation and economic and financial stability; it is unlikely that financial technology varies greatly across industrialized countries.

CHAPTER 4

Review Questions

1. In a discount bond, the borrower repays face value at maturity; in a simple loan, the borrower repays the stated principal plus interest at maturity.
3. The yield to maturity is the interest rate that equates value of asset today with present value of future payments. It can be derived from present-value formulas.
5. The total rate of return includes current interest payment plus capital gain; it equals current yield plus percentage change in price.
7. According to the Fisher hypothesis, the nominal interest rate moves one-for-one with expected inflation. While there is broad support for the proposition that nominal interest rates move in response to changes in expected inflation, the Fisher effect, narrowly defined, is not supported exactly by U.S. data.

Analytical Problems

9. With a discount rate of 10%, the present value of the Yankees' offer is: $3,000,000 + ($6,000,000/1.1) + ($7,000,000/$1.1^2$) + ($8,000,000/1.1^3) = $20,250,188. The present value of the Giants' offer is: $6,000,000 + ($5,500,000/1.1) + ($6,000,000/$1.1^2$) + ($6,000,000/1.1^3) = $20,466,566. So, based on the present value criterion, the Giants are making the more valuable offer. With a discount rate of 5%, the present value of the Yankees' offer is: $3,000,000 + ($6,000,000/1.05) + ($7,000,000/$1.05^2$) + ($8,000,000/1.05^3) = $21,974,193. The present value of the Giants' offer is: $6,000,000 + ($5,500,000/1.05) + ($6,000,000/$1.05^2$) + ($6,000,000/1.05^3) = $21,863,298. So, the Yankees' offer is more valuable.
11. The present value is $857.
13. Option (a) has the highest present value.
15. At an initial interest rate of 7%, the bond's value is $700/1.07 + 700/(1.07)^2 + 700/(1.07)^3 + 700/(1.07)^4 + 10{,}000/(1.07)^4 = 654.21 + 611.41 + 571.41 + 549.43 + 7849.02 =$ $10,235.48. At an interest rate of 5%, the bond's value is $700/1.05 + 700/1.05^2 + 700/1.05^3 + 700/1.05^4 + 10{,}000/1.05^4 = 666.67 + 634.92 + 604.69 + 575.89 + 8227.02 =$ $10,709.19. Hence the bond's value rises as the yield falls.
17. The present value of two one-year subscriptions is $60 + $60/1.10 = $114.55. The present value of a two-year subscription is $115. Hence you prefer the one-year subscription

today. There is a complication, however—the price next year is unknown.

19. The current yield is 2/55, or 3.6%. The capital gain is 5/55, or 9.1%. The total rate of return is 12.7%.
21. Because of higher inflation in the mid 1970s, stock prices declined in real terms.
23. The actual real interest rate will differ from the expected real interest rate if the actual inflation rate differs from the expected inflation rate. The longer the term of a loan, the greater the concern of the lender that the actual real interest rate might differ from the expected real interest rate.
25. In the first institution's case, there should be little effect because of short maturities of the assets. In the second institution's case, however, there will be a major loss of net worth on account of capital loss on long maturities.

CHAPTER 5

Review Questions

1. The five key determinants of portfolio choice are wealth, relative return, relative risk, relative liquidity, and relative cost of acquiring information.
3. The difference lies in the attitude toward risk relative to return. A risk-loving individual is more likely to hold stocks and options. A risk-averse individual is more likely to hold bonds and cash. A risk-neutral individual cares only about an asset's expected return and not its risk.
5. The saying states the benefit of diversification. It means that one can reduce portfolio risk by owning many different assets.
7. Mutual funds provide small investors with diversification, which lowers their risk from investing in equities.
9. Market risk refers to the risk in the returns on assets generally, whereas idiosyncratic risk relates to the risk in an individual asset. Idiosyncratic risk can be reduced through diversification.
11. The variability of the return on an individual stock should be greater than that for the market portfolio. The reason is that individual returns are imperfectly correlated.

Analytical Problems

13. Asset 1 yields 6% after taxes; asset 2 yields 6%; asset 3 offers the highest return, yielding 6.5%.
15. The interest rate is lower because investors do not like the call provision (the government calls the bond only if the current market interest rate is below the rate on the bond). Hence investors prefer noncallable bonds and will pay more for them, so the interest rate is lower.
17. They offer greater liquidity. Some people (who wanted to invest for the long term) did not like having to reinvest coupon payments with unknown interest rates; they preferred the second part. Others preferred the steady income stream but did not want to have to reinvest the principal; they preferred the first part.
19. a. Your rates of return are 20%, −10%, 35%, −15%, 27.5%, and −12.5%, respectively.
    b. Your rates of return are now 15%, −15%, 30%, −20%, 22.5%, and −17.5%, respectively. You are now less likely to hold both stocks and may be more likely to hold riskier Lowrunner stock.
21. a. You are more willing (higher wealth).
    b. You are less willing (higher risk).
    c. You are more willing (higher return).
    d. You are less willing (alternative asset has increased liquidity).

CHAPTER 6

Review Questions

1. a. The bond demand curve shifts to the right in response to a fall in current income or a rise in expected future income.
   b. The bond demand curve shifts to the right in response to a rise in current income or a fall in expected future income.
   c. The loanable funds demand curve shifts to the left in response to a fall in expected future profitability or a rise in corporate taxes.
   d. The loanable funds supply curve shifts to the right in response to a rise in bonds' liquidity or to an increase in the expected return on bonds.
3. You would not expect the real interest rate to be the same in all small open economies because of transactions costs and because some countries impose barriers to interna-

tional borrowing and lending.

5. In a small open economy and a large open economy, domestic lending and borrowing need not be equal. The difference between domestic lending and borrowing is international lending—if desired domestic lending exceeds desired domestic borrowing—or international borrowing—if desired domestic borrowing exceeds desired domestic lending.
7. Shifts in domestic lending and borrowing in a small open economy have no effect on the world real interest rate, while such shifts in a large open economy can affect the world real interest rate.

Analytical Problems

9. The shift in the bond supply curve is greater than the shift in the bond demand curve, so the price of bonds falls, and the interest rate rises. In a small open economy, there is no such effect, as the world real interest rate is given.
11. In a small open economy, the real interest rate is unaffected in each case.
    a. Domestic borrowing rises.
    b. Domestic borrowing falls.
    c. Domestic borrowing does not change.
    d. Domestic borrowing does not change.
13. a. Aggregate wealth rises.
    b. Aggregate wealth rises.
    c. The increase in the real interest rate increases saving and wealth.
15. a. Net expected profitability falls, so the demand for loanable funds falls.
    b. Expected profitability rises, so the demand for loanable funds rises.
    c. The increase in the expected after-tax real interest rate reduces the demand for loanable funds.
17. The country with social insurance should have lower levels of saving and, all else being equal, lower wealth.
19. The bond supply curve shifts to the right in response to the increase in stock prices. In a closed or large open economy (assuming no shift in the bond demand curve), the interest rate will rise.
21. Not necessarily; the *expected* real interest rate likely was positive, but actual inflation exceeded expected inflation.

CHAPTER 7

Review Questions

1. The bonds have different times to maturity.
3. Long-term yields fall below current short-term yields.
5. In the preferred habitat theory, term premiums account for the upward bias in the slope.
7. U.S. Treasury bonds have no default risk.
9. The taxable bond pays a higher before-tax interest rate.
11. A recession raises default risk. The phenomenon is known as a flight to quality.
13. Factors include default risk, liquidity, and taxability. In the latter case, information cost is an additional factor.
15. If more investors were willing to purchase these bonds as a result of Milken's arguments, then their liquidity would have increased.

Analytical Problems

17. The current two-year rate is 4%. The current three-year rate is 5%.
19. a. $\$1000(1.06^4) = \$1262.48$;
    b. $\$1000(1.055^3)(1.09) = \$1279.92$;
    c. $\$1000(1.05^2)(1.07)(1.09) = \$1285.85$;
    d. $\$1000(1.04)(1.065)(1.07)(1.09) = \$1291.79$.
    You should choose option (d).
21. In 1981, investors expected short-term yields to decline. In 1984, investors expected short-term yields to rise.
23. The analyst must be arguing that either an increase in expected inflation or an increase in borrowing will increase the yield on long-term bonds relative to the yield on short-term bonds.
25. The coupon on the state bond will not be subject to tax, so its pre-tax yield will also be 8%. The \$75 coupon on the federal perpetuity will be subject to a tax of \$29.70. If its after-tax yield is 8%, its price must be $\$45.30/.08 = \$566.25$. Therefore, its pre-tax yield must be $\$75/\$566.25 = 13.25\%$.
27. Federal income tax rates were lower in the 1980s than in the 1970s.
29. Liquidity is an important consideration; as a young firm, Fred's may have only a thin market for its assets.

31. According to expectations theory, it should not; but according to preferred habitat theory or segmented markets theory, it should, because the Fed is unlikely to have any reason to prefer a particular maturity (at least for its long-run portfolio).
33. The expected future short-term rate is higher, so the borrower gets the same rate over the two-year period.

CHAPTER 8

Review Questions

1. This idea is the nominal interest rate parity condition.
3. A fall in the value of the yen lowers the foreign currency price of Japanese exports and raises the yen price of foreign imports to Japan. This would increase demand for Japanese businesses that export or that compete domestically with foreign imports. Japanese consumers would be hurt by higher prices of foreign imports.
5. The euro has appreciated; the Japanese yen and British pound have depreciated.
7. The yen/dollar rate is 300 yen/dollar. The euro/dollar rate is 550/500 = 1.1 euros/dollar.
9. The dollar should appreciate, as demand for U.S.-produced goods rises.
11. The dollar should appreciate, as funds flow into the United States.
13. The new common European currency is the euro. England is not participating in the move to a common currency. When a country gives up its domestic currency it loses control over its domestic money supply (and monetary policy). Some persons may also be reluctant to give up a domestic currency for political reasons.

Analytical Problems

15. Both appreciate relative to the dollar.
17. It is not a sure thing. A depreciation in the value of the dollar versus the yen could wipe out the apparent gain from higher U.S. interest rates.
19. You should invest at home.
21. The United States should benefit from greater investment flow from Japan.
23. a. $EX_r = EX(P)/P_f$ = (200 yen/\$)(\$16/CD)/(3500 yen/CD) = 8/9.
    b. $EX_r = EX(P)/P_f$ = (2 pounds/\$)(\$16/CD)/(6 pounds/CD) = 4/3.
25. $\Delta EX^e/EX = -1\%$, so $EX^e = 247.5$ yen/dollar.
27. In this case, the difference is maturity (preferred habitat) versus country (currency premium) for assets that are otherwise perfect substitutes. The preference arises because of differences in risk, liquidity, or information across countries versus across maturities. A "segmented markets" analogue is inconsistent with large observed capital flows.
29. Portfolio investors would prefer to invest in German bonds if inflation were lower in Germany (so that the total return is higher) or if the pound were expected to depreciate.

CHAPTER 9

Review Questions

1. The difference is trade today (spot transaction) versus trade in future (forward transaction). A futures contract offers greater liquidity and lower information costs.
3. A hedge transaction reduces risk for the hedger; in speculation, a trader accepts increased risk to try to profit.
5. Options work like life insurance; by paying a small premium, you can hedge against changes in your asset's value.
7. The exchanges guarantee all contracts, so information and search costs are reduced, thereby permitting anonymous trading.
9. At a price of 60, the put is in the money; at a price of 70, neither is in the money; at a price of 80, the call is in the money.
11. You might well disagree, as these markets provide useful risk-sharing benefits, promoting liquidity and the transmission of information.
13. You could buy a put option, which gives the option of selling the underlying security. If the market price of the stock drops below the strike price of the option, you would be able to profit by buying the stock in the market and reselling it at the higher strike price.

Analytical Problems

15. Investors who bought put options would benefit by being able to purchase stock at prices below the strike price in their options contracts. Investors who sold put options would be hurt by having to buy stock at prices above their current market values.
17. Because Tropicana is purchasing oranges, they would be better off if orange prices were low. They could hedge the risk of an increase in orange prices by buying futures contracts.
19. You could buy put options. If interest rates rise, your Treasury bonds lose value, but you make money on the put option; if interest rates fall, your Treasury bonds rise in value, and your puts are worthless.
21. You could buy Treasury put options.

CHAPTER 10

Review Questions

1. Rational expectations make use of all available information. In a market in which investors and traders have rational expectations the market price of an asset equals its fundamental value.
3. When traders and investors use all available information in forming expectations of future rates of return and the cost of trading is low, the equilibrium price of a financial instrument is equal to the optimal forecast based on the available information.
5. There is a bubble. In the future, the bubble is likely to burst. Yes, bubbles have burst many times; the latest prominent examples occurred in 1987 in the United States and in 1991–1992 in Japan.
7. Not always. Usually, an informed trader can profit from noise traders, but only if they do not make the equilibrium price deviate from fundamental value.
9. Fads are characterized by overreaction to good or bad news, so prices do not reflect fundamental value. Someone could profit by investing when there is bad news and selling when there is good news.

Analytical Problems

11. Active portfolio management raises trading costs and provides a lower total return.
13. No; this seasonality in returns is not consistent with efficient markets. An investor could profit by buying at the end of December, and selling at the end of January.
15. Darts are cheaper (but don't balance risk).
17. At a 4% discount rate, you would be willing to pay $(1 + i)D/(i - g) = 1.04 \times \$7/(0.04 - 0.02) = \$364$. At a 3% discount rate, you would be willing to pay $1.03 \times \$7/(0.03 - 0.02) = \$721$. If Bigbuck's dividends grow at only 1% per year you would be willing to pay $1.04 \times \$7/(0.04 - 0.01) = \$242.67$.
19. In this case, you could adopt a contrarian strategy: Buy after bad news, sell after good news.

CHAPTER 11

Review Questions

1. Financial intermediaries are able to take advantage of economies of scale to reduce transactions costs.
3. Moral hazard occurs when borrowers make different use of borrowed funds than they would have made with their own; adverse selection occurs when bad risks are more likely to accept a financial contract than are good risks. Each makes information asymmetric: the lender may not know what the borrower will do with the funds because of moral hazard, and the lender may not know the riskiness of the borrower because of adverse selection.
5. The "lemons problem" refers to the adverse selection problem that arises from asymmetric information. Because potential investors have difficulty in distinguishing good borrowers from bad borrowers, they offer good borrowers terms they are reluctant to accept. Because banks specialize in gathering information, they are able to overcome this problem.
7. Such provisions are restrictive covenants; banks use them in order to reduce moral hazard problems.
9. A large firm with many shares is more likely to suffer principal-agent problems because organizing challenges to management is more costly.

Analytical Problems

11. The problem is adverse selection. It is likely that only a lemon would be sold so fast. A buyer could circumvent the problem by hav-

ing a mechanic inspect the car or by getting a guarantee from the dealer (or trusting the dealer's reputation).

13. Moral hazard is less likely to be a problem in (b). Note that you can use this question to explain why large companies often provide stock options as part of executives' compensation packages.
15. Asymmetric information owing to moral hazard and adverse selection makes information costs for external funds higher than for internal funds. No; it depends upon the extent to which problems are solved by debt finance, takeover or threat of takeover, high internal net worth, or greater shareholder control.
17. You would not be happy in the first case because higher default risk reduces the bond's price. In the second case, you would be happy because lower default risk raises the bond's price.
19. No, because business cycles are less pronounced in Japan than in the United States.

CHAPTER 12

Review Questions

1. The five main groups of financial institutions are securities market institutions (investment banks, brokers and dealers, and organized exchanges); investment institutions (mutual funds and finance companies); contractual savings institutions (insurance companies and pension funds); government financial institutions; and depository institutions (commercial banks, savings institutions, and credit unions).
3. No, the NYSE is a secondary market. You are buying the shares of stock from someone else, not from IBM.
5. E-trading is on-line trading conducted over the Internet. Combined with the competition from electronic trading, the effect of e-trading has been to reduce the value of seats on the major stock exchanges.
7. Moral hazard describes the situation where those with insurance take on greater risks than they would have in the absence of insurance. Insurance companies use a variety of methods to reduce moral hazard problems, including deductibles, coinsurance, restrictive covenants, limits on individual claims paid, reserving the right to cancel policies, and the hiring of claims adjustors to investigate claims.
9. Predicting property and casualty losses is more difficult than predicting deaths.
11. Banks address adverse selection by specializing in gathering information about the credit risk of borrowers and by custom-tailoring loans (e.g., including collateral and covenants).
13. Mutual funds pool resources to invest in a diversified portfolio (allowing risk sharing). They also lower transactions costs of investing, increasing liquidity. Mutual funds do not make commercial loans; they pass funds through to existing direct instruments. There is less need for regulation because they just pass funds through, as long as information is made available to investors.

Analytical Problems

15. These institutions pool risk of death and investment risk that individuals may not be able to do. Self-insurance would be more costly for individuals.
17. Such a country is more likely to develop significant markets in mutual funds. The funds would help savers more than borrowers because mutual funds just buy well-known assets, they do not make commercial loans.
19. If the stock market is efficient, an actively managed fund is unlikely to generate high enough returns to offset its additional costs, so the index fund would be preferred.
21. Yes, past performance is not necessarily a guide to future returns; risk levels may be different; transactions costs may be different; sales loads may be different; liquidity may be different; and taxability may be different.

CHAPTER 13

Review Questions

1. A bank's liabilities, principally deposits and borrowings, are its sources of funds. Its assets, principally loans and securities, are its uses of those funds.
3. Banks are able to offer small savers deposit insurance. This gives them an advantage over other intermediaries in acquiring funds from small savers.

5. Banks borrow (unsecured) from each other at the federal funds rate; repos are secured by underlying securities.
7. The three types of risk faced by banks are credit risk (the risk of default); liquidity risk (the risk of running out of cash when needed); and interest rate risk (the risk that changes in interest rates affect the value of the bank's portfolio).
9. The interest rate charged depends on the default risk of the loans, the opportunity cost of funds, and the cost of funds.
11. Banks manage assets and liabilities to reduce liquidity risk. To meet these goals they mix lending through the federal funds market and repurchase agreements (RPs), and keep enough cash to meet needs without sacrificing too much return by using CDs, RPs, Eurodollars, and federal funds.
13. Off-balance-sheet banking activities include trading in derivative assets, selling liquidity and information services, and securitizing loans. Banks have participated in these activities to capitalize on the transactions-cost and information-cost advantages to augment income.

Analytical Problems

15. Yes, there would still need to be transactions services and a payments system even if there were no need for commercial lending by banks.
17. If depositors had full information on borrowers, there would not be a bank run started by the unfounded fear that bad loans had been made; this would be possible if bankers had private information. However, a run could start for other reasons, such as bad economic times.
19. Banks welcome it because the action reduces the implicit tax on reserves (because reserves pay no interest); banks can then lend the freed reserves at a positive interest rate. In the second case, no, since they would not reduce their level of reserves.
21. First: assets: −\$1000 in reserves, liabilities: −\$1000 in checkable deposits; Melon: assets: +\$1000 in reserves, liabilities: +\$1000 in checkable deposits.
23. No, because with such a large proportion of assets in the form of loans—and no securities—it has no defense against a liquidity crisis; also, with no equity cushion, a small bad event could cause the bank to fail.
25. \$5 million excess reserves; reserves \$10 million, securities \$40 million, loans \$140 million, deposits \$140 million, capital \$50 million; −\$4 million excess reserves, so borrow \$4 million; same as before but reserves \$14 million, borrowings from banks \$2 million, borrowings from Fed \$2 million.
27. $MV = \Sigma PV_t = \$1100/1.1 + \$1210/1.1^2 + \$1331/1.1^3 = \$3000$. Duration $= d = \Sigma t(PV_t/MV) = 1(\$1000/\$3000) + 2(\$1000/\$3000) + 3(\$1000/\$3000) = 1/3 + 2/3 + 3/3 = 2$. $(MV/MV = -d\,[i/(1 + i)] = -2(0.02/1.1) = -0.036$, so the market value falls 3.6%.
29. $GAP = d^A - d^L(L/A) = 13 - 7(93/100) = 6.49$.

CHAPTER 14

Review Questions

1. Under the dual banking system, some banks have national charters, while others have state charters. There are different sets of regulations for national versus state banks that allow specialization by different types of banks.
3. Historically, political concerns over large banks have been fueled by the public's fear of large banks. These concerns led to the creation of the Federal Reserve System, federal deposit insurance, and branching restrictions.
5. No, it would be efficient. Bank runs may cause contagion, which could lead to the failure of solvent banks.
7. Under the payoff method, the bank's goodwill is lost, but the purchase and assumption method maintains goodwill; purchase and assumption may be attractive to other banks wanting to diversify; the payoff method often costs less because only insured depositors are covered, whereas under the purchase and assumption method uninsured depositors do not lose anything.
9. *Branching Restrictions:* The McFadden Act kept national banks from expanding into other states—owing to fear of the monopoly power of large banks. *Activities Restrictions:* The Glass-Steagall Act kept banks from engaging in nonbank activities (investment

banking and brokerage)—to restrict risks taken by banks. Neither regulation seems likely to survive in the future.

11. Banks tried to use bank holding companies (regulated by the Bank Holding Company Act of 1956), nonbank banks (regulated by the Competitive Equality Banking Act of 1987), and ATMs to expand geographically. Most states have allowed at least regional banking.
13. The Glass-Steagall Act of 1933 forced the separation of commercial and investment banking. It was enacted to prevent conflicts of interest in banks. Its restrictions, whittled away in various ways over the years, were repealed by the Gramm-Leach-Bliley Financial Act of 1999.
15. Banks can (1) finance growth opportunities in sectors in which information problems are important; (2) make sure that managers of large-scale enterprises are working to maximize the long-run value of those firms; and (3) reduce costs of financial distress for firms having difficulty meeting their current obligations to banks and other creditors.

Analytical Problems

17. Bankers attempted to deal with the problem of bank runs by operating clearing houses, the members of which agreed to lend funds to banks threatened by a run. A clearing house could deal effectively with localized runs, but could not deal effectively with a common shock, such as a financial panic, that affected most members simultaneously.
19. The Fed was concerned about a contagion effect that might have arisen from the failure of Long-Term Capital Management. Because the Fed helped to arrange for the creditors of Long-Term Capital Management to keep the company in operation, it may have increased the moral hazard problem.
21. You do not care, because you are fully insured. You pull at least $100,000 out of the bank. No, because runs can occur, as they did at Continental Illinois Bank in 1984.
23. Possibly. Before the introduction of federal deposit insurance, depositor discipline forced banks to have a lot of capital; with deposit insurance, depositors are no longer concerned about the banks' level of capital.

CHAPTER 15

Review Questions

1. A lender of last resort should (a) lend to solvent banks that are threatened by a run and (b) have a large source of funds to handle large, common shocks.
3. a. The Penn Central default caused a temporary shock to the supply of funds to commercial paper issuers, as lenders questioned the default risk on commercial paper. This could have disrupted the supply of funds to firms (and thus caused reduced output) if the Fed had not stepped in to accelerate bank lending to firms.
   b. The stock market crash of 1987 could have caused markets to shut down owing to illiquidity of market makers. This would have reduced the flow of information about firms that had issued stock, making it difficult for them to raise funds for investment. The Fed's action prevented a loss of information and allowed smooth working of the system.
5. Innovations to circumvent deposit-rate ceilings included the use of negotiable CDs, repos or overnight Eurodollars, and ATS and NOW accounts.
7. The sudden rise in interest rates in the late 1970s and early 1980s led to big capital losses at S&Ls, which had loaned long-term and borrowed short-term. The problems were magnified owing to the interaction of deregulation, undiscovered fraud, lax supervision, and failure to close insolvent institutions (which assumed additional risks) made losses greater.
9. FIRREA was passed to end the S&L crisis. The act replaced the FSLIC with a new deposit insurance fund, the Savings Association Insurance Fund, organized by the FDIC; it formed the Resolution Trust Corporation to handle thrift insolvencies; it authorized the Office of Thrift Supervision to supervise and examine S&Ls; it raised the deposit insurance premiums of S&Ls; and it reregulated investment activities of S&Ls.
11. A "narrow bank" is one that takes deposits and invests them in safe assets. There is no default risk (except for possible fraud), so

there is no need for deposit insurance in a narrow banking system.

13. If a firm goes bankrupt with an underfunded plan, retirees may lose all their income, and the PBGC is by itself inadequate to cover all possibly underfunded plans. This issue is significant because, in the event that many firms fail at the same time (as in a major recession), the bailout of pension plans could be perhaps as large as the S&L crisis.

Analytical Problems

15. Although the Fed had been established as a lender of last resort to help stabilize the banking system, it also felt obliged to maintain a fixed exchange rate under the gold standard. After England left the gold standard in 1931, the Fed took actions (including raising the discount rate) that increased interest rates in order to attract foreign investors and, thereby, maintain the fixed exchange rate. The higher discount rate made it difficult for banks to borrow from the Fed. Hence, the Fed appears to have put its responsibility to maintain the gold standard ahead of its responsibility to maintain the stability of the banking system.
17. You could pay U.S. depositors to move their money to accounts outside the United States so that you could avoid reserve requirements.
19. You would follow strategy (b), as you will surely be closed if you follow strategy (a). Strategy (b) loses money, on average, but its losses are covered by the insurance fund. If you get lucky, the S&L will make money and survive. The consequence of this moral hazard situation is that a socially bad decision is made—one that is inefficient, as it channels funds inappropriately. A regulator could prevent this occurrence by shutting down the S&L before it reaches this point.
21. Here is one possibility: If it is solvent, you could lend to the big bank to get it to cover its securitized mortgages and end the crisis; if it is not solvent, the bank must be shut down, however. In this case, you could organize other banks together to convince them to cover the large banks' losses, paving the way for this by offering discount loans at below-market interest rates.

CHAPTER 16

Review Questions

1. The international banking market exists to satisfy the demand for banking services (risk sharing, liquidity, and information) with lower transactions costs than could be provided by domestic banks, especially with regard to international trade.
3. The leading financial centers are located in the United Kingdom, Japan, the United States, and Switzerland.
5. IBFs are subsidiaries of U.S. banks that do not conduct banking operations in the United States, but cater to customers who trade internationally. They can branch across state lines, do not have to hold required reserves, and are not subject to interest rate ceilings; hence they can be more competitive with foreign banks.
7. A currency swap is the exchange of debt instruments denominated in different currencies. Using currency swaps allows firms to borrow in their own countries so that borrowing costs are lower (because information about the company is more available) and then swap the payments to obtain foreign currency.
9. There is an information problem because trading partners are in a foreign country, so there is limited information about their credit worthiness. Banks and their customers use the bankers' acceptance, in which a bank guarantees repayment by the borrowing firm, earning a fee for its investment in information collecting and monitoring.
11. In a loan syndication individual banks hold fractions of a loan. Loan syndication is often used with Euroloans because they are quite large and would result in a lack of diversification for a single commercial bank.
13. The problem of interest rate risk is reflected in a mismatch of the duration of assets and liabilities. The problem of exchange rate risk is reflected in the mismatch in the value of currencies of assets and liabilities. Possible risk management strategies include hedging with futures or options and using currency swaps.
15. U.K. regulations that banks could not use pounds for overseas loans led to use of the U.S. dollar. Binding Regulation Q interest rate ceilings in the United States led to U.S. banks

acquiring dollar deposits overseas. The role of the lender of last resort becomes complicated in Eurocurrency markets—large multinational banks have deposits and loans in many countries, so which country should be the lender of last resort for these banks is not clear.

Analytical Problems

17. No; bankers' acceptances are negotiable and often sold in the market, just like any other financial asset.
19. Ichi-ball's bank writes a letter of credit and sends it to Big Ball to pay for the balls. When Big Ball ships the baseballs from the United States to Japan, it presents the letter of credit to its own bank in the United States, which pays it in dollars. Big Ball's bank issues a time draft and sends it to Ichi-ball's bank. Ichi-ball's bank pays Big Ball's bank. All that remains is for Ichi-ball to pay off its bank at some point in the future; in the meantime, the bankers' acceptance, which is a liability of Ichi-ball's bank, exists and can be traded in the market.

CHAPTER 17

Review Questions

1. Principal assets include (1) U.S. government securities, held to earn interest, and (2) discount loans to banks, usually due to banks' short-run financing needs. Principal liabilities include (1) currency, held by the nonbank public for transactions purposes, and (2) reserves, held by banks as vault cash or as deposits with the Fed.
3. Currency in circulation = Currency outstanding − Vault cash. Currency in circulation is part of the monetary base.
5. To increase the money supply, the Fed can conduct open market purchase or increase the volume of discount loans. To decrease the money supply, the Fed can conduct open market sales or reduce the volume of discount loans.
7. A single bank has to take into account that funds it loans out may leave the bank, reducing its reserves. For the system as a whole, funds that are loaned out only reduce the total reserves in the system if those funds are converted into currency.
9. (*C/D*) would have declined steadily.
11. The Fed should increase the monetary base by 10% − 2% = 8%.

Analytical Problems

13. Assets: Δ Loans = +\$100,000; Liabilities: Δ Deposits = +\$100,000; Assets: Δ Reserves = −\$100,000; Liabilities: Δ Deposits = −\$100,000; Δ Assets = 0; Δ Loans = +\$100,000; Δ Reserves = −\$100,000; Δ Liabilities = 0.
15. Required reserves: $(0.14 \times 300) + (0.03 \times 200) = 42 + 6 = 48$; $0.16 \times 300 = 48$. Excess reserves are 0 in both cases.
17. If the elimination of deposit insurance made depositors more concerned about the safety of bank deposits, then we might see a return to larger fluctuations in the currency-deposit ratio, *C/D*, destabilizing the money multiplier and reducing the Fed's control over the money supply.
19. a. $RR = (0.03 \times 30) + (0.12 \times 150) = 18.9$. $ER = 0$.
    b. Assets: Reserves = 23.9, Securities = 26.1; everything else the same. Total reserves are now 23.9; since *RR* still equal 18.9, $ER = 5$.
    c. Assets: Loans = 155; Liabilities: Checkable deposits = 185; everything else the same as in (b). $RR = 19.5$, $R = 23.9$, $ER = 4.4$.
    d. Assets: Reserves = 18.9; Liabilities: Checkable deposits = 180; everything else the same as in (c). $RR = 18.9 = R$, so $ER = 0$.
21. $(1 + 100/800)/(100/800 + 0.20 + 40/800) = 3$.
23. No, the demand for U.S. dollars rises, as the United States is a safe haven for wealth.
25. The money multiplier is 1; the Fed cannot affect the money supply beyond the change in the monetary base.
27. a. $B = C + R = [(0.06 + 0.14) \times 2000] + (0.2 \times 2000) = 400 + 400 = 800$; $M1 = C + D = 2400$; $M2 = M1 + N + MM = 2400 + (1.5 \times 2000) + (0.5 \times 2000) = 6400$. Bank A required reserves are \$300 million × 0.14 = \$42 million; total

reserves are \$48 million; excess reserves are \$6 million. Economy required reserves are \$2000 billion × 0.14 = \$280 billion; total reserves are \$400 billion; excess reserves are \$120 billion.

b. Using multiplier formulas: *M1* multiplier = (1 + *C/D*)/[(*C/D*) + (*R/D*) + (*ER/D*)] = 1.2/(0.2 + 0.14 + 0.06) = 3; *M2* multiplier = [(1 + *C/D*) + (*N/D*) + (*MM/D*)]/[(*C/D*) + (*R/D*) + (*ER/D*)] = (1 + 0.2 + 1.5 + 0.5)/(0.2 + 0.14 + 0.06) = 3.2/0.4 = 8.

c. Bank A's balance sheet is unchanged; required reserves = \$300 million, so excess reserves = 0. *M1* multiplier = (1 + *C/D*)/[(*C/D* + (*R/D*) + *ER/D*)] = 1.2/(0.2 + 0.16) = 3 1/3; *M2* multiplier = [1 + (*C/D*) + (*N/D*) + (*MM/D*)]/[(*C/D*) + (*R/D*) + (*ER/D*)] = 3.2/0.36 = 8 8/9. (Notice that other variables can be calculated, given the same ratios defined above: Since *B* = 800, and given the multipliers, we can derive *M1* = \$2666 2/3 billion, *M2* = \$7111 1/9 billion; *N* + *MM* = *M2* − *M1* = \$4444 4/9 billion; *N/D* + *MM/D* = 2 implies that *D* = \$2222 = 2/9 billion; *C/D* = 0.2 implies that *C* = \$444 4/9 billion; *B* = *R* + *C* implies that *R* = \$355 5/9 billion, since *B* is unchanged at \$800 billion.)

d. Bank A loses \$1.5 million in securities and gains \$1.5 million in reserves. Required reserves are \$42 million, as in part (a). Total reserves are \$49.5 million, so Bank A has \$7.5 million in excess reserves. The new monetary base is \$888 8/9 billion. (*Additional effects*: Multipliers for *M1* and *M2* are 3 and 6, as in (b), so with *B* = \$888 8/9 billion, *M1* = \$2666 2/3 billion, *M2* = \$7111 1/9 billion; so *M1*, *M2*, *N*, *MM*, *D*, and *C* are all the same as in (c), but now reserves are higher (888 − 8/9) − 444 4/9 = \$444 4/9 billion) than in part (c).)

CHAPTER 18

Review Questions

1. Sources of the monetary base are enumerated in Eq. (18.3). Uses of the monetary base are enumerated in Eq. (18.1).
3. Items (a), (c), and (e) are assets of the Fed. Items (b), (d), (f), (g), and (h) are liabilities of the Fed.
5. The Fed's largest asset is its security holdings; its largest liability is Federal Reserve Notes outstanding.
7. If the central bank is not independent, it is likely to monetize the debt, causing inflation. If the central bank is independent, it will not monetize the debt, and inflation may be low even if deficits are high.
9. The start of the Korean War substantially increased government spending and borrowing. The Fed was obliged to buy large quantities of Treasury securities in order to peg the interest rate on them. The Fed was afraid that the consequent increases in the monetary base would cause an acceleration in the inflation rate.

Analytical Problems

11. The Federal Reserve float rises \$1 billion; the monetary base rises \$1.75 billion. (Just add up sources of the base and subtract uses of the base in Eq. (18.3).)
13. Deposit withdrawals need not cause the monetary base to change. An increase in the currency-deposit ratio, *C/D*, would cause the money multiplier and, therefore, the money supply to fall. The Fed could make discount loans to help banks deal with the withdrawals. An increase in discount loans would increase the monetary base. The Fed might not want to take action to offset this increase in the base if the increase in the base were offsetting the decline in the money multiplier.
15. The monetary base will not necessarily grow by less than it would without the deal (if the Fed has not let the size of the deficit affect monetary policy).
17. Federal Reserve float equals \$2 billion. The Fed loses interest on float. Accordingly, if Federal Reserve float were reduced, the Fed would hold more securities, earning more interest.
19. There is no change in the monetary base (this is called a "sterilized intervention")—the Fed has \$100 million more of foreign-exchange reserves and \$100 million less of securities.
21. The rise in the deficit tends to raise interest rates. To stabilize interest rates, the Fed must increase the monetary base, thereby monetizing the debt.

CHAPTER 19

Review Questions

1. Congress passed the Federal Reserve Act in order to deal with recurring financial panics. The Panic of 1907 had a particular impact on Congressional thinking.
3. The FOMC consists of members of the Board of Governors, the president of the Federal Reserve Bank of New York, and presidents of four other Federal Reserve Banks.
5. The Fed's independence is enhanced by long, overlapping, nonrenewable terms of office and independent financing. The Constitution does not protect the Fed.
7. The Federal Open Market Committee guides the Fed's open market operations.
9. No; stock in Federal Reserve Banks pays only a flat 6% dividend, so there is no opportunity for high profits; in any event, only member banks can own the stock.
11. This observation does apply to the Federal Reserve System. Although in some respects power within the system appears to be decentralized, in fact, power within the system is highly centralized.
13. This is not necessarily true; monetary policy is a type of public policy and so should be the responsibility of elected officials. Also, the Fed's independence may make it more difficult to coordinate monetary and fiscal policy.

Analytical Problems

15. Less developed countries often have more trouble marketing governmental debt than do industrial countries. As a result it is often difficult for a central bank to act independently in a less developed country. Research has shown that the more independent a central bank is, the lower the inflation will be. So, on these grounds we would expect the average inflation rate in less developed countries to be higher than in industrial countries.
17. The Fed is operating a political business cycle to get incumbents reelected. The conclusion would change, as the weakening economy justifies the monetary easing; doubts remain, however, that the Fed would have eased monetary policy as much if an election were not coming up.
19. This might appear to contradict the public-interest view, but it could be that Fed policymakers really were pursuing what they believed were correct policies. As discussed in later chapters, in the early 1970s, policymakers and staff at the Fed (like most macroeconomists at that time) did not understand the difference between short-run and long-run tradeoffs between inflation and unemployment. Having never before faced large supply shocks such as those caused by OPEC in the 1970s, the Fed's response didn't give enough attention to reducing inflation. In other words, the Fed tried to pursue socially beneficial policies but lacked the knowledge to do so successfully.
21. Reduce independence: The President of the United States would have much more control over the FOMC; it would be more accountable, as all members of the FOMC would be political appointees, whereas the Federal Reserve bank presidents are not; would lose information about regional concerns, except as they are communicated through political channels (currently at each FOMC meeting there is a "go around" at which each Federal Reserve bank president discusses conditions in each district).
23. Because the European Central Bank is newly created it may feel that it is particularly important to demonstrate its independence from European politicians. It may be particularly inclined to demonstrate its independence of political pressure from Germany, the most economically powerful state in Europe.
25. This is not true. The Fed may feel that its independence is necessary to carry out the public interest, so it mobilizes groups that support it to help guarantee its independence.

CHAPTER 20

Review Questions

1. When the Fed was set up its main purpose was to use discount loans to stop bank panics. It only began using open market operations during the 1920s.
3. The Fed has greater control over open market operations, considers them to be more flexible, and considers them to be easier to implement than its other monetary policy tools.

5. More banks borrow; they can profit from borrowing at the lower discount rate and lending at the higher federal funds rate. Although the Fed's policing activities prevent banks from doing this directly, they can do it indirectly by varying their transactions over time.
7. False. It is too powerful, and thus isn't of much use in making small changes in policy.
9. No; it can carry forward a deficit of up to 4% of its required reserves.
11. Otherwise, banks could profit from borrowing at the discount rate, which is generally lower than the federal funds rate; the Fed would not need to do so if the discount rate were higher than the federal funds rate.
13. A *Fed watcher* is someone who interprets what the Fed is doing and possibly predicts what the Fed is likely to do in the future.
15. (1) In the principal-agent view, the Fed issues vague announcements in order to avoid accountability. (2) In the cheap-talk view, the Fed issues vague announcements because, if it were more precise and people believed it, the Fed would have an incentive to change its actions. Political pressure could be a factor, especially to the extent that the Fed is vague because being precise would raise the ire of politicians.
17. Dynamic operations are for implementing monetary policy. Defensive operations are for offsetting minor disturbances to the economy that are unrelated to the business cycle.

Analytical Problems

19. The money supply decreases by 8 × $1 billion, or $8 billion.
21. The Fed will use defensive open market operations to increase money supply, offsetting the seasonal demand without a change in interest rates.
23. No; it is necessary to keep the discount rate in line with other interest rates. (Keeping the discount rate fixed when other interest rates were rising would be an expansionary policy.) What matters is the relationship among interest rates (especially between the federal funds rate and the discount rate) not the levels of the interest rates.
25. The Fed's supply of reserves would become a vertical line. An open market purchase would have a larger effect on the equilibrium exchange rate.
27. The answer is given away by the question. Just do the exercise to write out the supply and demand schedules to determine the equilibrium.

CHAPTER 21

Review Questions

1. The principal goals of monetary policy are to stabilize the price level, promote high employment, promote economic growth, stability in financial markets and institutions, promote interest rate stability, and promote stability in foreign-exchange markets.
3. If the demand for money becomes less stable, the links between changes in the money supply and changes in nominal GDP will also become less stable. This would reduce the desirability of selecting a monetary aggregate as an intermediate target.
5. An indicator is a financial variable whose movements reveal information about present or prospective conditions in financial markets or the economy. Targets are variables that the Fed can influence directly and that help achieve monetary policy goals. An indicator can be used as a target. An example would be William McChesney Martin's use of free reserves as a target.
7. A zero unemployment rate isn't attainable because some frictional unemployment always occurs in the process of job search and matching.
9. The use of operating targets allows for quicker response if the intermediate target is being missed.
11. When the economy expanded, putting upward pressure on interest rates, the Fed had to expand the money supply to try to keep interest rates low. This action in turn put upward pressure on inflation.
13. The Fed targeted nonborrowed reserves, allowing the federal funds rate to vary more. The lack of increased monetary control was the result of financial deregulation at the same

time, combined with a recession and, later, credit controls.

15. The usefulness of commodity prices as an intermediate target is limited because they are not sufficiently related to inflation.
17. The choice of an operating target must match the choice of an intermediate target for controllability.

Analytical Problems

19. *Tools:* (d) and (i); *operating targets:* (b), (e), and (f); *intermediate targets:* (a) and (g); *goal variables:* (c) and (h).
21. The economic expansion puts upward pressure on interest rates; to keep interest rates fixed, the Fed uses expansionary policy, so the economy grows even faster. A possible change would be to adjust targets to conditions—if there is no evidence of a change in economic strength, a rise in interest rates means an increased money demand, which it makes sense to accommodate with increased money supply; but if there is evidence that the economy is stronger, a rise in interest rates should be met with a rise in the target interest rate to avoid procyclical policy.
23. The simple rule would be valid when the relationship of *M2* with goal variables such as real output growth and inflation is stable and predictable. Problems arise when the relationship is affected by other events; then the growth rate of *M2* may need to change over time.
25. False. When money demand increases, with reserves fixed, interest rates increase, but the money supply doesn't change (except to the extent that the multiplier changes with changes in the interest rate).
27. It does matter. For instance, when the federal government's budget has been in deficit, the Fed has sometimes come under pressure to keep interest rates from rising by engaging in open market operations.
29. Interest rate targets are not useful for this purpose if the targets do not adjust frequently. For example, if interest rate targets are fixed, then in a recession, demand for money falls, reducing interest rates, and the Fed tightens to raise interest rates, further reducing money supply and worsening the economy further.

CHAPTER 22

Review Questions

1. U.S. international reserves and the monetary base both increase by $3 billion. This is an unsterilized intervention.
3. The Japanese central bank sells yen and buys dollars; the Fed sells yen and buys dollars.
5. The appreciation makes exports more expensive, while depreciation raises the cost of imports.
7. It is an accounting device for keeping track of private and government flows of funds between the United States and foreign countries.
9. If Japan has a trade surplus, its exports exceed its imports.
11. U.S. inflation rose, and the United States had persistent balance-of-payments deficits. The United States did not have enough gold to cover foreign holdings of dollar assets.
13. Devaluing or revaluing calls into question a country's economic policies. Exporters complain about revaluations, and importers complain about devaluations. Speculative attacks often force the exchange rate to change.
15. False. This situation depends on the promise of the United States to exchange dollars for gold; with continued balance-of-payments deficits, the U.S. gold stock would eventually disappear, as could have happened under Bretton Woods.
17. The IMF lends to countries with short-term balance-of-payments problems so they will not come under speculative attack and can maintain their exchange rate. This approach is similar to the Fed's lender-of-last-resort function that lets banks handle short-run liquidity problems in order to avoid runs that would force liquidation of assets.

Analytical Problems

19. The world's trade balance should be zero. But, in fact, it is a trade surplus because of statistical discrepancies.
21. Gold flows out of the country.
23. A failure by Brazil to balance its budget would put pressure on the central bank to monetize some of the debt. This would make it difficult to maintain a pegged exchange rate against the

dollar. To defend the pegged exchange rate, the Brazilian central bank has to buy its currency with dollars. The funds from the IMF would increase its ability to do so, but the IMF would be reluctant to provide the funds unless the Brazilian government were willing to take steps to make defending the peg viable.

25. You would expect the pound to depreciate. To profit from this knowledge, you would sell pound assets and buy yen assets. Such a collective effort to do so would constitute a speculative attack on the pound.
27. The net balance is \$45 billion + \$20 billion, or \$65 billion.
29. Merchandise imports equal −\$1 million. Net unilateral transfers equal +\$1 million. There is no change in the current account balance.

CHAPTER 23

Review Questions

1. Real money balances equal nominal money balances divided by the price level.
3. Because of how velocity is defined. That velocity was constant.
5. No; changes in velocity depend on the availability of near-money substitutes, which in turn depends on the financial system and regulation in each country.
7. Fisher ignored the effect of the interest rate on the demand for money.
9. The interest rate, which is the opportunity cost of holding money, affects money demand in the Baumol-Tobin approach.
11. Individuals expect capital gain on bonds, so they reduce their demand for money.
13. The relevant income concept in Friedman's approach is permanent income—expected present value of future income. Permanent income is not directly measurable, so proxies must be developed.
15. A weighted monetary aggregate sums monetary assets using weights according to how liquid the assets are in order to approximate the "moneyness" of different assets. Such aggregates have closer relationships with other economic variables than do the simple sum aggregates.

Analytical Problems

17. a. $MV = PY$, so $M = PY/V =$ \$2 trillion. $P = 1$, so $M/P =$ \$2 trillion.
    b. Assume that V is constant, and assume no change in Y. Hence $P = MV/Y =$ \$2.5 trillion × 3/\$6 trillion = 7.5/6 = 1 1/4; so the price level rises 25%.
19. Because of a decline in confidence in the banking system, depositors withdrew large amounts from banks and held the funds in cash. Nominal interest rates dropped to very low levels.
21. Real money demand will rise by 10%. (Note that, as $M^d = k\,(PY)$, $M^d/P = kY$.)
23. Inflation would have been higher, because velocity declined in the 1980s, owing to financial innovation and a decline in interest rates.
25. To represent a good deal, you must be avoiding service charges of at least \$1000 × (8% − 3%), or \$50.
27. According to the liquidity preference theory, the interest rate rises, reducing money demand and increasing velocity.
29. Money demand functions would break down completely. There is no longer any transactions demand for money, so you would have to redefine money as a collection of assets. At the same time, all financial assets would become very liquid, so you could call them all money.
31. Financial innovation is difficult to quantify. You could reduce the effect of this problem on forecasts of money demand by trying to guess at some quantitative measure for S.

CHAPTER 24

Review Questions

1. The *LM* curve shifts down to the right; the *IS* curve and *FE* line are unaffected.
3. The *IS* curve is directly shifted by a change in fiscal policy in a closed economy. An increase in government spending shifts the *IS* curve up to the right.
5. In a general equilibrium, all markets in the economy are in equilibrium at the same time; *IS*, *LM*, and *FE* all intersect at the same point.

7. The two principal determinants of investment are the expected future profitability of capital and the expected real interest rate.
9. If data show that there is no relationship across countries between their levels of saving and investment, the economies must be open, since domestic saving does not equal investment. If domestic saving and investment are highly correlated, the economies are closed.
11. The *FE* line shows output produced by fully employed resources in the economy; it is vertical because output produced today depends on current factors in place, which are not affected by the current real interest rate.
13. Because they believe that prices are much more flexible in the long run than in the short run.

Analytical Problems

15. The fall in desired investment shifts the *IS* curve down to the left.
17. The *FE* line will shift to the left by a greater amount than expected. The result will be that the actual inflation rate will be less than the expected inflation rate.
19. Desired investment declines because the new tax reduces the profitability of investment. The real interest rate is unaffected because Puny is a small open economy. Puny's current account balance rises because saving is unaffected and investment declines; hence saving is greater than investment, and Puny lends funds internationally.
21. There is no effect in any case because the *FE* line determines current output (none of the events causes the *FE* line to shift) and the *IS* curve is horizontal for a small open economy, so the real interest rate never changes.
23. a. An upward shift of the *IS* curve causes the price level to rise.
    b. A downward shift of the *IS* curve causes the price level to fall.
    c. A rightward shift of the *FE* line causes the price level to fall.
    d. A leftward shift of the *FE* line causes the price level to rise.
    e. A downward shift of the *LM* curve causes the price level to rise.
25. The Asian financial crisis reduced U.S. exports to the countries affected and increased U.S. imports from those countries. The result was a shift of the *IS* curve to the left. The Fed attempted to offset this by an expansionary monetary policy, shifting the *LM* curve to the right.
27. In a small open economy, if the world interest rate declines, the *LM* curve must shift down to the right to restore equilibrium. Hence the price level must fall.
29. The new development increases current productivity, so the *FE* line shifts to the right. The price level falls to restore equilibrium. In the new equilibrium, real interest rate is lower, and current output is higher.
31. a. As a result of the fall in government saving, the *IS* curve shifts up to the right, so the price level rises (to shift the *LM* curve up to the left to restore equilibrium at higher real interest rate).
    b. Because Germany and the United States are both large open economies, Germany also experiences a higher real interest rate and higher price level.
    c. To mitigate the increase in the price level, the U.S. Fed or the German Bundesbank could reduce money supply. Such an action would shift the *LM* curve up to the left, reducing upward pressure on the price level.

CHAPTER 25

Review Questions

1. Along the *AD* curve, there is a negative relationship between the price level and aggregate output. A higher price level reduces real money balances. If nothing else changes, the real interest rate rises, reducing consumption and investment, so aggregate demand declines.
3. In the new classical model, a rise in the price level can increase the aggregate quantity of output supplied in the short run. Firms confuse part of the rise in prices with increases in relative prices, so they increase output.
5. The *LRAS* curve is vertical because output isn't affected by changes in the price level in the long run.

7. The *SRAS* curve slopes upward in the new Keynesian model, indicating that the increase in aggregate demand is a result of the increase in government purchases and raises output in the short run.

Analytical Problems

9. Yes. $MV = PY \rightarrow M/P = (1/V)Y$. If P increases and V is constant, then Y must decline. This establishes the inverse relationship between P and Y necessary for a downward-sloping *AD* curve.
11. In the short run (in the new Keynesian view), the rise in income taxes reduces desired consumption, shifting the *AD* curve to the left and reducing output and the price level. In the long run, the *SRAS* curve shifts to the right, reducing the price level further and restoring full-employment output.
15. a. With no perception of inflation, $\pi = \pi^e$, and $u = 4\%$.
    b. If $\pi = 4\%$ and $\pi^e = 8\%$, $2u = 12\%$, or $u = 6\%$.
    c. If $\pi = 8\%$ and $\pi^e = 4\%$, $2u = 4\%$, or $u = 2\%$.
17. A thrift campaign reduces desired consumption, shifting the *AD* curve to the left. In the short run, output falls. In the long run, the price level falls to restore equilibrium at the full-employment level of output.
19. Recall that aggregate demand equals $C + I + G$. An increase in government purchases reduces desired saving, shifting the saving curve to the left in the saving-investment diagram. If desired investment is very sensitive to changes in the real interest rate, private investment may fall sufficiently to offset much of the fiscal stimulus. That is, the fall in I may offset the stimulative effect on aggregate demand of an increase in G.
21. The *proponents'* claim focuses on aggregate supply: If the infrastructure program makes private labor and capital inputs more productive, the *LRAS* curve shifts to the right. The *opponents'* claim focuses on aggregate demand: In the short run, the increase in government purchases reduces desired saving and raises the real interest rate, possibly crowding out private investment.
23. All else being equal, the increase in the interest rate paid on bank deposits raises money demand and shifts the *AD* curve to the left. In the long run, the price level falls.

CHAPTER 26

Review Questions

1. A business cycle is an episode in which an expansion of current output toward a peak is followed by a contraction in current output toward a trough; they affect economic well-being, and it may be possible to design policies to reduce their severity.
3. Money is nonneutral because of the cost of changing prices by firms with price greater than marginal cost, so prices are sticky; money is nonneutral because wages and prices are set in advance, so prices are sticky.
5. Money is neutral in the short run in the real business cycle model because prices are flexible. Business cycle movements reflect shocks to productivity.
7. In the new classical model, money is nonneutral because of misperceptions. In the new Keynesian model, money is nonneutral because of price stickiness. Both models assume rational expectations about the price level or inflation, so unexpected changes in the money supply affect output. In the new Keynesian model, even expected changes in the money supply affect output in the short run.
9. New classical economists believe changes in the money supply can have an effect on real output only if the changes are unexpected. Therefore, they believe an attempt to carry out a stabilization would be either ineffective (if the policy were announced) or counterproductive (if it were implemented without being announced).
11. a. *Data lag:* Data are not available quickly.
    b. *Recognition lag:* It may take some time to recognize trends in the data.
    c. *Legislation lag:* Legislative action is a time-consuming process.
    d. *Implementation lag:* Carrying out policy changes takes time.
    e. *Impact lag:* It takes time for a policy change to affect the economy.
13. The correlation of money growth and output growth in the real business cycle model is an example of reverse causation: Output growth causes money to grow.

Analytical Problems

15. a. Do nothing, if the *AD* shift were anticipated.
    b. You could stabilize output by increasing the money supply, shifting the *AD* curve to the right, but you would probably not do so to preserve your long-run credibility.
17. The policy will be ineffective in the new classical view; the *AD* and *SRAS* curves will shift by the same amount, resulting in a higher price level, but no increase in output. The policy will result in a short-run increase in output in the new Keynesian view; the *SRAS* will not shift by as much as the *AD*, resulting in a short-run equilibrium at a higher level of output.
19. The increase in business taxes reduces desired investment, shifting the *AD* curve to the left. Output and the price level fall in the short run. With an unexpected increase in the nominal money supply, the Fed could shift the *AD* curve back to the right, restoring the original output and price levels.
21. The increase in expected future output decreases desired saving, shifting the *AD* curve to the right. The Fed could use contractionary monetary policy to shift the *AD* curve back to the left.
23. a. Contractionary—10; Expansionary—12.
    b. If the economy was good six months ago, following a contractionary policy gives a misery index of 10 if the current state is good (90% chance) and a misery index of 13 if the current state is bad (10% chance), so the average misery index is 0.90(10) + 0.10(13) = 10.3. If the economy was good six months ago, following an expansionary policy gives a misery index of 14 if the current state is good (90% chance) and a misery index of 12 if the current state is bad (10% chance), so the average misery index is 0.90(14) + 0.10(12) = 13.8. If the economy was bad six months ago, following a contractionary policy gives a misery index of 10 if the current state is good (75% chance) and a misery index of 13 if the current state is bad (25% chance), so the average misery index is 0.75(10) + 0.25(13) = 10.75. If the economy was bad six months ago, following an expansionary policy gives a misery index of 14 if the current state is good (75% chance) and a misery index of 12 if the current state is bad (25% chance), so the average misery index is 0.75(14) + 0.25(12) = 13.5. Thus policy should be contractionary (10.3 < 13.8) if the economy was in good shape six months ago; it should also be contractionary (10.75 < 13.5) if the economy was in bad shape six months ago.
    c. This situation makes the argument for being contractionary in either state more convincing.
    d. Lags make activist policy more difficult to carry out; in this example, policy should always be contractionary.

CHAPTER 27

Review Questions

1. Banks reduce costs of asymmetric information in lending.
3. Internal funds are a cheaper source of finance than external funds for many firms, owing to asymmetric information (insiders know more than outsiders about the firm's prospects).
5. A financial panic period is characterized by violent fluctuations in financial markets, bank runs, and bankruptcies of many firms. During a financial panic, bank lending falls as depositors withdraw funds from the banking system, thus magnifying the decline in economic activity.
7. The Carter credit controls were "too effective" in reducing credit availability, as they led to a recession.
9. In the money view, the credit market *per se* is not important, since banks are just passive intermediaries. Monetary policy affects the economy through effects on the real interest rate determined in a money market. In a credit view, banks are specialized providers of financial services. Bank loans are special, and monetary policy affects the economy through both the money market and the credit market.
11. The more liquid assets a household or business has, the less likely it is to have to sell illiquid assets to meet current obligations.
13. Both channels are important. Evidence of a role for the bank lending channel is provided by Gertler and Gilchrist, who find that small (bank-dependent) firms are more affected by

monetary policy than are large firms; and Kashyap, Stein, and Wilcox find that commercial paper issuance rises when bank loans decline with contractionary monetary policy.

15. In a credit crunch, the federal funds rate should decline as there is less demand for reserves. The volume of bank lending declines as banks reduce loans to many borrowers; the volume of nonbank lending rises as businesses turn elsewhere for funds. If the volume of nonbank lending declines, this suggests that there is a recession, not a credit crunch.
17. The statement is true to the extent that banks are passive intermediaries in the money view and that bank loans are special in the credit view. However, in the credit view, the public's decisions matter also.

Analytical Problems

19. The financial weakness of borrowers is greater in recession.
21. False. In the bank lending or balance sheet channels, contractionary monetary policy could lead to a credit crunch that reduces the real interest rate.
23. The credit restrictions shift the *AD* curve to the left, resulting in a lower level output and a lower price level than would have prevailed otherwise.
25. The real interest rate will rise more under the money channel. The bank lending channel has an offsetting effect because of the fall in money demand.
27. In the early 1990s the Fed cut interest rates aggressively only after the economy had begun to contract, whereas in late 1998 the Fed acted quickly when signs of a credit crunch appeared. One possible reason for the difference in the Fed's reaction is that the inflation rate had increased in the late 1980s and there had been a temporary spike in oil prices during the Gulf War. Therefore, the Fed may have been reluctant to pursue an expansionary policy too soon for fear of the negative consequences for inflation. In late 1998, the inflation rate was low and stable.

CHAPTER 28

Review Questions

1. Costs of expected inflation arise because expected inflation (1) taxes money holdings and leads to shoe leather costs, (2) distorts saving and investment decisions because of the interaction of inflation and the tax code, and (3) leads to menu costs of changing prices. Costs of unexpected inflation arise because unexpected inflation (1) leads to redistribution of wealth and (2) distorts price signals.
3. Over the long run, the principal cause of inflation is sustained growth of the nominal money supply.
5. People holding money lose purchasing power because of inflation, just as if they were taxed on their money balances.
7. Because of structural and frictional unemployment, we would never expect the unemployment rate to be zero.
9. Because of rapid money creation by the German government. Because of the enormous tax on money balances imposed by the hyperinflation, the demand for real money balances declined drastically. The hyperinflation ended suddenly in the Fall of 1923 as a result of a strong government commitment to reduce the rate of growth of the money supply.
11. In the new classical view, the best strategy for reducing inflation is cold turkey. The monetary authority announces and implements a sudden reduction in money growth.
13. In the new Keynesian view, sticky prices mean that adjustment to slower money growth does not occur quickly; thus output declines in the short run, causing a recession. Rather than a cold turkey approach, new Keynesians recommend using a gradual policy of reducing the money growth rate.
15. The statements are true in the short run but not in the long run.
17. If people believe policymakers' announcements, they will adjust their behavior to the lower inflation rate, and the costs of disinflation will be lower.

Analytical Problems

19. Deflation hurts debtors when it is unexpected. Those economic historians who argue that deflation was not a problem for U.S. farmers in the late nineteenth century believe that since it went on for decades it must have been expected and, therefore, it ought to have been incorporated into the nominal interest rates farmers were paying.
21. In this case, the public would not worry that the Fed would monetize the debt to keep interest rates from rising. This result enhances the Fed's credibility that it will be able to maintain disinflation because it reduces political pressure to inflate away the debt.
23. The Fed could implement a contractionary monetary policy to shift the *AD* curve to the left. Otherwise, the *SRAS* curve shifts up over time, restoring full employment output at a higher price level.
25. Increased optimism shifts the *AD* curve to the right, increasing output and the price level in the short run; in the long run, output is at its full employment level and the price level is higher.
27. If the Fed wants annual inflation to be 4%, the nominal money supply should grow at an annual rate of 5%. If the Fed wants annual inflation to be 1%, the nominal money supply should grow at an annual rate of 1%.
29. In all cases the expected real return is 3%. (a) The realized real return is −2%, so borrowers are better off; (b) the realized return is 8%, so lenders are better off; (c) the realized return is 3%, so neither party is better off.
31. In the short run, policymakers can trade off more inflation for higher output, but there is no long-run trade-off. In both approaches, an unexpected increase in money supply raises inflation and increases output in the short run. In the new Keynesian model, in the short run even an expected increase in money supply raises inflation and increases output. An anticipated increase in money supply doesn't affect output in a new classical model. In the long run, the economy returns to full employment output in both models.
33. If the Fed does nothing in response to the adverse aggregate demand shift, both output and the price level fall in the short run. If the Fed uses expansionary policy, the price level is higher in the long run.
35. Because prices adjust slowly in the new Keynesian approach, the monetary contraction brings on a recession, with falling output, higher unemployment, and the inflation rate falling only slowly.

Index

Note: Page numbers followed by n indicate footnotes.

Accommodating policy, 750
Account, money as unit of, 17
Actuaries, 290
Adaptive expectations, 236
Adjustable-rate mortgages (ARMs), 332, 392
Adjustment credit loans, 519
Adverse selection, 260–264
  financial intermediaries and, 270
  insurance and, 290
  lemons problems and, 261–262
  reducing information costs and, 262–264
Aetna, 289
Agency offices, 414
Agents, 265
Aggregate demand, 629–630, 662
  changes in, price level fluctuations and, 742–743
  equilibrium in, 677–681
  output in long run and, 679
  shocks to, during 1964-1969, 682, 683
  tax cuts and, 666
Aggregate demand (*AD*) curve, 662–667
  deriving, 663–664
  shifts of, 664–667
Aggregate supply, 668
  equilibrium in, 677–681
Aggregate supply (*AS*) curve, 668–676
  long-run, 674, 675–676, 677
  shifts in, 674–676, 677
  short-run, 668–675
Akerlof, George A., 260n
Alesina, Alberto, 486
Allstate, 289
Altman, Robert, 416
American Stock Exchange (AMEX), 44, 218, 283, 285
Announcement effect, 521–522
Annuities, 293
Anonymity premium, 452
Appreciation, of currencies, 179–180, 587n
Arab-Israeli conflict of 1973, 682
Arbitrage pricing theory (APT), 109
Arena, Roberta, 340
Argentina, inflation in, 19
Armey, Dick, 159, 600
Asian financial crisis, 2, 234, 585, 586, 597, 722. *See also* Japan, financial crisis in
  European bonds and, 160
Asset(s), 18, 37
  of banks, 313, 316–317, 331
  of Fed, 436–437, 472–473
  liquidity of. *See* Liquidity
  luxury, 100
  necessity, 100
  reserve, official, 580–581
  returns on. *See* Rate of return; Return(s)
  serving as money, 19–20, 22
Asset management, by banks, 323–325
Asset market(s), shifts in demand curve originating in, 665
Asset market equilibrium, 640–641
Asymmetric information, 40–41, 238, 260
  adverse selection and, 260–264
  moral hazard and, 264–269
Atchison, Topeka, and Santa Fe Railroad, 88
Attrill, Ray, 206
Auction markets, 44
Auriti, Giancinto, 622
Automated teller machines (ATMs), 23, 363
Automatic transfer system (ATS) accounts, 388

Bacchetta, Philippe, 636n
Bahamas, 413
Baker, George F., 355
Baker, Gerard, 709
Baker, James, 576
Balance sheet(s)
  of banks, 313
  of Fed, 471–474
Balance sheet channel, 715, 727–732
Balance-of-payments accounts, 578–580
Balance-of-payments surplus or deficit, 581
Ban, Hideyasu, 734
Bank(s), 312–342. *See also* Banking
  central. *See* Central bank(s); Federal Reserve System (Fed)
  changing activities of, 333–339
  commercial bank loans and, 65
  consolidation of, 376–377
  deposit insurance and. *See* Deposit insurance
  Federal Reserve, 493–495
  information problems in lending and, 715–722
  international. *See* International bank(s); International banking
  Internet, 340–341
  investment, 280–281
  main, in Japan, 372
  member, of Federal Reserve, 495
  national, 347
  nonbank, 363
  profits of, 313–320

regulation of. *See* Banking regulation
relationship with borrowers, 325–333
relationship with savers, 320–325
reserves and. *See* Reserve(s)
state, 347
Bank assets, 313, 316–317, 331
Bank failures, 317–318
of commercial banks, 395–397
deposit insurance and, 356–360
during Great Depression, 382
of savings and loans, 391–393
Bank for International Settlements (BIS), 425
Bank holding companies (BHCs), 349–350, 362–363
Bank Holding Company Act of 1956, 362–363
Bank holiday, 382
Bank Insurance Fund, stability of, 358
Bank lending channel, 715, 724–727, 729–732
Bank liabilities, 313–315, 331
Bank loans
from commercial banks, 65
demand for, 730
supply of, 730
Bank net worth, 313, 317
Bank of America, 361, 363
Bank of Canada, 562
Bank of China, 415
Bank of Credit and Commerce International (BCCI), 415, 416, 429
Bank of England, 416
discount policy of, 519–520
independence of, 505
monetary policy of, 564
Bank of Japan, 504
credibility of, 755
discount policy of, 522
independence of, 505
monetary policy of, 563–564
open market operations of, 517–518
reserve requirements of, 527
Bank of New England, 398
Bank of the United States, 347, 492
Second, 347, 492
Bank of Tokyo, 403
Bank of Tokyo-Mitsubishi, 278
Bank One, 340
Bank reserves, 436
Bank runs, 352–353
BankAmerica, 278, 425
Bankers' acceptances, 60–61, 418–419
Bankers Trust, 278, 374, 425
Banking. *See also* Bank(s)
changing nature of, 369–371
integration in Europe, 374
international, 338–339. *See also* International bank(s); International banking
merchant, 281
narrow, 398
in United States. *See* U.S. banking industry
outside United States, 368, 371–374
universal, 366
Banking Act of 1933, 364–365, 367–368, 385, 497
Banking Act of 1935, 497, 523
Banking panics, 355
Banking regulation, 348–368, 380–408
anticompetitive, 361–368, 385–391
branching restrictions and, 361–364
consolidation and, 361–364
deposit insurance and, 354, 356–360, 391–403
Fed as lender of last resort and, 355–356, 381–385
of Japanese banks, 371–372
lessons for other industries from, 404–405
pattern of, 381
restrictions on scope of activities and, 364–365, 366
outside United States, 371–372
Banking restrictions, 354–355
Banks for Cooperatives, 301
Baring, Peter, 223
Barings P.L.C., 223, 224
Barro, Robert J., 131, 666n
Barta, Patrick, 308–309
Barter, 15–16
Barth, James R., 368n
Basis risk, 217
Basle capital standards of 1988, 400–401
Basle Committee, 416, 426, 428–429
Bat Masterson, 88
Baumol, William J., 612
BBVA, 340
Beenz.com, 30
Behavioral finance theories, 242
Bequest saving, 125
Berger, Allen N., 364n, 369
Bernanke, Ben, 584, 694, 720, 721
Beta, 107
BFG, 340
Bid-asked spread, 84
Birch, David, 30
Black, Fischer, 220
Blinder, Alan S., 561n, 694
Board of Governors, of Fed, 495–496, 497
Boehne, Edward G., 368n, 434
Boesky, Ivan, 52, 272
Bond(s)
corporate, 63–65
coupon, 70, 77–78
discount, 70, 76–77
Eurobonds, 423, 424
government, 63
indexed, 90–91
municipal, 156, 159
oversubscription and, 82
perpetual (consol), 78n
trading, 284–285

Bond markets
  Asian financial crisis and, 160
  changes in equilibrium interest rates in, 121–135
  interest rate determination in, 116–121
  international, growth of, 51
Bond prices
  inflation and, 88
  yields and, 80–86
Bond ratings, 52, 126, 148, 149, 281
Booking sites, 422
Book-value measures, 400
Borrowers, 36–37
  banks' relationships with, 325–333
  matching with savers, 41–43, 258–260
  monetary policy effects of, 729–730
Borrowing
  by banks, 315
  by government, bond supply and, 130–132, 133
Bowie, David, 50
Boyd, John H., 370
BP, 226
Bracket creep, 746
Brady, Nicholas, 248
Brady Task Force, 248, 250
Bramwell, Elizabeth, 112–113
Branches, foreign, of U.S. banks, 413
Branching restrictions, on banks, 361–364
Brauchli, Marcus W., 504n
Bretton Woods system, 584–591
  U.S. abandonment of, 589–591
Britain. *See* Bank of England; United Kingdom
Broker(s), 282
Brokered deposits, 392
Brumbaugh, R. Dan, Jr., 368n
Bubbles, 248, 248n
Buchanan, James, 502
Budget deficits, European Central Bank and, 488–489
Buffett, Warren, 250
Bundesbank, 595
  credibility of, 759
  monetary policy of, 562–563
Burns, Arthur, 496, 552, 553, 559, 706, 760
Bush, George H. W., 501, 503, 706, 714, 762
Bush, George W., 116, 206, 297, 709
Business cycle
  interest rates and, 132–134
  money and output and, 690–694
  political, 502–503
  real business cycle view and, 680–681
  stabilization policies and, 700–704
  in United States, 681–684

Call options, 217
Call Reports, 349
CAMELS rating, 349
Campeau, Robert, 396
Canada, monetary policy in, 562
Capital
  expected profitability of, bond supply and, 127, 133
  international mobility of, 192–194
Capital account, 580, 581
  monetary base and, 480
Capital account balance, 580
Capital adequacy management, 321–322
Capital asset pricing model (CAPM), 109
Capital controls, 575–576
Capital gains, 81
Capital inflow, 580
Capital losses, 81
Capital market(s), 44
Capital market, international, 6
Capital market instruments, 62–65
Capital outflow, 580
Capital requirements, for banks, 359–360, 400–401, 425–426
Caprio, Gerald, 368n
Captive insurance subsidiaries, 291
Caramanico, Franco, 622
Carter, Jimmy, 501, 503, 553, 720, 752, 758
Cash
  electronic (digital), 24, 30–31
  vault, 316, 436
Cash items in process of collection, 316
Cash markets, 45
Cash value, 293
Catte, Pietro, 577
Cayman Islands, 413
Central bank(s), 204, 278, 491–510. *See also* European Central Bank (ECB); Federal Reserve System (Fed)
  fiat money and, 21–22
  independence of, 503–506, 508–509
  intervention by, 427
Central bank credibility, 706, 754–760
  price controls and, 760
  rules versus discretion and, 758–760
  strategies for building, 755–758
Central bank money, 562
Certificates of deposit (CDs), 61, 314
  negotiable, 388
Chandler, Clay, 504n
Charles Schwab, 282
Chase Manhattan, 23, 50, 278, 425
Check(s), 22–23
  electronic, 23
Checkable deposits, 314
  choice of currency over, 450–452
Chemical Bank, 23, 278, 425
Chicago Board Options Exchange, 218
China
  central bank of, 415
  privatization in, 274–275
Chrysler, 367
Churning, 243
Circuit breakers, 250

CIRRUS, 363
Cirrus network, 23
Citibank, 61, 319, 388
Citicorp, 306, 367–368, 415, 425
Citigroup, 278, 306, 415
Citron, Robert L., 222
Clearing House for Interbank Payments and Settlements (CHIPs), 384
Clifford, Clark, 416
Clinton, Bill, 2, 305, 491
Closed economies, 136–137
  IS curve and, 659–660
Closed-end mutual funds, 286
Coins, as asset of Fed, 473
Coinsurance, 292
Cold turkey, 752–753
Collateral, 263
  banks' requirement for, 328
Commercial bank(s), 299–300, 304. *See also* Bank(s); Banking
  failures during 1980s, 395–397
  regulation of, 349–350
Commercial bank loans, 65
Commercial paper, 60
Commodities Futures Trading Commission
(CFTC), 52, 54, 212, 224
Commodity money, 21
Commodity prices, as monetary policy target, 558
Common shocks, 356
Community Reinvestment Act of 1977 (CRA), 327
Compensating balances, 328
Competition, in banking industry, 369
  restriction of, 361–368, 385–391
Competitive Equality Banking Act of 1987, 363, 394
Compounding, 73
Confinity, 30
Consol bonds, 78n
Consult Hyperion, 30
Consumer preferences, long-run exchange rates and, 185–186
Contagion, 352–353
Continental Illinois Bank collapse, 358, 396, 397, 521
Contractual saving institutions, 289–295
Convenience yield, 614
Convertible bonds, 64
Corporate bonds, 63–65
Corporate restructuring firms, 271–272
Corporate taxes, bond supply and, 127, 129–130, 133
Correspondent banking, 316
Cosmo Credit Corporation, 403
Cost(s)
  of acquiring information. *See* Information costs
  historical, 400
  of inefficiency in financial markets, 251–253
  of inflation, 746–749
  transactions. *See* Transactions costs
Cost of living adjustments (COLAs), 671n
Cost-push inflation, 749–750
Coupon bonds
  timing of payments on, 70
  yield to maturity of, 77–78
Credibility. *See* Central bank credibility
Credit controls, 720
Credit crunches, 555, 714, 720–722, 732, 733, 734–735
    of 1966, 387
  aggregate demand during 1990–1991 and, 683–684
Credit derivatives, 233
Crédit Lyonnais, 397, 508
Credit market instruments. *See* Coupon bonds; Debt instruments; Discount bonds; Fixed-payment loans; Simple loans
Credit rationing, 262, 328–329
Credit risk, 326–330, 376–377
Credit unions, 300–301, 304
  regulation of, 350–351
Credit-risk analysis, 326–328
Credit-scoring systems, 327
Crow, John, 562
CS First Boston, 280, 283
Currencies, 16
  appreciation and depreciation of, 179–180, 587n
  devaluation of, 587–589, 590
  exchange rates and. *See* Exchange rate(s)
  international reserve, 585, 592–593
  revaluation of, 587
Currency board, 598
Currency in circulation, 436
Currency outstanding
  as liability of Fed, 473
  monetary base and, 478–479
Currency premiums, 202–203
Currency swaps, 231, 232–233, 417–418
Currency/deposit (C/D) ratio, 450–453
Current account, 579–580, 581
Current account balance, 579, 635
Current output, 637
Current yield, 81
Customers, in Euromarkets, 422–423

Daiichi Kangyo, 372
Daimler-Benz, 373
Daimler-Chrysler, 373
Daiwa Bank, 429
Day trading, 285
Dealers, 282
Debelle, Guy, 560n
Debit cards, 23
Debt, 41–42
  floating-rate, 331–332
  intermediate-term, 42
  long-term, 42
  monetizing, 483
  moral hazard and, 321
  short-term, 42

Debt deflation, 268
Debt financing, moral hazard in, 266–269
Debt instruments
present value and, 72–75
timing of payments and, 69–72
yield to maturity and, 75–79
Deductibles, 291–292
Default, 42
Default risk, 147–152
changes in, 149–152
measuring, 147–148, 149
Default risk premium, 147–152
changes in, 149–152
Default swaps, 233, 338
Default-risk-free instruments, 147
Defensive transactions, 514
Deferred availability cash items, as liability of Fed, 473–474
Deferred payment, money as standard of, 18–19
Defined benefit plans, 297
Defined contribution plans, 296
Deflation, 19
Delegated monitors, 272
Deleveraging, 281
Demand
aggregate. *See* Aggregate demand
for bank loans, 730–732
for currencies, exchange rates and, 183
for money. *See* Money demand
Demand curve
aggregate, 662–667
interest rates in bond market and, 117–118, 122–127, 128
Demand deposits, 347
Demand elasticity, wealth, 99
Demand-pull inflation, 749, 750–751
Department of Education, 305
Department of Veterans Affairs (VA), 305
Deposit insurance, 315, 354, 356–360, 397–398
crisis of 1980s and, 7, 391–403
in international banking, 426–427
private, 399
risk-based pricing of, 399
Deposit multiplier. *See* Simple deposit multiplier
Depository institutions, 299–301
deposits by, as liability of Fed, 474
Depository Institutions Deregulation and Monetary Control Act of 1980 (DIDMCA), 389, 392, 395, 495, 523, 526
Depreciation, of currencies, 179–180, 587n
Derivative instruments, 210–228
of banks, 332–333, 338
forward transactions and, 211
futures, 212–217, 332–333
options, 217–221, 332–333
swaps, 230–233, 332, 417–418
Derivative markets, 45, 210–211, 221–225
anonymous trading and information in, 224–225
benefits for financial system, 221–225
standardization and liquidity in, 224
Determinants of portfolio choice, 97–104
costs of acquiring information, 102, 104
expected returns on assets, 100–101
liquidity of assets, 102
risk associated with asset returns, 101–102, 103
wealth, 99–100
Deutsche Bank, 278, 373
Deutsche Borse, 285
Devaluation, 587–589, 590
Digital cash, 24, 30–31
Direct finance, 41, 47
Discount bonds
timing of payments on, 70
yield to maturity of, 76–77
Discount brokers, 282
Discount loans, 315
as assets of Fed, 437, 472
monetary base and, 476
money multiplier and, 455–456
open market operations compared with, 441–443
reserves and, 440–441
Discount policy, 518–522
benefits of, 520–522
drawbacks of, 522
in other countries, 522
Discount rate, 437, 529, 531
Discount window
policing, 519–520
using, 518
Discretion strategy, for monetary policy, 758–760
Disinflation, 752–754
Disintermediation, 387, 721
Diversification, 39, 105
by banks, 326
in international markets, 110
Dividends, 42
Dixon, Don, 392
Dodd, David, 251
Dollar
foreign-exchange value of, as monetary policy target, 558
as international reserve currency, 592–593
Dollarization, 598
Domenici, Pete, 159
Dornbusch, Rudiger, 708
Dotsey, Michael, 169
Drexel Burnham Lambert, 281
Dreyfus, 278, 286
Dual banking system, 347
Duisenberg, Wim, 491, 506, 508, 509, 600
Dun and Bradstreet, 263
Duration, of bank assets and liabilities, 331
Duration gap, 331
Dynamic transactions, 514

Eastern Europe. *See also* specific countries
collapse of economic system in, 3, 16
former, collapse of economic system in, 258
Eccles, Marriner, 500
Eckel, Catherine, 112–113
Economic analysis, 9–11
Economic fluctuations. *See* Business cycle; Great Depression
Economic growth, as monetary policy goal, 541
Economic Recovery Act of 1981, 705
Economies of scale, 259
Edge Act corporations, 413
Edge Act of 1919, 413
Edwards, Franklin R., 303n
Efficiency
actual, in financial markets, 244–251
costs of inefficiency in financial markets and, 251–253
efficient markets hypothesis and, 234, 237–244
Efficient markets hypothesis, 234, 237–244
Eisenhower, Dwight D., 482
Elasticity of demand, wealth, 99
Electronic cash (e-cash), 24, 30–31
Electronic checks, 23
Electronic communications networks (ECNs), 285
Electronic funds transfer systems, 23–24
Electronic money (e-money), 23–24
Electronic trading (e-trading), 285
Elizabeth II, Queen of England, 223
Employee Retirement Income Security Act of 1974 (ERISA), 297–298, 405
Employee stock ownership plans (ESOPs), 296–297
Employment. *See also* Unemployment
high, as monetary policy goal, 540–541
Employment Act of 1946, 540
Engel, Charles, 246
England. *See* Bank of England; United Kingdom
Equation of exchange, 608
Equilibrium
in aggregate demand and aggregate supply, 677–681
in asset markets, 640–641
in foreign-exchange market, 192–196
general, 628
interest rates at, 121–135
long-run, 679–680
price-level adjustment and, 650–652
shifts in *FE* line and, 649, 651–652
shifts in *IS* curve and, 648–649, 650–651
shifts in *LM* curve and, 649–650, 652
short-run, 678
Equity, 42
Equity financing, moral hazard in, 264–266
Equity premium, 102
Euro, 20, 204, 593
exchange rate for, 206–207
Fed bolstering of, 600–601
Euro Interbank Offer Rate (EURIBOR), 423
Eurobonds, 51, 367, 423, 424
Eurocurrency deposits, 422
Eurodollar(s), 61, 421
Eurodollar market, 422
Euroequities, 51
Euromarkets, 420–424
Europe. *See also* specific countries
fixed exchange rates in, 593–595, 598–599
integration of banking in, 374
European Central Bank (ECB), 204, 576, 594, 698
budget deficits and, 488–489
credibility of, 759
discount policy of, 522
independence of, 505, 506–507, 508–509
monetary policy of, 564
reserve requirements of, 527
European Community (EC), 204, 374
European Monetary Institute (EMI), 594
European Monetary System (EMS), 593, 598
European monetary union, 593–595, 598–599, 698
European System of Central Banks (ESCB), 507
Excess reserves, 319–320, 436
money multiplier and, 454–455
Exchange
money and, 14–20
money as medium of, 16–17
Exchange(s), 44, 283–284
Exchange rate(s), 178–205
aggregate demand and, 699
consequences of changes in, 197
determination in long run, 183–188
determination in short run, 188–196
expected, changes in, 200–201
fixed, 582–591, 593–595, 598–599
flexible, 591–593
fluctuations in, 196–204
foreign-exchange market intervention and, 572–576, 577
forward, 183
nominal, 179, 180–182
real, 180–182
Exchange rate regimes, 582–599
Exchange rate risk, 415–417
Exchange-rate mechanism (ERM), 593–594, 598
Executive Life Insurance Company, 405
Exercise price, 217
Expectations
adaptive, 236
rational, 235–237, 701
Expectations theory, of term structure of interest rates, 162–166, 170
Expectations-augmented Phillips curve, 769
Expected exchange rate, changes in, 200–201
Expected income, national saving and, 630–631
Expected inflation
bond supply and, 130, 133
costs of, 746–747

demand for bonds and, 123–124, 128
domestic, exchange rate fluctuation and, 198–199
interest rates and, 134–136
shifts in *LM* curve and, 646, 647
Expected price, determining, 238–239
Expected price level, short-run aggregate supply curve shifts and, 675
Expected productivity of capital, national investment and, 631
Expected profitability, bond supply and, 127, 133
Expected real interest rate, 88
national investment and, 631
national saving and, 630–631
Expected returns
currency/deposit ratio and, 451
demand for bonds and, 123–124, 128
money demand and, 614
short-run exchange rates and, 190–192
Expiration dates, of options, 218
Extended credit loans, 519

Face value, 70
of bonds, price and, 80–82
Fads, 247
Fair, Ray, 749
Fama, Eugene, 244
Farm Credit System, 63, 301
Farmers Home Administration (FmHA), 305
Fazzari, Steven M., 265
FE line, 647
shifts in, 649, 651–652
Fed watching, 512, 527–533
discount rate and, 529, 531
federal funds market and, 527–528
open market operations and, 516–517, 528, 530
reserve requirements and, 529–530, 532
Federal budgetary deficit, monetary base and, 481–486
Federal deposit insurance, 315, 354, 356–360, 397–398
crisis of 1980s and, 391–403
Federal Deposit Insurance Corporation (FDIC), 54, 325, 354, 356–358, 359, 397, 398, 399–400, 401
Federal Deposit Insurance Corporation Improvement Act of 1991 (FDICIA), 358–359, 399, 400, 401
Federal funds, 61
Federal funds market, 315, 527–528
Federal funds rate, 61, 315, 531–535
Federal Home Loan Bank(s), 350
Federal Home Loan Bank Board (FHLBB), 393
Federal Home Loan Bank System (FHLBS), 350
Federal Home Loan Mortgage Corporation (FHLMC; "Freddie Mac"), 65, 301, 304, 308–309
Federal Housing Administration (FHA), 305
Federal Intermediate Credit Banks, 301
Federal Land Banks, 301
Federal National Mortgage Association ("Fannie Mae;" FNMA), 65, 172–173, 301, 304, 308–309
Federal Open Market Committee (FOMC), 492, 494–495, 496–497, 497, 553
Federal Reserve Act of 1913, 418–419, 492, 523
Federal Reserve banks, 493–495
Federal Reserve float, 475, 476–478
Federal Reserve Notes, 20, 21, 22, 436
Federal Reserve repurchase agreements, 514
Federal Reserve System (Fed), 9, 54, 492–505. *See also* Fed watching
assets of, 436–437
balance sheet of, 471–474
banks of, 493–495
barriers between banks and securities companies and, 367
Board of Governors of, 495–496
chairman of, 496, 501
conflict with treasury, 500–501
creation of, 348, 354, 356, 492–493
credibility of, 755. *See also* Central bank credibility
factors motivating, 501–503
Federal Open Market Committee of, 496–497
during Great Depression, 381–383
independence of, 499–500, 503–505
as lender of last resort, 355–356, 381–385, 520–521
liabilities of, 435–436
member banks of, 495
monetary base and. *See* Monetary base
money supply and, 53
power and authority within, 497–498
successes in recent years, 383–385
supervisory role of, 401–402
Federal Savings and Loan Insurance Corporation (FSLIC), 350, 354, 394
Fedwire system, 384
Fee income, of banks, 334–339
Feldstein, Martin, 636n
Fiat money, 21–22
Fidelity, 38, 286, 287, 367
Finance companies, 288–289, 304
Financial Accounting Standards Board, accounting principles set by, 265
Financial analysis, efficient markets hypothesis and, 242–243
Financial distress, 728–729
Financial futures, 45
Financial innovation, 49, 50, 334
Financial institutions (intermediaries), 3, 7–8, 37
change in activities of, 6
depository institutions, 299–301, 474
functions performed by, 45–46, 48
governmental, 301–305
information costs and, 269–272
information problems in lending and, 716
insurance companies, 289–295, 404–405
investment institutions, 285–289
pension funds, 295–299, 304, 405

removal of regulatory lines separating, 305–307
securities market institutions, 279–285
Financial Institutions Reform, Recovery, and Enforcement Act of 1989 (FIRREA), 394, 395
Financial instruments, 4, 60–65
Financial integration, 49
Financial intermediation, 46, 48
Financial market(s), 3, 5–6, 37, 41–45
globalization of, 50–51
primary, 41–43
secondary, 43–45
Financial market and institution stability, as monetary policy goal, 541–542
Financial panics, 719–720
Financial regulation, 51–55
Financial services, 5
Financial system, 4, 35–58
competition and change in, 48–51
financial intermediaries in, 45–48
financial markets in, 41–45
of Japan, 56–57
key services provided by, 38–41
purpose of, 35–38
regulation in, 51–55
stability of, 52–53
Fiorello, James, 734
First American Bankshares, 416
First Boston Corporation, 281, 364
First Chicago, 425
First National Bank of Boston, 23, 364
First Network Savings Bank, 392
First Republic Bank of Dallas, 396
First-e, 340
Fiscal policy
shifts during early 1980s, 705–706
shifts during early 1990s, 706–707
Fischer, Stanley, 746
Fisher, Irving, 89, 608, 609
Fisher, Peter, 600
Fisher hypothesis, 89, 135
Fixed exchange rate systems, 582–591, 593–595, 598–599
Bretton Woods system and, 584–591
in Europe, 593–595, 598–599
Fixed-payment loans
timing of payments on, 71–72
yield to maturity of, 78–79
Flexible exchange rate systems, 591–593
Flight to quality, 151–152
Float, Federal Reserve, 475, 476–478
Floating-rate debt, 331–332
Ford, 367
Forecasting
risk structure of interest rates for, 158–159
term structure of interest rates for, 168–170
Foreign bank branches, 414–415
Foreign bonds, 51
Foreign deposits
as liability of Fed, 473
monetary base and, 480
Foreign-exchange market(s), 182–183. *See also* Exchange rate(s)
currency premiums in, 202–203
equilibrium in, 192–196
Foreign-exchange market intervention, 570–576
exchange rate and, 572–576
exchange rates and, 577
money supply and, 570–572
Foreign-exchange market stability, as monetary policy goal, 542
Forward rate, 183
Forward transactions, 183, 211
401(k) plans, 298–299
Franklin National Bank crisis, 383, 521
Free Banking period, 347, 348
Free reserves, 551
Free riders, 263
Freedom National Bank, 398
Free-rider problem, 263
French, Kenneth, 110
Frictional unemployment, 541, 750
Friedman, Milton, 459, 525, 614, 617–618, 692–693, 730, 739, 767–768
Full Employment and Balanced Growth Act of 1978, 500, 540, 553, 749
Full employment (FE) line, 637–639
Full employment output, 638, 670
Fundamental value, 236
Futures, 212–217, 332–333
index arbitrage and, 221
Futures contracts, 212, 226–227
Futures prices, 212–214
Fuyo, 372

Galli, Giampaolo, 577
Garn-St. Germain Act of 1982, 389–390, 395
Geithner, Timothy, 600
General Account, 479–480
General Accounting Office (GAO), 305
General directives, 513
General equilibrium, 628
General Motors, 367
General Motors Acceptance Corporation (GMAC), 288
Gensaki market, 518
Germany
banking in, 373–374, 426
central bank of, 562–563, 595, 759
inflation in, 540, 748
interest rates in, 199
postwar growth of economy of, 371
speculative attack and, 595
Gertler, Mark, 370, 730
Ghoten, Toyoo, 592n

Gibbons, David, 376
Gilchrist, Simon, 730
Glassman, James K., 255
Glass-Steagall Act of 1933, 364–365, 367–368, 385, 497
Globalization. *See also* International entries
 of financial markets, 50–51
 trends toward, 7
Gold
 as asset of Fed, 473
 monetary base and, 478
Gold standard, 582–584
Goldfeld, Stephen, 621
Goldman Sachs, 280, 281
Goods market, 628
 shifts in demand curve originating in, 665–666
Gordon, Robert J., 654, 760
Gore, Al, 116
Government
 intervention in banking industry, 354–368
 regulation by. *See* Regulation
Government allocation, 16
Government bonds, 63
Government borrowing, bond supply and, 130–132, 133
Government budget constraint, 482–483, 485–486
Government financial institutions, 301–305
Government National Mortgage Association ("Ginnie Mae;" GNMA), 63, 65, 301
Government purchases, national saving and, 631
Government securities, as assets of Fed, 437
Gradualism, 754
Graham, Benjamin, 251
Gramm-Leach-Bliley Financial Services Modernization Act of 1999, 306–307, 368, 402
Gray, Edwin, 393
"Great Contraction," 693
Great Depression, 53
 Federal Reserve System's actions following crash of October 1929 and, 381–383
 financial panic and, 720
 financial regulation and, 53
 flight to quality during, 151
 global banking crisis and, 721
 money multiplier and money supply during, 459
Greenbacks, market for, 243
Greenspan, Alan, 384, 464, 491, 496, 497, 539, 555, 562, 566–567, 600, 654, 706, 708, 709, 714, 739, 763
Guinnane, Timothy W., 243
Gulf War
 credit crunch following, 683–684
 saving and investment and, 637

Hamilton, Alexander, 347, 492
Hammack, Beth, 172
Hanwa Bank, 403
Harvey, Campbell R., 168–169
Hassett, Kevin, 255
Havrilesky, Thomas, 503n
Hayami, Masaru, 491
Hedge funds, 302–303
Hedging, 214
HFC Bank, 340
High employment, as monetary policy goal, 540–541
Highly leveraged transactions (HLTs), 396
Himmelberg, Charles P., 266n, 271
Historical costs, 400
Hitler, Adolf, 540
Hokkaido Takushoku Bank, 403
Hong Kong, 413
Hoover, Herbert, 543n
Horioka, Charles, 636n
Horner, Sidney, 445n
Households, savings of, 47
Hubbard, R. Glenn, 265, 266n, 271, 303n, 726n, 731n
Humphrey-Hawkins Act of 1978, 500, 540, 553, 749
Hunt, H. L., 384
Hunt, Herbert, 384, 521
Hunt, Nelson Baker, 384, 521
Hyperinflation, 19, 540, 748–749
Hysteresis, 679

Ibbotson, Roger C., 102n, 103n
Ibison, David, 735
IBM, 102, 236
Icahn, Carl, 272
Idiosyncratic risk, 106
Impact lag, 543, 703
Implementation lag, 703
In the money, defined, 220
Income, 18
 expected, national saving and, 630–631
 money demand and, 614
 national saving and, 630
 permanent, 617
Index arbitrage, 221
Indexed bonds, 90–91
Indicators, 551
Indonesia, financial crisis in, 597
Inflation, 18–19, 739–761. *See also* Hyperinflation
 central bank credibility and, 754–760
 cost-push, 749–750
 costs of, 746–749
 demand-pull, 749, 750–751
 expected. *See* Expected inflation
 Fed's attempt to avoid, 762–763
 long-term bond prices and, 88
 monetary policy and, 749–751
 price level changes and, 739–745
 reducing, costs of, 752–754
 uncertainty about, 748–749
 unemployment versus, 766–771
 unexpected, costs of, 747
Inflation targets, 560–561
Inflation-indexed Treasury securities, 88

Information, 5, 40–41
anonymous trading and, 224–225
asymmetric, 40–41, 260
government regulation of access to, 52
money demand and, 615
provision by international banks, 418–420, 421
symmetric, 260
Information costs, 102, 104
changes in, 154–156
currency/deposit ratio and, 452
demand for bonds and, 126, 128
depository institutions and, 300
diversification in international markets and, 110
falling prices and, 268
financial intermediaries and, 269–272
inefficiency and, 252–253
interest rates and, 153–156
measuring, 154
reducing, 262–264
Information lag, 543
Information problems, 715–722
credit controls and credit crunches and, 720–722
financial intermediaries and, 716
financial panics and, 719–720
net worth and, 716–717, 718–719
Input costs, short-run aggregate supply curve shifts and, 675
Insider information, 242, 282
Insider trading, 52
Institutional barriers, diversification in international markets and, 110
Insurance companies, 289–295, 304
regulation of, 404–405
Interest, 42
Interest rate(s). *See also* Theory of portfolio allocation
aggregate demand and, 699
business cycle and, 132–134
discount rate, 437, 529, 531
Fed emphasis on after 1982, 554–556
federal funds rate, 61, 315, 531–535
foreign, exchange rate fluctuation and, 199–200
money demand and, 612–613
nominal, 87–88, 89–91
real. *See* Real interest rate
risk structure of, 146–159
as targets, 545–547
term structure of, 159–170
during wartime, 131
Interest rate parity, 194–196
Interest rate risk, banks' management of, 330–333
Interest rate stability, as monetary policy goal, 542
Interest rate swaps, 231–232, 332
Intermediate targets, 543–544, 547–550
Intermediate-term debt, 42
International bank(s), 411–430
Euromarkets and, 420–424
exchange rate risk and, 415–417
financial regulation in, 424–427
organization of, 412–415
services provided by, 417–420
International Bank for Reconstruction and Development (IBRD), 585, 586
International banking
discount policy and, 522
leaders in, 415
off-balance sheet activities and, 338–339
open market operations and, 517–518
reserve requirements and, 527
International Banking Act of 1978, 415
International banking facilities (IBFs), 414
International capital market, 6
International capital mobility, 192–194
International comparisons, of monetary policy, 562–564
International coordination, of banking, 427
International markets, diversification in, 110
International Monetary Fund (IMF), 585, 586, 597
International Organization of Securities Commissions (IOSCO), 425
International reserve(s), 570
International reserve currencies, 585, 592–593
International transaction currency, 420
Internet banks, 340–341
Intrinsic value, 218, 220
Investment incentives for, 684
national, determinants of, 631
Investment banks, 280–281, 304
Investment Company Act of 1940, 287, 303n
Investment institutions, 285–289
Investment strategies, efficient markets hypothesis and, 241–244
Ip, Greg, 535
IS curve, 629
constructing, 632–633, 634
derivation of, 659–661
for open economy, 634–635
shifts of, 636–637, 648–649, 650–651
IS-LM-FE model, 627–656
assumptions of, 628–637
equilibrium explained by, 648–650
FE line and, 647, 649, 651–652
full employment line and, 637–639, 640
IS curve and. *See IS* curve
LM curve and, 639–646
money, output, and prices in long run and, 652–653
price-level adjustment and, 650–652
Italy, speculative attack and, 595
Items in process of collection, as assets of Fed, 472–473
ITT, 231–232
iX, 285

Jackson, Andrew, 347, 492
James, Harold, 584, 721
January effect, 245–426

Japan
- banking in, 338–339, 371–373, 412–413, 415, 426
- central bank of. *See* Bank of Japan
- credit crunch in, 734–735
- financial crisis in, 7, 234, 249, 403, 406–407, 686–687
- financial system of, 56–57
- postwar growth of economy of, 371
- stabilization policy in, 703

Jerram, Richard, 686
J. P. Morgan, 364, 425

Kahn, George A., 560n
Kashyap, Anil K., 364n, 369, 730–731
Keating, Charles, 393
"Keating Five" scandal, 393
Keiretsu, 372
Keynes, John Maynard, 614, 615–618, 670
King, Robert G., 271, 733n
Kizu Credit Corporation, 403
Kodak, 189
Kravis, Henry, 272
Kroszner, Randall, 364n
Krugman, Paul, 597
Kulish, Nicholas, 535
Kuttner, Kenneth N., 731n
Kyle, Albert, 247

La Porta, Rafael, 271
Labor costs, short-run aggregate supply curve shifts and, 675
Lafontaine, Oskar, 488
Lags in the policymaking and implementation process, 702
Laibson, David, 242
Lakonishok, Josef, 251
Large open economies
- interest rates and, 138–142
- *IS* curve and, 634–635, 661

Large-denomination time deposits, 315
Law of large numbers, 290
Law of one price, 186–187
Leading indicators, 159
Leeson, Nick, 223
Legal tender, 21
Legislative lag, 703
Lehman Brothers, 281
Lemons problems, 261–262
Lender of last resort, 355–356, 381–385, 520–521
Lending, information problems in, 715–722
Letts, Phillip, 30
Levine, Ross, 271, 368n, 733n
Liabilities, 37
- of banks, 313–315, 331
- of Fed, 435–436, 473–474

Liability management, by banks, 323–325
Life insurance companies, 289, 292–293, 294
Life-cycle considerations, saving and, 125
Lincoln Savings and Loan, 393
Lintner, John, 109
Liquidity, 5, 18, 39–40, 102
- currency/deposit ratio and, 451
- demand for bonds and, 126, 128
- interest rates and, 152–153
- money demand and, 615
- reserve requirements and, 525
- in secondary markets, 282–285
- standardization and, 224

Liquidity preference theory, 615–618
Liquidity premium, 153
Liquidity risk, banks' relationships with savers and, 323–325
LM curve, 639–646
- asset market equilibrium and, 640–641
- constructing, 641–644
- shifts of, 645–646, 649–650, 652

Load funds, 286
Loan(s)
- bank, 65, 730
- as bank asset, 316–317
- credit, adjustment, 519
- discount. *See* Discount loans
- in Euromarkets, 423–424
- extended credit, 519
- Fed control of availability of, 519
- fixed-payment, 71–72, 78–79
- losses on, 319
- seasonal credit, 519
- simple, 69, 76
- writing off losses on, 319

Loan certificates, 355
Loan commitments, 336
Loan guarantees, 305
Loan loss reserve, 319
Loan officers, 327
Loan sales, 336–337
Loan syndication, 423–424
Loanable funds, interest rates in bond market and, 118–121
Local government bonds, 63
Lombard rate, 563
London Interbank Offer Rate (LIBOR), 332, 423
London Stock Exchange, 44, 285
Long position, 212
Long Term Capital Management, 203, 224, 302–303, 356, 385, 426, 597, 722
Long-run aggregate supply (*LRAS*) curve, 674, 675–676, 677
Long-run equilibrium, 679–680
Long-run exchange rates, 183–188
Long-run Phillips curve, 770
Long-Term Credit Bank of Japan, 403
Long-term debt, 42
Lopez-di-Silanes, Florencio, 271

Louvre Accord, 557, 576
Love, Inessa, 271
Lucas, Robert E., Jr., 668
Luxury assets, 100

M1 aggregate, 26
M2 aggregate, 27
  money supply process for, 469–470
M3 aggregate, 27, 562
McCain, John, 562
McCarran-Ferguson Act of 1945, 405
McFadden Act of 1927, 355, 361
Mack, Connie, 542
Main banks, in Japan, 372
Maintenance periods, 524
Maisel, Sherman J., 497–498
Malaysia, financial crisis in, 597
Margin requirements, 252, 496
Market(s)
  auction, 44
  for bonds. *See* Bond markets
  capital, 44
  cash, 45
  derivative, 45
  Euromarkets, 420–424
  foreign-exchange, 182–183. *See also* Exchange rate(s)
  goods, 628
  money, 44, 628
  for nonmoney assets, 628
  offshore, 413
  over-the-counter, 44–45, 284
Market equilibrium, in bond market, 119–135
Market interest rates, 116–143
  equilibrium, changes in, 121–135
  international capital market and, 136–142
  supply and demand in bond market and loanable funds and, 116–121
Market risk, 106
Marketable securities, 316
Market-value accounting, 400
Marking to market, 214
Markowitz, Harry, 105
Martin, William McChesney, 482, 496, 551
Massachusetts Investors Trust, 286
Masson, Paul, 560n
Matched sale-purchase transactions, 514
Maturity, 42
  yield to, 75–79
Mean reversion, 246
Medium of exchange, money as, 16–17
Mellon Bank, 278
Meltzer, Allan, 586
Member banks, of Fed, 495
Menem, Carlos, 19
Menu costs, 747
Merchant banking, 281
Merrill Lynch, 38, 71, 222, 280, 282, 283, 367, 384
Merton, Robert, 220, 302
Metropolitan Life, 306
Mexican financial crisis, 585, 596
Mieno, Yasushi, 504, 703
Milken, Michael, 52, 281
Miller, G. William, 496, 501, 553, 706
Misperception theory, 668, 669
Mitsubishi, 372
Mitsubishi Bank, 403
Mitsui, 372
Monetarists, 552
Monetary aggregates, 25–28
  growth targets for, 610
  as targets, 544, 545–547
Monetary base, 435–443, 471–486
  balance sheet of Fed and, 471–474
  changes in, 475–481
  determining, 474–475
  disturbances of, defensive open market operations and, 530–531
  Fed assets and, 436–437
  Fed liabilities and, 435–436
  Fed manipulation of, 437–441
  federal budget deficit and, 481–486
  open market operations and discount loans and, 441–443
Monetary control, reserve requirements and, 525–526
Monetary neutrality, 680
Monetary policy, 9, 512–536, 539–565, 569–602
  balance of payments and, 577–582
  balance sheet channel for, 715, 727–732
  bank lending channel for, 715, 724–727, 729–732
  borrowers and, 729–730
  discount policy and, 518–522, 529, 531
  exchange rate regimes and, 582–599
  federal funds market and, 527–528
  federal funds rate and, 531–533, 531–535
  foreign-exchange intervention and, 570–576
  goals of, 539–542
  inflation and, 749
  international comparison of, 562–564
  money channel for, 715, 722–723, 724–727
  open market operations and, 512–518, 528, 530
  politics and, 556
  price level fluctuations and, 741–742
  problems in achieving goals of, 542–550
  procyclical, 552
  record of, 550–557
  reserve requirements and, 522–527, 529–530, 532
  shifts during early 1980s, 705–706
  shifts during early 1990s, 706–707
  targets and. *See* Targets
Monetary policy goals, 539–542
Monetary theory, 9
Monetizing the debt, 483

Money, 8–9
assets serving as, 19–20, 22
commodity, 21
demand for. *See* Money demand
electronic, 23–24
fiat, 21–22
functions of, 16–19
neutrality of, 652, 692
output and, in short run, 690–710
supply of. *See* Money supply; Money supply process
velocity of, 608–613
Money center banks, 363
Money channel, 715, 722–723, 724–727
Money demand, 606–624
measuring, 619–621
model of, 618–621
portfolio allocation motives and, 614–618
quantity theory of, 609
transactions motives and, 606–613
Money demand function, 609, 619, 620
Money market(s), 44, 628
Money market deposit accounts (MMDAs), 314, 390
Money market instruments, 60–62
Money market mutual funds, 286–287
Money supply, 9
control of, 53
expected changes in, 695, 696
growth of, predicting, 461–463
measuring, 25–29
prediction of, money multiplier and, 456–463
slowdown in growth of, 464–465
unexpected changes in, 695, 696
Money supply process, 434–466
deriving, 456–463
excess reserves and discount loans and, 453–456
for *M2*, 469–470
monetary base and, 435–443
simple deposit multiplier and, 443–453
Monitoring, by banks, 329
Moody's Investor Service, 263
bond ratings of, 52, 148, 149
Moral hazard, 264–269
banks' relationships with savers and, 321–322
in debt financing, 266–269
in equity financing, 264–266
financial intermediaries and, 270–272
insurance and, 290
Mørck, Randall, 266n
Morgan, J. P., 355, 364, 492
Morgan, Peter, 686
Morgan Guaranty Trust Company, 522
Morgan Stanley, 364
Morris, Charles S., 246
Mortgages, 65
Multiple deposit contraction, 448–450
Multiple deposit expansion, 443–448
Munchau, Wolfgang, 489
Municipal bonds, 156, 159
Muth, John, 236n
Mutual funds, 285–288, 304
Mutual insurance companies, 292

Naqvi, Swaleh, 416
Narrow banking, 398
National Association of Insurance Commissioners, 405
National Association of Securities Dealers (NASD), 284
National Association of Securities Dealers' Automated Quotation (NASDAQ) system, 284
National bank(s), 347
National Banking Act of 1863, 326n, 347, 354–355, 523
National Banking Act of 1864, 326n
National Banking Period, 355
National Bureau of Economic Research, 159
National Credit Union Administration (NCUA), 54, 350
National Credit Union Share Insurance Fund (NCUSIF), 350
National Futures Association, 224
National investment, determinants of, 631
National Market System, 284
National Monetary Commission, 492
National saving, determinants of, 630–631
NationsBank, 278, 361, 363
Natural rate of unemployment, 541, 750–751
Navy Federal Credit Union, 350
Necessity assets, 100
Negotiable certificates of deposit, 61, 388
Negotiable order of withdrawal (NOW) accounts, 314, 388
Net worth, 263–264
of banks, 313, 317
information problems in lending and, 716–717, 718–719
moral hazard and, 321
Neuer Markt exchange, 284
Neutrality of money, 652
New classical view, 668–670
of disinflation, 752–753
of money and output, 694–696
of stabilization policies, 700–701
New Keynesian view, 670–674
of disinflation, 753–754
of money and output, 696–700
of stabilization policies, 701–704
New York Clearing House, 355–356
New York Stock Exchange (NYSE), 44, 218, 248, 283, 285
Newton, Isaac, 248n
Nikon, 189
Nixon, Richard, 503
Noise traders, 247–248
No-load funds, 286

Nominal exchange rate, 179, 180–182
Nominal GDP, as monetary policy target, 557–558
Nominal interest rate(s), 87–88, 89–91
Nominal interest rate parity condition, 194–196
Nominal return, shifts in *LM* curve and, 645–646
Nonbank banks, 363
Nonbank offices, 363
Nonmoney asset market, 628
Nontransaction deposits, 314–315
Nonusage fees, 336
Noyer, Christian, 506
Nunn, Sam, 159
NYCE, 363

Obstfeld, Maurice, 577
Obuchi, Keizo, 686
Odean, Terence, 112–113
Off-balance-sheet activities, 334–339
Off-balance-sheet lending, 335
Office of the Comptroller of the Currency (OCC), 54, 349, 367, 376, 397, 401
Office of Thrift Supervision (OTS), 54, 350, 394, 401
Official reserve assets, 580–581
Official settlements balance, 581
Offshore markets, 413
Okun, Arthur M., 767n
Okun's law, 766–767
O'Neill, Paul, 576, 654
Open economies
  interest rates and, 137–142
  IS curve and, 634–635, 661
Open market operations, 437–440, 512–518
  compared with other policy tools, 516
  discount loans compared with, 441–443
  Fed watching and, 516–517, 528, 530
  FOMC statements and, 517
  implementing, 513–515
  in other countries, 517–518
Open market purchases, 437–439
Open market sales, 439–440
Open Market Trading Desk, 513, 515
Open-end mutual funds, 286
Operating targets, 544, 545, 550
Option(s), 45, 217–221, 332–333
  managing risk using, 220–221
  pricing, 218, 220
Option premium, 218
Options contracts, 217
Orange County, California bankruptcy, 63, 222, 224
Organization of Petroleum Exporting Countries (OPEC), 422–423, 682
Output
  current, 637
  full employment, 638, 670
  money and, in short run, 690–710
  unemployment rate and, 766–770
Outright purchases and sales, 514
Overnight Eurodollars, 388
Oversubscription, 82
Over-the-counter (OTC) markets, 44–45, 284

Palia, Darius, 266n, 731n
Panic of 1907, 356
Par value, 70
Parrish, Klara, 560n
Passbook accounts, 314
Payments, timing of, on debt instruments, 69–72
Payments system, 20–25, 384
Payments system factors, 611–612
Payoff method, for resolving bank failures, 391
PayPal, 30
Penn Central Railroad default, 151, 383, 521
Penn Square Bank, 391n
Pension Benefit Guaranty Corporation (PBGC; "Penny Benny"), 298, 405
Pension funds, 295–299, 304
  regulation of, 405
Permanent income, 617
Perpetual bonds, 78n
Petersen, Bruce C., 265
Phelps, Edmund, 767–768
Philippines, financial crisis in, 597
Phillips, A. W., 766
Phillips, Michael M., 601
Phillips curve, 766–771
  expectations-augmented, 769
  long-run, 770
  output changes and unemployment rate and, 766–770
  short-run, 769–771
  simple, 767
Pickens, T. Boone, 272
Plan funding, 297
Plaza Accord, 556–557, 576, 593
Poland, shock therapy in, 676
Political business cycle, 502–503
Politics, monetary policy and, 556
Pollution permits, 226–227
Portfolio(s), 39. *See also* Determinants of portfolio choice
  churning, 243
  gender and allocation decisions and, 112–113
Portfolio allocation. *See also* Theory of portfolio allocation
  currency/deposit ratio and, 450–452
  efficient markets hypothesis and, 242–243
  velocity and, 613
Portfolio allocation motives, 614–618
Poterba, James, 110
Precautionary motive, 616
Precautionary saving, 125
Preferences, long-run exchange rates and, 185–186

Preferred habitat theory, 166–168, 170
Premiums
  currency, 202–203
  for insurance, 289, 290–291
  liquidity, 153, 154
  option, 218
  risk, 108–109, 147–152, 154–156
  risk-based, 290–291
  term, 167
Present value, 72–75
Price(s)
  of bonds, 80–86, 88
  exercise, 217
  expected, determining, 238–239
  of futures, 212–214
  of options, 218, 220
pricing anomalies and, 245–426
  shock, aggregate demand and, 699
  sticky, 670–674
  strike, 217
Price changes
  anticipated, hedging and, 216
  efficient markets hypothesis and, 239–241
  excessive, costs of, 251–252
  information costs and, 268
  predicting, 244
Price controls, central bank credibility and, 760
Price indexes, 19, 181
Price levels. *See also* Inflation
  adjustment of, equilibrium and, 650–652
  changes in, 739–745
  long-run exchange rates and, 184
Price stability, as monetary policy goal, 540
Price takers, 671
Primary markets, 41–43
Prime rate, 328
Principal (amount borrowed), 42
Principal-agent problem, 265–266
Principal-agent view, of Fed motivation, 502–503
Private placements, 289–290
Privatization, in China, 274–275
Procyclical monetary policy, 552
Productivity, long-run exchange rates and, 184–185
Productivity growth, 654–655
Profitability, expected, bond supply and, 127, 133
Program trading, 250
Property and casualty insurance companies, 289, 291, 293–294
Prudential, 289
Public interest view, of Fed motivation, 502
Public pension plans, 298
Purchasing power, 18–19
Purchasing power parity (PPP) theory, 187–188
Put options, 217
Putnam Management Company, 286
Quantity theory of money demand, 609
Quotas, for imports, 186
Quotations, for options, 219
Rahnman, Bayan, 735
Random walk, 237n
Rate of return
  expected, portfolio choice and, 100–101
  real, 90
  total, 86–87
Rational expectations, 235–237
  stabilization policies and, 701
Reagan, Ronald, 248, 394, 500–501, 705
Real business cycle view, 680–681
  of stabilization policies, 700
Real exchange rate, 180–182
Real interest rate, 88–91
  domestic, exchange rate fluctuation and, 196, 197
  expected, 88, 631
  world, 137
Real interest rate parity condition, 195, 196
Real money balances, 607–609
  shifts in *LM* curve and, 645
Real rate of return, 90
Rebecchini, Salvatore, 577
Recessions, 691. *See also* Business cycle
  Fed's attempt to prevent, 709
  interest rates during, 132–134
  of 1990-1991, 731, 732
Recognition lag, 703
Regulation, 51–55
  of banking. *See* Banking regulation
  of insurance companies, 295, 404–405
  in international banking, 424–427
  of mutual fund industry, 287
  of pension plans, 297–298, 405
  separating financial institutions, 305–307
Regulation Q, 385–391, 389–390, 392, 421–422
Reinvestment risk, 86
Repurchase agreements (repos; RPs), 61, 315, 388
Required reserve(s), 316, 436
Required reserve ratio, 436
Reserve(s)
  bank, 436
  as bank asset, 316
  banking system's response to increase in, 444–448
  bank's response to increase in, 443–444
  excess, 319–320, 436
  free, 551
  international, 570
  as liability of Fed, 436
  loan loss, 319
  required, 316, 436
  secondary, 316
Reserve accounts, 316
Reserve Bank of New Zealand, credibility of, 759
Reserve requirements, 522–527
  changes in, 523–524

criticism of, 524–526
measurement and compliance with, 524
in other countries, 527
Resolution Funding Corporation, 394
Resolution Trust Corporation (RTC), 394
Restrictive covenants, 267, 292, 329
Return(s)
expected, demand for bonds and, 123–124, 128
nominal, shifts in LM curve and, 645–646
rate of. *See* Rate of return
risks associated with, 101–102
Return on assets (ROA), 322
Return on equity (ROE), 322
Revaluation, 587
Reverse causation, 692
Reverse repos, 514
Ricardian equivalence proposition, 666
Ricardo, David, 666n
Riegle-Neal Interstate Banking and Branching Efficiency Act of 1994, 363, 401, 414
Risk, 5
amount of, 103
associated with asset returns, 101–102
basis, 217
credit, 326–330, 376–377
currency/deposit ratio and, 451
default, 147–152
demand for bonds and, 124–125, 128
exchange rate, 415–417
idiosyncratic (unsystematic), 106
interest rate, 330–333
managing using options, 220
managing with futures, 214–217
market (systematic), 106
money demand and, 615
pooling, 290
reinvestment, 86
Risk premiums, 147–152, 154–156
changes in, 154–156
modeling, 108–109
Risk sharing, 5, 39
Risk structure of interest rates, 146–159
default risk and, 147–152
forecasting using, 158–159
information costs and, 153–156
liquidity and, 152–153
taxation and, 156–158
Risk-averse savers, 101–102
Risk-based premiums, 290–291
Risk-loving savers, 101
Risk-neutral savers, 101
Rogoff, Kenneth, 758n
Rolnick, Arthur J., 348n
Romer, Christina, 693–694
Romer, David, 612n, 693–694
Roosevelt, Franklin Delano, 382
Rosen, Harvey S., 243
Rules strategy, for monetary policy, 758, 759–760
Russian financial crisis, 2, 403
Sakaiya, Taichi, 686
Sanwa, 372
Sargent, Thomas J., 752
Savastano, Miguel, 560n
Savers, 36
matching with borrowers, 41–43, 258–260
relationship with banks, 320–325
Saving(s)
changes in wealth and, 125
of households, 47
international mobility of, 636
national, determinants of, 630–631
Savings and loan institutions (S&Ls)
credit crunch of 1966 and, 387
crisis of 1980s and, 391–393
regulation of, 350
Savings Association Insurance Fund (SAIF), 350, 394
Savings institutions, 300, 304. *See also* Savings and loan institutions (S&Ls)
regulation of, 350
Scalise, Joseph M., 364n, 369
Schleifer, Andrei, 251, 266n, 271
Schlesinger, Arthur M., Jr., 543n
Scholes, Myron, 220, 302
Schwartz, Anna J., 459, 692–693, 730
Seasonal credit loans, 519
SEB, 340
Second Bank of the United States, 347, 492
Secondary loan participations, 336–337
Secondary markets, 43–45
Secondary reserves, 316
Securities. *See also* specific types of securities
as assets of Fed, 472
monetary base and, 476
Securities Act of 1933, 52, 287
Securities Amendment Act of 1975, 284
Securities and Exchange Acts of 1933 and 1934, 281
Securities and Exchange Commission (SEC), 52, 54, 281
accounting principles set by, 265
disclosure required by, 262
regulation of brokers and dealers by, 282
Rule 415 of, 281
Securities firms, 304
barriers between banks and, 367
Securities market institutions, 279–285
investment banks, 280–282
secondary markets and, 282–285
Securitization, 50, 369–370
Segmented markets theory, 161–162
Seignorage, 598
Semistrong-form efficiency, 245n
Sharma, Sunil, 560n
Sharpe, William, 105, 109

Shell, 226
Shiller, Robert J., 246, 248n
Shock prices, aggregate demand and, 699
Shock therapy, 676
Shoe leather costs, 746
Short position, 212
Short run, money and output in, 690–710
Short-run aggregate supply (*SRAS*) curve, 668–675
Short-run equilibrium, 678
Short-run exchange rates, 188–196
Short-run Phillips curve, 769–771
Short-term debt, 42
Siegel, Jeremy, 92
Signaling Fed policy, 521–522
Silver market, 384
Simec, 622
Simple deposit multiplier, 443–450
  multiple deposit contraction and, 448–450
  multiple deposit expansion and, 443–448
Simple loans
  timing of payments on, 69
  yield to maturity of, 76
Simple Phillips curve, 767
Sims, G. Thomas, 601
Singapore, 413
Sinquefield, Rex A., 102n, 103n
Small open economies
  interest rates and, 137–138
  IS curve and, 635, 661
Small-denomination time deposits, 315
Small-firm effect, 245
Smithsonian Conference, 590
Social security, 297
South Korea, financial crisis in, 597
Soviet Union, former, collapse of economic system in, 3, 16, 258
Spain, speculative attack and, 595
Special Drawing Rights (SDRs), 591
  as asset of Fed, 473
  monetary base and, 478
Specialists, 248, 285
Specialization, 15
Speculative attack, 587–589, 590
Speculative motive, 615–616
Speculators, 214
Spot market transactions, 183
Spot price, 212–214
Spot transactions, 211
Stabilization policies, 700–704
Stagflation, 662, 683
Standard & Poor's Corporation, 263
  bond ratings of, 52, 126, 148, 149
Standard of deferred payment, money as, 18–19
Standardization, 224
Standby letters of credit (SLCs), 335
State bank(s), 347
State banking commissions, 54
State government bonds, 63
State insurance commissions, 54
State Street Investment Corporation, 286
Statistical discrepancy, 581
Stein, Jeremy, 730–731
Steinberg, Bruce, 464
Sterilized foreign-exchange intervention, 574–575, 577
Stevenson, Richard W., 465
Stewart, Rod, 50
Sticky prices, 670–674
Stock(s), 63
Stock exchanges, 283–284
Stock insurance companies, 292
Stock market(s)
  adverse selection and, 265
  Chinese, 274
  international, growth of, 51
Stock market crash of October 1929, 381–383
Stock market crash of October 1987, 356, 384–385, 521
  index arbitrage and, 221
  market efficiency and, 247–248
  specialists and, 284
Store of value, money as, 17–18
Stored-value cards, 24
Straddles, 223
Strike price, 217
STRIPS (Separate Trading of Registered Interest and Principal of Securities), 71
Strong-form efficiency, 245n
Structural unemployment, 541, 750
Student Loan Marketing Association ("Sallie Mae;" SLMA), 231–232, 304–305
Subsidiary U.S. banks, 414
Sumita, Satoshi, 504
Sumitomo, 372
Summers, Lawrence H., 600, 762
Super-NOW accounts, 314
Superregional banks, 363
Supply
  aggregate, 668, 677–681. *See also* Aggregate supply (*AS*) curve
  of bank loans, 730–732
  of currencies, exchange rates and, 183
Supply curve, interest rates in bond market and, 119, 127, 129–132
Supply shocks
  during 1973-1975 and 1995-2000, 682–683
  price level fluctuations and, 743
  short-run aggregate supply curve shifts and, 675
  Swap(s), 230–233, 332
  currency, 417
  default, 338
Swap facilitators, 231

Sylla, Richard, 445n
Symmetric information, 260
Syndicates, 280
Systematic risk, 106

T-accounts, 318
Tagliabue, John, 623
Takeda, Yoneo, 56
Targets, 543–550
  inflation, 560–561
  intermediate, 543–544, 547–550
  monetary aggregates and interest rates as, 545–547
  during 1951–1970, 551–552
  during 1970–1979, 552–553
  during 1979–1982, 553–554
  during 1982–1990s, 554–557
  operating, 544, 545, 550
Tariffs, 186
Tax Reform Act of 1986, 294n
Taxes
  aggregate demand and, 666
  exemptions and, yield differences related to, 157–158, 159
  interest rates and, 156–158
  measuring differences in, 156–157
  pension plans and, 296n
  raising, monetary base and, 483–484
  transaction, 252
Tax-exempt bonds, 100
Taylor, John B., 559
Taylor rule, 558–559
Tennessee Valley Authority (TVA), 82
Term, 42
Term life insurance, 293
Term premium, 167
Term structure of interest rates, 159–170
  expectations theory of, 162–166, 170
  forecasting using, 168–170
  preferred habitat theory of, 166–168, 170
  segmented markets theory of, 161–162
Thailand, financial crisis in, 597
Thaler, Richard, 242
Thatcher, Margaret, 679
Theory of portfolio allocation, 97–111
  determinants of portfolio choice and, 97–104
  diversification and, 104–107
Thrifts. *See* Savings and loan institutions (S&Ls)
Thurow, Lester, 762
TIGR (Treasury Investment Growth Receipt), 71
Time deposits, 315
TIPS (Treasury Inflation Protection Securities), 90–91, 92–93
Tobin, James, 105, 612
Tokyo Stock Exchange, 44
Tombstones, 283
Tomlinson, Steven, 116n
Too-big-to-fail policy, 397–398
Total rate of return, 86–87
Total return swaps, 233
Trade balance, 579
Trade barriers, long-run exchange rates and, 186
Trading mechanisms, efficient markets hypothesis and, 248, 250
Transaction taxes, 252
Transactions costs, 259–260
  depository institutions and, 300
  hedging and, 216–217
  reduction by international banks, 417–418
Transactions motives, 606–613, 616
  real money balances and, 607–609
  velocity and, 608–613
Travelers, 278, 306, 367–368
Treasury, Fed conflict with, 500–501
Treasury bills (T-bills), 60
Treasury bonds
  buying, monetary base and, 485
  future of, 172–173
  selling, monetary base and, 484–485
  trading, 284–285
Treasury currency in circulation, 435–436
Treasury deposits
  as liability of Fed, 473
  monetary base and, 479–480
Treasury securities, 63
Treasury strips, 71
Treasury tax and loan accounts, 479–480
Trichet, Jean-Claude, 508
Truman, Ted, 600
Trump, Donald, 396
Tullock, Gordon, 502

Uchitelle, Louis, 465
Underground economy, 452
Underwriting, 280–281
Unemployment
  frictional, 541, 750
  inflation versus, 766–771
  natural rate of, 541, 750–751
  structural, 541, 750
Unexpected inflation, costs of, 747
Unit of account, money as, 17
United Kingdom. *See* also Bank of England
  banking in, 338
  foreign exchange value of pound and, 201
  hysteresis in, 679
  speculative attack and, 595
United Negro College Fund, 398
U.S. banking industry, 346–378
  agencies regulating, 348–351
  government intervention in, 354–368
  origins of, 347–348

overseas organization of U.S. banks and, 413–414
reasons for regulating, 351–354
U.S. government agency securities, 63. *See also* Treasury entries
Universal banking, 366
Unsterilized foreign-exchange intervention, 571, 572–574
Unsystematic risk, 106
Upfront fees, 336
Urban league, 398
Usury ceilings, 389

Value, money as store of, 17–18
Value investing, efficient markets versus, 250–251
Value Line, 263
Value-at-risk (VAR) approach, 338
Vanguard, 286, 287
Vanguard Group, 92
Vault cash, 316, 436
Velocity of money, 608–613
Venture capital firms, 271
Venture capital funds, 303
Vesting, 296
Vishny, Robert, 251, 266n, 271
Volcker, Paul, 496, 500–501, 539, 553–554, 559, 576, 592n, 705, 739, 752, 758

Wall Street Journal
bond prices and yields in, 84–85
exchange rates in, 185
futures listings in, 213
monetary base data in, 477
Walt Disney Company, 88
War, interest rates and, 131
Washington State Public Power System default, 152
Weak-form efficiency, 245n
Wealth, 18
changes in, 125
currency/deposit ratio and, 451
demand for bonds and, 122–123, 128
money demand and, 614
portfolio choice and, 99–100
Wealth elasticity of demand, 99
Weber, Warren E., 348n
Wessel, David, 655
Whole life insurance, 293
Wilcox, David, 730–731
Wilcox, James A., 368n
Willard, Kristen L., 243
Willman, John, 429
Wilson, Woodrow, 356, 492
Wingspan, 340
Without recourse, defined, 336
Woodward, Bob, 116
Working Group on Financial Markets, 250
World Bank, 585, 586
World real interest rate, 137
Writing off loan losses, 319

Yield(s), of bonds, 80–86
Yield curve, 160, 161
as monetary policy target, 558
Yield to maturity, 75–79

Zedillo, Ernesto, 596